The Greek Code of Civil Procedure

Presidential Decree 503/1985

Daniel A. Webber & John A. O'Shea

The Greek Code of Civil Procedure

Presidential Decree 503/1985

Daniel A. Webber & John A. O'Shea

LEX GRAECA

LEX GRAECA

The Greek Code of Civil Procedure
Presidential Decree 503/1985

1 3 5 7 9 10 8 6 4 2

First edition published 2023

Lex Graeca
London

ISBN: 978-1-8384106-4-3

Note to Readers – Disclaimer

This publication is designed to provide an accurate and authoritative translation of the legislation covered. Appropriate diligence has been shown in preparing the translation and the translated legal provisions are as they stand on the date of publication.

It is sold on the understanding that the publisher is not engaged in providing legal or advisory/ consultancy or other such professional services in general and in relation to the matters translated in particular. If legal advice or other expert assistance is required, the services of a competent professional person in the jurisdiction concerned should be sought.

Readers should also be aware more recent developments and amendments to the original Greek legislation may have occurred since the time of publication and primary sources in Greek should always be consulted in cooperation with your legal advisors to ensure that they are basing decisions on the most recent version of the legislation.

No responsibility for loss caused to any individual or organization acting on or refraining from action as a result of the translated material in this publication can be accepted by Lex Graeca or the authors.

Acknowledgments

This work spanned many years and would have been impossible without the generous and selfless contributions of many individuals, to whom the authors owe a tremendous debt of gratitude and who, at the very least, must be named and thanked individually. Therefore, our deepest thanks to Alexandros Koliopoulos, John Sortikos, Natalia Alexiou, Penny Mitsopoulou. We must also thank Professor Panayiotopoulos for his insightful introduction and feedback.

We hope this book proves to be a useful, practical resource for readers and another step on the long road towards producing authoritative translations of the main codes of the Greek legal system. Any errors remain our own, and we welcome any comments and feedback regarding our work (info@lexgraeca.com).

Table of Contents

Introduction

The Greek Code of Civil Procedure (GCCivP) entered into force on 16 September 1968. At the time, it was a truly progressive legislative instrument, being the outcome of a lengthy drafting project launched in the mid-1930s by the Drafting Committee of the Code and the Reform Committee, comprising some of the most eminent academics and judges of the era. As attested by the ten volumes of Minutes from the two Committees, the final text of the initial Code was the result of an extensive review and balancing of the trends of procedural law at that time, yet frequently adopting progressive legislative solutions, some of which survive even today. Naturally, the Code relied heavily on the German Code of Civil Procedure (ZPO) as a comparative standard, which was, at the time, the most modern and widely praised codification of procedural law around. Nevertheless, the drafters would often not hesitate to deviate from the German original, incorporating provisions and institutions from other laws, such as, for example, French law.

The GCCivP has undergone many amendments in the 55 years since its enactment. At times for the sake of addressing pressing needs of judicial practice, at others for the purpose of expediting the administration of justice, and, more recently, for the sake of balancing and addressing the grave dilemmas imposed by the economic crisis that has been affecting the Greek economy since the late 2000s, the legislature intervened repeatedly, introducing amendments to the initial legislative text. Such interventions had started almost at the outset, in 1971 with Legislative Decree 958/1971, and carried on with unabated intensity throughout the 55 years the Code has remained in force; in fact, there are very few years in the course of that period without even a single amendment to the Code. Despite the justified concerns one could have about continuous modifications to a legal text as fundamental as the GCCivP, the repeated amendments have not, in fact, hurt the consistency of the Code's legislative framework. On the contrary, many of these amendments have definitely contributed to the modernisation of the Code and its harmonisation with European and international trends in procedural law.

Although the GCCivP presents significant interest, the international community's access to the text was by definition limited, since it was only available in Greek and not in translation, official or otherwise. Additionally, the language barrier has, until now, prevented international scholars from carrying out comparative research on Greek procedural law. Certain attempts to provide translations of the Code into English or German in the past either bore no fruit or have become completely outdated, given the repeated legislative amendments to the

GCCivP.

A further challenge to be addressed in any attempt to provide an accurate and concise translation of the GCCivP is the fact that an accurate conveying of the text of the Greek original in English is not always possible, as many Greek legal terms lack an exact equivalent in English, as well as the fact that sometimes the corresponding legal term in English does not cover the exact same terrain as the Greek term. Therefore, an accurate translation of the GCCivP into English would require a legal scholar who is a native speaker of English and possesses exceptional knowledge of Greek law, a combination truly difficult to achieve.

Thus, one cannot but applaud the difficult task that Messrs Daniel Webber and John O'Shea undertook and executed with diligence and care, providing the legal community with an accurate and truly functional and useable translation of the Greek Code of Civil Procedure, updated even to the most recent amendments passed up to late 2023. Their work definitely fills a void in the international bibliography, particularly in the field of comparative law, not to mention the exceptional quality of the translation which successfully addresses the challenges of rendering a Greek legal text into English. In undertaking this endeavour, the authors had the foresight to make the GCCivP available for international scholars, for which the Greek legal community should be grateful.

Thessaloniki, 25 October 2023

Panayiotis S. Yiannopoulos
Associate Professor (Democritus University Thrace)

Foreword

John A. O'Shea & Daniel A. Webber

The *Quadricodex*

This book is the second instalment in the *Quadricodex*, a series of translations of the four major codes underpinning the Greek legal system, namely the Civil Code, the Penal Code, the Code of Civil Procedure and the Code of Criminal Procedure. We have taken the liberty of naming our series after the *Tetravivlos* or *Tetrakodikas*, the popular title given to the compendium of the aforesaid codes. It is our sincere hope that we will publish the translations of the two remaining Codes in the coming years.

Purpose

As is the case with other *Lex Graeca* publications, the translation of Presidential Decree No 503/1985, the Greek Code of Civil Procedure (hereinafter GCCivP), aims to serve a dual purpose: to satisfy a clear and present need for English-language versions of Greek codes and legislation, on the one hand, and to set a standard in terms of language, quality, accuracy and promptness for such translations, on the other. It is our intention that all further instalments in the *Lex Graeca* series continue to adhere to this standard.

The overarching aim of *Lex Graeca* publications is to clarify Greek law for an international audience. That audience is diverse, consisting of:

- legal practitioners, who might be engaged to provide legal advice to their foreign clients or explain sections of statutes;
- legal translators, who might be called upon to translate sections of the Code or need a reference text for terminology and style purposes;
- businesspeople, who have already invested in Greece or are interested in doing so, as well as foreign shareholders in Greek businesses;
- academics, particularly comparative lawyers, who thus far have had little access to information in English about the Greek legal system; and
- the general public, who might be interested in reading about the way Greek laws are structured and the topics touched upon.

The more specific aim of the *Quadricodex* series is to make available for the first time a thoroughly researched English-language translation of the four major statutory texts governing almost every aspect of the Greek legal reality, exhaustively researched and consistent in the terminology used across all four instalments.

In making these texts available in English, another aim is to create momentum for international investors in Greece, facilitating their understanding of Greek law through plain-language translations of the latest business-related laws and the general framework of rules which apply in the country.

A more specific goal of the GCCivP is to aid both legal practitioners advising clients who find themselves involved in litigation in Greece and any such persons themselves, where they do not speak Greek and/or are unfamiliar with the stages of Greek legal proceedings, so that they stand aware of their rights and obligations.

Background

In historical terms, only a few serious attempts have been made to translate any of the codes into English. The first was a translation of the Penal Code (number 18 in the American Series of Foreign Penal Codes) by Nicholas Lolis and published in 1973, when Greece remained under the military junta of the Colonels. The next (and only one, to date, concerning civil law) was the daunting Civil Code, translated by Constantine Taliadoros and published in 1982. The last and most recent was the translation of the Penal Code by Vasiliki Chalkiadaki and Emmanouil Billis, published in 2017.

It is not our intention to cast aspersions on any of these translations – nor, indeed, are aspersions required in certain cases – but we would be remiss in our duty to translators, scholars and laypersons alike if we were not to advise caution and judicious use of any existing translations of the codes, as their quality ranges from serviceable to poor. In any case, it must be noted that even the most recent translations are no longer useful, given that recent legislative revisions, if not upheavals, have rendered them mostly obsolete.

To our knowledge, and barring certain sections found translated online, but with little information as to the process followed and of varying quality, this is the first translation of the GCCivP into the English language. The translation stage began in January 2022 and the first draft was completed in April of the same year.

A painstaking editing process ensued, lasting two years in total and consisting of countless hours of back-and-forth between the translators and consulting sessions with Greek attorneys practising law, including translation of the latest amendments to the Code, passed in just February 2023 as part of Law 5023/2023, and another round of consulting.

Compared to our other publications, the GCCivP was a far more arduous task, for two major reasons: firstly, the fact that, contrary to the Greek Code of Criminal Procedure (GCCP), which was radically overhauled by enacting a new Law (4260/2019) and whose translation we published in 2022, the GCCivP has been gradually amended since 1985; secondly, the fact that, while gradual, these amendments were countless in number over the decades since its enactment. Rather than wait for the inevitable next round of amendments, given the propensity of the Greek legislature to amend and supplement laws and the frequency at which such amendments are promulgated, we decided that this latest round of amendments would be the last we would translate before going to press. It goes without saying that, should further changes be made to the GCCivP, we will be prepared to translate them and publish a second edition of this book, having comprehensively addressed the bulk of the Code.

Methodology

The translation and editing were carried out to the highest professional standards and in accordance with current standard practices, so as to ensure consistency and quality throughout the text. The translation process consisted of four stages (**Research and Compilation, Preparation of Source Text, Translation, Review**) which are outlined below:

i) Research and Compilation

The preliminary stage of our process involved three steps:

- Familiarising ourselves with the actuality of legal proceedings in Greece.
- Identifying the texts (historical and recent) on which sections of the GCCivP were based, consisting mainly of relevant EU Directives and foreign Codes of Civil Procedure from various European countries (including Italy, Belgium, Austria, and others), and tracking down authoritative English-language versions of such Codes.
- Consulting the explanatory memoranda of the various laws that amended the Code over the years, the most recent being in 2023.

Having identified the relevant texts, we compiled them and leveraged their terminology in order to:
a) identify such sections and, where appropriate, reproduce or at least adhere to the official English-language text;
b) ensure consistency in both the style applied and the terminology used throughout the translation;
c) identify problematic terms in the target text (TT) not only to be discussed and resolved in the context of this publication, but also to be highlighted for research purposes; and
d) identify issues with the source text (ST), examples of which will be discussed below.

It is self-evident that translations of foreign Codes are just that – translations rather than authoritative, authentic versions of the texts, despite the scholarship involved in their production. We therefore consulted them with a view towards background research and generic illumination of key terms and concepts rather than as a source to be mined for material to use.

As intimated below, the source text presented a host of translational issues to be overcome, given the polysemic nature of Greek legal terminology, so the reference texts were of tertiary importance. The main secondary text we consulted was the Greek Civil Code (GCC) and the numerous analyses of both GCCivP and the GCC published over the decades by eminent Greek jurists. These works are, inevitably in large part, in Greek and served to illuminate issues concerning procedural reality in the Greek courts rather than point out candidate terms in English, given the paucity of English-language scholarship on modern Greek law, a situation which is gradually improving. Additionally, the terminology used in the scant English language works we consulted was both vertically and horizontally inconsistent, i.e. inconsistent both within a single work and across multiple works.

ii) Preparation of Source Text

The second stage of our work, particularly with a view to facilitating the bilingual two-page layout of the book, consisted of identifying the proper version of the source text (i.e. compiling a version that included the very latest amendments to the GCCivP) to use and then editing it for our purposes. This editing was a two-step process:

a) Pagination

This step concerned achieving a logical layout of the book while adhering to an environmentally friendly, space-saving approach. Our conclusion was to insert a page break in the text at every Book rather than every Chapter of the Code.

b) Editing of original text for readability purposes

Where the original text included a list under the subparagraph of an article, we opted to insert a line break in the original so as to have the items on the list one under the other rather than as parts of long, uninterrupted paragraphs, the sole purpose being to enhance readability and ease of reference. An example can be found in Article 1 of the Code:

Original:

> *"Άρθρο 1.*
> *Στη δικαιοδοσία των τακτικών πολιτικών δικαστηρίων ανήκουν: α) Οι διαφορές του ιδιωτικού δικαίου, εφόσον ο νόμος δεν τις έχει υπαγάγει σε άλλα δικαστήρια, β) οι υποθέσεις εκούσιας δικαιοδοσίας που ο νόμος έχει υπαγάγει σ' αυτά, γ) οι υποθέσεις δημόσιου δικαίου που ο νόμος έχει υπαγάγει σ' αυτά και δ) οι διοικητικές διαφορές που δεν υπάγονται στη δικαιοδοσία διοικητικών δικαστηρίων."*

Translation:

> "Article 1.
> The following shall fall under the jurisdiction of the ordinary civil courts:
> a) private law disputes, where they are not subject by law to other courts;
> b) non-contentious proceedings subject by law to ordinary civil courts;
> c) public law cases subject by law to ordinary civil courts; and
> d) administrative disputes not subject to the jurisdiction of administrative courts."
> A final minor step was making corrections to the source text in the rare cases where this was necessary, e.g. adding a stress to the word *"πως"* to change it to an adverb (*"πώς"*) in Article 978(2).

iii) Translation

The translation process was carried out according to the exacting requirements and specifications of modern-day professional translation in terms of style and terminology. Given the size of the GCCivP, it was an arduous task, compounded by the frequent amendments to the Code and, as noted above, took several years, given our day-to-day work as legal translators.

Moreover, we made use of the following standard translation strategies:

a) Explicitation

A major issue in the field of legal translation is explicitation, i.e. the introduction of additional information to convey meaning inherent in a source-text word or phrase. At first glance, this might seem an obvious strategy when called upon to translate a text. However, the demands of legal translation in terms of conciseness, accuracy and, where possible, one-for-one equivalence, particularly in the case of a comparativist approach, might make explicitation a less likely candidate. Nevertheless, we have opted to employ explicitation where we felt it necessary and have signified such instances with the use of square brackets in order to provide the additional information we felt was necessary for a fuller understanding of the law, particularly by laypeople having to grasp the intricacies of a legal system and language that are foreign to them.

Examples include:
Article 15(9) (emphasis our own)

*"[...] οι διαφορές από σύμβαση μεταφοράς προσώπων με οποιοδήποτε **μέσο** [...]"*

Our translation (emphasis our own):

"disputes arising from a contract to carry persons using any ***means [of transport]***"

Article 133(2) (emphasis our own):

*"[...] Η παραγγελία για επίδοση δίνεται εγγράφως **κάτω από*** το έγγραφο που επιδίδεται."

Our translation (emphasis our own):

"[...] The order for service shall be made out in writing ***[at the end of]*** the document being served."

In both the examples above, explicitation was chosen in order to clarify a term in the source text but in a way that would not drastically alter the form and content of the original provision.

Other issues which we considered as part of the overall translation strategy are:

b) Gender-neutral language

Where the Greek text opted for the masculine as the default, we opted for several strategies widely utilised[1] by translation professionals to render sex and gender irrelevant as a consideration which changing the core meaning of the source text[2]:

- A gender-neutral term, e.g. Article 902(2)(a):

  "πρόεδροι"

  "chairpersons"

- A singular noun with plural pronouns, e.g. Article 63(1):

  [...] Όποιος είναι ικανός για οποιαδήποτε δικαιοπραξία μπορεί να παρίσταται στο δικαστήριο με το δικό του όνομα. [...]

  [...] Any person with capacity to enter into any legal transaction may appear before the court in their own name. [...]

- A plural noun where the meaning in the ST is intentionally abstract and is not referring to a single specific individual, e.g. Article 66:

  "Αλλοδαπό πρόσωπο που δεν έχει σύμφωνα με το δίκαιο της ιθαγένειάς του ικανότητα για δικαστική παράσταση με το δικό του όνομα, θεωρείται πως έχει ικανότητα να παρίσταται στα ελληνικά δικαστήρια αν έχει αυτή την ικανότητα σύμφωνα με το ελληνικό δίκαιο."

Our translation:

"Foreigners who, under their national law, do not have capacity to appear before the court in their own name shall be deemed to have capacity to appear before Greek courts if they have such capacity under Greek law."

---

1 https://www.europarl.europa.eu/cmsdata/151780/GNL_Guidelines_EN.pdf

2 Xanthaki, Helen (2020), Gender inclusive legislative drafting in English: A drafter's response to Emily Grabham, *feminists@law*, Vol 10, No 2 (2020), available at: https://journals.kent.ac.uk/index.php/feministsatlaw/article/view/952/1842

c) Easified language

This aspect of the task we set ourselves was one of the hardest and most time-consuming to address during both the translation and the editing of the Code. Our objective was to publish a comprehensively researched text that offers, to the greatest extent possible, equivalence of terms used in the Greek legal system – belonging to the civil law family – and terms established in the English-speaking legal world – mostly belonging to the common law family. The conundrum facing any translator working in this pair of languages (and legal systems) is immediately apparent.

Nevertheless, in our approach towards using easified language, we opted to minimise the use of Latin legal terms, employing them only where we deemed it necessary, and to use terms more immediately accessible and understandable to a layperson rather than a jurist.
The conventions we followed to achieve an easified-language result by and large adhered to common sense, as we understand it, and to the rules prescribed by the European Commission[3], with a view not to simplify or radically reformulate the ST, but to ensure that the TT is clear and comprehensible, reflecting the actual wording and intention of the ST and also being able to be read as a standalone text free from any of the hallmarks of mediocre translations (stunted syntax, excessive adherence to the structure of the original sentence, etc., all of which are by-and-large hallmarks of the translations of the Greek codes to date).

In more concrete terms, the choices we made concerned:

d) Syntax

- Changing word order to reflect what is normal in English-language texts, i.e. Subject-Verb-Object syntax where possible, e.g. Article 3(2):

  "Εξαιρούνται από τη δικαιοδοσία των ελληνικών δικαστηρίων οι αλλοδαποί που έχουν ετεροδικία, εκτός αν πρόκειται για τις διαφορές που υπάγονται στις διατάξεις του άρθρου 29."

Our translation:

> "Foreign nationals enjoying immunity are exempt from the jurisdiction of the Greek courts, save in cases of disputes falling under the provisions of Article 29."

- Joining sentences where a full stop or a semicolon would not make sense, e.g. Article 783:

  "Αρμόδιο κατά το νόμο να κηρύξει και να άρει την αφάνεια, καθώς και να μεταβάλει το χρόνο της έναρξής της είναι το δικαστήριο της τελευταίας κατοικίας που είχε στην Ελλάδα εκείνος που εξαφανίστηκε και, αν δεν υπάρχει κατοικία, της τελευταίας διαμονής του στην Ελλάδα. Αν δεν υπάρχει ούτε διαμονή, το δικαστήριο της πρωτεύουσας του κράτους."

Our translation:

> "The court competent in law to issue and reverse a declaration of a person as absent and to change the time such absence commenced is the court of the last place of domicile of the person who disappeared in Greece and, where there is no such place of domicile, their last place of residence in Greece and, where there is no such place of residence, the court of the capital."

---

3 How to Write Clearly, https://op.europa.eu/en/publication-detail/-/publication/c2dab20c-0414-408d-87b5-dd3c6e5dd9a5

- Splitting sentences where we considered this served the purpose of clarity, e.g. in Article 2:

  "Τα πολιτικά δικαστήρια απαγορεύεται να επεμβαίνουν σε διοικητικές διαφορές ή υποθέσεις που υπάγονται σε διοικητικά δικαστήρια ή αρχές, όπως επίσης απαγορεύεται τα διοικητικά δικαστήρια ή αρχές να επεμβαίνουν σε διαφορές ή υποθέσεις του ιδιωτικού δικαίου και επιτρέπεται μόνο η εξέταση των ζητημάτων που ανακύπτουν παρεμπιπτόντως."

Our translation:

"Civil courts shall not intervene in administrative disputes or cases subject to administrative courts or authorities. Furthermore, administrative courts or authorities shall not intervene in private law disputes or cases, and may only examine issues which arise incidentally."

- Changing passive-voice syntax to active-voice where advisable, e.g. in Article 808(2):

  "Η δημοσίευση διαθήκης από προξενική αρχή γίνεται από τον πρόξενο [...]"

Our translation:

"In cases of probate granted by consular authorities, the consul shall grant probate [...]"

Vocabulary:

When in doubt and presented with a multitude of terminological choices, we opted for the most readily understandable term. An indicative —and by no means exhaustive list— is presented below, and should be understood as conventions on our part for the sake of consistency across all relevant texts, with a view to easified language and clarity:

- A court's decision on individual matters is a "ruling", whereas its final decision on the subject matter of the case is a "judgment".
- *"Αρμοδιότητα"* (competence) and *"δικαιοδοσία"* (jurisdiction) are used somewhat interchangeably in the source text, therefore we have rendered them accordingly in the translation (the latter being always "jurisdiction", but the former being "competence" at times and "jurisdiction" at others, depending on the context and intended meaning).
- *"Προσωπική κράτηση"* has been rendered as "personal detention" instead of "coercive detention".
- The term *"ελεύθερη συμβίωση"* has been rendered as "free union", as the term "concubinage" would not be considered easified. In all cases, it should be understood to mean "a romantic relationship where [different-sex] partners live together".
- Similarly, the term *"συμβίωση"* (literally "co-habitation") has been rendered as "living together", as the legal definition of the Greek term covers much more than just residing in the same house, such as the pursuit of common goals, taking an interest in the other's life, etc., i.e. literally "living" "together".
- When *"εδάφιο"* refers to a sentence within a standalone paragraph, it has been rendered as "sentence", and when it refers to an entire subparagraph among others of a paragraph, it has been rendered as "subparagraph".
- The term *"χωρισμός από τραπέζης και κοίτης"* has been rendered as "legal separation" rather than *"a mensa et thoro"* or "from bed and board", as also discussed in the Euphemism section of this Foreword.
- The term *"τυχαία κατάταξη"* means ranking without preference, rather than "random ranking".
- References to the *"ΚΠολΔ"*, i.e. the Code of Civil Procedure, are rendered as "to this Code".
- *"Κληρονομιά"* and *"κληρονομία"* are used somewhat interchangeably. Depending on context, they have been rendered either as "inheritance" or as "estate", in the sense of the pool of assets making up the estate.
- *"Δέσμευση"* has been rendered as "freezing" of accounts. We are aware of Regulation (EU) No 655/2014 concerning European Account 'Preservation' Orders, but have chosen a more familiar word.

iv) Review

The final (but by no means shortest) step in our process was to review the translation, discuss and resolve any issues that arose and highlight any problems we considered worthy of inclusion in the Issues section of this Foreword.
This stage was particularly time-consuming, consisting of several passes of revisions and corrections, and involved reaching out to experts to explicate terms and clarify processes. Considering the effort involved, we are exceptionally satisfied with the final result and are confident in its quality and utility for readers.

Issues

In previous Lex Graeca publications, we categorised the issues we identified into broad categories and provided indicative examples of each problem. Given the importance of the GCCivP both for translating and scholarship purposes, we decided to note and reproduce a broad selection of all the issues that we faced in our efforts, with the hope that they are resolved in future amendments and drive further research into the Greek text. We remain at the disposal of the Greek legislature for a full list of all the issues identified.

The six specific categories into which we classified each issue are as follows:
a) **Citation / Typographic / Capitalisation errors**
b) **Vague / Obscure language**
c) **Problematic syntax / Odd word choices**
d) **Polysemic terms/ambiguous language**
e) **Acronyms & official translations and names of entities**
f) **Elegant variation - Euphemisms**

a) Citation / Typographic / Capitalisation errors

i) Citation errors

Where citation errors were identified in the source text, we decided not to alter the Greek but to use explicitation brackets to correct the error in the translation. One such example can be found in Article 571(2) (emphasis our own):

> *"[...] Η αίτηση υποβάλλεται μέσα σε προθεσμία εξήντα (60) ημερών από την επίδοση της διάταξης και κατατίθεται στη γραμματεία του Αρείου Πάγου, η οποία συντάσσει σχετική έκθεση στο βιβλίο της παραγράφου **3**. [...]"*

Our translation (emphasis our own):

> "[...] The application shall be submitted within a deadline of 60 days from the date the order was served, and shall be filed with the registry of the Supreme Court, which shall enter a relevant report in the [special] register referred to in paragraph ***[4]***. [...]"

While paragraph 3 of Article 571 makes no reference to any register, paragraph 4 makes reference to special registers for the entry of council orders and applications, therefore we inferred that this must be a citation error and the legislator must have meant paragraph 4 rather than 3.

Another example can be found in Article 747(2) (emphasis our own):

> *"Το δικόγραφο της αίτησης ή η έκθεση πρέπει να περιέχει, εκτός από όσα ορίζονται στο άρθρο **118 ή 117**"*

This is the only instance where Articles are cited in descending rather than ascending order and is curious to say the least. We decided that, since this does not particularly impact the comprehension of the text, we would render the text in descending order as well to reflect the Greek text.

One more example can be found in Article 796(2) (emphasis our own):

> *"[...] αυτό οφείλει να συντάσσει χωρίς καθυστέρηση την **κατά την τέταρτη παράγραφο** του άρθρου 747 πράξη του [...]"*

Article 747 being cited has four separate, numbered paragraphs. It is, therefore, striking why the Greek legislator would choose to use the wording usually reserved for subparagraphs when citing paragraph 4. We have chosen to render the text in a more appropriate manner (emphasis our own):

> "[...] the court is obligated to draft its decision under ***Article 747(4)*** without delay [...]"

Another example can be found in Article 1019(3) (emphasis our own):

> *"Αν πριν από την έκδοση της κατά την παρ. 1 απόφασης, είχαν αναγγελθεί δανειστές με τα προσόντα αυτοτελούς κατάσχεσης, κατά τα άρθρ. 972 παρ. 2 εδάφ. β' και **1006 παρ. 1 εδάφ. α'**, η ανατροπή επέρχεται ως προς αυτούς μόνο αν οι ως άνω προθεσμίες είχαν συμπληρωθεί και ως προς αυτούς από τις αναγγελίες τους."*

When consulting Article 1006(1), one is somewhat surprised to see that it consists of a single sentence. Therefore, the reference to "the first subparagraph" of Article 1006(1) cannot but be an error and we have disregarded it in our translation (emphasis our own):

> "If, prior to the judgment referred to in paragraph 1 being handed down, a claim is lodged by creditors able to request attachment on their own in accordance with the second subparagraph of Article 972(2) and ***Article 1006(1)***, the reversal shall take place with regard to the foregoing only if the aforesaid deadlines had also lapsed with regard to them from the date they are lodged."

One final example can be found in Article 951(1), which cites Article 62(2) (emphasis our own):

> *"Όταν πρόκειται για ένωση προσώπων του **άρθρου 62 παρ. 2**, η αναγκαστική εκτέλεση γίνεται στην κοινή περιουσία τους."*

However, Article 62 consists of a single paragraph and two sentences. Given that the second sentence concerns groupings of persons, we believe that this is a citation error and that the legislator meant the second subparagraph of Article 62 rather than Article 62(2), and have rendered it accordingly through use of explicitation brackets (emphasis our own):

> "In cases of a grouping of persons referred to in ***[the second sentence of]*** Article 62, compulsory enforcement shall concern their joint assets."

ii) Typographic errors

Where typographic errors or conventions that do not carry over in translation were encountered in the original document, we highlighted the issue using explicitation brackets in the translation. One such example can be found in Article 559(10) (emphasis our own):

> *"αν το δικαστήριο* ***<u>παρά το νόμο</u>*** *δέχτηκε πράγματα που έχουν ουσιώδη επίδραση στην έκβαση της δίκης ως αληθινά χωρίς απόδειξη"*

The underlined phrase should have been in the dative ("παρά τω νόμω"). Our translation of thus stands as follows (emphasis our own):

> "***<u>[in breach of the law]</u>***, the court accepted things that materially impact the outcome of the proceedings as true without the taking of evidence [...]"

A final example of odd punctuation can be seen in Article 800(6), where the standard phrase "κεκλεισμένων των θυρών" (in camera) appears between quotation marks (emphasis our own):

> *"Το δικαστήριο μπορεί να διατάξει, η κύρια διαδικασία τέλεσης της υιοθεσίας να διεξάγεται* ***<u>«κεκλεισμένων των θυρών»</u>***."

This paragraph was introduced by virtue of Law 2447/1996 and, having consulted the relevant Government Gazette issue, we confirmed that this is indeed how the legislator intended for the paragraph to read. Nevertheless, we consider it odd, especially given that the exact same phrase is used frequently throughout the Code (e.g., Articles 110(2), 114(1), 256, etc.) without quotation marks. We therefore rendered it as we would expect to see it, in italics (given that we use a Latin term) but without quotation marks (emphasis our own):

> "The court may order that the main proceedings for granting adoption be held ***<u>in camera</u>***."

iii) Capitalisation errors

Greek legal texts, perhaps under the influence of the German language, are notorious for capitalising the initial letters of certain terms. While it is standard practice to capitalise terms only after having given a definition (as is often the case in contracts, with a list of terms provided at the beginning of the document to be used in capitalised form thereafter for purposes of specification and disambiguation), the GCCivP is yet another example of such unnecessary and arbitrary capitalisation.

One characteristic example is the word *"δικαστήριο"* (court). It can be found in both the lower case (e.g., Article 1), but curiously appears in the upper case in Article 423(2) and Article 632(1).

Another example is the odd capitalisation of the term *"Τεχνολογίας Πληροφορίας και Επικοινωνίας"* (information and communication technologies) in Article 468(4). While it is common practice to capitalise scientific disciplines in Greek, it would nevertheless make no sense to reproduce the capitalisation in English and it has been rendered in lower case.

One final example is the term *"κώδικας"* (code). In almost all cases, it appears in the upper case. However, in Article 809, it appears in the lower case (emphasis our own):

> *"Οι γραμματείς των ειρηνοδικείων και των προξενικών αρχών τηρούν βιβλία των διαθηκών που δημοσιεύονται και των αντιγράφων τους που οι γραμματείες αυτές φυλάγουν, καθώς και των αντιγράφων που κατατίθενται ή φυλάγονται κατά την παράγραφο 6 του άρθρου 808 του* ***<u>κώδικα</u>*** *αυτού."*

Given that it appears everywhere else in the upper case, we considered this a typographic error and have rendered it in the upper case in English through use of explicitation brackets (emphasis our own):

> "Court of the peace registrars and consular authority secretaries shall keep registers of wills granted probate and their copies kept at such registries and secretariats, as well as the copies filed or kept in accordance with Article 808(6) of this ***[C]ode***."

Lastly, while books, chapters and titles within this Code have headings, the general rule is that individual articles do not have headings. However, we observe that some of the more recent amendments have started introducing headings for articles, perhaps inspired by the valuable "article-by-article interpretations" of the Code penned by teams of lawyers over the year and which were so helpful in our process of translating this text.

b) Vague / Obscure language

The richness of the modern Greek language belies the many pitfalls and shortcomings awaiting the unseasoned translator. The GCCivP features numerous examples of vague language and obscure terminology not encountered elsewhere that required extensive discussions with Greek legal practitioners to help us threefold by explaining the term, helping us understand what the actual situation in a court of law would be, and enabling us to identify the best candidate term for translation. A few examples are given below to highlight such issues:

- In Article 495, we encountered the term *"δημόσιο ταμείο"* in the following context:

Original text (emphasis our own):

> *"Σε περίπτωση ολικής ή μερικής νίκης του καταθέσαντος, το δικαστήριο με την απόφασή του διατάσσει να επιστραφεί το παράβολο σε αυτόν, αλλιώς διατάσσει να εισαχθεί στο **δημόσιο ταμείο**."*

Our translation (emphasis our own):

> "If the person who filed the legal remedy is successful in whole or in part, the court shall order reimbursement of the procedural fee to the said person in the judgment it hands down, otherwise it shall order that it be paid to the ***tax office***."

A context-blind, word-for-word translation of the Greek term would be "public/state fund". However, this would have no meaning for either Greek or English speakers, nor would it reflect the actuality of life in Greece. Having consulted legal practitioners, we are assured that this means the tax office to which persons, both natural and legal, belong and must pay their debts and taxes.

A related issue first appears in Article 716:

Original text (emphasis our own):

> *"Σε κατάσχεση στα χέρια του οφειλέτη χρημάτων ή άλλων πραγμάτων που κατά το νόμο επιδέχονται κατάθεση, ο δικαστικός επιμελητής τα αφαιρεί και χωρίς καθυστέρηση **τα καταθέτει δημοσίως**."*

Our translation (emphasis our own):

> "In cases of attachment of monies or other things which, by law, can be deposited and which are held by the debtor, the court process server shall remove such monies or things and ***deposit them with the state*** without delay."

As above, a word-for-word translation would be "shall deposit them publicly". However, the term *"δημοσίως"* does not function as an adverb; rather, it means with the *"δημόσιο"* (Greek State), and we have therefore rendered it accordingly.

- In Article 79(1), we encountered the term "αντιποιείται" in the following context:

Original text (emphasis our own):

> *"Αν τρίτος* ***αντιποιείται*** *ολόκληρο ή ένα μέρος από το αντικείμενο της δίκης που εκκρεμεί ανάμεσα σε άλλους, έχει δικαίωμα να παρέμβει κυρίως στον πρώτο βαθμό."*

Our translation (emphasis our own):

> "If a third party ***has an interest in*** all or part the subject-matter of proceedings pending between other parties, said third party has the right to intervene primarily at first instance."

The verb *"αντιποιούμαι"* normally has a negative connotation and means to arrogate, to misappropriate or to impersonate. Indeed, most Greek speakers would be familiar with it in the context of Article 175 of the Penal Code, which provides for the crime of impersonating a state official. However, in this context, it is being used with a neutral connotation to mean "have a right to something / have an interest in something / claim something" and we have therefore rendered it accordingly.

- The term *"ατελώς"* is first encountered in Article 128(4)(b) in the following context:

Original text (emphasis our own):

> *"το αργότερο την επομένη εργάσιμη ημέρα μετά τη θυροκόλληση, αντίγραφο του εγγράφου, που συντάσσεται* ***ατελώς****, πρέπει να παραδοθεί [...]"*

Our translation (emphasis our own):

> "no later than the working day after constructive service, a copy of the document, prepared ***free of official charges***, must be delivered [...]"

The term is used in common Greek parlance as somewhat synonymous with "gratis" or "free of charge". However, there is a more nuanced meaning to the term, as it means free of any procedural fees or official state charges. There may, indeed, be other charges involved, e.g., the cost of photocopying a document, payable to a photocopy store, which is indeed borne by the person obligated to produce a photocopy.

- In Article 802(5), we encountered the term *"υπενθυμίζεται"* in the following context:

Original text (emphasis our own):

> *"Στη γνωστοποίηση* ***υπενθυμίζεται*** *οπωσδήποτε στον συμπαραστατούμενο το δικαίωμά του να ασκήσει ένδικα μέσα."*

Our translation (emphasis our own):

> "The notification must ***[inform]*** the person under legal guardianship of their right to file legal remedies."

A straightforward translation of the Greek verb would be "remind". This forms part of the legal fiction (most frequently encountered in the context of notarial instruments) that every citizen must be familiar with the law and this is just a "reminder" of the relevant provisions. However, we do not believe this fiction is clear to English speakers and have chosen a more appropriate verb, rendered in explicitation brackets.

- In Article 828, we encountered the term *"χωροφυλακής"* in the following context:

Original text (emphasis our own):

> *"[...] αν τη σφράγιση την ενεργεί συμβολαιογράφος, υπάλληλος της γραμματείας, διοικητής του σταθμού* ***χωροφυλακής*** *ή πρόεδρος της κοινότητας, την παραλαμβάνει και την παραδίδει [...]"*

Our translation (emphasis our own):

> "[...] if the sealing is being effected by a notary public, registry clerk, commander of the ***gendarmerie*** station or president of a community, the person in question shall collect it and deliver it without delay to the court of the peace [...]"

There has been no gendarmerie in Greece for 40 years, as the corps was merged with the City Police before both were abolished pursuant to Law 1481/1984. Nevertheless, we have chosen to render the Greek term accordingly and consider it an oversight on the part of the legislator.

- In Article 15, we encountered the term *"πταισματοδικείο"* in the following context:

Original text (emphasis our own):

> "οι διαφορές που αφορούν τις απαιτήσεις των δικηγόρων ή των καθολικών διαδόχων τους για τις αμοιβές και τα έξοδά τους, εφόσον πρόκειται για υπηρεσίες τους σε δίκες στο ειρηνοδικείο ή στο ***πταισματοδικείο***,"

Our translation (emphasis our own):

> "disputes concerning the claims of lawyers or their universal successors with regard to their fees and costs, in cases of services provided in proceedings conducted before the court of the peace or the ***petty offences court***;"

The concept of petty offences (and, by extension, petty offences courts) was abolished pursuant to Article 468 of the new Penal Code (Law 4619/2019). However, the legislator seems to have overlooked the Code of Civil Procedure and was remiss in changing the text. Nevertheless, we have translated the term accordingly.

- Finally, in Article 75 of the Law Introducing the Code of Civil Procedure, we encountered the abbreviation *"β.δ."* which stands for *"βασιλικό διάταγμα"* (Royal Decree) in the following context:

Original text (emphasis our own):

> *"Με* ***β.δ.*** *που εκδίδεται ύστερα από πρόταση του υπουργού δικαιοσύνης, θα κωδικοποιηθούν σε ενιαίο κείμενο οι διατάξεις του κώδικα πολιτικής δικονομίας και του εισαγωγικού του νόμου, όπως ισχύουν τώρα και όπως τροποποιούνται και συμπληρώνονται από το νόμο αυτόν και θα μεταβληθεί και η αρίθμηση των άρθρων τους."*

Our translation (emphasis our own):

> "The provisions of the Code of Civil Procedure and the Law Introducing the Code, as currently in force and as amended and supplemented by this Law, shall be codified into a single text and the numbering of their Articles shall be changed pursuant to a ***Royal Decree*** issued on a proposal from the Minister of Justice."

The monarchy was abolished pursuant to the referenda of 1973 and 1974, therefore any reference to a Royal Decree and requirement for such a Royal Decree, in the present, in order to change the numbering of Articles cannot but be a failure on the part of the legislator to update the text and keep track of important legal changes. As above, we chose to render the term accordingly despite the error.

Nevertheless, this entire (sub-)category of issues was interesting to address and is akin to insects perpetually preserved in amber.

c) Problematic syntax / Odd word choices

The GCCivP is no exception to the odd and esoteric language often found in Greek statutes. Certain examples which we had to discuss both among ourselves and with legal practitioners in order to resolve are presented below as an illustration of our methodology when such issues arose, which was quite often:

- Article 495(3) (emphasis our own):

  "Εκείνος που ασκεί το ένδικο μέσο της έφεσης, της αναίρεσης ***και*** *της αναψηλάφησης, υποχρεούται να καταθέσει παράβολο, που επισυνάπτεται στην έκθεση που συντάσσει ο γραμματέας, ως εξής (...)"*

This is an issue arising frequently both within the GCCivP (and in Articles 114(4), 539(1), 553(1) and others) and in Greek law in general, where the legislator uses the Greek conjunction "και" ("and") instead of "ή" ("or") where the meaning is definitively disjunctive. Thus, in the example presented above, the meaning is certainly not that a person has filed all four legal remedies, but that they have filed either of them. We have therefore rendered it as follows using explicitation brackets (emphasis our own):

> "The person filing the legal remedy of appeal, cassation ***[or]*** application for re-opening proceedings is obligated to pay the following procedural fee, the receipt for which shall be appended to the report prepared by the registrar (...)"

- Article 122A(9) (emphasis our own):

  "Με κοινή απόφαση των Υπουργών Δικαιοσύνης και Ψηφιακής Διακυβέρνησης, εξειδικεύονται οι όροι δημιουργίας και λειτουργίας της ηλεκτρονικής εφαρμογής για την επίδοση εγγράφων με ηλεκτρονικά μέσα και καθορίζεται κάθε αναγκαία, τεχνική ή άλλη λεπτομέρεια για την εφαρμογή ***του παρόντος****."*

The emphasised term is usually translated as "hereof" or "of this [document]". In this case, the "this" cannot but mean the Article in question and not the entire document, i.e. the entire Code. We have therefore rendered it as follows using explicitation brackets (emphasis our own):

> "A joint decision of the Minister of Justice and the Minister of Digital Governance shall specify the terms of creation and operation of the electronic application for the service of documents using electronic means and set out all necessary, technical or other details required to give effect to this ***[Article]***."

- Article 424 (emphasis our own):

  "Ένορκη βεβαίωση σε δίκη για την οποία δίδεται δεν λαμβάνεται υπόψη, ούτε για συναγωγή δικαστικών τεκμηρίων, ***όταν****: (...) δ)* ***όταν*** *παραβιάζεται το δεύτερο εδάφιο του άρθρου 421. (...)"*

This is a syntactical oversight on the part of the legislator, given that the term "όταν" ("when") is already used before the colon and therefore there is no need to repeat it in any of the items making up the list. We have omitted it from our translation:

> "An affidavit prepared for a specific set of proceedings shall not be taken into consideration [during those proceedings], not even in order to establish judicial presumptions, where: (...) d) the second sentence of Article 421 is infringed. (...)"

- Article 536(1) (emphasis our own):

  "Το δευτεροβάθμιο δικαστήριο δεν μπορεί να εκδώσει απόφαση ***επιβλαβέστερη*** *για τον εκκαλούντα χωρίς ο εφεσίβλητος να ασκήσει δική του έφεση ή αντέφεση."*

The use of the comparative is striking when there is nothing against which the judgment is being compared. In this instance, we are called upon to tease out the intended meaning and, following consultation with lawyers, we have rendered it as follows using explicitation brackets (emphasis our own):

> "The second-instance court may not hand down a judgment that places the appellant at a greater disadvantage ***[than the first-instance judgment]*** without the respondent having filed their own appeal or cross-appeal."

- Article 728(1) (emphasis our own):

  "Το δικαστήριο μπορεί να επιδικάσει προσωρινά, ως ασφαλιστικό μέτρο, εν όλω ή εν μέρει, απαιτήσεις: (...) στ) αποζημίωσης, σε περίπτωση, που ένα πρόσωπο ***θανατώνεται****, υπέρ εκείνων που το πρόσωπο αυτό κατά τον χρόνο του θανάτου του είχε από τον νόμο υποχρέωση να διατρέφει, (...)."*

The verb used is *"θανατώνω"* (to put a person/animal to death) in the active voice. Already an odd word choice, in this instance it is being used in the passive voice, i.e. "when one is put to death". Wishing to steer clear of any insinuation that this is an execution or that there was malice involved, we chose a more appropriate term in our translation (emphasis our own):

> "The court may provisionally award, as an interim measure, whether in whole or in part, claims concerning (...) f) compensation, where a person ***is killed***, payable to those whom the person who was killed was obligated to maintain at the time of their death; (...)".

- A final example of problematic syntax and odd word choice can be found in Article 965(3) (emphasis our own):

  "Ο υπερθεματιστής έχει υποχρέωση να καταβάλει στον υπάλληλο του πλειστηριασμού το πλειστηρίασμα σε μετρητά ή με μεταφορά πίστωσης στον ειδικό τραπεζικό επαγγελματικό λογαριασμό του υπαλλήλου του πλειστηριασμού ή με επιταγή έκδοσης τράπεζας που λειτουργεί νόμιμα στην Ελλάδα, ***την τρίτη εργάσιμη μέρα*** *από τον πλειστηριασμό και αμέσως μετά του παραδίδεται το κατακυρωμένο πράγμα."*

The text quite unequivocally says "on the third day" and an incautious translator might translate it as such. However, it seemed odd to us that the legislator would set so exact a date, where something has to happen exactly three days after something else, especially in a text riddled with deadlines and abstract time periods. Having consulted lawyers, we are confident that the intended meaning is "by the third day", and have rendered it as such in our translation using explicitation brackets (emphasis our own):

> "The highest bidder is obligated to pay the auction price to the auctioneer in cash or by transferring that amount into the special business account held by the auctioneer or by providing a letter of guarantee issued by a bank lawfully operating in Greece ***[by]*** the third working day after the auction, and the awarded thing shall then be immediately handed over to the highest bidder."

d) Polysemic terms

Perhaps the most egregious problem facing translators from Greek into English is the plethora of polysemic terms to convey often completely unrelated concepts. There are numerous examples we could cite, but for the purpose of saving space and illustrating the issue, we will note but four:

- *Εταιρία*
In modern Greek, this term most commonly means a commercial company. However, it may also refer to a partnership in the sense of a personal partnership, where the partners are personally liable (i.e. general and limited partnerships, etc.). Depending on the context, is has been rendered either as "partnership" (Article 27(1)) or as "company" (Article 788).

- *Δικαίωμα*
Depending on the context, this noun can mean "right", as translated in Article 9, or "fee", as translated in Article 15(12).

- *Κατάστημα*
This term most commonly means a shop or store (Article 124). However, depending on context, it may mean a military facility (Article 32), a police facility (Article 128(4)(b)) or a court building (Article 819).

- *Κατάσχεση*
This term is one of the most complicated issues we had to address. In our translation of the Code of Criminal Procedure, it was clear that this concerned "seizure" of things. However, in a civil context, we considered the term "attachment" more appropriate (Article 707). This comes with two provisos. The first concerns *"κατάσχεση εις χείρας τρίτου"*, which has been rendered as "garnishment" and is applicable when the thing to be attached is in the possession of a third party, e.g., money held in a bank account, where the third party is the bank. The second concerns ships and aircraft, where, under the international treaties and conventions signed by Greece, the appropriate term is "arrest" (Article 709).

e) Acronyms, official translations and names of entities

Whenever we encountered acronyms, e.g. *"ΦΕΚ"* (Government Gazette Issue), *"ΑΚ"* (Civil Code), *"ΠΚ"* (Penal Code), etc., we chose not to use existing or create new acronyms in English, but rather to type out the full translation of the term being abbreviated, both in order to save readers from having to consult a table of abbreviations and acronyms and for reasons of clarity. In any event, it should be noted that the number of acronyms used in the GCCivP is rather low.

A more ponderous question, which was also discussed extensively in our Foreword to the translation of the Code of Criminal Procedure, is the use of official names of entities. The most characteristic example of this issue concerns the *Άρειος Πάγος,* the Greek court of cassation and Supreme Court. According to its official website and the official English translation of the Hellenic Constitution , the full name of the court in English is the unwieldy "Supreme Civil and Criminal Court [of Greece]".
Taking a number of factors into account, such as the fact that transliterating the Ancient Greek name as "Areios Pagos" would be nonsensical to English-speaking readers not familiar with the Greek legal system, especially those presented with a contextless extract of our translation, or the fact that, as intimated above, the "official" name is unwieldy, especially when repeated often in the same sentence, we chose to abbreviate it to "Supreme Court", as a more readily recognisable term. We opted not to use the term "court of cassation" (whether or not capitalised) as that is more a descriptor of its function, which is clearly worded in Article 10 of the Code of Criminal Procedure.

The official English-language version of the Hellenic Constitution is often a point of concern for translators. In theory, it should serve as the standard for all terminology and style when translating Greek legal texts into English. In practice, however, the translational choices made give pause when considering whether or not to incorporate its terminology.

To provide a few examples:
- *"Όργανα"* is translated as "organs", whereas we have rendered the term as "bodies", considering "organs" to be too literal, inappropriate and unestablished a translation.
- *"Δικαστικοί λειτουργοί"* is ambiguously translated as both "judicial functionaries" (a term we have also used in our translation) and the generic term "magistrates".
- Similarly, *"τακτικοί δικαστές"* is translated as both "ordinary judges" and "regular judges".

Given the above (and other) issues, the obvious path was to cherry-pick terms we considered usable and disregard any inconsistencies in the official translation of the Constitution, consistently using a single term we found most appropriate in each case.

Another example concerns the name of the Ministry of Justice. At times it appears as the *Υπουργείο "Δικαιοσύνης"* (Article 5(1), Article 689), at times as *"Δικαιοσύνης, Διαφάνειας και Ανθρωπίνων Δικαιωμάτων"* (Article 53(2), Article 505(2), Article 571(1)). We consider this an oversight on the part of the legislator, failing to keep up with the ever-changing name of Greek Ministries, a separate problem unto itself, as discussed in our Foreword to the translation of the Greek Code of Private Maritime Law.

f) Elegant variation - Euphemisms

The first part of this category stands in contrast to the previous category. Whereas before we were facing a single term having several possible meanings, we now have to consider the problem of several terms being used interchangeably, often within the same Article of the Code, but with their meaning remaining unaltered. This might well be an example of elegant variation, as defined by the brothers Fowler in the early 20th century, but in legal texts, in particular, one cannot but wonder if employing this

strategy could cause more harm than good. There are numerous examples to be found in the GCCivP. Depending on context:
- *"άσκηση"*, *"κίνηση"* and *"έναρξη"* all mean initiation/institution of proceedings;
- *"διαδικασία"* and *"δίκη"* both mean trial/proceedings;
- *"πραγματικά γεγονότα"* and *"πραγματικά περιστατικά"* both mean actual facts;
- *"τίτλος παραστατικός αξίας"*, *"χρεόγραφο"* and *"αξιόγραφο"* all mean security, with the latter being the hypernym and the former two being hyponyms.

Our solution was to use a single term when faced with such synonymous usage, so as to streamline both our translation and the glossary.

The second part of this category concerns the use of euphemism throughout the GCCivP. Examples include various grammatical forms of the following terms:
- *"χωρισμός από τραπέζης και κοίτης"* ("*a mensa et thoro*", "from bed and board"): this term euphemistically refers to legal separation of spouses.
- *"προσκαλώ"* ("to invite", most commonly in Modern Greek): this verb is often used when one is "invited" by an authority to do something, e.g. in Article 686(4). Depending on context, though, this "invitation" may be a euphemism and the intended meaning is far stricter: this is a command issued that compels one to do something, e.g. summoned by the court registrar to appear in court (Article 686(4) judge to give precise testimony (Article 225), ordered by a Court of the Peace judge to attend a settlement intervention (Article 209), notified by the court to lodge a claim (Article 843) or notified by an auctioneer to pay the auction price (Article 965).
- *"αποβιώνω"* ("to pass away"); however, it should be noted that *"πεθαίνω"* ("to die") is also used — in fact, the latter appears far more frequently than the former.

Finally, a further issue that is compounded by the combination of all the above issues (a meta-issue, perhaps) is the fact that consulting or reproducing our translation of the Code without referring to the introduction for a better understanding, if not resolution, of the translational issues we faced could result in risk.

In memoriam - Kostas Beys

ΠΡΟΕΔΡΙΚΟ ΔΙΑΤΑΓΜΑ ΥΠ' ΑΡΙΘ. 503/1985
ΦΕΚ 182/Α/24-10-1985
Κώδικας Πολιτικής Δικονομίας και Εισαγωγικός του Νόμος.

Έχοντας υπόψη:
Τις διατάξεις του άρθρου 36 παρ. 2 εδαφ. γ' και 3 του Ν. 1406/83 (ΦΕΚ 182 Α') με πρόταση του Υπουργού Δικαιοσύνης, αποφασίζουμε:

Άρθρο μόνο.
Τα κείμενα του Κώδικα Πολίτικης Δικονομίας και του Εισαγωγικού του Νόμου, όπως ήδη ισχύουν και μεταγλωττίστηκαν στη δημοτική από την επιτροπή του άρθρου 36 παρ. 1 του Ν.1406/1983, έχουν ως εξής:

ΚΩΔΙΚΑΣ ΠΟΛΙΤΙΚΗΣ ΔΙΚΟΝΟΜΙΑΣ

ΠΡΩΤΟ ΒΙΒΛΙΟ
ΓΕΝΙΚΕΣ ΔΙΑΤΑΞΕΙΣ

ΚΕΦΑΛΑΙΟ Α'
Δικαιοδοσία των πολιτικών δικαστηρίων.

Άρθρο 1
Στη δικαιοδοσία των τακτικών πολιτικών δικαστηρίων ανήκουν:
α) Οι διαφορές του ιδιωτικοί δικαίου, εφόσον ο νόμος δεν τις έχει υπαγάγει σε άλλα δικαστήρια,
β) οι υποθέσεις εκούσιας δικαιοδοσίας που ο νόμος έχει υπαγάγει σ' αυτά,
γ) οι υποθέσεις δημόσιου δικαίου που ο νόμος έχει υπαγάγει σ' αυτά και
δ) οι διοικητικές διαφορές που δεν υπάγονται στη δικαιοδοσία διοικητικών δικαστηρίων.

Άρθρο 2
Τα πολιτικά δικαστήρια απαγορεύεται να επεμβαίνουν σε διοικητικές διαφορές ή υποθέσεις που υπάγονται σε διοικητικά δικαστήρια ή αρχές, όπως επίσης απαγορεύεται τα διοικητικά δικαστήρια ή αρχές να επεμβαίνουν σε διαφορές ή υποθέσεις του ιδιωτικού δικαίου και επιτρέπεται μόνο η εξέταση των ζητημάτων που ανακύπτουν παρεμπιπτόντως.

Άρθρο 3
1. Στη δικαιοδοσία των πολιτικών δικαστηρίων υπάγονται Έλληνες και αλλοδαποί, εφόσον υπάρχει αρμοδιότητα ελληνικού δικαστηρίου.
2. Εξαιρούνται από τη δικαιοδοσία των ελληνικών δικαστηρίων οι αλλοδαποί που έχουν ετεροδικία, εκτός αν πρόκειται για τις διαφορές που υπάγονται στις διατάξεις του άρθρου 29.

Άρθρο 4
Τα δικαστήρια ερευνούν την έλλειψη δικαιοδοσίας και αυτεπαγγέλτως στις περιπτώσεις των άρθρων 1 και 2 στις περιπτώσεις του άρθρου 3 την ερευνούν αυτεπαγγέλτως, αν ο εναγόμενος δεν παρίσταται στη συζήτηση ή αν πρόκειται για διαφορές που αφορούν ακίνητα που βρίσκονται στο εξωτερικό. Το δικαστήριο απορρίπτει την αγωγή ή την αίτηση, αν δεν έχει δικαιοδοσία.

Άρθρο 5
1. Αν είναι ανάγκη να γίνουν διαδικαστικές πράξεις στο εξωτερικό, τα δικαστήρια έχουν τη δυνατότητα να ζητήσουν να γίνουν είτε από τις ελληνικές προξενικές αρχές του εξωτερικού, είτε από τις αρμόδιες αλλοδαπές αρχές. Στην τελευταία περίπτωση μεσολαβεί για τη διαβίβαση της αίτησης το Υπουργείο Δικαιοσύνης, εκτός αν διεθνείς συμβάσεις ορίζουν διαφορετικά.
2. Η πράξη της αλλοδαπής αρχής είναι έγκυρη, αν έγινε σύμφωνα με τις διατάξεις του δικού της δικαίου ή αν είναι σύμφωνη προς τις διατάξεις του ελληνικού δικαίου.

PRESIDENTIAL DECREE No 503/1985
GOVERNMENT GAZETTE, SERIES I, ISSUE 182/24-10-1985
Code of Civil Procedure and Law Introducing It.

Having regard to:
The provisions of Article 36(2)(c) and (3) of Law 1406/1983 (Government Gazette, Series I, Issue 182), on a proposal from the Minister of Justice, we [hereby] decide [as follows]:

Sole article.

The texts of the Code of Civil Procedure and of the Law Introducing It, as already in force and recast in demotic Greek by the committee referred to in Article 36(1) of Law 1406/1983, read as follows:

CODE OF CIVIL PROCEDURE

BOOK I
GENERAL PROVISIONS

CHAPTER I
Jurisdiction of the civil courts

Article 1

The following fall under the jurisdiction of the ordinary civil courts:
a) private law disputes, where they are not subject by law to other courts;
b) non-contentious proceedings subject by law to ordinary civil courts;
c) public law cases subject by law to ordinary civil courts; and
d) administrative disputes not subject to the jurisdiction of administrative courts.

Article 2

Civil courts shall not intervene in administrative disputes or cases subject to administrative courts or authorities. Furthermore, administrative courts or authorities shall not intervene in private law disputes or cases, and may only examine issues which arise incidentally.

Article 3

1. Where Greek courts are competent [to try a matter], Greeks and foreign nationals are subject to the jurisdiction of the civil courts.
2. Foreign nationals enjoying immunity from jurisdiction are exempt from the jurisdiction of the Greek courts, save in cases of disputes falling under the provisions of Article 29.

Article 4

The courts shall examine even *ex officio* lack of jurisdiction in the cases of Articles 1 and 2; in the cases of Article 3, the courts shall examine lack of jurisdiction *ex officio* where the defendant does not attend the hearing or where the disputes concern immovables located abroad. Where the court does not have jurisdiction, it shall dismiss the action or application.

Article 5

1. If it is necessary for procedural steps to be taken abroad, the courts may request that they be taken either by Greek consular authorities abroad or by the competent foreign authorities. In the latter case, the Ministry of Justice shall intervene [to ensure] transmission of the request, unless otherwise required under international treaties and conventions.
2. Steps by foreign authorities are valid if taken in accordance with the provisions of the laws of that state or are consistent with the provisions of Greek law.

Άρθρο 6

1. Τα ελληνικά δικαστήρια οφείλουν να ενεργούν ορισμένες διαδικαστικές πράξεις της δικαιοδοσίας τους που τους ζητούν αλλοδαπές αρχές, εκτός αν διεθνείς συμβάσεις ορίζουν διαφορετικά ή η εκτέλεσή τους είναι αντίθετη στη δημόσια τάξη.

2. Τα ελληνικά δικαστήρια, όταν εκτελούν τις αιτήσεις αυτές, ενεργούν και αυτεπαγγέλτως, εφαρμόζοντας τις διατάξεις του ελληνικού δικαίου, εκτός αν διεθνείς συμβάσεις ορίζουν διαφορετικά.

ΚΕΦΑΛΑΙΟ Β'
Προσδιορισμός της αξίας του αντικειμένου της δίκης.

Άρθρο 7

Όταν η αρμοδιότητα των δικαστηρίων ή η διαδικασία ή το παραδεκτό ένδικου μέσου καθορίζεται από την αξία του αντικειμένου της διαφοράς, εφαρμόζονται οι ακόλουθες διατάξεις.

Άρθρο 8

Ο προσδιορισμός της αξίας του αντικειμένου της διαφοράς ανήκει στην ελεύθερη κρίση του δικαστηρίου το οποίο, αν χρειάζεται, μπορεί να διατάξει απόδειξη.

Άρθρο 9

Για την εκτίμηση του αντικειμένου της διαφοράς λαμβάνεται υπόψη το αίτημα της αγωγής. Δεν συνυπολογίζονται οι παρεπόμενες αιτήσεις για καρπούς, τόκους και έξοδα. Συνυπολογίζονται περισσότερες απαιτήσεις που επιδιώκονται με την ίδια αγωγή. Σε περίπτωση ομοδικίας, αν πρόκειται για διαιρετά δικαιώματα, λαμβάνεται υπόψη το αίτημα κάθε ενάγοντος ή το αιτούμενο από κάθε εναγόμενο, και αν οι απαιτήσεις υπάγονται στην καθ' ύλην αρμοδιότητα διαφόρων δικαστηρίων, αρμόδιο είναι το ανώτερο από αυτά. Σε περίπτωση επικουρικής σώρευσης αγωγών, η αξία του αντικειμένου της διαφοράς προσδιορίζεται από το ανώτερο ως προς την αξία αίτημα.

Άρθρο 10

Για τον υπολογισμό της αξίας λαμβάνεται υπόψη ο χρόνος που ασκείται η αγωγή.

Άρθρο 11

Η αξία του αντικειμένου της διαφοράς προσδιορίζεται

1) για τη νομή και την κυριότητα, από την αξία του πράγματος και για την ψιλή κυριότητα, από το μισό της αξίας του πράγματος,

2) για το ενέχυρο, την υποθήκη, την εγγύηση και κάθε άλλη ασφάλεια, από την αξία που έχει η ασφαλιζόμενη απαίτηση, αν όμως το πράγμα που δόθηκε για ασφάλεια έχει μικρότερη αξία, λαμβάνεται υπόψη αυτή,

3) για την πραγματική δουλεία, από την αξία που έχει η δουλεία για το δεσπόζον κτήμα, εκτός αν το ποσό, κατά το οποίο η δουλεία ελαττώνει την αξία του δουλεύοντος κτήματος, είναι μεγαλύτερο, οπότε λαμβάνεται υπόψη αυτό,

4) για την προσωπική δουλεία, από το μισό της αξίας του κτήματος,

5) για τη διανομή, από την αξία του αντικειμένου που πρέπει να διανεμηθεί,

6) για τις διαφορές που αφορούν την ύπαρξη, τη διάρκεια, την εκτέλεση ή την ακυρότητα μισθωτικής σύμβασης, από το μίσθωμα ενός έτους' αν όμως η διάρκεια της μίσθωσης είναι μικρότερη, λαμβάνεται υπόψη το ποσό του μισθώματος για το χρονικό αυτό διάστημα,

7) για τις έννομες σχέσεις, από τις οποίες πηγάζουν περιοδικές παροχές, από την αξία της ετήσιας παροχής, και ειδικότερα από το δεκαπλάσιο της ετήσιας παροχής, αν η επέλευση του γεγονότος από το οποίο εξαρτάται η παύση της παροχής είναι βέβαιη, αβέβαιος όμως ο χρόνος της, και αν οι παροχές διαρκούν απεριόριστα, από το εικοσαπλάσιο της ετήσιας παροχής. Αν οι παροχές έχουν ορισμένη διάρκεια, λαμβάνεται υπόψη το σύνολο των μελλοντικών παροχών, αλλά ποτέ πάνω από το δεκαπλάσιο της ετήσιας παροχής.

Article 6

1. Greek courts are obligated to take certain procedural steps under their jurisdiction requested by foreign authorities, unless otherwise required under international treaties and conventions or taking is contrary to public policy.
2. When executing such requests, the Greek courts shall also act *ex officio*, applying the provisions of Greek law, unless otherwise required under international treaties and conventions.

CHAPTER II
Determination of the value of the subject-matter of the proceedings

Article 7

When the competence of the courts or the procedure or admissibility of a legal remedy is determined by the value of the subject-matter of the dispute, the following provisions shall apply.

Article 8

The value of the subject-matter of the dispute shall be freely determined by the court which, if necessary, may order the taking of evidence.

Article 9

The form of order sought in the action shall be taken into account when assessing the subject-matter of the dispute. Ancillary applications on fruits, interest and costs shall not be taken into account [when determining the above value]. Several claims being pursued by means of the same action shall be taken into account [when determining the above value]. In cases of joinder, where the case concerns divisible rights, the form of order sought by each plaintiff or the form of order sought from each defendant shall be taken into account [when determining the above value], and if the claims are subject to the jurisdiction *ratione materiae* of different courts, the superior of these courts shall have jurisdiction. In cases of joinder of actions in respect of their alternative bases, the value of the subject-matter of the dispute shall be determined by the form of order sought with the highest value.

Article 10

The time the action is filed shall be taken into account when calculating the value.

Article 11

The value of the subject-matter of the dispute shall be determined[:]
1) regarding possession and ownership, by the value of the thing, while regarding bare ownership, by half the value of the thing;
2) regarding pledges, mortgages, guarantees and any other collateral, by the value of the secured claim, but if the thing provided as collateral has a lower value, that value shall be taken into account;
3) regarding real easements, by the value of the easement for the dominant tenement, unless the amount by which the easement decreases the value of the servient tenement is greater, in which case that amount shall be taken into account;
4) regarding personal easements, by half the value of the tenement;
5) regarding partition, by the value of the thing that must be partitioned;
6) regarding disputes concerning the existence, term, performance or nullity of a lease agreement, by one year's rent, but if the term of the lease is shorter, the rent amount for that period of time shall be taken into account;
7) regarding legal relationships from which periodically recurring dues arise, by the value of the annual dues and, specifically, 10 times the annual dues if the occurrence of the event on which the cessation of the dues depends is certain but the time of occurrence is uncertain, and 20 times the annual dues if the dues have an indefinite duration. If the dues have a fixed duration, all future dues shall be taken into account, but never more than 10 times the annual dues.

ΚΕΦΑΛΑΙΟ Γ'
Καθ' ύλην αρμοδιότητα

Άρθρο 12

1. Δύο μόνο βαθμοί δικαιοδοσίας των πολιτικών δικαστηρίων υπάρχουν, των οποίων την τήρηση το δικαστήριο εξετάζει και αυτεπαγγέλτως.
2. Αυτοτελής αίτηση δεν επιτρέπεται να υποβληθεί απευθείας σε δευτεροβάθμιο δικαστήριο, εκτός αν ο νόμος ορίζει διαφορετικά.

Άρθρο 13

Για την εκδίκαση των υποθέσεων που υπάγονται στα πολιτικά δικαστήρια είναι αρμόδια σε πρώτο βαθμό τα ειρηνοδικεία, τα μονομελή πρωτοδικεία και τα πολυμελή πρωτοδικεία.

Άρθρο 14

Στην αρμοδιότητα των ειρηνοδικείων υπάγονται:
1. α) όλες οι διαφορές που μπορούν να αποτιμηθούν σε χρήματα και που η αξία του αντικειμένου τους δεν υπερβαίνει το ποσό των είκοσι χιλιάδων (20.000) ευρώ,
β) όλες οι διαφορές, κύριες ή παρεπόμενες, από σύμβαση μίσθωσης, καθώς και οι διαφορές του άρθρου 601 του Αστικού Κώδικα, εφόσον σε όλες τις περιπτώσεις αυτές το συμφωνημένο μηνιαίο μίσθωμα δεν υπερβαίνει τα εξακόσια (600) ευρώ.
γ) οι διαφορές ανάμεσα στους ιδιοκτήτες ορόφων ή διαμερισμάτων από τη σχέση της οροφοκτησίας και οι διαφορές ανάμεσα στους διαχειριστές ιδιοκτησίας κατ' ορόφους και στους ιδιοκτήτες ορόφων και διαμερισμάτων που αφορούν κοινόχρηστες δαπάνες, εφόσον η αξία του αντικειμένου τους δεν υπερβαίνει το ποσό των είκοσι χιλιάδων (20.000) ευρώ.
2. Στην αρμοδιότητα των μονομελών πρωτοδικείων υπάγονται όλες οι διαφορές που μπορούν να αποτιμηθούν σε χρήματα και που η αξία του αντικειμένου τους είναι πάνω από είκοσι χιλιάδες (20.000) ευρώ, δεν υπερβαίνει όμως το ποσό των διακοσίων πενήντα χιλιάδων (250.000) ευρώ.

Άρθρο 15

Στην αρμοδιότητα των ειρηνοδικείων υπάγονται ανεξάρτητα από την αξία του αντικειμένου της διαφοράς:
1) οι διαφορές από επίμορτη αγροληψία που αφορούν την παράδοση της χρήσης του μισθίου ή την απόδοση της για οποιοδήποτε λόγο,
2) οι διαφορές που αφορούν ζημίες σε δέντρα, κλήματα, καρπούς, σπαρτά, ρίζες και γενικά φυτά, που έγιναν με παράνομη βοσκή ζώων ή με οποιοδήποτε άλλον τρόπο,
3) οι διαφορές που προκύπτουν από τις διατάξεις των άρθρων 1003 έως 1009, 1018 έως 1020 και 1023 έως 1031 του Αστικού Κώδικα, καθώς και εκείνες που αναφέρονται σε ζημίες που προκλήθηκαν από την παράβασή τους,
4) οι διαφορές που αφορούν τον καθορισμό των αποστάσεων που επιβάλλουν οι νόμοι και οι κανονισμοί ή οι επιτόπιες συνήθειες για το φύτεμα δέντρων ή φυτειών ή για την ανέγερση φραχτών ή για τη διάνοιξη τάφρων,
5) οι διαφορές που αφορούν την παρεμπόδιση της ελεύθερης χρήσης δρόμων και μονοπατιών, καθώς και τις ζημίες που προκαλούνται από την παρεμπόδιση αυτή,
6) οι διαφορές που αφορούν τη χρήση του τρεχούμενου νερού ή την παρεμπόδιση της χρήσης του,
7) οι διαφορές που προκύπτουν από τις διατάξεις των άρθρων 834 έως 839 του Αστικού Κώδικα,
8) οι διαφορές που αφορούν απαιτήσεις των προσώπων που αναφέρονται στα άρθρο 834 και 839 του Αστικού Κώδικα, ή των καθολικών διαδόχων τους, εναντίον των πελατών τους ή των καθολικών διαδόχων τους,
9) οι διαφορές από σύμβαση μεταφοράς προσώπων με οποιοδήποτε μέσο, για τις απαιτήσεις που έχουν από αυτήν οι μεταφορείς ή οι πράκτορες ή οι καθολικοί διάδοχοι τους,

CHAPTER III
Jurisdiction *ratione materiae*

Article 12

1. There are only two instances of civil courts, and the court shall also verify the instance [of each case] *ex officio*.
2. Unless otherwise provided for by law, an application cannot be filed on its own directly with a second-instance court.

Article 13

The courts of the peace, single-member courts of first instance and multi-member courts of first instance have jurisdiction to try at first instance cases subject to the civil courts.

Article 14

Courts of the peace have jurisdiction over:
1. a) all disputes that can be expressed in monetary terms and whose subject-matter has a value not exceeding the amount of 20,000 euros;
b) all disputes, whether principal or ancillary, arising from lease agreements, as well as disputes under Article 601 of the Civil Code, where the monthly rent agreed upon in all such cases does not exceed 600 euros;
c) disputes between storey or apartment owners arising from the joint ownership relationship and disputes between building managers and storey and apartment owners concerning service charges, where the value of their subject-matter does not exceed the amount of 20,000 euros.
2. Single-member courts of first instance have jurisdiction over all disputes that can be expressed in monetary terms and whose subject-matter has a value exceeding 20,000 euros but not exceeding 250,000 euros.

Article 15

Courts of the peace have jurisdiction over the following disputes, irrespective of the value of their subject-matter:
1) disputes arising from sharecropping that concern the hand-over or return of use of a leased property for any reason;
2) disputes concerning damage to trees, vineyards, fruits, crops, roots and plants in general arising through illegal grazing of animals or any other manner;
3) disputes arising from the provisions of Articles 1003 to 1009, 1018 to 1020 and 1023 to 1031 of the Civil Code, as well as disputes concerning losses arising from the infringement of those provisions;
4) disputes concerning the determination of distances imposed by laws and regulations or local customs concerning the planting of trees or crops or the erection of fences or the digging of ditches;
5) disputes concerning obstruction of free use of roads and pathways and losses arising due to such reasons;
6) disputes concerning the use of running water or obstruction of its use;
7) disputes arising from the provisions of Articles 834 to 839 of the Civil Code;
8) disputes concerning claims [brought] by the persons referred to in Articles 834 and 839 of the Civil Code or their universal successors against their guests or the universal successors of such guests;
9) disputes arising from a contract to carry persons using any means [of transport] with regard to claims under such contract [brought] by the carriers or agents or the universal successors of such carriers or agents;

10) οι διαφορές που αφορούν τις απαιτήσεις των σωματείων και των συνεταιρισμών εναντίον των μελών τους ή των καθολικών διαδόχων τους, για την εισφορά που τους οφείλουν, καθώς και οι διαφορές που αφορούν τις απαιτήσεις που έχουν εναντίον των σωματείων και των συνεταιρισμών τα μέλη ή οι καθολικοί διάδοχοι τους για χρηματική ή άλλη παροχή,
11) οι διαφορές που αφορούν τις απαιτήσεις των δικηγόρων ή των καθολικών διαδόχων τους για τις αμοιβές και τα έξοδά τους, εφόσον πρόκειται για υπηρεσίες τους σε δίκες στο ειρηνοδικείο ή στο πταισματοδικείο,
12) οι διαφορές που αφορούν δικαιώματα ή αποζημιώσεις ή έξοδα των μαρτύρων που εξετάστηκαν σε οποιοδήποτε δικαστήριο ή σε διαιτητές, καθώς και εκείνες που αφορούν τα δικαιώματα ή αποζημιώσεις ή έξοδα των διερμηνέων, των μεσεγγυούχων και των φυλάκων, με οποιοδήποτε τρόπο και αν διορίστηκαν, και των καθολικών διαδόχων όλων αυτών,
13) οι διαφορές που προκύπτουν από πώληση ζώων, εξαιτίας πραγματικών ελαττωμάτων ή έλλειψη συμφωνημένων ιδιοτήτων,
14) (Καταργήθηκε)

Άρθρο 16

Στην αρμοδιότητα των μονομελών πρωτοδικείων υπάγονται, ακόμη και αν η αξία του αντικειμένου της διαφοράς υπερβαίνει τις διακόσιες πενήντα χιλιάδες (250.000)ευρώ:
1) οι διαφορές από μίσθωση πράγματος ή άλλου προσοδοφόρου αντικειμένου ή από επίμορτη αγροληψία που δεν υπάγονται στην αρμοδιότητα των ειρηνοδικείων,
2) οι διαφορές από παροχή εξαρτημένης εργασίας ή και από οποιαδήποτε άλλη αιτία με αφορμή την εργασία αυτή, ανάμεσα στους εργαζομένους ή τους διαδόχους τους ή εκείνους στους οποίους ο νόμος δίνει δικαιώματα από την παροχή της εργασίας των πρώτων και στους εργοδότες ή τους διαδόχους τους,
3) οι διαφορές από παροχή εξαρτημένης εργασίας ή και από οποιαδήποτε άλλη αιτία, με αφορμή την εργασία αυτή, ανάμεσα σε εκείνους που εργάζονται από κοινού στον ίδιο εργοδότη,
4) οι διαφορές ανάμεσα στους επαγγελματίες ή τους βιοτέχνες, είτε μεταξύ τους είτε με τους πελάτες τους, από την παροχή εργασίας ή ειδών που κατασκεύασαν αυτοί,
5) οι διαφορές από συλλογική σύμβαση εργασίας ή από διατάξεις που εξομοιώνονται με διατάξεις συλλογικής σύμβασης, είτε ανάμεσα σε αυτούς, που δεσμεύονται από αυτές, είτε ανάμεσα σε αυτούς και τρίτους,
6) οι διαφορές ανάμεσα σε οργανισμούς κοινωνικής ασφάλισης και στους ασφαλισμένους σε αυτούς ή τους διαδόχους τους ή εκείνους που κατά το νόμο έχουν δικαιώματα από τη σχέση ασφάλισης,
7) οι διαφορές που αφορούν τις αμοιβές, τις αποζημιώσεις και τα έξοδα δικηγόρων, εκτός από εκείνες που αναφέρονται στο άρθρο 15 αρ. 11, συμβολαιογράφων, άμισθων δικαστικών επιμελητών, γιατρών, οδοντογιατρών, διπλωματούχων μαιών, κτηνιάτρων, μηχανικών και χημικών διπλωματούχων ανώτατων και ανώτερων σχολών, μεσιτών που έχουν διοριστεί νόμιμα, ή των καθολικών διαδόχων όλων αυτών, όπως και αν χαρακτηρίζεται η σχέση από την οποία προκύπτουν και ανεξάρτητα από το αν υπάρχει ή όχι συμφωνία για τον καθορισμό της αμοιβής ή για τον τρόπο της πληρωμής της,
8) οι διαφορές που αφορούν απαιτήσεις διαιτητών, εκτελεστών διαθηκών, διαχειριστών σε ιδιοκτησία κατά ορόφους ή διαχειριστών που διορίστηκαν από δικαστική αρχή, εκκαθαριστών εταιριών ή νομικών προσώπων ή κληρονομιών ή των καθολικών διαδόχων όλων αυτών για τις αμοιβές και τα έξοδά τους, ανεξάρτητα από το αν υπάρχει ή όχι συμφωνία για τον καθορισμό της αμοιβής ή για τον τρόπο της πληρωμής της,
9) οι διαφορές που αφορούν το ποσοστό ή την πληρωμή του ασφαλίστρου,
10) οι διαφορές που αφορούν τις αμοιβές, τις αποζημιώσεις και τα έξοδα των πραγματογνωμόνων, των διαιτητών πραγματογνωμόνων και των εκτιμητών, με οποιοδήποτε τρόπο και αν διορίστηκαν, ή των καθολικών διαδόχων τους,
11) οι διαφορές που αφορούν απαιτήσεις αποζημίωσης οποιοσδήποτε μορφής για ζημίες από αυτοκίνητο, ανάμεσα στους δικαιούχους ή τους διαδόχους τους και εκείνους που έχουν υποχρέωση για αποζημίωση ή τους διαδόχους τους, όπως και οι απαιτήσεις από σύμβαση ασφάλισης αυτοκινήτου, ανάμεσα στις ασφαλιστικές εταιρίες και τους ασφαλισμένους ή τους διαδόχους τους,
12) οι διαφορές από προσβολή της νομής ή κατοχής κινητών ή ακινήτων.

10) disputes concerning the claims of associations and cooperatives against their members or the universal successors of such members with regard to the dues owed to such associations and cooperatives, as well as with regard to claims by members or their universal successors with regard to monetary or other benefits against such associations and cooperatives;
11) disputes concerning the claims of lawyers or their universal successors with regard to their fees and costs, in cases of services provided in proceedings conducted before the court of the peace or the petty offences court;
12) disputes concerning the fees or compensation or costs of witnesses examined before any court or arbitrators, as well as those of interpreters, sequestrators and custodians appointed or the universal successors of all the foregoing;
13) disputes arising from the sale of animals due to actual defects or absence of properties agreed upon.
14) [Repealed]

Article 16

Single-member courts of first instance have jurisdiction over the following disputes, even if the value of their subject-matter exceeds 250,000 euros:
1) disputes arising from the leasing of a thing or other revenue-generating object or sharecropping which are not subject to the jurisdiction of the courts of the peace;
2) disputes arising from the provision of salaried labour or any other cause arising from said labour between workers or their successors or those on whom the law confers rights from the provision of the labour of the former[, on the one hand,] and their employers or their successors[, on the other];
3) disputes arising from the provision of salaried labour or any other cause arising from said labour between persons who work together for the same employer;
4) disputes between professionals or artisans, whether with each other or with their customers, with regard to the provision of labour or goods they manufactured;
5) disputes arising from a collective bargaining agreement or provisions treated as equivalent to collective bargaining agreement provisions, whether between persons bound by them or between them and third parties;
6) disputes between social security organisations and persons insured with them or their successors or those who, by law, derive rights from the insurance relationship;
7) disputes concerning the fees, compensation and costs of lawyers, save those referred to in Article 15(11), notaries public, non-stipendiary court process servers, physicians, dentists, certified midwives, veterinarians, engineers and certified chemists holding degrees from superior and higher schools, lawfully appointed real estate brokers or the universal successors of all the foregoing, irrespective of how the relationship from which they arise is characterised and regardless of whether or not there is an agreement on setting the fee or the manner of its payment;
8) disputes concerning claims [brought] by arbitrators, executors of wills, building managers or court-appointed administrators, liquidators of companies or legal persons or estates, or the universal successors of all the foregoing with regard to their fees and costs, regardless of whether or not there is an agreement on setting the fee or the manner of its payment;
9) disputes concerning the percentage or payment of insurance premiums;
10) disputes concerning the fees, compensation and costs of experts, expert arbitrators and valuers, irrespective of how they were appointed, or the universal successors of such persons;
11) disputes concerning compensation claims of any kind for damage caused by a car between the beneficiaries or their successors and those obligated to pay compensation or their successors, as well as claims arising from a car insurance policy between insurance companies and their policyholders or their successors;
12) disputes arising from infringement of possession or detentorship of movables or immovables.

Άρθρο 17

Στην αρμοδιότητα των μονομελών πρωτοδικείων υπάγονται πάντοτε:
1) οι διαφορές που αφορούν το διαζύγιο, την ακύρωση του γάμου, την αναγνώριση της ύπαρξης ή της ανυπαρξίας του γάμου, τις σχέσεις των συζύγων κατά τη διάρκεια του γάμου, οι οποίες πηγάζουν από αυτόν, καθώς και εκείνες του άρθρου 592 αρ. 2.
2) οι διαφορές που αναφέρονται στο άρθρο 592 αρ. 3, καθώς και εκείνες που αφορούν τη ρύθμιση της οικογενειακής στέγης και την κατανομή των κινητών μεταξύ των συζύγων σε περίπτωση διακοπής της συμβίωσης,
3) με την επιφύλαξη του άρθρου 14 παράγραφος 1 περίπτωση γ', οι διαφορές ανάμεσα στους ιδιοκτήτες ορόφων ή διαμερισμάτων από τη σχέση της οροφοκτησίας, καθώς και οι διαφορές ανάμεσα στους διαχειριστές ιδιοκτησίας κατ' ορόφους και στους ιδιοκτήτες ορόφων και διαμερισμάτων και
4) οι διαφορές που αφορούν την ακύρωση αποφάσεων της γενικής συνέλευσης σωματείων ή συνεταιρισμών.

Άρθρο 17Α

Στην αρμοδιότητα των μονομελών πρωτοδικείων υπάγονται και οι εφέσεις κατά των αποφάσεων των ειρηνοδικείων της περιφέρειάς τους. Στην περίπτωση αυτή τα μονομελή πρωτοδικεία συγκροτούνται από πρόεδρο πρωτοδικών ή έναν από τους αρχαιότερους κατά διορισμό πρωτοδίκες που ορίζεται με πράξη του προϊσταμένου ή του εκτελούντος χρέη προϊσταμένου προέδρου πρωτοδικών.

Άρθρο 18

Στην αρμοδιότητα των πολυμελών πρωτοδικείων υπάγονται όλες οι διαφορές, για τις οποίες δεν είναι αρμόδια τα ειρηνοδικεία ή τα μονομελή πρωτοδικεία.

Άρθρο 19

Στην αρμοδιότητα των μονομελών εφετείων υπάγονται οι εφέσεις κατά των αποφάσεων των μονομελών πρωτοδικείων και στην αρμοδιότητα των τριμελών εφετείων υπάγονται οι εφέσεις κατά των αποφάσεων των πολυμελών πρωτοδικείων της περιφέρειάς τους.

Άρθρο 20

1. Στην αρμοδιότητα του Αρείου Πάγου υπάγονται οι αναιρέσεις κατά αποφάσεων οποιουδήποτε πολιτικού δικαστηρίου.
2. Στην αρμοδιότητα του Αρείου Πάγου ανήκουν επίσης, εφόσον δεν έχουν οριστεί άλλα δικαστήρια,
α) οι αιτήσεις για παραπομπή, σε περίπτωση εξαίρεσης των δικαστών πολυμελούς πολιτικού δικαστηρίου,
β) οι αιτήσεις για καθορισμό δικαστηρίου, αν δεν υπάρχει πια το δικαστήριο που είχε εκδώσει την απόφαση που προσβλήθηκε με ένδικο μέσο.

Άρθρο 20Α

1. Οποιοδήποτε ένδικο βοήθημα ή μέσο που ασκήθηκε ενώπιον οποιουδήποτε πολιτικού δικαστηρίου μπορεί να εισαχθεί στην πλήρη ολομέλεια του Αρείου Πάγου με απλή πράξη τριμελούς επιτροπής, που αποτελείται από τον Πρόεδρό του, τον αρχαιότερο Αντιπρόεδρο και τον Πρόεδρο του αρμόδιου καθ' ύλην Τμήματος, ύστερα από αίτημα ενός εκ των διαδίκων που κατατίθεται ενώπιον της η ύστερα από προδικαστικό ερώτημα που υποβάλλεται από το δικαστήριο της ουσίας, με απόφαση που δεν υπόκειται σε ένδικα μέσα, όταν με αυτό τίθεται νέο δυσχερές ερμηνευτικό νομικό ζήτημα γενικότερου ενδιαφέροντος που έχει συνέπειες για ευρύτερο κύκλο προσώπων. Τα ως άνω ένδικα βοηθήματα ή μέσα μπορούν να εισαχθούν και απευθείας στην πλήρη ολομέλεια του Αρείου Πάγου με απλή πράξη του Εισαγγελέα του Αρείου Πάγου. Η πλήρης ολομέλεια του Αρείου Πάγου εκδίδει την απόφασή της σε προθεσμία έξι (6) μηνών. Η ως άνω διαδικασία δεν εφαρμόζεται όταν εκκρεμεί αναίρεση για το νομικό αυτό ζήτημα.

Article 17

Single-member courts of first instance always have jurisdiction over the following disputes:
1) disputes concerning divorce, annulment of marriage, recognition of existence or non-existence of marriage, relations between spouses during the marriage arising from the marriage, as well as those referred to in Article 592(2);
2) the disputes referred to in Article 592(3), as well as disputes concerning allocation of the family residence and of movables to each spouse if the spouses cease living together [in wedlock];
3) without prejudice to Article 14(1)(c), disputes between storey or apartment owners arising from the joint ownership relationship, as well as disputes between building managers and storey and apartment owners; and
4) disputes concerning the annulment of decisions made by the general meetings of associations or cooperatives.

Article 17A

Single-member courts of first instance also have jurisdiction over appeals against judgments handed down by the courts of the peace in their district. In this case, the single-member court of first instance shall be composed of a presiding judge of the court of first instance or one of the most senior judges of the court of first instance in order of appointment, designated in a decision issued by the head or the acting head presiding judge of the court of first instance.

Article 18

Multi-member courts of first instance have jurisdiction over all disputes not falling under the jurisdiction of courts of the peace or single-member courts of first instance.

Article 19

Single-member courts of appeal have jurisdiction over appeals [filed] against judgments handed down by the single-member courts of first instance; [however] three-member courts of appeal have jurisdiction over appeals [filed] against judgments handed down by the multi-member courts of first instance in their district.

Article 20

1. The Supreme Court has jurisdiction over applications for cassation [filed] against judgments handed down by any civil court.
2. Where no other courts have been designated, the Supreme Court also has jurisdiction over
a) applications for remittal in cases of exemption of the judges of a multi-member civil court;
b) applications for the appointment of a court, if the court that had handed down the judgment being contested by legal remedies no longer exists.

Article 20A

1. Any form of relief or legal remedy filed with any civil court may be brought before the Supreme Court sitting in full court by means of a simple decision issued by a three-member committee consisting of the President [of the Supreme Court], its most senior Vice-President and the President of the Chamber with jurisdiction *ratione materiae*, following a request filed by one of the parties in the proceedings before the committee or following a request for a preliminary ruling filed by the trial court, by means of a judgment not subject to legal remedies when it raises a new, complex legal interpretation issue of general interest with ramifications for a wider circle of persons. The above forms of relief or legal remedies may also be brought before the Supreme Court sitting in full court by means of a simple decision issued by the Supreme Court Public Prosecutor. The Supreme Court sitting in full court shall hand down a judgment within a deadline of six months. The above procedure does not apply when an application for cassation regarding this legal issue is pending.

2. Τα αιτήματα των διαδίκων υπογράφονται επί ποινή απαραδέκτου από δικηγόρο και συνοδεύονται από παράβολο τριακοσίων (300) ευρώ, το οποίο καταπίπτει υπέρ του Δημοσίου σε περίπτωση απόρριψης του αιτήματος. Το ύψος του ποσού μπορεί να αναπροσαρμόζεται με κοινή απόφαση των Υπουργών Οικονομικών και Δικαιοσύνης. Πριν από την έκδοση της πράξης, η Επιτροπή καλεί όλους τους διαδίκους, να εμφανισθούν ενώπιόν της και να εκθέσουν τις απόψεις τους αυτοπροσώπως ή με υπόμνημα, που κατατίθεται σε οριζόμενη από αυτήν προθεσμία.
3. Η πράξη της Επιτροπής ή του Εισαγγελέα του Αρείου Πάγου δημοσιεύεται σε δύο (2) ημερήσιες εφημερίδες των Αθηνών και συνεπάγεται την αναστολή της εκδίκασης των εκκρεμών υποθέσεων, στις οποίες τίθεται το ίδιο ζήτημα, με απόφαση των κατά περίπτωση επιλαμβανομένων δικαστηρίων της ουσίας. Η αναστολή δεν καταλαμβάνει την προσωρινή δικαστική προστασία.
4. Στη δίκη ενώπιον της πλήρους ολομέλειας του Αρείου Πάγου μπορεί να παρέμβει κάθε διάδικος σε εκκρεμή δίκη, στην οποία τίθεται το ίδιο ως άνω ζήτημα, και να προβάλει τους ισχυρισμούς του σχετικά με το ζήτημα αυτό. Για την εν λόγω παρέμβαση δεν καταλογίζεται δικαστική δαπάνη, η δε μη άσκησή της δεν δημιουργεί δικαίωμα άσκησης ανακοπής ή τριτανακοπής.
5. Μετά από την επίλυση του ζητήματος, η πλήρης ολομέλεια του Αρείου Πάγου παραπέμπει το ένδικο μέσο ή βοήθημα στο αρμόδιο δικαστήριο. Η απόφαση της πλήρους ολομέλειας του Αρείου Πάγου δεσμεύει τους διαδίκους της ενώπιόν του δίκης, στους οποίους περιλαμβάνονται και οι παρεμβάντες.
6. Μετά από την επίλυση του ζητήματος κατά την παρ. 1, οι υποθέσεις, των οποίων είχε ανασταλεί η εκδίκαση, επαναφέρονται για συζήτηση σε νέα δικάσιμο με κλήση, η οποία κατατίθεται με επιμέλεια οποιουδήποτε διαδίκου στη γραμματεία του αρμόδιου δικαστηρίου.

Άρθρο 21

Αρμόδιο να δικάσει την ανακοπή ερημοδικίας ή την αναψηλάφηση είναι το δικαστήριο που έχει εκδώσει την προσβαλλόμενη απόφαση.

ΚΕΦΑΛΑΙΟ Δ'
Κατά τόπον αρμοδιότητα

Άρθρο 22

Κατά τόπον αρμόδιο είναι το δικαστήριο, στην περιφέρεια του οποίου, έχει την κατοικία του ο εναγόμενος, εκτός αν ο νόμος ορίζει διαφορετικά.

Άρθρο 23

1. Αν ο εναγόμενος δεν έχει κατοικία ούτε στην Ελλάδα ούτε στο εξωτερικό, αρμόδιο δικαστήριο είναι εκείνο στην περιφέρεια του οποίου έχει τη διαμονή του. Αν ο τόπος όπου διαμένει δεν είναι γνωστός, αρμόδιο είναι το δικαστήριο, στην περιφέρεια του οποίου είχε την τελευταία κατοικία του στην Ελλάδα και αν δεν είχε κατοικία, την τελευταία διαμονή του.
2. Αν ο εναγόμενος έχει ειδική κατοικία, είναι αρμόδιο και το δικαστήριο, στην περιφέρεια του οποίου βρίσκεται αυτή.

Άρθρο 24

Έλληνες που έχουν προνόμιο ετεροδικίας, καθώς και οι κρατικοί υπάλληλοι που είναι διορισμένοι στο εξωτερικό, υπάγονται στην αρμοδιότητα του δικαστηρίου στην περιφέρεια του οποίου κατοικούσαν πριν από την αποστολή τους, και αν πριν από την αποστολή τους δεν είχαν κατοικία, στα δικαστήρια της πρωτεύουσας του κράτους. Το ίδιο ισχύει για τη σύζυγο και τα τέκνα τους.

2. The motions of the parties in the proceedings shall be signed by a lawyer, on penalty of inadmissibility, and accompanied by a procedural fee [receipt] of 300 euros, which shall be forfeited to the Greek State if the motion is dismissed. The fee amount may be adjusted pursuant to a joint decision issued by the Minister of Finance and the Minister of Justice. Prior to issuing its decision, the committee shall summon all the parties in the proceedings to appear before it and present their views in person or by means of a memorandum filed within the deadline set by the committee.
3. The decision issued by the committee or the Supreme Court Public Prosecutor shall be published in two daily newspapers circulating in Athens and shall result in the stay of the hearing of the pending cases in which the same issue has arisen, [effected] by means of a ruling of the relevant trial court. The stay shall not extend to interim relief.
4. During proceedings before the Supreme Court sitting in full court, any party in pending proceedings where the same aforesaid issue has arisen may intervene and put forth their arguments regarding the issue in question. No court costs shall be ordered for the intervention in question, while any failure to file such intervention shall not give rise to a right to file an opposition or institute third-party proceedings.
5. After the issue has been resolved, the Supreme Court sitting in full court shall remit the legal remedy or form of relief to the competent court. The ruling of the Supreme Court sitting in full court shall be binding on the parties in the proceedings before it, including intervenors.
6. After the issue referred to in paragraph 1 has been resolved, the case whose hearing had been stayed shall resume on a new hearing date by means of a summons, filed by any party in the proceedings with the registry of the competent court.

Article 21

The court that had handed down the judgment being contested shall be competent to try the opposition against a default judgment or application for re-opening proceedings.

CHAPTER IV
Jurisdiction *ratione loci*

Article 22

Unless otherwise provided for in law, the court in whose district the defendant has their place of domicile has jurisdiction *ratione loci*.

Article 23

1. If the defendant has no place of domicile in Greece or abroad, the court in whose district the defendant has their place of residence has jurisdiction. If the place of residence of the defendant is unknown, the court in whose district the defendant had their last place of domicile in Greece, and, absent such, their last place of residence, has jurisdiction.
2. If the defendant has a special place of domicile, the court in whose district that place of domicile is located has jurisdiction.

Article 24

Greek citizens who enjoy the privilege of immunity from jurisdiction, as well as state officials appointed abroad, are subject to the jurisdiction of the court in whose district they were domiciled prior to being dispatched abroad, and, absent such, the courts of the capital of the state. The foregoing also apply to the spouse and children of such officials.

Άρθρο 25

1. Το δημόσιο υπάγεται στην αρμοδιότητα του δικαστηρίου, στην περιφέρεια του οποίου είναι η έδρα της αρχής η οποία, σύμφωνα με το νόμο, το εκπροσωπεί στις δίκες που έχει κάθε φορά.

2. Τα μη φυσικά πρόσωπα που έχουν ικανότητα να είναι διάδικοι, υπάγονται στην αρμοδιότητα του δικαστηρίου στην περιφέρεια του οποίου βρίσκεται η έδρα ή υποκατάστημά τους, εφόσον πρόκειται για διαφορές που αφορούν την εκμετάλλευσή του.

Άρθρο 26

Δικηγόροι και συμβολαιογράφοι υπάγονται στην αρμοδιότητα του δικαστηρίου, στην περιφέρεια του οποίου ασκούν τα καθήκοντά τους.

Άρθρο 27

1. Διαφορές από την εταιρική σχέση ανάμεσα σε μια εταιρία και στους εταίρους της ή ανάμεσα στους εταίρους μεταξύ τους υπάγονται στην αποκλειστική αρμοδιότητα του δικαστηρίου, στην περιφέρεια του οποίου η εταιρία έχει την έδρα της.

2. Στην αρμοδιότητα του δικαστηρίου που ορίζει η παρ. 1 υπάγονται και οι διαφορές που δημιουργούνται μετά τη διάλυση και την εκκαθάριση της εταιρίας και αφορούν τη διανομή της εταιρικής περιουσίας, εφόσον η αγωγή ασκηθεί μέσα σε δύο χρόνια από την περάτωση της διανομής.

Άρθρο 28

Διαφορές που αφορούν τη διαχείριση, η οποία διεξάγεται ύστερα από εντολή δικαστηρίου, υπάγονται στην αποκλειστική αρμοδιότητα του δικαστηρίου που έδωσε την εντολή και αν την εντολή την έδωσε άλλη δικαστική αρχή, στην αρμοδιότητα του δικαστηρίου, στην περιφέρεια του οποίου έχει την έδρα της η αρχή αυτή.

Άρθρο 29

1. Διαφορές που αφορούν εμπράγματα δικαιώματα επάνω σε ακίνητα, τη νομή ή την κατοχή τους, διαίρεση κοινού, κανονισμό ορίων, απαιτήσεις κατά οποιουδήποτε διακατόχου, αποζημίωση για αναγκαστική απαλλοτρίωση, καθώς και διαφορές από μίσθωση ακινήτου ή δικαιώματος που συνδέεται με την εκμετάλλευσή του ή από επίμορτη αγροληψία, υπάγονται στην αποκλειστική αρμοδιότητα του δικαστηρίου, στην περιφέρεια του οποίου βρίσκεται το ακίνητο.

2. Αν το ακίνητο βρίσκεται στις περιφέρειες περισσότερων δικαστηρίων, ο ενάγων έχει το δικαίωμα επιλογής.

Άρθρο 30

1. Διαφορές που αφορούν την αναγνώριση κληρονομικού δικαιώματος ή διανομή κληρονομίας, απαιτήσεις του κληρονόμου εναντίον του νομέα ή του κατόχου της κληρονομίας, απαιτήσεις από κληροδοτήματα ή απαιτήσεις από άλλες διατάξεις αιτία θανάτου ή απαιτήσεις από νόμιμη μοίρα ή απαιτήσεις εναντίον εκτελεστών διαθήκης για την εκτέλεση των διατάξεών της, υπάγονται στην αποκλειστική αρμοδιότητα του δικαστηρίου, στην περιφέρεια του οποίου ο κληρονομούμενος, όταν πέθανε, είχε την κατοικία του, και αν δεν είχε κατοικία τη διαμονή του.

2. Απαιτήσεις μεταξύ των κληρονόμων έως τη διανομή της κληρονομιάς, απαιτήσεις τρίτων εξαιτίας χρεών του κληρονομουμένου ή της κληρονομίας, καθώς και εμπράγματες απαιτήσεις για κινητά που δεν περιλαμβάνονται στην παράγραφο 1 υπάγονται, για δύο χρόνια από το θάνατο του κληρονομουμένου, στην αποκλειστική αρμοδιότητα του δικαστηρίου, στην περιφέρεια του οποίου είχε αυτός την κατοικία του και, αν δεν είχε κατοικία, τη διαμονή του.

Article 25

1. The Greek State is subject to the jurisdiction of the court in whose district the authority which, by law, represents the Greek State in proceedings from time to time is seated.
2. Non-natural persons who have capacity to be parties in legal proceedings are, where disputes concern their operation, subject to the jurisdiction of the court in whose district their registered offices or branch is located.

Article 26

Lawyers and notaries public are subject to the jurisdiction of the court in whose district they perform their duties.

Article 27

1. Disputes arising from the relationship between a partnership and its partners, or among the partners themselves, are subject to the exclusive jurisdiction of the court in whose district the partnership is seated.
2. The court referred to in paragraph 1 also has jurisdiction over disputes which arise after the partnership has been wound up and liquidated and concern the distribution of the assets of the partnership, where the action is filed within two years from the date said distribution was completed.

Article 28

Disputes concerning court-ordered administration are subject to the exclusive jurisdiction of the court that issued the order, and where a different judicial authority issued the order, to the jurisdiction of the court in whose district said authority has its seat.

Article 29

1. Disputes concerning rights *in rem* in immovables, possession or detentorship of immovables, division of a jointly owned immovable, determination of boundaries, claims against any holder of possession, compensation in cases of expropriation, as well as disputes arising from the lease of an immovable or right relating to its operation or from sharecropping are subject to the exclusive jurisdiction of the court in whose district the immovable is located.
2. If the immovable is located in the districts of several courts, the plaintiff has the right of choice.

Article 30

1. Disputes concerning the recognition of an inheritance right or sharing-out of an estate, claims [brought] by an heir against the possessor or detentor of an estate, claims arising from bequests or claims under other provisions *mortis causa* or claims due to reserved portion [of an estate] or claims against executors of a will regarding the execution of its dispositions are subject to the exclusive jurisdiction of the court in whose district the deceased had their place of domicile and, absent such, their place of residence at the time of their death.
2. Claims between heirs until the estate is shared out, claims [brought] by third parties due to debts of the deceased or the estate, as well as claims *in rem* concerning movables not included in paragraph 1 are subject, for two years from the date the deceased person died, to the exclusive jurisdiction of the court in whose district the deceased had their place of domicile and, absent such, their place of residence at the time of their death.

Άρθρο 31

1. Δίκες που έχουν μεταξύ τους σχέση κυρίου και παρεπομένου, ιδίως οι παρεμπίπτουσες αγωγές, οι αγωγές για εγγύηση, οι παρεμβάσεις, και άλλες όμοιες υπάγονται στην αποκλειστική αρμοδιότητα του δικαστηρίου της κύριας δίκης.

2. Στην αρμοδιότητα του πολυμελούς πρωτοδικείου που δικάζει την κύρια δίκη υπάγονται οι παρεπόμενες υποθέσεις της αρμοδιότητας του μονομελούς και του ειρηνοδικείου, και στην αρμοδιότητα του μονομελούς Πρωτοδικείου που δικάζει την κύρια δίκη υπάγονται οι παρεπόμενες υποθέσεις της αρμοδιότητας του ειρηνοδικείου.

3. Αν πρόκειται για κύριες δίκες που είναι συναφείς μεταξύ τους, έχει αποκλειστική αρμοδιότητα το δικαστήριο που είχε επιληφθεί πρώτο, και εφαρμόζεται ανάλογα η διάταξη της παραγράφου 2.

Άρθρο 32

Δημόσιοι υπάλληλοι υπάγονται και στην αρμοδιότητα του δικαστηρίου, στην περιφέρεια του οποίου ασκούν τα καθήκοντά τους. οι στρατιωτικοί υπάγονται και στην αρμοδιότητα του δικαστηρίου, στην περιφέρεια του οποίου βρίσκεται η μονάδα, το κατάστημα ή η υπηρεσία όπου υπηρετούν.

Άρθρο 33

Διαφορές που αφορούν την ύπαρξη ή το κύρος δικαιοπραξίας εν ζωή, και όλα τα δικαιώματα που πηγάζουν από αυτήν, μπορούν να εισαχθούν και στο δικαστήριο, στην περιφέρεια του οποίου βρίσκεται ο τόπος όπου καταρτίστηκε η δικαιοπραξία ή όπου πρέπει να εκπληρωθεί η παροχή. Στο ίδιο δικαστήριο μπορούν να εισαχθούν και οι διαφορές για αρνητικό διαφέρον, καθώς και για αποζημίωση εξαιτίας πταίσματος κατά τις διαπραγματεύσεις.

Άρθρο 34

Οι ανταγωγές μπορούν να εισαχθούν στο δικαστήριο όπου εκκρεμεί η αγωγή, εφόσον υπάγονται στην καθ' ύλην αρμοδιότητα του ίδιου ή κατώτερου δικαστηρίου.

Άρθρο 35

Διαφορές από αδικοπραξία μπορούν να εισαχθούν και στο δικαστήριο του τόπου όπου συνέβη το ζημιογόνο γεγονός ή επίκειται η επέλευσή του.

Άρθρο 36

Διαφορές από διαχείριση που έγινε χωρίς δικαστική εντολή μπορούν να εισαχθούν και στο δικαστήριο στην περιφέρεια του οποίου έγινε η διαχείριση.

Άρθρο 37

1. Όταν ενάγονται περισσότερα πρόσωπα που συνδέονται με το δεσμό της ομοδικίας, αρμόδιο είναι το δικαστήριο στην περιφέρεια του οποίου έχει την κατοικία του, και αν δεν έχει κατοικία, τη διαμονή του, οποιοσδήποτε από τους ομοδίκους.

2. Διαφορές ανάμεσα στα ίδια πρόσωπα, οι οποίες έχουν την ίδια βάση και αφορούν εμπράγματα δικαιώματα επάνω σε ακίνητα που βρίσκονται στις περιφέρειες διαφορετικών δικαστηρίων, μπορούν να εισαχθούν σε ένα από τα δικαστήρια αυτά.

Άρθρο 38

Απαιτήσεις εναντίον προσώπων που έχουν ικανότητα δικαστικής παράστασης και, εξαιτίας ειδικών συνθηκών, έχουν σε ορισμένο τόπο διαμονή με μακρότερη διάρκεια, όπως είναι ιδίως οι υπάλληλοι, οι υπηρέτες, οι σπουδαστές, οι μαθητές, εφόσον το αντικείμενό τους είναι περιουσιακό, μπορούν να εισαχθούν και στο δικαστήριο, στην περιφέρεια του οποίου βρίσκεται ο τόπος διαμονής τους.

Article 31

1. Proceedings [predicated on each other] and, in particular, incidental actions, actions concerning guarantees, interventions and others treated as such are subject to the exclusive jurisdiction of the court of the main proceedings.
2. The multi-member court of first instance trying the main proceedings has jurisdiction over ancillary matters falling under the jurisdiction of the single-member [court of first instance] and the court of the peace, while the single-member court of first instance trying the main proceedings has jurisdiction over ancillary matters falling under the jurisdiction of the court of the peace.
3. Where there are related main proceedings, the court first seised of the matter has exclusive jurisdiction and the provisions of paragraph 2 apply *mutatis mutandis*.

Article 32

Civil servants are also subject to the jurisdiction of the court in whose district they perform their duties; military personnel are also subject to the jurisdiction of the court in whose district the unit, facility or service where they serve is located.

Article 33

Disputes concerning the existence or validity of legal transactions *inter vivos* and all rights deriving from such transactions may also be brought before the court in whose district the place where the legal transaction was entered into or where the obligation must be performed is located. Disputes concerning reliance damages, as well as disputes concerning compensation due to *culpa in contrahendo*, may be brought before the same court.

Article 34

Cross-actions may be brought before the court before which the action is pending provided they are subject to the jurisdiction *ratione materiae* of the same or a lower court.

Article 35

Tortious disputes may also be brought before the court of the place where the loss event occurred or its occurrence is imminent.

Article 36

Disputes arising due to non-court-ordered administration may also be brought before the court in whose district such administration took place.

Article 37

1. Where there are several persons linked by joinder, the court in whose district any of the joined parties has their place of domicile and, absent such, their place of residence has jurisdiction.
2. Disputes between the same persons which have the same basis and concern rights *in rem* in immovables located in the districts of different courts may be brought before any one of those courts.

Article 38

Claims [brought] against persons who have capacity to appear before the courts and, due to special circumstances, have their place of residence in a specific location for a prolonged period of time, such as, in particular, employees, servants, students, pupils, where such claims concern property, may also be brought before the court in whose district the said persons have their place of residence.

Άρθρο 39

Γαμικές διαφορές μπορούν να εισαχθούν και στο δικαστήριο, στην περιφέρεια του οποίου βρίσκεται ο τόπος της τελευταίας κοινής διαμονής των συζύγων.

Άρθρο 39Α
Ειδική δωσιδικία διατροφών

Διαφορές που αφορούν αξιώσεις διατροφής μπορούν να εισαχθούν και στο δικαστήριο του τόπου όπου έχει την κατοικία του ή τη διαμονή του ο δικαιούχος της διατροφής.

Άρθρο 40

1. Δίκες εναντίον προσώπων που δεν έχουν κατοικία στην Ελλάδα, εφόσον το αντικείμενό τους είναι περιουσιακό, μπορούν να εισαχθούν και στο δικαστήριο, στην περιφέρεια του οποίου υπάρχει περιουσία του εναγομένου ή βρίσκεται το επίδικο αντικείμενο.
2. Αν η περιουσία συνίσταται σε χρηματικές απαιτήσεις του εναγομένου εναντίον τρίτου, θεωρείται πως η περιουσία βρίσκεται στον τόπο της κατοικίας του τρίτου.

Άρθρο 40Α

[Καταργήθηκε]

Άρθρο 41

Ανάμεσα σε περισσότερα αρμόδια δικαστήρια, ο ενάγων έχει το δικαίωμα επιλογής· η προτεραιότητα μεταξύ τους κανονίζεται από το χρόνο που ασκήθηκε η αγωγή.

ΚΕΦΑΛΑΙΟ Ε'
Παρέκτασις της αρμοδιότητος.

Άρθρο 42

1. Πρωτοβάθμιο τακτικό δικαστήριο που δεν είναι κατά τόπον αρμόδιο μπορεί, με ρητή ή σιωπηρή συμφωνία των διαδίκων, να γίνει αρμόδιο, εκτός αν πρόκειται για διαφορές που δεν έχουν περιουσιακό αντικείμενο. Η συμφωνία πρέπει να είναι ρητή, όταν πρόκειται για διαφορές για τις οποίες ισχύει αποκλειστική αρμοδιότητα.
2. Θεωρείται πως υπάρχει σιωπηρή συμφωνία, αν ο εναγόμενος παρίσταται στο ακροατήριο στη συζήτηση και δεν προτείνει έγκαιρα την ένσταση αναρμοδιότητας.

Άρθρο 43

Η συμφωνία των διαδίκων με την οποία τακτικό δικαστήριο γίνεται αρμόδιο για μελλοντικές διαφορές είναι έγκυρη μόνο αν είναι έγγραφη και αναφέρεται σε ορισμένη έννομη σχέση, από την οποία θα προέλθουν οι διαφορές.

Άρθρο 44

Οι συμφωνίες κατά τα άρθρα 42 και 43 δημιουργούν αποκλειστική αρμοδιότητα, εκτός αν από την ίδια τη συμφωνία προκύπτει το αντίθετο.

ΚΕΦΑΛΑΙΟ ΣΤ'
Έρευνα της αρμοδιότητος.

Άρθρο 45

Το δικαστήριο που ήταν καθ' ύλην και κατά τόπον αρμόδιο όταν ασκήθηκε η αγωγή, είναι αρμόδιο έως την περάτωση της δίκης, ακόμη και αν, στη διάρκειά της, μεταβληθούν τα πραγματικά περιστατικά που καθορίζουν την αρμοδιότητα.

Article 39

Matrimonial disputes may also be brought before the court in whose district the spouses had their last joint residence.

Article 39A
Special jurisdiction in cases of maintenance

Disputes concerning maintenance claims may also be brought before the court where the person entitled to maintenance has their place of domicile or residence.

Article 40

1. Proceedings concerning property against persons who do not have their place of domicile in Greece may also be brought before the court in whose district the defendant has assets or the thing at issue is located.
2. If the asset consists of monetary claims of the defendant against a third party, the asset shall be deemed
to be located where the third party has their place of domicile.

Article 40A

[Repealed]

Article 41

Where there are several competent courts, the plaintiff has the right of choice; priority between said courts shall be set in accordance with the time the action was filed.

CHAPTER V
Prorogation of jurisdiction

Article 42

1. An ordinary court of first instance that does not have jurisdiction *ratione loci* may, pursuant to an express or tacit agreement between the parties in the proceedings, acquire jurisdiction, save in cases of disputes that do not concern property. This agreement must be express in cases of disputes where exclusive jurisdiction applies.
2. A tacit agreement shall be deemed to exist if the defendant appears in court to attend the hearing and does not raise a plea of lack of jurisdiction in good time.

Article 43

An agreement between the parties in the proceedings whereby an ordinary court acquires jurisdiction over future disputes shall be valid only if it is drawn up in writing and refers to a specific legal relationship from which the disputes will arise.

Article 44

Unless otherwise stipulated therein, the agreements referred to in Articles 42 and 43 establish exclusive jurisdiction.

CHAPTER VI
Examination of jurisdiction

Article 45

The court which had jurisdiction *ratione materiae* and *ratione loci* when the action was filed has jurisdiction until the conclusion of the proceedings, even if the actual facts determining jurisdiction change during the course of the proceedings.

Άρθρο 46

Αν το δικαστήριο δεν είναι καθ' ύλην ή κατά τόπον αρμόδιο, αποφαίνεται γι' αυτό αυτεπαγγέλτως και προσδιορίζει το αρμόδιο δικαστήριο, στο οποίο παραπέμπει την υπόθεση. Η παραπεμπτική απόφαση, όταν τελεσιδικήσει, είναι υποχρεωτική, τόσο για την αναρμοδιότητα του δικαστηρίου που παρέπεμψε, όσο και για την αρμοδιότητα του δικαστηρίου στο οποίο γίνεται η παραπομπή. Οι συνέπειες που έχει η άσκηση της αγωγής διατηρούνται.

Άρθρο 47

Απόφαση πολυμελούς ή μονομελούς πρωτοδικείου δεν προσβάλλεται με ένδικο μέσο για το λόγο ότι η υπόθεση ανήκει στην αρμοδιότητα του κατώτερου δικαστηρίου. Το ίδιο εφαρμόζεται αναλόγως και για την απόφαση κατώτερου δικαστηρίου που παραπέμπει την υπόθεση σε ανώτερο.

ΚΕΦΑΛΑΙΟ Ζ'

Παραπομπή από δικαστηρίου εις δικαστήριον.

Άρθρο 48

Παραπομπή από ένα δικαστήριο σε άλλο, ισόβαθμο και ομοειδές γίνεται με αίτηση:

1) αν από ένα δικαστήριο εξαιρεθούν τόσοι δικαστές, ώστε οι υπόλοιποι να μην αρκούν για τη νόμιμη συγκρότηση του δικαστηρίου.

2) αν, εξαιτίας ασθένειας ή από οποιοδήποτε άλλο λόγο, δεν υπάρχει ο αριθμός τον δικαστών που απαιτείται από το νόμο για τη συγκρότηση του δικαστηρίου,

3) αν από τη συζήτηση της υπόθεσης σε ορισμένο τόπο προκύπτει κίνδυνος για την κοινή ασφάλεια.

Άρθρο 49

Την παραπομπή έχει δικαίωμα να ζητήσει οποιοσδήποτε διάδικος και αυτεπαγγέλτως ο πρόεδρος του δικαστηρίου ή του συμβουλίου διεύθυνσης του δικαστηρίου εφαρμόζοντας αναλόγως τις διατάξεις του άρθρου 307, στις περιπτώσεις 1 και 2 του άρθρου 48 και μόνον ο Εισαγγελέας του Αρείου Πάγου στην περίπτωση 3 του ίδιου άρθρου.

Άρθρο 50

1. Για την παραπομπή, στις περιπτώσεις 1 και 2 του άρθρου 48, έχει αρμοδιότητα:

1) το πολυμελές πρωτοδικείο, αν πρόκειται για παραπομπή από ειρηνοδικείο σε ειρηνοδικείο,

2) το εφετείο, αν πρόκειται για παραπομπή από μονομελές ή πολυμελές πρωτοδικείο σε μονομελές ή πολυμελές πρωτοδικείο,

3) ο Άρειος Πάγος, σε κάθε άλλη περίπτωση. Για την παραπομπή στην περίπτωση 3 του άρθρου 48 έχει αρμοδιότητα πάντοτε ο Άρειος Πάγος.

Άρθρο 51

Η αίτηση για παραπομπή γίνεται με έγγραφο που κατατίθεται στη γραμματεία του αρμόδιου δικαστηρίου και δικάζεται κατά τη διαδικασία που τηρείται στο δικαστήριο αυτό, χωρίς να χρειάζεται παραπομπή της υπόθεσης σε εισηγητή. Για την παραδοχή της αίτησης αρκεί πιθανολόγηση των λόγων για τους οποίους ζητείται η παραπομπή.

Article 46

If the court does not have jurisdiction *ratione materiae* or *ratione loci*, it shall issue a ruling on the matter *ex officio* and specify the court which has jurisdiction, to which it shall remit the case. Once rendered *de jure* non-appealable, the remittal ruling shall be binding, regarding both the lack of jurisdiction of the court that remitted the case and the jurisdiction of the court to which the case was remitted. The consequences of filing the action shall persist.

Article 47

A judgment handed down by a multi-member or single-member court of first instance may not be contested by a legal remedy on the grounds that the case falls under the jurisdiction of a lower court. This also applies *mutatis mutandis* to judgments handed down by a lower court remitting the case to a higher court.

CHAPTER VII
Remittal from court to court

Article 48

Remittal by one court to a similar court of equal instance is done by means of an application if:
1) such a number of judges of one court are exempted that the remaining judges do not suffice for its lawful constitution;
2) due to illness or any other reason, the number of judges required by law for the constitution of the court is not achieved;
3) the hearing of the case at a specific location gives rise to a public security risk.

Article 49

Remittal may be requested by any party in the proceedings and *ex officio* by the presiding judge of the court or the court management board, the provisions of Article 307 applying *mutatis mutandis*, in the cases referred to tin Article 48(1) and (2), and only by the Supreme Court Public Prosecutor in the case referred to in Article 48(3).

Article 50

1. With regard to remittal, in the cases referred to in Article 48(1) and (2), jurisdiction lies with:
1) the multi-member court of first instance, in cases of remittal from [one] court of the peace to [another] court of the peace;
2) the court of appeal, in cases of remittal from a single- or multi-member court of first instance to a single- or multi-member court of first instance;
3) the Supreme Court, in all other cases. With regard to remittal in the case referred to in Article 48(3), the Supreme Court always has jurisdiction.

Article 51

The application for remittal takes the form of a document filed with the registry of the competent court and shall be tried under the procedure followed by that court, with no need to refer the case to a reporting judge. In order for the application to be accepted, it shall suffice for the grounds on which remittal is being requested to satisfy the balance of probabilities test.

ΚΕΦΑΛΑΙΟ Η'
Εξαίρεσις δικαστών και υπαλλήλων της γραμματείας.

Άρθρο 52

1. *Δικαστές, εισαγγελείς και υπάλληλοι της γραμματείας, με οποιαδήποτε ιδιότητα και αν ενεργούν, μπορούν να προτείνουν την εξαίρεσή τους ή να εξαιρεθούν από οποιοδήποτε διάδικο:*

α) αν είναι διάδικοι ή συνδέονται με έναν από τους διαδίκους ως συνδικαιούχοι, συνυπόχρεοι ή είναι υπόχρεοι σε αποζημίωση ή έχουν άμεσο ή έμμεσο συμφέρον στη δίκη,

β) αν συνδέονται με κάποιο διάδικο σε ευθεία γραμμή, με συγγένεια εξ αίματος ή εξ αγχιστείας ή με υιοθεσία, αν είναι συγγενείς σε πλάγια γραμμή με συγγένεια εξ αίματος έως τον τέταρτο βαθμό ή με συγγένεια εξ αγχιστείας έως το δεύτερο βαθμό, αν είναι ή υπήρξαν σύζυγοι ή μνηστήρες ενός από τους διαδίκους,

γ) αν είναι συγγενείς εξ αίματος ή εξ αγχιστείας, σε ευθεία γραμμή ή συνδέονται με υιοθεσία, ή είναι συγγενείς εξ αίματος ή εξ'αγχιστείας σε πλάγια γραμμή έως το δεύτερο βαθμό προσώπου, το οποίο παίρνει μισθό ή άλλη χορηγία με χρηματική αξία είτε για τις υπηρεσίες που παρέχει είτε για οποιοδήποτε άλλο λόγο από φυσικό ή νομικό πρόσωπο ή οποιασδήποτε μορφής εταιρία που έχουν άμεσο ή έμμεσο ιδιωτικό συμφέρον στην έκβαση της δίκης,

δ) αν στην ίδια υπόθεση εξετάστηκαν ως μάρτυρες ή παραστάθηκαν ως δικηγόροι ή γενικά ως πληρεξούσιοι ή παραστάθηκαν ή μπορούν να παραστούν ως νόμιμοι αντιπρόσωποι κάποιου από τους διαδίκους,

ε) αν διεξήγαγαν την υπόθεση, από την οποία προήλθε η διαφορά ή έχουν ενεργήσει στη δίκη ως πραγματογνώμονες ή σύμβουλοι ή διαιτητές ή έχουν συντάξει το έγγραφο που προσβάλλεται ή είχαν μετάσχει στη σύνθεση του δικαστηρίου του οποίου η απόφαση έχει προσβληθεί με έφεση ή αναίρεση,

στ) αν έχουν προκαλέσει ή προκαλούν υπόνοια μεροληψίας, ιδίως αν έχουν με κάποιο διάδικο ιδιαίτερη φιλία, ιδιαίτερες σχέσεις καθηκόντων ή εξάρτησης, έριδα ή έχθρα.

2. *Οι εισαγγελείς δεν εξαιρούνται, όταν ενεργούν ως διάδικοι.*

Άρθρο 53

1. *Είναι απαράδεκτη η αίτηση για την εξαίρεση ολόκληρου του δικαστηρίου του Αρείου Πάγου ή όλων των μελών της εισαγγελίας του ή τόσων αρεοπαγιτών, ώστε με τον αριθμό που απομένει να μην είναι δυνατή η νόμιμη συγκρότηση του δικαστηρίου αυτού.*

2. *Οι διατάξεις της παρ. 1 εφαρμόζονται και όταν η αίτηση για την εξαίρεση αφορά όλα τα εφετεία, τα πρωτοδικεία ή τα ειρηνοδικεία του κράτους.*

3. *Η αίτηση εξαίρεσης είναι απαράδεκτη αν δεν συνοδεύεται από παράβολο εκατό (100) ευρώ, το οποίο επιστρέφεται αν γίνει αυτή ολικά ή μερικά δεκτή. Το ύψος του ποσού αναπροσαρμόζεται με κοινή απόφαση των Υπουργών Οικονομικών και Δικαιοσύνης, Διαφάνειας και Ανθρωπίνων Δικαιωμάτων.*

Άρθρο 54

Αρμόδιο να αποφανθεί για την εξαίρεση είναι το δικαστήριο στο οποίο υπηρετεί ο εξαιρούμενος. Σε περίπτωση εξαίρεσης δικαστή μονομελούς πρωτοδικείου ή ειρηνοδικείου, είναι αρμόδιο το πολυμελές πρωτοδικείο, στην περιφέρεια του οποίου υπάγονται τα δικαστήρια αυτά. Σε περίπτωση εξαίρεσης υπαλλήλου γραμματείας, είναι αρμόδιος ο προϊστάμενος του δικαστηρίου στο οποίο υπηρετεί ο εξαιρούμενος.

CHAPTER VIII
Exemption of judges and registry clerks

Article 52

1. Judges, public prosecutors and registry clerks, acting in any capacity, may propose their own exemption or their exemption [may be proposed] by any party in the proceedings if:
a) they are parties in the proceedings, or are associated with any of the parties in the proceedings as joint bearers of a right, joint bearers of an obligation, or persons obligated to pay compensation, or have a direct or indirect interest in the proceedings;
b) they are related to any party in the proceedings directly by blood or marriage or adoption, if they are related co-laterally by blood up to the fourth degree or by marriage up to the second degree, or if they were married or engaged to any of the parties in the proceedings;
c) they are directly related by blood or marriage or related by adoption, or are related by blood or marriage co-laterally up to the second degree to a person drawing a salary or monetary amounts either for the services they provide or any other reason from any natural or legal person or company of any form with a direct or indirect private interest in the outcome of the proceedings;
d) they were examined as a witness or appeared as lawyers or, in general, as authorised representatives or appeared or can appear as the lawful proxies of any of the parties in the proceedings regarding the same case;
e) they conducted the case from which the dispute arose or acted in the proceedings as experts or advisors or arbitrators, or drafted the document being contested, or had participated in the composition of the court that handed down the judgment being contested by means of appeal or application for cassation;
f) they have caused or cause suspicion of bias, particularly if they share a particular friendship, particular relationship of duty or dependence, contention or enmity with any party in the proceedings.
2. Public prosecutors shall not be exempted when acting as parties in the proceedings.

Article 53

1. Applications to exempt the entire Supreme Court or all the members of the public prosecutor's office at the Supreme Court or Supreme Court Judges where the number remaining would not allow that court to be lawfully constituted are inadmissible.
2. The provisions of paragraph 1 also apply where the application for exemption concerns all courts of appeal, courts of first instance or courts of the peace of the state.
3. Applications for exemption are inadmissible if not accompanied by a procedural fee receipt for 100 euros, which shall be refunded if the application is accepted in whole or in part. The fee amount shall be adjusted by a joint decision issued by the Minister of Finance and the Minister of Justice, Transparency and Human Rights.

Article 54

The court where the person whose exemption is being sought serves has jurisdiction to rule on the exemption. In cases of exemption of a judge of a single-member court of first instance or court of the peace, the multi-member court of first instance within whose district the said courts lie has jurisdiction. In cases of exemption of a registry clerk, the head of the court where the person whose exemption is being sought serves is competent to rule on the exemption.

Άρθρο 55

1. Δικαστές πολυμελών δικαστηρίων και εισαγγελείς, αν υπάρχει λόγος εξαίρεσής τους, οφείλουν να το δηλώσουν στον πρόεδρο του δικαστηρίου.

2. Υπάλληλοι της γραμματείας των πολυμελών δικαστηρίων, αν υπάρχει λόγος εξαίρεσής τους, οφείλουν να το δηλώσουν στον προϊστάμενο της γραμματείας.

3. Δικαστές μονομελών πρωτοδικείων και ειρηνοδίκες, καθώς και υπάλληλοι της γραμματείας τους, αν υπάρχει λόγος εξαίρεσής τους, οφείλουν να το δηλώσουν στον πρόεδρο του πολυμελούς πρωτοδικείου και να απόσχουν από τα καθήκοντά τους εωσότου αυτό αποφασίσει.

4. Το δικαστήριο αποφασίζει χωρίς τη συμμετοχή εκείνου που υπέβαλε τη δήλωση και χωρίς συζήτηση στο ακροατήριο.

Άρθρο 56

Το αρμόδιο δικαστήριο έχει εξουσία να αποφασίσει για την εξαίρεση των προσώπων που αναφέρονται στο άρθρο 52 και αυτεπαγγέλτως, ύστερα από πρόταση του προέδρου ή του εισαγγελέα, έχοντας τη δυνατότητα να ακούσει και τον εξαιρούμενο.

Άρθρο 57

1. Η εξαίρεση προτείνεται από τον διάδικο πέντε ημέρες πριν από τη συζήτηση στο ακροατήριο, ενώ αργότερα έως ότου περατωθεί η συζήτηση στο ακροατήριο, μόνο αν πιθανολογείται ότι η περίπτωση ή οι λόγοι της εξαίρεσης προέκυψαν ή έγιναν γνωστοί στον διάδικο μετά την πάροδο της πενθήμερης προθεσμίας. Στην τελευταία περίπτωση, αν η εξαίρεση γίνει δεκτή, μπορούν, ύστερα από αίτηση, να κηρυχθούν άκυρες οι πράξεις της διαδικασίας στις οποίες είχε συμπράξει εκείνος του οποίου ζητείται η εξαίρεση.

2. Δεν επιτρέπεται αίτηση εξαίρεσης:

α) όλων των μελών του δικαστηρίου, στο οποίο υπηρετούν πράγματι περισσότεροι από πέντε δικαστές,

β) μελών του δικαστηρίου ή του γραμματέα του δικαστηρίου, το οποίο αποφασίζει για την αίτηση εξαίρεσης κατά το άρθρο 54,

γ) περισσοτέρων των οκτώ δικαστών για κάθε δικαστήριο στο οποίο υπηρετούν πράγματι τουλάχιστον δώδεκα δικαστές,

δ) περισσοτέρων των τεσσάρων δικαστών για κάθε δικαστήριο, στο οποίο υπηρετούν πράγματι τουλάχιστον επτά δικαστές και περισσοτέρων των δύο όταν υπηρετούν πράγματι λιγότεροι από επτά δικαστές,

ε) μελών του δικαστηρίου, το οποίο αποφασίζει για την παραπομπή της αίτησης εξαίρεσης από δικαστήριο σε δικαστήριο κατά το άρθρο 50.

3. Αίτηση εξαίρεσης, η οποία υποβάλλεται παρά τα οριζόμενα στην προηγούμενη παράγραφο, είναι απαράδεκτη και απορρίπτεται από το ίδιο το δικαστήριο, του οποίου ζητείται η εξαίρεση μελών του. Η αίτηση αυτή δεν αποτελεί λόγο αποχής από την άσκηση των καθηκόντων τους για τα πρόσωπα των οποίων ζητείται η εξαίρεση.

Άρθρο 58

1. Η αίτηση για την εξαίρεση που υποβάλλεται έως την έναρξη της συζήτησης γίνεται με την κατάθεση εγγράφου στη γραμματεία του αρμόδιου δικαστηρίου. Στην αίτηση πρέπει να αναφέρονται οι λόγοι της εξαίρεσης, διαφορετικά είναι απαράδεκτη.

2. Η αίτηση για την εξαίρεση ανακοινώνεται χωρίς υπαίτια καθυστέρηση στον εξαιρούμενο για να λάβει θέση και συζητείται το αργότερο έως την εκδίκαση της υπόθεσης, κατά τη διαδικασία που εφαρμόζει το δικαστήριο που τη δικάζει, χωρίς συμμετοχή του εξαιρουμένου. Οι διάδικοι καλούνται να παραστούν στη συζήτηση με την επιμέλεια της γραμματείας του δικαστηρίου. Ο εξαιρούμενος, από τότε που θα του ανακοινωθεί ότι έχει υποβληθεί η αίτηση, οφείλει να απέχει από κάθε ενέργεια, εκτός αν προκύπτει κίνδυνος από την αναβολή.

Article 55

1. Judges at multi-member courts and public prosecutors must, where there are grounds for their exemption, declare this fact to the presiding judge of the court.
2. Registry clerks of multi-member courts must, where there are grounds for their exemption, declare this fact to the head of the registry.
3. Judges at single-member courts of first instance and court of the peace judges, as well as registry clerks at such courts must, where there are grounds for their exemption, declare this fact to the presiding judge of the multi-member court of first instance and abstain from their duties until the court decides on the matter.
4. The court shall decide on the matter without the participation of the person who submitted the declaration and without a courtroom hearing.

Article 56

The competent court also has the power to decide *ex officio* on exemption of the persons referred to in Article 52, on a proposal from the presiding judge or the public prosecutor, and may allow the person being exempted to be heard.

Article 57

1. The exemption shall be proposed by the party in the proceedings five days prior to the courtroom hearing, and at a later stage until the courtroom hearing is concluded only if it is considered likely on the balance of probabilities that the case of, or the grounds for, the exemption arose or were made known to the party in the proceedings after the five-day deadline had elapsed. In the latter case, if the exemption is accepted, the procedural steps to which the person whose exemption is being sought had contributed may, following an application, be declared invalid.
2. Applications for exemption may not be filed against:
a) all the members of a court where more than five judges actually serve;
b) members of the court or the registrar of the court deciding on the application for exemption under Article 54;
c) more than eight judges for each court where at least 12 judges actually serve;
d) more than four judges for each court where at least seven judges actually serve, and more than two judges when fewer than seven judges actually serve;
e) members of a court deciding to remit the application for exemption from [one] court to [another] court in accordance with Article 50.
3. An application for exemption filed notwithstanding the provisions of the preceding paragraph is inadmissible and shall be dismissed by the same court of whose members the exemption is being sought. This application does not constitute grounds for the persons whose exemption is being sought to abstain from their duties.

Article 58

1. The application for exemption filed by the commencement of the hearing takes the form of a document filed with the registry of the competent court. The application must, on penalty of inadmissibility, set out the grounds for exemption.
2. The application for exemption shall be sent without undue delay to the person being exempted for them to express their opinion, and shall be heard no later than the hearing date of the case, in accordance with the procedure applied by the court trying the case, without the participation of the person being exempted. The parties in the proceedings shall be summoned to attend the hearing by the court registry. From the time they are notified that the application has been submitted, the person being exempted must refrain from all [procedural] steps, unless [time-barring] risks arise from the postponement.

Άρθρο 59

Η αίτηση για την εξαίρεση, όταν υποβάλλεται κατά τη διάρκεια της συζήτησης στο ακροατήριο, γίνεται με δήλωση που καταχωρίζεται στα πρακτικά και αναφέρει τους λόγους της εξαίρεσης. στα πολυμελή δικαστήρια συζητείται αμέσως, χωρίς συμμετοχή του εξαιρουμένου. Ο εξαιρούμενος, από τότε που θα μάθει ότι έχει υποβληθεί η αίτηση, οφείλει να απέχει από κάθε ενέργεια, εκτός αν προκύπτει κίνδυνος από την αναβολή.

Άρθρο 60

1. Η απόφαση για την αίτηση της εξαίρεσης εκδίδεται αμέσως με απλή πιθανολόγηση των λόγων της εξαίρεσης. Η απόφαση για την εξαίρεση υπαλλήλου της γραμματείας καταχωρίζεται κάτω από την αίτηση.
2. Σε περίπτωση που η αίτηση γίνει δεκτή, δεν επιδικάζονται έξοδα.
3. Όταν η αίτηση εξαίρεσης κατά ενός, περισσοτέρων ή όλων των μελών του δικαστηρίου, κρίνεται ότι είναι αόριστη ως προς τα πραγματικά γεγονότα ή προδήλως ανεπίδεκτη εκτίμησης ή ασκείται καταχρηστικά, απορρίπτεται στην ίδια συνεδρίαση από την ίδια σύνθεση του δικαστηρίου στο οποίο υποβάλλεται.

Άρθρο 61

Αν η αίτηση για την εξαίρεση δικαστή μονομελούς πρωτοδικείου ή ειρηνοδίκη γίνει δεκτή και το δικαστήριο δεν μπορεί να συγκροτηθεί, το πολυμελές πρωτοδικείο, με την ίδια απόφαση για την εξαίρεση παραπέμπει την υπόθεση σε άλλο μονομελές πρωτοδικείο ή ειρηνοδικείο της περιφέρειάς του.

ΚΕΦΑΛΑΙΟΝ Θ'
Διάδικοι.

Άρθρο 62

Όποιος έχει την ικανότητα να είναι υποκείμενο δικαιωμάτων και υποχρεώσεων έχει και την ικανότητα να είναι διάδικος. Ενώσεις προσώπων που επιδιώκουν κάποιο σκοπό, χωρίς να είναι σωματεία, καθώς και εταιρίες που δεν έχουν νομική προσωπικότητα, μπορούν να είναι διάδικοι.

Άρθρο 63

1. Όποιος είναι ικανός για οποιαδήποτε δικαιοπραξία μπορεί να παρίσταται στο δικαστήριο με το δικό του όνομα. Όποιος έχει περιορισμένη ικανότητα για δικαιοπραξία ή βρίσκεται, κατά το χρόνο που επιχειρεί συγκεκριμένη δήλωση της βούλησής του, σε κατάσταση που δεν επιτρέπει να είναι αυτή έγκυρη, μπορεί να παρίσταται στο δικαστήριο με το δικό του όνομα, μόνο όπου κατά το ουσιαστικό δίκαιο έχει ικανότητα για δικαιοπραξία ή όπου ο νόμος επιτρέπει την αυτοπρόσωπη παράστασή του.
2. Στα ασφαλιστικά μέτρα για να αποτραπεί επικείμενος κίνδυνος από την αναβολή μπορεί να παρίσταται και όποιος δεν είναι, ικανός για δικαιοπραξία.

Άρθρο 64

1. Όσοι είναι ανίκανοι να παρίστανται στο δικαστήριο με το δικό τους όνομα εκπροσωπούνται από τους νόμιμους αντιπροσώπους τους.
2. Τα νομικά πρόσωπα παρίστανται στο δικαστήριο με όποιον τα εκπροσωπεί. Στις περιπτώσεις που χρειάζεται προηγούμενη άδεια για τη διεξαγωγή της δίκης, η απεριόριστη χορήγησή της περιλαμβάνει και τη δίκη κατ' έφεση, αναψηλάφηση και αναίρεση.
3. Οι ενώσεις προσώπων που επιδιώκουν κάποιο σκοπό, χωρίς να αποτελούν σωματείο, καθώς και οι εταιρίες που δεν έχουν νομική προσωπικότητα, παρίστανται στο δικαστήριο με τα πρόσωπα, στα οποία έχει ανατεθεί η διαχείριση των υποθέσεών τους.
4. Αν δεν υπάρχει διάταξη που ρυθμίζει τη δικαστική παράσταση των προσώπων που αναφέρονται στις παραγράφους 1 έως 3, τα πρόσωπα αυτά εκπροσωπούνται από όποιους τα αντιπροσωπεύουν στις συναλλακτικές τους σχέσεις.

Article 59

When filed during the courtroom hearing, the application for exemption takes the form of a statement entered in the transcript setting out the grounds for exemption; in cases of multi-member courts, the application shall be heard immediately without the participation of the person whose exemption is being sought. Upon being made aware that the application has been filed, the person whose exemption is being sought must refrain from all [procedural] steps, unless [time-barring] risks arise from the postponement.

Article 60

1. The decision on the application for exemption shall be issued immediately simply by considering that the grounds for exemption satisfy the balance of probabilities test. The decision to exempt a registry clerk shall be recorded below the application.
2. Where the application is accepted, no costs shall be awarded.
3. When an application for exemption filed against one or more or all the members of the court is deemed factually vague or manifestly incapable of being assessed or abusive, it shall be dismissed during the same sitting by the same composition of the court with which it was filed.

Article 61

Where the application for the exemption of a single-member court of first instance judge or a court of the peace judge is accepted and the court cannot be constituted, the multi-member court of first instance shall, in the same decision concerning the exemption, remit the case to a different single-member court of first instance or court of the peace within its district.

CHAPTER IX
Parties in proceedings

Article 62

Any person who can be vested with rights and obligations also has capacity to be a party in proceedings. Groupings of persons which, while not being associations, pursue a specific purpose, as well as partnerships without legal personality, may be parties in proceedings.

Article 63

1. Any person with capacity to enter into any legal transaction may appear before the court in their own name. Any person who has limited capacity to enter into a legal transaction or who, at the time that they make a specific declaration of will, is in a condition that does not allow said declaration to be valid, may appear before the court in their own name only where, under substantive law, they have capacity to enter into a legal transaction or where the law permits an appearance in person.
2. In cases of interim measures to prevent an imminent danger due to adjournment, a person not capable of entering into a legal transaction may also appear before the court.

Article 64

1. Persons who lack capacity to appear in court in their own name shall be represented by their lawful proxies.
2. Legal persons shall appear before the court through their representatives. Where prior leave is required to conduct proceedings, the unlimited conferral of such leave shall also include those concerning appeals, applications to re-open cases and cassation.
3. Groupings of persons which, while not being associations, pursue a specific purpose, as well as partnerships without legal personality, shall appear in court through the persons to whom management of their affairs has been assigned.
4. If there is no provision regulating the appearance of the persons referred to in paragraphs 1 to 3 before the courts, they shall be represented by the persons who represent them in their dealings.

Άρθρο 65

1. Πράξεις για την εξώδικη ενέργεια των οποίων από το νόμιμο αντιπρόσωπο του διαδίκου απαιτείται, κατά τους ορισμούς του ουσιαστικού δικαίου, ειδική εξουσιοδότηση είναι ισχυρές, και χωρίς αυτήν, ως διαδικαστικές πράξεις, αν έχει δοθεί γενική εξουσιοδότηση για τη διεξαγωγή της δίκης.
2. Ο συμβιβασμός, η αναγνώριση ή η παραίτηση από το δικαίωμα της αγωγής και η συμφωνία για διαιτησία είναι ανίσχυρες, χωρίς εξουσιοδότηση για την ενέργεια των πράξεων αυτών.

Άρθρο 66

Αλλοδαπό πρόσωπο που δεν έχει σύμφωνα με το δίκαιο της ιθαγένειάς του ικανότητα για δικαστική παράσταση με το δικό του όνομα, θεωρείται πως έχει ικανότητα να παρίσταται στα ελληνικά δικαστήρια αν έχει αυτή την ικανότητα σύμφωνα με το ελληνικό δίκαιο.

Άρθρο 67

1. Αν υπάρχουν ελλείψεις σχετικά με την ικανότητα των διαδίκων για δικαστική παράσταση με το δικό τους όνομα ή σχετικά με τη νόμιμη εκπροσώπησή τους και την άδεια ή εξουσιοδότηση που απαιτείται για τη διεξαγωγή της δίκης, εφόσον μπορούν να συμπληρωθούν, το δικαστήριο αναβάλλει την πρόοδο της δίκης και ορίζει προθεσμία για τη συμπλήρωση των ελλείψεων. Αν από την αναβολή απειλείται κίνδυνος για τα συμφέροντα του διαδίκου, το δικαστήριο μπορεί να επιτρέψει σ' αυτόν ή στον αντιπρόσωπό του να συνεχίσει τη δίκη ή να ενεργήσει τις διαδικαστικές πράξεις που χρειάζονται για να αποφευχθεί ο κίνδυνος, δεν έχει όμως την εξουσία να εκδώσει οριστική απόφαση προτού συμπληρωθούν οι ελλείψεις ή προτού περάσει η προθεσμία που έταξε για το σκοπό αυτόν. Το κύρος των πράξεων που επιτράπηκαν, εξαρτάται από την εμπρόθεσμη συμπλήρωση των ελλείψεων.
2. Αν η συμπλήρωση των ελλείψεων είναι αδύνατη ή πέρασε άπρακτη η προθεσμία που ορίστηκε για το σκοπό αυτόν, το δικαστήριο προχωρεί στην εκδίκαση της υπόθεσης.

Άρθρο 68

Δικαστική προστασία έχει δικαίωμα να ζητήσει όποιος έχει άμεσο έννομο συμφέρον.

Άρθρο 69

1. Επιτρέπεται να ζητηθεί δικαστική προστασία και
α) αν η παροχή που δεν εξαρτάται από αντιπαροχή συνδέεται με την επέλευση χρονικού σημείου, προτού επέλθει το χρονικό αυτό σημείο,
β) στην περίπτωση του άρθρου 378 του Αστικού Κώδικα,
γ) αν ο ενάγων ζητεί να του παραδοθεί ένα πράγμα και, για την περίπτωση που δεν του παραδοθεί το ίδιο το πράγμα, ζητεί το διαφέρον,
δ) αν η γένεση ή η άσκηση του δικαιώματος εξαρτάται από την έκδοση της απόφασης,
ε) αν το δικαίωμα εξαρτάται από την πλήρωση αίρεσης ή την επέλευση γεγονότος,
στ) σε κάθε άλλη περίπτωση, αν υπάρχει βάσιμος φόβος ότι ο οφειλέτης θα αποφύγει την έγκαιρη εκπλήρωση της παροχής.
2. Στην περίπτωση του εδάφ.α' της προηγούμενης παραγράφου ο εναγόμενος καταδικάζεται να καταβάλει τα χρήματα ή να παραδώσει το πράγμα μόλις επέλθει το χρονικό σημείο. Στην περίπτωση του εδάφ.γ' καταδικάζεται να πληρώσει αποζημίωση, αν δεν βρεθεί το πράγμα στο στάδιο της εκτέλεσης. Στην περίπτωση του εδάφ.ε' καταδικάζεται στην παροχή, μόλις πληρωθεί η αίρεση ή επέλθει το γεγονός και αυτό διαπιστωθεί με τον τρόπο που ορίζει η απόφαση.

Άρθρο 70

Όποιος έχει έννομο συμφέρον να αναγνωριστεί η ύπαρξη ή μη ύπαρξη κάποιας έννομης σχέσης, μπορεί να εγείρει σχετική αγωγή.

Article 65

1. Steps which, in order to be taken extra-judicially by the lawful proxy of the party in the proceedings, require special authorisation under the [provisions] of substantive law shall function as procedural steps even without said authorisation if general authorisation to conduct proceedings has been granted.
2. Settlement, acknowledgement or waiver of the right to an action and an arbitration agreement do not generate effects without authorisation to take said steps.

Article 66

Foreigners who, under their national law, do not have capacity to appear before the court in their own name shall be deemed to have capacity to appear before Greek courts if they have such capacity under Greek law.

Article 67

1. If there are defects concerning the ability of the parties in the proceedings to appear in court in their own name or concerning their lawful representation and the leave or authorisation required to conduct proceedings, where these defects can be rectified, the court shall stay the proceedings and set a deadline for rectifying the defects. If the stay imperils the interests of the party in the proceedings, the court may allow the party or their proxy to continue the proceedings or take the procedural steps necessary to avert such peril, but shall not have the power to hand down a final judgment before the defects have been rectified or before the deadline it set for this purpose has lapsed. The validity of permitted steps shall be predicated on the defects being rectified in good time.
2. If the defects cannot be rectified or the deadline set for this purpose lapses without the relevant steps having been taken, the court shall proceed with hearing the case.

Article 68

Any person with a direct legitimate interest shall have the right to request judicial protection.

Article 69

1. Judicial protection may also be requested[:]
a) if the performance not predicated on counter-performance is associated with the lapse of a point in time, before said point in time elapses;
b) in the case referred to in Article 378 of the Civil Code;
c) if the plaintiff requests that a thing be handed over to them and, where the thing itself is not handed over, they seek damages;
d) if the emergence or exercise of the right depends on a judgment being handed down;
e) if the right depends on a condition being fulfilled or an event occurring;
f) in all other cases, if there is a well-founded fear that the debtor will avoid performing the obligation in good time.
2. In the case referred to in subparagraph (a) of the preceding paragraph, the defendant shall be ordered to pay the money or hand over the thing once the point in time elapses. In the case referred to in subparagraph (c), the defendant shall be ordered to pay compensation if the thing is not found during the enforcement stage. In the case referred to in subparagraph (e), the defendant shall be ordered to provide performance once the condition is fulfilled or the event occurs and this is ascertained in the manner set out in the judgment.

Article 70

Any person who has a legitimate interest in the recognition of the existence or non-existence of a legal relationship may file an action in respect of that matter.

Άρθρο 71

Δικαστική προστασία μπορεί να ζητήσει όποιος επιδιώκει τη σύσταση, τη μεταβολή ή την κατάργηση έννομης σχέσης στις περιπτώσεις που ορίζει ο νόμος.

Άρθρο 72

Οι δανειστές έχουν δικαίωμα να ζητήσουν δικαστική προστασία ασκώντας τα δικαιώματα του οφειλέτη τους εφόσον εκείνος δεν τα ασκεί, εκτός αν συνδέονται στενά με το πρόσωπό του.

Άρθρο 73

Το δικαστήριο εξετάζει και αυτεπαγγέλτως, σε κάθε στάση της δίκης, αν υπάρχουν οι προϋποθέσεις των άρθρων 62 έως 72.

ΚΕΦΑΛΑΙΟ Ι'
Ομοδικία.

Άρθρο 74

Περισσότερα πρόσωπα μπορούν να ασκήσουν αγωγή ή να εναχθούν από κοινού, ως ομόδικοι, εκτός από τις περιπτώσεις που ορίζουν άλλες διατάξεις,
1) αν, σχετικά με το αντικείμενο της διαφοράς, έχουν κοινό δικαίωμα ή κοινή υποχρέωση ή αν τα δικαιώματα ή οι υποχρεώσεις τους στηρίζονται στην ίδια πραγματική και νομική αιτία, ή
2) αν αντικείμενο της διαφοράς είναι ομοειδείς απαιτήσεις ή υποχρεώσεις που στηρίζονται σε όμοια, κατά τα ουσιώδη στοιχεία της, ιστορική και νομική βάση και συγχρόνως το δικαστήριο έχει αρμοδιότητα για τον καθένα από τους εναγομένους

Άρθρο 75

1. Κάθε ομόδικος, εφόσον ο νόμος δεν ορίζει διαφορετικά, ενεργεί στη δίκη ανεξάρτητα από τους άλλους. Οι πράξεις και οι παραλείψεις κάθε ομοδίκου δεν βλάπτουν, ούτε ωφελούν τους άλλους.
2. Κάθε ομόδικος έχει δικαίωμα να επισπεύσει τη δίκη. Το δικαστήριο, αν κρίνει αναγκαία την ενιαία διεξαγωγή της δίκης, έχει το δικαίωμα να διατάξει το διάδικο που επισπεύδει τη διαδικασία να καλέσει και τους ομοδίκους που δεν κάλεσε.

Άρθρο 76

1. Όταν η διαφορά επιδέχεται ενιαία μόνο ρύθμιση ή η ισχύς της απόφασης που θα εκδοθεί επεκτείνεται σε όλους τους ομοδίκους ή όταν οι ομόδικοι μόνο από κοινού μπορούν να ασκήσουν αγωγή ή να εναχθούν ή, εξαιτίας των περιστάσεων που συνοδεύουν την υπόθεση, δεν μπορούν να υπάρξουν αντίθετες αποφάσεις απέναντι στους ομοδίκους, οι πράξεις του καθενός ωφελούν και βλάπτουν τους άλλους. οι ομόδικοι που μετέχουν νόμιμα στη δίκη ή έχουν προσεπικληθεί, αν δεν παραστούν, θεωρούνται ότι αντιπροσωπεύονται από εκείνους που παρίστανται.
2. Η διάταξη της παρ. 1 δεν εφαρμόζεται στο συμβιβασμό, στην αναγνώριση, στην παραίτηση από τη δίκη και στη συμφωνία για διαιτησία.
3. Οι απόντες ομόδικοι καλούνται σε κάθε μεταγενέστερη διαδικαστική πράξη.
4. Η άσκηση των ένδικων μέσων από κάποιον από τους ομοδίκους της παρ. 1 έχει αποτέλεσμα και για τους άλλους.

Άρθρο 77

Στις περιπτώσεις του άρθρου 76, αν οι ομόδικοι προτείνουν αντιφατικούς ισχυρισμούς, το δικαστήριο εκτιμά ελεύθερα την επιρροή τους στη διαδικασία και στην απόφαση, και μπορεί να καθορίσει τα αποτελέσματά τους χωριστά για κάθε ομόδικο.

Article 71

Any person seeking the establishment, change or negation of a legal relationship may request legal protection in the cases provided for in law.

Article 72

Creditors have the right to request judicial protection by exercising the rights of their debtor, where the latter does not exercise them, unless said rights are closely associated with the person of the debtor.

Article 73

The court may, at any stage of the proceedings, also examine *ex officio* whether the conditions laid down in Articles 62 to 72 are met.

CHAPTER X
Joinder

Article 74

Several persons may sue or be sued as joined parties, save where otherwise provided,
1) if, with regard to the subject-matter of the dispute, they have a common right or common obligation, or if their rights or obligations have the same factual and legal cause; or
2) if the subject-matter of the dispute concerns similar claims or obligations with the same factual and legal basis in terms of merits, and, at the same time, the court has jurisdiction over each of the defendants.

Article 75

1. Unless provided otherwise in law, each joined party shall act independently of each other during the proceedings. The acts and omissions of each joined party shall neither harm nor benefit the others.
2. Each joined party shall have the right to expedite the proceedings. If the court deems joinder of proceedings necessary, it shall have the right to order to the party expediting the proceedings to summon the joined parties who have not been summoned.

Article 76

1. Where the dispute may only be resolved in a single manner [for all joined parties], or the effect of the judgment to be handed down extends to all the joined parties, or the joined parties can only sue or be sued jointly, or, due to the circumstances particular to the case, there can be no contrary judgments concerning the joined parties, the acts of each joined party shall harm or benefit the others. Where joined parties who legitimately participate in the proceedings or who have been impleaded do not appear before the court, the parties appearing shall be deemed to be their proxies.
2. The provisions of paragraph 1 shall not apply to settlement, acknowledgement, discontinuation of proceedings and arbitration agreements.
3. Joined parties who are absent shall be summoned [to attend] all subsequent procedural steps.
4. The filing of legal remedies by any of the joined parties referred to in paragraph 1 also generates effects for the others.

Article 77

In the cases referred to in Article 76, if the joined parties make contradictory assertions, the court shall freely weigh up how they impact the proceedings and the judgment, and may determine their outcomes separately for each joined party.

Άρθρο 78

Αν λείπουν οι προϋποθέσεις της ομοδικίας, το δικαστήριο διατάζει το χωρισμό.

ΚΕΦΑΛΑΙΟ ΙΑ'
Συμμετοχή τρίτων στη δίκη.

Άρθρο 79

1. Αν τρίτος αντιποιείται ολόκληρο ή ένα μέρος από το αντικείμενο της δίκης που εκκρεμεί ανάμεσα σε άλλους, έχει δικαίωμα να παρέμβει κυρίως στον πρώτο βαθμό.
2. Όποιος παρεμβαίνει κατά την παράγραφο 1 δεν έχει δικαίωμα να ζητήσει να τεθεί εκτός δίκης οποιοσδήποτε από τους αρχικούς διαδίκους, εκτός αν ο νόμος ορίζει διαφορετικά ή αν συμφωνούν σ' αυτό όλοι οι διάδικοι.

Άρθρο 80

Αν σε δίκη που εκκρεμεί μεταξύ άλλων τρίτος έχει έννομο συμφέρον να νικήσει κάποιος διάδικος, έχει δικαίωμα, έως την έκδοση αμετάκλητης απόφασης, να ασκήσει πρόσθετη παρέμβαση για να υποστηρίξει το διάδικο αυτόν.

Άρθρο 81

1. Η κύρια και η πρόσθετη παρέμβαση, ανεξάρτητα από το αν γίνεται εκούσια ή ύστερα από προσεπίκληση ή ανακοίνωση, ασκείται σύμφωνα με τις διατάξεις που ισχύουν για την αγωγή και κοινοποιείται σε όλους τους διαδίκους. Το δικόγραφο της παρέμβασης πρέπει να περιέχει, εκτός από τα στοιχεία που απαιτούνται για κάθε δικόγραφο
α) αναγραφή των διαδίκων και της διαφοράς που εκκρεμεί,
β) προσδιορισμό του έννομου συμφέροντος που έχει ο παρεμβαίνων στην εκκρεμή δίκη, καθώς και του δικαιώματος με βάση το οποίο αντιποιείται το επίδικο,
γ) σε περίπτωση πρόσθετης παρέμβασης, καθορισμό του διαδίκου για την υποστήριξη του οποίου γίνεται η παρέμβαση.
2. Η άσκηση της κύριας παρέμβασης έχει τα αποτελέσματα που έχει και η άσκηση της αγωγής.
3. Ο παρεμβαίνων καλείται στις επόμενες διαδικαστικές πράξεις από το διάδικο που επισπεύδει τη δίκη. Σε περίπτωση πρόσθετης παρέμβασης έχει δικαίωμα να προτείνει την έλλειψη κλήτευσης και ο διάδικος για την υποστήριξη του οποίου ασκήθηκε η παρέμβαση.

Άρθρο 82

Όποιος προσθέτως παρεμβαίνει έχει δικαίωμα να ενεργήσει όλες τις διαδικαστικές πράξεις που επιτρέπονται στη δίκη προς το συμφέρον εκείνου για την υποστήριξη του οποίου ασκήθηκε η παρέμβαση και έχει την υποχρέωση να δεχτεί τη δίκη στη θέση που βρίσκεται κατά το χρόνο της παρέμβασής του. Οι πράξεις που ενεργεί είναι ισχυρές, εφόσον δεν είναι αντίθετες προς τις πράξεις του διαδίκου, για την υποστήριξη του οποίου άσκησε την παρέμβαση. Αποφάσεις και δικόγραφα που επιδίδονται στους κύριους διαδίκους πρέπει να επιδίδονται και σε εκείνον που άσκησε πρόσθετη παρέμβαση.

Άρθρο 83

Αν η ισχύς της απόφασης στην κύρια δίκη εκτείνεται και στις έννομες σχέσεις εκείνου που άσκησε πρόσθετη παρέμβαση προς τον αντίδικό του, εφαρμόζονται οι διατάξεις των άρθρων 76 έως 78.

Article 78

If the requirements for joinder are not met, the court shall order that the proceedings be split.

CHAPTER XI

Participation of third parties in the proceedings

Article 79

1. If a third party has an interest in all or part the subject-matter of proceedings pending between other parties, said third party has the right to intervene primarily at first instance.

2. Any person intervening under paragraph 1 does not have the right to request that any of the initial parties in the proceedings be excluded from the proceedings, unless otherwise provided for in law or all the parties in the proceedings agree on the matter.

Article 80

Where, in proceedings pending between other parties, a third party has a legitimate interest in a specific party winning, said third party has the right, until an irrevocable judgment is handed down, to file a permissive intervention in support of that party in the proceedings.

Article 81

1. Main and permissive interventions, regardless of whether they were filed voluntarily or following an impleader or third-party notice, shall be filed in accordance with the provisions applicable to actions and shall be communicated to all the parties in the proceedings. In addition to the information required for all procedural documents, the intervention must contain[:]

a) an indication of the parties in the proceedings and the pending dispute;

b) specification of the legitimate right of the intervenor in the pending proceedings, as well as the right based on which the intervenor is opposing the subject-matter of the dispute;

c) in the case of a permissive intervention, designation of the party in the proceedings in support of whom the intervention is filed.

2. Filing a main intervention generates the same effects as filing an action.

3. The intervenor shall be summoned [in the context of] subsequent procedural steps by the party expediting the proceedings. In the case of a permissive intervention, the party in the proceedings in support of whom the intervention was filed also has the right to propose that summonsing be omitted.

Article 82

The permissive intervenor has the right to take all the procedural steps permitted during proceedings to benefit the person in support of whom the intervention was filed, and the obligation to accept the proceedings, whatever their stage was at the time the intervention was filed. The steps taken are valid provided they are not contrary to the steps taken out by the party in the proceedings in support of whom the intervention was filed. Judgments and procedural documents that are served on the main parties in the proceedings must also be served on the permissive intervenor.

Article 83

If the binding effect of the judgment handed down in the main proceedings also extends to the legal relationships between the permissive intervenor and their opponent, the provisions of Articles 76 to 78 apply.

Άρθρο 84

Όποιος άσκησε πρόσθετη παρέμβαση, στις σχέσεις του με διάδικο για την υποστήριξη του οποίου άσκησε την παρέμβαση, δεν έχει δικαίωμα να ισχυριστεί ότι το δικαστήριο έκρινε εσφαλμένα τη διαφορά έτσι όπως του υποβλήθηκε. Έχει δικαίωμα να προτείνει ότι ο διάδικος, για την υποστήριξη του οποίου άσκησε την παρέμβαση, διεξήγαγε τη δίκη κατά τρόπο πλημμελή, αλλά μόνο όταν είτε εξαιτίας της στάσης, στην οποία βρισκόταν η δίκη, όταν άσκησε την παρέμβασή του, είτε από τις πράξεις του διαδίκου, για την υποστήριξη του οποίου άσκησε την παρέμβαση, εμποδίστηκε να προτείνει ισχυρισμούς ή όταν ο διάδικος, για την υποστήριξη του οποίου άσκησε την παρέμβαση, παρέλειψε από δόλο ή από βαριά αμέλεια να προτείνει ισχυρισμούς που ήταν άγνωστοι σε εκείνον που άσκησε την παρέμβαση.

Άρθρο 85

Όποιος άσκησε πρόσθετη παρέμβαση έχει δικαίωμα, αν συμφωνούν όλοι οι διάδικοι, να συμμετάσχει στη δίκη ως κύριος διάδικος, οπότε παίρνει τη θέση του διαδίκου για την υποστήριξη του οποίου άσκησε την παρέμβαση και εκείνος τίθεται εκτός δίκης. Η απόφαση που θα εκδοθεί δεν ισχύει εναντίον του αρχικού διαδίκου που με τη συναίνεση όλων των διαδίκων τέθηκε εκτός δίκης.

Άρθρο 86

Στις περιπτώσεις του άρθρου 76, αν μόνο ένας ή μερικοί από τους ομοδίκους ασκούν την αγωγή, ενώ οι άλλοι δεν θέλουν να συμπράξουν μαζί τους, οι πρώτοι έχουν δικαίωμα να προσεπικαλέσουν τους τελευταίους για τη συζήτηση της υπόθεσης. Το ίδιο δικαίωμα έχει και ο εναγόμενος, αν μόνο ένας ή κάποιοι από τους ομοδίκους άσκησαν εναντίον του την αγωγή ή αν ο ενάγων άσκησε την αγωγή μόνο εναντίον ενός ή μερικών από τους ομοδίκους.

Άρθρο 87

Όποιος ενάγεται με εμπράγματη αγωγή, αν κατέχει το επίδικο πράγμα ή αν ασκεί εμπράγματο δικαίωμα στο όνομα άλλου, έχει δικαίωμα να τον προσεπικαλέσει στη δίκη.

Άρθρο 88

Ο ενάγων, ο εναγόμενος και όποιος άσκησε κύρια παρέμβαση έχουν δικαίωμα να προσεπικαλέσουν στη δίκη εκείνους από τους οποίους έχουν δικαίωμα να απαιτήσουν αποζημίωση σε περίπτωση ήττας.

Άρθρο 89

Η προσεπίκληση ασκείται σύμφωνα με τις διατάξεις που ισχύουν για την αγωγή και κοινοποιείται στον προσεπικαλούμενο. Η άσκηση της προσεπίκλησης έχει τα αποτελέσματα που έχει και η άσκηση της αγωγής.

Άρθρο 90

Αν υπάρχει περίπτωση να προσεπικαλέσει ένας διάδικος κάποιον τρίτο και το δικαστήριο κρίνει αναγκαία την παρέμβασή του στη δίκη, έχει εξουσία να διατάξει και αυτεπαγγέλτως την προσεπίκλησή του, με απόφαση που ορίζει με την επιμέλεια ποιου διαδίκου θα γίνει η προσεπίκληση καθώς και το χρόνο, κατά τον οποίο πρέπει να γίνει. Η προσεπίκληση που διατάχθηκε επιτρέπεται να γίνει και με την επιμέλεια οποιουδήποτε άλλου διαδίκου.

Article 84

With respect to their relationships with the party in the proceedings in support of whom the intervention was filed, the permissive intervenor does not have the right to assert that the court erred in ruling on the dispute in the form in which it was submitted. The intervenor has the right to propose that the party in the proceedings in support of whom the intervention was filed conducted the proceedings in an irregular manner, but only when, either due to the stage of the proceedings when the intervention was filed or due to the steps taken by the party in the proceedings in support of whom the intervention was filed, the intervenor was hindered from making assertions or when the party in the proceedings in support of whom the intervention was filed failed, due to *dolus* or gross negligence, to make assertions that were unknown to the intervenor.

Article 85

If all the parties in the proceedings agree, the permissive intervenor has the right to participate in the proceedings as a main party in the proceedings, in which case the intervenor shall take the place of the party in the proceedings in support of whom the intervention was filed, and that party shall be excluded from the proceedings. The judgment to be handed down shall not have effect vis-à-vis the initial party in the proceedings who was excluded from the proceedings with the consent of all the parties.

Article 86

In the cases referred to in Article 76, if only one or certain of the joined parties file the action while others do not wish to collaborate with them, the former shall have the right to implead the latter [to participate in] the hearing of the case. The defendant also has the same right if only one or certain of the joined parties filed an action against the defendant or if the plaintiff filed the action against only one or certain of the joined parties.

Article 87

Where any person sued in an action *in rem* enjoys detentorship over the thing at issue or exercises a right *in rem* in the name of another person, the former has the right to implead the latter in the proceedings.

Article 88

The plaintiff, the defendant and the main intervenor has the right to implead those with the right to seek compensation in the event of an unsuccessful outcome in the proceedings.

Article 89

Impleaders shall be filed in accordance with the provisions applicable to actions, and shall be communicated to the impleaded party. Filing an impleader generates the same effects as filing an action.

Article 90

If it is necessary for a party in the proceedings to implead a third party and the court deems that third party's intervention in the proceedings necessary, the court shall also have the power to order *ex officio* that that third party be impleaded by means of a ruling specifying which party in the proceedings will be responsible for filing the impleader and when. The impleader ordered may also be filed by any other party in the proceedings.

Άρθρο 91

1. Με την επιφύλαξη του άρθρου 238, όποιος έχει έννομο συμφέρον δικαιούται να ανακοινώσει τη δίκη σε τρίτους, ώσπου να εκδοθεί από το πρωτοβάθμιο δικαστήριο οριστική απόφαση για την ουσία της υπόθεσης.
2. Η ανακοίνωση γίνεται με δικόγραφο, που πρέπει να αναφέρει και την αιτία, για την οποία γίνεται η ανακοίνωση, καθώς και τη στάση στην οποία βρίσκεται η δίκη. Η ανακοίνωση ασκείται σύμφωνα με τις διατάξεις που ισχύουν για την αγωγή και κοινοποιείται στον τρίτο.
3. Η ανακοίνωση δεν δίνει σε εκείνον που ανακοινώνει τη δίκη το δικαίωμα να ζητήσει αναβολή της δίκης ή παράταση των προθεσμιών της.

Άρθρο 92

Ο τρίτος στον οποίο έγινε η ανακοίνωση έχει δικαίωμα να συμμετάσχει στη δίκη, σύμφωνα με τις διατάξεις που ισχύουν για την παρέμβαση. Αν εκείνος προς τον οποίο έγινε η ανακοίνωση δεν συμμετάσχει στη δίκη, και η ανακοίνωση έγινε πριν από την συζήτηση στο ακροατήριο, δεν έχει το δικαίωμα να ασκήσει τριτανακοπή εναντίον της απόφασης που θα εκδοθεί.

Άρθρο 93

Αν παρέμβει στη δίκη τρίτος, αντιποιούμενος επίδικη απαίτηση, με αντικείμενο που μπορεί να κατατεθεί, εφόσον ο εναγόμενος το καταθέσει δημόσια και παραιτηθεί από το δικαίωμα να το αναλάβει, το δικαστήριο ύστερα από αίτηση του εναγομένου τον θέτει εκτός δίκης.

Άρθρο 93Α.

(Καταργήθηκε)

ΚΕΦΑΛΑΙΟ ΙΒ'
Πληρεξουσιότης.

Άρθρο 94

1. Στα πολιτικά δικαστήρια οι διάδικοι έχουν υποχρέωση να παρίστανται με πληρεξούσιο δικηγόρο.
2. Επιτρέπεται η δικαστική παράσταση διαδίκου χωρίς πληρεξούσιο δικηγόρο:
α) στο ειρηνοδικείο, εφόσον πρόκειται για μικροδιαφορές
β) για να αποτραπεί επικείμενος κίνδυνος.
3. Στις περιπτώσεις της παρ. 2 ο δικαστής έχει δικαίωμα, εκτιμώντας τις ιδιαίτερες περιστάσεις, να υποχρεώσει το διάδικο να προσλάβει δικηγόρο.

Άρθρο 95

Αν στην ίδια δίκη εκπροσωπούν το διάδικο περισσότεροι πληρεξούσιο δικηγόροι, έχουν δικαίωμα να ενεργούν είτε από κοινού είτε ο καθένας χωριστά. Αντίθετος όρος του πληρεξούσιου εγγράφου δεν ισχύει απέναντι στον αντίδικο, εκτός αν το πληροφορήθηκε με κοινοποίηση.

Άρθρο 96

1. Η πληρεξουσιότητα δίνεται είτε με συμβολαιογραφική πράξη είτε με προφορική δήλωση, που καταχωρίζεται στα Πρακτικά ή στην έκθεση είτε με ιδιωτικό έγγραφο, εφόσον η υπογραφή εκείνου που παρέχει την πληρεξουσιότητα βεβαιώνεται από δημόσια, δημοτική ή άλλη αρμόδια αρχή ή από δικηγόρο. Η πληρεξουσιότητα μπορεί να αφορά ορισμένες ή όλες τις δίκες εκείνου που την παρέχει και πρέπει να αναγράφει τα ονόματα των δικαστικών πληρεξουσίων και σε περίπτωση που δικαστικός πληρεξούσιος ενεργεί ως εταίρος ή συνεργάτης δικηγορικής εταιρείας και την επωνυμία της δικηγορικής εταιρείας, κατά περίπτωση.

Article 91

1. Without prejudice to Article 238, any person with a legitimate interest shall be entitled to issue a third-party notice until such time as the first-instance court hands down a final judgment on the merits of the case.
2. The notice shall be effected by means of a procedural document, which must also set out the reason for the notice, as well as what stage the proceedings are at. The notice shall be issued in accordance with the provisions applicable to actions, and shall be communicated to the third party.
3. The notice does not give the person issuing the third-party notice the right to request adjournment of the proceedings or an extension to the [procedural] deadlines.

Article 92

The third party notified shall have the right to participate in the proceedings in accordance with the provisions applicable to interventions. If said third party does not participate in the proceedings and the notice was given prior to the hearing in court, they do not have the right to institute third-party proceedings against the judgment to be handed down.

Article 93

If a third party intervenes in proceedings asserting an interest in a disputed claim concerning a thing that can be placed in deposit, provided the defendant places it in deposit and waives the right to take it back into their possession, the court, at the request of the defendant, shall exclude the latter from the proceedings.

Article 93A

[Repealed]

CHAPTER XII
Power [of representation]

Article 94

1. Parties in proceedings before civil courts shall appear with an authorised lawyer.
2. A party in proceedings may appear before the court without an authorised lawyer:
a) in cases of small claims before a court of the peace;
b) in order to avert an imminent danger.
3. In cases falling under paragraph 2, the judge shall have the right, taking the particular circumstances into consideration, to order the party in the proceedings to engage a lawyer.

Article 95

If several authorised lawyers represent one party in the same proceedings, they have the right to act either jointly or individually. A term to the contrary in the power of attorney does not generate effects vis-à-vis the opponent, unless the latter was made aware of it by means of notification.

Article 96

1. Power of representation shall be conferred by means of a notarial instrument, a verbal statement recorded in the transcript or the report, or a private document, where the signature of the person conferring power of attorney is attested by a public, municipal or other competent authority or by a lawyer. The power of representation may concern some or all of the proceedings involving the person conferring it, and [the document] must indicate the names of the advocates and where the advocate acts as the partner or associate of a law firm, the name of the law firm, as appropriate.

2. Η πληρεξουσιότητα μιας αρχής μπορεί να δοθεί σε δικηγόρο ή σε δικηγορική εταιρεία και με έγγραφό της που περιέχει τα στοιχεία που αναγράφονται στην παρ. 1.
3. Κατά τη διαδικασία ενώπιον του Αρείου Πάγου και στις περιπτώσεις του άρθρου 98 η πληρεξουσιότητα δίνεται μόνο με συμβολαιογραφική πράξη ή με προφορική δήλωση, που καταχωρίζεται στα Πρακτικά ή στην έκθεση. Ειδικά, για τις εργατικές διαφορές η πληρεξουσιότητα μπορεί να δίνεται με ιδιωτικό έγγραφο, το οποίο φέρει βεβαίωση του γνησίου της υπογραφής του διαδίκου από Κέντρο Εξυπηρέτησης Πολιτών ή οποιαδήποτε άλλη δημόσια ή δημοτική αρχή.

Άρθρο 97

1. Η πληρεξουσιότητα παρέχει στον πληρεξούσιο το δικαίωμα να παριστά στο δικαστήριο εκείνον που έδωσε την πληρεξουσιότητα, να ενεργεί όλες τις κύριες ή παρεπόμενες πράξεις που αφορούν τη διεξαγωγή της δίκης, στις οποίες περιλαμβάνεται η άσκηση αγωγών, ανταγωγών, παρεμβάσεων, προσεπικλήσεων και ένδικων μέσων, να λαμβάνει ασφαλιστικά μέτρα και να επιδιώκει την εκτέλεση καθώς και να παρίσταται στις αντίστοιχες δίκες που δημιουργούνται από τις πράξεις αυτές.
2. Περιορισμός της πληρεξουσιότητας ισχύει μόνο αν δηλώθηκε ρητά, όταν χορηγήθηκε.
3. Η πληρεξουσιότητα για όλες τις δίκες παύει να ισχύει μετά πέντε χρόνια από τη χορήγησή της.

Άρθρο 98

Η πληρεξουσιότητα που δίνεται κατά το άρθρο 96 δεν περιλαμβάνει, εκτός αν το αναφέρει ειδικά,
α) το δικαίωμα να ασκηθεί αγωγή κακοδικίας, καθώς και να διεξαχθεί δίκη που αφορά γαμικές διαφορές ή σχέσεις των τέκνων με τους γονείς τους,
β) το δικαίωμα να συμφωνηθεί συμβιβασμός και διαιτησία, να γίνει αναγνώριση, παραίτηση από το δικαίωμα της αγωγής ή των ένδικων μέσων, καθώς και την προσβολή εγγράφου ως πλαστού.

Άρθρο 99

Ο διάδικος, όταν εμφανίζεται μαζί με πληρεξούσιο, έχει δικαίωμα να ανακαλεί αμέσως τις ομολογίες εκείνου.

Άρθρο 100

Η πληρεξουσιότητα παύει:
1) όταν πεθάνει ο πληρεξούσιος ή μεταβληθεί η ικανότητά του για δικαστική παράσταση,
2) όταν περατωθεί η δίκη ή η πράξη, για την οποία είχε δοθεί η πληρεξουσιότητα,
3) όταν ο πληρεξούσιος δικηγόρος παραιτηθεί ή παυθεί περισσότερο από τρεις μήνες ή εκπέσει από το λειτούργημά του,
4) όταν ανακληθεί η πληρεξουσιότητα,
5) όταν ο πληρεξούσιος παραιτηθεί από την πληρεξουσιότητα.

Άρθρο 101

Σε περίπτωση θανάτου εκείνου που έδωσε την πληρεξουσιότητα ή μεταβολής της ικανότητας για δικαστική παράσταση του ίδιου ή του νόμιμου αντιπροσώπου του, η πληρεξουσιότητα εξακολουθεί και παύει μόνο όταν διακοπεί η δίκη για έναν από τους λόγους αυτούς.

2. An authority may also confer power of representation upon a lawyer or a law firm by means of a document containing the information referred to in paragraph 1.
3. During proceedings before the Supreme Court and in the cases referred to in Article 98, power of representation shall be conferred only by means of a notarial instrument or a verbal statement recorded in the transcript or the report. In cases of labour disputes, specifically, power of representation may be conferred by means of a private document bearing an attestation of the authenticity of the signature of the party in the proceedings [affixed by] a Citizen Service Centre or by any other public or municipal authority.

Article 97

1. Power of representation shall grant the authorised [lawyer] the right to represent before the court the person conferring such power, to takes all principal or ancillary steps concerning the conduct of the proceedings, including the filing of actions, cross-actions, interventions, impleaders and legal remedies, to adopt interim measures and seek enforcement, and to appear at the corresponding proceedings instituted by means of said steps.
2. Any limitations on the power of representation are valid only if expressly declared when [said power] was conferred.
3. The effective term of the power of representation for all proceedings expires five years after it was conferred.

Article 98

Unless otherwise specifically stated, power of representation conferred in accordance with Article 96 shall not include:
a) the right to file an action for miscarriage of justice, as well as the right to conduct proceedings concerning matrimonial disputes or parent-child relationships;
b) the right to agree upon a settlement and arbitration, the right to acknowledge or discontinue the action or legal remedies, and the right to contest the authenticity of a document.

Article 99

When appearing with an authorised [lawyer], a party in the proceedings has the right to immediately recant the authorised [lawyer's] statements.

Article 100

Power of representation shall cease:
1) when the authorised [lawyer] dies or their ability to appear before the courts changes;
2) upon the conclusion of the proceedings or the step for which the power of representation had been conferred;
3) when the authorised lawyer resigns or is suspended for longer than three months or is disbarred;
4) when the power of representation is revoked;
5) when the authorised [lawyer] relinquishes the power of representation.

Article 101

In the event of death of the person who conferred power of representation or a change in the ability of that person or their lawful proxy to appear before the court, the power of representation shall persist and shall only cease when the proceedings are stayed on any of these grounds.

Άρθρο 102

1. Η παύση της πληρεξουσιότητας για τη διεξαγωγή δίκης ή την ενέργεια ορισμένων διαδικαστικών πράξεων, που προκλήθηκε με την ανάκλησή της ή με την παραίτηση του πληρεξουσίου, ισχύει απέναντι στον αντίδικο μόνο από τότε που του κοινοποιείται η ανάκληση ή η παραίτηση ή από τη δήλωση που καταχωρίζεται στα πρακτικά· όπου ο νόμος απαιτεί να διοριστεί άλλος πληρεξούσιος δικηγόρος, η παύση ισχύει από τότε που θα γνωστοποιηθεί στον αντίδικο και ο διορισμός του νέου πληρεξουσίου.
2. Η παύση που επέρχεται με ανάκληση της πληρεξουσιότητας πρέπει να κοινοποιηθεί και στον ανακαλούμενο πληρεξούσιο, καθώς και στο συμβολαιογράφο που είχε συντάξει το πληρεξούσιο έγγραφο ο οποίος είναι υποχρεωμένος να σημειώσει την ανάκληση στο πρωτότυπο του πληρεξούσιου εγγράφου.

Άρθρο 103

Επί ένα μήνα μετά την παύση της πληρεξουσιότητας που προκλήθηκε με παραίτηση του πληρεξουσίου, αν δεν ανέλαβε τη διεξαγωγή της δίκης αντικαταστάτης, ο πληρεξούσιος που παραιτήθηκε έχει δικαίωμα και υποχρέωση να ενεργεί στη δίκη μόνο τις πράξεις που είναι αναγκαίες για να προστατευθούν τα συμφέροντα εκείνου που έδωσε την πληρεξουσιότητα και να αποτραπούν επιβλαβείς συνέπειες εξαιτίας της παραίτησης.

Άρθρο 104

Για τις προπαρασκευαστικές πράξεις και τις κλήσεις έως την συζήτηση στο ακροατήριο θεωρείται ότι υπάρχει πληρεξουσιότητα ενώ για τη συζήτηση στο ακροατήριο απαιτείται ρητή πληρεξουσιότητα, και αν δεν υπάρχει κηρύσσονται άκυρες όλες οι πράξεις, ακόμη και εκείνες που είχαν γίνει προηγουμένως. Το δικαστήριο εξετάζει αυτεπαγγέλτως, σε κάθε στάση της δίκης, την έλλειψη πληρεξουσιότητας, καθώς και την υπέρβασή της.

Άρθρο 105

1. Αν αυτός που παρίσταται ως πληρεξούσιος δεν αποδεικνύει την ύπαρξη πληρεξουσιότητας, το δικαστήριο μπορεί να ορίσει σύντομη προθεσμία για τη συμπλήρωση της έλλειψης και να επιτρέψει σε εκείνον που δεν αποδεικνύει την πληρεξουσιότητά του να συμμετάσχει στη δίκη προσωρινά. Το κύρος των πράξεων που επιτράπηκαν εξαρτάται από την εμπρόθεσμη συμπλήρωση της έλλειψης.
2. Η οριστική απόφαση δεν επιτρέπεται να εκδοθεί προτού συμπληρωθεί η έλλειψη ή πριν παρέλθει η προθεσμία που ορίστηκε.
3. Αν δεν συμπληρώθηκε η έλλειψη μέσα στην προθεσμία που ορίστηκε, το δικαστήριο προχωρεί στην εκδίκαση της υπόθεσης και καταδικάζει εκείνον που παραστάθηκε χωρίς πληρεξουσιότητα να πληρώσει τα έξοδα που προκλήθηκαν από την παράστασή του αυτή.

ΚΕΦΑΛΑΙΟ ΙΓ'
Θεμελιώδεις δικονομικές αρχές.

Άρθρο 106

Το δικαστήριο ενεργεί μόνο ύστερα από αίτηση διαδίκου και αποφασίζει με βάση τους πραγματικούς ισχυρισμούς που προτείνουν και αποδεικνύουν οι διάδικοι και τις αιτήσεις που υποβάλλουν, εκτός αν ο νόμος ορίζει διαφορετικά.

Άρθρο 107

Το δικαστήριο διατάζει και αυτεπαγγέλτως τη διεξαγωγή απόδειξης με οποιαδήποτε κατάλληλα αποδεικτικά μέσα που επιτρέπει ο νόμος, και αν δεν τα επικαλέστηκαν οι διάδικοι.

Article 102

1. Cessation of the power to conduct proceedings or take procedural steps due to the power of representation being revoked or the authorised [lawyer] having relinquished said power generates effects vis-à-vis the opponent only from the date the revocation or relinquishment is communicated to the opponent or from the date the declaration was entered into the transcript; where the law requires appointment of a different authorised lawyer, the cessation shall take effect from the date the opponent is also notified of the appointment of the new authorised [lawyer].
2. Cessation due to the power of representation being revoked must also be notified to the authorised [lawyer] whose power has been revoked and to the notary public who had drawn up the power of attorney, who is obligated to note the revocation on the original document.

Article 103

For one month after the power of representation ceased to apply due to relinquishment, unless a replacement has undertaken to conduct the proceedings, the authorised [lawyer] who relinquished the power of representation has the right and obligation to participate in the proceedings by taking only those steps necessary to protect the interests of the person who conferred the power of representation and to prevent harmful effects due to said relinquishment.

Article 104

Power of representation shall be deemed to apply with regard to preparatory steps and summonses until the time of the courtroom hearing, whereas express power of representation shall be required for the courtroom hearing, and, absent such, all steps shall be declared void, including those previously taken. The court may examine *ex officio*, at any stage of the proceedings, the lack of power of representation, as well as instances of *ultra vires*.

Article 105

1. If the person appearing in court as an authorised [lawyer] cannot prove the existence of the power of representation, the court may set a short deadline to rectify the defect and permit the person who cannot prove their power of representation to participate in the proceedings on a provisional basis. The validity of permitted steps is dependent on the defects being rectified in good time.
2. A final judgment may not be handed down before the defect has been rectified or the deadline set has elapsed.
3. If the defect is not rectified within the deadline set, the court shall hear the case and order the person who appeared without power of representation to pay the costs incurred due to said appearance.

CHAPTER XIII
Fundamental procedural principles

Article 106

Unless otherwise provided for in law, the court shall act only following an application filed by a party in the proceedings, and shall rule on the basis of the factual assertions put forth and proven by the parties in the proceedings and the applications they file.

Article 107

The court shall also order *ex officio* the taking of evidence using any appropriate means of evidence permitted by law, even if the parties in the proceedings did not invoke them.

Άρθρο 108

Οι διαδικαστικές πράξεις ενεργούνται με πρωτοβουλία και επιμέλεια των διαδίκων, εκτός αν ο νόμος ορίζει διαφορετικά.

Άρθρο 109

1. Δεν επιτρέπεται να αφαιρεθεί από κανέναν, χωρίς τη θέλησή του, ο δικαστής που ορίζει ο νόμος γι' αυτόν.
2. Το αρμόδιο δικαστήριο δεν μπορεί να μεταβιβάσει τη δικαιοδοσία του, εκτός αν ο νόμος ορίζει διαφορετικά. Μόνο ειδικές διαδικαστικές πράξεις μπορούν να ανατεθούν και σε άλλα δικαστήρια ή δικαστές, στις περιπτώσεις που ορίζει ο νόμος.

Άρθρο 110

1. Οι διάδικοι έχουν τα ίδια δικαιώματα και τις ίδιες υποχρεώσεις και είναι ίσοι ενώπιον του δικαστηρίου.
2. Οι διάδικοι έχουν δικαίωμα να παρίστανται σε όλες τις συζητήσεις της υπόθεσης, ακόμη και όταν γίνονται κεκλεισμένων των θυρών και πρέπει για το σκοπό αυτό να καλούνται σύμφωνα με τις διατάξεις του νόμου.
3. Οι διάδικοι έχουν υποχρέωση να εμφανίζονται αυτοπροσώπως στο δικαστήριο, όταν τους καλεί για το σκοπό αυτό.

Άρθρο 111

1. Η διαδικασία στο ακροατήριο στηρίζεται στην έγγραφη προδικασία.
2. Καμιά κύρια ή παρεμπίπτουσα αίτηση για δικαστική προστασία δεν μπορεί να εισαχθεί στο δικαστήριο χωρίς να τηρηθεί προδικασία, εκτός αν ο νόμος ορίζει διαφορετικά. Η αίτηση που έχει εισαχθεί χωρίς προδικασία απορρίπτεται ως απαράδεκτη και αυτεπαγγέλτως.

Άρθρο 112

Η προδικασία και η διαδικασία έξω από το ακροατήριο δεν είναι δημόσιες, επιτρέπεται όμως να προσέρχονται σε αυτές οι διάδικοι, οι νόμιμοι αντιπρόσωποι και οι πληρεξούσιοί τους.

Άρθρο 113

1. Οι συνεδριάσεις όλων των πολιτικών δικαστηρίων γίνονται δημόσια. Η διάσκεψη για την έκδοση της απόφασης γίνεται μυστικά.
2. Όποιος διευθύνει τη διαδικασία ορίζει κατά την κρίση του τον αριθμό των προσώπων που μπορούν να μείνουν στην αίθουσα των συνεδριάσεων και έχει την εξουσία να διατάξει τον αποκλεισμό των ανηλίκων, εκείνων που οπλοφορούν, καθώς και εκείνων που εμφανίζονται με τρόπο ανάρμοστο και αντίθετο προς την τάξη και την ευπρέπεια της συνεδρίασης.

Άρθρο 114

1. Αν η διεξαγωγή της συζήτησης θα μπορούσε να είναι επιβλαβής για τα χρηστά ήθη ή τη δημόσια τάξη, το δικαστήριο μπορεί να διατάξει και αυτεπαγγέλτως τη διεξαγωγή ολόκληρης της συζήτησης ή ενός μέρους της κεκλεισμένων των θυρών· οι διάδικοι, οι νόμιμοι αντιπρόσωποι, οι πληρεξούσιοι και οι τεχνικοί σύμβουλοί τους έχουν δικαίωμα να παρίστανται. Το δικαστήριο μπορεί να διατάξει να παραμείνουν στο ακροατήριο τα πρόσωπα που έχουν εντολή να τηρούν την τάξη, οι μάρτυρες και οι πραγματογνώμονες καθώς και να επιτρέψει, ύστερα από αίτηση διαδίκου, να παραμείνουν στο ακροατήριο έως τρία πρόσωπα της εκλογής του.
2. Η απόφαση της παραγράφου 1 δεν επιτρέπεται να εκδοθεί χωρίς προηγούμενη ακρόαση των διαδίκων ή των πληρεξουσίων τους και του εισαγγελέα, αν αυτός παρίσταται. Η συζήτηση γίνεται δημόσια, εκτός αν το δικαστήριο κρίνει σκόπιμο να γίνει και αυτή κεκλεισμένων των θυρών.
3. Η απόφαση που διατάζει να γίνει η συζήτηση κεκλεισμένων των θυρών καθώς και η απόφαση για την υπόθεση δημοσιεύονται σε δημόσια συνεδρίαση.
4. Ο εισαγγελέας που ήταν παρών καθώς και οι διάδικοι έχουν δικαίωμα να ασκήσουν αμέσως και αυτοτελώς τα ένδικα μέσα της έφεσης και της αναίρεσης εναντίον της απόφασης που διέταξε να γίνει η συζήτηση κεκλεισμένων των θυρών. Τα ένδικα αυτά μέσα δεν αναστέλλουν τη συζήτηση της υπόθεσης.

Article 108

Unless otherwise provided for in law, procedural steps shall be taken at the initiative and care of the parties in the proceedings.

Article 109

1. No person may be deprived of the judge assigned to them by law against their will.
2. Unless otherwise provided for in law, the competent court may not transfer its jurisdiction. Only special procedural steps may be assigned to other courts or judges in the cases provided for in law.

Article 110

1. The parties in the proceedings have the same rights and the same obligations, and are equal before the court.
2. The parties in the proceedings have the right to attend all hearings of the case, even when conducted *in camera*, and for this purpose must be summoned in accordance with the provisions of the law.
3. The parties in the proceedings are obligated to appear before the court in person when summoned for this purpose.

Article 111

1. Courtroom proceedings are based on the written preliminary procedure.
2. Unless otherwise provided for in law, no main or incidental application for judicial protection can be filed with the court without complying with the preliminary procedure. Any application filed without [complying with] the preliminary procedure shall be dismissed *ex officio* as inadmissible.

Article 112

The preliminary procedure and procedure outside the courtroom are not public, but may be attended by the parties in the proceedings, their lawful proxies and authorised [lawyers].

Article 113

1. The sittings of all civil courts are public. Deliberations in order to hand down a judgment take place in secret.
2. The person directing the course of the hearing shall set, at their discretion, the number of persons who may remain in the courtroom, and has the power to order the exclusion of juveniles, persons who are armed, as well as persons comporting themselves in a manner which is inappropriate and contrary to the order and propriety of the sitting.

Article 114

1. Where conducting the hearing would be injurious to morality or public policy, the court may also order *ex officio* that the entire hearing or part thereof take place *in camera*; the parties in the proceedings, their lawful proxies, authorised [lawyers] and technical advisors have the right to be present. The court may order that the persons charged with keeping order, witnesses and experts remain in the courtroom, and, following an application by a party in the proceedings, permit up to three persons of that party's choosing to remain in the courtroom.
2. The ruling referred to in paragraph 1 may not be issued unless the parties in the proceedings or their authorised [lawyers] and the public prosecutor, if present, have not first been heard. The hearing shall take place in public, unless the court deems it expedient that it take place *in camera*.
3. The ruling ordering a hearing *in camera* and the judgment concerning the case shall be made public in open court.
4. The public prosecutor present and the parties in the proceedings have the right to immediately and separately file the legal remedies of appeal [or] cassation against the ruling ordering that the hearing take place *in camera*. [The act of filing] such legal remedies does not stay the hearing of the case.

Άρθρο 115

1. Η διαδικασία πριν από τη δημόσια συνεδρίαση και έξω από το ακροατήριο είναι πάντοτε έγγραφη.
2. Αν δεν ορίζεται διαφορετικά, στον πρώτο βαθμό, καθώς και στις υποθέσεις της εκούσιας δικαιοδοσίας η προφορική συζήτηση είναι υποχρεωτική.
3. Με την επιφύλαξη των υποθέσεων των μικροδιαφορών, η κατάθεση προτάσεων είναι υποχρεωτική.

Άρθρο 116

1. Οι διάδικοι, οι νόμιμοι αντιπρόσωποι και οι πληρεξούσιοί τους οφείλουν να τηρούν τους κανόνες των χρηστών ηθών και της καλής πίστης, να αποφεύγουν ενέργειες που φανερά οδηγούν στην παρέλκυση της δίκης, να εκθέτουν τα πραγματικά γεγονότα που αναφέρονται στην υπόθεση, έτσι ακριβώς όπως τα γνωρίζουν με πληρότητα και σύμφωνα με την αλήθεια, αποφεύγοντας διφορούμενες και ασαφείς εκφράσεις.
2. Το δικαστήριο, οι διάδικοι, οι πληρεξούσιοι δικηγόροι και οι νόμιμοι εκπρόσωποι των διαδίκων οφείλουν να συμβάλλουν με την εν γένει δικονομική τους συμπεριφορά και ιδίως με την επιμελή διεξαγωγή της δίκης, την εμπρόθεσμη επιχείρηση διαδικαστικών πράξεων, την έγκαιρη προβολή ισχυρισμών και προσαγωγή αποδεικτικών μέσων στην επίσπευση της δίκης και στην ταχεία επίλυση της διαφοράς.

Άρθρο 116Α

Το δικαστήριο ενθαρρύνει σε κάθε στάση της δίκης και σε κάθε διαδικασία τη συμβιβαστική επίλυση της διαφοράς, την επιλογή της διαμεσολάβησης ως μέτρο εξώδικης επίλυσης της διαφοράς, υποστηρίζει σχετικές πρωτοβουλίες των διαδίκων και μπορεί να διατυπώνει προτάσεις συμβιβασμού με συνεκτίμηση της πραγματικής και νομικής κατάστασης.

ΚΕΦΑΛΑΙΟΝ ΙΔ'
Εκθέσεις.

Άρθρο 117

1. Ουσιώδη προαπαιτούμενα για κάθε έκθεση είναι:
α) να συντάσσεται όταν γίνεται η πράξη με την παρουσία όσων συμπράττουν,
β) να αναφέρει τον τόπο και το χρόνο που γίνεται η πράξη, το όνομα, το επώνυμο, το πατρώνυμο, την κατοικία, τη διεύθυνση, καθώς και τον αριθμό φορολογικού μητρώου κάθε προσώπου που είναι παρόν,
γ) να διαβάζεται στους παρόντες διαδίκους και στα άλλα πρόσωπα που συμπράττουν και να επιβεβαιώνεται από αυτούς,
δ) να υπογράφεται από το δικαστή ή δικαστικό υπάλληλο που τη συνέταξε, από το γραμματέα που συνέπραξε, από τους παρόντες διαδίκους και τα άλλα πρόσωπα που συνέπραξαν ή να αναφέρεται η άρνηση ή η αδυναμία τους να υπογράψουν.
2. Η σύνταξη της έκθεσης μπορεί να γίνεται και με ηλεκτρονικά μέσα.

ΚΕΦΑΛΑΙΟ ΙΕ'
Δικόγραφα.

Άρθρο 118

Τα δικόγραφα που επιδίδονται από έναν διάδικο σε άλλον ή υποβάλλονται στο δικαστήριο πρέπει να αναφέρουν:
1) το δικαστήριο ή τον δικαστή, ενώπιον του οποίου διεξάγεται η δίκη ή η διαδικαστική πράξη,
2) το είδος του δικογράφου,

Article 115

1. The procedure prior to the public sitting and outside the courtroom is always conducted in writing.
2. Unless otherwise provided for, oral hearings are mandatory at first instance and in cases heard under non-contentious proceedings.
3. With the exception of cases involving small claims, pleadings must be filed.

Article 116

1. The parties in the proceedings, their lawful proxies and their authorised [lawyers] are obligated to comply with the rules of morality and good faith, refrain from steps that clearly lead to the proceedings being protracted, set out the true facts to which the case relates precisely as they know them, and do so fully and truthfully, avoiding equivocal and vague expressions.
2. The court, the parties in the proceedings, the parties' authorised lawyers and the parties' lawful representatives are obligated to contribute towards expediting the proceedings and resolving the dispute swiftly through their overall procedural comportment and, in particular, by conducting the proceedings diligently, taking procedural steps within deadlines, and making assertions and producing means of evidence in good time.

Article 116A

At every stage of the proceedings and during every procedure, the court shall encourage resolution of the dispute by settlement and the option of mediation as a means of resolving the dispute out of court, shall support such initiatives by the parties in the proceedings, and may propose settlements, taking the factual and legal circumstances into consideration.

CHAPTER XIV
Reports

Article 117

1. The essential prerequisites for every report are as follows:
a) it must be prepared when the step is taken in the presence of everyone involved in its preparation;
b) it must indicate the time and place where the step is taken, the first name, last name, father's name, place of domicile, address and tax identification number of every person present;
c) it must be read to the parties in the proceedings who are present and the other persons involved, and must be confirmed by them;
d) it must be signed by the judge or officer of the court who prepared it, by the registrar involved, by the parties in the proceedings who were present and the other persons involved, or must indicate their refusal or inability to sign.
2. The report may also be prepared using electronic means.

CHAPTER XV
Procedural documents

Article 118

Procedural documents served by one party in the proceedings on another or filed with the court must indicate:
1) the court before which or judge before whom the proceedings or procedural step is taken;
2) the type of procedural document;

3) το όνομα, το επώνυμο, το πατρώνυμο, την κατοικία και τη διεύθυνση όλων των διαδίκων και των νόμιμων αντιπροσώπων τους, καθώς και τον αριθμό φορολογικού μητρώου του διαδίκου που επιδίδει ή υποβάλλει το δικόγραφο και αν πρόκειται για νομικά πρόσωπα, την επωνυμία, τη διεύθυνση της έδρας τους, καθώς και τον αριθμό του φορολογικού μητρώου τους,
4) το αντικείμενο του δικογράφου, κατά τρόπον σαφή, ορισμένο και ευσύνοπτο και
5) τη χρονολογία και την υπογραφή του διαδίκου ή του νομίμου αντιπροσώπου ή του δικαστικού πληρεξουσίου του και, όταν είναι υποχρεωτική η παράσταση με δικηγόρο, την υπογραφή του δικηγόρου. Η υπογραφή μπορεί να τεθεί και με μόνη την ηλεκτρονική επαλήθευση της ταυτότητας των παραπάνω προσώπων, όπως ο νόμος ορίζει.

Άρθρο 119

1. Τα δικόγραφα της αγωγής, της ανακοπής ερημοδικίας, της έφεσης, της αναίρεσης, της αναψηλάφησης, της τριτανακοπής, της ανακοπής εναντίον εξώδικων και δικαστικών πράξεων, της κύριας και πρόσθετης παρέμβασης, της ανακοίνωσης και της προσεπίκλησης πρέπει να περιέχουν, εκτός από τα στοιχεία που αναφέρονται στο άρθρο 118, και ακριβή καθορισμό της διεύθυνσης, και ιδίως οδό και αριθμό της κατοικίας ή του γραφείου ή του καταστήματος του διαδίκου που ενεργεί τη διαδικαστική πράξη, του νόμιμου αντιπροσώπου του και του δικαστικού πληρεξουσίου του. Τα δικόγραφα περιέχουν επίσης τις διευθύνσεις ηλεκτρονικού ταχυδρομείου των πληρεξούσιων δικηγόρων.

2. Η διάταξη της παρ. 1 εφαρμόζεται και στο δικόγραφο της δήλωσης για την εκούσια επανάληψη της δίκης, καθώς και στις προτάσεις που υποβάλλονται για πρώτη φορά σε κάθε δικαστήριο, εφόσον ο διάδικος δεν είχε κοινοποιήσει δικόγραφο από εκείνα που αναφέρονται στην παρ. 1.

3. Κάθε μεταβολή της διεύθυνσης πρέπει να γνωστοποιείται με τα δικόγραφα που κοινοποιεί ο ένας διάδικος στον άλλον ή με τις προτάσεις ή με χωριστό δικόγραφο που κατατίθεται στη γραμματεία του δικαστηρίου, στο οποίο εκκρεμεί η υπόθεση, επισυνάπτεται στη δικογραφία και κοινοποιείται στον αντίδικο.

4. Τα δικόγραφα κάθε φύσεως, είναι δυνατόν να υποβάλλονται και με ηλεκτρονικά μέσα, εφόσον φέρουν ισοδύναμη της ιδιόχειρης ηλεκτρονική υπογραφή ή σφραγίδα. Κατά τον ίδιο τρόπο είναι δυνατό να υποβάλλονται και τα επικαλούμενα με τις προτάσεις αποδεικτικά μέσα. Το δικόγραφο που έχει υποβληθεί με ηλεκτρονικά μέσα θεωρείται ότι κατατέθηκε, εφόσον επιστραφεί στον αποστολέα του εγγράφου από το δικαστήριο ηλεκτρονική απόδειξη, που θα φέρει ισοδύναμη της ιδιόχειρης ηλεκτρονική υπογραφή ή σφραγίδα και θα περιέχει και την έκθεση κατάθεσης. Δεν απαιτείται η παραπάνω υπογραφή ή σφραγίδα, αν υφίσταται ηλεκτρονικό σύστημα επικοινωνιών στα δικαστήρια, στο οποίο έχουν πρόσβαση προεγγεγραμμένοι χρήστες με πιστοποίηση ταυτότητας, το οποίο επιτρέπει την επαλήθευση της ταυτότητας αυτών, την υποβολή του δικογράφου ηλεκτρονικά και την αυτοματοποιημένη αποστολή σε αυτούς αντιγράφου του κατατεθειμένου δικογράφου.

Άρθρο 120

Η επίδοση εγγράφου που αφορά την εκκρεμή δίκη, καθώς και η επίδοση της οριστικής απόφασης, που γίνεται στη διεύθυνση της κατοικίας ή του γραφείου ή του καταστήματος, η οποία είχε αναφερθεί σύμφωνα με το άρθρο 119, είναι έγκυρη, ακόμη και αν ο αποδέκτης της επίδοσης δεν είχε ή δεν έχει πια εκεί την κατοικία ή το γραφείο ή το κατάστημά του.

Άρθρο 121

Αν δεν τηρηθούν οι διατάξεις των παραγράφων 1 και 2 του άρθρου 119, επιτρέπεται να γίνουν όλες οι επιδόσεις στον αντίκλητο, ακόμη και εκείνες που πρέπει να γίνουν στον ίδιο το διάδικο. Αν δεν υπάρχει αντίκλητος ή υπάρχει αλλά είναι άγνωστη η διεύθυνσή του, καθώς και του διαδίκου, οι επιδόσεις αυτές μπορεί να γίνουν στη γραμματεία του δικαστηρίου ενώπιον του οποίου διεξάγεται η δίκη. Για την κρίση αν είναι άγνωστη η διεύθυνση του διαδίκου ή του αντικλήτου, όταν υπάρχει, αρκεί και απλή πιθανολόγηση.

3) the first name, last name, father's name, [place of] domicile and address of all the parties in the proceedings and their lawful proxies, as well as the tax identification number of the party in the proceedings serving or filing the procedural document and, in the case of legal persons, their corporate name, the address of their registered offices and their tax identification number;
4) the subject-matter of the procedural document, in a clear, specific and concise manner; and
5) the date and signature of the party in the proceedings or their lawful proxy or their advocate and, when appearance with a lawyer is mandatory, the signature of the lawyer. The signature may also be placed with electronic verification of the identities of the aforesaid persons alone, as provided for in law.

Article 119

1. Procedural documents (actions, oppositions against a default judgment, appeals, applications for cassation, applications for re-opening proceedings, third-party proceedings, oppositions against extra-judicial and judicial acts, main and permissive interventions, third-party notices and impleaders) must also contain, in addition to the information referred to in Article 118, the precise designation of the address and, in particular, the street and number of the residence or office or store of the party in the proceedings taking the procedural step, their lawful proxy and their advocate. Procedural documents shall also contain the e-mail addresses of the authorised lawyers.
2. The provisions of paragraph 1 also apply to the procedural document known as statement for voluntary repetition of the proceedings and to pleadings first filed with each court, provided the party in question had not notified any of the procedural documents referred to in paragraph 1.
3. Any change in address must be notified by means of procedural documents sent by one party in the proceedings to another, or pleadings, or a separate procedural document filed with the registry of the court before which the case is pending, shall be attached to the case-file and notified to the opponent.
4. All manner of procedural documents may also be submitted using electronic means, provided they bear an electronic signature equivalent to a handwritten one or a seal. Means of evidence invoked in pleadings may also be submitted in the same manner. Procedural documents submitted using electronic means shall be deemed to have been filed if the court sends an electronic receipt to the sender of the document bearing an electronic signature equivalent to a handwritten one or a seal and containing the filing report. The above signature or seal shall not be required if an electronic communications system is in place at the courts, accessible to preregistered users with identity certification allowing for verification of their identity, electronic submission of procedural documents and automated dispatch of a copy of the filed procedural document to such users.

Article 120

Service of a document concerning pending proceedings and service of the final judgment effected at the address of the residence or office or store that had been indicated in accordance with Article 119 is valid even if the person served did not or no longer has their residence or office or store there.

Article 121

Where the provisions of Article 119(1) and (2) are not complied with, all documents may be served on process agents, including those that must be served on parties in the proceedings themselves. If there is no process agent or if there is a process agent but their address and that of the party in the proceedings are unknown, such documents may be served on the registry of the court before which the proceedings are being conducted. With regard to the ruling on whether the address of the party in the proceedings or the process agent, where there is one, is unknown, it shall simply suffice for the balance of probabilities test to be satisfied.

ΚΕΦΑΛΑΙΟ ΙΣΤ'
Επιδόσεις.

Άρθρο 122

1. Η επίδοση κάθε εγγράφου γίνεται με δικαστικό επιμελητή διορισμένο στο δικαστήριο, στην περιφέρεια του οποίου έχει την κατοικία ή τη διαμονή του, όταν γίνεται η επίδοση, εκείνος προς τον οποίο αυτή απευθύνεται.
2. Οι επιδόσεις που γίνονται με την επιμέλεια του δικαστηρίου μπορούν να γίνουν και από ποινικό κλητήρα της περιφέρειας ή από όργανο της ελληνικής αστυνομίας ή της δασοφυλακής, ή από το γραμματέα του δήμου.
3. Αν δεν υπάρχει δικαστικός επιμελητής στον τόπο της επίδοσης ή αν κατά την κρίση του εισαγγελέα πρωτοδικών ή του ειρηνοδίκη της περιφέρειας όπου πρόκειται να γίνει η επίδοση είναι δύσκολη η μετάβαση του δικαστικού επιμελητή στον τόπο αυτόν, η επίδοση μπορεί να γίνει και από ποινικό κλητήρα της περιφέρειας ή από όργανο της ελληνικής αστυνομίας ή της δασοφυλακής ή από τον γραμματέα του δήμου που ορίζεται από τον προαναφερόμενο εισαγγελέα ή ειρηνοδίκη.
4. Με διατάγματα που εκδίδονται με πρόταση του υπουργού δικαιοσύνης μπορεί να καθιερωθεί και η επίδοση με το ταχυδρομείο ή με τηλεγράφημα ή τηλέφωνο, όλων ή μερικών από τα προαναφερόμενα έγγραφα και παράλληλα να οριστεί ο τρόπος με τον οποίο θα γίνεται και θα αποδεικνύεται η επίδοση.
5. [Καταργείται]

Άρθρο 122Α
Επίδοση με ηλεκτρονικά μέσα

1. Επίδοση εγγράφου είναι δυνατόν να διενεργείται και με ηλεκτρονικά μέσα από πιστοποιημένο για τον σκοπό αυτόν δικαστικό επιμελητή, διορισμένο στο δικαστήριο, στην περιφέρεια του οποίου έχει την κατοικία ή τη διαμονή του ή την έδρα του, κατά τον χρόνο διενέργειας της επίδοσης, το φυσικό ή νομικό πρόσωπο προς το οποίο αυτή απευθύνεται.
2. Τα δικόγραφα είναι δυνατόν να επιδίδονται, σύμφωνα με την παρ. 1, και με ηλεκτρονικά μέσα, εφόσον φέρουν εγκεκριμένη ηλεκτρονική υπογραφή κατά την έννοια της περ. 20 του άρθρου 2 του ν. 4727/2020 (Α' 184). Η επίδοση με ηλεκτρονικά μέσα θεωρείται συντελεσμένη μόνο εφόσον επιστραφεί στον διενεργούντα την επίδοση δικαστικό επιμελητή, ηλεκτρονική απόδειξη παραλαβής του εγγράφου, η οποία φέρει εγκεκριμένη ηλεκτρονική υπογραφή, κατά την έννοια της περ. 20 του άρθρου 2 του ν. 4727/2020, του προσώπου προς το οποίο γίνεται η επίδοση. Επί ποινή ακυρότητας, η ηλεκτρονική απόδειξη περιέχεται στην έκθεση επίδοσης την οποία συντάσσει ο δικαστικός επιμελητής σύμφωνα με το άρθρο 139 ΚΠολΔ. Η επίδοση θεωρείται ανυπόστατη αν η ηλεκτρονική απόδειξη δεν περιέλθει στον διενεργούντα την επίδοση μέσα σε είκοσι τέσσερις (24) ώρες από την αποστολή. Συνέπεια του ανυπόστατου της ηλεκτρονικής επίδοσης είναι η αυτοδίκαιη διενέργειά της με φυσικό τρόπο επίδοσης, όπως ορίζουν τα άρθρα 122 επ.
3. Με την επιφύλαξη της παρ. 4, φυσικό πρόσωπο ή, στην περίπτωση νομικού προσώπου, ο νόμιμος εκπρόσωπός αυτού, που επιθυμεί να αποστέλλει ή να λαμβάνει έγγραφα με ηλεκτρονικά μέσα υποχρεούται να δηλώσει μία μοναδική ηλεκτρονική διεύθυνση στο Εθνικό Μητρώο Επικοινωνίας (Ε.Μ.Επ.) του άρθρου 17 του ν. 4704/2020 (Α' 133). Αν πρόκειται για κάτοικο εξωτερικού ή νομικό πρόσωπο με έδρα στην αλλοδαπή, η δήλωση υποβάλλεται στο ανωτέρω Μητρώο.
4. Η επίδοση με ηλεκτρονικά μέσα, όπως ορίζεται στις παρ. 1 έως 3, με παραλήπτη το Δημόσιο, πιστωτικό ίδρυμα, ίδρυμα πληρωμών, κατάστημα ηλεκτρονικού χρήματος ή ασφαλιστική εταιρεία διενεργείται στην εκάστοτε αρμόδια αποκεντρωμένη υπηρεσία ή κεντρικό υποκατάστημα της περιφέρειας, όπου κατά τον χρόνο επίδοσης, έχει την έδρα του, ο διενεργών την επίδοση δικαστικός επιμελητής. Σε περίπτωση μη ύπαρξης αρμόδιας αποκεντρωμένης υπηρεσίας ή κεντρικού υποκαταστήματος της περιφέρειας, η επίδοση διενεργείται στην κεντρική έδρα των φορέων του πρώτου εδαφίου. Για τον σκοπό αυτόν, οι νόμιμοι εκπρόσωποι των νομικών προσώπων υποχρεούνται να δηλώνουν την ηλεκτρονική τους διεύθυνση στο Ε.Μ.Επ., όπως επίσης και το όνομα του αντιπροσώπου, εκπροσώπου ή υπαλλήλου που είναι εξουσιοδοτημένος να παραλαμβάνει ηλεκτρονικά το έγγραφο που επιδίδεται.

CHAPTER XVI
Service [of process]

Article 122

1. All documents shall be served by a court process server appointed at the court in whose district the addressee has their place of residence or domicile at the time the document is being served.
2. Documents served by the court may also be served by a bailiff serving at the criminal courts of the district or a Hellenic Police officer or forest ranger, or by the secretary of the Municipality.
3. Where there is no court process server at the place of service or where, in the view of the court of first instance public prosecutor or the court of the peace judge of the district where service is to take place, it is difficult for a court process server to travel to that location, the document may also be served by a bailiff serving at the criminal courts of the district or a Hellenic Police officer or forest ranger, or by the secretary of the Municipality, designated by the aforesaid public prosecutor or court of the peace judge.
4. Service by post or telegram or telephone of some or all of the aforementioned documents may also be instituted pursuant to decrees issued on a proposal from the Minister of Justice; such decrees shall also designate how service will take place and be proven.
5. [Repealed]

Article 122A
Service using electronic means

1. Documents may also be served using electronic means by a court process server who has been certified for this purpose, is appointed at the court in whose district the natural person to whom the document is addressed has their place of residence or domicile or the legal person to whom the document is addressed has its registered offices at the time of service.
2. Procedural documents may also be served, in accordance with Article 1, using electronic means, provided they bear an approved electronic signature, within the meaning of Article 2(20) of Law 4727/2020 (Government Gazette, Series I, Issue 184). Service using electronic means shall be deemed to have been effected only if the person served dispatches an electronic acknowledgement of receipt of the document bearing an approved electronic signature, within the meaning of Article 2(20) of Law 4727/2020, to the court process server effecting service. On penalty of nullity, the electronic acknowledgement shall be included in the service report prepared by the court process server in accordance with Article 139 of this Code. Service shall be deemed to be void if the person effecting service does not receive the electronic acknowledgement within 24 hours of the time it was sent. As a result of electronic service being void, service must be automatically effected using physical means, in accordance with Articles 122 *et seq.*
3. Without prejudice to the paragraph 4, any natural person or, in the case of a legal person, its lawful representative who wishes to send or receive documents using electronic means is obligated to declare a single e-mail address to the National Communication Register referred to in Article 17 of Law 4704/2020 (Government Gazette, Series I, Issue 133). In cases of a person resident abroad or a legal person with registered offices abroad, the declaration shall be submitted to the aforementioned Register.
4. Where the recipient is the Greek State, a credit institution, a payment institution, an electronic money institution or an insurance company, service using electronic means, as defined in paragraphs 1 to 3, shall be effected at the competent decentralised department or central branch in the district where the court process server effecting service has their offices at the time of service in each case. Where there is no competent decentralised department or central branch in the district, service shall be effected at the headquarters of the bodies referred to in the first subparagraph. For this purpose, the lawful representatives of legal persons are obligated to declare their e-mail address to the National Communication Register, as well as the name of the proxy, representative or employee authorised to electronically receive the document served.

5. [Καταργείται]
6. Αντικατάσταση ή κατάργηση της ηλεκτρονικής διεύθυνσης που έχει καταχωριστεί γίνεται σύμφωνα με το άρθρο 17 του ν. 4704/2020.
7. Η επίδοση στον αντίκλητο πληρεξούσιο δικηγόρο, σύμφωνα με τις παρ. 1 και 3 του άρθρου 143, μπορεί να γίνεται και στη διεύθυνση ηλεκτρονικού ταχυδρομείου που περιέχεται σε δικόγραφο, σύμφωνα με την παρ. 1 του άρθρου 119 ΚΠολΔ.
8. Στις περιπτώσεις ηλεκτρονικής επίδοσης οι δικονομικές προθεσμίες παρατείνονται κατά μία (1) ημέρα.
9. Με κοινή απόφαση των Υπουργών Δικαιοσύνης και Ψηφιακής Διακυβέρνησης, εξειδικεύονται οι όροι δημιουργίας και λειτουργίας της ηλεκτρονικής εφαρμογής για την επίδοση εγγράφων με ηλεκτρονικά μέσα και καθορίζεται κάθε αναγκαία, τεχνική ή άλλη λεπτομέρεια για την εφαρμογή του παρόντος.
10. [Καταργείται]

Άρθρο 123

1. Η επίδοση γίνεται με την επιμέλεια του διαδίκου ύστερα από παραγγελία που δίνεται είτε από τον ίδιο ή τον πληρεξούσιό του, είτε, με αίτησή της, από τον αρμόδιο δικαστή, και προκειμένου για πολυμελή δικαστήρια από τον πρόεδρό τους.
2. Η παραγγελία για επίδοση δίνεται εγγράφως κάτω από το έγγραφο που επιδίδεται.

Άρθρο 124

1. Η επίδοση επιτρέπεται οπουδήποτε βρεθεί το πρόσωπο προς το οποίο πρόκειται να γίνει.
2. Αν το πρόσωπο έχει στον τόπο όπου πρόκειται να γίνει η επίδοση κατοικία, κατάστημα, γραφείο ή εργαστήριο, είτε μόνο του είτε με άλλον ή εργάζεται εκεί ως υπάλληλος, εργάτης ή υπηρέτης, η επίδοση σε άλλο μέρος δεν μπορεί να γίνει χωρίς τη συναίνεσή του.
3. Η επίδοση δεν επιτρέπεται να γίνει σε εκκλησία, την ώρα που γίνεται ιεροτελεστία ή άλλη θρησκευτική τελετή ή προσευχή, ούτε σε αίθουσα δικαστηρίου όταν αυτό συνεδριάζει.

Άρθρο 125

1. Η επίδοση δεν επιτρέπεται να γίνει νύχτα, Σάββατο ή Κυριακή ή άλλη εορτή που ορίζεται από το νόμο ως αργία, χωρίς να συναινεί ο παραλήπτης ή χωρίς άδεια του αρμόδιου δικαστή στον οποίο εκκρεμεί η υπόθεση και, αν πρόκειται για πολυμελή δικαστήρια, του προέδρου τους. Αν δεν εκκρεμεί δίκη, η άδεια δίνεται από τον ειρηνοδίκη, στην περιφέρεια του οποίου πρόκειται να γίνει η επίδοση.
2. Η νύχτα θεωρείται ότι διαρκεί από τις 7 το βράδυ έως τις 7 το πρωί.
3. Η άδεια που δίνεται στις περιπτώσεις της παραγράφου 1 πρέπει να σημειώνεται στο έγγραφο που επιδίδεται και στην έκθεση της επίδοσης.

Άρθρο 126

1. Η επίδοση γίνεται:
α) προσωπικά σε εκείνον στον οποίο απευθύνεται το έγγραφο,
β) για πρόσωπα που δεν έχουν ικανότητα δικαστικής παράστασης, στο νόμιμο αντιπρόσωπό τους,
γ) για νομικά πρόσωπα ή άλλες ενώσεις προσώπων, στον εκπρόσωπό τους, σύμφωνα με το νόμο ή το καταστατικό,
δ) για το δημόσιο, σε εκείνους που το εκπροσωπούν σύμφωνα με το νόμο.
2. Αν υπάρχουν περισσότεροι νόμιμοι αντιπρόσωποι, αρκεί η επίδοση σε έναν από αυτούς.

5. [Repealed]
6. Any e-mail address registered shall be replaced or removed in accordance with Article 17 of Law 4704/2020.
7. Documents may also be served on authorised lawyers who are process agents, in accordance with the provisions of Article 143(1) and (3), at the e-mail address contained in a procedural document, in accordance with Article 119(1) of this Code.
8. In cases of electronic service, procedural deadlines shall be extended by one day.
9. A joint decision of the Minister of Justice and the Minister of Digital Governance shall specify the terms of creation and operation of the electronic application for the service of documents using electronic means and set out all necessary, technical or other details required to give effect to this [Article].
10. [Repealed]

Article 123

1. Documents shall be served by the party in the proceedings [effecting service] following an order issued either by that party or their authorised representative, or, following a request for service, by the competent judge and, in the case of multi-member courts, by their presiding judge.
2. The order for service shall be made out in writing [at the end of] the document being served.

Article 124

1. Service may be effected at any location where the person being served is found.
2. If the person being served has their residence, store, office or workshop at the place where service is to be effected, either alone or with another person, or works there as an employee, worker or servant, service cannot be effected at a different location without their consent.
3. Service may not be effected at a church during a ritual or other religious ceremony or prayer, nor at a courtroom during a sitting.

Article 125

1. Service may not be effected at night-time, on Saturdays or Sundays or other holiday designated by law as a bank holiday without the consent of the recipient or without leave of the competent judge before whom the case is pending and, in the case of multi-member courts, their presiding judge. If no proceedings are pending, such leave shall be granted by the court of the peace judge in whose district service is to be effected.
2. Night-time is considered to last from 7 in the evening to 7 in the morning.
3. Leave granted in the cases referred to in paragraph 1 must be noted on the document served and in the service report.

Article 126

1. Service shall be effected:
a) personally to addressee of the document;
b) to the lawful proxies of persons who do not have capacity to appear before the courts;
c) to the representatives of legal persons or other groupings of persons, in accordance with the law or their statutes;
d) with regard to the Greek State, to the persons who represent it in accordance with the law.
2. If there is more than one lawful proxy, service on one such proxy shall suffice.

Άρθρο 127

1. Η επίδοση συνίσταται στην παράδοση του εγγράφου στα χέρια του προσώπου προς το οποίο γίνεται.
2. Αν η επίδοση γίνεται στο νόμιμο αντιπρόσωπο περισσότερων ανίκανων προσώπων ή στον αντίκλητο περισσοτέρων, αρκεί να του παραδοθεί ένα μόνο αντίγραφο ή πρωτότυπο του εγγράφου που πρέπει να επιδοθεί.

Άρθρο 128

1. Αν ο παραλήπτης δεν βρίσκεται στην κατοικία του, το έγγραφο παραδίδεται σε έναν από τους ενήλικους συνοίκους του, που έχουν συνείδηση των πράξεών τους και δεν συμμετέχουν στη δίκη ως αντίδικοί του.
2. Κατοικία, με την έννοια της παραγράφου 1, είναι το σπίτι ή το διαμέρισμα που είναι προορισμένο για διημέρευση ή διανυκτέρευση του παραλήπτη, ακόμη και αν για πολύ μικρό χρονικό διάστημα δεν χρησιμοποιείται για το σκοπό αυτόν.
3. Σύνοικοι θεωρούνται εκείνοι που διαμένουν στο ίδιο διαμέρισμα, οι θυρωροί πολυκατοικιών και τα μέλη της οικογένειάς που συνοικούν μαζί τους, οι διευθυντές ξενοδοχείων και οικοτροφείων, καθώς και το υπηρετικό και υπαλληλικό προσωπικό τους, όχι όμως οι ένοικοι άλλου διαμερίσματος ή δωματίου της ίδιας κατοικίας.
4. Αν κανείς από όσους αναφέρονται στην παράγραφο 1 δεν βρίσκεται στην κατοικία,
α) το έγγραφο πρέπει να κολληθεί στην πόρτα της κατοικίας και σε ενσφράγιστο φάκελο, επί του οποίου θα υπάρχουν μόνο τα στοιχεία του δικαστικού επιμελητή και του προς όν η επίδοση, μπροστά σε ένα μάρτυρα. Σε περιπτώσεις πολυκατοικιών, οι οποίες είναι κλειστές και δεν είναι δυνατόν να κολληθεί το έγγραφο στην πόρτα της κατοικίας, η επικόλληση μπορεί να γίνεται κατά τα ανωτέρω και στην κεντρική είσοδο της πολυκατοικίας,
β) το αργότερο την επομένη εργάσιμη ημέρα μετά τη θυροκόλληση, αντίγραφο του εγγράφου, που συντάσσεται ατελώς, πρέπει να παραδοθεί στα χέρια του προϊσταμένου του αστυνομικού τμήματος ή σταθμού της περιφέρειας της κατοικίας και αν λείπει ο προϊστάμενος, στον αξιωματικό ή υπαξιωματικό υπηρεσίας ή στο σκοπό του αστυνομικού καταστήματος. Σε όλες αυτές τις περιπτώσεις η παράδοση βεβαιώνεται με απόδειξη που συντάσσεται ατελώς κάτω από την έκθεση της επίδοσης που αναφέρεται στο άρθρο 140 παράγραφος 1. Η απόδειξη αυτή πρέπει να αναφέρει την ημερομηνία που έγινε η παράδοση, και το ονοματεπώνυμο, καθώς και την ιδιότητα εκείνου που παρέλαβε το αντίγραφο, ο οποίος υπογράφει την απόδειξη και τη σφραγίζει με την υπηρεσιακή σφραγίδα. Το αντίγραφο που παραδόθηκε φυλάγεται σε ιδιαίτερο φάκελο στο υπηρεσιακό γραφείο, όπου υπηρετεί εκείνος που το παρέλαβε,
γ) το αργότερο την επόμενη εργάσιμη ημέρα από την παράδοση, σύμφωνα με την περίπτωση β', εκείνος που ενήργησε την επίδοση του εγγράφου πρέπει να ταχυδρομήσει σε εκείνον προς τον οποίο απευθύνεται η επίδοση έγγραφη ειδοποίηση στην οποία πρέπει να αναφέρεται το είδος του εγγράφου που επιδόθηκε, η διεύθυνση της κατοικίας, όπου έγινε η θυροκόλλησή του, η ημερομηνία της θυροκόλλησης, η αρχή στην οποία παραδόθηκε το αντίγραφο, καθώς και η ημερομηνία της παράδοσης. Η ειδοποίηση ταχυδρομείται με έξοδα εκείνου που ζητεί να γίνει η επίδοση. Το γεγονός ότι ταχυδρομήθηκε η ειδοποίηση βεβαιώνεται με απόδειξη, την οποία συντάσσει και υπογράφει ατελώς, κάτω από την επιδοτήρια έκθεση της παραγράφου 1 του άρθρου 140, εκείνος που ενεργεί την επίδοση. Η βεβαίωση πρέπει να αναφέρει το ταχυδρομικό γραφείο, με το οποίο έστειλε την ειδοποίηση, και τον υπάλληλο που την παρέλαβε, ο οποίος προσυπογράφει τη βεβαίωση. Ύστερα από προφορική αίτηση του παραλήπτη, η αρχή στην οποία είχε παραδοθεί το αντίγραφο, σύμφωνα με την άνω περίπτωση β' του παρόντος, του το παραδίδει, με έγγραφη απόδειξη που συντάσσεται ατελώς.

Άρθρο 129

1. Αν ο παραλήπτης της επίδοσης δεν βρίσκεται στο κατάστημα, το γραφείο ή το εργαστήριο, που προβλέπει το άρθρο 124 παρ. 2, το έγγραφο παραδίδεται στα χέρια του διευθυντή του καταστήματος, του γραφείου ή του εργαστηρίου ή σε έναν από τους συνεταίρους, συνεργάτες, υπαλλήλους ή υπηρέτες, εφόσον έχουν συνείδηση των πράξεών τους και δεν συμμετέχουν στη δίκη ως αντίδικοι του παραλήπτη της επίδοσης.
2. Αν κανένα από τα πρόσωπα που αναφέρονται στην παράγραφο 1 δεν βρίσκεται στο κατάστημα, στο γραφείο ή στο εργαστήριο, εφαρμόζονται όσα ορίζονται το άρθρο 128 παρ. 4.

Article 127

1. Service consists of delivery of the document into the hands of the person on whom service is effected.
2. Where service is being effected on the lawful proxy of several persons lacking legal capacity or the process agent of several persons, delivery of a single copy or original version of the document to be served suffices.

Article 128

1. If the recipient is not at their residence, the document shall be delivered to an adult co-habitant who is in command of their faculties and is not participating in the proceedings as an opponent [of the recipient].
2. "Residence", within the meaning of paragraph 1, meanσ a house or apartment intended for the recipient to spend the day or night, even if it is not used for that purpose for a very short period of time.
3. "Co-habitants" means those residing in the same apartment, the caretaker of apartment buildings and their co-habitant relatives, the managers of hotels and dormitories, as well as their servants and employees, but not the residents of a different apartment or room within the same residence.
4. If none of the persons referred to in paragraph 1 is at the residence[:]
a) the document must be affixed on the door of the residence, in a sealed envelope bearing only the particulars of the court process server and the person being served, in the presence of a witness. In cases of apartment buildings where [the main entrance doors] are closed and the document cannot be posted on the door of the residence, the document may be posted in accordance with the foregoing at the central entrance of the apartment building;
b) no later than the working day after constructive service, a copy of the document, prepared free of official charges, must be delivered into the hands of the commanding officer of the police department or station of the district where the residence is located and, if the commander is absent, to the officer or non-commissioned officer on duty or to the guard of the police department. In all these cases, delivery shall be attested by a receipt prepared free of official charges [at the end of] the service report referred to in Article 140(1). This receipt must indicate the date of the delivery and the full name and capacity of the person who received the copy, who shall sign the receipt and place an official seal. The copy delivered shall be kept in a special dossier at the office where the recipient serves;
c) no later than the working day after delivery, in accordance with point (b), the person who served the document must post a written notice to the person being served indicating the type of document served, the address of the residence where constructive service of the document was affected, the date of constructive service, the authority to which the copy was delivered, and the date of delivery. The notice shall be posted at the expense of the person requesting service. The fact that the notice was posted shall be attested by a receipt, prepared and signed, free of official charges, [at the end of] the service report referred to in Article 140(1) by the person effecting service. The attestation must indicate the post office from which the notice was sent and the post office clerk who received it, who shall countersign the attestation. Following a verbal request by the recipient, the authority to which the copy was delivered in accordance with point (b) above shall deliver it to the recipient and prepare a written receipt free of official charges.

Article 129

1. If the recipient of the document to be served is not at the store, office or workshop referred to in Article 142(2), the document shall be delivered into the hands of the manager of the store, office or workshop or one of the partners, associates, employees or servants, provided they are in command of their faculties and and are not participating in the proceedings as opponents of the recipient.
2. If none of the persons referred to in paragraph 1 is at the store, office or workshop, the provisions of Article 128(4) apply.

Άρθρο 130

1. Αν ο παραλήπτης της επίδοσης ή τα πρόσωπα που αναφέρονται στα άρθρα 128 και 129 αρνηθούν να παραλάβουν το έγγραφο ή να υπογράψουν την έκθεση της επίδοσης ή αν δεν μπορούν να την υπογράψουν, το όργανο της επίδοσης επικολλά το έγγραφο στην πόρτα της κατοικίας, του γραφείου, του καταστήματος ή του εργαστηρίου, μπροστά σε ένα μάρτυρα.

2. Αν ο παραλήπτης της επίδοσης δεν έχει κατοικία, γραφείο, κατάστημα ή εργαστήριο και είτε αρνείται να παραλάβει το έγγραφο είτε δεν μπορεί ή αρνείται να υπογράψει την έκθεση της επίδοσης και η άρνηση του παραλήπτη ή η αδυναμία του βεβαιώνεται και από ένα μάρτυρα που προσλαμβάνεται από το όργανο της επίδοσης για το σκοπό αυτόν, το έγγραφο παραδίδεται στα χέρια των προσώπων που αναφέρονται στο άρθρο 128 παράγραφος 4 εδάφιο β'.

Άρθρο 131

Αν ο παραλήπτης της επίδοσης νοσηλεύεται σε νοσοκομείο ή κρατείται σε φυλακή και δεν είναι δυνατή η επικοινωνία μαζί του σύμφωνα με βεβαίωση της διεύθυνσης του νοσοκομείου ή της φυλακής, που σημειώνεται στην έκθεση της επίδοσης, η επίδοση μπορεί να γίνει στο διευθυντή του νοσοκομείου ή της φυλακής, ο οποίος είναι υποχρεωμένος να παραδώσει το έγγραφο στα χέρια εκείνου προς τον οποίον γίνεται η επίδοση.

Άρθρο 132

1. Αν εκείνος προς τον οποίο πρέπει να γίνει η επίδοση υπηρετεί σε εμπορικό πλοίο που βρίσκεται σε ελληνικό λιμάνι, αν απουσιάζει ή αρνείται να παραλάβει το έγγραφο ή αρνείται ή δεν μπορεί να υπογράψει την έκθεση, η επίδοση γίνεται στον πλοίαρχο του πλοίου ή στον αναπληρωτή του και αν απουσιάζουν ή αρνούνται και αυτοί να το παραλάβουν, η επίδοση γίνεται στο λιμενάρχη, ο οποίος είναι υποχρεωμένος να ειδοποιήσει εκείνον προς τον οποίο γίνεται η επίδοση.

2. Αν εκείνος προς τον οποίο πρέπει να γίνει η επίδοση υπηρετεί σε εμπορικό πλοίο που δεν βρίσκεται σε ελληνικό λιμάνι, η επίδοση γίνεται στην κατοικία του, σύμφωνα με το άρθρο 128 και αν δεν έχει κατοικία, γίνεται σύμφωνα με τις διατάξεις για την επίδοση σε πρόσωπο άγνωστης διαμονής. Σε κάθε περίπτωση η επίδοση γίνεται και στα γραφεία του πλοιοκτήτη στην Ελλάδα ή διαφορετικά, στα γραφεία του πράκτορα του πλοίου σε ελληνικό λιμάνι, εφόσον υπάρχουν.

Άρθρο 133

1. Για πρόσωπα που ανήκουν σε μία από τις ακόλουθες κατηγορίες και βρίσκονται σε ενεργή υπηρεσία, αν δεν είναι δυνατή η επίδοση στους ίδιους ή στους συγγενείς ή υπηρέτες, που συνοικούν μαζί τους, γίνεται, σύμφωνα με τις παραγράφους 3 και 4 του ίδιου άρθρου 128 καθώς και

α) για εκείνους που υπηρετούν γενικά στις ένοπλες δυνάμεις της ξηράς, στο διοικητή της μονάδας ή του καταστήματος ή της υπηρεσίας, όπου ανήκει ο παραλήπτης της επίδοσης. Αν είναι άγνωστη η μονάδα, το κατάστημα ή η υπηρεσία, η επίδοση γίνεται στον αρχηγό του αντίστοιχου κλάδου,

β) για αξιωματικούς, υπαξιωματικούς και ναύτες του πολεμικού ναυτικού, στον αρχηγό του γενικού επιτελείου ναυτικού,

γ) για αξιωματικούς, υπαξιωματικούς και σμηνίτες της πολεμικής αεροπορίας, στον αρχηγό του γενικού επιτελείου αεροπορίας,

δ) για αξιωματικούς και υπαξιωματικούς της αστυνομίας πόλεων, της χωροφυλακής και του λιμενικού σώματος καθώς και για αστυφύλακες, χωροφύλακες και λιμενοφύλακες, στον προϊστάμενο της υπηρεσίας τους,

ε) για εκείνους που ανήκουν στο προσωπικό των φάρων, των φανών και των σηματοφόρων, στο λιμενάρχη της περιφέρειας, όπου ασκούν τα καθήκοντά τους.

2. Οι αναφερόμενοι στην παράγραφο 1 α' έως ε', όταν λάβουν το έγγραφο, είναι υποχρεωμένοι να το στείλουν χωρίς υπαίτια καθυστέρηση σε εκείνον στον οποίο πρέπει να γίνει η επίδοση με το πιο γρήγορο και πιο ασφαλές μέσο.

Article 130

1. If the recipient of the document to be served or the persons referred to in Articles 128 and 129 refuse to receive the document or sign the service report or are unable to sign, the person effecting service shall affix the document to the door of the residence, office, store or workshop, in the presence of a witness.

2. If the recipient of the document to be served does not have a residence, office, store or workshop and either refuses to receive the document or is unable or refuses to sign the service report and the recipient's refusal or inability is also attested by a witness enlisted by the person effecting service for this purpose, the document shall be delivered into the hands of the persons referred to in Article 128(4)(b).

Article 131

If the recipient of the document to be served is being treated at a hospital or detained in prison and communication with them is not possible, in accordance with an attestation prepared by the management of the hospital or the prison and noted on the service report, service may be effected to the hospital director or the prison governor, who is obligated to deliver the document into the hands of the person being served.

Article 132

1. If the person being served is serving on a merchant ship at a Greek port and is away or refuses to receive the document or refuses or is unable to sign the report, the document shall be served on the master of the ship or their substitute and, if they are also away or also refuse to receive it, the document shall be served on the harbour master, who is obligated to notify the person being served.

2. If the person being served is serving on a merchant ship not at a Greek port, the document shall be served at their residence, in accordance with Article 128 and, if they have no residence, the document shall be served in accordance with the provisions concerning service on a person of no known residence. In all cases, the document may also be served at the offices of the owner-operator in Greece, otherwise at the offices of the ship's agent at a Greek port, where such offices exist.

Article 133

1. With regard to persons belonging to any of the following categories who are in active service, if it is not possible to serve documents on such persons or their relatives or servants or co-habitants, such documents shall be served in accordance with Article 128(3) and (4), as well as[:]

a) for persons generally serving in the Hellenic Army, on the commander of the unit or facility or department to which the person being served belongs. If the unit, facility or department is unknown, service shall be effected on the chief of the respective branch;

b) for officers, non-commissioned officers and sailors of the Hellenic Navy, on the Chief of the Hellenic Navy General Staff;

c) for officers, non-commissioned officers and airmen of the Hellenic Air Force, on the Chief of the Hellenic Air Force General Staff;

d) for officers and non-commissioned officers of city police forces, the gendarmerie and Hellenic Coast Guard, as well as for police constables, gendarmes and coast guards, on the commanding officer of their department;

e) for persons belonging to lighthouse, lighting and semaphore personnel, on the harbour master of the district where they perform their duties.

2. When the persons referred to in paragraph 1(a) to (e) receive the document, they shall be obligated to send it without undue delay to the person being served using the swiftest and most secure means.

Άρθρο 134

1. Αν το πρόσωπο στο οποίο γίνεται η επίδοση διαμένει ή έχει την έδρα του στο εξωτερικό, η επίδοση γίνεται στον εισαγγελέα του δικαστηρίου, στο οποίο εκκρεμεί ή πρόκειται να εισαχθεί η δίκη ή σ' αυτό που εξέδωσε την επιδιδόμενη απόφαση και για δίκες στο ειρηνοδικείο, στον εισαγγελέα του πρωτοδικείου, στην περιφέρεια του οποίου υπάγεται το ειρηνοδικείο. Για έγγραφα που αφορούν την εκτέλεση, η επίδοση γίνεται στον εισαγγελέα πρωτοδικών, στην περιφέρεια του οποίου γίνεται η εκτέλεση, και για εξώδικες πράξεις, στον εισαγγελέα της τελευταίας στο εσωτερικό κατοικίας ή γνωστής διαμονής του παραλήπτη της επίδοσης και αν δεν υπάρχει κατοικία ή γνωστή διαμονή στο εσωτερικό, η επίδοση γίνεται στον εισαγγελέα πρωτοδικών της πρωτεύουσας.
2. Στις περιπτώσεις της παραγράφου 1 η παραγγελία για επίδοση πρέπει να περιέχει με ακρίβεια τον τόπο και τη διεύθυνση του παραλήπτη της επίδοσης.
3. Ο εισαγγελέας, όταν παραλάβει το έγγραφο, οφείλει να το αποστείλει χωρίς υπαίτια καθυστέρηση στον Υπουργό των Εξωτερικών ο οποίος έχει την υποχρέωση να το διαβιβάσει σε εκείνον προς τον οποίον γίνεται η επίδοση.

Άρθρο 135

1. Αν είναι άγνωστος ο τόπος ή η ακριβής διεύθυνση διαμονής εκείνου προς τον οποίο πρέπει να γίνει η επίδοση, εφαρμόζονται οι διατάξεις της παραγράφου 1 του άρθρου 134 και συγχρόνως δημοσιεύεται σε δύο ημερήσιες εφημερίδες, από τις οποίες η μία πρέπει να εκδίδεται στην Αθήνα και η άλλη στην έδρα του δικαστηρίου, διαφορετικά και η άλλη πρέπει να εκδίδεται στην Αθήνα, ύστερα από υπόδειξη του εισαγγελέα στον οποίο γίνεται η επίδοση, περίληψη του δικογράφου που κοινοποιήθηκε· η περίληψη συντάσσεται και υπογράφεται από εκείνον που ενεργεί την επίδοση και πρέπει να αναφέρεται το ονοματεπώνυμο των διαδίκων, το είδος του δικογράφου που επιδόθηκε, το αίτημά του και, προκειμένου για απόφαση, το διατακτικό, το δικαστήριο στο οποίο εκκρεμεί ή πρόκειται να εισαχθεί η δίκη ή τον υπάλληλο που ενεργεί την εκτέλεση και, αν εκείνος προς τον οποίο γίνεται η επίδοση καλείται να εμφανιστεί ή να ενεργήσει ορισμένη πράξη, πρέπει να αναφέρεται ο τόπος και ο χρόνος εμφάνισης, καθώς και το είδος της πράξης.
2. Όποιος επισπεύδει την επίδοση σε πρόσωπο άγνωστης διαμονής μπορεί να δημοσιεύσει σε εφημερίδες προσκλήσεις προς καθέναν που γνωρίζει τον τόπο και τη συγκεκριμένη διεύθυνση διαμονής εκείνου προς τον οποίο πρέπει να γίνει η επίδοση, να ανακοινώσει ενυπογράφως τα στοιχεία αυτά, με αναφορά της συγκεκριμένης διεύθυνσής του, στη γραμματεία του πρωτοδικείου Αθηνών ή του πρωτοδικείου της τελευταίας κατοικίας ή διαμονής του· ως προς τις εφημερίδες εφαρμόζεται ανάλογα η παράγραφος 1 του άρθρου αυτού· ο προσδιορισμός τους γίνεται από τον εισαγγελέα που είναι αρμόδιος σύμφωνα με το άρθρο 134 παρ. 1, ύστερα από αίτηση εκείνου που επισπεύδει την επίδοση. Οι δημοσιεύσεις γίνονται σε εμφανές μέρος των εφημερίδων και μάλιστα σε δύο φύλλα που απέχουν μεταξύ τους οκτώ ημέρες. Στις προσκλήσεις που δημοσιεύονται με τον τρόπο αυτόν δεν είναι απαραίτητο να αναφέρεται ο λόγος για τον οποίο ζητούνται τα στοιχεία. Αν, ύστερα από οκτώ ημέρες, μετά την τελευταία δημοσίευση, δεν φτάνει ανακοίνωση σε καμιά από τις γραμματείες αυτές, ισχύει το τεκμήριο ότι ο τόπος ή η συγκεκριμένη διεύθυνση διαμονής του παραλήπτη της επίδοσης είναι άγνωστα και η ανταπόδειξη αποκλείεται.
3. Οι διατάξεις της παραγράφου 1 εφαρμόζονται και στις περιπτώσεις που το υπουργείο εξωτερικών βεβαιώσει ότι δεν είναι δυνατή η αποστολή του εγγράφου σε πρόσωπο που διαμένει ή εδρεύει στο εξωτερικό.

Άρθρο 136

1. Η επίδοση θεωρείται ότι συντελέστηκε, προκειμένου για πρόσωπα που αναφέρονται στα άρθρα 131 έως 134, μόλις παραδοθεί το έγγραφο στις αρχές ή τα πρόσωπα που ορίζονται εκεί, ανεξάρτητα από το χρόνο της αποστολής και παραλαβής του, και για τα πρόσωπα άγνωστης διαμονής η επίδοση θεωρείται ότι ολοκληρώθηκε από τη δημοσίευση της περίληψης σύμφωνα με το άρθρο 135 παρ. 1.
2. Στις επιδόσεις του άρθρο 128 παρ. 4 η επίδοση θεωρείται ότι συντελέστηκε με τη θυροκόλληση του εγγράφου στην πόρτα της κατοικίας εκείνου προς τον οποίο γίνεται η επίδοση, με την προϋπόθεση ότι έγιναν όσα ορίζονται στην παράγραφο αυτή με τα στοιχεία β' και γ'.

Article 134

1. If the person being served is resident or seated abroad, the document shall be served on the public prosecutor of the court before which the proceedings are pending, or before which the proceedings will be conducted, or before the court that handed down the judgment being served; with regard to proceedings before the court of the peace, on the court of first instance public prosecutor within whose district the court of the peace falls. Documents concerning enforcement shall be served on the court of first instance public prosecutor in whose district enforcement is taking place, while extra-judicial documents shall be served on the public prosecutor of the last domestic domicile or known residence of the person being served, and, absent such, on the court of first instance public prosecutor of the capital.
2. In the cases referred to in paragraph 1, the order for service must accurately indicate the location and address of the person being served.
3. Upon receiving the document, the public prosecutor must send it without undue delay to the Minister of Foreign Affairs, who is obligated to forward it to the person being served.

Article 135

1. If the place of residence or precise address of the person being served is unknown, the provisions of Article 134(1) apply, and a summary of the procedural document notified shall be concurrently published in two daily newspapers, of which one must be published in Athens and the other at the seat of the court, otherwise both must be published in Athens, following a recommendation by the public prosecutor served; the summary shall be prepared and signed by the person effecting service and must indicate the full names of the parties in the proceedings, the type of procedural document served, the form of order sought and, in cases of judgments, the operative part of the judgment, the court before which the proceedings are pending or are to be conducted or the officer effecting enforcement and, if the person being served is being summoned to appear or to take a specific step, it must also indicate the time and place of appearance, as well as the type of step to be taken.
2. The person initiating service on a person of no known residence may publish notices in newspapers, addressed to any person familiar with the location and specific address of the residence of the person being served, to provide a signed document containing the information in question, making reference to the specific address of the person being served, at the registry of the Athens Court of First Instance or the court of first instance of the last domicile or residence of the person being served. Paragraph 1 of this Article shall apply *mutatis mutandis* to newspapers, which shall be designated by the public prosecutor competent under Article 134(1), following a request by the person requesting service. Such notices shall be published in a prominent section of the newspapers and, in fact, in two issues published eight days apart. Notices published in this manner need not indicate the reasons why information is being sought. If these registries receive no information after eight days have elapsed since the last publication, it shall be presumed that the person being served had no known place of residence or specific address, and counter-evidence is precluded.
3. The provisions of paragraph 1 also apply in cases where the Ministry of Foreign Affairs attests that it was not possible to send the document to a person resident or seated abroad.

Article 136

1. Service on the persons referred to in Articles 131 to 134 shall be deemed to have been effected as soon as the document is delivered to the authorities or persons designated therein, irrespective of the time of dispatch and receipt, while service on persons of no known residence shall be deemed to be complete upon publication of the summary in accordance with Article 135(1).
2. In the cases referred to in Article 128(4), constructive service of the document shall be considered as [consisting of] affixing the document to the door of the residence of the person being served, provided the steps set forth in [Article 128(4)(b) and (c)] were taken.

Άρθρο 137

Η επίδοση σε εκείνους που έχουν τη διαμονή ή την έδρα τους στο εξωτερικό μπορεί να γίνει και με τις διατυπώσεις του αλλοδαπού νόμου, από τα όργανα που αυτός ορίζει.

Άρθρο 138

Αν τα γραφεία ή καταστήματα που αναφέρονται στα άρθρα 128 παρ. 4 στοιχείο β', 131, 132 και 133, είναι κλειστά ή οι αρχές ή τα πρόσωπα που αναφέρονται σ' αυτά αρνούνται να παραλάβουν το επιδιδόμενο έγγραφο ή να υπογράψουν την έκθεση της επίδοσης, όποιος ενεργεί την επίδοση συντάσσει σχετική έκθεση και παραδίδει το επιδιδόμενο έγγραφο στον εισαγγελέα πρωτοδικών, στην αρμοδιότητα του οποίου ανήκει ο τόπος της επίδοσης, ο οποίος αποστέλλει το έγγραφο σε εκείνον που είχε αρνηθεί να το παραλάβει ή να υπογράψει την έκθεση. Στην περίπτωση αυτή εφαρμόζεται το άρθρο 136.

Άρθρο 139

1. Όποιος ενεργεί την επίδοση συντάσσει έκθεση, η οποία εκτός από όσα απαιτεί το άρθρο 117, πρέπει να περιέχει και

α) την παραγγελία για επίδοση,

β) σαφή καθορισμό του εγγράφου που επιδόθηκε και των προσώπων που αφορά,

γ) μνεία της ημέρας και της ώρας της επίδοσης,

δ) μνεία του προσώπου στο οποίο παραδόθηκε το έγγραφο και τον τρόπο που επιδόθηκε σε περίπτωση απουσίας ή άρνησης του παραλήπτη ή των προσώπων που ορίζονται στα άρθρα 128 έως 135 και 138.

2. Η έκθεση υπογράφεται από εκείνον που ενεργεί την επίδοση, καθώς και από εκείνον που παραλαμβάνει το έγγραφο και σε περίπτωση άρνησης ή αδυναμίας του, υπογράφεται και από το μάρτυρα που είχε προσληφθεί για το σκοπό αυτόν.

3. Όποιος ενεργεί την επίδοση σημειώνει πάνω στο επιδιδόμενο έγγραφο την ημέρα και την ώρα της επίδοσης και υπογράφει. Η σημείωση αυτή αποτελεί απόδειξη υπέρ εκείνου προς τον οποίο έγινε η επίδοση. Αν υπάρχει διαφορά ανάμεσα στην έκθεση της επίδοσης και στη σημείωση, υπερισχύει η έκθεση.

Άρθρο 140

1. Η έκθεση του άρθρου 139 συντάσσεται σε δύο πρωτότυπα, από τα οποία το ένα παραδίδεται σε εκείνον που είχε δώσει την παραγγελία της επίδοσης, ενώ το άλλο, ατελώς, φυλάγεται από το όργανο της επίδοσης. Για την επίδοση γίνεται περιληπτική σημείωση σε ειδικό βιβλίο που τηρεί το όργανο της επίδοσης.

2. Ο δικαστικός επιμελητής οφείλει να δίνει αντίγραφα από το πρωτότυπο που έχει στο αρχείο του, ύστερα από αίτησή τους, σε όποιον είχε δώσει την παραγγελία για επίδοση και σε εκείνον προς τον οποίο απευθύνεται και σε καθέναν που έχει έννομο συμφέρον, αν ο πρόεδρος πρωτοδικών της περιφέρειας, όπου έγινε η επίδοση, το εγκρίνει με σημείωσή του πάνω στην αίτηση.

3. Αν η επίδοση έγινε από τα όργανα που αναφέρονται στο άρθρο 122 παρ. 2 και 3, τα όργανα αυτά καταθέτουν το δεύτερο πρωτότυπο στο γραφείο του δήμου ή της κοινότητας στην περιφέρεια του οποίου έγινε η επίδοση, όπου φυλάγεται σε ιδιαίτερο φάκελο, από τον οποίο ο αρμόδιος υπάλληλος του δήμου ή της κοινότητας εκδίδει τα αντίγραφα, σύμφωνα με όσα ορίζονται στην προηγούμενη παράγραφο. Τα όργανα που αναφέρονται στο άρθρο 122 παρ. 2 και 3 δεν τηρούν το ειδικό βιβλίο της παραγράφου 1 του άρθρου αυτού.

Article 137

Service on persons resident or seated abroad may also be effected under for the formalities laid down in the law of the country in question and by the bodies designated in such law.

Article 138

If the offices or stores referred to in Articles 128(4)(b), 131, 132 and 133 are closed or the authorities or persons referred to therein refuse to receive the document being served or to sign the service report, the person effecting service shall prepare a relevant report and deliver the document being served on the court of first instance public prosecutor within whose jurisdiction the place of service lies, and the latter shall send the document to the person who had refused to receive it or to sign the report. In this case, the provisions of Article 136 shall apply.

Article 139

1. The person effecting service shall prepare a report which, in addition to the requirements of Article 117, must also contain[:]
a) the order for service;
b) a clear designation of the document served and the persons it concerns;
c) reference to the date and time of service;
d) reference to the person to whom the document was delivered and the manner in which it was served if the recipient or the persons specified in Articles 128 to 135 and 138 were away or refused to accept the document.
2. The report shall be signed by the person effecting service and the person receiving the document; if the latter refuses or is unable to sign, the report shall also be signed by the witness enlisted for this purpose.
3. The person effecting service shall note the date and time of service on the document being served and affix their signature to it. This note constitutes proof for the person served. Where there are differences between the service report and the note, the report takes precedence.

Article 140

1. The report referred to in Article 139 shall be prepared in two original copies, one of which shall be delivered to the person who ordered service, while the other shall be kept, free of official charges, by the person who effected service. A summary note concerning service shall be entered in a special register kept by the person effecting service.
2. Court process servers are obligated to provide copies of the original document in their records to the person who ordered service and the addressee, following a request from them, as well as any person with a legitimate interest, if approved by the presiding judge of the court of first instance of the district where service was effected, by means of a note on the application.
3. If service was effected by the persons referred to in Article 122(2) and (3), they shall file the second original counterpart with the offices of the municipality or community in the district where service was effected, where it shall be kept in a special dossier from which the competent employee of the municipality or community shall issue copies in accordance with the provisions of the preceding paragraph. The persons referred to in Article 122(2) and (3) are not obligated to keep the special register referred to in paragraph 1 of this Article.

Άρθρο 141

1. Στις περιπτώσεις που η επίδοση γίνεται αυτεπαγγέλτως την παραγγελία δίνει η γραμματεία η οποία οφείλει να επιβλέψει για την πραγματοποίηση της επίδοσης και να φροντίσει να αρθούν οι ενδεχόμενες ελλείψεις.
2. Ύστερα από έγγραφη αίτηση οποιουδήποτε διαδίκου, ο γραμματέας μπορεί να επιτρέψει να γίνει η επίδοση με την επιμέλεια του αιτούντος, ορίζοντας την προθεσμία, μέσα στην οποία ο διάδικος αυτός πρέπει να προσκομίσει την έκθεση της επίδοσης. Αν ο διάδικος δεν την προσκομίσει μέσα στην προθεσμία, η επίδοση γίνεται με την επιμέλεια της γραμματείας.
3. Η επίδοση για το διάδικο που τη ζήτησε θεωρείται ότι έγινε από την υποβολή της αίτησης.

Άρθρο 142

1. Κάθε διάδικος ή άλλος ενδιαφερόμενος μπορεί να διορίσει αντίκλητο για να παραλαμβάνει τα έγγραφα που του κοινοποιούνται. Ο διορισμός γίνεται για όλες ή ορισμένες από τις δικαστικές ή εξώδικες επιδόσεις που του απευθύνονται και αφορούν μία ή περισσότερες ή όλες τις υποθέσεις του. Ο διορισμός γίνεται με δήλωση στη γραμματεία του πρωτοδικείου της κατοικίας του και αν τη δήλωση την κάνει κάτοικος του εξωτερικού γίνεται στη γραμματεία του πρωτοδικείου της πρωτεύουσας. Στη δήλωση αναφέρεται με ακρίβεια η διεύθυνση της κατοικίας ή του γραφείου του αντικλήτου. Η δήλωση γίνεται αυτοπροσώπως ή με ειδικό πληρεξούσιο. ο αρμόδιος υπάλληλος της γραμματείας συντάσσει έκθεση που υπογράφει ο ίδιος και εκείνος που κάνει τη δήλωση και καταχωρίζεται σε ευρετήριο με την αλφαβητική σειρά των επωνύμων.
2. Με τον τρόπο της παραγράφου 1 γίνεται και η αντικατάσταση ή η ανάκληση του αντικλήτου, η οποία σημειώνεται κάτω από την πράξη του διορισμού. Το ίδιο ισχύει και όταν ο αντίκλητος δηλώσει παραίτηση.
3. Η εξουσία του αντικλήτου παύει
α) όταν πεθάνει,
β) όταν περατωθεί η υπόθεση ή η πράξη για την οποία διορίστηκε,
γ) δυο πλήρεις ημέρες μετά την ανάκληση του αντικλήτου ή την παραίτησή του.
4. Μπορεί να διοριστεί έγκυρα αντίκλητος και με ρήτρα σε σύμβαση. Στον αντίκλητο που διορίστηκε με τον τρόπο αυτόν, και μάλιστα στη διεύθυνσή του που αναφέρεται στη σύμβαση, ύστερα από παραγγελία του αντισυμβαλλομένου ή των καθολικών ή ειδικών διαδόχων του, γίνεται η επίδοση όλων των εξώδικων ή διαδικαστικών πράξεων που έχουν σχέση με τη σύμβαση, στις οποίες περιλαμβάνονται και οι αποφάσεις ή πράξεις που επιβάλλουν αυτοπρόσωπη ενέργεια από τον παραλήπτη της επίδοσης, εκτός αν η σύμβαση έχει ρητά διαφορετική ρύθμιση. Σε περίπτωση αμφιβολίας η επίδοση στον αντίκλητο που διορίστηκε με σύμβαση, είναι δυνητική. Η παράγραφος 3 εφαρμόζεται και γι' αυτούς τους αντίκλητους, αλλά ανάκληση ή η παραίτηση ισχύει απέναντι στον αντισυμβαλλόμενο ή στους καθολικούς ή ειδικούς διαδόχους του μόνο από την κοινοποίησή της σ' αυτούς και μόνο αν, περιέχει διορισμό άλλου αντικλήτου στην ίδια πόλη, με σημείωση της συγκεκριμένης διεύθυνσής του. Τα ίδια ισχύουν και σε περίπτωση που μεταβληθεί η διεύθυνση του διορισμένου αντικλήτου, η οποία είχε δηλωθεί στη σύμβαση ή στο μεταγενέστερο διορισμό του.
5. Ο αρμόδιος γραμματέας στέλνει αντίγραφα των δηλώσεων των παραγράφων 1 και 2 στο γραμματέα του πρωτοδικείου Αθηνών, ο οποίος τα καταχωρίζει σε ευρετήριο με την αλφαβητική σειρά των επωνύμων.

Άρθρο 143

1. Ο δικαστικός πληρεξούσιος που διορίστηκε σύμφωνα με το άρθρο 96, είναι αυτοδικαίως και αντίκλητος για όλες τις επιδόσεις που αναφέρονται στη δίκη στην οποία είναι πληρεξούσιος, έως και την έκδοση αμετάκλητης απόφασης, εκτός αν με δικόγραφο γνωστοποιηθεί στους λοιπούς διαδίκους η αντικατάστασή του. Σε περίπτωση που ο δικαστικός πληρεξούσιος ενεργεί ως εταίρος ή συνεργάτης δικηγορικής εταιρείας, αντίκλητος θεωρείται και η δικηγορική εταιρεία.

Article 141

1. Where service is effected *ex officio*, the order shall be issued by the registry, which shall supervise execution of service and shall ensure that any defects are rectified.
2. Following an application in writing by any party in the proceedings, the registrar may allow service by the applicant, setting a deadline within which the party in question must produce the service report. If the applicant does not produce the report within the deadline, service shall be effected by the registry.
3. With regard to the party in the proceedings that requested it, service shall be deemed to have been effected from the date the application is submitted.

Article 142

1. Any party in the proceedings or other interested party may appoint a process agent to receive documents notified to them. This appointment may take place for all or certain judicial or extra-judicial documents to be served on them and concerning one, several or all of their cases, and shall be effected by means of a statement made before the registry of the court of first instance of their place of residence and, if the statement is being made by a person resident abroad, before the registry of the court of first instance of the capital. The address of the process agent's residence or office must be precisely indicated in this statement. The statement shall be made in person or using a special power of attorney. The competent registry clerk shall prepare a report which shall be signed by the said clerk and the person making the statement, and entered into an index of the surnames [of the persons in question], kept in alphabetical order.
2. Process agents shall be replaced or removed in the manner set forth in paragraph 1, with a note made beneath the appointment document. This also applies where the process agent tenders their resignation.
3. The power of the process agent shall cease[:]
a) when they die;
b) when the case or [procedural step] for which they were appointed is concluded;
c) two full days after the process agent was removed or resigned.
4. A process agent may also be validly appointed by means of a contractual clause. All [documents concerning] extra-judicial and procedural steps relating to the contract shall be served on the process agent appointed in this manner and at the address indicated in the contract following an order issued by the counterparty or their universal successors or specific successors, including rulings or acts requiring steps to be taken in person by the person being served, unless expressly provided for otherwise in the contract. In case of doubt, service on the process agent appointed by means of a contract is possible. Paragraph 3 also applies to such process agents, but their removal or resignation shall take effect vis-à-vis the counterparty or their universal successors or specific successors only from the date of its notification to them and only if it contains the appointment of a different process agent in the same city and indicates their specific address. The same also applies in the event of a change in the address of the appointed process agent as declared in the contract or their subsequent appointment.
5. The competent registrar shall send copies of the statements referred to in paragraphs 1 and 2 to the registrar of the Athens Court of First Instance, who shall enter them in an index of the surnames [of the persons in question], kept in alphabetical order.

Article 143

1. Advocates appointed in accordance with Article 96 are automatically also process agents for all service of process relating to the proceedings for which they have power of representation until an irrevocable judgment has been handed down, unless their replacement is notified to the other parties in the proceedings by means of a procedural document. Where the advocate is a partner or associate in a law firm, that law firm shall also be deemed to be the process agent.

2. Η επίδοση μπορεί να γίνει και στον αντίκλητο, εκτός αν πρόκειται για αποφάσεις ή πράξεις πού επιβάλλουν αυτοπρόσωπη ενέργεια του ενδιαφερομένου, οι οποίες πρέπει να επιδίδονται στον ίδιο.
3. Η επίδοση της κλήσης για την συζήτηση αγωγής ή ένδικου μέσου μπορεί να γίνει και σε όποιον τα έχει υπογράφει ως πληρεξούσιος.
4. Η επίδοση σε πρόσωπο που έχει τη διαμονή ή την έδρα του στο εξωτερικό ή είναι άγνωστης διαμονής πρέπει να γίνεται υποχρεωτικά στον αντίκλητο, εφόσον αναφέρεται στον κύκλο των υποθέσεων για τις οποίες έχει γίνει ο διορισμός, του, και όταν ακόμη πρόκειται για αποφάσεις ή πράξεις που επιβάλλουν αυτοπρόσωπη ενέργεια του παραλήπτη της επίδοσης.

ΚΕΦΑΛΑΙΟ ΙΖ'
Προθεσμίες.

Άρθρο 144

1. Οι προθεσμίες που ορίζονται από το νόμο ή τα δικαστήρια αρχίζουν από την επόμενη ημέρα μετά την επίδοση ή μετά τη συντέλεση του γεγονότος που αποτελεί την αφετηρία της προθεσμίας και λήγουν στις 7 το βράδυ της τελευταίας ημέρας και αν αυτή είναι κατά το νόμο εξαιρετέα, την ίδια ώρα της επόμενης μη εξαιρετέας ημέρας.
2. Οι προθεσμίες που αρχίζουν με την επίδοση εγγράφου, τρέχουν εναντίον και εκείνου με παραγγελία του οποίου έγινε η επίδοση.
3. Το Σάββατο θεωρείται για τον παρόντα Κώδικα εξαιρετέα και μη εργάσιμη ημέρα.

Άρθρο 145

1. Η προθεσμία που προσδιορίζεται σε έτη λήγει μόλις περάσει η αντίστοιχη ημερομηνία του τελευταίου έτους.
2. Η προθεσμία που προσδιορίζεται σε μήνες λήγει μόλις περάσει η ημέρα του τελευταίου μήνα που αντιστοιχεί αριθμητικά στην ημέρα έναρξης, και αν δεν υπάρχει αντιστοιχία, τότε υπολογίζεται η τελευταία ημέρα του μήνα.
3. Προθεσμία μισού έτους ισχύει ως προθεσμία έξι μηνών και προθεσμία μισού μήνα ισχύει ως προθεσμία δεκαπέντε ημερών.
4. Αν η προθεσμία προσδιορίζεται σε ώρες, δεν συνυπολογίζονται οι ημέρες που μεσολαβούν και είναι κατά το νόμο εξαιρετέες.
5. Αν η ορισμένη προθεσμία αποτελείται από μήνες και ημέρες, υπολογίζονται πρώτα οι μήνες και μετά προσθέτονται οι ημέρες.

Άρθρο 146

1. Αν κάποιος διάδικος πεθάνει ενώ διαρκεί η προθεσμία αυτή, διακόπτεται.
2. Αν η προθεσμία που διακόπηκε είχε αρχίσει με τη επίδοση εγγράφου, η νέα προθεσμία αρχίζει με τη νέα επίδοση σ' αυτούς που κατά το νόμο διαδέχθηκαν εκείνον που πέθανε. Αν η προθεσμία που διακόπηκε είχε αρχίσει με κάποιο άλλο γεγονός, η νέα προθεσμία αρχίζει με την επίδοση σχετικής δήλωσης στα παραπάνω πρόσωπα.
3. Η διακοπή της δίκης που επέρχεται κατά τη διάρκεια κάποιας προθεσμίας διακόπτει και την προθεσμία και η νέα προθεσμία αρχίζει με την επανάληψη της δίκης.

Άρθρο 147

1. Οι συντηρητικές αποδείξεις που έχουν επιτραπεί διεξάγονται σε όλη τη διάρκεια των διακοπών.
2. Το χρονικό διάστημα από 1 έως 31 Αυγούστου δεν υπολογίζεται για τις προθεσμίες των άρθρων 503, 518 παρ. 1, 545 παρ. 1 και 2, 564 παρ. 1 και 2, καθώς και των άρθρων 153, 215 παρ. 2, 237 παρ. 1, 2, 3 και 9 και 238 παρ. 1, 260 παρ. 2, 468 παρ. 1 και 2 εδάφια πρώτο και τρίτο, 598, 632 παρ. 2, 633 παρ. 2, 642, 715 παρ. 5, 729 παρ. 5, 847 παρ. 1, 926 παρ. 2, 934 παρ. 1 στοιχ. α΄ και β΄, 943 παρ. 4, 955, 966 παρ. 2 και 3, 971 παρ. 1, 972 παρ. 1 στοιχ. β΄, 973, 974, 979 παρ. 2, 985 παρ. 1, 986, 988 παρ. 1, 995 και 997 παρ. 2.
3. Το χρονικό διάστημα των δικαστικών διακοπών δεν υπολογίζεται στην προθεσμία του άρθρου 938 παράγραφος 4.

2. Service may also be effected on the process agent, unless it concerns judgments or acts which require steps to be taken in person by the interested party and which must be served on them.
3. A summons for the hearing of an action or legal remedy may also be served on any person signing them as authorised [lawyer].
4. Service on persons resident or seated abroad or of no known residence must be effected on the process agent, if referred to in the set of affairs for which he or she was appointed, even in cases of rulings or acts requiring steps to be taken in person by the person being served.

CHAPTER XVII
Deadlines

Article 144

1. Deadlines set by law or courts commence on the day following the date of service or the occurrence of the event marking the beginning of the deadline, and expire at 7 in the evening of the final day, and if the final day is a public holiday, at the same time on the next [working day].
2. Deadlines starting upon the service of a document also apply against the person who ordered service.
3. For the purposes of this Code, Saturdays are considered a public holiday and non-working day.

Article 145

1. A deadline specified in years lapses on expiry of the corresponding date in the final year.
2. A deadline specified in months lapses on expiry of the day of the final month numerically corresponding to the commencement date and if no such correspondence exists, it is specifid as the final day of that month.
3. A deadline of half a year operates as a deadline of six months, while a deadline of half a month operates as a deadline of fifteen days.
4. If a deadline is specified in hours, the intervening days that are public holidays under law are not taken into account.
5. If the deadline set is comprised of months and days, the months are calculated first and the days are added subsequently.

Article 146

1. If a party in the proceedings dies during this deadline, the deadline is interrupted.
2. If the interrupted deadline had commenced upon service of a document, the new deadline commences upon the new service on the persons who succeeded the deceased person in accordance with law. If the interrupted deadline had commenced following some other event, the new deadline commences upon service of a relevant declaration on the above persons.
3. A stay of proceedings occurring during a deadline also interrupts the deadline, and the new deadline commences upon resumption of the proceedings.

Article 147

1. Where the preservation/recording of evidence has been permitted, [the relevant steps shall continue to be taken] throughout the judicial vacations.
2. The period between 1 and 31 August shall not be taken into account for the purposes of the deadlines referred to in Articles 503, 518(1), 545(1) and (2), 564(1) and (2), as well as Articles 153, 215(2), 237(1) and (2), 238(1), 598, 632(2), 633(2), 642, 715(5), 729(5), 847(1), 926(2), 934(1)(a) and (b), 943(4), 955, 966(2) and (3), 971(1), 972(1)(b), 973, 974, 979(2), 985(1), 986, 988(1), 995 and 997(2).
3. The period of judicial vacations shall not be taken into account for the purposes of the deadline referred to in Article 938(4).

Άρθρο 148

Οι προθεσμίες που ορίζει ο νόμος ή ο δικαστής και αφορούν τη διαδικασία μπορούν να παραταθούν από τους διαδίκους, με συμφωνία αυτών, μόνο εφόσον συμφωνεί ο δικαστής ή από τον ίδιο τον δικαστή, ο οποίος σταθμίζει τις ειδικές κάθε φορά περιστάσεις. Η δυνατότητα αυτή δεν ισχύει για τις προθεσμίες ένδικων μέσων.

Άρθρο 149

[Καταργήθηκε]

Άρθρο 150

1. Ο πρόεδρος του δικαστηρίου, ο δικαστής του μονομελούς πρωτοδικείου ή ο ειρηνοδίκης, εφόσον πιθανολογούνται σπουδαίου λόγοι, μπορούν με απόφασή τους ύστερα από αίτηση κάποιου διαδίκου, που δικάζεται κατά τη διαδικασία των άρθρων 686 επ., να διατάξουν τη σύντμηση των νόμιμων προθεσμιών, με εξαίρεση τις προθεσμίες για τη άσκηση ένδικων μέσων.
2. Οι διάδικοι μπορούν να συμφωνήσουν τη σύντμηση των νόμιμων ή δικαστικών προθεσμιών.

Άρθρο 151

Η παρέλευση νόμιμης ή δικαστικής προθεσμίας συνεπάγεται έκπτωση από το δικαίωμα να επιχειρηθεί η πράξη για την οποία είχε οριστεί η προθεσμία, εκτός αν ο νόμος ορίζει διαφορετικά.

ΚΕΦΑΛΑΙΟ ΙΗ'
Επαναφορά των πραγμάτων στην προηγούμενη κατάσταση.

Άρθρο 152

1. Αν κάποιος διάδικος δεν μπόρεσε να τηρήσει κάποια προθεσμία εξαιτίας ανώτερης βίας ή δόλου του αντιδίκου του, έχει δικαίωμα να ζητήσει την επαναφορά των πραγμάτων στην προηγούμενη κατάσταση.
2. Πταίσμα του δικαστικού πληρεξουσίου ή του νόμιμου αντιπροσώπου του αιτούντος διαδίκου δεν αποτελεί λόγο για την επαναφορά των πραγμάτων στην προηγούμενη κατάσταση.
3. Η αίτηση για την επαναφορά των πραγμάτων στην προηγούμενη κατάσταση δεν μπορεί να στηριχθεί σε περιστατικά τα οποία ο δικαστής, όταν εξέταζε την αίτηση για παράταση της προθεσμίας ή για αναβολή, είχε κρίνει ανεπαρκή για τη χορήγηση της παράτασης ή της αναβολής.

Άρθρο 153

Η επαναφορά πρέπει να ζητηθεί μέσα σε προθεσμία τριάντα ημερών από την ημέρα της άρσης του εμποδίου που συνιστούσε την ανώτερη βία ή της γνώσης του δόλου.

Άρθρο 154

Η επαναφορά ζητείται από το δικαστήριο στο οποίο εκκρεμεί η κύρια δίκη ή, αν δεν υπάρχει εκκρεμοδικία, ζητείται από το δικαστήριο που είναι αρμόδιο να αποφασίσει, για το αν ασκήθηκε εμπρόθεσμα η πράξη για την ενέργεια της οποίας είχε ταχθεί η προθεσμία.

Article 148

Deadlines set by law or a judge that concern the procedure may be extended by the parties in the proceedings by means of an agreement between them only if the judge agrees, or by the judge themselves, taking the specific circumstances of each case into consideration. This does not apply to deadlines for legal remedies.

Article 149

[Repealed]

Article 150

1. Where the presiding judge of the court, the single-member court of first instance judge or the court of the peace judge, considers that, on the balance of probabilities, there are serious grounds, they may issue a decision, following an application filed by a party in the proceedings and tried under the procedure referred to in Articles 686 *et seq.*, ordering that the statutory deadlines be curtailed, save for deadlines for filing legal remedies.
2. The parties in the proceedings may agree to curtail statutory or court-ordered deadlines.

Article 151

Unless otherwise provided for in law, the lapse of a statutory or court-ordered deadline results in forfeiture of the right to take the steps for which the deadline had been set.

CHAPTER XVIII
Restoration of a prior state of affairs

Article 152

1. If a party in the proceedings could not comply with a deadline due to force majeure or *dolus* on the part of their opponent, they have the right to request restoration of a prior state of affairs.
2. Fault on the part of the advocate or lawful proxy of the applicant party in proceedings does not constitute grounds for restoration of a prior state of affairs.
3. The application for restoration of a prior state of affairs may not rely on facts which the judge, when examining the application to extend the deadline or grant deferral, had ruled insufficient for granting such extension or deferral.

Article 153

Restoration of a prior state of affairs must be requested within a deadline of 30 days from the day the obstacle constituting force majeure or knowledge of the *dolus* ceased to exist.

Article 154

Restoration of a prior state of affairs shall be requested at the court where the main proceedings are pending or, if there is no *lis pendens*, at the court competent to rule on whether the steps for which the deadline had been set were taken in good time.

Άρθρο 155

1. Η αίτηση για την επαναφορά ασκείται με τα δικόγραφα που κοινοποιεί ο ένας διάδικος στον άλλον ή με τις προτάσεις ή με χωριστό δικόγραφο που κατατίθεται σύμφωνα με τις διατάξεις για την άσκηση της αγωγής και κοινοποιείται στον αντίδικο. Όταν στις περιπτώσεις των άρθρων 237 και 238 υποβάλλεται με τις προτάσεις και αίτημα επαναφοράς στην προηγούμενη κατάσταση, αυτές κατατίθενται στη γραμματεία του δικαστηρίου, εφόσον ο διάδικος έχει ενημερώσει προηγουμένως τον αντίδικό του περί της ενέργειάς του αυτής, με την αποστολή ηλεκτρονικού μηνύματος στη δηλωθείσα ηλεκτρονική διεύθυνση, η αποτύπωση του οποίου προσκομίζεται στον σχετικό φάκελο. Στην περίπτωση αυτή η αντίκρουση από τον αντίδικο γίνεται σε προθεσμία είκοσι (20) ημερών από την κατάθεση των εκπρόθεσμων προτάσεων.

2. Η αίτηση της παρ. 1 πρέπει να αναφέρει τους λόγους για τους οποίους δεν ήταν δυνατό να τηρηθεί η προθεσμία, καθώς και τα αποδεικτικά μέσα για την εξακρίβωση της αλήθειας τους και να περιέχει την πράξη που παραλείφθηκε ή να αναφέρει ότι έχει ήδη ενεργηθεί και εφόσον για την άσκηση της πράξης χρειάζεται ιδιαίτερος τύπος, πρέπει να αναφέρεται και ότι τηρήθηκε ο τύπος.

Άρθρο 156

Η συζήτηση της αίτησης γίνεται μαζί με τη συζήτηση της κύριας υπόθεσης, εφόσον είναι εκκρεμής, το δικαστήριο όμως μπορεί να διατάξει τη χωριστή εκδίκασή τους.

Άρθρο 157

Η άσκηση της αίτησης δεν αναστέλλει την πρόοδο της κύριας δίκης ή την εκτέλεση της απόφασης που εκδίδεται, εκτός αν το δικαστήριο που έχει αρμοδιότητα σύμφωνα με το άρθρο 154, διατάξει την αναστολή της προόδου της δίκης ή της εκτέλεσης, ύστερα από πρόταση διαδίκου που υποβάλλεται κατά την εκδίκαση της αίτησης.

Άρθρο 158

Δεν επιτρέπεται να υποβληθεί αίτηση για την επαναφορά των πραγμάτων στην προηγούμενη κατάσταση, αν χάθηκε η προθεσμία του άρθρου 153 από οποιοδήποτε λόγο.

ΚΕΦΑΛΑΙΟ ΙΘ'
Ακυρότητες

Άρθρο 159

Η παράβαση διάταξης που ρυθμίζει τη διαδικασία και ιδίως τον τύπο κάποιας διαδικαστικής πράξης συνεπάγεται ακυρότητα, την οποία απαγγέλλει το δικαστήριο

1) αν την τήρηση της διάταξης απαιτεί ρητά ο νόμος με την ποινή της ακυρότητας,

2) αν για την παράβαση αυτή επιτρέπεται αναίρεση ή αναψηλάφηση,

3) σε κάθε άλλη περίπτωση, αν ο δικαστής κρίνει ότι η παράβαση προκάλεσε στο διάδικο που την προτείνει βλάβη η οποία δεν μπορεί να αποκατασταθεί διαφορετικά παρά μόνο με την κήρυξη της ακυρότητας.

Άρθρο 160

1. Η ακυρότητα δεν μπορεί να απαγγελθεί χωρίς πρόταση του διαδίκου, εκτός αν ο νόμος παρέχει στο δικαστήριο την εξουσία να εξετάσει αυτεπαγγέλτως αν τηρήθηκε η διάταξη.

2. Δεν έχει δικαίωμα να προτείνει την ακυρότητα εκείνος που είχε ενεργήσει την προσβαλλόμενη σαν άκυρη πράξη ή εκείνος του οποίου η συμπεριφορά προκάλεσε την ακυρότητα ή εκείνος που, αφού είχε γίνει η άκυρη πράξη, παραιτήθηκε ρητώς ή σιωπηρώς από την πρόταση της ακυρότητας.

3. Η πρόταση της ακυρότητας είναι απαράδεκτη, αν δεν γίνει κατά την πρώτη διαδικαστική πράξη, ύστερα από εκείνη που προσβάλλεται ως άκυρη, εκτός αν ο νόμος δίνει στο δικαστήριο την εξουσία να εξετάσει αυτεπαγγέλτως αν τηρήθηκε η διάταξη ή αν εξαιτίας της ακυρότητας μπορεί να ζητηθεί αναίρεση.

Article 155

1. The application for restoration of a prior state of affairs may be filed by means of the procedural documents communicated by one party in the proceedings to the other, or the pleadings, or a separate procedural document filed in accordance with the provisions on filing actions, and shall be notified to the opponent. When an application for restoration of a prior state of affairs is submitted together with the pleadings in the cases referred to in Articles 237 and 238, they shall be filed with the registry of the court, provided the party in the proceedings has previously notified the opponent of this step by sending an e-mail message to the e-mail address declared, with a print-out of said message included in the relevant dossier. In this case, the opponent shall file a rebuttal within a deadline of 20 days from the date the late pleadings were filed.
2. The application referred to in paragraph 1 must set out the reasons for which it was not possible to meet the deadline, as well as the means of evidence to establish the veracity of said reasons, and must contain the step omitted or make reference to the fact that it has already been taken and, if the taking that step requires specific formalities to be observed, reference to the fact that the formalities were observed.

Article 156

The application shall be heard at the hearing of the main case, where it is pending; however, the court may order that they be heard separately.

Article 157

[The act of] filing an application shall not stay the main proceedings or the enforcement of a judgment handed down, unless the competent court under Article 154 orders stay of proceedings or enforcement following a motion by a party in the proceedings submitted during the hearing of the application.

Article 158

An application for restoration of a prior state of affairs may not be submitted where the deadline set forth in Article 153 is missed for any reason.

CHAPTER XIX
Nullities

Article 159

Failure to comply with a provision regulating the procedure and, in particular, the form of a procedural step shall result in nullity, which shall be pronounced by the court if[:]
1) compliance with the provision is expressly required by law on penalty of nullity;
2) an application for cassation or re-opening proceedings is permitted for the failure in question;
3) in all other cases, the judge rules that the failure caused harm to the party in the proceedings pleading it, which can be rectified only by declaration of nullity and in no other manner.

Article 160

1. Nullity cannot be pronounced without having been pleaded by a party in the proceedings, unless the law empowers the court to examine *ex officio* whether the provision was complied with.
2. Nullity may not be pleaded by the person who took the step being contested as null and void, or the person whose conduct caused the nullity, or the person who, after the null and void step had been taken, explicitly or tacitly waived the plea of nullity.
3. The plea of nullity shall be inadmissible if it does not take place during the first procedural step after the one being contested as null and void, unless the law empowers the court to examine *ex officio* whether the provision was complied with or if cassation can be requested due to the nullity.

Άρθρο 161

Το δικαστήριο, όταν απαγγέλλει την ακυρότητα, διατάζει αυτεπαγγέλτως να επαναληφθεί η πράξη μέσα σε ορισμένη προθεσμία, αν κρίνει ότι αυτό είναι δυνατό, εκτός αν έχει ήδη επέλθει έκπτωση από το δικαίωμα ή απαράδεκτο.

ΚΕΦΑΛΑΙΟ Κ'
Εγγυοδοσία

Άρθρο 162

Το δικαστήριο διατάζει εγγυοδοσία στις περιπτώσεις που προβλέπει ο νόμος, με την επιφύλαξη ότι οι διάδικοι δεν έχουν συμφωνήσει διαφορετικά, εκτιμώντας ελεύθερα και καθορίζοντας το μέγεθος της ποσότητας που πρέπει να δοθεί, καθώς και την προθεσμία μέσα στην οποία πρέπει να γίνει η παροχή αυτή.

Άρθρο 163

Η εγγυοδοσία γίνεται με την κατάθεση μετρητών χρημάτων στο ταμείο παρακαταθηκών και δανείων. Το γραμμάτιο της κατάθεσης πρέπει να κατατεθεί, μέσα στην προθεσμία του άρθρου 162, στη γραμματεία του δικαστηρίου που διέταξε την εγγυοδοσία.

Άρθρο 164

Το δικαστήριο, όταν διατάζει εγγυοδοσία, μπορεί ύστερα από αίτηση του υπόχρεου, να επιτρέψει, αντί για μετρητά χρήματα να δοθεί
1) με τίτλους παραστατικούς αξίας, στους οποίους πρέπει να είναι προσαρτημένα τα μη ληξιπρόθεσμα τοκομερίδια ή οι μη απαιτητές μερισματαποδείξεις,
2) με εγγυητική επιστολή αξιόχρεης τράπεζας,
3) με εγγραφή υποθήκης σε ακίνητα που βρίσκονται στην Ελλάδα. Οι παραστατικοί αξίας τίτλοι και τα ακίνητα υπολογίζονται για την εγγύηση στα τρία τέταρτα της αξίας τους.

Άρθρο 165

1. Η εγγυοδοσία με τίτλους παραστατικούς αξίας γίνεται με την κατάθεσή τους στο ταμείο παρακαταθηκών και δανείων. Αν πρόκειται για εγγυοδοσία με ονομαστικούς τίτλους, το ταμείο παρακαταθηκών και δανείων ανακοινώνει χωρίς υπαίτια καθυστέρηση την κατάθεση αυτή στην ανώνυμη εταιρία που τους έχει εκδώσει, η οποία αμέσως το σημειώνει στα βιβλία της.
2. Το γραμμάτιο που βεβαιώνει την κατάθεση των τίτλων, η εγγυητική επιστολή της αξιόχρεης τράπεζας και το πιστοποιητικό εγγραφής της υποθήκης πρέπει να κατατεθούν, μέσα στην προθεσμία του άρθρου 162, στη γραμματεία του δικαστηρίου που διέταξε την εγγυοδοσία. Το μονομελές πρωτοδικείο ή το ειρηνοδικείο, όταν αυτό διέταξε την εγγυοδοσία, μπορεί να παρατείνει την προθεσμία αυτή για δεκαπέντε ημέρες, δικάζοντας κατά τη διαδικασία των άρθρων 686 επ.

Άρθρο 166

Από την κατάθεση ως εγγυοδοσίας των χρημάτων ή των παραστατικών αξίας τίτλων εκείνος υπέρ του οποίου έγινε η εγγύηση αποκτά δικαίωμα ενεχύρου επάνω σ' αυτά για την απαίτηση για την οποία δόθηκε η εγγύηση.

Άρθρο 167

Αν μετά τη χορήγηση της εγγύησης γίνει φανερό ότι είναι ανεπαρκής ή αν μεσολαβήσουν νέα γεγονότα που δικαιολογούν την αντικατάστασή της, μπορεί να ζητηθεί συμπλήρωση ή αντικατάσταση από το μονομελές πρωτοδικείο ή το ειρηνοδικείο, όταν αυτό είχε διατάξει την εγγυοδοσία, κατά τη διαδικασία των άρθρων 686 επ. Η σχετική αίτηση δεν αναστέλλει την πρόοδο της κύριας δίκης.

Article 161

When pronouncing nullity, the court shall order *ex officio* that the step be repeated within a specific deadline, where it rules this is possible, unless the right has already been forfeited or inadmissibility has already occurred.

CHAPTER XX
Provision of surety

Article 162

The court shall order provision of surety in the cases provided for in law, provided the parties in the proceedings have not agreed otherwise, ruling at its unfettered discretion and designating the amount, and setting the deadline within which it is to be provided.

Article 163

Surety shall be provided by depositing cash with the Consignment Deposits and Loans Fund. The deposit note must be filed with the registry of the court that ordered the provision of surety within the deadline laid down in Article 162.

Article 164

When the court orders provision of surety, it may, following an application filed by the person obligated to provide surety, allow surety to be provided instead of cash by means of[:]
1) securities to which the non-overdue interest coupons or dividend coupons not yet due and payable must be appended;
2) a letter of guarantee issued by a solvent bank;
3) registration of a mortgage on immovables situated in Greece. Securities and immovables shall be calculated at three quarters of their value for the purposes of surety.

Article 165

1. Surety in the form of securities is provided by depositing them with the Consignment Deposits and Loans Fund. In cases of surety in the form of registered [share] certificates, the Consignment Deposits and Loans Fund shall announce said deposit without undue delay to the société anonyme that issued them, which shall immediately record this fact in its registers.
2. The note attesting deposit of the certificates, the letter of guarantee issued by a solvent bank and the mortgage registration certificate must be filed with the registry of the court that ordered [payment of] surety within the deadline laid down in Article 162. Where provision of surety was ordered by a single-member court of first instance or a court of the peace, the court may extend this deadline by 15 days, trying the matter under the procedure set forth in Articles 686 *et seq.*

Article 166

As of the date the money or certificates were deposited as surety, the person for whose benefit the surety was provided shall acquire a pledge thereon regarding the claim for which the surety was provided.

Article 167

If it becomes apparent after the surety was provided that it is insufficient or if new events occur that justify its replacement, the single-member court of first instance or the court of the peace may be petitioned, where it had ordered provision of surety in accordance with the procedure laid down in Articles 686 *et seq*, to order that the surety be supplemented or replaced. The [act of filing the] application in question shall not stay the main proceedings.

Άρθρο 168

Αν πάψει η αιτία για την οποία δόθηκε η εγγύηση, αυτή αίρεται και αν πραγματοποιηθεί ο λόγος για τον οποίο δόθηκε, επέρχεται κατάπτωση της εγγύησης υπέρ εκείνου, για τον οποίο είχε δοθεί. Σχετικά αποφασίζει το μονομελές πρωτοδικείο ή το ειρηνοδικείο, όταν αυτό είχε διατάξει την εγγύηση, κατά τη διαδικασία των ασφαλιστικών μέτρων.

Άρθρο 169

Το δικαστήριο, ύστερα από αίτηση του εναγομένου ή του διαδίκου εναντίον του οποίου ασκήθηκε κύρια παρέμβαση ή ένδικο μέσο, μπορεί να υποχρεώσει σε εγγυοδοσία τον ενάγοντα, ή το διάδικο που άσκησε κύρια παρέμβαση ή ένδικο μέσο, για τα έξοδα της διαδικασίας που γίνεται στο ίδιο δικαστήριο, αν αυτό κρίνει ότι υπάρχει προφανής κίνδυνος αδυναμίας να εκτελεστεί η ενδεχόμενη καταδίκη του στα έξοδα.

Άρθρο 170

Δεν επιτρέπεται εγγυοδοσία, σύμφωνα με το άρθρο 169,
1) αν ο ενάγων ή ο διάδικος που άσκησε κύρια παρέμβαση ή ένδικο μέσο έχει το ευεργέτημα της πενίας,
2) σε περίπτωση ανταγωγής,
3) στις γαμικές διαφορές, στις διαφορές που αναφέρονται στις σχέσεις γονέων και τέκνων και γενικά στις μη περιουσιακές διαφορές,
4) στις διαφορές διατροφής,
5) στις διαφορές από συναλλαγματικές ή άλλους τίτλους εις διαταγή,
6) στις εργατικές διαφορές και στις διαφορές από αμοιβές για την παροχή εργασίας.

Άρθρο 171

Ο εναγόμενος ή ο διάδικος εναντίον του οποίου ασκήθηκε κύρια παρέμβαση δεν έχει υποχρέωση να απαντήσει στην αγωγή ή στην κύρια παρέμβαση ώσπου να κατατεθεί η εγγύηση που διατάχθηκε. Το δικαστήριο δεν προχωρεί στη συζήτηση του ένδικου μέσου, ώσπου να κατατεθεί η εγγύηση που διέταξε σχετικά με το ένδικο μέσο.

Άρθρο 172

Αν η προθεσμία που ορίστηκε για την εγγυοδοσία περάσει άπρακτη, το δικαστήριο, ύστερα από αίτηση εκείνου που είχε ζητήσει την εγγύηση, αποφασίζει ότι ανακλήθηκε η αγωγή ή η κύρια παρέμβαση ή το ένδικο μέσο.

ΚΕΦΑΛΑΙΟ ΚΑ'
Δικαστικά έξοδα

Άρθρο 173

1. *Όποιος προκαλεί κύρια ή παρεμπίπτουσα δίκη προκαταβάλλει τα τέλη για τις συζητήσεις της δίκης αυτής.*
2. *Όποιος προσβάλλει απόφαση με ένδικο μέσο προκαταβάλλει τα τέλη για την συζήτησή του.*
3. *Ο διάδικος που προκαλεί διαδικαστική πράξη προκαταβάλλει τα έξοδα και τα τέλη της.*
4. *Σε δίκες διατροφής, όποιος έχει υποχρέωση σύμφωνα με το νόμο ή με δικαιοπραξία να δώσει διατροφή, προκαταβάλλει και τα, κατά την κρίση του δικαστή, έξοδα και τέλη του ενάγοντος, έως το ποσό των τριακοσίων (300) ευρώ.*

Article 168

If the reason for which the surety was given ceases to exist, [the obligation to provide surety] shall be lifted and if the reason for which it was given occurs, it shall be forfeited to the person for whom it had been provided. The single-member court of first instance or the court of the peace shall rule on the matter, where it had ordered the surety under interim measures proceedings.

Article 169

Following an application by the defendant or the party in the proceedings against whom a main intervention or legal remedy was filed and where the court considers that there is a clear risk that it will not be possible to enforce any costs ordered, it may order the plaintiff to [pay] a surety, or the party in the proceedings who filed a main intervention or legal remedy to pay the costs of the procedure taking place before the same court.

Article 170

Provision of surety shall not be permitted, in accordance with Article 169[:]
1) if the plaintiff or the party in the proceedings who filed a main intervention or legal remedy is receiving legal aid;
2) in the case of a cross-action;
3) in matrimonial disputes, in disputes concerning parent-child relationships, and in non-property disputes in general;
4) in maintenance disputes;
5) in disputes arising from bills of exchange or other notes payable to order;
6) in labour disputes and disputes concerning pay for the provision of labour.

Article 171

The defendant or party in the proceedings against whom the main intervention was filed is not obligated to respond to the action or main intervention before the surety ordered has been deposited. The court shall not conduct a hearing on the legal remedy before the surety it ordered with regard to the legal remedy has been deposited.

Article 172

If the deadline set for provision of surety lapses without the relevant steps having been taken, the court, following an application by the person who had requested the surety, shall rule that the action or the main intervention or the legal remedy was withdrawn.

CHAPTER XXI
Court costs

Article 173

1. The person who institutes main or incidental proceedings shall pay in advance the fees for hearing those proceedings.
2. The person who contests a judgment by filing a legal remedy shall pay in advance the fees for the hearing of that legal remedy.
3. The party in the proceedings who causes a procedural step to be taken shall pay its costs and fees in advance.
4. In maintenance proceedings, the person obligated in law or by legal transaction to pay maintenance shall also pay the plaintiff's costs and fees in advance, up to the amount of 300 euros, as determined by the judge.

5. *Στις υποθέσεις που αφορούν σε ενήλικο θύμα των εγκλημάτων που ορίζονται στα άρθρα 323, 323Α και 351 του ΠΚ ή σε ανήλικο θύμα των πράξεων που αναφέρονται στα άρθρα 323Α παρ. 4, 323Β εδάφιο α', 324, 336, 338, 339, 342, 343, 345, 346, 347, 348, 348Α, 348Β, 348Γ, 349 , 351 και 351Α του ΠΚ, ο εναγόμενος προκαταβάλλει τα κατά την κρίση του δικαστή έξοδα και τέλη του ενάγοντος (θύματος) έως το ποσό των εξακοσίων (600) ευρώ.*

Άρθρο 174

1. *Όταν ο νόμος δεν προσδιορίζει με ακρίβεια τα έξοδα και τέλη που πρέπει να προκαταβληθούν για κάποια διαδικαστική πράξη ή συζήτηση, τα προσδιορίζει ο δικαστής, στον οποίο εκκρεμεί η δίκη και, όταν πρόκειται για πολυμελές δικαστήριο, ο πρόεδρος, με πράξη που γράφεται επάνω στη σχετική αίτηση και κοινοποιείται στον υπόχρεο για να τα προκαταβάλλει.*

2. *Η απόδειξη της προκαταβολής των τελών και εξόδων που έγινε σύμφωνα με το άρθρο 173 πρέπει να προσάγεται στο γραμματέα, όταν συζητείται η υπόθεση ή όταν επιχειρείται η πράξη.*

Άρθρο 175

Ο υπόχρεος σε προκαταβολή των τελών και εξόδων, αν την παραλείψει, θεωρείται ότι δεν εμφανίστηκε.

Άρθρο 176

Ο διάδικος που νικήθηκε καταδικάζεται να πληρώσει τα έξοδα. Θεωρείται ότι νικήθηκε και εκείνος, του οποίου απορρίφθηκε η αίτηση, ως προς το μέρος που ο αντίδικος δεν είχε ομολογήσει ή αναγνωρίσει.

Άρθρο 177

Αν ο εναγόμενος δεν προκάλεσε με τη στάση του την άσκηση της αγωγής και αμέσως μετά την άσκησή της την αποδέχεται ή ομολογεί πλήρως τη βάση της, το δικαστήριο επιβάλλει τα έξοδα στον ενάγοντα.

Άρθρο 178

1. *Σε περίπτωση μερικής νίκης και μερικής ήττας κάθε διαδίκου, το δικαστήριο κατανέμει τα έξοδα ανάλογα με την έκταση της νίκης ή της ήττας του καθενός.*

2. *Στις περιπτώσεις της παραγράφου 1, ο δικαστής μπορεί να επιβάλλει το σύνολο των εξόδων σε βάρος του ενός μόνο διαδίκου, αν το μέρος που απορρίφθηκε από την αίτηση του άλλου διαδίκου είναι ελάχιστο και δεν έδωσε αφορμή για να αυξηθούν τα έξοδα ή αν ο καθορισμός του μεγέθους της απαίτησης είχε εξαρτηθεί από την κρίση του δικαστή ή από την εκτίμηση πραγματογνωμόνων.*

Άρθρο 179

Το δικαστήριο μπορεί να συμψηφίσει όλα τα έξοδα ή ένα μέρος τους, μόνο όταν πρόκειται για διαφορές ανάμεσα σε συζύγους ή σε συγγενείς εξ αίματος έως και τον δεύτερο βαθμό ή όταν η ερμηνεία του κανόνα δικαίου που εφαρμόσθηκε ήταν ιδιαίτερα δυσχερής. Το δικαστήριο μπορεί επίσης να συμψηφίσει ένα μέρος των εξόδων, εάν, κατ' εκτίμηση των περιστάσεων, υπήρχε εύλογη αμφιβολία για την έκβαση της δίκης.

Άρθρο 180

1. *Αν καταδικασθούν περισσότεροι, είτε είναι ομόδικοι είτε όχι, να πληρώσουν τα έξοδα, ενέχονται κατά ίσα μέρη, το δικαστήριο όμως μπορεί κατά την κρίση του, να κατανείμει τα έξοδα με βάση το μερίδιο που αναλογεί σε καθέναν επάνω στο επίδικο αντικείμενο.*

2. *Τα έξοδα της ιδιαίτερης πράξης ή της ιδιαίτερης διαδικασίας που προκάλεσε ένας μόνο ομόδικος, επιβάλλονται αποκλειστικά σε βάρος του.*

3. *Αν καταδικάστηκαν περισσότεροι ως συνοφειλέτες εις ολόκληρον, έχουν εις ολόκληρον υποχρέωση και για την πληρωμή των εξόδων, εφόσον η απόφαση δεν ορίζει διαφορετικά, με την επιφύλαξη της διάταξης της παραγράφου 2.*

5. In cases concerning an adult victim of the crimes referred to in Articles 323, 323A or 351 of the Penal Code or a juvenile victim of the acts referred to in Articles 323A(4), the first subparagraph of Article 323B, Articles 324, 336, 338, 339, 342, 343, 345, 346, 347, 348, 348A, 348B, 348C, 349, 351 and 351A of the Penal Code, the defendant shall pay the plaintiff's (victim's) costs and fees in advance, up to the amount of 600 euros, as determined by the judge.

Article 174

1. Where the law does not precisely specify the costs and fees that must be paid in advance for a procedural step or hearing, these shall be set by the judge before whom the proceedings are pending and, in the case of a multi-member court, by the presiding judge, by means of a decision recorded on the relevant application and notified to the person obligated to pay said costs and fees in advance.
2. The receipt for the advance payment of fees and costs effected in accordance with Article 173 must be submitted to the registrar when the case is heard or the step is taken.

Article 175

Where the person obligated to pay fees and costs in advance fails to do so, they shall be deemed not to have entered an appearance.

Article 176

The unsuccessful party in the proceedings shall be ordered to pay costs. A party whose application was dismissed shall also be considered unsuccessful insofar as the opponent had made no admission or acknowledgment.

Article 177

If the defendant did not cause the action to be filed through their conduct and immediately after it is filed he or she accepts it or fully admits its basis, the court shall order the plaintiff to pay costs.

Article 178

1. Where each party in the proceedings is partly successful and partly unsuccessful, the court shall allocate the costs in accordance with the extent to which each party was successful or unsuccessful.
2. In the cases referred to in paragraph 1, the judge may order just a single party in the proceedings to pay all costs if the part of the other party's application dismissed is minimal and did not result in an increase in costs, or if the amount of the claim was determined by the judge or following an estimate by experts.

Article 179

The court may offset all or part of the costs only in cases of disputes between spouses or blood relatives up to the second degree or if the interpretation of the legal norms applied was particularly difficult. The court may also offset part of the costs if, taking circumstances into account, there was reasonable doubt concerning the outcome of the proceedings.

Article 180

1. If several parties are ordered to pay costs, whether or not they are joined parties, the costs shall be shared equally among them; however, the court may, at its discretion, allocate the costs based on the share corresponding to each party in the contested matter.
2. The court shall order the costs for a specific act or specific procedure caused by a single joined party to be paid by that party.
3. If several parties were found by the court to be severally liable debtors, they are jointly obligated to pay the costs, unless otherwise provided for in the judgment, without prejudice to the provisions of paragraph 2.

Άρθρο 181

1. Σε περίπτωση κύριας παρέμβασης τα έξοδα της κύριας δίκης και της παρέμβασης, αν η τελευταία γίνει δεκτή, επιβάλλονται κατά ίσα μέρη σε βάρος των αρχικών διαδίκων.
2. Αν η κύρια παρέμβαση απορριφθεί ως απαράδεκτη ή άκυρη, όποιος άσκησε την παρέμβαση καταδικάζεται στα έξοδα των αρχικών διαδίκων τα οποία προκλήθηκαν από την άσκησή της.
3. Αν η κύρια παρέμβαση απορριφθεί στην ουσία, τα έξοδά της επιβάλλονται σε βάρος εκείνου που άσκησε την παρέμβαση, ενώ τα έξοδα της κύριας δίκης επιβάλλονται, κατά ίσα μέρη, σε βάρος εκείνου που άσκησε την παρέμβαση και του αρχικού διαδίκου που νικήθηκε.
4. Οι διατάξεις των άρθρων 178 έως 180 εφαρμόζονται και στην περίπτωση αυτή.

Άρθρο 182

1. Σε πρόσθετη παρέμβαση τα έξοδα που προκλήθηκαν από αυτήν σε περίπτωση νίκης του διαδίκου για το συμφέρον του οποίου ασκήθηκε η παρέμβαση επιβάλλονται σε βάρος του αντιδίκου, ενώ σε περίπτωση ήττας του καθώς και σε κάθε άλλη περίπτωση, σε βάρος εκείνου που άσκησε την πρόσθετη παρέμβαση.
2. Οι διατάξεις των άρθρων 178 έως 180 εφαρμόζονται και στην περίπτωση αυτή.
3. Στις περιπτώσεις που εκείνος ο οποίος άσκησε πρόσθετη παρέμβαση θεωρείται ομόδικος εφαρμόζονται οι διατάξεις του άρθρου 180.

Άρθρο 183

Τα έξοδα που προκάλεσε η άσκηση και η εκδίκαση ένδικου μέσου επιβάλλονται, σε περίπτωση που απορριφθεί, σε βάρος του διαδίκου που το άσκησε, ενώ σε περίπτωση που γίνει δεκτό, σε βάρος του διαδίκου που νικήθηκε· οι διατάξεις των άρθρων 176 έως 182 εφαρμόζονται και στην περίπτωση αυτή.

Άρθρο 184

Τα έξοδα της ερήμην δίκης, καθώς και εκείνα που προκάλεσε η αναβολή της συζήτησης ή της ενέργειας κάποιας διαδικαστικής πράξης, επιβάλλονται σε βάρος του διαδίκου που δικάστηκε ερήμην ή που ζήτησε την αναβολή. Αν η ερημοδικία κριθεί άκυρη ή η αναβολή προκλήθηκε από υπαιτιότητα του αντιδίκου, τα έξοδα επιβάλλονται σε βάρος του.

Άρθρο 185

Όλα τα έξοδα ή ένα μέρος τους μπορούν να επιβληθούν σε βάρος του διαδίκου που νίκησε,
1) αν ο δικαστής κρίνει ότι ο διάδικος αυτός δεν τήρησε το καθήκον της αλήθειας,
2) αν καθυστερημένα πρότεινε επιθετικό ή αμυντικό μέσο ή επέφερε αποδεικτικό μέσο, ενώ ο δικαστής κρίνει ότι μπορούσε να το προτείνει ή να το φέρει νωρίτερα,
3) αν έγινε υπαίτιος για την ακυρότητα διαδικαστικής πράξης ή της συζήτησης.

Άρθρο 186

1. Υπάλληλοι της γραμματείας των δικαστηρίων, δικηγόροι, συμβολαιογράφοι, δικαστικοί επιμελητές, πληρεξούσιοι ή αντιπρόσωποι των διαδίκων, μάρτυρες και πραγματογνώμονες μπορούν να καταδικαστούν να πληρώσουν τα έξοδα, ύστερα από αίτηση των διαδίκων ή και αυτεπαγγέλτως,
α) όταν έγιναν υπαίτιοι, από βαριά αμέλεια ή από δόλο, ακυρότητας διαδικαστικής πράξης ή συζήτησης ή αναβολής της ή αν προξένησαν περιττά έξοδα, και
β) όταν τα ορίζει ρητώς ο νόμος.
2. Η απόφαση μπορεί να προσβληθεί με ανακοπή, σύμφωνα με τα άρθρα 583 επ.

Article 181

1. Where there is a main intervention, the initial parties in the proceedings shall be ordered to equally share the costs of the main proceedings and the intervention, where the latter is accepted.
2. If the main intervention is dismissed as inadmissible or null and void, the intervenor shall be ordered to pay the costs of the initial parties in the proceedings incurred by filing the intervention.
3. If the main intervention is dismissed on its merits, the intervenor shall be ordered to pay costs, while the intervenor and the initial party in the proceedings who was unsuccessful shall equally share the costs of the main proceedings.
4. The provisions of Articles 178 to 180 also apply in such cases.

Article 182

1. Where there is a permissive intervention, the relevant costs incurred shall be paid by the opponent, if the party in the proceedings in support of whom the intervention was filed is successful, and where the latter is unsuccessful and in all other cases, by the permissive intervenor.
2. The provisions of Articles 178 to 180 also apply in such cases.
3. Where the permissive intervenor is considered a joined party, the provisions of Article 180 apply.

Article 183

Where a legal remedy was filed, adjudicated and dismissed, the relevant costs shall be paid by the party in the proceedings who filed [the legal remedy], and where the legal remedy was accepted, by the party in the proceedings who was unsuccessful; the provisions of Articles 176 to 182 also apply in this case.

Article 184

The costs of proceedings held *in absentia* and those incurred due to adjournment of the hearing or the taking of a procedural step shall be paid by the party in the proceedings who was tried *in absentia* or who requested the adjournment. Where the default judgment is annulled or adjournment was due to the opponent's fault, the latter shall be ordered to pay costs.

Article 185

The party in the proceedings who was successful may be ordered to pay all or part of the costs if:
1) the judge rules that the party in question failed to adhere to the duty of truth;
2) the party in question raised a plea or adduced means of evidence that the judge rules the party in question could have raised or adduced at an earlier time;
3) the party in question was responsible for the nullity of a procedural step or the hearing.

Article 186

1. Court registry clerks, lawyers, notaries public, court process servers, authorised representatives or proxies of parties in the proceedings, witnesses and experts may be ordered to pay costs, either following an application by the parties in the proceedings or *ex officio*[:]
a) when they were responsible, due to gross negligence or *dolus*, for the nullity of a procedural step, or the hearing, or its adjournment, or if they caused needless expense; and
b) when expressly provided for in law.
2. The decision may be contested by means of opposition, in accordance with Articles 583 *et seq.*

Άρθρο 187

Με την επιφύλαξη αντίθετης συμφωνίας των ενδιαφερομένων, τα έξοδα του δικαστικού συμβιβασμού επιβαρύνουν εξίσου τους διαδίκους, ενώ τα έξοδα της καταργούμενης δίκης συμψηφίζονται.

Άρθρο 188

1. Αν γίνει ανάκληση διαδικαστικής πράξης ή παραίτηση είτε από αυτήν είτε από όλη τη δίκη, τα έξοδα επιβάλλονται σε βάρος του διαδίκου που ανακαλεί ή παραιτείται.

2. Σε περίπτωση αποδοχής της αγωγής ή ένδικου μέσου, τα έξοδα της δίκης, που τερματίζεται με την αποδοχή, επιβάλλονται σε βάρος του διαδίκου που αποδέχεται, με την επιφύλαξη της διάταξης του άρθρου 177.

Άρθρο 189

1. Αποδίδονται μόνο τα δικαστικά και εξώδικα έξοδα που ήταν απαραίτητα για τη διεξαγωγή και υπεράσπιση της δίκης και ιδίως

α) τα τέλη χαρτοσήμου για τη σύνταξη των αποφάσεων, των δικογράφων, των δικαστικών εκθέσεων και των άλλων εγγράφων της δίκης και για τη ενέργεια των διαδικαστικών πράξεων,

β) το τέλος δικαστικού ενσήμου,

γ) η αμοιβή των δικηγόρων ή άλλων δικαστικών πληρεξουσίων και των δικαστικών υπαλλήλων, σύμφωνα με τις διατιμήσεις που ισχύουν,

δ) τα ποσά που καταβάλλονται στους μάρτυρες για έξοδα και αποζημίωση, καθώς και στους πραγματογνώμονες για έξοδα και αμοιβή, σύμφωνα με τις διατιμήσεις που ισχύουν,

ε) τα ποσά που καταβλήθηκαν για την προσαγωγή άλλων αποδεικτικών μέσων, καθώς και τα έξοδα ταξιδιού και αλληλογραφίας που κατέβαλε ο διάδικος για να εμφανιστεί στη δίκη.

2. Δεν αποδίδονται τα έξοδα που έγιναν

α) από απείθεια, απροσεξία ή σφάλμα του ίδιου του διαδίκου

β) από υπερβολική πρόνοιά του.

Άρθρο 190

1. Για τον προσδιορισμό και την εκκαθάριση του ποσού των εξόδων που πρέπει να αποδοθούν, κάθε διάδικος πρέπει να επισυνάψει στη δικογραφία, έως την συζήτηση στο ακροατήριο, κατάλογο των εξόδων και να φέρει, έως το τέλος της συζήτησης, τις παρατηρήσεις του για τον κατάλογο εξόδων που έχει υποβάλει ο αντίδικός του.

2. Ο κατάλογος της παραγράφου 1 μπορεί να περιληφθεί και στις προτάσεις που υποβάλλονται κατά τη συζήτηση στο ακροατήριο. Στις περιπτώσεις των άρθρων 237 και 238 ο κατάλογος υποβάλλεται μόνο με τις προτάσεις.

3. Για την εκκαθάριση των εξόδων αρκεί πιθανολόγηση.

Άρθρο 191

1. Όταν το δικαστήριο αποφασίζει οριστικά για ολόκληρη την κύρια ή την παρεμπίπτουσα δίκη ή για ένα μέρος της, πρέπει, εφόσον έχει υποβληθεί ο κατάλογος του άρθρου 190, να περιλάβει διάταξη στην απόφαση για την υποχρέωση της πληρωμής των εξόδων, καθορίζοντας και το ποσό τους.

2. Αν δεν υποβληθεί ο κατάλογος εξόδων, το δικαστήριο προχωρεί στην εκκαθάρισή τους, αν έχει υποβληθεί αίτημα για την επιδίκασή τους.

3. Αν η απόφαση δεν περιέχει διάταξη για τα έξοδα, μπορεί να υποβληθεί σχετική αίτηση στο ίδιο δικαστήριο.

Article 187

Without prejudice to an agreement between the interested parties to the contrary, the costs of a court settlement shall be shared equally among the parties in the proceedings, while the costs of quashed proceedings shall be offset.

Article 188

1. If a procedural step is revoked or if a procedural step or the entire proceedings are discontinued, the party in the proceedings effecting revocation or discontinuance shall be ordered to pay costs.
2. If the action or legal remedy is accepted, the accepting party in the proceedings shall be ordered to pay the costs of the proceedings ending with such acceptance, without prejudice to the provisions of Article 177.

Article 189

1. Only the judicial and extra-judicial costs necessary for the conduct and defence of the proceedings shall be paid and, in particular[:]
a) stamp duty for preparing judgments, procedural documents, court reports and other documents relating to the proceedings and for taking procedural steps;
b) judicial claims duty;
c) the fees of lawyers or other legal representatives and officers of the courts, in accordance with the applicable tariffs;
d) the amounts paid to witnesses for costs and compensation, as well as experts for costs and fees, in accordance with the applicable tariffs;
e) the amounts paid for the adduction of other means of evidence, as well as the travel and correspondence costs incurred by the party in the proceedings in order to appear in court.
2. There shall be no reimbursement of costs incurred[:]
a) due to contempt, oversight or error by the party in the proceedings;
b) due to an excess of caution on their part.

Article 190

1. In order to calculate and finalise the costs to be reimbursed, each party in the proceedings must append a list of the costs to the case-file by the date of the courtroom hearing, and make observations on the list of costs presented by the opponent by the end of the hearing.
2. The list referred to in paragraph 1 may also be included in the pleadings filed during the courtroom hearing. In the cases referred to in Articles 237 and 238, the list shall only be filed together with the pleadings.
3. The balance of probabilities test shall suffice for finalising the costs.

Article 191

1. If the list referred to in Article 190 has been filed, when the court hands down a final judgment regarding the main or incidental proceedings or part of such proceedings, it must include an order in its judgment regarding the payment of costs and specify their amount.
2. If the list of costs has not been filed, the court shall finalise them if an application for their award has been filed.
3. If the judgment contains no order concerning costs, a relevant application may be filed with the same court.

Άρθρο 192

Σε περίπτωση αποδοχής ή ανάκλησης διαδικαστικής πράξης ή παραίτησης, είτε από αυτήν είτε από ολόκληρη τη δίκη, αν εκδίδεται οριστική απόφαση, εφαρμόζονται όσα ορίζονται στο άρθρο 191, διαφορετικά η εκκαθάριση των εξόδων γίνεται κατά τη διαδικασία των περιουσιακών διαφορών των άρθρων 614 επ. από το μονομελές πρωτοδικείο ή από το ειρηνοδικείο, για τις δίκες που διεξάγονται σε αυτό.

Άρθρο 193

Δεν επιτρέπεται προσβολή της απόφασης με ένδικο μέσο ως προς τα έξοδα, αν δεν περιλαμβάνει και την ουσία της υπόθεσης.

ΚΕΦΑΛΑΙΟ ΚΒ'
Ευεργέτημα πενίας.

Άρθρο 194

1. Το ευεργέτημα της πενίας παρέχεται σε όποιον αποδεδειγμένα δεν μπορεί να καταβάλει τα έξοδα της δίκης και τα παράβολα χωρίς να περιορισθούν από αυτό τα απαραίτητα μέσα για τη διατροφή του ίδιου και της οικογένειας του.

2. Το ευεργέτημα της πενίας μπορεί να δοθεί και σε νομικά πρόσωπα κοινωφελή ή που δεν επιδιώκουν κερδοσκοπικό σκοπό καθώς και σε ομάδες προσώπων που έχουν την ικανότητα να είναι διάδικοι, αν αποδεικνύουν ότι με την προκαταβολή των εξόδων γίνεται πια αδύνατη ή προβληματική η εκπλήρωση του σκοπού τους.

3. Η διάταξη της παραγράφου 2 εφαρμόζεται και σε ομόρρυθμες ή ετερόρρυθμες εταιρίες, καθώς και σε συνεταιρισμούς, εφόσον η καταβολή των εξόδων δεν μπορεί να γίνει ούτε από το ταμείο τους ούτε από τα μέλη, χωρίς να περιοριστούν τα απαραίτητα μέσα για τη διατροφή των ίδιων και της οικογένειάς τους.

4. Το ευεργέτημα της πενίας δίνεται μόνο εφόσον η δίκη δεν παρουσιάζεται φανερά άδικη ή ασύμφορη.

Άρθρο 195

Με τις προϋποθέσεις του άρθρου 194 μπορεί να δοθεί το ευεργέτημα της πενίας σε αλλοδαπούς και σε πρόσωπα που αποδεδειγμένα δεν έχουν ιθαγένεια.

Άρθρο 196

1. Το ευεργέτημα της πενίας δίνεται ύστερα από αίτηση, από τον ειρηνοδίκη, το δικαστή του μονομελούς πρωτοδικείου ή τον πρόεδρο του δικαστηρίου στο οποίο εκκρεμεί ή πρόκειται να εισαχθεί η δίκη και, αν πρόκειται για πράξεις που είναι άσχετες με δίκη, από τον ειρηνοδίκη της κατοικίας του αιτούντος.

2. Η αίτηση πρέπει να αναφέρει συνοπτικά το αντικείμενο της δίκης ή της πράξης, τα αποδεικτικά μέσα που υπάρχουν για την κύρια υπόθεση, καθώς και τα στοιχεία που βεβαιώνουν την συνδρομή των προϋποθέσεων του άρθρου 194.

3. Στην αίτηση πρέπει να επισυνάπτονται:

α) πιστοποιητικό, ατελώς, του δημάρχου όπου είναι η κατοικία ή η μόνιμη διαμονή του αιτούντος, το οποίο βεβαιώνει την επαγγελματική, οικονομική και οικογενειακή κατάστασή του, καθώς και όσα ορίζονται στο άρθρο 194 παράγραφοι 1 έως 3, και

β) πιστοποιητικό, ατελώς, του οικονομικού εφόρου της κατοικίας ή της μόνιμης διαμονής του αιτούντος το οποίο βεβαιώνει αν ο αιτών υπέβαλε κατά την τελευταία τριετία δήλωση φόρου εισοδήματος ή οποιουδήποτε άλλου άμεσου φόρου, καθώς και την εξακρίβωσή της, ύστερα από έλεγχο.

Article 192

Where a procedural step is accepted or revoked or where a procedural step or the entire proceedings are discontinued and a final judgment is handed down, the provisions of Article 191 apply, otherwise the costs shall be finalised in accordance with the procedure for property disputes laid down in Articles 614 *et seq.* by the single-member court of first instance or the court of the peace for proceedings conducted before it.

Article 193

Judgments may not be contested by means of a legal remedy with regard to costs if the legal remedy does not also concern the merits of the case.

CHAPTER XXII
Legal aid

Article 194

1. Legal aid shall be granted to any person who demonstrably cannot pay the court costs and procedural fees without this limiting the means necessary to support themselves and their family.
2. Legal aid may also be granted to legal persons pursuing public-benefit or non-profit objectives, as well as groups of persons who have capacity to be parties in legal proceedings, where they prove that paying the costs in advance makes it impossible or problematic to achieve their objectives.
3. The provisions of paragraph 2 also apply to general or limited partnerships, as well as cooperatives, where payment of costs cannot be effected either from their own funds or from their members without limiting the means necessary to support themselves and their families.
4. Legal aid shall be granted only if the proceedings do not appear to be manifestly unjustified or disadvantageous.

Article 195

Subject to the conditions laid down in Article 194, legal aid may also be granted to foreign nationals and persons who are demonstrably stateless.

Article 196

1. Legal aid shall be granted, following an application, by the court of the peace judge, the single-member court of first instance judge or the presiding judge of the court before which the proceedings are pending or are to be brought and, with regard to steps unrelated to the proceedings, by the court of the peace judge of the district where the applicant is domiciled.
2. The application must concisely cite the subject-matter of the proceedings or the step, the means of evidence available for the main case, as well as information confirming that the conditions laid down in Article 194 are met.
3. The following must be appended to the application:
a) a certificate, issued free of official charges, by the mayor of the place where the applicant is domiciled or permanently resident, confirming their occupational, financial and marital status, as well as the information referred to in Article 194(1) to (3); and
b) a certificate, issued free of official charges, by the tax inspector of the place where the applicant is domiciled or permanently resident, attesting whether the applicant filed an income tax return or any other direct tax return during the last three years, as well as verification of the said return following an audit.

Άρθρο 197

1. Όταν δικάζεται η αίτηση, δεν είναι υποχρεωτική η παράσταση με δικηγόρο και μπορεί να διαταχθεί η κλήτευση του αντιδίκου του αιτούντος. Για την παραδοχή της αίτησης αρκεί πιθανολόγηση, το δικαστήριο μπορεί όμως να ζητήσει και αυτεπαγγέλτως συμπληρωματικές αποδείξεις, να εξετάσει μάρτυρες, καθώς και τον αιτούντα, με όρκο ή χωρίς όρκο, επίσης να ζητήσει πληροφορίες από τον δικαστή της υπόθεσης και γνώμη δικηγόρου ότι η διεξαγωγή της δίκης δεν εμφανίζεται φανερά άδικη ή ασύμφορη.
2. Ο δικαστής που δικάζει την αίτηση, όταν διατάζει να κλητευθεί ο αντίδικος του αιτούντος, μπορεί να ορίσει ότι η εκδίκαση της αίτησης θα συνεχιστεί ατελώς.

Άρθρο 198

Το ευεργέτημα της πενίας δίνεται χωριστά για κάθε δίκη, ισχύει για κάθε βαθμό για κάθε δικαστήριο και περιλαμβάνει την αναγκαστική εκτέλεση της απόφασης.

Άρθρο 199

1. Όποιος έλαβε το ευεργέτημα της πενίας απαλλάσσεται προσωρινά από την υποχρέωση να καταβάλει τα έξοδα της δίκης και γενικά της διαδικασίας, ιδίως τα τέλη χαρτοσήμου, το τέλος δικαστικού ενσήμου, το τέλος του απογράφου και τις προσαυξήσεις τους, τα παράβολα, τα δικαιώματα των συμβολαιογράφων και των δικαστικών επιμελητών, των μαρτύρων και άλλων δικαστικών πληρεξουσίων, καθώς και από την υποχρέωση εγγυοδοσίας για τα έξοδα αυτά.
2. Με την απόφαση που χορηγεί το ευεργέτημα της πενίας μπορεί να οριστεί ότι ο άπορος απαλλάσσεται προσωρινά από την προκαταβολή ενός μέρους από τα έξοδα αυτά.
3. Η παραχώρηση του ευεργετήματος της πενίας δεν επηρεάζει την υποχρέωση να πληρωθούν τα έξοδα που επιδικάστηκαν στον αντίδικο.

Άρθρο 200

1. Ύστερα από αίτηση του διαδίκου, η απόφαση που χορηγεί το ευεργέτημα της πενίας ή και μεταγενέστερη απόφαση διορίζει έναν δικηγόρο, ένα συμβολαιογράφο και ένα δικαστικό επιμελητή, με την εντολή να υπερασπιστούν τον άπορο, να τον εκπροσωπήσουν στο δικαστήριο και να του δώσουν τη βοήθεια που χρειάζεται για να γίνουν οι διάφορες πράξεις. Αυτοί έχουν υποχρέωση να δεχτούν την εντολή και να δίνουν τη βοήθειά τους στον άπορο χωρίς αξίωση προκαταβολής αμοιβής δικαιωμάτων.
2. Ο διορισμός δικηγόρου με την απόφαση ισχύει ως παροχή δικαστικής πληρεξουσιότητας από τον άπορο, στην έκταση που ορίζει το άρθρο 97, εκτός αν η απόφαση ύστερα από αίτηση του απόρου, την περιορίζει ή την επεκτείνει.

Άρθρο 201

Το ευεργέτημα της πενίας παύει με το θάνατο του φυσικού προσώπου ή με τη διάλυση του νομικού προσώπου ή της εταιρίας ή άλλης ομάδας προσώπων. Πράξεις που δεν επιδέχονται αναβολή μπορούν να ενεργηθούν και αργότερα με βάση το ευεργέτημα που δόθηκε.

Άρθρο 202

Το ευεργέτημα της πενίας μπορεί να ανακληθεί ή να περιοριστεί με απόφαση του αρμοδίου δικαστή, ύστερα από πρόταση του εισαγγελέα ή και αυτεπαγγέλτως, εφόσον αποδεικνύεται ότι οι προϋποθέσεις της παροχής του είτε δεν υπήρχαν εξαρχής, είτε έπαψαν να υπάρχουν αργότερα, είτε μεταβλήθηκαν.

Article 197

1. When the application is heard, appearance with a lawyer is not mandatory, and the court may order that the applicant's opponent be summonsed. The application shall be accepted if, on the balance of probabilities, it is considered likely to succeed; however, the court may request supplementary evidence *ex officio*, examine witnesses as well as the applicant, whether or not under oath, and request information from the judge seised of the case and the opinion of a lawyer that conducting the proceedings does not appear manifestly unjustified or disadvantageous.
2. When ordering that the applicant's opponent be summonsed, the judge hearing the application may rule that adjudication of the application shall continue free of official charges.

Article 198

Legal aid shall be granted separately for each set of proceedings, apply at every instance and before every court, and cover compulsory enforcement of the judgment.

Article 199

1. Any person who was granted legal aid shall be provisionally released from the obligation to pay the costs of the proceedings and the procedure in general and, in particular, stamp duty, judicial stamp duty, enforcement precept duty and surcharges thereto, procedural fees, the fees of notaries public and court process servers, witnesses and other legal representatives, as well as the obligation to provide surety for such costs.
2. The ruling granting legal aid may specify that the financially challenged person is provisionally released from advance payment of part of such costs.
3. The granting of legal aid shall not affect the obligation to pay the costs awarded to the opponent.

Article 200

1. Following an application by a party in the proceedings, the ruling granting legal aid or a subsequent ruling shall also appoint a lawyer, a notary public and a court process server with the mandate to defend the financially challenged person, represent them in court and provide them with the assistance necessary to take the various steps [required]. The above persons are obligated to accept the mandate and provide their assistance to the financially challenged person without [being entitled to] claim advance payment of fees and charges.
2. The appointment of a lawyer by the [above] ruling shall function as conferral of judicial power of attorney by the financially challenged person, to the extent provided for in Article 97, unless, following an application filed by the financially challenged person, the ruling handed down restricts or extends this power.

Article 201

Legal aid ceases upon the death of the natural person or the dissolution of the legal person or partnership or other group of persons. Steps that cannot be deferred may also be taken at a later time on the basis of the aid granted.

Article 202

Legal aid may be revoked or restricted by a ruling of the competent judge, on a proposal from the public prosecutor or even *ex officio*, where it is proven that the requirements for granting it were either not met from the outset, or ceased to be met at a later time, or changed.

Άρθρο 203

1. Η εκκαθάριση των εξόδων της δίκης, όταν είχε προηγηθεί ευεργέτημα πενίας, γίνεται σύμφωνα με τα άρθρα 190 έως 193 και περιλαμβάνει όσα έξοδα δεν είχαν προκαταβληθεί προσωρινά σύμφωνα με το άρθρο 199.

2. Αν η απόφαση επιβάλλει τα έξοδα σε βάρος του αντιδίκου του απόρου, η είσπραξη των τελών χαρτοσήμου, του δικαστικού ενσήμου, του απογράφου και του αντιγράφου, καθώς και των προσαυξήσεών τους γίνεται σύμφωνα με το νόμο για την είσπραξη των δημοσίων εσόδων, ενώ εκείνων που οφείλονται στον άπορο, τους δικηγόρους ή άλλους δικαστικούς πληρεξούσιους και στους άλλους δικαστικούς υπαλλήλους επιδικάζονται στα πρόσωπα αυτά και εισπράττονται κατά τις διατάξεις της αναγκαστικής εκτέλεσης. Με τον ίδιο τρόπο γίνεται η είσπραξη των εξόδων, αν επιβληθούν σε βάρος του απόρου, αμέσως μόλις πάψουν να υπάρχουν όλες ή μερικές από τις προϋποθέσεις για την παροχή του ευεργετήματος της πενίας και βεβαιωθεί αυτό με τον τρόπο που ορίζει το άρθρο 202.

Άρθρο 204

Αν οι διάδικοι ή οι νόμιμοι αντιπρόσωποί τους πέτυχαν την παροχή του ευεργετήματος της πενίας με αναληθείς δηλώσεις και στοιχεία, ο δικαστής, που αποφασίζει την ανάκληση του ευεργετήματος, τους καταδικάζει σε χρηματική ποινή από εκατό (100) ευρώ έως διακόσια (200) ευρώ που περιέρχεται στο δημόσιο ως δημόσιο έσοδο, χωρίς να αποκλείεται υποχρέωσή τους να καταβάλουν τα ποσά από τα οποία είχαν απαλλαγεί, ούτε και η ποινική τους δίωξη. Αντίγραφο της απόφασης αυτής γνωστοποιείται αμέσως στο Υπουργείο Οικονομικών με επιμέλεια της γραμματείας.

ΚΕΦΑΛΑΙΟ ΚΓ'
Ποινές.

Άρθρο 205

Το δικαστήριο αυτεπαγγέλτως, με την οριστική απόφαση του, επιβάλλει στον διάδικο ή στον νόμιμο αντιπρόσωπό του ή στο δικαστικό του πληρεξούσιο, ανάλογα με την ευθύνη καθενός, χρηματική ποινή από χίλια (1.000) ευρώ έως δύο χιλιάδες πεντακόσια (2.500) ευρώ, που περιέρχεται στο δημόσιο ως δημόσιο έσοδο, αν προκύψει από τη δίκη που έγινε, ότι, αν και το γνώριζαν:
1) άσκησαν προφανώς αβάσιμη αγωγή, ανταγωγή ή παρέμβαση ή προφανώς αβάσιμο ένδικο μέσο ή
2) διεξήγαγαν τη δίκη παρελκυστικά ή δεν τήρησαν τους κανόνες των χρηστών ηθών ή της καλής πίστης ή το καθήκον της αλήθειας.
Αντίγραφο της απόφασης αυτής γνωστοποιείται αμέσως στο Υπουργείο Οικονομικών με επιμέλεια της γραμματείας.

Άρθρο 206

Ο δικαστής μπορεί, ύστερα από αίτηση ενός διαδίκου ή και αυτεπαγγέλτως, να διατάξει να διαγραφούν από τα δικόγραφα ή τις προτάσεις των διαδίκων εξυβριστικές ή άλλες ανάρμοστες φράσεις και να επιβάλλει, αν έγιναν στο ακροατήριο ασυγχώρητες παραδρομές και παραβάσεις, πειθαρχικές ποινές σε υπαλλήλους της γραμματείας, συμβολαιογράφους και δικαστικούς επιμελητές.

Άρθρο 207

1. Αν όταν ενεργείται κάποια πράξη, είτε στο ακροατήριο είτε και έξω από αυτό, γίνει θόρυβος ή εκδηλωθεί ανυπακοή στα μέτρα που έχουν ληφθεί ή στις διαταγές που δόθηκαν, ο δικαστής και, αν πρόκειται για πολυμελές δικαστήριο, ο πρόεδρος έχει εξουσία να επιβάλλει σε αυτόν που θορυβεί ή στον παραβάτη είτε χρηματική ποινή από εκατό (100) ευρώ έως πεντακόσια (500) ευρώ είτε την απομάκρυνσή του από τον τόπο όπου ενεργείται η πράξη είτε κράτηση 24 ωρών.

2. Αν αυτός που θορυβεί ή ο παραβάτης είναι δικηγόρος, το δικαστήριο, είτε πρόκειται για συνεδρίαση στο ακροατήριο, είτε πρόκειται για ενέργεια πράξης έξω από αυτό, εφαρμόζει το άρθρο 155 του Κώδικα Δικηγόρων.

3. Οι πράξεις αυτές μπορούν να ανακληθούν από εκείνον που τις έχει εκδώσει.

4. Κατά τις συνεδριάσεις των δικαστηρίων στο ακροατήριο εφαρμόζονται και τα άρθρα 116 και 117 του Κώδικα Ποινικής Δικονομίας.

Article 203

1. Where legal aid had been granted, court costs shall be finalised in accordance with Articles 190 to 193 and shall include any costs not provisionally paid in advance in accordance with Article 199.
2. If the judgment orders the opponent of the financially challenged person to pay costs, [then] the stamp duty, judicial stamp duty, enforcement precept duty and copy duty as well as surcharges thereto shall be collected in accordance with the law on the collection of public revenues, while the costs payable to the financially challenged person, the lawyers or other legal representatives and other officers of the court shall be awarded to such persons and collected in accordance with the provisions on compulsory enforcement. If the financially challenged person is ordered to pay costs, such costs shall be collected in the same manner immediately after all or certain of the requirements for granting legal aid cease to be met and this is confirmed in the manner set forth in Article 202.

Article 204

If the parties in the proceedings or their lawful proxies procured legal aid through misrepresentations and false information, the judge deciding on revoking the aid shall order them to pay a monetary penalty ranging from 100 to 200 euros, which shall accrue to the Greek State as public revenue; this neither precludes their obligation to pay the amounts from which they had been released nor their criminal prosecution. A copy of this ruling shall be immediately notified to the Ministry of Finance by the [court] registry.

CHAPTER XXIII
Penalties

Article 205

In its final judgment, the court shall impose *ex officio* a monetary penalty on the party in the proceedings or their lawful proxy or their legal representative, depending on each person's liability, ranging from 1,000 to 2,500 euros, which shall accrue to the Greek State as public revenue, if it arises from the proceedings conducted that they knowingly:
1) filed a manifestly unfounded action, cross-action or intervention, or a manifestly unfounded legal remedy; or
2) conducted the proceedings in a dilatory manner or failed to comply with the rules of morality or good faith or the duty of truth.
A copy of this ruling shall be immediately notified to the Ministry of Finance by the [court] registry.

Article 206

Following an application filed by a party in the proceedings or even *ex officio*, the judge may order that abusive and inappropriate phrases be stricken from procedural documents or the pleadings of the parties in the proceedings and, if inexcusable errors and violations took place in the courtroom, shall impose disciplinary sanctions on registry clerks, notaries public and court process servers.

Article 207

1. If there is commotion or disobedience against measures taken or orders issued during the conduct of any act, whether inside or outside the courtroom, the judge and, in the case of a multi-member court, the presiding judge shall be empowered to impose either a monetary penalty ranging from 100 to 500 euros on the person causing the commotion or the offender, or eject him or her from the place where the act is being conducted, or detain him or her for 24 hours.
2. Where the person causing a commotion or the offender is a lawyer, the court, whether in cases of a courtroom hearing or the conduct of any act outside the courtroom, shall apply Article 155 of the Lawyers' Code.
3. These decisions may be revoked by the [judge] who issued them.
4. During courtroom sittings, Articles 116 and 117 of the Code of Criminal Procedure also apply.

ΔΕΥΤΕΡΟ ΒΙΒΛΙΟ
ΔΙΑΔΙΚΑΣΙΑ ΣΤΑ ΠΡΩΤΟΒΑΘΜΙΑ ΔΙΚΑΣΤΗΡΙΑ

ΚΕΦΑΛΑΙΟ Α'
Απόπειρα Συμβιβασμού

Άρθρο 208

[Καταργείται]

Άρθρο 209

1. Όποιος έχει την πρόθεση να ασκήσει αγωγή μπορεί πριν από την κατάθεσή της να ζητήσει τη συμβιβαστική επέμβαση του αρμόδιου για την εκδίκαση της αγωγής ειρηνοδίκη. Για το σκοπό αυτόν υποβάλλεται αίτηση προς τον ειρηνοδίκη, στην οποία πρέπει να αναγράφεται συνοπτικά το αντικείμενο της διαφοράς, ή εμφανίζονται αυθόρμητα οι ενδιαφερόμενοι ενώπιον του.
2. Ο ειρηνοδίκης, όταν υποβληθεί αίτηση συμβιβασμού καλεί ενώπιόν του το συντομότερο σε ορισμένη ημέρα και ώρα όλους τους ενδιαφερομένους. Η πρόσκληση του ειρηνοδίκη πρέπει να αναφέρει με συντομία τη διαφορά. Αν προσέλθουν αυθόρμητα όλοι οι ενδιαφερόμενοι, ο ειρηνοδίκης μπορεί αμέσως να προχωρήσει σε συμβιβαστική επέμβαση. Η συμβιβαστική επέμβαση του ειρηνοδίκη δεν είναι ανάγκη να γίνεται δημόσια, όμως για την επέμβαση αυτή τηρούνται πρακτικά.
3. Αν αυτός που υπέβαλε την αίτηση δεν εμφανιστεί, η αίτηση θεωρείται ότι δεν υποβλήθηκε ποτέ και καταδικάζεται αυτός στα δικαστικά έξοδα. Αν δεν εμφανιστεί κάποιος από αυτούς που κλήθηκαν, αναφέρεται αυτό στα πρακτικά και η συμβιβαστική επέμβαση του ειρηνοδίκη θεωρείται ότι απέτυχε.

Άρθρο 210

1. Ο ειρηνοδίκης κατά τη συμβιβαστική επέμβαση εξετάζει μαζί με τους ενδιαφερομένους ολόκληρη τη διαφορά χωρίς να δεσμεύεται από το ισχύον δικονομικό και ουσιαστικό δίκαιο, εκτιμά ελεύθερα τα διάφορα πραγματικά περιστατικά και προσπαθεί να βρει τρόπο συμβιβασμού. Ιδίως έχει το δικαίωμα να διατάζει αυτοψία, πραγματογνωμοσύνη, την προσαγωγή οποιουδήποτε εγγράφου, την προσωπική εμφάνιση των διαδίκων και μπορεί να εξετάζει μάρτυρες, έστω και χωρίς όρκο, και γενικά να ενεργεί οποιοδήποτε πράξη για να διευκρινιστεί η διαφορά.
2. Ο συμβιβασμός μπορεί να αφορά ολόκληρη τη διαφορά ή μόνο μέρος της.

Άρθρο 211

[Καταργείται]

Άρθρο 212

1. Για τις ενέργειες του ειρηνοδίκη προς συμβιβασμό γίνεται σύντομη αναφορά στα πρακτικά.
2. Αν η συμβιβαστική επέμβαση αποτύχει, γίνεται σχετική αναφορά στα πρακτικά και σημειώνεται από τον ειρηνοδίκη ο λόγος της αποτυχίας.
3. Αν επιτευχθεί συμβιβασμός αναγράφονται λεπτομερώς στο πρακτικό όλοι οι όροι του.
4. Ο συμβιβασμός που έγινε σύμφωνα με τα άρθρα 208 και επόμενα έχει όλα τα αποτελέσματα του δικαστικού συμβιβασμού.

BOOK II
PROCEDURE BEFORE FIRST-INSTANCE COURTS

CHAPTER I
Attempt to Reach Settlement

Article 208

[Repealed]

Article 209

1. Any person who intends to file an action may, prior to doing so, request that the court of the peace judge competent to hear the action intervene for the purpose of reaching a settlement. For this purpose, an application shall be filed with the court of the peace judge, summarily citing the subject-matter of the dispute, or the interested parties shall appear of their own volition before the said judge.
2. When an application for a settlement is filed, the court of the peace judge shall summon all the interested parties to appear before him or her as soon as possible, specifying the date and time. The summons issued by the court of the peace judge must contain a summary of the dispute. If all interested parties appear voluntarily, the court of the peace judge may immediately proceed with the settlement intervention. The settlement intervention by the court of the peace judge need not take place in public, but a transcript shall be kept.
3. If the applicant fails to appear, the application shall be deemed to never have been filed and that person shall be ordered to pay court costs. If any of the persons summoned fails to appear, this shall be noted in the transcript and the settlement intervention by the court of the peace judge shall be deemed unsuccessful.

Article 210

1. During the [attempt to reach a] settlement, the court of the peace judge, together with the interested parties, shall examine the entire dispute, without being bound by the procedural and substantive law in force, freely assess the various actual facts and try to reach a settlement. In particular, the court of the peace judge shall have the right to order an inspection, expert evidence, production of any document, personal appearance by the parties in the proceedings, and may examine witnesses, even without an oath, and generally take any steps in order to clarify the dispute.
2. The settlement may concern all or only part of the dispute.

Article 211

[Repealed]

Article 212

1. The steps taken by the court of the peace judge to reach a settlement shall be summarised in the transcript.
2. If the settlement intervention proves unsuccessful, this shall be recorded in the transcript and the court of the peace judge shall note the reason for failure.
3. If a settlement is achieved, all its terms shall be recorded in detail in the [settlement] report.
4. Settlements achieved in accordance with Articles 208 *et seq.* generate all the [same] effects [as] a court settlement.

Άρθρο 213

Η αίτηση συμβιβαστικής επέμβασης θεωρείται ότι δεν υποβλήθηκε ποτέ, αν δεν συντρέχουν οι προϋποθέσεις του ουσιαστικού δικαίου για να είναι έγκυρος ο συμβιβασμός. Στην περίπτωση αυτή γίνεται σχετική σημείωση στα πρακτικά.

Άρθρο 214

Η υποβολή αίτησης για συμβιβαστική επέμβαση του ειρηνοδίκη έχει όλες τις συνέπειες της άσκησης αγωγής, εφόσον αυτή ασκηθεί μέσα σε τρεις μήνες από την αποτυχία της συμβιβαστικής επέμβασης.

Άρθρο 214Α

1. Οι διάδικοι μπορούν να συμβιβάζονται, μετά την επέλευση της εκκρεμοδικίας μέχρι την έκδοση τελεσίδικης απόφασης και χωρίς να υφίσταται στάση της δίκης, όταν αντικείμενό της είναι ιδιωτικού δικαίου διαφορά, για την οποία επιτρέπεται κατά το ουσιαστικό δίκαιο να συνομολογηθεί συμβιβασμός.
2. Για το συμβιβασμό συντάσσεται ατελώς πρακτικό, που περιλαμβάνει το περιεχόμενο της συμφωνίας τους και ιδίως το είδος του αναγνωριζόμενου δικαιώματος, το ποσό της οφειλόμενης παροχής και τους τυχόν όρους υπό τους οποίους θα εκπληρωθεί, καθώς και πρόβλεψη για τα δικαστικά έξοδα. Το πρακτικό συντάσσεται σε τόσα αντίτυπα όσοι και οι διάδικοι ή ομάδες διαδίκων, που αντιδικούν, χρονολογείται και υπογράφεται από αυτούς ή από τους δικηγόρους τους αν έχουν ειδική πληρεξουσιότητα κατά το άρθρο 98 περίπτωση β'.
3. Κάθε διάδικος μπορεί, προσκομίζοντας το πρακτικό σε πρωτότυπο, να ζητήσει την επικύρωσή του από το δικαστή ή τον πρόεδρο του δικαστηρίου, ενώπιον του οποίου εκκρεμεί η αγωγή ή το ένδικο μέσο. Το πρακτικό επικυρώνεται αφού διαπιστωθεί ότι:
α) η διαφορά είναι δεκτική συμβιβαστικής επίλυσης,
β) το πρακτικό έχει υπογραφεί σύμφωνα με όσα προαναφέρονται και
γ) από αυτό προκύπτει σαφώς το είδος του αναγνωριζόμενου δικαιώματος και το ποσό της οφειλόμενης παροχής, καθώς και οι τυχόν όροι εκπλήρωσής της. Αν η διαφορά περιλαμβάνει και καταψήφιση, το πρακτικό αποτελεί από την επικύρωσή του τίτλο εκτελεστό και περιάπτεται με τον εκτελεστήριο τύπο από το αρμόδιο για την επικύρωσή του δικαστήριο. Αν η διαφορά έχει χαρακτήρα απλώς αναγνωριστικό, το πρακτικό αποδεικνύει το δικαίωμα. Με την επικύρωση του πρακτικού επέρχεται κατάργηση της δίκης.

Αρθρο 214Β
Δικαστική μεσολάβηση

1. Διαφορές ιδιωτικού δικαίου μπορούν να επιλυθούν και με προσφυγή σε δικαστική μεσολάβηση. Η προσφυγή στη δικαστική μεσολάβηση, η οποία είναι προαιρετική, μπορεί να γίνει πριν από την άσκηση της αγωγής ή και κατά τη διάρκεια της εκκρεμοδικίας.
2. Σε κάθε πρωτοδικείο και εφετείο ορίζονται, για δύο έτη, με δυνατότητα ανανέωσης για ένα επιπλέον έτος, ένας ή περισσότεροι από τους υπηρετούντες προέδρους πρωτοδικών και εφετών ή από τους αρχαιότερους πρωτόδικες και εφέτες, ως μεσολαβητές μερικής ή πλήρους απασχόλησης.

Article 213

If the requirements of substantive law necessary for the settlement to be valid are not met, the application for settlement shall be deemed never to have been filed. In this case, a relevant note shall be made in the transcript.

Article 214

[The act of] filing an application for settlement by a court of the peace judge generates all the [same] effects as filing an action, provided the action is filed within three months from the [date the attempt to reach a] settlement proved unsuccessful.

Article 214A

1. The parties in the proceedings may reach a settlement after the occurrence of *lis pendens* and until a *de jure* non-appealable judgment is handed down and without the proceedings being suspended, when the proceedings concern a private law dispute in which, according to substantive law, a settlement may be reached.

2. With regard to the settlement, a report shall be prepared free of official charges and shall include the contents of the agreement between the parties and, in particular, the type of right acknowledged, the amount owed and any conditions under which it shall be paid, as well as a provision regarding court costs. The report shall be prepared in as many counterparts as there are parties in the proceedings or groups of litigants, dated and signed by the said parties or their lawyers if they have special authorisation in accordance with Article 98(b).

3. Any party in the proceedings may present the original report and request its certification by the judge or presiding judge of the court before whom the action or legal remedy is pending. The report shall be certified once it has been ascertained that:

a) the dispute is amenable to settlement;

b) the report has been signed in accordance with the foregoing; and

c) the type of right acknowledged, the amount owed and any conditions under which it shall be paid clearly emerge from the report. If the dispute also includes a request for performance, the report, as of its certification, shall constitute an enforceable title and shall be endorsed as an enforcement order by the court competent to certify it. If the only thing sought in the dispute is a declaratory judgment, the report shall [serve as] proof of the right. Upon certification of the report, the proceedings shall be quashed.

Article 214B
Judicial mediation

1. Private-law disputes may also be resolved through recourse to judicial mediation. Recourse to judicial mediation, which is optional, may take place prior to the action being filed or even during *lis pendens*.

2. At each court of first instance and court of appeal, one or more among the presiding judges of the court of first instance and presiding judges of the court of appeal or among the most senior court of first instance judges and court of appeal judges shall be appointed as part-time or full-time mediators for two years, with the possibility of renewal for an additional year.

3. Η δικαστική μεσολάβηση περιλαμβάνει ξεχωριστές και κοινές ακροάσεις και συζητήσεις των μερών και των πληρεξούσιων δικηγόρων τους με τον μεσολαβητή δικαστή, ο οποίος και μπορεί να απευθύνει στα μέρη μη δεσμευτικές προτάσεις επίλυσης της διαφοράς. Κάθε ενδιαφερόμενος μπορεί, μετά ή δια πληρεξουσίου δικηγόρου, να προσφεύγει στον κατά τόπον αρμόδιο δικαστή μεσολαβητή υποβάλλοντας γραπτώς το αίτημά του.

4. Το δικαστήριο στο οποίο είναι εκκρεμής η υπόθεση μπορεί σε κάθε στάση της δίκης, ανάλογα με την περίπτωση και λαμβάνοντας υπόψη όλες τις περιστάσεις της υπόθεσης, να καλεί τα μέρη να προσφύγουν στη δικαστική μεσολάβηση για την επίλυση της διαφοράς τους και ταυτόχρονα, αν συμφωνούν τα μέρη, να αναβάλει την εκδίκαση της υπόθεσης σε σύντομη δικάσιμο και πάντως όχι πέραν του εξαμήνου.

5. Αν τα μέρη καταλήξουν σε συμφωνία συντάσσεται πρακτικό μεσολάβησης. Το πρακτικό υπογράφεται από τον μεσολαβητή, τα μέρη και τους πληρεξουσίους δικηγόρους τους και το πρωτότυπό του κατατίθεται στη γραμματεία του πρωτοδικείου όπου διεξήχθη η μεσολάβηση. Κατά την κατάθεση ο ενδιαφερόμενος υποβάλλει παράβολο υπέρ του Δημοσίου, το ύψος και η αναπροσαρμογή του οποίου καθορίζονται με κοινή απόφαση των Υπουργών Οικονομικών και Δικαιοσύνης, Διαφάνειας και Ανθρωπίνων Δικαιωμάτων. Από την κατάθεση στη γραμματεία του πρωτοδικείου, το πρακτικό μεσολάβησης, εφόσον περιέχει συμφωνία των μερών για ύπαρξη αξίωσης, αποτελεί εκτελεστό τίτλο, σύμφωνα με το άρθρο 904 παράγραφος 2 εδάφιο γ' Κ.Πολ.Δ.

6. Η μεσολάβηση πρέπει να διεξάγεται κατά τρόπο που να μην παραβιάζει το απόρρητο αυτής, εκτός αν τα μέρη συμφωνήσουν άλλως. Πριν από την έναρξη της διαδικασίας όλοι οι συμμετέχοντες δεσμεύονται εγγράφως να τηρήσουν το απόρρητο της διαδικασίας.

Άρθρο 214Γ
Προσφυγή σε διαδικασία διαμεσολάβησης

Το δικαστήριο προτείνει στους διαδίκους την προσφυγή σε διαδικασία διαμεσολάβησης αν αυτό ενδείκνυται με βάση τις περιστάσεις της υποθέσεως, όπως ο νόμος ορίζει. Σε περίπτωση αποδοχής της πρότασης η συζήτηση της υπόθεσης αναβάλλεται για χρονικό διάστημα τριών (3) έως έξι (6) μηνών.

ΚΕΦΑΛΑΙΟ Β
Άσκηση της αγωγής.

Άρθρο 215

1. Η αγωγή ασκείται με κατάθεση δικογράφου στη γραμματεία του δικαστηρίου στο οποίο απευθύνεται και με επίδοση αντιγράφου της στον εναγόμενο. Η κατάθεση του δικογράφου μπορεί να γίνεται και με ηλεκτρονικά μέσα σύμφωνα με την παράγραφο 4 του άρθρου 119. Κάτω από το δικόγραφο που κατατέθηκε συντάσσεται έκθεση στην οποία αναφέρεται η ημέρα, ο μήνας και το έτος της κατάθεσης, καθώς και το ονοματεπώνυμο του καταθέτη. Η έκθεση μπορεί να συντάσσεται και με ηλεκτρονικά μέσα σύμφωνα με την παράγραφο 2 του άρθρου 117. Αναφορά του δικογράφου της αγωγής που κατατέθηκε γίνεται χωρίς καθυστέρηση σε ειδικό βιβλίο με αλφαβητικό ευρετήριο. Στο βιβλίο αυτό αναγράφονται με αύξοντα αριθμό και χρονολογική σειρά οι αγωγές που κατατίθενται και αναφέρονται τα ονοματεπώνυμα των διαδίκων, η χρονολογία της κατάθεσης και το αντικείμενο της διαφοράς. Στη γραμματεία κάθε δικαστηρίου τηρείται και ηλεκτρονικό αρχείο αγωγών.

2. Στην περίπτωση του άρθρου 237, η αγωγή επιδίδεται στον εναγόμενο μέσα σε προθεσμία τριάντα (30) ημερών από την κατάθεσή της και αν αυτός ή κάποιος από τους ομοδίκους διαμένει στο εξωτερικό ή είναι άγνωστης διαμονής μέσα σε προθεσμία εξήντα (60) ημερών. Αν η αγωγή δεν επιδοθεί μέσα στην προθεσμία αυτή, θεωρείται ως μη ασκηθείσα.

3. Judicial mediation involves separate and joint hearings and discussions between the parties and their authorised lawyers [on the one hand] and the mediator judge [on the other], who may present the parties with non-binding proposals to resolve the dispute. Any interested party may seek recourse to the mediator judge with jurisdiction *ratione loci*, with or via their authorised lawyer, by filing a request in writing.
4. The court before which the case is pending may, at any stage of the proceedings, depending on and taking all the circumstances of the case into consideration, call upon the parties to seek recourse to mediation to resolve their dispute and, at the same time, if the parties agree, may defer adjudication of the case for a short period and, in all cases, no more than six months.
5. If the parties reach an agreement, a mediation report shall be prepared. The report shall be signed by the mediator, the parties and their authorised lawyers, and the original report shall be filed with the registry of the court of first instance where the mediation took place. When filing the report, the interested party shall pay a procedural fee to the Greek State, the amount of which shall be specified in a joint decision of the Minister of Finance and the Minister of Justice, Transparency and Human Rights. Provided it contains an agreement between the parties on the existence of a claim, the mediation report shall constitute an enforceable title, in accordance with Article 904(2)(c) of this Code, as of its filing with the registry of the court of first instance.
6. Unless otherwise agreed upon by the parties, the mediation must be conducted in a manner that does not breach its secrecy. Prior to its commencement, all participants shall be bound in writing to observe the secrecy of the process.

Article 214C
Use of mediation

The court shall propose that the parties in the proceedings use mediation, where appropriate according to the circumstances of the case, as required by law. Where the proposal is accepted, the hearing of the case shall be adjourned for a period of three to six months.

CHAPTER II
Filing actions

Article 215

1. Actions are filed by submitting a procedural document to the registry of the court to which the action is addressed and by serving a copy of the action on the defendant. The procedural document may also be filed using electronic means, in accordance with Article 119(4). A report shall be prepared at the end of the procedural document filed, indicating the day, month and year of filing, as well as the full name of the person filing it. The report may also be prepared using electronic means, in accordance with Article 117(2). The procedural document of the action filed shall be recorded without delay in a special register with an index kept in alphabetical order. Actions filed shall be recorded in this register by incremental number and in chronological order, listing the full names of the parties in the proceedings, the date of filing and the subject-matter of the dispute. A database of actions shall also be kept at the registry of every court.
2. In accordance with Article 237, the action shall be served on the defendant within a deadline of 30 days from the date it was filed, and if the defendant or any of the joined parties resides abroad or has no known place of residence, within a deadline of 60 days. If the action is not served within that deadline, it shall be deemed not to have been filed.

Άρθρο 216

1. Η αγωγή εκτός από τα στοιχεία που ορίζονται στα άρθρα 118 ή 117 πρέπει να περιέχει
α) σαφή έκθεση των γεγονότων που θεμελιώνουν σύμφωνα με το νόμο την αγωγή και δικαιολογούν την άσκησή της από τον ενάγοντα κατά του εναγομένου,
β) ακριβή περιγραφή του αντικειμένου της διαφοράς,
γ) ορισμένο αίτημα.
2. Στην αγωγή αναφέρεται
α) προκειμένου για δίκες περιουσιακών σχέσεων η χρηματική αξία του επιδίκου αντικειμένου και
β) τα στοιχεία που θεμελιώνουν την αρμοδιότητα του δικαστηρίου.

Άρθρο 217

Οι διατάξεις για την αγωγή εφαρμόζονται και σε κάθε δικόγραφο εισαγωγικό δίκης, εκτός αν ορίζει διαφορετικά ο νόμος.

Άρθρο 218

1. Περισσότερες αιτήσεις του ιδίου ενάγοντος κατά του ιδίου εναγόμενου οι οποίες πηγάζουν από την ίδια ή διαφορετική αιτία, αφορούν το ίδιο ή διαφορετικό αντικείμενο και στηρίζονται στον ίδιο ή διαφορετικό λόγο μπορούν να ενωθούν στο ίδιο δικόγραφο αγωγής
α) αν δεν είναι αντιφατικές μεταξύ τους,
β) αν στο σύνολό τους υπάγονται λόγω ποσού στο δικαστήριο όπου εισάγονται,
γ) αν υπάγονται στην τοπική αρμοδιότητα του ίδιου δικαστηρίου,
δ) αν υπάγονται στο ίδιο είδος διαδικασίας,
ε) αν η σύγχρονη εκδίκαση τους δεν επιφέρει σύγχυση.
2. Αν ενωθούν περισσότερες αιτήσεις χωρίς να συντρέχουν οι προϋποθέσεις της παραγρ. 1, διατάσσεται ύστερα από αίτηση ή και αυτεπαγγέλτως ο χωρισμός και στην περίπτωση καθ' ύλην ή κατά τόπον αναρμοδιότητας εφαρμόζονται τα άρθρα 46 και 47.

Άρθρο 219

1. Αγωγή υπό αίρεση δεν επιτρέπεται, μπορεί όμως ο ενάγων για την περίπτωση που απορριφθεί η πρώτη βάση ή αίτηση της αγωγής να τη στηρίξει σε άλλη βάση ή να υποβάλει άλλη αίτηση που στηρίζεται στην ίδια ή σε άλλη βάση.
2. Η επιβοηθητική σύμφωνα με την παράγραφο 1 άσκηση αγωγής μπορεί γίνει με το ίδιο ή άλλο δικόγραφο.
3. Οι διατάξεις της παραγράφου 1 εφαρμόζονται και στην ανταγωγή.

Άρθρο 220

1. Αγωγές, στις οποίες περιλαμβάνονται και αναγνωριστικές ή ανακοπές εμπράγματες, μικτές ή νομής, εκτός από τα ασφαλιστικά μέτρα νομής, καθώς και αγωγές διάρρηξης δικαιοπραξίας ως καταδολιευτικής, όταν αφορούν ακίνητα, εγγράφονται ύστερα από αίτηση του ενάγοντος ή ανακόπτοντος στα βιβλία διεκδικήσεων του γραφείου της περιφέρειας όπου βρίσκεται το ακίνητο μέσα σε τριάντα ημέρες από την κατάθεσή τους, διαφορετικά απορρίπτονται και αυτεπαγγέλτως ως απαράδεκτες.
2. Αν οι αγωγές και ανακοπές που εγγράφηκαν στα βιβλία διεκδικήσεων είναι φανερά αβάσιμες, διατάσσεται η διαγραφή τους, κατά τη διαδικασία των άρθρων 740 επ. Στη συζήτηση κλητεύεται υποχρεωτικά αυτός που έχει καταθέσει την αγωγή ή ανακοπή που πρέπει να διαγραφεί. Μετά την παρέλευση δεκαετίας από την κατάθεση, η διαγραφή μπορεί να διαταχθεί και χωρίς κλήτευση, αν κατά την κρίση του δικαστηρίου αυτή είναι δύσκολη.
3. Με διατάγματα που εκδίδονται ύστερα από πρόταση του υπουργού της δικαιοσύνης ορίζεται ο τρόπος που τηρούνται τα βιβλία διεκδικήσεων.

Article 216

1. In addition to the information specified in Articles 118 or 117, the action must contain[:]
a) a clear statement of the facts which establish the action in law and justify the action being filed by the plaintiff against the defendant;
b) a precise description of the subject-matter of the dispute;
c) a specific form of order sought.
2. The action shall include[:]
a) in proceedings concerning property relationships, the monetary value of the subject-matter at issue; and
b) the facts establishing the jurisdiction of the court.

Article 217

Unless otherwise provided for in law, the provisions on actions also apply to all procedural documents instituting proceedings.

Article 218

1. Several applications by the same plaintiff against the same defendant arising from the same or a different cause, concerning the same or a different subject-matter and relying on the same or different grounds, may be joined in the same action[:]
a) if they do not contradict each other;
b) if, considered overall, they fall under the jurisdiction of the court with which they are filed due to their amount;
c) if they fall under the jurisdiction *ratione loci* of the same court;
d) if they are subject to the same type of procedure;
e) if their simultaneous adjudication does not cause confusion.
2. If several applications are joined without the conditions laid down in paragraph 1 being met, the court shall order that the proceedings be split following an application or even *ex officio*, and where there is no jurisdiction *ratione materiae* or *ratione loci*, Articles 46 and 47 apply.

Article 219

1. Actions subject to a condition are not permitted; however, where the first ground of, or form of order sought in, the action is dismissed, the plaintiff may rely on a different ground or file a different application relying on the same or a different ground.
2. Filing an action with an alternative form of order sought in accordance with paragraph 1 may take place by means of the same or a different procedural document.
3. The provisions of paragraph 1 also apply to cross-actions.

Article 220

1. Actions for a declaratory judgment or oppositions *in rem*, mixed actions or actions for possession, save interim measures concerning possession, and Paulian actions, shall, where they concern immovables, be registered, following an application by the plaintiff or party filing the opposition, in the claims registers of the [cadastral] office of the district where the immovable is located within 30 days of the date such actions were filed, otherwise they shall be automatically dismissed as inadmissible.
2. If the actions and oppositions registered in claims registers are manifestly unfounded, the court shall order that they be struck out, in accordance with the procedure laid down in Articles 740 *et seq.* The person who filed the action or opposition that must be struck out shall necessarily be summonsed to the hearing. After 10 years have elapsed from the filing, the court may order that they be struck out even without a summons, where it considers such summonsing difficult.
3. The manner in which claims registers are kept shall be specified in decrees issued on a proposal from the Minister of Justice.

ΚΕΦΑΛΑΙΟ Γ'
Συνέπειαι ασκήσεως της αγωγής.

Άρθρο 221

1. Με την άσκηση της αγωγής σύμφωνα με το άρθρο 215, η κατάθεσή της έχει ως συνέπεια
α) εκκρεμοδικία,
β) το αμετάβλητο της δικαιοδοσίας και αρμοδιότητας του δικαστηρίου,
γ) την προτίμηση ανάμεσα σε περισσότερα αρμόδια δικαστήρια,
και η επίδοσή της έχει ως συνέπεια τα αποτελέσματα που το ουσιαστικό δίκαιο ορίζει ότι επέρχονται από την έγερση της αγωγής.
2. Εκκρεμοδικία συνεπάγεται και η υποβολή, ενώ διαρκεί η δίκη, αίτησης με την οποία επιδιώκεται καταψήφιση, αναγνώριση ή διάπλαση, καθώς και η πρόταση ένστασης συμψηφισμού.

Άρθρο 222

1. Όταν επέλθει εκκρεμοδικία και όσο αυτή διαρκεί, δεν μπορεί να γίνει σε οποιοδήποτε δικαστήριο νέα δίκη για την ίδια επίδικη διαφορά ανάμεσα στους ίδιους διαδίκους, εφόσον εμφανίζονται με την ίδια ιδιότητα.
2. Αν κατά τη διάρκεια της εκκρεμοδικίας ασκηθεί άλλη αγωγή, ανταγωγή ή κύρια παρέμβαση ή προταθεί ένσταση συμψηφισμού για την ίδια επίδικη διαφορά, αναστέλλεται και αυτεπαγγέλτως η εκδίκασή της εωσότου περατωθεί η πρώτη δίκη.

Άρθρο 223

Όταν επέλθει η εκκρεμοδικία, είναι απαράδεκτη η μεταβολή του αιτήματος της αγωγής. Κατ' εξαίρεση μπορεί ο ενάγων με τις προτάσεις ή με δήλωση στα πρακτικά εωσότου περατωθεί η δίκη στον πρώτο βαθμό να περιορίσει το αίτημα της αγωγής ή να ζητήσει:
1) τα παρεπόμενα του κύριου αντικειμένου της αγωγής και
2) αντί γι' αυτό που ζητήθηκε αρχικά άλλο αντικείμενο ή το διαφέρον εξαιτίας μεταβολής που επήλθε.

Άρθρο 224

Είναι απαράδεκτο να μεταβληθεί η βάση της αγωγής. Με τις προτάσεις που κατατίθενται ενώπιον του πρωτοβάθμιου δικαστηρίου ή με προφορική δήλωση που καταχωρίζεται στα πρακτικά, μπορεί ο ενάγων να συμπληρώσει, να διευκρινίσει ή να διορθώσει τους ισχυρισμούς του, αρκεί να μη μεταβάλλεται η βάση της αγωγής.

Άρθρο 225

1. Η επέλευση της εκκρεμοδικίας δεν στερεί τους διαδίκους από την εξουσία να μεταβιβάσουν το επίδικο πράγμα ή δικαίωμα ή να συστήσουν εμπράγματο δικαίωμα.
2. Η μεταβίβαση του επίδικου πράγματος ή δικαιώματος ή η σύσταση εμπράγματου δικαιώματος δεν επιφέρει καμιά μεταβολή στη δίκη. Ο ειδικός διάδοχος έχει δικαίωμα να ασκήσει παρέμβαση.
3. Αν ο ενάγων μεταβίβασε το επίδικο πράγμα ή δικαίωμα ή σύστησε εμπράγματο δικαίωμα, δεν μπορεί να προταθεί εναντίον του έλλειψη νομιμοποίησης, εκτός αν η απόφαση που θα εκδοθεί δεν δεσμεύει τον ειδικό διάδοχο.

CHAPTER III
Effects of filing actions

Article 221

1. Once an action has been submitted in accordance with Article 215, its filing results in[:]

a) *lis pendens*;

b) immutability of the jurisdiction and competence of the court;

c) preference among several equally competent courts,

and its service generates the effects which, according to substantive law, arise once the action has been filed.

2. *Lis pendens* also arises if, during the proceedings, an application is filed seeking performance, a declaratory judgment or a formative judgment, or if a plea for offsetting is raised.

Article 222

1. When *lis pendens* occurs and while it persists, new proceedings cannot take place before any court regarding the same dispute between the same parties in the proceedings, provided they appear in the same capacities.

2. If a different action, cross-action or main intervention is filed or a plea for offsetting is made with regard to the same dispute during *lis pendens*, its adjudication shall be stayed even *ex officio* until the first proceedings have concluded.

Article 223

Once *lis pendens* has occurred, changes to the form of order sought in the action are inadmissible. By way of exception, in their pleadings or by means of a statement [recorded] in the transcript until the first-instance proceedings have concluded, the plaintiff may limit the form of order sought in the action or seek:

1) the claims ancillary to the main subject-matter of the action; and

2) a different subject-matter than the one originally sought or damages due to a change that occurred.

Article 224

Changes to the basis of the action are inadmissible. In the pleadings filed with the first-instance court or by means of a verbal statement recorded in the transcript, the plaintiff may supplement, clarify or correct their assertions, provided the basis of the action is not changed.

Article 225

1. Occurrence of *lis pendens* does not deprive the parties in the proceedings of the power to transfer the thing or right at issue or establish a right *in rem*.

2. Transfer of the thing or right at issue or establishment of a right *in rem* results in no changes to the proceedings. Specific successors have the right to file an intervention.

3. If the plaintiff transferred the thing or right at issue or established a right *in rem*, lack of legal standing cannot be pleaded against them, unless the judgment handed down is not binding on the specific successor.

ΚΕΦΑΛΑΙΟ Δ'
Εισαγωγή της αγωγής για συζήτηση.

Άρθρο 226

1. Το πρωτότυπο της αγωγής που κατατέθηκε φυλάσσεται στο αρχείο του δικαστηρίου.

2. Αμέσως μετά την κατάθεση της αγωγής ο γραμματέας, με βάση τη σημείωση στο πρωτότυπο της αγωγής της ημέρας και ώρας συζήτησής της, την εγγράφει στο πινάκιο του δικαστηρίου, όπου σημειώνει το όνομα και το επώνυμο των διαδίκων και των πληρεξουσίων τους, καθώς και το αντικείμενο της δίκης. Στην περίπτωση του άρθρου 237, κατά τη σύνταξη της έκθεσης κατάθεσης της αγωγής ο γραμματέας θέτει στο πρωτότυπο και στα αντίγραφα ευδιάκριτη σημείωση στην οποία αναγράφεται η προθεσμία κατάθεσης των προτάσεων για τον ενάγοντα και τον εναγόμενο και επισημαίνεται ότι εκπρόθεσμες προτάσεις δεν λαμβάνονται υπόψη.

3. Το πινάκιο είναι βιβλίο με αριθμημένες σελίδες, μονογραφημένες από τον πρόεδρο του δικαστηρίου ή τον ειρηνοδίκη, στο οποίο καταχωρίζονται οι υποθέσεις που θα συζητηθούν σε κάθε δικάσιμο. Στα δικαστήρια που έχουν ενταχθεί στο ολοκληρωμένο σύστημα διαχείρισης δικαστικών υποθέσεων το πινάκιο τηρείται και ηλεκτρονικά. Ο πρόεδρος του δικαστηρίου ή ο ειρηνοδίκης ορίζει τον αριθμό των υποθέσεων που θα εκδικασθούν σε κάθε δικάσιμο.

4. Ο δικαστής που διευθύνει τη συζήτηση σημειώνει στο πινάκιο αν η συζήτηση έγινε κατ' αντιμωλία ή ερήμην ή αναβλήθηκε ή ματαιώθηκε. Αν η συζήτηση αναβληθεί, ο γραμματέας οφείλει αμέσως μετά το τέλος της συνεδρίασης να μεταφέρει την υπόθεση στη σειρά των υποθέσεων που πρέπει να συζητηθούν κατά τη δικάσιμο που ορίσθηκε. Κλήση του διαδίκου για εμφάνιση στη δικάσιμο αυτή δεν χρειάζεται και η αναγραφή της υπόθεσης στο πινάκιο ισχύει ως κλήτευση όλων των διαδίκων. Αν ματαιωθεί η συνεδρίαση για οποιονδήποτε λόγο, οι υποθέσεις που είναι γραμμένες σ' αυτήν μεταφέρονται με επιμέλεια των διαδίκων στις επόμενες συνεδριάσεις, ακόμη και με υπέρβαση του ορισμένου αριθμού, και ο αντίδικος αυτού που επισπεύδει τη συζήτηση καλείται πάντοτε στη νέα δικάσιμο. Στην περίπτωση αυτή η εγγραφή, η κλήση και η επίδοσή της γίνονται ατελώς. Το ίδιο ισχύει και όταν είναι αναγκαία η ανασυζήτηση της υπόθεσης.

Ελλείψεις ή σφάλματα του πινακίου, ως προς τα στοιχεία των διαδίκων, των εκδικαζόμενων υποθέσεων και τη σήμανσή του, συμπληρώνονται κατά την εκφώνηση της υπόθεσης ύστερα από προφορική αίτηση οποιουδήποτε διαδίκου.

5. Κάθε αίτημα προτίμησης που υποβάλλεται από διάδικο για ορισμό ημέρας συζήτησης αίτησης, αγωγής ή ενδίκου μέσου ενώπιον παντός δικαστηρίου, οιασδήποτε διαδικασίας, διαφορετικής από εκείνη που, κατά τη νόμιμη σειρά, πρέπει να προσδιοριστεί ή έχει ήδη προσδιοριστεί, υποβάλλεται εγγράφως. Στην αίτηση πρέπει, με ποινή απαραδέκτου, να περιέχονται οι λόγοι της προτίμησης και ο αρμόδιος δικαστής αποφαίνεται σχετικά, με αιτιολογημένη πράξη του.

Άρθρο 227

1. Αν υπάρχουν τυπικές παραλείψεις που μπορούν να αναπληρωθούν, ο πρόεδρος οποιουδήποτε πολυμελούς δικαστηρίου ή ο εισηγητής ή ο δικαστής μονομελούς δικαστηρίου καλεί να τις συμπληρώσει και μετά τη συζήτηση τον πληρεξούσιο δικηγόρο ή το διάδικο εφόσον, παρίσταται αυτοπροσώπως τάσσοντας εύλογη κατά την κρίσιν του προθεσμία.

2. Η πρόσκληση γίνεται και τηλεφωνικώς, ο δε γραμματέας βεβαιώνει με σημείωση στο εσωτερικό του φακέλου της δικογραφίας τον χρόνο της ειδοποίησης, τα ζητούμενα στοιχεία και την προθεσμία. Αν η τηλεφωνική πρόσκληση είναι αδύνατη ή δυσχερής, αποστέλλεται έγγραφο, αντίγραφο του οποίου τηρείται στο φάκελο της δικογραφίας. Στο αντίγραφο αυτό σημειώνεται η ημερομηνία αποστολής του εγγράφου. Η πρόσκληση μπορεί επίσης να γίνει με αποστολή από τον γραμματέα ηλεκτρονικού μηνύματος στη διεύθυνση ηλεκτρονικού ταχυδρομείου του διαδίκου.

CHAPTER IV
Bringing actions [before the court] for a hearing

Article 226

1. The original action filed shall be kept in the court archives.

2. Immediately after the action is filed, the registrar, based on the note of the day and time of its hearing made on the original action, shall enter it in the court case register, noting the first and last names of the parties in the proceedings and their [authorised lawyers], as well as the subject-matter of the proceedings. In accordance with Article 237, when preparing the action filing report, the registrar shall make a clearly legible note on the original and the copies, indicating the deadline for the plaintiff and the defendant to file pleadings and stressing that late pleadings will be disregarded.

3. The case register comprises numbered pages, initialled by the presiding judge of the court or the court of the peace judge, in which the cases to be heard on each hearing date are recorded. At courts included in the integrated court case management system, the case register shall also be kept in electronic form. The presiding judge of the court or the court of the peace judge shall set the number of cases to be heard on each hearing date.

4. The judge directing the course of the hearing shall note in the case register whether the hearing took place having heard both sides or *in absentia*, or was adjourned or unable to go ahead. If the hearing is adjourned, immediately after the sitting the registrar shall be obligated to move the case to the list of cases to be heard on the hearing date set. Parties in the proceedings need not be summoned to enter an appearance on that hearing date, and [the act of] entering a case in the case register functions as a summons of all the parties in the proceedings. If the sitting is unable to go ahead for any reason, the cases scheduled shall be moved by the parties in the proceedings to subsequent sittings, even if this entails the number of cases set being exceeded, and the opponent of the party expediting the hearing shall always be summoned to appear on the new hearing date. In such cases, the entry [in the register], the summons and its service shall be free of official charges. This also applies where it is necessary to re-hear the case.

Following a verbal request by any party in the proceedings, defects or errors in the case register regarding the particulars of the parties in the proceedings, the cases to be heard and the affixation of stamps in the register shall be supplemented during the calling of cases.

5. Any preferential request filed by a party in the proceedings to set a hearing date for an application, action or legal remedy before any court, under any procedure, other than the date which must be specified or has already been specified in proper order shall be filed in writing. On penalty of inadmissibility, the application must include the reasons for such preference and the competent judge shall issue a reasoned decision on the matter.

Article 227

1. If there are procedural oversights that can be rectified, the presiding judge of any multi-member court or the reporting judge or the single-member court judge shall request the authorised lawyer or the party in the proceedings, if appearing in person, to rectify such oversights even after the hearing, setting a deadline which the judge considers reasonable in their view.

2. This request may also be made by telephone, with the registrar attesting on the inside of the case-file the time of notification, the information requested and the deadline. If a request by telephone is impossible or difficult, a document shall be sent and a copy shall be kept in the case-file. This copy shall indicate the date the document was sent. The request may also be made by e-mail sent by the registrar to the e-mail address of the party in the proceedings.

Άρθρο 228

Αν δεν ορίζεται διαφορετικά, η προθεσμία για την κλήτευση των διαδίκων είναι τριάντα (30) ημέρες και, αν ο διάδικος που καλείται ή κάποιος από τους ομοδίκους διαμένει στο εξωτερικό ή είναι άγνωστης διαμονής, εξήντα (60) ημέρες πριν από τη συζήτηση.

Άρθρο 229

[Καταργείται]

Άρθρο 230

1. Οι διατάξεις του άρθρου 228 του Κώδικα Πολιτικής Δικονομίας εφαρμόζονται και για τον προσδιορισμό κάθε άλλης δικασίμου.
2. Δικαίωμα να επισπεύσει συζήτηση έχει οποιοσδήποτε διάδικος.

Άρθρο 231

[Καταργείται]

Άρθρο 232

1. Ο Πρόεδρος του πολυμελούς πρωτοδικείου, ο δικαστής του μονομελούς ή ο ειρηνοδίκης μπορούν ύστερα από αίτηση των διαδίκων, που υποβάλλεται με την αγωγή ή και αυτοτελώς πριν από την ορισμένη δικάσιμο:
α) [Καταργείται]
β) να ζητήσουν εγγράφως από δημόσια αρχή την προσαγωγή ή αποστολή εγγράφου, που βρίσκεται στην κατοχή της,
γ) να διατάξουν την προσαγωγή εγγράφων που βρίσκονται στην κατοχή ενός των διαδίκων ή τρίτου εντός προθεσμίας που ορίζει το δικαστήριο. Ο τρίτος δεν υποχρεούται στην προσαγωγή αν συντρέχουν λόγοι για τους οποίους δεν υπάρχει υποχρέωση μαρτυρίας ή υπάρχει δικαίωμα αρνήσεως μαρτυρίας ή η προσαγωγή θα συνιστούσε ιδιαίτερη επιβάρυνση για τον τρίτο.
2. Αν ο διάδικος ή ο τρίτος κληθεί και αδικαιολόγητα δεν προσκομίσει τα έγγραφα της παρ. 1 εδάφιο γ', καταδικάζεται, εκτός από τα δικαστικά έξοδα και σε χρηματική ποινή εκατό (100) ευρώ έως διακοσίων (200) ευρώ, που περιέρχεται στο δημόσιο ως δημόσιο έσοδο. Η άρνηση του διαδίκου ή του τρίτου να προσκομίσει τα έγγραφα εκτιμάται ελεύθερα από το δικαστήριο. Αντίγραφο της απόφασης με την οποία καταδικάζεται ο διάδικος ή ο τρίτος γνωστοποιείται αμέσως στο Υπουργείο Οικονομικών με επιμέλεια της γραμματείας.

ΚΕΦΑΛΑΙΟ Ε
Συζήτηση στο ακροατήριο.

Άρθρο 233

1. Η διαδικασία αρχίζει με την εκφώνηση από το δικαστή των υποθέσεων από το πινάκιο με την σειρά που είναι γραμμένες. Ο δικαστής διευθύνει τη συζήτηση, δίνει το λόγο στα πρόσωπα που μετέχουν σ' αυτήν, τον αφαιρεί σε περίπτωση παράβασης των διατάξεων που τη ρυθμίζουν ή των οδηγιών του, εξετάζει τους διαδίκους, τους νόμιμους αντιπροσώπους τους, τους μάρτυρες και τους πραγματογνώμονες, κηρύσσει τη συζήτηση περατωμένη, όταν σύμφωνα με την κρίση του η υπόθεση διευκρινίστηκε όσο χρειάζεται και δημοσιεύει την απόφαση.
2. [Καταργείται]
3. [Καταργείται]
4. [Καταργείται]

Article 228

Unless otherwise specified, the deadline for summonsing the parties in the proceedings is 30 days, and if the party being summoned or any of the joined parties resides abroad or has no known place of residence, is 60 days prior to the hearing.

Article 229

[Repealed]

Article 230

1. The provisions of Article 228 of this Code also apply when setting any other hearing date.
2. All parties in the proceedings have the right to expedite a hearing.

Article 231

[Repealed]

Article 232

1. Following an application by the parties in the proceedings filed with the action or separately prior to the hearing date set, the presiding judge of the multi-member court of first instance, the single-member court judge or the court of the peace judge may:
a) [Repealed]
b) issue a written request to a public authority to present or send a document in its possession;
c) order documents in the possession of one of the parties in the proceedings or a third party to be presented within a deadline set by the court. The third party is not obligated to adduce the documents if there are grounds on which there is no obligation to give testimony, or there is a right to refuse to give testimony, or presenting such would constitute a particular burden for the third party.
2. If the party in the proceedings or the third party is summoned and unreasonably fails to present the documents referred to in paragraph 1(c), they shall be ordered to pay both the court costs and a monetary penalty ranging from 100 to 200 euros, which shall accrue to the Greek State as public revenue. Refusal by the party in the proceedings or the third party to present the documents shall be weighed up by the court at its unfettered discretion. A copy the ruling ordering the party in the proceedings or the third party [to pay the above court costs and monetary penalty] shall be immediately notified to the Ministry of Finance by the registry.

CHAPTER V
Hearing in court

Article 233

1. The proceedings begin with the judge calling the cases from the case register in the order in which they have been entered. The judge directing the course of the hearing shall give the floor to the persons participating in the proceedings, forbid them to speak if they infringe the provisions regulating proceedings or the instructions of the judge, examine the parties in the proceedings, their lawful proxies, the witnesses and experts, declare the hearing closed when, at their discretion, the case has been sufficiently clarified, and hand down the judgment.
2. [Repealed]
3. [Repealed]
4. [Repealed]

Άρθρο 234

1. Κάθε μέλος του δικαστηρίου έχει δικαίωμα με την άδεια του δικαστή που διευθύνει τη συζήτηση να απευθύνει ερωτήσεις στους διαδίκους, τους νόμιμους αντιπροσώπους τους, τους μάρτυρες και τους πραγματογνώμονες και να απαιτεί την ανάγνωση εγγράφων.

2. Το δικαίωμα της παραγράφου 1 έχουν και οι διάδικοι, οι νόμιμοι αντιπρόσωποι, οι πληρεξούσιοι και οι τεχνικοί σύμβουλοί τους, αφού ζητήσουν και λάβουν άδεια από το δικαστή που διευθύνει. Η υποβολή των ερωτήσεων μπορεί να γίνει απευθείας ή μέσω του δικαστή που διευθύνει τη συζήτηση, ο οποίος μπορεί και να τις απαγορεύσει, αν τις κρίνει άσκοπες ή ανεπίτρεπτες. Επίσης μπορεί να απαγορεύσει και την ανάγνωση εγγράφων, αν την κρίνει περιττή.

Άρθρο 235

Στα πολυμελή δικαστήρια, αν η διαταγή που αφορά τη διευκρίνιση της υπόθεσης από το δικαστή ο οποίος διευθύνει τη συζήτηση ή η ερώτηση που υπέβαλε αυτός ή άλλο μέλος του δικαστηρίου αποκρούεται από κάποιο πρόσωπο που μετέχει στη συζήτηση ως ανεπίτρεπτη, αποφαίνεται γι' αυτό το δικαστήριο. Το ίδιο εφαρμόζεται και στην περίπτωση που απαγορεύεται ερώτηση ή ανάγνωση εγγράφου.

Άρθρο 236

Ο δικαστής που διευθύνει τη συζήτηση πρέπει να φροντίζει με την υποβολή ερωτήσεων ή με άλλο τρόπο να εκφράζονται σαφώς για όλα τα ουσιώδη πραγματικά γεγονότα τα πρόσωπα που μετέχουν στη συζήτηση, να υποβάλλουν τις αναγκαίες προτάσεις και αιτήσεις, να συμπληρώνουν τους ισχυρισμούς που υποβλήθηκαν ελλιπώς και αορίστως με προφορική δήλωση που καταχωρίζεται στα πρακτικά και γενικά να παρέχουν τις αναγκαίες διασαφήσεις για την εξακρίβωση της αλήθειας των προβαλλόμενων ισχυρισμών.

Άρθρο 237

1. Μέσα σε ενενήντα (90) ημέρες από τη λήξη της προθεσμίας για την επίδοση της αγωγής κατά την παρ. 2 του άρθρου 215, οι διάδικοι οφείλουν να καταθέσουν τις προτάσεις και να προσκομίσουν όλα τα αποδεικτικά μέσα και τα διαδικαστικά έγγραφα που επικαλούνται με αυτές. Μέσα στην ίδια προθεσμία κατατίθενται το αποδεικτικό επίδοσης της αγωγής, καθώς και τα πληρεξούσια έγγραφα προς τους δικηγόρους κατά το άρθρο 96. Σε περίπτωση έλλειψης των πληρεξουσίων εγγράφων εφαρμόζεται το άρθρο 227. Αν δεν κατατεθούν τα πληρεξούσια έγγραφα μέσα στην προθεσμία που θα ταχθεί, το δικαστήριο εκδίδει οριστική απόφαση επί της αγωγής. Το δικαστικό ένσημο κατατίθεται το αργότερο μέχρι τη συζήτηση της υπόθεσης. Η προθεσμία του πρώτου εδαφίου παρατείνεται σε εκατόν είκοσι (120) ημέρες από τη λήξη της προθεσμίας επίδοσης της αγωγής για όλους τους διαδίκους, αν ο εναγόμενος ή κάποιος από τους ομοδίκους του διαμένει στο εξωτερικό ή είναι άγνωστης διαμονής.

2. Οι αμοιβαίες αντικρούσεις γίνονται με προσθήκη στις προτάσεις, η οποία κατατίθεται μέσα στις επόμενες δεκαπέντε (15) ημέρες από τη λήξη της παραπάνω προθεσμίας. Νέοι ισχυρισμοί με την προσθήκη μπορεί να προταθούν και νέα αποδεικτικά μέσα να προσκομισθούν μόνο για την αντίκρουση ισχυρισμών που περιέχονται στις προτάσεις. Εκπρόθεσμες προτάσεις και προσθήκες δεν λαμβάνονται υπόψη.

Article 234

1. Every member of the bench, with the permission of the judge directing the course of the hearing, has the right to put questions to the parties in the proceedings, their lawful proxies, witnesses and experts, and request that documents be read out.

2. After having requested and received permission from the judge directing the course of the hearing, the parties in the proceedings, their lawful proxies, their authorised representatives and their technical advisors shall also have the right referred to in paragraph 1. Questions may be put either directly or via the judge directing the course of the hearing, who may also prohibit questions [from being answered] if they deem them unnecessary or impermissible. The judge may also prohibit the reading of documents if they deem it superfluous.

Article 235

If, [during proceedings before] multi-member courts, a person participating in the hearing challenges an order concerning clarification of the case by the judge directing the course of the hearing or a question put by the judge or another member of the bench as impermissible, the [entire bench] shall rule on the matter. The same also applies in cases where a question or the reading out of a document is prohibited.

Article 236

The judge directing the course of the hearing must ensure that, through the questions put or in any other manner, the persons participating in the hearing clearly express their views on all the essential actual facts, file the necessary pleadings and applications, supplement any insufficiently and vaguely made assertions with verbal statements to be entered in the transcript, and generally provide the necessary clarifications to establish the truth of the assertions made.

Article 237

1. Within 90 days of the deadline for service of the action lapsing in accordance with Article 215(2), the parties in the proceedings shall be obligated to file pleadings and adduce all the means of evidence and documents concerning the procedure invoked in their pleadings. Proof of service of the action and powers of attorney authorising lawyers in accordance with Article 96 shall be filed within the same deadline. If the powers of attorney contain defects, Article 227 applies. If the powers of attorney are not filed within the deadline set, the court shall hand down a final judgment regarding the action. The judicial stamp duty shall be paid no later than the date on which the case is heard. If the defendant or any of the joined parties resides abroad or has no known place of residence, the deadline set in the first subparagraph shall be extended to 120 days from when the deadline for service of the action on all the parties in the proceedings lapses.

2. Rebuttals from both sides shall take the form of additional pleadings filed within 15 days from the date the aforesaid deadline lapses. New assertions may be made in the additional pleadings and new means of evidence may be adduced only in order to rebut assertions contained in the pleadings. Pleadings and additions filed late shall be disregarded.

3. Στην περίπτωση έκδοσης παραπεμπτικής απόφασης λόγω καθ' ύλην ή κατά τόπον αναρμοδιότητας ή λόγω μη εισαγωγής της υπόθεσης κατά την προσήκουσα διαδικασία, οι ως άνω προθεσμίες των ενενήντα (90) ή εκατόν είκοσι (120) ημερών για την κατάθεση των προτάσεων αρχίζουν από την κατάθεση της κλήσης για τον προσδιορισμό δικασίμου. Το ίδιο ισχύει, αν το δικαστήριο κηρύξει απαράδεκτη τη συζήτηση της αγωγής. Στις περιπτώσεις των άρθρων 249 και 250 οι διάδικοι μπορούν να καταθέτουν συμπληρωματικές προτάσεις το αργότερο μέχρι τη νέα συζήτηση της υπόθεσης, δίχως να προτείνονται νέοι ισχυρισμοί και νέα αποδεικτικά μέσα με την επιφύλαξη της παρ. 5 του παρόντος.
4. Η κατάθεση γίνεται στον αρμόδιο υπάλληλο της γραμματείας, που βεβαιώνει με επισημείωση τη χρονολογία της κατάθεσης των προτάσεων και των αντικρούσεων. Η κατάθεση των προτάσεων και των αντικρούσεων γίνεται μέχρι τη δωδεκάτη (12.00) ώρα της τελευταίας ημέρας της προθεσμίας για την κατάθεσή τους. Κάθε διάδικος δικαιούται να πάρει ατελώς με δική του δαπάνη αντίγραφα των προτάσεων και των αντικρούσεων των αντιδίκων του και των εγγράφων που έχουν προσκομίσει. Το δικαίωμα αυτό μπορεί να ασκηθεί και από τον δικηγόρο που υπογράφει την αγωγή, την παρέμβαση ή τις προτάσεις ή από τρίτο πρόσωπο εξουσιοδοτημένο από τον δικηγόρο αυτόν.
5. Ισχυρισμοί που γεννήθηκαν μετά την παρέλευση της προθεσμίας για την κατάθεση των προτάσεων και της προθεσμίας αντίκρουσης ή αποδεικνύονται εγγράφως ή με δικαστική ομολογία του αντιδίκου μπορούν να προταθούν με προσθήκη στις προτάσεις το αργότερο είκοσι (20) ημέρες πριν από την ορισθείσα συζήτηση. Το πρώτο εδάφιο εφαρμόζεται και στις περιπτώσεις των άρθρων 249 και 250. Η αντίκρουση γίνεται το αργότερο δέκα (10) ημέρες πριν από την ορισθείσα συζήτηση. Στην ίδια προθεσμία του πρώτου εδαφίου της παρούσας παραγράφου ο Πρόεδρος του Πολυμελούς Πρωτοδικείου, ο δικαστής του Μονομελούς Πρωτοδικείου ή ο ειρηνοδίκης μπορούν, ύστερα από αίτηση των διαδίκων που υποβάλλεται με την αγωγή ή και αυτοτελώς πριν από την ορισμένη δικάσιμο, να καλέσουν εγγράφως τους διαδίκους ή τους νομίμους αντιπροσώπους τους να εμφανιστούν αυτοπροσώπως κατά τη συζήτηση για να τους υποβληθούν ερωτήσεις και να δώσουν διασαφήσεις για την υπόθεση.
6. Μέσα σε δεκαπέντε (15) ημέρες από την παρέλευση της προθεσμίας της παρ. 2 με πράξη του Προέδρου του τριμελούς συμβουλίου ή του αρμόδιου δικαστή, ορίζεται, σύμφωνα με τον κανονισμό του δικαστηρίου, ο δικαστής και για τις υποθέσεις αρμοδιότητας του πολυμελούς πρωτοδικείου, η σύνθεση του δικαστηρίου για την εκδίκαση της υπόθεσης. Στην τελευταία περίπτωση ο Πρόεδρος του Πολυμελούς Πρωτοδικείου ορίζει τον εισηγητή. Συγχρόνως ορίζεται ημέρα και ώρα συζήτησης στο ακροατήριο σε χρόνο όχι μεγαλύτερο από τριάντα (30) ημέρες από την παρέλευση της δεκαπενθήμερης προθεσμίας του πρώτου εδαφίου. Κατ' εξαίρεση, αν ο προβλεπόμενος από τον κανονισμό του δικαστηρίου αριθμός υποθέσεων, που ανατίθεται σε κάθε δικαστή, καλυφθεί, ο ορισμός δικαστή και χρόνου συζήτησης της υπόθεσης γίνεται στον απολύτως αναγκαίο χρόνο. Η εγγραφή της υπόθεσης στο οικείο πινάκιο, το οποίο μπορεί να τηρείται και ηλεκτρονικά, γίνεται με πρωτοβουλία του γραμματέα και ισχύει ως κλήτευση όλων των διαδίκων. Με πρωτοβουλία επίσης του γραμματέα μπορεί να γνωστοποιείται η δικάσιμος που ορίστηκε με αποστολή ηλεκτρονικού μηνύματος στη διεύθυνση ηλεκτρονικού ταχυδρομείου των διαδίκων. Κατά την ορισμένη δικάσιμο δεν εξετάζονται μάρτυρες και η υπόθεση συζητείται και χωρίς την παρουσία των διαδίκων ή των πληρεξούσιων δικηγόρων τους. Αναβολή της συζήτησης κατά το άρθρο 241 δεν επιτρέπεται.
7. Με την επιφύλαξη της παρ. 8, μετά τη συζήτηση εκδίδεται η οριστική απόφαση με βάση τα στοιχεία του φακέλου της δικογραφίας.

3. Where a remittal decision is issued due to lack of jurisdiction *ratione materiae* or *ratione loci* or due to failure to bring the case for a hearing under the proper procedure, the above deadlines of 90 or 120 days for filing pleadings shall commence upon filing of summons to set a hearing date. This also applies if the court declares the hearing of the action inadmissible. Without prejudice to paragraph 5 of this Article, in the cases referred to in Articles 249 and 250, the parties in the proceedings may file supplementary pleadings no later than the next hearing of the case, without making new assertions and [adducing] new means of evidence.

4. The filing shall be made with the competent registry clerk, who shall make a note confirming the date of filing of the pleadings and rebuttals. Pleadings and rebuttals shall be filed no later than 12:00 noon on the final day of the deadline for their filing. All parties in the proceedings are entitled to receive copies of the pleadings and rebuttals of their opponents and the documents they have adduced free of official charges [but] at their own expense. This right may also be exercised by the lawyer signing the action, intervention or pleadings or by a third party authorised by the said lawyer.

5. Assertions [whose factual basis] arose after the deadline for filing pleadings and the deadline for filing rebuttals lapsed or which are proven in writing or by an admission made by the opponent in court may be made in the form of additional pleadings no later than 20 days prior to the hearing date set. The first subparagraph also applies in the cases referred to in Articles 249 and 250. The rebuttal shall be filed no later than 10 days prior to the hearing date set. Within the same deadline set in the first subparagraph of this paragraph, the presiding judge of the multi-member court of first instance, the single-member court of first instance judge or the court of the peace judge may, following an application by the parties in the proceedings filed with the action or even separately prior to the hearing date specified, summon the parties in the proceedings or their lawful proxies in writing to appear in person during the hearing in order to answer questions and provide clarifications regarding the case.

6. Within 15 days of the deadline set in paragraph 2 lapsing, the president of the three-member management board or the competent judge shall issue a decision designating, in accordance with the statute of the court, the judge and, for cases falling under the jurisdiction of the multi-member court of first instance, the composition of the court to try the case. In the latter case, the presiding judge of multi-member court of first instance shall appoint the reporting judge. Moreover, a date and time for a courtroom hearing shall be set no later than 30 days from the 15-day deadline referred to in the first subparagraph lapsing. By way of exception, if the number of cases provided for in the statute of the court to be assigned to each judge is reached, the judge and time for the hearing of the case shall be designated within the allotted time. The case shall be entered in the pertinent case register, which may also be kept in electronic form, by the registrar and its entry shall function as summonsing all the parties in the proceedings. The hearing date set may also be notified by the registrar by e-mail sent to the e-mail addresses of the parties in the proceedings. On the hearing date set, witnesses shall not be examined and the case shall be heard even without the presence of the parties in the proceedings or their authorised lawyers. Adjournment of the hearing under Article 241 shall not be permitted.

7. Without prejudice to paragraph 8, a final judgment shall be handed down after the hearing on the basis of the information contained in the case-file.

8. Αν από τη μελέτη του φακέλου της δικογραφίας κρίνεται απολύτως αναγκαία η εξέταση μαρτύρων στο ακροατήριο, ενός από κάθε πλευρά από εκείνους, που έδωσαν ένορκη βεβαίωση ή σε περίπτωση ανυπαρξίας αυτών, από τους προτεινόμενους από κάθε πλευρά, ή η εξέταση των διαδίκων, με απλή διάταξη του δικαστηρίου, διατάσσεται η επανάληψη της συζήτησης στο ακροατήριο σε χρόνο όχι συντομότερο από δεκαπέντε (15) ημέρες, για την εξέταση των μαρτύρων ή των διαδίκων ενώπιον του ήδη ορισμένου δικαστή, στον τόπο και στην ημέρα και ώρα που ορίζεται με τη διάταξη αυτή μέσα στο ίδιο δικαστικό έτος, εκτός αν αυτό είναι χρονικά αδύνατο. Αν ο χρόνος εξέτασης των μαρτύρων δεν επαρκεί, επιτρέπεται μόνο διακοπή για άλλη ημέρα και ώρα ενώπιον του ίδιου δικαστή, με προφορική ανακοίνωση που καταχωρίζεται στα πρακτικά και επέχει θέση κλήτευσης όλων των διαδίκων, συμπεριλαμβανομένων και εκείνων που δεν παρίστανται. Αν ο χρόνος εξέτασης των μαρτύρων οριστεί για οποιοδήποτε λόγο μέσα στο επόμενο δικαστικό έτος και η εξέταση των μαρτύρων ενώπιον του ίδιου δικαστή δεν είναι δυνατή, η υπόθεση διαγράφεται από τη χρέωση του συγκεκριμένου δικαστή και ακολουθεί νέα χρέωση για την εξέταση των μαρτύρων και την έκδοση της απόφασης. Στη θέση της διαγραφείσας υπόθεσης, στον εισηγητή ή στον δικαστή του μονομελούς πρωτοδικείου ή του ειρηνοδικείου ανατίθεται άλλη υπόθεση. Με τη διάταξη του πρώτου εδαφίου, το δικαστήριο μπορεί να διατάξει αυτοψία ή πραγματογνωμοσύνη στην οποία προσδιορίζονται ο τόπος, ο χρόνος, τα ονόματα των πραγματογνωμόνων, το θέμα της πραγματογνωμοσύνης, η προθεσμία για την κατάθεση της γνωμοδότησης των πραγματογνωμόνων, που δεν μπορεί να είναι μεγαλύτερη από εξήντα (60) ημέρες, καθώς και κάθε άλλο χρήσιμο στοιχείο. Η καταχώριση της διάταξης στο οικείο βιβλίο του δικαστηρίου, το οποίο μπορεί να τηρείται και ηλεκτρονικά, επέχει θέση κλήτευσης όλων των διαδίκων. Η καταχώριση της διάταξης μπορεί επίσης να γνωστοποιείται με πρωτοβουλία του γραμματέα με αποστολή ηλεκτρονικού μηνύματος στη διεύθυνση ηλεκτρονικού ταχυδρομείου των διαδίκων. Ο δικαστής που έχει οριστεί ως εισηγητής ή ο πρωτοδίκης ή ο ειρηνοδίκης αποφασίζει για όλα τα σχετικά με την απόδειξη διαδικαστικά ζητήματα. Με την ολοκλήρωση της διαδικασίας εξέτασης των μαρτύρων ή των διαδίκων ή την κατάθεση της έκθεσης αυτοψίας ή της έκθεσης πραγματογνωμοσύνης θεωρείται συντελεσμένη και η επανάληψη της συζήτησης. Η άνω διάταξη ανακαλείται είτε αυτεπαγγέλτως είτε με αίτηση των διαδίκων.

9. Μέσα σε οκτώ (8) εργάσιμες ημέρες από την εξέταση των μαρτύρων ή των διαδίκων ή τη διενέργεια της αυτοψίας ή της πραγματογνωμοσύνης οι διάδικοι δικαιούνται με προσθήκη να προβούν μόνο σε αξιολόγηση των αποδείξεων αυτών. Μετά το πέρας της συζήτησης ο Πρόεδρος του Δικαστηρίου ή επί πολυμελούς συνθέσεως ο Εισηγητής δύνανται να ζητούν από τους διαδίκους να προσκομίσουν σε ηλεκτρονική μορφή αντίγραφο του δικογράφου της αγωγής, των προτάσεων και της προσθήκης.

10. Μετά την περάτωση της δίκης οι διάδικοι οφείλουν να αναλάβουν όλα τα σχετικά έγγραφά τους. Ο γραμματέας βεβαιώνει στις προτάσεις κάθε διαδίκου ότι ανέλαβε τα έγγραφά του. Αν υπάρχει σπουδαίος λόγος, ο πρόεδρος του δικαστηρίου επιτρέπει στον διάδικο να αναλάβει ορισμένο έγγραφο και πριν από την περάτωση της δίκης. Αν το έγγραφο αυτό είναι αναγκαίο, η ανάληψη επιτρέπεται μόνο αφού κατατεθεί επικυρωμένο αντίγραφο. Οι προτάσεις παραμένουν στο αρχείο του δικαστηρίου.

11. Η κατάθεση των προτάσεων, καθώς και της προσθήκης, μπορεί να γίνεται και με ηλεκτρονικά μέσα σύμφωνα με την παρ. 4 του άρθρου 119. Επίσης, με ηλεκτρονικά μέσα μπορεί να υποβάλλονται και τα σχετικά έγγραφα που επικαλούνται με τις προτάσεις τους οι διάδικοι.

12. Το δικαστήριο, ύστερα από αίτηση των διαδίκων ή αυτεπαγγέλτως, μπορεί να αποφασίσει, οι διάδικοι και οι πληρεξούσιοι δικηγόροι τους, κατά τη διάρκεια της συζήτησης, να παρίστανται σε άλλον τόπο και να ενεργούν εκεί διαδικαστικές πράξεις. Η συζήτηση αυτή μεταδίδεται ταυτόχρονα με ήχο και εικόνα στην αίθουσα συνεδρίασης του δικαστηρίου και στον τόπο, όπου παρίστανται οι διάδικοι και οι πληρεξούσιοι δικηγόροι τους.

8. If, having examined the case-file, [the court] deems it absolutely necessary to examine witnesses in court, one for each side of those [parties] who submitted an affidavit or, absent such, of those nominated by each side, or to examine the parties in the proceedings, then the court shall issue an ordinary decree for the courtroom hearing to resume after at least 15 days have elapsed, for the purpose of examining the witnesses or the parties in the proceedings before the judge already designated, at the place, date and time set in that decree, and within the same judicial year, unless time does not permit. If the time for examining the witnesses is insufficient, the hearing may be stayed until a different date and time before the same judge by means of a verbal notice entered in the transcript and functioning as summonsing of all the parties in the proceedings, including those not present. If for any reason the time for examining the witnesses is scheduled to take place during the following judicial year and it is not possible for witnesses to be examined before the same judge, the case shall be removed from the case-load of the judge in question and assigned to a new judge who will examine the witnesses and hand down judgment. The reporting judge or single-member court of first instance judge or court of the peace judge shall be assigned a different case in place of the one removed. In the decree referred to in the first subparagraph, the court may order an inspection or expert evidence, specifying the place, time, names of experts, subject-matter of expert evidence, deadline for the experts to file their opinion, which shall be no later than 60 days, as well as all other useful information. The [act of] entering the decree in the pertinent register of the court, which may also be kept in electronic form, functions as summonsing of all the parties in the proceedings. The entry of the decree may also be notified by the registrar by e-mail sent to the e-mail addresses of the parties in the proceedings. The judge appointed as reporting judge or the court of first instance judge or the court of the peace judge shall rule on all procedural issues concerning evidence. Once the witnesses or the parties in the proceedings have been examined or the inspection report or expert evidence report has been filed, the resumed hearing shall also be deemed to have concluded. The above decree may be revoked either *ex officio* or following an application by the parties in the proceedings.

9. Within 8 working days of the witnesses or the parties in the proceedings being examined or the inspection taking place or expert evidence being prepared, the parties in the proceedings shall be entitled to file an addition [to the pleadings] only for the purpose of evaluating such evidence. After the hearing has ended, the presiding judge of the court or, in the case of a multi-member court, the reporting judge may request that the parties in the proceedings submit a copy of the action, the pleadings and supplementary pleadings in electronic form.

10. After the proceedings have concluded, the parties in the proceedings are responsible for taking back all their relevant documents. The registrar shall confirm in the pleadings of each party that they took back their documents. Where there is a serious reason, the presiding judge of the court may permit a party in the proceedings to take back a specific document even before the proceedings has concluded. If the document in question is necessary [for the proceedings], it may only be taken back after a certified copy has been filed. Pleadings shall remain in the court archives.

11. Pleadings and additions may also be filed using electronic means, in accordance with Article 119(4). Exhibits invoked by the parties in their pleadings may also be submitted using electronic means.

12. The court may, following an application by the parties in the proceedings or *ex officio*, decide that the parties in the proceedings and their authorised lawyers must, during the hearing, be present at a specific place and take procedural steps there. Audio and video of this hearing shall be simultaneously broadcast to the courtroom and to the place where the parties in the proceedings and their authorised lawyers are located.

13. Το δικαστήριο, ύστερα από αίτηση των διαδίκων ή αυτεπαγγέλτως, μπορεί να αποφασίσει την εξέταση μαρτύρων, πραγματογνωμόνων και διαδίκων χωρίς αυτοί να παρίστανται στην αίθουσα συνεδρίασής του, η δε σχετική απόφαση του δικαστηρίου δεν υπόκειται σε ένδικα μέσα. Η εξέταση μεταδίδεται ταυτοχρόνως με ήχο και εικόνα στην αίθουσα συνεδρίασης του δικαστηρίου και στον τόπο εξέτασης των μαρτύρων, πραγματογνωμόνων και διαδίκων. Η εξέταση αυτή, η οποία θεωρείται ότι διεξάγεται ενώπιον του δικαστηρίου, έχει την ίδια αποδεικτική ισχύ με την εξέταση στο ακροατήριο.

Άρθρο 238

1. Παρεμπίπτουσες αγωγές, ανταγωγές, παρεμβάσεις, προσεπικλήσεις και ανακοινώσεις στην περίπτωση του άρθρου 237 κατατίθενται και επιδίδονται σε όλους τους διαδίκους μέσα σε προθεσμία εξήντα (60) ημερών από την κατάθεση της αγωγής. Παρεμβάσεις μετά από προσεπίκληση ή ανακοίνωση κατατίθενται και επιδίδονται σε όλους τους διαδίκους μέσα σε προθεσμία ενενήντα (90) ημερών από την κατάθεση της αγωγής. Αν ο αρχικός εναγόμενος ή κάποιος από τους ομοδίκους του διαμένει στο εξωτερικό ή είναι άγνωστης διαμονής, οι ως άνω προθεσμίες παρατείνονται σε ενενήντα (90) και εκατόν είκοσι (120) ημέρες, αντίστοιχα, από την κατάθεση της αγωγής. Η κατάθεση των προτάσεων γίνεται σε προθεσμία εκατόν είκοσι (120) ημερών και στην περίπτωση του προηγούμενου εδαφίου σε προθεσμία εκατόν ογδόντα (180) ημερών από την κατάθεση της αγωγής. Για την προσθήκη ισχύει η παρ. 2 του άρθρου 237 ΚΠολΔ.

2. Μέσα στην προθεσμία της κατάθεσης των προτάσεων προσκομίζονται και όλα τα αποδεικτικά μέσα και διαδικαστικά έγγραφα που οι διάδικοι επικαλούνται με αυτές.

Άρθρο 239

[Καταργείται]

Άρθρο 240

Για την επαναφορά ισχυρισμών που υποβλήθηκαν σε προηγούμενη συζήτηση στο ίδιο ή ανώτερο δικαστήριο αρκεί η επανυποβολή τους με σύντομη περίληψη και αναφορά στις σελίδες των προτάσεων της προηγούμενης συζήτησης που τους περιέχουν· οι προτάσεις της προηγούμενης συζήτησης προσκομίζονται απαραιτήτως σε επικυρωμένο αντίγραφο.

Άρθρο 241

1. Ύστερα από αίτηση του διαδίκου και αν ακόμη δεν κατατέθηκαν προτάσεις ή αυτές κατατέθηκαν εκπρόθεσμα, μπορεί να αναβληθεί η συζήτηση της υπόθεσης μόνο μία φορά, ανά βαθμό δικαιοδοσίας, σε μεταγενέστερη δικάσιμο, εφόσον υπάρχει σπουδαίος κατά την κρίση του δικαστηρίου λόγος, με απλή σημείωση στο πινάκιο.

Σε περίπτωση αποχής των δικηγόρων, οι υποθέσεις αναβάλλονται υποχρεωτικά σε δικάσιμο που ανακοινώνει το δικαστήριο εντός αποκλειστικής προθεσμίας ενενήντα (90) ημερών ή σε άλλη εμβόλιμη δικάσιμο.

2. Το δικαστήριο μπορεί να επιδικάσει, με απόφαση που καταχωρίζεται στα πρακτικά, δικαστική δαπάνη σε βάρος εκείνου που ζήτησε την αναβολή, με αίτηση του αντιδίκου του, 70 έως 400 ευρώ.

3. Για την υποβολή αιτήματος αναβολής ο διάδικος καταβάλλει παράβολο υπέρ του Ταμείου Χρηματοδότησης Δικαστικών Κτιρίων (ΤΑ.Χ.ΔΙ.Κ.) ως εξής:

α) είκοσι (20) ευρώ, ενώπιον Ειρηνοδικείου και Μονομελούς Πρωτοδικείου,

β) τριάντα (30) ευρώ, ενώπιον του Πολυμελούς Πρωτοδικείου,

γ) σαράντα (40) ευρώ, ενώπιον του Εφετείου.

Σε κοινό αίτημα αναβολής περισσότερων διαδίκων, καταβάλλεται ένα παράβολο το οποίο επιμερίζεται ισομερώς. Δεν υπέχουν υποχρέωση καταβολής παραβόλου το Δημόσιο, τα νομικά πρόσωπα δημοσίου δικαίου (Ν.Π.Δ.Δ.) και οι οργανισμοί τοπικής αυτοδιοίκησης (Ο.Τ.Α.). Δεν καταβάλλεται παράβολο σε περίπτωση αποχής των δικηγόρων. Το παράβολο επιστρέφεται αν το αίτημα της αναβολής απορριφθεί από το δικαστήριο.

13. The court may, following an application by the parties in the proceedings or *ex officio*, decide that witnesses, experts and parties in the proceedings be examined without being physically present in court; this decision are not subject to legal remedies. Audio and video of the examination shall be simultaneously broadcast to the courtroom and to the place where the witnesses, the experts and the parties in the proceedings are being examined. This examination, which shall be deemed to be conducted before the court, has the same probative value as examination in court.

Article 238

1. In the case referred to in Article 237, incidental actions, cross-actions, interventions, impleaders and [third-party] notices shall be filed and served on all parties in the proceedings within a deadline of 60 days from the date the action was filed. Interventions following an impleader or [third-party] notice shall be filed and served on all parties in the proceedings within a deadline of 90 days from the date the action was filed. If the initial defendant or any of their joined parties resides abroad or has no known place of residence, the above deadlines shall be extended to 90 and 120 days from the date the action was filed. Pleadings shall be filed within a deadline of 120 days and, in the case referred to in the preceding subparagraph, 180 days from the date the action was filed. Article 237(2) of this Code applies to additions [to the pleadings].
2. Within the deadline for filing pleadings, all means of evidence and procedural documents the parties in the proceedings invoked in the pleadings must also be adduced.

Article 239

[Repealed]

Article 240

In order to reiterate assertions made during a previous hearing before the same or a higher court, it shall suffice to re-state them in the form of a brief summary and cite the pages in the pleadings filed during the previous hearing that contain them; a certified copy of the pleadings filed during the previous hearing must be adduced.

Article 241

1. Following an application by the party in the proceedings, even if pleadings were not filed or were filed late, the hearing of the case may be adjourned once only per instance for a later hearing date where, in the view of the court, there is a serious reason, with a simple note [to that effect] made in the case register.
Where lawyers are abstaining [from their duties], cases shall be adjourned for a hearing date announced by the court within a fixed deadline of 90 days or another ad hoc hearing date.
2. Following an application filed by the opponent, the court, by means of a ruling entered in the transcript, may order the person who requested adjournment to pay court costs ranging from 70 to 400 euros.
3. In order to file a motion for adjournment, the party in the proceedings shall pay a procedural fee for the Court Buildings Financing Fund as follows:
a) 20 euros for cases before with the court of the peace and the single-member court of first instance;
b) 30 euros for cases before the multi-member court of first instance;
c) 40 euros for cases before the court of appeal.
Where several parties file a joint motion for adjournment, a single procedural fee shall be paid, shared equally among them. The Greek State, bodies governed by public law and local government authorities are not obligated to pay this fee. The fee shall not be paid in cases where lawyers are abstaining [from their duties]. The fee shall be reimbursed if the motion for adjournment is dismissed by the court.

Άρθρο 242

1. Η συζήτηση αρχίζει μετά την εκφώνηση των ονομάτων των διαδίκων και τη δήλωση των παραστάσεών τους. Οι διάδικοι που παρίστανται νόμιμα έχουν δικαίωμα να αναπτύξουν στο ακροατήριο προφορικά τους ισχυρισμούς τους.

2. Αν δεν ορίζεται διαφορετικά, στις περιπτώσεις που η προφορική συζήτηση δεν είναι υποχρεωτική οι διάδικοι μπορούν να συμφωνήσουν με κοινή δήλωση, που υπογράφεται από τους πληρεξούσιους δικηγόρους ότι δε θα παραστούν κατά την εκφώνηση. Τέτοια δήλωση μπορεί να γίνει και από έναν ή ορισμένους μόνο πληρεξουσίους. Η δήλωση αυτή παραδίνεται στην περίπτωση κοινής δήλωσης από έναν τουλάχιστον πληρεξούσιο δικηγόρο και στην περίπτωση μονομερούς δήλωσης από τον πληρεξούσιο δικηγόρο, στον αρμόδιο γραμματέα το αργότερο την παραμονή της δικασίμου και σημειώνεται αμέσως στο πινάκιο. Στις παραπάνω περιπτώσεις η συζήτηση περατώνεται με μόνη την εκφώνηση της υπόθεσης. Μόνο δήλωση βίαιης διακοπής της δίκης είναι παραδεκτή. Μπορεί όμως το δικαστήριο, αν προβάλλονται άλλοι διαδικαστικοί ισχυρισμοί, να αναβάλει την υπόθεση σε σύντομη δικάσιμο με πρακτικό στο οποίο καταχωρίζονται και οι ισχυρισμοί αυτοί. Στη δικάσιμο αυτή καλούνται όσοι διάδικοι δεν ήταν παρόντες κατά την αναβολή, ενώ οι παρόντες οφείλουν να εμφανιστούν χωρίς κλήτευση και αν δεν παραστούν κατά τη νέα δικάσιμο δικάζονται εξαρχής ερήμην.

Άρθρο 243

Όλες οι συζητήσεις στο ακροατήριο γίνονται ενώπιον του ίδιου ειρηνοδίκη ή δικαστή του μονομελούς πρωτοδικείου που εκδίδει και την οριστική απόφαση. Αν ο δικαστής αυτός κωλύεται πρόσκαιρα, η συζήτηση αναβάλλεται για άλλη σύντομη δικάσιμο. Αν ο δικαστής έπαψε να υπηρετεί στο δικαστήριο ή βρίσκεται με άδεια που πρόκειται να διαρκέσει περισσότερο από ένα μήνα, ορίζεται αναπληρωτής και η συζήτηση γίνεται ενώπιόν του.

Άρθρο 244

[Καταργείται]

Άρθρο 245

1. Το δικαστήριο μπορεί, αυτεπαγγέλτως ή ύστερα από αίτηση κάποιου διαδίκου, να διατάξει οτιδήποτε μπορεί να συντελέσει στη διάγνωση της διαφοράς και ιδιαίτερα την αυτοπρόσωπη εμφάνιση των διαδίκων ή των νόμιμων αντιπροσώπων τους στο ακροατήριο για την υποβολή ερωτήσεων και την παροχή διασαφήσεων σχετικών με την υπόθεση.

2. [Καταργείται]

Άρθρο 246

Το δικαστήριο σε κάθε στάση της δίκης μπορεί, αυτεπαγγέλτως ή ύστερα από αίτηση κάποιου διαδίκου, να διατάξει την ένωση και συνεκδίκαση περισσότερων εκκρεμών ενώπιόν του δικών ανάμεσα στους ίδιους ή διαφορετικούς διαδίκους, αν υπάγονται στην ίδια διαδικασία και κατά την κρίση του διευκολύνεται ή επιταχύνεται η διεξαγωγή της δίκης ή επέρχεται μείωση των εξόδων.

Άρθρο 247

1. Το δικαστήριο σε κάθε στάση της δίκης μπορεί αυτεπαγγέλτως ή ύστερα από αίτηση κάποιου διαδίκου να διατάξει να συζητηθούν χωριστά περισσότερες αιτήσεις που υποβλήθηκαν με το ίδιο δικόγραφο.

2. Αν ο εναγόμενος ασκεί ανταγωγή, το δικαστήριο μπορεί να διατάξει να γίνει χωριστή συζήτηση της αγωγής και της ανταγωγής, αν κατά την κρίση του διευκολύνεται ή επιταχύνεται η διεξαγωγή της δίκης.

Article 242

1. The hearing commences after the names of the parties in the proceedings have been read out and they have entered an appearance. Parties duly present have the right to verbally expound on their assertions in court.

2. Unless otherwise provided for, where a verbal hearing is not mandatory, the parties in the proceedings may agree, by means of a joint statement signed by their authorised lawyers, that they will not enter an appearance when [the names] are read out. This statement may also be made by only one or certain authorised lawyers. Where a joint statement is made, it shall be delivered by at least one authorised lawyer and, where a unilateral statement is made by an authorised lawyer, it shall be delivered by that lawyer to the competent registrar no later than the eve of the hearing date and shall be immediately noted in the case register. In the above cases, the hearing shall conclude only with the calling of the case. Only a statement of forced discontinuation of the proceedings shall be admissible. However, if other procedural assertions are made, the court may adjourn the case for a close hearing date by means of a report that records those assertions. All the parties in the proceedings not present at the time of adjournment shall be summoned to appear on that hearing date, while those present shall be obligated to appear without a summons and, if they fail to appear on the new hearing date, shall be tried *in absentia* from the outset of the proceedings.

Article 243

All courtroom hearings shall take place before the same court of the peace judge or single-member court of first instance judge who shall also hand down the final judgment. If this judge is temporarily indisposed, the hearing shall be adjourned for a close hearing date. If the judge is no longer serving at the court or is on leave for more than one month, a substitute shall be appointed and the hearing shall take place before them.

Article 244

[Repealed]

Article 245

1. The court may, following an application filed by a party in the proceedings or *ex officio*, order anything that could contribute towards establishing the facts of the dispute and, in particular, the appearance in person of the parties in their proceedings or of their lawful proxies in court in order to answer questions and provide clarifications regarding the case.

2. [Repealed]

Article 246

At any time, the court may, following an application filed by a party in the proceedings or *ex officio*, order the joinder of several cases pending before it involving the same or different parties in the proceedings, if they are subject to the same proceedings and where this, in its view, would facilitate or expedite the conduct of the proceedings or result in decreased costs.

Article 247

1. At any time, the court may, following an application filed by a party in the proceedings or *ex officio*, order the separate hearing of several applications filed by means of the same procedural document.

2. If the defendant files a cross-action, the court may order that the action and cross-action be heard separately where this, in its view, would facilitate or expedite the conduct of the proceedings.

Άρθρο 248

Το δικαστήριο μπορεί, αυτεπαγγέλτως ή ύστερα από αίτηση κάποιου διαδίκου, να διατάξει στην περίπτωση περισσότερων αυτοτελών μέσων επίθεσης ή άμυνας που αφορούν την ίδια αίτηση, η συζήτηση να γίνει διαδοχικά ή να περιοριστεί σε ένα ή ορισμένα μόνο από αυτά, αν κατά την κρίση του διευκολύνεται ή επιταχύνεται η διεξαγωγή της δίκης.

Άρθρο 249

Αν η διάγνωση της διαφοράς εξαρτάται ολικά ή εν μέρει από την ύπαρξη ή ανυπαρξία μιας έννομης σχέσης ή την ακυρότητα ή τη διάρρηξη μιας δικαιοπραξίας που συνιστά αντικείμενο άλλης δίκης εκκρεμούς σε πολιτικό ή διοικητικό δικαστήριο ή από ζήτημα που πρόκειται να κριθεί ή κρίνεται από διοικητική αρχή, το δικαστήριο μπορεί αυτεπαγγέλτως ή ύστερα από αίτηση κάποιου διαδίκου να διατάξει την αναβολή της συζήτησης εωσότου περατωθεί τελεσίδικα ή αμετάκλητα η άλλη δίκη ή εωσότου εκδοθεί από τη διοικητική αρχή απόφαση που δεν θα μπορεί να προσβληθεί. Αν η διοικητική αρχή δεν έχει ακόμη ασχοληθεί με την υπόθεση, το δικαστήριο ορίζει προθεσμία, μέσα στην οποία ο διάδικος οφείλει να προκαλέσει με αίτηση την ενέργεια της αρχής.

Άρθρο 250

Αν είναι εκκρεμής ποινική αγωγή που επηρεάζει τη διάγνωση της διαφοράς, το δικαστήριο μπορεί, αυτεπαγγέλτως ή ύστερα από αίτηση κάποιου διαδίκου, να διατάξει την αναβολή της συζήτησης εωσότου περατωθεί αμετάκλητα η ποινική διαδικασία.

Άρθρο 251

[Καταργείται]

Άρθρο 252

1. Αν μάρτυρας, πραγματογνώμονας ή κάποιος από τους παριστάμενους διαδίκους ή τους νόμιμους αντιπροσώπους τους που εμφανίζεται αυτοπροσώπως στη συζήτηση ή την επιχείρηση διαδικαστικής πράξης αγνοεί την ελληνική γλώσσα, προσλαμβάνεται διερμηνέας. Αν πρόκειται για γλώσσα ελάχιστα γνωστή, μπορεί να προσληφθεί διερμηνέας του διερμηνέα.
2. Η κατάθεση του μάρτυρα γράφεται στα πρακτικά ή στην έκθεση σε μετάφραση.
3. Οι διερμηνείς διορίζονται από το δικαστή και στα πολυμελή δικαστήρια από τον πρόεδρο του δικαστηρίου και εφόσον δεν έχουν ορκιστεί ως διερμηνείς, ορκίζονται σύμφωνα με το άρθρο 408 ότι θα ασκήσουν το καθήκον τους πιστά και με ακρίβεια και μπορούν να εξαιρεθούν για τους ίδιους λόγους που μπορούν να εξαιρεθούν και οι πραγματογνώμονες.

Άρθρο 253

1. Αν μάρτυρας ή πραγματογνώμονας ή κάποιος από τους διαδίκους ή τους νόμιμους αντιπροσώπους τους που παρίστανται στη συζήτηση ή την επιχείρηση διαδικαστικής πράξης είναι κωφός ή πρόσωπο με σοβαρή αναπηρία λόγου, η συνεννόηση μαζί του γίνεται ως εξής: Οι ερωτήσεις και οι τυχόν παρατηρήσεις υποβάλλονται προς τον κωφό εγγράφως και ο κωφός επιλέγει να απαντήσει είτε προφορικώς είτε εγγράφως, σύμφωνα με τον προσφορότερο τρόπο επικοινωνίας για τον ίδιο. Προς το πρόσωπο με σοβαρή αναπηρία λόγου οι ερωτήσεις και οι παρατηρήσεις υποβάλλονται προφορικά και αυτός απαντά εγγράφως. Οι γραπτές ερωτήσεις, παρατηρήσεις και απαντήσεις καταχωρίζονται στα πρακτικά ή στην έκθεση.
2. Αν ο κωφός ή το πρόσωπο με σοβαρή αναπηρία λόγου δεν ξέρει να διαβάζει και να γράφει, ο δικαστής διορίζει έναν ή δύο διερμηνείς, που εκλέγονται κατά προτίμηση ανάμεσα στα πρόσωπα που είναι συνηθισμένα να συνεννοούνται μαζί του.

Article 248

The court may, following an application filed by a party in the proceedings or *ex officio* and in the case of several separate pleas that concern the same application, order that the hearing take place consecutively or be limited to just one of said pleas where this, in its view, would facilitate or expedite the conduct of the proceedings.

Article 249

Where the determination of the dispute depends in whole or in part on the existence or non-existence of a legal relationship or the nullity of or overturning a legal transaction that constitutes the subject-matter of different proceedings pending before a civil or administrative court or an issue to be ruled or being ruled upon by an administrative authority, the court, following an application filed by a party in the proceedings or *ex officio*, may order that the hearing be stayed until a *de jure* non-appealable or irrevocable judgment has been handed down in the other proceedings or until the administrative authority has issued a decision that cannot be contested. If the administrative authority has not yet addressed the matter, the court shall set a deadline within which the party in the proceedings is obligated to require the authority to act by filing an application.

Article 250

If criminal proceedings affecting the determination of the dispute are ongoing, the court may, following an application filed by a party in the proceedings or *ex officio*, order that the hearing be stayed until an irrevocable judgment has been handed down in the criminal proceedings.

Article 251

[Repealed]

Article 252

1. An interpreter shall be engaged if a witness, expert or any of the parties in the proceedings or their lawful proxies appearing in person at the hearing or when procedural steps are being taken does not speak the Greek language. In the case of languages of lesser diffusion, an interpreter for the interpreter may be engaged.
2. The testimony given by the witness shall be entered in the transcript or the report in translated form.
3. Interpreters shall be appointed by the judge and, at multi-member courts, by the presiding judge of the court; if they have not been sworn in as interpreters, they shall take an oath in accordance with Article 408 to perform their duties accurately and faithfully, and they may exempted on the same grounds on which experts may be exempted.

Article 253

1. If a witness, expert or any of the parties in the proceedings or their lawful proxies appearing in person at the hearing or when procedural steps are being taken is deaf or has a serious speech impediment, communication with them shall take place as follows: questions and any observations shall be put to deaf persons in writing, and answers shall be given verbally; questions and observations shall be put verbally to mute persons and they shall answer in writing; questions and observations shall be put to deaf and mute persons in writing and they shall also answer in writing; written questions, observations and answers shall be recorded in the transcript or the report.
2. If the person who is deaf or has a serious speech impediment cannot read and write, the judge shall appoint one or two interpreters preferably appointed from among the persons accustomed to communicating with them.

Άρθρο 254

1. Το δικαστήριο μπορεί να διατάξει την επανάληψη της συζήτησης, η οποία έχει κηρυχθεί περατωμένη, όταν κατά τη μελέτη της υπόθεσης ή τη διάσκεψη παρουσιάζονται κενά ή αμφίβολα σημεία που χρειάζονται συμπλήρωση ή επεξήγηση. Η απόφαση μνημονεύει απαραιτήτως τα ειδικά θέματα που αποτελούν αντικείμενο της επαναλαμβανόμενης συζήτησης. Η συζήτηση αυτή θεωρείται συνέχεια της προηγουμένης.
2. Στην επαναλαμβανόμενη συζήτηση, η οποία ορίζεται το συντομότερο δυνατό, οι διάδικοι κλητεύονται τριάντα (30) τουλάχιστον ημέρες πριν από αυτήν.
3. Η υπόθεση εκδικάζεται από τον ίδιο δικαστή και από την ίδια σύνθεση επί πολυμελούς δικαστηρίου, εκτός αν αυτό είναι για φυσικούς ή νομικούς λόγους αδύνατο. Σε προθεσμία τριών (3) εργασίμων ημερών από τη συζήτηση της υπόθεσης μπορεί να κατατεθεί προσθήκη επί των ζητημάτων της παρ. 1. Νέοι ισχυρισμοί και νέα αποδεικτικά μέσα δεν επιτρέπονται.

Άρθρο 255

Αν για να τηρηθεί η τάξη διατάχθηκε η απομάκρυνση προσώπου που μετέχει στη συζήτηση ή τη διαδικαστική πράξη από τον τόπο όπου διεξάγεται, η διαδικασία συνεχίζεται σαν να ήταν η αποχώρηση εκούσια.

Άρθρο 256

Για την προφορική συζήτηση στο ακροατήριο συντάσσονται από το γραμματέα και με τις οδηγίες του δικαστή που διευθύνει τη συζήτηση πρακτικά, που πρέπει να περιέχουν
α) τον τόπο και το χρόνο της συζήτησης,
β) τα ονοματεπώνυμα των δικαστών, του εισαγγελέα, του γραμματέα, του διερμηνέα, των διαδίκων που εμφανίστηκαν, των νόμιμων αντιπροσώπων και των πληρεξουσίων τους,
γ) αν η συζήτηση έγινε δημόσια ή κεκλεισμένων των θυρών,
δ) όσα έγιναν κατά τη συζήτηση και ιδίως τις ερωτήσεις που υποβλήθηκαν και τις απαντήσεις σ' αυτές, τους ισχυρισμούς, τις αιτήσεις και τις δηλώσεις των διαδίκων, εκτός αν είναι υποχρεωτική η υποβολή προτάσεων, οπότε αρκεί η αναφορά σ' αυτές, τις καταθέσεις των μαρτύρων, των πραγματογνωμόνων και των διαδίκων ή των νόμιμων αντιπροσώπων τους που εξετάστηκαν, εφόσον δεν εξετάστηκαν προηγουμένως ή απομακρύνονται από την προηγούμενη κατάθεσή τους, τις γνωμοδοτήσεις των πραγματογνωμόνων, εφόσον δεν υποβλήθηκαν εγγράφως, οπότε αρκεί η αναφορά σ' αυτές, το πόρισμα της αυτοψίας και
ε) τη δημοσίευση των αποφάσεων.
2. Τα πρακτικά μπορούν να τηρηθούν και στενογραφικά. Το στενογραφημένο πρωτότυπο μεταφράζεται από αυτόν που το τήρησε και προσαρτάται στα πρακτικά.
3. Ενώπιον των δικαστηρίων, συμπεριλαμβανομένων και των ειρηνοδικείων, μπορεί να εφαρμοστεί και το σύστημα τήρησης πρακτικών των συζητήσεων με φωνοληψία.

Άρθρο 257

Το σχέδιο των πρακτικών διαβάζεται στους διαδίκους ή τους πληρεξουσίους τους ύστερα από αίτησή τους υποχρεωτικά αν περιλαμβάνουν αναγνώριση, συμβιβασμό, παραίτηση ή ομολογία και σε κάθε άλλη περίπτωση κατά την κρίση του δικαστηρίου. Η ανάγνωση αυτή αναφέρεται στα πρακτικά.

Άρθρο 258

1. Τα πρακτικά υπογράφονται από το δικαστή που διευθύνει τη συζήτηση και από το γραμματέα.
2. Αν ο δικαστής που διεύθυνε τη συζήτηση κωλύεται ή έπαψε να είναι μέλος του δικαστηρίου, υπογράφει αντί γι' αυτόν ο αρχαιότερος κατά το διορισμό από τους δικαστές που έλαβαν μέρος στη συζήτηση και αν όλοι αυτοί κωλύονται, υπογράφει μόνο ο γραμματέας. Τα κωλύματα αναφέρονται στα πρακτικά.
3. Οι διατάξεις της παραγράφου 2 εφαρμόζονται αναλόγως και σε μονομελή δικαστήρια.

Article 254

1. When, during the examination of the case or deliberations, there are gaps or uncertainties that must be supplemented or explained, the court may order the re-opening of a hearing declared concluded. This decision must cite the specific issues constituting the subject-matter of the re-opened hearing. The hearing shall be deemed a continuation of the previous hearing.
2. Parties in the proceedings shall be summonsed at least 30 days prior to attend the re-opened hearing, set for the closest date possible.
3. The case shall be tried by the same judge or the same composition in the case of a multi-member court, unless this is not possible on actual or legal grounds. Within a deadline of three working days from the hearing of the case, an addition [to the pleadings] may be filed with regard to the issues referred to in paragraph 1. New assertions and new means of evidence are not permitted.

Article 255

If a person participating in the hearing or the procedural step was ordered to be removed from the place where the step was being taken or for the purpose of keeping order, the procedure shall continue as if this removal was voluntary.

Article 256

With regard to the verbal hearing in court, the registrar shall prepare a transcript according to the instructions of the judge directing the course of the hearing, which shall contain:
a) the place and time of the hearing;
b) the full names of the judges, the public prosecutor, the registrar, the interpreter, the parties who entered an appearance, their lawful proxies and their authorised representatives;
c) whether the hearing took place in open court or *in camera*;
d) everything that occurred during the hearing and, in particular, the questions put and answers given, the assertions, [motions] and statements of the parties in the proceedings (unless the filing of pleadings is mandatory, in which case reference thereto shall suffice), the testimony given by witnesses, experts and the parties in the proceedings or their lawful proxies under examination (provided they were not previously examined or they differ from their previous testimony), the opinions of the experts (provided they were not filed in writing, in which case reference thereto shall suffice), the findings of the inspection; and
e) the handing down of rulings/judgments.
2. Transcripts may also be kept in stenographic form. The original stenographic document shall be transcribed by the person who prepared it and shall be appended to the transcript.
3. A system for keeping audio transcripts may also be used in court, including courts of the peace.

Article 257

The draft transcript shall be read to the parties in the proceedings or their proxies, following a request on their part, if the transcript contains an acknowledgement, settlement, discontinuation or admission and in all other cases, at the discretion of the court. The fact that the reading took place shall be cited in the transcript.

Article 258

1. The transcript shall be signed by the judge directing the course of the hearing and the registrar.
2. If the judge directing the course of the hearing is indisposed or ceases to be a member of the court, the transcript shall be signed by the most senior of the judges in order of appointment who participated in the hearing instead and, if all such judges are indisposed, only by the registrar. The impediments shall be cited in the transcript.
3. The provisions of paragraph 2 also apply to single-member courts *mutatis mutandis*.

Άρθρο 259

1. Τα πρακτικά αποτελούν πλήρη απόδειξη ως προς τη συζήτηση και το περιεχόμενό της.

2. Αν κατά την ανάγνωση των πρακτικών διατυπώθηκε από την πλευρά των διαδίκων, των νόμιμων αντιπροσώπων ή των πληρεξουσίων τους αντίρρηση για την ακρίβεια της διατύπωσης των αναγνωρίσεων, συμβιβασμών, παραιτήσεων, ομολογιών ή άλλων δηλώσεων, το μέρος αυτό των πρακτικών εκτιμάται ελεύθερα από το δικαστή.

3. Η τήρηση των διατυπώσεων της προφορικής συζήτησης μπορεί να αποδειχθεί μόνο με τα πρακτικά.

Άρθρο 260

1. Αν κατά την εκφώνηση της υπόθεσης δεν εμφανίζονται όλοι οι διάδικοι ή εμφανίζονται, αλλά δεν μετέχουν κανονικά στη συζήτηση, η συζήτηση ματαιώνεται.

2. Στην τακτική διαδικασία και στις δίκες των ειδικών διαδικασιών, αν οι διάδικοι δεν λάβουν κανονικά μέρος στη δίκη ή δεν εμφανιστούν στο ακροατήριο, η συζήτηση της υπόθεσης ματαιώνεται. Αν παρέλθουν ενενήντα (90) ημέρες από τη ματαίωση χωρίς να ζητηθεί ο προσδιορισμός νέας συζήτησης, η υπόθεση διαγράφεται από το πινάκιο από τον γραμματέα με εντολή του διευθύνοντος το δικαστήριο και η δίκη καταργείται. Για τη νέα συζήτηση της τακτικής διαδικασίας εφαρμόζονται αναλόγως οι προθεσμίες της παρ. 2 του άρθρου 215 και των παρ. 1 και 2 του άρθρου 237.

3. Η με οποιονδήποτε τρόπον ματαίωση της συζήτησης της υπόθεσης αποτελεί διαδικαστική πράξη του δικαστηρίου.

4. Όταν οι υποθέσεις που είναι γραμμένες στο πινάκιο δεν εισάγονται προς συζήτηση συνεπεία λόγων ανώτερης βίας ορίζεται αυτεπαγγέλτως, με πράξη του διευθύνοντος το δικαστήριο, ημέρα και ώρα συζήτησης στο ακροατήριο σε σύντομη κατά το δυνατόν δικάσιμο. Η εγγραφή της υπόθεσης στο οικείο πινάκιο, το οποίο μπορεί να τηρείται και ηλεκτρονικά, γίνεται με πρωτοβουλία του γραμματέα και ισχύει ως κλήτευση όλων των διαδίκων. Με πρωτοβουλία του γραμματέα μπορεί να γνωστοποιείται η νέα δικάσιμος με αποστολή ηλεκτρονικού μηνύματος στη διεύθυνση ηλεκτρονικού ταχυδρομείου των διαδίκων ή με ανάρτηση στην πύλη ψηφιακών υπηρεσιών δικαστηρίων solon.gov.gr για όσα δικαστήρια και διαδικασίες έχουν ενταχθεί στο εν λόγω σύστημα.

Άρθρο 261

Κάθε διάδικος οφείλει να απαντά με σαφήνεια γενικά ή ειδικά για την αλήθεια ή όχι των πραγματικών ισχυρισμών του αντιδίκου του. Εφόσον δεν αμφισβητήθηκε η αλήθεια κάποιου πραγματικού ισχυρισμού, απόκειται στο δικαστή να κρίνει σε συνδυασμό με την τυχόν γενική άρνηση και το σύνολο των ισχυρισμών των διαδίκων, αν συνάγεται ομολογία ή άρνηση.

Άρθρο 262

1. Η ένσταση πρέπει να περιλαμβάνει ορισμένη αίτηση και σαφή έκθεση των γεγονότων που τη θεμελιώνουν. Ο ενιστάμενος μπορεί να συμπληρώσει, να διευκρινίσει ή να διορθώσει τους ισχυρισμούς του με προφορική δήλωση που καταχωρίζεται στα πρακτικά.

2. Ενστάσεις από δικαίωμα τρίτου επιτρέπονται μόνο στις περιπτώσεις που ορίζει ο νόμος.

Άρθρο 263

Κατά τη συζήτηση και στις περιπτώσεις των άρθρων 237 και 238 με τις προτάσεις πρέπει να προτείνονται, με ποινή απαραδέκτου:

α) η αναρμοδιότητα, εκτός αν δεν επιτρέπεται παρέκταση,
β) η υπαγωγή της διαφοράς σε διαιτησία,
γ) η έλλειψη εγγυοδοσίας,
δ) η μη καταβολή των εξόδων της προηγούμενης δίκης,
ε) η ύπαρξη προθεσμίας για την αποποίηση κληρονομιάς,
στ) η προσεπίκληση ομοδίκων ή υπόχρεων για αποζημίωση.

Article 259

1. Transcripts constitute proof in full with regard to the hearing and its content.
2. If the parties in the proceedings, their lawful proxies or their authorised representatives raised objections during the hearing of the transcript regarding the accuracy of the wording of the acknowledgements, settlements, waivers, admissions or other statements, this part of the transcript shall be freely weighed up by the judge.
3. The fact that the formalities of oral hearings were complied with shall be proven only by means of the transcript.

Article 260

1. If, during the calling of the case, all the parties in the proceedings fail to appear, or do appear but fail to participate in the hearing in the manner required, the hearing is unable to go ahead.
2. Under the ordinary procedure and at proceedings conducted in accordance with special procedure, if the parties failed to participate in the hearing in the manner required or failed to appear in court, the hearing of the case is unable to go ahead. If 90 days elapse from the date the case was unable to go ahead and no request to set a new hearing [date] was filed, the case shall be stricken from the case register by the registrar at the order of the person directing the court, and the proceedings shall be quashed. The deadlines laid down in Article 215(2) and Article 237(1) and (2) apply *mutatis mutandis* to the new hearing under the ordinary procedure.
3. [Ruling] in any manner that the hearing of the case is unable to go ahead constitutes a procedural step taken by the court.
4. When the cases entered in the case register are not brought to be heard due to force majeure, the person directing the court shall issue an act *ex officio* setting a day and time for the courtroom hearing on the nearest possible hearing date. The case shall be entered in the pertinent case register, which may also be kept in electronic form, by the registrar and its entry shall function as summonsing all the parties in the proceedings. The new hearing date may be notified by the registrar by e-mail sent to the e-mail addresses of the parties in the proceedings or via a post on the solon.gov.gr digital court services portal for those courts and procedures included in the system in question.

Article 261

All parties in the proceedings must respond clearly in general or in particular about the truth or otherwise of the factual assertions made by the opponent. Where the truth of a factual assertion is not contested, it is up to the judge to decide, taking into account any general denial and all assertions made by the parties in the proceedings, whether [this fact] can be inferred to constitute admission or denial.

Article 262

1. Pleas must contain a specific form of order sought and clearly present the substantiating facts. The party raising the plea may supplement, clarify or rectify their assertions by means of a verbal statement recorded in the transcript.
2. Pleas arising from third-party rights are permitted only where provided for in law.

Article 263

During the hearing and in the cases referred to in Articles 237 and 238, the following must be pleaded in the pleadings, on penalty of inadmissibility:
a) lack of jurisdiction, unless prorogation is not permitted;
b) bringing the dispute to arbitration;
c) lack of provision of surety;
d) non-payment of the costs of the previous proceedings;
e) existence of a deadline [within which] to repudiate an inheritance;
f) impleading of joined parties or persons liable to pay compensation.

Άρθρο 264

Αν η διαφορά υπάγεται σε διαιτησία, το δικαστήριο παραπέμπει την υπόθεση στη διαιτησία, διατηρούνται όμως οι συνέπειες της άσκησης της αγωγής. Αν πάψει να ισχύει η συμφωνία της διαιτησίας, η υπόθεση επαναφέρεται με κλήση.

Άρθρο 265

Ο κληρονόμος που ενάγεται για απαίτηση κατά της κληρονομίας, εφόσον έχει ακόμη το δικαίωμα να την αποποιηθεί, μπορεί να ζητήσει αναβολή της συζήτησης. Αν το δικαστήριο δεχτεί την αίτηση αναβάλλει τη συζήτηση εωσότου περάσει η προθεσμία για την αποποίηση της κληρονομίας.

Άρθρο 266

Αν ο εναγόμενος προσεπικάλεσε τους ομοδίκους ή τους υπόχρεους για αποζημίωση ή το νομέα και αυτοί δεν εμφανίστηκαν κατά τη συζήτηση, μπορεί να ζητήσει την αναβολή της συζήτησης εωσότου περάσει η προθεσμία για εμφάνιση που παρέχεται σ' αυτόν που έχει προσεπικληθεί. Αν το δικαστήριο δεχτεί την αίτηση, αναβάλλει τη συζήτηση εωσότου περάσει η προθεσμία.

Άρθρο 267

Στις περιπτώσεις του άρθρου 263 το δικαστήριο, αν κρίνει ότι διευκολύνεται ή επιταχύνεται η διεξαγωγή της δίκης, μπορεί να προχωρήσει σε ιδιαίτερη συζήτηση και να εκδώσει ιδιαίτερη απόφαση πριν εξετάσει την ουσία της υπόθεσης. Το ίδιο ισχύει και ως προς την έλλειψη δικαιοδοσίας, την εκκρεμοδικία, την ικανότητα διαδίκου ή την ικανότητα διεξαγωγής της δίκης στο όνομα του διαδίκου ή τη νόμιμη παράσταση ή την εξουσιοδότηση του νόμιμου αντιπροσώπου.

Άρθρο 268

1. Μετά την εκκρεμοδικία ο εναγόμενος μπορεί να ασκήσει ανταγωγή.

2. Στην περίπτωση αναγκαστικής ομοδικίας επιτρέπεται ανταγωγή μόνο όταν ασκείται από όλους ή εναντίον όλων των ομοδίκων.

3. Δεν μπορεί να ασκηθεί ανταγωγή για υπόθεση που υπάγεται σε ειδική διαδικασία, αν η αγωγή δικάζεται κατά τη γενική ή άλλη ειδική διαδικασία και αντίστροφα.

4. Η ανταγωγή ασκείται με χωριστό δικόγραφο. Μετά την άσκηση της ανταγωγής, η δωσιδικία της διατηρείται και αν η κύρια αγωγή απορριφθεί ή ο ενάγων την ανακαλέσει ή παραιτηθεί από αυτήν.

Άρθρα 269-270Α

[Καταργούνται]

Article 264

If the dispute can be brought to arbitration, the court shall remit the case to arbitration, but the effects of filing the action shall persist. If the arbitration agreement ceases to apply, proceedings on the case shall resume following a summons.

Article 265

Where an action is filed against an heir with regard to their inheritance and the heir still has the right to repudiate the inheritance, they may request that the hearing be adjourned. If the court accepts the application, it shall adjourn the hearing until the deadline within which they may repudiate the inheritance has lapsed.

Article 266

If the defendant impleaded the joined parties or persons liable to pay compensation or the possessor and they failed to appear during the hearing, the defendant may request an adjournment of the hearing until the deadline for appearance set for the person impleaded has lapsed. If the court accepts the application, it shall adjourn the hearing until the deadline has lapsed.

Article 267

In the cases referred to in Article 263, where the court rules that this would facilitate or expedite the proceedings, it may hold a separate hearing and issue a specific judgment [thereon] before examining the case on its merits. This also applies with regard to lack of jurisdiction, *lis pendens*, the capacity of the party or the ability to conduct the proceedings in the name of the party, or the lawful appearance or authorisation of the lawful proxy.

Article 268

1. After *lis pendens* [has ended], the defendant may file a cross-action.

2. In cases of compulsory joinder, a cross-action is permitted only when filed by or against all the joined parties.

3. A cross-action may not be filed in a case subject to a special procedure if the action is being tried under the general or a different special procedure and vice versa.

4. Cross-actions shall be filed by means of a separate procedural document. After the cross-action has been filed, its jurisdictional effects persist even if the main action is dismissed or the plaintiff withdraws or discontinues [the cross-action].

Articles 269-270A

[Repealed]

Άρθρο 271

1. Αν ο εναγόμενος δεν λάβει μέρος κανονικά στη δίκη, το δικαστήριο εξετάζει αυτεπαγγέλτως, αν η αγωγή και η κλήση για συζήτηση επιδόθηκαν σε αυτόν νόμιμα και εμπρόθεσμα.
2. Αν η αγωγή και η κλήση για συζήτηση επιδόθηκαν νόμιμα και εμπρόθεσμα, η υπόθεση συζητείται ερήμην του εναγομένου. Διαφορετικά κηρύσσεται απαράδεκτη η συζήτηση και στην περίπτωση των άρθρων 237 και 238 θεωρείται ως μη ασκηθείσα η αγωγή.
3. Στην περίπτωση ερημοδικίας του εναγομένου, οι περιεχόμενοι στην αγωγή πραγματικοί ισχυρισμοί του ενάγοντος θεωρούνται ομολογημένοι, εκτός αν πρόκειται για γεγονότα για τα οποία δεν επιτρέπεται ομολογία, και η αγωγή γίνεται δεκτή, εφόσον κρίνεται νομικά βάσιμη και δεν υπάρχει ένσταση που εξετάζεται αυτεπαγγέλτως.

Άρθρο 272
Ερημοδικία ενάγοντος. Πότε απορρίπτεται η αγωγή. Τύχη της ανταγωγής.

1. Αν η συζήτηση γίνεται με επιμέλεια του ενάγοντος και αυτός δεν λάβει μέρος κανονικά στη δίκη, το δικαστήριο συζητεί την υπόθεση χωρίς αυτόν και απορρίπτει την αγωγή.
2. Αν η συζήτηση γίνεται με την επιμέλεια του εναγόμενου ή εκείνου που άσκησε κύρια ή πρόσθετη παρέμβαση, εφαρμόζονται οι διατάξεις του άρθρου 271, και σε περίπτωση ερημοδικίας του ενάγοντος απορρίπτεται η αγωγή.
3. Αν ο εναγόμενος άσκησε ανταγωγή εφαρμόζονται οι διατάξεις του άρθρου 271.

Άρθρο 273

Αν εκείνος που άσκησε κύρια παρέμβαση δεν λάβει μέρος κανονικά στη δίκη, εφαρμόζονται οι διατάξεις του άρθρου 272.

Άρθρο 274

1. Αν εκείνος που άσκησε πρόσθετη παρέμβαση δεν λάβει μέρος κανονικά στη δίκη, η διαδικασία προχωρεί σαν να μην είχε ασκηθεί η πρόσθετη παρέμβαση. Όποιος άσκησε πρόσθετη παρέμβαση μπορεί να παρίσταται στις επόμενες στάσεις της δίκης και στις επόμενες διαδικαστικές πράξεις, πρέπει δε να καλείται νόμιμα για αυτό.
2. Αν εκείνος που άσκησε πρόσθετη παρέμβαση λάβει μέρος κανονικά στη δίκη, τότε:

α) αν δεν λάβουν μέρος κανονικά στη δίκη και οι δύο αρχικοί διάδικοι ή ο αντίδικος εκείνου υπέρ του οποίου ασκήθηκε η παρέμβαση, το δικαστήριο συζητεί την υπόθεση ερήμην του αντιδίκου εκείνου υπέρ του οποίου ασκήθηκε η παρέμβαση και εφαρμόζονται οι διατάξεις των άρθρων 271 και 272,
β) αν δεν λάβει μέρος κανονικά στη δίκη μόνο εκείνος υπέρ του οποίου ασκήθηκε η παρέμβαση, το δικαστήριο συζητεί την υπόθεση ερήμην του μεταξύ εκείνου που άσκησε την παρέμβαση και του αντιδίκου εκείνου υπέρ του οποίου ασκήθηκε η παρέμβαση.
3. Αν εκείνος που άσκησε πρόσθετη παρέμβαση, συμμετάσχει στη δίκη ως κύριος διάδικος αλλά δεν λάβει μέρος σ' αυτήν κανονικά, επέρχονται ως προς αυτόν οι συνέπειες της απουσίας του διαδίκου τη θέση του οποίου ανέλαβε.

Άρθρο 275

Αν δεν έλαβαν μέρος κανονικά στη δίκη αυτοί που έχουν προσεπικληθεί κατά το άρθρο 86 ή εκείνος που προσεπικάλεσε, αλλά έλαβαν μέρος κανονικά οι ομόδικοι που προσεπικλήθηκαν, εφαρμόζονται οι διατάξεις του άρθρου 76. Αν δεν έλαβαν μέρος κανονικά στη δίκη αυτοί που έχουν προσεπικληθεί και εκείνος που προσεπικάλεσε, οι ομόδικοι που προσεπικλήθηκαν υπόκεινται στις ίδιες συνέπειες στις οποίες υπόκειται και εκείνος που προσεπικάλεσε.

Article 271

1. If the defendant fails to participate in the proceedings in the manner required, the court shall examine *ex officio* whether the action and the summons to the hearing were served on the defendant duly and in good time.
2. If the action and the summons to the hearing were served duly and in good time, the case shall be heard in the defendant's absence, otherwise the hearing shall be declared inadmissible and, in the cases referred to in Articles 237 and 238, the action shall be deemed never to have been filed.
3. Where the defendant fails to enter an appearance, the factual assertions made by the plaintiff in the action shall be deemed to have been admitted [by the defendant], unless they concern facts for which admission is not permitted, and the action shall be accepted if deemed well-founded in law and there are no pleas [which must be] examined *ex officio*.

Article 272

Failure of the plaintiff to enter an appearance. When the action is dismissed. What happens to cross-actions.

1. If the hearing is expedited by the plaintiff and they fail to participate in the proceedings in the manner required, the court shall hear the case in the plaintiff's absence and dismiss the action.
2. If the hearing is expedited by the defendant or the main or permissive intervenor, the provisions of Article 271 apply and, if the plaintiff fails to enter an appearance, the action shall be dismissed.
3. If the defendant filed a cross-action, the provisions of Article 271 apply.

Article 273

If the main intervenor fails to participate in the proceedings in the manner required, the provisions of Article 272 apply.

Article 274

1. If the permissive intervenor fails to participate in the proceedings in the manner required, proceedings shall go ahead as if the permissive intervention had not been filed. The permissive intervenor may appear during subsequent stages of the proceedings and subsequent procedural steps, and must be duly summoned to do so.
2. If the permissive intervenor participates in the proceedings in the manner required, then:
a) if the two initial parties in the proceedings or the opponent of the person in support of whom the intervention was filed fail to participate in the proceedings in the manner required, the court shall hear the case in the absence of the opponent of the person in support of whom the intervention was filed, and the provisions of Articles 271 and 272 apply;
b) if only the person in support of whom the intervention was filed fails to participate in the proceedings in the manner required, the court shall hear the case in the absence of that person between the intervenor and the opponent of the person in support of whom the intervention was filed.
3. If the permissive intervenor is a main party in the proceedings but fails to participate in the proceedings in the manner required, the consequences of absence of the party in the proceedings whose place that person took shall apply to them.

Article 275

If the persons impleaded in accordance with Article 86 or the person who impleaded them fail to participate in the proceedings in the manner required but the joined parties who were impleaded participated in the manner required, the provisions of Article 76 apply. If the persons impleaded and the person who impleaded them fail to participate in the proceedings in the manner required, the joined parties who were impleaded shall be subject to the same consequences as the person who impleaded them.

Άρθρο 276

1. Αν αυτός που έχει προσεπικληθεί κατά το άρθρο 87 δεν λάβει μέρος κανονικά στη δίκη ή λάβει αλλά δεν κάνει δήλωση για τη σχέση του με το επίδικο ή αμφισβητήσει τους ισχυρισμούς του εναγομένου που τον προσεπικάλεσε ο τελευταίος μπορεί να αποδεχτεί την αγωγή.

2. Αν αυτός που έχει προσεπικληθεί κατά το άρθρο 87 αναγνωρίσει ως αληθείς τους ισχυρισμούς του εναγομένου που τον προσεπικάλεσε, έχει δικαίωμα, αν εκείνος συναινεί, να λάβει μέρος στη δίκη ως κύριος διάδικος, στη θέση του εναγομένου. Στην περίπτωση αυτή ο εναγόμενος τίθεται εκτός δίκης, η απόφαση όμως που θα εκδοθεί ισχύει και εναντίον του.

Άρθρο 277

Αν ο ενάγων, ο εναγόμενος ή εκείνος που έχει ασκήσει κύρια παρέμβαση προσεπικάλεσε τους υπόχρεους σε αποζημίωση, τότε:

1) αν δεν λάβουν μέρος κανονικά στη δίκη αυτοί που έχουν προσεπικληθεί και εκείνος που έχει προσεπικαλέσει δικάζονται ερήμην,

2) αν οι κύριοι διάδικοι λάβουν μέρος κανονικά στη δίκη αλλά απουσιάζουν αυτοί που έχουν προσεπικληθεί, συζητείται η υπόθεση μεταξύ των πρώτων κατ' αντιμωλίαν, ενώ αυτοί που έχουν προσεπικληθεί δικάζονται ερήμην,

3) αν λάβουν μέρος κανονικά στη δίκη αυτοί που έχουν προσεπικληθεί και απουσιάζει ο κύριος διάδικος που τους προσεπικάλεσε, οι πρώτοι έχουν το δικαίωμα είτε να λάβουν τη θέση του κύριου διαδίκου και να συζητήσουν την υπόθεση με τον αντίδικο, είτε απλώς να ασκήσουν παρέμβαση. Στη δεύτερη περίπτωση η διαδικασία προχωρεί σαν να μην είχε ασκηθεί η πρόσθετη παρέμβαση και το δικαστήριο δικάζει ερήμην τον απόντα προσεπικαλέσαντα διάδικο,

4) αν λάβουν μέρος κανονικά στη δίκη οι κύριοι διάδικοι και αυτοί που έχουν προσεπικληθεί, οι τελευταίοι έχουν το δικαίωμα να αρνηθούν την προσεπίκληση ή να ασκήσουν απλώς παρέμβαση ή να πάρουν τη θέση εκείνου που τους προσεπικάλεσε και να συζητήσουν την υπόθεση με τον αντίδικο.

Άρθρο 278

Αν στις περιπτώσεις του άρθρου 277 αυτοί που έχουν προσεπικληθεί λάβουν τη θέση εκείνου που τους προσεπικάλεσε, χάνουν το δικαίωμα να αμφισβητήσουν την υποχρέωση για αποζημίωση και η υπόθεση συζητείται μεταξύ αυτών και των υπόλοιπων διαδίκων, ενώ εκείνος που προσεπικάλεσε τίθεται εκτός δίκης. Η απόφαση ισχύει και εναντίον του προσεπικαλούντος που τέθηκε εκτός της δίκης, ο οποίος μπορεί να εξακολουθήσει να μετέχει στη δίκη σαν να έχει ασκήσει πρόσθετη παρέμβαση.

Άρθρο 279

[Καταργείται]

Article 276

1. If the person impleaded under Article 87 fails to participate in the proceedings in the manner required or does participate but makes no statement regarding their relationship to the subject-matter at issue or disputes the assertions made by the defendant who impleaded them, the defendant may accept [that] the action [stands].

2. If the person impleaded under Article 87 acknowledges the assertions made by the defendant who impleaded him or her as true, that person has the right, if the defendant consents, to participate in the proceedings as the main party, taking the place of the defendant. In this case, the defendant shall be removed from the proceedings, but the judgment to be handed down shall also apply to them.

Article 277

If the plaintiff, the defendant or the main intervenor impleaded the persons liable to pay compensation, then:

1) if they fail to participate in the proceedings in the manner required, the persons who were impleaded and the person who impleaded them shall be tried *in absentia*;

2) if the main parties in the proceedings participate in the proceedings in the manner required but the persons impleaded are absent, the case shall be heard between the former with both sides being heard, while those who were impleaded shall be tried *in absentia*;

3) if the persons who were impleaded participate in the proceedings in the manner required and the main party in the proceedings who impleaded them is absent, the former have the right either to take the place of the main party in the proceedings and attend the hearing of the case with the opponent or to simply file an intervention. In the latter case, the procedure shall go ahead as if the permissive intervention had not been filed and the court shall try *in absentia* the party in the proceedings who filed the impleader but is absent;

4) if the main parties in the proceedings and the persons who were impleaded participate in the proceedings in the manner required, the latter have the right to deny the impleader or simply file an intervention or take the place of the person who impleaded them and participate in the hearing of the case with the opponent.

Article 278

If, in the cases referred to in Article 277, the persons who were impleaded take the place of the person who impleaded them, they shall forfeit the right to dispute the obligation to pay compensation, and the case shall be heard between them and the other parties, while the person who impleaded them shall be removed from the proceedings. The judgment shall also apply to the person who filed the impleader and was removed from the proceedings, who may continue participating in the proceedings as if they had filed a permissive intervention.

Article 279

[Repealed]

Άρθρο 280

1. Αν διάδικος που δεν εμφανίστηκε κατά την εκφώνηση της υπόθεσης, προσέλθει κατά τη διάρκεια της συζήτησης και λάβει μέρος κανονικά σ' αυτήν, θεωρείται ότι δικάζεται κατ' αντιμωλίαν και είναι υποχρεωμένος να δεχτεί τη συζήτηση στο σημείο που βρίσκεται.
2. Θεωρείται, ότι δεν εμφανίζεται ο διάδικος που ζητεί μόνο αναβολή, η οποία δεν έγινε δεκτή από το δικαστήριο.
3. Αν διάδικος που εμφανίστηκε κατά την εκφώνηση της υπόθεσης υποβάλει αίτηση αναβολής της συζήτησης, η οποία απορρίφθηκε από το δικαστήριο, χωρίς να έχει απαντήσει στην ουσία, θεωρείται ότι δεν μετέχει κανονικά στην παραπέρα συζήτηση.
4. Ο διάδικος που αποχωρεί εκούσια μετά την έναρξη της κατ' ουσίαν συζήτησης θεωρείται ότι δικάζεται κατ' αντιμωλίαν.

Άρθρο 281

Συζήτηση θεωρείται εκείνη κατά την οποία εκφωνήθηκε η υπόθεση και άρχισε η εκδίκασή της, ανεξάρτητα από το αν το δικαστήριο άρχισε ή όχι να εξετάζει την ουσία της.

ΚΕΦΑΛΑΙΟ ΣΤ'
Παρεμπίπτοντα.

Άρθρο 282

1. Παρεμπίπτον ζήτημα είναι οτιδήποτε μπορεί να εμποδίσει, διακόψει ή καταργήσει ή οπωσδήποτε επηρεάζει την τακτική πρόοδο της κύριας δίκης, στην οποία περιλαμβάνεται και η εκτέλεση.
2. Τα παρεμπίπτοντα ζητήματα προϋποθέτουν κύρια διαφορά και ένα τουλάχιστον διάδικο τον οποίο ενδιαφέρει η απόφαση για την κύρια διαφορά και το παρεμπίπτον ζήτημα.

Άρθρο 283

1. Η παρεμπίπτουσα αγωγή ανάμεσα στους ίδιους διαδίκους στο ίδιο δικαστήριο πρέπει να περιέχει μεταγενέστερη αίτηση του ενός ή του άλλου διαδίκου.
2. Οι παρεμπίπτουσες αγωγές μπορούν να ασκηθούν σε κάθε στάση της δίκης και κατ' έφεση, εκτός αν περιέχουν αυτοτελή αίτηση.

Άρθρο 284

Το δικαστήριο, με οποιαδήποτε διαδικασία και αν δικάζει, εξετάζει τα παρεμπίπτοντα ζητήματα ακόμη και όταν είναι αναρμόδιο να τα εκδικάσει.

Άρθρο 285

Τα παρεμπίπτοντα ζητήματα ή οι παρεμπίπτουσες αγωγές συνεκδικάζονται με την κυρία δίκη. Αν ο δικαστής κρίνει ότι η κύρια δίκη είναι ώριμη για να εκδοθεί οριστική απόφαση, ενώ το παρεμπίπτον ζήτημα πρέπει να εξεταστεί, εκδίδει απόφαση για την κύρια δίκη και παραπέμπει το παρεμπίπτον σε ιδιαίτερη συζήτηση.

Article 280

1. If a party in the proceedings did not appear when the case was called [but] does appear during the hearing and participates in the proceedings in the manner required, the hearing shall be deemed to be held with both sides being heard, and the said party is obligated to accept the progress of the hearing from its current stage.
2. A party in the proceedings who merely requests an adjournment which is not accepted by the court shall be deemed not to have entered an appearance.
3. If a party in the proceedings appeared when the case was called and filed an application to adjourn the hearing without [having filed pleadings on the merits of the case], and the court dismissed this request, the court shall deem that party to be no longer participating in the hearing in the manner required.
4. When a party in the proceedings voluntarily leaves after the hearing on the merits of the case has commenced, the hearing shall be deemed to be held with both sides being heard.

Article 281

There is a hearing when the case was called and its adjudication commenced, irrespective of whether or not the court began examining its merits.

CHAPTER VI
Incidental issues

Article 282

1. Incidental issues are any issues that can hinder, suspend, quash or in any way affect the normal progress of the main proceedings, including enforcement.
2. Incidental issues require that there is a main dispute and at least one party in the proceedings to whom the judgment in the main dispute and the ruling concerning the incidental issue relate.

Article 283

1. An incidental action between the same parties in the proceedings before the same court must include a subsequent form of order sought by one or the other party in the proceedings.
2. Incidental actions can be filed at any stage of the proceedings and on appeal, unless they relate to a standalone form of order sought.

Article 284

Irrespective of the procedure under which it is trying the case, the court shall examine incidental issues even when it lacks jurisdiction to adjudicate them.

Article 285

Incidental issues or incidental actions shall be tried together with the main proceedings. If the judge rules that the main proceedings are ready for a final judgment to be handed down, but the incidental issue must be [further] examined, they shall hand down judgment regarding the main proceedings and remit the incidental issue to be heard separately.

ΚΕΦΑΛΑΙΟ Ζ'
Διακοπή και επανάληψη της δίκης.

Άρθρο 286

Η δίκη διακόπτεται αν, έως ότου τελειώσει η συζήτηση, μετά την οποία εκδίδεται η οριστική απόφαση:
α) πεθάνει κάποιος διάδικος ή νόμιμος αντιπρόσωπός του ή συμβεί άλλη μεταβολή στο πρόσωπο κάποιου από αυτούς, η οποία επηρεάζει την ικανότητα της δικαστικής παράστασής του ή την εξουσία εκπροσώπησης του νόμιμου αντιπροσώπου, εκτός αν πρόκειται για θάνατο ή άλλες μεταβολές στο πρόσωπο του νόμιμου αντιπροσώπου ανώνυμης εταιρίας, εταιρίας περιορισμένης ευθύνης, νομικού προσώπου δημοσίου δικαίου, σωματείου ή ιδρύματος,
β) επέλθει περίπτωση αποκατάστασης κληρονομιάς ή κληροδοσίας,
γ) πτωχεύσει κάποιος διάδικος, εφόσον η δίκη αφορά την πτωχευτική περιουσία ή πεθάνει ή αντικατασταθεί ο σύνδικος ή εκδοθεί τελεσίδικη απόφαση για επικύρωση του πτωχευτικού συμβιβασμού ή για αποκατάσταση, εφόσον έχουν ως αποτέλεσμα την ανάληψη της διαχείρισης της περιουσίας από τον πτωχό που συμβιβάστηκε ή αποκαταστάθηκε,
δ) πεθάνει, απολυθεί, εκπέσει, παραιτηθεί από το λειτούργημά του ή χάσει γενικά την ικανότητα για εκπροσώπηση και υπεράσπιση του διαδίκου ο δικαστικός πληρεξούσιος κάποιου διαδίκου ή νόμιμου αντιπροσώπου διαδίκου, εκτός αν ο διάδικος ή ο νόμιμος αντιπρόσωπός του έχει στη δίκη περισσότερους δικαστικούς πληρεξούσιους που έλαβαν μέρος σε αυτήν.

Άρθρο 287

1. Η διακοπή επέρχεται από τη γνωστοποίηση προς τον αντίδικο του λόγου της διακοπής με επίδοση δικογράφου ή με τις προτάσεις ή με προφορική δήλωση στο ακροατήριο ή εκτός του ακροατηρίου κατά την επιχείρηση της διαδικαστικής πράξης. Η γνωστοποίηση γίνεται από πρόσωπο που έχει δικαίωμα να επαναλάβει τη δίκη.
2. Τη γνωστοποίηση της παραγράφου 1 μπορεί να κάνει και αυτός που ήταν κατά τη στιγμή που επήλθε ο λόγος της διακοπής πληρεξούσιος του διαδίκου ή του νόμιμου αντιπροσώπου, στο πρόσωπο του οποίου επήλθε ο λόγος αυτός.

Άρθρο 288

Στην περίπτωση αναγκαστικής ομοδικίας, ο θάνατος ενός από τους ομοδίκους ή άλλο γεγονός του άρθρου 286 που επέρχεται στο πρόσωπο ενός ομοδίκου, έχει ως αποτέλεσμα τη διακοπή της δίκης ως προς όλους τους διαδίκους.

Άρθρο 289

Κάθε διαδικαστική πράξη, εκτός από την έκδοση της απόφασης, αν γίνει μετά τη διακοπή της δίκης και πριν από την επανάληψή της, είναι άκυρη, εκτός αν την ενεργήσει ο διάδικος υπέρ του οποίου επήλθε η διακοπή.

Άρθρο 290

Η επανάληψη της δίκης που έχει διακοπεί μπορεί να γίνει εκούσια με ρητή ή σιωπηρή δήλωση του διαδίκου υπέρ του οποίου επήλθε η διακοπή.

CHAPTER VII
Interruption and resumption of proceedings

Article 286

The proceedings shall be interrupted if, before the end of the hearing after which the final judgment is to be handed down:

a) a party in the proceedings or their lawful proxy dies or another change occurs to their person affecting their capacity to be a party in proceedings or the power of representation of the lawful proxy, save in cases of death or other changes to the person of the lawful proxy of a société anonyme, a limited liability company, a body governed by public law, an association or foundation;

b) an heir or legatee is appointed;

c) a party in the proceedings becomes bankrupt, provided the proceedings concern the bankruptcy estate, or the administrator dies, or is substituted, or a *de jure* non-appealable judgment is handed down on certification of the bankruptcy composition or substitution, where this results in the management of the estate being undertaken by the bankrupt person who entered into composition or was substituted;

d) the advocate or the lawful proxy of a party in the proceedings dies, is dismissed, forfeits their capacity, resigns from their profession or generally loses the ability to represent and defend the party, save where the party or their lawful proxy has several legal representatives in the proceedings who participated in the said proceedings.

Article 287

1. Proceedings shall be interrupted from the notification of the reason for interruption to the opponent by means of service of a procedural document, or the pleadings, or a verbal statement — whether made in or out of court — when a procedural step is being taken. Notification shall be effected by the person who has the right to request that proceedings resume.

2. The notification referred to in paragraph 1 may also be effected by the person who, at the time the reason for interruption occurred, was the authorised [lawyer] of the party in the proceedings or their lawful proxy, and to whom the reason relates.

Article 288

In cases of compulsory joinder, death of any of the joined parties or a different event referred to in Article 286 involving a joined party, shall result in interruption of the proceedings with regard to all parties.

Article 289

Save the handing down of judgment, any procedural step taken after proceedings were interrupted and before they resumed is null and void, unless taken by the party for whom the proceedings were interrupted.

Article 290

The interrupted proceedings may resume by means of an explicit or tacit statement by the party for whom the proceedings were interrupted.

Άρθρο 291

1. Ο αντίδικος του διαδίκου υπέρ του οποίου επήλθε η διακοπή της δίκης και ο ομόδικός του μπορούν να προκαλέσουν την επανάληψη της δίκης που έχει διακοπεί προσκαλώντας τον για το σκοπό αυτό με κοινοποίηση δικογράφου. Μπορούν να κοινοποιήσουν την πρόσκληση και πριν από τη γνωστοποίηση του γεγονότος που προκάλεσε τη διακοπή θεωρώντας ότι αυτή επήλθε.
2. Η δίκη επαναλαμβάνεται αυτοδικαίως τριάντα ημέρες μετά την κοινοποίηση της πρόσκλησης. Η προθεσμία αυτή μπορεί να παραταθεί ως έξι το πολύ μήνες από το δικαστή, και στην περίπτωση πολυμελούς δικαστηρίου από τον πρόεδρο, που δικάζουν κατά τη διαδικασία των άρθρων 686 επ.

Άρθρο 292

Ο κληρονόμος, ο κληροδόχος ή ο καταπιστευματοδόχος δεν μπορούν να κληθούν για να επαναληφθεί η δίκη που έχει διακοπεί πριν περάσει η προθεσμία της αποποίησης ή πριν χάσουν με οποιοδήποτε άλλο τρόπο το δικαίωμα της αποποίησης.

ΚΕΦΑΛΑΙΟ Η'
Κατάργηση και περάτωση της δίκης.

Άρθρο 293

1. Οι διάδικοι μπορούν σε κάθε στάση της δίκης να συμβιβάζονται, εφόσον συντρέχουν οι προϋποθέσεις του ουσιαστικού δικαίου. Ο συμβιβασμός γίνεται με δήλωση ενώπιον του δικαστηρίου ή του εισηγητή δικαστή ή συμβολαιογράφου και επιφέρει αυτοδίκαιη κατάργηση της δίκης. Ο συμβιβασμός αυτός, καθώς και εκείνος που περιέχεται στα πρακτικά των παραγράφων 3 του άρθρου 214Α και 5 του άρθρου 214Β, καλύπτει τον τύπο του συμβολαιογραφικού εγγράφου, που προβλέπεται από το ουσιαστικό δίκαιο, και μπορεί να χρησιμοποιηθεί ως τίτλος προς εγγραφή ή εξάλειψη υποθήκης.
2. Συμβιβασμός που έγινε με άλλο τρόπο δεν επιφέρει κατάργηση της δίκης και κρίνεται κατά τις διατάξεις του ουσιαστικού δικαίου.

Άρθρο 294

Ο ενάγων μπορεί να παραιτηθεί από το δικόγραφο της αγωγής χωρίς συναίνεση του εναγομένου πριν αυτός προχωρήσει στη συζήτηση της ουσίας της υπόθεσης και στην περίπτωση των άρθρων 237 και 238 πριν από την κατάθεση προτάσεων από τον εναγόμενο. Η παραίτηση που γίνεται αργότερα είναι απαράδεκτη, εφόσον ο εναγόμενος προβάλλει αντίρρηση και πιθανολογεί ότι έχει έννομο συμφέρον η δίκη να περατωθεί με έκδοση οριστικής απόφασης.

Άρθρο 295

1. Η παραίτηση από το δικόγραφο της αγωγής έχει ως αποτέλεσμα ότι η αγωγή θεωρείται πως δεν ασκήθηκε. Ο περιορισμός του αιτήματος θεωρείται ως μερική παραίτηση από το δικόγραφο.
2. Αν η αγωγή ασκηθεί πάλι, ο εναγόμενος μπορεί να αρνηθεί να απαντήσει στην αγωγή εωσότου καταβληθούν τα έξοδα της πρώτης δίκης, εκτός αν για την πρώτη δίκη είχε παραχωρηθεί στον ενάγοντα το ευεργέτημα της πενίας.

Άρθρο 296

Ο ενάγων μπορεί να παραιτηθεί από το δικαίωμα που ασκήθηκε με την αγωγή, εφόσον συντρέχουν οι προϋποθέσεις του ουσιαστικού δικαίου, χωρίς συναίνεση του εναγομένου. Η παραίτηση είναι απαράδεκτη, εφόσον ο εναγόμενος προβάλλει αντιρρήσεις και πιθανολογεί ότι έχει έννομο συμφέρον η δίκη να περατωθεί με έκδοση οριστικής απόφασης.

Article 291

1. The opponent of the party for whom the proceedings were interrupted and their joined party may cause the interrupted proceedings to be resumed, inviting that party [to resume the proceedings] by notifying a procedural document [to them] to that end. The above persons may notify the invitation even before the event that caused the interruption has been disclosed, taking the view that it has already occurred.
2. The proceedings automatically resume 30 days after the invitation was notified. This deadline may be extended for a maximum of six months by the judge and, in the case of a multi-member court, by the presiding judge, trying the matter under the procedure laid down in Articles 686 *et seq.*

Article 292

An heir, legatee or trustee may not be called upon to resume the interrupted proceedings before the deadline for repudiation [of an inheritance] lapses or before they lose the right of repudiation in any other manner.

CHAPTER VIII
Discontinuation and conclusion of proceedings

Article 293

1. Where the requirements of substantive law are met, the parties in the proceedings may enter into a settlement at any stage of the proceedings. The settlement shall be effected by means of a statement made before the court or the reporting judge or a notary public, and results in automatic discontinuation of the proceedings. This settlement, as well as the settlement entered in the transcript in accordance with Article 214A(3) and Article 214B(5), shall take the form of a notarial instrument provided for in substantive law, and may be used as a title for the registration or extinguishment of a mortgage.
2. A settlement reached in any other manner does not result in discontinuation of the proceedings, and shall be adjudicated in accordance with the provisions of substantive law.

Article 294

The plaintiff may discontinue the action without the consent of the defendant before the hearing on the merits of the case commences and, where Articles 237 and 238 apply, before the defendant files pleadings. Discontinuation effected at a later stage is be inadmissible if the defendant raises objections and argues, on the balance of probabilities, that they have a legitimate interest in the proceedings concluding and a final judgment being handed down.

Article 295

1. Discontinuation of an action results in the action being deemed never to have been filed. Reduction in the scope of the form of order sought shall be deemed partial discontinuation of the [action].
2. If the action is filed anew, the defendant may refuse to respond to the action until the costs of the first set of proceedings have been paid, unless the plaintiff had been granted legal aid for the first set of proceedings.

Article 296

Where the requirements of substantive law are met, the plaintiff may, without the consent of the defendant, waive the right exercised by filing the action. Discontinuation is inadmissible if the defendant raises objections and argues, on the balance of probabilities, that they have a legitimate interest in the proceedings concluding and a final judgment being handed down.

Άρθρο 297

Η παραίτηση κατά τα άρθρα 294 και 296 γίνεται ή με δήλωση που καταχωρίζεται στα πρακτικά ή με δικόγραφο που επιδίδεται στον αντίδικο του παραιτουμένου ή με δήλωση στις προτάσεις.

Άρθρο 298

Ο εναγόμενος μπορεί να αποδεχτεί την αγωγή αναγνωρίζοντας ολικά ή εν μέρει το δικαίωμα που έχει ασκηθεί με αυτήν, εφόσον συντρέχουν οι προϋποθέσεις κατά το ουσιαστικό δίκαιο. Η αποδοχή γίνεται είτε κατά το άρθρο 297 είτε σιωπηρά με πράξεις από τις οποίες συνάγεται σαφώς. Αν γίνει αποδοχή, εκδίδεται απόφαση σύμφωνα με αυτήν.

Άρθρο 299

Οι διατάξεις των άρθρων 294 έως 298 εφαρμόζονται και στην ανταγωγή, την κύρια και πρόσθετη παρέμβαση, την προσεπίκληση, την ανακοίνωση, τα ένδικα μέσα, την ανακοπή κατά εξώδικων και δικαστικών πράξεων, την τριτανακοπή και σε οποιαδήποτε άλλη διαδικαστική πράξη.

ΚΕΦΑΛΑΙΟ Θ'
Απόφαση.

Άρθρο 300

Η απόφαση εκδίδεται μόνο από το δικαστή που έλαβε μέρος στη σύνθεση του δικαστηρίου κατά τη συζήτηση, ύστερα από την οποία εκδίδεται, και στα πολυμελή δικαστήρια ύστερα από διάσκεψη και ψηφοφορία όλων των δικαστών που έλαβαν μέρος στη συζήτηση.

Άρθρο 301

1. Τη διάσκεψη τη διευθύνει ο πρόεδρος και την εισήγηση κάνει ο δικαστής που ο πρόεδρος όρισε εισηγητή· η διάσκεψη γίνεται είτε αμέσως μετά τη συζήτηση, είτε αργότερα, σε ημέρα που ορίζει ο πρόεδρος.
2. Τη σειρά της συζήτησης και της ψηφοφορίας ορίζει ο πρόεδρος.
3. Στην ψηφοφορία πρώτος ψηφίζει ο νεότερος κατά το διορισμό δικαστής, ύστερα ο αμέσως αρχαιότερος και τελευταίος ο πρόεδρος.

Άρθρο 302

1. Σε περίπτωση διαφωνίας επικρατεί η γνώμη της πλειοψηφίας. Αν το ζητήσει η μειοψηφία, η γνώμη της καταχωρίζεται στο αιτιολογικό της απόφασης με τον τύπο της αμφιβολίας, καθώς και στο πρακτικό της διάσκεψης. Στην απόφαση του Αρείου Πάγου καταχωρίζεται μόνο η γνώμη της πλειοψηφίας και στο πρακτικό της διάσκεψης η γνώμη της μειοψηφίας.
2. Αν κατά την ψηφοφορία σχηματιστούν περισσότερες από δύο γνώμες, εκείνοι που αποτελούν την ασθενέστερη μειοψηφία οφείλουν να προσχωρήσουν σε μία από τις επικρατέστερες γνώμες. Αν περισσότερες από τις ασθενέστερες γνώμες συγκεντρώνουν ισοψηφία, γίνεται ψηφοφορία για να αποκλειστεί η μία από αυτές και τότε εκείνοι που την ακολουθούν οφείλουν να προσχωρήσουν σε μία από τις άλλες γνώμες εωσότου σχηματιστεί πλειοψηφία.
3. Αν επέλθει ισοψηφία, προσλαμβάνεται και άλλος δικαστής και η υπόθεση συζητείται πάλι στο ακροατήριο.

Άρθρο 303

Αν στη διάσκεψη διχαστούν οι ψήφοι, συντάσσεται πρακτικό, που υπογράφεται από τον πρόεδρο, εκείνους που μειοψήφησαν και το γραμματέα. Αν κάποιος από αυτούς πέθανε ή έπαψε να είναι τοποθετημένος στο δικαστήριο ή έχει άδεια, αυτό αναφέρεται στο πρακτικό και υπογράφουν οι υπόλοιποι.

Article 297

Discontinuation in accordance with Articles 294 and 296 shall be effected by means of a statement recorded in the transcript, or a procedural document served on the opponent of the discontinuing party, or a statement in the pleadings.

Article 298

Where the requirements of substantive law are met, the defendant may accept the action by acknowledging the right thereby exercised in whole or in part. Acceptance shall take place either in accordance with Article 297 or tacitly by means of steps from which such acceptance can be clearly inferred. If acceptance takes place, a judgment shall be handed down in accordance with such acceptance.

Article 299

The provisions of Articles 294 to 298 also apply to cross-actions, main and permissive interventions, impleaders, third-party notices, legal remedies, oppositions against extra-judicial and judicial acts, third-party proceedings and any other procedural step.

CHAPTER IX
Judgment

Article 300

A judgment shall be handed down only by the judge who participated in the composition of the court during the hearing, after which a judgment is handed down, while at multi-member courts, a judgment shall be handed down after all the judges who participated in the hearing have deliberated and voted.

Article 301

1. Deliberations shall be directed by the presiding judge, and the report shall be presented by the reporting judge designated by the presiding judge; deliberations shall take place either immediately after the hearing or on a subsequent date to be set by the presiding judge.
2. The presiding judge shall determine the order of the hearing and the voting.
3. The most junior judge in order of appointment shall vote first, followed by the next most senior judge, with the presiding judge casting the final vote.

Article 302

1. Where opinions diverge, the majority opinion shall prevail. If requested by the minority, their opinion shall be recorded in the reasoning of the judgment in the form of doubts, as well as in the deliberation report. In Supreme Court judgments, only the majority opinion shall be recorded, while the minority opinion shall be recorded in the deliberation report.
2. If more than two [minority] opinions emerge during the voting process, those constituting the smallest minority must endorse one of the prevailing opinions. If there are several smaller [minority] opinions and they reach a tied vote, voting shall take place to exclude one of these opinions, and those who hold it shall be obligated to endorse one of the other opinions until a majority is reached.
3. In the event of a tied vote, an additional judge shall also be enlisted and the case shall be heard anew in court.

Article 303

If there a split vote during deliberations, a report shall be prepared, signed by the presiding judge, the dissenting judges and the registrar. If any of the above persons dies or no longer serves at that court or is on leave, this shall be noted in the report and it shall be signed by the others.

Άρθρο 304

1. Αφού περατωθεί η ψηφοφορία, ο εισηγητής δικαστής συντάσσει την απόφαση σε ηλεκτρονική μορφή. Αν πρόκειται για αποφάσεις του Μονομελούς Πρωτοδικείου και του Ειρηνοδικείου, την απόφαση συντάσσει σε ηλεκτρονική μορφή και ακολούθως χρονολογεί και υπογράφει την αποτύπωσή της σε υλική μορφή ο δικαστής που εκδίδει την απόφαση.
2. Η απόφαση της παραγράφου 1 δημοσιεύεται σε δημόσια συνεδρίαση. Ο δικαστής που παραδίδει την απόφαση σε ηλεκτρονική μορφή, παραδίδει ομοίως και το πρωτότυπο της απόφασης με πλήρες το περιεχόμενο που προβλέπεται στο άρθρο 305.

Άρθρο 305

Το πρωτότυπο της απόφασης πρέπει να αναφέρει:
1) τη σύνθεση του δικαστηρίου και, αν πρόκειται για πολυμελή δικαστήρια, το όνομα του εισηγητή δικαστή,
2) το ονοματεπώνυμο, το πατρώνυμο, την κατοικία, τη διεύθυνση και τον αριθμό φορολογικού μητρώου των διαδίκων και των νόμιμων αντιπροσώπων και αν πρόκειται για νομικά πρόσωπα την επωνυμία τους, τη διεύθυνση της έδρας τους και τον αριθμό φορολογικού μητρώου τους και αναφέρεται αν αυτοί έχουν παραστεί και αν υπέβαλαν προτάσεις,
3) το ονοματεπώνυμο, το πατρώνυμο, την κατοικία και τη διεύθυνση των δικαστικών πληρεξουσίων τους και σε περίπτωση που δικαστικός πληρεξούσιος παρίσταται ως εταίρος ή συνεργάτης δικηγορικής εταιρείας, κατά το άρθρο 55 του Κώδικα περί Δικηγόρων [ν. 4194/2013 (Α' 208)], αναγράφονται και η επωνυμία και η διεύθυνση της δικηγορικής εταιρείας,
4) σύντομη περίληψη του αντικειμένου και της πορείας της δίκης,
5) το αιτιολογικό και το διατακτικό της απόφασης και
6) ότι η απόφαση δημοσιεύθηκε.

Άρθρο 306

1. Όποιος είχε διευθύνει τη συζήτηση και ο γραμματέας υπογράφουν το πρωτότυπο της απόφασης.
2. Αν όποιος είχε διευθύνει τη συζήτηση πέθανε ή έπαψε να είναι τοποθετημένος στο δικαστήριο ή βρίσκεται σε άδεια, υπογράφει στη θέση του ο αρχαιότερος κατά το διορισμό από τους δικαστές που έλαβαν μέρος στη συζήτηση. Αν όλοι τους κωλύονται, υπογράφει ο προϊστάμενος του δικαστηρίου και, αν ούτε αυτός υπάρχει, υπογράφει μόνο ο γραμματέας.
3. Τα κωλύματα της παραγράφου 2 αναφέρονται στο πρωτότυπο της απόφασης.

Άρθρο 307

Αν για οποιονδήποτε λόγο που παρουσιάστηκε μετά το τέλος της συζήτησης είναι αδύνατο να εκδοθεί η απόφαση, η συζήτηση επαναλαμβάνεται αφού οριστεί νέα δικάσιμος και κοινοποιηθεί κλήση. Ο ορισμός της δικασίμου μπορεί να γίνει και η κλήση για τη συζήτηση μπορεί να κοινοποιηθεί με την επιμέλεια είτε κάποιου διαδίκου, είτε της γραμματείας του δικαστηρίου. Το ίδιο εφαρμόζεται και όταν το δικαστήριο διατάζει να επαναληφθεί η συζήτηση. Σε όλες τις πιο πάνω περιπτώσεις, οι κλήσεις για συζήτηση και τα αποδεικτικά της επίδοσης συντάσσονται ατελώς.
Μόλις συμπληρωθεί το οκτάμηνο, ο Πρόεδρος του Τριμελούς Συμβουλίου Επιθεώρησης των Δικαστηρίων επιλαμβάνεται και ερευνά αν είναι δικαιολογημένη ή μη η καθυστέρηση. Όταν αυτή κριθεί δικαιολογημένη, παρέχεται στον δικαστή προθεσμία δύο (2) μηνών για τη δημοσίευση των αποφάσεων που καθυστερούν πέραν του οκταμήνου. Σε περίπτωση αδικαιολόγητης καθυστέρησης, όπως και όταν παρέλθει η προθεσμία των δύο (2) μηνών που χορηγήθηκε, κατά το προηγούμενο εδάφιο, χωρίς να έχουν δημοσιευθεί οι αποφάσεις που καθυστερούν, ο δικαστής υποχρεούται να επιστρέψει τη δικογραφία, άλλως αυτή αφαιρείται αμέσως με πράξη του δικαστή που διευθύνει το δικαστήριο ή του Προέδρου του τριμελούς συμβουλίου διεύθυνσης αυτού. Για τις υποθέσεις αυτές ορίζεται δικάσιμος για νέα συζήτηση, υποχρεωτικώς, εντός τριών (3) μηνών για τις υποθέσεις ειδικών διαδικασιών και έξι (6) μηνών για τις υποθέσεις τακτικής διαδικασίας, από τη συμπλήρωση των παραπάνω προθεσμιών των οκτώ ή των δέκα (10) μηνών.

Article 304

1. Once voting has concluded, the reporting judge shall prepare the judgment in electronic form. In cases of judgments handed down by the single-member court of first instance and by the court of the peace, the judge handing down the judgment shall prepare it in electronic form, print it, date it and sign it.

2. The judgment referred to in paragraph 1 shall be handed down in open court. The judge delivering the judgement in electronic form shall also deliver the original judgment with the full content provided for in Article 305.

Article 305

The original judgment must set out:

1) the composition of the court and, in cases of multi-member courts, the name of the reporting judge;

2) the full name, father's name, place of domicile, address and tax identification number of [each of] the parties in the proceedings and the lawful proxies and, in cases of legal persons, their name, address of their registered offices and tax identification number, indicating whether they entered an appearance and whether they filed pleadings;

3) the full name, father's name, place of domicile and address of their advocates and, where the advocate is appearing as a partner or associate of a law firm, in accordance with Article 55 of the Lawyers' Code (Law 4194/2013, Government Gazette, Series I, Issue 208), the name and address of the law firm as well;

4) a short summary of the subject-matter and progress of the proceedings;

5) the reasoning and operative part of the judgment; and

6) the fact that the judgment was handed down.

Article 306

1. The person who directed the course of the hearing and the registrar shall sign the original judgment.

2. If the person who directed the course of the hearing dies or no longer serves at that court or is on leave, the most senior of the judges in order of appointment who participated in the hearing shall sign in their stead. If all such judges are indisposed, the judgment shall be signed by the head of the court and, absent such, only by the registrar.

3. The impediments referred to in paragraph 2 shall be indicated in the original judgment.

Article 307

If a judgment cannot be handed down for any reason which occurs after the hearing has ended, the hearing shall resume after a new hearing date has been set and a summons has been sent. The hearing date may be set and the summons for the hearing may be sent either by a party in the proceedings or by the court registry. This also applies where the court orders the re-opening of the hearing. In all the above cases, summonses for the hearing and proof of service shall be prepared free of official charges. Once eight months have elapsed, the chairperson of the Three-Member Court Inspection Council shall become seised of the matter and inquire into whether or not the delay is justified. Where it is deemed justified, the judge shall be given a two-month deadline to hand down judgments which were delayed by more than eight months. In cases of undue delay and when the two-month deadline given under the preceding subparagraph lapses without the judgments delayed having been handed down, the judge shall be obligated to return the case-file, otherwise it shall be removed immediately by means of a decision issued by the judge directing the court or the president of its three-member management board. After the above deadlines of eight or ten months have elapsed, a date shall be set for hearing these cases anew within three months for cases under special procedures, and six months for cases under the ordinary procedure.

Επιφυλασσομένων των διατάξεων των προηγούμενων εδαφίων, εάν διαπιστωθεί μετά το τέλος της συζήτησης ότι η διάσκεψη δεν μπορεί να ολοκληρωθεί εντός ευλόγου χρόνου για λόγους ανωτέρας βίας, όπως μεταξύ άλλων αναρρωτικής άδειας δικαστικού λειτουργού, μέλους της σύνθεσης του δικαστηρίου, ο δικαστής που διευθύνει το δικαστήριο ή ο Πρόεδρος του Τριμελούς Συμβουλίου Διοίκησης μπορεί να αποφασίσει την επανάληψη της συζήτησης. Στην περίπτωση αυτή εφαρμόζονται οι διατάξεις των προηγούμενων εδαφίων σχετικά με τον ορισμό δικασίμου, την κλήση προς συζήτηση και τα αποδεικτικά επίδοσης. Οι διάδικοι μπορούν να καταθέτουν συμπληρωματικές προτάσεις στο ακροατήριο, εφόσον είχαν παραστεί στην αρχική συζήτηση. Νέοι ισχυρισμοί και νέα αποδεικτικά μέσα δεν επιτρέπονται.

Άρθρο 308

1. Το δικαστήριο εκδίδει οριστική απόφαση, αν κρίνει πως η υπόθεση είναι ώριμη γι' αυτό. Συμφωνία των διαδίκων για μη έκδοση απόφασης μετά τη συζήτηση δεν παράγει έννομες συνέπειες.
2. Σε περίπτωση που σωρεύονται αγωγές ή που συνεκδικάζονται υποθέσεις, το δικαστήριο μπορεί, είτε να εκδώσει οριστική απόφαση για τις ώριμες υποθέσεις, είτε να αναβάλει να αποφασίσει οριστικά, εωσότου γίνουν όλες ώριμες, αν το κρίνει σκόπιμο για την καλύτερη διάγνωση της διαφοράς.

Άρθρο 309

Οι αποφάσεις που αποφαίνονται οριστικά σε κύρια ή παρεμπίπτουσα αίτηση δεν μπορούν μετά τη δημοσίευσή τους να ανακαλούνται από το δικαστήριο που τις εξέδωσε. Όσες δεν κρίνουν οριστικά μπορούν είτε αυτεπαγγέλτως είτε με πρόταση κάποιου διαδίκου που υποβάλλεται μόνο στη διάρκεια της συζήτησης της υπόθεσης και όχι αυτοτελώς, να ανακληθούν σε κάθε στάση της δίκης από το δικαστήριο που τις εξέδωσε εωσότου εκδοθεί οριστική απόφαση. Το δικαστήριο δεν έχει υποχρέωση να απαντά σε πρόταση για ανάκληση και όταν ακόμη αυτή υποβάλλεται με τρόπο παραδεκτό.

Άρθρο 310

1. Οι αποφάσεις επιδίδονται με επιμέλεια των διαδίκων.
2. Όταν πρόκειται για μη οριστικές αποφάσεις, η παρουσία κατά τη δημοσίευση των διαδίκων ή των νόμιμων αντιπροσώπων τους που διεξάγουν τη δίκη ή των πληρεξούσιων δικηγόρων τους ισοδυναμεί με επίδοση.

Άρθρο 311

[Καταργείται]

Άρθρο 312

1. Το περιεχόμενο της απόφασης αποτελεί πλήρη απόδειξη για ό,τι αφορά την εμφάνιση και την εκπροσώπηση των διαδίκων, για την προβολή προφορικά στο ακροατήριο ισχυρισμών και την υποβολή αιτήσεων καθώς και για τη γνώμη που έχει εκφέρει το δικαστήριο.
2. Η κατά την παράγραφο 1 αποδεικτική δύναμη του περιεχομένου της απόφασης μπορεί να ανατραπεί με το πρακτικό της συζήτησης ή με την προσβολή της απόφασης ως πλαστής.

Άρθρο 313

1. Μπορεί να επιδιωχθεί με αγωγή ή ένσταση η αναγνώριση της ανυπαρξίας μιας δικαστικής απόφασης μόνο στις ακόλουθες περιπτώσεις:
α) αν την εξέδωσαν πρόσωπα που δεν είχαν δικαστική ιδιότητα,
β) αν πολιτικό δικαστήριο αποφάσισε για αντικείμενο που δεν υπάγεται στη δικαιοδοσία των πολιτικών δικαστηρίων,
γ) αν δεν δημοσιεύθηκε,
δ) αν εκδόθηκε σε δίκη που είχε διεξαχθεί κατά ανύπαρκτου φυσικού ή νομικού προσώπου,
ε) αν εκδόθηκε κατά προσώπου που έχει το προνόμιο της ετεροδικίας.

Without prejudice to the provisions of the preceding subparagraphs, if it is found after the hearing has concluded that deliberations cannot be completed within a reasonable period of time due to force majeure, including but not limited to medical leave of a judicial functionary who sat on the bench, then the judge directing the court or the president of the three-member management board may order the re-opening of the hearing. In this case, the provisions of the preceding subparagraphs on setting a hearing date, the summons for the hearing and proof of service apply. The parties in the proceedings may file supplementary pleadings in court, provided they had entered an appearance during the initial hearing. New assertions and new means of evidence shall not be permitted.

Article 308

1. The court shall hand down a final judgment if it rules that proceedings have progressed sufficiently to enable it to do so. An agreement between the parties in the proceedings for no judgment to be handed down after the hearing generates no legal effects.
2. Where actions are cumulated or cases are joined, the court may either hand down a final judgment if proceedings have progressed sufficiently to enable it to do so, or defer handing down a final judgment until this is so, if it deems this expedient to better determine the dispute.

Article 309

Judgments making a final determination on main or incidental applications cannot be subsequently revoked by the court that handed them down. Judgments not containing a final ruling may, either *ex officio* or following a motion by a party in the proceedings made only during the hearing of the case and not separately, be revoked at any stage of the proceedings by the court that handed down them until such time as a final judgment is handed down. The court is not obligated to respond to a motion for revocation, even when made admissibly.

Article 310

1. Judgments shall be served by the parties in the proceedings.
2. In cases of non-final judgments, the presence of the parties in the proceedings or their lawful proxies initiating the proceedings or their authorised lawyers when the judgment is handed down is equivalent to service.

Article 311

[Repealed]

Article 312

1. The content of the judgment constitutes proof in full regarding the appearance and representation of the parties in the proceedings, the verbal presentation of assertions in court and the filing of applications, as well as the opinion expressed by the court.
2. The probative value of the content of the judgment referred to in paragraph 1 may be overturned by the hearing transcript or the authenticity of the judgment being contested.

Article 313

1. Acknowledgement of non-existence of a court judgment may be sought by means of an action or plea only in the following cases:
a) if it was handed down by persons not holding a judicial capacity;
b) if a civil court ruled on a matter that was not within the jurisdiction of the civil courts;
c) if it was not handed down;
d) if it was handed down during proceedings conducted against a non-existent natural or legal person;
e) if it was handed down against a person enjoying the privilege of immunity from jurisdiction.

2. Η αγωγή της παραγράφου 1 αποκλείεται αν η απόφαση έχει προσβληθεί με ένδικα μέσα.
3. Η αγωγή της παραγράφου 1 υπάγεται στο πολυμελές πρωτοδικείο της γενικής δωσιδικίας του εναγομένου.

Άρθρο 314

Το δικαστήριο που δικάζει την αγωγή του άρθρου 313 μπορεί ύστερα από αίτηση κάποιου διαδίκου, που μπορεί να υποβληθεί και με τις προτάσεις, να διατάξει να ανασταλεί η εκτέλεση της απόφασης, ολικά ή εν μέρει. Το δικαστήριο μπορεί, αν ένας διάδικος το ζητήσει με τον ίδιο τρόπο, να ανακαλέσει αυτή την απόφαση εωσότου εκδοθεί η οριστική απόφαση.

ΚΕΦΑΛΑΙΟ Ι'
Διαδικασία διόρθωσης και ερμηνείας αποφάσεων.

Άρθρο 315

Αν από παραδρομή κατά τη σύνταξη της απόφασης περιέχονται λάθη γραφικά ή λογιστικά ή το διατακτικό της διατυπώθηκε κατά τρόπο ελλιπή ή ανακριβώς, το δικαστήριο που την έχει εκδώσει μπορεί, αν το ζητήσει κάποιος διάδικος ή και αυτεπαγγέλτως, να τη διορθώσει με νέα απόφασή του.

Άρθρο 316

Αν απόφαση είναι διατυπωμένη με τρόπο που γεννά αμφιβολίες ή είναι ασαφής, το δικαστήριο που την έχει εκδώσει μπορεί, αν το ζητήσει κάποιος διάδικος, να την ερμηνεύσει με νέα του απόφαση έτσι που η έννοιά της να γίνει αναμφίβολη, η ερμηνεία όμως δεν μπορεί ποτέ να αλλάξει το διατακτικό της απόφασης που ερμηνεύεται.

Άρθρο 317

1. Η αίτηση διόρθωσης ή ερμηνείας μιας απόφασης πρέπει εκτός από όσα ορίζει το άρθρο 118, να αναφέρει με σαφήνεια και τα λάθη ή τις παραλείψεις ή τις ανακρίβειες που ζητείται να διορθωθούν η τα αμφίβολα σημεία ή τις ασάφειες που ζητείται να ερμηνευθούν.
2. Η αίτηση κατατίθεται στη γραμματεία του δικαστηρίου που εξέδωσε την απόφαση και συντάσσεται σχετική έκθεση.
3. Αν ο πρόεδρος ή ο δικαστής του μονομελούς πρωτοδικείου ή ο ειρηνοδίκης θεωρούν αναγκαίο να διορθωθεί η απόφαση, κινούν αυτεπαγγέλτως τη διαδικασία διόρθωσης.

Άρθρο 318

1. Η συζήτηση γίνεται κατά τη διαδικασία με την οποία εκδόθηκε η απόφαση που διορθώνεται ή ερμηνεύεται, και αφού κληθούν οκτώ (8) τουλάχιστον ημέρες πριν από τη συζήτηση όλοι οι διάδικοι που αναφέρονται στην απόφαση. Αν τη διόρθωση την προκαλεί το δικαστήριο αυτεπαγγέλτως, η κλήση των διαδίκων γίνεται με την επιμέλεια της γραμματείας του δικαστηρίου.
2. Αν κατά τη συζήτηση της αίτησης δεν εμφανίζεται κάποιος διάδικος που κλητεύθηκε νόμιμα, η διαδικασία προχωρεί σαν να ήταν παρόντες όλοι οι διάδικοι και, αν δεν κλητεύθηκε νόμιμα, η συζήτηση αναβάλλεται και το δικαστήριο διατάζει να κλητευθεί.

Άρθρο 319

Οι αποφάσεις που εκδίδονται σε αιτήσεις για διόρθωση ή ερμηνεία μιας απόφασης μπορούν να προσβληθούν με όλα τα ένδικα μέσα με τα οποία θα μπορούσε να προσβληθεί η απόφαση που ζητήθηκε να διορθωθεί ή να ερμηνευθεί, εκτός από την ανακοπή ερημοδικίας.

2. The action referred to in paragraph 1 shall be precluded if the judgment has [already] been contested by legal remedies.
3. The action referred to in paragraph 1 shall be filed with the multi-member court of first instance of the defendant's general forum.

Article 314

The court trying the action referred to in Article 313 may, following an application filed by a party in the proceedings that can also be submitted together with the pleadings, order stay of enforcement of the judgment, whether in whole or in part. If requested by a party in the proceedings in the same manner, the court may revoke this judgment until such time as a final judgment has been handed down.

CHAPTER X
Procedure for rectifying and interpreting judgments

Article 315

If the judgment erroneously contains lexical or mathematical errors made during its preparation or its operative part was worded incompletely or inaccurately, the court that handed down it may, if requested to do so by a party in the proceedings or *ex officio*, rectify it by means of a new judgment.

Article 316

If a judgment is worded in a manner that gives rise to doubts or is vague, the court that handed it down may, if requested to do so by a party in the proceedings, interpret it by means of a new judgment so that its meaning becomes unequivocal; however, the interpretation may never change the operative part of the judgment being interpreted.

Article 317

1. In addition to meeting the requirements laid down in Article 118, the application to rectify or interpret a judgment must clearly cite the errors, omissions or inaccuracies whose rectification is being requested or the uncertain or vague sections whose interpretation is being requested.
2. The application shall be filed with the registry of the court that handed down the judgment, and a relevant report shall be prepared.
3. If the presiding judge or the single-member court of first instance judge or the judge of the peace consider it necessary to rectify a judgment, they shall initiate the rectification procedure *ex officio*.

Article 318

1. The hearing shall be conducted in accordance with the procedure under which the judgment being rectified or interpreted was handed down, and after all the parties in the proceedings named in the judgment have been summoned at least eight days prior to the hearing. If rectification is initiated by the court *ex officio*, the parties in the proceedings shall be summoned by the court registry.
2. If a party in the proceedings who was duly summonsed fails to appear during the hearing of the application, the procedure shall go ahead as if all the parties in the proceedings were present, and if that party was not duly summonsed, the hearing shall be adjourned and the court shall order that person to be summonsed.

Article 319

Judgments handed down on applications to rectify or interpret a judgment may be contested by means of all legal remedies with which the judgment whose rectification or interpretation is being requested could be contested, save opposition against a default judgment.

Άρθρο 320

Η διορθωτική ή ερμηνευτική απόφαση σημειώνεται στο πρωτότυπο της απόφασης που διορθώνεται ή ερμηνεύεται, και πρέπει στα αντίγραφα, τα απόγραφα ή τα αποσπάσματά της να αναγράφεται ο αριθμός και η ημερομηνία της διορθωτικής ή ερμηνευτικής απόφασης.

ΚΕΦΑΛΑΙΟ ΙΑ'
Δεδικασμένον.

Άρθρο 321

Όσες οριστικές αποφάσεις των πολιτικών δικαστηρίων δεν μπορούν να προσβληθούν με ανακοπή ερημοδικίας και έφεση είναι τελεσίδικες και αποτελούν δεδικασμένο.

Άρθρο 322

1. Το δεδικασμένο εκτείνεται στο ουσιαστικό ζήτημα που κρίθηκε, αν η απόφαση έκρινε οριστικά για μια έννομη σχέση που έχει προβληθεί με αγωγή, ανταγωγή, κύρια παρέμβαση ή ένσταση συμψηφισμού. Το δεδικασμένο εκτείνεται επίσης και στο δικονομικό ζήτημα που κρίθηκε οριστικά.

2. Αν προβλήθηκε ένσταση συμψηφισμού, η απόφαση που αποφαίνεται για την ύπαρξη ή όχι της ανταπαίτησης η οποία προτάθηκε σε συμψηφισμό αποτελεί δεδικασμένο μόνο έως το ποσό για το οποίο προβλήθηκε η ένσταση του συμψηφισμού, εκτός αν κρίθηκε ολόκληρο το ποσό της ανταπαίτησης, οπότε το δεδικασμένο εκτείνεται σ' αυτό.

Άρθρο 323

Με την επιφύλαξη αυτών που ορίζουν διεθνείς συμβάσεις, απόφαση αλλοδαπού πολιτικού δικαστηρίου ισχύει και αποτελεί δεδικασμένο στην Ελλάδα χωρίς άλλη διαδικασία εφόσον

1) αποτελεί δεδικασμένο σύμφωνα με το δίκαιο του τόπου όπου εκδόθηκε,

2) η υπόθεση κατά τις διατάξεις του ελληνικού δικαίου υπαγόταν στη δικαιοδοσία των δικαστηρίων του κράτους στο οποίο ανήκει το δικαστήριο που εξέδωσε την απόφαση,

3) ο διάδικος που νικήθηκε δεν στερήθηκε το δικαίωμα της υπεράσπισης και γενικά της συμμετοχής στη δίκη, εκτός αν η στέρηση έγινε σύμφωνα με διάταξη που ισχύει και για τους υπηκόους του κράτους στο οποίο ανήκει το δικαστήριο που εξέδωσε την απόφαση,

4) δεν είναι αντίθετη προς απόφαση ελληνικού δικαστηρίου που εκδόθηκε στην ίδια υπόθεση και αποτελεί δεδικασμένο για τους διαδίκους μεταξύ των οποίων εκδόθηκε η απόφαση του αλλοδαπού δικαστηρίου και

5) δεν είναι αντίθετη προς τα χρηστά ήθη ή προς τη δημόσια τάξη.

Άρθρο 324

Δεδικασμένο υπάρχει μεταξύ των ίδιων προσώπων με την ίδια ιδιότητα μόνο για το δικαίωμα που κρίθηκε και εφόσον πρόκειται για το ίδιο αντικείμενο και την ίδια ιστορική και νομική αιτία.

Άρθρο 325

Το δεδικασμένο ισχύει υπέρ και κατά:

1) των διαδίκων,

2) εκείνων που έγιναν διάδοχοί τους όσο διαρκούσε η δίκη ή μετά το τέλος της,

3) εκείνων που νέμονται ή κατέχουν το επίδικο πράγμα στο όνομα κάποιου διαδίκου ή διαδόχου του, αδιάφορο αν πρόκειται για σχέσεις εμπράγματες ή ενοχικές. Το δεδικασμένο δεν ισχύει απέναντι σε εκείνον που απέκτησε δικαιώματα σύμφωνα με τις διατάξεις του ουσιαστικού δικαίου με μεταβίβαση από μη δικαιούχο.

Article 320

The rectifying or interpreting judgment shall be noted on the original judgment being rectified or interpreted, and its copies, enforcement precepts or excerpts must cite the number and date of the rectifying or interpreting judgment.

CHAPTER XI
Res judicata

Article 321

Final judgments that were handed down by the civil courts and cannot be contested by opposition against a default judgment and appeal are *de jure* non-appealable and have the force of *res judicata*.

Article 322

1. *Res judicata* extends to the fundamental issue ruled upon, if the judgment contained a definitive ruling on a legal relationship contested by means of an action, cross-action, main intervention or plea of offsetting. *Res judicata* also extends to the procedural matter definitively ruled upon.
2. If a plea of offsetting was raised, the judgment ruling on whether or not the cross-action whose offsetting was proposed exists has the force of *res judicata* only up to the amount for which the plea of offsetting was raised, unless the entire amount of the cross-action was ruled upon, in which case *res judicata* extends to that amount.

Article 323

Without prejudice to the provisions of international treaties and conventions, judgments handed down by foreign civil courts have effect and the force of *res judicata* in Greece without any further procedure if[:]
1) it has the force of *res judicata* under the law of the place where it was handed down;
2) the case, under the provisions of Greek law, fell under the jurisdiction of the courts of the state to which the court that handed down the judgment belongs;
3) the unsuccessful party in the proceedings was not deprived of the right to participate in the proceedings, unless such deprivation took place in accordance with a provision that also applies to the citizens of the state to which the court that handed down the judgment belongs;
4) it does not contravene a judgment handed down by a Greek court on the same case that has the force of *res judicata* for the parties in the proceedings for whom the judgment was handed down by the foreign court; and
5) it is not contrary to morality or public policy.

Article 324

Res judicata exists between the same persons [acting] in the same capacity only for the right ruled upon and provided it concerns the same subject-matter with the same factual background and legal cause.

Article 325

Res judicata functions in favour of and against:
1) the parties in the proceedings;
2) those who succeeded them during or after the proceedings;
3) those who, in the name of a party in the proceedings or their successor, have possession or detentorship of the thing at issue, whether or not it concerns real or contractual relationships. *Res judicata* does not function vis-à-vis persons who acquired rights under the provisions of substantive law by means of transfer from a person not entitled [to the thing in question].

Άρθρο 326

1. Η απόφαση που εκδόθηκε υπέρ του υπόχρεου να αποκαταστήσει κληρονομιά ή κληροδότημα και εναντίον ενός τρίτου, η οποία αφορά την περιουσία που υπόκειται σε αποκατάσταση ή κάποιο αντικείμενο της αποτελεί δεδικασμένο και υπέρ του καταπιστευματοδόχου.

2. Η απόφαση που εκδόθηκε κατά του υποχρέου να αποκαταστήσει κληρονομιά ή κληροδότημα και υπέρ ενός τρίτου, η οποία αφορά αντικείμενο της περιουσίας που υπόκειται σε αποκατάσταση, αποτελεί δεδικασμένο και κατά του καταπιστευματοδόχου μόνο αν εκείνος που έχει υποχρέωση να αποκαταστήσει έχει εξουσία να διαθέσει το επίδικο αντικείμενο χωρίς τη συναίνεση του καταπιστευματοδόχου.

Άρθρο 327

1. Η απόφαση που εκδόθηκε σε δίκη μεταξύ του κηδεμόνα σχολάζουσας κληρονομίας ή του εκκαθαριστή κληρονομίας ή του εκτελεστή διαθήκης που έχει δικαίωμα να διεξάγει τη δίκη και τρίτου, η οποία αφορά δικαιώματα ή υποχρεώσεις της κληρονομίας, αποτελεί δεδικασμένο και απέναντι στους κληρονόμους.

2. Η απόφαση που εκδόθηκε μεταξύ των κληρονόμων που έχουν δικαίωμα διεξαγωγής της δίκης και τρίτου, η οποία αφορά δικαιώματα και υποχρεώσεις της κληρονομίας, αποτελεί δεδικασμένο και απέναντι στον εκτελεστή της διαθήκης.

Άρθρο 328

1. Η απόφαση που εκδόθηκε μεταξύ του δανειστή και του πρωτοφειλέτη και απορρίπτει την αγωγή επειδή το χρέος είναι ανύπαρκτο, αποτελεί δεδικασμένο και υπέρ του εγγυητή.

2. Η απόφαση που εκδόθηκε μεταξύ του δανειστή και του εγγυητή και απορρίπτει την αγωγή επειδή το χρέος είναι ανύπαρκτο, αποτελεί δεδικασμένο και υπέρ του πρωτοφειλέτη.

Άρθρο 329

Η απόφαση που εκδόθηκε μεταξύ νομικού προσώπου και τρίτου και αφορά δικαιώματα ή υποχρεώσεις του νομικού προσώπου αποτελεί δεδικασμένο και απέναντι στα μέλη του ως προς τα δικαιώματα ή τις υποχρεώσεις του νομικού προσώπου.

Άρθρο 330

Το δεδικασμένο εκτείνεται στις ενστάσεις που προτάθηκαν, καθώς και σε εκείνες που μπορούσαν να προταθούν και δεν προτάθηκαν. Από τις ενστάσεις που δεν προτάθηκαν εξαιρούνται εκείνες που στηρίζονται σε αυτοτελές δικαίωμα που μπορεί να ασκηθεί και με κύρια αγωγή.

Άρθρο 331

Το δεδικασμένο εκτείνεται και στα ζητήματα που κρίθηκαν παρεμπιπτόντως και αποτελούν αναγκαία προϋπόθεση του κύριου ζητήματος, αν το δικαστήριο ήταν καθ' ύλην αρμόδιο να αποφασίσει για τα παρεμπίπτοντα αυτά ζητήματα.

Άρθρο 332

Το δεδικασμένο λαμβάνεται υπόψη από το δικαστήριο και αυτεπαγγέλτως.

Άρθρο 333

1. Οι διάδικοι και οι διάδοχοί τους δεν μπορούν να προσβάλουν την απόφαση για δόλο κάποιου διαδίκου ή τρίτου παρά μόνο στις περιπτώσεις κατά τις οποίες επιτρέπεται αναψηλάφηση.

2. Τρίτοι απέναντι στους οποίους ισχύει το δεδικασμένο μπορούν να το προσβάλουν μόνο εξαιτίας δόλου των διαδίκων.

Article 326

1. A judgment handed down in favour of a party liable for substitution of an heir or legatee and against a third party with regard to the estate subject to substitution or any part thereof also has the force of *res judicata* for the trustee.
2. A judgment handed down against a party liable for substitution of an heir or legatee and in favour of a third party, where this judgment concerns part of the estate subject to substitution, also has the force of *res judicata* against the trustee only if the person under a duty of substitution has the power to dispose of the part at issue without the consent of the trustee.

Article 327

1. A judgment handed down in proceedings between the curator of an unclaimed estate or the liquidator of an estate or the executor of a will who also has the right to bring proceedings against a third party concerning rights or obligations of the estate also has the force of *res judicata* vis-à-vis the heirs.
2. A judgment handed down [in proceedings] between heirs with the right to bring proceedings and a third party concerning rights and obligations of the estate also has the force of *res judicata* vis-à-vis the executor of the will.

Article 328

1. A judgment handed down [in proceedings] between a creditor and a principal debtor dismissing the action due to non-existence of the debt also has the force of *res judicata* for the guarantor.
2. A judgment handed down [in proceedings] between a creditor and a guarantor dismissing the action due to non-existence of the debt also has the force of *res judicata* for the principal debtor.

Article 329

A judgment handed down [in proceedings] between a legal person and a third party concerning rights or obligations of the legal person also has the force of *res judicata* vis-à-vis its members with regard to the rights or obligations of the legal person.

Article 330

Res judicata extends to the pleas raised, as well as those that could have been raised but were not. Of the pleas not raised, those relying on an independent right that can also be exercised through a main action are excluded.

Article 331

Res judicata also extends to the issues that were ruled upon incidentally and constitute a necessary condition for the principal issue, if the court had jurisdiction *ratione materiae* to rule on such incidental issues.

Article 332

The court shall also take *res judicata* into consideration *ex officio*.

Article 333

1. The parties in the proceedings and their successors may not contest a judgment on grounds of *dolus* by a party in the proceedings or a third party save only in cases where an application for re-opening is permitted.
2. Third parties to whom *res judicata* applies may only contest it on grounds of *dolus* by the parties in the proceedings.

Άρθρο 334

1. Κάθε διάδικος έχει δικαίωμα να ζητήσει να μεταρρυθμιστεί τελεσίδικη ή ανέκκλητη απόφαση, που καταδικάζει σε καταβολή περιοδικών παροχών, οι οποίες οφείλονται κατά το νόμο από οποιαδήποτε αιτία και γίνονται απαιτητές στο μέλλον, αν μεσολάβησε ουσιαστική μεταβολή των συνθηκών επάνω στις οποίες βασίστηκε η απαγγελία της καταδίκης. Το ίδιο ισχύει και για περιοδικές παροχές που οφείλονται σύμφωνα με κάποια δικαιοπραξία εφόσον το ποσό ή η διάρκεια της καταβολής τους ορίστηκε από το δικαστήριο, και μόνο για το ποσό ή τη διάρκειά της.
2. Μεταβολή των συνθηκών θεωρείται και η ουσιώδης μετά την απόφαση αυξομείωση του τιμαρίθμου της ζωής.
3. Η μεταβολή των συνθηκών λαμβάνεται υπόψη μόνο εφόσον έγινε σε χρόνο στον οποίο εκείνος που ζητεί να μεταρρυθμιστεί η απόφαση δεν μπορούσε να προβάλει τη μεταβολή στην αρχική δίκη.
4. Η μεταρρύθμιση μπορεί να ζητηθεί μόνο με αγωγή που εισάγεται στο αρμόδιο δικαστήριο.
5. Η μεταρρύθμιση μπορεί να ζητηθεί και να απαγγελθεί μόνο για το χρόνο μετά την έγερση της αγωγής.

ΚΕΦΑΛΑΙΟ ΙΒ'
Απόδειξη.

ΤΙΤΛΟΣ Ι.
Γενικές διατάξεις.

Άρθρο 335

Αντικείμενο απόδειξης είναι μόνο τα πραγματικά γεγονότα που έχουν ουσιώδη επιρροή στην έκβαση της δίκης.

Άρθρο 336

1. Πραγματικά γεγονότα τα οποία είναι τόσο πασίγνωστα ώστε να μην υπάρχει εύλογη αμφιβολία ότι είναι αληθινά λαμβάνονται υπόψη αυτεπαγγέλτως και χωρίς απόδειξη.
2. Πραγματικά γεγονότα γνωστά στο δικαστήριο από άλλη δικαστική ενέργειά του λαμβάνονται υπόψη αυτεπαγγέλτως και χωρίς απόδειξη, αν η αλήθεια τους ισχύει απέναντι σε όλους.
3. Με βάση αποδεδειγμένα πραγματικά γεγονότα το δικαστήριο μπορεί να βγάλει συμπεράσματα για άλλα γεγονότα.
4. Το δικαστήριο λαμβάνει αυτεπαγγέλτως υπόψη τα διδάγματα της κοινής πείρας και χωρίς απόδειξη.

Άρθρο 337

Το δικαστήριο λαμβάνει υπόψη αυτεπαγγέλτως και χωρίς απόδειξη το δίκαιο που ισχύει σε αλλοδαπή πολιτεία, τα έθιμα και τα συναλλακτικά ήθη και, αν δεν τα γνωρίζει, μπορεί να διατάξει απόδειξη ή να χρησιμοποιήσει όποιο μέσο κρίνει κατάλληλο χωρίς να περιορίζεται στις αποδείξεις που προσάγουν οι διάδικοι.

Άρθρο 338

1. Κάθε διάδικος οφείλει να αποδείξει τα πραγματικά γεγονότα που είναι αναγκαία για να υποστηρίξει την αυτοτελή αίτηση ή ανταίτησή του.
2. Όταν ο νόμος ορίζει κάποιο τεκμήριο για την ύπαρξη ενός πραγματικού γεγονότος, επιτρέπεται αντίθετη απόδειξη, αν δεν ορίζεται διαφορετικά.

Article 334

1. Any party in the proceedings may request that a *de facto* or *de jure* non-appealable judgment ordering periodically recurring dues which are owed by law on any grounds and which become payable in the future be amended if, in the interim, there was a supervening material change in the conditions on which the pronouncement of the judgment was based. This also applies to periodically recurring dues owed on the basis of a legal transaction, where the amount or duration of the dues was set by the court, and only with regard to the said amount or duration.
2. A material increase or decrease in the consumer price index shall also be deemed to be a change in conditions.
3. The change in conditions shall be taken into consideration only where it occurred at a time when the person requesting that the judgment be amended could not have pleaded the change during the initial proceedings.
4. The amendment may be requested only by means of an action filed with the competent court.
5. The amendment may be requested and pronounced only in relation to the period after the action was filed.

CHAPTER XII
Evidence

TITLE I
General provisions

Article 335

Only the actual facts exerting a material influence on the outcome of the proceeding shall be proven through the evidence-gathering process.

Article 336

1. Actual facts so widely known that there is no reasonable doubt that they are true shall be taken into consideration *ex officio* and without evidence.
2. Actual facts that are known to the court through other judicial steps it took shall be taken into consideration *ex officio* and without evidence if their factuality applies *erga omnes*.
3. The court may, on the basis of proven actual facts, draw conclusions regarding other facts.
4. The court shall take the teachings of common experience into consideration *ex officio* and without evidence.

Article 337

The court shall also take the law applicable in a foreign state, custom and business practices into consideration *ex officio* and without evidence and, if it is not aware of the foregoing, may order evidence or use any means deemed appropriate, without restricting itself to the evidence adduced by the parties in the proceedings.

Article 338

1. All parties in the proceedings are obligated to prove the actual facts necessary to support their standalone applications or cross-applications.
2. Where the law provides for a presumption on the existence of an actual fact, evidence to the contrary is permitted, unless otherwise provided for [in law].

Άρθρο 339

Αποδεικτικά μέσα είναι η ομολογία, η αυτοψία, η πραγματογνωμοσύνη, τα έγγραφα, η εξέταση των διαδίκων, οι μάρτυρες, τα δικαστικά τεκμήρια και οι ένορκες βεβαιώσεις.

Άρθρο 340

1. Το δικαστήριο λαμβάνει υπόψη τα αποδεικτικά μέσα που πληρούν τους όρους του νόμου, σύμφωνα με την προβλεπόμενη αποδεικτική δύναμη του καθενός. Λαμβάνει επίσης υπόψη και εκτιμά ελεύθερα και αποδεικτικά μέσα που δεν πληρούν τους όρους του νόμου, με την επιφύλαξη των άρθρων 393 και 394.

2. Εκτός από τις περιπτώσεις που ορίζει ρητά ο νόμος, το δικαστήριο κρίνει ελεύθερα τα αποδεικτικά μέσα και αποφασίζει κατά συνείδηση αν οι ισχυρισμοί είναι αληθινοί. Στην απόφαση πρέπει να αναφέρονται οι λόγοι που οδήγησαν το δικαστή να σχηματίσει την πεποίθηση του.

Άρθρα 341-345

[Καταργούνται]

Άρθρο 346

Τα αποδεικτικά μέσα που έχει προσκομίσει ένας διάδικος λαμβάνονται υπόψη από το δικαστήριο και για την απόδειξη των ισχυρισμών άλλου διαδίκου.

Άρθρο 347

Όπου ο νόμος θεωρεί αρκετή την πιθανολόγηση το δικαστήριο δεν έχει υποχρέωση να εφαρμόσει τις διατάξεις που ισχύουν για την αποδεικτική διαδικασία, τα αποδεικτικά μέσα και τη δύναμή τους, αλλά λαμβάνει υπόψη οποιαδήποτε μέσα κρίνει κατάλληλα για να σχηματιστεί πιθανότητα σχετικά με την αλήθεια των πραγματικών περιστατικών.

Άρθρο 348

Αν συμφωνούν οι διάδικοι ή υπάρχει κίνδυνος να χαθεί ή να δυσκολευθεί η χρήση κάποιου αποδεικτικού μέσου ή πρόκειται να διαπιστωθεί η τωρινή κατάσταση ενός πράγματος ή έργου, μπορεί να ζητηθεί να γίνει συντηρητική απόδειξη για συγκεκριμένο ισχυρισμό και πριν αρχίσει η δίκη.

Άρθρο 349

1. Η αίτηση για συντηρητική απόδειξη υποβάλλεται στο δικαστήριο το αρμόδιο να δικάσει την κύρια δίκη· αν ο κίνδυνος είναι άμεσος, μπορεί να υποβληθεί και σε κάθε άλλο δικαστήριο που μπορεί να αποφασίσει γρηγορότερα. Η αίτηση συζητείται κατά τη διαδικασία των άρθρων 686 επ. Όταν πρόκειται για πολυμελές δικαστήριο, τη δικάσιμο ορίζει ο πρόεδρος.

2. Η αίτηση πρέπει να περιέχει:

α) το όνομα και την κατοικία του αντιδίκου,

β) τα πραγματικά γεγονότα για τα οποία θα γίνει η συντηρητική απόδειξη,

γ) το αποδεικτικό μέσο με το οποίο θα διεξαχθεί,

δ) το λόγο για τον οποίο υπάρχει κίνδυνος να χαθεί ή να δυσκολευθεί η χρήση του αποδεικτικού μέσου. Ο λόγος αυτός αρκεί να πιθανολογείται.

Article 339

The means of evidence are admission, inspection, expert evidence, documents, examination of the parties in the proceedings, witness [testimony], judicial presumptions and affidavits.

Article 340

1. The court shall take into consideration the means of evidence that meet the requirements laid down in law, in accordance with the probative value of each means, as such is provided for [in law]. Without prejudice to Articles 393 and 394, the court shall also take into consideration and freely weigh up means of evidence that do not meet the requirements laid down in law.
2. Save in the cases expressly provided for in law, the court shall freely consider the means of evidence and rule on whether the assertions are true according to the best of its knowledge and belief. In [their] judgments, judges must cite the grounds that led them to form their [judicial] conviction.

Articles 341-345

[Repealed]

Article 346

Means of evidence adduced by one party in the proceedings shall also be taken into consideration by the court as evidence of the assertions made by a different party.

Article 347

Where the law considers the balance of probabilities test sufficient, the court shall not be obligated to apply the provisions on the taking of evidence, the means of evidence and their value, but shall take into account any means it considers suitable to establish probability concerning the truth of the actual facts.

Article 348

If the parties in the proceedings agree, or there is a risk of loss or difficulty in using some means of evidence, or the current state of a thing or work is to be ascertained, preservation/recording of evidence may be requested for a specific assertion even before the proceedings commence.

Article 349

1. The application for preservation/recording of evidence shall be filed with the court competent to hear the main proceedings and, where the risk is imminent, it may be filed with any other court that can issue a ruling more quickly. The application shall be heard in accordance with the procedure laid down in Articles 686 *et seq.* At multi-member courts, the hearing date shall be set by the presiding judge.
2. The application must contain:
a) the name and [address] of the opponent;
b) the actual facts regarding which preservation/recording of evidence shall be conducted;
c) the means of evidence by which evidence shall be preserved/recorded;
d) the reason for which there is a risk of loss or difficulty in using that means of evidence. The balance of probabilities test shall be sufficient with regard to this reason.

Άρθρο 350

1. Αν το δικαστήριο επιτρέψει τη συντηρητική απόδειξη, ορίζει με την απόφασή του τα πραγματικά γεγονότα για τα οποία θα διεξαχθεί, τα αποδεικτικά μέσα και το χρόνο μέσα στον οποίο πρέπει να περατωθεί, και, αν κρίνει ότι η κλήτευση του αντιδίκου είναι δυνατή, ορίζει και την προθεσμία της.
2. Αν η αίτηση έχει υποβληθεί σε δικαστήριο αναρμόδιο να δικάσει την κυρία δίκη, το δικαστήριο αυτό μπορεί, αν ο κίνδυνος δεν είναι άμεσος, να παραπέμψει την αίτηση στο δικαστήριο το αρμόδιο για την κύρια δίκη.

Άρθρο 351

Όταν δικάζει τη διαφορά, το δικαστήριο έχει υποχρέωση να λάβει υπόψη του τη συντηρητική απόδειξη που έχει διεξαχθεί, ανεξάρτητα από το αν ο κίνδυνος πραγματοποιήθηκε.

ΤΙΤΛΟΣ II.
Ομολογία

Άρθρο 352

1. Η ομολογία του διαδίκου, προφορική ή γραπτή, ενώπιον του δικαστηρίου που δικάζει τη δίκη ή του εντεταλμένου δικαστή, αποτελεί πλήρη απόδειξη εναντίον εκείνου που ομολόγησε.
2. Το δικαστήριο εκτιμά ελεύθερα την εξώδικη ομολογία.

Άρθρο 353

Η αποδεικτική δύναμη της ομολογίας δεν επηρεάζεται από το ότι, εκτός από το επιζήμιο πραγματικό γεγονός για εκείνον που ομολογεί, περιέχει και άλλο πραγματικό γεγονός που τον ωφελεί και αποτελεί αυτοτελή ισχυρισμό. Αν το πραγματικό γεγονός, το ωφέλιμο για εκείνον που ομολογεί, δεν είναι αυτοτελές, το δικαστήριο εκτιμά ελεύθερα την ομολογία.

Άρθρο 354

Όποιος ομολόγησε μπορεί να ανακαλέσει την ομολογία του μόνο αν αυτός αποδείξει ότι δεν ανταποκρίνεται στην αλήθεια.

ΤΙΤΛΟΣ III.
Αυτοψία

Άρθρο 355

Το δικαστήριο διατάζει αυτοψία αν θεωρεί αναγκαία την αντίληψη του αντικειμένου της απόδειξης με τις δικές του αισθήσεις.

Άρθρο 356

1. Το δικαστήριο που αποφασίζει να ενεργήσει αυτοψία μπορεί να διατάξει να γίνει ταυτόχρονα και πραγματογνωμοσύνη ή και εξέταση μαρτύρων.
2. Αν μαζί με την αυτοψία διατάχθηκε και πραγματογνωμοσύνη, ο διορισμός και η όρκιση των πραγματογνωμόνων μπορούν να γίνουν και κατά την αυτοψία από εκείνον που την ενεργεί.

Article 350

1. If the court permits the preservation/recording of evidence, it shall issue a ruling specifying the actual facts for which this shall take place, the means of evidence for which evidence shall be preserved/ recorded and the time within which this must be completed and, if it rules that it is possible to summons the opponent, shall set a deadline.
2. If the application is filed with a court that lacks jurisdiction to hear the main proceedings and if the risk is not imminent, that court may refer the application to the court with jurisdiction to hear the main proceedings.

Article 351

When trying the dispute, the court shall be obligated to take the preservation/recording of evidence ordered into consideration, regardless of whether or not the risk occurred.

TITLE II
Admission

Article 352

1. An admission made by a party in the proceedings, whether verbally or in writing, before the court conducting the proceedings or a delegated judge constitutes proof in full against the person making the admission.
2. Admissions made out of court shall be freely weighed up by the court.

Article 353

The probative value of an admission is not affected by the fact that it contains not only the adverse actual fact for the person making the admission, but also another actual fact that is beneficial for that person and constitutes a separate assertion. If the actual fact that is beneficial for the person making the admission is not separate, the court shall freely weigh up the admission.

Article 354

The person who made the admission may recant their admission only if they prove that the admission is not factual.

TITLE III
Inspection

Article 355

The court shall order an inspection if it considers this necessary [for the judges] to understand the subject-matter of the evidence using [their] own senses.

Article 356

1. The court that decides to conduct an inspection may also order the preparation of expert evidence or the examination of witnesses at the same time.
2. If the preparation of expert evidence was ordered together with the inspection, the experts may appointed and sworn in during the inspection by the person conducting it.

Άρθρο 357

Ο δικαστής που θα ενεργήσει την αυτοψία ορίζει τον τόπο, την ημέρα και την ώρα της διεξαγωγής της. Αν ο δικαστής που ενεργεί την αυτοψία ή, αν πρόκειται για πολυμελές δικαστήριο, ο πρόεδρός του, κρίνει πως είναι αδύνατο ή δύσκολο να μεταφερθεί το αντικείμενο της αυτοψίας στον τόπο των συνεδριάσεων, ορίζει τόπο κατάλληλο για τη διεξαγωγή της, όπου πηγαίνει εκείνος που την ενεργεί.

Άρθρο 358

Όποιος ενεργεί την αυτοψία μπορεί, αν το κρίνει σκόπιμο, κατά την ενέργειά της να καταρτίσει σχέδια ή ιχνογραφήματα, να πάρει φωτογραφίες ή άλλες απεικονίσεις ή να εφαρμόσει επιτόπου τίτλους ή να προβεί σε τεχνικές ενέργειες, είτε ο ίδιος είτε διαμέσου ενός υπαλλήλου της γραμματείας του δικαστηρίου ή του πραγματογνώμονα που είναι ήδη διορισμένος ή που διορίζεται γι' αυτό το σκοπό. Με τον ίδιο τρόπο μπορεί να κάνει και αναπαράσταση του αποδεικτέου γεγονότος και ενδεχομένως φωτογράφιση ή άλλη απεικόνιση της αναπαράστασης.

Άρθρο 359

1. Η αυτοψία, αν γίνεται στο ακροατήριο, αναφέρεται στα πρακτικά, ενώ, αν γίνεται έξω από το ακροατήριο, συντάσσεται σχετική έκθεση. Στα πρακτικά ή την έκθεση πρέπει να αναφέρεται το αντικείμενο της αυτοψίας, καθώς και η αντίληψη που σχημάτισε από την αυτοψία το δικαστήριο ή ο δικαστής.
2. Αν διορίστηκαν πραγματογνώμονες, πρέπει στα πρακτικά ή την έκθεση να αναγράφονται τα ονόματά τους, καθώς και αν αυτοί ενήργησαν την πραγματογνωμοσύνη. Επίσης πρέπει να αναφέρεται η γνωμοδότηση των πραγματογνωμόνων, εφόσον δεν την υπέβαλαν εγγράφως, οπότε αρκεί να γίνει αναφορά σ' αυτήν.
3. Αν εξετάστηκαν μάρτυρες, οι καταθέσεις τους πρέπει να περιλαμβάνονται στα πρακτικά ή την έκθεση.
4. Η γραπτή γνωμοδότηση των πραγματογνωμόνων, καθώς και τα τυχόν σχέδια, ιχνογραφήματα, φωτογραφίες, αναπαραστάσεις και γενικά τα βοηθήματα που το δικαστήριο ή ο δικαστής είχε υπόψη ενεργώντας την αυτοψία, επισυνάπτονται στα πρακτικά ή την έκθεση.

Άρθρο 360

Αν η αυτοψία γίνεται στο ακροατήριο, η υπόθεση συζητείται αμέσως κατόπιν. Αν γίνεται έξω από το ακροατήριο, η έκθεση που συντάσσεται για την αυτοψία κατατίθεται ή αποστέλλεται μαζί με τα συνημμένα της στη γραμματεία του δικαστηρίου που δικάζει την υπόθεση.

Άρθρο 361

Οι διάδικοι οφείλουν να βοηθούν για την ενέργεια της αυτοψίας και να κάνουν ό,τι είναι αναγκαίο για τη διεξαγωγή της.

Άρθρο 362

Αν αντικείμενο της αυτοψίας είναι διάδικος ή τρίτος, αυτός οφείλει να ανεχθεί την αυτοψία, εκτός αν συντρέχει σπουδαίος λόγος, και ιδίως αν θίγεται η υγεία ή η αξιοπρέπεια του, δεν μπορούν όμως να ληφθούν εναντίον του εξαναγκαστικά μέτρα. Εκείνος που ενεργεί την αυτοψία πρέπει να λάβει όλα τα μέτρα για να εξασφαλιστεί εντελώς η υγεία και η αξιοπρέπεια του προσώπου όσο γίνεται η αυτοψία.

Άρθρο 363

1. Αν αντικείμενο της αυτοψίας είναι κινητό που το κατέχει διάδικος ή τρίτος, αυτός οφείλει να το παρουσιάσει και να το επιδείξει σε εκείνον που ενεργεί την αυτοψία.
2. Αν αντικείμενο της αυτοψίας είναι ακίνητο που κατέχει διάδικος η τρίτος, αυτός έχει υποχρέωση να επιτρέψει την επίσκεψη του ακινήτου για να γίνει η αυτοψία. Επίσης ο διάδικος ή ο τρίτος που κατέχει ακίνητο οφείλει να επιτρέψει την επίσκεψη του αν μέσα στο ακίνητο βρίσκεται κινητό που είναι αντικείμενο αυτοψίας εφόσον η μεταφορά του είναι αδύνατη ή δύσκολη.

Article 357

The judge who will carry out the inspection shall set the place, date and time at which it will be conducted. If the judge conducting the inspection or, in the case of a multi-member court, its presiding judge, rules that it is impossible or difficult to transport who/what is being inspected to the place where the court sits, they shall designate a place suitable for the inspection to be conducted, and go there.

Article 358

During the inspection and where they deem it expedient, the person conducting the inspection may, either themselves or via a court clerk or an expert already appointed or specifically appointed for this purpose, prepare plans or sketches, take photographs or prepare other depictions or affix labels on site or take technical steps. The same person may re-enact the event to be proven or possibly take photographs or render any other depiction of the re-enactment in the same manner.

Article 359

1. Where the inspection is conducted in court, this shall be noted in the transcript, and where it is conducted out of court, a relevant report shall be prepared. The transcript or the report must mention the subject-matter of the inspection, as well as the view that the court or the judge formed as a result of the inspection.
2. If experts were appointed, the transcript or the report must mention their names and whether or not they were the ones who prepared the expert evidence. Furthermore, the opinion given by the experts must be mentioned, unless they submitted it in writing, in which case reference thereto shall suffice.
3. If witnesses were examined, their testimonies must be included in the transcript or the report.
4. The opinion given by experts in writing, as well as any plans, sketches, photographs, re-enactments and, generally, the aids taken into consideration by the court or the judge when conducting the inspection shall be attached to the transcript or the report.

Article 360

If the inspection is conducted in court, the case shall be heard immediately after [the inspection]. If the inspection is conducted out of court, the inspection report prepared shall be filed with or sent together with its attachments to the registry of the court trying the case.

Article 361

The parties in the proceedings are obligated to assist in carrying out the inspection and take any steps necessary for its conduct.

Article 362

If the inspection concerns a party in the proceedings or a third party, the person in question is obligated to tolerate the inspection, unless there are serious grounds and, in particular, if their health or dignity are prejudiced, but coercive measures may not be taken against them. The person conducting the inspection must take all measures to fully safeguard the health and dignity of the [aforesaid] person during the inspection.

Article 363

1. If the inspection concerns a movable held by a party in the proceedings or a third party, the person in question shall be obligated to produce and demonstrate it to the person conducting the inspection.
2. If the inspection concerns an immovable held by a party in the proceedings or a third party, the person in question shall be obligated to allow the immovable to be visited in order for the inspection to be conducted. Furthermore, the party in the proceedings or third party with detentorship of an immovable shall be obligated to allow the immovable to be visited if it contains a movable that is the subject of an inspection, where transporting it is impossible or difficult.

Άρθρο 364

Ο διάδικος ή τρίτος που κατέχει το αντικείμενο της αυτοψίας ή που είναι ο ίδιος αντικείμενο της αυτοψίας πρέπει τρεις ημέρες πριν ενεργηθεί η αυτοψία να κληθεί να παραστεί σ' αυτήν.

Άρθρο 365

1. Αν ο διάδικος ή ο τρίτος αρνείται για λόγο σπουδαίο κατά την κρίση εκείνου που ενεργεί την αυτοψία να παρουσιάσει και να επιδείξει ένα κινητό ή να επιτρέψει την επίσκεψη ενός ακινήτου ή να υποβάλει τον εαυτό του σε αυτοψία, η αυτοψία ματαιώνεται.

2. Αν ο διάδικος ή ο τρίτος που κατέχει το κινητό ή το ακίνητο δεν παρίσταται την ημέρα και ώρα που ορίστηκε για την αυτοψία ή αν εκείνος που την ενεργεί κρίνει πως αρνείται αδικαιολόγητα να παρουσιάσει και να επιδείξει το κινητό ή να επιτρέψει την επίσκεψη του ακινήτου, μπορεί με απόφαση που εκδίδει αμέσως να διατάξει να αφαιρεθεί βίαια το κινητό και να του προσκομιστεί ή να ανοιχθούν βίαια οι θύρες του ακινήτου για να γίνει η αυτοψία.

3. Η βίαιη αφαίρεση κινητού και η παρουσίασή του σ' αυτόν που ενεργεί την αυτοψία γίνεται κατά τις διατάξεις που ισχύουν για την αναγκαστική εκτέλεση από δικαστικό επιμελητή, που αμέσως μετά την αυτοψία επιστρέφει το κινητό στον κάτοχο, από τον οποίο το αφαίρεσε. Το βίαιο άνοιγμα των θυρών του ακινήτου γίνεται σύμφωνα με τις διατάξεις που ισχύουν για την αναγκαστική εκτέλεση.

4. Αν δεν είναι δυνατό να γίνει αμέσως η αφαίρεση του κινητού ή να ανοιχθούν οι θύρες, εκείνος που κάνει την αυτοψία μπορεί με απόφασή του που την εκδίδει αμέσως να αναβάλει την αυτοψία για ορισμένη ημέρα και ώρα στην οποία οι διάδικοι ή ο τρίτος οφείλουν να παραστούν χωρίς κλήτευση.

Άρθρο 366

Αν η αυτοψία δεν μπόρεσε να γίνει επειδή κάποιος διάδικος απουσίασε ή αρνήθηκε να φέρει και να επιδείξει το κινητό που κατέχει ή να επιτρέψει την επίσκεψη ακινήτου που βρίσκεται στην κατοχή του ή να υποβληθεί ο ίδιος σε αυτοψία, το δικαστήριο που αποφάσισε την αυτοψία κρίνει ελεύθερα αν το αντικείμενο της απόδειξης για το οποίο διατάχθηκε η αυτοψία πρέπει να θεωρηθεί αποδεδειγμένο.

Άρθρο 367

Διάδικοι ή τρίτοι που εμποδίζουν αδικαιολόγητα την αυτοψία με την απουσία τους την ημέρα και ώρα που ορίστηκε για την ενέργεια της ή με την άρνησή τους να φέρουν και να επιδείξουν ένα κινητό ή να επιτρέψουν την επίσκεψη ενός ακινήτου ή να υποβάλουν τον εαυτό τους σε αυτοψία καταδικάζονται σε αποζημίωση, στα δικαστικά έξοδα, καθώς και σε χρηματική ποινή κατά τις διατάξεις του άρθρου 205.

ΤΙΤΛΟΣ IV.
Πραγματογνωμοσύνη

Άρθρο 368

1. Το δικαστήριο μπορεί να διορίσει έναν ή περισσότερους πραγματογνώμονες, αν κρίνει πως πρόκειται για ζητήματα που απαιτούν για να γίνουν αντιληπτά ειδικές γνώσεις επιστήμης ή τέχνης.

2. Το δικαστήριο οφείλει να διορίσει πραγματογνώμονες, αν το ζητήσει κάποιος διάδικος και κρίνει ότι χρειάζονται ιδιάζουσες γνώσεις επιστήμης ή τέχνης.

Άρθρο 369

Οι πραγματογνώμονες βοηθούν το δικαστήριο με τη γνωμοδότησή τους στα ζητήματα που έθεσε. Αν είναι ανάγκη, το δικαστήριο διατάζει να παραστούν οι πραγματογνώμονες κατά την ενέργεια όλων ή ορισμένων διαδικαστικών πράξεων.

Article 364

The party in the proceedings or third party with detentorship of what is being inspected or who is themselves being inspected must be summoned three days beforehand to appear at the inspection.

Article 365

1. If the party in the proceedings or the third party refuses, on serious grounds acceptable to the person conducting the inspection, to produce and demonstrate a movable or to allow an immovable to be visited or to submit to inspection, the inspection shall be cancelled.
2. If the party in the proceedings or the third party with detentorship of the movable or the immovable is not present on the day and time set for the inspection or if the person conducting it considers that the party in question is unjustifiably refusing to produce and demonstrate the movable or to allow the immovable to be visited, the person conducting the inspection may issue a decision immediately ordering that the movable be forcibly removed and brought before them or that the doors of the immovable be forcibly opened in order to conduct the inspection.
3. The forcible removal of a movable and its presentation to the person conducting the inspection shall be carried out in accordance with the provisions applicable to compulsory enforcement by a court process server, who shall return the movable immediately after the inspection to the detentor from whom it was removed. The forcible opening of the doors of the immovable shall be carried out in accordance with the provisions applicable to compulsory enforcement.
4. If the movable cannot be removed or the doors cannot be opened immediately, the person conducting the inspection may issue a decision immediately ordering postponement of the inspection for a specific day and time on which the parties in the proceedings or the third party shall be obligated to appear without being summonsed.

Article 366

If the inspection could not be conducted because a party in the proceedings was absent or refused to bring and demonstrate the movable in their detentorship or allow the immovable in their detentorship to be visited or to submit to inspection, the court that ordered the inspection shall freely rule on whether the evidentiary issue for which inspection was ordered must be deemed to have been proven.

Article 367

Parties in the proceedings or third parties who unjustifiably obstruct the inspection through their absence on the day and time set for it being carried out, or their refusal to bring and demonstrate a movable, or allow an immovable to be visited, or submit to inspection shall be ordered to pay compensation, court costs and a monetary penalty in accordance with the provisions of Article 205.

TITLE IV
Expert evidence

Article 368

1. The court may appoint one or more experts where it considers that there are matters which, in order to be understood, require specialised knowledge of the state of the art [of the relevant discipline].
2. The court must appoint experts if so requested by a party in the proceedings and if it considers that specialised knowledge of the state of the art [of the relevant discipline] is required.

Article 369

Experts shall assist the court by providing an opinion on the issues put to them. Where necessary, the court shall order the experts to appear at all or certain of the procedural steps being taken.

Άρθρο 370

1. Το δικαστήριο που δικάζει την υπόθεση μπορεί να αναθέσει το διορισμό των πραγματογνωμόνων ή και τον ορισμό του αριθμού τους σε άλλο δικαστήριο, που ενεργεί σύμφωνα με αίτηση ή παραγγελία, ή σε εντεταλμένο δικαστή.

2. Τους πραγματογνώμονες μπορεί να τους αντικαταστήσει για εύλογη αιτία το δικαστήριο που τους διόρισε με αίτηση των διαδίκων ή αυτεπαγγέλτως κατά τη διαδικασία των άρθρων 686 επ.

Άρθρο 371

Σε κάθε δικαστήριο τηρείται κατάλογος πραγματογνωμόνων. Ο τρόπος που καταρτίζονται και τηρούνται οι κατάλογοι ορίζεται με διατάγματα, που εκδίδονται με πρόταση του Υπουργού της Δικαιοσύνης.

Άρθρο 372

Το δικαστήριο ορίζει τους πραγματογνώμονες από τον κατάλογο πραγματογνωμόνων, αν όμως δεν υπάρχει κατάλογος ή αν το δικαστήριο το κρίνει σκόπιμο, διορίζει τα πρόσωπα που κρίνει κατάλληλα για το σκοπό αυτόν.

Άρθρο 373

Δεν μπορούν να εγγραφούν στον κατάλογο πραγματογνωμόνων, ούτε να διοριστούν πραγματογνώμονες
1) όσοι καταδικάστηκαν για κακούργημα ή πλημμέλημα και στερήθηκαν τα πολιτικά τους δικαιώματα κατά τα άρθρα 59 έως 63 του Ποινικού Κώδικα, καθώς και όσοι παραπέμφθηκαν με βούλευμα για τέτοιες πράξεις,
2) όσοι στερήθηκαν την άδεια να ασκούν το επάγγελμά τους για όσο καιρό διαρκεί αυτή η στέρηση,
3) όσοι έχουν στερηθεί το δικαίωμα να διαθέτουν ελεύθερα την περιουσία τους,
4) οι δικαστές, οι εισαγγελείς και οι υπάλληλοι της γραμματείας των δικαστηρίων.

Άρθρο 374

Όσοι είναι γραμμένοι στον κατάλογο πραγματογνωμόνων, καθώς και όσοι ασκούν νόμιμα ένα επάγγελμα στον κύκλο του οποίου περιλαμβάνεται το θέμα της πραγματογνωμοσύνης, οφείλουν να εκτελέσουν τα καθήκοντα που τους αναθέτει η απόφαση· όσοι δεν ανήκουν σ' αυτές τις κατηγορίες μπορούν να αποποιηθούν το διορισμό τους, εφόσον δεν δήλωσαν πως τον δέχονται ή δεν έδωσαν το νόμιμο όρκο.

Άρθρο 375

Αντίγραφο της απόφασης που διορίζει ή αντικαθιστά πραγματογνώμονες κοινοποιείται μόλις δημοσιευθεί στους διαδίκους και τους πραγματογνώμονες με επιμέλεια της γραμματείας του δικαστηρίου ή του δικαστή που την έχει εκδώσει.

Άρθρο 376

Οι πραγματογνώμονες μπορούν να ζητήσουν οι ίδιοι να εξαιρεθούν, ή να εξαιρεθούν από διάδικο
1) αν συντρέχει κάποιος από τους λόγους του άρθρου 52 παρ. 1 εδ. α' έως γ' και στ',
2) αν είναι δημόσιοι υπάλληλοι και η προϊσταμένη τους αρχή τους απαγόρευσε εγγράφως να ενεργήσουν την πραγματογνωμοσύνη για λόγους που αφορούν την υπηρεσία τους,
3) αν συντρέχει άλλος σπουδαίος λόγος.

Άρθρο 377

1. Την εξαίρεση την προτείνει ο πραγματογνώμονας ή ένας από τους διαδίκους με γραπτή αίτηση που υποβάλλεται στο δικαστήριο ή στον εντεταλμένο δικαστή που διόρισε τους πραγματογνώμονες. Η αίτηση κατατίθεται στη γραμματεία του δικαστηρίου μέσα σε πέντε ημέρες αφότου κοινοποιήθηκε η απόφαση που διορίζει τους πραγματογνώμονες. Αργότερα η αίτηση για εξαίρεση είναι απαράδεκτη, εκτός αν ο λόγος της εξαίρεσης προέκυψε κατόπιν.

2. Η αίτηση για εξαίρεση μπορεί να γίνει και με δήλωση στη γραμματεία του δικαστηρίου ή στον εντεταλμένο δικαστή που διορίζει τους πραγματογνώμονες.

3. Η αίτηση για εξαίρεση πρέπει να περιέχει τους λόγους της εξαίρεσης, αλλιώς είναι απαράδεκτη.

Article 370

1. The court trying the case may assign the appointment of experts or the determination of their number to a different court acting on an application or order, or to a delegated judge.
2. Experts may be substituted for a serious reason by the court that appointed them on an application by the parties in the proceedings or *ex officio* in accordance with the procedure laid down in Articles 686 *et seq.*

Article 371

A list of experts shall be kept at every court. The manner in which lists are prepared and kept shall be specified in decrees issued on a proposal from the Minister of Justice.

Article 372

The court shall designate experts from the list of experts, but if there is no list or where it so deems expedient, the court shall appoint the persons deemed suitable for this purpose.

Article 373

The following persons may not be included in the list of experts or be appointed as experts[:]
1) those convicted of a felony or misdemeanour and deprived of their civil rights under Articles 59 to 63 of the Penal Code, and those committed to trial on the basis of a judicial council decision for such acts;
2) those deprived of the licence to engage in their profession for the duration of the said deprivation;
3) those deprived of the right to freely dispose of their property;
4) judges, public prosecutors and court registry clerks.

Article 374

Those included in the list of experts and those who lawfully engage in a profession relevant to the expert evidence shall be obligated to perform the duties assigned in the decision. Those who do not fall into the above categories may renounce their appointment if they have not declared that they accept it or have not taken the oath prescribed by law.

Article 375

Upon being issued, a copy of the decision appointing or substituting experts shall be communicated to the parties in the proceedings and the experts by the registry of the court or by the judge who issued it.

Article 376

Experts themselves or a party in the proceedings may request that such experts be exempted[:]
1) if any of the grounds referred to in Article 52(1)(a) to (c) and (f) apply;
2) if they are civil servants and they were prohibited in writing by their superiors from preparing expert evidence on service-related grounds;
3) if other serious grounds apply.

Article 377

1. The exemption shall be requested by the expert or a party in the proceedings by means of an application in writing filed with the court which or the delegated judge who appointed the experts. The application shall be filed with the court registry within five days of notification of the decision appointing the experts. Subsequent applications for exemption are inadmissible, unless the grounds for exemption arose at a later time.
2. The application for exemption may also be effected by means of a declaration made to the registry of the court which or the delegated judge who appointed the experts.
3. On penalty of inadmissibility, the application for exemption must contain the grounds for exemption.

Άρθρο 378

1. Η αίτηση για εξαίρεση εισάγεται για να συζητηθεί στο δικαστήριο ή στον εντεταλμένο δικαστή που διόρισε τους πραγματογνώμονες, και δικάζεται κατά τη διαδικασία των άρθρων 686 επ.· όταν πρόκειται για πολυμελές δικαστήριο, τη δικάσιμο ορίζει ο πρόεδρος.
2. Αν η εξαίρεση γίνει δεκτή, το δικαστήριο ή ο εντεταλμένος δικαστής διορίζει με την ίδια απόφαση άλλον πραγματογνώμονα για να αντικαταστήσει εκείνον που εξαιρέθηκε.

Άρθρο 379

1. Το δικαστήριο που δικάζει την υπόθεση δίνει στους πραγματογνώμονες τις αναγκαίες οδηγίες για τον τρόπο με τον οποίο θα εκτελέσουν τα καθήκοντά τους και ορίζει ιδίως
α) αν κρίνει αναγκαίο να παραστούν σε διαδικαστικές πράξεις και σε ποιες,
β) αν η πραγματογνωμοσύνη θα ενεργηθεί ενώπιόν του ή από μόνους τους πραγματογνώμονες.
2. Τις εξουσίες της παραγράφου 1 έχει και το δικαστήριο που ύστερα από αίτηση ή παραγγελία ενεργεί διαδικαστικές πράξεις που αναφέρονται στην πραγματογνωμοσύνη ή ο εντεταλμένος δικαστής, εφόσον δεν όρισε διαφορετικά το δικαστήριο που δικάζει την υπόθεση.

Άρθρο 380

1. Οι πραγματογνώμονες μπορούν να λάβουν γνώση των στοιχείων της δικογραφίας που είναι χρήσιμα για τη διεξαγωγή της πραγματογνωμοσύνης.
2. Το δικαστήριο του άρθρου 379 ή ο δικαστής μπορούν να επιτρέψουν στους πραγματογνώμονες να ζητήσουν, πριν συντάξουν τη γνωμοδότησή τους, διευκρινίσεις από τους διαδίκους ή πληροφορίες από τρίτους ή να καταρτίσουν σχέδια ή ιχνογραφήματα, να πάρουν φωτογραφίες ή άλλες απεικονίσεις ή να κάνουν επιτόπια εφαρμογή τίτλων ή τεχνικές ενέργειες ή να εξετάσουν έγγραφα ή βιβλία εμπόρων ή επαγγελματιών.

Άρθρο 381

Τις αποφάσεις των άρθρων 379 και 380 παρ. 2 τις λαμβάνει το δικαστήριο ύστερα από αίτηση των διαδίκων ή των πραγματογνωμόνων ή και αυτεπαγγέλτως, χωρίς να κλητευθούν προηγουμένως οι διάδικοι ή οι πραγματογνώμονες.

Άρθρο 382

1. Αν το δικαστήριο διέταξε να παραστούν οι πραγματογνώμονες κατά την ενέργεια ορισμένων διαδικαστικών πράξεων, τους κοινοποιείται πριν από τρεις ημέρες κλήση για να παραστούν σ' αυτές.
2. Οι πραγματογνώμονες, όταν παρίστανται στις συνεδριάσεις, έχουν δικαίωμα με την άδεια εκείνου που διευθύνει τη συζήτηση να υποβάλουν ερωτήσεις στους διαδίκους, τους νόμιμους αντιπροσώπους τους και τους μάρτυρες και να ζητούν να διαβαστούν έγγραφα.

Άρθρο 383
Γνωμοδότηση πραγματογνωμόνων - Στοιχεία που πρέπει να περιέχει. Κατάθεση της εκθέσεως πραγματογνωμοσύνης.

1. Αν διατάχθηκε έγγραφη γνωμοδότηση, το δικαστήριο ορίζει προθεσμία μέσα στην οποία πρέπει να την υποβάλουν οι πραγματογνώμονες. Ο δικαστής ή στα πολυμελή δικαστήρια ο πρόεδρος του δικαστηρίου μπορούν, αν το ζητήσουν οι πραγματογνώμονες, χωρίς την προηγούμενη κλήτευση των διαδίκων, να παρατείνουν την προθεσμία, αν κρίνουν ότι δεν είναι αρκετή για να καταρτιστεί η γνωμοδότηση.
2. Αν υπάρχουν περισσότεροι πραγματογνώμονες, ενεργούν όλες τις πράξεις που χρειάζονται για την πραγματογνωμοσύνη και καταρτίζουν τη γραπτή τους γνωμοδότηση από κοινού. Για το σκοπό αυτόν συνέρχονται, όταν τους καλεί οποιοσδήποτε από αυτούς.

Article 378

1. The application for exemption shall be brought for a hearing before the court that or the delegated judge who appointed the experts, and shall be tried under the procedure laid down in Articles 686 *et seq.* In the case of a multi-member court, the hearing date shall be set by the presiding judge.
2. If the exemption is accepted, the court or the delegated judge shall appoint a different expert to substitute the one exempted in that same decision.

Article 379

1. The court trying the case shall provide the experts with the necessary instructions on how they will perform their duties and shall specify, in particular[:]
a) whether it deems their appearance during procedural steps necessary and, if so, during which steps;
b) whether the expert evidence shall be prepared in the presence of the court or by the experts alone.
2. Unless otherwise specified by the court trying the case, the powers referred to in paragraph 1 shall also be vested in the court which, following an application or an order, shall take procedural steps which concern the expert evidence, or in the delegated judge.

Article 380

1. Experts may take cognisance of the information in the case-file useful for preparing the expert evidence.
2. The court referred to in Article 379 or the judge may allow the experts, prior to preparing their opinion, to request clarifications from the parties in the proceedings or information from third parties or prepare plans or sketches, take photographs or prepare other depictions, or affix labels on site or take technical steps or examine documents or ledgers held by merchants or professionals.

Article 381

The court shall issue the decisions referred to in Articles 379 and 380(2) following an application by the parties in the proceedings or the experts or *ex officio*, without summonsing the parties in the proceedings or the experts beforehand.

Article 382

1. If the court ordered the experts to appear during specific procedural steps, a summons to appear shall be notified to them three days beforehand.
2. When appearing at sittings, experts have the right, with the permission of the person directing the course of the hearing, to put questions to the parties in the proceedings, their lawful proxies and the witnesses, and to request that documents be read out.

Article 383

Expert opinions - Information they must contain. Filing of the expert evidence report.

1. If a written opinion was ordered, the court shall set a date within which the experts must submit this opinion. The judge or, in cases of multi-member courts, the presiding judge of the court may, if so requested by the experts and without previously summonsing the parties in the proceedings, extend the deadline if the judge considers that it does not suffice for the opinion to be prepared.
2. If there are several experts, they shall take all the steps required for the preparation of expert evidence and prepare their written opinion jointly. To this end, the experts shall convene a meeting when called by any one of them.

3. Η έγγραφη γνωμοδότηση πρέπει να αναφέρει τις ενέργειες των πραγματογνωμόνων και τη γνώμη καθενός αιτιολογημένη, και να υπογράφεται από αυτούς. Αν κάποιος ή κάποιοι από τους πραγματογνώμονες δεν παρουσιάζονται όταν γίνεται η πραγματογνωμοσύνη ή αρνούνται να υπογράψουν την έγγραφη γνωμοδότηση, αυτό σημειώνεται στη γνωμοδότηση.
4. Η έγγραφη γνωμοδότηση κατατίθεται από τους πραγματογνώμονες ή από εκείνον που εξουσιοδότησαν γι' αυτό στη γραμματεία του δικαστηρίου που τους διόρισε και συντάσσεται σχετική έκθεση. Αν η γνωμοδότηση κατατέθηκε στη γραμματεία του δικαστηρίου που ενεργεί ύστερα από αίτηση ή παραγγελία ή του δικαστηρίου όπου υπηρετεί ο εντεταλμένος δικαστής, η έκθεση στέλνεται αμέσως στη γραμματεία του δικαστηρίου που δικάζει την υπόθεση.

Άρθρο 384

Το δικαστήριο ή ο δικαστής του άρθρου 379 μπορούν, αφού οι πραγματογνώμονες υποβάλουν τη γνωμοδότηση τους, να διατάξουν να δοθούν γι' αυτήν διευκρινίσεις ή άλλες πληροφορίες, οπότε εφαρμόζονται τα άρθρα 382 και 383.

Άρθρο 385

1. Πριν από κάθε ενέργεια οι πραγματογνώμονες ορκίζονται σύμφωνα με τις διακρίσεις του άρθρου 408, ότι θα εκτελέσουν ευσυνειδήτως τα καθήκοντά τους.
2. Η όρκιση των πραγματογνωμόνων γίνεται ενώπιον του δικαστηρίου που δικάζει την υπόθεση ή του δικαστηρίου ή του δικαστή που ορίζεται από το πρώτο, και συντάσσεται έκθεση γι' αυτήν.

Άρθρο 386

Αν ο διορισμένος πραγματογνώμονας οφείλει να εκτελέσει τα καθήκοντα που του ανατέθηκαν και αρνηθεί αδικαιολόγητα ή παραλείψει οποτεδήποτε να τα εκτελέσει, εκτός από την υποχρέωσή του για αποζημίωση, καταδικάζεται χωρίς κλήτευση ύστερα από αίτηση κάποιου διαδίκου, από το δικαστήριο που δικάζει την υπόθεση ή το δικαστήριο ή το δικαστή που τον διόρισε, στα δικαστικά έξοδα με τα οποία ο διάδικος που έκανε την αίτηση επιβαρύνεται εξαιτίας της αποχής ή της άρνησης του πραγματογνώμονα. Το δικαστήριο μπορεί να επιβάλει αυτεπαγγέλτως και χρηματική ποινή σύμφωνα με τις διατάξεις του άρθρου 205.

Άρθρο 387

Το δικαστήριο εκτιμά ελεύθερα τη γνωμοδότηση των πραγματογνωμόνων.

Άρθρο 388

Το δικαστήριο που δικάζει την υπόθεση, αν κρίνει πως υπάρχει λόγος, μπορεί ύστερα από αίτηση των διαδίκων ή και αυτεπαγγέλτως να διατάξει νέα πραγματογνωμοσύνη ή την επανάληψη ή τη συμπλήρωση της πραγματογνωμοσύνης από τους ίδιους ή άλλους πραγματογνώμονες.

Άρθρο 389

[Καταργείται]

Άρθρο 390

Το δικαστήριο εκτιμά ελεύθερα τις γνωμοδοτήσεις προσώπων που έχουν ειδικές γνώσεις επιστήμης ή τέχνης σε ζητήματα που αφορούν εκκρεμή δίκη, οι οποίες συντάχθηκαν ύστερα από αίτηση κάποιου διαδίκου και προσάγονται από αυτόν.

Άρθρο 391

1. Αν το δικαστήριο διορίζει πραγματογνώμονες, κάθε διάδικος μπορεί να διορίσει από ένα τεχνικό σύμβουλο που έχει την ικανότητα να διοριστεί πραγματογνώμονας.
2. Ο τεχνικός σύμβουλος που διορίζεται από τους διαδίκους δεν είναι υποχρεωμένος να αποδεχτεί το διορισμό και η αμοιβή του πληρώνεται από το διάδικο που τον διόρισε.

3. The written opinion must mention the steps taken by the experts and the reasoned opinion of each one, and must be signed by them. If one or more of the experts fail to appear during the preparation of the expert evidence or refuse to sign the written opinion, this shall be noted in the opinion.
4. The written opinion shall be filed by the experts or the person authorised by them with the registry of the court that appointed them, and a relevant report shall be prepared. If the opinion was filed with the registry of the court acting on an application or order or with the registry of the court where the delegated judge serves, the report shall be sent immediately to the registry of the court trying the case.

Article 384

Once the experts have submitted their opinion, the court or the judge referred to in Article 379 may order that they provide clarifications or other information, in which case Articles 382 and 383 apply.

Article 385

1. Before taking any action, experts shall take an oath, according to the distinctions set forth in Article 408, to conscientiously perform their duties.
2. Experts shall take an oath before the court trying the case or the court or judge appointed by the first court, and a report on the oath-taking shall be prepared.

Article 386

If the expert appointed is obligated to perform the duties assigned to them and unjustifiably refuses or fails to perform them at any time, in addition to their obligation to pay compensation, they shall be ordered, without being summonsed and following an application filed by a party in the proceedings, by the court trying the case or the court or judge who appointed them, to pay the court costs incurred by the party that filed the application due to the expert's abstention or refusal. The court may also impose a monetary penalty *ex officio* in accordance with the provisions of Article 205.

Article 387

The court shall freely weigh up the opinion provided by the experts.

Article 388

Where it considers that there are grounds for doing so, the court trying the case may, following an application filed by the parties in the proceedings or *ex officio*, order the preparation of new expert evidence or repetition or supplementation of the expert evidence by the same or other experts.

Article 389

[Repealed]

Article 390

The court shall freely weigh up the opinions provided by persons with specialised knowledge of the state of the art [of the relevant discipline], with regard to matters concerning pending proceedings, that were prepared following an application filed by a party in the proceedings and are adduced by that party.

Article 391

1. If the court appoints experts, each party in the proceedings may appoint [only] one technical advisor qualified to be appointed as an expert.
2. The technical advisor appointed by [each] party in the proceedings is not obligated to accept their appointment, and their fee shall be paid by the party who appointed them.

Άρθρο 392

1. Ο διορισμός των τεχνικών συμβούλων γίνεται εγγράφως ή προφορικώς με δήλωση, είτε ενώπιον του δικαστηρίου ή του εντεταλμένου δικαστή, η οποία καταχωρίζεται στα πρακτικά ή στην έκθεση, είτε ενώπιον της γραμματείας του δικαστηρίου και συντάσσεται έκθεση.

2. Οι τεχνικοί σύμβουλοι των διαδίκων τους βοηθούν με τις τεχνικές γνώσεις τους, μπορούν να παρίστανται σε όλες τις διαδικαστικές πράξεις όπου παρίστανται οι πραγματογνώμονες, και έχουν τις εξουσίες των άρθρων 380 παρ. 1 και 382 παρ. 2.

3. Οι τεχνικοί σύμβουλοι των διαδίκων μπορούν, αφού οι πραγματογνώμονες υποβάλουν τη γνωμοδότησή τους και πριν συζητηθεί η υπόθεση, να αναπτύξουν τις γνώμες τους για τη γνωμοδότηση των πραγματογνωμόνων προφορικά ενώπιον του δικαστηρίου ή να τις υποβάλλουν εγγράφως, καθώς και να υποβάλουν ερωτήσεις και στους πραγματογνώμονες.

ΤΙΤΛΟΣ V.
Μάρτυρες

Άρθρο 393

1. Δεν επιτρέπεται να αποδειχθούν με μάρτυρες συμβάσεις ή συλλογικές πράξεις, καθώς και πρόσθετα σύμφωνα, προγενέστερα, σύγχρονα ή μεταγενέστερα δικαιοπραξίας που έχει συνταχθεί εγγράφως όταν η αξία του αντικειμένου τους υπερβαίνει τα τριάντα χιλιάδες (30.000) ευρώ, έστω και αν δεν είναι αντίθετα προς το περιεχόμενο του εγγράφου.

2. Δεν επιτρέπεται η απόδειξη με μάρτυρες κατά του περιεχομένου εγγράφου.

3. Η εξέταση των μαρτύρων μπορεί να γίνει και με τηλεδιάσκεψη.

Άρθρο 394

1. Εξαιρετικά επιτρέπεται η απόδειξη με μάρτυρες:
α) αν υπάρχει αρχή έγγραφης απόδειξης που πηγάζει από έγγραφο που έχει αποδεικτική δύναμη,
β) αν υπήρχε φυσική ή ηθική αδυναμία να αποκτηθεί έγγραφο,
γ) αν αποδεικνύεται ότι το έγγραφο που είχε συνταχθεί χάθηκε τυχαία, και
δ) αν από την φύση της δικαιοπραξίας ή τις ειδικές συνθήκες κάτω από τις οποίες έγινε και ιδίως όταν πρόκειται για εμπορικές συναλλαγές, δικαιολογείται η απόδειξη με μάρτυρες.

2. Όταν ο νόμος ή τα μέρη ορίζουν ότι για τη δικαιοπραξία χρειάζεται έγγραφο είτε ως συστατικός είτε ως αποδεικτικός τύπος, η απόδειξη της δικαιοπραξίας με μάρτυρες επιτρέπεται μόνο στην περίπτωση της παραγράφου 1 εδάφ. γ'.

Άρθρο 395

Όταν η απόδειξη με μάρτυρες αποκλείεται, δεν επιτρέπεται ούτε και η απόδειξη με δικαστικά τεκμήρια.

Άρθρο 396

Με την επιφύλαξη των άρθρων 237 και 238, το δικαστήριο οφείλει να εξετάσει έναν τουλάχιστον από τους προτεινόμενους και παριστάμενους μάρτυρες για κάθε πλευρά. Σε περίπτωση ομοδικίας μπορεί να εξετασθεί ένας μάρτυρας για κάθε ομόδικο, αν τούτο κριθεί απαραίτητο λόγω διαφορετικών συμφερόντων.

Άρθρο 397

[Καταργείται]

Article 392

1. Technical advisors shall be appointed in writing or verbally by means of a statement made either before the court or the delegated judge, which shall be entered in the transcript or the report, or before the court registry, in which case a report shall be prepared.
2. The technical advisors of the parties in the proceedings shall use their technical knowledge to assist them, may appear during all the procedural steps during which experts also appear, and are vested with the powers referred to in Articles 380(1) and 382(2).
3. After the experts have submitted their opinion and before the case is heard, the technical advisors of the parties in the proceedings may verbally expound on their own views regarding the opinion submitted by the experts before the court or submit their views in writing, and put questions to the experts.

TITLE V
Witnesses

Article 393

1. Agreements or collective decisions, as well as addenda prior, simultaneous or subsequent to a legal transaction concluded in writing may not be proven by witness testimony where their value exceeds 30,000 euros, even if such does not conflict with the content of the document.
2. Witnesses are not permitted to give evidence against the contents of a document.
3. Witnesses may also be examined via teleconference.

Article 394

1. By way of exception, evidence given by witness testimony shall be permitted if:
a) there is rudimentary evidence in writing arising from a document with probative value;
b) it was physically or ethically impossible to obtain a document;
c) it is proven that the document prepared was accidentally lost; and
d) this is justified from the nature of the legal transaction or the specific conditions under which it was entered into, and particularly in cases of commercial dealings.
2. Where the law or the parties stipulate that a legal transaction requires a document either as a formality or as proof thereof, proving a legal transaction through witness testimony shall only be allowed in the case referred to in paragraph 1(c).

Article 395

When evidence may not be given in the form of witness testimony, evidence in the form of judicial presumptions shall not be allowed either.

Article 396

Without prejudice to Articles 237 and 238, the court shall be obligated to examine at least one of the witnesses nominated by and appearing for each side. In the case of joinder, one witness for each joined party may be examined, where this is deemed necessary due to diverging interests.

Article 397

[Repealed]

Άρθρο 398

1. Όποιος καλείται να εξεταστεί ως μάρτυρας οφείλει να προσέλθει και να καταθέσει για τα πραγματικά γεγονότα που γνωρίζει.

2. Αν εκείνος που κλητεύτηκε να εξεταστεί μάρτυρας δεν προσέλθει αδικαιολόγητα, το δικαστήριο ή ο δικαστής με απόφασή του που καταχωρίζεται στα πρακτικά ή στην έκθεση τον καταδικάζουν να πληρώσει τα έξοδα που προξενήθηκαν από την απουσία του και μπορεί να τον καταδικάσουν και σε χρηματική ποινή σύμφωνα με το άρθρο 20**5.** Αν η απουσία του μάρτυρα πιθανολογείται ως δικαιολογημένη, το ίδιο δικαστήριο ή ο ίδιος δικαστής μπορούν να ανακαλέσουν την απόφαση αυτή, εφόσον το ζητήσει ο μάρτυρας μέσα σε είκοσι ημέρες αφότου του επιδόθηκε η απόφαση.

Άρθρο 399

Δεν εξετάζονται ως μάρτυρες:

1) οι κληρικοί για όσα έμαθαν κατά την εξομολόγηση,

2) πρόσωπα τα οποία όταν έγινε το πραγματικό γεγονός που πρέπει να αποδειχθεί δεν είχαν το αισθητήριο για να το αντιληφθούν ή δεν έχουν την ικανότητα να ανακοινώσουν αυτό που αντιλήφθηκαν,

3) πρόσωπα που, όταν έγινε το πραγματικό γεγονός που πρέπει να αποδειχθεί, βρίσκονταν σε κατάσταση ψυχικής ή διανοητικής διαταραχής που περιόριζε αποφασιστικά τη λειτουργία της κρίσης και της βούλησής τους ή που βρίσκονται σε μια τέτοια κατάσταση, όταν πρόκειται να εξετασθούν.

Άρθρο 400

Δεν εξετάζονται, όταν κληθούν ως μάρτυρες:

1) οι κληρικοί, δικηγόροι, συμβολαιογράφοι, γιατροί, φαρμακοποιοί, νοσοκόμοι, μαίες, ψυχολόγοι, οι βοηθοί τους, καθώς και οι σύμβουλοι των διαδίκων, για τα πραγματικά γεγονότα που τους εμπιστεύτηκαν ή που διαπίστωσαν κατά την άσκηση του επαγγέλματός τους για τα οποία έχουν καθήκον εχεμύθειας, εκτός αν το επιτρέψει εκείνος που τους τα εμπιστεύθηκε και εκείνος τον οποίο αφορά το απόρρητο,

2) δημόσιοι υπάλληλοι και στρατιωτικοί εν ενεργεία ή όχι, για πραγματικά γεγονότα για τα οποία υπάρχει καθήκον εχεμύθειας, εκτός αν ο αρμόδιος υπουργός επιτρέψει να εξεταστούν.

Άρθρο 401

Έχουν δικαίωμα να αρνηθούν να εξεταστούν ως μάρτυρες:

1) οι κληρικοί, δικηγόροι, συμβολαιογράφοι, γιατροί, φαρμακοποιοί, νοσοκόμοι, μαίες, ψυχολόγοι, οι βοηθοί τους, καθώς και σύμβουλοι των διαδίκων, για τα γεγονότα που έμαθαν κατά την άσκηση του επαγγέλματός τους,

2) οι συγγενείς κάποιου από τους διαδίκους εξ αίματος ή εξ αγχιστείας ή υιοθεσίας έως και τον τρίτο βαθμό σε ευθεία ή σε πλάγια γραμμή, εκτός αν έχουν τον ίδιο βαθμό συγγένειας με όλους τους διαδίκους, οι σύζυγοι και μετά τη λύση του γάμου, καθώς και οι μνηστευμένοι.

Άρθρο 402

Ο μάρτυρας δεν έχει υποχρέωση να καταθέσει

1) περιστατικά που μπορούν να δικαιολογήσουν τη δίωξη για αξιόποινη πράξη είτε του ίδιου είτε κάποιου προσώπου που συνδέεται μαζί του κατά το άρθρο 401 αριθ. 2, ή που θίγουν την τιμή του, ή την τιμή των προσώπων αυτών,

2) περιστατικά που αποτελούν επαγγελματικό ή καλλιτεχνικό απόρρητο.

Άρθρο 403

1. Στην περίπτωση του άρθρου 399, η απαγόρευση να εξεταστεί ο μάρτυρας λαμβάνεται υπόψη αυτεπαγγέλτως ή αφού το ζητήσει κάποιος από τους διαδίκους.

2. Ο διάδικος οφείλει να προτείνει το λόγο της μη εξέτασης του μάρτυρα κατά το άρθρο 400 πριν ορκιστεί.

Article 398

1. Any person summoned to be examined as a witness is obligated to appear and testify regarding the actual facts of which he or she has knowledge.
2. If a person summonsed to be examined as a witness fails to appear without justification, the court or the judge shall issue a ruling, entered in the transcript or the report, ordering that person to pay the costs caused by their absence, and may also order them to pay a monetary penalty in accordance with Article 205. If, on the balance of probabilities, the absence of the witness is deemed justified, the same court or judge may revoke this ruling, provided the witness made such a request within 20 days of the ruling being served on them.

Article 399

The following persons shall not be examined as witnesses:
a) priests regarding anything they learned of during [the sacrament of] confession;
b) persons who, when the actual fact to be proven occurred, did not possess the senses necessary to perceive it or who lack the ability to disclose what they perceived;
c) persons who, when the actual fact to be proven occurred, were in a state of mental or emotional disorder that decisively limited the functioning of their judgement and will or who are in such a state when they are about to be examined.

Article 400

The following persons shall not be examined when summoned as witnesses:
1) priests, lawyers, notaries public, physicians, pharmacists, nurses, midwives, psychologists, their assistants, as well as the advisors of the parties in the proceedings, regarding actual facts which were entrusted to them or which they ascertained while carrying on their profession, regarding which [actual facts] they have a duty of confidentiality, unless permitted by the person who entrusted them [with these actual facts] and the person whom the confidentiality concerns;
2) civil servants and military personnel, whether or not in active service, concerning actual facts regarding which they have a duty of confidentiality, unless the competent Minister allows such persons to be examined.

Article 401

The following persons have the right to refuse to be examined as witnesses:
1) priests, lawyers, notaries public, physicians, pharmacists, nurses, midwives, psychologists, their assistants, as well as the advisors of the parties in the proceedings, regarding facts they learned of while carrying on their profession;
2) persons related to any of the parties in the proceedings by blood or marriage or adoption up to the third degree, whether directly or co-laterally, unless they are related to the same degree to all the parties in the proceedings; spouses and former spouses; as well as persons engaged to be married.

Article 402

Witnesses are not obligated to give testimony regarding[:]
1) facts that could lead to prosecution for a punishable offence either of the witness or a person related to them under Article 401(2) or that prejudice their honour or the honour of such persons;
2) facts constituting a trade or artistic secret.

Article 403

1. In the case referred to in Article 399, the prohibition on examining witnesses shall be taken into consideration *ex officio* or when requested by a party in the proceedings.
2. The party in the proceedings is obligated to put forth grounds for not examining the witness under Article 400 before the witness takes an oath.

3. Ο μάρτυρας οφείλει να προτείνει το λόγο του άρθρου 401 για τον οποίο έχει δικαίωμα να αρνηθεί να μαρτυρήσει, καθώς και το λόγο του άρθρου 402 για τον οποίο δεν έχει υποχρέωση να καταθέσει.
4. Το δικαστήριο ή ο δικαστής ενώπιον του οποίου διεξάγεται η μαρτυρική απόδειξη αποφασίζουν για τις περιπτώσεις των παραγράφων 1, 2 και 3, και αρκεί για αυτό η πιθανολόγηση.
5. [Καταργείται]

Άρθρο 404

Μάρτυρας που εμφανίζεται και αρνείται να καταθέσει, αν και υποχρεούται, μπορεί να καταδικαστεί από το δικαστήριο ή το δικαστή ενώπιον του οποίου διεξάγεται η απόδειξη, σε χρηματική ποινή κατά το άρθρο 205.

Άρθρο 405

Αν επιβάλλεται για ειδικούς λόγους να εξεταστούν ως μάρτυρες πρόσωπα που δεν συμπλήρωσαν το δέκατο τέταρτο έτος της ηλικίας τους ή που έχασαν τα πολιτικά τους δικαιώματα επειδή έχουν καταδικαστεί, τα πρόσωπα αυτά εξετάζονται χωρίς να ορκιστούν.

Άρθρο 406

1. [Καταργείται]
2. Υπουργοί, αρχιερείς, πρεσβευτές και άλλοι διπλωματικοί υπάλληλοι ξένου κράτους επιφορτισμένοι με διπλωματική αποστολή εξετάζονται στην κατοικία τους, εκτός αν προτιμούν να προσέλθουν στο δικαστήριο. Στην κατοικία τους εξετάζονται επίσης και οι μάρτυρες που εμποδίζονται από αρρώστια ή γεράματα να εμφανιστούν.

Άρθρο 407

Πριν εξεταστεί ο μάρτυρας ερωτάται για το όνομα και το επώνυμο, τον τόπο που γεννήθηκε, την ηλικία, την κατοικία και το επάγγελμά του. Επίσης ερωτάται για την τυχόν συγγένειά του με τους διαδίκους και για κάθε άλλο περιστατικό που μπορεί να αποτελέσει λόγο για να μην εξεταστεί, ή να διαφωτίσει για τις σχέσεις του με τους διαδίκους και για την αξιοπιστία του.

Άρθρο 408

1. Πριν εξεταστεί ο μάρτυρας οφείλει να ορκισθεί. Προς τούτο ερωτάται, αν προτιμά να δώσει θρησκευτικό ή πολιτικό όρκο.
2. Ο τύπος του χριστιανικού όρκου είναι: «Ορκίζομαι ενώπιον του Θεού να πω ευσυνείδητα όλη την αλήθεια και μόνο την αλήθεια, χωρίς να προσθέσω ούτε να κρύψω τίποτε». Αν ο μάρτυρας πιστεύει σε γνωστή θρησκεία ή δόγμα, που ορίζει άλλο τύπο όρκου, δίνει τον όρκο σύμφωνα με αυτόν τον τύπο.
3. Ο πολιτικός όρκος δίνεται ως διαβεβαίωση με τον εξής τύπο: «Δηλώνω στην τιμή και στη συνείδησή μου πως θα πω όλη την αλήθεια και μόνο την αλήθεια, χωρίς να προσθέσω ούτε να κρύψω τίποτε».
4. Οι κληρικοί κάθε θρησκεύματος ορκίζονται διαβεβαιώνοντας στην ιεροσύνη τους.
5. Αν ο μάρτυρας είναι πρόσωπο με σοβαρή αναπηρία στα άνω άκρα, επαναλαμβάνει τον όρκο που διαβάζει ο δικαστής.
6. Κωφοί, ή πρόσωπα με σοβαρή αναπηρία λόγου ορκίζονται σύμφωνα με τις διατάξεις του άρθρου 253.

3. Witnesses are obligated to put forth the grounds referred to in Article 401 on which they have the right to refuse to give testimony, as well as the grounds referred to in Article 402 on which they are not obligated to give testimony.
4. The court or the judge before which or whom witness testimony is taking place shall rule on the cases referred to in paragraphs 1, 2 and 3, and the balance of probabilities test shall suffice in this respect.
5. [Repealed]

Article 404

Witnesses who appear and refuse to testify even though obligated to do so may be ordered by the court or judge before which or whom evidence is being taken to pay a monetary penalty in accordance with Article 205.

Article 405

If the examination of persons who have not attained the age of 14 or who were deprived of their civil rights due to conviction is necessary for special reasons, these persons shall be examined without taking an oath.

Article 406

1. [Repealed]
2. Ministers, senior clerics, ambassadors and other diplomatic staff of foreign states engaging in diplomatic missions shall be examined at their residence, unless they prefer to appear before the court. Witnesses who are impeded from appearing due to illness or old age shall also be examined at their residence.

Article 407

Before being examined, witnesses shall be asked to state their first name, last name, place of birth, age, place of domicile and occupation. They shall also be asked whether they are related to the parties in the proceedings and whether there is any fact that could constitute grounds to not examine them, or could enlighten the court on their relationships with the parties in the proceedings and their credibility.

Article 408

1. Before being examined, witnesses are obligated to take an oath. To this end, they shall be asked whether they prefer to take a religious or secular oath.
2. The religious oath takes the following form: “I swear before God to conscientiously tell the whole truth and nothing but the truth, without adding or concealing anything”. If the witness is a member of a known religion or denomination prescribing a different form of oath, the witness shall take an oath in accordance with that form.
3. The secular oath shall be given as an affirmation in the following form: “I declare on my honour and my conscience that I shall tell the whole truth and nothing but the truth, without adding or concealing anything”.
4. Priests of all religions shall take on oath by providing assurances in light of their clerical status.
5. If the witness has a serious disability involving the upper limbs, they shall repeat the oath read by the judge.
6. Persons who are deaf or have a serious speech impediment shall take oaths in accordance with the provisions of Article 253.

Άρθρο 409

1. Οι μάρτυρες εξετάζονται χωριστά και μόνο αν κριθεί απαραίτητο μπορούν να εξεταστούν σε αντιπαράσταση με άλλους μάρτυρες ή και με τους διαδίκους. Οι μάρτυρες καταθέτουν προφορικά και μπορούν, κατά την κρίση του δικαστή, να χρησιμοποιούν σημείωμα για να βοηθήσουν τη μνήμη τους.
2. Ο μάρτυρας οφείλει να δηλώσει πώς έμαθε αυτά που καταθέτει, και αν πρόκειται για γεγονότα για τα οποία δεν έχει άμεση αντίληψη, οφείλει να δηλώνει και το πρόσωπο από το οποίο πληροφορήθηκε όσα καταθέτει.
3. Το δικαστήριο μπορεί να απαγορεύει τις ερωτήσεις των διαδίκων ή των πληρεξουσίων τους προς το μάρτυρα, αν είναι έκδηλα άσκοπες ή έξω από το θέμα και κηρύσσει περαιωμένη την εξέταση του μάρτυρα, όταν κρίνει ότι κατέθεσε όλα όσα γνωρίζει για τα αποδεικτέα.

Άρθρο 410

Οι καταθέσεις μαρτύρων καταχωρίζονται στα πρακτικά, στα οποία πρέπει να αναφέρονται η όρκιση του μάρτυρα και οι τυχόν ενστάσεις των διαδίκων.

Άρθρο 411

Το δικαστήριο μπορεί ύστερα από αίτηση ή και αυτεπαγγέλτως να διατάξει να εξεταστεί και πάλι ένας μάρτυρας, αν αυτό χρειάζεται για να συμπληρωθεί ή να διευκρινιστεί η κατάθεση ή αν το δικαστήριο κρίνει πως ο μάρτυρας αρνήθηκε αδικαιολόγητα να καταθέσει επάνω σε ορισμένο θέμα. Στις περιπτώσεις αυτές ο μάρτυρας δεν ορκίζεται και πάλι.

Άρθρο 412

[Καταργείται]

Άρθρο 413

Οι σχετικές διατάξεις με τους μάρτυρες εφαρμόζονται και όταν, για να αποδειχθούν περασμένα πραγματικά γεγονότα, εξετάζονται πρόσωπα που τα αντιλήφθηκαν με βάση τις ειδικές γνώσεις τους.

Άρθρο 414

[Καταργείται]

ΤΙΤΛΟΣ VI.
Εξέταση των διαδίκων

Άρθρο 415

1. Το δικαστήριο μπορεί να εξετάσει έναν ή περισσότερους διαδίκους για την αλήθεια των πραγματικών γεγονότων.
2. Αν ο διάδικος είναι πρόσωπο ανίκανο να παρίσταται στο δικαστήριο, μπορεί κατά την κρίση του δικαστηρίου να εξεταστεί είτε εκείνος που τελεί υπό επιμέλεια, εκτός αν δεν έχει συνείδηση των πράξεών του ή αν δεν συμπλήρωσε το δέκατο τέταρτο έτος της ηλικίας του, είτε ο νόμιμος αντιπρόσωπός του είτε και οι δύο.
3. Αν ο διάδικος είναι νομικό πρόσωπο, μπορεί να εξεταστεί όποιος το εκπροσωπεί στο δικαστήριο ή κάποιο άλλο μέλος της διοίκησής του.
4. Αν διεξάγει τη δίκη ο σύνδικος πτώχευσης, μπορούν να εξεταστούν είτε ο σύνδικος είτε ο πτωχός είτε και οι δύο.

Article 409

1. Witnesses shall be examined separately and, only if deemed necessary, may be cross-examined with other witnesses or the parties in the proceedings. Witnesses shall give verbal testimony and may, at the discretion of the judge, use notes to aid their memories.
2. Witnesses shall be obligated to state how they learned what they are testifying to, and in the case of facts of which they have no direct knowledge, they must state the person from whom they learned what they are testifying to.
3. The court may prohibit the answering of questions put by the parties in the proceedings or their proxies to the witness if they are manifestly unnecessary or off-topic, and shall declare the testimony given the witness complete when it considers that the witness has testified all they know regarding the matters to be proven.

Article 410

Witness testimonies shall be entered in the transcript, which must also cite the taking of an oath by the witness and any pleas raised by the parties in the proceedings.

Article 411

Following an application or *ex officio*, the court may order the re-examination of a witness, where necessary to supplement or clarify the testimony or where the court considers that the witness unjustifiably refused to testify with regard to a specific matter. In such cases, the witness in question need not take an oath again.

Article 412

[Repealed]

Article 413

The provisions concerning witnesses also apply when, in order to prove actual facts that occurred in the past, persons who became aware of them on the basis of their specialised knowledge are being examined.

Article 414

[Repealed]

TITLE VI
Examination of the parties in the proceedings

Article 415

1. The court may examine one or more parties in the proceedings to establish the truth of the actual facts.
2. If the party in the proceedings lacks capacity to be a party in proceedings, the court may, at its discretion, order the examination of the person under custodianship, unless they are not in command of their faculties or have not attained the age of 14, or order the examination of their lawful proxy, or both.
3. If the party in the proceedings is a legal person, any person representing it before the court or another member of its management team may be examined.
4. If a bankruptcy administrator is bringing proceedings, either the administrator or the bankrupt person or both may be examined.

Άρθρο 416

Η εξέταση των διαδίκων διατάσσεται ύστερα από αίτηση κάποιου από τους διαδίκους ή αυτεπαγγέλτως και διεξάγεται κατά τις διατάξεις για την εξέταση μαρτύρων.

Άρθρο 417

1. *Οι διάδικοι εξετάζονται χωρίς να ορκιστούν, εκτός αν το δικαστήριο κρίνει σκόπιμο να διατάξει να εξεταστεί με όρκο ο διάδικος για όλα ή μερικά από τα αμφισβητούμενα γεγονότα. Το δικαστήριο μπορεί επίσης να καλέσει το διάδικο που εξετάστηκε ήδη χωρίς όρκο να βεβαιώσει με όρκο την κατάθεσή του ολόκληρη ή μέρος της. Ο δικαστής επισημαίνει τη δυνατότητα αυτήν στο διάδικο που εξετάζεται πριν να αρχίσει η εξέτασή του. Η ένορκη εξέταση δεν επιτρέπεται σχετικά με γεγονότα που αποτελούν για εκείνον που ορκίζεται πράξη αξιόποινη ή ανήθικη.*

2. *Δεν μπορούν να εξεταστούν με όρκο για το ίδιο γεγονός οι διάδικοι που αντιδικούν.*

Άρθρο 418

Δεν εξετάζονται με όρκο όσοι έχουν καταδικαστεί τελεσίδικα για ψευδορκία ή για ψευδομαρτυρία.

Άρθρο 419

1. *Η μη εμφάνιση κάποιου διαδίκου στη δικάσιμο που ορίστηκε για την εξέτασή του ή η άρνησή του να καταθέσει δεν εμποδίζει να εξεταστεί άλλος διάδικος που εμφανίστηκε.*

2. *Δεν επιτρέπεται να χρησιμοποιηθούν εξαναγκαστικά μέτρα για να υποχρεωθεί ο διάδικός να προσέλθει και να εξεταστεί.*

Άρθρο 420

Το δικαστήριο εκτιμά ελεύθερα την κατάθεση των διαδίκων, ένορκη ή χωρίς όρκο, την αδικαιολόγητη μη εμφάνιση του διαδίκου που κλητεύθηκε να εξεταστεί, με όρκο ή χωρίς όρκο, την άρνησή του να καταθέσει ή να απαντήσει στις ερωτήσεις που του υπέβαλαν, καθώς και τη διαφορά ανάμεσα στην ένορκη και τη χωρίς όρκο προηγούμενη κατάθεσή του.

ΤΙΤΛΟΣ VII.
Όρκος

Άρθρο 421

Οι διάδικοι μπορούν να προσκομίσουν προαποδεικτικώς ένορκες βεβαιώσεις, εφόσον αυτές λαμβάνονται ενώπιον του ειρηνοδίκη ή συμβολαιογράφου ή δικηγόρου της έδρας του δικαστηρίου ή της κατοικίας ή της διαμονής του μάρτυρα ή ενώπιον του προξένου της κατοικίας ή της διαμονής του μάρτυρα κατά τη διαδικασία των άρθρων 422 έως 424. Η ένορκη βεβαίωση, που λαμβάνεται ενώπιον δικηγόρου, δεν μπορεί να ληφθεί ενώπιον των πληρεξουσίων δικηγόρων των διαδίκων. Αμέσως μετά τη λήψη της ένορκης βεβαίωσης, ο δικηγόρος ενώπιον του οποίου αυτή δόθηκε την αποστέλλει ηλεκτρονικά στον δικηγορικό σύλλογο στον οποίο ανήκει και λαμβάνει ηλεκτρονική απόδειξη λήψης. Με την ηλεκτρονική απόδειξη η ένορκη βεβαίωση αποκτά βέβαιη χρονολογία και μοναδικό αριθμό. Ο δικηγόρος χορηγεί αντίγραφα της ένορκης βεβαίωσης μαζί με την ως άνω ηλεκτρονική απόδειξη λήψης. Όμοια αντίγραφα χορηγεί και ο οικείος δικηγορικός σύλλογος μέσω της διαδικτυακής πύλης portal.olomeleia.gr. Τα αρχεία των ένορκων βεβαιώσεων που λαμβάνονται ενώπιον δικηγόρου τηρούνται στους οικείους δικηγορικούς συλλόγους, σύμφωνα με αποφάσεις των διοικητικών τους συμβουλίων.

Article 416

Examination of the parties in the proceedings shall be ordered following an application filed by any party in the proceedings or *ex officio*, and shall be conducted in accordance with the provisions on the examination of witnesses.

Article 417

1. The parties in the proceedings shall be examined without taking an oath, unless the court deems it expedient to order the examination of a party in the proceedings under oath for all or certain of the disputed facts. The court may also summon a party in the proceedings already examined without having taken an oath to confirm all or part of their testimony under oath. The judge shall stress this option to the party in the proceedings being examined before their examination begins. Examination under oath shall not be allowed with regard to facts which, for the person taking the oath, constitute a punishable or immoral act.
2. Opposing parties may not be examined under oath with regard to the same fact.

Article 418

Persons found by a *de jure* non-appealable judgment to have committed perjury or to have given false testimony shall not be examined under oath.

Article 419

1. Failure of a party in the proceedings to appear on the hearing date set for their examination or refusal by that party to testify shall not hinder the examination of a different party in the proceedings who appeared before the court.
2. Coercive measures may not be used to compel a party in the proceedings to appear and be examined.

Article 420

The court shall freely weigh up the testimony given by the parties in the proceedings, whether or not under oath, the unjustified absence of a party in the proceedings summonsed to testify, whether or not under oath, their refusal to testify or answer the questions put to them, as well as discrepancies between their sworn testimony and unsworn prior testimony.

TITLE VII
Oaths

Article 421

Prior to the taking of evidence, the parties in the proceedings may adduce affidavits, provided these were prepared in the presence of a court of the peace judge, or notary public or lawyer [registered in the district] of the court or the place of residence or domicile of the witness, or in the presence of the consul at the place of residence or domicile of the witness, in accordance with the procedure laid down in Articles 422 to 424. Affidavits to be prepared in the presence of a lawyer may not be prepared in the presence of the authorised lawyers of the parties in the proceedings. Immediately after preparing the affidavit, the lawyer in whose presence it was prepared shall send it using electronic means to the bar association to whom they belong and obtain an electronic acknowledgement of receipt. The electronic acknowledgement contains a timestamp and a unique number [specific] to the affidavit. The lawyer shall issue copies of the affidavit together with the aforesaid electronic acknowledgement of receipt. Exact copies may also be issued by the local bar association via the 'portal.olomeleia.gr' website. The records of affidavits prepared in the presence of lawyers shall be kept at the local bar associations in accordance with decisions made by their boards of directors.

Άρθρο 422
Επίδοση κλήσης

1. Ο διάδικος που επιδιώκει τη λήψη ένορκης βεβαίωσης, σύμφωνα με όσα ορίζονται στο προηγούμενο άρθρο, επιδίδει δύο (2) τουλάχιστον εργάσιμες ημέρες πριν από την βεβαίωση στον αντίδικο κλήση, η οποία αναφέρει την αγωγή, το ένδικο βοήθημα ή μέσο, που αφορά η βεβαίωση, τόπον, ημέρα και ώρα που θα δοθεί, το ονοματεπώνυμο, το επάγγελμα και τη διεύθυνση της κατοικίας του μάρτυρα.
2. Κατά τη βεβαίωση παρίστανται, εφόσον το επιθυμούν, οι διάδικοι.
3. Δεν επιτρέπεται η λήψη ένορκων βεβαιώσεων πάνω από τριών (3) για κάθε διάδικο και δυο (2) για την αντίκρουση, για κάθε βαθμό δικαιοδοσίας.

Άρθρο 423

1. Οι διατάξεις των άρθρων 393, 394, 398 παράγραφος 2, 399, 400, 402, 405, 407, 408, 409 παρ. 2, 411 και 413 εφαρμόζονται αναλόγως.
2. Ενστάσεις και αιτήσεις εξαίρεσης εκείνου, που δίδει τη βεβαίωση, καταχωρίζονται στο προοίμιο της ένορκης βεβαίωσης κρίνονται όμως από το Δικαστήριο.

Άρθρο 424

Ένορκη βεβαίωση σε δίκη για την οποία δίδεται δεν λαμβάνεται υπόψη, ούτε για συναγωγή δικαστικών τεκμηρίων, όταν:
α) δεν έχει γίνει εμπρόθεσμη κλήση του αντιδίκου,
β) δίδεται ενώπιον άλλου από τα αναφερόμενα στο άρθρο 421 όργανα ή σε διαφορετικό τόπο, ημέρα και ώρα από αυτήν που αναφέρεται στην κλήση,
γ) η κλήση δεν αναφέρει το ονοματεπώνυμο του μάρτυρα, την αγωγή, το ένδικο βοήθημα ή μέσο, που αφορά η βεβαίωση, τον τόπο, την ημέρα και την ώρα που θα δοθεί, και
δ) όταν παραβιάζεται το δεύτερο εδάφιο του άρθρου 421. Ένορκη βεβαίωση κατά παράβαση των λοιπών διατάξεων λαμβάνεται υπόψη, εκτός αν συντρέχει δικονομική βλάβη του αντιδίκου.

Άρθρα 425-431

[Καταργούνται]

ΤΙΤΛΟΣ VIII.
Έγγραφα

Άρθρο 432

Τα έγγραφα έχουν αποδεικτική δύναμη όταν έχουν συνταχθεί σύμφωνα με τους νόμιμους τύπους, έχουν τα στοιχεία τα απαραίτητα για το κύρος τους, δεν είναι τεμαχισμένα, τρυπημένα ή διαγραμμένα, δεν έχουν ξυσίματα ή εξαλείψεις ή δεν είναι με άλλον τρόπο αλλαγμένα σε ουσιώδη μέρη τους, και μπορούν να διαβαστούν.

Άρθρο 433

Ο τεμαχισμός, η διάτρηση ή η διαγραφή ενός εγγράφου τεκμαίρεται ότι έγινε για να εκμηδενιστεί η αποδεικτική του δύναμη, εκτός αν αποδειχθεί το αντίθετο.

Article 422
Service of a summons

1. The party in the proceedings seeking to prepare an affidavit in accordance with the provisions of the preceding Article shall serve a summons on the opponent at least two working days prior to the [preparation of the] affidavit, citing the action, the form of relief or legal remedy the affidavit concerns, the place, date and time it will be served, the full name, occupation, and the residential address of the witness.

2. If they so desire, the parties in the proceedings may be present during the [preparation of the] affidavit.

3. No more than three affidavits may be prepared by each party in the proceedings and two for the rebuttal at each instance.

Article 423

1. The provisions of Articles 393, 394, 398(2), 399, 400, 402, 405, 407, 408, 409(2), 411 and 413 apply *mutatis mutandis*.

2. Objections and applications to exclude the person giving the affidavit shall be recorded in the introduction to the affidavit, but shall be ruled upon by the court.

Article 424

An affidavit prepared for a specific set of proceedings shall not be taken into consideration [during those proceedings], not even in order to establish judicial presumptions, where:

a) the opponent was not summoned in good time;

b) the affidavit was prepared in the presence of persons other than those referred to in Article 421 or at a different place, date and time than those cited in the summons;

c) the summons does not cite the full name of the witness, the action, the form of relief or legal remedy the affidavit concerns, the place, date and time it will be prepared; and

d) the second sentence of Article 421 is infringed. Affidavits prepared in breach of the other provisions shall be taken into consideration, unless this would entail a procedural disadvantage for the opponent.

Articles 425-431

[Repealed]

TITLE VIII
Documents

Article 432

Documents have probative value when they are prepared in accordance with legal form, contain the information necessary for their validity, are not shredded, perforated or have had content expunged, they do not contain erased or redacted sections or have not been otherwise altered in terms of their material sections, and are legible.

Article 433

The shredding, perforation or expungement of the content of a document shall be presumed to have taken place in order to negate its probative value, unless the contrary is proven.

Άρθρο 434

Αν σε ένα έγγραφο υπάρχουν μεταβολές, όποιος το χρησιμοποιεί ως αποδεικτικό μέσο πρέπει να αποδείξει πως οι μεταβολές έγιναν από εκείνον που έχει εκδώσει το έγγραφο ή από εκείνον κατά του οποίου πρόκειται να χρησιμεύσει ως απόδειξη ή από εκείνον στον οποίο περιήλθε το δικαίωμα ή ότι έγιναν με τη συγκατάθεσή τους.

Άρθρο 435

Αν ένα έγγραφο χαθεί ή γίνει δυσανάγνωστο ή άχρηστο, εκείνος που διεξάγει την απόδειξη μπορεί να αποδείξει ή ότι το έγγραφο υπάρχει νόμιμα συνταγμένο ή το περιεχόμενό του ή και τα δύο, με κάθε αποδεικτικό μέσο και αν ακόμη πρόκειται για σχέση που για να συσταθεί επιβάλλεται από το νόμο ή από τα μέρη να συνταχθεί έγγραφο.

Άρθρο 436

1. Αν το έγγραφο που προσκομίστηκε αναφέρεται σε άλλο έγγραφο, προσάγεται και αυτό, εκτός αν εκείνο που προσκομίστηκε αντικατέστησε το έγγραφο που αναφέρεται ή περιλαμβάνει όλο το ουσιώδες περιεχόμενό του.

2. Αν το έγγραφο που προσκομίστηκε έχει περιεχόμενο διαφορετικό από το αναφερόμενο έγγραφο, προτιμάται το περιεχόμενο του τελευταίου.

Άρθρο 437

Σε περίπτωση συντηρητικής απόδειξης με έγγραφο το δικαστήριο μπορεί, εκτός από τα άλλα μέτρα, να επιτρέψει να ληφθεί επικυρωμένο αντίγραφο που ισχύει σαν πρωτότυπο αν το πρωτότυπο χαθεί, ή να διατάξει να προσκομιστεί το έγγραφο για να αποδειχθεί η γνησιότητά του.

Άρθρο 438

Έγγραφα που έχουν συνταχθεί κατά τους νόμιμους τύπους από δημόσιο υπάλληλο ή λειτουργό ή πρόσωπο που ασκεί δημόσια υπηρεσία ή λειτουργία αποτελούν πλήρη απόδειξη για όλους ως προς όσα βεβαιώνονται στο έγγραφο ότι έγιναν από το πρόσωπο που συνέταξε το έγγραφο ή ότι έγιναν ενώπιόν του, αν το πρόσωπο αυτό είναι καθ' ύλην και κατά τόπον αρμόδιο να κάνει αυτή τη βεβαίωση. Ανταπόδειξη επιτρέπεται μόνο με προσβολή του έγγραφου ως πλαστού.

Την ίδια ισχύ έχουν και τα ηλεκτρονικά δημόσια έγγραφα των παρ. 3 και 6 του άρθρου 13 του νόμου για την Ψηφιακή Διακυβέρνηση.

Άρθρο 439

Έγγραφα συνταγμένα από αλλοδαπό δημόσιο υπάλληλο ή λειτουργό ή πρόσωπο που ασκεί δημόσια υπηρεσία ή λειτουργία καθ' ύλην και κατά τόπον αρμόδιο, τα οποία θεωρούνται ως δημόσια έγγραφα στον τόπο όπου εκδόθηκαν, έχουν την αποδεικτική δύναμη που ορίζει το άρθρο 438.

Άρθρο 440

Τα έγγραφα που αναφέρονται στα άρθρα 438 και 439 αποτελούν πλήρη απόδειξη για όλους ως προς όσα βεβαιώνονται σ' αυτά, την αλήθεια των οποίων όφειλε να διαπιστώσει εκείνος που έχει συντάξει το έγγραφο, επιτρέπεται όμως ανταπόδειξη.

Άρθρο 441

1. Τα έγγραφα που συντάσσονται σύμφωνα με τα άρθρα 438 και 439 για τη σύσταση ή τη βεβαίωση δικαιοπραξίας αποτελούν πλήρη απόδειξη για όλους ως προς το περιεχόμενο των δικαιοπρακτικών δηλώσεων των μερών επιτρέπεται όμως ανταπόδειξη.

2. Όσα ορίζονται στην παράγραφο 1 ισχύουν και για όσα αναφέρονται αφηγηματικά στο έγγραφο, εφόσον έχουν άμεση σχέση με το κύριο αντικείμενο του εγγράφου. Όσα δεν έχουν άμεση σχέση θεωρούνται ως αρχή έγγραφης απόδειξης.

Article 434

If a document contains changes, the person using it as means of evidence must prove that the changes were made by the person who issued the document, or the person against whom it is to be used as evidence, or the person who acquired the right, or that the changes were made with their consent.

Article 435

If a document is lost or becomes illegible or useless, the party presenting the evidence may prove that the document or its content or both exist in duly prepared form using any means of evidence, even in cases of a relationship where the law or the parties require the preparation of a document in order for such relationship to be established.

Article 436

1. If the document adduced cites a different document, that document shall also be produced, unless the one adduced replaces the document cited or contains all its essential content.
2. If the content of the document adduced is different from the content of the document cited, the content of the latter shall be preferred.

Article 437

In the case of preservation/recording of evidence by documentary means, the court may, in addition to the other measures [provided for], allow the creation of a certified copy, which shall function as the original if the original is lost, or order that the document be adduced for the purpose of proving its authenticity.

Article 438

Documents prepared in accordance with legal form by a civil servant or functionary or person discharging a public service or function constitute proof in full *erga omnes* concerning the fact that everything attested in the document was done by or in the presence of the person who prepared the document, if the person in question is locally and materially competent to make such attestation. Counter-evidence shall only be permitted by contesting the authenticity of the document.
Electronic public documents prepared in accordance with Article 13(3) and (6) of the law on digital governance generate the same effects.

Article 439

Documents which are prepared by a materially and locally competent foreign civil servant or functionary or person discharging a public service or function and which are considered public documents at the place where they were issued have the probative value provided for in Article 438.

Article 440

The documents referred to in Articles 438 and 439 constitute proof in full *erga omnes* concerning what was attested therein, the truth of which the person who prepared the document was obligated to ascertain; however, counter-evidence shall be allowed.

Article 441

1. Documents prepared in accordance with Articles 438 and 439 regarding the establishment or attestation of a legal transaction constitute proof in full *erga omnes* concerning the content of the transactional representations made by the parties; however, counter-evidence shall be allowed.
2. The provisions of paragraph 1 also apply to all narrative information in the document, provided such information is directly related to the main subject-matter of the document. Anything not directly related shall be deemed to be rudimentary evidence in writing.

Άρθρο 442

Το έγγραφο που δεν συγκεντρώνει τις προϋποθέσεις των άρθρων 438 και 439 δεν έχει την αποδεικτική δύναμη δημόσιου εγγράφου, αλλά μπορεί να ισχύσει σαν ιδιωτικό έγγραφο με τους όρους του άρθρου 443.

Άρθρο 443

Για να έχει αποδεικτική δύναμη ιδιωτικό έγγραφο πρέπει να έχει την ιδιόχειρη υπογραφή του εκδότη ή αντί για υπογραφή ένα σημάδι που αυτός έβαλε και επικυρώθηκε από συμβολαιογράφο ή άλλη δημόσια αρχή, που επιβεβαιώνει πως το σημάδι έχει τεθεί αντί για την υπογραφή και ότι ο εκδότης δήλωσε ότι δεν μπορεί να υπογράψει.

Άρθρο 444

1. Ιδιωτικά έγγραφα θεωρούνται και

α) τα βιβλία που έμποροι και επαγγελματίες τηρούν κατά τον εμπορικό νόμο ή άλλες διατάξεις,

β) τα βιβλία που δικηγόροι, συμβολαιογράφοι, δικαστικοί επιμελητές, γιατροί, φαρμακοποιοί και μαίες τηρούν κατά τις ισχύουσες διατάξεις,

γ) φωτογραφικές ή κινηματογραφικές αναπαραστάσεις, φωνοληψίες και κάθε άλλη μηχανική απεικόνιση.

2. Μηχανική απεικόνιση, κατά την έννοια της παραγράφου 1, είναι και κάθε μέσο το οποίο χρησιμοποιείται από υπολογιστή ή περιφερειακή μνήμη υπολογιστή, με ηλεκτρονικό, μαγνητικό ή άλλο τρόπο, για εγγραφή, αποθήκευση, παραγωγή ή αναπαραγωγή στοιχείων, που δεν μπορούν να διαβαστούν άμεσα, όπως επίσης και κάθε μαγνητικό, ηλεκτρονικό ή άλλο υλικό στο οποίο εγγράφεται οποιαδήποτε πληροφορία, εικόνα, σύμβολο ή ήχος, αυτοτελώς ή σε συνδυασμό, εφόσον τα μέσα και τα υλικά αυτά προορίζονται ή είναι πρόσφορα να αποδείξουν γεγονότα που έχουν έννομη σημασία.

Άρθρο 445

Έγγραφα ιδιωτικά, συνταγμένα σύμφωνα με τους νόμιμους τύπους, εφόσον η γνησιότητά τους αναγνωρίσθηκε ή αποδείχθηκε, αποτελούν πλήρη απόδειξη ότι η δήλωση που περιέχουν προέρχεται από τον εκδότη του εγγράφου, επιτρέπεται όμως ανταπόδειξη. Με τους ίδιους όρους αυτά αποτελούν πλήρη απόδειξη και ως προς το περιεχόμενο των δικαιοπρακτικών δηλώσεων.

Άρθρο 446

Το ιδιωτικό έγγραφο αποκτά βέβαιη χρονολογία ως προς τους τρίτους μόνο όταν το θεωρήσει συμβολαιογράφος ή άλλος δημόσιος υπάλληλος αρμόδιος κατά το νόμο ή όταν πεθάνει ένας από εκείνους που το υπέγραψαν ή όταν το ουσιώδες περιεχόμενό του αναφερθεί σε δημόσιο έγγραφο ή όταν υπάρξει άλλο γεγονός που κάνει με ανάλογο τρόπο βέβαιη τη χρονολογία. Η θεώρηση γίνεται με τη σημείωση επάνω στο έγγραφο της λέξης «θεωρήθηκε» και της χρονολογίας.

Άρθρο 447

Το ιδιωτικό έγγραφο αποτελεί απόδειξη υπέρ του εκδότη μόνο αν το προσκόμισε ο αντίδικος ή αν πρόκειται για τα βιβλία που αναφέρονται στις περιπτώσεις α' και β' της παραγράφου 1 του άρθρου 444.

Article 442

A document that does not meet the requirements laid down in Articles 438 and 439 does not have the probative value of a public document, but may function as a private document under the conditions laid down in Article 443.

Article 443

In order to have probative value, a private document must bear the handwritten signature of the author or, instead of a signature, a mark by the author, certified by a notary public or other public authority confirming that the mark was affixed instead of a signature and that the author declared that they are unable to affix their signature.

Article 444

1. The following are also considered private documents[:]
a) ledgers/registers kept by merchants and professionals in accordance with the Commercial Law or other provisions;
b) ledgers/registers kept by lawyers, notaries public, court process servers, physicians, pharmacists and midwives, in accordance with the provisions in force;
c) photographic, video, audio recordings and any other mechanically displayed means.
2. "Mechanically displayed means", within the meaning of paragraph 1, also includes any medium used by a computer or peripheral computer memory via electronic, magnetic or other means to record, store, produce or reproduce data that cannot be directly read, as well as any magnetic, electronic or other material on which any information, image, symbol or sound is recorded, whether independently or in combined form, where such media and materials are intended or suitable for proving facts of legal importance.

Article 445

Provided their authenticity has been acknowledged or proven, private documents prepared in accordance with legal form constitute proof in full that the representation they contain originates from the author of the document; however, counter-evidence shall be allowed. They also constitute proof in full under the same conditions with regard to the content of transactional representations.

Article 446

A private document shall be deemed to be time-stamped vis-à-vis third parties only when certified by a notary public or other civil servant authorised in law, or one of the persons who signed it dies, or its material content is cited in a public document, or a different event that similarly constitutes a time-stamp occurs. A document is time-stamped by noting the word "certified" and the date on it.

Article 447

A private document constitutes proof in favour of the author only if adduced by the opponent or the ledgers referred to in Article 444(1)(a) and (b) are concerned.

Άρθρο 448

1. Τα βιβλία που αναφέρονται στις περιπτώσεις α' και β' της παραγράφου 1 του άρθρου 444, εφόσον είναι συνταγμένα σύμφωνα με τους νόμιμους τύπους, αποτελούν μεταξύ εμπόρων ή άλλων προσώπων υποχρεωμένων να τηρούν όμοια βιβλία πλήρη απόδειξη για όσα αναφέρονται σε αυτά, αλλά επιτρέπεται η ανταπόδειξη. Κατά προσώπων όμως που δεν έχουν υποχρέωση να τηρούν αυτά τα βιβλία αποτελούν πλήρη απόδειξη για το μέγεθος της απαίτησης, όταν η ύπαρξή της είναι αποδεδειγμένη με άλλο τρόπο, και μόνο για ένα έτος αφότου γίνει η εγγραφή, εκτός αν ο υπόχρεος αναγνώρισε με την υπογραφή του το περιεχόμενο.
2. Τα έγγραφα που αναφέρονται στην περίπτωση γ' της παραγράφου 1 του άρθρου 444 αποτελούν πλήρη απόδειξη για τα γεγονότα ή πράγματα που αναγράφουν, επιτρέπεται όμως ανταπόδειξη.
3. Οι απεικονίσεις της παραγράφου 2 του άρθρου 444 αποτελούν πλήρη απόδειξη με την επιφύλαξη του άρθρου 445.

Άρθρο 449

1. Αντίγραφα των οποίων η ακρίβεια βεβαιώνεται από τον αρμόδιο υπάλληλο έχουν αποδεικτική δύναμη ίση με το πρωτότυπο.
2. Φωτογραφίες ή φωτοτυπίες εγγράφων έχουν αποδεικτική δύναμη ίση με το πρωτότυπο, εφόσον η ακρίβειά τους βεβαιώνεται από πρόσωπο που είναι κατά το νόμο αρμόδιο να εκδίδει αντίγραφα.
3. Τα ακριβή ηλεκτρονικά αντίγραφα, τα ψηφιοποιημένα ηλεκτρονικά αντίγραφα και οι εκτυπώσεις αυτών έχουν αποδεικτική δύναμη ακριβούς αντιγράφου, κατά τα οριζόμενα στο άρθρο 14 του νόμου για την Ψηφιακή Διακυβέρνηση.

Άρθρο 450

1. Κάθε διάδικος οφείλει να επιδείξει τα έγγραφα που χρησιμοποίησε ή επικαλέστηκε στη δίκη.
2. Κάθε διάδικος ή τρίτος έχει υποχρέωση να επιδείξει τα έγγραφα που κατέχει και που μπορούν να χρησιμεύσουν για απόδειξη, εκτός αν συντρέχει σπουδαίος λόγος που δικαιολογεί τη μη επίδειξή τους. Σπουδαίος λόγος συντρέχει ιδίως στις περιπτώσεις που επιτρέπεται να αρνηθεί κανείς να μαρτυρήσει.

Άρθρο 451

1. Η επίδειξη μπορεί να ζητηθεί, εφόσον έχει την υποχρέωση αυτή ένας τρίτος, με παρεμπίπτουσα αγωγή, ενώ αν έχει την υποχρέωση διάδικος, και με τις προτάσεις. Αν δεν είναι υποχρεωτική η κατάθεση προτάσεων, η αίτηση για την επίδειξη υποβάλλεται με δήλωση που καταχωρίζεται στα πρακτικά.
2. Η συζήτηση και η απόδειξη γίνονται κατά τις γενικές διατάξεις.
3. Αν είναι δύσκολη για σπουδαίους λόγους η προσαγωγή του εγγράφου στο ακροατήριο ή από τη σπουδαιότητα ή τη φύση του υπάρχει κίνδυνος να χαθεί ή να υποστεί βλάβη, το δικαστήριο μπορεί να ορίσει να προσαχθεί το έγγραφο ενώπιον ενός από τα μέλη του δικαστηρίου που δικάζει την υπόθεση ή ενώπιον άλλου δικαστηρίου ή να εξεταστεί από εντεταλμένο δικαστή, που πηγαίνει στον τόπο όπου βρίσκεται το έγγραφο, ή να επιτρέψει να προσαχθεί επικυρωμένη φωτοτυπία ή φωτογραφία ή επικυρωμένο αντίγραφό του.

Άρθρο 452

1. Η εκτέλεση της απόφασης που διατάζει την επίδειξη γίνεται κατά τις διατάξεις που αφορούν την εκτέλεση για την ικανοποίηση απαιτήσεων που συνίστανται στην απόδοση και στην παράδοση πράγματος ή την ενέργεια πράξης.
2. Το άρθρο 366 εφαρμόζεται και εδώ.
3. Τα άρθρα 450 και 451 εφαρμόζονται και όταν το έγγραφο βρίσκεται σε δημόσια αρχή ή δημόσιο όργανο ή άλλο υπάλληλο νομικού προσώπου δημόσιου ή ιδιωτικού δικαίου, εκτός αν πρόκειται για έγγραφα που ανάγονται σε απόρρητα του κράτους σχετικά με την ασφάλεια και τις διεθνείς σχέσεις του.

Article 448

1. Where prepared in accordance with legal form, the ledgers/registers referred to in Article 444(1) (a) and (b) constitute proof in full concerning their contents between merchants or other persons obligated to keep such ledgers/registers; however, counter-evidence shall be allowed. Nevertheless, they constitute proof in full of the amount of a claim against persons not obligated to keep such ledgers/ registers, where the existence of said claim is otherwise proven, and only for one year after the entry was made, unless the person obligated to keep the ledger/register acknowledged the content by affixing their signature.
2. The documents referred to in Article 444(1)(c) constitute proof in full concerning the facts or things they concern; however, counter-evidence shall be allowed.
3. The [mechanically displayed] means referred to in Article 444(2) constitute proof in full, without prejudice to Article 445.

Article 449

1. Copies whose exactness is confirmed by the competent employee have probative value equal to that of the original.
2. Photographs or photocopies of documents have probative value equal to that of the original, provided their exactness is confirmed by a person authorised in law to issue copies.
3. Exact electronic copies, digitised electronic copies and their print-outs have the probative value of an exact copy, in accordance with the provisions of Article 14 of the Law on Digital Governance.

Article 450

1. Every party in the proceedings is obligated to adduce the documents used or relied upon during proceedings.
2. Every party in the proceedings or third party is obligated to disclose the documents which they hold and which can be useful as evidence, unless there are serious grounds justifying their non-disclosure. In particular, there are serious grounds in cases where one is allowed to refuse to testify.

Article 451

1. Disclosure may be requested by means of an incidental action where a third party is obligated to do so, and by means of the pleadings where a party in the proceedings is obligated to do so. If the filing of pleadings is not mandatory, the application for disclosure shall be filed by means of a statement entered in the transcript.
2. The hearing and taking of evidence shall be conducted in accordance with the general provisions.
3. If there is a good reason why it is difficult to produce the document in court or if the document is at risk of being lost or damaged due to its importance or nature, the court may order the document to be brought before one of the members of the court trying the case or a different court or to be examined by a delegated judge who will visit the location where the document is situated, or allow a certified photocopy or photograph or certified copy of the document in question to be produced.

Article 452

1. The ruling ordering disclosure shall be enforced in accordance with the provisions concerning enforcement for satisfaction of claims involving a thing being returned and delivered or a step being taken.
2. Article 366 also applies in this case.
3. Articles 450 and 451 also apply when the document is being held by a public authority or public body or other employee of a body governed by public or private law, except for documents that concern confidential information of the state relating to its security and international relations.

Άρθρο 453

1. Ιδιωτικό έγγραφο το οποίο θέλει να μεταχειριστεί ο διάδικος για απόδειξη πρέπει να υποβάλλεται στο πρωτότυπο με όλο το περιεχόμενό του. Το δικαστήριο κατά την κρίση του μπορεί να λάβει υπόψη επικυρωμένο αντίγραφο του εγγράφου ή τηλεγράφημα που έχει επιδοθεί.

2. Αν πρόκειται να διεξαχθεί απόδειξη με βιβλίο ή άλλο εκτενές έγγραφο που περιέχει περισσότερα θέματα τα οποία δεν έχουν συνάφεια με τη δίκη, μπορεί να υποβληθεί επικυρωμένο απόσπασμα που περιέχει τα μέρη του εγγράφου τα οποία έχουν συνάφεια με τη δίκη.

Άρθρο 454

Αν το έγγραφο που προσάγεται έχει συνταχθεί σε ξένη γλώσσα, υποβάλλεται μαζί και επίσημη μετάφρασή του επικυρωμένη από το υπουργείο εξωτερικών ή άλλο αρμόδιο κατά το νόμο πρόσωπο ή από την πρεσβεία ή το προξενείο της Ελλάδας στη χώρα, στην περιοχή της οποίας έχει συνταχθεί το έγγραφο ή από την πρεσβεία στην Ελλάδα ή το προξενείο της ίδιας χώρας. Σε οποιαδήποτε περίπτωση το δικαστήριο μπορεί να διατάξει να μεταφραστεί το έγγραφο στα ελληνικά από πραγματογνώμονα.

Άρθρο 455

Τα δημόσια έγγραφα θεωρούνται γνήσια και επιτρέπεται μόνο να προσβληθούν ως πλαστά. Το δικαστήριο μπορεί, αν έχει αμφιβολίες ως προς τη γνησιότητα του εγγράφου, να ζητήσει αυτεπαγγέλτως εξηγήσεις από εκείνον που φέρεται ως εκδότης του εγγράφου.

Άρθρο 456

Το δικαστήριο μπορεί με βάση τις συντρέχουσες περιστάσεις να θεωρήσει γνήσιο χωρίς απόδειξη ξένο δημόσιο έγγραφο. Για το σκοπό αυτόν μπορεί να θεωρήσει επαρκή την επικύρωσή του από το υπουργείο εξωτερικών ή από πρεσβευτή ή πρόξενο της Ελλάδας.

Άρθρο 457

1. Τη γνησιότητα ιδιωτικού εγγράφου, εφόσον αμφισβητείται, πρέπει να την αποδείξει εκείνος που το επικαλείται και το προσάγει, εκτός αν είναι τόσο φανερά αλλαγμένο ώστε το δικαστήριο να μπορεί να διαπιστώσει αμέσως και ασφαλώς ότι δεν είναι γνήσιο.

2. Εκείνος κατά του οποίου προσάγεται ιδιωτικό έγγραφο οφείλει να δηλώσει αμέσως αν αναγνωρίζει ή αρνείται τη γνησιότητα της υπογραφής, διαφορετικά το έγγραφο θεωρείται αναγνωρισμένο.

3. Αν αναγνωριστεί ή αποδειχθεί η γνησιότητα της υπογραφής, θεωρείται ότι έχει διαπιστωθεί η γνησιότητα του περιεχομένου με την επιφύλαξη της προσβολής του ως πλαστού.

4. Σε φωτογραφικές ή κινηματογραφικές αναπαραστάσεις, φωνοληψίες και κάθε άλλη μηχανική απεικόνιση τη γνησιότητά τους, εφόσον αμφισβητείται, οφείλει να την αποδείξει εκείνος που τις επικαλείται και τις προσάγει.

Άρθρο 458

Η απόδειξη της γνησιότητας ιδιωτικού εγγράφου μπορεί να γίνει με κάθε αποδεικτικό μέσο.

Article 453

1. A private document that a party in the proceedings wishes to use as evidence must be submitted in its original form and with its entire content. The court may, at its discretion, take into consideration a certified copy of the document or a telegram which was served.

2. If a ledger/register or other long document containing numerous subjects not relevant to the proceedings is to be used as evidence, a certified excerpt containing the parts of the document relevant to the proceedings may be submitted.

Article 454

If the document produced was prepared in a foreign language, an official translation shall also be submitted, certified by the Ministry of Foreign Affairs, or other person authorised in law, or the embassy or consulate of Greece in the country in whose territory the document was prepared, or by the embassy or consulate of that country in Greece. In all cases, the court may order that the document be translated into Greek by an expert.

Article 455

Public documents shall be deemed to be authentic, and may only be challenged by contesting their authenticity. If the court has doubts concerning the authenticity of the document, the court may request *ex officio* explanations from the person purported to be the author of the document.

Article 456

On the basis of the specific circumstances, the court may consider a foreign public document to be authentic without [requiring] proof [of this]. To this end, the court may consider that certification by the Ministry of Foreign Affairs or a Greek ambassador or consul suffices.

Article 457

1. Where the authenticity of a private document is disputed, [its] authenticity must be proven by the party relying on and producing the document, unless the document has been so obviously altered that the court cannot but immediately and assuredly ascertain that it is not authentic.

2. The person against whom a private document is produced is obligated to immediately declare whether they acknowledge or deny the authenticity of the signature, otherwise the document shall be deemed to be acknowledged.

3. If the authenticity of the signature is acknowledged or proven, the authenticity of the content shall be deemed to be ascertained, without prejudice to any challenge to its authenticity.

4. Where the authenticity of photographic, video, audio recordings and any other mechanically displayed means is being disputed, the person relying on and producing them is obligated to prove their authenticity.

Article 458

The authenticity of a private document may be proven using any means of evidence.

Άρθρο 459

1. Αν πρόκειται να γίνει παραβολή εγγράφων, εκείνος που διεξάγει την απόδειξη οφείλει πέντε ημέρες πριν από την ορισμένη για την παραβολή ημέρα να κοινοποιήσει στον αντίδικο κατάλογο των εγγράφων προς τα οποία θα γίνει η παραβολή ή να καταθέσει τα πρωτότυπα στη γραμματεία του δικαστηρίου.
2. Αν δεν υπάρχουν ή δεν είναι δυνατό να προσαχθούν εύκολα αναμφισβητήτως γνήσια έγγραφα, μπορεί ο διάδικος ή τρίτος, του οποίου αμφισβητείται η γνησιότητα της γραφής ή της υπογραφής, να υποχρεωθεί να γράψει ενώπιον του δικαστηρίου ή εντεταλμένου δικαστή με υπαγόρευσή τους ορισμένο κείμενο προς το οποίο θα γίνει η παραβολή. Το κείμενο αυτό επισυνάπτεται στα πρακτικά ή στην έκθεση. Το δικαστήριο εκτιμά ελεύθερα την άρνηση του διαδίκου ή του τρίτου να γράψει ή την προσπάθειά του να αλλοιώσει τη γραφή του.
3. Αν τα έγγραφα που πρόκειται να παραβληθούν τα κατέχει ο αντίδικος ή τρίτος, μπορεί να ζητηθεί η επίδειξή τους. Για την παραβολή εφαρμόζονται οι διατάξεις οι σχετικές με την αυτοψία και την πραγματογνωμοσύνη.

Άρθρο 460

Κάθε έγγραφο μπορεί να προσβληθεί ως πλαστό, τα ιδιωτικά και όταν με παραβολή προς άλλα αποδείχθηκαν γνήσια.

Άρθρο 461

Αν η πλαστογραφία αποδίδεται σε ορισμένο πρόσωπο, μπορεί να προταθεί σε οποιοδήποτε στάση της δίκης με κύρια ή παρεμπίπτουσα αγωγή ή με τις προτάσεις, όπως και με τους τρόπους που προβλέπει ο Κώδικας Ποινικής Δικονομίας.

Άρθρο 462

Αν δημιουργούνται σοβαρές υπόνοιες πλαστογραφίας εναντίον ορισμένου προσώπου, το δικαστήριο μπορεί, εφόσον το έγγραφο που προσβάλλεται ως πλαστό είναι κατά την κρίση του ουσιώδες για τη διάγνωση της υπόθεσης, είτε να αναβάλει τη δίκη έως το τέλος της ποινικής δίκης, είτε να διατάξει αποδείξεις για την πλαστότητα.

Άρθρο 463

Όποιος προβάλλει ισχυρισμούς για την πλαστότητα εγγράφου είναι ταυτόχρονα υποχρεωμένος να προσκομίσει τα έγγραφα που αποδεικνύουν την πλαστότητα και να αναφέρει ονομαστικά τους μάρτυρες και τα άλλα αποδεικτικά μέσα, αλλιώς οι ισχυρισμοί του είναι απαράδεκτοι.

Άρθρο 464

Αν έγγραφο προσβάλλεται παρεμπιπτόντως ως πλαστό χωρίς να αποδίδεται η πλαστογραφία σε ορισμένο πρόσωπο, το δικαστήριο διατάζει αποδείξεις μόνο αν εκείνος που προσκόμισε το έγγραφο επιμένει να το χρησιμοποιήσει και το έγγραφο είναι κατά την κρίση του δικαστηρίου ουσιώδες για τη διάγνωση της υπόθεσης.

Άρθρο 465

1. Η γραμματεία του δικαστηρίου στέλνει αμέσως αντίγραφο κάθε απόφασης που κηρύσσει έγγραφο πλαστό ή ανακαλεί ή μεταρρυθμίζει την απόφαση αυτή στον εισαγγελέα του δικαστηρίου και στη δημόσια αρχή που το έχει εκδώσει.
2. Το έγγραφο που κηρύχθηκε πλαστό δεν αποδίδεται στο διάδικο αλλά παραμένει στο αρχείο του δικαστηρίου. Στην περίπτωση αυτή ο γραμματέας σημειώνει επάνω στο έγγραφο ή σε πρόσθεμα ότι κηρύχθηκε πλαστό, καθώς και την απόφαση που κήρυξε την πλαστότητα.
3. Στην περίπτωση που θα εκδοθεί αντίγραφο, το αντίγραφο περιλαμβάνει και τη σημείωση που αναφέρεται στην προηγούμενη παράγραφο.

Article 459

1. If documents are to be compared, the person using them as evidence is obligated to notify a list of the documents to be compared to the opponent or to file the original documents with the court registry five days prior to the day set for the comparison.
2. If indisputably authentic documents do not exist or cannot be easily produced, the party in the proceedings or the third party the authenticity of whose handwriting or signature is being disputed may be obligated to write a specific text before the court or delegated judge, dictated by the latter, to be used for the purpose of comparison. This text shall be attached to the transcript or the report. The court shall freely weigh up the refusal by the party in the proceedings or the third party to write or any attempt to alter their handwriting.
3. If the documents to be compared are being held by the opponent or a third party, their disclosure may be requested. The provisions concerning inspections and expert evidence apply to the comparison.

Article 460

The authenticity of any document may be contested, [including] private documents proven to be authentic when compared to others.

Article 461

If forgery is attributed to a specific person, it may be pleaded at any stage of the proceedings by means of a main or incidental action or the pleadings, and in the manner set forth in the Code of Criminal Procedure.

Article 462

If there are serious suspicions of forgery against a specific person, the court may, where the document whose authenticity is being contested is essential, in the view of the court, for determining the case, either stay proceedings until the criminal proceedings in question have ended or order the taking of evidence regarding the forgery.

Article 463

Any person alleging that a document is forged is also obligated to adduce the documents proving the forgery and name the witnesses and other means of evidence, otherwise their allegations shall be inadmissible.

Article 464

If the authenticity of a document is being contested incidentally without attributing forgery to a specific person, the court shall order the taking of evidence only if the person who adduced the document insists on using it and the document is, in the view of the court, essential for determining the case.

Article 465

1. The court registry shall immediately send a copy of any ruling declaring a document to be forged or revoking or amending this ruling to the public prosecutor of the court and the public authority that issued the document in question.
2. The document declared to be forged shall not be returned to the party in the proceedings but shall be kept in the court archives. In this case, the registrar shall note on the document or a cover page that it was declared to be forged, as well as the ruling declaring it as such.
3. Where a copy is issued, the copy shall also contain the note referred to in the preceding paragraph.

ΚΕΦΑΛΑΙΟ ΙΓ'
Ειδικές διατάξεις για τις μικροδιαφορές

Άρθρο 466

1. Αν το αντικείμενο της διαφοράς υπάγεται στο ειρηνοδικείο και αφορά απαιτήσεις, καθώς και δικαιώματα επάνω σε κινητά πράγματα ή τη νομή τους και η αξία του δεν είναι μεγαλύτερη από πέντε χιλιάδες (5.000) ευρώ, εφαρμόζονται τα άρθρα 467 έως 471.

2. Τα άρθρα 467 έως 471 εφαρμόζονται και όταν η αξία του αντικειμένου της διαφοράς είναι μεγαλύτερη από πέντε χιλιάδες (5.000) ευρώ, αν ο ενάγων δηλώσει ότι δέχεται προς ικανοποίηση του, αντί για το αντικείμενο που ζητεί με την αγωγή χρηματικό ποσό όχι μεγαλύτερο από πέντε χιλιάδες (5.000) ευρώ. Στην περίπτωση αυτή ο εναγόμενος καταδικάζεται διαζευκτικά να καταβάλει είτε το αντικείμενο που ζητείται με την αγωγή είτε την αποτίμηση του σύμφωνα με την απόφαση που θα εκδώσει ο ειρηνοδίκης.

Άρθρο 467

Ο ενάγων είναι υποχρεωμένος να ασκήσει με την ίδια αγωγή όλες τις απαιτήσεις του κατά του εναγομένου, οι οποίες δεν εξαρτώνται από αίρεση ή προθεσμία, εφόσον το σύνολό τους δεν υπερβαίνει τις πέντε χιλιάδες (5.000) ευρώ. Αν τις ασκήσει χωριστά, οι αγωγές δεν απορρίπτονται, αλλά οι σχετικές δαπάνες, εκτός της πρώτης, βαρύνουν τον ενάγοντα.

Άρθρο 468

1. Η αγωγή κατατίθεται στη γραμματεία του ειρηνοδικείου και επιδίδεται στον εναγόμενο μέσα σε προθεσμία δέκα (10) ημερών από την κατάθεσή της. Αν ο εναγόμενος διαμένει στο εξωτερικό ή είναι άγνωστης διαμονής η αγωγή επιδίδεται σε προθεσμία τριάντα (30) ημερών από την κατάθεσή της. Το δεύτερο εδάφιο της παρ. 2 του άρθρου 215 εφαρμόζεται αναλόγως.

2. Μέσα σε είκοσι (20) ημέρες από τη λήξη της προθεσμίας για την επίδοση της αγωγής, οι διάδικοι προσκομίζουν στο ειρηνοδικείο τα αποδεικτικά τους μέσα και ο εναγόμενος υποβάλλει με έγγραφο υπόμνημα τους ισχυρισμούς του. Μέχρι δύο (2) ένορκες βεβαιώσεις, επιτρέπονται και χωρίς κλήση του αντιδίκου. Εντός προθεσμίας πέντε (5) ημερών από τη λήξη της ως άνω προθεσμίας οι διάδικοι μπορούν να καταθέσουν έγγραφη προσθήκη- αντίκρουση. Νέοι ισχυρισμοί με την προσθήκη μπορεί να προταθούν και νέα αποδεικτικά μέσα να προσκομισθούν μόνο για την αντίκρουση ισχυρισμών που περιέχονται στο ως άνω υπόμνημα. Εκπρόθεσμα αποδεικτικά μέσα και ισχυρισμοί των διαδίκων δεν λαμβάνονται υπόψη.

3. Παρεμβάσεις και ανταγωγές κατατίθενται και επιδίδονται στους διαδίκους μέσα σε προθεσμία είκοσι (20) ημερών από την κατάθεση της αγωγής. Η προθεσμία αυτή παρατείνεται κατά είκοσι (20) ημέρες αν ο εναγόμενος διαμένει στο εξωτερικό ή είναι άγνωστης διαμονής. Η προσκομιδή των αποδεικτικών μέσων και το έγγραφο υπόμνημα των ισχυρισμών στις περιπτώσεις του δεύτερου εδαφίου γίνονται σε προθεσμία τριάντα (30) ή πενήντα (50) ημερών, αντίστοιχα, από την κατάθεση της αγωγής και η έγγραφη προσθήκη- αντίκρουση στην προθεσμία του τρίτου εδαφίου της παρ. 2.

4. Η προηγούμενη διαδικασία μπορεί να γίνει και με χρήση τυποποιημένων εγγράφων ή Τεχνολογίας Πληροφορίας και Επικοινωνίας. Με κοινή απόφαση των Υπουργών Δικαιοσύνης και Ψηφιακής Διακυβέρνησης καθορίζονται οι λεπτομέρειες για την εφαρμογή της παρούσας με χρήση Τεχνολογίας Πληροφορίας και Επικοινωνίας. Με απόφαση του Υπουργού Δικαιοσύνης καθορίζεται το περιεχόμενο των τυποποιημένων εγγράφων.

5. Αμέσως μετά την παρέλευση των ως άνω προθεσμιών προσδιορίζεται αρμοδίως η ημέρα συζήτησης με εγγραφή της υπόθεσης σε πινάκιο. Τα εδάφια πέμπτο και έκτο της παρ. 6 του άρθρου 237 ισχύουν αναλόγως.

CHAPTER XIII
Special provisions on small claims

Article 466

1. If the subject-matter of the dispute falls within the jurisdiction of the court of the peace and concerns claims and rights over movables or their possession and their value does not exceed 5,000 euros, Articles 467 to 471 apply.
2. Article 467 to 471 also apply where the value of the subject-matter of the dispute exceeds 5,000 euros if the plaintiff declares that they accept, as satisfaction, a monetary sum not exceeding 5,000 euros instead of the form of order being sought in the action. In this case, the defendant shall be ordered, disjunctively, to either return the subject-matter being requested in the action or pay the value set in the judgment to be handed down by the court of the peace judge.

Article 467

The plaintiff is obligated to bring all their claims against the defendant that are not subject to conditions or a term in the same action, provided these claims do not exceed 5,000 euros in total. If the plaintiff brings them separately, the actions shall not be dismissed, but the relevant costs, except for those of the first action, shall be borne by the plaintiff.

Article 468

1. The action shall be filed with the registry of the court of the peace and served on the defendant within a deadline of 10 days from its filing. If the defendant has their place of domicile abroad or has no known place of residence, the action shall be served within a deadline of 30 days from its filing. The second subparagraph of Article 215(2) applies *mutatis mutandis*.
2. Within 20 days of the deadline for service of the action lapsing, the parties in the proceedings shall adduce their means of evidence before the court of the peace, and the defendant shall submit their assertions by means of a written statement. No more than two affidavits are allowed even where the opponent has not been summoned. Within 5 days of the aforesaid deadline lapsing, the parties in the proceedings may file an addition [to the pleadings] - rebuttal in writing. New assertions may be put forth in the addition and new means of evidence may be adduced only in order to rebut assertions contained in the aforesaid statement. Means of evidence and assertions submitted late by the parties in the proceedings shall be disregarded.
3. Interventions and cross-actions shall be filed and served on the parties in the proceedings within a deadline of 20 days from the date the action is filed. This deadline shall be extended by 20 days if the defendant has their place of domicile abroad or has no known place of residence. In the cases provided for in the second subparagraph, the means of evidence and the written statement containing allegations shall be adduced within a deadline of 30 or 50 days, respectively, from the filing of the action and the addition [to the pleadings] - rebuttal in writing within the deadline laid down in the third subparagraph of paragraph 2.
4. The above procedure may also be carried out using standardised documents or information and communication technologies. Details on the application of this paragraph using information and communication technologies shall be specified in a joint decision issued by the Minister of Justice and the Minister of Digital Governance. The information to be included in standardised documents shall be specified in a decision issued by the Minister of Justice.
5. Immediately after the above deadlines have lapsed, the hearing date shall be duly set with entry of the case in the case register. The fifth and sixth subparagraphs of Article 237(6) apply *mutatis mutandis*.

Άρθρο 469

1. Κατά την ορισμένη δικάσιμο η υπόθεση συζητείται με την παρουσία των διαδίκων. Αν αυτοί συμφωνούν, μπορούν να καταθέσουν κοινή δήλωση κατά την παρ. 2 του άρθρου 242. Το τελευταίο εδάφιο της παρ. 6 του άρθρου 237, το άρθρο 260, η παρ. 3 του άρθρου 271, οι παρ. 1 και 2 του άρθρου 272 και το άρθρο 501 εφαρμόζονται αναλόγως. Μετά το πέρας της συζήτησης ο Πρόεδρος του Δικαστηρίου δύναται να ζητεί από τους διαδίκους να προσκομίσουν σε ηλεκτρονική μορφή αντίγραφο του δικογράφου της αγωγής, του υπομνήματος και της προσθήκης.
2. Ο ειρηνοδίκης λαμβάνει υπόψη και αποδεικτικά μέσα που δεν πληρούν τους όρους του νόμου. Οι παριστάμενοι κατά τη συζήτηση διάδικοι μπορούν, κατά την κρίση του ειρηνοδίκη, να εξετάζονται κατ' άρθρο 415 ή να παρέχουν διασαφήσεις για την υπόθεση, οι δε ενόρκως βεβαιώσαντες να καταθέτουν συμπληρωματικώς, εφόσον είναι παρόντες και ο ειρηνοδίκης κρίνει τούτο απολύτως αναγκαίο. Νέοι ισχυρισμοί μπορούν να προταθούν μόνον εάν αποδεικνύονται εγγράφως ή με δικαστική ομολογία του αντιδίκου ή προέκυψαν μεταγενέστερα, αποδεικνυόμενοι με την προσκομιδή μέχρι δύο (2) ενόρκων βεβαιώσεων.

Άρθρα 470

[Καταργούνται]

ΚΕΦΑΛΑΙΟ ΙΔ'
Ειδικές διατάξεις για τη λογοδοσία

Άρθρο 473

Όποιος ασκεί αγωγή για λογοδοσία ή για την παράδοση καταλόγου με τα στοιχεία ομάδας αντικειμένων μπορεί να περιλάβει στην αγωγή αίτημα για την καταβολή του καταλοίπου του λογαριασμού ή για την απόδοση των αντικειμένων της ομάδας, χωρίς να προσδιοριστούν τα αντικείμενα στο δικόγραφο της αγωγής ή για την καταβολή ορισμένου ελλείμματος, στην περίπτωση που δεν θα κατατεθεί ο λογαριασμός ή ο κατάλογος με τα δικαιολογητικά. Τα ίδια αιτήματα μπορούν να υποβληθούν και με παρεμπίπτουσα αγωγή.

Άρθρο 474

Η απόφαση που διατάζει λογοδοσία ή παράδοση καταλόγου των στοιχείων ομάδας αντικειμένων ορίζει προθεσμία μέσα στην οποία ο λογαριασμός ή ο κατάλογος πρέπει να κατατεθεί με τα δικαιολογητικά στη γραμματεία του δικαστηρίου.

Άρθρο 475

1. Για την κατάθεση του λογαριασμού ή του καταλόγου συντάσσεται έκθεση. Τα έγγραφα αυτά και τα δικαιολογητικά αποτελούν στοιχεία του φακέλου της δικογραφίας.
2. Μετά την κατάθεση του λογαριασμού ή του καταλόγου η υπόθεση εισάγεται για συζήτηση, κατά την οποία οι διάδικοι υποβάλλουν τις παρατηρήσεις τους, προσδιορίζουν σαφώς τα κονδύλια του λογαριασμού ή τα στοιχεία του καταλόγου, τα οποία αμφισβητούν, τις ελλείψεις ή τις παραλείψεις τους και γενικά προβάλλουν όλα τα μέσα επίθεσης και άμυνας που αφορούν το λογαριασμό ή τον κατάλογο.

Άρθρο 476

Αν με το λογαριασμό ή τον κατάλογο που έχει κατατεθεί ομολογείται υποχρέωση για καταβολή ορισμένου ποσού ή για απόδοση ορισμένων αντικειμένων, το δικαστήριο ύστερα από σχετική αίτηση καταδικάζει τον εναγόμενο να καταβάλει το ποσό ή να αποδώσει τα αντικείμενα με βάση την ομολογία που περιέχεται στο λογαριασμό ή τον κατάλογο, επιφυλάσσεται όμως για όσα επιπλέον πρέπει να καταβληθούν ή να αποδοθούν.

Article 469

1. On the hearing date set, the case shall be heard in the presence of the parties in the proceedings. If the parties agree, they may file a joint statement in accordance with Article 242(2). The final subparagraph of Article 237(6), Article 260, Article 271(3), Article 272(1) and (2) and Article 501 apply *mutatis mutandis*. After the hearing has ended, the presiding judge of the court may request that the parties in the proceedings submit a copy of the action, memorandum and supplementary pleadings in electronic form.

2. The court of the peace judge shall also take into consideration means of evidence that do not meet statutory requirements. The parties in the proceedings appearing during the hearing may, at the discretion of the court of the peace judge, be examined in accordance with Article 415 or provide clarifications regarding the case, and the persons who submitted affidavits may give supplementary testimony, if they are present and the court of the peace judge considers this absolutely necessary. New assertions may only be put forth if proven in writing or by admission made by the opponent in court or arose at a later stage, proven by submission of no more than two affidavits.

Articles 470-472

[Repealed]

CHAPTER XIV

Special provisions regarding rendering of account

Article 473

Any person filing an action for an account to be rendered or for a list containing information on a group of things to be delivered may include a claim in the action for payment of the remainder of the account or for return of the things comprising the group without the things being specified in the procedural document of the action or for the payment of a specific shortfall, where the account or the list with the supporting documents is not filed. The same claims may also be brought in an incidental action.

Article 474

The judgment ordering rendering of an account or delivery of a list containing information on a group of things shall set a deadline within which the account or list must be filed, together with the supporting documents, with the court registry.

Article 475

1. A report shall be prepared with regard to the filing of the account or the list. These documents and the supporting documents constitute part of the case-file.

2. After the account or the list has been filed, the case shall be brought for a hearing, during which the parties in the proceedings shall submit their observations, clearly specify the amounts in the account or information on the list which they dispute, their defects or omissions, and generally put forth all pleas concerning the account or list.

Article 476

If an obligation for payment of a specific amount or return of specific things is admitted in the account or list filed, the court, following a relevant application, shall order the defendant to pay the amount or return the things on the basis of the admission contained in the account or list, but shall reserve judgment on any additional amounts or things that must be paid or returned.

Άρθρο 477

1. Αν δεν κατατεθούν μέσα στην προθεσμία που όρισε η απόφαση ο λογαριασμός ή ο κατάλογος, η απόφαση γίνεται οριστική ως προς την υποχρέωση λογοδοσίας ή την υποβολή του καταλόγου.
2. Αν ζητήθηκε κατά το άρθρο 473 να καταβληθεί ορισμένο έλλειμμα και το έλλειμμα πιθανολογείται, το δικαστήριο με την απόφαση που διατάζει τη λογοδοσία μπορεί να καταδικάσει τον εναγόμενο, για την περίπτωση που δεν θα καταθέσει εμπρόθεσμα το λογαριασμό ή τον κατάλογο με τα δικαιολογητικά, να καταβάλει το κατά την κρίση του έλλειμμα. Το δικαστήριο μπορεί, αν το κρίνει αναγκαίο, να διατάξει απόδειξη για το πιθανό έλλειμμα.

ΚΕΦΑΛΑΙΟ ΙΕ'
Ειδικές διατάξεις για τη διανομή

Άρθρο 478

Όταν υπάρχει κοινωνία, η αγωγή διανομής απευθύνεται κατά όλων των κοινωνών, αλλιώς απορρίπτεται ως απαράδεκτη.

Άρθρο 479

Στην αγωγή διανομής το δικαστήριο προσδιορίζει τη μερίδα κάθε κοινωνού, τα αντικείμενα που πρέπει να διανεμηθούν και τις απαιτήσεις κάθε κοινωνού από την κοινωνία, καθώς και από τη συνεισφορά.

Άρθρο 480

1. Το δικαστήριο αποφασίζει την αυτούσια διανομή, αν είναι δυνατή η διαίρεση του διανεμητέου σε μέρη ανάλογα προς τις μερίδες των κοινωνών, δίχως να μειώνεται η αξία του.
2. Αν τα διανεμητέα αντικείμενα είναι περισσότερα και η αυτούσια διανομή όλων ή μερικών από αυτά είναι αδύνατη ή ασύμφορη, είναι όμως δυνατή η κατανομή τους σε μέρη ανάλογα προς τις μερίδες των κοινωνών, το δικαστήριο μπορεί να αποφασίσει την αυτούσια διανομή με τον τρόπο αυτόν.
3. Αν ορισμένοι κοινωνοί ζήτησαν να λάβουν κοινή μερίδα, η μερίδα αυτή λογίζεται ως ενιαία. Στο μέρος που περιέρχεται σ' αυτούς με την αυτούσια διανομή συνιστάται κοινωνία κατά το λόγο των μερίδων τους.

Άρθρο 480Α

1. Κάθε συγκύριος οικοπέδου στο οποίο υπάρχει οικοδομή ή χωριστές οικοδομές, έχει το δικαίωμα να ζητήσει την αυτούσια διανομή του οικοπέδου με σύσταση χωριστής ιδιοκτησίας κατ' ορόφους ή μέρη ορόφων ή με σύσταση χωριστής ιδιοκτησίας σε διακεκριμένα μέρη του ενιαίου οικοπέδου, στα οποία έχουν ανεγερθεί οι χωριστές οικοδομές με την επιφύλαξη των πολεοδομικών διατάξεων. Το δικαστήριο αποφασίζει τη διανομή με τον τρόπο αυτόν, αν είναι εφικτή και δεν αντιβαίνει στο συμφέρον των λοιπών συγκυρίων. Η απόφαση που διατάζει τη διανομή κατά τον τρόπο αυτόν προσδιορίζει τα χωριστά μέρη της οικοδομής που αναλογούν στις μερίδες των συγκυρίων και τα επιδικάζει σ' αυτούς. Αν με τη διανομή αυτή περιέρχονται σε κάποιον συγκύριο περισσότερες αυτοτελείς ιδιοκτησίες, η απόφαση καθορίζει το ποσοστό της συγκυριότητας που αναλογεί σε καθεμιά από τις ιδιοκτησίες αυτές.
2. Αν πρόκειται για οικόπεδο ακάλυπτο και οικοδομήσιμο και η αυτούσια διαίρεσή του είναι ανέφικτη ή ασύμφορη, το δικαστήριο μπορεί να αποφασίσει την αυτούσια διανομή του με σύσταση χωριστής ιδιοκτησίας σε διακεκριμένα μέρη του ενιαίου οικοπέδου στα οποία θα είναι δυνατή η ανέγερση χωριστών οικοδομημάτων, με την επιφύλαξη των πολεοδομικών διατάξεων. Οι διατάξεις της προηγούμενης παραγράφου εφαρμόζονται αναλόγως.
3. Η παράγραφος 3 του προηγούμενου άρθρου εφαρμόζεται αναλόγως και στην περίπτωση της διανομής με σύσταση χωριστών ιδιοκτησιών.

Article 477

1. If the account or list is not filed within the deadline set in the judgment, the judgment becomes final with regard to the obligation to render account or submit the list.
2. If payment of a specific shortfall was requested in accordance with Article 473 and the shortfall is considered likely on the balance of probabilities, in its judgment ordering rendering of account, the court may order the defendant, if they fail to file the account or list together with the supporting documents in good time, to pay the shortfall [computed] at the discretion of the court. Where deemed necessary, the court may order the taking of evidence with regard to the possible shortfall.

CHAPTER XV
Special provisions regarding partition

Article 478

When there is a community of rights, the action for partition shall be brought against all the members of that community, otherwise it shall be dismissed as inadmissible.

Article 479

During [the hearing of] the action for partition, the court shall specify the share of each member, the things that must be partitioned and the claims of each member from the community, as well as from their contributions.

Article 480

1. The court shall order partition *in natura*, where it is possible to divide the partitionable thing into parts in proportion to the shares of the community members without impairing its value.
2. If there are several partitionable things and partition *in natura* of all or certain of them is impossible or disadvantageous but they can be allocated in parts in proportion to the shares of the community members, the court may order partition *in natura* in this manner.
3. If specific community members requested to receive a joint share, that share shall be deemed to be a single share. Where partition *in natura* is ordered, a community of rights shall be established in proportion to their shares in the part devolving to them.

Article 480A

1. Each joint owner of a plot on which a building or separate buildings have been erected has the right to request partition *in natura* of the plot by establishing separate properties by floors or parts of floors, or by establishing a separate property on discrete sections of the single plot on which the separate buildings have been erected, subject to urban planning provisions. The court shall order partition in this manner where it is feasible and is not contrary to the interests of the other joint owners. The judgment ordering partition in this manner shall specify the separate parts of the building corresponding to the shares of the joint owners, and shall award them the said parts. If several separate properties devolve to a joint owner through such partition, the judgment shall specify the joint ownership percentage corresponding to each of these properties.
2. Where an undeveloped plot is fit for building on and its partition *in natura* is infeasible or disadvantageous, the court may order its partition *in natura* by establishing a separate property on discrete sections of the single plot on which the erection of separate structures will be possible, subject to urban planning provisions. The provisions of the preceding paragraph apply *mutatis mutandis*.
3. Paragraph 3 of the preceding Article also applies *mutatis mutandis* in the case of partition by establishing separate properties.

Άρθρο 481

Στις περιπτώσεις των άρθρων 480 και 480Α το δικαστήριο
1) δεν είναι υποχρεωμένο να διατάξει απόδειξη, αν κρίνει ότι η αυτούσια διανομή είναι προδήλως δυνατή, αδύνατη ή ασύμφορη και
2) μπορεί για την εξίσωση άνισων μερών να αποφασίσει ότι οι κοινωνοί που λαμβάνουν ορισμένα μέρη θα καταβάλουν σε άλλους κοινωνούς ορισμένο χρηματικό ποσό ή να συστήσει δουλεία σε ορισμένα μέρη υπέρ άλλων κοινωνών.

Άρθρο 482

1. Κατά το σχηματισμό των μερών πρέπει, όσο είναι δυνατό, να αποφεύγεται η κατάτμηση των ακινήτων και η διανομή των επιχειρήσεων.
2. Για να σχηματιστούν τα μέρη λαμβάνεται υπόψη η αξία των αντικειμένων που πρέπει να διανεμηθούν κατά το χρόνο του σχηματισμού τους. Το δικαστήριο καθορίζει την αξία με βάση τις αποδείξεις που έχουν διεξαχθεί χωρίς να διατάζει γι' αυτό νέες αποδείξεις στην περίπτωση που έχει κατόπιν μεταβληθεί η αξία.

Άρθρο 483

1. Αν στην κοινωνία υπάρχει εμπορική, βιομηχανική, βιοτεχνική, μεταλλευτική, γεωργική, κτηνοτροφική ή άλλη επιχείρηση που αποτελεί οικονομικό σύνολο, το δικαστήριο μπορεί με αίτηση κάποιου από τους κοινωνούς να επιδικάσει ολόκληρη την επιχείρηση που πρέπει να διανεμηθεί σε εκείνον που το ζητεί έναντι καταβολής χρηματικού ποσού ίσου προς την αγοραία αξία της επιχείρησης. Για να καθοριστεί η αξία εφαρμόζονται οι διατάξεις της παρ. 2 του άρθρου 482. Αν περισσότεροι κοινωνοί ζητήσουν να επιδικαστεί σ' αυτούς η επιχείρηση, το δικαστήριο την επιδικάζει, σε εκείνον που κατά την κρίση του είναι πιο ικανός να τη συνεχίσει κατά τρόπο επωφελή.
2. Η αίτηση πρέπει να υποβάλλεται μέχρι τη συζήτηση στο ακροατήριο.
3. Η αίτηση ενός ή περισσότερων κοινωνών για επιδίκαση ολόκληρης της επιχείρησης ως οικονομικού συνόλου, είτε η επιχείρηση αποτελεί το μοναδικό περιουσιακό στοιχείο της κοινωνίας, είτε ένα από τα στοιχεία που την αποτελούν, μπορεί, αν συντρέχουν σοβαροί λόγοι για τους οποίους δικαιολογείται να μη γίνει η διανομή της, να υποβληθεί στο δικαστήριο της διανομής και πριν από κάθε εκκαθάριση η άσκηση της αγωγής για διανομή της κοινής περιουσίας και να δικαστεί από το ίδιο δικαστήριο αυτοτελώς. Το άρθρο 220 εφαρμόζεται και εδώ.

Άρθρο 484

1. Αν η κατά τα άρθρ. 480 και 480Α διανομή είναι ανέφικτη ή ασύμφορη, το δικαστήριο διατάζει την πώληση με πλειστηριασμό.
2. Η διαδικασία του πλειστηριασμού αρχίζει με την περιγραφή των επικοίνων κατά το άρθρο 954 και διεξάγεται όπως ορίζουν τα άρθρα 959 επ.. Εφαρμόζεται επίσης το άρθρο 955 παράγραφος 2 εδάφιο β', η προθεσμία του οποίου αρχίζει από την κατάρτιση της έκθεσης περιγραφής. Στην έκθεση περιγραφής αναφέρονται το όνομα και το επώνυμο, το επάγγελμα και η κατοικία όλων των κοινωνών. Με την καταβολή του πλειστηριάσματος επέρχεται απόσβεση της υποθήκης ή του ενεχύρου που υπάρχει στα πράγματα τα οποία πλειστηριάστηκαν.

Άρθρο 485

Αν η αυτούσια διανομή είναι κατά ένα μόνο μέρος δυνατή, το δικαστήριο μπορεί να αποφασίσει κατά ένα μέρος την αυτούσια διανομή και κατά ένα μέρος την πώληση με πλειστηριασμό.

Article 481

In the cases referred to in Articles 480 and 480A, the court[:]

a) shall not be obligated to order the taking of evidence where it considers that partition *in natura* is manifestly possible, impossible or disadvantageous; and

b) may, in order to equalise unequal parts, order the community members receiving specific parts to pay other members a specific monetary amount or establish an easement on certain parts to benefit other members.

Article 482

1. Insofar as it is possible, the segmentation of immovables and the partition of enterprises must be avoided when creating the parts.

2. When creating the parts, account shall be taken of the value of the things to be partitioned at the time of partitioning. The court shall set the value on the basis of evidence taken without ordering the taking of new evidence in cases where the value changed at a later stage.

Article 483

1. If the community contains a commercial, industrial, craft, mining, agricultural, livestock farming or other enterprise constituting an economic unit, the court may, following an application filed by any of the community members, award the entire enterprise to be partitioned to the person requesting it in return for payment of a monetary sum equal to the market value of the enterprise. The provisions of Article 482(2) apply when determining the value. If several community members request that the enterprise be awarded to them, the court shall award the enterprise to the member who, in the view of the court, is most capable to continue its operation in a beneficial manner.

2. The application must be filed by the date of the courtroom hearing.

3. An application filed by one or more community members to be awarded the entire enterprise as an economic unit, whether the enterprise constitutes the sole asset of the community or [just] one of its assets, may, where there are serious grounds justifying its non-partition, be filed with the court trying the partition, even before any liquidation or filing of an action for partition of the joint property, and tried independently by the same court. Article 220 also apply in this case.

Article 484

1. If the partition referred to in Articles 480 and 480A is infeasible or disadvantageous, the court shall order sale by auction.

2. The auction process shall commence with a description of the jointly owned assets, in accordance with Article 954, and shall be conducted in accordance with the provisions of Articles 959 *et seq.* The second subparagraph of Article 955(2) also applies, with the deadline set therein commencing upon the preparation of the description report. The description report shall mention the first name, last name, occupation and residence of all community members. Upon payment of the auction price, [any] mortgage or pledge registered on the things auctioned shall be extinguished.

Article 485

If partition *in natura* is possible only for one part, the court may order partition *in natura* of that part and sale by auction of another part.

Άρθρο 486

1. Αν τα μέρη που σχηματίσθηκαν κατά τα άρθρ. 480 ή 480Α είναι ίσα, η αυτούσια διανομή τους μεταξύ των κοινωνών γίνεται με κλήρωση. Αν όμως η διανομή με κλήρωση μπορεί να οδηγήσει σε τεμαχισμό της ιδιοκτησίας κάποιου από τους κοινωνούς ή είναι προδήλως αντίθετη προς το συμφέρον του, το δικαστήριο μπορεί, ύστερα από σχετική αίτηση, να επιδικάσει σε κάθε κοινωνό ή στις ομάδες των κοινωνών που ζήτησαν να λάβουν κοινή μερίδα ό,τι τους αναλογεί, δίχως κλήρωση.

2. Αν τα μέρη που σχηματίσθηκαν κατά τα άρθρ. 480 ή 480Α είναι άνισα, η αυτούσια διανομή γίνεται με επιδίκασή τους στους συγκυρίους ή στις ομάδες εκείνων που ζήτησαν κοινή μερίδα, κατά το λόγο των μερίδων τους.

Άρθρο 487

1. Η απόφαση του πολυμελούς δικαστηρίου, με την οποία διατάζεται αυτούσια διανομή με κλήρωση και σχηματίζονται τα μέρη, παραπέμπει την υπόθεση σε εντεταλμένο δικαστή για να γίνει η κλήρωση ενώπιόν του. Αν η απόφαση παρέλειψε την παραπομπή, μπορεί να ζητηθεί η συμπλήρωσή της.

2. Ο ειρηνοδίκης ή ο δικαστής του μονομελούς πρωτοδικείου ή ο εντεταλμένος δικαστής ορίζει, με αίτηση κάποιου από τους διαδίκους, ημέρα και ώρα κατά την οποία γίνεται ενώπιόν του η κλήρωση, αφού κληθούν όλοι οι διάδικοι.

3. Ο δικαστής ενώπιον του οποίου γίνεται η κλήρωση ορίζει κατά την κρίση του την προθεσμία που πρέπει να περάσει από την κοινοποίηση της κλήσης έως την ημέρα της κλήρωσης, καθώς και τον τρόπο της κλήρωσης.

4. Κατά την ημέρα και την ώρα που έχει οριστεί καταρτίζονται τόσοι κλήροι όσα είναι τα μέρη που σχημάτισε η απόφαση και τοποθετούνται στην κληρωτίδα. Από την κληρωτίδα εξάγεται για κάθε κοινωνό ο αριθμός κλήρων που αναλογεί στη μερίδα του.

5. Η κλήρωση γίνεται και αν απουσιάζει κάποιος διάδικος ή και όλοι οι διάδικοι, εφόσον αποδεικνύεται ότι κλητεύθηκαν νόμιμα.

6. Για τον καταρτισμό των κλήρων και την κλήρωση συντάσσεται έκθεση στην οποία πρέπει να αναφέρεται ο τρόπος που καταρτίστηκαν οι κλήροι και έγινε η κλήρωση και να ορίζονται ακριβώς τα μέρη που έλαχαν σε κάθε κοινωνό.

Άρθρο 488

1. Αν όλοι οι διάδικοι είναι σύμφωνοι, η κλήρωση μπορεί να γίνει ενώπιον συμβολαιογράφου. Ο συμβολαιογράφος συντάσσει έκθεση στην οποία πρέπει να αναφέρονται όλοι όσοι ήταν παρόντες κατά την κλήρωση, να βεβαιώνεται η συμφωνία των κοινωνών για να γίνει η κλήρωση ενώπιον του συμβολαιογράφου, να αναφέρεται ο τρόπος που σχηματίστηκαν οι κλήροι, η κλήρωση, καθώς και τα μέρη που έλαχαν σε κάθε κοινωνό.

2. Αν όλοι οι διάδικοι είναι σύμφωνοι, αντί για κλήρωση μπορεί να γίνει διανομή των μερών που σχηματίστηκαν από την απόφαση η οποία διέταξε την αυτούσια διανομή μεταξύ των κοινωνών χωρίς κλήρωση και να συνταχθεί γι' αυτό έκθεση ενώπιον του συμβολαιογράφου.

Άρθρο 489

1. Με τη διανομή κάθε κοινωνός γίνεται δικαιούχος του μέρους που περιήλθε σ' αυτόν.

2. Για τη μεταβίβαση στους κοινωνούς της κυριότητας των διανεμόμενων ακινήτων, για τη σύστασή της χωριστής ιδιοκτησίας, σύμφωνα με το άρθρο 480Α, καθώς και για τη σύσταση υπέρ κοινωνού, τη μεταβίβαση σ' αυτόν ή την κατάργηση εμπράγματου δικαιώματος απαιτείται μεταγραφή της τελεσίδικης δικαστικής απόφασης που διατάζει την αυτούσια διανομή, και σε περίπτωση κλήρωσης και της σχετικής έκθεσης.

Article 486

1. If the parts created under Article 480 or Article 480A are equal, partition *in natura* among the community members shall be done by drawing lots. However, if the partition by drawing lots could lead to segmentation of the property of one of the community members or is manifestly contrary to the interests of that member, the court, following a relevant application, may award whatever corresponds to each community member or groups of members who asked to receive a common share without drawing lots.
2. If the parts created under Article 480 or Article 480A are unequal, partition *in natura* shall be done by awarding them to the joint owners or groups of members who requested a common share in proportion to their shares.

Article 487

1. The judgment handed down by the multi-member court ordering partition *in natura* by drawing lots and creating parts shall remit the case to a delegated judge in order for lots to be drawn in their presence. If the judgment did not contain a remittal order, supplementation of the judgment may be requested.
2. Following an application filed by any of the parties in the proceedings, the court of the peace judge or single-member court of first instance judge or delegated judge shall set a day and time for lots to be drawn in their presence, after all the parties in the proceedings have been summoned.
3. The judge in whose presence lots are to be drawn shall, at their discretion, set the deadline that must elapse between the notification of the summons and the day lots are to be drawn, as well as the manner in which lots will be drawn.
4. On the day and time set, a number of lots equal to the parts formed pursuant to the judgment shall be prepared and placed in the drawing apparatus. The number of lots corresponding to the share of each community member shall be drawn from the drawing apparatus.
5. Lots shall be drawn even if one or all the parties in the proceedings are absent, where it has been proven that they were duly summonsed.
6. A report shall be prepared on the preparation and drawing of lots, indicating how the lots were prepared and the drawing was conducted, and precisely specifying the parts drawn for each community member.

Article 488

1. If all the parties in the proceedings agree, lots may be drawn in the presence of a notary public. The notary public shall prepare a report citing all the persons present during the drawing of lots, attesting the fact that the community members agreed to lots being drawn in the presence of a notary public, the manner in which the lots were created, the drawing of lots, as well as the parts drawn for each community member.
2. If all the parties in the proceedings agree, instead of a lot, the parts created pursuant to the judgment ordering partition *in natura* may be partitioned among the community members without lots being drawn, and a report to that effect shall be drawn up in the presence of the notary public.

Article 489

1. Following the partition, each community member becomes owner of the part that devolved to them.
2. Transfer of ownership of partitioned immovables to the community members, the establishment of a separate property in accordance with Article 480A, as well as the establishment of a right *in rem* in favour of a community member, the transfer of that right to that member or the elimination of that right shall require registration of the *de jure* non-appealable court judgment ordering partition *in natura* and, in the case of drawing of lots, the relevant report.

Άρθρο 490

Κάθε κοινωνός έχει δικαίωμα να ζητήσει και λάβει στην κατοχή του τα αποδεικτικά έγγραφα των δικαιωμάτων πάνω στα μέρη που περιήλθαν σ' αυτόν. Αν τα έγγραφα αυτά αφορούν περισσότερα μέρη, ανήκουν σ' εκείνον που έλαβε το μεγαλύτερο από αυτά. Οι άλλοι κοινωνοί έχουν δικαίωμα να λάβουν με έξοδά τους αντίγραφα επικυρωμένα από δημόσια αρχή. Σε περίπτωση διαφωνίας αποφασίζει το δικαστήριο.

Άρθρο 491

1. Στη δίκη διανομής προσεπικαλούνται υποχρεωτικά με επιμέλεια εκείνου που επισπεύδει τη συζήτηση όσοι έχουν δικαίωμα υποθήκης ή ενεχύρου ή επικαρπίας, καθώς και όσοι έχουν επιβάλει συντηρητική ή αναγκαστική κατάσχεση στη μερίδα κάποιου από τους κοινωνούς.

2. Αν δεν έγινε η προσεπίκληση που αναφέρεται στην παρ. 1, το δικαστήριο, με αίτηση κάποιου από τους διαδίκους ή αυτεπαγγέλτως, αναβάλλει τη συζήτηση και ορίζει προθεσμία μέσα στην οποία πρέπει να προσεπικληθεί εκείνος που έχει δικαίωμα υποθήκης ή ενεχύρου ή επικαρπίας ή εκείνος που έχει επιβάλει συντηρητική ή αναγκαστική κατάσχεση. Αν η προθεσμία περάσει άπρακτη, η αγωγή απορρίπτεται ως απαράδεκτη.

Άρθρο 492

1. Από την τελεσιδικία της απόφασης που διατάζει τη διανομή, σύμφωνα με τα άρθρ. 480, 480Α και 486, η υποθήκη ή το ενέχυρο περιορίζονται στα μέρη που περιήλθαν στον οφειλέτη. Ο περιορισμός της υποθήκης σημειώνεται στο βιβλίο υποθηκών. Ο περιορισμός του ενέχυρου σημειώνεται, εφόσον τηρούνται για τη σύστασή του δημόσια βιβλία.

2. Αν ως συνέπεια του περιορισμού που αναφέρεται στην παρ. 1 δεν ασφαλίζεται επαρκώς η απαίτηση του ενυπόθηκου ή του ενεχυρούχου δανειστή, μπορεί με αίτησή του το δικαστήριο που διατάζει τη διανομή να συστήσει υποθήκη ή ενέχυρο σε άλλα αντικείμενα, τα οποία με τη διανομή περιέρχονται στον οφειλέτη του. Η αίτηση μπορεί να υποβληθεί και μετά την τελεσιδικία της απόφασης και την ενέργεια της διανομής.

3. Αν η απόφαση που διατάζει τη διανομή για να εξισωθούν τα μέρη υποχρεώνει κάποιον από τους κοινωνούς να καταβάλει χρηματικό ποσό στον κοινωνό που η μερίδα του βαρύνεται με υποθήκη ή ενέχυρο, το δικαστήριο με αίτηση του δανειστή διατάζει να καταβληθεί σ' αυτόν το χρηματικό ποσό για να εξοφληθεί, ολικά ή εν μέρει, η απαίτησή του και αν η απαίτηση που ασφαλίζεται δεν είναι ληξιπρόθεσμη.

Άρθρο 493

Από την τελεσιδικία της απόφασης που διατάζει τη διανομή, σύμφωνα με τα άρθρ. 480, 480Α και 486, αντικείμενο επικαρπίας γίνονται όσα περιήλθαν στον ψιλό κύριο.

Άρθρο 494

1. Η συντηρητική ή αναγκαστική κατάσχεση δεν εμποδίζει τη δικαστική διανομή.

2. Μετά την τελεσιδικία της απόφασης που διατάζει την αυτούσια διανομή ή συντηρητική ή η αναγκαστική κατάσχεση στη μερίδα ενός από τους κοινωνούς περιορίζεται στο μέρος που περιήλθε σ' αυτόν.

Article 490

Each community member has the right to request and receive the documentary evidence concerning the rights over the parts that devolved to them. If such documentary evidence concerns several parts, it shall belong to the person who received the largest part. The other community members have the right to receive copies certified by a public authority at their own expense. Where a dispute arises, the court shall rule on the matter.

Article 491

1. Persons with a right of mortgage or pledge or usufruct and persons who have procured preventive or compulsory attachment concerning the share of one of the community members must be impleaded in the partition proceedings by the person expediting the hearing.
2. If the impleading referred to in paragraph 1 does not take place, the court, following an application filed by any of the parties in the proceedings or *ex officio*, shall adjourn the hearing and set a deadline within which the person who has a right of mortgage or pledge or usufruct or the person who procured preventive or compulsory attachment must be impleaded. If the deadline lapses without the relevant steps having been taken, the action shall be dismissed as inadmissible.

Article 492

1. Once the judgment ordering partition in accordance with Articles 480, 480A and 486 has become *de jure* non-appealable, the mortgage or pledge shall be limited to the parts that devolved to the debtor. Limiting of the mortgage shall be noted in the mortgage register. Limiting of the pledge shall be noted, provided public registers concerning its establishment are kept.
2. If the limiting referred to in paragraph 1 results in the claim of the mortgagee or the pledgee not being sufficiently secured, following an application filed by the latter, the court ordering the partition may establish a mortgage or pledge on other things which devolve to their debtor through the partition. The application may be filed even after the judgment has become *de jure* non-appealable and the partition has been effected.
3. If the judgment ordering partition obligates one of the community members, for the purpose of equalising parts, to pay a monetary sum to the community member whose share is encumbered with a mortgage or pledge, the court, following an application filed by the creditor, shall order the monetary sum to be paid to the creditor in order for their claim to be paid, whether in whole or in part, provided the claim secured is not overdue.

Article 493

Once the judgment ordering partition in accordance with Articles 480, 480A and 486 becomes *de jure* non-appealable, whatever devolved to the bare owner becomes subject to usufruct.

Article 494

1. Preventive or compulsory attachment does not hinder court-ordered partitioning.
2. After the judgment ordering partition *in natura* becomes *de jure* non-appealable, preventive or compulsory attachment concerning the share of one of the community members is limited to the part that devolved to them.

ΤΡΙΤΟ ΒΙΒΛΙΟ
ΕΝΔΙΚΑ ΜΕΣΑ ΚΑΙ ΑΝΑΚΟΠΕΣ

ΚΕΦΑΛΑΙΟ Α'
Γενικές διατάξεις.

Άρθρο 495

1. Τα ένδικα μέσα της ανακοπής ερημοδικίας, της έφεσης, της αναψηλάφησης και της αναίρεσης ασκούνται με δικόγραφο που κατατίθεται στο πρωτότυπο στη γραμματεία του δικαστηρίου που έχει εκδώσει την προσβαλλόμενη απόφαση ή στη γραμματεία του πρωτοδικείου της μεταβατικής έδρας, αν προσβάλλεται απόφαση εφετείου που συνεδρίασε σε μεταβατική έδρα.
2. Για την κατάθεση συντάσσεται έκθεση στο βιβλίο που τηρείται σύμφωνα με το άρθρο 496, την οποία υπογράφει και αυτός που καταθέτει. Στο δικόγραφο που κατατίθεται σημειώνεται ο αριθμός της έκθεσης και η χρονολογία της και βεβαιώνονται με την υπογραφή εκείνου που συντάσσει την έκθεση.
3. Εκείνος που ασκεί το ένδικο μέσο της έφεσης, της αναίρεσης και της αναψηλάφησης, υποχρεούται να καταθέσει παράβολο, που επισυνάπτεται στην έκθεση που συντάσσει ο γραμματέας, ως εξής:
Α. Για το ένδικο μέσο της έφεσης:
α) κατά απόφασης Ειρηνοδικείου παράβολο ποσού εβδομήντα πέντε (75) ευρώ,
β) κατά απόφασης Μονομελούς Πρωτοδικείου παράβολο ποσού εκατό (100) ευρώ,
γ) κατά απόφασης Πολυμελούς Πρωτοδικείου παράβολο ποσού εκατόν πενήντα (150) ευρώ.
Β. Για το ένδικο μέσο της αναίρεσης:
α) κατά απόφασης Ειρηνοδικείου παράβολο ποσού διακοσίων πενήντα (250) ευρώ,
β) κατά απόφασης Μονομελούς Πρωτοδικείου παράβολο ποσού τριακοσίων (300) ευρώ,
γ) κατά απόφασης Πολυμελούς Πρωτοδικείου παράβολο ποσού τετρακοσίων (400) ευρώ,
δ) κατά απόφασης Εφετείου παράβολο ποσού τετρακοσίων πενήντα (450) ευρώ.
Γ. Για το ένδικο μέσο της αναψηλάφησης:
α) κατά αποφάσεων ειρηνοδικείων, μονομελών και πολυμελών πρωτοδικείων παράβολο ποσού τετρακοσίων (400) ευρώ,
β) κατά αποφάσεων Εφετείου και του Αρείου Πάγου παράβολο ποσού πεντακοσίων (500) ευρώ.
Σε περίπτωση που ασκήθηκε ένα ένδικο μέσο από ή κατά περισσότερων διαδίκων κατατίθεται ένα παράβολο από τους εκκαλούντες, αναιρεσείοντες ή αιτούντες. Το ύψος του ποσού αναπροσαρμόζεται με κοινή απόφαση των Υπουργών Οικονομικών και Δικαιοσύνης, Διαφάνειας και Ανθρωπίνων Δικαιωμάτων. Σε περίπτωση που δεν κατατεθεί το παράβολο, το ένδικο μέσο απορρίπτεται από το δικαστήριο ως απαράδεκτο. Σε περίπτωση ολικής ή μερικής νίκης του καταθέσαντος, το δικαστήριο με την απόφασή του διατάσσει να επιστραφεί το παράβολο σε αυτόν, αλλιώς διατάσσει να εισαχθεί στο δημόσιο ταμείο. Η υποχρέωση της παρούσας παραγράφου δεν ισχύει για τις διαφορές των άρθρων 614 αριθμ. 3 και 5, και 592 αριθμ. 1 και 3.
4. Το δεύτερο εδάφιο της παρ. 9 του άρθρου 237, περί προσκόμισης εγγράφων σε ηλεκτρονική μορφή, εφαρμόζεται αναλόγως και για τα ένδικα μέσα και τις ανακοπές του παρόντος κεφαλαίου.

Άρθρο 496

1. Η γραμματεία των δικαστηρίων τηρεί χωριστό βιβλίο για καθένα από τα ένδικα μέσα που αναφέρονται στο άρθρο 495 παρ. 1· ο τρόπος που τηρείται το βιβλίο και οι άλλες λεπτομέρειες ορίζονται με διάταγμα.

BOOK III
LEGAL REMEDIES AND OPPOSITIONS

CHAPTER I
General provisions

Article 495

1. The legal remedies of opposition against a default judgment, appeal, application for re-opening proceedings, and cassation shall be filed by means of procedural document with the registry of the court that handed down the judgment being contested or, where a judgment handed down by a court of appeal sitting in a circuit is being contested, the registry of the court of first instance of that circuit.
2. A report on the filing shall be entered in the register kept in accordance with Article 496, and shall be signed by the person filing the procedural document. The number and date of the report shall be noted in the procedural document being filed and attested by the signature of the person preparing the report.
3. The person filing the legal remedy of appeal, cassation [or] application for re-opening proceedings is obligated to pay the following procedural fee, the receipt for which shall be appended to the report prepared by the registrar:
A. For the legal remedy of appeal:
a) against a judgment handed down by a court of the peace, a fee of 75 euros;
b) against a judgment handed down by a single-member court of first instance, a fee of 100 euros;
c) against a judgment handed down by a multi-member court of first instance, a fee of 150 euros.
B. For the legal remedy of cassation:
a) against a judgment handed down by a court of the peace, a fee of 250 euros;
b) against a judgment handed down by a single-member court of first instance, a fee of 300 euros;
c) against a judgment handed down by a multi-member court of first instance, a fee of 400 euros.
d) against a judgment handed down by a court of appeal, a fee of 450 euros.
C. For the legal remedy of application for re-opening proceedings:
a) against judgments handed down by courts of the peace, single- and multi-member courts of first instance, a fee of 400 euros;
b) against judgments handed down by courts of appeal and the Supreme Court, a fee of 500 euros.
Where a legal remedy was filed by or against several parties in the proceedings, a single procedural fee shall be paid by the appellants, cassationers or applicants. The fee amount shall be adjusted by a joint decision issued by the Minister of Finance and the Minister of Justice, Transparency and Human Rights. If the fee is not paid, the court shall dismiss the legal remedy as inadmissible. If the person who filed the legal remedy is successful in whole or in part, the court shall order reimbursement of the procedural fee to the said person in the judgment it hands down, otherwise it shall order that it be paid to the tax office. The obligation laid down in this paragraph does not apply to the disputes referred to in Article 614(3) and (5) and Article 592(1) and (3).
4. The second subparagraph of Article 237(9) on the submission of documents in electronic form also applies *mutatis mutandis* to the legal remedies and oppositions referred to in this Chapter.

Article 496

1. Court registries shall keep a separate register for each of the legal remedies referred to in Article 495(1); the manner in which each register is kept and other details shall be specified in a decree.

2. Ο αρμόδιος υπάλληλος της γραμματείας κάθε δικαστηρίου είναι υποχρεωμένος, μόλις προσαχθεί δικόγραφο ένδικου μέσου για κατάθεση, να συντάξει χωρίς καθυστέρηση και μπροστά σε εκείνον που έφερε το δικόγραφο, την έκθεση της κατάθεσης, και να την καταχωρίσει στο βιβλίο που αναφέρεται στην παρ. 1. Στην περίπτωση που θα προσαχθούν πολλά δικόγραφα είναι υποχρεωμένος, τηρώντας τη σειρά με την οποία προσέρχονται οι αιτούντες, να συντάξει όλες τις εκθέσεις την ίδια ημέρα.

Άρθρο 497

Το πρωτότυπο του ενδίκου μέσου ή η έκθεση που συντάχθηκε φυλάσσονται στο αρχείο του δικαστηρίου.

Άρθρο 498

1. Κάθε διάδικος μπορεί μετά την άσκηση του ένδικου μέσου, φέρνοντας αντίγραφο του ένδικου μέσου και της απόφασης που προσβάλλεται στη γραμματεία του δικαστηρίου προς το οποίο το ένδικο μέσο απευθύνεται, να ζητήσει να προσδιοριστεί δικάσιμος και να φέρει για συζήτηση την υπόθεση με κλήση, κάτω από το αντίγραφο του δικογράφου που έχει κατατεθεί ή και αυτοτελώς, η οποία επιδίδεται στον αντίδικο.

Ο προσδιορισμός δικασίμου, σύμφωνα με το προηγούμενο εδάφιο, προκειμένου για εφέσεις κατά αποφάσεων των πολυμελών και μονομελών πρωτοδικείων που εκδικάζονται στις μεταβατικές έδρες των εφετείων της περιφερείας τους, γίνεται κατ' εντολήν του οικείου προέδρου εφετών από τον προϊστάμενο του πρωτοδικείου τούτου.

2. Η προθεσμία για την κλήτευση των διαδίκων είναι τριάντα (30) ημέρες και, αν ο διάδικος που καλείται ή κάποιος από τους ομοδίκους διαμένει στο εξωτερικό ή είναι άγνωστης διαμονής, εξήντα (60) ημέρες πριν από τη συζήτηση. Κατά τα λοιπά για τον προσδιορισμό δικασίμου ισχύουν οι διατάξεις του άρθρου 226.

3. Οι διατάξεις του παρ. 1 και 2 εφαρμόζονται και για τον προσδιορισμό κάθε άλλης δικασίμου.

Άρθρο 499

Τα ένδικα μέσα μπορούν, να ασκηθούν, και πριν από την επίδοση της απόφασης, ακόμη και την ίδια ημέρα της δημοσίευσής της.

Άρθρο 500

Τα αποτελέσματα τον ένδικων μέσων αρχίζουν από τη σύνταξη της έκθεσης της κατάθεσής τους.

ΚΕΦΑΛΑΙΟ Β'
Ανακοπή ερημοδικίας

Άρθρο 501

Ανακοπή κατά απόφασης που έχει εκδοθεί ερήμην επιτρέπεται, αν εκείνος που δικάσθηκε ερήμην δεν κλητεύθηκε καθόλου ή δεν κλητεύθηκε νόμιμα ή εμπρόθεσμα ή αν συντρέχει λόγος ανώτερης βίας.

Άρθρο 502

1. Δικαίωμα ανακοπής ερημοδικίας έχουν ο ενάγων, ο εναγόμενος, ο εκκαλών, ο εφεσίβλητος ή εκείνος που άσκησε κύρια παρέμβαση, εφόσον δικάστηκαν ερήμην, οι καθολικοί διάδοχοί τους, καθώς και οι μετά την άσκηση της αγωγής ειδικοί διάδοχοί τους.

2. Όποιος άσκησε πρόσθετη παρέμβαση και δεν έλαβε μέρος κανονικά στη δίκη, και όταν θεωρείται ομόδικος του διαδίκου υπέρ του οποίου άσκησε την παρέμβαση, δεν έχει δικαίωμα να ασκήσει ανακοπή, εκτός αν ανέλαβε τη δίκη.

3. Όποιος άσκησε πρόσθετη παρέμβαση μπορεί να ασκήσει το δικαίωμα της ανακοπής του διαδίκου υπέρ του οποίου είχε παρέμβει.

2. When a procedural document for a legal remedy is filed, the competent registry clerk at each court is obligated to prepare a filing report without delay and in the presence of the person bearing the procedural document, and to enter the report in the register referred to in paragraph 1. Where numerous procedural documents are presented, the clerk is obligated to prepare all the reports on the same day in the order in which applicants appear.

Article 497

The original of the legal remedy or the report prepared shall be kept in the court archives.

Article 498

1. After a legal remedy has been filed, any party in the proceedings, presenting a copy of the legal remedy and the judgment being contested to the registry of the court to which the legal remedy is addressed, may request that a hearing date be set and bring the case for a hearing by means of a summons, [placed] at the end of the copy of the procedural document filed or even by serving a separate summons on the opponent.

In cases of appeals against judgments handed down by single- and multi-member courts of first instance heard at the circuits of the courts of appeal in their district, the hearing date shall be set, in accordance with the preceding subparagraph, at the order of the competent presiding appeal judge by the [judge] in charge of the court of first instance in question.

2. The deadline for summonsing the parties in the proceedings is 30 days, and if the party being summoned or any of the joined parties resides abroad or has no known place of residence, 60 days prior to the hearing. In all other respects, the provisions of Article 226 apply to setting hearing dates.

3. The provisions of paragraphs 1 and 2 also apply to setting any other hearing dates.

Article 499

Legal remedies may be filed before the judgment is served, even on the day it is handed down.

Article 500

Legal remedies generate effects from the date on which the filing report is prepared.

CHAPTER II
Opposition against a default judgment

Article 501

Opposition against a default judgment shall be allowed if the person tried *in absentia* was not summonsed at all, or was not duly summonsed, or was not summonsed in good time, or reasons of force majeure apply.

Article 502

1. Plaintiffs, defendants, appellants, respondents [in appeal], main intervenors, if they were tried *in absentia*, their universal successors, as well as their specific successors after the action was filed, have the right to file an opposition against a default judgment.

2. Permissive intervenors who did not participate in the proceedings in the manner required, even when considered to be joined parties of the party in the proceedings in support of whom they filed the intervention, do not have the right to file an opposition, unless they take over the proceedings.

3. Permissive intervenors may exercise the right of opposition enjoyed by the party in the proceedings in support of whom they intervened.

Άρθρο 503

1. Αν ο διάδικος που δικάστηκε ερήμην διαμένει στην Ελλάδα, η προθεσμία της ανακοπής είναι δεκαπέντε ημέρες και αρχίζει από την επίδοση της απόφασης.
2. Αν ο διάδικος που δικάστηκε ερήμην έχει άγνωστη διαμονή, η προθεσμία της ανακοπής είναι εξήντα ημέρες και αρχίζει από την τελευταία δημοσίευση κατά το άρθρο 135 παρ. 1 της περίληψης της έκθεσης για την επίδοση της απόφασης. Η περίληψη περιλαμβάνει το όνομα και το επώνυμο, καθώς και την ιδιότητα εκείνου που επιδίδει, τα ονόματα, τα επώνυμα και τις κατοικίες των διαδίκων, τον αριθμό και τη χρονολογία της απόφασης, το δικαστήριο που την εξέδωσε και σύντομη αναφορά του διατακτικού της.
3. Οι διατάξεις της παρ. 2 εφαρμόζονται και όταν ο διάδικος που δικάστηκε ερήμην διαμένει στο εξωτερικό.

Άρθρο 504

[Καταργείται]

Άρθρο 505

1. Το έγγραφο της ανακοπής πρέπει να περιέχει τα στοιχεία, που απαιτούνται κατά τα άρθρ. 118 έως 120 και τους λόγους της ανακοπής.
2. Ο ανακόπτων οφείλει να προκαταβάλει στη γραμματεία του δικαστηρίου κατά την κατάθεση της ανακοπής το παράβολο που όρισε η ερήμην απόφαση και ανέρχεται για κάθε ανακόπτοντα:
α) σε ποσό που δεν μπορεί να είναι μικρότερο από εκατόν είκοσι (120) ευρώ και μεγαλύτερο από διακόσια (200) ευρώ, αν αυτή εκδίδεται από το Ειρηνοδικείο,
β) σε ποσό που δεν μπορεί να είναι μικρότερο από εκατόν πενήντα (150) ευρώ και μεγαλύτερο από διακόσια πενήντα (250) ευρώ, αν αυτή εκδίδεται από το Μονομελές Πρωτοδικείο, ή
γ) σε ποσό που δεν μπορεί να είναι μικρότερο από διακόσια (200) ευρώ και μεγαλύτερο από τριακόσια (300) ευρώ, όταν εκδίδεται από το Πολυμελές Πρωτοδικείο ή το Εφετείο.
Το ύψος του ποσού αναπροσαρμόζεται με κοινή απόφαση των Υπουργών Οικονομικών και Δικαιοσύνης, Διαφάνειας και Ανθρωπίνων Δικαιωμάτων. Σε περίπτωση που δεν κατατεθεί το παράβολο, το ένδικο μέσο απορρίπτεται από το δικαστήριο ως απαράδεκτο. Σε περίπτωση ολικής ή μερικής νίκης του καταθέσαντος, το δικαστήριο με την απόφασή του διατάσσει να επιστραφεί το παράβολο σε αυτόν, αλλιώς διατάσσει να εισαχθεί στο δημόσιο ταμείο.

Άρθρο 506

[Καταργείται]

Άρθρο 507

1. Αν η συζήτηση της ανακοπής γίνεται με επιμέλεια του ανακόπτοντος και αυτός δεν εμφανιστεί κατά τη συζήτηση ή εμφανιστεί αλλά δεν μετέχει νόμιμα στη δίκη, το δικαστήριο απορρίπτει την ανακοπή.
2. Αν η συζήτηση της ανακοπής γίνεται με επιμέλεια εκείνου κατά του οποίου στρέφεται η ανακοπή και ο ανακόπτων δεν εμφανιστεί κατά τη συζήτηση ή εμφανιστεί αλλά δεν μετέχει νόμιμα σ' αυτήν, το δικαστήριο ενεργεί όπως ορίζεται στο άρθρο 271 και σε περίπτωση ερημοδικίας απορρίπτει την ανακοπή.
3. [Καταργείται]

Article 503

1. If the party in the proceedings who was tried *in absentia* resides in Greece, the deadline for the opposition is 15 days, starting on the date the judgment was served.
2. If the party in the proceedings who was tried *in absentia* has no known place of residence, the deadline for the opposition is 60 days, starting from the date of the most recent publication of the summary of the report on service of the judgment in accordance with Article 135(1). The summary shall include the first name, last name and capacity of the server, the first names, last names and residential addresses of the parties in the proceedings, the number and date of the judgment, the court that handed it down and a brief reference to its operative part.
3. The provisions of paragraph 2 also apply where the party in the proceedings who was tried *in absentia* resides abroad.

Article 504

[Repealed]

Article 505

1. The opposition document must contain the information required by Articles 118 to 120 and the grounds for opposition.
2. When filing the opposition, the opposing party must pay the procedural fee set in the default judgment in advance to the court registry, amounting for each opposing party:
a) to a sum of no less than 120 euros and no more than 200 euros if the default judgment was handed down by a court of the peace;
b) to a sum of no less than 150 euros and no more than 250 euros if the default judgment was handed down by a multi-member court of first instance; or
c) to a sum of no less than 200 euros and no more than 300 euros if the default judgment was handed down by a multi-member court of first instance or a court of appeal.
The fee amount shall be adjusted by a joint decision issued by the Minister of Finance and the Minister of Justice, Transparency and Human Rights. If the procedural fee is not paid, the court shall dismiss the legal remedy as inadmissible. If the person who filed the legal remedy is successful in whole or in part, the court shall order in the judgment it hands down that the procedural fee be reimbursed to the said person, otherwise it shall order that it be paid to the tax office.

Article 506

[Repealed]

Article 507

1. If the opposition is brought for hearing by the opposing party and they fail to appear during the hearing or appears but does not participate in the proceedings in the manner required, the court shall dismiss the opposition.
2. If the opposition is brought for hearing by the subject of the opposition and the opposing party fails to appear during the hearing or appears but does not participate in the proceedings in the manner required, the court shall take the steps provided for in Article 271 and, in the case of failure to enter an appearance, shall dismiss the opposition.
3. [Repealed]

Άρθρο 508

[Καταργείται]

Άρθρο 509

1. Αν η ανακοπή ασκήθηκε εμπρόθεσμα και κατά τις νόμιμες διατυπώσεις και το δικαστήριο πιθανολογεί ότι είναι βάσιμοι οι λόγοι που προτάθηκαν, εξαφανίζει την απόφαση που ανακόπηκε και τις πράξεις που ενεργήθηκαν μετά την απόφαση αυτή, διατάσσει να επιστραφεί το παράβολο και αμέσως προχωρεί στην εξέταση της διαφοράς, αφού οι διάδικοι επανέλθουν στην κατάσταση που υπήρχε πριν από την απόφαση που εξαφανίστηκε. Αλλιώς απορρίπτει την ανακοπή και διατάσσει να εισαχθεί το παράβολο στο δημόσιο ταμείο.

2. Η κατάθεση των προτάσεων γίνεται έως την έναρξη της συζήτησης και η κατάθεση της προσθήκης σε αυτές έως τη δωδέκατη ώρα της τρίτης εργάσιμης ημέρας μετά τη συζήτηση. Το ίδιο ισχύει για τις διαδικαστικές πράξεις της ανταγωγής, της προσεπίκλησης, της ανακοίνωσης και της παρέμβασης.

Άρθρο 510

Αν κατά τη συζήτηση της ανακοπής δεν εμφανισθεί ή εμφανισθεί αλλά δεν μετέχει νόμιμα σ' αυτήν εκείνος κατά του οποίου στρέφεται η ανακοπή, η διαδικασία προχωρεί σαν να ήταν και αυτός παρών.

ΚΕΦΑΛΑΙΟ Γ'

Έφεση

Άρθρο 511

Με έφεση μπορούν να προσβληθούν οι αποφάσεις των ειρηνοδικείων, των μονομελών και των πολυμελών πρωτοδικείων.

Άρθρο 512

Οι αποφάσεις των ειρηνοδικείων σε διαφορές που εκδικάζονται κατά τη διαδικασία των άρθρων 466 έως 471 είναι ανέκκλητες.

Άρθρο 513

1. Έφεση επιτρέπεται μόνο κατά των αποφάσεων που εκδίδονται στον πρώτο βαθμό:

α)εκείνων που παραπέμπουν την υπόθεση στο αρμόδιο δικαστήριο λόγω αναρμοδιότητας,

β)των οριστικών αποφάσεων που περατώνουν όλη τη δίκη ή μόνο τη δίκη για την αγωγή ή για την ανταγωγή.

Κατά των αποφάσεων που έχουν εκδοθεί ερήμην επιτρέπεται από τη δημοσίευσή τους. Αν η απόφαση είναι εν μέρει οριστική, δεν επιτρέπεται έφεση ούτε κατά των οριστικών διατάξεων πριν εκδοθεί οριστική απόφαση στη δίκη.

2. Αν προσβληθεί με έφεση η οριστική απόφαση θεωρείται ότι μαζί έχουν προσβληθεί και οι μη οριστικές που είχαν προηγουμένως εκδοθεί και αν η έφεση δεν απευθύνεται ρητώς εναντίον τους.

3. [Καταργείται]

Άρθρο 514

Δεύτερη έφεση από τον ίδιο διάδικο κατά της ίδιας απόφασης ως προς το ίδιο ή άλλο κεφάλαιο δεν επιτρέπεται.

Άρθρο 515

[Καταργείται]

Article 508

[Repealed]

Article 509

1. If the opposition was filed in good time and in accordance with legal formalities and the court considers it likely, on the balance of probabilities, that the grounds put forth are well-founded, it shall set aside the judgment opposed and the steps taken after the said judgment, shall order that the procedural fee be reimbursed and shall immediately examine the dispute, after the state of affairs that existed prior to the judgment set aside has been restored for the parties in the proceedings; otherwise the court shall dismiss the opposition and order that the procedural fee be paid to the tax office.
2. Pleadings shall be filed by the commencement of the hearing, and additions to the pleadings shall be filed by twelve noon on the third working day after the hearing. This also applies to cross-actions, impleaders, third-party notices and interventions.

Article 510

If the subject of the opposition fails to appear during the hearing of the opposition or appears but does not participate in the hearing in the manner required, the procedure shall go ahead as if they were present.

CHAPTER III
Appeal

Article 511

Appeals may be filed to contest judgments handed down by courts of the peace, single-, and multi-member courts of first instance.

Article 512

Judgments handed down by courts of the peace on disputes tried under the procedure laid down in Articles 466 to 471 are *de facto* non-appealable.

Article 513

1. Appeals may only be filed against the following first-instance judgments:
a) those remitting the case to the competent court due to lack of jurisdiction;
b) final judgments concluding the entire proceedings or only the proceedings concerning the action or cross-action.
Appeals may only be filed against default judgments from the date the judgments were handed down. If the judgment is final only in part, an appeal may not be filed against final orders before a final judgment is handed down in the proceedings.
2. If the final judgment is contested by means of appeal, non-final judgments previously handed down shall also be deemed to be contested, even if the appeal was not expressly filed against them.
3. [Repealed]

Article 514

A second appeal may not be filed by the same party in the proceedings against the same judgment with regard to the same or a different matter.

Article 515

[Repealed]

Άρθρο 516

1. Δικαίωμα έφεσης έχουν, εφόσον νικήθηκαν ολικά ή εν μέρει στην πρωτόδικη δίκη, ο ενάγων, ο εναγόμενος, εκείνοι που άσκησαν κύρια ή πρόσθετη παρέμβαση, οι προσεπικληθέντες, οι καθολικοί διάδοχοί τους, οι ειδικοί διάδοχοί τους εφόσον απέκτησαν την ιδιότητα αυτή μετά την άσκηση της αγωγής και οι εισαγγελείς πρωτοδικών, αν ήταν διάδικοι.

2. Έφεση έχει δικαίωμα να ασκήσει και ο διάδικος που νίκησε, εφόσον έχει έννομο συμφέρον.

Άρθρο 517

Η έφεση απευθύνεται κατά εκείνων που ήταν διάδικοι στην πρωτόδικη δίκη ή των καθολικών διαδόχων ή των κληροδόχων τους. Αν υπάρχει αναγκαστική ομοδικία, η έφεση πρέπει να απευθύνεται κατά όλων των ομοδίκων, αλλιώς απορρίπτεται ως απαράδεκτη.

Άρθρο 518

1. Αν ο εκκαλών διαμένει στην Ελλάδα, η προθεσμία της έφεσης είναι τριάντα ημέρες. αν διαμένει στο εξωτερικό ή η διαμονή του είναι άγνωστη, εξήντα ημέρες· και στις δύο περιπτώσεις η προθεσμία αρχίζει από την επίδοση της απόφασης που περατώνει τη δίκη.

2. Αν δεν επιδοθεί η απόφαση, η προθεσμία της έφεσης είναι δύο έτη, που αρχίζει από τη δημοσίευση της απόφασης που περατώνει τη δίκη.

3. Αν ο διάδικος που δικαιούται να ασκήσει έφεση πέθανε, η προθεσμία της έφεσης αρχίζει από την επίδοση της απόφασης που περατώνει τη δίκη στους καθολικούς διαδόχους ή τους κληροδόχους.

Άρθρο 519

1. Όσο διαρκεί η προθεσμία της έφεσης δεν μπορεί να εκτελεστεί η απόφαση του πρωτοβάθμιου δικαστηρίου. Κάθε πράξη που ενεργείται κατά τη διάρκεια της προθεσμία της έφεσης είναι άκυρη, επιτρέπεται όμως να ληφθούν ασφαλιστικά μέτρα.

2. Σε οριστικές αποφάσεις προσωρινά εκτελεστές η εκτέλεση δεν αναστέλλεται, εκτός αν πρόκειται να γίνει κατά τρίτου.

Άρθρο 520

1. Το έγγραφο της έφεσης πρέπει να περιέχει τα στοιχεία που απαιτούνται κατά τα άρθρα 118 έως 120 και τους λόγους της έφεσης.

2. Πρόσθετοι λόγοι έφεσης ως προς τα κεφάλαια της απόφασης που έχουν προσβληθεί με την έφεση και εκείνα που αναγκαστικά συνέχονται με τα κεφάλαια αυτά ασκούνται μόνο με ιδιαίτερο δικόγραφο που κατατίθεται στη γραμματεία του δευτεροβάθμιου δικαστηρίου και, αφού συνταχθεί έκθεση κάτω από το δικόγραφο αυτό, κοινοποιείται στον εφεσίβλητο τριάντα ημέρες πριν από τη συζήτηση της έφεσης.

Άρθρο 521

1. Η έφεση που έχει ασκηθεί εμπρόθεσμα και νόμιμα αναστέλλει την εκτέλεση της απόφασης. Κάθε πράξη που ενεργείται μετά την άσκηση της έφεσης είναι άκυρη, επιτρέπεται όμως να ληφθούν ασφαλιστικά μέτρα.

2. Σε αποφάσεις προσωρινά εκτελεστές, δεν αναστέλλεται η εκτέλεση, εκτός αν πρόκειται να γίνει κατά τρίτου.

3. Το ανασταλτικό αποτέλεσμα διαρκεί εωσότου εκδοθεί η οριστική απόφαση για την έφεση ή καταργηθεί με άλλο τρόπο η δευτεροβάθμια δίκη.

Article 516

1. The following persons have the right of appeal, provided they were unsuccessful, whether in whole or in part, during first-instance proceedings: the plaintiff, the defendant, the main or permissive intervenor, impleaded persons, their universal successors, their specific successors, provided they acquired this capacity after the action was filed, and court of first instance public prosecutors, if they were parties in the proceedings.
2. The successful party in the proceedings also has the right to file an appeal, where they have a legitimate interest.

Article 517

The appeal shall be brought against the persons who were parties in the first-instance proceedings or their universal successors or legatees. In cases of compulsory joinder, the appeal must be brought against all the joined parties, otherwise it shall be dismissed as inadmissible.

Article 518

1. If the appellant resides in Greece, the deadline for [filing] the appeal is 30 days, and if the appellant resides abroad or has no known place of residence, 60 days; in both cases, the deadline shall commence from the date on which the judgment concluding the proceedings was served.
2. If the judgment is not served, the deadline for [filing] the appeal is two years, starting from the date the judgment concluding the proceedings was handed down.
3. If the party in the proceedings entitled to file an appeal has died, the deadline for [filing] the appeal commences from the date the judgment concluding the proceedings was served on their universal successors or legatees.

Article 519

1. During the period in which appeals may be filed, the judgment handed down by the first-instance court may not be enforced. Any steps taken during the period in which appeals may be filed are null and void; however, interim measures are permitted.
2. In cases of provisionally enforceable final judgments, enforcement shall not be stayed, unless it is to take place against a third party.

Article 520

1. The appeal document must contain the information required by Articles 118 to 120 and the grounds for appeal.
2. Additional grounds of appeal regarding the heads of the judgment being contested by the appeal and those necessarily related to such heads shall only be filed in a separate procedural document, which shall be submitted to the registry of the second-instance court and, after a report is prepared below it, shall be notified to the respondent 30 days before the hearing of the appeal.

Article 521

1. Appeals filed lawfully and in good time shall stay enforcement of the judgment. Any steps taken after the appeal was filed are null and void; however, interim measures are permitted.
2. In cases of provisionally enforceable judgments, enforcement shall not be stayed, unless it is to take place against a third party.
3. The suspensive effect shall last until a final judgment is handed down on the appeal or the second-instance proceedings are otherwise discontinued.

Άρθρο 522

Με την άσκηση της έφεσης η υπόθεση μεταβιβάζεται στο δευτεροβάθμιο δικαστήριο μέσα στα όρια που καθορίζονται από την έφεση και τους πρόσθετους λόγους.

Άρθρο 523

1. Ο εφεσίβλητος μπορεί, και αφού περάσει η προθεσμία της έφεσης, να ασκήσει αντέφεση ως προς τα κεφάλαια της απόφασης που προσβάλλονται με την έφεση και ως προς εκείνα που συνέχονται αναγκαστικά με αυτά, και αν ακόμη αποδέχτηκε την απόφαση ή παραιτήθηκε από την έφεση.
2. Η αντέφεση ασκείται μόνο με ιδιαίτερο δικόγραφο που κατατίθεται στη γραμματεία του δευτεροβάθμιου δικαστηρίου και, αφού συνταχθεί έκθεση κάτω από αυτό, κοινοποιείται στον εκκαλούντα τριάντα ημέρες πριν από τη συζήτηση της έφεσης.
3. Αν η έφεση απορριφθεί ως εκπρόθεσμα ή απαράδεκτη ή τυπικά άκυρη, απορρίπτεται και η αντέφεση, εκτός αν ασκήθηκε ενώ διαρκούσε η προθεσμία της έφεσης για τον αντεκκαλούντα, οπότε ισχύει ως αυτοτελής έφεση. Η παραίτηση από την έφεση ή η απόρριψή της ως αβάσιμης δεν επηρεάζει την αντέφεση.

Άρθρο 524

1. Στη διαδικασία της δευτεροβάθμιας δίκης εφαρμόζονται οι διατάξεις των άρθρων 227, 233 έως 236, των παρ. 8 και 10 έως 13 του άρθρου 237, 240 έως 312, περ. α΄ έως γ΄ της παρ. 1 του άρθρου 591 και παρ. 4 του άρθρου 591, με την επιφύλαξη της ισχύος του άρθρου 591 για τις ειδικές διαδικασίες. Η κατάθεση των προτάσεων γίνεται έως την έναρξη της συζήτησης και η κατάθεση της προσθήκης σε αυτές έως τη δωδέκατη ώρα της τρίτης εργάσιμης ημέρας μετά τη συζήτηση.
2. Η προφορική συζήτηση είναι υποχρεωτική μόνο στην περίπτωση του άρθρου 528. Η κατάθεση των προτάσεων και της προσθήκης σε αυτές γίνεται στις προθεσμίες του εδαφίου β' της παρ. 1.
3. Σε περίπτωση ερημοδικίας του εκκαλούντος η έφεση απορρίπτεται, εφόσον είναι παραδεκτή. Το ίδιο ισχύει σε περίπτωση ερημοδικίας του εφεσιβλήτου ως προς την αντέφεση.
4. Σε περίπτωση ερημοδικίας του εφεσιβλήτου ως προς την έφεση η διαδικασία προχωρεί σαν να ήταν και αυτός παρών. Το ίδιο ισχύει και σε περίπτωση ερημοδικίας του εκκαλούντος ως προς την αντέφεση. Ο παριστάμενος διάδικος υποχρεούται μέσα σε πέντε(5) ημέρες από τη συζήτηση να προσκομίσει αντίγραφα του εισαγωγικού δικογράφου και των προτάσεων του αντιδίκου του, που κατατέθηκαν στην πρωτοβάθμια δίκη, καθώς και τα πρακτικά και τις εκθέσεις που λήφθηκαν κατ' αυτήν. Διαφορετικά κηρύσσεται απαράδεκτη η συζήτηση.
5. Τους Εισαγγελείς Πρωτοδικών, αν έχουν την ιδιότητα του εκκαλούντος ή του εφεσιβλήτου, εκπροσωπεί ο Εισαγγελέας Εφετών.

Άρθρο 525

1. Κάθε αίτηση που έχει υποβληθεί στον πρώτο βαθμό δικαιοδοσίας μπορεί να αποτελέσει αντικείμενο της έφεσης και της δευτεροβάθμιας δίκης και αν δεν έχει αποφανθεί γι' αυτήν το πρωτοβάθμιο δικαστήριο.
2. Είναι απαράδεκτη η υποβολή νέας αίτησης, όπως και η άσκηση ανταγωγής για πρώτη φορά στη δευτεροβάθμια δίκη ακόμη και αν ο αντίδικος συναινεί. Το απαράδεκτο λαμβάνεται και αυτεπαγγέλτως υπόψη.
3. Επιτρέπεται στη δευτεροβάθμια δίκη να υποβληθούν με τις προτάσεις αιτήσεις για παρεπόμενες απαιτήσεις που γεννήθηκαν μετά τη συζήτηση κατά την οποία εκδόθηκε η προσβαλλόμενη απόφαση ή αιτήσεις για αποκατάσταση των πραγμάτων στην κατάσταση που υπήρχε πριν από την εκτέλεση της απόφασης.

Article 522

Once the appeal has been filed, the case shall devolve to the second-instance court within the limits laid down in the appeal and additional grounds.

Article 523

1. Even after the deadline for [filing] the appeal has lapsed, the respondent may file a cross-appeal regarding the heads of the judgment being contested in the appeal and those necessarily related to such heads, even if they accepted the judgment or [had] waived [the right to file an] appeal.
2. The cross-appeal shall be filed only by means of a separate document, which shall be filed with the registry of the second-instance court and, after a report is prepared below it, shall be notified to the respondent 30 days before the hearing of the appeal.
3. If the appeal is dismissed as late or inadmissible or formally null and void, the cross-appeal shall also be dismissed, unless it was filed in the period during which appeals could be filed by the cross-appellant, in which case it shall function as a separate appeal. Discontinuation of the appeal or its dismissal as unfounded shall not affect the cross-appeal.

Article 524

1. The provisions of Articles 227, 233 to 236, 237(8) and (10) to (13), 240 to 312, 591(1)(a) to (c) and 591(4) apply to the second-instance proceedings, without prejudice to the effect of Article 591 concerning special procedures. Pleadings shall be filed by the commencement of the hearing, and additions to the pleadings shall be filed by twelve noon on the third working day after the hearing.
2. Oral hearings shall be mandatory only in the case referred to in Article 528. Pleadings and additions to such pleadings shall be filed within the deadlines laid down in the second subparagraph of paragraph 1.
3. If the appellant fails to enter an appearance, the appeal, if admissible, shall be dismissed. The same shall apply if the respondent fails to enter an appearance with regard to the cross-appeal.
4. If the respondent fails to enter an appearance with regard to the appeal, the procedure shall go ahead as if they were present. The same shall also apply if the appellant fails to enter an appearance with regard to the cross-appeal. The party in the proceedings entering an appearance is obligated to adduce copies of the procedural document instituting proceedings, the pleadings filed by the opponent during the first-instance proceedings and the transcripts and reports prepared during those proceedings within five days of the hearing, otherwise the hearing shall be declared inadmissible.
5. Where court of first instance public prosecutors appear in the capacity of appellant or respondent, they shall be represented by the court of appeal public prosecutor.

Article 525

1. Any application filed during first-instance proceedings may constitute the subject-matter of an appeal in second-instance proceedings, even if the first-instance court has not ruled on said application.
2. Any new application or cross-action which was filed for the first time during the second-instance proceedings shall be inadmissible, even if the opponent consents. Inadmissibility shall also be taken into account *ex officio*.
3. Ancillary claims that arose after the hearing during which the judgment being contested was handed down may be raised or applications for restoring a prior state of affairs before enforcement of the judgment may be included in the pleadings during second-instance proceedings.

Άρθρο 526

Είναι απαράδεκτη στην κατ' έφεση δίκη κάθε μεταβολής της βάσης, του αντικειμένου και του αιτήματος της αγωγής και αν ο αντίδικος συναινεί. Το απαράδεκτοι λαμβάνεται υπόψη και αυτεπαγγέλτως. Επιτρέπεται εξαιτίας γεγονότων που επήλθαν μετά την έκδοση της πρωτόδικης απόφασης να ζητηθεί αντί για το αντικείμενο που ζητήθηκε αρχικά άλλο ή η αξία του ή το διαφέρον.

Άρθρο 527

Είναι απαράδεκτη η προβολή στην κατ' έφεση δίκη πραγματικών ισχυρισμών που δεν προτάθηκαν στην πρωτόδικη δίκη, εκτός αν:

1) προτείνονται από τον εφεσίβλητο, ενάγοντα, εναγόμενο ή εκείνον που είχε παρέμβει, ως υπεράσπιση κατά της έφεσης και δεν μεταβάλλεται με τους ισχυρισμούς αυτούς η βάση της αγωγής ή της παρέμβασης, ή προτείνονται από εκείνον που παρεμβαίνει για πρώτη φορά στην κατ' έφεση δίκη με πρόσθετη παρέμβαση, θεωρείται όμως αναγκαίος ομόδικος του αρχικού διαδίκου,

2) γεννήθηκαν μετά τη συζήτηση στο πρωτοβάθμιο δικαστήριο,

3) λαμβάνονται υπόψη αυτεπαγγέλτως ή μπορούν να προταθούν σε κάθε στάση της δίκης,

4) το δικαστήριο κρίνει ότι δεν προβλήθηκαν εγκαίρως με τις προτάσεις ή, στην περίπτωση της παρ. 5 του άρθρου 237 και της παρ. 1 του άρθρου 238, με τις συμπληρωματικές προτάσεις από δικαιολογημένη αιτία· αυτό ισχύει και για την ένσταση κατάχρησης δικαιώματος,

5) προέκυψαν για πρώτη φορά μεταγενέστερα και

6) αποδεικνύονται εγγράφως ή με δικαστική ομολογία του αντιδίκου.

Το απαράδεκτο λαμβάνεται υπόψη και αυτεπαγγέλτως.

Άρθρο 528

Αν ασκηθεί έφεση από τον διάδικο που δικάσθηκε ερήμην, η εκκαλούμενη απόφαση εξαφανίζεται μέσα στα όρια που καθορίζονται από την έφεση και τους πρόσθετους λόγους, ανεξάρτητα από τη διαδικασία που τηρήθηκε. Ο εκκαλών δικαιούται να προβάλει όλους τους ισχυρισμούς που μπορούσε να προτείνει πρωτοδίκως.

Άρθρο 529

1. Στην κατ' έφεση δίκη επιτρέπεται να γίνει επίκληση και προσαγωγή νέων αποδεικτικών μέσων. Εξέταση νέων μαρτύρων για ζητήματα για τα οποία εξετάσθηκαν μάρτυρες στην πρωτόδικη δίκη επιτρέπεται, αν αυτό επιβάλλεται κατά την κρίση του δικαστηρίου.

2. Το δευτεροβάθμιο δικαστήριο μπορεί να αποκρούσει τα αποδεικτικά μέσα που προσάγονται πρώτη φορά σ' αυτό ως απαράδεκτα, αν κατά την κρίση του ο διάδικος δεν τα είχε προσκομίσει στην πρωτόδικη δίκη από πρόθεση στρεψοδικίας ή από βαριά αμέλεια.

Άρθρο 530

1. Αν κατά την πρωτόδικη δίκη εξετάστηκε με όρκο ο διάδικος, δεν επιτρέπεται στην κατ' έφεση δίκη η ένορκη εξέταση του αντιδίκου για το ίδιο πραγματικό γεγονός.

2. Αν κατά την πρωτόδικη δίκη διάδικος αρνήθηκε να εξεταστεί με όρκο, από την κρίση του δευτεροβάθμιου δικαστηρίου εξαρτάται να επιτρέψει ή όχι την εξέτασή του κατά τη δευτεροβάθμια δίκη.

Άρθρο 531

[Καταργείται]

Article 526

Any change to the basis of, subject-matter of and form of order sought in the action shall be inadmissible during appeal proceedings, even if the opponent consents. Inadmissibility shall also be taken into account *ex officio*. Due to events that occurred after the first-instance judgment was handed down, it is permissible to request, instead of the thing initially requested, something different, the value of the thing initially requested, or damages.

Article 527

During second-instance proceedings, it is not permissible to present factual assertions not made in first-instance proceedings, unless:

1) they are made by the respondent, the plaintiff, the defendant or the person who had intervened as a defence against the appeal and the basis of the action or intervention is not changed by the said assertions, or they are made by the person who first intervened during the appeal proceedings by means of a permissive intervention, but who is considered a compulsorily joined party of the initial party in the proceedings;

2) they arose after the hearing before the first-instance court;

3) they are taken into account *ex officio* or may be made during any stage of the proceedings;

4) the court rules that they were not presented in good time in the pleadings or, in the cases referred to in Article 237(5) and 238(1), in the supplementary pleadings for a serious reason; this also applies to pleas of abuse of right;

5) they first arose at a later stage; [or]

6) they are proven in writing or by admission made by the opponent in court. Inadmissibility shall also be taken into account *ex officio*.

Article 528

If an appeal is filed by a party in the proceedings tried *in absentia*, the judgment being contested shall be set aside within the limits laid down in the appeal and the additional grounds, irrespective of the procedure followed. The appellant is entitled to make all the assertions they could have made at first instance.

Article 529

1. During appeal proceedings, new means of evidence may be adduced and relied upon. Where deemed necessary at the discretion of the court, new witnesses may be examined with regard to matters for which witnesses were examined during first-instance proceedings.

2. The second-instance court may dismiss the means of evidence first adduced before it as inadmissible if, in its view, the party in the proceedings had not adduced them during the first-instance proceedings due to chicanery or gross negligence.

Article 530

1. If a party in the proceedings was examined under oath during first-instance proceedings, the opponent may not be examined under oath with regard to the same actual fact during appeal proceedings.

2. If a party in the proceedings refused to be examined under oath during first-instance proceedings, the second-instance court shall decide, at its discretion, whether or not to examine that person during second-instance proceedings.

Article 531

[Repealed]

Άρθρο 532

Αν λείπει κάποια από τις προϋποθέσεις του παραδεκτού της έφεσης, ιδίως αν η έφεση δεν ασκήθηκε εμπρόθεσμα και κατά τις νόμιμες διατυπώσεις, το δικαστήριο την απορρίπτει ως απαράδεκτη και αυτεπαγγέλτως.

Άρθρο 533

1. Αν το δευτεροβάθμιο δικαστήριο κρίνει ότι η έφεση είναι παραδεκτή, εξετάζει το παραδεκτό και το βάσιμο των λόγων της.
2. Το δευτεροβάθμιο δικαστήριο εφαρμόζει το νόμο που ίσχυε όταν δημοσιεύθηκε η πρωτόδικη απόφαση.

Άρθρο 534

Αν το αιτιολογικό της απόφασης που έχει προσβληθεί με έφεση κρίνεται εσφαλμένο, αλλά το διατακτικό της ορθό, το δευτεροβάθμιο δικαστήριο αντικαθιστά τις αιτιολογίες και απορρίπτει την έφεση.

Άρθρο 535

1. Αν ο λόγος της έφεσης κριθεί βάσιμος, η απόφαση που προσβάλλεται εξαφανίζεται και το δευτεροβάθμιο δικαστήριο κρατεί την υπόθεση και τη δικάζει κατ' ουσίαν.
2. Αν η προσβαλλόμενη απόφαση εξαφανίζεται για αναρμοδιότητα του πρωτοβάθμιου δικαστηρίου, η υπόθεση παραπέμπεται στο αρμόδιο δικαστήριο και εφαρμόζονται οι διατάξεις του άρθρου 46. Αν πρόκειται για κατά τόπον αναρμοδιότητα και κριθεί αρμόδιο άλλο πρωτοβάθμιο δικαστήριο που υπάγεται στην περιφέρεια του δευτεροβάθμιου δικαστηρίου το οποίο δικάζει την έφεση, αυτό μπορεί ή να παραπέμψει την υπόθεση στο αρμόδιο δικαστήριο ή να την κρατήσει και να τη δικάσει κατ' ουσίαν.

Άρθρο 536

1. Το δευτεροβάθμιο δικαστήριο δεν μπορεί να εκδώσει απόφαση επιβλαβέστερη για τον εκκαλούντα χωρίς ο εφεσίβλητος να ασκήσει δική του έφεση ή αντέφεση.
2. Οι διατάξεις της παρ. 1 δεν εφαρμόζονται όταν το δευτεροβάθμιο δικαστήριο μετά την εξαφάνιση της πρωτόδικης απόφασης δικάζει την υπόθεση κατ' ουσίαν.

Άρθρο 537

Αν περισσότεροι νικήθηκαν με την ίδια απόφαση και για τους ίδιους λόγους και ένας μόνο άσκησε έφεση, η απόφαση που δέχεται την έφεση ισχύει και υπέρ των ομοδίκων που δεν άσκησαν έφεση, εφόσον δεν αποδέχτηκαν την πρωτόδικη απόφαση.

ΚΕΦΑΛΑΙΟ Δ'
Αναψηλάφηση

Άρθρο 538

Με αναψηλάφηση, μπορούν να προσβληθούν οι αποφάσεις των ειρηνοδικείων, των μονομελών και των πολυμελών πρωτοδικείων, των εφετείων και του Αρείου Πάγου εφόσον δικάζει κατ' ουσίαν.

Article 532

If any of the requirements for admissibility of the appeal is not met and, in particular, if the appeal was not filed in good time and in accordance with legal formalities, the court may also dismiss the appeal as inadmissible *ex officio*.

Article 533

1. If the second-instance court rules that the appeal is admissible, it shall examine whether the grounds [of appeal] are admissible and well-founded.
2. The second-instance court instance shall apply the law that was in force when the first-instance judgment was handed down.

Article 534

If the reasoning of the judgment contested by means of appeal are found to be erroneous but its operative part correct, the second-instance court shall replace the reasoning and dismiss the appeal.

Article 535

1. If the court rules that the grounds of appeal are well-founded, the judgment being contested shall be set aside and the second-instance court shall stand seised of the case and try it on its merits.
2. If the judgment being contested is set aside due to lack of jurisdiction of the first-instance court, the case shall be remitted to the court with jurisdiction, and the provisions of Article 46 apply. In the case of lack of jurisdiction *ratione loci* and where a different first-instance court belonging to the district of the second-instance court trying the appeal is found to have jurisdiction, that second-instance court may either remit the case to the competent court or stand seised of it and try it on its merits.

Article 536

1. The second-instance court may not hand down a judgment that places the appellant at a greater disadvantage [than the first-instance judgment] without the respondent having filed their own appeal or cross-appeal.
2. The provisions of paragraph 1 do not apply when the second-instance court, having set aside the first-instance judgment, tries the case on its merits.

Article 537

If several persons were unsuccessful following the same judgment and on the same grounds and only one of them filed an appeal, the judgment accepting the appeal also applies to the joined parties who did not file an appeal, provided they did not accept the first-instance judgment.

CHAPTER IV
Re-opening proceedings

Article 538

Judgments handed down by courts of the peace, single- and multi-member courts of first instance, courts of appeal and the Supreme Court, where trying cases on their merits, may be contested by means of an application for re-opening proceedings.

Άρθρο 539

1. Αναψηλάφηση επιτρέπεται μόνο κατά των οριστικών αποφάσεων που περατώνουν τη δίκη και δεν μπορούν να προσβληθούν με ανακοπή ερημοδικίας και έφεση. Αν η απόφαση είναι κατά ένα μέρος οριστική, δεν επιτρέπεται αναψηλάφηση ούτε κατά των οριστικών διατάξεων πριν εκδοθεί η οριστική απόφαση στη δίκη.

2. Αν προσβληθεί με αναψηλάφηση η οριστική απόφαση θεωρούνται ότι έχουν προσβληθεί και οι μη οριστικές αποφάσεις που έχουν εκδοθεί προηγουμένως και αν η αναψηλάφηση δεν απευθύνεται ρητώς κατά των αποφάσεων αυτών.

Άρθρο 540

Αν η ανακοπή ερημοδικίας απορρίφθηκε, η αναψηλάφηση απευθύνεται κατά της απόφασης που απέρριψε την ανακοπή, οπότε θεωρείται ότι έχει προσβληθεί και η απόφαση κατά της οποίας είχε στραφεί η ανακοπή ερημοδικίας, εφόσον δεν πέρασε η προθεσμία για την άσκηση αναψηλάφησης κατά της απόφασης αυτής.

Άρθρο 541

Δεύτερη αναψηλάφηση από τον ίδιο διάδικο κατά της ίδιας απόφασης ως προς το ίδιο ή άλλο κεφάλαιο δεν επιτρέπεται.

Άρθρο 542

1. Δικαίωμα αναψηλάφησης έχουν, εφόσον νικήθηκαν ολικά ή εν μέρει στη δίκη που εκδόθηκε η προσβαλλόμενη απόφαση, ο ενάγων, ο εναγόμενος, ο εκκαλών, ο εφεσίβλητος, ο αναιρεσείων, ο αναιρεσίβλητος, εκείνοι που παρενέβησαν κυρίως και προσθέτως, οι προσεπικληθέντες, οι καθολικοί διάδοχοί τους, οι ειδικοί διάδοχοί τους που απέκτησαν την ιδιότητα αυτή μετά την άσκηση της αγωγής, καθώς και οι εισαγγελείς, αν ήταν διάδικοι.

2. Αναψηλάφηση έχει δικαίωμα να ασκήσει και ο διάδικος που νίκησε, εφόσον έχει έννομο συμφέρον.

Άρθρο 543

Η αναψηλάφηση απευθύνεται κατά εκείνων που ήταν διάδικοι στη δίκη στην οποία εκδόθηκε η προσβαλλόμενη απόφαση ή κατά των καθολικών διαδόχων τους ή των κληρονόμων τους. Αν υπάρχει αναγκαστική ομοδικία, η αναψηλάφηση πρέπει να απευθύνεται κατά όλων των ομοδίκων, αλλιώς απορρίπτεται ως απαράδεκτη.

Άρθρο 544
Αναψηλάφηση

Αναψηλάφηση επιτρέπεται μόνο:

1) αν στην ίδια υπόθεση εκδόθηκαν, μεταξύ των ίδιων διαδίκων που είχαν παραστεί με την ίδια ιδιότητα, από το ίδιο ή διαφορετικά δικαστήρια αποφάσεις που αντιφάσκουν μεταξύ τους,

2) αν διάδικος δεν εκπροσωπήθηκε νόμιμα στη δίκη, εφόσον ύστερα δεν εγκρίθηκε ρητά ή σιωπηρά η διεξαγωγή της δίκης,

3) αν το ίδιο πρόσωπο είχε παραστεί ως διάδικος στο όνομά του ή εκπροσώπησε διαδίκους με περισσότερες ιδιότητες, οι οποίοι είχαν αντίθετα συμφέροντα στη δίκη,

Article 539

1. Applications for re-opening proceedings shall be allowed only against final judgments which conclude proceedings and which cannot be contested by an opposition against a default judgment [or] an appeal. If the judgment is [only] partially final, an application for re-opening proceedings shall not be allowed against final rulings before a final judgment is handed down during proceedings.
2. If the final judgment is contested by means of an application for re-opening proceedings, non-final judgments previously handed down shall also be deemed to be contested, even if the application for re-opening proceedings is not expressly brought against such judgments.

Article 540

If the opposition against a default judgment was dismissed, the application for re-opening proceedings shall be brought against the judgment that dismissed the opposition, in which case the judgement against which the opposition against a default judgment had been filed shall also be deemed to be contested, provided the deadline for filing an application for re-opening proceedings against that judgment has not lapsed.

Article 541

A second application for re-opening proceedings may not be filed by the same party in the proceedings against the same judgment with regard to the same or different heads [of the judgment].

Article 542

1. The following persons shall, provided they were unsuccessful, whether in whole or in part, during proceedings where the judgment being contested was handed down, have the right to file an application for re-opening proceedings: the plaintiff, the defendant, the appellant, the respondent [in appeal], the cassationer, the cassationee, main or permissive intervenors, impleaded persons, their universal successors, their specific successors, provided they acquired this capacity after the action was filed, and public prosecutors, provided they were parties in the proceedings.
2. The successful party in the proceedings also has the right to file an application for re-opening proceedings, where they have a legitimate interest.

Article 543

The application for re-opening proceedings shall be brought against the persons who were parties in the proceedings in which the judgment being contested was handed down or their universal successors or heirs. In cases of compulsory joinder, the application for re-opening proceedings must be brought against all the joined parties, otherwise it shall be dismissed as inadmissible.

Article 544
Re-opening proceedings

Applications for re-opening proceedings shall be permitted only if:
1) with regard to the same case involving the same parties in the proceedings who had appeared in the same capacities, the same court or different courts had handed down judgments contradicting each other;
2) a party was not duly represented in the proceedings, where the manner in which the proceedings were conducted was not explicitly or implicitly approved at a later stage;
3) the same person had appeared as a party in the proceedings in their own name or represented parties in the proceedings in several capacities who had opposing interests in the [outcome of the] proceedings;

4) αν κάποιος είχε παραστεί ως πληρεξούσιος διαδίκου χωρίς πληρεξουσιότητα, εφόσον δεν εγκρίθηκε ύστερα η διεξαγωγή της δίκης,
5) αν η προσβαλλόμενη απόφαση είναι πλαστή, είτε διότι γράφει ψευδώς ότι το δικαστήριο συγκροτήθηκε από τον αναγκαίο σύμφωνα με τον νόμο αριθμό δικαστών, είτε διότι, όπως προκύπτει από το πρακτικό της διάσκεψης, δεν εκδόθηκε με την πλειοψηφία που απαιτεί ο νόμος ή δεν έχει τις υπογραφές που ορίζει ο νόμος και δεν είναι δυνατή η υπογραφή της από τα πρόσωπα αυτά,
6) αν η προσβαλλόμενη απόφαση στηρίζεται σε ψευδή κατάθεση μάρτυρα ή διαδίκου, σε ψευδή έκθεση ή κατάθεση πραγματογνώμονα, σε ψευδή όρκο διαδίκου ή ενόρκως βεβαιώσαντος ή σε πλαστά έγγραφα, εφόσον το ψεύδος ή η πλαστότητα αναγνωρίστηκαν με αμετάκλητη απόφαση ποινικού δικαστηρίου και, αν πρόκειται για κατάθεση διαδίκου, και με δικαστική ή δημόσια, προφορική ή έγγραφη, ομολογία του δια του τύπου και λοιπών ΜΜΕ ή μέσω του διαδικτύου. Αν η άσκηση της ποινικής αγωγής ή η πρόοδος της ποινικής διαδικασίας είναι αδύνατη, η αναγνώριση γίνεται με απόφαση που εκδίδεται σε κύρια αγωγή, η οποία ασκείται μέσα σε έξι (6) μήνες από την έκδοση της προσβαλλόμενης απόφασης και, αν η αδυναμία επήλθε κατόπιν, μέσα σε έξι (6) μήνες από αυτήν,
7) αν ο διάδικος που ζητεί την αναψηλάφηση βρήκε ή πήρε στην κατοχή του μετά την έκδοση της προσβαλλόμενης απόφασης νέα κρίσιμα έγγραφα, από τα οποία προκύπτει ισχυρισμός που προβλήθηκε ή που δεν μπορούσε να προβληθεί και τα οποία δεν μπορούσε να τα προσκομίσει εγκαίρως από ανώτερη βία ή τα οποία κατακράτησε ο αντίδικός του ή τρίτος που είχε συνεννοηθεί με τον αντίδικό του και των οποίων την ύπαρξη αγνοούσε, όπως αγνοούσε και την κατοχή τους από τον αντίδικο ή τον τρίτο κατά τη διάρκεια της δίκης,
8) αν η προσβαλλόμενη απόφαση στηρίζεται σε απόφαση πολιτικού, ποινικού ή διοικητικού δικαστηρίου, η οποία ανατράπηκε αμετάκλητα ύστερα από την τελευταία συζήτηση, μετά την οποία εκδόθηκε η απόφαση που προσβάλλεται,
9) αν ο διάδικος κλήτευσε στη δίκη τον αντίδικό του ως άγνωστης διαμονής, αν και γνώριζε τη διαμονή του,
10) αν το περιεχόμενο της προσβαλλόμενης απόφασης επηρεάστηκε ουσιωδώς από δωροληψία ή από άλλη εκ προθέσεως παράβαση καθήκοντος συμπράττοντος στην έκδοση της δικαστή, εφόσον η δωροληψία ή η παράβαση καθήκοντος αποδεικνύονται με αμετάκλητη απόφαση ποινικού δικαστηρίου. Αν η άσκηση της ποινικής αγωγής ή η πρόοδος της ποινικής διαδικασίας είναι αδύνατη, η αναγνώριση της δωροληψίας ή της παράβασης καθήκοντος γίνεται με απόφαση που εκδίδεται σε κύρια αγωγή, η οποία ασκείται μέσα σε έξι (6) μήνες από την έκδοση της προσβαλλόμενης απόφασης, και αν η αδυναμία επήλθε κατόπιν, μέσα σε έξι (6) μήνες από αυτήν.

Άρθρο 545

1. Αν εκείνος που ζητεί την αναψηλάφηση διαμένει στην Ελλάδα, η προθεσμία της αναψηλάφησης είναι εξήντα ημέρες.
2. Αν εκείνος που ζητεί την αναψηλάφηση διαμένει στο εξωτερικό ή η διαμονή του είναι άγνωστη, η προθεσμία της αναψηλάφησης είναι εκατόν είκοσι ημέρες.
3. Η προθεσμία της αναψηλάφησης αρχίζει
α) στην περίπτωση του άρθρου 544 αρ.1 από την επίδοση της νεότερης από τις αντιφατικές αποφάσεις,
β) στην περίπτωση του άρθρου 544 αρ.2 από την επίδοση της προσβαλλόμενης απόφασης στο διάδικο που έχει γίνει ικανός ή σε εκείνον που νόμιμα τον αντιπροσωπεύει,
γ) στην περίπτωση του άρθρου 544 αριθ.4 από την επίδοση της προσβαλλόμενης απόφασης προσωπικά σε εκείνον που ζητεί την αναψηλάφηση,

4) a person had appeared as the proxy of a party in the proceedings without a power of attorney, where the manner in which the proceedings were conducted was not approved at a later stage;
5) the judgment being contested is inauthentic, either because it falsely states that the court was comprised of the number of judges necessary in law, or because it is clear from the deliberation report that it was not handed down with the majority required by law, or it does not bear the signatures required by law and it was not possible for it to be signed by the persons in question;
6) the judgment being contested relies on false testimony by a witness or a party in the proceedings, a false report or testimony by an expert, a false oath taken by a party in the proceedings or a party who submitted an affidavit or counterfeit documents, where the falsehood or forgery was acknowledged by means of an irrevocable judgment handed down by a criminal court and, in the case of testimony by a party in the proceedings, admission in court or public, whether verbal or in writing, in the press and other media or the internet. If it is not possible to institute criminal proceedings or for the criminal procedure to progress, such acknowledgement shall take place in a judgment handed down on a main action, filed within six months from the date the judgment being contested was handed down and, if the impossibility arose at a later stage, within six months of the date [when impossibility arose];
7) after the judgment being contested was handed down, the party in the proceedings requesting re-opening of proceedings found or took possession of [a)] new, essential documents from which an assertion arises that was made or could not have been made and which that party was not able to adduce due to force majeure, or [b)] such documents which were retained by the opponent or a third party following an understanding reached with the opponent, and whose existence the party requesting re-opening was unaware of, just as they were unaware of their possession by the opposing party or third party during the proceedings;
8) the judgment being contested is based on a judgment handed down by a civil, criminal or administrative court that was irrevocably overturned after the final hearing, following which the judgment being contested was handed down;
9) the party in the proceedings summonsed their opponent to trial as having no known place of residence, despite knowing their place of residence;
10) the content of the judgment being contested was materially affected by passive bribery or other intentional breach of duty by a judge involved in handing it down, where the passive bribery or breach of duty are proven by means of an irrevocable judgment handed down by a criminal court. If the filing of the criminal action or the progression of the criminal procedure is not possible, acknowledgement of the passive bribery or breach of duty shall take place in a judgment handed down with regard to a main action filed within six months of the date the judgment being contested was handed down and, if the impossibility arose at a later stage, within six months of that date.

Article 545

1. If the person requesting re-opening of proceedings resides in Greece, the deadline for [filing the application for] re-opening proceedings is 60 days.
2. If the person requesting re-opening of proceedings resides abroad or has no known place of residence, the deadline for [filing the application for] re-opening proceedings is 120 days.
3. The deadline for [filing the application for] re-opening proceedings shall commence[:]
a) in the case referred to in Article 544(1), from the date of service of the most recent of the contradictory judgments;
b) in the case referred to in Article 544(2), from the date of service of the judgment being contested on the party in the proceedings who has acquired legal capacity or the person who is duly representing that party;
c) in the case referred to in Article 544(4), from the date of service of the judgment being contested on the person requesting re-opening of proceedings insofar as it concerns them;

δ) στην περίπτωση του άρθρου 544 αριθ.6 από το αμετάκλητο της απόφασης με την οποία αναγνωρίζεται η ψευδομαρτυρία, η ψευδορκία ή η πλαστότητα,
ε) στην περίπτωση του άρθρου 544 αριθ.7 από την ημέρα που εκείνος ο οποίος ζητεί την αναψηλάφηση έμαθε ότι υπάρχουν νέα κρίσιμα έγγραφα,
στ) στην περίπτωση του άρθρου 544 αριθ.8 από την ημέρα που εκείνος ο οποίος ζητεί την αναψηλάφηση έμαθε την απόφαση που ανατράπηκε,
ζ) στις περιπτώσεις του άρθρου 544 αριθ.3, 5 και 9 από την επίδοση της προσβαλλόμενης απόφασης.
η) στην περίπτωση του άρθρου 544 αριθ. 10 από το αμετάκλητο της απόφασης με την οποία αναγνωρίζεται η δωροληψία ή η παράβαση καθήκοντος του δικαστή.
4. Στις περιπτώσεις της παραγράφου 3 εδάφια δ', ε', στ' και η', η προθεσμία δεν αρχίζει αν δεν επιδοθεί προηγουμένως η προσβαλλόμενη απόφαση, αλλιώς αρχίζει από την επίδοση και το αμετάκλητο ή τη γνώση των κρίσιμων εγγράφων ή της απόφασης που ανατράπηκε. Τα γεγονότα που αποτελούν την αφετηρία της προθεσμίας των εδαφίων αυτών, πρέπει να αποδεικνύονται με έγγραφο ή με δικαστική ομολογία.
5. Αν η απόφαση δεν επιδόθηκε, η προθεσμία της αναψηλάφησης είναι τρία χρόνια από τη δημοσίευση της προσβαλλόμενης απόφασης, εφόσον είναι τελεσίδικη ή ανέκκλητη, αλλιώς από την ημέρα που έγινε τελεσίδικη. Στις περιπτώσεις όμως του άρθρου 544 αριθ. 6 και 10, η αναψηλάφηση είναι απαράδεκτη μετά την παρέλευση ενός έτους από τη δημοσίευση της αμετάκλητης απόφασης των ποινικών ή των πολιτικών δικαστηρίων. Η προθεσμία αυτή δεν αρχίζει πριν από την επίδοση της προσβαλλόμενης απόφασης.
6. Αν εκείνος που δικαιούται να ασκήσει αναψηλάφηση πέθανε, η προθεσμία της αναψηλάφησης αρχίζει μόνο από την επίδοση της απόφασης στους καθολικούς διαδόχους ή τους κληροδόχους.

Άρθρο 546

1. Η προθεσμία της αναψηλάφησης, καθώς και η άσκησή της, δεν αναστέλλει την εκτέλεση της προσβαλλόμενης απόφασης, εκτός αν πρόκειται για αποφάσεις οι οποίες εκδίδονται στις γαμικές διαφορές που αναφέρονται στο άρθρο 592 αριθμ. 1 ή στις διαφορές που αφορούν τις σχέσεις γονέων και τέκνων, οι οποίες αναφέρονται στο άρθρο 592 αριθμ. 2 ή διατάζουν την εξάλειψη υποθήκης ή προσημείωσης ή κατάσχεσης ή κηρύσσουν έγγραφο πλαστό και εφόσον σε όλες τις περιπτώσεις αυτές η προθεσμία αρχίζει από την επίδοση της προσβαλλόμενης απόφασης. Μπορεί όμως το δικαστήριο που δικάζει την αναψηλάφηση με αίτηση κάποιου από τους διαδίκους που υποβάλλεται με τις προτάσεις να διατάξει σε περίπτωση εξάλειψης υποθήκης, προσημείωσης ή κατάσχεσης την άρση του ανασταλτικού αποτελέσματος με παροχή ανάλογης εγγύησης.
2. Το δικαστήριο που δικάζει την αναψηλάφηση μπορεί, με αίτηση κάποιου από τους διαδίκους που υποβάλλεται με τις προτάσεις, να διατάξει να ανασταλεί η εκτέλεση της προσβαλλόμενης απόφασης, ολικά ή εν μέρει, με παροχή ανάλογης εγγύησης ή και χωρίς εγγύηση. Η απόφαση αυτή μπορεί να ανακληθεί από το δικαστήριο εωσότου εκδοθεί η οριστική απόφαση για την Αναψηλάφηση, ύστερα από αίτηση κάποιου από τους διαδίκους που υποβάλλεται κατά τον ίδιο τρόπο.
3. Με τους όρους των παρ. 1 και 2 μπορεί να διαταχθεί η αναστολή της ισχύος της προσβαλλόμενης απόφασης.

d) in the care referred to in Article 544(6), from the date the judgment acknowledging the false testimony, perjury or forgery became irrevocable;
e) in the case referred to in Article 544(7), from the date the person requesting re-opening of proceedings became aware of the existence of new, essential documents;
f) in the case referred to in Article 544(8), from the date the person requesting re-opening of proceedings became aware of the judgment that was overturned;
g) in the cases referred to in Article 544(3), (5) and (9), from the date of service of the judgment being contested;
h) in the care referred to in Article 544(10), from the date the judgment acknowledging the passive bribery or breach of duty by the judge became irrevocable.
4. In the cases referred to in subparagraphs (d), (e), (f) and (h) of paragraph 3, the deadline shall not commence unless the contested judgment was previously served, otherwise it shall commence from [the date of] service and irrevocability of the judgment, or knowledge of the essential documents or of the overturned judgment.The events constituting the starting point of the deadline referred to in those subparagraphs must be proven by means of a document or admission made in court.
5. If the judgment was not served, the deadline for [filing an application for] re-opening proceedings is three years from the date of the judgment being contested was handed down, where it is *de jure* non-appealable or *de facto* non-appealable, otherwise from the date it became *de jure* non-appealable. However, in the cases referred to in Article 544(6) and (10), [the application for] re-opening proceedings shall be inadmissible after one year has elapsed from the date the criminal or civil courts handed down the irrevocable judgment. This deadline shall not commence before the judgment being contested has been served.
6. If the person entitled to file an application for re-opening proceedings has died, the deadline for re-opening proceedings shall commence only from the date of service of the judgment on their universal successors or legatees.

Article 546

1. The [fact that the] deadline for filing an application for re-opening proceedings [has commenced] and the [act of] filing such an application shall not stay enforcement of the judgment being contested, except in cases of judgments handed down in the matrimonial disputes referred to in Article 592(1) or the disputes concerning parent-child relationships referred to in Article 592(2), or judgments that order the extinguishment of a mortgage, or prenotation of mortgage, or attachment or declaring a document to be forged, provided, in all the above cases, the deadline commences from the date the judgment being contested was served. However, the court trying the application for re-opening proceedings, following a request by any of the parties in the proceedings in their pleadings, may, in the case of extinguishment of mortgage, or prenotation of mortgage, or attachment, order the suspensive effect to be lifted where a corresponding surety is provided.
2. The court trying the application for re-opening proceedings may, following a request by any of the parties in the proceedings in their pleadings, order stay of enforcement of the judgment being contested, either in whole or in part, whether or not a corresponding surety is provided. This [order] may be revoked by the court up to the time a final judgment is handed down on the application for re-opening proceedings, following a request made in the same manner by any of the parties in the proceedings.
3. Stay of the effect of the judgment being contested may be ordered under the conditions laid down in paragraphs 1 and 2.

Άρθρο 547

1. Το έγγραφο της αναψηλάφησης πρέπει να περιέχει τα στοιχεία που απαιτούνται κατά τα άρθρα 118 έως 120, να αναφέρει την προσβαλλόμενη απόφαση, τους λόγους της αναψηλάφησης, τα γεγονότα από τα οποία προκύπτει η τήρηση της προθεσμίας, αίτηση για εξαφάνιση, ολική ή εν μέρει, της προσβαλλόμενης απόφασης, καθώς και η αίτηση για την ουσία της υπόθεσης.
2. Πρόσθετοι λόγοι αναψηλάφησης ως προς τα ίδια κεφάλαια της απόφασης, όπως και εκείνα που αναγκαστικά συνέχονται μαζί τους, ασκούνται μόνο με ιδιαίτερο δικόγραφο που κατατίθεται στη γραμματεία του δικαστηρίου προς το οποίο απευθύνεται η αναψηλάφηση και, αφού συνταχθεί έκθεση κάτω από αυτό, κοινοποιείται σε εκείνον κατά του οποίου στρέφεται η αναψηλάφηση τριάντα ημέρες πριν από τη συζήτησή της.

Άρθρο 548

Στη διαδικασία της κατ' αναψηλάφηση δίκης εφαρμόζονται οι διατάξεις των άρθρων 227, 233 έως 236, των παρ. 10 έως 13 του άρθρου 237, 240 έως 312, εδάφια πρώτο έως τρίτο της παρ. 1 του άρθρου 591 και της παρ. 4 του άρθρου 591, με την επιφύλαξη της ισχύος του άρθρου 591 για τις ειδικές διαδικασίες. Η κατάθεση των προτάσεων γίνεται έως την έναρξη της συζήτησης και η κατάθεση της προσθήκης σε αυτές έως τη δωδέκατη ώρα της τρίτης εργάσιμης ημέρας μετά τη συζήτηση.

Άρθρο 549

1. Αν το δικαστήριο κρίνει ότι η αναψηλάφηση είναι παραδεκτή, έχει ασκηθεί εμπρόθεσμα και κατά τις νόμιμες διατυπώσεις, εξετάζει τους λόγους της και αν θεωρήσει κάποιον από αυτούς παραδεκτό και βάσιμο, τη δέχεται και εξαφανίζοντας την προσβαλλόμενη απόφαση εξετάζει την ουσία της υπόθεσης μέσα στα όρια που καθορίζονται από την αναψηλάφηση, αλλιώς απορρίπτει την αναψηλάφηση.
2. Αν η αναψηλάφηση έγινε δεκτή επειδή έχουν εκδοθεί αντιφατικές αποφάσεις, το δικαστήριο εξαφανίζει την τελευταία απόφαση.

Άρθρο 550

Το δικαστήριο που δικάζει την αναψηλάφηση, αν υποβληθεί αίτηση με το κύριο ή το πρόσθετο δικόγραφο της αναψηλάφησης, διατάζει με την απόφαση που δέχεται την αναψηλάφηση, την επαναφορά των πραγμάτων στην κατάσταση που υπήρχε πριν από την εκτέλεση της απόφασης, η οποία εξαφανίστηκε.

Άρθρο 551

Κατά της απόφασης που εκδίδεται στην αναψηλάφηση επιτρέπονται ένδικα μέσα μόνο εφόσον η απόφαση που είχε εκδοθεί στην αρχική δίκη μπορούσε να προσβληθεί με ένδικα μέσα.

ΚΕΦΑΛΑΙΟ Ε'
Αναίρεση

Άρθρο 552

Με αναίρεση μπορούν να προσβληθούν οι αποφάσεις των ειρηνοδικείων, των μονομελών και των πολυμελών πρωτοδικείων, καθώς και των εφετείων.

Article 547

1. The application for re-opening proceedings must contain the information required by Articles 118 to 120, refer to the judgment being contested, the grounds for re-opening proceedings, the events proving compliance with the deadline, a request to set aside the judgment being contested, whether in whole or in part, as well a request concerning the merits of the case.
2. Additional grounds for re-opening proceedings regarding the same heads of the judgment, as well as those necessarily related to such heads, shall only be filed by a separate procedural document, which shall be submitted to the registry of the court to which [the application for] re-opening proceedings is addressed and, after a report is prepared at its end, shall be notified to the respondent, 30 days before the hearing of the [application].

Article 548

The provisions of Articles 227, 233 to 236, 237(10) to (13), 240 to 312, the first to third subparagraphs of Article 591(1) and Article 591(4) apply to the re-opened proceedings, without prejudice to the effect of Article 591 concerning special procedures. Pleadings shall be filed by the commencement of the hearing, and additions to the pleadings shall be filed by twelve noon on the third working day after the hearing.

Article 549

1. If the court rules that [the application for] re-opening proceedings is admissible, was brought in good time and is in accordance with legal formalities, it shall examine the grounds and, if it considers any of the grounds admissible and well-founded, it shall accept the application, set aside the judgment being contested, and try the case on its merits within the limits set out in the application, otherwise it shall dismiss the application.
2. If [the application for] re-opening proceedings was accepted because contradictory judgments had been handed down, the court shall set aside the most recent judgment.

Article 550

If so requested in the main or additional procedural document for re-opening proceedings, the court trying the application shall order, in the judgment accepting the application, restoration of the state of affairs which existed prior to enforcement of the judgment that was set aside.

Article 551

Legal remedies may be filed against the judgment handed down on the application for re-opening proceedings only if the judgment that had been handed down during the initial proceedings could have been contested by legal remedies.

CHAPTER V
Cassation

Article 552

Applications for cassation may be filed to contest judgments handed down by courts of the peace, single- and multi-member courts of first instance, as well as courts of appeal.

Άρθρο 553

1. Αναίρεση επιτρέπεται μόνο κατά των αποφάσεων που δεν μπορούν να προσβληθούν με ανακοπή ερημοδικίας και έφεση

α) εκείνων που παραπέμπουν την υπόθεση στο αρμόδιο δικαστήριο εξαιτίας καθ' ύλην αναρμοδιότητας και εκείνων που έχουν εκδοθεί κατά παράβαση του άρθρου 46 από το δικαστήριο στο οποίο έγινε η παραπομπή,

β) των οριστικών αποφάσεων που περατώνουν όλη τη δίκη ή μόνο τη δίκη για την αγωγή ή για την ανταγωγή. Αν η απόφαση είναι κατά ένα μέρος οριστική, δεν επιτρέπεται αναίρεση ούτε κατά των οριστικών διατάξεων, πριν εκδοθεί οριστική απόφαση στη δίκη.

2. Αν προσβληθεί με αναίρεση η οριστική απόφαση, θεωρούνται ότι έχουν προσβληθεί και οι μη οριστικές που έχουν εκδοθεί προηγουμένως, και αν δεν απευθύνεται ρητώς εναντίον τους η αναίρεση.

Άρθρο 554

Αν η ανακοπή ερημοδικίας απορρίφθηκε, η αναίρεση απευθύνεται κατά της απόφασης που απέρριψε την ανακοπή, οπότε θεωρείται ότι η αναίρεση απευθύνεται και κατά της ερήμην απόφασης κατά της οποίας είχε απευθυνθεί η ανακοπή, εφόσον δεν πέρασε η προθεσμία για την άσκηση αναίρεσης κατά της απόφασης αυτής.

Άρθρο 555

Δεύτερη αναίρεση από τον ίδιο διάδικο κατά της ίδιας απόφασης, ως προς το ίδιο ή άλλο κεφάλαιο, δεν επιτρέπεται.

Άρθρο 556

1. Δικαίωμα αναίρεσης έχουν, εφόσον νικήθηκαν ολικά ή εν μέρει στη δίκη που εκδόθηκε η προσβαλλόμενη απόφαση, ο ενάγων, ο εναγόμενος, ο εκκαλών, ο εφεσίβλητος, εκείνος που ζητεί την αναψηλάφηση, εκείνος κατά του οποίου στρέφεται η αναψηλάφηση, εκείνοι που είχαν ασκήσει κύρια ή πρόσθετη παρέμβαση, οι προσεπικληθέντες, οι καθολικοί διάδοχοι και οι ειδικοί διάδοχοι, εφόσον απέκτησαν την ιδιότητα αυτή μετά την άσκηση της αγωγής, καθώς και οι εισαγγελείς, μόνο αν ήταν διάδικοι.

2. Αναίρεση δικαιούται να ασκήσει και ο διάδικος που νίκησε, εφόσον έχει έννομο συμφέρον.

Άρθρο 557

Ο Εισαγγελέας του Αρείου Πάγου δικαιούται να ζητήσει την αναίρεση υπέρ του νόμου κάθε απόφασης, ακόμη και αν δεν μπορούν να ασκήσουν αναίρεση κατά της απόφασης αυτής οι διάδικοι, για κάθε λόγο και χωρίς περιορισμό προθεσμίας. Η απόφαση που εκδίδεται για την αναίρεση αυτή δεν παράγει αποτελέσματα για τους διαδίκους, εκτός αν στηρίζεται σε υπέρβαση δικαιοδοσίας ή έλλειψη καθ' ύλην αρμοδιότητας.

Άρθρο 558

Η αναίρεση απευθύνεται κατά εκείνων οι οποίοι ήταν διάδικοι στη δίκη κατά την οποία εκδόθηκε η προσβαλλόμενη απόφαση ή των καθολικών διαδόχων τους ή των κληροδόχων τους. Αν υπάρχει αναγκαστική ομοδικία, η αναίρεση πρέπει να απευθύνεται κατά όλων των ομοδίκων, αλλιώς απορρίπτεται ως απαράδεκτη.

Article 553

1. Cassation shall be allowed only against the following judgments which cannot be contested by opposition against a default judgment [or] appeal[:]
a) those remitting the case to the competent court due to lack of jurisdiction *ratione materiae* and those handed down in breach of Article 46 by the court to which the case was remitted;
b) final judgments concluding the entire proceedings or only the proceedings on the action or cross-action. If the judgment is [only] partially final, applications for cassation shall not be allowed against final orders, before a final judgment is handed down in the proceedings.
2. If the final judgment is contested by means of an application for cassation, non-final judgments previously handed down shall also be deemed to be contested, even if the application for cassation is not expressly brought against these judgments.

Article 554

If the opposition against a default judgment was dismissed, the application for cassation shall be brought against the judgment that dismissed the opposition, in which case the application for cassation shall be deemed to also be brought against the default judgment against which the opposition had been filed, provided the deadline for filing the application for cassation against that judgment has not lapsed.

Article 555

A second application for cassation may not be filed by the same party in the proceedings against the same judgment with regard to the same or a different matter.

Article 556

1. The following persons shall, provided they were unsuccessful, whether in whole or in part, during proceedings where the judgment being contested was handed down, have the right to file an application for cassation: the plaintiff, the defendant, the appellant, the respondent, the person [filing an application for] re-opening proceedings, the respondent [in those re-opening proceedings], main or permissive intervenors, impleaded persons, their universal successors and their specific successors, provided they acquired this capacity after the action was filed, and public prosecutors, only if they were parties in the proceedings.
2. The successful party in the proceedings also has the right to file an application for cassation, where they have a legitimate interest.

Article 557

The Supreme Court Public Prosecutor has the right, on any grounds and without being subject to any deadline, to request cassation of any judgment in the interests of ensuring proper application of the law in the future, even if the parties in the proceedings cannot file an application for cassation against that judgment. The judgment handed down on such [application for] cassation does not generate effects for the parties in the proceedings, unless it concerns overstepping of jurisdiction or lack or jurisdiction *ratione materiae*.

Article 558

An [application for] cassation shall be brought against the persons who were parties in the proceedings in which the judgment being contested was handed down or their universal successors or legatees. In cases of compulsory joinder, the [application for] cassation must be brought against all the joined parties, otherwise it shall be dismissed as inadmissible.

Άρθρο 559

Αναίρεση επιτρέπεται μόνο

1) αν παραβιάστηκε κανόνας του ουσιαστικού δικαίου, στον οποίο περιλαμβάνονται και οι ερμηνευτικοί κανόνες των δικαιοπραξιών, αδιάφορο αν πρόκειται για νόμο ή έθιμο, ελληνικό ή ξένο, εσωτερικού ή διεθνούς δικαίου. Η παράβαση των διδαγμάτων της κοινής πείρας αποτελεί λόγο αναίρεσης μόνο αν τα διδάγματα αυτά αφορούν την ερμηνεία κανόνων δικαίου ή την υπαγωγή των πραγματικών γεγονότων σ' αυτούς,

2) αν το δικαστήριο δεν είχε τη νόμιμη σύνθεση ή έλαβε μέρος στη σύνθεσή του δικαστής του οποίου είχε γίνει δεκτή η εξαίρεση ή κατά του οποίου είχε ασκηθεί αγωγή κακοδικίας,

3) αν το δικαστήριο απέρριψε την αίτηση για εξαίρεση δικαστή, αν και ο δικαστής αυτός, σύμφωνα με τα πραγματικά περιστατικά που δέχτηκε η απόφαση, έπρεπε κατά το νόμο να εξαιρεθεί,

4) αν το δικαστήριο έχει υπερβεί τη δικαιοδοσία των πολιτικών δικαστηρίων,

5) αν το δικαστήριο σε περίπτωση καθ' ύλην αρμοδιότητας εσφαλμένα δέχτηκε ότι είναι αρμόδιο ή αναρμόδιο, με την επιφύλαξή των διατάξεων του άρθρου 47 ή αν το δικαστήριο στο οποίο παραπέμφθηκε η υπόθεση παραβίασε τις διατάξεις του άρθρου 46,

6) αν παρά το νόμο και ιδίως παρά τις σχετικές με την επίδοση διατάξεις ο διάδικος δικάστηκε ερήμην,

7) αν παράνομα αποκλείστηκε η δημοσιότητα της διαδικασίας,

8) αν το δικαστήριο παρά το νόμο έλαβε υπόψη πράγματα που δεν προτάθηκαν ή δεν έλαβε υπόψη πράγματα που προτάθηκαν και έχουν ουσιώδη επίδραση στην έκβαση της δίκης,

9) αν το δικαστήριο επιδίκασε κάτι που δεν ζητήθηκε ή επιδίκασε περισσότερα από όσα ζητήθηκαν ή άφησε αίτηση αδίκαστη,

10) αν το δικαστήριο παρά το νόμο δέχτηκε πράγματα που έχουν ουσιώδη επίδραση στην έκβαση της δίκης ως αληθινά χωρίς απόδειξη,

11) αν το δικαστήριο έλαβε υπόψη αποδεικτικά μέσα που ο νόμος δεν επιτρέπει ή παρά το νόμο έλαβε υπόψη αποδείξεις που δεν προσκομίστηκαν ή δεν έλαβε υπόψη αποδεικτικά μέσα που οι διάδικοι επικαλέστηκαν και προσκόμισαν,

12) αν το δικαστήριο παραβίασε τους ορισμούς του νόμου σχετικά με τη δύναμη των αποδεικτικών μέσων,

13) αν το δικαστήριο εσφαλμένα εφάρμοσε τους ορισμούς του νόμου ως προς το βάρος της απόδειξης,

14) αν το δικαστήριο παρά το νόμο κήρυξε ή δεν κήρυξε ακυρότητα, έκπτωση από δικαίωμα ή απαράδεκτο,

15) αν παρά το νόμο ανακλήθηκε οριστική απόφαση,

16) αν το δικαστήριο κατά παράβαση του νόμου δέχτηκε ότι υπάρχει ή ότι δεν υπάρχει δεδικασμένο ή ότι υπάρχει δεδικασμένο με βάση απόφαση που εξαφανίστηκε ύστερα από ένδικο μέσο ή αναγνωρίστηκε ως ανύπαρκτη,

17) αν η ίδια απόφαση περιέχει αντιφατικές διατάξεις,

18) αν το δικαστήριο της παραπομπής δεν συμμορφώθηκε προς την αναιρετική απόφαση,

19) αν η απόφαση δεν έχει νόμιμη βάση και ιδίως αν δεν έχει καθόλου αιτιολογίες ή έχει αιτιολογίες αντιφατικές ή ανεπαρκείς σε ζήτημα που ασκεί ουσιώδη επίδραση στην έκβαση της δίκης,

20) αν το δικαστήριο παραμόρφωσε το περιεχόμενο εγγράφου με το να δεχτεί πραγματικά γεγονότα προφανώς διαφορετικά από εκείνα που αναφέρονται στο έγγραφο αυτό.

Article 559

Cassation shall be permitted only if[:]

1) a rule of substantive law was infringed, including the interpretative rules for legal transactions, irrespective of whether these constitute law or custom, Greek or foreign, national or international law. Infringements of the teachings of common experience shall constitute grounds for cassation only if such teachings concern the interpretation of legal norms or the subsumption of actual facts to such norms;

2) the court was not lawfully comprised or a judge whose exemption had been accepted or against whom an action for miscarriage of justice had been brought took part in its composition;

3) the court dismissed the application concerning the exemption of a judge, even though that judge, in light of the actual facts accepted in the judgment, should have been exempted in law;

4) the court overstepped the jurisdiction of the civil courts;

5) in the case of jurisdiction *ratione materiae*, the court erroneously accepted that it did or did not have jurisdiction, without prejudice to the provisions of Article 47, or if the court to which the case was remitted breached the provisions of Article 46;

6) in breach of the law and, in particular, the provisions relating to service [of documents], the party in the proceedings was tried *in absentia*;

7) the public nature of proceedings was unlawfully precluded;

8) in breach of the law, the court took into account things not pleaded or did not take into account things which were pleaded and which materially impact the outcome of the proceedings;

9) the court awarded something not requested or awarded more than what was requested or failed to consider a form of order sought;

10) [in breach of the law], the court accepted things that materially impact the outcome of the proceedings as true without the taking of evidence;

11) the court took into account means of evidence not permitted in law or, in breach of the law, the court took into account evidence not adduced or did not take into account means of evidence that the parties in the proceedings adduced and relied upon;

12) the court infringed the statutory provisions concerning the probative value of means of evidence;

13) the court misapplied the statutory provisions concerning the burden of proof;

14) in breach of the law, the court declared or did not declare nullity, forfeiture of a right or inadmissibility;

15) in breach of the law, a final judgment was revoked;

16) in breach of the law, the court accepted that there is *res judicata*, or that there is no *res judicata,* or that there is *res judicata* on the basis of a judgment which was later set aside following the filing of a legal remedy or which was acknowledged to be non-existent;

17) a single judgment contains contradictory orders;

18) the remittal court did not comply with the judgment ordering cassation;

19) the judgment has no legal basis and, in particular, if it contains no reasoning whatsoever or contains contradictory or insufficient reasoning with regard to a matter materially impacting the outcome of the proceedings;

20) the court distorted the content of a document by accepting actual facts manifestly different from those referred to in that document.

Άρθρο 560

Κατά των αποφάσεων των ειρηνοδικείων, καθώς και των αποφάσεων των πρωτοδικείων που εκδίδονται σε εφέσεις κατά των αποφάσεων των ειρηνοδικείων, επιτρέπεται αναίρεση μόνο:

1) αν παραβιάστηκε κανόνας του ουσιαστικού δικαίου, στον οποίο περιλαμβάνονται και οι ερμηνευτικοί κανόνες των δικαιοπραξιών, αδιάφορο αν πρόκειται για νόμο ή έθιμο, ελληνικό ή ξένο, εσωτερικού ή διεθνούς δικαίου. Η παράβαση των διδαγμάτων της κοινής πείρας αποτελεί λόγο αναίρεσης μόνο αν τα διδάγματα αυτά αφορούν την ερμηνεία κανόνων δικαίου ή την υπαγωγή των πραγματικών γεγονότων σε αυτούς. Ο λόγος αυτός αναίρεσης δεν μπορεί να προβληθεί σε μικροδιαφορές,

2) αν το δικαστήριο δεν συγκροτήθηκε, όπως ορίζει ο νόμος ή δίκασε δικαστής του οποίου είχε γίνει δεκτή η εξαίρεση,

3) αν το δικαστήριο δέχτηκε ή δεν δέχτηκε τη δικαιοδοσία των πολιτικών δικαστηρίων ή δεν είχε καθ' ύλην αρμοδιότητα,

4) αν παράνομα αποκλείστηκε η δημοσιότητα της διαδικασίας,

5) αν το δικαστήριο παρά τον νόμο έλαβε υπόψη πράγματα που δεν προτάθηκαν ή δεν έλαβε υπόψη πράγματα που προτάθηκαν και έχουν ουσιώδη επίδραση στην έκβαση της δίκης,

6) αν η απόφαση δεν έχει νόμιμη βάση και ιδίως αν δεν έχει καθόλου αιτιολογίες ή έχει αιτιολογίες αντιφατικές ή ανεπαρκείς σε ζήτημα που ασκεί ουσιώδη επίδραση στην έκβαση της δίκης.

Άρθρο 561

1. Η εκτίμηση από το δικαστήριο της ουσίας πραγματικών γεγονότων και ιδιαίτερα του περιεχομένου εγγράφων δεν υπόκειται στον έλεγχο του Αρείου Πάγου, εκτός αν παραβιάστηκαν κανόνες δικαίου, στους οποίους περιλαμβάνονται και οι ερμηνευτικοί ή αν υπάρχει λόγος αναίρεσης κατά το άρθρο 559 αριθ. 19 και 20.

2. Η εκτίμηση του περιεχομένου διαδικαστικών εγγράφων της ίδιας ή άλλης δίκης, ιδίως αγωγών, παρεμβάσεων, ένδικων μέσων, προτάσεων ή δικαστικών αποφάσεων, ελέγχεται από τον Άρειο Πάγο.

Άρθρο 562

1. Είναι απαράδεκτος λόγος αναίρεσης κατά απόφασης του δικαστηρίου της παραπομπής, εφόσον με τον λόγο αυτόν προσβάλλεται η απόφαση κατά το τμήμα της εκείνο κατά το οποίο συμμορφώθηκε προς την αναιρετική.

2. Είναι απαράδεκτος λόγος αναίρεσης που στηρίζεται σε ισχυρισμό, ο οποίος δεν προτάθηκε νόμιμα στο δικαστήριο της ουσίας, εκτός αν πρόκειται:

α) για παράβαση που δεν μπορεί να προβληθεί στο δικαστήριο της ουσίας,

β) για σφάλμα που προκύπτει από την ίδια την απόφαση,

γ) για ισχυρισμό που αφορά στη δημόσια τάξη, ή το δεδικασμένο.

3. Κανείς δεν μπορεί να δημιουργήσει λόγο αναίρεσης από τις δικές του πράξεις ή από πράξεις προσώπων που ενεργούν στο όνομά του, εκτός αν πρόκειται για λόγους που αφορούν τη δημόσια τάξη.

4. Κατ' εξαίρεση ο Άρειος Πάγος εξετάζει αυτεπαγγέλτως, λόγο αναίρεσης από εκείνους που αναφέρονται στους αριθμούς 1, 4, 14, 16, 17 και 19 του άρθρου 559. Ο Άρειος Πάγος με απλή διάταξή του, αν υπάρχουν λόγοι, οι οποίοι λαμβάνονται υπόψη αυτεπαγγέλτως κατά το πρώτο εδάφιο, καλεί τους διαδίκους να διατυπώσουν με υπόμνημα τις απόψεις τους στην οριζόμενη από αυτόν προθεσμία. Η γνωστοποίηση της διάταξης αυτής γίνεται με επιμέλεια του γραμματέα με αποστολή ηλεκτρονικού μηνύματος στη διεύθυνση ηλεκτρονικού ταχυδρομείου των διαδίκων. Η απόφαση δεν εκδίδεται πριν από τη συμπλήρωση της προθεσμίας αυτής.

Article 560

Cassation against judgments handed down by the courts of the peace and judgments handed down by courts of first instance on appeals against judgments handed down by the courts of the peace shall be permitted only if:

1) a rule of substantive law was infringed, including the interpretative rules for legal transactions, irrespective of whether these constitute law or custom, Greek or foreign, national or international law. Infringements of the teachings of common experience shall constitute grounds for cassation only if such teachings concern the interpretation of legal norms or the subsumption of actual facts to such norms. This ground of cassation cannot be relied upon in [cases of] small claims;

2) the court was not constituted in accordance with the law or a judge whose exemption had been accepted tried the case;

3) the court accepted or did not accept the jurisdiction of the civil courts or did not have jurisdiction *ratione materiae*;

4) the public nature of proceedings was unlawfully precluded;

5) in breach of the law, the court took into account things not pleaded or did not take into account things which were pleaded and which materially impact the outcome of the proceedings;

6) the judgment has no legal basis and, in particular, if it contains no reasoning whatsoever or contains contradictory or insufficient reasoning with regard to a matter materially impacting the outcome of the proceedings.

Article 561

1. The trial court's weighing up of the actual facts and, in particular, of the content of documents is not subject to review by the Supreme Court, unless legal norms were breached, including interpretative rules, or if there are grounds for cassation under Article 559(19) and (20).

2. The weighing up of the content of procedural documents of the same or a different set of proceedings, particularly actions, interventions, legal remedies, pleadings or court judgments, is subject to review by the Supreme Court.

Article 562

1. Grounds of cassation against a judgment handed down by the remittal court shall be inadmissible where those grounds contest the judgment insofar as it complied with the judgment ordering cassation.

2. Grounds of cassation shall be inadmissible where those grounds rely on assertions not lawfully pleaded before the trial court, unless they concern:

a) an infringement that cannot be raised before the trial court;

b) an error arising from the judgment itself;

c) an assertion concerning public policy or *res judicata*.

3. No person may cause grounds for cassation to arise through their own acts or acts carried out by persons acting in their name, except for reasons relating to public policy.

4. By way of exception, the Supreme Court shall examine *ex officio* the grounds of cassation referred to in Article 559(1), (4), (14), (16), (17) and (19). By means of a simple order and where there are grounds, which shall be taken into account *ex officio* in accordance with the first subparagraph, the Supreme Court shall summon the parties in the proceedings to set out their views in a memorandum filed within the deadline set by [the Supreme Court]. This order shall be notified by the [Supreme Court] registrar by electronic message sent to the e-mail addresses of the parties in the proceedings. A judgment shall not be handed down before this deadline has lapsed.

Άρθρο 563

1. Η αίτηση αναίρεσης υπάγεται στον Άρειο Πάγο, ο οποίος δικάζει σε ολομέλεια ή σε τμήμα.

2. Στην αρμοδιότητα της ολομέλειας του Αρείου Πάγου υπάγονται

α) αιτήσεις αναίρεσης υπέρ του νόμου,

β) αιτήσεις αναίρεσης κατά αποφάσεων πολιτικών δικαστηρίων που παραπέμπονται για εκδίκαση στην ολομέλεια με κοινό πρακτικό του Προέδρου και του Εισαγγελέα του Αρείου Πάγου ή με απόφαση του τμήματος που δικάζει. Η παραπομπή μπορεί να γίνει για όλους ή για μερικούς μόνο από τους λόγους της αναίρεσης, αν σε κάθε περίπτωση κριθεί ότι δημιουργούνται ζητήματα με γενικότερο ενδιαφέρον ή ότι τούτο είναι αναγκαίο για την ενότητα της νομολογίας. Το τμήμα που δικάζει είναι υποχρεωμένο να παραπέμψει την εκδίκαση της υπόθεσης στην ολομέλεια αν η απόφασή του για την αίτηση αναίρεσης, αναιρετική ή απορριπτική, λαμβάνεται με πλειοψηφία μιας ψήφου ή αν αρνείται να εφαρμόσει νόμο ως αντισυνταγματικό. Αν όμως το ζήτημα της συνταγματικότητας έχει ήδη κριθεί με απόφαση της ολομέλειας, η παραπομπή είναι δυνητική.

3. Αν η παραπομπή στην ολομέλεια γίνεται με πρακτικό του προέδρου και του εισαγγελέα του Αρείου Πάγου, ο πρόεδρος ορίζει συγχρόνως δικάσιμο της ολομέλειας τηρώντας τις διατάξεις των παρ. 3 και 4 του άρθρου 568.

Άρθρο 564

1. Αν ο αναιρεσείων διαμένει στην Ελλάδα, η προθεσμία της αναίρεσης είναι τριάντα ημέρες και αρχίζει από την επίδοση της απόφασης.

2. Αν ο αναιρεσείων διαμένει στο εξωτερικό ή η διαμονή του είναι άγνωστη, η προθεσμία της αναίρεσης είναι εξήντα (60) ημέρες και αρχίζει από την επίδοση της απόφασης.

3. Αν η απόφαση δεν επιδόθηκε, η προθεσμία της αναίρεσης είναι δύο (2) έτη και αρχίζει από τη δημοσίευση της απόφασης που περατώνει τη δίκη.

4. Αν εκείνος που έχει δικαίωμα να ασκήσει αναίρεση πέθανε, η προθεσμία της αναίρεσης αρχίζει μόνο από την επίδοση της απόφασης που περατώνει τη δίκη στους καθολικούς διαδόχους ή τους κληροδόχους.

Άρθρο 565

1. Η προθεσμία της αναίρεσης, καθώς και η άσκησή της, δεν αναστέλλει την εκτέλεση της προσβαλλόμενης απόφασης. Στις γαμικές διαφορές που αναφέρονται στο άρθρο 592 αριθμ. 1, στις διαφορές του άρθρου 592 αριθμ. 2, που αφορούν σχέσεις γονέων και τέκνων, καθώς και σε δίκες που αφορούν εξάλειψη υποθήκης, προσημείωσης ή κατάσχεσης ή κηρύσσουν έγγραφο πλαστό, η προθεσμία της αναίρεσης, καθώς και η άσκησή της, αναστέλλει την εκτέλεση.

2. Αν από την εκτέλεση της απόφασης πιθανολογείται κίνδυνος βλάβης, της οποίας η αποκατάσταση δεν είναι εύκολη, μπορεί να διαταχθεί με αίτηση κάποιου από τους διαδίκους η ολική ή εν μέρει αναστολή της εκτέλεσης της προσβαλλόμενης απόφασης, με τον όρο παροχής ανάλογης εγγύησης ή και χωρίς απόφασης, με τον όρο παροχής ανάλογης εγγύησης ή και χωρίς εγγύηση ή να εξαρτηθεί η εκτέλεση της απόφασης από την παροχή εγγύησης από το διάδικο που έχει νικήσει. Για την αίτηση αποφαίνεται, συνεδριάζοντας ως συμβούλιο χωρίς υποχρεωτική κλήτευση των διαδίκων το αρμόδιο πολιτικό τμήμα, το οποίο συγκροτείται από τρία μέλη, στα οποία περιλαμβάνεται υποχρεωτικά ο εισηγητής της υπόθεσης. Η απόφαση της αναστολής μπορεί κατά τον ίδιο τρόπο να ανακληθεί με αίτηση κάποιου από τους διαδίκους έως την συζήτηση της αναίρεσης. Κατόπιν επιτρέπεται μόνο κατά την συζήτησή της.

Article 563

1. Applications for cassation are filed with the Supreme Court, which shall try the matter sitting in full court or as a chamber.

2. The Supreme Court, sitting in full court, has jurisdiction for[:]

a) applications for cassation in the interests of ensuring proper application of the law in the future;

b) applications for cassation against judgments handed down by civil courts, which are remitted for adjudication to the full court by means of a joint report prepared by the President of the Supreme Court and the Supreme Court Public Prosecutor or a decision by the chamber trying the case. Remittal is possible on some or all of the grounds of cassation, provided, in all cases, it is ruled that issues of broader interest arise or this is necessary for reasons of case-law consistency. The chamber trying the case is obligated to remit adjudication of the case to the full court if its judgment on the application for cassation, whether accepting or dismissing the application, is made with a single-vote majority or if it refuses to apply a law as unconstitutional. However, if the issue of constitutionality has already been determined in a judgment handed down by the Supreme Court sitting in full court, remittal shall be optional.

3. Where remittal to the full court is effected by means of a report prepared by the President of the Supreme Court and the Supreme Court Public Prosecutor, the President shall also set a hearing date before the full court, in compliance with the provisions of Article 568(3) and (4).

Article 564

1. If the cassationer resides in Greece, the deadline for filing the application for cassation is 30 days, commencingon the date the judgment was served.

2. If the cassationer resides abroad or has no known place of residence, the deadline for the application for cassation is 60 days, commencing on the date the judgment was served.

3. If the judgment was not served, the deadline for the application for cassation is two years, starting on the date the judgment concluding the proceedings was handed down.

4. If the person entitled to file an application for cassation has died, the deadline for filing the application for cassation shall commence only from the date the judgment concluding the proceedings was served on their universal successors or legatees.

Article 565

1. The [fact that the] deadline for [filing an application for] cassation [has commenced] and [the act of] filing the application for cassation shall not stay enforcement of the judgment being contested. In the matrimonial disputes referred to in Article 592(1) or the disputes concerning parent-child relationships referred to in Article 592(2) or in proceedings which concern extinguishment of a mortgage or prenotation of mortgage or attachment or declaring a document to be forged, the [fact that the] deadline for [filing an application for] cassation [has commenced] and [the act of] filing the application for cassation shall stay enforcement.

2. If enforcement of the judgment is considered likely on the balance of probabilities to give rise to risk of harm whose restitution is difficult, following an application filed by any of the parties in the proceedings, an order may be issued to stay enforcement of the judgment being contested, whether in whole or in part, on condition that a corresponding surety is provided, or even without surety, or to predicate enforcement of the judgment on the provision of surety by the successful party in the proceedings. The competent civil chamber, sitting in council, shall rule on the application, without summonsing the parties in the proceedings being mandatory; the chamber shall be comprised of three members, one of whom must be the reporting judge in the case. The decision staying [enforcement] may be revoked in the same manner following an application filed by any of the parties in the proceedings by the hearing of the [application for] cassation and, subsequently, only during the hearing.

Άρθρο 566

1. Το έγγραφο της αναίρεσης πρέπει να περιέχει τα στοιχεία που απαιτούνται κατά τα άρθρα 118 έως 120, να αναφέρει την προσβαλλόμενη απόφαση, τους λόγους της αναίρεσης, αίτηση για την αναίρεση, ολική ή εν μέρει της προσβαλλόμενης απόφασης και αίτηση για την ουσία της υπόθεσης.

2. Αν με το ίδιο αναιρετήριο προσβάλλονται δύο ή περισσότερες αποφάσεις πρωτοβάθμιου και δευτεροβάθμιου δικαστηρίου, η κατάθεσή του πρέπει να γίνεται στο καθένα από τα δικαστήρια αυτά.

Άρθρο 567

1. Όταν ασκούν αναίρεση εισαγγελείς, πρόσθετους λόγους μπορεί να ασκήσει και ο εισαγγελέας του Αρείου Πάγου.

2. Η αναίρεση που ασκεί ο εισαγγελέας του Αρείου Πάγου διαβιβάζεται στη γραμματεία του Αρείου Πάγου. Με τον ίδιο τρόπο και χωρίς περιορισμό προθεσμίας ασκούνται και οι πρόσθετοι λόγοι αναίρεσης.

Άρθρο 568

1. Για να προσδιοριστεί δικάσιμος ο διάδικος που επισπεύδει τη συζήτηση προσάγει στη γραμματεία του Αρείου Πάγου επικυρωμένο αντίγραφο της αναίρεσης, των προσβαλλόμενων αποφάσεων, των εισαγωγικών εγγράφων της κύριας δίκης ή των παρεμπιπτουσών δικών και των προτάσεων του ίδιου και των άλλων διαδίκων, αν είναι απαραίτητες για να διαγνωστεί η βασιμότητα των λόγων αναίρεσης που περιέχονται στο κύριο δικόγραφο ή στο πρόσθετο αναιρετήριο, καθώς και συμβολαιογραφικό πληρεξούσιο του εντολέα του. Δύο αντίγραφα των εγγράφων αυτών κατατίθενται ατελώς.

2. Η γραμματεία του Αρείου Πάγου υποβάλλει χωρίς καθυστέρηση τα έγγραφα που κατατέθηκαν στον πρόεδρο του Αρείου Πάγου, ο οποίος ορίζει το αρμόδιο τμήμα, και ο πρόεδρος του τμήματος με απλή σημείωση στο αντίγραφο της αναίρεσης που έχει κατατεθεί ορίζει:

α) δικάσιμο της υπόθεσης,

β) την προθεσμία μέσα στην οποία πρέπει να επιδοθεί η κλήση για συζήτηση,

γ) εισηγητή αρεοπαγίτη προς τον οποίον διαβιβάζεται ο φάκελος της δικογραφίας για τους σκοπούς του άρθρου 571.

3. Η δικάσιμος ορίζεται σε χρόνο που παρέχει επαρκή προθεσμία για την επίδοση και την προπαρασκευή της συζήτησης της υπόθεσης.

4. Αν ο αναιρεσείων επισπεύδει τη συζήτηση η κλήση συντάσσεται κάτω από το αντίγραφο του δικογράφου που έχει κατατεθεί και επιδίδεται με επιμέλειά του στους αντιδίκους τουλάχιστον εξήντα ημέρες πριν από τη δικάσιμο, αν όλοι οι διάδικοι που καλούνται διαμένουν στην Ελλάδα, και τουλάχιστον ενενήντα ημέρες, αν κάποιος από του διαδίκους διαμένει στο εξωτερικό ή η διαμονή του είναι άγνωστη. Αν ο αναιρεσίβλητος επισπεύδει τη συζήτηση ή την επισπεύδει άλλος διάδικος εκτός από τον αναιρεσείοντα, η κλήση επιδίδεται μέσα στην ίδια προθεσμία με επιμέλεια εκείνου που επισπεύδει τη συζήτηση, στον αναιρεσείοντα και τους άλλους διαδίκους.

Άρθρο 569

1. Πρόσθετοι λόγοι αναίρεσης είναι παραδεκτοί, και αν η αίτηση της αναίρεσης δεν περιέχει λόγο τυπικά παραδεκτό και ορισμένο.

Article 566

1. An application for cassation must contain the information required by Articles 118 to 120, a reference to the judgment being contested, the grounds of cassation, a request to quash the judgment being contested, whether in whole or in part, as well as a request concerning the merits of the case.
2. If two or more judgments handed down by a first-instance and second-instance court are being contested in the same application for cassation, it must be filed with each of those courts.

Article 567

1. When public prosecutors file applications for cassation, the Supreme Court Public Prosecutor may also file additional grounds [of cassation].
2. Applications for cassation filed by the Supreme Court Public Prosecutor shall be forwarded to the registry of the Supreme Court. Additional grounds of cassation shall also be filed in the same manner and without being subject to any deadline.

Article 568

1. In order for a hearing date to be set, the party in the proceedings expediting the hearing shall provide the registry of the Supreme Court with a certified copy of the application for cassation, the judgments being contested, the documents instituting the main proceedings or incidental proceedings and the pleadings by that party and the other parties in the proceedings, where necessary to determine whether the grounds of cassation included in the main procedural document or the additional [grounds of] cassation are well-founded, as well as a notarial power of attorney from their principal. Two copies of these documents shall be filed free of official charges.
2. The registry of the Supreme Court shall submit the documents filed without delay to the President of the Supreme Court, who shall designate the competent chamber, and the president of the chamber shall set the following, making a simple note on the copy of the application for cassation filed:
a) a hearing date for the case;
b) the deadline within which the summons for the hearing must be served;
c) a Supreme Court Judge as reporting judge to whom the case-file shall be forwarded for the purposes of Article 571.
3. A hearing date shall be set so as to provide a sufficient deadline for service and preparation of the hearing of the case.
4. If the hearing is being expedited by the cassationer, the summons shall be drafted at the end the copy of the procedural document which was filed and shall be served by the cassationer on the opponents at least 60 days prior to the hearing date, if all the parties in the proceedings being summonsed reside in Greece, and at least 90 days [prior to the hearing date] if any party in the proceedings resides abroad or has no known place of residence. If the hearing is being expedited by the cassationee or any party in the proceedings other than the cassationer, the summons shall be served on the cassationer and the other parties in the proceedings within the same deadline by the party expediting the hearing.

Article 569

1. Additional grounds of cassation shall be admissible even if the grounds set forth in the application for cassation are not formally admissible and specific.

2. Οι πρόσθετοι λόγοι αναίρεσης ως προς τα ίδια κεφάλαια της προσβαλλόμενης απόφασης και τα κεφάλαια εκείνα που αναγκαστικά συνέχονται με αυτά, ασκούνται μόνο με δικόγραφο που κατατίθεται στη γραμματεία του Αρείου Πάγου, τριάντα (30) τουλάχιστον πλήρεις ημέρες πριν από τη συζήτηση της αναίρεσης, όπως αυτή ορίζεται στο άρθρο 281, κάτω από το οποίο συντάσσεται έκθεση. Αντίγραφο του δικογράφου των πρόσθετων λόγων επιδίδεται πριν από την ίδια προθεσμία στον αναιρεσίβλητο και τους άλλους διαδίκους. Η επίδοση μπορεί να γίνει και στον πληρεξούσιο δικηγόρο του αναιρεσιβλήτου, αν αυτός επισπεύδει τη συζήτηση. Αντίγραφα των προσθέτων λόγων, τα οποία εκδίδονται ατελώς, αφού κατατεθούν από τον αναιρεσείοντα, παραδίδονται από τον γραμματέα του Αρείου Πάγου ένα στον εισηγητή της υπόθεσης για τους σκοπούς του άρθρου 571 και ένα στον Εισαγγελέα του Αρείου Πάγου μέσα στην παραπάνω προθεσμία των τριάντα ημερών. Τα ίδια εφαρμόζονται και όταν τη συζήτηση επισπεύδει ο αναιρεσίβλητος ή ο άλλος διάδικος εκτός από τον αναιρεσείοντα.

Άρθρο 570

1. Οι διάδικοι δεν είναι υποχρεωμένοι να καταθέσουν προτάσεις, εκτός αν προβάλλονται ενστάσεις ως προς το παραδεκτό και το εμπρόθεσμο της αίτησης της αναίρεσης και των πρόσθετων λόγων. Σε αυτή την περίπτωση, ο προβάλλων τις ενστάσεις διάδικος καταθέτει τις προτάσεις του είκοσι (20) τουλάχιστον ημέρες πριν από τη δικάσιμο. Σε κάθε άλλη περίπτωση, οι διάδικοι έχουν δικαίωμα να καταθέτουν υπόμνημα έως τη δωδέκατη ώρα της τρίτης εργάσιμης ημέρας μετά τη συζήτηση, εφόσον παρέστησαν σε αυτή.

2. Νέοι ισχυρισμοί των διαδίκων και νέα αποδεικτικά μέσα για την ουσιαστική εκδίκαση της υπόθεσης από τον Άρειο Πάγο μετά την αναίρεση υποβάλλονται σύμφωνα με τις διατάξεις που ισχύουν για τα δικαστήρια της ουσίας.

3. Μέσα στην προθεσμία της παρ. 1 οφείλουν όλοι οι διάδικοι να καταθέσουν στη γραμματεία του Αρείου Πάγου τα έγγραφα που χρησιμεύουν για να υποστηριχθεί ή να αποκρουστεί η αναίρεση. Η κατάθεση και η ημερομηνία της βεβαιώνεται με σημείωση επάνω στο φάκελο της δικογραφίας.

4. Τα αντίγραφα των διαδικαστικών εγγράφων των διαδίκων, των αντιδίκων τους ή των άλλων διαδίκων, τα οποία προσάγονται, υποβάλλονται ατελώς, νόμιμα επικυρωμένα.

Άρθρο 571

1. Αν ο εισηγητής κρίνει ότι η αναίρεση είναι απαράδεκτη ή ότι όλοι οι λόγοι της, αρχικοί και πρόσθετοι, είναι απαράδεκτοι ή προδήλως αβάσιμοι, εισηγείται προφορικώς σε τριμελές συμβούλιο, απαρτιζόμενο από τον Πρόεδρο του Αρείου Πάγου ή το νόμιμο αναπληρωτή του και από δύο Αρεοπαγίτες, χωρίς κλήτευση των διαδίκων, την απόρριψη της αναίρεσης. Αν το συμβούλιο αποδεχθεί ομόφωνα την πρόταση του εισηγητή, εκδίδει διάταξη με την οποία ματαιώνεται η συζήτηση της υπόθεσης. Με την ίδια διάταξη επιδικάζεται στον αναιρεσίβλητο δικαστική δαπάνη, αν αυτός είχε καταθέσει προτάσεις, ενώ η αμοιβή του πληρεξούσιου δικηγόρου του υπολογίζεται στο μισό του ελάχιστου ορίου και ορίζεται παράβολο τριακοσίων (300) έως εννιακόσια (900) ευρώ. Επί εργατικών υποθέσεων το παράβολο μπορεί να μειωθεί έως το ποσό των διακοσίων (200) ευρώ. Τα ποσά των δύο προηγούμενων εδαφίων μπορούν να αυξομειώνονται με κοινή απόφαση των Υπουργών Οικονομικών και Δικαιοσύνης, Διαφάνειας και Ανθρωπίνων Δικαιωμάτων. Με επιμέλεια του γραμματέα σημειώνεται ο αριθμός της διάταξης του συμβουλίου στο πινάκιο και στο φάκελο της υπόθεσης και επιδίδεται κυρωμένο αντίγραφό της στον αναιρεσείοντα ή στο δικηγόρο που υπογράφει την αναίρεση ή τους πρόσθετους λόγους μέσα σε τριάντα (30) ημέρες από την έκδοσή της.

2. Additional grounds of cassation regarding the same heads of the judgment being contested, as well as those necessarily related to such heads, shall only be filed by means of a procedural document submitted to the registry of the Supreme Court at least 30 full days prior to the hearing of the application for cassation, as [a hearing is] defined in Article 281, at the end of which a report shall be drafted. A copy of the procedural document containing additional grounds of cassation shall be served within the same deadline on the cassationee and the other parties in the proceedings. The procedural document may also be served on the authorised lawyer of the cassationee, if they are expediting the hearing. After copies of the additional grounds of cassation filed by the cassationer have been issued free of official charges, the registrar of the Supreme Court shall deliver one copy to the reporting judge in the case for the purposes of Article 571 and one copy to the Supreme Court Public Prosecutor within the aforesaid 30-day deadline. This also applies where the hearing is being expedited by the cassationee or [any] party in the proceedings other than the cassationer.

Article 570

1. The parties in the proceedings are not obligated to file pleadings, unless they raise pleas regarding the admissibility and timeliness of the application for cassation and the additional grounds [of cassation]. In this case, the party in the proceedings raising such pleas shall file pleadings at least 20 days prior to the hearing date. In all other cases, the parties in the proceedings have the right to file a memorandum by twelve noon on the third working day after the hearing, provided they entered an appearance at said hearing.
2. Where the Supreme Court is to try the case on its merits following cassation, the parties in the proceedings shall make new assertions and adduce new means of evidence in accordance with the provisions applicable to trial courts.
3. Within the deadline set in paragraph 1, all the parties in the proceedings must have filed the documents used to support or rebut the application for cassation with the registry of the Supreme Court. The filing and its date shall be attested by means of a note made on the case-file.
4. Copies of the procedural documents of the parties in the proceedings, their opponents or the other parties in the proceedings that are adduced shall be submitted free of official charges and duly certified.

Article 571

1. If the reporting judge considers that the application for cassation is inadmissible or that all its grounds, whether initial or additional, are inadmissible or manifestly unfounded, they shall verbally propose dismissal of the application for cassation to a three-member council comprised of the President of the Supreme Court or their lawful substitute and two Supreme Court Judges, without summonsing the parties in the proceedings. If the council unanimously accepts the proposal made by the reporting judge, it shall order that the hearing of the case be terminated. The same order shall award court costs to the cassationee, if he or she filed pleadings, while the fee of their authorised lawyer shall be computed at half the minimum limit, and a procedural fee between 300 and 900 euros shall be set. In labour law cases, the procedural fee may be reduced to the sum of 200 euros. The sums referred to in the two preceding subparagraphs may be increased or decreased by joint decision of the Minister of Finance and the Minister of Justice, Transparency and Human Rights. The registrar shall note the number of the council order in the case register and on the case-file, and a certified copy of the order shall be served on the cassationer or the lawyer signing the application for cassation or the additional grounds [of cassation] within 30 days from the date the order was issued.

2. Αν εκδοθεί διάταξη της προηγούμενης παραγράφου, με την οποία ματαιώνεται η συζήτηση της υπόθεσης, μπορεί ο αναιρεσείων να ζητήσει με αίτηση του να συζητηθεί η υπόθεση στο ακροατήριο. Η αίτηση υποβάλλεται μέσα σε προθεσμία εξήντα (60) ημερών από την επίδοση της διάταξης και κατατίθεται στη γραμματεία του Αρείου Πάγου, η οποία συντάσσει σχετική έκθεση στο βιβλίο της παραγράφου 3. Στην αίτηση επισυνάπτεται με ποινή απαραδέκτου διπλότυπο της αρμόδιας δημόσιας οικονομικής υπηρεσίας, από το οποίο προκύπτει η κατάθεση του παραβόλου που έχει ορισθεί με τη διάταξη. Ο αριθμός και η χρονολογία της έκθεσης σημειώνονται στο πρωτότυπο της αίτησης από τον συντάσσοντα την έκθεση, ο οποίος υπογράφει τη σχετική σημείωση. Η υπόθεση συζητείται κατά την ορισθείσα δικάσιμο. Στη σύνθεση του δικαστηρίου δεν μετέχουν τα μέλη του συμβουλίου της παραγράφου 1. Αν το δικαστήριο κρίνει παραδεκτή την αίτηση, ακυρώνει τη διάταξη του συμβουλίου και δικάζει την αναίρεση. Αν το δικαστήριο απορρίψει την αίτηση για συζήτηση της υπόθεσης στο ακροατήριο ως απαράδεκτη ή κρίνει μεν παραδεκτή την αίτηση, απορρίψει όμως στο σύνολό της την αναίρεση, διατάσσει συγχρόνως την εισαγωγή του παραβόλου στο δημόσιο ταμείο ως δημόσιο έσοδο. Αλλιώς το παράβολο επιστρέφεται στον καταθέσαντα. Αν δεν υποβληθεί εμπρόθεσμα αίτηση για συζήτηση της υπόθεσης στο ακροατήριο ή η υποβληθείσα αίτηση απορριφθεί ως απαράδεκτη η αίτηση αναίρεσης θεωρείται πως δεν ασκήθηκε.

3. Αν ο εισηγητής δεν εισηγηθεί την απόρριψη της αναίρεσης ή δεν εκδοθεί απορριπτική διάταξη του συμβουλίου σύμφωνα με την παρ. 1 ή αν ο αναιρεσείων υποβάλει αίτηση να συζητηθεί η υπόθεση στο ακροατήριο, σύμφωνα με την παρ. 2, η υπόθεση συζητείται κατά την ορισθείσα δικάσιμο.

4. Οι διατάξεις του συμβουλίου που εκδίδονται σύμφωνα με το άρθρο αυτό και οι αιτήσεις για συζήτηση της υπόθεσης στο ακροατήριο καταχωρίζονται σε ειδικά βιβλία που τηρούνται στη γραμματεία του Αρείου Πάγου.

Άρθρο 572

1. Οι διατάξεις των άρθρων 568 έως 571 εφαρμόζονται και όταν η συζήτηση επισπεύδει ο εισαγγελέας του Αρείου Πάγου ή ο εισαγγελέας εφετών ή ο εισαγγελέας πρωτοδικών.

2. Η συζήτηση δεν είναι απαράδεκτη σε αναίρεση που έχει ασκήσει ο εισαγγελέας του Αρείου Πάγου, αν δεν κληθούν οι διάδικοι, εκτός μόνο από τις περιπτώσεις εκείνες που η αναίρεση παράγει αποτελέσματα και γι' αυτούς.

Άρθρο 573

1. Στη διαδικασία της δίκης για την αναίρεση εφαρμόζονται οι διατάξεις των άρθρων 233 έως 236, 242 παρ. 2, 245, 246, 252 έως 261, 286 έως 308, 310 και 312 έως 334.

2. Τους εισαγγελείς, όταν έχουν την ιδιότητα του διαδίκου, εκπροσωπεί ο εισαγγελέας του Αρείου Πάγου.

Άρθρο 574

Μετά την εκφώνηση της υπόθεσης αρχίζει η συζήτηση στο ακροατήριο και αγορεύουν, εφόσον το ζητήσουν, οι πληρεξούσιοι των διαδίκων. Ο εισαγγελέας του Αρείου Πάγου, όταν παρίσταται, αγορεύει τελευταίος, εκτός αν είναι διάδικος ή εκπροσωπεί αναιρεσείοντα εισαγγελέα.

2. If an order cancelling the hearing of the case is issued in accordance with the preceding paragraph, the cassationer may file an application requesting that the case be heard in court. The application shall be submitted within a deadline of 60 days from the date the order was served, and shall be filed with the registry of the Supreme Court, which shall enter a relevant report in the [special] register referred to in paragraph [4]. On penalty of inadmissibility, a duplicate receipt, issued by the competent tax office, showing that the procedural fee set in the order has been deposited shall be attached to the application. The number and date of the report shall be noted on the original of the application by the author of the report, who shall sign the note in question. The case shall be heard on the hearing date set. The members of the council referred to in paragraph 1 shall not participate in the composition of the court. If the court considers that the application is admissible, it shall annul the order issued by the council and try the application for cassation. If the court dismisses the application for the hearing of the case in court as inadmissible or considers that the application is admissible but dismisses the application for cassation in its entirety, it shall simultaneously order payment of the procedural fee to the tax office as public revenue, otherwise the procedural fee shall be reimbursed to the person who deposited it. If an application for the hearing of the case in court is not submitted in good time or the application submitted is dismissed as inadmissible, the application for cassation shall be deemed not to have been filed.
3. If the reporting judge does not propose dismissal of the application for cassation, or the council does not issue an order dismissing it in accordance with paragraph 1, or if the cassationer submits an application for the hearing of the case in court in accordance with paragraph 2, the case shall be heard on the hearing date set.
4. Council orders issued in accordance with this Article and applications for the hearing of the case in court shall be entered in special registers kept at the registry of the Supreme Court.

Article 572

1. The provisions of Articles 568 to 571 also apply where the hearing is being expedited by the Supreme Court Public Prosecutor or a court of appeal public prosecutor or a court of first instance public prosecutor.
2. The hearing shall not be inadmissible in cases of applications for cassation filed by the Supreme Court Public Prosecutor if the parties in the proceedings are not summonsed, except only in those cases where cassation also generates effects for said parties.

Article 573

1. The provisions of Articles 233 to 236, 242(2), 245, 246, 252 to 261, 286 to 308, 310 and 312 to 334 apply to cassation proceedings.
2.When a public prosecutor is a party in the proceedings, they shall be represented by the Supreme Court Public Prosecutor.

Article 574

After the calling of the case, the courtroom hearing commences and, if so requested, the authorised lawyers of the parties in the proceedings present oral arguments. The Supreme Court Public Prosecutor, where present, shall present oral arguments last, unless they are a party in the proceedings or are representing a public prosecutor who is a cassationer.

Άρθρο 575

Με αίτηση του εισαγγελέα ή κάποιου από τους διαδίκους ή και αυτεπαγγέλτως το δικαστήριο μπορεί να αναβάλει τη συζήτηση της υπόθεσης μόνο μία (1) φορά σε μεταγενέστερη δικάσιμο, που ορίζεται αμέσως με επισημείωση στο πινάκιο. Τα εδάφια τρίτο και τέταρτο της παραγράφου 4 του άρθρου 226 εφαρμόζονται και εδώ. Σε κάθε περίπτωση αναβολής της συζήτησης το δικαστήριο μπορεί να διατηρήσει την, κατά το άρθρο 565 παράγραφος 2, αναστολή. Για την υποβολή αιτήματος αναβολής ο διάδικος καταβάλλει παράβολο υπέρ του Ταμείου Χρηματοδότησης Δικαστικών Κτιρίων (ΤΑ.Χ.ΔΙ.Κ.) ποσού πενήντα (50) ευρώ. Σε κοινό αίτημα αναβολής περισσότερων διαδίκων, καταβάλλεται ένα παράβολο το οποίο επιμερίζεται ισομερώς. Δεν υπέχουν υποχρέωση καταβολής παραβόλου το Δημόσιο, τα νομικά πρόσωπα δημοσίου δικαίου (Ν.Π.Δ.Δ.) και οι οργανισμοί τοπικής αυτοδιοίκησης (Ο.Τ.Α.). Δεν καταβάλλεται παράβολο σε περίπτωση αποχής των δικηγόρων. Το παράβολο επιστρέφεται αν το αίτημα της αναβολής απορριφθεί από το δικαστήριο.

Άρθρο 576

1. Αν ο διάδικος που επισπεύδει τη συζήτηση δεν εμφανιστεί ή εμφανιστεί αλλά δεν λάβει μέρος με τον τρόπο που ορίζει ο νόμος, ο Άρειος Πάγος συζητεί την υπόθεση σαν να ήταν παρόντες οι διάδικοι.

2. Αν ο αντίδικος εκείνου που επέσπευσε τη συζήτηση δεν εμφανιστεί η εμφανιστεί αλλά δεν λάβει μέρος σ' αυτήν με τον τρόπο που ορίζει ο νόμος ο Άρειος Πάγος εξετάζει αυτεπαγγέλτως αν κλητεύθηκε νόμιμα και εμπρόθεσμα. Αν η κλήση για τη συζήτηση δεν επιδόθηκε καθόλου ή δεν επιδόθηκε νόμιμα ή εμπρόθεσμα, ο Άρειος Πάγος κηρύσσει απαράδεκτη τη συζήτηση και η υπόθεση επαναφέρεται για τη συζήτηση με νέα κλήτευση. Στην αντίθετη περίπτωση προχωρεί στη συζήτηση παρά την απουσία εκείνου που έχει κλητευθεί.

3. Αν μετέχουν περισσότεροι στη δίκη για την αναίρεση και δεν κλητεύθηκε κάποιος από αυτούς, η συζήτηση κηρύσσεται απαράδεκτη για όλους. Σε περίπτωση απλής ομοδικίας, αν κάποιος δεν εκπροσωπηθεί από πληρεξούσιο δικηγόρο, η υπόθεση χωρίζεται και η συζήτηση της αίτησης αναίρεσης χωρεί νομίμως, ως προς όσους εκπροσωπούνται από πληρεξούσιο δικηγόρο ή έχουν κλητευθεί νομίμως και κηρύσσεται απαράδεκτη ως προς τους λοιπούς.

4. Κατά των αποφάσεων που εκδίδονται κατά τις παραγρ. 1 έως 3 δεν επιτρέπεται ανακοπή ερημοδικίας.

Άρθρο 577

1. Το δικαστήριο πρώτα συζητεί για το παραδεκτό της αναίρεσης.

2. Αν η αναίρεση δεν ασκήθηκε νόμιμα ή αν λείπει κάποια προϋπόθεση για να είναι παραδεκτή, ο Άρειος Πάγος την απορρίπτει και αυτεπαγγέλτως.

3. Αν ο Άρειος Πάγος κρίνει νόμιμη και παραδεκτή την αναίρεση, εξετάζει το παραδεκτό και το βάσιμο των λόγων της.

Άρθρο 578

Αν το αιτιολογικό της προσβαλλόμενης απόφασης κρίνεται εσφαλμένο αλλά το διατακτικό της ορθό, ο Άρειος Πάγος απορρίπτει την αναίρεση, εκτός αν υπάρχει έννομο συμφέρον να αποτραπεί δεδικασμένο, οπότε αναιρείται η απόφαση μόνο ως προς την εσφαλμένη αιτιολογία της.

Article 575

The court may, following an application by the public prosecutor or any party in the proceedings or even *ex officio*, adjourn the hearing of the case once only for a later hearing date set immediately by means of a note in the case register. The third and fourth subparagraphs of Article 226(4) also apply in this case. Where any hearing is adjourned, the court may retain in effect the stay referred to in Article 565(2). In order to file an application for adjournment, the party in the proceedings shall pay a procedural fee of 50 euros for the Court Buildings Financing Fund. Where several parties make a joint motion for adjournment, a single procedural fee shall be paid, shared equally among them. The Greek State, bodies governed by public law and local government authorities are not obligated to pay this procedural fee. The procedural fee shall not be paid in cases where lawyers are abstaining [from their duties]. The procedural fee shall be reimbursed if the motion for adjournment is dismissed by the court.

Article 576

1. If the party in the proceedings expediting the hearing fails to appear or appears but does not participate in the manner prescribed by law, the Supreme Court shall hear the case as if the parties in the proceedings were present.

2. If the opponent of the party expediting the hearing fails to appear or appears but does not participate in the hearing in the manner prescribed by law, the Supreme Court shall examine *ex officio* whether the opponent was summonsed duly and in good time. If the summons to the hearing was not served at all or was not served duly and in good time, the Supreme Court shall declare the hearing inadmissible and proceedings on the case shall resume following new summonsing; otherwise the Supreme Court shall proceed with the hearing despite the absence of the person summonsed.

3. If several parties are participating in the cassation proceedings and one of them was not summonsed, the hearing shall be declared inadmissible for all parties. In the event of permissive joinder, if a person is not represented by an authorised lawyer, the case shall be split and the hearing of the application of cassation shall take place lawfully with regard to those who are represented by an authorised lawyer or were lawfully summonsed, and declared inadmissible with regard to the other [joined parties].

4. Opposition against a default judgment shall not be allowed against judgments handed down in accordance with paragraphs 1 to 3.

Article 577

1. The [Supreme Court] shall first examine the admissibility of the application for cassation.

2. If the application for cassation was not duly filed or a requirement for its admissibility is not met, the Supreme Court may also dismiss the application *ex officio*.

3. If the Supreme Court rules that the application for cassation is lawful and admissible, it shall examine whether its grounds are admissible and well-founded.

Article 578

If the reasoning of the judgment being contested is found to be erroneous but its operative part correct, the Supreme Court shall dismiss the application for cassation, unless there is a legitimate interest to avert *res judicata*, in which case the judgment shall be quashed only with regard to the erroneous grounds.

Άρθρο 579

1. Αν αναιρεθεί η απόφαση, οι διάδικοι επανέρχονται στην κατάσταση που υπήρχε πριν από την απόφαση που αναιρέθηκε και η διαδικασία πριν από την απόφαση αυτή ακυρώνεται μόνο εφόσον στηρίζεται στην παράβαση για την οποία έγινε δεκτή η αναίρεση. Κάθε απόφαση που στηρίζεται σ' αυτήν που αναιρέθηκε αναιρείται, εφόσον οι λόγοι της αναίρεσης αναφέρονται και σ' αυτήν.

2. Αν αποδεικνύεται προαποδεικτικώς εκούσια ή αναγκαστική εκτέλεση της απόφασης που αναιρέθηκε, ο Άρειος Πάγος, αν υποβληθεί αίτηση με το αναιρετήριο ή με τις προτάσεις ή με αυτοτελές δικόγραφο που κατατίθεται στη γραμματεία του Αρείου Πάγου ως την παραμονή της συζήτησης, διατάζει με την αναιρετική απόφαση την επαναφορά των πραγμάτων στην κατάσταση που υπήρχε πριν από την εκτέλεση.

Άρθρο 580

1. Αν ο Άρειος Πάγος αναιρέσει την απόφαση για υπέρβαση δικαιοδοσίας, τα πολιτικά δικαστήρια δεν έχουν δικαίωμα να ασχοληθούν πια με την υπόθεση. Στην περίπτωση αυτή αναιρείται και η πρωτόδικη απόφαση που έχει τυχόν επικυρωθεί με την απόφαση που αναιρέθηκε, εφόσον και αυτή ενέχει υπέρβαση δικαιοδοσίας.

2. Αν ο Άρειος Πάγος αναιρέσει την απόφαση για παράβαση των διατάξεων των σχετικών με την αρμοδιότητα, παραπέμπει την υπόθεση στο δικαστήριο που κρίνει αρμόδιο.

3. Αν ο Άρειος Πάγος αναιρέσει την απόφαση για οποιονδήποτε άλλο λόγο, εκτός από εκείνους που αναφέρονται στις παραγράφους 1 και 2, μπορεί να κρατήσει την υπόθεση και να την δικάσει, αν κατά την κρίση του δεν χρειάζεται άλλη διευκρίνιση. Στην αντίθετη περίπτωση παραπέμπει την υπόθεση σε ιδιαίτερη συζήτηση και, αν πρόκειται για τους λόγους που αναφέρονται στους αριθμούς 1, 2, 3, 6 έως 17, 19 και 20 του άρθρου 559, μπορεί να παραπέμψει την υπόθεση για περαιτέρω εκδίκαση σε άλλο δικαστήριο ισόβαθμο και ομοειδές προς εκείνο το οποίο εξέδωσε την απόφαση που αναιρέθηκε ή στο ίδιο αν είναι δυνατή η σύνθεσή του από άλλους δικαστές. Αν, όμως, αναιρεθεί η απόφαση του τελευταίου αυτού δικαστηρίου, δικάζει αυτός την ουσία της υπόθεσης. Στην περίπτωση αυτή η υπόθεση εισάγεται με κλήση στο ίδιο τμήμα.

4. Οι αποφάσεις της ολομέλειας και των τμημάτων του Αρείου Πάγου δεσμεύουν τα δικαστήρια που ασχολούνται με την ίδια υπόθεση ως προς τα νομικά ζητήματα που έλυσαν.

5. Αν ο Άρειος Πάγος δικάζοντας σε ολομέλεια, απορρίψει τους λόγους αναίρεσης που παραπέμφθηκαν στην ολομέλεια και υπάρχουν και άλλοι λόγοι αναίρεσης που δεν έχουν παραπεμφθεί, η υπόθεση αναπέμπεται στο τμήμα που την παρέπεμψε, στο οποίο συζητείται με κλήση σύμφωνα με όσα ορίζονται στο άρθρο 568. Αν αναιρέσει την απόφαση, παραπέμπει την υπόθεση για περαιτέρω εκδίκαση, σύμφωνα με όσα ορίζονται στην παράγραφο 3.

Άρθρο 581

1. Στο δικαστήριο της παραπομπής η υπόθεση εισάγεται και συζητείται με κλήση. Δεν είναι απαραίτητο να επιδοθεί η αναιρετική απόφαση.

2. Η υπόθεση συζητείται μέσα στα όρια που διαγράφονται με την αναιρετική απόφαση και αφού κατατεθούν προτάσεις κατά το άρθρο 524 παράγραφος 1 εδάφιο β'.

3. Η διάταξη της παρ. 2 του αρ. 579 εφαρμόζεται και στο δικαστήριο της παραπομπής.

Article 579

1. If the judgment is quashed, the state of affairs that existed prior to the quashed judgment shall be restored for the parties in the proceedings, and the proceedings prior to this judgment shall be annulled only if they relied on the breach for which the application for cassation was accepted. Any judgments relying on the judgment quashed shall also be quashed, where the grounds of cassation also relate to it.

2. Where voluntary or compulsory enforcement of the quashed judgment is proven during the preliminary taking of evidence and a request is submitted in the application for cassation, or in the pleadings, or in a separate procedural document filed with the registry of the Supreme Court by the eve of the hearing, the Supreme Court shall include an order in its judgment on cassation to restore the affairs to their state prior to enforcement.

Article 580

1. If the Supreme Court quashes the judgment due to overstepping of jurisdiction, the civil courts no longer have the right to be seised of the case. In this case, any first-instance judgment certified by means of the quashed judgment, provided it also involves overstepping of jurisdiction, shall also be quashed.

2. If the Supreme Court quashes the judgment due to infringement of the provisions on jurisdiction, it shall remit the case to the court it deems to have jurisdiction.

3. If the Supreme Court quashes the judgment on any grounds other than those referred to in paragraphs 1 and 2, it may hold over the case and try it if, in its view, no further clarifications are required; otherwise it shall remit the case to a separate hearing and, in cases of the grounds referred to in Article 559(1), (2), (3), (6) to (17), (19) and (20), it may remit the case for further adjudication to another similar court of equal instance as the one that handed down the judgment that was quashed or to the same court if it can be composed of other judges. However, if the judgment handed down by the aforementioned court is quashed, the Supreme Court shall try the case on its merits, and the case shall be brought by means of summons before the same chamber.

4. Judgments handed down by the Supreme Court sitting in full court or its chambers are binding on courts seised of the same case with regard to the legal issues resolved.

5. If the Supreme Court, sitting in full court, dismisses the grounds of cassation remitted to the full court and there are other grounds of cassation not remitted, the case shall be referred back to the chamber that remitted it, where it shall be heard following a summons [served] in accordance with the provisions of Article 568. If the Supreme Court quashes the judgment, it shall remit the case for further adjudication in accordance with the provisions of paragraph 3.

Article 581

1. The case shall be brought and heard before the remittal court following a summons. The judgment ordering cassation need not be served.

2. The case shall be heard within the limits set out in the judgment ordering cassation and after pleadings have been filed in accordance with the second subparagraph of Article 524(1).

3. The provisions of Article 579(2) also apply to the remittal court.

Άρθρο 582

Η αναιρετική απόφαση σημειώνεται στο περιθώριο του πρωτοτύπου της απόφασης που αναιρέθηκε. Για το σκοπό αυτόν η γραμματεία του Αρείου Πάγου οφείλει να ειδοποιεί χωρίς καθυστέρηση τη γραμματεία του δικαστηρίου που την εξέδωσε η οποία είναι υποχρεωμένη να κάνει τη σημείωση αυτή χωρίς αναβολή.

ΚΕΦΑΛΑΙΟ ΣΤ'
Ανακοπή και τριτανακοπή.

Άρθρο 583

Αν κάποιος δεν έλαβε μέρος ή δεν προσκλήθηκε σε δικαστική ή εξώδικη πράξη που του προκαλεί βλάβη ή θέτει σε κίνδυνο τα έννομα συμφέροντά του, μπορεί να ασκήσει ανακοπή κατά της πράξης αυτής.

Άρθρο 584

Η ανακοπή εισάγεται στο δικαστήριο της γενικής δωσιδικίας του ανακόπτοντος με την επιφύλαξη των διατάξεων των ειδικών δωσιδικιών.

Άρθρο 585

1. Οι διατάξεις για την άσκηση της αγωγής, την εισαγωγή της για συζήτηση και τη συζήτηση στο ακροατήριο εφαρμόζονται και στην ανακοπή.

2. Το έγγραφο της ανακοπής πρέπει να περιέχει, εκτός από τα στοιχεία που αναφέρονται στα άρθρα 118 έως 120, και τους λόγους της. Νέοι λόγοι μπορούν να προταθούν μόνο με πρόσθετο δικόγραφο που κατατίθεται στη γραμματεία του δικαστηρίου προς το οποίο απευθύνεται η ανακοπή, κάτω από το οποίο συντάσσεται έκθεση, και κοινοποιείται στον αντίδικο μέσα σε εξήντα ημέρες (60) από την κατάθεση της ανακοπής ή, όταν πρόκειται για ειδικές διαδικασίες, οκτώ (8) τουλάχιστον ημέρες πριν από τη συζήτηση.

Άρθρο 586

1. Με τις προϋποθέσεις του άρθρου 583 μπορεί να ασκηθεί τριτανακοπή κατά της οριστικής απόφασης που εκδόθηκε μεταξύ άλλων.

2. Τριτανακοπή μπορεί να ασκήσει και ο τρίτος που δεσμεύεται από το δεδικασμένο, εφόσον επικαλείται δόλο ή συμπαιγνία των διαδίκων.

Άρθρο 587

Η τριτανακοπή εισάγεται στο δικαστήριο που εξέδωσε την προσβαλλόμενη απόφαση και παρεμπιπτόντως στο δικαστήριο στο οποίο εκκρεμεί η κύρια δίκη, αν το δικαστήριο αυτό είναι ισόβαθμο ή ανώτερο από εκείνο που εξέδωσε την προσβαλλόμενη απόφαση.

Article 582

The judgment ordering cassation shall be cited in the margin of the original judgment that was quashed. To this end, the registry of the Supreme Court is obligated to notify without delay the registry of the court that handed it down, which is obligated to include this citation immediately.

CHAPTER VI
Opposition and third-party proceedings

Article 583

If a person did not take part in or was not invited to [be present during] a judicial or extra-judicial act that prejudices or places at risk their legitimate interests, they may file an opposition against said act.

Article 584

The opposition shall be brought before the court of general forum of the opposing party, without prejudice to the provisions relating to special forum.

Article 585

1. The provisions on actions being filed, brought for a hearing and heard in court also apply to oppositions.
2. The opposition document must contain the information required by Articles 118 to 120, and the grounds for opposition. New grounds may be pleaded only by means of an additional procedural document filed with the registry of the court to which the opposition is addressed, at the end of which a report shall be drafted, and it shall be notified to the opponent within 60 days from the opposition being filed or, in cases of special procedures, at least 8 days prior to the hearing.

Article 586

1. Third-party proceedings may be brought against the final judgment handed down with regard to other parties under the conditions laid down in Article 583.
2. Third-party proceedings may also be brought by a third party bound by *res judicata*, where said party invokes *dolus* or collusion by the parties in the proceedings.

Article 587

[An application for] third-party proceedings shall be [filed] before the court that handed down the judgment being contested [or] incidentally before the court before which the main proceedings are pending, if that court is of the same instance or superior to the one that handed down the judgment being contested.

Άρθρο 588

1. Η τριτανακοπή απευθύνεται κατά όλων των διαδίκων μεταξύ των οποίων εκδόθηκε η προσβαλλόμενη απόφαση, εκτός αν ασκείται μετά την εκτέλεσή της, οπότε μπορεί να απευθυνθεί μόνο κατά του διαδίκου που νίκησε.

2. Οι διατάξεις του άρθρου 585 εφαρμόζονται και στην τριτανακοπή.

Άρθρο 589

Η άσκηση της τριτανακοπής δεν αναστέλλει την εκτέλεση της προσβαλλόμενης απόφασης. Το δικαστήριο στο οποίο εκκρεμεί η τριτανακοπή και, αν πρόκειται για πολυμελές δικαστήριο, ο πρόεδρος μπορούν, ύστερα από αίτηση του τριτανακόπτοντος που δικάζεται κατά τη διαδικασία των άρθρων 686 επ., να διατάξουν την αναστολή της εκτέλεσης με τον όρο εγγυοδοσίας ή και χωρίς αυτόν, αν πιθανολογείται ότι από την εκτέλεση της απόφασης θα προκληθεί ουσιώδης βλάβη στα συμφέροντα του τριτανακόπτοντος. Το δικαστήριο ή ο πρόεδρος μπορεί να εμποδίσει με σημείωμά του την εκτέλεση ώσπου να εκδοθεί η απόφαση για την αίτηση αναστολής. Η απόφαση αυτή μπορεί να ανακληθεί με τον ίδιο τρόπο ως την έκδοση της οριστικής απόφασης για την τριτανακοπή.

Άρθρο 590

Το δικαστήριο, αν κρίνει την τριτανακοπή παραδεκτή και βάσιμη, ακυρώνει ή ανάλογα με τις περιστάσεις αποφαίνεται ότι είναι ανενεργός η προσβαλλόμενη απόφαση ως προς τον τριτανακόπτοντα. Η απόφαση διατηρεί την ισχύ της μεταξύ των αρχικών διαδίκων, εκτός αν πρόκειται για αδιαίρετο δίκαιο.

Article 588

1. [The application for] third-party proceedings shall concern all the parties in the proceedings for whom the judgment being contested was handed down, unless it is filed after enforcement, in which case it may be filed only against the successful party in the proceedings.
2. The provisions of Article 585 also apply to [applications for] third-party proceedings.

Article 589

[The act of] filing an application for third-party proceedings shall not stay enforcement of the judgment being contested. The court before which the third-party proceedings are pending and, in the case of a multi-member court, its presiding judge may, following an application filed by the third party and tried under the procedure laid down in Articles 686 *et seq.*, order stay of enforcement, whether or not under the condition of provision of surety, where it is considered likely on the balance of probabilities that enforcement of the judgment will materially harm the interests of the third party. The court or the presiding judge may prevent enforcement by means of a written note until a judgment has been handed down on the application for stay. This decision may be revoked in the same manner up to the time a final judgment has been handed down in the third-party proceedings.

Article 590

If it deems the [application for] third-party proceedings admissible and well-founded, the court shall annul the judgment being contested or, depending on circumstances, rule that it generates no effects with regard to the third party. The judgment shall remain in effect with regard to the initial parties in the proceedings, except in cases of [compulsory joinder].

ΤΕΤΑΡΤΟ ΒΙΒΛΙΟ
ΕΙΔΙΚΕΣ ΔΙΑΔΙΚΑΣΙΕΣ

ΚΕΦΑΛΑΙΟ Α'

Άρθρο 591

1. Τα άρθρα 1 έως 590 εφαρμόζονται και στις ειδικές διαδικασίες, εκτός αν αντιβαίνουν προς τις ειδικές διατάξεις των διαδικασιών αυτών. Αν στις ειδικές αυτές διατάξεις δεν ορίζεται διαφορετικά:
α) Η προθεσμία για την κλήτευση των διαδίκων είναι τριάντα (30) ημέρες και αν ο διάδικος που καλείται ή κάποιος από τους ομοδίκους διαμένει στο εξωτερικό ή είναι άγνωστης διαμονής, εξήντα (60) ημέρες πριν από τη συζήτηση.
β) Η παρέμβαση, η προσεπίκληση και η ανακοίνωση ασκούνται, με ποινή απαραδέκτου, με δικόγραφο, που κατατίθεται στη γραμματεία του δικαστηρίου, στο οποίο εκκρεμεί η δίκη και επιδίδεται στους διαδίκους τουλάχιστον δέκα (10) ημέρες πριν από τη συζήτηση, η οποία ορίζεται υποχρεωτικά κατά την ημερομηνία συζήτησης της κύριας υπόθεσης. Παρέμβαση μετά από προσεπίκληση ή ανακοίνωση κατατίθεται και επιδίδεται στους διαδίκους, τουλάχιστον πέντε (5) ημέρες πριν από τη συζήτηση.
γ) Οι προτάσεις κατατίθενται το αργότερο κατά τη συζήτηση.
δ) Τα περιεχόμενα στις προτάσεις μέσα επίθεσης και άμυνας προτείνονται συνοπτικώς και προφορικά και καταχωρίζονται στα πρακτικά συζητήσεως, διαφορετικά είναι απαράδεκτα.
ε) Οι διάδικοι το αργότερο κατά τη συζήτηση στο ακροατήριο προσάγουν όλα τα αποδεικτικά τους μέσα.
στ) Οι διάδικοι μπορούν έως τη δωδέκατη ώρα της πέμπτης εργάσιμης ημέρας από τη συζήτηση να καταθέσουν προσθήκη στις προτάσεις τους, με την οποία αξιολογούνται οι αποδείξεις, προτείνονται ισχυρισμοί και προσκομίζονται ένορκες βεβαιώσεις, έγγραφα και γνωμοδοτήσεις κατά το άρθρο 390 μόνο για την αντίκρουση ισχυρισμών που προτάθηκαν.
ζ) Ανταγωγή, αντέφεση και πρόσθετοι λόγοι έφεσης και αναψηλάφησης ασκούνται με ποινή απαραδέκτου με δικόγραφο, που κατατίθεται στη γραμματεία του δικαστηρίου, στο οποίο απευθύνονται και επιδίδεται στον αντίδικο τουλάχιστον οκτώ (8) ημέρες πριν από τη συζήτηση, η οποία ορίζεται υποχρεωτικά κατά την ημερομηνία συζήτησης της κύριας υπόθεσης.
2. Ενώπιον των πρωτοβάθμιων δικαστηρίων η συζήτηση είναι προφορική. Με εξαίρεση τις διαφορές από την οικογένεια, τον γάμο και την ελεύθερη συμβίωση, οι διάδικοι μπορούν, κατ' εφαρμογήν της παρ. 2 του άρθρου 242, να συμφωνήσουν μόνο με κοινή δήλωση ότι δεν θα παραστούν στη συζήτηση. Η δήλωση υπογράφεται από τους πληρεξουσίους δικηγόρους όλων των μερών, κατατίθεται με τις προτάσεις το αργότερο ως την παραμονή της δικασίμου και ισχύει μόνο για τη συγκεκριμένη δικάσιμο.
3. Το δικαστήριο ζητεί τις αναγκαίες πληροφορίες και διασαφήσεις από τους διαδίκους ή τους εκπροσώπους τους και τους εξετάζει κατά την κρίση του σύμφωνα με τα άρθρα 415 επ.
4. Το δικαστήριο, αν είναι αναγκαίο, διατάσσει αυτοψία ή πραγματογνωμοσύνη κατ' ανάλογη εφαρμογή της παρ. 8 του άρθρου 237.
5. Η οριστική απόφαση εκδίδεται με βάση τα αποδεικτικά μέσα που οι διάδικοι έχουν προσκομίσει και τις αποδείξεις που έχουν διεξαχθεί στο ακροατήριο.
6. Αν η υπόθεση δεν υπάγεται στη διαδικασία κατά την οποία έχει εισαχθεί, το δικαστήριο αποφαίνεται γι' αυτό αυτεπαγγέλτως και διατάζει την εκδίκαση της υπόθεσης, κατά τη διαδικασία σύμφωνα με την οποία δικάζεται.
7. Κατά την εκδίκαση της ανακοπής ερημοδικίας, της έφεσης και της αναψηλάφησης, εφαρμόζονται οι διατάξεις που ισχύουν για την εκδίκαση της υπόθεσης, επί της οποίας εκδόθηκε η απόφαση που προσβάλλεται με το ένδικο μέσο. Σε περίπτωση ερημοδικίας του ανακόπτοντος, του εκκαλούντος, του αντεκκαλούντος ή του αιτούντος την αναψηλάφηση, το αντίστοιχο ένδικο μέσο απορρίπτεται. Η αναίρεση εκδικάζεται σύμφωνα με τις γενικές διατάξεις, εκτός αν προβλέπεται διαφορετικά στις διατάξεις των άρθρων 591 έως 645.
8. Τα άρθρα 466 έως 471 δεν εφαρμόζονται στις ειδικές διαδικασίες.

BOOK IV
SPECIAL PROCEDURES

CHAPTER I

Article 591

1. Articles 1 to 590 also apply to special procedures, unless they conflict with the specific provisions concerning said procedures. Unless otherwise stipulated in these specific provisions:
a) the deadline for summonsing the parties in the proceedings is 30 days, and if the party being summoned or any of the joined parties resides abroad or has no known place of residence, 60 days prior to the hearing;
b) on penalty of inadmissibility, interventions, impleaders and third-party notices shall be brought by means of a procedural document filed with the registry of the court before which the proceedings are pending and served on the parties in the proceedings at least 10 days prior to their hearing, the date of which must be set on the date the main case is heard. An intervention after an impleader or third-party notice shall be filed and served on the parties in the proceedings at least five days prior to the hearing;
c) pleadings shall be filed during the hearing at the latest;
d) the pleas contained in the pleadings shall be concisely put forth verbally and entered in the hearing transcript, otherwise they shall be inadmissible;
e) the parties in the proceedings shall produce all their means of evidence during the courtroom hearing at the latest;
f) the parties in the proceedings may file an addition to their pleadings, by twelve noon on the fifth working day after the date of the hearing, in which they weigh up the evidence, make assertions and adduce affidavits, documents and opinions, in accordance with Article 390, only to rebut assertions made;
g) on penalty of inadmissibility, cross-actions, cross-appeals and additional grounds of appeal and of applications for re-opening proceedings shall be brought by means of a procedural document filed with the registry of the court to which they are addressed and served on the opponent at least eight days prior to their hearing, the date of which must be set on the date the main case is heard.
2. Hearings before first-instance courts shall take place orally. With the exception of disputes concerning family, marriage and free unions, the parties in the proceedings may, pursuant to Article 242(2) and only by means of a joint statement, agree not to appear during the hearing. The statement shall be signed by the authorised lawyers of all the parties, filed with their pleadings no later than the eve of the hearing date, and is effective only for that specific hearing date.
3. The court shall request the necessary information and clarifications from the parties in the proceedings or their representatives and examine them, at its discretion, in accordance with Articles 415 *et seq.*
4. Where necessary, the court shall order an inspection or expert evidence, with Article 237(8) applying *mutatis mutandis*.
5. The final judgment shall be handed down on the basis of the means of evidence adduced and the evidence taken in court.
6. If the case is not subject to the procedure under which it was brought, the court shall rule on the matter *ex officio* and order adjudication of the case under the appropriate procedure.
7. During the adjudication of an opposition against a default judgment, an appeal [or] an application for re-opening proceedings, the provisions on adjudication of the case on which the judgment being contested by means of the legal remedy was handed down apply. If the opposing party, the appellant, the cross-appellant or the person applying for re-opening of proceedings fails to enter an appearance, the legal remedy in question shall be dismissed. Applications for cassation shall be tried in accordance with the general provisions, unless otherwise provided for in the provisions of Articles 519 to 645.
8. Articles 466 to 471 do not apply to special procedures.

ΚΕΦΑΛΑΙΟ Β'
ΔΙΑΦΟΡΕΣ ΑΠΟ ΤΗΝ ΟΙΚΟΓΕΝΕΙΑ, ΤΟ ΓΑΜΟ ΚΑΙ ΤΗΝ ΕΛΕΥΘΕΡΗ ΣΥΜΒΙΩΣΗ

ΤΙΤΛΟΣ Ι
ΥΠΑΓΟΜΕΝΕΣ ΔΙΑΦΟΡΕΣ

Άρθρο 592

Κατά την ειδική διαδικασία των οικογενειακών διαφορών δικάζονται οι γαμικές διαφορές, οι διαφορές από την ελεύθερη συμβίωση, οι διαφορές από τις σχέσεις γονέων και τέκνων, και οι λοιπές οικογενειακές διαφορές που ορίζονται στην παράγραφο 3 του άρθρου αυτού:

1. *Οι γαμικές διαφορές αφορούν:*

α) το διαζύγιο,

β) την ακύρωση γάμου,

γ) την αναγνώριση της ύπαρξης ή της ανυπαρξίας γάμου,

δ) τις σχέσεις των συζύγων κατά τη διάρκεια του γάμου, οι οποίες πηγάζουν από αυτόν, εκτός από τις υπαγόμενες στην παράγραφο 3 του άρθρου αυτού. Στην ίδια κατηγορία εντάσσονται και οι διαφορές που προκύπτουν από το ν. 3719/2008 για την ελεύθερη συμβίωση.

2. *Οι διαφορές από τις σχέσεις γονέων και τέκνων αφορούν:*

α) την προσβολή της πατρότητας,

β) την προσβολή της μητρότητας,

γ) την αναγνώριση ότι υπάρχει ή δεν υπάρχει σχέση γονέα και τέκνου ή γονική μέριμνα,

δ) την αναγνώριση ότι υπάρχει ή δεν υπάρχει ή είναι άκυρη η εκούσια αναγνώριση ενός τέκνου χωρίς γάμο των γονέων του ή η εξομοίωσή του με τέκνο γεννημένο σε γάμο λόγω επιγενόμενου γάμου των γονέων του, καθώς και την προσβολή της εκούσιας αναγνώρισης,

ε) την αναγνώριση ότι υπάρχει ή δεν υπάρχει ή είναι άκυρη υιοθεσία ή τη λύση της,

στ) την αναγνώριση ότι υπάρχει ή δεν υπάρχει επιτροπεία.

3. *Οι λοιπές οικογενειακές διαφορές αφορούν:*

α) τον καθορισμό, τη μείωση ή την αύξηση της συνεισφοράς του καθενός από τους συζύγους για τις ανάγκες της οικογένειας, της διατροφής που οφείλεται λόγω γάμου, διαζυγίου ή συγγένειας, των δαπανών τοκετού και της διατροφής της άγαμης μητέρας, καθώς και της διατροφής της μητέρας από την κληρονομική μερίδα που έχει επαχθεί στο τέκνο που αυτή κυοφορεί,

β) την άσκηση της γονικής μέριμνας αναφορικά με το τέκνο κατά τη διάρκεια του γάμου, και σε περίπτωση διαζυγίου ή ακύρωσης του γάμου ή όταν πρόκειται για τέκνο χωρίς γάμο των γονέων του, τη διαφωνία των γονέων κατά την κοινή άσκηση από αυτούς της γονικής τους μέριμνας, καθώς και την επικοινωνία των γονέων και των λοιπών ανιόντων με το τέκνο,

γ) τη ρύθμιση της χρήσης της οικογενειακής στέγης και της κατανομής των κινητών μεταξύ συζύγων,

δ) κάθε άλλη περιουσιακού δικαίου διαφορά, που απορρέει από τη σχέση των συζύγων, ή των γονέων και τέκνων.

4. *Σε περίπτωση διαζυγίου και κατά την ίδια διαδικασία της παραγράφου 1 μπορεί να ενωθεί ή συνεκδικασθεί η απαίτηση του αναίτιου συζύγου για ηθική βλάβη.*

ΤΙΤΛΟΣ ΙΙ
ΚΟΙΝΕΣ ΔΙΑΤΑΞΕΙΣ

Άρθρο 593

Οι διαφορές που αναφέρονται στο άρθρο 592 αριθμ. 1 και 2 εισάγονται μόνο με κύρια ή παρεμπίπτουσα αγωγή.

CHAPTER II
DISPUTES CONCERNING FAMILY, MARRIAGE AND FREE UNIONS

TITLE I
DISPUTES COVERED

Article 592

Matrimonial disputes, disputes arising from free unions, disputes arising from parent-child relationships and the other family disputes provided for in paragraph 3 of this Article shall be tried under the special family disputes procedure:

1. Matrimonial disputes concern:

a) divorce;

b) annulment of marriage;

c) recognition of the existence or non-existence of a marriage;

d) relationships between spouses during the marriage arising from that marriage, except for those subject to paragraph 3 of this Article. Disputes arising under Law 3719/2008 with regard to free unions also belong to this category.

2. Disputes arising from parent-child relationships concern:

a) contesting of paternity;

b) contesting of maternity;

c) recognition of the existence or non-existence of a parent-child relationship or parental responsibility;

d) recognition of the existence or non-existence or nullity of voluntary recognition of a child born out of wedlock or their treatment as a child born in wedlock due to subsequent marriage of the parents, as well as contesting voluntary recognition;

e) recognition of the existence or non-existence or nullity of adoption or its dissolution;

f) recognition of the existence or non-existence of tutorship.

3. Other family disputes concern:

a) the computation, decrease or increase of each spouse's contribution towards the needs of the family, maintenance owed due to marriage, divorce or family relationship, the costs of childbirth and maintenance of a single mother, as well as maintenance for the mother from the share in the estate that has devolved to the child she is carrying;

b) the exercise of parental responsibility over the child during the marriage and, in the case of divorce or annulment of the marriage or a child born out of wedlock, disagreements between the parents on their joint exercise of parental responsibility, as well as access of the parents and other relatives in the ascendant line to the child;

c) regulation of use of the family home and distribution of movables between the spouses;

d) any other dispute under property law deriving from the marital or parent-child relationship.

4. In cases of divorce and under the procedure laid down in paragraph 1, a claim for [compensation due to] moral damage brought by the spouse not at fault may be joined [to the same procedural document] or heard together with the divorce proceedings.

TITLE II
COMMON PROVISIONS

Article 593

The disputes referred to in Article 592(1) and (2) shall be brought only by means of a main or incidental action.

Άρθρο 594

Οι ανήλικοι που συνάπτουν γάμο και τα πρόσωπα που βρίσκονται σε επικουρική δικαστική συμπαράσταση μπορούν να ασκούν μόνοι τους τις κατά το άρθρο 592 αγωγές και να εμφανίζονται στο δικαστήριο, όταν αυτές εκδικάζονται, χωρίς τη συγκατάθεση οποιουδήποτε άλλου προσώπου.

Άρθρο 595

Αν κατά τη συζήτηση στο ακροατήριο δεν εμφανισθεί ή εμφανισθεί και δεν λάβει νόμιμα μέρος κάποιος από τους διαδίκους, η διαδικασία προχωρεί σαν να ήταν παρόντες όλοι οι διάδικοι.

Άρθρο 596

Στις διαφορές που αναφέρονται στο άρθρο 592 αριθμ. 1 και 2, αν πεθάνει ο ένας από τους διαδίκους πριν καταστεί αμετάκλητη η απόφαση η δίκη καταργείται ως προς το κύριο αντικείμενό της. Σε δίκες που αφορούν την ύπαρξη ή την ανυπαρξία ή την ακύρωση γάμου, αν οι κληρονόμοι έχουν δικαίωμα να ασκήσουν την αγωγή, η δίκη διακόπτεται.

Άρθρο 597

1. Στις διαφορές που αναφέρονται στο άρθρο 592 η μη προσέλευση, η παράλειψη ή η άρνηση διαδίκου να καταθέσει ή να απαντήσει στις ερωτήσεις που του υποβάλλονται ή να δηλώσει για την αλήθεια πραγματικών περιστατικών ή για τη γνησιότητα εγγράφου, όπως και η ομολογία, λαμβάνονται υπόψη σε συνδυασμό με τις άλλες αποδείξεις και εκτιμώνται ελεύθερα.

2. Στις διαφορές που αναφέρονται στο άρθρο 592 δεν επιτρέπεται:

1) να εξεταστούν με όρκο οι διάδικοι,

2) να εξεταστούν ως μάρτυρες τα τέκνα τους, γνήσια, νομιμοποιημένα, θετά και αναγνωρισμένα, τα τέκνα της γυναίκας που γεννήθηκαν χωρίς γάμο, καθώς και οι σύζυγοι και οι κατιόντες τους.

Άρθρο 598

Στις διαφορές που αναφέρονται στο άρθρο 592 αριθμ.1,2 και 3 περίπτωση β', η προθεσμία της αναψηλάφησης, σύμφωνα με τις διατάξεις του άρθρου 545 παράγραφος 3 εδάφια δ', ε' και στ', είναι έξι (6) μήνες και αρχίζει από την επίδοση της προσβαλλόμενης απόφασης.

Άρθρο 599

Στις διαφορές που αναφέρονται στο άρθρο 592 οι διάδικοι έχουν το δικαίωμα να παραιτηθούν από τα ένδικα μέσα μόνο μετά την έκδοση της οριστικής απόφασης. Η παραίτηση γίνεται με δήλωση στη γραμματεία του δικαστηρίου που εξέδωσε την απόφαση και με επίδοση αντιγράφου της έκθεσης στον αντίδικο.

Άρθρο 600

Αν η διάγνωση διαφοράς εξαρτάται, ολικά ή εν μέρει,

α) από την ύπαρξη ή ανυπαρξία ή από την ακύρωση γάμου ή

β) από κάποια από τις διαφορές που αναφέρονται στο άρθρο 592 αριθμ. 2,

το δικαστήριο αναβάλλει, με αίτηση ή και αυτεπαγγέλτως, τη συζήτηση ωσότου εκδοθεί αμετάκλητη απόφαση, σχετικά με την αγωγή αυτή. Αν δεν έχει ακόμη ασκηθεί η αγωγή αυτή, το δικαστήριο ορίζει προθεσμία για την άσκησή της. Αν η προθεσμία περάσει άπρακτη, η συζήτηση μπορεί να συνεχισθεί και ο σχετικός ισχυρισμός θεωρείται ότι δεν έχει προβληθεί.

Article 594

Juveniles who enter into marriage and persons under assisted legal guardianship may file the actions referred to in Article 592 themselves and appear in court when they are tried without [requiring] the consent of any other person.

Article 595

If any of the parties in the proceedings fails to appear during the courtroom hearing or appears but does not participate in the manner required, the procedure shall go ahead as if all the parties in the proceedings were present.

Article 596

In the disputes referred to in Article 592(1) and (2), if one of the parties in the proceedings dies before the judgment becomes irrevocable, the proceedings shall be quashed as to their main subject-matter. In proceedings concerning the existence or non-existence or annulment of a marriage, if the heirs have the right to file the action, the proceedings shall be stayed.

Article 597

1. In the disputes referred to in Article 592, [the court] shall take into account, in conjunction with the other evidence, and freely weigh up any failure by a party to appear and failure or refusal by that party to testify or answer the questions put to them or speak to the truth of actual facts or the authenticity of a document, as well as admissions.
2. In the disputes referred to in Article 592, it shall not be permitted:
1) to examine the parties in the proceedings under oath;
2) to examine as witnesses their children, whether legitimate, legitimised, adopted [or] recognised, the children of a woman that were born out of wedlock, as well as their spouses and descendants.

Article 598

In the disputes referred to in Article 592(1), (2) and (3)(b), the deadline for re-opening proceedings, in accordance with the provisions of Article 545(3)(d), (e) and (f), is six months and shall commence from the date the judgment being contested is served.

Article 599

In the disputes referred to in Article 592, the parties in the proceedings have the right to discontinue the legal remedies only after the final judgment has been handed down. Discontinuation shall be effected by means of a statement made to the registry of the court that handed down the judgment and service of a copy of the report on the opponent.

Article 600

If the determination of a dispute depends, whether in whole or in part,
a) on the existence or non-existence or annulment of a marriage; or
b) on any of the disputes referred to in Article 592(2),
the court shall adjourn the hearing, following an application or even *ex officio*, until an irrevocable judgment has been handed down on that action. If said action has yet to be filed, the court shall set a deadline for filing the action. If the deadline lapses without the relevant steps having been taken, the hearing may resume and the relevant assertion shall be deemed not to have been made.

Άρθρο 601

1. Τα ελληνικά δικαστήρια έχουν δικαιοδοσία να εκδικάζουν τις διαφορές του άρθρου 592 αριθμ. 1, αν ο ένας από τους συζύγους είναι Ελληνας, και αν ακόμη δεν έχει ούτε είχε κατοικία ή διαμονή στην Ελλάδα ή αν ήταν κατά την τέλεση του γάμου Έλληνας και απέβαλε λόγω του γάμου την ελληνική ιθαγένεια.
2. Τα ελληνικά δικαστήρια έχουν δικαιοδοσία να εκδικάζουν τις διαφορές που αναφέρονται στο άρθρο 592 αρ. 2, αν ο πατέρας ή η μητέρα ή το τέκνο είναι Έλληνες και αν ακόμη δεν έχουν ούτε είχαν κατοικία ή διαμονή στην Ελλάδα.
3. Αν δεν υπάρχει δικαστήριο κατά τόπον αρμόδιο για να δικάσει τις διαφορές που αναφέρονται στις παραγράφους 1 και 2, αρμόδια είναι τα δικαστήρια της πρωτεύουσας του κράτους.

Άρθρο 602

1. Αποτελούν δεδικασμένο που ισχύει υπέρ και εναντίον όλων, εφόσον δεν μπορούν να προσβληθούν με αναίρεση και αναψηλάφηση, αποφάσεις οι οποίες:
α) απαγγέλλουν ακύρωση γάμου ή διαζύγιο ή αναγνωρίζουν την ύπαρξη ή όχι έγκυρου γάμου ή απορρίπτουν τέτοιες αγωγές και
β) δέχονται ή απορρίπτουν αγωγές που αφορούν διαφορές οι οποίες αναφέρονται στο άρθρο 592 αρ. 2.
2. Το δεδικασμένο από τις αποφάσεις της περίπτωσης β' της παραγράφου 1 δεν ισχύει για τον τρίτο που δεν έλαβε μέρος στη δίκη και επικαλείται για τον εαυτό του σχέση γονέα και τέκνου ή γονική μέριμνα.

ΤΙΤΛΟΣ III
ΔΙΑΤΑΞΕΙΣ ΓΙΑ ΤΙΣ ΓΑΜΙΚΕΣ ΔΙΑΦΟΡΕΣ

Άρθρο 603

1. Η αγωγή για την αναγνώριση της ύπαρξης ή της ανυπαρξίας ή την ακύρωση γάμου, που ασκείται από τον ένα σύζυγο, απευθύνεται κατά του άλλου και, αν αυτός έχει πεθάνει, κατά των κληρονόμων του, αλλιώς απορρίπτεται ως απαράδεκτη.
2. Η αγωγή που αναφέρεται στην παράγραφο 1, όταν ασκείται από τον εισαγγελέα ή κάποιον που έχει συμφέρον, απευθύνεται και κατά των δύο συζύγων, και αν έχει πεθάνει ο ένας κατά των κληρονόμων του, αλλιώς απορρίπτεται ως απαράδεκτη.

Άρθρο 604

1. Στις περιπτώσεις που ο εισαγγελέας μπορεί να ασκήσει την αγωγή για την ακύρωση γάμου έχει το δικαίωμα, ακόμη και αν δεν άσκησε αυτός την αγωγή, να λάβει μέρος στη δίκη έχοντας όλα τα δικαιώματα του διαδίκου.
2. Η γραμματεία του δικαστηρίου έχει την υποχρέωση να γνωστοποιεί στον εισαγγελέα του δικαστηρίου τις δικασίμους των αγωγών για την ακύρωση γάμου, όπως και τις αποφάσεις που εκδίδονται στις αγωγές αυτές. Η παράλειψη της γνωστοποίησης δεν επιφέρει ακυρότητα της διαδικασίας.

Άρθρο 605

1. Τα ελληνικά δικαστήρια δεν έχουν δικαιοδοσία να εκδικάσουν τις διαφορές που αναφέρονται στο άρθρο 592 αρ. 1, αν και οι δύο σύζυγοι κατά το χρόνο που ασκείται η αγωγή είναι αλλοδαποί, ή αν κατά το δίκαιο της κοινής ιθαγένειας και των δύο συζύγων, ή κατά το δίκαιο της ιθαγένειας του ενός από αυτούς δεν αναγνωρίζεται η δικαιοδοσία άλλου κράτους για την εκδίκαση των σχετικών διαφορών. Τα ελληνικά δικαστήρια, ωστόσο, έχουν δικαιοδοσία να δικάσουν αγωγές διαζυγίου, όταν ο γάμος είναι έγκυρος κατά το ελληνικό δίκαιο, αλλά ανυπόστατος ή άκυρος κατά το δίκαιο της ιθαγένειας και των δύο ή του ενός συζύγου.
2. Η ισχύς των αποφάσεων των ελληνικών δικαστηρίων που δεν μπορούν να προσβληθούν με ανακοπή ερημοδικίας, έφεση, αναψηλάφηση και αναίρεση δεν μπορεί να αμφισβητηθεί για το λόγο ότι παραβιάσθηκε η διάταξη της παραγράφου 1.

Article 601

1. Greek courts have jurisdiction to try the disputes referred to in Article 592(1) if one of the spouses is Greek, even if they do not or did not have their place of domicile or residence in Greece or if they were Greek at the time of marriage and lost their Greek nationality due to said marriage.
2. Greek courts have jurisdiction to try the disputes referred to in Article 592(2) if the father or mother or child is Greek, even if they do not or did not have their place of domicile or residence in Greece.
3. If there is no court with jurisdiction *ratione loci* to try the disputes referred to in paragraphs 1 and 2, the courts of the capital have jurisdiction.

Article 602

1. The following judgments have the effect of *res judicata erga omnes*, where they cannot be contested by means of cassation and an application for re-opening proceedings:
a) those pronouncing annulment of a marriage or divorce or recognising the existence or non-existence of a valid marriage or dismissing such actions; and
b) those accepting or dismissing actions concerning the disputes referred to in Article 592(2).
2. The *res judicata* of the judgments referred to in case (b) of paragraph 1 does not apply to a third party who did not participate in the proceedings and invokes a parent-child relationship or parental responsibility as regards themselves.

TITLE III
PROVISIONS ON MATRIMONIAL DISPUTES

Article 603

1. An action for recognition of the existence or non-existence or annulment of a marriage shall be brought by one spouse against the other and, if the latter has died, against their heirs, otherwise it shall be dismissed as inadmissible.
2. Where the action referred to in paragraph 1 is brought by the public prosecutor or a person with an interest [in doing so], it shall be brought against both spouses and, if one has died, against their heirs, otherwise it shall be dismissed as inadmissible.

Article 604

1. In cases where the public prosecutor may file an action for annulment of marriage, the public prosecutor is entitled, even if they did not file the action, to participate in the proceedings with all the rights of a party in the proceedings.
2. The court registry is obligated to notify the public prosecutor of the court of the hearing dates for actions for annulment of marriage and the judgments handed down on such actions. Failure to notify shall not result in nullity of the procedure.

Article 605

1. Greek courts do not have jurisdiction to try the disputes referred to in Article 592(1) if both spouses are foreigners at the time the action is filed or if the law of the state of the two spouses' common nationality or the law of the state of nationality of one of the spouses does not recognise the jurisdiction of a different state to try such disputes. However, Greek courts have jurisdiction to try actions for divorce when the marriage is valid under Greek law but non-existent or null and void under the law of the state of nationality of both spouses or one spouse.
2. The validity of judgments handed down by Greek courts that cannot be contested by opposition against a default judgment, appeal, application for re-opening proceedings and application for cassation may not be disputed on grounds that the provisions of paragraph 1 were infringed.

ΤΙΤΛΟΣ IV
ΔΙΑΤΑΞΕΙΣ ΓΙΑ ΤΙΣ ΔΙΑΦΟΡΕΣ ΑΠΟ ΤΙΣ ΣΧΕΣΕΙΣ ΓΟΝΕΩΝ ΚΑΙ ΤΕΚΝΩΝ

Άρθρο 606

1. Στις δίκες που αναφέρονται στο άρθρο 592 αριθμ. 2 και αφορούν την υιοθεσία, το θετό τέκνο που συμπλήρωσε το δέκατο έκτο της ηλικίας του έχει πλήρη ικανότητα να ασκεί αυτοπροσώπως τη σχετική αγωγή, να παρίσταται αυτοπροσώπως στο δικαστήριο με την ιδιότητα του ενάγοντος ή του εναγομένου, να επιχειρεί όλες τις διαδικαστικές πράξεις και να ασκεί ή να παραιτείται από ένδικα μέσα.
2. Στις δίκες της παραγράφου 1 έχουν εφαρμογή και οι διατάξεις των άρθρων 744, 747 παράγραφος 4, 748 παράγραφοι 2 και 5 και 759 παράγραφος 3.

Άρθρο 607

1. Αν ένας διάδικος, χωρίς να έχει ειδικούς λόγους υγείας, αρνείται να υποβληθεί στις πρόσφορες ιατρικές εξετάσεις με γενικά αναγνωρισμένες επιστημονικές μεθόδους, που του επιβλήθηκαν από το δικαστήριο ως αναγκαίο αποδεικτικό μέσο για τη διαπίστωση της πατρότητας ή της μητρότητας, οι ισχυρισμοί του αντιδίκου του λογίζονται ότι έχουν αποδειχθεί, ως προς την ύπαρξη βιολογικών στοιχείων, τα οποία καθιστούν κατά την επιστήμη, πιθανή ή σφόδρα πιθανή την πατρότητα ή τη μητρότητα.
2. Αν το δικαστήριο διατάσσει την υποβολή στις εξετάσεις της προηγούμενης παραγράφου και τρίτων που δεν είναι διάδικοι, μπορεί με την ίδια απόφασή του να απειλεί την επιβολή σε αυτούς, για την περίπτωση που θα παρεμπόδιζαν αδικαιολόγητα τη διενέργεια των εξετάσεων με την απουσία τους κατά την ημέρα και ώρα που ορίσθηκαν για το σκοπό αυτόν ή με την άρνησή τους να υποβληθούν σ' αυτές, χρηματική ποινή εκατό (100) έως πεντακοσίων (500) ευρώ που περιέρχεται στο δημόσιο ως δημόσιο έσοδο. Αντίγραφο της απόφασης αυτής γνωστοποιείται αμέσως στο Υπουργείο Οικονομικών με επιμέλεια της γραμματείας.
3. Κατά τη διενέργεια των εξετάσεων των δύο προηγούμενων παραγράφων, πρέπει να λαμβάνονται όλα τα μέτρα ώστε να εξασφαλίζονται πλήρως η υγεία και η αξιοπρέπεια του εξεταζομένου. Ο διάδικος ή ο τρίτος, του οποίου διατάσσεται η εξέταση, πρέπει να κληθεί δέκα (10) ημέρες πριν από τη διενέργειά της για να παραστεί σε αυτήν.

Άρθρο 608

Αγωγή για την αναγνώριση της ύπαρξης ή μη σχέσης γονέα και τέκνου μπορεί να ασκηθεί και στον τόπο, όπου ο ενάγων έχει την κατοικία του κατά το χρόνο που ασκείται η αγωγή.

Άρθρο 609

1. Η αγωγή για την προσβολή της πατρότητας τέκνου γεννημένου σε γάμο απευθύνεται:
α) αν ασκείται από τον σύζυγο της μητέρας ή έναν από τους γονείς του, κατά του τέκνου ή του ειδικού επιτρόπου του και της μητέρας του,
β) αν ασκείται από το τέκνο, κατά της μητέρας και του συζύγου της,
γ) αν ασκείται από τη μητέρα, κατά του τέκνου ή του ειδικού επιτρόπου του και κατά του συζύγου.
Αν έχει πεθάνει κάποιο από τα παραπάνω πρόσωπα, η αγωγή απευθύνεται κατά των κληρονόμων του αποβιώσαντος, εκτός αν πεθάνει το ίδιο το τέκνο, διαφορετικά απορρίπτεται ως απαράδεκτη.
2. Η αγωγή για την προσβολή της μητρότητας απευθύνεται:
α) αν ασκείται από την τεκμαιρόμενη μητέρα, κατά της κυοφόρου γυναίκας και του συζύγου της, αν είναι έγγαμη, καθώς και κατά του τέκνου ή του ειδικού επιτρόπου του,
β) αν ασκείται από την κυοφόρο γυναίκα, κατά της τεκμαιρόμενης μητέρας και του συζύγου της, αν είναι έγγαμη, καθώς και κατά του τέκνου.

TITLE IV
PROVISIONS ON DISPUTES ARISING FROM PARENT-CHILD RELATIONSHIPS

Article 606

1. In the proceedings referred to in Article 592(2) that concern adoption, the adopted child who has attained the age of 18 has full capacity to file the relevant action themselves, to appear in court in person in the capacity of plaintiff or defendant, to take all procedural steps and to file or discontinue legal remedies.
2. The provisions of Articles 744, 747(4), 748(2) and (5) and 759(3) also apply to the proceedings referred to in paragraph 1.

Article 607

1. If a party in the proceedings, without invoking special health-related reasons, refuses to undergo the appropriate medical examinations [carried out using] generally recognised scientific methods that were ordered by the court as a means of evidence necessary to establish paternity or maternity, the assertions made by the opponent shall be deemed to be proven with regard to the existence of biological facts which, according to science, render paternity or maternity probable or highly probable.
2. If the court orders third parties who are not parties in the proceedings to undergo the examinations referred to in the preceding paragraph, it may, in the same decision, threaten to impose on them a monetary penalty ranging from 100 to 500 euros, which shall accrue to the Greek State as public revenue, where they unjustifiably obstruct the conduct of the examinations by being absent on the date and time set for this purpose or by refusing to undergo said examinations. A copy of this decision shall be immediately notified to the Ministry of Finance by the registry.
3. When the examinations referred to in the two preceding paragraphs are being conducted, all measures must be taken to fully safeguard the health and dignity of the person undergoing the examination. The party in the proceedings or third party whose examination is ordered must be summoned 10 days beforehand to attend the examination.

Article 608

An action for recognition of the existence or non-existence of a parent-child relationship may also be filed at the place where the plaintiff has their place of domicile at the time the action is filed.

Article 609

1. An action contesting the paternity of a child born in wedlock shall be brought:
a) against the child or the guardian *ad litem* and mother of the child, where it is brought by the spouse of the mother or one of the child's parents;
b) against the mother and her spouse, where it is brought by the child;
c) against the child or their guardian *ad litem* and the spouse, where it is brought by the mother.
If any of the above persons has died, the action shall be brought against the heirs of the deceased person, unless the child dies, otherwise it shall be dismissed as inadmissible.
2. An action contesting maternity shall be brought:
a) against the pregnant woman and her spouse, if she is married, and against the child or their guardian *ad litem*, where it is brought by the presumed mother;
b) against the presumed mother and her spouse, if she is married, and against the child, where it is brought by the pregnant woman.

3. Η αγωγή για την αναγνώριση της ύπαρξης ή μη ύπαρξης σχέσης γονέα και τέκνου, γονικής μέριμνας, εκούσιας αναγνώρισης ή εξομοίωσης λόγω επιγενόμενου γάμου των γονέων του ενός τέκνου που γεννήθηκε χωρίς γάμο τους με τέκνο γεννημένο σε γάμο ή ακυρότητας εκούσιας αναγνώρισης ή παρόμοιας εξομοίωσης, απευθύνεται:
α) αν την ασκεί ο ένας γονέας, κατά του άλλου γονέα και του τέκνου,
β) αν την ασκεί το τέκνο, κατά των δύο γονέων,
γ) αν την ασκεί τρίτος, κατά των δύο γονέων και του τέκνου.
Σε περίπτωση που έχει πεθάνει κάποιος από αυτούς, απευθύνεται κατά των κληρονόμων του και στην περίπτωση που η αναγνώριση έγινε από τον παππού ή τη γιαγιά η αγωγή απευθύνεται και εναντίον τους, αλλιώς απορρίπτεται.
4. Η αγωγή για την προσβολή εκούσιας αναγνώρισης απευθύνεται κατά των προσώπων που συνέπραξαν σε αυτήν ή των κληρονόμων τους και όταν δεν ασκεί την αγωγή το τέκνο ή οι κατιόντες του, και κατ' αυτών, αλλιώς απορρίπτεται.
5. Η αγωγή για την αναγνώριση της ύπαρξης ή μη ύπαρξης ή ακυρότητας ή λύσης της υιοθεσίας απευθύνεται:
α) αν την ασκεί ο θετός γονέας, κατά του θετού τέκνου,
β) αν την ασκεί το θετό τέκνο, κατά του θετού γονέα,
γ) αν την ασκεί τρίτος, κατά του θετού γονέα και του θετού τέκνου.
Σε περίπτωση που έχει πεθάνει κάποιος από αυτούς η αγωγή απευθύνεται κατά των κληρονόμων του, αλλιώς απορρίπτεται.
6. Η αγωγή για την αναγνώριση της ύπαρξης ή μη ύπαρξης επιτροπείας απευθύνεται, αν την ασκεί ο επίτροπος, κατά του επιτροπευομένου και όταν την ασκεί ο επιτροπευόμενος ή ένας τρίτος, κατά του επιτρόπου, αλλιώς απορρίπτεται. Η απόφαση παράγει τις έννομες συνέπειές της όταν επέλθει τελεσιδικία.

ΤΙΤΛΟΣ V
ΔΙΑΤΑΞΕΙΣ ΓΙΑ ΤΙΣ ΛΟΙΠΕΣ ΟΙΚΟΓΕΝΕΙΑΚΕΣ ΔΙΑΦΟΡΕΣ

Άρθρο 610

Οι διαφορές του άρθρου 592 αρ. 3 μπορούν να σωρευτούν με τις διαφορές των αρ. 1 και 2 του ίδιου άρθρου.

Άρθρο 611

Το δικαστήριο είναι υποχρεωμένο, κατά τη συζήτηση στο ακροατήριο της αγωγής και πριν από κάθε συζήτηση να προσπαθήσει να επιλύσει συμβιβαστικά τη διαφορά, ύστερα από ακρόαση όσων από τους διαδίκους παρίστανται. Ο συμβιβασμός πρέπει να αποβλέπει στο συμφέρον του τέκνου, αλλιώς δεν δεσμεύει το δικαστήριο.

Άρθρο 612

1. Το δικαστήριο στις διαφορές του άρθρου 592 αριθμ. 3 περίπτωση β' πριν από την έκδοση της απόφασής του, ανάλογα με την ωριμότητα του τέκνου, λαμβάνει υπόψη τη γνώμη του. Μπορεί αν αποφασίσει τη διενέργεια πραγματογνωμοσύνης, να ορίζει ελεύθερα το χρόνο διεξαγωγής της, χωρίς να δεσμεύεται από χρονικούς περιορισμούς.
2. Για την επικοινωνία με το τέκνο ορίζονται και καταχωρίζονται, στα πρακτικά του αρμόδιου δικαστηρίου, ο χρόνος και ο τόπος της συνάντησης, καθώς και, ο δικαστής που θα επικοινωνήσει με το τέκνο. Με διαταγή του δικαστηρίου, που καταχωρίζεται επίσης στα πρακτικά, καλείται να παρουσιάσει το τέκνο όποιος διαμένει μαζί του. Σε περίπτωση ερημοδικίας κάποιου διαδίκου, το δικαστήριο ορίζει χρόνο επίδοσης αντιγράφου των πρακτικών στον απολειπόμενο διάδικο. Η επικοινωνία του δικαστή με το τέκνο γίνεται ιδιαιτέρως και δεν επιτρέπεται να είναι παρόν σε αυτήν άλλο πρόσωπο, εκτός αν ο δικαστής κρίνει διαφορετικά. Για το περιεχόμενο της συνομιλίας δεν συντάσσεται έκθεση.

3. An action for recognition of the existence or non-existence of a parent-child relationship, parental responsibility, voluntary recognition or treatment of a child born out of wedlock as a child born in wedlock due to subsequent marriage of the parents or nullity of voluntary recognition or similar treatment shall be brought:
a) against the other parent and child, where it is brought by one parent;
b) against both parents, where it is brought by the child;
c) against both parents and the child, where it is brought by a third party.
If one of the above persons has died, the action shall be brought against the heirs of the deceased person, and where recognition was done by the grandfather or grandmother, the action shall also be brought against them, otherwise it shall be dismissed.
4. An action contesting voluntary recognition shall be brought against the persons who procured it or their heirs, and where the action is not brought by the child or their descendants, it shall also be brought against the above persons, otherwise it shall be dismissed.
5. An action for recognition of the existence or non-existence or nullity or dissolution of adoption shall be brought:
a) against the adopted child, where it is brought by the adoptive parent;
b) against the adoptive parent, where it is brought by the adopted child;
c) against the adoptive parent and the adopted child, where it is brought by a third party.
If one of the above persons has died, the action shall be brought against their heirs, otherwise it shall be dismissed.
6. An action for recognition of the existence or non-existence of tutorship shall be brought against the ward, when filed by the tutor, and against the tutor, when filed by the ward or a third party, otherwise it shall be dismissed. The judgment generates legal effects when it becomes *de jure* non-appealable.

TITLE V
PROVISIONS ON OTHER FAMILY DISPUTES

Article 610
The disputes referred to in Article 592(3) may be joined to the disputes referred to in Article 592(1) and (2).

Article 611
When the action is heard in court and before the hearing commences, the court is obligated to attempt to resolve the dispute via settlement, after having heard the parties in the proceedings who have entered an appearance. The settlement must be reached with a view to the best interests of the child, otherwise it is not binding on the court.

Article 612
1. Before handing down judgment on the disputes referred to in Article 592(3)(b), the court, depending on how mature the child is, shall take their opinion into account. The court may decide to order expert evidence and freely set the time at which it will be prepared, without being bound by time restrictions.
2. With regard to contact with the child, the time and place of the meeting and the judge who will contact the child shall be specified and recorded in the transcript of the competent court. By order of the court, which shall also be recorded in the transcript, any person residing with the child shall be called upon to produce the child. If any party in the proceedings fails to enter an appearance, the court shall set a time for a copy of the transcript to be served on the absent party. Contact between the judge and the child shall take place in private and no other person may attend, unless the judge rules otherwise. No report shall be prepared on the content of the discussion.

Άρθρο 613

Με την απόφαση, με την οποία ανατίθεται η επιμέλεια του προσώπου του τέκνου στον ένα γονέα, διατάσσεται αυτεπαγγέλτως και η απόδοση ή παράδοση του τέκνου σ' αυτόν, και η απόφαση εκτελείται κατά τις διατάξεις του άρθρου 950 του ΚΠολΔ.

ΚΕΦΑΛΑΙΟ Γ
ΠΕΡΙΟΥΣΙΑΚΕΣ ΔΙΑΦΟΡΕΣ

ΤΙΤΛΟΣ Ι
ΥΠΑΓΟΜΕΝΕΣ ΔΙΑΦΟΡΕΣ

Άρθρο 614

Κατά την ειδική διαδικασία των περιουσιακών διαφορών δικάζονται οι μισθωτικές διαφορές, οι διαφορές από οριζόντια ή κάθετη ιδιοκτησία, οι εργατικές διαφορές, οι διαφορές επαγγελματιών και οργανισμών κοινωνικής ασφάλισης, οι διαφορές από αμοιβές, οι διαφορές για ζημιές από αυτοκίνητα, οι διαφορές από δημοσιεύματα ή ραδιοτηλεοπτικές εκπομπές και οι διαφορές από πιστωτικούς τίτλους:

1. Μισθωτικές διαφορές είναι οι κύριες ή παρεπόμενες διαφορές από μίσθωση κάθε είδους πράγματος ή άλλου προσοδοφόρου αντικειμένου ή από επίμορτη αγροληψία.

2. Διαφορές από οριζόντια ή κάθετη ιδιοκτησία είναι οι διαφορές ανάμεσα στους ιδιοκτήτες οριζοντίων ή καθέτων ιδιοκτησιών από τη σχέση της ιδιοκτησίας, καθώς και οι διαφορές ανάμεσα στους διαχειριστές οριζόντιας ή κάθετης ιδιοκτησίας και στους ιδιοκτήτες.

3. Εργατικές διαφορές είναι:

α) οι διαφορές από παροχή εξαρτημένης εργασίας ή και από οποιοδήποτε άλλη αιτία με αφορμή την παροχή της εργασίας αυτής μεταξύ των εργαζομένων ή των διαδόχων τους ή εκείνων που κατά το νόμο έχουν δικαίωμα από την παροχή εργασίας τους και των εργοδοτών ή των διαδόχων τους,

β) οι διαφορές από την παροχή εξαρτημένης εργασίας ή και από οποιοδήποτε άλλη αιτία με αφορμή την παροχή της εργασίας αυτής μεταξύ εκείνων που εργάζονται μαζί στον ίδιο εργοδότη,

γ) οι διαφορές από συλλογική σύμβαση εργασίας ή από διατάξεις που εξομοιώνονται προς διατάξεις συλλογικής σύμβασης μεταξύ εκείνων που υπάγονται στις διατάξεις αυτές ή μεταξύ αυτών και τρίτων,

δ) οι παρεμπίπτουσες αγωγές κατά δικονομικών εγγυητών στις δίκες που αφορούν τις διαφορές των περιπτώσεων α' και β' της παρούσας παραγράφου, καθώς και

ε) οι αγωγές κατά ομοδίκων των εναγομένων στις δίκες που αφορούν τις διαφορές των περιπτώσεων α' και β' της παρούσας παραγράφου, εφόσον εναχθούν από κοινού ή προσεπικληθούν.

4. Διαφορές επαγγελματιών και οργανισμών κοινωνικής ασφάλισης είναι:

α) οι διαφορές μεταξύ επαγγελματιών ή βιοτεχνών μεταξύ τους ή μεταξύ αυτών και των πελατών τους, από την παροχή εργασίας ή ειδών που αυτοί κατασκεύασαν και

β) οι διαφορές μεταξύ οργανισμών κοινωνικής ασφάλισης και των ασφαλισμένων στους οργανισμούς αυτούς ή των διαδόχων τους ή εκείνων που κατά το νόμο έχουν δικαιώματα από την ασφαλιστική σχέση.

5. Διαφορές από αμοιβές είναι:

α) οι διαφορές για τις αμοιβές, τις αποζημιώσεις και τα έξοδα δικηγόρων, συμβολαιογράφων, άμισθων δικαστικών επιμελητών, γιατρών, οδοντογιατρών, κτηνιάτρων, διπλωματούχων μαιών, μηχανικών και χημικών διπλωματούχων ανώτατων και ανώτερων σχολών, νόμιμα διορισμένων μεσιτών ή των καθολικών διαδόχων όλων αυτών και των πελατών τους ή των καθολικών διαδόχων τους, όπως και αν χαρακτηρίζεται η μεταξύ τους σχέση και ανεξάρτητα από το αν υπάρχει ή όχι συμφωνία για τον καθορισμό της αμοιβής ή τον τρόπο της καταβολής της,

Article 613

The judgment awarding custody of the child to one parent shall also *ipso jure* contain an order for the return or handing over of the child to that parent, and the judgment shall be enforced in accordance with the provisions of Article 950 of this Code.

CHAPTER III
PROPERTY DISPUTES

TITLE I
DISPUTES COVERED

Article 614

Lease disputes, disputes arising from horizontal or vertical properties, labour disputes, disputes involving professionals and social security organisations, disputes concerning pay, disputes concerning damage involving [motor vehicles], disputes arising from publications or radio or television broadcasts and disputes arising from securities shall be tried under the special procedure for property disputes:

1. Lease disputes are main or ancillary disputes arising from a lease of any manner of thing or other revenue-generating article or sharecropping.

2. Disputes arising from horizontal or vertical properties are disputes between the owners of horizontal or vertical properties arising from the ownership relationship, as well as disputes between building managers and the owners of a horizontal or vertical property.

3. Labour disputes are:

a) disputes arising from employment or any other cause relating to the provision of labour between [on the one hand] workers or their successors or those on whom the law confers rights from the provision of labour by the former and [on the other] their employers or their successors;

b) disputes arising from employment or any other cause relating to the provision of labour between persons who work together for the same employer;

c) disputes arising from a collective bargaining agreement or provisions treated as equivalent to collective agreement provisions, whether between persons bound by them or between such persons and third parties;

d) ancillary actions against third parties joined in proceedings as guarantors concerning the disputes referred to in cases (a) and (b) of this paragraph; and

e) actions against the joined parties of defendants in proceedings concerning the disputes referred to in cases (a) and (b) of this paragraph, if sued jointly or impleaded.

4. Disputes involving professionals and social security organisations are:

a) disputes between professionals or artisans, whether between them or between such persons and their customers, with regard to the provision of labour or goods they manufactured; and

b) disputes between social security organisations and persons insured by them or their successors or those who, by law, derive rights from the insurance relationship.

5. Disputes concerning pay are:

a) disputes concerning fees, compensation and costs between [on the one hand] lawyers, notaries public, non-stipendiary court process servers, physicians, dentists, veterinarians, certified midwives, engineers and certified chemists holding degrees from superior and higher schools, lawfully appointed real estate brokers or the universal successors of all the foregoing and [on the other] their customers or their universal successors, irrespective of how the relationship between them is characterised and regardless of whether or not there is an agreement on setting the fee or the manner of its payment;

β) οι διαφορές για τις αμοιβές, τις αποζημιώσεις και τα έξοδα διαιτητών, διαμεσολαβητών, εκτελεστών διαθήκης, κηδεμόνων σχολάζουσας κληρονομιάς, διαχειριστών σε ιδιοκτησίες κατ' ορόφους ή διαχειριστών που διορίζονται από δικαστική αρχή, εκκαθαριστών εταιριών ή νομικών προσώπων ή κληρονομιών ή των καθολικών διαδόχων όλων αυτών και των προσώπων που έχουν την υποχρέωση να καταβάλουν ή των καθολικών διαδόχων τους, ανεξάρτητα από το αν υπάρχει ή όχι συμφωνία για τον καθορισμό της αμοιβής ή τον τρόπο καταβολής της και
γ) οι διαφορές για τις αμοιβές, τις αποζημιώσεις και τα έξοδα των μαρτύρων που εξετάσθηκαν ενώπιον οποιουδήποτε δικαστηρίου ή διαιτητών, όπως και των πραγματογνωμόνων, διαιτητών πραγματογνωμόνων, εκτιμητών, διερμηνέων, μεσεγγυούχων και φυλάκων, όπως και αν διορίσθηκαν ή των καθολικών διαδόχων όλων αυτών και των προσώπων που έχουν την υποχρέωση καταβολής ή των καθολικών διαδόχων τους.
6. Διαφορές για ζημίες από αυτοκίνητα είναι οι διαφορές που αφορούν απαιτήσεις αποζημίωσης οποιοσδήποτε μορφής για ζημίες που έχουν προκληθεί από αυτοκίνητο μεταξύ των δικαιούχων ή των διαδόχων τους και εκείνων που έχουν την υποχρέωση να καταβάλουν αποζημίωση ή των διαδόχων τους, όπως και απαιτήσεις από σύμβαση ασφάλισης αυτοκινήτου μεταξύ των ασφαλιστικών εταιριών και των ασφαλισμένων ή των διαδόχων τους.
7. Διαφορές από δημοσιεύματα ή ραδιοτηλεοπτικές εκπομπές είναι οι κάθε φύσεως διαφορές που αφορούν σε αποζημιώσεις οποιοσδήποτε μορφής περιουσιακής ζημίας ή ηθικής βλάβης, που προκλήθηκε δια του τύπου ή με ραδιοφωνικές ή τηλεοπτικές εκπομπές, ή μέσω διαδικτύου και γενικά κάθε άλλο σύγχρονο μέσο διάδοσης πληροφοριών και ειδήσεων όπως και οι συναφείς προς αυτές αξιώσεις προστασίας της προσωπικότητας των προσβληθέντων.
8. Διαφορές από πιστωτικούς τίτλους είναι οι διαφορές από συναλλαγματικές, γραμμάτια εις διαταγήν, επιταγές, ανώνυμες ομολογίες και τοκομερίδια ομολογιακών δανείων, αποθετήρια, ενεχυρόγραφα και πιστωτικούς γενικά τίτλους για πληρωμή υποχρεώσεων, οι οποίες προκύπτουν άμεσα από τον τίτλο και αφορούν τους δικαιούχους και τους υποχρέους ή τους καθολικούς διαδόχους τους.

ΤΙΤΛΟΣ II
ΔΙΑΤΑΞΕΙΣ ΓΙΑ ΤΙΣ ΜΙΣΘΩΤΙΚΕΣ ΔΙΑΦΟΡΕΣ

Άρθρο 615
Το δικαστήριο δικαιούται να ορίσει προθεσμία για την παράδοση ή την απόδοση της χρήσης του μισθίου έως τριάντα (30) ημέρες από τη δημοσίευση της απόφασης.

Άρθρο 616
Αποφάσεις που αφορούν την απόδοση της χρήσης μισθίου ακινήτου εκτελούνται και κατά των υπομισθωτών, καθώς και κατά οποιουδήποτε αντλεί τα δικαιώματά του από το μισθωτή ή κατέχει το μίσθιο για αυτόν.

Άρθρο 617
1. Αν εξαφανισθεί απόφαση που διατάσσει παράδοση ή απόδοση της χρήσης μισθίου και η απόφαση έχει εκτελεσθεί, εκείνος κατά του οποίου έγινε η εκτέλεση, δικαιούται να ζητήσει την επανεγκατάστασή του στο μίσθιο.
2. Η επανεγκατάστασή μπορεί να ζητηθεί με αίτηση που υποβάλλεται και με τις προτάσεις στο δικαστήριο που εξαφάνισε την απόφαση ως το τέλος της συζήτησης στο ακροατήριο ή με αγωγή που απευθύνεται προς τον ειρηνοδίκη και δικάζεται κατά την παρούσα διαδικασία, η απόφαση όμως του ειρηνοδίκη δεν προσβάλλεται με κανένα ένδικο μέσο. Η αγωγή πρέπει να ασκηθεί μέσα σε τρεις (3) μήνες από την ημέρα που η απόφαση, η οποία εξαφάνισε την απόφαση που διατάσσει την παράδοση ή απόδοση της χρήσης μισθίου, έγινε αμετάκλητη.
3. Η απόφαση που διατάσσει την επανεγκατάστασή εκτελείται και κατά οποιουδήποτε αντλεί τα δικαιώματά του από εκείνον κατά του οποίου διατάχθηκε η επανεγκατάσταση.

b) disputes concerning fees, compensation and costs between [on the one hand] arbitrators, mediators, executors of wills, curators of unclaimed estates, building managers or court-appointed administrators, liquidators of companies or legal persons or estates or the universal successors of all the foregoing and [on the other] the persons obligated to make such payment or their universal successors, irrespective of whether or not there is an agreement on setting the fee or the manner of its payment; and
c) disputes concerning fees, compensation and costs between [on the one hand] witnesses examined before any court or arbitrators, as well as experts, expert arbitrators, valuers, interpreters, sequestrators and custodians, irrespective of the manner of their appointment, or the universal successors of all the foregoing and [on the other] the persons obligated to make such payment or their universal successors.
6. Disputes concerning damage involving [motor vehicles] are disputes that concern compensation claims of any kind for damage caused by a [motor vehicle] between the beneficiaries or their successors and those obligated to pay compensation or their successors, as well as claims arising from a [motor vehicle] insurance policy between insurance companies and their policyholders or their successors.
7. Disputes arising from publications or radio or television broadcasts are disputes of any manner concerning compensation for any manner of monetary damage or moral damage caused by means of the press or radio or television broadcasts or the internet and, generally, using any other modern means of dissemination of information and news, as well as related actions for the protection of the right of personality of the affected persons.
8. Disputes arising from securities are disputes arising from bills of exchange, promissory notes, cheques, bearer bonds and bond loan coupons, depositary receipts, warrants and, generally, securities for the payment of obligations that directly arise from the security and concern the beneficiaries and the parties liable for payment or their universal successors.

TITLE II
PROVISIONS ON LEASE DISPUTES

Article 615

The court may set a deadline of no more than 30 days from the date the judgment was handed down for handing back or returning use of a leased property.

Article 616

Judgments concerning return of use of a leased property are also enforceable against sublessees and any person deriving rights from the lessee or holding the leased property for the lessee.

Article 617

1. If a judgment ordering handing back or return of use of a leased property is quashed and the judgment has [already] been enforced, the person enforcement concerned is entitled to request they be allowed to return to the leased property.
2. Return to the leased property may be requested in an application filed together with the pleadings before the court that quashed the judgment by the end of the courtroom hearing or in an action addressed to the court of the peace judge and tried under this procedure; however, the judgment to be handed down by the court of the peace judge cannot be contested by any legal remedy. The action must be filed within three months from the day the judgment quashing the judgment ordering handing back or return of use of the leased property became irrevocable.
3. The judgment ordering return to the leased property is also enforceable against any person deriving rights from the person against whom such return was ordered.

Άρθρο 618
Η καταβολή ενώπιον του ειρηνοδικείου ή του μονομελούς πρωτοδικείου έως το τέλος της συζήτησης στο ακροατήριο όλων των ληξιπρόθεσμων μισθωμάτων που οφείλονται έως την ημέρα της συζήτησης και των δικαστικών εξόδων που ορίζονται αμέσως από το δικαστή, καταργεί τη δίκη για την απόδοση της χρήσης του μισθίου για καθυστέρηση μισθωμάτων από δυστροπία. Η διάταξη αυτή δεν εφαρμόζεται, αν υπάρχει επανειλημμένη καθυστέρηση από δυστροπία.

Άρθρο 619
Η άσκηση αγωγής για την απόδοση της χρήσης μισθίου ισχύει ως καταγγελία της σύμβασης, σύμφωνα με τις διατάξεις του ουσιαστικού δικαίου.

Άρθρο 620
Οι τελεσίδικες αποφάσεις για τις διαφορές του άρθρου 17 παρ. 3 αποτελούν δεδικασμένο.

ΤΙΤΛΟΣ ΙΙΙ
ΔΙΑΤΑΞΕΙΣ ΓΙΑ ΤΙΣ ΕΡΓΑΤΙΚΕΣ ΔΙΑΦΟΡΕΣ

Άρθρο 621
1. Οι διαφορές που αναφέρονται στο άρθρο 614 αριθμ. 3 μπορεί να εισαχθούν και στο δικαστήριο του τόπου όπου ο εργαζόμενος παρέχει ή, σε περίπτωση λύσης της σχέσης, παρείχε την εργασία του κατά τον αμέσως πριν από τη λήξη χρόνο.
2. Στις διαφορές που αναφέρονται στην παράγραφο 1, μπορούν να εναγάγουν ή να εναχθούν μαζί περισσότεροι εργαζόμενοι και όταν τα δικαιώματα ή οι υποχρεώσεις τους προέρχονται μόνο από την ίδια νομική αιτία. Στις διαφορές που αναφέρονται στην παράγραφο 1, αν κατά τη συζήτηση στο ακροατήριο δεν εμφανιστεί κάποιος διάδικος ή εμφανιστεί και δεν λάβει νόμιμα μέρος στη συζήτηση, η διαδικασία προχωρεί σαν να ήταν παρόντες όλοι οι διάδικοι.
3. Η συζήτηση των αγωγών και των τακτικών ένδικων μέσων επί των διαφορών για άκυρη απόλυση, μισθούς υπερημερίας και καθυστερούμενους μισθούς προσδιορίζεται υποχρεωτικά μέσα σε εξήντα (60) ημέρες από την κατάθεσή τους. Αν αναβληθεί η συζήτηση, αυτή προσδιορίζεται υποχρεωτικά μέσα σε τριάντα (30) ημέρες. Η απόφαση του δικαστηρίου δημοσιεύεται υποχρεωτικά μέσα σε τριάντα (30) ημέρες από τη συζήτηση της αγωγής ή του τακτικού ένδικου μέσου.

Άρθρο 622
1. Στις διαφορές που αναφέρονται στο προηγούμενο άρθρο, αναγνωρισμένα επαγγελματικά σωματεία εργαζομένων ή εργοδοτών, αναγνωρισμένες ενώσεις τους ή επιμελητήρια έχουν το δικαίωμα:
1) να ασκούν υπέρ των μελών τους τα δικαιώματα που απορρέουν από συλλογική σύμβαση ή άλλες διατάξεις που εξομοιώνονται προς διατάξεις συλλογικής σύμβασης, εκτός αν τα μέλη έχουν ρητώς εκδηλώσει την αντίθεσή τους· έχουν πάντως το δικαίωμα να παρέμβουν,
2) να παρέμβουν μέχρι την έκδοση αμετάκλητης απόφασης υπέρ διαδίκου, εφόσον είναι μέλος τους ή μέλος κάποιας από τις οργανώσεις που αποτελούν την ένωση,
3) να παρέμβουν σε κάθε δίκη που αφορά την ερμηνεία ή την εφαρμογή συλλογικής σύμβασης εργασίας στην οποία μετέχουν ή διάταξης που εξομοιώνεται προς τις διατάξεις τέτοιας συλλογικής σύμβασης, για την προστασία του συλλογικού συμφέροντος που παρουσιάζει η έκβαση της δίκης.
4) να παρεμβαίνουν υπέρ διαδίκου, ο οποίος ασκεί τα δικαιώματα που απορρέουν από την εκάστοτε ισχύουσα νομοθεσία για την τήρηση της αρχής της ίσης μεταχείρισης των φύλων και την καταπολέμηση των διακρίσεων με βάση το φύλο στην εργασία και ιδίως από τον ν. 3896/2010 (Α' 207), σε οποιοδήποτε στάδιο της δίκης και στην κατ' αναίρεση δίκη, εφόσον η διαφορά δικάζεται κατά την ειδική διαδικασία των εργατικών διαφορών.

Article 618

Payment made before the court of the peace or the single-member court of first instance by the end of the hearing of all overdue rent owed up to the day of the hearing and of the court costs set at that time by the judge shall result in discontinuation of the proceedings for return of use of the leased property on grounds of delayed [payment of] rent due to intransigence. This provision does not apply where there are repeated delays due to intransigence.

Article 619

[The act of] filing an action for return of use of a leased property functions as notice of termination of the agreement, in accordance with the provisions of substantive law.

Article 620

De jure non-appealable judgments handed down in the disputes referred to in Article 17(3) have the effect of *res judicata*.

TITLE III
PROVISIONS ON LABOUR DISPUTES

Article 621

1. The disputes referred to in Article 614(3) may also be brought before the court of the place where the worker is providing labour or, where employment has ended, provided labour during the period immediately before employment ended.
2. In the disputes referred to in paragraph 1, several workers may sue or be sued together when their rights or obligations stem only from the same legal cause. In the disputes referred to in paragraph 1, if any of the parties in the proceedings fails to appear during the courtroom hearing or appears and fails to participate in the hearing in the manner required, the procedure shall go ahead as if all the parties in the proceedings were present.
3. The hearing [date] of actions and ordinary legal remedies concerning disputes for null and void dismissal, default salaries and delayed salaries must be set within 60 days of the date such actions or remedies were filed. If the hearing is adjourned, [the new hearing] date must be set within 30 days. The court judgment must be handed down within 30 days of the date the action or ordinary legal remedy was heard.

Article 622

1. In the disputes referred to in the preceding Article, recognised professional trade unions or employer organisation, recognised associations of such unions or organisations, or chambers may:
1) exercise rights deriving from a collective bargaining agreement or provisions treated as equivalent to collective agreement provisions on behalf of their members, unless their members have expressly opposed this. Nevertheless, they shall have the right to intervene [in proceedings];
2) intervene on behalf of a party in the proceedings up to the time an irrevocable judgment is handed down, provided that party is a member thereof or a member of one of the organisations comprising the association;
3) intervene in any proceedings concerning the interpretation or application of a collective bargaining agreement to which they are party or a provision treated as equivalent to collective agreement provisions, for the protection of a collective interest which the outcome of the proceedings concerns;
4) intervene on behalf of a party in the proceedings exercising rights deriving from the legislation in force from time to time on compliance with the principle of equal treatment of the sexes and combating discrimination at work on the basis of sex and, in particular, from Law 3896/2010 (Government Gazette, Series I, Issue 207), at any stage of the proceedings and in cassation proceedings, where the dispute is being tried under the special procedure for labour disputes.

ΤΙΤΛΟΣ IV
ΔΙΑΤΑΞΕΙΣ ΓΙΑ ΤΙΣ ΔΙΑΦΟΡΕΣ ΑΠΟ ΑΜΟΙΒΕΣ

Άρθρο 622Α

1. Διαφορές για τις αμοιβές, τις αποζημιώσεις και τα έξοδα δικηγόρων, συμβολαιογράφων, και άμισθων δικαστικών επιμελητών μπορούν να εισαχθούν και στο δικαστήριο του τόπου όπου είναι διορισμένοι.

2. Διαφορές για τις αμοιβές, τις αποζημιώσεις και τα έξοδα γιατρών, οδοντογιατρών, κτηνιάτρων, μηχανικών και χημικών διπλωματούχων ανώτατων και ανώτερων σχολών και νόμιμα διορισμένων μεσιτών, μπορούν να εισαχθούν και στο δικαστήριο του τόπου όπου ασκούν το επάγγελμά τους.

3. Διαφορές για τις αμοιβές, τις αποζημιώσεις και τα έξοδα διαιτητών, διαμεσολαβητών και διαιτητών πραγματογνωμόνων μπορούν να εισαχθούν και στο δικαστήριο του τόπου όπου έχει διεξαχθεί η διαιτησία, η διαμεσολάβηση ή η διαιτητική πραγματογνωμοσύνη.

4. Διαφορές για τις αμοιβές, τις αποζημιώσεις και τα έξοδα εκτελεστών διαθήκης, εκκαθαριστών κληρονομιάς και κηδεμόνων σχολάζουσας κληρονομιάς μπορούν να εισαχθούν και στο δικαστήριο της κληρονομιάς.

5. Διαφορές για τις αμοιβές, τις αποζημιώσεις και τα έξοδα των μαρτύρων που εξετάσθηκαν και των διερμηνέων που διορίσθηκαν από δικαστήρια ή διαιτητές υπάγονται και στο ειρηνοδικείο της έδρας του δικαστηρίου από το οποίο εξετάσθηκαν ή διορίσθηκαν ή στο οποίο έχει κατατεθεί η διαιτητική απόφαση.

6. Διαφορές για τις αμοιβές, τις αποζημιώσεις και τα έξοδα των πραγματογνωμόνων που διορίσθηκαν από δικαστήρια ή από διαιτητές υπάγονται και στο ειρηνοδικείο ή το μονομελές πρωτοδικείο της έδρας του δικαστηρίου το οποίο τους διόρισε ή στο οποίο κατέθεσαν τη διαιτητική απόφαση.

ΤΙΤΛΟΣ V
ΔΙΑΤΑΞΕΙΣ ΓΙΑ ΤΙΣ ΔΙΑΦΟΡΕΣ ΑΠΟ ΠΙΣΤΩΤΙΚΟΥΣ ΤΙΤΛΟΥΣ

Άρθρο 622Β

1. Οι διαφορές του άρθρου 614 αριθμ. 8 υπάγονται στην αρμοδιότητα του ειρηνοδικείου εφόσον η αξία του αντικειμένου της διαφοράς δεν υπερβαίνει το ποσό των είκοσι χιλιάδων (20.000) ευρώ και στην αρμοδιότητα του μονομελούς πρωτοδικείου αν υπερβαίνει το ποσό αυτό.

2. Το αργότερο κατά τη συζήτηση στο ακροατήριο πρέπει να προσάγονται υποχρεωτικά οι πιστωτικοί τίτλοι, διαφορετικά η αγωγή απορρίπτεται αυτεπαγγέλτως ως απαράδεκτη.

3. Στις διαφορές της παραγράφου 1 άσκηση ανταγωγής δεν επιτρέπεται και αν ασκηθεί απορρίπτεται αυτεπαγγέλτως ως απαράδεκτη, εκτός αν η ανταγωγή είναι συναφής με την κύρια αγωγή.

4. Η απόφαση που δέχεται ή απορρίπτει την αγωγή μπορεί να προσβληθεί με ένδικα μέσα, εκτός από ανακοπή ερημοδικίας.

ΚΕΦΑΛΑΙΟ Δ'
ΔΙΑΤΑΓΕΣ

ΤΙΤΛΟΣ I
ΔΙΑΤΑΓΗ ΠΛΗΡΩΜΗΣ

Άρθρο 623

Κατά τις διατάξεις των άρθρων 624 έως 636 μπορεί να ζητηθεί η έκδοση διαταγής πληρωμής για χρηματικές απαιτήσεις ή απαιτήσεις παροχής χρεογράφων, εφόσον πρόκειται για ιδιωτικού δικαίου διαφορά και η απαίτηση, καθώς και το οφειλόμενο ποσό αποδεικνύονται με δημόσιο ή ιδιωτικό έγγραφο, ή με απόφαση ασφαλιστικών μέτρων, η οποία εκδόθηκε μετά από ομολογία ή αποδοχή της αίτησης του οφειλέτη.

TITLE IV
PROVISIONS ON PAY DISPUTES

Article 622A

1. Disputes concerning the fees, compensation and costs of lawyers, notaries public and non-stipendiary court process servers may also be brought before the court of the place where such persons are appointed.
2. Disputes concerning the fees, compensation and costs of physicians, dentists, veterinarians, engineers and certified chemists holding degrees from superior and higher schools and lawfully appointed real estate brokers may also be brought before the court of the place where such persons carry on their profession.
3. Disputes concerning the fees, compensation and costs of arbitrators, mediators and expert arbitrators may also be brought before the court of the place where the arbitration or mediation was carried out or the arbitration-related expert evidence was prepared.
4. Disputes concerning the fees, compensation and costs of executors of wills, liquidators of estates and curators of unclaimed estates may also be brought before the court ruling on the inheritance.
5. Disputes concerning the fees, compensation and costs of witnesses examined and court-appointed interpreters or arbitrators may also be heard by to the court of the peace within the district of the court which examined or appointed them or with which the arbitration award was filed.
6. Disputes concerning the fees, compensation and costs of court-appointed experts or arbitrators may also be heard by the court of the peace or single-member court of first instance within the district of the court which appointed them or with which they filed the arbitration award.

TITLE V
PROVISIONS ON SECURITIES DISPUTES

Article 622B

1. The disputes referred to in Article 614(8) fall under the jurisdiction of the court of the peace, provided the value of their subject-matter does not exceed 20,000 euros, and under the jurisdiction of the single-member court of first instance if it does exceed said sum.
2. The securities must be produced no later than during the courtroom hearing, otherwise the action shall be dismissed *ex officio* as inadmissible.
3. In the disputes referred to in paragraph 1, a cross-action may not be filed; if one is filed, it shall be dismissed *ex officio* as inadmissible, unless it is related to the main action.
4. The judgment accepting or dismissing the action may be contested by legal remedies, except opposition against a default judgment.

CHAPTER IV
ORDERS

TITLE I
PAYMENT ORDER

Article 623

Issuance of a payment order may be requested under the provisions of Articles 624 to 636 with regard to monetary claims or claims for handing over securities, provided it concerns a private-law dispute and the claim and amount owed are proven by means of a public or private document or a judgment granting interim measures handed down after the debtor made an admission or accepted the application.

Άρθρο 624

1. Η έκδοση διαταγής πληρωμής μπορεί να ζητηθεί μόνον αν η απαίτηση δεν εξαρτάται από αίρεση, προθεσμία, όρο ή αντιπαροχή και το ποσό χρημάτων ή χρεογράφων που οφείλεται είναι ορισμένο.

2. Δεν είναι δυνατόν να εκδοθεί διαταγή πληρωμής, και αν εκδοθεί είναι άκυρη, αν η επίδοσή της πρέπει να γίνει σε πρόσωπο που η διαμονή του είναι άγνωστη, εκτός αν έχει αντίκλητο νόμιμα διορισμένο, σύμφωνα με το άρθρο 142 ΚΠολΔ.

Άρθρο 625

Αρμόδιος να εκδώσει διαταγή πληρωμής είναι για απαίτηση της αρμοδιότητας του ειρηνοδικείου ο ειρηνοδίκης και για κάθε άλλη απαίτηση ο δικαστής του μονομελούς πρωτοδικείου. Για την έκδοση διαταγής πληρωμής δεν γίνεται συζήτηση στο ακροατήριο.

Άρθρο 626

1. Η διαταγή πληρωμής εκδίδεται ύστερα από αίτηση του δικαιούχου της απαίτησης. Η αίτηση κατατίθεται στη γραμματεία του δικαστηρίου και συντάσσεται κάτω από αυτήν έκθεση.

2. Η αίτηση πρέπει να περιέχει:

α) όσα ορίζουν τα άρθρα 117 ή 118 και η παράγραφος 1 του άρθρου 119,

β) αίτηση για την έκδοση διαταγής πληρωμής και

γ) την απαίτηση και το ακριβές ποσό των χρημάτων ή των χρεογράφων με τους τυχόν οφειλόμενους τόκους των οποίων ζητείται η καταβολή.

3. Στην αίτηση πρέπει να αναφέρονται και να επισυνάπτονται και όλα τα έγγραφα από τα οποία προκύπτει η απαίτηση και το ποσό της.

Άρθρο 627

Ο δικαστής αποφασίζει το ταχύτερο σχετικά με την αίτηση, χωρίς να καλέσει τον οφειλέτη, έχει όμως το δικαίωμα:

α) να καλεί τον αιτούντα για να του δώσει εξηγήσεις σχετικά με την αίτηση,

β) να υποδείξει στον αιτούντα τις αναγκαίες συμπληρώσεις ή διορθώσεις της αίτησης,

γ) αν ο αιτών επικαλείται ιδιωτικά έγγραφα, να ζητεί βεβαίωση της υπογραφής από συμβολαιογράφο ή μάρτυρες που εξετάζονται ενώπιον του.

Άρθρο 628

1. Ο δικαστής απορρίπτει την αίτηση:

α) αν δεν συντρέχουν οι νόμιμες προϋποθέσεις για την έκδοση διαταγής πληρωμής,

β) αν ο αιτών δεν δίνει τις εξηγήσεις που του ζήτησε ή αρνείται να συμμορφωθεί προς τις υποδείξεις για τη συμπλήρωση ή διόρθωση της αίτησής του ή για τη βεβαίωση των υπογραφών ιδιωτικών εγγράφων.

2. Η απόρριψη σημειώνεται κάτω από την αίτηση και αναφέρεται με συντομία ο λόγος της απόρριψης.

3. Σε περίπτωση απόρριψης της αίτησης δεν αποκλείεται η άσκηση αγωγής ή η υποβολή νέας αίτησης.

Άρθρο 629

Ο δικαστής δέχεται την αίτηση κατά το μέρος που κατά την κρίση του είναι νομικά και πραγματικά βάσιμη, διατάσσει τον οφειλέτη να πληρώσει το οφειλόμενο ποσό και τον καταδικάζει στη δικαστική δαπάνη. Κατά το μέρος που η αίτηση απορρίπτεται, εφαρμόζεται η διάταξη της παραγράφου 3 του άρθρου 628.

Article 624

1. Issuance of a payment order may be requested only if the claim is not subject to a condition, term, proviso or counter-performance and the amount of monies or securities owed is specific.
2. A payment order may not be issued — and shall be null and void if issued — if it must be served on a person of no known place of residence, unless that person has a duly appointed process agent in accordance with Article 142 of this Code.

Article 625

Court of the peace judges are competent to issue a payment order for a claim falling under the jurisdiction of the court of the peace, and single-member court of first instance judges for all other claims. A courtroom hearing need not be held to issue a payment order.

Article 626

1. The payment order shall be issued following an application by the person entitled to the claim. The application shall be filed with court registry and a report shall be drafted at its end.
2. The application must contain:
a) the information required under Articles 117 or 118 and Article 119(1);
b) a request to issue a payment order; and
c) the claim and exact amount of the monies or securities plus any interest whose payment is being requested.
3. The application must also refer to all the documents on which the claim and its amount are based, and said documents must be attached to said application.

Article 627

The judge shall rule on the application as soon as possible, without summoning the debtor, but has the right:
a) to summon the applicant to provide explanations regarding the application;
b) to indicate to the applicant any necessary additions or corrections to the application;
c) if the applicant is relying on private documents, to request that the authenticity of the signature thereon be verified by a notary public or witnesses examined in the presence of [the notary public].

Article 628

1. The judge shall dismiss the application:
a) if the requirements provided for in law for issuing a payment order are not met;
b) if the applicant does not give the explanations requested or refuses to comply with the instructions to supplement or correct their application or to verify the authenticity of the signatures on private documents.
2. The dismissal shall be noted at the end of the application and contain a summary of the grounds for dismissal.
3. Dismissal of an application does not preclude filing an action or a new application.

Article 629

The judge shall accept the application insofar as, in their view, it is legally and factually well-founded and shall order the debtor to pay the amount owed and the court costs. Insofar as the application is dismissed, the provisions of Article 628(3) apply.

Άρθρο 630

Η διαταγή πληρωμής καταρτίζεται εγγράφως και πρέπει να περιέχει:
α) το ονοματεπώνυμο του δικαστή που εκδίδει τη διαταγή πληρωμής,
β) το ονοματεπώνυμο, το πατρώνυμο, την κατοικία, τη διεύθυνση, καθώς και τον αριθμό φορολογικού μητρώου εκείνου που ζήτησε την έκδοση της διαταγής και αν πρόκειται για νομικό πρόσωπο την επωνυμία, τη διεύθυνση της έδρας του και τον αριθμό φορολογικού μητρώου
γ) το ονοματεπώνυμο, το πατρώνυμο, την κατοικία, τη διεύθυνση, καθώς και αν αυτό είναι εφικτό τον αριθμό φορολογικού μητρώου εκείνου κατά του οποίου στρέφεται η αίτηση και αν πρόκειται για νομικό πρόσωπο την επωνυμία, τη διεύθυνση της έδρας του, καθώς και αν αυτό είναι εφικτό τον αριθμό φορολογικού του μητρώου,
δ) την αιτία της πληρωμής,
ε) το ποσό των χρημάτων ή των χρεογράφων που πρέπει να καταβληθεί,
στ) διαταγή πληρωμής,
ζ) υπόμνηση σε εκείνον κατά του οποίου στρέφεται ότι έχει το δικαίωμα να ασκήσει ανακοπή μέσα στην προθεσμία που ορίζεται στο άρθρο 636 και
η) υπογραφή του δικαστή.

Άρθρο 630Α

Η διαταγή πληρωμής επιδίδεται σε εκείνον κατά του οποίου στρέφεται μέσα σε προθεσμία δύο (2) μηνών από την έκδοσή της. Αν η επίδοση δεν γίνει μέσα στην προθεσμία του προηγούμενου εδαφίου, η διαταγή πληρωμής παύει αυτοδικαίως να ισχύει. Μέσα στην ίδια προθεσμία αντίγραφο της σχετικής έκθεσης επίδοσης κατατίθεται στη γραμματεία του δικαστηρίου, ο δικαστής του οποίου εξέδωσε τη διαταγή πληρωμής. Ο αρμόδιος γραμματέας υποχρεούται να καταχωρίσει τη χρονολογία της επίδοσης στο οικείο βιβλίο δημοσιεύσεων.

Άρθρο 631

Η διαταγή πληρωμής αποτελεί τίτλο εκτελεστό. Κατ' εξαίρεση αναστέλλεται η εκτελεστότητα διαταγής πληρωμής που εκδόθηκε κατά προσώπου με άγνωστη διαμονή ή με διαμονή ή έδρα στο εξωτερικό όσο διαρκεί η προθεσμία για την άσκηση ανακοπής σύμφωνα με το άρθρο 632, επιτρέπεται όμως να ληφθούν ασφαλιστικά μέτρα σύμφωνα με το άρθρο 724.

Άρθρο 632

1. Ο οφειλέτης κατά του οποίου στρέφεται η διαταγή πληρωμής έχει το δικαίωμα να ασκήσει ανακοπή, η οποία απευθύνεται στο καθ' ύλην αρμόδιο Δικαστήριο του τόπου έκδοσης της διαταγής πληρωμής. Αντίγραφα των εγγράφων τα οποία αποδεικνύουν την απαίτηση παραμένουν στη γραμματεία του δικαστηρίου μέχρι την πάροδο της προθεσμίας για την άσκηση ανακοπής κατά την παρούσα παράγραφο.
2. Η προθεσμία για την άσκηση της ανακοπής είναι δεκαπέντε (15) εργάσιμες ημέρες αν η διαταγή πληρωμής έχει εκδοθεί κατά προσώπου που έχει την διαμονή ή την έδρα του στην Ελλάδα και τριάντα (30) εργάσιμες ημέρες αν η διαταγή πληρωμής έχει εκδοθεί κατά προσώπου που έχει τη διαμονή ή την έδρα του στο εξωτερικό ή η διαμονή του είναι άγνωστη. Η ανακοπή εκδικάζεται κατά τη διαδικασία των περιουσιακών διαφορών των άρθρων 614 επ..
3. Με την επιφύλαξη του άρθρου 631 η άσκηση της ανακοπής δεν αναστέλλει την εκτέλεση της διαταγής πληρωμής. Το δικαστήριο όμως, ο δικαστής του οποίου εξέδωσε τη διαταγή πληρωμής, μπορεί, κατά τη διαδικασία των άρθρων 686 επ., να χορηγήσει αναστολή με ή και χωρίς εγγύηση, ώσπου να εκδοθεί οριστική απόφαση για την ασκηθείσα ανακοπή. Η αναστολή αυτή δεν εμποδίζει την λήψη ασφαλιστικών μέτρων σύμφωνα με το άρθρο 724.

Article 630

Payment orders shall be drawn up in writing and must contain:

a) the full name of the judge issuing the payment order;

b) the full name, father's name, place of residence, address and tax identification number of the person who requested that the order be issued and, in the case of a legal person, its name, registered offices and tax identification number;

c) the full name, father's name, place of residence, address and, where feasible, the tax identification number of the addressee and, in the case of a legal person, its name, registered offices and, where feasible, its tax identification number;

d) the reason for the payment;

e) the amount of monies or securities payable;

f) a payment order;

g) a reminder to the addressee that they have the right to file an opposition within the deadline laid down in Article 636; and

h) the judge's signature.

Article 630A

A payment order shall be served on its addressee within a deadline of two months from being issued. If service is not effected within the deadline laid down in the preceding subparagraph, the payment order shall automatically cease to be effective. Within the same deadline, a copy of the relevant service report shall be filed with the registry of the court whose judge issued the payment order. The competent registrar is obligated to enter the date of service in the pertinent service register.

Article 631

A payment order constitutes an enforceable title. By way of exception, the enforceability of a payment order issued against a person of no known place of residence or who resides or is seated abroad shall be stayed until the deadline for filing an opposition in accordance with Article 632 has lapsed; however, interim measures may be granted in accordance with Article 724.

Article 632

1. The debtor against whom the payment order was issued has the right to file an opposition addressed to the court with jurisdiction *ratione materiae* of the place where the payment order was issued. Copies of the documents proving the claim shall remain at the court registry until the deadline for filing the opposition referred to in this paragraph has lapsed.

2. The deadline for filing an opposition is 15 working days if the payment order was issued against a person who resides or is seated in Greece, and 30 working days if the payment order was issued against a person who resides or is seated abroad or has no known place of residence. The opposition shall be tried under the procedure on property disputes laid down in Articles 614 *et seq.*

3. Without prejudice to Article 631, [the act of] filing an opposition shall not stay enforcement of the payment order. However, the court whose judge issued the payment order may, under the procedure laid down in Articles 686 *et seq.*, grant a stay, whether or not with surety, until a final judgment has been handed down on the opposition filed. This stay shall not hinder the granting of interim measures in accordance with Article 724.

4. Αν ασκηθεί εμπρόθεσμα έφεση κατά της οριστικής απόφασης, το δικαστήριο που εξέδωσε την απόφαση που προσβάλλεται μπορεί, δικάζοντας κατά τη διαδικασία των άρθρων 686 επ., έως τη συζήτηση της έφεσης, μετά από αίτηση του οφειλέτη, και εφόσον πιθανολογείται η ευδοκίμηση της έφεσης, να αναστείλει ολικά ή εν μέρει την εκτέλεση, ώσπου να εκδοθεί οριστική απόφαση, με τον όρο να δοθεί εγγύηση, η οποία ορίζεται από την απόφαση που διατάσσει την αναστολή ή και χωρίς εγγύηση. Με τις ίδιες προϋποθέσεις το δικαστήριο που δικάζει την έφεση μπορεί, σε κάθε στάση της δίκης, ύστερα από αίτηση του οφειλέτη η οποία υποβάλλεται με το δικόγραφο της έφεσης ή με τις προτάσεις, να αναστείλει την εκτέλεση σύμφωνα με το προηγούμενο εδάφιο.
5. Η δυνατότητα αναστολής της εκτέλεσης κατά την παράγραφο 4 του παρόντος άρθρου παρέχεται και στην περίπτωση που δεν είχε χορηγηθεί αναστολή της εκτέλεσης σύμφωνα με την παράγραφο 3.
6. Με την ανακοπή κατά της διαταγής πληρωμής μπορεί να σωρευθεί και αίτημα ακυρώσεως των πράξεων εκτελέσεως, οι οποίες ενεργούνται με βάση αυτήν, αν συντρέχουν και οι προϋποθέσεις του άρθρου 218 ΚΠολΔ.
7. Αν ο ανακόπτων δεν λάβει μέρος κανονικά στη δίκη, το δικαστήριο συζητεί την υπόθεση χωρίς αυτόν και απορρίπτει την ανακοπή.

Άρθρο 633

1. Αν η ανακοπή έχει ασκηθεί εμπρόθεσμα και νόμιμα και οι λόγοι της είναι νόμιμοι και βάσιμοι, το δικαστήριο ακυρώνει τη διαταγή πληρωμής. Διαφορετικά απορρίπτει την ανακοπή και επικυρώνει τη διαταγή πληρωμής.
2. Αν δεν έχει ασκηθεί εμπρόθεσμα ανακοπή, εκείνος υπέρ του οποίου έχει εκδοθεί η διαταγή πληρωμής μπορεί να επιδώσει πάλι τη διαταγή στον οφειλέτη, ο οποίος έχει το δικαίωμα να ασκήσει την ανακοπή μέσα σε προθεσμία δεκαπέντε (15) εργασίμων ημερών από τη νέα επίδοση. Στην περίπτωση αυτή δεν χορηγείται η αναστολή εκτέλεσης, που προβλέπεται στις παρ. 3 και 4 του προηγούμενου άρθρου. Αν περάσει άπρακτη και η παραπάνω προθεσμία, η διαταγή πληρωμής αποκτά δύναμη δεδικασμένου και είναι δυνατό να προσβληθεί μόνο με αναψηλάφηση.
3. Εάν η διαταγή πληρωμής που έχει εκτελεστεί, ακυρωθεί εν όλω ή εν μέρει με τελεσίδικη δικαστική απόφαση επί της ανακοπής, το δικαστήριο διατάζει, εάν το ζητήσει εκείνος κατά του οποίου έγινε η εκτέλεση, την επαναφορά των πραγμάτων στην κατάσταση που βρισκόταν πριν εκτελεστεί η ακυρωθείσα διαταγή πληρωμής. Η αίτηση υποβάλλεται είτε με τα δικόγραφα της έφεσης και των προσθέτων λόγων είτε με τις ενώπιον του εφετείου προτάσεις του ανακόπτοντος. Η εκτέλεση της απόφασης πρέπει να προαποδεικνύεται.

Άρθρο 634

1. Η επίδοση διαταγής πληρωμής διακόπτει την παραγραφή και την αποσβεστική προθεσμία.
2. Αν ακυρωθεί η διαταγή πληρωμής, η παραγραφή ή η αποσβεστική προθεσμία θεωρείται ότι έχει ανασταλεί από την επίδοση της διαταγής πληρωμής ώσπου να εκδοθεί τελεσίδικη απόφαση για την ανακοπή.

Άρθρο 635

Η επίδοση της ανακοπής των άρθρων 632 και 633 και των αιτήσεων αναστολής του άρθρου 632 μπορεί να γίνει είτε στον δικηγόρο που υπέγραψε την αίτηση για την έκδοση της διαταγής πληρωμής είτε στη διεύθυνση εκείνου κατά του οποίου στρέφονται, η οποία αναφέρεται στη διαταγή πληρωμής, εκτός αν γνωστοποιηθεί με δικόγραφο μεταβολή που τυχόν έχει επέλθει.

Άρθρο 636

Σε περίπτωση επίδοσης στο εξωτερικό, για την έναρξη της προθεσμίας ανακοπής των άρθρων 632 και 633 παράγραφος 2, η επίδοση θεωρείται ότι συντελέσθηκε κατά τον χρόνο που προβλέπει το δίκαιο του κράτους της διαμονής του παραλήπτη ή κατά τον χρόνο της πραγματικής παραλαβής, η οποία αποδεικνύεται με έγγραφο ή δικαστική ομολογία.

4. If an appeal is filed in good time against the final judgment, the court that handed down the judgment being contested may, by the hearing of the appeal, trying the matter under the procedure laid down in Articles 686 *et seq.*, following an application filed by the debtor, and, where it is considered likely on the balance of probabilities that the appeal will be successful, stay enforcement in whole or in part until a final judgment has been handed down, whether with surety, to be set in the judgment ordering the stay, or even without surety. Under the same conditions, the court trying the appeal may, during any stage of the proceedings and following an application by the debtor submitted with the appeal or the pleadings, stay enforcement in accordance with the preceding subparagraph.
5. Stay of enforcement in accordance with paragraph 4 of this Article is also possible if enforcement had not been stayed in accordance with paragraph 3.
6. A request to annul enforcement steps carried out on the basis of the payment order may be joined to the opposition against the payment order if the conditions laid down in Article 218 of this Code are also met.
7. If the opposing party does not participate in the proceedings in the manner required, the court shall hear the case in the opposing party's absence and dismiss the opposition.

Article 633

1. If the opposition was filed duly and in good time and its grounds are lawful and well-founded, the court shall annul the payment order, otherwise it shall dismiss the opposition and confirm the payment order.
2. If an opposition was not filed in good time, the person who procured the payment order may serve the order on the debtor anew, and the debtor has the right to file an opposition within a deadline of 15 working days from the date of second service. In this case, the stay of enforcement provided for in paragraphs 3 and 4 of the preceding Article shall not be granted. If the above deadline also lapses without the relevant steps having been taken, the payment order acquires the force of *res judicata* and may only be contested by means of an application for re-opening proceedings.
3. If a payment order that has been enforced is annulled in whole or in part by means of a *de jure* non-appealable court judgment on the opposition, the court shall, where requested by the debtor, order that affairs be restored to their state prior to enforcement of the annulled payment order. The application shall be submitted either with the appeal and the additional grounds or with the pleadings of the opposing party filed with the court of the appeal. Enforcement of the judgment must be proven beforehand.

Article 634

1. Service of the payment order interrupts the time-barring period and exclusive deadline.
2. If the payment order is annulled, the time-barring period and exclusive deadline shall be deemed to be suspended from the date the payment order was served until a *de jure* non-appealable judgment has been handed down on the opposition.

Article 635

The opposition referred to in Articles 632 and 633 and applications to stay [enforcement] referred to in Article 632 may be served either on the lawyer who signed the application to issue the payment order or at the address of the person against whom the foregoing were filed, as indicated in the payment order, unless any change that may have occurred is notified by means of a procedural document.

Article 636

In cases of service abroad, for the purposes of commencement of the deadline for the opposition laid down in Article 632 and 633(2), service shall be deemed to be effected at the time provided for in the law of the state where the recipient resides or at the time of actual receipt, proven by means of a document or admission made in court.

Άρθρο 636Α

1. Με την επιφύλαξη του δεύτερου εδαφίου της παρ. 2 του άρθρου 621 μπορεί να ζητηθεί η έκδοση διαταγής πληρωμής οφειλόμενου μισθού κατά τις διατάξεις των άρθρων 623 έως 636, εφόσον η σύναψη της σύμβασης εξαρτημένης εργασίας και το ύψος του μισθού αποδεικνύονται με δημόσιο ή ιδιωτικό έγγραφο ή με απόφαση ασφαλιστικών μέτρων, η οποία εκδόθηκε μετά από ομολογία ή αποδοχή της αίτησης από τον οφειλέτη, και εφόσον έχει επιδοθεί έγγραφη όχληση με δικαστικό επιμελητή δεκαπέντε (15) τουλάχιστον ημέρες πριν από την κατάθεση της αίτησης. Η εργασία που αντιστοιχεί στον μισθό για τον οποίο ζητείται η έκδοση διαταγής πληρωμής, τεκμαίρεται ότι έχει παρασχεθεί.

2. Η αίτηση για την έκδοση διαταγής πληρωμής υποβάλλεται και στον κατά τόπο αρμόδιο δικαστή της παρ. 1 του άρθρου 621.

3. Η συζήτηση της ανακοπής κατά διαταγής πληρωμής, που εκδόθηκε για απαιτήσεις της παρ. 1, προσδιορίζεται κατά προτεραιότητα στη συντομότερη διαθέσιμη δικάσιμο και πάντως όχι πέραν των τριών (3) μηνών από την κατάθεσή της. Αν αναβληθεί η συζήτηση, αυτή προσδιορίζεται υποχρεωτικά μέσα σε τριάντα (30) ημέρες.

4. Τυχόν ειδικότερες διατάξεις που ισχύουν για τις διαφορές του άρθρου 614 αριθμ. 3, σχετικά με την καταβολή δικαστικού ενσήμου, τέλους απογράφου, παραβόλου και κάθε άλλου τέλους ή φόρου, ισχύουν ανάλογα και για τη διαταγή πληρωμής του παρόντος άρθρου, την ανακοπή που ασκείται κατ' αυτής, καθώς και για τα ένδικα μέσα και βοηθήματα που ασκούνται κατά της απόφασης επί της ανακοπής.

ΤΙΤΛΟΣ II
ΔΙΑΤΑΓΗ ΑΠΟΔΟΣΗΣ ΤΗΣ ΧΡΗΣΗΣ ΜΙΣΘΙΟΥ

Άρθρο 637

Κατά τις διατάξεις των άρθρων 638 έως 645, στην περίπτωση καθυστέρησης του μισθώματος από δυστροπία, μπορεί να ζητηθεί η έκδοση διαταγής απόδοσης της χρήσης μισθίου ακινήτου, αν η έναρξη της μίσθωσης αποδεικνύεται εγγράφως, και εφόσον έχει επιδοθεί έγγραφη όχληση με δικαστικό επιμελητή δεκαπέντε (15) τουλάχιστον ημέρες πριν από την κατάθεση της αίτησης. Η καταβολή των μισθωμάτων εντός του δεκαπενθήμερου, αποδεικνυόμενη εγγράφως, αποκλείει την έκδοση διαταγής απόδοσης της χρήσης του μισθίου, εκτός αν υπάρχει επανειλημμένη καθυστέρηση από δυστροπία. Επίδοση έγγραφης όχλησης απαιτείται μόνο την πρώτη φορά.

Άρθρο 638

Αρμόδιος για την έκδοση της διαταγής απόδοσης της χρήσης του μισθίου είναι ο ειρηνοδίκης στις περιπτώσεις που αυτός έχει αρμοδιότητα κατά το άρθρο 14 παράγραφος 1 περίπτωση β' και ο δικαστής του μονομελούς πρωτοδικείου σε κάθε άλλη περίπτωση. Η αίτηση υποβάλλεται στο κατά το άρθρο 29 κατά τόπο αρμόδιο δικαστήριο.

Άρθρο 639

1. Η διάταξη της παραγράφου 1 του άρθρου 626 εφαρμόζεται αναλόγως.

2. Η αίτηση πρέπει να περιλαμβάνει, εκτός από τα στοιχεία του άρθρου 117 ή 118, και εκείνα της παραγράφου 1 του άρθρου 119, καθώς και:

α) αίτημα να εκδοθεί διαταγή απόδοσης της χρήσης του μισθίου ακινήτου και μνεία του τόπου όπου βρίσκεται με περιγραφή του,

β) επίκληση του εγγράφου από το οποίο αποδεικνύεται η μίσθωση,

γ) επίκληση της κατά το άρθρο 637 ΚΠολΔ περίπτωσης σύμφωνα με την οποία ζητείται η απόδοση της χρήσης του μισθίου με μνεία των αναγκαίων περιστατικών, καθώς και της έκθεσης επίδοσης.

3. Στην αίτηση επισυνάπτεται το έγγραφο από το οποίο αποδεικνύεται η μίσθωση, η έκθεση επίδοσης της όχλησης, καθώς και κάθε άλλο σχετικό έγγραφο. Ο δικαστής μπορεί να καλέσει τον αιτούντα να βεβαιώσει και ενόρκως τα περιστατικά που απαιτούνται για την έκδοση της διαταγής.

4. Η διάταξη του άρθρου 627 εφαρμόζεται αναλόγως.

Article 636A

1. Without prejudice to the second subparagraph of Article 621(2), issuance of a payment order concerning a salary owed under the provisions of Articles 623 to 636 may be requested if the signing of the employment contract and the salary amount are proven by means of a public or private document or a judgment granting interim measures that was handed down after the debtor's admission or acceptance of the application, and provided a written notice has been served by a court process server at least 15 days prior to the application being filed. It shall be presumed that the work corresponding to the salary for which issuance of a payment order is being requested was provided.

2. The application for a payment order may also be submitted to the judge with the jurisdiction *ratione loci* referred to in Article 621(1).

3. The hearing of an opposition filed against a payment order issued with regard to claims referred to in paragraph 1 shall be given priority and set for the nearest hearing date available and, in all cases, no later than three months after it was filed. If the hearing is adjourned, the hearing date must be set within 30 days.

4. Any more specific provisions applicable to the disputes referred to in Article 614(3) concerning payment of judicial stamp duty, enforcement precept duty, fees and all other duties or taxes apply *mutatis mutandis* to the payment order referred to in this Article, the opposition filed against it, as well as the legal remedies and forms of relief filed against the judgment handed down on the opposition.

TITLE II
ORDER FOR RETURN OF USE OF A LEASED PROPERTY

Article 637

An order for return of use of a leased property may be requested under the provisions of Articles 638 to 645 in the case of delayed [payment of] rent due to intransigence, if it is proven in writing that the lease has commenced and where a written notice has been served by a court process server at least 15 days prior to the application being filed. Except in the case of repeated delays due to intransigence, an order for return of use of a leased property may not be issued if [all] the rent [due] is paid within the 15-day period, proven in writing. Service of a written notice is only required the first time.

Article 638

Competence to issue the order for return of use of a leased property shall lie with court of the peace judges, where they have jurisdiction under Article 14(1)(b), and single-member court of first instance judges in all other cases. The application shall be filed with the court with jurisdiction *ratione loci* under Article 29.

Article 639

1. The provisions of Article 626(1) apply *mutatis mutandis*.

2. In addition to the information required under Articles 117 or 118 and Article 119(1), the application must also contain:

a) a request to issue an order for return of use of a leased property and reference to the place where the property is located and a description thereof;

b) statement of reliance on the document proving [that there is a] lease;

c) statement of reliance of the case provided for in Article 637 of this Code under which return of use of the leased property is being requested, setting out the necessary facts, as well as the service report.

3. The document proving [that there is a] lease, the service report concerning the notice and all other relevant documents shall be attached to the application. The judge may summon the applicant to attest under oath to the facts required to issue the order.

4. The provisions of Article 627 apply *mutatis mutandis*.

Άρθρο 640

1. Αν η αίτηση είναι νόμιμη και τα απαιτούμενα σε κάθε περίπτωση περιστατικά αποδεικνύονται εγγράφως, ο δικαστής εκδίδει διαταγή με την οποία υποχρεώνει τον καθ' ου να αποδώσει στον αιτούντα τη χρήση του μισθίου και τον καταδικάζει στα δικαστικά έξοδα.

2. Η διαταγή καταρτίζεται εγγράφως και περιέχει:

α) το ονοματεπώνυμο του δικαστή που την εκδίδει,

β) το ονοματεπώνυμο, το πατρώνυμο, την κατοικία, τη διεύθυνση, καθώς και τον αριθμό φορολογικού μητρώου εκείνου που ζήτησε την έκδοση της διαταγής και αν πρόκειται για νομικό πρόσωπο την επωνυμία, τη διεύθυνση της έδρας του και τον αριθμό φορολογικού μητρώου

γ) το ονοματεπώνυμο, το πατρώνυμο, την κατοικία, τη διεύθυνση, καθώς και αν αυτό είναι εφικτό τον αριθμό φορολογικού μητρώου εκείνου κατά του οποίου στρέφεται η αίτηση και αν πρόκειται για νομικό πρόσωπο την επωνυμία, τη διεύθυνση της έδρας του, καθώς και αν αυτό είναι εφικτό τον αριθμό φορολογικού μητρώου,

δ) περιγραφή του μισθίου,

ε) την αιτία της απόδοσης με έκθεση των αναγκαίων περιστατικών και μνεία της έκθεσης επίδοσης της όχλησης,

στ) διαταγή απόδοσης της χρήσης του μισθίου,

ζ) υπόμνηση στον καθ' ου ότι η διαταγή αποτελεί τίτλο εκτελεστό που μπορεί να εκτελεστεί μετά την πάροδο είκοσι (20) ημερών από την προς αυτόν επίδοση και ότι δικαιούται να ασκήσει κατ' αυτής ανακοπή μέσα σε προθεσμία δεκαπέντε (15) εργάσιμων ημερών από την επίδοση και

η) υπογραφή του δικαστή που την εξέδωσε.

3. Η διαταγή αποτελεί τίτλο εκτελεστό. Η εκτέλεση μπορεί να πραγματοποιηθεί αφού παρέλθουν είκοσι (20) ημέρες από την επίδοσή αντιγράφου εξ απογράφου με επιταγή προς εκτέλεση, χωρίς να απαιτείται προηγούμενη επίδοση αντιγράφου της. Η διαταγή εκτελείται και κατά των προσώπων που αναφέρονται στο άρθρο 616.

Άρθρο 641

1. Ο δικαστής απορρίπτει την αίτηση:

α) αν δεν συντρέχουν οι απαιτούμενες προϋποθέσεις για την έκδοσή της και

β) αν ο αιτών δεν δίνει τις τυχόν ζητούμενες από αυτόν εξηγήσεις ή δεν προβαίνει στις υποδεικνυόμενες συμπληρώσεις ή διορθώσεις της αίτησης ή δεν παρέχει τις τυχόν ζητούμενες από αυτόν βεβαιώσεις της υπογραφής ιδιωτικών εγγράφων ή αν, μολονότι έχει κληθεί να βεβαιώσει ενόρκως τα κατά το άρθρο 639 περιστατικά, δεν προβαίνει στη βεβαίωση αυτή.

2. Η απόρριψη της αίτησης σημειώνεται κάτω από την αίτηση με σύντομη έκθεση του λόγου.

3. Η απόρριψη της αίτησης δεν εμποδίζει την υποβολή νέας ούτε την άσκηση αγωγής.

Άρθρο 642

Ο καθ' ου η διαταγή δικαιούται να ασκήσει ανακοπή ενώπιον του καθ' ύλην αρμοδίου για την εκδίκαση της αγωγής απόδοσης του μισθίου δικαστηρίου, μέσα σε προθεσμία δεκαπέντε (15) εργάσιμων ημερών από την επίδοση της διαταγής. Η ανακοπή εκδικάζεται ως μισθωτική διαφορά.

Άρθρο 643

Η άσκηση της ανακοπής δεν αναστέλλει την εκτέλεση της διαταγής. Ο δικαστής όμως που την εξέδωσε μπορεί, ύστερα από αίτηση του ανακόπτοντος, η οποία εκδικάζεται κατά τα άρθρα 686 επ., να χορηγήσει αναστολή, είτε με εγγυοδοσία υπέρ του καθ' ου η ανακοπή είτε χωρίς εγγυοδοσία, έως την έκδοση οριστικής απόφασης επί της ανακοπής.

Article 640

1. If the application is lawful and the facts required in each case are proven in writing, the judge shall issue an order obligating the respondent to return use of the leased property to the applicant and pay the court costs.

2. The order shall be drawn up in writing and must contain:

a) the full name of the judge issuing the order;

b) the full name, father's name, place of residence, address and tax identification number of the person who requested that the order be issued and, in the case of a legal person, its name, registered offices and tax identification number;

c) the full name, father's name, place of residence, address and, where feasible, the tax identification number of the respondent and, in the case of a legal person, its name, registered offices and, where feasible, its tax identification number;

d) a description of the leased property;

e) the reason for return, setting out the necessary facts and making reference to the service report concerning notice;

f) an order for return of use of the leased property;

g) a reminder to the respondent that the order constitutes an enforceable title that may be enforced after 20 days have elapsed from the date of service on them, and that they may file an opposition against it within a deadline of 15 working days from the date of service; and

h) the signature of the judge who issued it.

3. The order constitutes an enforceable title. Enforcement may be carried out after 20 days have elapsed from the date a copy of the enforcement precept with an enforcement order was served, without prior service of a copy of the order being required. The order is also enforceable against the persons referred to in Article 616.

Article 641

1. The judge shall dismiss the application:

a) if the requirements necessary for issuing it are not met;

b) if the applicant fails to give any explanations requested, or fails to supplement or correct the application as indicated, or fails to provide any verification of the authenticity of signatures on private documents requested, or fails to provide such verification of authenticity despite having been summoned to attest to the facts under oath in accordance with Article 639.

2. Dismissal shall be noted at the end of the application and contain a summary of the grounds.

3. Dismissal shall not hinder a new application being filed or an action being brought.

Article 642

The defendant named in the order is entitled to file an opposition with the court with jurisdiction *ratione materiae* to try the action for return of the leased property within a deadline of 15 working days from the date the order was served. The opposition shall be tried as a lease dispute.

Article 643

[The act of] filing an opposition shall not stay enforcement of the order. However, the judge who issued it may, following an application filed by the opposing party and tried in accordance with Articles 686 *et seq.*, grant a stay, whether or not with provision of surety in favour of the defendant named in the order, until a final judgment has been handed down on the opposition.

Άρθρο 644

1. Αν η ανακοπή ασκήθηκε νόμιμα και εμπρόθεσμα και οι λόγοι της είναι νόμιμοι και βάσιμοι, το δικαστήριο ακυρώνει τη διαταγή απόδοσης της χρήσης του μισθίου, διαφορετικά απορρίπτει την ανακοπή και επικυρώνει τη διαταγή.

2. Η διάταξη του άρθρου 634 εφαρμόζεται αναλόγως.

3. Η παρ. 3 του άρθρου 633 εφαρμόζεται και σε περίπτωση ακύρωσης με τελεσίδικη δικαστική απόφαση επί της ανακοπής της διαταγής απόδοσης του μισθίου που έχει εκτελεσθεί.

Άρθρο 645

Στην αίτηση για την έκδοση διαταγής απόδοσης της χρήσης μισθίου μπορεί να σωρευτεί και αίτημα καταβολής των οφειλόμενων μισθωμάτων, κοινόχρηστων δαπανών, τελών και λογαριασμών κοινής ωφέλειας, εφόσον το ύψος τους αποδεικνύεται από δημόσια ή ιδιωτικά έγγραφα, ιδίως λογαριασμούς κοινοχρήστων και οργανισμών κοινής ωφέλειας. Στην περίπτωση αυτή εφαρμόζονται αναλόγως οι διατάξεις των άρθρων 638 έως 645, 624, 626 παρ. 2 και 3, 630 στοιχ. γ, δ και ε και 634.

Άρθρα 646 – 681Δ

[Καταργούνται].

Article 644

1. If the opposition was filed duly and in good time and its grounds are lawful and well-founded, the court shall annul the order for return of use of the leased property, otherwise it shall dismiss the opposition and confirm the order.
2. The provisions of Article 634 apply *mutatis mutandis*.
3. Article 633(3) shall also apply in cases of annulment by means of a *de jure* non-appealable court judgment on the opposition filed against the order for return of a leased property that has [already] been enforced.

Article 645

A request for payment of [all] rent owed, building service charges, duties and utility bills may be joined to the application for an order for return of use of a leased property, provided the amounts of the foregoing are proven by means of public or private documents and, in particular, building service charge and utility company bills. The provisions of Articles 638 to 645, 624, 626(2) and (3), 630(c), (d) and (e) and 634 apply *mutatis mutandis* in this case.

Articles 646 – 681D

[Repealed]

ΠΕΜΠΤΟ ΒΙΒΛΙΟ
ΑΣΦΑΛΙΣΤΙΚΑ ΜΕΤΡΑ

ΚΕΦΑΛΑΙΟ Α'
Γενικές διατάξεις.

Άρθρο 682

1. Κατά την ειδική διαδικασία των άρθρων 683 έως 703 τα δικαστήρια, σε επείγουσες περιπτώσεις ή για να αποτραπεί επικείμενος κίνδυνος, μπορούν να διατάζουν ασφαλιστικά μέτρα για την εξασφάλιση ή διατήρηση ενός δικαιώματος ή τη ρύθμιση μιας κατάστασης και να τα μεταρρυθμίζουν ή να τα ανακαλούν. Το δικαίωμα είναι δυνατό να εξαρτάται από αίρεση ή προθεσμία ή να αφορά μέλλουσα απαίτηση.
2. Τα ασφαλιστικά μέτρα μπορούν να διαταχθούν και κατά τη διάρκεια της δίκης που αφορά την κύρια υπόθεση.

Άρθρο 683

1. Τα ασφαλιστικά μέτρα διατάσσονται από τα μονομελή πρωτοδικεία.
2. Αν η κύρια υπόθεση υπάγεται στην καθ' ύλην αρμοδιότητα των ειρηνοδικείων, τα ασφαλιστικά μέτρα διατάσσονται από αυτά.
3. Τα ειρηνοδικεία είναι αρμόδια και για την εγγραφή ή άρση προσημείωσης υποθήκης.
4. Τα ασφαλιστικά μέτρα διατάσσονται και από το καθ' ύλην αρμόδιο δικαστήριο που βρίσκεται πλησιέστερα προς τον τόπο όπου πρόκειται να εκτελεστούν.
5. Αν το δικαστήριο δεν είναι καθ' ύλην ή κατά τόπον αρμόδιο, αποφαίνεται γι' αυτό αυτεπαγγέλτως και απορρίπτει την αίτηση.

Άρθρο 684

Αν η κύρια υπόθεση είναι εκκρεμής σε πολυμελές πρωτοδικείο ή σε δευτεροβάθμιο δικαστήριο, τα ασφαλιστικά μέτρα διατάσσονται και από το δικαστήριο αυτό.

Άρθρο 685

Δεν ισχύει συμφωνία διαιτησίας σε υποθέσεις που αφορούν ασφαλιστικά μέτρα.

Άρθρο 686

1. Η αίτηση πρέπει να κατατεθεί στη γραμματεία του δικαστηρίου.
2. Η γραμματεία του δικαστηρίου υποβάλλει αμέσως την αίτηση στον δικαστή του μονομελούς πρωτοδικείου ή τον ειρηνοδίκη, ο οποίος ορίζει τόπο, ημέρα και ώρα για τη συζήτησή της, διατάζει την κλήση εκείνων κατά των οποίων απευθύνεται η αίτηση, ορίζει τον τρόπο κατά τον οποίο θα γνωστοποιηθεί σε αυτούς η κλήση, καθώς και το χρονικό διάστημα που πρέπει να μεσολαβήσει κατά την κρίση του μεταξύ της επίδοσης της κλήσης και της συζήτησης.
3. Ως τόπος συζήτησης μπορεί να οριστεί και η κατοικία του δικαστή που δικάζει την υπόθεση ή άλλος κατά την κρίση του κατάλληλος για την ταχύτερη εκδίκαση της υπόθεσης. Η συζήτηση μπορεί να οριστεί και Κυριακή ή εορτή.
4. Η γνωστοποίηση γίνεται με επίδοση εγγράφου που εκδίδεται από τη γραμματεία του δικαστηρίου, στο οποίο αναγράφεται ο τόπος, η ημέρα και η ώρα της συζήτησης ή με τηλεγραφική ή με τηλεφωνική πρόσκληση της γραμματείας του δικαστηρίου ή με ηλεκτρονικά μέσα με δαπάνες του αιτούντος. Ο δικαστής του μονομελούς πρωτοδικείου ή ο ειρηνοδίκης μπορεί συγχρόνως με την επίδοση της κλήσης να διατάξει και την επίδοση αντιγράφου της αίτησης.
5. Κατά τη συζήτηση της κύριας υπόθεσης η αίτηση μπορεί να υποβληθεί και με τις προτάσεις. Στην περίπτωση του άρθρου 684 η αίτηση δικάζεται μόνον κατά τη συζήτηση της κύριας υπόθεσης.

BOOK V
INTERIM MEASURES

CHAPTER I
General provisions

Article 682

1. Under the special procedure laid down in Articles 683 to 703, the court may, in urgent circumstances or to avert imminent danger, order interim measures to safeguard or preserve a right or regulate a situation, and amend or revoke such measures. The right may be subject to a condition or term, or concern a future claim.
2. Interim measures may also be ordered during the proceedings in the main case.

Article 683

1. Interim measures shall be ordered by single-member courts of first instance.
2. If the courts of the peace have jurisdiction *ratione materiae* over the main case, they shall [be the ones to] order interim measures.
3. Courts of the peace shall also be competent to register or remove prenotations of mortgage.
4. Interim measures may also be ordered by the court with jurisdiction *ratione materiae* nearest to the place where the measures are to be enforced.
5. If the court does not have jurisdiction *ratione materiae* or *ratione loci*, it shall issue a ruling on that matter *ex officio* and dismiss the application.

Article 684

If the main case is pending before a multi-member court of first instance or a second-instance court, interim measures may also be ordered by that court.

Article 685

Arbitration agreements do not apply to cases concerning interim measures.

Article 686

1. The application must be filed with the court registry.
2. The court registry shall immediately submit the application to the single-member court of first instance judge or the court of the peace judge, who shall set a place, date and time for its hearing, order the summoning of the persons to whom the application is addressed, set the manner in which the summons will be notified to them and the period that, in their view, must elapse between service of the summons and the hearing.
3. The place of the hearing may even be set as the place of domicile of the judge trying the case or any other place deemed appropriate, in their view, for the fastest adjudication of the case. The hearing may also be set for a Sunday or holiday.
4. Notification shall be effected by means of service of a document issued by the court registry indicating the place, date and time of the hearing or by telegram or telephone call from the registry or by electronic means, at the expense of the applicant. The single-member court of first instance judge or court of the peace judge may also order that a copy of the application be served together with the summons.
5. During the hearing of the main case, the application may also be submitted together with the pleadings. In the case referred to in Article 684, the application shall be tried only during the hearing of the main case.

6. Στη διαδικασία των ασφαλιστικών μέτρων στο μονομελές πρωτοδικείο ή στο ειρηνοδικείο η πρόσθετη παρέμβαση μπορεί να ασκηθεί και προφορικά.
7. Αν κατά τη συζήτηση της αίτησης ή της ανταίτησης στο ακροατήριο δεν εμφανιστεί κάποιος διάδικος ή εμφανιστεί και δεν λάβει νόμιμα μέρος στη συζήτηση, η διαδικασία προχωρεί σαν να ήταν παρόντες όλοι οι διάδικοι.
8. Η αίτηση για εγγραφή συναινετικής προσημείωσης ή ανάκλησης συναινετικής προσημείωσης κατατίθεται στη γραμματεία του δικαστηρίου. Η αίτηση μπορεί να κατατεθεί και τα δικαιολογητικά έγγραφα να υποβληθούν ηλεκτρονικά κατά την παρ. 2 του άρθρου 117 και την παρ. 4 του άρθρου 119.

Άρθρο 687

1. Σε εξαιρετικά κατεπείγουσες περιπτώσεις ή όταν επίκειται άμεσος κίνδυνος, το δικαστήριο μπορεί να συζητήσει την αίτηση χωρίς να κλητεύσει εκείνον κατά του οποίου απευθύνεται.
2. Αν ο αιτών και εκείνοι κατά των οποίων απευθύνεται η αίτηση εμφανιστούν εκούσια ενώπιον του δικαστή του μονομελούς πρωτοδικείου ή του ειρηνοδίκη, η αίτηση συζητείται αμέσως.

Άρθρο 688

1. Στην αίτηση με την οποία ζητείται να διαταχθούν ασφαλιστικά μέτρα πρέπει να ορίζεται το μέτρο το οποίο ζητείται και να αναφέρονται συνοπτικά τα πραγματικά περιστατικά που πιθανολογούν το δικαίωμα για την εξασφάλιση ή διατήρηση του οποίου ζητείται η λήψη του μέτρου ή για την κατάσταση της οποίας ζητείται η ρύθμιση με το μέτρο αυτό, καθώς και τον επικείμενο κίνδυνο ή την επείγουσα περίπτωση. Σε χρηματικές απαιτήσεις πρέπει να αναφέρεται το οφειλόμενο χρηματικό ποσό ή η χρηματική αξία του αντικειμένου που οφείλεται.
2. Στην αίτηση για μεταρρύθμιση ή ανάκληση ασφαλιστικού μέτρου πρέπει να αναφέρονται οι λόγοι για τους οποίους ζητείται η μεταρρύθμιση ή η ανάκλησή του.

Άρθρο 689

Η απόφαση ασφαλιστικών μέτρων κατά αλλοδαπού δημοσίου δεν εκτελείται χωρίς προηγούμενη άδεια του Υπουργού Δικαιοσύνης, διαφορετικά η εκτέλεση είναι άκυρη.

Άρθρο 690

1. Σε υποθέσεις που αφορούν ασφαλιστικά μέτρα αρκεί η πιθανολόγηση των ισχυρισμών.
2. Ο δικαστής του μονομελούς πρωτοδικείου ή ο ειρηνοδίκης δικάζει την αίτηση χωρίς τη σύμπραξη γραμματέα, εκτός αν κρίνει αναγκαία την τήρηση πρακτικών. Αν δεν συμπράττει γραμματέας, ο δικάζων μπορεί να επιτρέψει τη μαγνητοφώνηση της διαδικασίας, μετά το πέρας της οποίας η μαγνητοταινία παραλαμβάνεται από αυτόν και, αφού εκδοθεί η απόφαση, φυλάσσεται στο αρχείο του δικαστηρίου.
3. Η συζήτηση για την εγγραφή συναινετικής προσημείωσης ή ανάκλησης συναινετικής προσημείωσης διεξάγεται εγγράφως, κατά παρέκκλιση της παρ. 2 του άρθρου 115 και οι διάδικοι μπορούν να παραστούν με δήλωση, σύμφωνα με την παρ. 2 του άρθρου 242.

Άρθρο 691

1. Το δικαστήριο μπορεί και αυτεπαγγέλτως να συγκεντρώσει όλα τα στοιχεία που απαιτούνται για το σχηματισμό της κρίσης του.
2. Η απόφαση που διατάζει ασφαλιστικά μέτρα πρέπει να ορίζει το ασφαλιστικό μέτρο, καθώς και το δικαίωμα, στην εξασφάλιση ή διατήρηση του οποίου αποβλέπει ή την κατάσταση την οποία ρυθμίζει.
3. Η απόφαση του δικαστηρίου περιέχει συνοπτική αιτιολογία ως προς την ύπαρξη ή ανυπαρξία του δικαιώματος του οποίου γίνεται επίκληση και τη συνδρομή ή μη επικείμενου κινδύνου ή επείγουσας περίπτωσης και δημοσιεύεται σε δημόσια συνεδρίαση μετά την περάτωση της ακροαματικής διαδικασίας.

6. During interim measures proceedings before the single-member court of first instance or the court of the peace, permissive interventions may also be made orally.
7. If any of the parties in the proceedings fails to appear during the courtroom hearing of the application or cross-application or appears but fails to participate in the hearing in the manner required, the procedure shall go ahead as if all the parties in the proceedings were present.
8. Applications for registration of consensual prenotation of mortgage or revocation of consensual prenotation shall be filed with the court registry. The application may be filed and the supporting documents may be submitted electronically, in accordance with Article 117(2) and Article 119(4).

Article 687

1. In exceptionally urgent circumstances or when there is imminent danger, the court may hear the application without summonsing the respondent.
2. If the applicant and the respondents appear voluntarily before the single-member court of first instance judge or the court of the peace judge, the application shall be heard immediately.

Article 688

1. The application requesting interim measures must specify the measure being requested and set out in summary form the actual facts on which it is considered likely, on the balance of probabilities, that there is a right for whose safeguarding or maintenance the specific interim measure is being requested, or that there is a right to seek regulation of a situation by means of the measure being requested, as well as the imminent danger or urgent circumstances. In [cases of] monetary claims, the monetary amount owed or monetary value of the thing owed must be indicated.
2. The application to amend or revoke an interim measure must set out the grounds on which its amendment or revocation is being requested.

Article 689

A judgment granting interim measures against a foreign state shall not be enforceable without prior permission of the Minister of Justice, otherwise enforcement shall be null and void.

Article 690

1. In cases concerning interim measures, it shall suffice for the assertions to be considered likely on the balance of probabilities.
2. The single-member court of first instance judge or court of the peace judge shall try the application without the involvement of a registrar, unless they deem it necessary to keep a transcript. If a registrar is not involved, the judge may allow the audio recording of the procedure, after the conclusion of which the recording shall be collected by the judge and, once the judgment has been handed down, shall be kept in the court archives.
3. Hearings on the registration or revocation of consensual prenotations [of mortgage] shall be conducted in writing, by way of derogation from Article 115(2), and the parties in the proceedings may enter an appearance by means of a statement, in accordance with Article 242(2).

Article 691

1. The court may also gather *ex officio* all the evidence necessary to form an opinion.
2. The judgment granting interim measures must specify the interim measure as well as the right it seeks to safeguard or preserve or the situation it regulates.
3. The court judgment shall contain concise reasoning on the existence or non-existence of the right being relied on and the existence or non-existence of an imminent danger or urgent circumstances, and shall be handed down in open court after the hearing has ended.

Άρθρο 691Α

1. Αν το δικαστήριο κρίνει ότι υπάρχει ανάγκη, έχει το δικαίωμα, μόλις κατατεθεί η αίτηση και ώσπου να εκδοθεί η απόφασή του, να εκδώσει και αυτεπαγγέλτως προσωρινή διαταγή, που καταχωρίζεται κάτω από την αίτηση ή στα πρακτικά, σχετικά με τα μέτρα που πρέπει να ληφθούν έως την έκδοση της απόφασής του για την εξασφάλιση ή τη διατήρηση του δικαιώματος ή τη ρύθμιση της κατάστασης.
2. Για την έκδοση προσωρινής διαταγής καλείται με οποιονδήποτε τρόπο ο καθ' ου η αίτηση, αν ο δικαστής κρίνει αναγκαία την εμφάνισή του. Αν γίνει δεκτό το αίτημα για έκδοση προσωρινής διαταγής, η σχετική αίτηση ασφαλιστικών μέτρων προσδιορίζεται για συζήτηση μέσα σε τριάντα (30) ημέρες. Αν η συζήτηση της αίτησης αναβληθεί, παύει αυτοδικαίως η ισχύς της προσωρινής διαταγής, εκτός αν αυτή παραταθεί από το δικαστήριο που δικάζει την αίτηση. Σε κάθε περίπτωση ο καθ' ου η αίτηση διατηρεί το δικαίωμα να ζητήσει την ανάκληση της προσωρινής διαταγής.
3. Η αίτηση ασφαλιστικών μέτρων επί της οποίας εκδόθηκε προσωρινή διαταγή που έχει ως αντικείμενο την απαγόρευση μεταβολής της πραγματικής ή νομικής κατάστασης ακινήτου ή πλοίου ή αεροσκάφους επιδίδεται στην αρμόδια αρχή και εγγράφεται στο αντίστοιχο βιβλίο, σύμφωνα με τις διατάξεις των άρθρων 713 και 714, οι οποίες εφαρμόζονται αναλόγως.

Άρθρο 692

1. Το δικαστήριο διατάζει τα ασφαλιστικά μέτρα που κατά την κρίση του αρμόζουν σε κάθε περίπτωση, και δεν έχει υποχρέωση να διατάξει το μέτρο που ζητείται.
2. Για την εξασφάλιση ή τη διατήρηση του ίδιου δικαιώματος μπορούν να διαταχθούν περισσότερα ασφαλιστικά μέτρα, αν είναι αναγκαίο.
3. Περισσότερα ασφαλιστικά μέτρα από όσα είναι αναγκαία για να αποφευχθεί επικείμενος κίνδυνος ή για να ρυθμιστεί επείγουσα περίπτωση δεν πρέπει να διατάσσονται και ανάμεσα σε περισσότερα πρέπει να προτιμάται εκείνο που είναι λιγότερο πιεστικό.
4. Τα ασφαλιστικά μέτρα δεν πρέπει να συνίστανται στην ικανοποίηση του δικαιώματος του οποίου ζητείται η εξασφάλιση ή η διατήρηση.
5. Τα ασφαλιστικά μέτρα δεν πρέπει να προσβάλλουν δικαιώματα τρίτων, ιδίως αν το ασφαλιζόμενο δικαίωμα εξαρτάται από αίρεση ή προθεσμία.
6. [Καταργείται]

Άρθρο 693

1. Αν το ασφαλιστικό μέτρο έχει διαταχθεί πριν από την άσκηση της αγωγής για την κύρια υπόθεση, ο δικαστής που το διατάσσει, μπορεί να ορίσει, κατά την κρίση του, προθεσμία για την άσκησή της, όχι όμως μικρότερη από εξήντα (60) ημέρες από τη δημοσίευση της απόφασης των ασφαλιστικών μέτρων.
2. Αν παρέλθει άπρακτη η προθεσμία της παραγράφου 1, αίρεται αυτοδικαίως το ασφαλιστικό μέτρο, εκτός αν ο αιτών μέσα στην προθεσμία αυτή επιδώσει διαταγή πληρωμής.

Άρθρο 694

1. Το δικαστήριο διατάζοντας ασφαλιστικά μέτρα έχει το δικαίωμα και αυτεπαγγέλτως να υποχρεώσει τον αιτούντα σε εγγυοδοσία.
2. Αν δεν χορηγηθεί η κατά την παρ. 1 εγγυοδοσία μέσα στην προθεσμία που όρισε το δικαστήριο, αίρεται αυτοδικαίως το ασφαλιστικό μέτρο.

Άρθρο 695

Η απόφαση των ασφαλιστικών μέτρων ισχύει προσωρινά και δεν επηρεάζει την κύρια υπόθεση.

Article 691A

1. Where the court deems it necessary, it has the right, as soon as the application is filed and before it hands down a judgment, to issue *ex officio* an interim order, which shall be recorded at the end of the application or in the transcript, concerning the measures that must be adopted until its judgment on safeguarding or preserving the right or regulating the situation has been handed down.

2. If the judge deems this necessary, the respondent shall be summoned in any manner [to appear at] the issuing of the interim order. If the request for an interim order is accepted, the hearing date of the application for interim measures in question shall be set within [the next] 30 days. If the hearing of the application is adjourned, the interim order shall automatically cease to be valid, unless its validity is extended by the court trying the application. In all cases, the respondent reserves the right to request that the interim order be revoked.

3. The application for interim measures on which an interim order was issued prohibiting any change to the actual or legal status of an immovable or ship or aircraft shall be served on the competent authority and entered in the corresponding register, in accordance with the provisions of Articles 713 and 714, which apply *mutatis mutandis*.

Article 692

1. The court shall order the interim measures which, in its view, are appropriate in each case, and shall not be obligated to order the measure requested.

2. Where necessary, several interim measures may be ordered to safeguard or preserve the same right.

3. The court must not order more interim measures than those necessary to avert an imminent danger or to regulate urgent circumstances, and, when it has the option of granting several measures, it must prefer the least onerous measure.

4. Interim measures must not entail satisfaction of the right whose safeguarding or preservation is being requested.

5. Interim measures must not infringe third-party rights, particularly if the right being protected is subject to a condition or term.

6. [Repealed]

Article 693

1. If the interim measure was ordered prior to the filing of the action concerning the main case, the judge ordering the measure may, at their discretion, set a deadline for filing the action, which shall not be shorter than 60 days from the date the judgment granting interim measures was handed down.

2. If the deadline set in paragraph 1 lapses without the relevant steps having been taken, the interim measure shall be lifted automatically, unless the applicant serves a payment order within that deadline.

Article 694

1. When ordering interim measures, the court also has the right *ex officio* to order the applicant to provide surety.

2. If the surety referred to in paragraph 1 is not paid within the deadline set by the court, the interim measure shall be lifted automatically.

Article 695

The judgment granting interim measures has temporary effect and does not affect the main case.

Άρθρο 696

1. Αν κάποιος δεν έλαβε μέρος ή δεν κλήθηκε κατά συζήτηση αίτησης στην οποία εκδόθηκε απόφαση που διέταξε ασφαλιστικά μέτρα ή μεταρρύθμισε ή ανακάλεσε απόφαση ασφαλιστικών μέτρων και έχει έννομο συμφέρον, δικαιούται να ζητήσει την ανάκληση ή τη μεταρρύθμιση της απόφασης από το δικαστήριο που την εξέδωσε.
2. [Καταργείται]
3. Το δικαστήριο που διέταξε ασφαλιστικά μέτρα, έως την συζήτηση της αγωγής που αφορά την κύρια υπόθεση, έχει δικαίωμα, με αίτηση όποιου έχει έννομο συμφέρον, να μεταρρυθμίσει ή να ανακαλέσει ολικά ή εν μέρει την απόφασή του εφόσον επήλθε μεταβολή των πραγμάτων που δικαιολογεί την ανάκληση ή τη μεταρρύθμισή της.

Άρθρο 697

Το αρμόδιο για την κύρια υπόθεση δικαστήριο όσο διαρκεί η εκκρεμοδικία μπορεί, με αίτηση του διαδίκου που έχει έννομο συμφέρον, η οποία υποβάλλεται και αυτοτελώς, να μεταρρυθμίσει ή να ανακαλέσει ολικά ή εν μέρει την απόφαση που δέχεται ή απορρίπτει αίτηση ασφαλιστικών μέτρων. Ο δικαστής, και στα πολυμελή δικαστήρια ο πρόεδρος, ορίζουν τη δικάσιμο και την προθεσμία κλήτευσης.

Άρθρο 698

1. Η απόφαση που διέταξε ασφαλιστικό μέτρο ανακαλείται ολικά ή εν μέρει
α) αν εκδοθεί οριστική απόφαση στη δίκη για την κύρια υπόθεση κατά εκείνου ο οποίος είχε ζητήσει το ασφαλιστικό μέτρο και γίνει τελεσίδικη,
β) αν εκδοθεί οριστική απόφαση που τον ωφελεί, και εκτελεστεί,
γ) αν συμφωνηθεί συμβιβασμός για την κύρια υπόθεση,
δ) αν περάσουν τριάντα ημέρες από την κατάργηση ή περάτωση της δίκης με άλλο τρόπο.
2. Η ανάκληση που αναφέρεται στην παρ. 1 γίνεται με αίτηση εκείνου που έχει έννομο συμφέρον, αν η κύρια υπόθεση είναι εκκρεμής, από το δικαστήριο στο οποίο εκκρεμεί, και σε κάθε άλλη περίπτωση από το δικαστήριο που διέταξε το ασφαλιστικό μέτρο.

Άρθρο 699

Αποφάσεις που δέχονται ή απορρίπτουν αιτήσεις ασφαλιστικών μέτρων ή αιτήσεις για ανάκληση ή για μεταρρύθμιση των μέτρων αυτών, δεν προσβάλλονται με κανένα ένδικο μέσο, εκτός αν ορίζεται διαφορετικά.

Άρθρο 700

1. Η απόφαση που διατάζει ασφαλιστικό μέτρο εκτελείται κατά τις διατάξεις της αναγκαστικής εκτέλεσης.
2. Η εκτέλεση του μέτρου που έχει διαταχθεί γίνεται χωρίς να εκδοθεί απόγραφο, με βάση αντίγραφο ή απόσπασμα της απόφασης που το διατάζει, χωρίς να απαιτείται προηγούμενη κοινοποίηση αντιγράφου της. Στις περιπτώσεις όμως των άρθρων 728 και 731 έως 735 απαιτείται η επίδοση επιταγής, και άλλη πράξη εκτέλεσης δεν μπορεί να γίνει πριν περάσουν είκοσι τέσσερις ώρες από την επίδοσή της.
3. Οι προσωρινές διαταγές που αναφέρονται στο άρθρο 691Α εκτελούνται μόλις καταχωριστούν, κάτω από την αίτηση ή στα πρακτικά, με βάση σημείωση του δικαστή που τις εξέδωσε και, αν πρόκειται για πολυμελές δικαστήριο, του προέδρου του.
4. Η εκτέλεση των διατάξεων των αποφάσεων για ασφαλιστικά μέτρα, που αφορούν τα δικαστικά έξοδα, γίνεται με βάση αντίγραφό τους και ύστερα από κοινοποίηση αντιγράφου της απόφασης σε εκείνον κατά του οποίου στρέφεται η αίτηση, είκοσι τέσσερις ώρες πριν από την εκτέλεση.

Article 696

1. If a party did not participate in or was not summoned to the application hearing where a judgment granting interim measures was handed down or amended or revoked and said party has a legitimate interest, they may request that the judgment granting interim measures be revoked or amended by the court that handed it down.

2. [Repealed]

3. Up until the hearing of the action in the main case, the court that ordered interim measures has the right, following an application filed by any person with a legitimate interest, to amend or revoke its judgment granting interim measures, whether in whole or in part, where there was a change in circumstances that justifies the judgment being amended or revoked.

Article 697

During *lis pendens*, the court with jurisdiction over the main case may, following an application by the party in the proceedings with a legitimate interest that may also be submitted separately, amend or revoke the judgment accepting or dismissing the application for interim measures, whether in whole or in part. The judge, and in cases of multi-member courts the presiding judge, shall set the hearing date and deadline for summonsing.

Article 698

1. The judgment granting interim measures shall be revoked in whole or in part[:]

a) if a final judgment is handed down during proceedings in the main case against the person who had requested the interim measure, and said judgment becomes *de jure* non-appealable;

b) if a final judgment benefiting said person is handed down and enforced;

c) if a settlement is agreed upon in the main case;

d) if 30 days elapse from the date the proceedings were discontinued or concluded in any other manner.

2. The revocation referred to in paragraph 1 shall be effected following an application filed by any person with a legitimate interest, if the main case is pending, by the court before which it is pending, and in all other cases by the court that ordered the interim measure.

Article 699

Unless otherwise provided for, judgments accepting or dismissing applications for interim measures or applications to revoke or amend such measures may not be contested by any legal remedy.

Article 700

1. Judgments granting interim measures shall be enforced in accordance with the provisions on compulsory enforcement.

2. The measure granted shall be enforced without an enforcement precept being issued, on the basis of a copy or excerpt of the judgment granting the measure, and without requiring prior notification of a copy thereof. However, in the cases referred to in Articles 728 and 731 to 735, an [enforcement] order must be issued, and no other enforcement steps may be taken before 24 hours have elapsed from its service.

3. The interim orders referred to in Article 691A shall be enforced upon being recorded at the end of the application or in the transcript, on the basis of a note prepared by the judge who issued them and, in the case of a multi-member court, by its presiding judge.

4. The orders concerning court costs contained in judgments granting interim measures shall be enforced on the basis of a copy of said orders, provided said copy has been notified to the respondent 24 hours prior to enforcement.

Άρθρο 701

Αν έχουν διαταχθεί ασφαλιστικά μέτρα με τον όρο της εγγυοδοσίας, δεν είναι δυνατό να εκτελεστεί η απόφαση που τα διατάζει πριν από την εγγυοδοσία.

Άρθρο 702

1. Διαφορές που αφορούν την εκτέλεση απόφασης που διατάζει ασφαλιστικά ή ανακαλεί ολικά ή εν μέρει απόφαση γι' αυτά δικάζονται από το δικαστήριο που εξέδωσε την απόφαση και εφαρμόζονται οι διατάξεις των άρθρων 686 επ.

2. Σε πολύ επείγουσες περιπτώσεις τις διαφορές που αναφέρονται στην παρ. 1 τις δικάζει το μονομελές πρωτοδικείο του τόπου όπου γίνεται η εκτέλεση της απόφασης και, όπου δεν υπάρχει μονομελές πρωτοδικείο, το ειρηνοδικείο, εφαρμόζοντας τις διατάξεις των άρθρων 686 έως 688, 690 έως 692, 695 και 699. Ανάκληση της απόφασης του μονομελούς πρωτοδικείου ή του ειρηνοδικείου μπορεί να ζητηθεί για οποιοδήποτε λόγο από το αρμόδιο κατά την παρ. 1 δικαστήριο.

3. Η εκτέλεση των αποφάσεων που διατάζουν ασφαλιστικά μέτρα, μπορεί, με αίτηση εκείνου που έχει έννομο συμφέρον, να περιοριστεί σε ορισμένα περιουσιακά στοιχεία, αν το δικαστήριο πιθανολογεί ότι τα στοιχεία αυτά είναι αρκετά για την εξασφάλιση ή τη διατήρηση του δικαιώματος.

Άρθρο 703

Αν απορριφθεί τελεσίδικα ως αβάσιμη η αγωγή για την κύρια υπόθεση, όποιος ζήτησε να διαταχθούν ασφαλιστικά μέτρα είναι υποχρεωμένος να καταβάλει αποζημίωση για τη ζημία που προξένησε από την εκτέλεση της απόφασης που τα διέταξε ή από την εγγύηση που δόθηκε, μόνο αν γνώριζε ή από βαριά αμέλεια αγνοούσε ότι δεν υπήρχε το δικαίωμα.

ΚΕΦΑΛΑΙΟ Β'
Εγγυοδοσία.

Άρθρο 704

Το δικαστήριο δικαιούται να διατάξει ως ασφαλιστικό μέτρο εγγυοδοσία του οφειλέτη υπέρ του αιτούντος για την εξασφάλιση χρηματικής απαίτησης ή απαίτησης που μπορεί να μετατραπεί σε χρήματα ή άλλου δικαιώματος.

Άρθρο 705

1. Αν διατάχθηκαν ασφαλιστικά μέτρα για να εξασφαλιστεί χρηματική απαίτηση ή απαίτηση που μπορεί να μετατραπεί σε χρήματα, το δικαστήριο που τα διέταξε ή το δικαστήριο που δικάζει την κύρια υπόθεση έχει υποχρέωση, με αίτηση όποιου έχει έννομο συμφέρον, να αντικαταστήσει τα ασφαλιστικά μέτρα που είχαν διαταχθεί με εγγυοδοσία υπέρ εκείνου που τα ζήτησε.

2. Αν διατάχθηκαν ασφαλιστικά μέτρα για να εξασφαλιστεί άλλο δικαίωμα, το δικαστήριο που τα διέταξε ή το δικαστήριο που δικάζει την κύρια υπόθεση, έχει το δικαίωμα, με αίτηση όποιου έχει έννομο συμφέρον, μεταρρυθμίζοντας τη σχετική απόφαση, να διατάξει εγγυοδοσία υπέρ εκείνου που τα ζήτησε μόνο αν κατά τις περιστάσεις εξασφαλίζεται πλήρως το δικαίωμα.

ΚΕΦΑΛΑΙΟ Γ'
Εγγραφή προσημείωσης υποθήκης.

Άρθρο 706

1. Το δικαστήριο δικαιούται να διατάξει ως ασφαλιστικό μέτρο την εγγραφή προσημείωσης υποθήκης.

2. Η απόφαση που διατάζει να εγγραφεί η προσημείωση υποθήκης πρέπει να ορίζει και το ποσό που ασφαλίζεται με την προσημείωση.

Article 701

If interim measures have been granted subject to provision of surety, the judgment in question may not be enforced prior to provision of said surety.

Article 702

1. Disputes concerning the enforcement of a judgment granting interim measures or revoking a judgment concerning such measures in whole or in part shall be tried by the court that handed down the judgment, and the provisions of Articles 686 *et seq.* apply.
2. In very urgent cases, the disputes referred to in paragraph 1 shall be tried by the single-member court of first instance of the place where the judgment is being enforced and, where there is no single-member court of first instance, the court of the peace, and the provisions of Articles 686 to 688, 690 to 692, and 695 to 699 apply. The court with jurisdiction under paragraph 1 may request that the judgment handed down by the single-member court of first instance or the court of the peace be revoked on any grounds.
3. The enforcement of judgments ordering interim measures may, following an application filed by any person with a legitimate interest, be restricted to specific assets, if the court considers it likely, on the balance of probabilities, that these assets suffice to safeguard or preserve the right.

Article 703

If the action regarding the main case is dismissed as unfounded by means of a *de jure* non-appealable judgment, the person who requested that interim measures be granted is obligated to pay compensation for the losses they caused through enforcement of the judgment that granted such measures or the surety provided, only if they knew or, through gross negligence were not aware, that the right did not exist.

CHAPTER II
Provision of surety

Article 704

The court may order provision of surety by the debtor for the applicant as an interim measure to safeguard a monetary claim or claim that can be [valued in monetary terms] or other right.

Article 705

1. If interim measures were granted to safeguard a monetary claim or claim that can be [valued in monetary terms], the court that ordered them or the court trying the main case is obligated, following an application filed by any person with a legitimate interest, to replace the interim measures granted with provision of surety for the person who requested the interim measures.
2. If interim measures were granted to safeguard an other right, the court that granted them or the court trying the main case has the right to amend the judgment in question, following an application filed by any person with a legitimate interest, and order provision of surety for the person who requested the interim measures only if the right is fully safeguarded under the circumstances.

CHAPTER III
Registration of prenotation of mortgage

Article 706

1. The court may order registration of prenotation of mortgage as an interim measure.
2. The judgment ordering registration of prenotation of mortgage must also specify the amount secured by the prenotation.

ΚΕΦΑΛΑΙΟ Δ'
Συντηρητική κατάσχεση.

Άρθρο 707

Το δικαστήριο δικαιούται να διατάξει ως ασφαλιστικό μέτρο τη συντηρητική κατάσχεση κινητών, ακινήτων, εμπράγματων δικαιωμάτων επάνω σ' αυτά, απαιτήσεων και γενικά όλων των περιουσιακών στοιχείων του οφειλέτη, είτε βρίσκονται στα χέρια του είτε στα χέρια τρίτου.

Άρθρο 708

Η απόφαση που διατάζει συντηρητική κατάσχεση πρέπει να καθορίζει το ποσό για το οποίο διατάσσεται.

Άρθρο 709

Συντηρητική κατάσχεση πλοίου ή αεροσκάφους μπορεί να γίνει μόνο αν στην απόφαση αναφέρεται ειδικά το πλοίο ή το αεροσκάφος στο οποίο πρόκειται να επιβληθεί.

Άρθρο 710

Δεν επιτρέπεται συντηρητική κατάσχεση πραγμάτων τα οποία είναι ακατάσχετα κατά τις διατάξεις της αναγκαστικής εκτέλεσης, καθώς και εκείνων που μπορούν να υποστούν άμεση φθορά.

Άρθρο 711

1. Η συντηρητική κατάσχεση κινητών ή εμπράγματων δικαιωμάτων επάνω σ' αυτά στα χέρια του οφειλέτη γίνεται κατά τις διατάξεις της αναγκαστικής κατάσχεσης, χωρίς να επιδοθεί προηγουμένως η απόφαση που διατάζει την κατάσχεση. Αντίγραφο ή περίληψη της έκθεσης της κατάσχεσης επιδίδεται σε εκείνον σε βάρος του οποίου επιβάλλεται η κατάσχεση, αν δεν ήταν παρών κατά την επιβολή της, το αργότερο την επόμενη ημέρα εφόσον έχει την κατοικία του στον τόπο της κατάσχεσης, διαφορετικά μέσα σε οκτώ ημέρες από αυτήν.

2. Αντίγραφο της έκθεσης κατάσχεσης επιδίδεται από τον δικαστικό επιμελητή στον γραμματέα του ειρηνοδικείου του τόπου της κατάσχεσης, ο οποίος είναι υποχρεωμένος να καταχωρίσει περίληψή της σε ειδικό βιβλίο με αλφαβητικό ευρετήριο εκείνων κατά των οποίων έχει επιβληθεί κατάσχεση.

Άρθρο 712

1. Η συντηρητική κατάσχεση απαιτήσεων ή κινητών στα χέρια τρίτου γίνεται με επίδοση στον τρίτο αντιγράφου της απόφασης που τη διατάζει με επιταγή να μην εξοφλήσει την απαίτηση ή να μην παραδώσει τα κινητά, καθώς και με επίδοση μέσα σε οκτώ ημέρες σε εκείνον κατά του οποίου στρέφεται η κατάσχεση εγγράφου στο οποίο αναφέρεται η κατάσχεση που έχει επιβληθεί στα χέρια του τρίτου, αλλιώς η κατάσχεση είναι άκυρη. Στην κατάσχεση αυτή εφαρμόζονται οι διατάξεις της αναγκαστικής κατάσχεσης απαιτήσεων ή κινητών σε χέρια τρίτου.

2. Ο τρίτος, εκείνος που επέβαλε την κατάσχεση και ο οφειλέτης έχουν όλες τις υποχρεώσεις και τα δικαιώματα που προβλέπουν οι διατάξεις της αναγκαστικής κατάσχεσης απαιτήσεων ή κινητών στα χέρια τρίτου, και εφαρμόζεται η διαδικασία για την άσκηση ή τη διαφύλαξή τους που ορίζεται στις διατάξεις αυτές.

CHAPTER IV
Preventive attachment, garnishment and arrest

Article 707

The court may order preventive attachment of movables, immovables, rights *in rem* thereon, claims and, generally, all the assets of the debtor, whether held by the debtor or a third party, as an interim measure.

Article 708

The judgment ordering preventive attachment must specify the amount for which it is being ordered.

Article 709

Preventive arrest of a ship or aircraft may only take place if the judgment specifically names the ship or aircraft which is to be arrested.

Article 710

Preventive attachment of things that are non-attachable/non-garnishable under the provisions on compulsory enforcement and things that can quickly become spoiled is not allowed.

Article 711

1. Preventive attachment of movables or rights *in rem* thereon held by the debtor shall be done in accordance with the provisions on compulsory enforcement, without the judgment ordering attachment having been previously served. A copy or summary of the attachment report shall be served on the person on whom attachment is imposed, if they were not present during its imposition, no later than the following working day, provided their place of residence is at the place where attachment took place, otherwise within eight days of the attachment.

2. A copy of the attachment report shall be served by the court process server on the registrar of the court of the peace of the place where attachment took place, who is obligated to enter a summary thereof in a special register with an alphabetical index of the persons on whom attachment has been imposed.

Article 712

1. Preventive garnishment of claims or movables shall be done by means of service of a copy of the judgment ordering garnishment on the third party, ordering them not to pay the claim or not to hand over the movables, as well as by means of service of a garnishment order on the person whom the garnishment concerns within eight days, otherwise the garnishment is null and void. The provisions on compulsory enforcement of claims or movables held by a third party apply to such garnishment.

2. The third party, the person who procured garnishment and the debtor have all the obligations and rights set out in the provisions on compulsory enforcement of claims or movables held by a third party, and the procedure on their exercise or safeguarding set out in said provisions apply.

Άρθρο 713

1. Η συντηρητική κατάσχεση πλοίου, αεροσκάφους ή εμπράγματου δικαιώματος επάνω σ' αυτά στα χέρια του οφειλέτη ή τρίτου γίνεται με επίδοση στον οφειλέτη αντιγράφου της απόφασης που διατάζει την κατάσχεση. Αν πρόκειται για κατάσχεση πλοίων νηολογημένων στην Ελλάδα ή αεροσκαφών που είναι γραμμένα σε μητρώο το οποίο τηρείται στην Ελλάδα, αντίγραφο της απόφασης επιδίδεται και στην αρχή που τηρεί το νηολόγιο ή το μητρώο. Αν η συντηρητική κατάσχεση γίνεται στα χέρια τρίτου, αντίγραφο της απόφασης που τη διατάζει επιδίδεται και στον τρίτο.
2. Η παραγγελία για την επίδοση αντιγράφου της απόφασης που διατάζει τη συντηρητική κατάσχεση πρέπει να προσδιορίζει το πλοίο, το αεροσκάφος ή το εμπράγματο δικαίωμα το οποίο κατάσχεται και το ποσό για το οποίο γίνεται η συντηρητική κατάσχεση.
3. Η αρχή που τηρεί το νηολόγιο ή το μητρώο αεροσκαφών εγγράφει τη συντηρητική κατάσχεση στο νηολόγιο ή στο μητρώο των αεροσκαφών. Για την εγγραφή, την εξάλειψη και τη σειρά των εγγραφών εφαρμόζονται οι διατάξεις της αναγκαστικής κατάσχεσης.

Άρθρο 714

1. Η συντηρητική κατάσχεση ακινήτου ή εμπράγματου δικαιώματος επάνω σ' αυτό στα χέρια του οφειλέτη γίνεται με κοινοποίηση αντιγράφου της απόφασης που διατάζει την κατάσχεση στον οφειλέτη και στην αρχή που είναι αρμόδια να τηρεί το βιβλίο κατασχέσεως της περιφέρειας του τόπου όπου βρίσκεται το ακίνητο.
2. Η παραγγελία για την επίδοση αντιγράφου της απόφασης που διατάζει τη συντηρητική κατάσχεση πρέπει να προσδιορίζει το ακίνητο ή το εμπράγματο δικαίωμα που κατάσχεται και το ποσό για το οποίο γίνεται η συντηρητική κατάσχεση.
3. Η αρχή που τηρεί το βιβλίο κατασχέσεων εγγράφει χωρίς υπαίτια καθυστέρηση τη συντηρητική κατάσχεση στο βιβλίο κατασχέσεων. Για την εγγραφή, την εξάλειψη και τη σειρά των εγγραφών εφαρμόζονται οι διατάξεις της αναγκαστικής κατάσχεσης.

Άρθρο 715

1. Απαγορεύεται και είναι άκυρη υπέρ εκείνου που επέβαλε την κατάσχεση η διάθεση των πραγμάτων που κατασχέθηκαν από εκείνον σε βάρος του οποίου έγινε η κατάσχεση. Σε χρηματικές απαιτήσεις η απαγόρευση ισχύει μόνο έως το ποσό για το οποίο έγινε η κατάσχεση.
2. Τα αποτελέσματα της κατάσχεσης που αναφέρονται στην παρ. 1 αρχίζουν
α) σε κατάσχεση κινητών ή εμπράγματων δικαιωμάτων επάνω σε κινητά στα χέρια του οφειλέτη, από την κατάσχεση, αν ήταν παρών κατά την επιβολή της, διαφορετικά από την επίδοση από το δικαστικό επιμελητή, σύμφωνα με το άρθρο 711,
β) σε κατάσχεση στα χέρια του τρίτου απαιτήσεων ή κινητών, από την επίδοση του εγγράφου που ανακοινώνει την κατάσχεση σε εκείνον κατά του οποίου στρέφεται, σύμφωνα με το άρθρο 712,
γ) σε κατάσχεση ακινήτου, πλοίου ή αεροσκάφους ή εμπράγματου δικαιώματος επάνω σ' αυτά, από την κοινοποίηση στον οφειλέτη της απόφασης που διατάζει την κατάσχεση.
3. Στη συντηρητική κατάσχεση ακινήτου, πλοίου, αεροσκάφους ή εμπράγματου δικαιώματος επάνω σ' αυτά η ακυρότητα που αναφέρεται στην παρ. 1 ισχύει ως προς τους τρίτους μόνο αν κατά το χρόνο της διάθεσης είχε γίνει η εγγραφή της κατάσχεσης στο βιβλίο κατασχέσεων, στο νηολόγιο ή στο μητρώο αεροσκαφών.
4. Αν έγινε κατάσχεση απαίτησης στα χέρια τρίτου, απαγορεύεται και είναι άκυρη υπέρ εκείνου που επέβαλε την κατάσχεση η εξόφληση από τον τρίτο της απαίτησης που έχει κατασχεθεί ή ο συμψηφισμός της με μεταγενέστερη απαίτηση. Αν έγινε κατάσχεση κινητών στα χέρια τρίτου, απαγορεύεται και είναι άκυρη υπέρ εκείνου που επέβαλε την κατάσχεση η απόδοση ή η διάθεση των κατασχεμένων.
5. Μέσα σε τριάντα ημέρες από την επίδοση στον οφειλέτη του εγγράφου για την κατάσχεση ο δανειστής οφείλει να ασκήσει εναντίον του αγωγή για την κύρια απαίτηση, που να απευθύνεται στο καθ' ύλη αρμόδιο δικαστήριο. Αν περάσει άπρακτη η προθεσμία αυτή, αίρεται αυτοδικαίως το ασφαλιστικό μέτρο. Δεν απαιτείται να ασκηθεί αγωγή, αν έχει ήδη ασκηθεί η αγωγή για την κύρια απαίτηση ή η συντηρητική κατάσχεση έγινε με βάση διαταγή πληρωμής ή αν επιδοθεί διαταγή πληρωμής μέσα στην παραπάνω προθεσμία.

Article 713

1. Preventive arrest of a ship, aircraft or right *in rem* thereon held by the debtor or a third party shall be done by means of service on the debtor of a copy of the judgment ordering arrest. In cases of arrest of ships registered in Greece or aircraft entered in a register kept in Greece, a copy of the judgment shall also be served on the authority which keeps the ship or aircraft registry. If the preventive arrest involves a third party, a copy of the judgment ordering it shall also be served on said third party.
2. The order to serve a copy of the judgment on preventive arrest must specify the ship, aircraft or right *in rem* being arrested and the amount for which the preventive arrest is taking place.
3. The authority which keeps the ship or aircraft registry shall enter the preventive arrest in said register. The provisions on compulsory enforcement apply to the registration, striking-out and order of entries.

Article 714

1. The preventive attachment of an immovable or right *in rem* thereon held by the debtor shall be done by notifying a copy of the judgment ordering attachment to the debtor and to the authority responsible for keeping the attachment register for the district where the immovable is located.
2. The order to serve a copy of the judgment on preventive attachment must specify the immovable or right *in rem* being attached and the amount for which preventive attachment is taking place.
3. The authority which keeps the attachment register shall enter the attachment in the attachment register without undue delay. The provisions on compulsory enforcement apply to the registration, striking-out and order of entries.

Article 715

1. The person whom attachment concerns may not dispose of the attached things, and any such disposal is null and void to the benefit of the person who procured attachment. In [cases of] monetary claims, the [above] prohibition shall only apply up to the amount for which attachment was effected.
2. The results of the attachment referred to in paragraph 1 shall commence[:]
a) from the date of attachment, in cases of attachment of movables or rights *in rem* on movables held by the debtor, if the latter was present during its imposition, otherwise from the date of service by the court process server, in accordance with Article 711;
b) from the date of service of the document notifying attachment on the person whom it concerns, in cases of attachment of claims or movables held by a third party, in accordance with Article 712;
c) from the date of notification of the judgment ordering attachment or arrest to the debtor, in cases of attachment of an immovable, or arrest of a ship or aircraft, or right *in rem* thereon.
3. In cases of preventive attachment of an immovable, or preventive arrest of a ship or aircraft, or right *in rem* thereon, the nullity referred to in paragraph 1 shall apply vis-à-vis third parties only if the attachment or arrest had been entered in the attachment register, ship registry or aircraft registry at the time of disposal.
4. If a claim was garnished, paying the attached claim or offsetting it against a subsequent claim is prohibited and null and void vis-à-vis the person who procured attachment. If movables were garnished, the return or disposal of the garnished movables is prohibited and null and void vis-à-vis the person who procured attachment.
5. Within 30 days of service of the attachment document on the debtor, the creditor is obligated to file an action against the debtor regarding the main claim before the court with jurisdiction *ratione materiae*. If this deadline lapses without the relevant steps having been taken, the interim measure shall be lifted automatically. An action need not be filed if the action regarding the main claim has already been filed or the preventive attachment took place on the basis of a payment order or if a payment order is served within the aforesaid deadline.

Άρθρο 716

1. Σε κατάσχεση κινητών στα χέρια του οφειλέτη ή τρίτου τα κινητά μένουν στα χέρια εκείνου που τα κατέχει κατά το χρόνο της κατάσχεσης, ο οποίος γίνεται μεσεγγυούχος.

2. Σε κατάσχεση στα χέρια του οφειλέτη χρημάτων ή άλλων πραγμάτων που κατά το νόμο επιδέχονται κατάθεση, ο δικαστικός επιμελητής τα αφαιρεί και χωρίς καθυστέρηση τα καταθέτει δημοσίως.

3. Σε κατάσχεση στα χέρια τρίτου χρημάτων ή άλλων πραγμάτων που κατά το νόμο επιδέχονται κατάθεση, ο τρίτος εφόσον είναι οφειλέτης έχει την υποχρέωση να τα καταθέσει δημοσίως αμέσως μετά την κατάσχεση αν η εναντίον του απαίτηση είναι ληξιπρόθεσμη, διαφορετικά μόλις λήξει η προθεσμία.

4. Οι διατάξεις των παρ. 2 και 3 δεν εφαρμόζονται, αν ο οφειλέτης ή τρίτος είναι το δημόσιο, νομικό πρόσωπο δημοσίου δικαίου ή τράπεζα.

Άρθρο 717

1. Το δικαστήριο με την απόφαση που διατάζει τη συντηρητική κατάσχεση ή και με μεταγενέστερη απόφασή του ή το δικαστήριο που δικάζει την κύρια υπόθεση και σε επείγουσες περιπτώσεις και ο ειρηνοδίκης του τόπου όπου βρίσκονται τα κατασχεμένα ή σε απαιτήσεις η κατοικία του τρίτου, έχει το δικαίωμα, με αίτηση όποιου έχει έννομο συμφέρον, να διορίσει μεσεγγυούχο άλλο πρόσωπο, εκτός από εκείνα που αναφέρονται στο άρθρο 716 και να διατάξει να παραδοθούν τα πράγματα ή να κατατεθεί σ' αυτόν το οφειλόμενο.

2. Το δικαστήριο που είναι αρμόδιο κατά την παρ. 1 με αίτηση όποιου έχει έννομο συμφέρον έχει δικαίωμα να διατάξει και οποιοδήποτε μέτρο είναι, κατά τις περιστάσεις πρόσφορο για την μεσεγγύηση.

3. Οι αιτήσεις που αναφέρονται στις παρ. 1 και 2 δικάζονται κατά τις διατάξεις του άρθρου 702 και οι αποφάσεις εκτελούνται αμέσως, χωρίς προηγούμενη επίδοσή τους.

4. Δεν είναι δυνατό να διοριστεί μεσεγγυούχος εκείνος που ζήτησε να διαταχθεί η συντηρητική κατάσχεση ή πρόσωπο που συνδέεται με αυτόν με σύμβαση εργασίας, εκτός αν συναινεί ο οφειλέτης.

Άρθρο 718

Οι διατάξεις για το μεσεγγυούχο στην περίπτωση της αναγκαστικής κατάσχεσης εφαρμόζονται και στους κατά τα άρθρα 716 και 717 μεσεγγυούχους.

Άρθρο 719

Αν τα κινητά πράγματα που έχουν κατασχεθεί στα χέρια του οφειλέτη ή τρίτου μπορούν να υποστούν φθορά ή η φύλαξή τους είναι σε σχέση με την αξία τους δαπανηρή, το δικαστήριο που είναι αρμόδιο κατά το άρθρο 171 διατάζει την εκποίησή τους. Το τίμημα από την εκποίηση είναι κατασχεμένο και κατατίθεται δημοσίως.

Άρθρο 720

1. Πλοίο το οποίο έχει κατασχεθεί συντηρητικώς απαγορεύεται να αποπλεύσει και αεροσκάφος να απογειωθεί.

2. Ο λιμενάρχης ή ο αερολιμενάρχης είναι υπεύθυνος για την αναχώρηση του πλοίου ή την απογείωση.

3. Το δικαστήριο το οποίο είναι αρμόδιο κατά το άρθρο 702, με αίτηση οποιουδήποτε έχει έννομο συμφέρον, μπορεί να επιτρέψει ένα ή περισσότερα ταξίδια του πλοίου που έχει κατασχεθεί συντηρητικώς ή μία ή περισσότερες πτήσεις του αεροσκάφους που έχει κατασχεθεί συντηρητικώς, με όποιους όρους θα έκρινε εύλογους και οπωσδήποτε με ασφάλιση του σκάφους για ανάλογο ποσό.

Article 716

1. In cases of attachment of movables held by the debtor or their garnishment, the movables shall continue to be held by the person holding them at the time of attachment/garnishment, who shall become the sequestrator.
2. In cases of attachment of monies or other things which, by law, can be deposited and which are held by the debtor, the court process server shall remove such monies or things and deposit them with the state without delay.
3. In cases of garnishment of monies or other things which, by law, can be deposited, the third party, where they are [also] a debtor, is obligated to deposit them with the state immediately after the garnishment if the claim against them is overdue, otherwise as soon as the deadline lapses.
4. The provisions of paragraph 2 do not apply if the debtor or third party is the Greek State, a body governed by public law or a bank.

Article 717

1. In the judgment ordering preventive attachment or in a subsequent judgment, the court that handed it down or the court trying the main case or, in urgent circumstances, the court of the peace judge of the place where the things are located or, in cases of claims, the place where the third party has their place of residence, may, following an application filed by any person with a legitimate interest, appoint a different person as sequestrator, other than the persons referred to in Article 716, and order that the things be handed over to or that the amount owed be deposited with the said sequestrator.
2. Following an application filed by any person with a legitimate interest, the court with jurisdiction under paragraph 1 may also order any measure which, under the circumstances, is expedient for the sequestration.
3. The applications referred to in paragraphs 1 and 2 shall be tried in accordance with the provisions of Article 702, and the judgments handed down shall be enforced immediately without having been previously served.
4. The person who requested preventive attachment or a person associated with them under an employment contract may not be appointed as sequestrator, unless the debtor consents.

Article 718

The provisions on sequestrators in cases of compulsory attachment also apply to the sequestrators referred to in Articles 716 and 717.

Article 719

If the attached movables held by the debtor or garnished movables can become spoiled or their safekeeping is costly in relation to their value, the court with jurisdiction under Article 171 shall order their sale. The sale proceeds shall be attached/garnished and deposited with the state.

Article 720

1. Any ship or aircraft made subject to preventive arrest is prohibited from leaving port or taking off.
2. The harbour master of airport manager shall be responsible for the departure of the ship or take-off of the aircraft.
3. Following an application filed by any person with a legitimate interest, the court with jurisdiction under Article 702 may allow the ship or aircraft made subject to preventive arrest [to make] one or more voyages or flights, under any conditions deemed reasonable and, in all cases, having insured the ship [or aircraft] for an appropriate amount.

Άρθρο 721

Συντηρητική ή αναγκαστική κατάσχεση μπορεί να επιβληθεί και σε αντικείμενα τα οποία έχουν ήδη κατασχεθεί συντηρητικώς.

Άρθρο 722

1. Όποιος έχει κατασχέσει συντηρητικώς κινητά ή ακίνητα ή εμπράγματα δικαιώματα επάνω σ' αυτά, αν η αγωγή για την κύρια υπόθεση γίνει δεκτή, και η σχετική απόφαση είναι εκτελεστή, έχει δικαίωμα, με βάση απόγραφο της απόφασης, να επιχειρήσει αναγκαστική εκτέλεση, χωρίς αναγκαστική κατάσχεσή τους.

2. Όποιος έχει κατασχέσει συντηρητικώς απαίτηση στα χέρια τρίτου γίνεται, από την τελεσιδικία της απόφασης που δέχεται την αγωγή για την κύρια υπόθεση, δικαιούχος ολόκληρης της απαίτησης ή μέρους της, ανάλογα με το περιεχόμενο της απόφασης.

3. Οι διαφορές που αναφέρονται στις παρ. 1 και 2 δικάζονται κατά τις διατάξεις του άρθρου 702 από το αρμόδιο, σύμφωνα με το άρθρο αυτό, δικαστήριο.

Άρθρο 723

Αν όσο ισχύει η συντηρητική κατάσχεση γίνει αναγκαστική εκτέλεση επάνω στα κατασχεμένα, εκείνος που έχει επιβάλει τη συντηρητική κατάσχεση μετέχει προσωρινά στη διανομή και κατατάσσεται τυχαίως, σύμφωνα με τις διατάξεις της αναγκαστικής εκτέλεσης.

Άρθρο 724

1. Ο δανειστής μπορεί με βάση οριστική απόφαση, καθώς και με διαταγή πληρωμής χρηματικών απαιτήσεων να ζητήσει εγγραφή προσημείωσης υποθήκης και να επιβάλει συντηρητική κατάσχεση στα χέρια του οφειλέτη ή τρίτου για το ποσό που επιδικάζεται με την απόφαση ή ορίζεται ότι πρέπει να καταβληθεί με τη διαταγή πληρωμής.

2. Το δικαστήριο που εξέδωσε την οριστική απόφαση ή τη διαταγή πληρωμής μπορεί με αίτηση εκείνου κατά του οποίου στρέφονται και κατά τη διαδικασία του άρθρου 702 παρ. 1, να αναστείλει ολικά ή εν μέρει την εκτέλεση των ασφαλιστικών μέτρων που αναφέρονται στην παρ. 1, αν πιθανολογείται η εξόφληση ή η ανυπαρξία, ολική ή εν μέρει, της απαίτησης για την οποία έχει εκδοθεί η οριστική απόφαση ή η διαταγή πληρωμής ή να περιορίσει την εκτέλεση σε ορισμένα περιουσιακά στοιχεία, αν πιθανολογείται ότι τα στοιχεία αυτά είναι επαρκή για την εξασφάλιση της απαίτησης.

ΚΕΦΑΛΑΙΟ Ε'
Δικαστική μεσεγγύηση

Άρθρο 725

1. Το δικαστήριο δικαιούται να διατάξει ως ασφαλιστικό μέτρο τη δικαστική μεσεγγύηση κινητών ή ακινήτων ή ομάδας πραγμάτων ή επιχείρησης, αν υπάρχει διαφορά σχετική με την κυριότητα, τη νομή ή την κατοχή ή οποιαδήποτε άλλη διαφορά σχετική με αυτά ή αν κατά τις διατάξεις του ουσιαστικού δικαίου μπορεί να ζητηθεί η μεσεγγύηση.

2. Το δικαστήριο δικαιούται να διατάξει ως ασφαλιστικό μέτρο τη δικαστική μεσεγγύηση εμπορικών ή επαγγελματικών βιβλίων, εγγράφων, δειγμάτων και κάθε άλλου πράγματος, αν ο αιτών έχει δικαίωμα να ζητήσει την επίδειξή τους κατά τις διατάξεις του ουσιαστικού δικαίου.

Article 721

Preventive or compulsory attachment may also be imposed on things that have already been made subject to preventive attachment.

Article 722

1. If the action in the main case is accepted and the relevant judgment is enforceable, any person who has procured preventive attachment of movables or immovables or rights *in rem* thereon has the right, on the basis of an enforcement precept of the judgment, to carry out compulsory enforcement with compulsory attachment of the foregoing.
2. From the date the judgment accepting the action in the main case becomes *de jure* non-appealable, any person who has procured preventive attachment of a claim held by a third party shall become entitled to all or part of the claim, depending on the content of the judgment.
3. The disputes referred to in paragraphs 1 and 2 shall be tried in accordance with the provisions of Article 702 by the court with jurisdiction under that Article.

Article 723

If the attached things are made subject to compulsory enforcement during the preventive attachment period, the person who procured preventive attachment shall temporarily participate in the partition and shall be ranked without preference, in accordance with the provisions on compulsory enforcement.

Article 724

1. The creditor may, on the basis of a final judgment [or] a payment order for monetary claims, request registration of prenotation of mortgage and procure preventive attachment [of things] held by the debtor or garnishment for the amount awarded in the judgment or specified as payable in the payment order.
2. The court that handed down the final judgment or issued the payment order may, following an application filed by the person they concern and under the procedure laid down in Article 702(1), stay enforcement of the interim measures referred to in paragraph 1 in whole or in part if it is considered likely, on the balance of probabilities, that the claim for which the final judgment was handed down or the payment order was issued has been paid in full or does not exist, whether in whole or in part, or limit enforcement to specific assets, if it is considered likely, on the balance of probabilities, that these assets suffice to safeguard the claim.

CHAPTER V
Judicial sequestration

Article 725

1. The court may order the interim measure of judicial sequestration of movables or immovables or groups of things or an enterprise if there is a dispute regarding ownership, possession or detentorship or any other dispute relating thereto, or if sequestration can be requested under the provisions of substantive law.
2. The court may order the interim measure of judicial sequestration of commercial or professional ledgers, documents, samples and any other thing if the applicant has the right to request their demonstration under the provisions of substantive law.

Άρθρο 726

1. Η απόφαση που διατάζει τη δικαστική μεσεγγύηση πρέπει να καθορίζει τα αντικείμενα τα οποία θέτει υπό μεσεγγύηση, να διορίζει μεσεγγυούχο και να διατάζει την παράδοσή τους σ' αυτόν. Αν τα πράγματα επιδέχονται κατά το νόμο κατάθεση, διατάζει τη δημόσια κατάθεσή τους.
2. Το δικαστήριο που διέταξε τη δικαστική μεσεγγύηση ή το δικαστήριο που δικάζει την κύρια υπόθεση μπορεί να διατάξει την αντικατάσταση του μεσεγγυούχου, καθώς και κάθε κατά την κρίση του, πρόσφορο μέτρο για τη μεσεγγύηση εφαρμόζοντας τις διατάξεις του άρθρου 702.
3. Μεσεγγυούχος μπορεί να διοριστεί και εκείνος που νέμεται ή κατέχει τα πράγματα και εκείνος που ζήτησε τη δικαστική μεσεγγύηση. Σε δικαστική μεσεγγύηση επιχείρησης, μεσεγγυούχος διορίζεται ο οφειλέτης. Αν συντρέχουν σπουδαίοι λόγοι, το δικαστήριο διορίζει άλλον μεσεγγυούχο.
4. Οι αποφάσεις που εκδίδονται κατά τις διατάξεις των παρ. 1 και 2 εκτελούνται αμέσως, χωρίς προηγούμενη επίδοσή τους.
5. Οι σχετικές με το μεσεγγυούχο διατάξεις στην περίπτωση αναγκαστικής κατάσχεσης εφαρμόζονται και στη δικαστική μεσεγγύηση.

Άρθρο 727

Τα άρθρα 709, 711, 713, 714, 715, 720, 721 και 722 παρ. 1 εφαρμόζονται και στη δικαστική μεσεγγύηση.

ΚΕΦΑΛΑΙΟ ΣΤ'
Προσωρινή επιδίκαση απαιτήσεων

Άρθρο 728

1. Το δικαστήριο μπορεί να επιδικάσει προσωρινά, ως ασφαλιστικό μέτρο, εν όλω ή εν μέρει, απαιτήσεις:
α) συνεισφοράς για τις ανάγκες της οικογένειας ή διατροφής οφειλόμενης από τον νόμο, από σύμβαση ή από διάταξη τελευταίας βούλησης,
β) καθυστερούμενων συντάξεων,
γ) καθυστερούμενων τακτικών ή έκτακτων αποδοχών οποιασδήποτε μορφής ή αμοιβών ή αποζημιώσεων που οφείλονται από την παροχή εργασίας ή εξόδων που έγιναν με αφορμή την εργασία,
δ) μισθών υπερημερίας ή αποζημίωσης για παράνομη καταγγελία της σύμβασης εργασίας ή για εργατικό ατύχημα ή που οφείλεται από τη σύμβαση εργασίας ή λόγω παραβάσεώς της,
ε) αποζημίωσης για τη μείωση ή την απώλεια της ικανότητας εργασίας λόγω τραυματισμού ή προσβολής με οποιοδήποτε τρόπο της υγείας ενός προσώπου από οποιαδήποτε αρρώστεια, καθώς και των εξόδων θεραπείας και ανάρρωσης,
στ) αποζημίωσης, σε περίπτωση, που ένα πρόσωπο θανατώνεται, υπέρ εκείνων που το πρόσωπο αυτό κατά τον χρόνο του θανάτου του είχε από τον νόμο υποχρέωση να διατρέφει,
ζ) σε κάθε άλλη περίπτωση που η προσωρινή επιδίκαση ορίζεται από τις διατάξεις του ουσιαστικού δικαίου.
2. Αν συντρέχει περίπτωση να μεταρρυθμιστεί τελεσίδικη ή ανέκκλητη απόφαση που καταδικάζει σε καταβολή περιοδικών παροχών, το δικαστήριο μπορεί να διατάξει προσωρινά να διακοπεί η καταβολή, να αυξηθεί ή να μειωθεί το ποσό κάθε παροχής.

Article 726

1. The judgment granting judicial sequestration must specify the things being sequestered, appoint a sequestrator and order that the things be handed over to them. If the things can, by law, be deposited, the court shall order that they be deposited with the state.
2. The court granting judicial sequestration or the court trying the main case may order replacement of the sequestrator, as well as any measure which, in its view, is expedient for the sequestration, and the provisions of Article 702 apply.
3. The person with possession or detentorship over the things and the person who requested judicial sequestration may also be appointed as sequestrator. In cases of judicial sequestration of an enterprise, the debtor shall be appointed as sequestrator. Where there are serious grounds, the court shall appoint a different sequestrator.
4. Judgments handed down under the provisions of paragraphs 1 and 2 shall be enforced immediately without prior service.
5. The provisions concerning sequestrators in cases of compulsory attachment also apply in cases of judicial sequestration.

Article 727

Articles 709, 711, 713, 714, 715, 720, 721 and 722(1) also apply to judicial sequestration.

CHAPTER VI
Provisional award of claims

Article 728

1. The court may provisionally award, as an interim measure, whether in whole or in part, claims concerning:
a) contributions for the needs of the family or maintenance owed in law, under a contract, or from testamentary disposition;
b) delayed pensions;
c) delayed ordinary or extraordinary earnings of any form or fees or compensation owed due to provision of labour or costs incurred for the purposes of labour;
d) default salaries or compensation for unlawful dismissal or occupational accident or owed under an employment contract or breach thereof;
e) compensation for impairment or loss of the ability to work due to injury or damage to the health of a person in any manner caused by any illness, as well as treatment and recuperation costs;
f) compensation, where a person is killed, payable to those whom the person who was killed was obligated to maintain at the time of their death;
g) all other cases where the provisional award is provided for in substantive law.
2. If a *de jure* or *de facto* non-appealable judgment ordering periodically recurring dues is to be amended, the court may order provisional cessation of payment [or] the increase or decrease of each amount owed.

Άρθρο 729

1. Η προσωρινή επιδίκαση απαίτησης περιοδικών παροχών γίνεται σε παροχές που πρέπει να πληρώνονται κατά μήνα.
2. Το ποσό που επιδικάζεται προσωρινά δεν μπορεί να υπερβεί συνολικά το μισό της πιθανολογούμενης απαίτησης, εκτός αν πρόκειται για διατροφή που πηγάζει από τον νόμο, από σύμβαση ή από διάταξη τελευταίας βούλησης ή για συνεισφορά για τις ανάγκες της οικογένειας ή για έξοδα θεραπείας ή ανάρρωσης ή για αποζημίωση λόγω στέρησης διατροφής ή για μισθούς υπερημερίας ή καθυστερούμενους μισθούς.
3. Απαγορεύεται η συντηρητική ή αναγκαστική κατάσχεση, ο συμψηφισμός και η εκχώρηση του ποσού που επιδικάζεται προσωρινά.
4. Τα άρθρα 694 και 705 δεν εφαρμόζονται σε προσωρινή επιδίκαση απαίτησης.
5. Μέσα σε εξήντα (60) ημέρες από τη επίδοση της απόφασης που επιδικάζει προσωρινά απαίτηση ή μεταρρυθμίζει προσωρινά απόφαση κατά το άρθρο 728 παρ. 2, εκείνος υπέρ του οποίου έγινε η προσωρινή επιδίκαση ή μεταρρύθμιση οφείλει να ασκήσει αγωγή για την απαίτηση που επιδικάστηκε ή για τη μεταρρύθμιση της απόφασης. Η απόφαση παύει αυτοδικαίως να ισχύει, αν περάσει άπρακτη η προθεσμία αυτή. Δεν απαιτείται να ασκηθεί αγωγή, αν αυτή έχει ασκηθεί.

Άρθρο 729Α

[Καταργείται]

Άρθρο 730

1. Η απόφαση που επιδικάζει προσωρινά την απαίτηση παύει αυτοδικαίως να ισχύει αν δημοσιευθεί οριστική απόφαση για την ουσία της κύριας υπόθεσης.
2. Αν απορριφθεί με τελεσίδικη απόφαση κατ' ουσίαν η αγωγή για την κύρια υπόθεση, το δικαστήριο που δικάζει την κύρια υπόθεση ή το δικαστήριο που διέταξε την προσωρινή επιδίκαση απαίτησης διατάζει, ύστερα από αίτηση, την απόδοση όσων έχουν καταβληθεί.
3. Το δικαστήριο που αναφέρεται στην παρ. 2 μπορεί να επιτρέψει για την απόδοση και την κατάσχεση ακατάσχετων πραγμάτων και απαιτήσεων στο μέτρο που επιτρέπεται για απαιτήσεις διατροφής συζύγου.

ΚΕΦΑΛΑΙΟ Ζ'
Προσωρινή ρύθμιση κατάστασης.

Άρθρο 731

Το δικαστήριο δικαιούται να διατάξει ως ασφαλιστικό μέτρο την ενέργεια, παράλειψη η ανοχή ορισμένης πράξης από εκείνον κατά του οποίου στρέφεται η αίτηση.

Άρθρο 732

Το δικαστήριο δικαιούται να διατάξει ως ασφαλιστικό μέτρο και κάθε μέτρο που κατά τις περιστάσεις είναι κατά την κρίση του πρόσφορο για την εξασφάλιση ή διατήρηση του δικαιώματος ή τη ρύθμιση κατάστασης.

Άρθρο 732Α
Προσωρινή απασχόληση εργαζομένου

Μέσα σε εξήντα (60) ημέρες από τη δημοσίευση της απόφασης που ρυθμίζει προσωρινά την κατάσταση κατά τα άρθρα 731 και 732, εκείνος, υπέρ του οποίου έγινε η προσωρινή ρύθμιση, οφείλει να ασκήσει αγωγή για την κύρια υπόθεση. Η απόφαση που διατάσσει ασφαλιστικά μέτρα κατά το πρώτο εδάφιο παύει αυτοδικαίως να ισχύει, αν περάσει άπρακτη η προθεσμία αυτή. Δεν απαιτείται να ασκηθεί αγωγή, αν έχει ασκηθεί πριν από τη δημοσίευση της παραπάνω απόφασης.

Article 729

1. The provisional award of claims concerning periodically recurring dues shall apply to dues payable on a monthly basis.
2. The amount provisionally awarded may not exceed half the total claim considered likely on the balance of probabilities, save in cases of maintenance [arising] in law, under a contract, or from testamentary disposition, or contributions for the needs of the family, or treatment or recuperation costs, or compensation due to deprivation of maintenance, or default or delayed salaries.
3. Preventive or compulsory attachment, offsetting and assignment of the amount provisionally awarded are prohibited.
4. Articles 694 and 705 do not apply to the provisional award of claims.
5. Within 60 days of service of the judgment provisionally awarding a claim or provisionally amending a judgment under Article 728(2), the person benefiting from the provisional award or amendment is obligated to file an action for the claim awarded or for amendment of the judgment. The judgment automatically ceases to be effective if this deadline lapses without the relevant steps having been taken. No action need be filed if an [action] has already been filed.

Article 729A

[Repealed]

Article 730

1. The judgment provisionally awarding the claim automatically ceases to be effective if a final judgment is handed down on the merits of the main case.
2. If the action in the main case is dismissed on its merits by a *de jure* non-appealable judgment, the court trying the main case or the court that ordered the provisional award of the claim shall, following an application, order that the amounts paid be returned.
3. The court referred to in paragraph 2 may also allow, for the purposes of [such] return, attachment of non-attachable and garnishment of non-garnishable things and claims to the extent permitted for spousal maintenance claims.

CHAPTER VII
Provisional regulation of a situation

Article 731

As an interim measure, the court may order that a specific step be taken, refrained from, or tolerated by the respondent.

Article 732

As an interim measure, the court may also order any measure which, under the circumstances and in its view, is expedient to safeguard or preserve the right or regulate the situation.

Article 732A
Provisional employment of a worker

Within 60 days of the date the judgment provisionally regulating a situation under Articles 731 and 732 is handed down, the person benefiting from provisional regulation is obligated to file an action in the main case. The judgment granting interim measures under the first subparagraph automatically ceases to be effective if this deadline lapses without the relevant steps having been taken. No action need be filed if an [action] had been filed prior to the date the aforesaid judgment was handed down.

Άρθρο 733

Ασφαλιστικά μέτρα σε κάθε είδους υποθέσεις νομής ή κατοχής διατάσσονται από το ειρηνοδικείο.

Άρθρο 734

1. Στην περίπτωση του προηγούμενου άρθρου επιδίδεται πάντοτε αντίγραφο της αίτησης με επισημείωση της πράξης που ορίζει τόπο και χρόνο για τη συζήτηση σε εκείνον κατά του οποίου στρέφεται η αίτηση.

2. Το ειρηνοδικείο για την προσωρινή ρύθμιση της νομής ή της κατοχής δικαιούται να διατάξει οποιοδήποτε ασφαλιστικό μέτρο κρίνει πρόσφορο και ιδίως να επιτρέψει ή να απαγορεύσει πράξεις νομής ή κατοχής ή να επιδικάσει νομή ή την κατοχή σε κάποιον από τους διαδίκους, είτε με παροχή είτε χωρίς παροχή εγγύησης.

3. Κατά της απόφασης του ειρηνοδικείου επιτρέπεται έφεση μέσα σε δέκα (10) ημέρες από την επίδοσή της. Η έφεση δικάζεται κατά την ίδια διαδικασία, εφαρμόζεται όμως και το άρθρο 226.

4. Η προθεσμία της έφεσης και η άσκησή της δεν αναστέλλουν την εκτέλεση της απόφασης του ειρηνοδικείου, εκτός αν η αναστολή διαταχθεί κατά το άρθρο 912.

5. Στα ασφαλιστικά μέτρα νομής ή κατοχής δεν εφαρμόζονται τα άρθρα 696 παρ. 3 και 697 και ο ειρηνοδίκης δικάζει με τη σύμπραξη γραμματέα που τηρεί πρακτικά.

Άρθρο 735

Το δικαστήριο έχει το δικαίωμα να διατάξει κάθε πρόσφορο ασφαλιστικό μέτρο που υπαγορεύεται από τις περιστάσεις, για τη ρύθμιση των σχέσεων των συζύγων από το γάμο και των σχέσεων γονέων και τέκνων. Ιδίως να διατάξει τη μετοίκηση ενός από τους συζύγους, να ορίσει ποια πράγματα δικαιούται αυτός να παραλάβει για τη χωριστή του εγκατάσταση, να καθορίσει τον τρόπο με τον οποίο ο κάθε σύζυγος θα χρησιμοποιεί το ακίνητο όπου διαμένουν ή τα έπιπλα και σκεύη που χρησιμοποιούν από κοινού, να ορίσει το γονέα στον οποίο ανήκει προσωρινά η άσκηση της γονικής μέριμνας, να αφαιρέσει από τους γονείς τη γονική μέριμνα εν όλω ή εν μέρει και να ρυθμίσει τα σχετικά με την επικοινωνία με το τέκνο. Σε υποθέσεις ενδοοικογενειακής βίας μπορεί να διατάσσεται ιδίως η απομάκρυνση του καθ` ου από την οικογενειακή κατοικία, η μετοίκησή του, η απαγόρευση να προσεγγίζει τους χώρους κατοικίας ή και εργασίας του αιτούντος, κατοικίες στενών συγγενών του, τα εκπαιδευτήρια των παιδιών και ξενώνες φιλοξενίας.

Άρθρο 736

[Καταργείται]

ΚΕΦΑΛΑΙΟ Η'

Σφράγιση, αποσφράγιση, απογραφή και δημόσια κατάθεση.

Άρθρο 737

Το δικαστήριο δικαιούται να διατάξει ως ασφαλιστικό μέτρο τη σφράγιση, την αποσφράγιση, την απογραφή ή τη δημόσια κατάθεση.

Article 733

Interim measures in all types of cases concerning possession or detentorship are ordered by the court of the peace.

Article 734

1. In the case of the preceding Article, a copy of the application shall always be served on the respondent, together with a note concerning the decision setting the place and time of the hearing.
2. In cases of provisional regulation of possession or detentorship, the court of the peace may order any interim measure it deems expedient and, in particular, to allow or prohibits acts of possession or detentorship or to award possession or detentorship to one of the parties in the proceedings, whether or not with provision of surety.
3. An appeal may be filed against the court of the peace judgment within 10 days of it being served. The appeal shall be tried under the same procedure; however, Article 226 also applies.
4. The [fact that the] deadline for [filing] an appeal [has commenced] and [the act of] filing an appeal shall not stay enforcement of the court of the peace judgment, unless such stay is ordered under Article 912.
5. Articles 696(3) and 697 do not apply to interim measures concerning possession or detentorship, and the court of the peace judge shall try the matter with the involvement of a registrar who keeps a transcript.

Article 735

The court has the right to order any expedient interim measure required under the circumstances to regulate spousal relationships arising from marriage and parent-child relationships. In particular, [the court may] order the rehousing of one of the spouses, specify which things that spouse is entitled to collect to set up their own home, specify the manner in which each spouse will use the immovable where they reside or the furniture and household effects they jointly use, designate the parent with provisional parental responsibility, remove parental responsibility from parents, whether in whole or in part, and regulate matters concerning access to the child. In cases of domestic violence, the court may, in particular, order removal of the respondent named in the application from the family home, order their rehousing, and prohibit them from approaching the places where the applicant lives and/or works, the homes of [the applicant's] close relatives, the children's schools and shelters.

Article 736

[Repealed]

CHAPTER VIII
Sealing, unsealing, inventory-taking and deposit with the state

Article 737

As an interim measure, the court may order sealing, unsealing, inventory-taking and deposit with the state.

Άρθρο 738

1. Κάθε διαφορά σχετική με τη σφράγιση, την αποσφράγιση, την απογραφή ή τη δημόσια κατάθεση, εφόσον διατάχθηκαν ως ασφαλιστικά μέτρα, δικάζεται από το δικαστήριο που τις διέταξε και, αν είναι πολυμελές, από το μονομελές πρωτοδικείο του τόπου όπου αυτές γίνονται.

2. Όποιος ενεργεί τη σφράγιση, την αποσφράγιση ή την απογραφή που έχει διαταχθεί αποφαίνεται αμέσως προσωρινά για τις διαφορές ή τις διενέξεις που ανακύπτουν κατά τη διάρκεια της ενέργειάς τους και η απόφασή του εκτελείται αμέσως. Όποιος έχει έννομο συμφέρον δικαιούται να ζητήσει την ανάκληση της απόφασης και των πράξεων που διενεργήθηκαν για την εκτέλεση κατά την παράγραφο 1.

ΚΕΦΑΛΑΙΟ Θ

Ευρωπαϊκή Διαταγή Δέσμευσης Λογαριασμού

Άρθρο 738Α

1. Αρμόδιος να εκδώσει Ευρωπαϊκή Διαταγή Δέσμευσης Λογαριασμού σύμφωνα με τον Κανονισμό 655/2014 είναι για απαίτηση της αρμοδιότητας ειρηνοδικείου ο ειρηνοδίκης και για κάθε άλλη απαίτηση ο δικαστής του μονομελούς πρωτοδικείου.

2. Ο δικαστής απορρίπτει εν όλω ή εν μέρει την αίτηση:

α) αν δεν συντρέχουν οι προϋποθέσεις του Κανονισμού για την έκδοση της διαταγής,

β) αν ο αιτών δεν υποβάλει τα στοιχεία που απαιτούνται σύμφωνα με το άρθρο 8 του Κανονισμού ή δεν συμπληρώνει ή διορθώνει την αίτηση εντός της προθεσμίας που όρισε ο δικαστής.

Η απορριπτική απόφαση περιέχει συνοπτική αιτιολογία και γνωστοποιείται επιμελεία του δικαστηρίου στον αιτούντα. Η γνωστοποίηση μπορεί να γίνεται και με ηλεκτρονικό μήνυμα στον πληρεξούσιο δικηγόρο του αιτούντος, με ηλεκτρονική υπογραφή και ηλεκτρονικό αποδεικτικό παραλαβής. Κατά της απορριπτικής απόφασης επιτρέπεται έφεση εντός τριάντα (30) ημερών από τη γνωστοποίησή της. Η έφεση εκδικάζεται από το αρμόδιο κατά τις γενικές διατάξεις δικαστήριο κατά τη διαδικασία του άρθρου 11 του Κανονισμού.

3. Ο οφειλέτης έχει τα δικαιώματα που προβλέπονται στα άρθρα 33 έως 38 του Κανονισμού. Με την επιφύλαξη των διατάξεων του Κανονισμού, για την εκτέλεση της Ευρωπαϊκής Διαταγής Δέσμευσης Λογαριασμού εφαρμόζονται οι διατάξεις της αναγκαστικής κατάσχεσης απαιτήσεων στα χέρια τρίτου και το πιστωτικό ίδρυμα, εκείνος που επέβαλε την κατάσχεση και ο οφειλέτης έχουν όλες τις υποχρεώσεις και τα δικαιώματα που προβλέπουν οι διατάξεις αυτές.

4. Αν η διαταγή δέσμευσης έχει εκδοθεί πριν από την άσκηση της αγωγής για την κύρια υπόθεση, η αγωγή πρέπει να ασκηθεί εντός τριάντα (30) ημερών από την επίδοση της διαταγής στον τρίτο. Αν παρέλθει άπρακτη η προθεσμία του προηγούμενου εδαφίου αίρεται αυτοδικαίως η δέσμευση, εκτός αν εκείνος που επέβαλε την κατάσχεση μέσα στην προθεσμία αυτή επιδώσει διαταγή πληρωμής για την ίδια απαίτηση.

5. Όποιος έχει επιδώσει Ευρωπαϊκή Διαταγή Δέσμευσης Λογαριασμού γίνεται, από την τελεσιδικία της απόφασης που δέχεται την αγωγή για την κύρια υπόθεση ή από την τελεσιδικία της διαταγής πληρωμής που επιδικάζει την ίδια απαίτηση, δικαιούχος ολόκληρης της απαίτησης ή μέρους της, ανάλογα με το περιεχόμενο της απόφασης ή της διαταγής πληρωμής.

6. Η ευθύνη του δανειστή που έχει επιτύχει την έκδοση Ευρωπαϊκής Διαταγής Δέσμευσης Λογαριασμού για τη ζημία που προξενήθηκε στον οφειλέτη διέπεται από τις διατάξεις των παραγράφων 1 και 2 του άρθρου 13 του Κανονισμού. Το άρθρο 703 εφαρμόζεται ανάλογα.

Article 738

1. All disputes concerning sealing, unsealing, inventory-taking and deposit with the state, where the foregoing were ordered as interim measures, shall be tried by the court that ordered them and, in the case of a multi-member court, by the single-member court of first instance where the foregoing are to take place.

2. The person carrying out the sealing, unsealing or inventory-taking ordered shall immediately issue a provisional decision on any disputes or differences which may arise [while those steps are being taken], and their decision shall be enforced immediately. Any person with a legitimate interest is entitled to request that the decision and enforcement steps taken in accordance with paragraph 1 be revoked.

CHAPTER IX
European Account Preservation Order

Article 738A

1. Court of the peace judges are competent to issue a European Account Preservation Order in accordance with Regulation (EU) No 655/2014 for a claim falling under the jurisdiction of the court of the peace, and single-member court of first instance judges for all other claims.

2. The judge shall dismiss the application in whole or in part if:

a) the requirements laid down in the Regulation and necessary for issuing the order are not met;

b) the applicant does not provide the information required under Article 8 of the Regulation or fails to complete or rectify the application within the deadline set by the judge.

The judgment dismissing the application shall contain concise reasoning and shall be notified to the applicant by the court. Notification may also be effected by means of an electronic message sent to the applicant's authorised lawyer, bearing an electronic signature and accompanied by electronic acknowledgement of receipt. An appeal may be filed against the judgment dismissing the application within 30 days of notification. The appeal shall be tried by the court with jurisdiction under the general provisions in accordance with the procedure laid down in Article 11 of the Regulation.

3. Debtors have the rights provided for in Articles 33 to 38 of the Regulation. Without prejudice to the provisions of the Regulation, the provisions on garnishment apply to the enforcement of European Account Preservation Orders, and the credit institution, the person who procured garnishment and the debtor have all the obligations and rights set out in said provisions.

4. If the preservation order had been issued before the action in the main case was filed, the action must be filed within 30 days from the date the order was served on the third party. If the deadline laid down in the preceding subparagraph lapses without the relevant steps having been taken, the preservation [order] shall be lifted automatically, unless the person who procured attachment serves a payment order regarding the same claim within that deadline.

5. From the date the judgment accepting the action in the main case or the payment order awarding the same claim becomes *de jure* non-appealable, any person who has served a European Account Preservation Order shall become entitled to all or part of the claim, depending on the content of the judgment or payment order.

6. The liability of the creditor who has obtained a European Account Preservation Order for the damage caused to the debtor is governed by the provisions of Article 13(1) and (2) of the Regulation. Article 703 applies *mutatis mutandis*.

ΕΚΤΟ ΒΙΒΛΙΟ
ΔΙΑΔΙΚΑΣΙΑ ΕΚΟΥΣΙΑΣ ΔΙΚΑΙΟΔΟΣΙΑΣ

ΚΕΦΑΛΑΙΟ Α'
Γενικές διατάξεις.

Άρθρο 739
Όλες οι υποθέσεις που αναφέρονται στα άρθρα 782 έως 866 υπάγονται στην ειδική διαδικασία των άρθρων 741 έως 781, καθώς και κάθε άλλη υπόθεση που υπάγεται με διάταξη νόμου στη διαδικασία αυτή.

Άρθρο 740
1. Στην αρμοδιότητα του Μονομελούς Πρωτοδικείου υπάγονται οι υποθέσεις οι οποίες αναφέρονται στο άρθρο 739, η θέση προσώπου σε ακούσια νοσηλεία, σύμφωνα με τις διατάξεις του ουσιαστικού δικαίου, καθώς και η ανακοπή των άρθρων 787 του παρόντος και 82 ΑΚ. Εξαιρούνται οι υποθέσεις που αφορούν την ιατρικώς υποβοηθούμενη αναπαραγωγή, οι οποίες υπάγονται στην αρμοδιότητα των Πολυμελών Πρωτοδικείων και εκείνες που από το νόμο υπάγονται στην αρμοδιότητα των Ειρηνοδικείων.
2. Στις υποθέσεις που αναφέρονται στο άρθρο 739 δεν επιτρέπεται παρέκταση της αρμοδιότητας.

Άρθρο 741
Τα άρθρα 1 έως 590 εφαρμόζονται και κατά τη διαδικασία των άρθρων 743 έως 781, εκτός αν είναι αντίθετα προς ειδικές διατάξεις ή δεν προσαρμόζονται στη διαδικασία αυτή.

Άρθρο 742
Οι ανήλικοι που έχουν συμπληρώσει το δέκατο έκτο έτος της ηλικίας τους έχουν την ικανότητα να παρίστανται στο δικαστήριο για υποθέσεις που αφορούν την προσωπική τους κατάσταση και να ασκούν κατά της απόφασης που εκδίδεται ένδικα μέσα και τριτανακοπή. Όταν παρίσταται ο ανήλικος, πρέπει να καλείται όποιος τον εκπροσωπεί νόμιμα.

Άρθρο 743
Η πληρεξουσιότητα δίνεται και με ιδιωτικό έγγραφο, κατά το άρθρο 96 παράγραφοι 1 και 3.

Άρθρο 744
Το δικαστήριο μπορεί και αυτεπαγγέλτως να διατάζει κάθε μέτρο πρόσφορο για την εξακρίβωση πραγματικών γεγονότων, ακόμη και εκείνων που δεν έχουν προταθεί και ιδιαίτερα γεγονότων που συντελούν στην προστασία των ενδιαφερομένων ή της έννομης σχέσης ή του γενικότερου κοινωνικού συμφέροντος.

Άρθρο 745
Έως την περάτωση και της τελευταίας συζήτησης στο πρωτοβάθμιο δικαστήριο επιτρέπεται η προβολή πραγματικών ισχυρισμών.

Άρθρο 746
Τα έξοδα επιβάλλονται σε βάρος του αιτούντος εφόσον η αίτηση έχει υποβληθεί για το συμφέρον του, αλλιώς σε βάρος εκείνου προς το συμφέρον του οποίου έχει υποβληθεί. Τα έξοδα μπορεί να επιβληθούν όλα ή κατά ένα μέρος σε βάρος του υπαιτίου για τη διεξαγωγή της δίκης.

BOOK VI
NON-CONTENTIOUS PROCEEDINGS

CHAPTER I
General provisions

Article 739
All the cases referred to in Articles 782 to 866 are subject to the special procedure laid down in Articles 741 to 781, as is any other case subject to said procedure under statutory provision.

Article 740
1. Single-member courts of first instance have jurisdiction over the cases referred to in Article 739, involuntary hospitalisation of persons, in accordance with the provisions of substantive law, as well as opposition under Articles 787 of this Code and Article 82 of the Civil Code. Cases concerning medically assisted reproduction that fall under the jurisdiction of multi-member courts of first instance and those that, by law, fall under the jurisdiction of the courts of the peace are excluded.
2. Prorogation of jurisdiction is not permitted in the cases referred to in Article 739.

Article 741
Articles 1 to 590 also apply during the procedure laid down in Articles 743 to 781, unless they are contrary to specific provisions or cannot be adapted to [fit] this procedure.

Article 742
Juveniles who have attained the age of 16 have capacity to appear in court in cases that concern their personal status, and may file legal remedies and bring third-party proceedings against the judgment handed down. When a juvenile enters an appearance, the person lawfully representing them must be summoned.

Article 743
Power of representation may also be conferred by means of a private document, in accordance with Article 96(1) and (3).

Article 744
The court may also order *ex officio* any measure expedient to ascertain actual facts, even those not pleaded, and particularly facts that help protect the interested parties or the legal relationship or wider societal interests.

Article 745
Factual assertions may be made no later than the conclusion of the final hearing before the first-instance court.

Article 746
Costs shall be imposed on the applicant, where the application was submitted in their interest, otherwise on the person in whose interest the application was submitted. The person responsible for initiating the proceedings may be ordered to pay all or part of the costs.

Άρθρο 747

1. Η αίτηση ασκείται με δικόγραφο που κατατίθεται στη γραμματεία του δικαστηρίου στο οποίο απευθύνεται.
2. Το δικόγραφο της αίτησης ή η έκθεση πρέπει να περιέχει, εκτός από όσα ορίζονται στο άρθρο 118 ή 117
α) ακριβή περιγραφή του αντικειμένου της υπόθεσης,
β) ορισμένο αίτημα,
γ) σαφή έκθεση των γεγονότων που δικαιολογούν το αίτημα κατά το κύριο αντικείμενο και τα παρεπόμενά του, καθώς και την εξουσία για την υποβολή του.
Στην αίτηση αναφέρονται ακόμη τα στοιχεία που θεμελιώνουν την αρμοδιότητα του δικαστηρίου.
3. Για την κατάθεση συντάσσεται έκθεση κάτω από το πρωτότυπο της αίτησης. Η έκθεση αναφέρει την ημέρα και την ώρα της κατάθεσης και το όνομα και το επώνυμο εκείνου που την κατέθεσε.
4. Όταν κατά το νόμο το δικαστήριο έχει την εξουσία να ενεργεί αυτεπαγγέλτως, μπορεί να διατάξει την εισαγωγή της υπόθεσης προς συζήτηση με πράξη του. Η πράξη πρέπει να περιλαμβάνει το αντικείμενο της υπόθεσης, υπογράφεται από αυτόν που την εκδίδει και αναφέρεται στο βιβλίο που τηρείται κατά το άρθρο 776.

Άρθρο 748

1. Η αίτηση υποβάλλεται χωρίς υπαίτια καθυστέρηση από τη γραμματεία στο δικαστήριο και αν πρόκειται για πολυμελές πρωτοδικείο, στον πρόεδρο, για να ορίσει δικάσιμο. Στην περίπτωση αυτή εφαρμόζεται το άρθρο 226.
2. Αντίγραφο της αίτησης με τη σημείωση για τον προσδιορισμό της δικασίμου πρέπει να κοινοποιείται στον εισαγγελέα πρωτοδικών της περιφέρειας του δικαστηρίου, στις περιπτώσεις των άρθρων 782, 783, 784, 796, 799, 800 και 801 ή να το διατάξει ο δικαστής που αναφέρεται στην παρ. 1.
3. Ο δικαστής που είναι αρμόδιος κατά την παράγραφο 1 μπορεί να διατάξει την κλήτευση τρίτων που έχουν έννομο συμφέρον από τη δίκη. Η κλήτευση γίνεται με κοινοποίηση αντιγράφου της αίτησης στο οποίο σημειώνεται ο προσδιορισμός της δικασίμου.
4. Ο δικαστής ορίζει την προθεσμία που κατά την κρίση του απαιτείται για τις κοινοποιήσεις που αναφέρονται στις παραγράφους 2 και 3.
5. Στις υποθέσεις που εισάγονται κατά την παρ. 4 του άρθρου 747, εκείνος που εξέδωσε την πράξη ορίζει δικάσιμο, κοινοποιεί αντίγραφο της πράξης στον εισαγγελέα και μπορεί να διατάξει την κλήτευση στη δίκη οποιουδήποτε έχει έννομο συμφέρον.

Άρθρο 749

Οι διατάξεις για τη διαμεσολάβηση και την απόπειρα συμβιβασμού δεν εφαρμόζονται.

Άρθρο 750

Ο εισαγγελέας πρωτοδικών δικαιούται να παρίσταται κατά τη συζήτηση στο ακροατήριο και ενώπιον του ειρηνοδικείου.

Άρθρο 751

Μεταβολή της αίτησης επιτρέπεται με άδεια του δικαστή, εφόσον κατά την κρίση του δεν βλάπτονται συμφέροντα εκείνων που μετέχουν στη δίκη ή τρίτων. Η μεταβολή αναφέρεται στο βιβλίο που τηρείται κατά το άρθρο 776.

Article 747

1. Applications shall be brought by means of a procedural document filed with the registry of the court to which the application is addressed.
2. In addition to the information specified in Articles 118 or 117, the application or the report must contain[:]
a) a precise description of the subject-matter of the case;
b) a specific request;
c) a clear statement of the facts justifying the request with regard to the main subject-matter and incidental matters, as well as the capacity to submit it.
The application must also set out the facts establishing the jurisdiction of the court.
3. A report on the filing shall be prepared at the end of the original of the application. The report shall indicate the date and time of filing, as well as the full name of the applicant.
4. When a court is empowered in law to act *ex officio*, it may issue a decision ordering that the case be brought for hearing. This decision must include the subject-matter of the case, be signed by the person issuing it and be included in the register kept in accordance with Article 776.

Article 748

1. In order for a hearing date to be set, the registry shall submit applications without undue delay to the court and, in the case of a multi-member court, to the presiding judge. In this case, the provisions of Article 226 apply.
2. A copy of the application with a note setting the hearing date must be notified to the court of first instance public prosecutor of the district of the court in the cases referred to in Articles 782, 783, 784, 796, 799, 800 and 801, or [its notification] must be ordered by the judge referred to in paragraph 1.
3. The judge competent under paragraph 1 may order that third parties with a legitimate interest in [the outcome of] the proceedings be summonsed. Summonsing shall be effected by means of notification of a copy of the application with a note setting the hearing date.
4. The judge shall set the deadline which, in their view, is necessary for the notifications referred to in paragraphs 2 and 3.
5. With regard to cases brought for a hearing in accordance with Article 747(4), the person who issued the decision shall set a hearing date, shall notify a copy of the decision to the public prosecutor, and may order that any person with a legitimate interest be summonsed to [participate in] the proceedings.

Article 749

The provisions on mediation and settlement attempts do not apply.

Article 750

The court of first instance public prosecutor may attend the courtroom hearing and appear before the court of the peace.

Article 751

The application may be changed with leave from the judge where, in their view, this does not prejudice the interests of those participating in the proceedings or third parties. The change shall be noted in the register kept in accordance with Article 776.

Άρθρο 752

1. Η κύρια παρέμβαση ασκείται με δικόγραφο και εφαρμόζονται για την παρέμβαση αυτή τα άρθρα 747, 748 και 751.
2. Η πρόσθετη παρέμβαση μπορεί να ασκηθεί και κατά τη συζήτηση στο ακροατήριο, χωρίς προδικασία.

Άρθρο 753

1. Κάθε διάδικος μπορεί να προσεπικαλεί τρίτο που έχει έννομο συμφέρον να προσέλθει στη δίκη. Το ίδιο μπορεί να πράξει και το δικαστήριο αυτεπαγγέλτως.
2. Η προσεπίκληση ασκείται με δικόγραφο και εφαρμόζονται τα άρθρα 747, 748 και 751. Αν το δικαστήριο διέταξε την προσεπίκληση, αυτή γίνεται με επιμέλεια του διαδίκου που ορίζεται στην απόφαση.

Άρθρο 754

Αν κατά την εκφώνηση της υπόθεσης στην ορισμένη για τη συζήτηση της αίτησης δικάσιμο δεν εμφανιστούν οι διάδικοι ή εμφανιστούν και δεν λάβουν κανονικά μέρος στη συζήτηση, η συζήτηση ματαιώνεται. Αν ο αιτών δεν εμφανιστεί ή εμφανιστεί αλλά δεν μετέχει κανονικά στη συζήτηση και εμφανισθεί ο καθ' ου η αίτηση ή ο τρίτος που έχει κλητευθεί ή έχει παρέμβει, η συζήτηση προχωρεί σαν να είχε εμφανιστεί ο αιτών και το δικαστήριο εξετάζει την υπόθεση κατ' ουσίαν.

Άρθρα 755-756

[Καταργούνται]

Άρθρο 757

Η παρουσία κατά τη δημοσίευση της απόφασης εκείνου στον οποίο πρέπει να επιδοθεί ή του νόμιμου αντιπροσώπου του που διεξάγει τη δίκη ή του πληρεξουσίου δικηγόρου του ισχύει ως επίδοση.

Άρθρο 758

1. Οι αποφάσεις που αποφαίνονται οριστικά, εφόσον δεν ορίζεται διαφορετικά, μπορούν με αίτηση διαδίκου, μετά τη δημοσίευσή τους, να ανακληθούν ή να μεταρρυθμιστούν από το δικαστήριο που τις εξέδωσε, αν προκύψουν νέα πραγματικά περιστατικά ή μεταβληθούν οι συνθήκες κάτω από τις οποίες εκδόθηκαν. Η ανάκληση ή μεταρρύθμιση γίνεται κατά τη διαδικασία των άρθρων 741 έως 781, αφού κληθούν οι διάδικοι της αρχικής δίκης και τα πρόσωπα τα οποία είχαν διοριστεί ή είχαν αντικατασταθεί ή παυθεί από την απόφαση για την άσκηση λειτουργήματος.
Η αίτηση ανάκλησης ή μεταρρύθμισης του πρώτου εδαφίου επιτρέπεται, επίσης, μετά την έκδοση οριστικής απόφασης του Ευρωπαϊκού Δικαστηρίου Δικαιωμάτων του Ανθρώπου με την οποία κρίνεται ότι η δικαστική απόφαση που δέχθηκε ή απέρριψε την αρχική αίτηση εκδόθηκε κατά παράβαση δικαιώματος που αφορά στον δίκαιο χαρακτήρα της διαδικασίας που τηρήθηκε ή διάταξης ουσιαστικού δικαίου της Ευρωπαϊκής Σύμβασης Δικαιωμάτων του Ανθρώπου, με την επιφύλαξη των όρων και περιορισμών που προβλέπονται στις επιμέρους διατάξεις της Ευρωπαϊκής Σύμβασης Δικαιωμάτων του Ανθρώπου περί προστασίας της εθνικής ασφάλειας, της δημόσιας τάξης, της πρόληψης του εγκλήματος, της προστασίας της υγείας ή ηθικής και της προστασίας των δικαιωμάτων και ελευθεριών των τρίτων. Στην περίπτωση αυτή η αίτηση ασκείται μέσα σε προθεσμία ενενήντα (90) ημερών, η οποία αρχίζει από την ημερομηνία που καθίσταται οριστική η απόφαση του Ευρωπαϊκού Δικαστηρίου Δικαιωμάτων του Ανθρώπου.
2. Η ανακλητική ή μεταρρυθμιστική απόφαση δεν έχει αναδρομική ισχύ, εκτός αν το ορίσει ειδικά το δικαστήριο.
3. Η ανακλητική ή μεταρρυθμιστική απόφαση σημειώνεται χωρίς υπαίτια καθυστέρηση στο βιβλίο που τηρείται κατά το άρθρο 776 και στο περιθώριο της απόφασης που ανακαλείται ή μεταρρυθμίζεται, με επιμέλεια της γραμματείας του δικαστηρίου.

Article 752

1. Main interventions are filed by means of a procedural document, and Articles 747, 748 and 751 apply to such interventions.
2. Permissive interventions may also be filed during the courtroom hearing without any preliminary procedure.

Article 753

1. Any party in the proceedings may implead a third party with a legitimate interest to participate in the proceedings. The court may also do the same *ex officio*.
2. Impleaders are filed by means of a procedural document, and Articles 747, 748 and 751 apply. If the court ordered the impleader, impleading shall be done by the party in the proceedings specified in the decision.

Article 754

If, when the case is called on the hearing date set for the hearing of the application, the parties in the proceedings fail to appear or do appear but do not participate in the hearing in the manner required, the the hearing shall be unable to go ahead. If the applicant fails to appear or does appear but does not participate in the hearing in the manner required and the respondent named in the application or the third party who was summonsed or who intervened appears, the hearing shall go ahead as if the applicant had entered an appearance and the court shall try the case on its merits.

Articles 755-756

[Repealed]

Article 757

The presence of the person on whom the judgment must be served or the lawful proxy of the person initiating the proceedings or their authorised lawyer when the judgment is handed down shall function as service.

Article 758

1. Unless otherwise provided for, final judgments may, following an application filed by a party in the proceedings after said judgments have been handed down, be revoked or amended by the court that handed them down if new actual facts emerge or the conditions under which the judgments were handed down change. Judgments shall be revoked or amended in accordance with the procedure laid down in Articles 741 to 781, after the parties in the initial proceedings and the persons who had been appointed or replaced or suspended from exercising a function pursuant to the judgment have been summoned.
The revocation or amendment application referred to in the first subparagraph may also be filed following a final judgment of the European Court of Human Rights ruling that the court judgment that accepted or dismissed the initial application was handed down in breach of a right concerning fairness of the procedure followed or a substantive provision of the European Convention on Human Rights, without prejudice to the conditions and restrictions envisaged in the individual provisions of the European Convention on Human Rights on the protection of national security, public policy, the prevention of crime, the protection of health or morals and the protection of the rights and freedoms of others. In this case, the application shall be filed within a deadline of 90 days commencing from the date on which the judgment of the European Court of Human Rights became final.
2. Unless specifically stipulated by the court, the revocation or amendment decision does not have retroactive effect.
3. The revocation or amendment decision shall be noted by the court registry without undue delay in the register kept in accordance with Article 776 and in the margin of the judgment being revoked or amended.

Άρθρο 759

1. Η απόδειξη που διατάζει το δικαστήριο διεξάγεται με την επιμέλεια κάποιου από τους διαδίκους.
2. Η διεξαγωγή αυτοψίας ή πραγματογνωμοσύνης μπορεί να γίνει και κατά τις διατάξεις της παρ. 4 του άρθρου 591.
3. Το δικαστήριο, ακόμη και αποκλίνοντας από τις διατάξεις που ρυθμίζουν την απόδειξη, διατάζει αυτεπαγγέλτως κάθε τι που κατά την κρίση του είναι απαραίτητο για την εξακρίβωση της αλήθειας των πραγματικών γεγονότων.
4. Οι διάδικοι προσάγουν κατά τη συζήτηση στο ακροατήριο όλα τα αποδεικτικά μέσα τα οποία θα χρησιμοποιήσουν για να αποδείξουν τους ισχυρισμούς τους.

Άρθρο 760

Το άρθρο 748 εφαρμόζεται και στα ένδικα μέσα. Αντί για τον εισαγγελέα που αναφέρεται στην παρ. 2 του άρθρου αυτού καλείται ο εισαγγελέας του δικαστηρίου που δικάζει το ένδικο μέσο.

Άρθρο 761

Έφεση έχουν το δικαίωμα να ασκήσουν και αν νίκησαν ο αιτών, εκείνος κατά του οποίου είχε στραφεί η αίτηση, εκείνοι που άσκησαν κύρια και πρόσθετη παρέμβαση, οι καθολικοί και ειδικοί διάδοχοί τους, καθώς και ο εισαγγελέας πρωτοδικών.

Άρθρο 762

Αν περισσότεροι έλαβαν μέρος στην πρωτόδικη δίκη, η έφεση που ασκεί ένας από αυτούς απευθύνεται κατά των άλλων ή των καθολικών διαδόχων ή των κληροδόχων τους.

Άρθρο 763

1. Προθεσμία της έφεσης και η άσκησή της δεν αναστέλλουν την ισχύ και την εκτέλεση της απόφασης.
2. Το δικαστήριο που δικάζει την υπόθεση μπορεί και αυτεπαγγέλτως, κατά την έκδοση της απόφασής του, να αναστείλει την ισχύ και την εκτέλεσή της, ώσπου να γίνει απρόσβλητη με έφεση.
3. Αν ασκηθεί έφεση, το δικαστήριο που εξέδωσε την απόφαση, όπως και το δικαστήριο που δικάζει την έφεση ή ο πρόεδρός του μπορούν κατά την κρίση τους, με αίτηση κάποιου από εκείνους που έλαβαν μέρος στην πρωτόδικη δίκη, να αναστείλουν την ισχύ και την εκτέλεσή της, μέχρι να εκδοθεί απόφαση στην έφεση. Η απόφαση που διατάζει την αναστολή σημειώνεται χωρίς υπαίτια καθυστέρηση στο βιβλίο που τηρείται κατά το άρθρο 776 και στο περιθώριο της απόφασης της οποίας αναστέλλεται η ισχύς και η εκτέλεση.

Άρθρο 764

1. Οι πρόσθετοι λόγοι της έφεσης και η αντέφεση ασκούνται και με τις προτάσεις.
2. Αν όταν εκφωνείται η υπόθεση, δεν εμφανιστεί κανείς διάδικος, η συζήτηση ματαιώνεται. Αν κάποιος από τους διαδίκους εμφανιστεί, το δικαστήριο εξετάζει την υπόθεση κατ' ουσίαν. Η παρ. 2 του άρθρου 242 εφαρμόζεται και εδώ.
3. Ανακοπή ερημοδικίας επιτρέπεται, αν όποιος δικάστηκε ερήμην δεν κλητεύθηκε καθόλου ή εμπρόθεσμα ή δεν κλητεύθηκε κανονικά ή αν συντρέχει λόγος ανώτερης βίας.

Άρθρο 765

Κατά τη δίκη στο εφετείο μπορούν να υποβληθούν νέοι πραγματικοί ισχυρισμοί και είναι δυνατή η επίκληση και η προσαγωγή νέων αποδεικτικών μέσων.

Article 759

1. Where the court orders that evidence be taken, such evidence shall be brought by any of the parties in the proceedings.

2. Inspections may also take place or expert evidence may also be prepared in accordance with the provisions of Article 591(4).

3. The court, even by way of derogation from the provisions regulating [the taking of] evidence, shall order *ex officio* anything which, in its view, is necessary to ascertain the truth of the actual facts.

4. During the courtroom hearing, the parties in the proceedings shall produce all the means of evidence they will use to prove their assertions.

Article 760

Article 748 also applies to legal remedies. Instead of the public prosecutor referred to in Article 748(2), the public prosecutor at the court trying the legal remedy shall be summoned.

Article 761

Even if successful, applicants, respondents, main and permissive intervenors, their universal successors and specific successors, as well as the court of first instance public prosecutor have the right to file an appeal.

Article 762

If several persons participated in the first-instance proceedings, an appeal filed by one of them shall be brought against the other persons or their universal successors or legatees.

Article 763

1. The [fact that the] deadline for [filing] an appeal [has commenced] and [the act of] filing an appeal shall not stay the effect and enforcement of the judgment.

2. The court trying the case may *ex officio*, when handing down its judgment, stay its effect and enforcement until it becomes non-appealable.

3. If an appeal is filed, the court that handed down the judgment and the court trying the appeal or its presiding judge may, at their discretion and following an application filed by any of the persons who participated in the first-instance proceedings, stay its effect and enforcement until a judgment is handed down on the appeal. The decision ordering stay shall be noted without undue delay in the register kept in accordance with Article 776 and in the margin of the judgment whose effect and enforcement are being stayed.

Article 764

1. Additional grounds of appeal and cross-appeal may also be filed with the pleadings.

2. If no party in the proceedings enters an appearance when the case is called, the hearing shall be cancelled. If any of the parties in the proceedings enters an appearance, the court shall try the case on its merits. Article 242(2) also apply in this case.

3. An opposition against a default judgment shall be permitted if the person tried *in absentia* was not summonsed at all, or was not summonsed in good time, or was not summonsed in the manner required, or reasons of force majeure apply.

Article 765

During proceedings before the court of appeal, new factual assertions may be put forth and new means of evidence may be adduced and relied upon.

Άρθρο 766

Αν γίνει δεκτή η έφεση και εξαφανιστεί ή μεταρρυθμιστεί η εκκαλούμενη απόφαση, η γραμματεία του δικαστηρίου που δίκασε την έφεση ειδοποιεί τη γραμματεία του δικαστηρίου που εξέδωσε την απόφαση που εξαφανίστηκε ή μεταρρυθμίστηκε, η οποία σημειώνει στο βιβλίο που τηρείται κατά το άρθρο 776 καθώς και στο περιθώριο της απόφασης του πρωτοβάθμιου δικαστηρίου, την απόφαση του δευτεροβάθμιου.

Άρθρο 767

Αναψηλάφηση δικαιούται να ασκήσουν ο αιτών, εκείνος κατά του οποίου στρέφεται η αίτηση, ο εκκαλών, ο εφεσίβλητος, ο αναιρεσείων, ο αναιρεσίβλητος, εκείνοι που άσκησαν κύρια και πρόσθετη παρέμβαση, οι καθολικοί και ειδικοί διάδοχοί τους και ο εισαγγελέας. Οι διατάξεις του άρθρου 762 εφαρμόζονται και εδώ.

Άρθρο 768

Αν γίνει δεκτή η αναψηλάφηση και εξαφανιστεί ή μεταρρυθμιστεί η απόφαση που έχει προσβληθεί, η γραμματεία του δικαστηρίου σημειώνει στο βιβλίο που τηρείται κατά το άρθρο 776 και στο περιθώριο της απόφασης που εξαφανίστηκε ή μεταρρυθμίστηκε την απόφαση που εκδόθηκε στην αναψηλάφηση.

Άρθρο 769

Αναίρεση έχουν δικαίωμα να ασκήσουν, και αν νίκησαν, ο αιτών, εκείνος κατά του οποίου στρέφεται η αίτηση, ο εκκαλών, ο εφεσίβλητος, εκείνοι που άσκησαν κύρια και πρόσθετη παρέμβαση και οι καθολικοί και ειδικοί διάδοχοί τους, καθώς και ο εισαγγελέας πρωτοδικών. Οι διατάξεις του άρθρου 762 εφαρμόζονται και εδώ.

Άρθρο 770

Το τμήμα του Αρείου Πάγου που αναφέρεται στο άρθρο 565 παρ. 2 μπορεί να διατάξει εκτός από την αναστολή της εκτέλεσης και την αναστολή της ισχύος της απόφασης.

Άρθρο 771

Αν διαταχθεί η αναστολή της ισχύος ή της εκτέλεσης απόφασης κατά το άρθρο 770, η γραμματεία του Αρείου Πάγου ειδοποιεί χωρίς υπαίτια καθυστέρηση τη γραμματεία του δικαστηρίου του οποίου η απόφαση αναστέλλεται, καθώς και τη γραμματεία του πρωτοβάθμιου δικαστηρίου. Η απόφαση της αναστολής σημειώνεται στο βιβλίο που τηρείται κατά το άρθρο 776, στο περιθώριο της αναιρεσιβαλλόμενης απόφασης καθώς και στο περιθώριο της απόφασης του πρωτοβάθμιου δικαστηρίου.

Άρθρο 772

Η αναιρετική απόφαση του Αρείου Πάγου σημειώνεται στο βιβλίο που τηρείται κατά το άρθρο 776, καθώς και στο περιθώριο της απόφασης του πρωτοβάθμιου δικαστηρίου. Για το σκοπό αυτό η γραμματεία του Αρείου Πάγου ειδοποιεί χωρίς υπαίτια καθυστέρηση τη γραμματεία του πρωτοβάθμιου δικαστηρίου, η οποία κάνει τη σχετική σημείωση.

Άρθρο 773

1. Για την άσκηση και την εκδίκαση της τριτανακοπής εφαρμόζονται οι διατάξεις των άρθρων 743 έως 759.

2. Νέοι λόγοι τριτανακοπής μπορούν να προστεθούν και με τις προτάσεις.

Άρθρο 774

Το δικαστήριο που δικάζει την τριτανακοπή δικαιούται κατά το άρθρο 589 να διατάξει εκτός από την αναστολή της εκτέλεσης και την αναστολή της ισχύος της απόφασης.

Article 766

If the appeal is accepted and the judgment being contested is quashed or amended, the registry of the court that tried the appeal shall notify the registry of the court that handed down the judgment that was quashed or amended, which shall note the judgment handed down by the second-instance court in the register kept in accordance with Article 776 and in the margin of the judgment handed down by the first-instance court.

Article 767

Applicants, respondents, appellants, respondents [in appeal], cassationers, cassationees, main and permissive intervenors, their universal successors and specific successors and the public prosecutor have the right to file an application for re-opening proceedings. The provisions of Article 762 also apply in this case.

Article 768

If the application for re-opening proceedings is accepted and the judgment contested is quashed or amended, the court registry shall note the judgment handed down in re-opened proceedings in the register kept in accordance with Article 776 and in the margin of the judgment quashed or amended.

Article 769

Even if successful, applicants, respondents, appellants, respondents [in appeal], main and permissive intervenors, their universal successors and specific successors, as well as the court of first instance public prosecutor have the right to file an application for cassation. The provisions of Article 762 also apply in this case.

Article 770

In addition to stay of enforcement, the chamber of the Supreme Court referred to in Article 565(2) may also order stay of the effect of the judgment.

Article 771

If stay of the effect or enforcement of a judgment is ordered under Article 770, the registry of the Supreme Court shall notify the registry of the court whose judgment is being stayed and the registry of the first-instance court without undue delay. The decision on stay shall be noted in the register kept in accordance with Article 776, in the margin of the judgment which the cassation proceedings concern and in the margin of the judgment handed down by the first-instance court.

Article 772

The judgment of the Supreme Court ordering cassation shall be noted in the register kept in accordance with Article 776 and in the margin of the judgment handed down by the first-instance court. To this end, the registry of the Supreme Court shall notify the registry of the first-instance court without undue delay, and the latter shall make the note in question.

Article 773

1. The provisions of Articles 743 to 759 apply to the bringing and adjudication of third-party proceedings.
2. New grounds for third-party proceedings may also be added in the pleadings.

Article 774

In addition to stay of enforcement, the court trying the third-party proceedings may also order stay of the effect of the judgment in accordance with Article 589.

Άρθρο 775

Αν ασκηθεί τριτανακοπή και γίνει δεκτή, η απόφαση που δέχεται την τριτανακοπή σημειώνεται χωρίς υπαίτια καθυστέρηση στο βιβλίο που τηρείται κατά τις διατάξεις του άρθρου 776 και στο περιθώριο της απόφασης που ακυρώνεται, με επιμέλεια της γραμματείας του δικαστηρίου.

Άρθρο 776

1. Σε κάθε πρωτοβάθμιο δικαστήριο τηρούνται βιβλία στα οποία καταχωρίζονται περιληπτικά:
α) οι αιτήσεις που υποβάλλονται κατά τη διαδικασία των άρθρων 740 έως 781 και οι αποφάσεις που εκδίδονται στις αιτήσεις αυτές,
β) οι αιτήσεις ανάκλησης ή μεταρρύθμισης των αποφάσεων, τα ένδικα μέσα που ασκούνται κατά των αποφάσεων, οι τριτανακοπές και οι σχετικές αποφάσεις,
γ) οι αποφάσεις με τις οποίες αναστέλλεται η ισχύς ή η εκτέλεση οποιοσδήποτε απόφασης.
2. Ο τρόπος που τηρούνται τα βιβλία και τα αλφαβητικά ευρετήρια, τα πιστοποιητικά που εκδίδονται με βάση τα βιβλία αυτά, καθώς και τα καθήκοντα των υπαλλήλων της γραμματείας σχετικά με την ενημέρωση των βιβλίων αυτών ορίζονται με διατάγματα που εκδίδονται με πρόταση του Υπουργού Δικαιοσύνης.

Άρθρο 777

Κάθε αντίγραφο ή απόσπασμα απόφασης στο περιθώριο της οποίας σημειώνεται η εξαφάνιση, η μεταρρύθμιση ή η αναστολή της ισχύος ή της εκτέλεσής της πρέπει να αναφέρει τη σημείωση αυτή.

Άρθρο 778

Αν στις υποθέσεις που αναφέρονται στο άρθρο 739 γίνει δεκτή ή απορριφθεί με οριστική απόφαση αίτηση, δεν είναι δυνατό να συζητηθεί νέα αίτηση των διαδίκων για το ίδιο αντικείμενο κατά τη διαδικασία των άρθρων 741 έως 781.

Άρθρο 779

Αν ανακληθεί ή μεταρρυθμιστεί ή εξαφανιστεί ή ανασταλεί η ισχύς μιας απόφασης, είναι ισχυρές οι καταβολές που έγιναν καλόπιστα από τον υπόχρεο ή τρίτο και δεν θίγονται τα δικαιώματα τα οποία απέκτησαν, καθώς και οι δικαιοπραξίες τις οποίες ενήργησαν τρίτοι καλόπιστα, με βάση την απόφαση, ώσπου να ισχύσει η απόφαση που ανακαλεί, μεταρρυθμίζει, εξαφανίζει ή αναστέλλει την ισχύ της προηγούμενης.

Άρθρο 780

Με την επιφύλαξη αυτών που ορίζουν διεθνείς συμβάσεις, απόφαση αλλοδαπού δικαστηρίου έχει στην Ελλάδα, χωρίς άλλη διαδικασία, την ισχύ που της αναγνωρίζει το δίκαιο του κράτους του δικαστηρίου που την εξέδωσε, εφόσον συντρέχουν οι εξής προϋποθέσεις:
1) αν η απόφαση εφάρμοσε τον ουσιαστικό νόμο που έπρεπε να εφαρμοστεί κατά το ελληνικό δίκαιο και εκδόθηκε από δικαστήριο που έχει δικαιοδοσία κατά το δίκαιο της πολιτείας της οποίας τον ουσιαστικό νόμο εφάρμοσε και
2) αν δεν είναι αντίθετη προς τα χρηστά ήθη ή προς τη δημόσια τάξη.

Άρθρο 781

1. Το δικαστήριο που δικάζει την αίτηση μπορεί σε οποιοδήποτε στάδιο της διαδικασίας, ύστερα από σχετικό αίτημα ή και αυτεπαγγέλτως, να εκδώσει προσωρινή διαταγή που καταχωρίζεται στα πρακτικά, με την οποία διατάζει τα αναγκαία ασφαλιστικά μέτρα έως την έκδοση της απόφασής του, για να εξασφαλιστεί ή να διατηρηθεί δικαίωμα ή να ρυθμιστεί κατάσταση.
2. Το δικαστήριο ανακαλεί οποτεδήποτε, ακόμη και αυτεπαγγέλτως, την προσωρινή διαταγή του.

Article 775

If third-party proceedings are brought and accepted, the judgment accepting the third-party proceedings shall be noted by the court registry without undue delay in the register kept in accordance with the provisions of Article 776 and in the margin of the judgment annulled.

Article 776

1. Registers shall be kept at every first-instance court in which the following shall be entered in summary form:

a) applications submitted under the procedure laid down in Articles 740 to 781 and the judgments handed down on such applications;

b) applications to revoke or amend judgments, the legal remedies filed against judgments, third-party proceedings and the relevant judgments;

c) decisions staying the effect or enforcement of any judgment.

2. The manner in which the registers and alphabetical indexes are kept, the certificates issued on the basis of such registers and the duties of registry clerks on keeping such registers up to date shall be specified in decrees issued on a proposal from the Minister of Justice.

Article 777

Any copy or excerpt of a judgment in the margins of which its annulment, amendment, or stay of effect or enforcement is noted must make reference to that note.

Article 778

If an application is accepted or dismissed by means of a final judgment in the cases referred to in Article 739, a new application filed by the parties in the proceedings on the same subject-matter under the procedure laid down in Articles 741 to 781 cannot be heard.

Article 779

If a judgment is revoked or amended or quashed or its effect is stayed, payments made in good faith by the debtor or third party shall remain effective, and the rights they acquired and the legal transactions entered into by third parties in good faith on the basis of the judgment shall not be prejudiced until the judgment revoking, amending, quashing or staying the effect of the previous judgment takes effect.

Article 780

Without prejudice to the provisions of international treaties and conventions, judgments handed down by foreign courts shall, without further procedure, have the effect in Greece recognised by the law of the state of the court that handed it down, provided the following conditions are met:

1) the judgment applied the substantive law that should have been applied under Greek law and was handed down by a court with jurisdiction under the law of the state whose substantive law it applied; and

2) it is not contrary to morality or public policy.

Article 781

1. The court trying the application may, at any stage of the proceedings, following a relevant request or even *ex officio*, issue an interim order, which shall be entered in the transcript, ordering the interim measures necessary to safeguard or preserve a right or regulate a situation until it has handed down a judgment.

2. The court may, even *ex officio*, revoke its interim order at any time.

ΚΕΦΑΛΑΙΟ Β'
Ειδικές διατάξεις.

Άρθρο 782

1. Όταν ο νόμος απαιτεί δικαστική απόφαση για να βεβαιωθεί ένα γεγονός με το σκοπό να συνταχθεί ληξιαρχική πράξη, η απόφαση εκδίδεται με αίτηση όποιου έχει έννομο συμφέρον ή του εισαγγελέα από το ειρηνοδικείο της περιφέρειας του ληξιάρχου ο οποίος θα συντάξει τη ληξιαρχική πράξη.
2. Η απόφαση πρέπει να βεβαιώνει και κάθε άλλο στοιχείο που πρέπει κατά το νόμο να περιέχει η ληξιαρχική πράξη, εκτός αν αυτό είναι αδύνατο.
3. Οι διατάξεις της παραγράφου 1 εφαρμόζονται και για τη διόρθωση ληξιαρχικής πράξης.

Άρθρο 783

Αρμόδιο κατά το νόμο να κηρύξει και να άρει την αφάνεια, καθώς και να μεταβάλει το χρόνο της έναρξής της είναι το δικαστήριο της τελευταίας κατοικίας που είχε στην Ελλάδα εκείνος που εξαφανίστηκε και, αν δεν υπάρχει κατοικία, της τελευταίας διαμονής του στην Ελλάδα. Αν δεν υπάρχει ούτε διαμονή, το δικαστήριο της πρωτεύουσας του κράτους.

Άρθρο 784

Αν την άρση της κατάστασης της αφάνειας ή τη μεταβολή του χρόνου της έναρξής της τη ζητεί κάποιος διάδικος, εφαρμόζονται οι διατάξεις του άρθρου 758. Αν τη ζητεί τρίτος, οι διατάξεις των άρθρων 773 έως 775.

Άρθρο 785

1. Η απόφαση που κηρύσσει την αφάνεια ή που μεταβάλλει το χρόνο της έναρξής της, εφόσον δεν είναι δυνατό να προσβληθεί με έφεση ή αναίρεση, ισχύει και παράγει αποτελέσματα υπέρ όλων και εναντίον όλων, πάντως τηρούνται οι λοιπές διατάξεις του άρθρου 47 του Αστικού Κώδικα.
2. Η απόφαση που δέχεται την αίτηση του αφάντου για να αρθεί η κατάσταση της αφάνειάς του δεν προσβάλλεται με έφεση, αναψηλάφηση ή αναίρεση.

Άρθρο 786

1. Όταν ζητείται κατά το νόμο να διοριστούν προσωρινή διοίκηση νομικού προσώπου ή εκκαθαριστές νομικού προσώπου ή εταιρίας που δεν έχει αποκτήσει νομική προσωπικότητα, αρμόδιο είναι το μονομελές πρωτοδικείο της περιφέρειας όπου έχει την έδρα του το νομικό πρόσωπο ή η εταιρία.
2. Στην περίπτωση που τα συμφέροντα των προσώπων τα οποία αποτελούν τη διοίκηση συγκρούονται προς τα συμφέροντα του νομικού προσώπου καλούνται κατά τη συζήτηση και τα πρόσωπα αυτά.
3. Το δικαστήριο μπορεί με αίτηση όποιου έχει έννομο συμφέρον να αντικαταστήσει την προσωρινή διοίκηση ή τους εκκαθαριστές για σπουδαίους λόγους. Κατά τη συζήτηση καλούνται και τα πρόσωπα αυτά.
4. Η ευθύνη των διορισμένων μελών της προσωρινής διοίκησης και των εκκαθαριστών περιορίζεται στις πράξεις ή παραλείψεις αυτών κατά τη διάρκεια της θητείας τους.

CHAPTER II
Special provisions

Article 782

1. Where the law requires a judgment to confirm a fact for the purpose of preparing a civil registry certificate, that judgment shall be handed down, following an application filed by any person with a legitimate interest or the public prosecutor, by the court of the peace of the district of the registrar who is to prepare the civil registry certificate.
2. The judgment must also confirm any other information which, by law, the civil registry certificate must contain, unless that is impossible.
3. The provisions of paragraph 1 also apply to corrections to civil registry certificates.

Article 783

The court competent in law to issue and reverse a declaration of a person as absent and to change the time such absence commenced is the court of the last place of domicile of the person who disappeared in Greece and, where there is no such place of domicile, their last place of residence in Greece and, where there is no such place of residence, the court of the capital.

Article 784

If reversing [the declaration of] a person's absence or changing the time such absence commenced is requested by a party in the proceedings, the provisions of Article 758 apply and, if it is being requested by a third party, the provisions of Articles 773 to 775 [apply].

Article 785

1. Where the judgment declaring the absence of a person or changing the time such absence commenced cannot be contested by means of appeal or an application for cassation, such judgment is valid and generates effects *erga omnes*; in all cases, the other provisions of Article 47 of the Civil Code apply.
2. A judgment accepting an application filed by the absentee to reverse [the declaration of] their absence may not be contested by means of appeal, application for re-opening proceedings or application for cassation.

Article 786

1. When the appointment of a temporary management team for a legal person or liquidators of a legal person or entity that has not acquired legal personality is requested in accordance with the law, the single-member court of first instance of the district where the legal person or company has its registered offices has jurisdiction.
2. Where the interests of the persons on the management team conflict with the interests of the legal person, said persons shall be summoned to appear during the hearing.
3. Following an application filed by any person with a legitimate interest, the court may replace the temporary management team or the liquidators for a serious reason. Those persons shall also be summoned to appear during the hearing.
4. The liability of the members of the temporary management team and the liquidators appointed is limited to their acts or omissions during their term in office.

Άρθρο 787

1. Όταν ζητείται κατά το νόμο να διαταχθεί η εγγραφή σωματείου στο βιβλίο που τηρείται για αυτό το σκοπό, ή η τροποποίηση του καταστατικού ή η εξουσιοδότηση για τη σύγκληση της συνέλευσης σωματείου και τη ρύθμιση της προεδρίας της ή η διάλυση σωματείου, αρμόδιος είναι ο Ειρηνοδίκης της περιφέρειας που έχει έδρα το σωματείο.

2. Δικαίωμα ανακοπής κατά της διαταγής που δέχεται αίτηση εγγραφής σωματείου ή τροποποίησης καταστατικού έχει ο εισαγγελέας πρωτοδικών αυτεπαγγέλτως ή κατόπιν αίτησης της εποπτεύουσας αρχής, καθώς και κάθε τρίτος που έχει έννομο συμφέρον.

Άρθρο 788

Όταν ζητείται κατά το νόμο να διαταχθεί από το δικαστήριο έλεγχος ανώνυμης εταιρίας, αρμόδιο είναι το δικαστήριο της περιφέρειας όπου έχει την έδρα της η εταιρία.

Άρθρο 789

Όταν ζητείται κατά το νόμο η σύγκληση της συνέλευσης, η αναγραφή ή η αναγγελία των θεμάτων της συνέλευσης συνεταιρισμού, το ειρηνοδικείο της περιφέρειας όπου έχει την έδρα του ο συνεταιρισμός, με αίτηση των συνεταίρων, χορηγεί σ' αυτούς την άδεια να συγκαλέσουν τη συνέλευση και να γνωστοποιήσουν τα θέματά της. Κατά τη συζήτηση καλούνται τα μέλη της διοίκησης του συνεταιρισμού.

Άρθρο 791

1. Όποιος τηρεί δημόσια βιβλία στα οποία καταχωρίζονται πράξεις ή αποφάσεις που έχουν σχέση με τη σύσταση, μεταβίβαση ή κατάργηση δικαιωμάτων ιδιωτικού δικαίου ή εγγράφονται ή εξαλείφονται κατασχέσεις ή εγγράφονται αγωγές ή ανακοπές ή γίνονται σημειώσεις γι' αυτές, αν αρνείται να ενεργήσει όπως του ζητείται, οφείλει, το αργότερο μέσα στην επόμενη από την υποβολή της αίτησης ημέρα, να σημειώσει περιληπτικά στο σχετικό βιβλίο την άρνησή του και τους λόγους της.

2. Η εκκρεμότητα που δημιουργείται με την άρνηση αίρεται με απόφαση του δικαστηρίου στην περιφέρεια του οποίου εδρεύει εκείνος που τηρεί τα βιβλία, με αίτηση οποιουδήποτε έχει έννομο συμφέρον.

3. Η απόφαση γνωστοποιείται με επιμέλεια της γραμματείας σε εκείνον που τηρεί τα βιβλία, ο οποίος είναι υποχρεωμένος να ενεργήσει όπως διατάσσεται και, σε περίπτωση απόρριψης της αίτησης, να το σημειώσει στο σχετικό βιβλίο.

4. Η εγγραφή, σημείωση ή εξάλειψη που ενεργείται ως συνέπεια απόφασης θεωρείται ότι έγινε από τότε που υποβλήθηκε η σχετική αίτηση σ' αυτόν που τηρεί τα δημόσια βιβλία.

5. Αν ο υπάλληλος που αναφέρεται στην παρ. 1 αρνείται να χορηγήσει αντίγραφο, περίληψη ή πιστοποιητικό, αποφασίζει για τη χορήγηση το δικαστήριο που αναφέρεται στην παρ. 2.

Άρθρο 792

Όταν κατά το νόμο απαιτείται άδεια δικαστηρίου για να εκποιηθεί ενέχυρο ή για να αποδοθεί με παροχή άλλης ασφάλειας ή άδεια για την άρνηση της απόδοσής του, η άδεια παρέχεται με απόφαση του ειρηνοδικείου της περιφέρειας όπου βρίσκεται το ενέχυρο.

Άρθρο 793

Αν κατά το νόμο δικαιούται κάποιος να ζητήσει το διορισμό μεσεγγυούχου ή φύλακα, ο διορισμός, η αντικατάσταση και η παύση τους γίνεται με απόφαση του ειρηνοδικείου της περιφέρειας όπου βρίσκονται τα πράγματα που πρέπει να φυλαχθούν.

Article 787

1. When the entry of an association in the register kept for this purpose or the amendment of its statutes or authorisation for the calling of the meeting of the association and the regulation of [matters concerning] its board or the dissolution of an association is being requested in accordance with the law, the court of the peace judge of the district where the association has its seat shall have jurisdiction.
2. The court of first instance public prosecutor, whether *ex officio* or following an application by the supervising authority, as well as any third party with a legitimate interest, have the right to file an opposition against the order accepting an application to register an association or amend its statutes.

Article 788

When a court is requested in accordance with the law order the audit of a société anonyme, the court of the district where that company has its registered offices has jurisdiction.

Article 789

When the calling of a meeting, the entry or announcement of the items on the agenda for the meeting of a cooperative is requested in accordance with the law, the court of the peace of the district where the cooperative has its registered offices shall, following an application filed by the members, grant them permission to call the meeting and make public the items on its agenda. The members of the cooperative's management team shall be summoned to attend the hearing.

Article 791

1. Any person who keeps public registers in which acts or decisions concerning the establishment, transfer or abolition of private-law rights are entered, or attachments are recorded or deleted, or actions or oppositions are recorded or notes thereon are made and who refuses to take the steps being requested is obligated, no later than the day following the date the application is filed, to record their refusal in the relevant register in summary form as well as the grounds for such refusal.
2. Following an application filed by any person with a legitimate interest, the delay resulting from such refusal shall be ended by a judgment of the court in whose district the person who keeps the registers is based.
3. The judgment shall be notified by the [court] registry to the person who keeps the registers, who is obligated to take the steps ordered and, if the application is rejected, to make a note to this effect in the relevant register.
4. Such entry, note or striking-out effected pursuant to the judgment shall be deemed to have taken place from the date the relevant application was filed with the person who keeps the public registers.
5. If the employee referred to in paragraph 1 refuses to issue a copy, summary or certificate, the court referred to in paragraph 2 shall rule on the issuing of such [documents].

Article 792

Where permission from a court is required in law for a pledge[d thing] to be sold or to be handed back with different collateral, or for refusing to hand back the pledge[d thing], said permission shall be granted by a judgment of the court of the peace in whose district the pledge[d thing] is located.

Article 793

If a person is entitled in law to request that a sequestrator or custodian be appoitned, such persons shall be appointed, replaced and removed by a judgment of the court of the peace in whose district the things to be safekept are located.

Άρθρο 794

Αν κατά το νόμο δικαιούται κάποιος να ζητήσει το διορισμό πραγματογνωμόνων, ο διορισμός, η αντικατάσταση και η παύση τους γίνεται με απόφαση του ειρηνοδικείου της περιφέρειας όπου πρόκειται να διεξαχθεί η πραγματογνωμοσύνη.

Άρθρο 795

Αν υπάρχει δικαίωμα επικαρπίας και ο κύριος του πράγματος έχει δικαίωμα κατά το νόμο να ζητήσει να διαταχθεί με δικαστική απόφαση η εκμίσθωσή του ή η ανάθεση της άσκησης της επικαρπίας σε διαχειριστή, οι ενέργειες αυτές, καθώς και η άρση της άσκησης της επικαρπίας, διατάσσονται από το δικαστήριο της περιφέρειας όπου βρίσκεται το πράγμα. Τα ίδια ισχύουν και για το διορισμό, την αντικατάσταση ή την παύση του διαχειριστή.

Άρθρο 796

1. Όταν ζητείται ο διορισμός, η αντικατάσταση ή η παύση επιτρόπου, ειδικού επιτρόπου ή προσωρινού επιτρόπου, αρμόδιο είναι το δικαστήριο στην περιφέρεια του οποίου έχει τη συνήθη διαμονή του εκείνος που πρόκειται να τεθεί ή που βρίσκεται σε επιτροπεία. Το ίδιο δικαστήριο είναι αρμόδιο και για το διορισμό, την αντικατάσταση ή την παύση των μελών του εποπτικού συμβουλίου. Αν ο ανήλικος, που έχει την ελληνική ιθαγένεια, δεν έχει τη συνήθη διαμονή του στην ημεδαπή, η σχετική αίτηση μπορεί να ασκηθεί στο δικαστήριο της τελευταίας συνήθους διαμονής του στην Ελλάδα, διαφορετικά στο δικαστήριο της πρωτεύουσας του κράτους.

2. Σε όλες τις περιπτώσεις όπου, κατά την ισχύουσα νομοθεσία για την επιτροπεία ανηλίκου, προβλέπεται η αυτεπάγγελτη ενέργεια του δικαστηρίου, αυτό οφείλει να συντάσσει χωρίς καθυστέρηση την κατά την τέταρτη παράγραφο του άρθρου 747 πράξη του, ώστε η υπόθεση να εισάγεται προς συζήτηση στη συντομότερη κατά το δυνατό δικάσιμο.

3. Η σχετική αίτηση ή η πράξη της τέταρτης παραγράφου του άρθρου 747 κοινοποιούνται υποχρεωτικά και στην αρμόδια κοινωνική υπηρεσία στις περιπτώσεις όπου ο νόμος προβλέπει ότι η σύνταξη και η υποβολή σχετικής έκθεσής της είναι υποχρεωτική. Η έκθεση της κοινωνικής υπηρεσίας πρέπει να κατατίθεται στη γραμματεία του δικαστηρίου τρεις ημέρες πριν από αυτήν που ορίστηκε για τη συζήτηση. Η έκθεση δεν είναι υποχρεωτική για τις περιπτώσεις του άρθρου 781.

4. Σε όλες τις περιπτώσεις όπου οι ισχύουσες διατάξεις για την επιτροπεία των ανηλίκων προβλέπουν την επικοινωνία του δικαστηρίου με τον ανήλικο και την ακρόασή του ή κρίνουν αναγκαία τη διεξαγωγή πραγματογνωμοσύνης, έχει εφαρμογή το άρθρο 612.

Άρθρο 797

Όταν σύμφωνα με το νόμο ζητείται να δοθεί άδεια να ενεργήσουν κάποια πράξη ο ανήλικος, αυτός που ασκεί τη γονική μέριμνα, ο επίτροπος ανηλίκου, ο δικαστικός συμπαραστάτης ενηλίκου, ο ίδιος ο ενήλικος που βρίσκεται σε κατάσταση δικαστικής συμπαράστασης, ο κληρονόμος από απογραφή, ο κηδεμόνας σχολάζουσας κληρονομιάς, ο εκκαθαριστής κληρονομιάς και ο εκτελεστής διαθήκης, αρμόδιο είναι το ειρηνοδικείο της συνήθους διαμονής του ανηλίκου ή αυτού που τελεί υπό δικαστική συμπαράσταση ή το δικαστήριο της κληρονομιάς. Για τις περιπτώσεις της δικαστικής επιμέλειας ξένων υποθέσεων αρμόδιο είναι το ειρηνοδικείο της συνήθους διαμονής αυτού που ζητεί το διορισμό του επιμελητή ή του τόπου όπου θα διεξαχθεί κυρίως η διαχείριση της υπόθεσης.

Άρθρο 798

Όταν ζητείται κατά το νόμο να χορηγηθεί άδεια για να ενεργηθεί πράξη εκτός από εκείνες που αναφέρονται στα άρθρα 792 και 797, αρμόδιο είναι το ειρηνοδικείο της κατοικίας και αν δεν υπάρχει κατοικία, της διαμονής του αιτούντος. Αν πρόκειται για εκποίηση πραγμάτων, το ειρηνοδικείο στην περιφέρεια του οποίου βρίσκονται τα πράγματα.

Article 794

If a person is entitled in law to request that experts be appointed, such experts shall be appointed, replaced and removed by a judgment of the court of the peace in whose district the expert evidence is to be prepared.

Article 795

If there is a right of usufruct and the [bare] owner of the thing has the right in law to request that its leasing or the assignment of exercise of [the right of] usufruct to a manager be ordered by court judgment, these steps as well as the removal of exercise of [the right of] usufruct shall be ordered by the court in whose district the thing is located. The same applies to the appointment, replacement or removal of the manager.

Article 796

1. Where it is requested that a tutor, guardian *ad litem* or interim guardian be appointed, replaced or removed, the court in whose district the place where the person who is to be placed or who has been placed under tutorship has their habitual residence is competent [to do so]. The same court is also competent to appoint, replace or remove the members of the supervisory board. If the juvenile who has Greek nationality does not have their place of habitual residence in Greece, the application in question may be filed with the court of the juvenile's last place of habitual residence in Greece, otherwise with the court of the capital.
2. In all cases where the legislation in force on tutorship of juveniles provides for steps to be taken *ex officio* by the court, the court is obligated to draft its decision under Article 747(4) without delay in order to bring the case for a hearing on the nearest hearing date possible.
3. The relevant application or decision referred to in Article 747(4) must also be notified to the competent social services, where the law stipulates that the drafting and submission of a relevant report is mandatory. The social services report must be filed with the court registry three days prior to the hearing date set. This report is not mandatory in the cases referred to in Article 781.
4. Article 612 applies in all cases where the provisions in force on tutorship of juveniles provide for contact between the court and the juvenile, and that they be heard, or deem the preparation of expert evidence necessary.

Article 797

Where it is requested in accordance with the law that permission be granted for the juvenile, the person exercising parental responsibility, the tutor of a juvenile, the legal guardian of an adult, the adult under legal guardianship, the heir under [the benefit of] inventory-taking, the curator of an unclaimed estate, the liquidator of an estate and the executor of a will [to enter into a legal transaction or take a legal step], the court of the peace of the place of habitual residence of the juvenile or the person under legal guardianship or the court ruling on the inheritance is competent [to grant such permission]. In cases of court-ordered custody of another's affairs, the court of the peace where the person requesting appointment of a custodian [of another's affairs] has their place of habitual residence or where the custody of the affairs will mainly take place has jurisdiction.

Article 798

When it is requiested in accordance with the law that permission be granted [to enter into transactions or take steps] other than those referred to in Articles 792 and 797, the court of the peace of the applicant's place of domicile or, where there is no such place of domicile, their place of residence, has jurisdiction and, in cases of sale of things, the court of the peace in whose district the things are located.

Άρθρο 799

Όταν ζητείται κατά το νόμο να χορηγηθεί άδεια για μεταθανάτια τεχνητή γονιμοποίηση ή για κυοφορία τέκνου από άλλη γυναίκα, αρμόδιο είναι το πολυμελές πρωτοδικείο, στην περιφέρεια του οποίου έχει τη συνήθη διαμονή της η αιτούσα ή εκείνη που θα κυοφορήσει το τέκνο.
Το δικαστήριο διατάζει να γίνει η συζήτηση κεκλεισμένων των θυρών, αν κρίνει ότι η δημοσιότητα πρόκειται να είναι επιβλαβής στα χρηστά ήθη ή ότι συντρέχουν ειδικοί λόγοι προστασίας της ιδιωτικής ή οικογενειακής ζωής των διαδίκων.

Άρθρο 800

1. Αρμόδιο για την τέλεση της υιοθεσίας είναι κάθε Μονομελές Πρωτοδικείο της Επικράτειας. Τα ελληνικά δικαστήρια έχουν δικαιοδοσία για την τέλεση της υιοθεσίας, αν ο υιοθετών ή ο υιοθετούμενος είναι ελληνικής ιθαγένειας, ακόμη και αν δεν έχουν τη συνήθη διαμονή τους στην Ελλάδα. Στην περίπτωση αυτή είναι αρμόδια τα δικαστήρια της πρωτεύουσας του Κράτους.
2. Οι συναινέσεις για την υιοθεσία δηλώνονται ενώπιον του δικαστηρίου που τελεί την υιοθεσία σε ιδιαίτερο γραφείο χωρίς δημοσιότητα.
Η ίδια διαδικασία τηρείται και όταν πρόκειται για την ακρόαση, από το δικαστήριο, του υποψήφιου να υιοθετηθεί ανηλίκου που δεν συμπλήρωσε το δέκατο έκτο έτος της ηλικίας του ή άλλων τέκνων του υποψήφιου θετού γονέα, στις περιπτώσεις που η ακρόαση αυτή προβλέπεται από το ουσιαστικό δίκαιο. Στην περίπτωση υιοθεσίας ανηλίκου που προστατεύεται από αρμόδια κοινωνική υπηρεσία ή αναγνωρισμένη κοινωνική οργάνωση, η συναίνεση των φυσικών γονέων για την τέλεση της υιοθεσίας μπορεί να δηλωθεί και ενώπιον δικαστηρίου ή δικαστή που έχουν λάβει σχετική εντολή.
3. Οι προθεσμίες της έφεσης, της αναίρεσης και της αναψηλάφησης εναντίον απόφασης που απαγγέλλει την υιοθεσία είναι, αν δεν επιδοθεί η απόφαση, ένα έτος και αρχίζουν σε κάθε περίπτωση από τη δημοσίευση της απόφασης.
4. Η προθεσμία της τριτανακοπής κατά της απόφασης που τελεί την υιοθεσία είναι έξι (6) μήνες από τη γνώση της υιοθεσίας και σε κάθε περίπτωση τρία (3) έτη από την τελεσιδικία της απόφασης. Ο φυσικός γονέας που, λόγω της εφαρμογής διατάξεων του ουσιαστικού δικαίου, δεν συναίνεσε στην υιοθεσία του παιδιού του έχει το δικαίωμα, προκειμένου να ασκήσει τριτανακοπή κατά της σχετικής δικαστικής απόφασης, να πληροφορείται τα στοιχεία αυτής της απόφασης από την αρμόδια κοινωνική υπηρεσία ή οργάνωση που συνέπραξε στην τέλεση της υιοθεσίας.
5. Οι ανήλικοι που έχουν συμπληρώσει το δέκατο έκτο έτος της ηλικίας τους έχουν την ικανότητα να παρίστανται αυτοπροσώπως στο δικαστήριο κατά την τέλεση της υιοθεσίας και να ασκούν ένδικα μέσα κατά της σχετικής απόφασης, ανεξάρτητα από το αντίστοιχο δικαίωμα του νόμιμου αντιπροσώπου τους.
6. Το δικαστήριο μπορεί να διατάξει, η κύρια διαδικασία τέλεσης της υιοθεσίας να διεξάγεται «κεκλεισμένων των θυρών».

Άρθρο 801

1. Όταν ζητείται ή πρόκειται να τεθεί αυτεπαγγέλτως ένα πρόσωπο σε δικαστική συμπαράσταση και να διοριστεί δικαστικός συμπαραστάτης ή ειδικός δικαστικός συμπαραστάτης, να αντικατασταθούν ή να παυθούν αυτά τα πρόσωπα, καθώς και να αρθεί η δικαστική συμπαράσταση, αρμόδιο είναι το δικαστήριο της συνήθους διαμονής του προσώπου. Το ίδιο δικαστήριο είναι αρμόδιο και για το διορισμό, την αντικατάσταση ή την παύση των μελών του εποπτικού συμβουλίου.
2. Αν Έλληνας δεν έχει συνήθη διαμονή στην ημεδαπή, αρμοδιότητα να τον θέσει σε δικαστική συμπαράσταση έχει το δικαστήριο της τελευταίας συνήθους διαμονής του στην Ελλάδα, διαφορετικά το δικαστήριο της πρωτεύουσας του κράτους. Αν έχει ήδη διοριστεί προσωρινός δικαστικός συμπαραστάτης από ημεδαπό δικαστήριο, το δικαστήριο αυτό είναι αρμόδιο και για την υποβολή, στη συνέχεια, στη δικαστική συμπαράσταση.

Article 799

When it is requested in accordance with the law that permission be granted for posthumous artificial insemination or for a surrogate to bear a child, the multi-member court of first instance in whose district the applicant or the surrogate has her place of habitual residence has jurisdiction.

The court shall order a hearing *in camera* if it deems that publicity would be injurious to morality or that special grounds apply for the protection of the private or family life of the parties in the proceedings.

Article 800

1. Every single-member court of first instance in Greece hase jurisdiction to grant adoptions. Greek courts have jurisdiction to grant adoptions if the adoptive parent or the adopted child has Greek nationality, even if they do not have their place of habitual residence in Greece. In this case, the courts of the capital have jurisdiction.

2. Consent regarding the adoption shall be declared before the court granting the adoption in a private office without publicity.

The same procedure shall also be followed in cases of a hearing of prospective adopted children, where they are juveniles under the age of 16, or the other children of the prospective adoptive parent by the court, where such hearing is provided for in substantive law. In the case of adoption of a juvenile under the protection of the competent social services or recognised organisation providing social support services, the consent of the biological parents to the granting of adoption may also be declared before a court or judge who has received relevant instructions.

3. The deadline for [filing an] appeal, [application for] cassation [or] application for re-opening proceedings against a judgment pronouncing adoption is one year if the judgment is not served, commencing in all events on the date the judgment was handed down.

4. The deadline for [bringing] third-party proceedings against a judgment granting adoption is six months from the date [the third party] became aware of the adoption and, in all events, three years from the date the judgment became *de jure* non-appealable. A biological parent who, due to application of provisions of substantive law, did not consent to the adoption of their child has the right, in order to institute third-party proceedings against the court judgment in question, to be informed of the details of this judgment by the competent social service or social organisation that was involved in granting the adoption.

5. Juveniles who have attained the age of 16 have capacity to appear in court in person during the granting of adoption and to file legal remedies against the judgment in question, notwithstanding the same right of their lawful proxy.

6. The court may order that the main proceedings for granting adoption be held *in camera*.

Article 801

1. Where it is requested that a person be placed or where a person is to be placed *ex officio* under legal guardianship and a legal guardian or guardian *ad litem* is to be appointed, replaced or removed, as well as where legal guardianship is requested or is to be reversed *ex officio*, the court where the person in question has their place of habitual residence is competent [to do so]. The same court is also competent to appoint, replace or remove the members of the supervisory board.

2. In the case of a Greek national who does not have their place of habitual residence in Greece, the court of that person's last place of habitual residence in Greece is competnet to place them under legal guardianship, otherwise the court of the capital is competent [to do so]. If an interim legal guardian has already been appointed by a Greek court, that court is also competnt to subsequently place the person in question under legal guardianship.

Άρθρο 802

1. Στις δίκες που αφορούν τη δικαστική συμπαράσταση ή την υποβολή προσώπου σε ακούσια νοσηλεία, το πρόσωπο αυτό, εφόσον έχει συμπληρώσει το δέκατο έκτο έτος της ηλικίας του, είναι πλήρως ικανό να παρίσταται στο δικαστήριο με το δικό του όνομα, να επιχειρεί όλες τις διαδικαστικές πράξεις, να επιχειρεί ή να δέχεται επιδόσεις κάθε είδους και να ασκεί ή να παραιτείται από ένδικα μέσα.
2. Σε δίκες για την υποβολή ενός προσώπου σε δικαστική συμπαράσταση, διατάσσεται υποχρεωτικώς η κλήτευση του ίδιου, καθώς και του τυχόν διορισμένου προσωρινού δικαστικού συμπαραστάτη του. Η δεύτερη παράγραφος του άρθρου 796 έχει εφαρμογή και εδώ.
3. Η διεξαγωγή ολόκληρης της συζήτησης, και ιδίως των αποδείξεων, γίνεται «κεκλεισμένων των θυρών», με εφαρμογή κατά τα λοιπά του άρθρου 114.
4. Κάθε σχετική απόφαση επιδίδεται, με την επιμέλεια του δικαστηρίου που την εξέδωσε, στα πρόσωπα που έλαβαν μέρος στη διαδικασία, στο δικαστικό συμπαραστάτη και στην αρμόδια κοινωνική υπηρεσία. Κατά τα λοιπά εφαρμόζεται η τέταρτη παράγραφος του άρθρου 805.
5. Το δικαστήριο γνωστοποιεί εγκαίρως στο πρόσωπο την απόφασή του, με την οποία το υποβάλλει σε δικαστική συμπαράσταση, ή διορίζει, αντικαθιστά ή παύει τον δικαστικό συμπαραστάτη. Στη γνωστοποίηση υπενθυμίζεται οπωσδήποτε στον συμπαραστατούμενο το δικαίωμά του να ασκήσει ένδικα μέσα. Η γνωστοποίηση παραλείπεται, αν υπάρχει προφανής αδυναμία του συμπαραστατούμενου να επικοινωνεί με το περιβάλλον ή βάσιμος κίνδυνος να προκληθεί βλάβη ή χειροτέρευση της υγείας του. Σε κάθε περίπτωση λαμβάνεται πρόνοια προστασίας της προσωπικότητάς του.

Άρθρο 803

1. Κατά της απόφασης που υποβάλλει ένα πρόσωπο σε δικαστική συμπαράσταση, διορίζει τον δικαστικό συμπαραστάτη, καθορίζει την έκταση των περιορισμών που επιβάλλονται στον συμπαραστατούμενο ή τροποποιεί το είδος και την έκταση της δικαστικής συμπαράστασης, ή που αρνείται την υποβολή στη δικαστική συμπαράσταση και το διορισμό δικαστικού συμπαραστάτη έχουν το δικαίωμα να ασκήσουν ένδικα μέσα όλα τα πρόσωπα που έλαβαν μέρος στη διαδικασία, σύμφωνα με το νόμο. Όταν η διαδικασία μπορεί να κινηθεί μόνο με αίτηση αυτού τον οποίο αφορά το μέτρο και αυτή απορρίφθηκε, δικαίωμα να ασκήσει ένδικα μέσα έχει μόνο το πρόσωπο αυτό. Ένδικα μέσα μπορεί να ασκήσει και ο δικαστικός συμπαραστάτης, στο όνομά του ή στο όνομα του συμπαραστατουμένου, κατά των αποφάσεων που αφορούν τον κύκλο των αρμοδιοτήτων του.
2. Παρέμβαση ή τριτανακοπή μπορούν να ασκήσουν μόνο τα πρόσωπα που νομιμοποιούνται να ζητήσουν την υποβολή του προσώπου σε δικαστική συμπαράσταση.
3. Το δικαστήριο μπορεί να παύσει τον δικαστικό συμπαραστάτη και με προσωρινή διαταγή του, σύμφωνα με το άρθρο 781, όταν πείθεται ότι συντρέχουν οι προϋποθέσεις για την παύση του, καθώς και ότι η αναβολή της λήψης του μέτρου συνεπάγεται επικείμενο κίνδυνο για τον συμπαραστατούμενο. Η σχετική απόφαση αρχίζει να ισχύει και με μόνη την κατάθεσή της στη γραμματεία του δικαστηρίου με σκοπό τη γνωστοποίησή της.

Άρθρο 804

1. Το δικαστήριο επικοινωνεί με αυτόν τον οποίο αφορά το μέτρο, ώστε να σχηματίσει άμεση αντίληψη για την κατάστασή του. Η προσωπική επικοινωνία μπορεί να γίνεται μέσα στο συνηθισμένο περιβάλλον του συμπαραστατέου, αν το ζητεί ο ίδιος ή αν αυτό διευκολύνει τη διευκρίνιση των πραγμάτων και δεν αντιτίθεται ο συμπαραστατέος. Η επικοινωνία παραλείπεται μόνο αν πιστοποιείται αρμοδίως ότι υπάρχει βάσιμος κίνδυνος για την υγεία του προσώπου, για το οποίο πρόκειται, ή αν αυτό βρίσκεται σε προφανή αδυναμία να επικοινωνήσει με το περιβάλλον. Κατά τα λοιπά έχει ανάλογη εφαρμογή η τέταρτη παράγραφος του άρθρου 612 παράγραφος 2.
2. Η διενέργεια πραγματογνωμοσύνης μπορεί, κατά την κρίση του δικαστηρίου, να παραλείπεται, αν προσκομίζεται βεβαίωση δημόσιας αρχής ή νομικού προσώπου δημοσίου δικαίου για την κατάσταση του συμπαραστατέου.

Article 802

1. In proceedings concerning the legal guardianship or involuntary hospitalisation of a person, the person in question, provided they have attained the age of 16, has full capacity to appear in court in their name, to take all procedural steps, to effect or accept service of any kind, and to file or discontinue legal remedies.

2. In proceedings concerning the placement of a person under legal guardianship, the court must necessarily summons the person in question and any interim legal guardian appointed for that person. Article 796(2) also applies in this case.

3. The entire hearing and the taking of evidence, in particular, shall be conducted *in camera*, and the provisions of Article 114 apply in all other respects.

4. All relevant judgments shall be served by the court that handed them down on the persons who took part in the proceedings, the legal guardian and the competent social services. In all other respects, Article 805(4) applies.

5. The court shall notify the person in question in good time of the judgment placing them under legal guardianship or appointing, replacing or removing the legal guardian. The notification must [inform] the person under legal guardianship of their right to file legal remedies. The notification shall be omitted if the person under legal guardianship is manifestly unable to communicate with their surroundings or there is a well-founded danger of their health being harmed or deteriorating. In all events, care shall be taken to protect the right of personality of the person in question.

Article 803

1. All the persons who took part in the proceedings in accordance with the law have the right to file legal remedies against the judgment placing a person under legal guardianship, appointing a legal guardian, specifying the extent of restrictions imposed on the person under legal guardianship or amending the type and extent of legal guardianship or refusing to place the person under legal guardianship and to appoint a legal guardian. Where the procedure can only be instituted following an application which was filed by the person whom the measure concerns and which was dismissed, only the person in question has the right to file legal remedies. Legal remedies against judgments concerning the legal guardian's remit may also be filed by the legal guardian either in their own name or that of the person under legal guardianship.

2. Only persons with standing to request the placement of a person under legal guardianship may file an opposition or initiate third-party proceedings.

3. The court may issue an interim order under Article 781 removing the legal guardian when it is convinced that the conditions for their removal are met and that delaying this measure would result in an imminent danger for the person under legal guardianship. The relevant judgment takes effect merely by being filed with the court registry for purposes of notification.

Article 804

1. The court shall contact the person whom the measure concerns in order to form a direct opinion on their situation. Personal contact may take place in the usual environment of the person to be placed under legal guardianship, if they so request or this would facilitate clarification of the matter and they do not object. Contact shall be omitted only if it is duly certified that there is a well-founded danger to the health of the person in question or if they are manifestly unable to communicate with their surroundings. In all other respects, the fourth [sub]paragraph of Article 612(2) applies *mutatis mutandis*.

2. The preparation of expert evidence may be omitted, at the discretion of the court, if a certificate issued by a state authority or a body governed by public law concerning the situation of the person to be placed under legal guardianship is adduced.

Άρθρο 805

1. Οι διατάξεις της πρώτης παραγράφου του άρθρου 801 ισχύουν και για το διορισμό του προσωρινού δικαστικού συμπαραστάτη. Για το διορισμό όμως προσωρινού δικαστικού συμπαραστάτη μετά την κίνηση της διαδικασίας για να τεθεί ένα πρόσωπο σε δικαστική συμπαράσταση, αρμόδιο είναι το δικαστήριο που δικάζει την κύρια υπόθεση. Η δεύτερη και η τρίτη παράγραφοι του άρθρου 802, καθώς και η πρώτη παράγραφος του άρθρου 804 εφαρμόζονται και για το διορισμό προσωρινού δικαστικού συμπαραστάτη πριν από την κίνηση της διαδικασίας της δικαστικής συμπαράστασης.
2. Προσωρινός δικαστικός συμπαραστάτης μπορεί να διοριστεί και με προσωρινή διαταγή του δικαστηρίου, σύμφωνα με το άρθρο 781, όταν από ιατρικό πιστοποιητικό συνάγεται ότι συντρέχουν, λόγω της κατάστασης της υγείας του προσώπου το οποίο αφορά το μέτρο, επείγοντες λόγοι υπέρ του διορισμού δικαστικού συμπαραστάτη και ότι απειλείται από την αναβολή κίνδυνος για τα συμφέροντά του. Η προσωρινή διαταγή εκδίδεται ύστερα από προηγούμενη ακρόαση του συμπαραστατέου και έκθεση της αρμόδιας κοινωνικής υπηρεσίας, εκτός αν επίκειται κίνδυνος από οποιαδήποτε αναβολή. Το β' εδάφιο της τρίτης παραγράφου του άρθρου 803 έχει εφαρμογή και εδώ.
3. Εφόσον το κρίνει απαραίτητο για τη διασφάλιση των συμφερόντων του συμπαραστατέου, το δικαστήριο που διόρισε τον προσωρινό δικαστικό συμπαραστάτη ορίζει ότι αυτός, εκτός από τις εξουσίες που του παρέχει το ουσιαστικό δίκαιο, παραστέκει τον συμπαραστατέο στη διενέργεια κάθε διαδικαστικής πράξης και την άσκηση ένδικων μέσων, τόσο κατά τη διεξαγωγή της κύριας δίκης για την υποβολή στη δικαστική συμπαράσταση, όσο και σε κάθε άλλη δίκη που αφορά το πρόσωπο ή την περιουσία του.
4. Αν διορίστηκε προσωρινός δικαστικός συμπαραστάτης, όλες οι επιδόσεις πρέπει να γίνονται σ' αυτόν και σ' εκείνον για τον οποίο διορίστηκε.
5. Ο διορισμός προσωρινού δικαστικού συμπαραστάτη για το χρονικό διάστημα μετά την έκδοση της απόφασης, με την οποία το πρόσωπο υποβλήθηκε σε δικαστική συμπαράσταση, καθώς και η διατήρηση ή αντικατάσταση, για το ίδιο χρονικό διάστημα, αυτού που είχε ήδη διοριστεί, γίνονται με την ίδια απόφαση, που απαγγέλλει την υποβολή στη δικαστική συμπαράσταση.

Άρθρο 806

Οι διατάξεις των παραγρ. 2 και 3 του άρθρου 763 δεν εφαρμόζονται στην περίπτωση αυτή.

Άρθρο 807

1. Για τη δημοσίευση δημόσιας ή μυστικής ή έκτακτης διαθήκης αρμόδιος είναι ο ειρηνοδίκης της περιφέρειας, όπου εδρεύει ο συμβολαιογράφος, ο οποίος τη συνέταξε ή στον οποίο έχει κατατεθεί, ενώ για τη δημοσίευση ιδιόγραφης διαθήκης και την κήρυξή της ως κύριας, ο ειρηνοδίκης στον οποίο προσάγεται για να δημοσιευθεί.
2. Αν η δημόσια διαθήκη έχει συνταχθεί σε προξενική αρχή ή έχει κατατεθεί στην αρχή αυτή μυστική ή έκτακτη διαθήκη, αρμόδιο για τη δημοσίευση είναι η προξενική αρχή στην οποία έχει συνταχθεί ή κατατεθεί. Οι προξενικές αρχές έχουν αρμοδιότητα να δημοσιεύουν και τις ιδιόγραφες διαθήκες που τους προσάγονται.

Άρθρο 808

1. Η δημοσίευση διαθήκης γίνεται με καταχώρησή της, ολόκληρης, στα πρακτικά του δικαστηρίου στα οποία βεβαιώνονται και όλα τα εξωτερικά ελαττώματά της.
2. Η δημοσίευση διαθήκης από προξενική αρχή γίνεται από τον πρόξενο ο οποίος συντάσσει πρακτικό που υπογράφεται από αυτόν και, αν πρόκειται για ιδιόγραφη διαθήκη, και από εκείνον που την παρέδωσε.

Article 805

1. The provisions of Article 801(1) also apply to the appointment of an interim legal guardian. However, after proceedings to place a person under legal guardianship have been instituted, the court trying the main case is competent to appoint an interim legal guardian. Article 802(2) and (3) and Article 804(1) also apply to the appointment of an interim legal guardian before legal guardianship proceedings have been instituted.

2. An interim legal guardian may also be appointed pursuant to an interim order issued by the court under Article 781 when it is concluded from a medical certificate that, due to the state of the health of the person whom the measure concerns, there are urgent grounds for appointing a legal guardian and that any delay would endanger that person's interests. The court shall issue the interim order after having first heard the person to be placed under legal guardianship and [examined] the report prepared by the competent social services, unless any delay would result in imminent danger. The second subparagraph of Article 803(3) also applies in this case.

3. Where deemed necessary to safeguard the interests of the person to be placed under legal guardianship, the court that appointed the interim legal guardian shall order that the guardian in question, in addition to the powers vested in them under substantive law, also support the person to be placed under legal guardianship in taking any procedural step and filing legal remedies, both during the main proceedings concerning their placement under legal guardianship and in any other proceedings that concern their person or property.

4. If an interim legal guardian has been appointed, all documents must be served on such guardian and the person for whom they were appointed.

5. The judgment pronouncing placement of a person under legal guardianship shall also provide for appointment of an interim legal guardian for the period after the judgment in question has been handed down, as well as retention or replacement of the guardian already appointed for the same period.

Article 806

The provisions of Article 763(2) and (3) do not apply in this case.

Article 807

1. In cases of a public or sealed or extraordinary will, the court of the peace judge in whose district the notary public who drafted the will or with whom it was filed is seated is competent to grant probate, and in cases of a holographic will and its declaration as valid, the court of the peace judge before whom it is produced for probate.

2. If the public will was prepared before a consular authority or a sealed or extraordinary will was filed with such an authority, the consular authority before which it was prepared or with which it was filed is competent. Consular authorities are also competent to grant probate for holographic wills produced before them.

Article 808

1. A will shall be granted probate by reproducing it in its entirety in the court transcript, in which all its physical defects shall also be attested.

2. In cases of probate granted by consular authorities, the consul shall grant probate and prepare a report which shall be signed by the consul and, in the case of a holographic will, by the person who presented the will.

3. Η κήρυξη ιδιόγραφης διαθήκης ως κυρίας γίνεται με πράξη του αρμόδιου για τη δημοσίευσή της ειρηνοδίκη, εφόσον πιθανολογηθεί γνησιότητα της γραφής και της υπογραφής του διαθέτη. Όταν η διαθήκη δημοσιεύθηκε από προξενική αρχή, αρμόδιος για να την κηρύξει κύρια είναι ο ειρηνοδίκης του δικαστηρίου της κληρονομιάς. Όταν με ιδιόγραφη διαθήκη ορίζεται αποκλειστικά κληρονόμος πρόσωπο που δεν είναι σύζυγος του διαθέτη ή δεν έχει με τον διαθέτη συγγενική σχέση τουλάχιστον τέταρτου βαθμού, διατάσσεται γραφολογική πραγματογνωμοσύνη προκειμένου να αποδειχθεί η γνησιότητα της γραφής και της υπογραφής του διαθέτη. Στην περίπτωση αυτή καλείται υποχρεωτικά, εξήντα (60) τουλάχιστον ημέρες πριν από τη συνεδρίαση, το Ελληνικό Δημόσιο.
4. Τα αντίγραφα των δημόσιων διαθηκών που δημοσιεύονται και τα πρωτότυπα των μυστικών ή έκτακτων ή ιδιόγραφων διαθηκών, με τα περικαλύμματά τους, χρονολογούνται και υπογράφονται από τον ειρηνοδίκη ή τον πρόξενο και φυλάγονται στο αρχείο του ειρηνοδικείου ή του προξενείου.
5. Αντίγραφα των πρακτικών δημοσίευσης της διαθήκης αποστέλλονται χωρίς υπαίτια καθυστέρηση, με επιμέλεια της γραμματείας του δικαστηρίου ή του προξενείου, στη γραμματεία του πρωτοδικείου Αθηνών, καθώς και στη γραμματεία του πρωτοδικείου της τελευταίας κατοικίας ή διαμονής του διαθέτη και φυλάγονται στα αρχεία τους.
6. Αντίγραφα διαθηκών και ανακλήσεων διαθηκών, που δημοσιεύθηκαν στο εξωτερικό, μπορεί να κατατεθούν σε ελληνική προξενική αρχή ή στη γραμματεία οποιουδήποτε ειρηνοδικείου. Η προξενική αρχή ή η γραμματεία που παραλαμβάνει τα αντίγραφα συντάσσει επάνω σε αυτά πράξη κατάθεσης, όπου αναγράφει όσα κατατέθηκαν, εκείνον που τα κατέθεσε και την ημερομηνία της κατάθεσης. Τα αντίγραφα αυτά πρέπει να είναι επικυρωμένα από την αλλοδαπή αρχή που δημοσίευσε τη διαθήκη. Αν είναι διατυπωμένες ολόκληρες ή εν μέρει σε ξένη γλώσσα, πρέπει να επισυνάπτεται, κατά την κατάθεσή τους, μετάφραση στην ελληνική γλώσσα του ξενόγλωσσου μέρους τους, που έχει γίνει από το Υπουργείο Εξωτερικών, ελληνική προξενική αρχή ή δικηγόρο. Αντίγραφά τους αποστέλλονται χωρίς καθυστέρηση, με επιμέλεια του προξένου που τα παρέλαβε ή της γραμματείας του δικαστηρίου, στη γραμματεία του πρωτοδικείου Αθηνών.

Άρθρο 809

Οι γραμματείς των ειρηνοδικείων και των προξενικών αρχών τηρούν βιβλία των διαθηκών που δημοσιεύονται και των αντιγράφων τους που οι γραμματείες αυτές φυλάγουν, καθώς και των αντιγράφων που κατατίθενται ή φυλάγονται κατά την παράγραφο 6 του άρθρου 808 του κώδικα αυτού. Η γραμματεία του πρωτοδικείου Αθηνών τηρεί βιβλία των διαθηκών που δημοσιεύονται από αυτό ή άλλα δικαστήρια και προξενικές αρχές, καθώς και των αντιγράφων τους που κατά την παράγραφο 6 του άρθρου 808 κατατίθενται στα άλλα δικαστήρια και τις προξενικές αρχές.

Άρθρο 810

Δικαστήριο της κληρονομίας είναι το ειρηνοδικείο στην περιφέρεια του οποίου ο κληρονομούμενος είχε κατά το χρόνο του θανάτου του την κατοικία του και, αν δεν είχε κατοικία, τη διαμονή του, και αν δεν είχε ούτε διαμονή, το ειρηνοδικείο της πρωτεύουσας του Κράτους.

Άρθρο 811

1. Το δικαστήριο της κληρονομίας, με αίτηση όποιου έχει έννομο συμφέρον ή και αυτεπαγγέλτως, μπορεί να διατάξει όποιο κατέχει διαθήκη να την καταθέσει. Το δικαστήριο μπορεί να επιβάλει στον κάτοχο της διαθήκης που δυστροπεί τις ποινές που προβλέπονται από το άρθρο 205.
2. Το δικαστήριο της κληρονομίας, με αίτηση όποιου έχει έννομο συμφέρον ή και αυτεπαγγέλτως, εφόσον πιθανολογείται ότι κάποιος κατέχει διαθήκη, μπορεί να τον υποχρεώσει να δώσει βεβαιωτικό όρκο.

3. A holographic will shall be declared valid by means of a decision of the court of the peace judge with jurisdiction to grant probate for the will, where the judge considers it likely on the balance of probabilities that the testator's handwriting and signature are authentic. Where a will was granted probate by a consular authority, the court of the peace judge of the court ruling on the inheritance is competent to declare it valid. Where a person who is not the spouse of the testator or is not a relative of the testator to at least the fourth degree is designated in a holographic will as the sole heir, handwriting expert evidence shall be ordered to prove the authenticity of the testator's handwriting and signature. In such cases, the Greek State must be summoned [to the hearing] at least 60 days prior to the sitting.
4. Copies of public wills granted probate and the originals of sealed or extraordinary or holographic wills and their dossiers shall be dated and signed by the court of the peace judge or the consul and kept in the archives of the court of the peace or the consulate.
5. Copies of will probate reports shall be sent by the court registry or consulate secretariat without undue delay to the registry of the Athens Court of First Instance and to the registry of the court of first instance where the testator had their final place of residence or domicile, and shall be kept in their archives.
6. Copies of wills and revocations of wills granted probate abroad may be filed with a Greek consular authority or the registry of any court of the peace. That consular authority or registry which receives such copies shall prepare a filing report upon those copies, noting everything filed, the person who filed them and the date of filing. Such copies must be certified by the foreign authority that granted probate for the will. If such wills or revocations are in a foreign language, whether in whole or in part, a translation of the foreign-language section prepared by the Ministry of Foreign Affairs, a Greek consular authority or a lawyer must be attached to them when they are filed. Copies shall be sent without delay to the registry of the Athens Court of First Instance by the consul who received them or the court registry.

Article 809

Court of the peace registrars and consular authority secretaries shall keep registers of wills granted probate and their copies kept at such registries and secretariats, as well as the copies filed or kept in accordance with Article 808(6) of this [C]ode. The registry of the Athens Court of First Instance shall keep registers of wills granted probate by the said court or other courts and consular authorities, as well as their copies filed with other courts and consular authorities in accordance with Article 808(6).

Article 810

The court ruling on the inheritance is the court of the peace in whose district the deceased person had their place of domicile at the time of death and, where they had no such place of domicile, their place of residence and, where they had no such place of residence, the court of the peace of the capital.

Article 811

1. Following an application filed by any person with a legitimate interest or even *ex officio*, the court ruling on the inheritance may order any person in possession of a will to file it. The court may impose the penalties provided for in Article 205 on any person in possession of a will who refuses to comply.
2. Following an application filed by any person with a legitimate interest or even *ex officio* and where it is considered likely on the balance of probabilities that a person is in possession of a will, the court ruling on the inheritance may order that person to take an attesting oath.

Άρθρο 812

Η δήλωση αποποίησης κληρονομιάς ή αποδοχής κληρονομιάς με το ευεργέτημα της απογραφής, αποδοχής ή αποποίησης του λειτουργήματος του εκτελεστή ή παραίτησης από αυτό και αποδοχής του διορισμού κηδεμόνα σχολάζουσας κληρονομίας ή παραίτησης από αυτόν γίνεται στη γραμματεία του δικαστηρίου της κληρονομίας.

Άρθρο 813

Όταν κατά το νόμο το δικαστήριο μπορεί να διορίσει ειδικό κηδεμόνα για τη διεξαγωγή δίκης, ο διορισμός, η αντικατάσταση και η παύση του γίνεται από το δικαστήριο της κληρονομίας. Από το ίδιο δικαστήριο γίνεται και η βεβαίωση ότι δεν υπάρχει άλλος κληρονόμος εκτός από το Δημόσιο.

Άρθρο 814

1. Όταν κατά το νόμο έχει κανείς το δικαίωμα να ζητήσει την εκκαθάριση κληρονομίας και το διορισμό εκκαθαριστή της, η εκκαθάριση της κληρονομίας διατάσσεται και ο διορισμός, η αντικατάσταση και η παύση του εκκαθαριστή γίνεται από το δικαστήριο της κληρονομίας. Από το ίδιο δικαστήριο παρατείνεται η προθεσμία για τη σύνταξη της απογραφής της κληρονομίας από τον εκκαθαριστή και γίνεται ο κανονισμός της σύμμετρης πληρωμής των δανειστών.

2. Αν εκείνος που πέθανε έχει κηρυχθεί σε κατάσταση πτώχευσης, δεν είναι δυνατό να διαταχθεί δικαστική εκκαθάριση της κληρονομίας του και η εκκαθάριση παύει, αν κηρυχθεί σε κατάσταση πτώχευσης κατά τη διάρκειά της.

Άρθρο 815

Όταν κατά το νόμο το δικαστήριο μπορεί να πάψει εκτελεστή διαθήκης, η παύση γίνεται από το δικαστήριο της κληρονομιάς. Το ίδιο δικαστήριο ορίζει προθεσμία δήλωσης αποδοχής του εκτελεστή και εκδίδει την απόφαση που προβλέπει ο νόμος σε περίπτωση περισσότερων εκτελεστών και ισοψηφίας τους.

Άρθρο 816

Όταν είναι δυνατό κατά το νόμο να οριστεί δικαστική προθεσμία για να κάνει δήλωση επιλογής όποιος βαρύνεται με κληροδότημα ή ο κληροδόχος ή τρίτος που ορίζεται με τη διαθήκη, η προθεσμία ορίζεται από το δικαστήριο της κληρονομιάς.

Άρθρο 817

1. Όταν κατά το νόμο ο κληρονόμος που έχει το ευεργέτημα της απογραφής έχει το δικαίωμα να παραχωρήσει την κληρονομική περιουσία προς τους δανειστές της κληρονομίας και τους κληροδόχους, το δικαστήριο της κληρονομίας διατάζει τη δικαστική εκκαθάριση της κληρονομικής περιουσίας που περιέχεται στον κληρονόμο, ο οποίος έχει το ευεργέτημα της απογραφής και διορίζει εκκαθαριστή της κληρονομίας.

2. Η δικαστική εκκαθάριση που αναφέρεται στην παρ. 1 διατάσσεται με αίτηση του κληρονόμου που έχει το ευεργέτημα της απογραφής και εφαρμόζονται οι διατάξεις για τη δικαστική εκκαθάριση της κληρονομίας και του άρθρου 814.

Άρθρο 818

1. Το δικαστήριο της κληρονομιάς είναι αρμόδιο να αποφασίζει, με αίτηση εκείνου που βαρύνεται με κληρονομικό καταπίστευμα, αν κατά το νόμο επιβάλλεται από τους κανόνες της τακτικής διαχείρισης να διαθέσει αντικείμενα της κληρονομιάς.

2. Το δικαστήριο που αναφέρεται στην παρ. 1, αν κρίνει ότι επιβάλλεται η διάθεση, μπορεί να ορίσει και τους όρους με τους οποίους πρέπει να γίνει. Η διάθεση αντικειμένων της κληρονομιάς χωρίς να τηρηθούν οι όροι αυτοί είναι άκυρη, εκτός αν όσοι αποκτούν δικαιώματα με βάση τη διάθεση αυτή προστατεύονται από το νόμο.

Article 812

Declarations of repudiation of an inheritance or acceptance of inheritance under benefit of inventory-taking, acceptance or refusal of the role of executor or relinquishment of such role, and acceptance of appointment as curator of an unclaimed estate or relinquishment of such appointment shall be made to the registry of the court ruling on the inheritance.

Article 813

Where the court may, in accordance with the law, appoint a special curator to conduct proceedings, said curator shall be appointed, replaced and removed by the court ruling on the inheritance. The same court shall also confirm that there is no heir other than the Greek State.

Article 814

1. Where a person has the right in accordance with the law to request that an estate be liquidated and a liquidator be appointed, the court ruling on the inheritance shall order the liquidation and appoint, replace and remove the liquidator. The same court shall extend the deadline for the liquidator to prepare an inventory of the estate, and shall regulate the *pari passu* payment of creditors.

2. If the deceased person had been declared bankrupt, judicial liquidation of their estate may not be ordered and the liquidation shall cease if bankruptcy is declared during said liquidation.

Article 815

Where a court may, in accordance with the law, remove the executor of a will, this removal shall be effected by the court ruling on the inheritance. The same court shall set a deadline for the executor to accept [their role as such], and shall hand down the judgment provided for in law where there are several executors and there is a tied vote between them.

Article 816

Where a court may, in accordance with the law, set a deadline for the person obligated to honour a bequest or a legatee or a third party designated in the will to declare their choice [concerning the bequest], the deadline shall be set by the court ruling on the inheritance.

Article 817

1. Where the heir with the benefit of inventory-taking has the right, in accordance with the law, to cede the estate to its creditors and legatees, the court ruling on the inheritance shall order judicial liquidation of the estate devolving to the heir who has the benefit of inventory-taking, and shall appoint a liquidator of the estate.

2. The judicial liquidation referred to in paragraph 1 shall be ordered following an application filed by the heir with the benefit of inventory-taking, and the provisions on judicial liquidation of estates and of Article 814 apply.

Article 818

1. Following an application filed by a person obligated to honour a testamentary trust, the court ruling on the inheritance is competent to rule if, in accordance with the law, that person is compelled by the rules of orderly management to dispose of contents of the estate.

2. If the court referred to in paragraph 1 rules that disposal is necessary, it may also specify the terms under which it must take place. Any disposal of contents of the estate without complying with such terms is null and void, unless the persons who acquire rights under said disposal are protected by law.

Άρθρο 819

Ο ειρηνοδίκης του δικαστηρίου της κληρονομίας με αίτηση του κληρονόμου ή του καταπιστευματοδόχου ή του κληροδόχου ή του εκτελεστή διαθήκης, η οποία αναρτάται για δέκα (10) ημέρες σε ειδικό χώρο του καταστήματος του Ειρηνοδικείου, χορηγεί το πιστοποιητικό για το κληρονομικό δικαίωμά του. Αν ασκηθεί μέσα στην παραπάνω προθεσμία παρέμβαση τρίτου, ο ειρηνοδίκης προσδιορίζει δικάσιμο για τη συζήτησή τους προκειμένου να εκδοθεί απόφαση επ' αυτών.

Το πιστοποιητικό (κληρονομητήριο) εκδίδεται από το γραμματέα του δικαστηρίου και παραδίδεται με απόδειξη παραλαβής του η οποία φυλάγεται στο αρχείο του δικαστηρίου. Αν την έκδοση του πιστοποιητικού τη διατάζει το δικαστήριο που δίκασε ύστερα από έφεση, το πιστοποιητικό το εκδίδει ο γραμματέας του πρωτοβάθμιου δικαστηρίου στον οποίο αποστέλλεται χωρίς υπαίτια καθυστέρηση αντίγραφο της απόφασης.

Άρθρο 820

1. Η διάταξη του ειρηνοδίκη και η απόφαση του δικαστηρίου της κληρονομίας που επιλαμβάνεται πρέπει να περιέχει:

α) το ονοματεπώνυμο του κληρονομουμένου,

β) τα ονοματεπώνυμα των κληρονόμων ή καταπιστευματοδόχων ή κληροδόχων στους οποίους παρέχεται,

γ) τις κληρονομικές μερίδες του καθενός ή τα αντικείμενα τα οποία περιέρχονται στον καθένα,

δ) τους όρους ή τους περιορισμούς με τους οποίους η κληρονομία, το καταπίστευμα ή η κληροδοσία περιέρχεται στον καθένα και, ιδιαίτερα αν πρόκειται για κληρονόμο, τα καταπιστεύματα και τα κληροδοτήματα που βαρύνουν την κληρονομία και

ε) τα ονοματεπώνυμα των εκτελεστών διαθήκης και τις εξουσίες που η διαθήκη τους παρέχει.

2. Αν το πιστοποιητικό χορηγείται σε εκτελεστή διαθήκης η πράξη του ειρηνοδίκη ή η απόφαση του δικαστηρίου πρέπει να περιέχει μόνο:

α) το ονοματεπώνυμο του κληρονομουμένου και

β) το ονοματεπώνυμο του εκτελεστή διαθήκης και τις εξουσίες που του παρέχει η διαθήκη.

Άρθρο 821

Όποιος στο πιστοποιητικό ονομάζεται κληρονόμος ή καταπιστευματοδόχος ή κληροδόχος ή εκτελεστής διαθήκης τεκμαίρεται ότι έχει τα δικαιώματα που αναφέρονται στο πιστοποιητικό αυτό και ότι δεν περιορίζεται από άλλες διατάξεις εκτός από εκείνες που αναγράφονται στο πιστοποιητικό.

Άρθρο 822

Κάθε δικαιοπραξία ή δικαστική πράξη όποιου στο πιστοποιητικό ονομάζεται κληρονόμος ή καταπιστευματοδόχος ή κληροδόχος ή εκτελεστής διαθήκης με τρίτον ή απέναντι σε τρίτον ή του τρίτου απέναντι σ' αυτούς είναι ισχυρή υπέρ του τρίτου, σε όση έκταση ισχύει το τεκμήριο του άρθρου 821, εκτός αν ο τρίτος γνώριζε την ανακρίβεια του πιστοποιητικού ή την υποβολή αίτησης για αφαίρεση ή κήρυξη ανίσχυρου του πιστοποιητικού ή την ανάκληση ή την τροποποίησή του.

Άρθρο 823

Αρμόδιο να διατάξει, με αίτηση οποιουδήποτε έχει έννομο συμφέρον ή και αυτεπαγγέλτως, να αφαιρεθεί, να κηρυχθεί ανίσχυρο, να τροποποιηθεί ή να ανακληθεί το πιστοποιητικό είναι το δικαστήριο της κληρονομίας.

Article 819

Following an application filed by the heir or the trustee or the legatee or the executor of a will, posted for 10 days at a special location within the building of the court of the peace, the court of the peace judge of the court ruling on the inheritance shall issue a certificate on the inheritance right of the aforesaid person. If a third party files an opposition within the above deadline, the court of the peace judge shall set a hearing date to hand down a judgment on those matters.

This certificate (certificate of inheritance) shall be issued by the court registrar and delivered with acknowledgement of receipt, which shall be kept in the court archives. If issuance of the certificate is ordered by the court which tried the matter following an appeal, the certificate shall be issued by the registrar of the first-instance court to whom a copy of the judgment shall be sent without undue delay.

Article 820

1. The order of the court of the peace judge and the judgment of the court ruling on the inheritance seised of the matter must contain:

a) the full name of the [deceased];

b) the full names of the heirs or trustees or legatees to whom it is issued;

c) the shares in the estate of each person or the things that devolve to each person;

d) the terms or restrictions under which the estate, trust or legacy devolves to each person and, particularly in the case of an heir, the trusts and legacies that encumber the estate; and

e) the full names of the executors of the will and the powers conferred upon them by the will.

2. If the certificate is issued to an executor of the will, the order of the court of the peace judge or the judgment of the court must contain only:

a) the full name of the [deceased]; and

b) the full name of the executor of the will and the powers conferred upon them by the will.

Article 821

Any person named in the certificate as heir or trustee or legatee or executor of the will shall be presumed to have the rights referred to in said certificate and not to be restricted by other [statutory] provisions save those referred to in the certificate.

Article 822

Any legal transaction or procedural step taken by any person named in the certificate as heir or trustee or legatee or executor of the will with a third party or vis-à-vis a third party or by a third party vis-à-vis the aforesaid persons generates effects to the benefit of the third party to the extent that the presumption referred to in Article 821 applies, unless the third party was aware of the inaccuracy of the certificate or the submission of an application to withdraw the certificate or to declare it null and void or to revoke or to amend it.

Article 823

Following an application filed by any person with a legitimate interest or even *ex officio*, the court ruling on the inheritance is competent to order that the certificate be withdrawn, declared null and void, amended or revoked.

Άρθρο 824

1. Η απόφαση που διατάζει την παροχή πιστοποιητικού είναι δυνατό να προσβληθεί με έφεση, μέσα σε προθεσμία είκοσι ημερών από τη δημοσίευσή της. Η προθεσμία της έφεσης και η άσκησή της αναστέλλουν την ισχύ της απόφασης και την έκδοση του πιστοποιητικού. Η απόφαση που διατάζει την παροχή πιστοποιητικού δεν προσβάλλεται με αναψηλάφηση, αναίρεση ή τριτανακοπή.
2. Η απόφαση που διατάζει την αφαίρεση του πιστοποιητικού ή το κηρύσσει ανίσχυρο ή εκείνη που το τροποποιεί ή το ανακαλεί μπορεί να προσβληθεί μόνο με τριτανακοπή μέσα στην προθεσμία που ορίζει το άρθρο 1965 Α.Κ.

Άρθρο 825
Ερμηνεία διαθήκης υπέρ του κράτους ή κοινωφελών σκοπών

Κάθε αμφιβολία ή αμφισβήτηση για την ερμηνεία διαθήκης ή άλλης πράξης με την οποία διαθέτονται περιουσιακά στοιχεία με κληρονομιά, κληροδοσία ή δωρεά υπέρ του κράτους ή κοινωφελών σκοπών, εφόσον αναφέρεται στον τρόπο της εκκαθάρισης και γενικά της διαχείρισης και της εκτέλεσης της περιουσίας που έχει διατεθεί για το κράτος ή για κοινωφελή σκοπό, υπάγεται στην αρμοδιότητα του Εφετείου της έδρας της Αποκεντρωμένης Διοίκησης που εποπτεύει την κοινωφελή περιουσία. Αν η κοινωφελής περιουσία υπάγεται στην εποπτεία του Υπουργού Οικονομικών, αρμόδιο είναι το Εφετείο Αθηνών.

Άρθρο 826

Ο ειρηνοδίκης, με αίτηση οποιουδήποτε έχει έννομο συμφέρον ή και αυτεπαγγέλτως, μπορεί, για να αποτραπεί κίνδυνος, να διατάξει τη σφράγιση πραγμάτων ορίζοντας συγχρόνως συμβολαιογράφο για να τη διενεργήσει. Αρμόδιος είναι ο ειρηνοδίκης της περιφέρειας όπου βρίσκονται τα πράγματα.

Άρθρο 827

1. Ο ειρηνοδίκης που διατάζει τη σφράγιση μπορεί να διατάξει κάθε πρόσφορο μέτρο για να επιτευχθεί η σφράγιση. Ο ειρηνοδίκης μπορεί να διατάξει η σφράγιση να γίνει και κατά τη νύχτα.
2. Δεν μπορούν να σφραγιστούν τα υπνοδωμάτια που χρησιμοποιούνται από εκείνους που στεγάζονται στο διαμέρισμα όπου γίνεται η σφράγιση.
3. Αντικείμενα που είναι αναγκαία για να χρησιμοποιούν εκείνοι που στεγάζονται στο διαμέρισμα όπου γίνεται η σφράγιση δεν σφραγίζονται και παραδίδονται σ' αυτούς.
4. Αντικείμενα των οποίων η σφράγιση είναι αδύνατη ή επιζήμια λόγω του είδους τους δεν σφραγίζονται και παραδίδονται για φύλαξη σε μεσεγγυούχο που διορίζει εκείνος που ενεργεί τη σφράγιση. Αν πρόκειται για αντικείμενα που μπορεί να υποστούν φθορά ο ειρηνοδίκης που διέταξε τη σφράγιση διατάζει την εκποίησή τους κατά τις διατάξεις για την αναγκαστική εκποίηση πραγμάτων τα οποία μπορούν να υποστούν φθορά.

Άρθρο 828

Αν κάποιος από εκείνους που παρευρίσκονται κατά τη σφράγιση ισχυρίζεται ότι υπάρχει διαθήκη ή άλλο σημαντικό έγγραφο, όποιος ενεργεί τη σφράγιση οφείλει να ερευνήσει αν υπάρχει. Αν τη σφράγιση την ενεργεί ο ειρηνοδίκης και βρεθεί η διαθήκη, την παραλαμβάνει και τη στέλνει χωρίς υπαίτια καθυστέρηση στο αρμόδιο για τη δημοσίευσή της δικαστήριο, και αν τη σφράγιση την ενεργεί συμβολαιογράφος, υπάλληλος της γραμματείας, διοικητής του σταθμού χωροφυλακής ή πρόεδρος της κοινότητας, την παραλαμβάνει και την παραδίδει χωρίς καθυστέρηση στον ειρηνοδίκη, ο οποίος τη στέλνει χωρίς υπαίτια καθυστέρηση στο αρμόδιο για τη δημοσίευση δικαστήριο. Αν βρεθεί άλλο σημαντικό έγγραφο, το παραλαμβάνει όποιος ενεργεί τη σφράγιση και ο ειρηνοδίκης διατάζει να παραδοθεί σ' αυτόν που δικαιούται να το κατέχει ή, ώσπου να εξακριβωθεί εκείνος που δικαιούται, να φυλάσσεται στο αρχείο της γραμματείας του ειρηνοδικείου.

Article 824

1. A judgment ordering issuance of a certificate may be contested by an appeal within a deadline of 20 days from the date the judgment is handed down. The [fact that the] deadline for [filing] an appeal [has commenced] and [the act of] filing the appeal shall stay the effect of the judgment and the issuance of the certificate. A judgment ordering issuance of a certificate may not be contested by means of an application for re-opening proceedings, cassation or third-party proceedings.
2. A judgment ordering that a certificate be withdrawn, or declaring it null and void, or amending it, or revoking it, may only be contested by means of third-party proceedings [instituted] within the deadline laid down in Article 1965 of the Civil Code.

Article 825
Interpretation of a will benefiting the Greek State or public-benefit purposes

Any doubts about or disputes concerning the interpretation of a will or other act devising assets by means of inheritance, legacy or donation benefiting the Greek State or public-benefit purposes, provided it makes reference to the manner of liquidation and general management and execution of the assets devised to the Greek State or a public-benefit purpose, fall under the jurisdiction of the court of appeal of the seat of the Decentralised Administration exercising powers of supervision over the estate intended for public-benefit purposes. If the estate intended for charitable purposes falls under the supervision of the Minister of Finance, the Athens Court of Appeal has jurisdiction.

Article 826

Following an application filed by any person with a legitimate interest or even *ex officio*, a court of the peace judge may, in order to avert a danger, order the sealing of things and appoint a notary public to effect said sealing. The court of the peace judge in whose district the things are located has jurisdiction.

Article 827

1. The court of the peace judge who orders the sealing may order any measures expedient for achieving such sealing. The court of the peace judge may also order that sealing take place at night-time.
2. The bedrooms used by the persons living in the dwelling where the sealing is taking place may not be sealed.
3. Things necessary for use by the persons living in the dwelling where the sealing is taking place shall not be sealed and shall be handed over to them.
4. Where it is impossible or harmful to seal things due their nature, they shall not be sealed, and shall be handed over for safekeeping to a sequestrator appointed by the person effecting the sealing. In cases of things that can become spoiled, the court of the peace judge who ordered the sealing shall order their sale in accordance with the provisions on forced sale of things that can become spoiled.

Article 828

If any of the persons present at the sealing claims that there is a will or other important document, the person effecting the sealing is obligated to search for it. If the sealing is being effected by a court of the peace judge and the will is found, the judge shall collect it and send it without undue delay to the court with jurisdiction to grant probate, and if the sealing is being effected by a notary public, registry clerk, commander of the gendarmerie station or president of a community, the person in question shall collect it and deliver it without delay to the court of the peace judge, who shall send it without undue delay to the court with jurisdiction to grant probate. If another important document is found, the person effecting the sealing shall collect it and the court of the peace judge shall order that it be handed over to the person entitled to have possession of it or, until it is ascertained who that person is, that it be kept in the archives of the registry of the court of the peace.

Άρθρο 829

1. Ο ειρηνοδίκης που διατάζει τη σφράγιση ορίζει μεσεγγυούχο των αντικείμενων που σφραγίζονται και κατά προτίμηση ορίζεται μεσεγγυούχος όποιος τα κατέχει.

2. Τα κλειδιά των αντικειμένων που σφραγίζονται παραλαμβάνει όποιος ενεργεί τη σφράγιση και τα παραδίδει, με έγγραφη απόδειξη, στη γραμματεία του ειρηνοδικείου.

3. Όποιος ενεργεί τη σφράγιση οφείλει να ερευνήσει αν έως τη σφράγιση έχει αφαιρεθεί κάποιο αντικείμενο, και να συγκεντρώνει κάθε σχετική πληροφορία.

Άρθρο 830

Για τη σφράγιση συντάσσεται έκθεση, η οποία εκτός από τα στοιχεία που απαιτούνται κατά το άρθρο 117 πρέπει να αναφέρει

1) την απόφαση του ειρηνοδίκη με την οποία διατάσσεται η σφράγιση,

2) περιγραφή των χώρων στους οποίους τοποθετήθηκαν οι σφραγίδες,

3) περιγραφή των εγγράφων που βρέθηκαν κατά το άρθρο 828 και αναφορά των προσώπων στα οποία παραδόθηκαν,

4) κάθε ισχυρισμό ή αμφισβήτηση εκείνων που παραβρέθηκαν κατά τη σφράγιση και κάθε τι που υπέπεσε στην αντίληψη εκείνου που έκανε τη σφράγιση και

5) βεβαίωση ότι εκείνος που έκανε τη σφράγιση παρέλαβε τα κλειδιά, ότι έκανε την έρευνα που αναφέρεται στο άρθρο 829 παρ. 3 και το αποτέλεσμά της. Αν στο διαμέρισμα το οποίο πρόκειται να σφραγιστεί δεν υπάρχουν κινητά πράγματα, αυτό σημειώνεται στην έκθεση.

Άρθρο 831

1. Αν η διατήρηση της σφράγισης δεν είναι αναγκαία ή πρόκειται να γίνει απογραφή, ο ειρηνοδίκης που διέταξε τη σφράγιση, με αίτηση οποιουδήποτε έχει έννομο συμφέρον ή και αυτεπαγγέλτως, διατάζει την αποσφράγιση. Αποσφράγιση και επανασφράγιση μπορεί να διαταχθεί και για να αποτραπεί κίνδυνος ή για άλλο σπουδαίο λόγο.

2. Ο ειρηνοδίκης κατά τη δικάσιμο που ο ίδιος ορίζει είναι υποχρεωμένος να διατάξει την κλήτευση εκείνου που ζήτησε τη σφράγιση, όπως και εκείνων που παραβρέθηκαν κατά την ενέργειά της, και αν η σφράγιση έγινε σε περιουσιακό στοιχείο κληρονομίας, μπορεί να διατάξει κλήτευση εκείνων που πιθανολογείται ότι είναι κληρονόμοι, καταπιστευματοδόχοι, κληροδόχοι και εκτελεστές διαθήκης.

Άρθρο 832

1. Αν η αποσφράγιση διατάσσεται για να γίνει απογραφή, ο ειρηνοδίκης ορίζει συμβολαιογράφο και πραγματογνώμονες κατά το άρθρο 838 παράγραφοι 2 έως 4.

2. Αν ο ειρηνοδίκης κρίνει ότι δεν είναι αναγκαία η διατήρηση της σφράγισης και δεν πρόκειται να γίνει απογραφή, με απόφασή του που διατάζει την αποσφράγιση ορίζει τον συμβολαιογράφο που θα την ενεργήσει.

Άρθρο 833

Ο ειρηνοδίκης με την απόφαση που διατάζει την αποσφράγιση ορίζει τα πρόσωπα στα οποία πρέπει να παραδοθούν τα αντικείμενα αφού γίνει αποσφράγιση. Αν η αποσφράγιση διατάχθηκε για να γίνει απογραφή, ο ειρηνοδίκης μπορεί να επιφυλαχθεί να ορίσει τα πρόσωπα αυτά μετά την ενέργεια της απογραφής. Ο ειρηνοδίκης μπορεί να ορίσει και μεσεγγυούχο για να παραλάβει, μετά την αποσφράγιση και την απογραφή, και να φυλάει τα αντικείμενα, ώσπου να αποφασιστεί σε όποιον πρέπει να παραδοθούν.

Article 829

1. The court of the peace judge ordering the sealing shall designate a sequestrator for the things sealed, with preference being given to the person in possession of the things in question.
2. The keys to things sealed shall be collected by the person effecting the sealing and delivered, with issuance of a written receipt, to the registry of the court of the peace.
3. Any person effecting sealing is obligated to check whether a thing had been removed by the time of the sealing and collect all relevant information.

Article 830

A report shall be prepared concerning the sealing and, in addition to the information required by Article 117, must include[:]
1) the decision of the court of the peace judge ordering the sealing;
2) a description of where the seals were placed;
3) a description of the documents found in accordance with Article 828 and reference to the persons to whom they were handed over;
4) any assertions or doubts by the persons present at the sealing and anything the person who effected the sealing became aware of; and
5) confirmation that the person who effected the sealing collected the keys, carried out the check referred to in Article 829(3) and the results of that check. If there are no movables in the dwelling to be sealed, this shall be noted in the report.

Article 831

1. If it is not necessary to retain the seal or if an inventory is to be taken, the court of the peace judge who ordered the sealing shall, following an application filed by any person with a legitimate interest or even *ex officio*, order unsealing. Unsealing and re-sealing may also be ordered to avert a danger or for other serious reason.
2. On the hearing date set by the court of the peace judge, that judge is obligated to order that the person who requested the sealing, as well as those present during the sealing, be summonsed, and if the sealing was effected on estate assets, may order that the persons considered likely on the balance of probabilities to be heirs, trustees, legatees and executors of a will be summonsed.

Article 832

1. If unsealing is ordered in order to take an inventory, the court of the peace judge shall designate a notary public and experts in accordance with Article 838(2) to (4).
2. If the court of the peace judge deems that it is not necessary to retain the seal and no inventory is to take place, they shall issue a decision ordering unsealing and designating a notary public for the unsealing.

Article 833

In the decision ordering unsealing, the court of the peace judge shall designate the persons to whom the things must be handed over after unsealing. If unsealing was ordered for the purpose of taking an inventory, the court of the peace judge may reserve the right to designate such persons after the inventory has been taken. The court of the peace judge may also designate a sequestrator to collect and safekeep the things after the unsealing and inventory-taking until it has been decided to whom they must be handed over.

Άρθρο 834

1. Όποιος ενεργεί την αποσφράγιση ορίζει την ημέρα και την ώρα που θα γίνει και καλεί εγγράφως ή προφορικώς να παραστούν στην αποσφράγιση όλοι οι διάδικοι που ήταν παρόντες στη συζήτηση για την αποσφράγιση ή οι πληρεξούσιοι που τους εκπροσώπησαν, οι πραγματογνώμονες και ο μεσεγγυούχος των αντικειμένων. Όταν γίνεται η αποσφράγιση μπορεί να παραστεί και οποιοσδήποτε έχει έννομο συμφέρον.

2. Σ' όποιον έλαβε την εντολή να ενεργήσει την αποσφράγιση παραδίδονται από τη γραμματεία, με έγγραφη απόδειξη, τα κλειδιά των αντικειμένων που σφραγίστηκαν.

Άρθρο 835

1. Όποιος ενεργεί την αποσφράγιση οφείλει να εξετάσει την κατάσταση των σφραγίδων που έχουν τεθεί.

2. Αν οι σφραγίδες που έχουν τεθεί δεν είναι άθικτες και την αποσφράγιση ενεργεί συμβολαιογράφος ή υπάλληλος της γραμματείας, διακόπτει κάθε παραπέρα ενέργεια και αυτό το αναφέρει αμέσως εγγράφως στον ειρηνοδίκη που διέταξε την αποσφράγιση.

3. Ο ειρηνοδίκης στις περιπτώσεις της παρ. 2 πηγαίνει χωρίς υπαίτια καθυστέρηση στον τόπο όπου έχουν τεθεί οι σφραγίδες, βεβαιώνει την κατάστασή τους και με απόφασή του διατάζει κάθε κατά την κρίση του πρόσφορο μέτρο.

Άρθρο 836

1. Η αποσφράγιση όταν γίνεται απογραφή ενεργείται βαθμιαία και όσο είναι αναγκαίο για να συνταχθεί η απογραφή. Αν η απογραφή δεν είναι δυνατό να τελειώσει την ίδια ημέρα, ο συμβολαιογράφος τη διακόπτει, ορίζει την ημέρα και την ώρα που θα την εξακολουθήσει και σφραγίζει τα αντικείμενα των οποίων η απογραφή δεν τελείωσε.

2. Μετά την ενέργεια της απογραφής τα αντικείμενα που απογράφηκαν παραδίδονται σε εκείνους που ορίζει η σχετική με την αποσφράγιση απόφαση και αν ο ειρηνοδίκης επιφυλάχθηκε με την απόφασή του να ορίσει τα πρόσωπα στα οποία πρέπει να παραδοθούν, ο συμβολαιογράφος τα ξανασφραγίζει.

Άρθρο 837

Για την αποσφράγιση συντάσσεται έκθεση, η οποία εκτός από ό,τι απαιτείται κατά το άρθρο 117 πρέπει να αναφέρει

1) την απόφαση του ειρηνοδίκη με την οποία διατάσσεται η αποσφράγιση,

2) βεβαίωση όποιου ενεργεί την αποσφράγιση ότι κάλεσε τα πρόσωπα που αναφέρονται στο άρθρο 834 και τον τρόπο με τον οποίο τα κάλεσε,

3) βεβαίωση όποιου ενεργεί την αποσφράγιση ότι οι σφραγίδες βρέθηκαν άθικτες,

4) κάθε αμφισβήτηση ή ισχυρισμό εκείνων που ήταν παρόντες στην αποσφράγιση και κάθε τι που υπέπεσε στην αντίληψη εκείνου που την ενεργεί και

5) τα πρόσωπα στα οποία παραδόθηκαν τα αντικείμενα.

Άρθρο 838

1. Ο ειρηνοδίκης, με αίτηση οποιουδήποτε έχει έννομο συμφέρον ή και αυτεπαγγέλτως, μπορεί να διατάξει να γίνει απογραφή πραγμάτων για να αποτραπεί κίνδυνος. Αρμόδιος είναι ο ειρηνοδίκης της περιφέρειας όπου βρίσκονται τα πράγματα.

2. Η απογραφή γίνεται από συμβολαιογράφο ο οποίος ορίζεται με την απόφαση που τη διατάζει. Αν κωλύεται ο συμβολαιογράφος, την απογραφή την ενεργεί ο νόμιμος αναπληρωτής του.

3. Ο ειρηνοδίκης που διατάζει την απογραφή ορίζει και δύο πραγματογνώμονες για να εκτιμήσουν τα αντικείμενα τα οποία θα απογραφούν.

4. Αν οι διάδικοι που είναι παρόντες στη συζήτηση υποδείξουν από κοινού συμβολαιογράφο και πραγματογνώμονες, ο ειρηνοδίκης ορίζει αυτούς που υποδείχθηκαν εκτός αν συντρέχουν σοβαροί λόγοι να μην οριστούν αυτοί.

Article 834

1. The person effecting unsealing shall set its time and date, and summon, whether verbally or in writing, all the parties present at the hearing concerning the unsealing or their authorised lawyers who represented them, the experts and the sequestrator of the things to attend the unsealing. Any person with a legitimate interest may also attend the unsealing.
2. The registry shall hand over the keys of the sealed things, with issuance of a written receipt, to the person ordered to effect the unsealing.

Article 835

1. The person effecting the unsealing shall be obligated to examine the condition of the seals placed.
2. If the seals placed are not intact and the unsealing is being effected by a notary public or a registry clerk, that person shall take no further steps and immediately report this fact in writing to the court of the peace judge who ordered the unsealing.
3. In the cases referred to in paragraph 2, the court of the peace judge shall visit the location where the seals were placed without undue delay, confirm their condition and issue a decision ordering any measure which they consider expedient.

Article 836

1. Where an inventory is to be taken, the unsealing shall be effected gradually and to the extent necessary for an inventory to be taken. If the inventory cannot be completed on the same day, the notary public shall interrupt it, set the date and time for its resumption and seal the things not yet taken into inventory.
2. After the inventory has been taken, the things taken into the inventory shall be handed over to the persons designated in the decision concerning the unsealing, and if the court of the peace judge reserved the right in their decision to designate such persons, the notary public shall re-seal them.

Article 837

A report shall be prepared on the unsealing and, in addition to the information required by Article 117, must include[:]
1) the decision of the court of the peace judge ordering the unsealing;
2) confirmation by the person effecting the unsealing that they summoned the persons referred to in Article 834 and the manner in which such persons were summoned;
3) confirmation by the person effecting the unsealing that the seals were found to be intact;
4) any doubts or assertions by the persons present at the unsealing and anything the person who effected the unsealing became aware of; and
5) the persons to whom the things were handed over.

Article 838

1. Following an application filed by any person with a legitimate interest or even *ex officio*, the court of the peace judge may order that an inventory of things be taken to avert a danger. The court of the peace judge in whose district the things are located has jurisdiction.
2. The inventory shall be taken by a notary public designated in the decision ordering it. If the notary public is indisposed, the inventory shall be taken by their lawful substitute.
3. The court of the peace judge ordering the taking of inventory shall also designate two experts to value the things to be taken into inventory.
4. If the parties in the proceedings present at the hearing jointly nominate a notary public and experts, the court of the peace judge shall designate those nominated, unless there are serious grounds for not designating such persons.

Άρθρο 839

1. Ο συμβολαιογράφος ορίζει την ημέρα και την ώρα που θα γίνει η απογραφή και καλεί εγγράφως ή προφορικώς τους διαδίκους που ήταν παρόντες κατά τη συζήτηση, μετά την οποία εκδόθηκε η απόφαση που διέταξε την απογραφή, καθώς και τους πραγματογνώμονες που έχουν οριστεί με την ίδια απόφαση να παραστούν κατά την απογραφή. Κατά την ενέργεια της απογραφής μπορεί να παραστεί όποιος έχει έννομο συμφέρον.

2. Οι πραγματογνώμονες που διορίστηκαν με την απόφαση που διατάζει την απογραφή δίνουν ενώπιον του συμβολαιογράφου τον όρκο που αναφέρεται στο άρθρο 385 παρ. 1.

Άρθρο 840

Για την απογραφή συντάσσεται έκθεση η οποία εκτός από ό,τι απαιτείται κατά το άρθρο 117, πρέπει να αναφέρει

1) την απόφαση με την οποία διατάσσεται η απογραφή,

2) τα ονόματα των πραγματογνωμόνων που είναι παρόντες και βεβαίωση του συμβολαιογράφου ότι έδωσαν τον όρκο που αναφέρεται στο άρθρο 839 παρ. 2,

3) βεβαίωση του συμβολαιογράφου ότι κάλεσε τα πρόσωπα που αναφέρονται στο άρθρο 834 και τον τρόπο με τον οποίο τα κάλεσε,

4) ακριβή περιγραφή των αντικειμένων και ακριβή εκτίμηση της αξίας τους από τους πραγματογνώμονες, κατά το χρόνο που συντάσσεται η απογραφή,

5) ακριβή περιγραφή όλων των αξιόγραφων και των μετρητών που βρέθηκαν,

6) ακριβή περιγραφή των εμπορικών ή οικιακών βιβλίων που βρέθηκαν, καθώς και όλων των εγγράφων που βρέθηκαν, και όλα αυτά τα μονογραφεί ο συμβολαιογράφος και

7) αν η απογραφή γίνεται ύστερα από αποσφράγιση, τα πρόσωπα στα οποία παραδίδονται τα αντικείμενα ή βεβαίωση ότι τα αντικείμενα που απογράφηκαν ξανασφραγίστηκαν.

Άρθρο 841

1. Κάθε διαφορά ή δυσχέρεια που προκύπτει κατά τη σφράγιση, την αποσφράγιση ή την απογραφή δικάζεται από τον ειρηνοδίκη που τις διέταξε.

2. Ο συμβολαιογράφος που ενεργεί τη σφράγιση, την αποσφράγιση και την απογραφή, αποφασίζει προσωρινά για τις διαφορές ή δυσχέρειες που παρουσιάζονται κατά τη διενέργειά τους και η απόφασή του καταχωρίζεται στην έκθεση και εκτελείται αμέσως. Οποιοσδήποτε έχει έννομο συμφέρον μπορεί να ζητήσει από τον ειρηνοδίκη που αναφέρεται στην παράγραφο 1, να ανακαλέσει την απόφαση αυτή και να επαναφέρει τα πράγματα στην προηγούμενη κατάσταση.

3. Οι αποφάσεις που εκδίδονται κατά την παράγραφο 1 έχουν προσωρινή ισχύ, δεν επηρεάζουν την κύρια υπόθεση και το δικαστήριο που είναι αρμόδιο να διατάξει ασφαλιστικά μέτρα μπορεί να τις τροποποιήσει ή να τις ανακαλέσει.

Άρθρο 842

Με διατάγματα που εκδίδονται με πρόταση του Υπουργού της Δικαιοσύνης μπορεί να οριστεί ο τρόπος που διενεργούνται η σφράγιση, η αποσφράγιση και η απογραφή.

Άρθρο 843

1. Στις περιπτώσεις που ορίζει ο νόμος, το δικαστήριο απευθύνει δημόσια πρόσκληση για την αναγγελία δικαιώματος ή απαίτησης.

2. Αρμόδιο είναι το ειρηνοδικείο της περιφέρειας της κατοικίας του αιτούντος ή, αν δεν έχει κατοικία, της διαμονής του.

Article 839

1. The notary public shall set the date and time of the inventory-taking and summon, whether verbally or in writing, the parties in the proceedings who were present at the hearing where the decision ordering the taking of inventory was issued, as well as the experts designated in the same decision to attend the taking of inventory. Any person with a legitimate interest may attend the taking of inventory.
2. The experts appointed in the decision ordering the taking of inventory shall take the oath referred to in Article 385(1) in the presence of the notary public.

Article 840

A report shall be prepared on the inventory taken and, in addition to the information required by Article 117, must include[:]
1) the decision ordering the taking of inventory;
2) the names of the experts present and a confirmation by the notary public that they took the oath referred to in Article 839(2);
3) confirmation by the notary public that they summoned the persons referred to in Article 834 and the manner in which such persons were summoned;
4) a precise description of the things and their precise valuation by the experts at the time the inventory was taken;
5) a precise description of all securities and cash found;
6) a precise description of all business or domestic ledgers found, as well as all documents found, all of which shall be initialled by the notary public; and
7) if the inventory is being taken following an unsealing, the persons to whom the things were handed over or confirmation that the things taken into inventory were re-sealed.

Article 841

1. Any dispute or difficulty that arose during sealing, unsealing or inventory-taking shall be tried by the court of the peace judge who ordered such steps.
2. The notary public effecting the sealing, unsealing [or] inventory-taking shall provisionally decide on the disputes or difficulties arising while these steps were being taken, and their decision shall be recorded in the report and enforced immediately. Any person with a legitimate interest may petition the court of the peace judge referred to in paragraph 1 to revoke this decision and to restore a prior state of affairs.
3. The decisions issued under paragraph 1 have provisional effect and do not affect the main case, and may be amended or revoked by the court with jurisdiction to order interim measures.

Article 842

The manner in which sealing, unsealing and inventory-taking are carried out may be laid down in [Presidential] decrees issued on a proposal from the Minister of Justice.

Article 843

1. In the cases provided for in law, the court shall issue a public call for the lodgement of any right or claim.
2. The court of the peace in whose district the applicant has their place of domicile or, where they have no domicile, place of residence has jurisdiction.

Άρθρο 844

1. Το δικαστήριο εξετάζει αν η αίτηση είναι παραδεκτή, και μπορεί να υποχρεώνει τον αιτούντα να βεβαιώσει με όρκο το περιεχόμενό της.
2. Αν το δικαστήριο κρίνει ότι η αίτηση είναι παραδεκτή, διατάζει να δημοσιευθεί πρόσκληση για την αναγγελία του δικαιώματος ή της απαίτησης. Η πρόσκληση πρέπει να περιέχει
α) το όνομα και την κατοικία του αιτούντος,
β) καθορισμό προθεσμίας για την αναγγελία και
γ) αναφορά της βλάβης που θα επέλθει αν η αναγγελία δεν γίνει εμπρόθεσμα.

Άρθρο 845

1. Η πρόσκληση για την αναγγελία δημοσιεύεται σε μία ή περισσότερες εφημερίδες που ορίζει το δικαστήριο, μία ή όσες φορές ορίζει η απόφαση.
2. Η προθεσμία για την αναγγελία αρχίζει από την τελευταία δημοσίευση και δεν μπορεί να είναι μικρότερη από εξήντα ημέρες.

Άρθρο 846

Οι αναγγελίες κατατίθενται στη γραμματεία του δικαστηρίου και συντάσσεται έκθεση. Η γραμματεία ειδοποιεί χωρίς υπαίτια καθυστέρηση όποιον ζήτησε να εκδοθεί διαταγή για τη δημοσίευση της πρόσκλησης, ώστε να λάβει γνώση της αναγγελίας.

Άρθρο 847

1. Μέσα σε τριάντα ημέρες από την παρέλευση της προθεσμίας για την αναγγελία, όποιος ζήτησε να εκδοθεί διαταγή για τη δημοσίευση της πρόσκλησης μπορεί να υποβάλει αίτηση για να εκδοθεί απόφαση που ορίζει τις συνέπειες αποκλεισμού του δικαιώματος ή της απαίτησης σύμφωνα με το νόμο.
2. Αναγγελία που γίνεται μετά την παρέλευση της προθεσμίας που έχει ταχθεί αλλά ως τη συζήτηση στο ακροατήριο, λαμβάνεται υπόψη.
3. Το δικαστήριο κατά τη συζήτηση μπορεί να διατάξει οτιδήποτε κρίνει πρόσφορο για να διευκρινιστεί η υπόθεση.
4. Αν μέσα στην προθεσμία της παρ. 1 δεν υποβληθεί αίτηση, το δικαστήριο, ύστερα από αίτηση που υποβάλλεται μέσα σε άλλες τριάντα ημέρες, μπορεί να ορίσει νέα προθεσμία για να υποβληθεί η αίτηση που αναφέρεται στην παράγραφο 1.

Άρθρο 848

1. Αν γίνει αναγγελία και αμφισβητηθεί το δικαίωμα ή η απαίτηση του αιτούντος, το δικαστήριο μπορεί είτε να αναστείλει τη διαδικασία ώσπου να λυθεί η αμφισβήτηση, είτε να εκδώσει απόφαση με την επιφύλαξη των δικαιωμάτων εκείνου που έχει αναγγελθεί.
2. Αν δεν έγινε αναγγελία, το δικαστήριο απαγγέλλει τις συνέπειες που ο νόμος ορίζει.
3. Περίληψη των αποφάσεων που εκδίδονται κατά τις παρ. 1 και 2 δημοσιεύεται κατά το άρθρο 845.

Άρθρο 849

1. Τριτανακοπή επιτρέπεται μόνο κατά αποφάσεων που απαγγέλλουν τις συνέπειες που ορίζει ο νόμος και μόνο εφόσον
α) η διαδικασία έγινε χωρίς να συντρέχουν οι προϋποθέσεις του νόμου,
β) παραβιάστηκαν διαδικαστικές διατάξεις και ιδιαίτερα εκείνες που αφορούν τις δημοσιεύσεις, τις προθεσμίες ή τις αναγγελίες,
γ) συντρέχουν οι προϋποθέσεις του άρθρου 544 περιπτ. 6.
2. Η τριτανακοπή που αναφέρεται στην παρ. 1 ασκείται μέσα σε προθεσμία δυο ετών από την τελευταία δημοσίευση της περίληψης της απόφασης.

Article 844

1. The court shall examine whether the application is admissible, and may order the applicant to confirm its content under oath.

2. If the court considers that the application is admissible, it shall order publication of a call for the lodgement of the right or claim. The call must contain[:]

a) the name and address of the applicant;

b) the deadline set for lodgement; and

c) reference to the harm that will occur if a claim is not lodged in good time.

Article 845

1. The call for lodging claims shall be published in one or more newspapers designated by the court, once or as many times as are specified in the decision.

2. The deadline for lodging claims commences on the date of the most recent publication and may not be shorter than 60 days.

Article 846

Claims shall be lodged with the court registry and a report shall be prepared. The registry shall notify without undue delay the person who requested that an order to publish a call be issued, so that they stand aware of the lodgement.

Article 847

1. Within 30 days of the lapse of the deadline for lodging claims, any person who requested that an order to publish a call be issued may file an application for a decision specifying the legal consequences of preclusion of the right or claim.

2. Claims lodged after the lapse of the deadline set but before the courtroom hearing shall be taken into account.

3. During the hearing, the court may order any steps expedient to clarify the case.

4. If an application is not filed within the deadline set in paragraph 1, the court may, following an application filed within a further 30-day period, set a new deadline for filing the application referred to in paragraph 1.

Article 848

1. If lodgement is made and the right or claim of the applicant is disputed, the court may either stay the proceedings until the dispute has been resolved or issue a decision without prejudice to the rights of the person who lodged the claim.

2. If no claim was lodged, the court shall issue a decision stating the legal consequences.

3. A summary of the decisions issued under paragraphs 1 and 2 shall be published in accordance with Article 845.

Article 849

1. Third-party proceedings are permitted only against decisions stating the legal consequences, and only where[:]

a) the procedure took place without the legal requirements being met;

b) procedural provisions were infringed and, in particular, those concerning publications, deadlines or lodgements;

c) the requirements laid down in Article 544(6) are met.

2. The third-party proceedings referred to in paragraph 1 must brought within a deadline of two years from the most recent publication of the summary of the decision.

Άρθρο 850

1. Κατά τη διαδικασία της πρόσκλησης μπορεί να κηρυχθεί αξιόγραφο ανίσχυρο και εφαρμόζονται και οι επόμενες ειδικές διατάξεις.

2. Η διαδικασία αυτή δεν εφαρμόζεται για τοκομερίδια, μερισματόγραφα καθώς και για άτοκα γραμμάτια πληρωτέα ενόψει.

Άρθρο 851

1. Σε τίτλους στον κομιστή ή τίτλους που μεταβιβάστηκαν με λευκή οπισθογράφηση, την έκδοση της διαταγής για τη δημοσίευση της πρόσκλησης δικαιούται να ζητήσει όποιος ήταν έως τώρα κομιστής του τίτλου που κλάπηκε, χάθηκε ή καταστράφηκε, και σε άλλα αξιόγραφα, όποιος μπορεί να ασκήσει δικαίωμα που πηγάζει από τα αξιόγραφα αυτά.

2. Αρμόδιο να εκδώσει τη διαταγή για τη δημοσίευση της πρόσκλησης είναι το ειρηνοδικείο του τόπου πληρωμής ο οποίος αναφέρεται στο αξιόγραφο. Αν δεν αναφέρεται τόπος πληρωμής, το ειρηνοδικείο της περιφέρειας όπου είναι η κατοικία ή η έδρα του εκδότη ή, αν δεν υπάρχει κατοικία, η διαμονή.

Άρθρο 852

Η αίτηση πρέπει να περιλαμβάνει το ουσιώδες περιεχόμενο του αξιογράφου που έχει κλαπεί, χαθεί ή καταστραφεί.

Άρθρο 853

Για να αποδειχθεί η κλοπή, η απώλεια ή η καταστροφή του αξιογράφου, καθώς και το δικαίωμα του αιτούντος να ζητήσει την έκδοση της διαταγής για τη δημοσίευση της πρόσκλησης, αρκεί πιθανολόγηση.

Άρθρο 854

1. Με την πρόσκληση καλείται ο κομιστής του αξιογράφου να αναγγείλει, το αργότερο ως το τέλος της προθεσμίας, τα δικαιώματά του και εφόσον κατέχει, το αξιόγραφο να το καταθέσει στη γραμματεία του δικαστηρίου. Η πρόσκληση πρέπει να ορίζει ως βλάβη, στην περίπτωση της παράλειψης της αναγγελίας, ότι το έγγραφο θα χάσει την ισχύ του.

2. Η πρόσκληση που αναφέρεται στην παρ. 1 δημοσιεύεται σύμφωνα με τις διατάξεις του άρθρου 845 παρ. 1, καθώς και στο δελτίο ανώνυμων εταιριών και εταιριών περιορισμένης ευθύνης της Εφημερίδας της Κυβερνήσεως και τοιχοκολλάται στην αίθουσα του Χρηματιστηρίου Αθηνών.

Άρθρο 855

Σε αξιόγραφα όπου κατά περιόδους καταβάλλονται, πρόσοδοι, η προθεσμία πρόσκλησης ορίζεται από το δικαστήριο αφού ληφθεί υπόψη ο χρόνος της κλοπής, της απώλειας ή της καταστροφής του αξιογράφου και ο χρόνος κατά τον οποίο αυτές οι πρόσοδοι μπορεί να απαιτηθούν.

Άρθρο 856

Αν ο κομιστής αναγγείλει το δικαίωμά του και καταθέσει το αξιόγραφο, η γραμματεία του δικαστηρίου καλεί χωρίς υπαίτια καθυστέρηση εκείνον που ζήτησε την έκδοση της διαταγής για τη δημοσίευση της πρόσκλησης ώστε να λάβει γνώση.

Άρθρο 857

Η απόφαση που εκδίδεται κατά το άρθρο 848 παρ. 2 κηρύσσει ανίσχυρο το αξιόγραφο με τα συνημμένα τοκομερίδια και μερισματόγραφα. Η απόφαση τοιχοκολλάται στην αίθουσα του Χρηματιστηρίου Αθηνών και εφαρμόζονται και οι διατάξεις του άρθρου 848 παρ. 3.

Article 850

1. Under the procedure for issuing calls, a security may be declared null and void, and the special provisions below also apply.
2. This procedure does not apply to interest coupons, dividend coupons and interest-free promissory notes payable on demand.

Article 851

1. In cases of bearer securities or securities transferred with a blank endorsement section, any person who, until that time, was the bearer of the security stolen, lost or destroyed is entitled to request that an order to publish a call be issued, and in cases of other securities, any person who can exercise a right deriving from said securities [is entitled to do so].
2. The court of the peace of the place of payment referred to in the security is competent to issue the order to publish a call. If no place of payment is referred to, the court of the peace in whose district the issuer has their place of domicile or registered offices or seat or, where there is no such place of domicile, their place of residence [is competent to do so].

Article 852

The application must include the essential information about the security that was stolen, lost or destroyed.

Article 853

In order to prove the theft, loss or destruction of the security, as well as the right of the applicant to request that an order to publish a call be issued, it shall suffice [for the court] to consider these likely on the balance of probabilities.

Article 854

1. In the call, the bearer of the security shall be required to make lodgement of their rights no later than the end of the deadline and, if they have the security in their possession, to deposit it with the court registry. The court must specify that, in the event of failure to make lodgement, the harm will be the loss of validity of the document.
2. The call referred to in paragraph 1 shall be published in accordance with the provisions of Article 845(1), as well as in the Sociétés Anonymes and Limited Liability Companies Bulletin of the Government Gazette, and shall be posted at the Athens Stock Exchange trading floor.

Article 855

In cases of securities where [amounts] are periodically payable, the deadline for the call shall be set by the court after having taken account of the time of theft, loss or destruction of the security and the time when such [amounts] may be claimed.

Article 856

If the bearer makes lodgement of their right and deposits the security, the court registry shall summon the person who requested that an order to publish a call be issued without undue delay so that they stand aware [of that fact].

Article 857

The decision issued under Article 848(2) shall declare the security and attached interest coupons and dividend coupons null and void. The ruling shall be posted at the Athens Stock Exchange trading floor, and the provisions of Article 848(3) shall apply.

Άρθρο 858

Όποιος ζήτησε να εκδοθεί απόφαση αποκλεισμού από δικαίωμα ή απαίτηση έχει δικαίωμα, από τότε που η απόφαση δεν μπορεί να προσβληθεί με έφεση και αναίρεση, να ασκήσει τα δικαιώματά του σύμφωνα με το ουσιαστικό δίκαιο.

Άρθρο 859

1. Το δικαστήριο ενώ διαρκεί η διαδικασία της πρόσκλησης δικαιούται να απαγορεύσει στον κομιστή του αξιογράφου οποιοδήποτε παροχή στην οποία περιλαμβάνεται και η παράδοση σ' αυτόν τοκομεριδίων και μερισματαποδείξεων που εκδίδονται μετά την απαγόρευση. Η απαγόρευση δεν αφορά τα τοκομερίδια και τα μερισματόγραφα που εκδόθηκαν πριν από τη δημοσίευση της. Απευθύνεται προς τον εκδότη ή και προς άλλα πρόσωπα, τα οποία μπορούν να δώσουν την παροχή και αναφέρει ότι άρχισε η διαδικασία της πρόσκλησης.
2. Η απαγόρευση μπορεί να αρθεί από το δικαστήριο και αυτεπαγγέλτως.
3. Η απαγόρευση και η άρση της δημοσιεύονται κατά το άρθρο 845.

Άρθρο 860

Το δικαστήριο μπορεί να διατάξει όποιους έχουν υποχρέωση που πηγάζει από το αξιόγραφο να καταθέσουν δημόσια το ποσό που οφείλεται ώσπου να εκδοθεί απόφαση σχετικά με τον αποκλεισμό του δικαιώματος ή της απαίτησης.

Άρθρο 861

Όταν ο νόμος υποχρεώνει κάποιον να δώσει βεβαιωτικό όρκο, αρμόδιο είναι το ειρηνοδικείο στην περιφέρεια του οποίου έχει την κατοικία του όποιος είναι υποχρεωμένος να δώσει τον όρκο.

Άρθρο 862

1. Η αίτηση με κλήση προς συζήτηση επιδίδεται προσωπικά στον υπόχρεο. Η διάταξη της παρ. 4 του άρθρου 143 εφαρμόζεται και εδώ.
2. Το ειρηνοδικείο με απόφαση του ορίζει προθεσμία μέσα στην οποία ο υπόχρεος οφείλει να δώσει τον όρκο.

Άρθρο 863

Δεν μπορεί να υποχρεωθεί να δώσει τον όρκο όποιος έχει ήδη δώσει τον ίδιο όρκο μέσα στην τελευταία τριετία ύστερα από αίτηση του ίδιου ή άλλου δανειστή, εκτός αν ο αιτών πιθανολογήσει ότι συντρέχουν ήδη οι προϋποθέσεις για νέα δόση του όρκου.

Άρθρο 864

Αν ο οφειλέτης δεν εμφανιστεί κατά την ημέρα που έχει οριστεί για να δώσει τον όρκο ή αφού εμφανιστεί αρνείται να τον δώσει, το ειρηνοδικείο, με αίτηση του δανειστή, διατάζει την προσωπική του κράτηση.

Άρθρο 865

1. Ο οφειλέτης, είτε έχει ήδη προσωποκρατηθεί είτε όχι, μπορεί με αίτηση προς το ειρηνοδικείο, να ζητήσει να του ορίσει το συντομότερο ημέρα για να δώσει τον όρκο. Για το σκοπό αυτό μπορεί να κληθεί και εκείνος που ζήτησε να δοθεί ο όρκος, αλλά αν δεν εμφανιστεί η δόση του όρκου δεν εμποδίζεται.
2. Όταν ο όρκος δοθεί, απολύεται εκείνος που έχει προσωποκρατηθεί και αν δεν έχει προσωποκρατηθεί ακόμη, ματαιώνεται η προσωπική κράτηση που έχει διαταχθεί.

Άρθρο 866

Η προσωπική κράτηση απαγγέλλεται και κατά εκείνων που εκπροσωπούν το νομικό πρόσωπο καθώς και κατά των νόμιμων αντιπροσώπων των προσώπων που έχουν ανάγκη από επιμέλεια. Δεν απαγγέλλεται κατά προσώπων που δεν υποβάλλονται σε προσωπική κράτηση.

Article 858

The person who requested issuance of a decision concerning preclusion of a right or claim is entitled, from the time the decision could no longer be contested by means of appeal and cassation, to exercise their rights under substantive law.

Article 859

1. During the procedure for issuing calls, the court is entitled to prohibit the bearer of the security from any performance, including handing over interest coupons and dividend coupons issued after that prohibition. The prohibition does not apply to interest coupons and dividend coupons issued prior to the decision [concerning prohibition]. [The decision concerning prohibition] shall be addressed to the issuer or other persons who can provide performance, and shall make reference to the fact that the procedure for issuing calls has commenced.
2. The prohibition may also be lifted *ex officio* by the court.
3. The prohibition and its lifting shall be published in accordance with Article 845.

Article 860

The court may order those with an obligation deriving from the security to deposit the amount owed with the state until a decision on the preclusion of the right or claim has been issued.

Article 861

Where a person is under a legal obligation to take an attesting oath, the court of the peace in whose district the person obligated to take the oath has their place of domicile has jurisdiction.

Article 862

1. The application with a summons to a hearing shall be served in person to the party in question. The provisions of Article 143(4) also apply in this case.
2. The court of the peace shall issue a decision laying down a deadline within which the party in question is obligated to take the oath.

Article 863

A person who has already taken the same oath within the last three years following an application by said person or another creditor cannot be obligated to take the oath, unless the applicant considers it likely on the balance of probabilities that the requirements for re-taking the oath are already met.

Article 864

If the debtor fails to appear on the day set for the oath to be taken or appears but refuses to take it, the court of the peace, following an application filed by the creditor, shall order that the debtor be detained.

Article 865

1. The debtor, whether or not detained, may file an application with the court of the peace requesting the nearest date be set for them to take the oath. To this end, the person who requested that the oath be taken may also be summoned, but if they fail to appear, this shall not hinder the oath being taken.
2. When the oath is taken, the detained person shall be released and, if not yet detained, the personal detention ordered shall be cancelled.

Article 866

Personal detention shall also be ordered against the persons representing a legal person and the lawful proxies of persons who require care. Personal detention may not be ordered against persons who are exempt from personal detention.

ΕΒΔΟΜΟ ΒΙΒΛΙΟ
ΔΙΑΙΤΗΣΙΑ

Άρθρο 867

Διαφορές ιδιωτικού δικαίου μπορούν να υπαχθούν σε διαιτησία με συμφωνία, αν εκείνοι που τη συνομολογούν έχουν την εξουσία να διαθέτουν ελεύθερα το αντικείμενο της διαφοράς. Οι διαφορές που αναφέρονται στο άρθρο 614 αρ. 3 δεν μπορούν να υπαχθούν σε διαιτησία.

Άρθρο 868

Συμφωνία για διαιτησία που αφορά μελλοντικές διαφορές είναι έγκυρη μόνο αν είναι έγγραφη και αναφέρεται σε ορισμένη έννομη σχέση από την οποία θα προέλθουν οι διαφορές.

Άρθρο 869

1. Η συμφωνία για διαιτησία καταρτίζεται εγγράφως. Έγγραφη θεωρείται η συμφωνία και αν καταρτίστηκε με ανταλλαγή ενυπόγραφων επιστολών, τηλεγραφημάτων, τηλετυπημάτων ή ενυπόγραφων τηλεομοιοτύπων. Αν αυτοί που συνομολόγησαν τη συμφωνία εμφανιστούν στους διαιτητές και λάβουν ανεπιφύλακτα μέρος στη διαιτητική διαδικασία, η έλλειψη εγγράφου θεραπεύεται.

2. Η συμφωνία για διαιτησία διέπεται από τις διατάξεις του ουσιαστικού δικαίου για τις συμβάσεις.

Άρθρο 870

1. Αν είναι εκκρεμής δίκη στα τακτικά πολιτικά δικαστήρια για τη διαφορά που συμφωνείται να επιλυθεί διαιτητικά, η υπαγωγή της στη διαιτησία πρέπει να προτείνεται κατά την πρώτη συζήτηση μετά τη συνομολόγηση της συμφωνίας, διαφορετικά είναι απαράδεκτη και εφαρμόζονται οι διατάξεις του άρθρου 264.

2. Η συμφωνία για διαιτησία μπορεί να γίνει και ενώπιον του δικαστηρίου ή του εντεταλμένου δικαστή κατά τη συζήτηση της υπόθεσης, οπότε το δικαστήριο παραπέμπει την υπόθεση στη διαιτησία και εφαρμόζονται οι διατάξεις του άρθρου 264.

Άρθρο 870Α

Αν ενώπιον του πολιτικού ή του διαιτητικού δικαστηρίου ανακύπτει ζήτημα κύρους της συμφωνίας διαιτησίας μεταξύ των διαδίκων, το μεταγενεστέρως επιληφθέν δικαστήριο αναστέλλει την εκδίκαση της ενώπιόν του δίκης μέχρι να εκδοθεί απόφαση από το πρώτο επιληφθέν δικαστήριο.

Άρθρο 871

1. Διαιτητές μπορούν να οριστούν ένας ή περισσότεροι, καθώς και ολόκληρο δικαστήριο.

2. Δεν μπορούν να οριστούν διαιτητές οι ανίκανοι για δικαιοπραξία, όποιοι έχουν περιορισμένη ικανότητα για δικαιοπραξία, όποιοι από καταδίκη έχουν στερηθεί την άσκηση των πολιτικών τους δικαιωμάτων και τα νομικά πρόσωπα.

BOOK VII
ARBITRATION

Article 867

Private-law disputes may be brought to arbitration by means of an agreement if the parties concluding the agreement can freely dispose of the subject-matter of the dispute. The disputes referred to in Article 614(3) may not be brought to arbitration.

Article 868

An arbitration agreement relating to future disputes is valid only if it is drawn up in writing and refers to a specific legal relationship from which such disputes will arise.

Article 869

1. Arbitration agreements shall be drawn up in writing. An agreement shall be deemed to be in writing if entered into by exchanging signed letters, telegrams, telexes or signed faxes. Any lack of a written document shall be remedied if the persons who entered into the agreement appear before arbitrators and unreservedly take part in the arbitration proceedings.
2. Arbitration agreement are governed by the provisions of substantive law applicable to contracts.

Article 870

1. Where proceedings are pending before the ordinary civil courts concerning a dispute agreed to be arbitrable, bringing the matter to arbitration must be pleaded during the hearing after the agreement has been entered into, otherwise the arbitration may not be admissibly brought for a hearing and the provisions of Article 264 apply.
2. The arbitration agreement may be entered into before the court or the delegated judge during the hearing of the case, in which case the court shall refer the matter to arbitration and the provisions of Article 264 apply.

Article 870A

If an issue concerning the validity of an arbitration agreement between the parties in the proceedings arises before the civil court or arbitration panel, the court last seised of the matter shall stay the proceedings before it until the court first seised of the matter has handed down a judgment.

Article 871

1. One or more arbitrators or even [judges selected from among all the judges comprising] the entire court may be appointed.
2. Persons unable to enter into legal transactions, persons with limited capacity to enter into legal transactions, persons who have been deprived of their civil rights due to a conviction and legal persons may not be appointed as arbitrators.

Άρθρο 871Α

1. Ο ορισμός δικαστικών λειτουργών ως διαιτητών ή επιδιαιτητών διέπεται από τις διατάξεις των επομένων παραγράφων.

2. Δικαστικός λειτουργός μπορεί να είναι μόνο μοναδικός διαιτητής (μονομελής διαιτησία) ή επιδιαιτητής. Δεν μπορεί να ασκήσει διαιτητικά έργα ο δικαστικός λειτουργός που δεν έχει συμπληρώσει πενταετή τουλάχιστον συνολική δικαστική υπηρεσία.

3. Αν η διαιτησία, κατά τη συμφωνία των μερών, προβλέπεται ότι θα διεξαχθεί από δικαστικό λειτουργό ορισμένου δικαστηρίου, αυτός είναι ο εκάστοτε εκ περιτροπής καλούμενος κατά τη σειρά αρχαιότητας μεταξύ των υπηρετούντων στο δικαστήριο αυτό προέδρων και δικαστών την ημέρα κατάθεσης της αίτησης. Το όνομα του δικαστικού αυτού λειτουργού γνωστοποιείται στον αιτούντα από τον πρόεδρο του δικαστηρίου ή από τον πρόεδρο του τριμελούς συμβουλίου που διευθύνει το δικαστήριο.

4. Ορισμός συγκεκριμένου δικαστικού λειτουργού ως διαιτητή ή επιδιαιτητή, είτε ονομαστικά είτε έμμεσα, με κριτήριο τη θέση ή ιδιότητα που έχει ή θα έχει στο μέλλον, είναι άκυρος. Η ακυρότητα αυτή δεν επιδρά στη συμφωνία για τη διαιτησία. Στην περίπτωση αυτή διαιτητής ή επιδιαιτητής είναι ο κατά την προηγούμενη παράγραφο καλούμενος από το δικαστήριο, στο οποίο ο συγκεκριμένος δικαστικός λειτουργός υπηρετούσε κατά την κατάρτιση της διαιτητικής συμφωνίας.

5. Αν η διαιτησία, κατά τη συμφωνία των μερών, προβλέπεται ότι θα διεξαχθεί από δικαστικό λειτουργό, χωρίς όμως να καθορίζεται με την ίδια ή με μεταγενέστερη συμφωνία το δικαστήριο από το οποίο θα προέλθει, θεωρείται ότι τα μέρη απέβλεψαν στο δικαστήριο του τόπου όπου καταρτίστηκε η συμφωνία για τη διαιτησία. Αν στον τόπο κατάρτισης της συμφωνίας λειτουργούν δικαστήρια διαφόρων δικαιοδοσιών ή βαθμών και δεν προκύπτει από τη συμφωνία εκείνο στο οποίο απέβλεψαν τα μέρη, θεωρείται ότι απέβλεψαν στο πολιτικό πρωτοδικείο και, αν πρόκειται για διοικητική διαφορά, στο διοικητικό πρωτοδικείο.

6. Σε κάθε δικαστήριο τηρείται από τη γραμματεία ιδιαίτερο βιβλίο, στο οποίο καταχωρίζονται για καθεμία από τις διαιτησίες και σε χωριστή στήλη, τα ονοματεπώνυμα των διαδίκων, καθώς και του μοναδικού διαιτητή ή επιδιαιτητή, οι χρονολογίες έκδοσης της απόφασης και της κατάθεσής της, καθώς και ο αριθμός της.

7. Ο κατά τις προηγούμενες διατάξεις καλούμενος δικαστικός λειτουργός υποχρεούται να διεξαγάγει τη διαιτησία η οποία αποτελεί μέρος των δικαστικών του καθηκόντων. Σε περίπτωση νόμιμου κωλύματος ή λόγου εξαίρεσης καλείται ο κατά σειράν επόμενος. Μεταγενέστερη μεταβολή στην υπηρεσιακή κατάσταση του δικαστικού λειτουργού δεν επιδρά στην ιδιότητά του ως μοναδικού διαιτητή ή επιδιαιτητή.

8. Οι διατάξεις των προηγούμενων παραγράφων εφαρμόζονται ανάλογα και όταν με τη συμφωνία των μερών προβλέπεται ότι ο διαιτητής ή ο επιδιαιτητής θα είναι εισαγγελικός λειτουργός.

Άρθρο 872

Αν με τη συμφωνία για διαιτησία δεν ορίζονται οι διαιτητές ή ο τρόπος του ορισμού τους, το κάθε μέρος ορίζει ένα διαιτητή. Συμφωνία με την οποία ορίζεται ότι το ένα από τα μέρη θα ορίσει διαιτητή και για το άλλο μέρος ή ότι τα μέρη μπορούν να ορίσουν άνισο αριθμό διαιτητών είναι άκυρη.

Article 871A

1. The appointment of judicial functionaries as arbitrators or presiding arbitrators is governed by the provisions of the paragraphs below.

2. A judicial functionary may only be a sole arbitrator (on a single-member arbitration panel) or a presiding arbitrator. A judicial functionary who has not completed a total of at least five years of judicial service may not engage in arbitration.

3. If, on the basis of the agreement of the parties, arbitration is to be carried out by a judicial functionary of a specific court, that judicial functionary shall be chosen by rotation in the order of seniority from among the presiding judges and judges serving at that court on the date the application is filed. The name of that judicial functionary shall be notified to the applicant by the president of the court or the president of the three-member management board of that court.

4. Appointment of a specific judicial functionary as arbitrator or presiding arbitrator, either by name or indirectly using the position or post they hold or will hold in the future, is not valid. Such invalidity has no impact on the arbitration agreement. In that case the arbitrator or presiding arbitrator shall be the person chosen by the court in accordance with the preceding paragraph where the specific judicial functionary served at the time the arbitration agreement was entered into.

5. If, on the basis of the agreement of the parties, arbitration is to be carried out by a judicial functionary, but without that agreement or a subsequent agreement specifying the court from which they will come, it shall be deemed that the parties specified the court at the place where the arbitration agreement was entered into. If there are courts of various jurisdictions or instances operating at the place where the agreement was entered into and the agreement does not indicate which court the parties intended, they shall be deemed to have intended the civil court of first instance and, if the matter is an administrative dispute, the administrative court of first instance.

6. The registry of each court shall keep a special register recording [the following information] for each arbitration in a separate column[:] the full names of the parties and of the sole arbitrator or presiding arbitrator, the dates on which the arbitration award was issued and the filing date, and the arbitration award number.

7. The judicial functionary chosen in accordance with the preceding provisions is obligated to conduct the arbitration as part of their judicial duties. In cases of legitimate impediment or grounds for exemption, the next judicial functionary in order shall be chosen. Any subsequent change in the service status of the judicial functionary shall not affect their capacity as the sole arbitrator or presiding arbitrator.

8. The provisions of the preceding paragraphs also apply *mutatis mutandis* when the agreement of the parties specifies that the arbitrator or presiding arbitrator will be a public prosecutor.

Article 872

If the arbitration agreement does not specify the arbitrators or the method for appointing them, each party shall appoint one arbitrator. An agreement which states that one of the parties shall also appoint an arbitrator for the other side or that the parties may appoint an uneven number of arbitrators is null and void.

Άρθρο 873

1. Αν οι διαιτητές δεν ορίζονται με τη συμφωνία για διαιτησία, αλλά είτε κατά τη συμφωνία είτε κατά το άρθρο 872 τους διαιτητές τους ορίζουν τα συμβαλλόμενα μέρη, το καθένα μπορεί να καλέσει το άλλο εγγράφως να ορίσει το διαιτητή ή τους διαιτητές, μέσα σε προθεσμία οκτώ τουλάχιστον ημερών και πρέπει να γνωστοποιήσει στο έγγραφο και το διαιτητή ή τους διαιτητές που το ίδιο ορίζει. Το μέρος στο οποίο απευθύνεται η κλήση οφείλει, μέσα στην οριζόμενη προθεσμία να ανακοινώσει σε εκείνον που το καλεί, το διαιτητή ή τους διαιτητές που αυτό ορίζει.
2. Σε κάθε διαιτητή γνωστοποιούνται τα ονόματα και οι διευθύνσεις του άλλου ή των άλλων διαιτητών.

Άρθρο 874

Αν οι διαιτητές είναι περισσότεροι και με τη συμφωνία για διαιτησία δεν ορίζεται διαφορετικά, οι διαιτητές οφείλουν να ορίσουν τον επιδιαιτητή μέσα σε δεκαπέντε ημέρες από την τελευταία κατά το άρθρο 873 παρ. 2 γνωστοποίηση και να το ανακοινώσουν στα μέρη που συνομολόγησαν τη συμφωνία.

Άρθρο 875

1. Αν ο διαιτητής που όρισε ένα από τα μέρη πεθάνει ή για οποιοδήποτε λόγο αρνείται ή κωλύεται να διενεργήσει τη διαιτησία ή εξαιρεθεί, το άλλο μέρος μπορεί να καλέσει εγγράφως το μέρος που όρισε αυτόν το διαιτητή να ορίσει άλλον, μέσα σε προθεσμία οκτώ τουλάχιστον ημερών. Το μέρος στο οποίο απευθύνεται η κλήση οφείλει μέσα στην οριζόμενη προθεσμία να ανακοινώσει σε εκείνον που το καλεί το διαιτητή που αυτό ορίζει.
2. Αν ο επιδιαιτητής που όρισαν οι διαιτητές πεθάνει ή για οποιοδήποτε λόγο αρνείται ή κωλύεται να διενεργήσει τη διαιτησία και οι διαιτητές δεν ορίσουν άλλον, καθένα από τα μέρη μπορεί να καλέσει εγγράφως τους διαιτητές να ορίσουν άλλον επιδιαιτητή, μέσα σε προθεσμία οκτώ ημερών και να το ανακοινώσουν στα μέρη που συνομολόγησαν τη συμφωνία.

Άρθρο 876

1. Αν κατά τη συμφωνία για διαιτησία τρίτος ορίζει το διαιτητή ή τους διαιτητές ή τον επιδιαιτητή, καθένα από τα μέρη και αν πρόκειται για τον επιδιαιτητή και καθένας από τους διαιτητές, μπορεί να καλέσει τον τρίτο εγγράφως να ορίσει, μέσα σε προθεσμία οκτώ τουλάχιστον ημερών, το διαιτητή ή τους διαιτητές ή τον επιδιαιτητή και να το ανακοινώσει σε εκείνον που καλεί και, αν πρόκειται για επιδιαιτητή, και στους διαιτητές.
2. Οι διατάξεις της παρ. 1 εφαρμόζονται και στην περίπτωση που ο διαιτητής ή επιδιαιτητής τον οποίο όρισε ο τρίτος πεθάνει ή για οποιοδήποτε λόγο αρνείται ή κωλύεται να διενεργήσει τη διαιτησία.

Άρθρο 877

Ο ορισμός διαιτητή από κάποιο από τα μέρη, ο ορισμός επιδιαιτητή από τους διαιτητές ή ο ορισμός των διαιτητών ή του επιδιαιτητή από τρίτον δεν ανακαλείται.

Άρθρο 878

1. Αν δεν οριστεί εμπρόθεσμα ο διαιτητής ή οι διαιτητές ή ο επιδιαιτητής και η συμφωνία για διαιτησία δεν ορίζει διαφορετικά, τους ορίζει με αίτηση το μονομελές πρωτοδικείο. Αρμόδιο είναι το μονομελές πρωτοδικείο, στην περιφέρεια του οποίου ορίζει η συμφωνία ότι θα διενεργηθεί η διαιτησία, διαφορετικά το μονομελές πρωτοδικείο της κατοικίας όποιου υποβάλλει την αίτηση ή, αν δεν υπάρχει κατοικία, της διαμονής του. Αν δεν υπάρχει και διαμονή, το μονομελές πρωτοδικείο της πρωτεύουσας του Κράτους.

Article 873

1. If the arbitrators are not specified in the arbitration agreement, but the contracting parties appoint their arbitrators in accordance with the agreement or in accordance with Article 872, each may invite the other in writing to appoint an arbitrator or arbitrators within a deadline of at least eight working days and must include in the document the name(s) of the arbitrator or arbitrators whom it has appointed. The recipient of the invitiation is obligated within that deadline to notify the sender of the invitation of the arbitrator or arbitrators appointed.
2. Each arbitrator shall be notified of the names and addresses of the other arbitrator(s).

Article 874

If there are several arbitrators and the arbitration agreement does not specify otherwise, the arbitrators are obligated to appoint a presiding arbitrator within 15 days from the last notification made in accordance with Article 873(2) and to notify the parties who entered into the agreement to this effect.

Article 875

1. If the arbitrator appointed by one of the parties dies or for any reason refuses to or is impeded from engaging in arbitration or is exempted, the other party may send a written invitation to the party who appointed the arbitrator to appoint another within a deadline of at least eight days. The recipient of the invitation is obligated within that deadline to notify the sender of the invitation of the arbitrator appointed.
2. If the presiding arbitrator appointed by the arbitrators dies or for any reason refuses to or is impeded from engaging in arbitration and the arbitrators do not appoint another, each of the parties may invite the arbitrators in writing to appoint another presiding arbitrator within a deadline of eight days and to notify the parties who entered into the agreement to this effect.

Article 876

1. If, in accordance with the arbitration agreement, a third party appoints the arbitrator or arbitrators or the presiding arbitrator, each of the parties, and in the case of the presiding arbitrator, each of the arbitrators, may invite the third party in writing to appoint the arbitrator or arbitrators or presiding arbitrator within a deadline of at least eight days and to notify the person so invited and, in the case of a presiding arbitrator, the arbitrators as well to this effect.
2. The provisions of paragraph 1 also apply if the arbitrator or presiding arbitrator appointed by a third party dies or for any reason refuses to or is impeded from engaging in arbitration.

Article 877

The appointment of an arbitrator by one of the parties, the appointment of a presiding arbitrator by the arbitrators or the appointment of arbitrators or the presiding arbitrator by a third party may not be revoked.

Article 878

1. If the arbitrator or arbitrators or presiding arbitrator is/are not appointed in good time and the arbitration agreement does not specify otherwise, they shall be appointed by the single-member court of first instance following an application to that end. Jurisdiction lies with the single-member court of first instance in whose district the agreement states that arbitration will take place, otherwise the single-member court of first instance where the applicant has their place of domicile or, where there is no such place of domicile, the place of residence. Where there is no such place of residence, jurisdiction lies with the single-member court of first instance of the capital.

2. Η παράγραφος 1 εφαρμόζεται και όταν ο διαιτητής ή ο επιδιαιτητής που όρισε το μονομελές πρωτοδικείο πεθάνει ή για οποιονδήποτε λόγο αρνείται ή κωλύεται να διενεργήσει τη διαιτησία.
3. Η αίτηση δικάζεται κατά τη διαδικασία των άρθρων 741 επ., και έχουν δικαίωμα να την υποβάλουν και τα μέρη που συνομολόγησαν τη συμφωνία για διαιτησία και αν πρόκειται για επιδιαιτητή και καθένας από τους διαιτητές. Η απόφαση δεν μπορεί να προσβληθεί με ένδικα μέσα. Αίτηση για ανάκληση ή για μεταρρύθμιση της απόφασης είναι απαράδεκτη μετά την έναρξη της διαιτητικής διαδικασίας.

Άρθρο 879

1. Σε κάθε πρωτοδικείο τηρείται κατάλογος διαιτητών τον οποίο καταρτίζει το πολυμελές πρωτοδικείο, σύμφωνα με όσα ορίζονται με διατάγματα που εκδίδονται με πρόταση του Υπουργού Δικαιοσύνης, Διαφάνειας και Ανθρωπίνων Δικαιωμάτων
2. Το μονομελές πρωτοδικείο ορίζει τους διαιτητές ή τον διαιτητή από τον κατάλογο των διαιτητών και, αν δεν υπάρχει κατάλογος ή αν συντρέχει κατά την κρίση του σοβαρός λόγος, ορίζει το κατάλληλο πρόσωπο.

Άρθρο 880

1. Όποιος ορίζεται ως διαιτητής ή επιδιαιτητής δεν είναι υποχρεωμένος να δεχτεί το διορισμό του.
2. Όποιος αποδέχτηκε τον ορισμό του ως διαιτητή ή επιδιαιτητή μπορεί για σοβαρό λόγο να αρνηθεί να εκπληρώσει τα καθήκοντα του, ύστερα από άδεια του δικαστηρίου. Η άδεια παρέχεται από το μονομελές πρωτοδικείο του τόπου της κατοικίας του ή αν δεν υπάρχει κατοικία της διαμονής του και αν δεν υπάρχει και διαμονή, από το μονομελές πρωτοδικείο της πρωτεύουσας του Κράτους, ύστερα από αίτηση του που δικάζεται κατά τη διαδικασία των άρθρων 741 επ.. Η απόφαση δεν προσβάλλεται με ένδικα μέσα, δεν ανακαλείται ούτε μεταρρυθμίζεται.

Άρθρο 881

Οι διαιτητές και ο επιδιαιτητής κατά την εκπλήρωση των καθηκόντων τους ευθύνονται μόνο για δόλο και βαριά αμέλεια.

Άρθρο 882

1. Το μέρος που καλεί για συζήτηση προκαταβάλλει το μισό της αμοιβής του διαιτητή ή των διαιτητών και του επιδιαιτητή, το οποίο ορίζεται στην επόμενη παράγραφο. Υποχρέωση προκαταβολής του ίδιου ποσοστού της αμοιβής έχει και κάθε άλλο μέρος, εφ' όσον με αίτημά του διευρύνεται το αντικείμενο της διαιτησίας. Το ποσό της προκαταβολής σε κάθε περίπτωση προσδιορίζεται από το διαιτητικό δικαστήριο με πράξη που καταχωρίζεται στην αίτηση ή στα πρακτικά. Σε εξαιρετικές περιπτώσεις ή για λόγους επιείκειας η προκαταβολή μπορεί, με την ίδια πράξη, να περιοριστεί σε ποσό μικρότερο από αυτό που προβλέπεται στο πρώτο εδάφιο, όχι όμως κάτω από το ένα τρίτο του ποσού της αμοιβής.
2. Το ύψος της συνολικής αμοιβής διαιτητών και επιδιαιτητών υπολογίζεται σε ποσοστό της αξίας του αντικειμένου της διαφοράς με βάση τον ακόλουθο πίνακα:
Για το τμήμα αξίας έως 500.000 δρχ. [χίλια πεντακόσια (1.500) ευρώ] 6%
Για το τμήμα αξίας 500.001 [1.500,01 ευρώ] έως 2.000.000 δρχ.[5.900 Ε] 5%
Για το τμήμα αξίας 2.000.001 [5.900,01 Ε] έως 5.000.000δρχ.[15.000 Ε] 4%
Για το τμήμα αξίας 5.000.001 [15.000,01 Ε]έως 10.000.000 δρχ.[29.000 Ε]3%
Για το τμήμα αξίας 10.000.001 [29.000,01Ε]έως 50.000.000 δρχ.[150.000Ε] 2%
Για το τμήμα αξίας 50.000.001 [150.000,01] και άνω 1%.
Αν το αντικείμενο της διαφοράς δεν είναι αποτιμητό σε χρήμα, η αμοιβή προσδιορίζεται από το διαιτητικό δικαστήριο κατά εύλογη κρίση.

2. Paragraph 1 also applies if the arbitrator or the presiding arbitrator appointed by the single-member court of first instance dies or for any reason refuses to or is impeded from engaging in arbitration.
3. The application shall be heard under the procedure laid down in Articles 741 *et seq.* and may also be filed by the parties who entered into the arbitration agreement and, in the case of the presiding arbitrator, by each of the arbitrators. The judgment may not be contested by any legal remedies. An application to revoke or amend the judgment shall be inadmissible after arbitration proceedings have commenced.

Article 879

1. Each court of first instance shall keep a list of arbitrators prepared by the multi-member court of first instance in accordance with the provisions of decrees issued on a proposal from the Minister of Justice, Transparency and Human Rights.
2. The single-member court of first instance shall appoint the arbitrator(s) from the list of arbitrators and, if there is no list or if it considers that there are serious grounds [for doing so], shall appoint the appropriate person.

Article 880

1. Persons appointed as arbitrators or presiding arbitrators are not obligated to accept their appointment.
2. Where there are serious grounds [for doing so], any person who has accepted their appointment as arbitrator or presiding arbitrator may refuse to perform their duties, with the court's permission. Permission shall be granted by the single-member court of first instance of their place of domicile or, where there is no such place of domicile, their place of residence and, where there is no such place of residence, by the single-member court of first instance of the capital, following an application heard under the procedure laid down in Articles 741 *et seq.* The decision in question may not be contested by legal remedies and may not be revoked or amended.

Article 881

The arbitrators and presiding arbitrator are only liable for *dolus* and gross negligence in the performance of their duties.

Article 882

1. The party who requests the hearing shall pay half the fees of the arbitrator or the arbitrators and presiding arbitrator in advance, as specified in the next paragraph. Any other party is obligated to pay the same percentage of the fee in advance, where they submit a request to extend the scope of the arbitration. In all cases, the advance payment amount shall be specified by the arbitration panel in a decision recorded on the application or in the transcript. In exceptional cases, or on grounds of clemency, the advance payment may be limited in the same decision to an amount lower than that specified in the first subparagraph, but may not be lower than 1/3 of the fee amount.
2. The total fee of the arbitrators and presiding arbitrators shall be calculated as a percentage of the value of the subject-matter of the dispute based on the table below:
For that part of the value up to 1,500 euros: 6%
For that part of the value from 1,500.01 euros up to 5,900 euros: 5%
For that part of the value from 5,900.01 euros up to 15,000 euros: 4%
For that part of the value from 15,000.01 euros up to 29,000 euros: 3%
For that part of the value from 29,000.01 euros up to 147,000 euros: 2%
For that part of the value greater than or equal to 147,000.01 euros: 1%
If the subject-matter of the dispute cannot be valued in monetary terms, the fee shall be set by the arbitration panel at its discretion.

Αν ο επιδιαιτητής είναι δικαστικός λειτουργός, η αμοιβή του ρυθμίζεται από το άρθρο 882Α και οι διαιτητές λαμβάνουν συνολικώς τα δύο τρίτα της κατά την παρούσα παράγραφο αμοιβής. Το ποσό της αμοιβής κατά διαιτητή ή επιδιαιτητή που δεν έχει την ιδιότητα δικαστικού λειτουργού δεν μπορεί να υπερβαίνει τα 15.000.000 εκτός αν η διαιτησία είναι διεθνής.

3. Με τη διαιτητική απόφαση γίνεται ο τελικός καθορισμός της αμοιβής και των εξόδων της διαιτησίας στα οποία περιλαμβάνεται και η αμοιβή του γραμματέα.

4. Σε εξαιρετικές περιπτώσεις, ιδίως σε πολύ απλές υποθέσεις ή για λόγους επιείκειας, οι διαιτητές μπορούν να περιορίσουν την αμοιβή τους έως το μισό. Με τη διαιτητική απόφαση κατανέμεται η συνολική αμοιβή μεταξύ διαιτητών και επιδιαιτητή. Αν τα μέρη αποφασίζουν τη ματαίωση της διαιτησίας, οφείλουν να το γνωστοποιήσουν εγγράφως στους διαιτητές, οι οποίοι στην περίπτωση αυτήν καθορίζουν τα έξοδα και αμοιβή μειωμένη, ανάλογη με την εργασία που είχε γίνει έως την ημέρα της ματαίωσης της διαιτησίας.

5. Η διαιτητική απόφαση ορίζει και το μέρος που θα επιβαρυνθεί με την αμοιβή και τα έξοδα, κατ' ανάλογη εφαρμογή των άρθρων 176 έως 180, 183 έως 185 και 188.

Σε κάθε περίπτωση η διαιτητική απόφαση μπορεί να ορίζει ότι τα μέρη είναι υπόχρεα εις ολόκληρο για την καταβολή της αμοιβής και των εξόδων, οπότε εφαρμόζονται οι διατάξεις των άρθρων 480 επ. του Αστικού Κώδικα.

6. Κάθε ενδιαφερόμενος έχει το δικαίωμα να προσφύγει εναντίον της διάταξης της διαιτητικής απόφασης που καθορίζει το ύψος της αμοιβής των διαιτητών και τα έξοδα ή να ζητήσει τον καθορισμό τους, αν δεν έχουν οριστεί. Η προσφυγή ασκείται μέσα σε τρεις (3) μήνες από την κατά το άρθρο 893 παρ. 2 κατάθεση της απόφασης και εκδικάζεται από το μονομελές πρωτοδικείο σύμφωνα με το άρθρο 622Α.

7. Στους διαιτητές και στον επιδιαιτητή, εάν δεν έχει ιδιότητα δικαστικού λειτουργού, καταβάλλεται ποσοστό ίσο με το 80% της αμοιβής τους. Το υπόλοιπο 20% καταβάλλεται συγχρόνως στο Ταμείο Χρηματοδοτήσεως Δικαστικών Κτιρίων (ΤΑ.Χ.ΔΙ.Κ.). Εάν το αντικείμενο της διαφοράς είναι αποτιμητό σε χρήμα, η καταβολή του κατά το προηγούμενο εδάφιο ποσοστού είναι προϋπόθεση για την κατά το άρθρο 893 κατάθεση της διαιτητικής αποφάσεως και την περιαφή του τύπου της εκτελέσεως. Ο περιορισμός της αμοιβής των διαιτητών ή επιδιαιτητών, δεν ισχύει σε διεθνείς διαιτησίες.

Άρθρο 882Α

1. Η αμοιβή δικαστικού ή εισαγγελικού λειτουργού ως μοναδικού διαιτητή ή ως επιδιαιτητή, κατανεμόμενη κατά τα οριζόμενα στην παράγραφο 2, δεν μπορεί να υπερβαίνει το πέντε τοις εκατό (5%) επί της μέχρι 5.900 ευρώ αξίας του αντικειμένου της διαφοράς, όπως αυτή προσδιορίζεται σύμφωνα με τα άρθρα 8 έως 11, το τέσσερα τοις εκατό (4%) επί του επιπλέον και μέχρι 15.000 ευρώ τμήματος της αξίας αυτής, το τρία τοις εκατό (3%) επί του περαιτέρω και μέχρι 29.000 ευρώ τμήματος αυτής, το δύο τοις εκατό (2%) επί του επιπλέον και μέχρι 150.000 ευρώ τμήματος αυτής και το ένα τοις εκατό (1%) επί του περαιτέρω τμήματος της αξίας, ούτε μπορεί να είναι ανώτερη των 44.000 ευρώ και επί διεθνών διαιτησιών των 59.000 ευρώ. Αν το αντικείμενο της διαφοράς δεν είναι αποτιμητό σε χρήμα, η αμοιβή του δικαστικού λειτουργού καθορίζεται από αυτόν, όχι όμως άνω του ορίου των 29.000 ευρώ. Στην περίπτωση αυτή, καθώς και όταν ο καθορισμός της αμοιβής στηρίζεται σε αποτίμηση του αντικειμένου της διαφοράς από το διαιτητή ή επιδιαιτητή, εφαρμόζονται οι διατάξεις της παρ. 6 του προηγούμενου άρθρ. 882. Το ποσό της αμοιβής διπλασιάζεται αν ο δικαστικός λειτουργός έχει βαθμό προέδρου εφετών, εφέτη, εισαγγελέα ή αντεισαγγελέα εφετών, Παρέδρου του Συμβουλίου της Επικρατείας ή του Ελεγκτικού Συνεδρίου και τριπλασιάζεται αν έχει βαθμό Αρεοπαγίτη ή Συμβούλου του Συμβουλίου της Επικρατείας ή του Ελεγκτικού Συνεδρίου και άνω, δεν μπορεί όμως να υπερβεί τα σαράντα τέσσερις χιλιάδες (44.000) ευρώ και προκειμένου περί διεθνών διαιτησιών τα πενήντα εννέα χιλιάδες (59.000) ευρώ.

2. Από το ποσό της αμοιβής ο δικαστικός λειτουργός λαμβάνει ποσοστό 35%, 25% καταβάλλεται συγχρόνως σε ειδικό λογαριασμό του Ταμείου Χρηματοδότησης Δικαστικών Κτιρίων (ΤΑ.Χ.ΔΙ.Κ.), το δε υπόλοιπο 40% κατατίθεται σε έντοκο λογαριασμό και περιέχεται σε κοινό ταμείο που τηρείται από τον οικείο πρόεδρο ή εισαγγελέα, ο οποίος τον Ιανουάριο κάθε τρίτου έτους κατανέμει το σύνολο των ποσών και των τόκων των δύο προηγούμενων ετών στους δικαστές ή τους εισαγγελείς που υπηρέτησαν στο δικαστήριο ή την εισαγγελία κατά τα εν λόγω δύο προηγούμενα έτη, ανάλογα με τη διάρκεια της υπηρεσίας τους κατά τη διετία αυτή.

If the presiding arbitrator is a judicial functionary, their fee shall be set in accordance with Article 882A, and the arbitrators shall receive a total of 2/3 of the fee specified in this paragraph. The fee of an arbitrator or presiding arbtirator who is not a judicial functionary may not exceed 44,000 euros unless the matter entails international arbitration.

3. The final level of the fee and arbitration costs, including the secretary's fee, shall be set in the arbitration award.

4. In exceptional cases, particularly in very straightforward cases or on grounds of clemency, the arbitrators may reduce their fee by up to half. The arbitration award shall allocate the total fee between the arbitrators and the presiding arbitrator. If the parties decide to end the arbitration, they are obligated to notify the arbitrators in writing to that effect, who, in this case, shall compute their expenses and reduced fee depending on the work done up until the date on which arbitration was ended.

5. The arbitration award shall also specify which party shall pay the fee and costs, and Articles 176 to 180, 183 to 185 and 188 apply *mutatis mutandis*.

In all cases, the arbitration award may stipulate that the parties are severally obligated to pay the fee and costs, in which case the provisions of Articles 480 *et seq.* of the Civil Code apply.

6. Each party concerned is entitled to seek recourse against the provision of the arbitration award setting the arbitrators' fees and costs or, if they have not been set, to request that they be set. Recourse shall be sought within three months from the date the award was filed in accordance with Article 893(2) and shall be adjudicated by the single-member court of first instance in accordance with Article 662A.

7. If the arbitrators and presiding arbitrator are not judicial functionaries, an amount equal to 80% of their fee shall be paid. At the same time, the remaining 20% shall be paid to the Court Buildings Financing Fund. If the subject-matter of the dispute can be valued in monetary terms, payment of the percentage referred to in the preceding subparagraph shall be a condition for the arbitration award to be filed in accordance with Article 893 and for an enforcement precept to be issued. The reduction in the fee of arbitrators or presiding arbitrators does not apply in matters entailing international arbitration.

Article 882A

1. The fee of the judicial functionary or public prosecutor as sole arbitrator or presiding arbitrator, allocated in accordance with paragraph 2, may not exceed 5% of the value of the subject-matter of the dispute up to 5,900 euros, as determined in accordance with Articles 8 to 11 [of this Code], 4% of the additional part of this value up to 15,000 euros, 3% of the additional part thereof up to 29,000 euros, 2% of the additional part thereof up to 150,000 euros, and 1% of the additional part of the value, nor may it exceed 44,000 euros and, in matters entailing international arbitration, 59,000 euros. Where the subject-matter of the dispute cannot be valued in monetary terms, the judicial functionary shall set their own fee, which may not exceed 29,000 euros. In this case, and where the fee is based on valuation of the subject-matter of the dispute by the arbitrator or presiding arbitrator, the provisions of Article 882(6) above shall apply. The fee shall be doubled if the judicial functionary holds the rank of presiding appeal judge, appeal judge, court of appeal public prosecutor or deputy public prosecutor, associate judge at the Council of State or Court of Audit, and shall be tripled if they hold the post of Supreme Court Judge or Councillor of the Council of State or the Court of Audit or above, but may not exceed 44,000 euros and, in matters entailing international arbitration, 59,000 euros.

2. Of that amount, 35% shall be received by the judicial functionary, 25% shall be paid at the same time into a special account of the Court Buildings Financing Fund and the remaining 40% shall be deposited in an interest-bearing account and held in a common fund kept by the competent presiding judge or public prosecutor who, in January of every third year, shall allocate all amounts and interest from the two previous years to the judges or public prosecutors who served at the court or the public prosecutor's office during the previous two years, pro rata to their length of service during that two-year period.

Εάν το αντικείμενο της διαφοράς είναι αποτιμητό σε χρήμα, η καταβολή των κατά το προηγούμενο εδάφιο ποσοστών είναι προϋπόθεση για την κατά το άρθρο 893 κατάθεση της διαιτητικής αποφάσεως και την περιαφή του τύπου της εκτελέσεως. Στην κατά την παρούσα παράγραφο διανομή μετέχουν και όσοι δεν έχουν συμπληρώσει την κατά το άρθρο 871Α, παρ. 2, εδάφ. β', πενταετία. Η πρώτη κατανομή μετά την έναρξη ισχύος του παρόντος θα γίνει τον Ιανουάριο του 1998.
Αντί της κατανομής το ποσοστό του 40% μπορεί, με απόφαση της Ολομέλειας του οικείου δικαστηρίου ή της εισαγγελίας, να διατίθεται, εν όλω ή εν μέρει, για σκοπούς συνδεόμενους με τη λειτουργία του δικαστηρίου ή για την αρωγή αναξιοπαθούντων δικαστικών λειτουργών και υπαλλήλων.
3. Οι διατάξεις των παρ. 1, 3, 4, 5 και 7 εδάφ. 3 του προηγούμενου άρθρ. 882, εκτός από τη διάταξη του εδάφ. β' της παρ. 4, εφαρμόζονται αναλόγως και στη διαιτητική αμοιβή δικαστικών λειτουργών.

Άρθρο 883

1. Εκείνοι που συναρμολόγησαν τη συμφωνία για διαιτησία μπορούν από κοινού να ανακαλέσουν τους διαιτητές καθώς και τον επιδιαιτητή.
2. Ο διαιτητής και ο επιδιαιτητής μπορούν να προτείνουν την εξαίρεσή τους ή να εξαιρεθούν από εκείνους που συνομολόγησαν την συμφωνία διαιτησίας για τους λόγους που αναφέρονται στο άρθρο 52 παρ. 1, καθώς και αν δεν μπορούν να είναι διαιτητές κατά το άρθρο 871 παρ. 2. Αν τους όρισε ένα από τα συμβαλλόμενα μέρη, η εξαίρεση μπορεί να ζητηθεί μόνο για τους λόγους που επήλθαν ή έγιναν γνωστοί σε εκείνον που ζητεί την εξαίρεση μετά τον ορισμό του διαιτητή ή του επιδιαιτητή. Για την εξαίρεση αποφαίνεται το δικαστήριο που είναι αρμόδιο κατά το άρθρο 878 παρ. 1 και τηρούνται οι διατάξεις των άρθρων 58 έως 60. Η απόφαση δεν προσβάλλεται με ένδικα μέσα και έως την έκδοσή της οι διαιτητές αναβάλλουν την εκδίκαση της υπόθεσης.

Άρθρο 884

Αν η διεξαγωγή της διαιτησίας ή η έκδοση της διαιτητικής απόφασης καθυστερεί και δεν ορίζεται με τη συμφωνία προθεσμίας για την έκδοσής της, το αρμόδιο κατά το άρθρο 878 παρ. 1 δικαστήριο με αίτηση ενός από τα μέρη τάσσει εύλογη προθεσμία για τον παραπάνω σκοπό. Η αίτηση δικάζεται κατά τη διαδικασία των άρθρων 741 επ. και η απόφαση δεν προσβάλλεται με ένδικα μέσα.

Άρθρο 885

Η συμφωνία παύει να ισχύει, εφόσον δεν ορίζεται διαφορετικά από την ίδια,
1) αν οι διαιτητές ή ο επιδιαιτητής που ορίστηκαν με τη συμφωνία ή κατόπιν όρισαν από κοινού οι συμβαλλόμενοι πεθάνουν ή δεν αποδεχτούν τον ορισμό τους και δεν έχουν οριστεί αντικαταστάτες ή ο τρόπος της αντικατάστασής τους,
2) αν περάσει η προθεσμία της ισχύος της συμφωνίας που ορίστηκε από την ίδια τη συμφωνία ή η προθεσμία για την έκδοση της διαιτητικής απόφασης ή η προθεσμία που τάσσεται κατά το άρθρο 884,
3) αν οι συμβαλλόμενοι συνομολογήσουν εγγράφως την κατάργηση της συμφωνίας.

Άρθρο 886

1. Η διαδικασία διεξάγεται ενώπιον των διαιτητών και του επιδιαιτητή που ενεργούν από κοινού. Οι διαιτητές αυτοί ορίζουν, κατά την ελεύθερη κρίση τους, τον τόπο και το χρόνο της διεξαγωγής της διαιτητικής διαδικασίας και τη διαιτητική διαδικασία, εκτός αν ορίζεται διαφορετικά στη συμφωνία διαιτησίας.
2. Κατά τη διαιτητική διαδικασία τα μέρη έχουν τα ίδια δικαιώματα και τις ίδιες υποχρεώσεις, τηρείται η αρχή της ισότητας και πρέπει να καλούνται τα μέρη να παραστούν κατά τις συζητήσεις, να αναπτύξουν, κατά την κρίση των διαιτητών, προφορικώς ή εγγράφως τους ισχυρισμούς τους και να προσκομίσουν τις αποδείξεις τους.
3. Ο επιδιαιτητής διευθύνει τη συζήτηση. Η παράσταση με δικηγόρο ή η εκπροσώπηση από δικηγόρο δεν μπορεί να αποκλειστεί.

If the subject-matter of the dispute can be valued in monetary terms, payment of the percentages referred to in the preceding subparagraph shall be a condition for the arbitration award to be filed in accordance with Article 893 and for an enforcement precept to be issued. All persons who have not completed the five years of service required under Article 871(A)(2)(b) shall also participate in the [allocation] referred to in this paragraph. The first allocation after this Code enters into force shall take place in January 1998.
Instead of distributing the 40%, the competent court, sitting in full court, or the public prosecutor's office may decide to make all or part of that amount available for purposes concerning the operation of the court or to assist judicial functionaries and employees facing hardship.
3. The provisions of Article 882(1), (3), (4), (5) and the third subparagraph of paragraph (7), except for the provisions of the second subparagraph of paragraph (4), also apply *mutatis mutandis* to the arbitration fee of judicial functionaries.

Article 883

1. The parties who entered into the arbitration agreement may jointly agree to remove the arbitrators and the presiding arbitrator.
2. The arbitrators and presiding arbitrator may propose that they be exempted, or may be exempted by the persons who entered into the arbitration agreement on the grounds set out in Article 52(1), as well as if they cannot be arbitrators in accordance with Article 871(2). If they were appointed by one of the contracting parties, exemption may be requested only on grounds which emerged or became known to the party requesting the exemption after the arbitrator or presiding arbitrator was appointed. The court with jurisdiction under Article 878(1) shall rule on the exemption, and the provisions of Articles 58 to 60 apply. The judgment may not be contested by legal remedies, and the arbitrators shall adjourn the hearing of the case until such judgment is handed down.

Article 884

If the arbitration proceedings or the issuance of an arbitration award is delayed and the agreement does not specify a deadline within which the award is to be issued, the court with jurisdiction under Article 878(1), following an application filed by one of the parties, shall set a reasonable deadline for this purpose. The application shall be heard under the procedure laid down Articles 741 *et seq.*, and the judgement may not be contested by legal remedies.

Article 885

Unless it stipulates otherwise, the arbitration agreement shall cease to apply[:]
1) if the arbitrators or presiding arbitrator appointed in the agreement or subsequently appointed jointly by the contracting parties die, or do not accept their appointment, and no replacements have been appointed, or the manner of their replacement has not been specified;
2) if the effective term of the agreement specified therein ends or if the deadline for issuing an arbitration award or the deadline set in Article 884 lapses;
3) if the contracting parties agree in writing to terminate the agreement.

Article 886

1. Proceedings shall be conducted before the arbitrators and the presiding arbitrator acting together. Unless otherwise specified in the arbitration agreement, the arbitrators shall determine, at their unfettered discretion, the place and time for arbitration proceedings and the arbitration procedure to be followed.
2. During arbitration proceedings, the parties have the same rights and same obligations, the principle of equality shall be complied with, and the parties must be summoned to appear at hearings, to expound on their assertions verbally or in writing, at the discretion of the arbitrators, and to adduce evidence.
3. The presiding arbitrator shall direct the course of the hearing. Appearance with a lawyer or representation by a lawyer cannot be precluded.

Άρθρο 887

1. Αν δεν ορίζεται διαφορετικά με τη συμφωνία διαιτησίας, η υπόθεση δικάζεται και αν τα συμβαλλόμενα μέρη ή ένα από αυτά δεν προσέλθουν ή δεν αναπτύξουν τους ισχυρισμούς τους ή δεν προσκομίσουν τις αποδείξεις τους.
2. Οι διαιτητές, αν δεν ορίζεται διαφορετικά από τη συμφωνία για διαιτησία, αποφαίνονται για τη δικαιοδοσία τους και εξετάζουν τα παρεμπίπτοντα ζητήματα.

Άρθρο 888

1. Μάρτυρες και πραγματογνώμονες μπορούν να εξεταστούν χωρίς όρκο ή ενόρκως. Οι διαιτητές δεν μπορούν να επιβάλουν ποινές ή να διατάξουν τη λήψη αναγκαστικών μέτρων για τη διεξαγωγή αποδείξεων, εκτός αν διαιτητής είναι δικαστήριο. Τέτοια μέτρα διατάζει, με αίτηση των διαιτητών, το ειρηνοδικείο το οποίο αποφασίζει αν η λήψη τους είναι νόμιμη. Οι συμβαλλόμενοι στη συμφωνία για διαιτησία μπορούν να εξεταστούν κατά τις διατάξεις των άρθρων 415 έως 420.
2. Η ενέργεια ορισμένων διαδικαστικών πράξεων μπορεί να ανατεθεί σε κάποιον από τους διαιτητές.
3. Οι διαιτητές μπορούν να ζητήσουν να διεξαχθούν αποδείξεις από το ειρηνοδικείο στην περιφέρεια του οποίου πρόκειται να διεξαχθεί η απόδειξη. Το ειρηνοδικείο αποφασίζει αν η διεξαγωγή της απόδειξης είναι νόμιμη και έχει όλες τις εξουσίες δικαστηρίου που διατάζει απόδειξη.

Άρθρο 889

1. Οι διαιτητές δεν μπορούν να διατάζουν, να μεταρρυθμίζουν ή να ανακαλούν ασφαλιστικά μέτρα.
2. Αν διατάχθηκε ασφαλιστικό μέτρο από το αρμόδιο δικαστήριο και ορίστηκε προθεσμία για την άσκηση αγωγής ή συντρέχει περίπτωση να εφαρμοστούν τα άρθρα 715 παρ. 5 και 729 παρ. 5, ο αιτών είναι υποχρεωμένος να προκαλέσει την έναρξη της διαιτητικής διαδικασίας μέσα στην προβλεπόμενη προθεσμία. Οι διατάξεις των άρθρων 693 παρ. 2, 715 παρ. 5 εδαφ. δεύτερο και 729 παρ. 5 εδαφ. δεύτερο εφαρμόζονται και στην περίπτωση αυτή.

Άρθρο 890

1. Αν δεν ορίζεται διαφορετικά από τη συμφωνία για διαιτησία, οι διαιτητές εφαρμόζουν τις διατάξεις του ουσιαστικού δικαίου.
2. Με τη συμφωνία για διαιτησία δεν μπορεί να αποκλειστεί η εφαρμογή διατάξεων δημόσιας τάξης.

Άρθρο 891

Αν οι διαιτητές είναι περισσότεροι και με τη συμφωνία για διαιτησία δεν ορίζεται διαφορετικά, αποφασίζουν όλοι από κοινού με τον επιδιαιτητή, κατά πλειοψηφία. Αν δεν σχηματιστεί πλειοψηφία, υπερισχύει η γνώμη του επιδιαιτητή.

Άρθρο 892

1. Η διαιτητική απόφαση πρέπει να συντάσσεται εγγράφως και να υπογράφεται ιδιοχείρως από τους διαιτητές. Μπορεί ακόμα να συντάσσεται και να υπογράφεται από τους διαιτητές και σε ηλεκτρονική μορφή με τη χρήση εγκεκριμένης ηλεκτρονικής υπογραφής κατά την έννοια της περ. 20 του άρθρου 2 του ν. 4727/2020 (Α' 184). Αν κάποιος από τους διαιτητές αρνείται ή κωλύεται να υπογράψει, πρέπει αυτό να βεβαιώνεται στο έγγραφο της απόφασης, καθώς και ότι εκείνος που αρνείται ή κωλύεται έλαβε μέρος στη διαιτητική διαδικασία και στη διάσκεψη, και να υπογράφεται από την πλειοψηφία των διαιτητών. Στη δεύτερη περίπτωση του άρθρου 891 αρκεί η υπογραφή από τον επιδιαιτητή. Με τη συμφωνία για διαιτησία μπορεί να οριστεί ότι η διαιτητική απόφαση υπογράφεται ιδιοχείρως ή με ηλεκτρονικά μέσα μόνο από τον επιδιαιτητή ή από αυτόν και κάποιον από τους διαιτητές.

Article 887

1. Unless otherwise specified in the arbitration agreement, the case shall be tried even if both the contracting parties or one of them fails to appear, or they do not expound on their assertions, or they do not adduce evidence.
2. Unless otherwise specified in the arbitration agreement, the arbitrators shall rule on matters concerning their jurisdiction and shall examine incidental issues.

Article 888

1. Witnesses and experts may be examined with or without taking an oath. The arbitrators may not impose penalties or order compulsory measures for the purpose of taking evidence, unless the arbitrator is [selected from among all the judges comprising the] entire court. The court of the peace, following an application from the arbitrators, shall order such measures and shall rule on whether taking such measures is lawful. The contracting parties to the arbitration agreement may be examined under the provisions of Articles 415 to 420.
2. The taking of certain procedural steps may be assigned to one of the arbitrators.
3. The arbitrators may request that evidence be taken by the court of the peace in whose district evidence is to be taken. The court of the peace shall rule on whether the taking of evidence is lawful, and shall have all the powers of a court ordering the taking of evidence.

Article 889

1. The arbitrators may not order, amend or revoke interim measures.
2. If interim measures were ordered by the competent court and a deadline was set for filing an action or there are grounds for applying Articles 715(5) and 729(5), the applicant is obligated to initiate arbitration proceedings within the deadline set. The provisions of Articles 693(2), the second subparagraph of Article 715(5) and the second subparagraph of Article 729(5) also apply in this case.

Article 890

1. Unless otherwise specified in the arbitration agreement, the arbitrators shall apply the provisions of substantive law.
2. The arbitration agreement may not preclude the application of public policy provisions.

Article 891

If there are several arbitrators and the arbitration agreement does not specify otherwise, they shall decide together with the presiding arbitrator by majority. If no majority can be achieved, the view of the presiding arbitrator shall be decisive.

Article 892

1. The arbitration award must be drafted in writing and signed in person by the arbitrators. The award may also be drafted and signed by the arbitrators in electronic form by using an approved electronic signature, within the meaning of Article 2(20) of Law 4727/2020 (Government Gazette, Series I, Issue 184). If one of the arbitrators refuses to or is impeded from signing, this must be confirmed in the award document, along with a statement that the person who refuses to or is impeded from signing took part in the arbitration proceedings and the deliberations, and the award decision must be signed by the majority of the arbitrators. In the second case of Article 891 the signature of the presiding arbitrator shall suffice. The arbitration agreement may specify that the arbitration award shall be signed in person or using electronic means only by the presiding arbitrator or by the presiding arbitrator and one of the arbitrators.

2. Η διαιτητική απόφαση πρέπει να αναφέρει:
α) το όνομα και το επώνυμο του επιδιαιτητή και των διαιτητών,
β) τον τόπο και το χρόνο της έκδοσής της,
γ) τα ονόματα και τα επώνυμα εκείνων που έλαβαν μέρος στη διαιτητική διαδικασία,
δ) τη συμφωνία για διαιτησία στην οποία βασίστηκε,
ε) το αιτιολογικό και
στ) το διατακτικό.
Με τη συμφωνία διαιτησίας μπορεί να οριστεί ότι η διαιτητική απόφαση αρκεί να αναφέρει τη συμφωνία διαιτησίας και το διατακτικό.

Άρθρο 893

1. Η διαιτητική απόφαση ολοκληρώνεται από τη στιγμή που θα υπογραφεί σύμφωνα με το άρθρο 892.
2. Ο διαιτητής ή, αν είναι περισσότεροι διαιτητές, ο επιδιαιτητής ή με εντολή του ένας από τους διαιτητές, είναι υποχρεωμένος, αν δεν ορίζεται διαφορετικά από τη συμφωνία διαιτησίας, να καταθέσει το πρωτότυπο της διαιτητικής απόφασης σε έγχαρτη ή ηλεκτρονική μορφή στη γραμματεία του μονομελούς πρωτοδικείου της περιφέρειας στην οποία εκδόθηκε και να παραδώσει αντίγραφά της σ' αυτούς που συνομολόγησαν τη συμφωνία διαιτησίας.

Άρθρο 894

Με αίτηση ενός από αυτούς που συνομολόγησαν τη συμφωνία, η οποία κοινοποιείται στους άλλους και στους διαιτητές μπορεί, με την τήρηση των διατάξεων των άρθρων 315 και 316, να γίνει διόρθωση ή ερμηνεία της διαιτητικής απόφασης από εκείνους που την εξέδωσαν. Το άρθρο 320 εφαρμόζεται και στην περίπτωση αυτή.

Άρθρο 895

1. Η διαιτητική απόφαση δεν προσβάλλεται με ένδικα μέσα.
2. Με τη συμφωνία διαιτησίας μπορεί να επιτραπεί προσφυγή κατά της διαιτητικής απόφασης σε άλλους διαιτητές, αλλά πρέπει να οριστούν συγχρόνως οι προϋποθέσεις, η προθεσμία και η διαδικασία για την άσκηση και την εκδίκασή της.

Άρθρο 896

Η διαιτητική απόφαση, αν με τη συμφωνία διαιτησίας δεν ορίζεται προσφυγή κατά το άρθρο 895 παρ. 2 ή πέρασε η ορισμένη για την προσφυγή προθεσμία, αποτελεί δεδικασμένο και εφαρμόζονται οι διατάξεις των άρθρων 322, 324 έως 330, 332 έως 334.

Άρθρο 897

Η διαιτητική απόφαση μπορεί να ακυρωθεί, ολικά ή εν μέρει, μόνο με δικαστική απόφαση για τους επόμενους λόγους:
1) αν η συμφωνία για τη διαιτησία είναι άκυρη,
2) αν εκδόθηκε αφού η συμφωνία για τη διαιτησία έπαψε να ισχύει,
3) αν εκείνοι που την εξέδωσαν ορίστηκαν κατά παράβαση των όρων της συμφωνίας για τη διαιτησία ή των διατάξεων του νόμου ή αν τα μέρη τους είχαν ανακαλέσει, ή αποφάνθηκαν αν και είχε γίνει δεκτή αίτηση εξαίρεσής τους,
4) αν εκείνοι που την εξέδωσαν ενέργησαν υπερβαίνοντας την εξουσία που τους παρέχει η συμφωνία για τη διαιτησία ή ο νόμος,
5) αν παραβιάστηκαν οι διατάξεις των άρθρων 886 παρ. 2, 891, 892,
6) αν είναι αντίθετη προς διατάξεις δημόσιας τάξης ή προς τα χρηστά ήθη,
7) αν είναι ακατάληπτη ή περιέχει αντιφατικές διατάξεις,
8) αν συντρέχει λόγος αναψηλάφησης κατά το άρθρο 544.

2. The arbitration award must state:
a) the first name and last name of the presiding arbitrator and the arbitrators;
b) the place and time at which it was issued;
c) the first names and last names of the persons who took part in the arbitration proceedings;
d) the arbitration agreement on which it was based;
e) the reasoning; and
f) the operative part.
The arbitration agreement may specify that it shall suffice for the arbitration award to make reference to the arbitration agreement and the operative part.

Article 893

1. The arbitration award shall become final upon being signed in accordance with Article 892.
2. Unless otherwise specified in the arbitration agreement, the arbitrator, or if there are several arbitrators, the presiding arbitrator, or, on their orders, one of the arbitrators, is obligated to file the original of the arbitration award in hard copy or electronic form with the registry of the single-member court of first instance in whose district it was issued, and to deliver copies of the award to the parties to the arbitration agreement.

Article 894

Following an application filed by one of the parties to the agreement, notified to the other parties and to the arbitrators, the arbitration award may, in compliance with the provisions of Articles 315 and 316, be corrected or interpreted by the persons who issued it. Article 320 shall also apply in such cases.

Article 895

1. The arbitration award may not be contested by legal remedies.
2. The arbitration agreement may allow recourse to other arbitrators against the arbitration award but it must, at the same time, also lay down the conditions, deadline and procedure for the filing and adjudication of such recourse.

Article 896

If the arbitration agreement does not specify recourse in accordance with Article 895(2) or the deadline set for recourse has lapsed, the arbitration award has the force of *res judicata* and the provisions of Articles 322, 324 to 330 and 332 to 334 apply.

Article 897

The arbitration award may be annulled in whole or in part only by a court judgment on the following grounds if:
1) the arbitration agreement was null and void;
2) it was issued after the arbitration agreement ceased to apply;
3) the persons who issued it were appointed in breach of the terms of the arbitration agreement or the provisions of law, or if the parties who appointed those persons had removed them, or if those persons issued an award even though an application for their exemption had been accepted;
4) the persons who issued it overstepped the powers conferred on them by the arbitration agreement or by law;
5) the provisions of Articles 886(2), 891 or 892 were infringed;
6) it is contrary to public policy provisions or morality;
7) it is incomprehensible or contains contradictory orders;
8) there are grounds for re-opening proceedings in accordance with Article 544.

Άρθρο 898

Αρμόδιο για την εκδίκαση της αγωγής ακύρωσης είναι το εφετείο στην περιφέρεια του οποίου εκδόθηκε η διαιτητική απόφαση. Η αγωγή εκδικάζεται κατά τη διαδικασία των περιουσιακών διαφορών των άρθρων 614 επ.. Αίτηση αναίρεσης προσδιορίζεται για συζήτηση μέσα σε τρεις (3) μήνες από την επίσπευση του προσδιορισμού.

Άρθρο 899

1. Την ακύρωση της διαιτητικής απόφασης έχουν δικαίωμα να ζητήσουν εκείνοι που συνομολόγησαν τη συμφωνία για τη διαιτησία και καθένας που έχει έννομο συμφέρον. Η αγωγή απευθύνεται εναντίον όλων όσων συνομολόγησαν τη συμφωνία διαιτησίας.

2. Η αγωγή για την ακύρωση της διαιτητικής απόφασης για τους λόγους που αναφέρονται στο άρθρο 897 αριθ. 1 έως 7 ασκείται μέσα σε προθεσμία τριών μηνών από την κοινοποίησή της, διαφορετικά είναι απαράδεκτη. Σε αγωγή ακύρωσης για τους λόγους που αναφέρονται στο άρθρο 897 αριθ. 8 εφαρμόζονται οι διατάξεις του άρθρου 545.

3. Η άσκηση της αγωγής δεν αναστέλλει την εκτέλεση της διαιτητικής απόφασης. Εφόσον η αγωγή ασκήθηκε παραδεκτά, το αρμόδιο δικαστήριο μπορεί, κατά τη διαδικασία των άρθρων 686 επ., να χορηγήσει αναστολή, με ή και χωρίς εγγύηση, ώσπου να εκδοθεί τελεσίδικη απόφαση επί της αγωγής, αν πιθανολογεί την ευδοκίμηση κάποιου λόγου ακύρωσης.

Άρθρο 900

Είναι άκυρη η παραίτηση από το δικαίωμα της άσκησης αγωγής για την ακύρωση διαιτητικής απόφασης πριν από την έκδοσή της.

Άρθρο 901

1. Μπορεί να επιδιωχθεί με αγωγή ή ένσταση η αναγνώριση της ανυπαρξίας διαιτητικής απόφασης μόνο στις ακόλουθες περιπτώσεις:

α) αν δεν συνομολογήθηκε συμφωνία διαιτησίας,

β) αν η απόφαση εκδόθηκε επάνω σε αντικείμενο που δεν μπορούσε να υπαχθεί σε διαιτησία,

γ) αν η απόφαση εκδόθηκε σε διαιτητική δίκη που έγινε κατά ανύπαρκτου φυσικού ή νομικού προσώπου.

2. Η αγωγή της παραγράφου 1 υπάγεται στο εφετείο, στην περιφέρεια του οποίου εκδόθηκε η διαιτητική απόφαση. Η αγωγή εκδικάζεται κατά την διαδικασία των περιουσιακών διαφορών των άρθρων 614 επ.. Αίτηση αναίρεσης προσδιορίζεται για συζήτηση μέσα σε τρεις (3) μήνες από την επίσπευση του προσδιορισμού.

3. Η άσκηση της αγωγής δεν αναστέλλει την εκτέλεση της διαιτητικής απόφασης. Εφόσον η αγωγή ασκήθηκε παραδεκτά, το αρμόδιο δικαστήριο μπορεί κατά τη διαδικασία των άρθρων 686 επ., να χορηγήσει αναστολή με εγγύηση ή και χωρίς εγγύηση, ώσπου να εκδοθεί τελεσίδικη απόφαση επί της αγωγής, αν πιθανολογεί την ευδοκίμηση κάποιου λόγου ανυπαρξίας.

Article 898

The court of appeal in whose district the arbitration award was issued has jurisdiction to hear the action for annulment. The action shall be tried under the procedure on property disputes laid down in Articles 614 *et seq.* The hearing date for an application for cassation shall be set within 3 months from the date on which the application for the proceedings was filed.

Article 899

1. The parties to the arbitration agreement and any person with a legitimate interest are entitled to request annulment of the arbitration award. The action shall be brought against all parties to the arbitration agreement.

2. The action to annul the arbitration award on the grounds set forth in Article 897(1) to (7) shall be filed within a deadline of 3 months from notification of the award, otherwise it shall be inadmissible. The provisions of Article 545 apply to actions for annulment on the grounds set forth in Article 897(8).

3. [The act of] filing an action shall not stay enforcement of the arbitration award. If the action was duly filed, the competent court may, under the procedure laid down in Articles 686 *et seq.*, stay [enforcement of the arbitration award], with or without surety, until a *de jure* non-appealable judgment on the action has been handed down, where it considers it likely on the balance of probabilities that any ground of annulment will succeed.

Article 900

Waiver of the right to file an action for annulment of an arbitration award before that award has been issued is invalid.

Article 901

1. Acknowledgement of non-existence of an arbitration award may be sought by means of an action or plea only in the following cases:

a) if no arbitration agreement was entered into;

b) if the award was issued on a matter which was not arbitrable;

c) if the award was issued in arbitration proceedings against a non-existent natural or legal person.

2. The action referred to in paragraph 1 shall be filed before the court of appeal in whose district the arbitration award was handed down. The action shall be tried under the procedure on property disputes laid down in Articles 614 *et seq.* The hearing date for an application for cassation shall be set within 3 months from the date on which the application to expedite the proceedings was filed.

3. [The act of] filing an action shall not stay enforcement of the arbitration award. If the action was duly filed, the competent court may, under the procedure laid down in Articles 686 *et seq.*, stay [enforcement of the arbitration award], with or without surety, until a *de jure* non-appealable judgment on the action has been handed down, where it considers it likely on the balance of probabilities that any ground of non-existence will succeed.

Άρθρο 902

1. Στα επιμελητήρια, στα χρηματιστήρια αξιών και εμπορευμάτων και στις επαγγελματικές ενώσεις προσώπων οι οποίες αποτελούν νομικά πρόσωπα δημοσίου δικαίου, μπορούν, με προηγούμενη γνωμοδότηση του διοικητικού τους συμβουλίου, να οργανώνονται μόνιμες διαιτησίες, με διατάγματα που εκδίδονται ύστερα από πρόταση του Υπουργού της Δικαιοσύνης και του Υπουργού που έχει την εποπτεία του επιμελητηρίου, του χρηματιστηρίου ή της ένωσης.

2. Τα διατάγματα της παρ. 1 ορίζουν ποιες διαφορές μπορούν να υπαχθούν στη διαιτησία κάθε επιμελητηρίου, χρηματιστηρίου ή ένωσης, καθώς και τις λεπτομέρειες για την οργάνωση της διαιτησίας. Στις διαιτησίες αυτές, εφαρμόζονται οι διατάξεις των άρθρων 867 έως 900. Τα ίδια διατάγματα μπορούν, κατ' απόκλιση από τις διατάξεις αυτές να ορίζουν

α) αντί για το μονομελές πρωτοδικείο να αποφασίζουν στις περιπτώσεις των άρθρων 878, 880 παρ. 2 και 884, ο πρόεδρος ή το διοικητικό συμβούλιο ή επιτροπή από συμβούλους του επιμελητηρίου, του χρηματιστηρίου ή της ένωσης,

β) την υποχρέωση εκλογής των διαιτητών και του επιδιαιτητή από κατάλογο διαιτητών που συντάσσεται κατά ορισμένα χρονικά διαστήματα από το επιμελητήριο, το χρηματιστήριο ή την ένωση,

γ) τη διαιτητική διαδικασία, σύμφωνα με τις διατάξεις του άρθρου 886 παρ. 2,

δ) το ουσιαστικό δίκαιο που πρέπει να εφαρμόζουν ο επιδιαιτητής και οι διαιτητές,

ε) τα στοιχεία που πρέπει να περιέχει η διαιτητική απόφαση, με την τήρηση όμως των διατάξεων του άρθρου 892 παρ. 2.

Άρθρο 903

Με επιφύλαξη αυτών που ορίζουν διεθνείς συμβάσεις, αλλοδαπή διαιτητική απόφαση αποτελεί δεδικασμένο, χωρίς άλλη διαδικασία, αν συντρέχουν οι ακόλουθες προϋποθέσεις:

1) αν η συμφωνία διαιτησίας στην οποία βασίστηκε η έκδοσή της είναι έγκυρη κατά το δίκαιο που τη διέπει,

2) αν το αντικείμενο της διαιτητικής απόφασης μπορεί να γίνει αντικείμενο συμφωνίας διαιτησίας κατά το ελληνικό δίκαιο,

3) αν η απόφαση δεν προσβάλλεται με ένδικα μέσα ή προσφυγή ή δεν εκκρεμεί διαδικασία αμφισβήτησης του κύρους της,

4) αν ο διάδικος που νικήθηκε δεν στερήθηκε κατά τη διαιτητική διαδικασία το δικαίωμα της υπεράσπισης,

5) αν η απόφαση δεν είναι αντίθετη με απόφαση ελληνικού δικαστηρίου που εκδόθηκε στην ίδια υπόθεση και αποτελεί δεδικασμένο για τους διαδίκους μεταξύ των οποίων εκδόθηκε η αλλοδαπή διαιτητική απόφαση,

6) αν η απόφαση δεν είναι αντίθετη προς τη δημόσια τάξη ή προς τα χρηστά ήθη.

Article 902

1. Chambers, securities and commodities exchanges and professional associations of persons which are bodies governed by public law may, with the prior opinion of their boards of directors, set up permanent arbitration panels by means of decrees issued on a proposal from the Minister of Justice and the Minister responsible for supervising the chamber, exchange or association.

2. The decrees referred to in paragraph 1 shall specify which disputes may be brought to arbitration before each chamber, stock exchange or association, and the details of how arbitration is to be organised. The provisions of Articles 867 to 900 apply to such arbitration proceedings. Those same decrees may, by way of derogation from those provisions, specify:

a) instead of the single-member court of first instance, that the chairperson or the board of directors or a committee of directors of the chamber, stock exchange or association shall decide on the matters referred to in Articles 878, 880(2) and 884;

b) the obligation to select the arbitrators and the presiding arbitrator from a list of arbitrators regularly compiled by the chamber, stock exchange or association;

c) the arbitration procedure in accordance with the provisions of Article 886(2);

d) the substantive law which the presiding arbitrator and arbitrators must apply;

e) the information the arbitration award must contain, provided, however, that the provisions of Article 892(2) are complied with.

Article 903

Without prejudice to the provisions of international treaties and conventions, a foreign arbitration award has the force of *res judicata* without further formalities where the following conditions are met:

1) if the arbitration agreement on which the issuance of the award was based is valid under the law governing it;

2) if the subject-matter of the arbitration award could form the subject-matter of an arbitration agreement under Greek law;

3) if the award is not contested by legal remedies or recourse, or no proceedings to contest its validity are pending;

4) if the unsuccessful party was not deprived of their right of defence during the arbitration proceedings;

5) if the award does not contravene a judgment handed down by a Greek court on the same case that has the force of *res judicata* for the parties in the proceedings for whom the foreign arbitration award was issued;

6) if the award is not contrary to public policy or morality.

ΟΓΔΟΟ ΒΙΒΛΙΟ
ΑΝΑΓΚΑΣΤΙΚΗ ΕΚΤΕΛΕΣΗ

ΚΕΦΑΛΑΙΟ Α'
Γενικές διατάξεις.

Άρθρο 904

1. Αναγκαστική εκτέλεση μπορεί να γίνει μόνο βάσει εκτελεστού τίτλου.

2. Εκτελεστοί τίτλοι είναι:

α) οι τελεσίδικες αποφάσεις καθώς και οι αποφάσεις κάθε ελληνικού δικαστηρίου που κηρύχθηκαν προσωρινά εκτελεστές,

β) οι διαιτητικές αποφάσεις,

γ) τα πρακτικά ελληνικών δικαστηρίων που περιέχουν συμβιβασμό ή προσδιορισμό δικαστικών εξόδων,

δ) τα συμβολαιογραφικά έγγραφα,

ε) οι διαταγές πληρωμής και απόδοσης της χρήσης μισθίου ακινήτου που εκδίδουν έλληνες δικαστές,

στ) οι αλλοδαποί τίτλοι που κηρύχθηκαν εκτελεστοί,

ζ) οι διαταγές και πράξεις που αναγνωρίζονται από το νόμο ως τίτλοι εκτελεστοί.

Άρθρο 905

1. Με επιφύλαξη αυτών που ορίζουν διεθνείς συμβάσεις και κανονισμοί της Ευρωπαϊκής Ένωσης μπορεί να γίνει στην Ελλάδα αναγκαστική εκτέλεση βασισμένη σε αλλοδαπό τίτλο από τότε που θα τον κηρύξει εκτελεστό απόφαση του μονομελούς πρωτοδικείου της περιφέρειας όπου βρίσκεται η κατοικία και, αν δεν έχει κατοικία, η διαμονή του οφειλέτη και, αν δεν έχει ούτε διαμονή, του μονομελούς πρωτοδικείου της πρωτεύουσας του Κράτους. Το μονομελές πρωτοδικείο δικάζει κατά τη διαδικασία των άρθρων 740 έως 781.

2. Το μονομελές πρωτοδικείο κηρύσσει εκτελεστό τον αλλοδαπό τίτλο, εφόσον είναι εκτελεστός κατά το δίκαιο του τόπου όπου εκδόθηκε και δεν είναι αντίθετος προς τα χρηστά ήθη ή προς τη δημόσια τάξη.

3. Αν ο αλλοδαπός τίτλος είναι δικαστική απόφαση, για να κηρυχθεί εκτελεστός πρέπει να συντρέχουν και οι όροι του άρθρου 323 αριθ. 2 έως 5.

4. Οι διατάξεις των παραγράφων 1 έως 3 εφαρμόζονται και για την αναγνώριση δεδικασμένου από απόφαση αλλοδαπού δικαστηρίου που αφορά την προσωπική κατάσταση.

Άρθρο 906

Οι αλλοδαπές διαιτητικές αποφάσεις κηρύσσονται εκτελεστές σύμφωνα με το άρθρο 905 παρ. 1, αν συντρέχουν οι προϋποθέσεις του άρθρου 903.

Άρθρο 907

Την προσωρινή εκτέλεση οριστικής απόφασης διατάζει το δικαστήριο, αν τη ζητήσει ο διάδικος που νίκησε.

BOOK VIII
COMPULSORY ENFORCEMENT

CHAPTER I
General provisions

Article 904

1. Compulsory enforcement is only be possible on the basis of an enforceable title.

2. The following are enforceable titles:

a) *de jure* non-appealable judgments as well as judgments handed down by any Greek court and declared provisionally enforceable;

b) arbitration awards;

c) transcripts of Greek court [proceedings] containing settlements or setting court costs;

d) notarial instruments;

e) orders for payment [or] return of use of a leased property issued by Greek judges;

f) foreign titles which have been declared enforceable; [and]

g) orders and decisions recognised in law as enforceable titles.

Article 905

1. Without prejudice to the provisions of international treaties and conventions and European Union regulations, compulsory enforcement may take place in Greece on the basis of a foreign title from the moment it is declared enforceable by a judgment handed down by the single-member court of first instance in whose district the debtor has their place of domicile and, where there is no such place of domicile, their place of residence and, where there is no such place of residence, by the single-member court of first instance of the capital. The single-member court of first instance shall try such matters under the procedure laid down in Articles 740 to 781.

2. The single-member court of first instance shall declare the foreign title enforceable provided it is enforceable under the law of the country where it was issued and it is not contrary to morality or public policy.

3. If the foreign title is a court judgment, the conditions laid down in Article 323(2) to (5) must also be met in order for it to be declared enforceable.

4. The provisions of paragraphs 1 to 3 also apply to the recognition of the *res judicata* of a judgment on personal status handed down by a foreign court.

Article 906

Foreign arbitration awards shall be declared enforceable in accordance with Article 905(1) if the conditions laid down in Article 903 are met.

Article 907

The court shall order provisional enforcement of a final judgment if so requested by the successful party in the proceedings.

Άρθρο 908

1. Το δικαστήριο μπορεί να κηρύξει προσωρινώς εκτελεστή την απόφαση ολικά ή εν μέρει σε κάθε περίπτωση που κρίνει πως συντρέχουν εξαιρετικοί λόγοι για αυτό ή ότι η καθυστέρηση στην εκτέλεση μπορεί να προκαλέσει σημαντική ζημία στο διάδικο που νίκησε. Ιδίως μπορεί να διαταχθεί προσωρινή εκτέλεση:

α) αν η απόφαση στηρίχθηκε σε αναγνώριση της απαίτησης ή σε δικαστική ομολογία ή σε δημόσιο ή αναγνωρισμένο ιδιωτικό έγγραφο,

β) αν πρόκειται για διατροφή από οποιοδήποτε αιτία,

γ) αν πρόκειται για απαιτήσεις από δικαιώματα πνευματικής ιδιοκτησίας,

δ) αν πρόκειται για αποζημίωση από άδικη πράξη,

ε) σε απαιτήσεις που πηγάζουν από τις σχέσεις που αναφέρουν τα άρθρα 614 αρ. 3 ή 728,

στ) σε εμπορικές διαφορές,

ζ) σε διαφορές σχετικές με τη νομή,

η) σε απαιτήσεις από ανώνυμους τίτλους.

2. Αν πιθανολογείται ότι η εκτέλεση θα βλάψει ανεπανόρθωτα το διάδικο που νικήθηκε, το δικαστήριο μπορεί να μην κηρύξει προσωρινά εκτελεστή την απόφαση.

Άρθρο 909

Προσωρινή εκτέλεση δεν μπορεί να διαταχθεί:

1) κατά του δημοσίου, των δήμων και των κοινοτήτων,

2) κατά οποιουδήποτε διαδίκου για τα δικαστικά έξοδα,

3) όταν κατά το ουσιαστικό δίκαιο για να επέλθουν οι έννομες συνέπειες της απόφασης απαιτείται αυτή να γίνει τελεσίδικη ή αμετάκλητη,

4) στις διαφορές του άρθρου 592 αρ. 2.

Άρθρο 910

Το δικαστήριο είναι υποχρεωμένο να κηρύξει την απόφαση προσωρινά εκτελεστή

1) σε απόδοση μισθίου,

2) σε καθυστέρηση μισθωμάτων,

3) σε απαίτηση από συναλλαγματική, γραμμάτιο εις διαταγήν ή τραπεζική επιταγή,

4) σε απαίτηση διατροφής από οποιαδήποτε αιτία και σε απαίτηση από καθυστερούμενους μισθούς, και στις δύο περιπτώσεις μόνο για το χρόνο μετά την άσκηση της αγωγής και για τρεις μήνες πριν από αυτήν.

Άρθρο 911

Στις περιπτώσεις του άρθρου 908 το δικαστήριο μπορεί, αν το ζητήσει ο διάδικος που νικήθηκε, να εξαρτήσει την προσωρινή εκτέλεση της απόφασης από την παροχή ανάλογης εγγύησης από το διάδικο που νίκησε, η οποία ορίζεται με την ίδια απόφαση, αν συντρέχουν σπουδαίοι λόγοι και ιδίως αν η οικονομική κατάσταση του διαδίκου που νίκησε ή άλλοι λόγοι, δημιουργούν τον κίνδυνο να μην είναι δυνατή η επαναφορά των πραγμάτων στην προηγούμενη κατάσταση σε περίπτωση που η απόφαση μεταρρυθμιστεί ή εξαφανιστεί. Το δικαστήριο μπορεί αντί για την εγγύηση να διατάξει να κατατεθεί δημόσια το χρηματικό ποσό ή το πράγμα που θα ληφθεί με την εκτέλεση, αν επιδέχεται κατάθεση, ώσπου να εκδοθεί η τελεσίδικη απόφαση.

Article 908

1. The court may declare a judgment provisionally enforceable, whether in whole or in part, where it considers that there are exceptional reasons for doing so or that any delay in enforcing the judgment may cause significant harm to the successful party in the proceedings. In particular, provisional enforcement may be ordered:

a) if the judgment was based on recognition of a claim or an admission made in court or a public or acknowledged private document;

b) if it concerns maintenance on any grounds;

c) if it concerns copyright claims;

d) if it concerns tortious compensation;

e) in cases of claims arising from the relationships referred to in Article 614(3) or Article 728;

f) in cases of commercial disputes;

g) in cases of disputes concerning possession;

h) in cases of claims arising from bearer securities.

2. If the court considers it likely on the balance of probabilities that enforcement will cause irreparable harm to the unsuccessful party in the proceedings, it may opt not to declare the judgment provisionally enforceable.

Article 909

Provisional enforcement may not be ordered:

1) against the Greek State, municipalities and communities;

2) against any party in the proceedings with regard to court costs;

3) when, under substantive law, the judgment must become *de jure* non-appealable or irrevocable in order for its legal effects to occur;

4) in the disputes referred to in Article 592(2).

Article 910

The court is obligated to declare the judgment provisionally enforceable:

1) in cases of return of a leased property;

2) in cases of rent in arrears;

3) in cases of claims arising from bills of exchange, promissory notes or cheques;

4) in cases of maintenance on any grounds and claims arising from salaries in arrears and, in both such cases, only for the year after the [date the] action was filed and for three months prior to that [date].

Article 911

In the cases referred to in Article 908, the court may, if so requested by the unsuccessful party in the proceedings, predicate provisional enforcement of the judgment on the successful party providing appropriate surety, to be specified in the same judgment, if there is a serious reason and, in particular, if the financial situation of the successful party or other grounds give rise to the risk of restoration of a prior state of affairs becoming impossible if the judgment were to be amended or set aside. Instead of surety, the court may order that the monetary sum or thing received through enforcement be deposited with the state, if it can be deposited, until such time as a *de jure* non-appealable judgment is handed down.

Άρθρο 912

1. Αν ασκηθεί εμπρόθεσμα ανακοπή ερημοδικίας ή έφεση κατά της απόφασης που κηρύχθηκε προσωρινά εκτελεστή σύμφωνα με τα άρθρα 908 ή 910 μπορεί έως τη συζήτηση στο ακροατήριο της ανακοπής ερημοδικίας ή της έφεσης να διαταχθεί, αν το ζητήσει ο διάδικος που νικήθηκε, και εφόσον πιθανολογείται η ευδοκίμηση της ανακοπής ερημοδικίας ή της έφεσης, να ανασταλεί ολικά ή εν μέρει, ώσπου να εκδοθεί οριστική απόφαση, με τον όρο να δοθεί εγγύηση, η οποία ορίζεται από την απόφαση που διατάσσει την αναστολή ή και χωρίς εγγύηση.
2. Την αναστολή της παρ. 1 διατάζει το δικαστήριο το οποίο εξέδωσε την απόφαση που προσβάλλεται. Η αίτηση συζητείται κατά τη διαδικασία των άρθρων 686 επ. Κατά τη συζήτηση καλείται υποχρεωτικά ο αντίδικος του αιτούντος.

Άρθρο 913

1. Το δικαστήριο που δικάζει την ανακοπή ερημοδικίας ή την έφεση μπορεί, σε κάθε στάση της δίκης, ύστερα από αίτηση του διαδίκου, η οποία υποβάλλεται μόνο με το δικόγραφο της ανακοπής ερημοδικίας ή της έφεσης ή με τις προτάσεις, να κηρύξει στις περιπτώσεις των άρθρων 908 και 910 προσωρινά εκτελεστή την απόφαση που προσβάλλεται, να διατάξει τα μέτρα που ορίζει το άρθρο 911, να αναστείλει την εκτέλεση κατά το άρθρο 912 ή να μεταρρυθμίσει την απόφαση κατά το ίδιο άρθρο. Οι διατάξεις του άρθρου 909 εφαρμόζονται και εδώ.
2. Το δικαστήριο μπορεί σε κάθε στάση της δίκης να ανακαλεί τις αποφάσεις της παρ. 1 ώσπου να εκδοθεί η οριστική απόφαση, αυτεπαγγέλτως ή ύστερα από αίτηση κάποιου διαδίκου, που υποβάλλεται με τις προτάσεις και όχι αυτοτελώς και, όταν δεν κατατίθενται προτάσεις, και με προφορική αίτηση που καταχωρίζεται στα πρακτικά.

Άρθρο 914

Αν το δικαστήριο δεχτεί την ανακοπή ερημοδικίας ή την έφεση οριστικά και κατ' ουσίαν και απορρίψει, ολικά ή εν μέρει, την αγωγή, την ανταγωγή ή την κύρια παρέμβαση, εφόσον αποδειχθεί ότι η απόφαση που προσβάλλεται εκτελέστηκε, διατάζει, αν το ζητήσει εκείνος κατά του οποίου έγινε η εκτέλεση, την επαναφορά των πραγμάτων στην κατάσταση που βρίσκονταν, πριν εκτελεστεί η απόφαση που εξαφανίστηκε ή μεταρρυθμίστηκε. Η αίτηση υποβάλλεται είτε με τα δικόγραφα της ανακοπής ή της έφεσης και των προσθέτων λόγων είτε με τις προτάσεις είτε με χωριστό δικόγραφο που κοινοποιείται στον αντίδικο. Η εκτέλεση της απόφασης πρέπει να προαποδεικνύεται.

Άρθρο 915

Αναγκαστική εκτέλεση που αφορά απαίτηση υπό αναβλητική αίρεση ή προθεσμία δεν μπορεί να γίνει πριν πληρωθεί η αίρεση ή περάσει η προθεσμία. Η πλήρωση της αίρεσης καθώς και η πάροδος της προθεσμίας, εφόσον η λήξη της δεν βρίσκεται ημερολογιακά, πρέπει να αποδεικνύεται με δημόσιο ή ιδιωτικό έγγραφο που έχει αποδεικτική δύναμη. Όταν η απόφαση ορίζει πως η εκτέλεση εξαρτάται από το αν θα συμβεί κάποιο γεγονός, το γεγονός αυτό πρέπει να αποδεικνύεται με έγγραφο δημόσιο ή ιδιωτικό που έχει αποδεικτική δύναμη.

Άρθρο 916

Αναγκαστική εκτέλεση δεν μπορεί να γίνει, αν από τον εκτελεστό τίτλο δεν προκύπτει η ποσότητα και η ποιότητα της παροχής.

Article 912

1. If an opposition against a default judgment or an appeal against the judgment declared provisionally enforceable in accordance with Article 908 or 910 is filed in good time, the court may order, by the date of the courtroom hearing of the opposition against the default judgment or the appeal, and where it is considered likely on the balance of probabilities that the opposition against the default judgment or the appeal will be successful, that [the judgment declared provisionally enforceable] be stayed, whether in whole or in part, until a final judgment is handed down, either on the condition that surety be provided, which shall be specified in the judgment ordering the stay, or without a surety.
2. The court that handed down the judgment being contested shall order the stay referred to in paragraph 1. The application shall be heard in accordance with the procedure laid down in Articles 686 *et seq.* The applicant's opponent must be summoned to the hearing.

Article 913

1. The court trying an opposition against a default judgment or the appeal may, during any stage of the proceedings, following an application by a party in the proceedings submitted only with the opposition against a default judgment, or with the appeal, or with the pleadings, declare the judgment being contested provisionally enforceable in the cases referred to in Articles 908 and 910, order the measures specified in Article 911, stay enforcement under Article 912 or amend the judgment in accordance with the same Article. The provisions of Article 909 also apply in such cases.
2. The court may, during any stage of the proceedings, revoke the judgments referred to in paragraph 1 until a final judgment has been handed down, whether *ex officio* or following an application by a party in the proceedings submitted with the pleadings and not separately and, where no pleadings are filed, by means of a verbal request entered in the transcript.

Article 914

If the court accepts the opposition against a default judgment or appeal on a final basis and on its merits and dismisses the action, cross-action or main intervention in whole or in part, it is proven that the judgment being contested was enforced and it is so requested by the party against whom the judgment was enforced, then the court shall order that affairs be restored to their state prior to enforcement of the judgment which was set aside or amended. The application shall be filed either with the opposition or the appeal and the additional grounds of appeal, or with the pleadings, or with a separate procedural document notified to the other party. Enforcement of the judgment must be proven beforehand.

Article 915

Compulsory enforcement concerning a claim subject to a suspensive condition or term may not take place before the condition has been fulfilled or the term has lapsed. Fulfilment of the condition or lapse of the term, provided that the expiry date cannot be worked out by reference to a calendar, must be proven by means of a public or private document with probative value. Where the judgment states that enforcement is predicated on whether an event will occur, that fact must be proven by means of a public or private document with probative value.

Article 916

Compulsory enforcement may not take place if the quality and quantity of the performance is not clear from the enforceable title.

Άρθρο 917

Όταν αντικείμενο της παροχής είναι πράγματα αντικαταστατά και πρέπει για την αναγκαστική εκτέλεση να οριστεί η αξία τους σε χρήμα, ο προσδιορισμός της αξίας του αντικειμένου της παροχής γίνεται με απόφαση του μονομελούς πρωτοδικείου, που δικάζει κατά τη διαδικασία των περιουσιακών διαφορών των άρθρων 614 επ.. Αν η παροχή επιδικάστηκε με απόφαση του ειρηνοδικείου, ο προσδιορισμός της αξίας γίνεται από αυτό, κατά την ίδια διαδικασία.

Άρθρο 918

1. Αναγκαστική εκτέλεση μπορεί να γίνει μόνο βάσει αντιγράφου του εκτελεστού τίτλου που έχει τον εκτελεστήριο τύπο (απόγραφο). Ο εκτελεστήριος τύπος συνίσταται στην έκδοσή του στο όνομα του Ελληνικού Λαού και στη διαταγή προς όλα τα αρμόδια όργανα να εκτελέσουν τον τίτλο.

2. Ο εκτελεστήριος τύπος δίνεται

α) σε αποφάσεις, διαταγές πληρωμής ή άλλες διαταγές ελληνικών δικαστηρίων, από το δικαστή που εξέδωσε την απόφαση ή τη διαταγή και αν πρόκειται για απόφαση πολυμελούς δικαστηρίου, από τον πρόεδρο,

β) σε Πρακτικά ελληνικών δικαστηρίων, από το δικαστή που δίκασε, και αν πρόκειται για πολυμελές δικαστήριο από τον πρόεδρο,

γ) σε συμβολαιογραφικά έγγραφα, από το συμβολαιογράφο,

δ) σε διαιτητικές αποφάσεις, από το δικαστή του μονομελούς πρωτοδικείου στη γραμματεία του οποίου έχουν κατατεθεί,

ε) σε αλλοδαπούς τίτλους, καθώς και στις αλλοδαπές διαιτητικές αποφάσεις, από το δικαστή του μονομελούς πρωτοδικείου που τους κήρυξε εκτελεστούς.

3. Ένα μόνο απόγραφο δίνεται στον καθένα από εκείνους που έχουν έννομο συμφέρον. Άλλο απόγραφο μπορεί να δοθεί, αν χαθεί εκείνο που δόθηκε ή για άλλο σοβαρό λόγο.

4. Απόγραφο δεν δίνεται, αν δεν μπορεί να γίνει εκτέλεση σύμφωνα με τα άρθρα 915 έως 917.

5. Αν ο αρμόδιος για την έκδοση απογράφου αρνηθεί να το δώσει, η έκδοση μπορεί να ζητηθεί από το μονομελές πρωτοδικείο στην περιφέρεια του οποίου εδρεύει ο αρμόδιος για την έκδοση του απογράφου, με την εφαρμογή της διαδικασίας των άρθρων 686 επ.

6. Ο υπάλληλος του πλειστηριασμού οφείλει να χορηγεί στον επισπεύδοντα επίσημα αντίγραφα του δικαιογράφου που εκτελείται και των επιδοτηρίων της επιταγής, με τα οποία μπορεί αυτός να ενεργήσει νέα εκτέλεση κατά του οφειλέτη και κατά κάθε άλλου υποχρέου, με κατάσχεση άλλης περιουσίας ή με προσωπική κράτηση, αν έχει απαγγελθεί.

Άρθρο 919

Η αναγκαστική εκτέλεση γίνεται

1) όταν πρόκειται για δικαστικές και διαιτητικές αποφάσεις, υπέρ και κατά των προσώπων, έναντι των οποίων ισχύει δεδικασμένο και κατά των προσώπων που απέκτησαν τη νομή ή κατοχή του επίδικου πράγματος κατά τη διάρκεια της δίκης ή μετά το τέλος της,

2) όταν πρόκειται για όλους τους άλλους εκτελεστούς τίτλους, υπέρ των δικαιούχων και κατά των υποχρέων που αναφέρονται σ' αυτούς, υπέρ και κατά των προσώπων που αναφέρονται στα άρθρα 325 έως 327, καθώς και κατά των προσώπων που απέκτησαν τη νομή ή κατοχή του πράγματος μετά τη σύνταξη του εγγράφου ή την έκδοση του τίτλου.

Άρθρο 920

Με βάση τον εκτελεστό τίτλο κατά της ομόρρυθμης ή ετερόρρυθμης εταιρίας μπορεί να γίνει αναγκαστική εκτέλεση και κατά των ομορρύθμων εταίρων.

Article 917

When the performance concerns fungible things and their monetary value must be specified for compulsory enforcement [to take place], the value of the performance shall be determined in a judgment handed down by the single-member court of first instance, trying the matter under the procedure on property disputes laid down in Articles 614 *et seq.* If performance was awarded by a judgment of the court of the peace, that court shall determine the value under the same procedure.

Article 918

1. Compulsory enforcement may only take place on the basis of a copy of the enforceable title which bears an enforcement form (enforcement precept). The enforcement form shall be issued in the name of the Greek people and include an order to all competent bodies to enforce the title.
2. The enforcement form shall be affixed to[:]
a) judgments, payment orders or other orders issued by Greek courts, by the judge who handed down the judgment or issued the order and, in the case of a judgment handed down by a multi-member court, by the presiding judge;
b) transcripts of Greek court [proceedings], by the trial judge and, in the case of a multi-member court, by the presiding judge;
c) notarial instruments, by the notary public;
d) arbitration awards, by the judge of the single-member court of first instance with whose registry such awards were filed;
e) foreign titles and foreign arbitration awards, by the single-member court of first instance judge who declared them enforceable.
3. A single enforcement precept shall be given to each person with a legitimate interest. A further enforcement precept may be given if the one given was lost or for other serious reason.
4. An enforcement precept shall not be given if enforcement cannot take place in accordance with Articles 915 to 917.
5. If the person competent to issue an enforcement precept refuses to do so, issuance may be requested from the single-member court of first instance in whose district the person competent to issue the enforcement precept is seated, under the procedure laid down in Articles 686 *et seq.*
6. Auctioneers must furnish the expediting party with official copies of the decision incorporating rights being enforced and the certificates of service of the order, which the latter may use for new enforcement steps to be taken against the debtor and any other liable party through attachment of other property or through personal detention, if such is ordered.

Article 919

Compulsory enforcement shall take place[:]
1) in cases of court judgments and arbitration awards, for and against persons with regard to whom there is *res judicata*, and against persons who acquired possession or detentorship of the thing at issue during or after the proceedings;
2) in cases of all other enforceable titles, for the beneficiaries and against the liable persons referred to in such titles, for and against the persons referred to in Articles 325 to 327, as well as against persons who acquired possession or detentorship of the thing after the document was drawn up or the title was issued.

Article 920

An enforceable title issued against a general or limited partnership may also serve as the basis for compulsory enforcement against the general partners.

Άρθρο 921

1. Η αναγκαστική εκτέλεση που άρχισε κατά του οφειλέτη συνεχίζεται μετά το θάνατό του αφότου ο κληρονόμος αποδεχτεί την κληρονομία ή αφότου περάσει η προθεσμία για την αποποίηση ή αφότου διοριστεί κηδεμόνας της σχολάζουσας κληρονομίας.

2. Όσο ο κληρονόμος έχει το δικαίωμα να αποποιηθεί την κληρονομία δεν μπορεί να γίνει αναγκαστική εκτέλεση για να ικανοποιηθεί απαίτηση κατά της κληρονομίας, εκτός αν έχει διοριστεί κηδεμόνας της σχολάζουσας κληρονομίας.

3. Αναγκαστική εκτέλεση για να ικανοποιηθούν απαιτήσεις κατά οφειλέτη που έγινε κληρονόμος δεν μπορεί να γίνει κατά της κληρονομίας, πριν αυτός την αποδεχτεί ή πριν περάσει η προθεσμία για να την αποποιηθεί.

4. Όταν σε αμφοτεροβαρείς συμβάσεις ο οφειλέτης έχει υποχρέωση παροχής με τον όρο ότι ο δανειστής θα εκπληρώσει ταυτόχρονα την αντιπαροχή που τον βαρύνει, η αναγκαστική εκτέλεση δεν μπορεί να προχωρήσει πριν γίνει η προσφορά της αντιπαροχής στον οφειλέτη, εκτός αν αποδεικνύεται με έγγραφο δημόσιο ή ιδιωτικό που έχει αποδεικτική δύναμη ότι εκπληρώθηκε ήδη η αντιπαροχή ή ότι ο οφειλέτης περιήλθε σε υπερημερία αποδοχής

Άρθρο 922

Όποιος έχει δικαίωμα να ενεργήσει αναγκαστική εκτέλεση μπορεί, όταν πρόκειται να την ενεργήσει, να ζητήσει την παροχή κληρονομητηρίου για το δικαίωμα εκείνου κατά του οποίου θα στραφεί η εκτέλεση.

Άρθρο 923

Αναγκαστική εκτέλεση κατά αλλοδαπού δημοσίου δεν μπορεί να γίνει χωρίς προηγούμενη άδεια του Υπουργού της Δικαιοσύνης.

Άρθρο 924

Η διαδικασία της αναγκαστικής εκτέλεσης αρχίζει από την επίδοση σε εκείνον κατά του οποίου στρέφεται η εκτέλεση αντιγράφου του απογράφου με επιταγή για εκτέλεση και στην περίπτωση του άρθρου 915 και αντιγράφου του αποδεικτικού εγγράφου που αναφέρεται στο άρθρο αυτό. Η επιταγή γράφεται κάτω από το αντίγραφο του απογράφου και πρέπει να ορίζει με ακρίβεια την απαίτηση. Όποιος επισπεύδει αναγκαστική εκτέλεση, έχει υποχρέωση να διορίσει, με την επιταγή που κοινοποιείται σε εκείνον κατά του οποίου γίνεται η εκτέλεση, αντίκλητο που να κατοικεί στην περιφέρεια του πρωτοδικείου του τόπου της εκτέλεσης, διαφορετικά αντίκλητος θεωρείται ο πληρεξούσιος δικηγόρος που υπογράφει την επιταγή. Στον αντίκλητο μπορούν να γίνουν όλες οι επιδόσεις και οι προσφορές που αφορούν την εκτέλεση.

Άρθρο 925

1. Ο καθολικός ή ειδικός διάδοχος του δικαιούχου δεν μπορεί να αρχίσει ή να συνεχίσει την αναγκαστική εκτέλεση πριν κοινοποιηθούν σε εκείνον κατά του οποίου στρέφεται η εκτέλεση η επιταγή και τα έγγραφα που τον νομιμοποιούν.

2. Όταν η αναγκαστική εκτέλεση που άρχισε πρόκειται να συνεχιστεί κατά κληρονόμου ή κηδεμόνα σχολάζουσας κληρονομίας, απαιτείται να τους επιδοθεί προηγουμένως η επιταγή.

Article 921

1. Compulsory enforcement initiated against the debtor shall continue following their death after their heir has accepted the inheritance, or after the deadline for repudiating the inheritance has lapsed, or after a curator has been appointed for the unclaimed estate.
2. So long as the heir has the right to repudiate the inheritance, compulsory enforcement in order to satisfy a claim against the estate cannot take place, unless a curator has been appointed for the unclaimed estate.
3. Compulsory enforcement to satisfy claims against a debtor who became an heir cannot take place against the estate before the debtor has accepted the inheritance or the deadline for repudiating it has lapsed.
4. Where, in cases of bilateral contracts, the debtor is obligated to provide performance on condition that the creditor will simultaneously provide counter-performance, compulsory enforcement may not proceed before such counter-performance has been offered to the debtor, unless it is proven by public or private document with probative value that such counter-performance has already been provided or that the debtor is in default of acceptance.

Article 922

Any person with the right to effect compulsory enforcement may, when intending to do so, request provision of a certificate of inheritance regarding the right of the person against whom enforcement will take place.

Article 923

Compulsory enforcement against a foreign state may not take place without prior permission of the Minister of Justice.

Article 924

The compulsory enforcement procedure shall commence when a copy of the enforcement precept with an enforcement order is served on the person enforcement concerns and, in the case referred to in Article 915, when a copy of the documentary evidence referred to in that Article is served. The order shall be written at the end the copy of the enforcement precept, and must precisely specify the claim. Any person expediting compulsory enforcement is obligated to appoint a process agent domiciled in the district of the court of first instance where the enforcement will take place by means of an order notified to the person enforcement concerns, otherwise the authorised lawyer signing the order shall be deemed to be the process agent. All documents concerning the enforcement may be served on the process agent and all offers may be sent to them.

Article 925

1. The universal successor or specific successor of the beneficiary may not initiate or continue compulsory enforcement before the order and their legitimation documents have been notified to the person enforcement concerns.
2. When compulsory enforcement that has commenced is to be continued against an heir or curator of an unclaimed estate, the order must have been served on them beforehand.

Άρθρο 926

1. Μετά την επίδοση της επιταγής δεν μπορεί με ποινή ακυρότητας να γίνει άλλη πράξη εκτέλεσης πριν περάσουν 3 εργάσιμες ημέρες από την επίδοση. Η προθεσμία αυτή πρέπει να τηρείται και όταν η αναγκαστική εκτέλεση συνεχίζεται κατά του κληρονόμου ή του κηδεμόνα σχολάζουσας κληρονομίας.
2. Όταν περάσει έτος από την επίδοση της επιταγής, δεν μπορεί να γίνει καμιά άλλη πράξη εκτέλεσης που να βασίζεται επάνω σ' αυτήν.

Άρθρο 927

Η αναγκαστική εκτέλεση γίνεται με επιμέλεια εκείνου που έχει δικαίωμα να την ενεργήσει, ο οποίος δίνει, επάνω στο απόγραφο, τη σχετική εντολή σε ορισμένο δικαστικό επιμελητή και ορίζει τον τρόπο και αν είναι δυνατό και τα αντικείμενα επάνω στα οποία θα γίνει η εκτέλεση. Αν πρόκειται για κατάσχεση κινητού ή ακινήτου, ορίζει ως υπάλληλο, ενώπιον του οποίου θα διενεργηθεί ηλεκτρονικά ο πλειστηριασμός, συμβολαιογράφο της περιφέρειας του τόπου όπου θα γίνει η κατάσχεση. Εάν, για οποιονδήποτε λόγο, δεν είναι δυνατό να ορισθεί συμβολαιογράφος του τόπου εκτέλεσης, τότε ο επισπεύδων περιλαμβάνει στην εντολή τη δήλωση να οριστεί συμβολαιογράφος διορισμένος στην περιφέρεια του συμβολαιογραφικού συλλόγου του τόπου εκτέλεσης ή, αν και αυτό δεν είναι δυνατό, του συμβολαιογραφικού συλλόγου της πρωτεύουσας του κράτους. Η εντολή πρέπει να χρονολογείται και να υπογράφεται από το δικαιούχο ή τον πληρεξούσιο του και δίνει την εξουσία να ενεργηθούν όλες οι πράξεις της εκτέλεσης, εκτός αν ορίζεται διαφορετικά σε αυτήν.

Άρθρο 928

Ο δικαστικός επιμελητής στον οποίο παραδόθηκε το απόγραφο με εντολή να ενεργήσει την εκτέλεση, έχει την εξουσία να δέχεται καταβολή και να δίνει γραπτή εξοφλητική απόδειξη, παραδίνοντας συνάμα και το απόγραφο, αν η παροχή εκπληρώθηκε εντελώς. Μπορεί να δεχτεί και μερική καταβολή για την οποία δίνει απόδειξη και την αναφέρει επάνω στο απόγραφο. Η μερική καταβολή δεν εμποδίζει την πρόοδο της εκτέλεσης.

Άρθρο 929

1. Ο δικαστικός επιμελητής έχει την εξουσία, εφόσον το απαιτεί ο σκοπός της αναγκαστικής εκτέλεσης, να εισέρχεται στην κατοικία ή και σε κάθε άλλο χώρο που βρίσκεται στην κατοχή εκείνου κατά του οποίου στρέφεται η εκτέλεση, να ανοίγει τις πόρτες και να κάνει έρευνες, καθώς και να ανοίγει κλειστά έπιπλα, σκεύη ή δοχεία.
2. Ο δικαστικός επιμελητής μπορεί να ζητεί τη βοήθεια της αρχής που είναι αρμόδια για την τήρηση της τάξης, η οποία οφείλει να παρέχει τη συνδρομή της.
3. Κατά τη νύχτα, τα Σάββατα, τις Κυριακές και τις ημέρες τις κατά νόμο εξαιρετέες δεν μπορεί να γίνει πράξη της αναγκαστικής εκτέλεσης, εκτός αν ο ειρηνοδίκης του τόπου της εκτέλεσης δώσει τη σχετική άδεια, κατά τη διαδικασία των άρθρων 686 επ..

Άρθρο 930

1. Αν κατά την αναγκαστική εκτέλεση προβληθεί αντίσταση ο δικαστικός επιμελητής μπορεί να χρησιμοποιήσει βία για να αποκρούσει την αντίσταση, καλώντας συνάμα γι' αυτό την αρχή που είναι αρμόδια για την τήρηση της τάξης.
2. Αν προβάλλεται ή απειλείται αντίσταση ή αν στον τόπο όπου πρόκειται να γίνει πράξη εκτέλεσης δεν βρίσκεται εκείνος κατά του οποίου στρέφεται η εκτέλεση ή πρόσωπο ενήλικο, από εκείνα που αναφέρονται στα άρθρα 128 παρ. 1 και 129 παρ. 1, ο δικαστικός επιμελητής προσλαμβάνει δύο ενήλικους μάρτυρες ή δεύτερο δικαστικό επιμελητή.

Article 926

1. After the order has been served and on penalty of nullity, no other enforcement steps may be taken before three working days from the date of service have elapsed. This deadline must also be complied with when compulsory enforcement is being continued against an heir or custodian of an unclaimed estate.

2. When one year has elapsed from the date of the order was served, no other enforcement steps based on that order may be taken.

Article 927

Compulsory enforcement shall be done by the person with the right to do so, who shall give instructions, added to the enforcement precept, to a specific court process server and specify the manner in which enforcement will take place and, if possible, the things which enforcement will concern. In cases of attachment of movables or immovables, the aforesaid person shall designate a notary public of the district where the attachment will take place as the auctioneer in whose presence the e-auction will take place. If a notary public from the place of enforcement cannot be designated for any reason, then the person procuring enforcement shall include in the instructions a statement to designate a notary public from the district of the notarial association of the place of enforcement and, if this is also not possible, from the notarial association of the capital. The instructions must be dated and signed by the beneficiary or their proxy, and shall grant power to take all enforcement steps, unless otherwise stipulated in the instructions.

Article 928

The court process server to whom the enforcement precept was delivered with instructions to carry out enforcement shall be empowered to accept payments and issue a written receipt for payment in full, and to hand over the enforcement precept if performance was provided in full. The court process server may also accept partial payment for which they shall issue a receipt and note this fact on the enforcement precept. Partial payment shall not hinder the progress of enforcement.

Article 929

1. If required for the purposes of the compulsory enforcement, the court process server shall be empowered to enter the residence or any other space of which the person enforcement concerns has detentorship, to open doors and carry out searches, as well as to open locked/closed furniture, household effects or containers.

2. The court process server may request help from the [police], which must provide assistance.

3. Compulsory enforcement steps may not be taken at night-time, on Saturdays, on Sundays and on statutory public holidays, unless the court of the peace judge of the place of enforcement gives such permission under the procedure laid down in Articles 686 *et seq.*

Article 930

1. If there is resistance against the compulsory enforcement, the court process server may use force to repel such resistance and summon the [police] to assist.

2. If there is resistance or the threat of resistance, or the person enforcement concerns or an adult person from among those referred to in Articles 128(1) and 129(1) is not present at the place where the enforcement steps are to be taken, the court process server shall enlist two adult witnesses or a second court process server.

Άρθρο 931

1. Ο δικαστικός επιμελητής συντάσσει έκθεση για κάθε πράξη της εκτελεστικής διαδικασίας. Αν η δικαστική εκτέλεση δεν πραγματώθηκε, ο δικαστικός επιμελητής συντάσσει σχετική έκθεση στην οποία αναφέρει και τους λόγους.

2. Για κάθε αξιόποινη πράξη που γίνεται κατά την αναγκαστική εκτέλεση ο δικαστικός επιμελητής οφείλει να συντάξει έκθεση και να την υποβάλει στον αρμόδιο εισαγγελέα.

Άρθρο 932

Τα έξοδα της αναγκαστικής εκτέλεσης βαρύνουν εκείνον κατά του οποίου στρέφεται η εκτέλεση και προκαταβάλλονται από εκείνον που την επισπεύδει.

Άρθρο 933

1. Αντιρρήσεις εκείνου κατά του οποίου στρέφεται η εκτέλεση και κάθε δανειστή του που έχει έννομο συμφέρον και αφορούν την εγκυρότητα του εκτελεστού τίτλου, τη διαδικασία της αναγκαστικής εκτέλεσης, ή την απαίτηση ασκούνται μόνο με ανακοπή, που εισάγεται στο ειρηνοδικείο, αν ο εκτελεστός τίτλος, έχει εκδοθεί από το δικαστήριο αυτό, και στο μονομελές πρωτοδικείο σε κάθε άλλη περίπτωση. Αν ασκηθούν περισσότερες ανακοπές με χωριστά δικόγραφα, με επιμέλεια της γραμματείας προσδιορίζονται και εκδικάζονται όλες υποχρεωτικά στην ίδια δικάσιμο. Πρόσθετοι λόγοι ανακοπής μπορούν να προταθούν μόνο με ιδιαίτερο δικόγραφο, που κατατίθεται στη γραμματεία του δικαστηρίου προς το οποίο απευθύνεται η ανακοπή, κάτω από το οποίο συντάσσεται έκθεση και κοινοποιείται στον αντίδικο, σε κάθε περίπτωση οκτώ (8) τουλάχιστον μέρες πριν τη συζήτηση. Η ανακοπή κατά του πλειστηριασμού απευθύνεται, με ποινή το απαράδεκτο, κατά του επισπεύδοντα δανειστή και του υπερθεματιστή. Επί κοινής δε πλειοδοσίας η ανακοπή ασκείται από όλους και κατά όλων των πλειοδοτών.

2. Η συζήτηση της ανακοπής προσδιορίζεται υποχρεωτικά μέσα σε εξήντα (60) ημέρες από την κατάθεσή της και η κλήτευση του καθ' ου η ανακοπή γίνεται είκοσι (20) ημέρες πριν από τη συζήτηση.

3. Αρμόδιο κατά τόπο είναι πάντοτε το δικαστήριο της περιφέρειας του τόπου της εκτέλεσης, εφόσον μετά την επίδοση της επιταγής ακολούθησαν και άλλες πράξεις της εκτελεστικής διαδικασίας, αλλιώς αρμόδιο είναι το δικαστήριο του άρθρου 584. Αν πρόκειται για εκτέλεση για την ικανοποίηση χρηματικών απαιτήσεων, τόπος εκτέλεσης είναι ο τόπος κατάσχεσης, ακόμη και εάν έχει οριστεί υπάλληλος του πλειστηριασμού συμβολαιογράφος που έχει την έδρα του σε άλλη περιφέρεια.

4. Αν ο εκτελεστός τίτλος είναι δικαστική απόφαση ή διαταγή πληρωμής, οι αντιρρήσεις είναι απαράδεκτες στην έκταση που ισχύει το δεδικασμένο σύμφωνα με τα άρθρα 330 και 633 παράγραφος 2 εδάφιο γ', αντίστοιχα.

5. Οι ισχυρισμοί που αφορούν την απόσβεση της απαίτησης, πρέπει να αποδεικνύονται μόνο με έγγραφα ή με δικαστική ομολογία.

6. Η απόφαση επί της ανακοπής εκδίδεται υποχρεωτικά μέσα σε προθεσμία εξήντα (60) ημερών από τη συζήτησή της.

Άρθρο 934

1. Ανακοπή σύμφωνα με το άρθρο 933 είναι παραδεκτή:

α) Αν αφορά ελαττώματα από τη σύνταξη της επιταγής προς εκτέλεση μέχρι και τη δημοσίευση του αποσπάσματος της κατασχετήριας έκθεσης κατά τα άρθρα 955 και 995 ή την απαίτηση ή σε περίπτωση κατάσχεσης στα χέρια τρίτου μέχρι και την επίδοση του κατασχετήριου εγγράφου στον καθ' ου, μέσα σε σαράντα πέντε (45) ημέρες από την ημέρα της κατάσχεσης. Σε περίπτωση άμεσης εκτέλεσης, η ανακοπή κατά της επιταγής προς εκτέλεση ασκείται μέσα σε τριάντα (30) ημέρες από την επίδοση της επιταγής.

Article 931

1. The court process server shall prepare a report on all enforcement procedure steps. If court-ordered enforcement was not carried out, the court process server shall prepare a relevant report and set out the reasons [for this fact].

2. The court process server is obligated to prepare a report on any punishable acts that occur during compulsory enforcement and submit it to the competent public prosecutor.

Article 932

The costs of compulsory enforcement shall be borne by the person enforcement concerns and paid in advance by the person procuring enforcement.

Article 933

1. Objections concerning the validity of the enforceable title, the compulsory enforcement procedure or the claim shall be lodged by the person enforcement concerns [or] any creditor thereof with a legitimate interest, only by means of an opposition filed with the court of the peace, if the enforceable title was issued by said court, and with the single-member court of first instance in all other cases. If several oppositions are filed by means of separate procedural documents, the registry shall set a single hearing date on which they shall all be heard. Additional grounds of opposition may be pleaded only by means of a separate procedural document filed with the registry of the court to which the opposition is addressed, at the end of which a report shall be drafted, and it shall be notified to the opponent at least eight days prior to the hearing in all events. On penalty of inadmissibility, an opposition against an auction shall be brought against the expediting creditor and highest bidder. In cases of joint bids, the opposition shall be filed by and against all bidders.

2. The hearing of the opposition must be set within 60 days of the date it was filed, and the respondent shall be summonsed 20 days prior to the hearing.

3. The court of the district where enforcement is being done always has jurisdiction *ratione loci* if other enforcement procedure steps were taken following service of the order, otherwise the court referred to in Article 584 has jurisdiction. In cases of enforcement for satisfaction of monetary claims, the place of attachment is the place of enforcement, even if a notary public seated in a different district has been designated as the auctioneer.

4. If the enforceable title is a court judgment or a payment order, objections shall be inadmissible to the extent that *res judicata* applies under Articles 330 and the third subparagraph of Article 633(2), respectively.

5. Assertions that a claim has been extinguished must be proven only by means of documentary evidence or admission made in court.

6. The judgment on the opposition must be handed down within a deadline of 60 days from the date of the hearing.

Article 934

1. An opposition filed in accordance with Article 933 shall be admissible if:

a) it concerns defects from the date the order for enforcement was drafted until the excerpt of the attachment report was published in accordance with Articles 955 and 995, or it concerns the claim, or, in the case of garnishment, until the garnishment order was served on the respondent, within 45 days of the date of garnishment. In cases of immediate enforcement, the opposition against the order for enforcement shall be filed within 30 days of the date the order was served;

β) Αν αφορά την εγκυρότητα της τελευταίας πράξης της εκτέλεσης, μέσα σε τριάντα (30) ημέρες αφότου η πράξη αυτή ενεργηθεί και αν πρόκειται για εκτέλεση για την ικανοποίηση χρηματικών απαιτήσεων, μέσα σε τριάντα (30) ημέρες από την ημέρα του πλειστηριασμού ή αναπλειστηριασμού αν πρόκειται για κινητά, και εξήντα (60) ημέρες αφότου μεταγραφεί η περίληψη της κατακυρωτικής έκθεσης, αν πρόκειται για ακίνητα.

2. Αν πρόκειται για εκτέλεση για την ικανοποίηση χρηματικών απαιτήσεων, τελευταία πράξη εκτέλεσης είναι η σύνταξη έκθεσης πλειστηριασμού και κατακύρωσης.

Άρθρο 935

Λόγοι ανακοπής που είναι ήδη γεννημένοι και μπορούν να προταθούν στη δίκη της ανακοπής σύμφωνα με το άρθρο 933 είναι απαράδεκτοι όταν προταθούν σε οποιαδήποτε μεταγενέστερη δίκη όπου ανακύπτει ζήτημα κύρους της αυτής ή άλλης πράξης της διαδικασίας αναγκαστικής εκτέλεσης.

Άρθρο 936

1. Τρίτος έχει δικαίωμα να ασκήσει ανακοπή κατά της αναγκαστικής εκτέλεσης, αν προσβάλλεται δικαίωμά του επάνω στο αντικείμενο της εκτέλεσης, το οποίο δικαιούται να αντιτάξει σε εκείνον κατά του οποίου έχει στραφεί η εκτέλεση και ιδίως:

α) δικαίωμα εμπράγματο που αποκλείει ή περιορίζει το δικαίωμα εκείνου κατά του οποίου στρέφεται η εκτέλεση,

β) απαγόρευση διάθεσης που έχει ταχθεί υπέρ αυτού και συνεπάγεται σύμφωνα με το νόμον την ακυρότητα της διάθεσης.

Έχει, επίσης, δικαίωμα να ασκήσει ανακοπή και ο νομέας, εκτός αν εκείνος υπέρ του οποίου γίνεται η εκτέλεση αποδείξει πως εκείνος κατά του οποίου στρέφεται έχει επάνω στο αντικείμενο που έχει κατασχεθεί εμπράγματο δικαίωμα επικρατέστερο από τη νομή. Η ανακοπή εισάγεται στο καθ' ύλην αρμόδιο δικαστήριο του τόπου όπου γίνεται η εκτέλεση.

2. Η ανακοπή πρέπει να απευθύνεται κατά του δανειστή και του οφειλέτη και αν πρόκειται για ακίνητο εγγράφεται στο βιβλίο διεκδικήσεων κατά το άρθρο 220. Η συζήτηση της ανακοπής προσδιορίζεται υποχρεωτικά μέσα σε εξήντα (60) ημέρες από την κατάθεσή της, μπορεί δε να επιδοθεί και στον πληρεξούσιο δικηγόρο που υπέγραψε την επιταγή του άρθρου 924 ή παρέσχε την εντολή για τη διενέργεια οποιασδήποτε διαδικαστικής πράξης της αναγκαστικής εκτέλεσης. Στην ανακοπή μπορεί να σωρευτεί και αίτημα απόδοσης του πράγματος.

3. Τρίτος που απέκτησε το δικαίωμα από τον καθ' ου η εκτέλεση με απαλλοτρίωση που διαρρήχθηκε ως καταδολιευτική κατά τα άρθρα 939 επ. του Αστικού Κώδικα, δεν μπορεί να αντιτάξει το δικαίωμα αυτό κατά του επισπεύδοντος που πέτυχε τη διάρρηξη ούτε κατά του υπερθεματιστή και των διαδόχων του.

Άρθρο 937

1. Στις δίκες τις σχετικές με την εκτέλεση:

α) έχει δικαίωμα να παρέμβει κάθε δανειστής εκείνου κατά του οποίου στρέφεται η εκτέλεση,

β) δεν επιτρέπεται η ανακοπή ερημοδικίας ούτε στο πρωτοβάθμιο ούτε και στο δευτεροβάθμιο δικαστήριο,

γ) η προθεσμία και η άσκηση του ενδίκου μέσου δεν αναστέλλουν την εκτέλεση της απόφασης.

2. Στις δίκες αυτές η προθεσμία της παραγράφου 2 του άρθρου 564 είναι εξήντα (60) ημέρες. Η δικάσιμος για τη συζήτηση της αναίρεσης δεν μπορεί να ορισθεί σύμφωνα με την παράγραφο 3 του άρθρου 568, σε χρόνο που υπερβαίνει τους έξι (6) μήνες. Οι προθεσμίες της παραγράφου 4 του άρθρου 568 είναι τουλάχιστον εξήντα (60) ημέρες σε κάθε περίπτωση. Αναβολή της συζήτησης, σύμφωνα με το άρθρο 575, δεν μπορεί να είναι κάθε φορά μεγαλύτερη από σαράντα πέντε (45) ημέρες.

3. Στις δίκες σχετικά με την εκτέλεση για την εκδίκαση των ανακοπών εφαρμόζονται οι διατάξεις της διαδικασίας των περιουσιακών διαφορών των άρθρων 614 επ., εκτός αν ορίζεται διαφορετικά.

b) it concerns the validity of the final enforcement step, within 30 days after the step in question was taken and, in the case of enforcement for the satisfaction of monetary claims, within 30 days from the date of the auction or repeat auction, in the case of movables, and 60 days after the entry of the summary of the award report [in the register], in the case of immovables.
2. In cases of enforcement for the satisfaction of monetary claims, the final enforcement step is the drafting of an auction and award report.

Article 935

Grounds for opposition that have already arisen and can be pleaded during opposition proceedings in accordance with Article 933 shall be inadmissible if pleaded in any subsequent proceedings where an issue concerning the validity of one step or any other step in the compulsory enforcement procedure arises.

Article 936

1. Any third party is entitled to file an opposition against compulsory enforcement if a right they have in the thing enforcement relates to is being infringed and they are entitled to assert such right against the person enforcement concerns and, in particular:
a) a right *in rem* precluding or restricting the right of the person enforcement concerns;
b) prohibition of disposal laid down for the benefit of that third party and which, in law, entails nullity of the disposal.
The possessor also has the right to file an opposition, unless the person for whose benefit enforcement is being done proves that the person enforcement concerns has a right *in rem* in the attached thing superior to possession. The opposition shall be filed before the court with jurisdiction *ratione materiae* of the place where enforcement is being done.
2. The opposition must be brought against the creditor and the debtor and, in the case of an immovable, shall be registered in the claims register referred to in Article 220. The hearing of the opposition must be set within 60 days from the date it was filed, and [the opposition document] may also be served on the authorised lawyer who signed the order referred to in Article 924 or gave instructions to take any step of the compulsory enforcement procedure. A claim for return of the thing may be joined to the opposition.
3. Any third party who obtained the right from the person enforcement concerns by means of alienation which was successfully challenged as fraudulent in accordance with Articles 939 *et seq.* of the Civil Code may not assert this right against the expediting party who successfully challenged the alienation or against the highest bidder and their successors.

Article 937

1. During enforcement proceedings:
a) any creditor of the person enforcement concerns has the right to intervene;
b) opposition against a default judgment before the first-instance and second-instance court shall not be allowed;
c) the [fact that the] deadline for [filing] a legal remedy [has commenced] and [the act of] filing the legal remedy shall not stay enforcement of the judgment.
2. In such proceedings, the deadline set in Article 564(2) is 60 days. The hearing of the application for cassation must be set, in accordance with Article 568(3), within six months from the date of the application. In all cases, the deadlines set in Article 568(4) shall be at least 60 days. Each adjournment of the hearing, in accordance with Article 575, may not be longer than 45 days.
3. Unless otherwise provided for, the provisions of the procedure on property disputes laid down in Articles 614 *et seq.* apply to the adjudication of oppositions during enforcement proceedings.

Άρθρο 938

1. Με εξαίρεση την κατάσχεση ακινήτων, ως προς τα οποία εφαρμόζεται η παρ. 2, όπως επίσης με εξαίρεση την κατάσχεση κινητών που υπόκεινται σε φθορά, με αίτηση του ανακόπτοντος μπορεί να διαταχθεί η αναστολή της αναγκαστικής εκτέλεσης με εγγύηση ή και χωρίς εγγύηση, αν το δικαστήριο κρίνει ότι η ενέργεια της αναγκαστικής εκτέλεσης θα προξενήσει ανεπανόρθωτη βλάβη στον αιτούντα και πιθανολογεί την ευδοκίμηση της ανακοπής. Επίσης μπορεί να διαταχθεί να προχωρήσει η αναγκαστική εκτέλεση αφού δοθεί εγγύηση. Η αίτηση ασκείται στο αρμόδιο κατά τα άρθρα 933 και 936 δικαστήριο και δικάζεται κατά τα άρθρα 686 επ.

2. Ειδικώς επί κατάσχεσης ακινήτου δεν εφαρμόζεται η παρ. 1, η δε άσκηση του ενδίκου μέσου δεν αναστέλλει την πρόοδο της εκτέλεσης, εκτός εάν το δικαστήριο του ενδίκου μέσου, μετά από αίτηση του ασκούντος αυτό, που υποβάλλεται με το ένδικο μέσο ή με τις προτάσεις, δικάζοντας με τη διαδικασία των άρθρων 686 επ., διατάξει την αναστολή με ή χωρίς παροχή εγγύησης, εφόσον κρίνει ότι η διενέργεια της αναγκαστικής εκτέλεσης θα προξενήσει ανεπανόρθωτη βλάβη στον αιτούντα και πιθανολογεί την ευδοκίμηση του ενδίκου μέσου. Επίσης μπορεί να διαταχθεί να προχωρήσει η αναγκαστική εκτέλεση αφού δοθεί εγγύηση.

3. Στις προηγούμενες περιπτώσεις είναι δυνατή η έκδοση σημειώματος με το οποίο εμποδίζεται η εκτέλεση μέχρι να εκδοθεί απόφαση επί της αίτησης αναστολής ή επί του ενδίκου μέσου.

4. Η αίτηση με την οποία ζητείται η αναστολή πλειστηριασμού είναι απαράδεκτη, αν δεν κατατεθεί το αργότερο πέντε (5) εργάσιμες ημέρες πριν από την ημέρα του πλειστηριασμού. Η απόφαση πρέπει να δημοσιεύεται έως τις 12.00 το μεσημέρι της Δευτέρας που προηγείται του πλειστηριασμού.

5. Η αναστολή των παρ. 1 και 2 ή η εγγυοδοσία μπορεί να διαταχθεί μόνο μέχρι να εκδοθεί η οριστική απόφαση επί της ανακοπής, ή η απόφαση επί του ενδίκου μέσου.

Άρθρο 939

1. Η απόφαση που διατάζει να ανασταλεί η αναγκαστική εκτέλεση ή απόσπασμά της γνωστοποιείται στα εκτελεστικά όργανα με επιμέλεια των διαδίκων ή της γραμματείας του δικαστηρίου. Σε επείγουσες περιπτώσεις η γνωστοποίηση μπορεί να γίνει από το δικαστήριο με υπηρεσιακό τηλεγράφημα, με ηλεκτρονικά μέσα ή προφορικά, αφού το όργανο της εκτέλεσης κληθεί να παρουσιαστεί στο δικαστήριο για να του γίνει η γνωστοποίηση και αυτό βεβαιωθεί με απλή σημείωση επάνω στην απόφαση της αναστολής.

2. Αφότου γίνει η γνωστοποίηση της παρ. 1 απαγορεύεται να ενεργηθεί οποιαδήποτε πράξη της αναγκαστικής εκτέλεσης, εκτός από εκείνες που έχει ειδικά επιτρέψει η απόφαση της αναστολής, και δεν τρέχουν οι προθεσμίες οι ορισμένες για την ενέργεια των απαγορευμένων πράξεων ενώ εκείνες που άρχισαν διακόπτονται.

3. Η εκτέλεση συνεχίζεται αφότου γνωστοποιηθεί η παύση της αναστολής που γίνεται με τους τρόπους της παρ. 1.

Άρθρο 940

1. Αν εξαφανιστεί ή μεταρρυθμιστεί απόφαση που είχε κηρυχθεί προσωρινά εκτελεστή και εκτελέστηκε, εκείνος κατά του οποίου είχε στραφεί η εκτέλεση έχει δικαίωμα, εκτός από την επαναφορά των πραγμάτων στην προηγούμενη κατάσταση σύμφωνα με το άρθρο 914, να ζητήσει από εκείνον που επέσπευσε την εκτέλεση αποζημίωση για τις ζημίες που προξενήθηκαν από την εκτέλεση, μόνο αν αυτός ήξερε ή αγνοούσε από βαριά του αμέλεια, ότι το δικαίωμα δεν υπήρχε.

2. Αν εξαφανιστεί ύστερα από άσκηση ένδικου μέσου τελεσίδικη απόφαση που εκτελέστηκε, εκείνος κατά του οποίου είχε στραφεί η εκτέλεση έχει δικαίωμα, εκτός από την επαναφορά των πραγμάτων στην προηγούμενη κατάσταση σύμφωνα με το άρθρο 914, να ζητήσει από εκείνον που επέσπευσε την εκτέλεση αποζημίωση για τις ζημίες που προήλθαν από την εκτέλεση, μόνο αν αυτός είχε δόλο ως προς τη μη ύπαρξη του δικαιώματος.

3. Αν ακυρωθεί αμετάκλητα η αναγκαστική εκτέλεση, εκείνος κατά του οποίου έγινε η εκτέλεση έχει δικαίωμα να ζητήσει από εκείνον που την επέσπευσε αποζημίωση για τις ζημίες που επήλθαν από την εκτέλεση, αν συντρέχουν οι προϋποθέσεις των άρθρων 914 ή 919 του Αστικού Κώδικα.

Article 938

1. With the exception of attachment of immovables, to which paragraph 2 applies, and attachment of movables that can become spoiled, the court may order stay of compulsory enforcement, with or without surety, following a request by the opposing party, if it considers that effecting compulsory enforcement will cause irreparable harm to the applicant and considers it likely on the balance of probabilities that the opposition will be successful. The court may also order that compulsory enforcement go ahead after surety has been provided. The application shall be filed with the court with jurisdiction under Articles 933 and 936 and tried in accordance with Articles 686 *et seq.*
2. Paragraph 1 does not apply specifically in cases of attachment of an immovable, while filing a legal remedy shall not stay the progress of enforcement, unless the court trying the legal remedy, following an application by the applicant submitted with the legal remedy or the pleadings, trying the matter under the procedure laid down in Articles 686 *et seq.*, orders a stay with or without surety if it considers that carrying out the compulsory enforcement will cause irreparable harm to the applicant and considers it likely on the balance of probabilities that the legal remedy will be successful. The court may also order that compulsory enforcement go ahead after surety has been provided.
3. In the aforesaid cases, a note may be issued blocking enforcement until a judgment has been handed down on the application for a stay or on the legal remedy.
4. An application requesting stay of an auction shall be inadmissible if it is not filed within five working days prior to the date of the auction. The judgment must be handed down no later than 12:00 pm on the Monday preceding the auction.
5. The stay referred to in paragraphs 1 and 2 or the provision of surety may be ordered only before a final judgment on the opposition or a judgment on the legal remedy has been handed down.

Article 939

1. The judgment ordering stay of compulsory enforcement or an excerpt from such judgment shall be notified to the enforcement officers by the parties in the proceedings or the court registry. In urgent circumstances, notification may be effected by the court by internal telegram, electronic means or verbally, after the enforcement officer has been summoned to appear before the court for notification and this is attested by means of an ordinary note made on the judgment ordering the stay.
2. After the notification referred to in paragraph 1 has been effected, all compulsory enforcement steps shall be prohibited, except for those specifically allowed in the judgment ordering the stay, the deadlines set for taking prohibited steps shall cease to apply, and any steps commenced shall cease.
3. Enforcement shall resume after cessation of the stay has been notified in the manner set forth in paragraph 1.

Article 940

1. If a judgment that was declared provisionally enforceable and was enforced is quashed or amended, the person enforcement concerns has the right, in addition to restoration of a prior state of affairs under Article 914, to request compensation for the losses incurred due to enforcement from the person who procured enforcement only if the latter knew or was not aware due to gross negligence that the right did not exist.
2. If a *de jure* non-appealable judgment that was enforced is quashed, the person enforcement concerns has the right, in addition to restoration of a prior state of affairs under Article 914, to request compensation for the losses incurred due to enforcement from the person who procured enforcement only if the latter acted with *dolus* in regard to the non-existence of the right.
3. In the event of irrevocable annulment of compulsory enforcement, the person enforcement concerns has the right to request compensation for the losses incurred due to enforcement from the person who procured enforcement if the conditions laid down in Article 914 or Article 919 of the Civil Code are met.

Άρθρο 940Α

Στο χρονικό διάστημα από 1 μέχρι 31 Αυγούστου δεν επιτρέπεται η διενέργεια οποιασδήποτε πράξης εκτέλεσης, συμπεριλαμβανομένης και της επιταγής προς εκτέλεση. Το προηγούμενο εδάφιο δεν εφαρμόζεται, όταν πρόκειται για πλοία και αεροσκάφη.

ΚΕΦΑΛΑΙΟ Β'
Μέσα της αναγκαστικής εκτέλεσης.

Άρθρο 941

1. Αν υπάρχει υποχρέωση να παραδοθεί ή να αποδοθεί ορισμένο κινητό πράγμα ή ποσότητα από ορισμένα κινητά πράγματα, ο δικαστικός επιμελητής αφαιρεί από εκείνον κατά του οποίου στρέφεται η εκτέλεση το πράγμα ή την ποσότητα των πραγμάτων που οφείλεται και τα παραδίδει σε εκείνον προς όφελος του οποίου γίνεται η εκτέλεση. Η παράγραφος 5 του άρθρου 943 εφαρμόζεται και στην αναγκαστική εκτέλεση για αφαίρεση κινητού.

2. Αν το πράγμα που οφείλεται δεν βρέθηκε, εκείνος κατά του οποίου στρέφεται η εκτέλεση υποχρεώνεται, κατά τη διαδικασία των άρθρων 861 έως 866, να δώσε βεβαιωτικό όρκο ότι δεν κατέχει το πράγμα και δεν γνωρίζει πού βρίσκεται. Το δικαστήριο μπορεί κατά τις περιστάσεις να ορίσει και διαφορετικά το περιεχόμενο του όρκου. Αρμόδιο δικαστήριο είναι το ειρηνοδικείο της περιφέρειας του τόπου της εκτέλεσης ή της κατοικίας εκείνου κατά του οποίου γίνεται η εκτέλεση και, αν δεν έχει κατοικία, της διαμονής του.

Άρθρο 942

Αν υπάρχει υποχρέωση παροχής ορισμένης ποσότητας πραγμάτων αντικαταστατών ή ανώνυμων χρεογράφων, ο δικαστικός επιμελητής, αν βρει στον οφειλέτη τέτοια πράγματα, αφαιρεί από αυτά την ποσότητα που οφείλεται και τα παραδίδει σε εκείνον υπέρ του οποίου γίνεται η εκτέλεση. Αν αυτό δεν κατορθωθεί, εφαρμόζονται οι διατάξεις του άρθρου 917.

Άρθρο 943

1. Αν υπάρχει υποχρέωση να παραδοθεί ή αν αποδοθεί ακίνητο, ο δικαστικός επιμελητής αποβάλλει εκείνον κατά του οποίου στρέφεται η εκτέλεση και εγκαθιστά εκείνον υπέρ του οποίου γίνεται η εκτέλεση.

2. Τα κινητά πράγματα που βρίσκονται στο ακίνητο και δεν είναι αντικείμενο της εκτέλεσης ο δικαστικός επιμελητής τα παραδίδει με απόδειξη σε εκείνον κατά του οποίου γίνεται η εκτέλεση. Αν αυτός απουσιάζει ή αρνείται να τα παραλάβει, ο δικαστικός επιμελητής τα παραδίδει είτε σε πρόσωπο που ανήκει στην οικογένεια εκείνου κατά του οποίου γίνεται η εκτέλεση είτε σε πρόσωπο που έχει εξουσία να τα παραλάβει.

3. Αν δεν υπάρχουν τα πρόσωπα της παραγράφου 2 ή αν αρνούνται να παραλάβουν τα κινητά πράγματα, ο δικαστικός επιμελητής τα παραδίδει σε μεσεγγυούχο τον οποίο διορίζει ο ίδιος και, ύστερα από άδεια του ειρηνοδίκη της περιφέρειας του τόπου της εκτέλεσης που δικάζει κατά τις διατάξεις των άρθρων 686 επ. πλειστηριάζει τα κινητά πράγματα. Ο ειρηνοδίκης που δίνει την άδεια ορίζει συνάμα τον τόπο, τον υπάλληλο, την ημέρα και ώρα του πλειστηριασμού. Εάν, για οποιονδήποτε λόγο, δεν είναι δυνατό να ορισθεί συμβολαιογράφος του τόπου όπου βρίσκονται τα κινητά, ως υπάλληλος του πλειστηριασμού μπορεί να οριστεί συμβολαιογράφος διορισμένος στην περιφέρεια του συμβολαιογραφικού συλλόγου του τόπου εκτέλεσης ή, αν και αυτό δεν είναι δυνατό, του συμβολαιογραφικού συλλόγου της πρωτεύουσας του κράτους. Ο πλειστηριασμός δεν μπορεί να οριστεί πριν περάσουν δέκα (10) ημέρες αφότου προσκληθεί εγγράφως εκείνος κατά του οποίου στρέφεται η εκτέλεση να παραλάβει τα πράγματα. Το πλειστηρίασμα κατατίθεται δημόσια, αφού αφαιρεθούν τα έξοδα.

4. Αν εκείνος κατά του οποίου στρέφεται η εκτέλεση δεν ήταν παρών, η έκθεση της εκτέλεσής του κοινοποιείται μέσα σε τριάντα ημέρες από τη σύνταξή της εφόσον αυτός έχει εγγράφως γνωστοποιήσει τη νέα διεύθυνσή του.

Article 940A

No enforcement steps, including orders for enforcement, may be taken between 1 and 31 August. The preceding subparagraph does not apply to ships and aircraft.

CHAPTER II
Means of compulsory enforcement

Article 941

1. If there is an obligation to hand over or return a specific movable or a quantity of specific movables, the court process server shall remove the thing or quantity of things owed from the person enforcement concerns and hand them over to the person for whose benefit enforcement is being done. Article 943(5) also applies in cases of compulsory enforcement to remove a movable.
2. If the thing owed was not found, the person enforcement concerns is obligated, under the procedure laid down in Articles 861 to 866, to take an attesting oath that they do not have the thing in their possession and are not aware of its whereabouts. The court may, considering the circumstances, specify a different wording for the oath. The competent court is the court of the peace of the district where enforcement is being done or where the person enforcement concerns has their place of domicile and, where they have no place of domicile, their place of residence.

Article 942

If there is an obligation to provide a specific quantity of fungible things or bearer shares, the court process server, where they find such things in the possession of the debtor, shall remove the quantity owed and hand over said quantity to the person for whose benefit enforcement is being done. If this is not achieved, the provisions of Article 917 apply.

Article 943

1. If there is an obligation to hand over or return an immovable, the court process server shall evict the person enforcement concerns and allow the person for whose benefit enforcement is being done to enter.
2. Any movables which are unrelated to the enforcement and are found at the immovable shall be handed over by the court process server to the person enforcement concerns, and a receipt shall be issued. If the latter is absent or refuses to accept them, the court process server shall hand them over either to a relative of the person enforcement concerns or to a person empowered to take receipt of them.
3. If the persons referred to in paragraph 2 do not exist or refuse to take receipt of the movables, the court process server shall hand them over to a sequestrator appointed by the court process server and, following permission by the court of the peace judge of the district where enforcement is taking place, trying the matter under the provisions of Articles 686 *et seq.*, shall auction the movables. The court of the peace judge granting permission shall also set the place, date and time of the auction and designate the auctioneer. If a notary public of the place where the movables are located cannot be designated for any reason, then a notary public from the district of the notarial association of the place of enforcement may be designated as auctioneer and, if this is also not possible, from the notarial association of the capital. The auction may not be set before 10 days have elapsed from the date on which the person enforcement concerns was invited to collect the things. After costs have been deducted, the auction price shall be deposited with the state.
4. If the person enforcement concerns was not present, the enforcement report shall be notified to them within 30 days of the date it was drafted, provided said person has notified their new address in writing.

5. Αναγκαστική εκτέλεση για απόδοση ακινήτου δεν επιτρέπεται να γίνει κατά το διάστημα
α) από 23 Δεκεμβρίου μέχρι 7 Ιανουαρίου του επομένου έτους,
β) από τη Μεγάλη Δευτέρα μέχρι την Κυριακή του Θωμά και
γ) την προηγουμένη και την επομένη εβδομάδα των εκλογών για την ανάδειξη βουλευτών, αντιπροσώπων στο Ευρωπαϊκό Κοινοβούλιο και Οργάνων Τοπικής Αυτοδιοίκησης. Η απαγόρευση αυτή ισχύει και για επαναληπτικές εκλογές και μόνο για τις περιφέρειες που διεξάγονται τέτοιες.
6. Στην περίπτωση του παρόντος άρθρου η αξίωση εκείνου κατά του οποίου έγινε η εκτέλεση, κατά του μεσεγγυούχου που διορίστηκε από τον δικαστικό επιμελητή, προς απόδοση των κινητών πραγμάτων, παραγράφεται ύστερα από έξι (6) μήνες από την αποβολή του.

Άρθρο 944

Οι διατάξεις του άρθρου 943 εφαρμόζονται και στα πλοία και τα αεροσκάφη.
Η έκθεση της εκτέλεσης κοινοποιείται χωρίς υπαίτια καθυστέρηση στο λιμενάρχη του λιμανιού όπου είναι λιμενισμένο το πλοίο ή στο διοικητή του αερολιμένα.

Άρθρο 945

1. Αν ο οφειλέτης δεν εκπληρώνει την υποχρέωσή του να ενεργήσει πράξη που μπορεί να γίνει και από τρίτο πρόσωπο, ο δανειστής έχει δικαίωμα να επιχειρήσει την πράξη με δαπάνη του οφειλέτη.
2. Το δικαστήριο, καταδικάζοντας τον οφειλέτη στην πράξη της παρ. 1, μπορεί, αν το ζητήσει ο δανειστής, να τον καταδικάσει ταυτόχρονα να προκαταβάλει το ποσό της δαπάνης για να επιχειρηθεί η πράξη από το δανειστή, υπό τον όρο ότι ο οφειλέτης δεν θα εκπληρώσει την υποχρέωσή του να ενεργήσει την πράξη. Το δικαίωμα του δανειστή να απαιτήσει ποσό μεγαλύτερο από εκείνο που επιδικάστηκε, αν η δαπάνη για να επιχειρηθεί η πράξη ήταν μεγαλύτερη, δεν επηρεάζεται.

Άρθρο 946

1. Αν ο οφειλέτης δεν εκπληρώνει την υποχρέωσή του να επιχειρήσει πράξη που δεν μπορεί να γίνει από τρίτο πρόσωπο και η επιχείρησή της εξαρτάται αποκλειστικά από τη βούληση του οφειλέτη, το δικαστήριο τον καταδικάζει να εκτελέσει την πράξη και στην περίπτωση που δεν την εκτελέσει τον καταδικάζει αυτεπαγγέλτως σε χρηματική ποινή έως πενήντα χιλιάδες (50.000) ευρώ υπέρ του δανειστή και σε προσωπική κράτηση έως ένα έτος.
2. Οι διατάξεις της παρ. 1 δεν εφαρμόζονται όταν η πράξη συνίσταται στην αποκατάσταση της έγγαμης συμβίωσης ή εξαρτάται από την ύπαρξη στο πρόσωπο του υποχρέου ιδιαιτέρων προϋποθέσεων για να ασκήσει τις τεχνικές, καλλιτεχνικές ή επιστημονικές ικανότητές του και η άρνησή του δεν οφείλεται σε δυστροπία του.

Άρθρο 947

1. Όταν ο οφειλέτης έχει υποχρέωση να παραλείψει ή να ανεχθεί πράξη, το δικαστήριο, για την περίπτωση που παραβεί την υποχρέωση του, απειλεί για κάθε παράβαση χρηματική ποινή έως εκατό χιλιάδες (100.000) ευρώ υπέρ του δανειστή και προσωπική κράτηση έως ένα έτος. Αν η απειλή της χρηματικής ποινής και της προσωπικής κράτησης δεν περιέχεται στην απόφαση που καταδικάζει τον οφειλέτη να παραλείψει ή να ανεχθεί πράξη, απαγγέλλεται από το μονομελές πρωτοδικείο. Το δικαστήριο αυτό είναι αρμόδιο να βεβαιώσει την παράβαση και να καταδικάσει στη χρηματική ποινή και στην προσωπική κράτηση. Στην τελευταία περίπτωση, δικάζει σύμφωνα με τη διαδικασία των περιουσιακών διαφορών των άρθρων 614 επ..
2. Αν το ζητήσει ο δανειστής, το δικαστήριο μπορεί, εκτός από την απειλή της χρηματικής ποινής και της προσωπικής κράτησης, να επιβάλει στον οφειλέτη να δώσει και εγγύηση για την παράλειψη ή την ανοχή της πράξης.
3. Αν ο οφειλέτης που έχει υποχρέωση να ανεχθεί πράξη προβάλει αντίσταση, ο δικαστικός επιμελητής παραμερίζει κάθε εμπόδιο και ενεργεί σύμφωνα με το άρθρο 930.

5. Compulsory enforcement for the return of an immovable may not take place during the period[:]
a) between 23 December [of one year] and 7 January of the following year;
b) from Monday before [Orthodox] Easter until the Sunday after [Orthodox] Easter; and
c) of the week prior to and the week subsequent to elections for members of parliament, members of the European Parliament and local government authorities. This prohibition also applies to run-off elections and only in the districts where such elections are being held.
6. In the case referred to in this Article, any claim of the person enforcement concerns against the sequestrator appointed by the court process server for return of movables shall become time-barred after six months have elapsed from the date that person was evicted.

Article 944

The provisions of Article 943 also apply to ships and aircraft.
The enforcement report shall be notified without undue delay to the harbour master of the harbour where the ship is berthed or to the airport manager.

Article 945

1. If the debtor fails to perform their obligation to take a step that can also be taken by a third party, the creditor has the right to take the step with the debtor bearing the costs.
2. When ordering the debtor to take the step referred to in paragraph 1, the court may, if so requested by the creditor, also order the debtor to pay in advance the expenses for the creditor to take the step, on condition that the debtor will not [also] perform their obligation to take the step. The right of the creditor to claim an amount higher than the one awarded, if the expenses for taking the step were higher, is not affected.

Article 946

1. If the debtor fails to perform their obligation to take a step that cannot be taken by a third party and taking it depends exclusively on the will of the debtor, the court shall order the debtor to take the step and, if the debtor fails to do so, shall *ex officio* order them to pay the creditor a monetary penalty of no more than 50,000 euros and order personal detention of no more than one year.
2. The provisions of paragraph 1 do not apply when the step involves the resumption of marital cohabitation or depends on the existence of specific conditions in order for the liable party to make use of their technical, artistic or scientific skills and their refusal is not due to intransigence.

Article 947

1. Where the debtor is obligated to abstain from or tolerate a step and they violate this obligation, the court shall threaten [the debtor with] a monetary penalty of up to 100,000 euros payable to the creditor and up to one year of personal detention for each violation. If the threat of monetary penalty and personal detention is not contained in the judgment ordering the debtor to abstain from or tolerate a step, it shall be pronounced by the single-member court of first instance. That court is competent to confirm the violation and order the monetary penalty and personal detention [for the debtor]. In the latter case, the court shall try the matter under the procedure on property disputes laid down in Articles 614 *et seq.*
2. If requested by the creditor, the court may, in addition to the threat of monetary penalty and personal detention, also order the debtor to provide surety for abstaining from or tolerating the step.
3. If there is resistance by the debtor obligated to tolerate a step, the court process server shall remove any obstacles and take the steps referred to in Article 930.

Άρθρο 948

Οι διατάξεις των άρθρων 941 έως 947 δεν θίγουν το δικαίωμα του δανειστή να απαιτήσει την αποζημίωση που προβλέπουν οι διατάξεις του ουσιαστικού δικαίου.

Άρθρο 949

Όταν κάποιος καταδικάζεται σε δήλωση βούλησης, η δήλωση αυτή θεωρείται ότι έγινε μόλις η απόφαση γίνει τελεσίδικη. Αν η καταδίκη σε δήλωση βούλησης εξαρτήθηκε από αντιπαροχή, η δήλωση βούλησης θεωρείται ότι έγινε από τη στιγμή που εκπληρώθηκε η αντιπαροχή ή επήλθε υπερημερία αποδοχής της.

Άρθρο 950

1. Με την απόφαση με την οποία διατάζεται η απόδοση ή παράδοση τέκνου, καταδικάζεται ο γονέας που έχει το τέκνο να εκτελέσει αυτήν την πράξη και με την ίδια απόφαση, για την περίπτωση που δεν την εκτελέσει, απαγγέλλεται αυτεπαγγέλτως χρηματική ποινή έως εκατό χιλιάδες (100.000) ευρώ υπέρ του αιτούντος την απόδοση ή παράδοση και σε προσωπική κράτηση έως ένα (1) έτος. Αν το τέκνο δεν βρεθεί, εφαρμόζονται οι διατάξεις των άρθρων 861 έως 866.

2. Αν παρεμποδίζεται το δικαίωμα της προσωπικής επικοινωνίας του γονέα με το τέκνο, το δικαστήριο, που ρυθμίζει το δικαίωμα της προσωπικής επικοινωνίας του γονέα με το τέκνο, καθορίζει τα χρονικά διαστήματα αυτής και απειλεί, και αυτεπάγγελτα, σε βάρος εκείνου που εμποδίζει κάθε φορά την επικοινωνία, για κάθε παράβαση, χρηματική ποινή έως δέκα χιλιάδες (10,000.00) ευρώ και προσωπική κράτηση έως ένα (1) έτος. Η παρεμπόδιση του δικαιώματος της προσωπικής επικοινωνίας του γονέα με το τέκνο διαπιστώνεται με έκθεση δικαστικού επιμελητή, ο οποίος παρευρίσκεται κατά τον ορισθέντα χρόνο έναρξης της επικοινωνίας.

3. [Καταργείται]

Άρθρο 951

1. Η αναγκαστική εκτέλεση για να ικανοποιηθεί χρηματική απαίτηση γίνεται με κατάσχεση περιουσίας εκείνου κατά του οποίου στρέφεται η εκτέλεση ή με αναγκαστική διαχείριση ή με προσωπική κράτηση. Όταν πρόκειται για ένωση προσώπων του άρθρου 62 παρ. 2, η αναγκαστική εκτέλεση γίνεται στην κοινή περιουσία τους.

2. Η κατάσχεση δεν επιτρέπεται να επεκταθεί σε περισσότερα από όσα χρειάζονται για να ικανοποιηθεί η απαίτηση και για να καλυφθούν τα έξοδα της εκτέλεσης.

Άρθρο 952

Αν με την κατάσχεση που έχει επιβληθεί δεν ικανοποιείται ή αν πιθανολογείται ότι με την κατάσχεση δεν μπορεί να ικανοποιηθεί εντελώς η απαίτηση του δανειστή, μπορεί με αίτηση του δανειστή να υποχρεωθεί ο οφειλέτης, κατά τη διαδικασία των άρθρων 861 έως 866, να υποβάλει αναλυτικό κατάλογο όλων των περιουσιακών του στοιχείων με ακριβή αναφορά του τόπου όπου αυτά βρίσκονται. Ως προς τις απαιτήσεις θα πρέπει να αναφέρονται η νομική αιτία, το αντικείμενο, ο οφειλέτης, οι τυχόν εξασφαλίσεις και τα τυχόν υπάρχοντα αποδεικτικά μέσα. Από τον κατάλογο θα πρέπει να προκύπτουν επίσης οι απαλλοτριώσεις ακινήτων που έλαβαν χώρα την τελευταία πενταετία πριν από την υποβολή της αίτησης. Ο οφειλέτης θα πρέπει να βεβαιώνει συγχρόνως με όρκο ότι ο κατάλογος περιέχει όλα τα περιουσιακά στοιχεία του, καθώς και τις ως άνω απαλλοτριώσεις, ότι δεν παραλείπει κανένα στοιχείο και ότι έκανε κάθε προσπάθεια, για να εξακριβώσει όλα τα περιουσιακά του στοιχεία.

Article 948

The provisions of Articles 941 to 947 do not prejudice the right of the creditor to claim the compensation provided for under substantive law provisions.

Article 949

If a person is ordered to make a declaration of will, this declaration shall be deemed to have been made the moment the judgment became *de jure* non-appealable. If the order to make a declaration of will was predicated on counter-performance, the declaration shall be deemed to have been made the moment the counter-performance was provided or [that the debtor] is in default of acceptance.

Article 950

1. A judgment ordering that a child be returned or handed over shall order the parent who has the child to take this step, and in case of failure to comply with this order, the same judgment may provide for the automatic imposition of a monetary penalty of up to 100,000 euros payable to the applicant requesting that the child be returned or handed over, and personal detention of up to one year. If the child is not found, the provisions of Articles 861 to 866 apply.

2. If the right of personal access between the parent and the child is obstructed, the court regulating the right of personal access between the parent and the child shall set the periods of access and *ex officio* threaten the person obstructing access with a monetary penalty of up to 10,000 euros and personal detention of up to one year for each violation. Obstruction of the right of personal access between the parent and the child shall be ascertained in a report prepared by a court process server who shall be present at the time set for access to commence.

3. [Repealed]

Article 951

1. Compulsory enforcement to satisfy a monetary claim shall be effected by means of attachment of the assets of the person enforcement concerns or by compulsory administration or personal detention. In cases of a grouping of persons referred to in [the second sentence of] Article 62, compulsory enforcement shall concern their joint assets.

2. Attachment may not extend to anything more than what is required to satisfy the claim and cover the enforcement costs.

Article 952

If the attachment imposed does not satisfy or it is considered likely on the balance of probabilities that the attachment cannot fully satisfy the claim of the creditor, the debtor may be obligated, following an application filed by the creditor and in accordance with the procedure laid down in Articles 861 to 866, to submit a detailed list of all their assets, with a precise reference to their location. With regard to the claims, the legal cause, the subject-matter, the debtor, any collateral and any existing means of evidence must be cited. This list must also indicate any alienation of immovables that occurred during the five years prior to submission of the application. At the same time, the debtor must attest under oath that the list contains all their assets and the aforesaid alienations, that they did not omit any asset, and that they made every effort to ascertain all of their assets.

ΚΕΦΑΛΑΙΟ Γ'
Κατάσχεση της κινητής περιουσίας του οφειλέτη.

Άρθρο 953

1. Κατάσχεση μπορεί να γίνει στα κινητά πράγματα που βρίσκονται στα χέρια του οφειλέτη, καθώς και στα χέρια μεσεγγυούχου κατά την έννοια του άρθρου 956 παράγραφος 1 ως συνέπεια προηγούμενης κατάσχεσης.

2. Οι διατάξεις για την κατάσχεση στα χέρια του οφειλέτη εφαρμόζονται και

α) όταν κινητά πράγματα του οφειλέτη βρίσκονται στα χέρια του δανειστή ή τρίτου πρόθυμου να τα αποδώσει,

β) όταν κατάσχεται εμπράγματο δικαίωμα του οφειλέτη επάνω σε ξένο κινητό πράγμα,

γ) όταν πρόκειται για κινητά πράγματα που είχαν μεταβιβαστεί από τον οφειλέτη σε τρίτο, εφόσον η κατάσχεση επιβάλλεται από δανειστή που πέτυχε τη διάρρηξη της μεταβίβασης ως καταδολιευτικής κατά τα άρθρα 939 επ. του Αστικού Κώδικα.

3. Εξαιρούνται από την κατάσχεση:

α) τα πράγματα που είναι απολύτως απαραίτητα για τις στοιχειώδεις ανάγκες διαβίωσης του οφειλέτη και της οικογένειάς του,

β) προκειμένου για πρόσωπα που με την προσωπική τους εργασία αποκτούν όσα τους χρειάζονται για να ζήσουν, τα πράγματα που είναι απαραίτητα για την εργασία τους,

γ) τα πάσης φύσεως βιβλία που δεν είναι εμπόρευμα, τα οποία, ως πολιτιστικά αγαθά, ο δικαστικός επιμελητής που διενεργεί την αναγκαστική εκτέλεση τα αφαιρεί και τα παραδίδει μετά από δημόσια πρόσκληση, σε πολιτιστικούς οργανισμούς αντί τιμήματος που συμφωνείται από τον επί του πλειστηριασμού υπάλληλο και αυτούς. Ο δικαστικός επιμελητής μπορεί να προβεί σε κάθε κατάλληλη ενέργεια για την εξασφάλιση δημοσιότητας. Αν διαφωνήσει εκείνος υπέρ του οποίου γίνεται ή εκείνος κατά του οποίου στρέφεται η εκτέλεση, αποφασίζει το ειρηνοδικείο του τόπου της εκτέλεσης, που δικάζει κατά τη διαδικασία των άρθρων 686 επ.

4. Αν τα κατασχεμένα πράγματα είναι ασφαλισμένα η κατάσχεση ισχύει και για την αποζημίωση που οφείλεται από την ασφάλιση.

Άρθρο 954

1. Η κατάσχεση, με την επιφύλαξη του άρθρου 956 παράγραφος 1 εδάφιο γ', γίνεται με την αφαίρεση του πράγματος από το δικαστικό επιμελητή και συντάσσεται σχετική έκθεση μπροστά σε ενήλικο μάρτυρα. Το κατασχεμένο το εκτιμά ο δικαστικός επιμελητής ή ο πραγματογνώμονας που ο επιμελητής προσλαμβάνει κατά την κρίση του για αυτόν τον σκοπό.

2. Η κατασχετήρια έκθεση πρέπει να περιέχει, εκτός από τα ουσιώδη που απαιτούνται από το άρθρο 117 και

α) ακριβή περιγραφή του κατασχεμένου πράγματος, ώστε να μη γεννιέται αμφιβολία για την ταυτότητά του,

β) αναφορά της εκτίμησης του κατασχεμένου που έκανε ο δικαστικός επιμελητής ή ο πραγματογνώμονας,

γ) τιμή πρώτης προσφοράς που πρέπει να είναι τουλάχιστον τα δύο τρίτα της αξίας, στην οποία εκτιμήθηκε το κατασχεμένο κινητό πράγμα,

δ) αναφορά του εκτελεστού τίτλου, στον οποίο βασίζεται η εκτέλεση, της επιταγής που επιδόθηκε στον οφειλέτη και του ποσού για το οποίο γίνεται η κατάσχεση,

ε) αναφορά της ημέρας του πλειστηριασμού, η οποία ορίζεται υποχρεωτικά σε πέντε (5) μήνες από την ημέρα περάτωσης της κατάσχεσης και όχι πάντως μετά την παρέλευση έξι (6) μηνών από την ημερομηνία αυτή, του τόπου του πλειστηριασμού, καθώς και του ονόματος του υπαλλήλου του πλειστηριασμού.

Εάν η παραπάνω προθεσμία συμπληρώνεται τον Αύγουστο, τότε για τον υπολογισμό της λαμβάνεται υπόψη ο επόμενος μήνας. Στην έκθεση αναφέρονται επίσης οι όροι που τυχόν έθεσε, σχετικά με τον πλειστηριασμό, ο υπέρ ου η εκτέλεση με την κατά το άρθρο 927 εντολή, καθώς επίσης και η τυχόν διενέργειά του ενώπιον συμβολαιογράφου διορισμένου στην περιφέρεια του συμβολαιογραφικού συλλόγου του τόπου εκτέλεσης ή του συμβολαιογραφικού συλλόγου της πρωτεύουσας του κράτους. Ο δικαστικός επιμελητής βεβαιώνει στην κατασχετήρια έκθεση τον λόγο της αδυναμίας ορισμού συμβολαιογράφου του τόπου εκτέλεσης ή της περιφέρειας του συμβολαιογραφικού συλλόγου του τόπου εκτέλεσης.

CHAPTER III
Attachment of the debtor's movables

Article 953

1. Attachment may concern the movables held by the debtor and by a sequestrator, within the meaning of Article 956(1), as the result of prior attachment.
2. The provisions on attachment [of movables] held by the debtor also apply[:]
a) when the debtor's movables are held by a creditor or a third party willing to return them;
b) when a debtor's right *in rem* in a movable owned by a third party is being attached;
c) in cases of movables transferred by the debtor to a third party, where attachment is procured by a creditor who successfully challenged the transfer as fraudulent in accordance with Articles 939 *et seq.* of the Civil Code.
3. The following shall be exempt from attachment:
a) the things absolutely necessary for the basic subsistence needs of the debtor and their family;
b) in cases of persons who earn their livelihood through personal labour, the things necessary for their labour;
c) all manner of books that are not merchandise, which, being cultural goods, the court process server carrying out compulsory enforcement shall remove and deliver, following a public notice, to cultural organisations for a price agreed upon between the auctioneer and said organisations. The court process server may take any appropriate steps to ensure publicity. If the person for whose benefit enforcement is being done or the person enforcement concerns disagrees, the court of the peace of the place of enforcement shall decide, trying the matter under the procedure laid down in Articles 686 *et seq.*
4. If the attached things are insured, the attachment shall also apply to the insurance compensation.

Article 954

1. Without prejudice to the third subparagraph of Article 956(1), attachment shall be done by means of removal of the thing by the court process server, and a relevant report shall be prepared in the presence of an adult witness. The attached things shall be valued by the court process server or the expert enlisted for this purpose by the court process server, at their discretion.
2. In addition to the essential information required under Article 117, the attachment report must also contain[:]
a) a precise description of the attached thing so that no doubts arise concerning its identity;
b) reference to the valuation of the attached thing done by the court process server or the expert;
c) a starting price, which must be at least 2/3 of the value assigned to the attached movable thing;
d) reference to the enforceable title on which enforcement is based, the order served on the debtor and the amount for which attachment is being done;
e) reference to the auction date, which must be set within five months of the date of completion of the attachment and, in all cases, no later than six months from that date, the place of the auction, as well as the name of the auctioneer.
If the above deadline lapses in August, the following month shall be taken into account for the above calculation. The report shall also make reference to any terms laid down with regard to the auction by the person for whose benefit enforcement was done in the instructions referred to in Article 927, as well as to the fact that the auction took place in the presence of a notary public from the district of the notarial association of the place of enforcement or from the notarial association of the capital. In the attachment report, the court process server shall confirm why a notary public of the place of enforcement or the district of the notarial association of the place of enforcement could not be appointed.

3. Την κατασχετήρια έκθεση υπογράφουν ο δικαστικός επιμελητής και ο μάρτυρας και αν είναι παρόντες εκείνος υπέρ του οποίου γίνεται και εκείνος κατά του οποίου στρέφεται η εκτέλεση την υπογράφουν και αυτοί. Αν κάποιος από αυτούς αρνηθεί να υπογράψει, η άρνησή του αναφέρεται στην έκθεση.
4. Ύστερα από ανακοπή του επισπεύδοντος ή του καθ' ου η εκτέλεση ή οποιουδήποτε άλλου έχει έννομο συμφέρον, το αρμόδιο κατά το άρθρο 933 δικαστήριο, δικάζοντας κατά τη διαδικασία των άρθρων 686 επ., μπορεί να διατάξει τη διόρθωση της έκθεσης και του αποσπάσματος αυτής, ιδίως ως προς την περιγραφή του κατασχεθέντος, την εκτίμηση και την τιμή πρώτης προσφοράς. Η ανακοπή είναι απαράδεκτη, αν δεν κατατεθεί το αργότερο δεκαπέντε (15) εργάσιμες ημέρες πριν από την ημέρα του πλειστηριασμού. Η απόφαση πρέπει να δημοσιεύεται έως τις 12:00' το μεσημέρι της όγδοης πριν από τον πλειστηριασμό ημέρας και αναρτάται την ίδια ημέρα με επιμέλεια της γραμματείας στην ιστοσελίδα δημοσιεύσεων πλειστηριασμών του Δελτίου Δικαστικών Δημοσιεύσεων του Ηλεκτρονικού Εθνικού Φορέα Κοινωνικής Ασφάλισης (e-ΕΦΚΑ).

Άρθρο 955

1. Αντίγραφο της κατασχετήριας έκθεσης επιδίδεται μόλις περατωθεί η κατάσχεση στον καθ' ου η εκτέλεση, αν ήταν παρών, και, αν αυτός αρνηθεί να παραλάβει το έγγραφο που του επιδίδεται, ο επιμελητής συντάσσει έκθεση για την άρνησή του. Αν είναι απών ή δεν είναι δυνατή η άμεση κατάρτιση του αντιγράφου, η επίδοση γίνεται το αργότερο την επομένη της ημέρας που περατώθηκε η κατάσχεση, εφόσον εκείνος κατά του οποίου στρέφεται η εκτέλεση έχει την κατοικία του στην περιφέρεια του δήμου όπου έγινε η κατάσχεση, διαφορετικά μέσα σε πέντε (5) ημέρες από την περάτωση της κατάσχεσης. Μέσα στην ίδια πενθήμερη προθεσμία η έκθεση επιδίδεται στον γραμματέα του ειρηνοδικείου του τόπου όπου έγινε η κατάσχεση, ο οποίος οφείλει να την καταχωρίσει σε ειδικό βιβλίο με αλφαβητικό ευρετήριο εκείνων κατά των οποίων γίνεται η κατάσχεση. Η παράλειψη των διατυπώσεων αυτών επιφέρει ακυρότητα της κατάσχεσης.
2. Ο δικαστικός επιμελητής οφείλει, μέσα σε οκτώ (8) ημέρες από την ημέρα της περάτωσης της κατάσχεσης, να καταθέσει στον υπάλληλο του πλειστηριασμού τον εκτελεστό τίτλο, την έκθεση της επίδοσης της επιταγής προς εκτέλεση, την κατασχετήρια έκθεση και τις εκθέσεις επίδοσής της στον οφειλέτη και τον γραμματέα του ειρηνοδικείου και, στην περίπτωση του άρθρου 956 παρ. 3, και το γραμμάτιο της δημόσιας κατάθεσης, ο οποίος συντάσσει έκθεση για όλα αυτά. Απόσπασμα της κατασχετήριας έκθεσης, που περιλαμβάνει τα ονοματεπώνυμα του υπέρ ου και του καθ' ου η εκτέλεση, καθώς και τον αριθμό φορολογικού μητρώου αυτών και αν πρόκειται για νομικά πρόσωπα την επωνυμία και τον αριθμό φορολογικού τους μητρώου, περιγραφή των κατασχεθέντων κινητών, την τιμή της πρώτης προσφοράς, του ποσού για το οποίο γίνεται η κατάσχεση, τους όρους του πλειστηριασμού, το όνομα και τη διεύθυνση του υπαλλήλου του πλειστηριασμού, καθώς και τον τόπο, την ημέρα και την ώρα του πλειστηριασμού, εκδίδεται από τον δικαστικό επιμελητή και δημοσιεύεται με επιμέλειά του μέχρι τη δέκατη ημέρα από την κατάσχεση στην ιστοσελίδα δημοσιεύσεων πλειστηριασμών του Δελτίου Δικαστικών Δημοσιεύσεων του Τομέα Ασφάλισης Νομικών του Ενιαίου Ταμείου Ανεξάρτητα Απασχολουμένων. Στο απόσπασμα περιλαμβάνεται και η τυχόν βεβαίωση του δικαστικού επιμελητή σχετικά με τη αδυναμία ορισμού συμβολαιογράφου του τόπου εκτέλεσης ή της περιφέρειας του συμβολαιογραφικού συλλόγου του τόπου εκτέλεσης. Το απόσπασμα αυτό επιδίδεται μέσα στην ίδια προθεσμία στον ενεχυρούχο δανειστή, εφόσον το ενέχυρο είναι γραμμένο σε δημόσιο βιβλίο. Ο πλειστηριασμός δεν μπορεί να γίνει χωρίς να τηρηθούν οι διατυπώσεις των προηγούμενων εδαφίων, διαφορετικά είναι άκυρος.

Άρθρο 956

1. Ο δικαστικός επιμελητής παραδίδει τα κατασχεμένα πράγματα για φύλαξη σε μεσεγγυούχο. Μεσεγγυούχος μπορεί να οριστεί εκείνος υπέρ του οποίου γίνεται η εκτέλεση, αν συναινεί εκείνος κατά του οποίου στρέφεται ή και εκείνος κατά του οποίου στρέφεται, αν συναινεί εκείνος υπέρ του οποίου γίνεται η εκτέλεση. Η ιδιότητα του κατά το προηγούμενο εδάφιο μεσεγγυούχου διατηρείται και για τις κατασχέσεις που ενδεχομένως θα ακολουθήσουν.

3. The attachment report shall be signed by the court process server and the witness and, if present, the person for whose benefit enforcement is being done and the person enforcement concerns. If any of the above persons refuses to sign the report, such refusal shall be noted in the report.
4. Following an opposition filed by the person procuring enforcement or the subject of the enforcement or by any other person with a legitimate interest, the court with jurisdiction under Article 933, trying the matter under the procedure laid down in Articles 686 *et seq.*, may order that the report and the report excerpt be corrected, particularly with regard to the description of the attached thing, the valuation and the starting price. The opposition shall be inadmissible if it is not filed within 15 working days prior to the date of the auction. The judgment must be handed down no later than 12:00 pm on the eighth day prior to the auction and uploaded on the same day, by the registry, to the auctions announcement website of the Court Announcements Bulletin of the e-National Social Security Fund.

Article 955

1. Upon completion of attachment, a copy of the attachment report shall be served on the person enforcement concerns, if present, and if they refuse to take receipt of the document being served, the court process server shall prepare a report on such refusal. If that person is absent or the copy cannot be prepared immediately, service shall be effected no later than the day after the date of completion of the attachment, where the person enforcement concerns has their place of domicile in the district of the municipality where the attachment took place, otherwise within five days of the date of completion of the attachment. Within the same five-day deadline, the report shall be served on the registrar of the court of the peace of the place where the attachment took place, who is obligated to enter it in a special register with an alphabetical index of persons enforcement concerns. Failure to comply with these formalities shall result in nullity of the attachment.
2. Within eight days of the date of completion of the attachment, the court process server is obligated to file with the auctioneer the enforceable title, the report on service of the order for enforcement, the attachment report and reports on the service of the attachment report on the debtor and the court of the peace registrar and, in the case referred to in Article 956(3), the note concerning deposit with the state, and the auctioneer shall prepare a report on all the foregoing. An excerpt of the attachment report, containing the full names of the person for whose benefit and against whom enforcement was done, as well as their tax identification numbers and, in the case of legal persons, their corporate names and tax identification numbers, a description of the attached movables, the starting price, the amount for which attachment is taking place, the auction terms, the name and address of the auctioneer, as well as the place, date and time of the auction shall be issued and published by a court process server no later than 10 days after the attachment, on the auction announcements website of the Court Announcements Bulletin of the Lawyers' Insurance Sector of the National Self-Employed Persons' Fund. The excerpt shall also contain any confirmation prepared by the court process server on the inability to appoint a notary public of the place of enforcement or the district of the notarial association of the place of enforcement. This excerpt shall be served within the same deadline on the pledgee, where the pledge is registered in a public register. Any auction not conducted in compliance with the formalities laid down in the preceding subparagraphs shall be null and void.

Article 956

1. The court process server shall hand over the attached things to a sequestrator for safekeeping. The person appointed as sequestrator may be the person for whose benefit enforcement is being done, with the consent of the person enforcement concerns, or may be the person enforcement concerns, with the consent of the person for whose benefit enforcement is being done. The capacity of sequestrator under the preceding subparagraph shall continue to be held even in the case of any subsequent attachment.

2. Αν κατασχέθηκαν πράγματα που η μεταφορά τους είναι δύσκολη ή μπορεί να τα βλάψει, ο δικαστικός επιμελητής τα αφήνει στον τόπο όπου έγινε η κατάσχεση.
3. Αν κατασχέθηκαν χρήματα ή άλλα πράγματα δεκτικά κατά το νόμο κατάθεσης, ο δικαστικός επιμελητής τα καταθέτει σύμφωνα με τα οριζόμενα στο άρθρο 965 παρ. 4.
4. Ο μεσεγγυούχος φυλάει τα κατασχεμένα πράγματα και δεν έχει εξουσία να τα χρησιμοποιεί. Αν η φύση του κατασχεμένου το επιβάλλει, ο μεσεγγυούχος, μετά από άδεια του ειρηνοδικείου της περιφέρειας του τόπου όπου έγινε η κατάσχεση, το οποίο δικάζει κατά τη διαδικασία των άρθρων 686 επ., ενεργεί και διαχειριστικές πράξεις. Ο μεσεγγυούχος έχει υποχρέωση να λογοδοτήσει και παραδίδει στον υπάλληλο του πλειστηριασμού το προϊόν της διαχείρισης.
5. Κάθε αμφισβήτηση για τον ορισμό του μεσεγγυούχο ή για ό,τι αφορά τη μεσεγγύηση, καθώς και η αίτηση για την αντικατάστασή του, εισάγεται, κατά τη διαδικασία των άρθρων 686 επ., στο ειρηνοδικείο της περιφέρειας του τόπου της εκτέλεσης. Το δικαστήριο μπορεί να ορίσει ως μεσεγγυούχο και εκείνον κατά του οποίου στρέφεται ή εκείνον υπέρ του οποίου γίνεται η εκτέλεση.
6. Αν ο μεσεγγυούχος αποβληθεί ή χάσει την κατοχή του πράγματος, το ειρηνοδικείο του τόπου της εκτέλεσης, δικάζοντας κατά τη διαδικασία των άρθρων 686 επ., διατάζει να του αποδοθεί το πράγμα.
7. Αν ο ασφαλιστικός κίνδυνος πραγματοποιήθηκε μετά την κατάσχεση, ο ασφαλιστής καταβάλλει στον υπάλληλο του πλειστηριασμού την αποζημίωση που οφείλεται. Ο ασφαλιστής έγκυρα καταβάλλει την αποζημίωση σε εκείνον κατά του οποίου στρέφεται η εκτέλεση, πριν ειδοποιηθεί εγγράφως από εκείνον που έκανε την κατάσχεση σχετικά με την επιβολή της.

Άρθρο 957

1. Αν τα κατασχεμένα είναι μόνο χρήματα εφαρμόζονται τα άρθρα 971 επ. Το ίδιο ισχύει αν τα κατασχεμένα είναι αλλοδαπά χρήματα τα οποία ο υπάλληλος του πλειστηριασμού μετατρέπει σε ελληνικό χρήμα.
2. Αν εκτός από τα χρήματα κατασχέθηκαν και άλλα πράγματα, η διανομή των χρημάτων γίνεται με μαζί με το πλειστηρίασμα.

Άρθρο 958

1. Αφότου γίνει η επίδοση αντιγράφου της κατασχετήριας έκθεσης κατά το άρθρο 955 παράγραφος 1, απαγορεύεται και είναι άκυρη υπέρ εκείνου που επέβαλε την κατάσχεση και των δανειστών που αναγγέλθηκαν η διάθεση του κατασχεμένου από εκείνον κατά του οποίου έγινε η κατάσχεση.
2. Η αναγκαστική κατάσχεση κινητών πραγμάτων δεν εμποδίζει την κατάσχεσή τους και από άλλο δανειστή. Κάθε διαδικασία αναγκαστικής εκτέλεσης διενεργείται ξεχωριστά και δεν επηρεάζει η μια την άλλη. Δεν επιτρέπεται η αναζήτηση των εξόδων της εκτέλεσης που προκατέβαλε εκείνος ο δανειστής, η εκτέλεση του οποίου δεν περατώθηκε.

Άρθρο 959

1. Τα κατασχεμένα πράγματα πλειστηριάζονται με ηλεκτρονικά μέσα ενώπιον συμβολαιογράφου της εφετειακής περιφέρειας του τόπου όπου έγινε η κατάσχεση. Εάν, για οποιονδήποτε λόγο, δεν είναι δυνατό να οριστεί συμβολαιογράφος του τόπου εκτέλεσης (κατάσχεσης), τα κατασχεμένα πράγματα πλειστηριάζονται ενώπιον συμβολαιογράφου της περιφέρειας του συμβολαιογραφικού συλλόγου του τόπου εκτέλεσης ή, αν και αυτό δεν είναι δυνατό, του συμβολαιογραφικού συλλόγου της πρωτεύουσας του Κράτους. Ο πλειστηριασμός των κατασχεμένων διενεργείται μέσω των ηλεκτρονικών συστημάτων πλειστηριασμού από τον πιστοποιημένο, για το σκοπό αυτόν, υπάλληλο του ηλεκτρονικού πλειστηριασμού. Ο πλειστηριασμός διενεργείται ενώπιον του ίδιου συμβολαιογράφου που ορίστηκε αρχικά και στην περίπτωση πολλαπλών κατασχέσεων.
2. Η κυριότητα, διοίκηση και διαχείριση των ηλεκτρονικών συστημάτων πλειστηριασμού ανήκει στους κατά τόπον αρμοδίους συμβολαιογραφικούς συλλόγους.

2. If transporting attached things is difficult or could result in them being damaged, the court process server shall leave them at the place where attachment took place.
3. If monies or other things which can, by law, be deposited were attached, the court process server shall deposit them in accordance with the provisions of Article 965(4).
4. The sequestrator shall safekeep the attached things and shall not be empowered to use them. Where required by the nature of the attached things, the sequestrator shall also take steps to manage them, with the permission of the court of the peace of the district where the attachment took place, trying the matter under the procedure laid down in Articles 686 *et seq.* The sequestrator is obligated to render account and hand over the proceeds of management to the auctioneer.
5. Any challenge concerning the sequestration or the designation of the sequestrator, as well as any application for their replacement, shall be brought, under the procedure laid down in Articles 686 *et seq.*, before the court of the peace of the district where enforcement took place. The court may also designate the person for whose benefit enforcement is being done or the person enforcement concerns as the sequestrator.
6. If the sequestrator is deprived of or loses possession of the thing, the court of the peace of the place of enforcement, trying the matter under the procedure laid down in Articles 686 *et seq.*, shall order that the thing be returned to them.
7. If the insurance risk occurred after the attachment, the insurer shall pay the auctioneer the insurance compensation due. Any payment of compensation by the insurer to the person enforcement concerns, before being notified in writing by the person who procured attachment with regard to imposition of such attachment, shall be valid.

Article 957

1. Articles 971 *et seq.* apply where the attached things only consist of monies. This also applies if the attached things consist of foreign monies, which the auctioneer shall convert into the currency of Greece.
2. If the attachment also concerned things other than monies, the monies shall be distributed together with the auction price.

Article 958

1. Once the copy of the attachment report has been served in accordance with Article 955(1), the person enforcement concerns is prohibited from disposing of the attached thing, and any such disposal is null and void vis-à-vis the person who procured the attachment and the creditors who lodged claims.
2. Compulsory attachment of movables does not prevent them from also being attached by a different creditor. Each compulsory enforcement procedure is separate and one does not affect the other. The costs of enforcement paid in advance by a creditor whose enforcement was not completed may not be recovered.

Article 959

1. Attached things shall be auctioned electronically in the presence of a notary public within the district of the court of appeal where the attachment took place. If a notary public from the place of enforcement (attachment) cannot be appointed for any reason, the attached things shall be auctioned in the presence of a notary public from the district of the notarial association of the place of enforcement or, if this is also not possible, from the notarial association of the capital. An e-auctioneer, certified for this purpose, shall auction the attached things using e-auction systems. Even where there are multiple attachment procedures, the auction shall also be conducted in the presence of the same notary public initially appointed.
2. E-auction systems shall be owned, managed and run by the locally competent notarial associations.

3. Τα ηλεκτρονικά συστήματα πλειστηριασμού περιέχουν όλα τα πληροφοριακά στοιχεία τα οποία περιλαμβάνονται στο απόσπασμα της κατασχετήριας έκθεσης.

4. Στον ηλεκτρονικό πλειστηριασμό λαμβάνουν μέρος υποψήφιοι πλειοδότες που έχουν προηγουμένως πιστοποιηθεί στα ηλεκτρονικά συστήματα πλειστηριασμών. Πλειοδοσία περισσότερων από κοινού είναι εφικτή, μόνο εάν χορηγηθεί σε οποιονδήποτε εξ αυτών ειδικό συμβολαιογραφικό πληρεξούσιο από τους λοιπούς ενδιαφερόμενους πλειοδότες και αυτός προβεί στη σχετική δήλωση συμμετοχής και υποβολής του πληρεξουσίου, πριν τον πλειστηριασμό, σύμφωνα με την παρ. 5. Στην περίπτωση αυτή, και εφόσον κατακυρωθεί στους περισσότερους πλειοδότες το πράγμα, αυτοί ενέχονται εις ολόκληρον για την καταβολή του πλειστηριάσματος.

5. Κάθε υποψήφιος πλειοδότης δηλώνει τη συμμετοχή του σε συγκεκριμένο πλειστηριασμό, σύμφωνα με τους όρους αυτού, αφού έχει καταβάλει την εγγύηση της παραγράφου 1 του άρθρου 965 και έχει υποβάλει ηλεκτρονικά το πληρεξούσιο της παραγράφου 2 του άρθρου 1003, επί κοινής δε πλειοδοσίας το κατά την παράγραφο 4 του παρόντος πληρεξούσιο μέχρι ώρα 15:00, δύο (2) εργάσιμες ημέρες πριν την ορισθείσα ημέρα του πλειστηριασμού. Οι προσφορές, με ποινή ακυρότητας, δεν πρέπει να περιλαμβάνουν αίρεση ή όρο, και είναι ανέκκλητες. Το τέλος χρήσης των συστημάτων για τη διενέργεια του ηλεκτρονικού πλειστηριασμού καταβάλλεται από τον υπερθεματιστή. Η κατάθεση της εγγύησης, του τέλους χρήσης των ηλεκτρονικών συστημάτων πλειστηριασμών και του πλειστηριάσματος γίνεται αποκλειστικά σε ειδικό ακατάσχετο επαγγελματικό λογαριασμό που θα διατηρείται σε ελληνικό τραπεζικό ίδρυμα από τον υπάλληλο του πλειστηριασμού. Σε περίπτωση πλειοδοσίας περισσοτέρων, σύμφωνα με την παρ. 4, η κατάθεση της εγγύησης και του τέλους χρήσης μπορεί να γίνει από οποιονδήποτε πλειοδότη είτε αυτός ενεργεί ατομικά είτε ως εκπρόσωπος των λοιπών. Κάθε υποψήφιος πλειοδότης, επί κοινής δε πλειοδοσίας ο εκπρόσωπος των λοιπών, διορίζει με ηλεκτρονική δήλωση αντίκλητο που κατοικεί στην περιφέρεια του πρωτοδικείου του τόπου της εκτέλεσης μέχρι ώρα 15:00 δύο (2) εργάσιμες ημέρες πριν την ορισθείσα ημέρα του πλειστηριασμού, διαφορετικά αντίκλητος θεωρείται ο γραμματέας του πρωτοδικείου του τόπου της εκτέλεσης. Το τελευταίο εδάφιο εφαρμόζεται, ακόμη και όταν ο πλειστηριασμός διενεργείται ενώπιον συμβολαιογράφου διορισμένου στην περιφέρεια του συμβολαιογραφικού συλλόγου του τόπου εκτέλεσης ή του συμβολαιογραφικού συλλόγου της πρωτεύουσας του Κράτους.

6. Ο υπάλληλος του ηλεκτρονικού πλειστηριασμού μετά το πέρας της προθεσμίας της προηγούμενης παραγράφου ελέγχει τα υποβαλλόμενα αρχεία, διαπιστώνει με πράξη του, μέχρι ώρα 17:00 της προηγούμενης του ηλεκτρονικού πλειστηριασμού ημέρας, την τήρηση των διατυπώσεων που ορίζονται στις προηγούμενες παραγράφους και υποβάλλει στα ηλεκτρονικά συστήματα πλειστηριασμών (ΗΛ. ΣΥ.ΠΛΕΙΣ.) κατάλογο των υποψήφιων πλειοδοτών που δικαιούνται να λάβουν μέρος.

7. Αν τα κατασχεμένα πράγματα βρίσκονται στην περιφέρεια περισσότερων ειρηνοδικείων, ο πλειστηριασμός διενεργείται, κατ' επιλογήν του επισπεύδοντος, στην περιφέρεια οποιουδήποτε εκ των άνω ειρηνοδικείων. Εάν ο πλειστηριασμός μπορεί να γίνει ηλεκτρονικά σε μία μόνο από αυτές, επιλέγεται υποχρεωτικά η περιφέρεια του συγκεκριμένου ειρηνοδικείου και αν, για οποιονδήποτε λόγο, δεν μπορεί να διενεργηθεί σε καμία από αυτές, επιλέγεται η περιφέρεια του συμβολαιογραφικού συλλόγου της πρωτεύουσας του κράτους. Αρμόδιο για την επίλυση των διαφορών που αναφύονται από τη διενέργεια του πλειστηριασμού είναι το δικαστήριο του τόπου εκτέλεσης.

8. Οι ηλεκτρονικοί πλειστηριασμοί διενεργούνται μόνο εργάσιμη ημέρα Τετάρτη ή Πέμπτη ή Παρασκευή, από τις 10:00' έως τις 12:00' και από τις 14:00' έως τις 16:00'. Σε υποβολή προσφοράς κατά το τελευταίο λεπτό του ηλεκτρονικού πλειστηριασμού, ήτοι από ώρα 11:59:00 έως 11:59:59 ή από ώρα 15:59:00 έως 15:59:59 δίδεται αυτόματη παράταση πέντε (5) λεπτών. Για κάθε προσφορά που υποβάλλεται κατά το τελευταίο λεπτό της παράτασης, δίδεται νέα αυτόματη παράταση πέντε (5) λεπτών, εφόσον υποβληθεί μεγαλύτερη προσφορά. Οι παρατάσεις μπορούν να συνεχισθούν για χρονικό διάστημα όχι μεγαλύτερο της μίας (1) ώρας από την ορισθείσα ώρα λήξης του ηλεκτρονικού πλειστηριασμού, οπότε ολοκληρώνεται η διαδικασία υποβολής προσφορών. Ηλεκτρονικός πλειστηριασμός δεν μπορεί να γίνει από την 1η Αυγούστου έως την 31η Αυγούστου, καθώς και την προηγούμενη και την επομένη εβδομάδα της ημέρας των εκλογών για την ανάδειξη βουλευτών, αντιπροσώπων στο Ευρωπαϊκό Κοινοβούλιο και Οργάνων Τοπικής Αυτοδιοίκησης. Η απαγόρευση αυτή ισχύει και για τις επαναληπτικές εκλογές και μόνο για τις Περιφέρειες που διεξάγονται τέτοιες, εκτός αν πρόκειται για πλοία, αεροσκάφη και για πράγματα που μπορούν να υποστούν φθορά.

3. E-auction systems shall include all the information contained in attachment report excerpts.
4. Prospective bidders who had been previously certified via e-auction systems may participate in the e-auction. Several bidders may submit joint bids only if any such bidder is granted special notarial power of attorney by the other interested bidders and, in accordance with paragraph 5, said bidder makes the relevant participation declaration and submits the power of attorney prior to the auction. In this case, and where the thing is awarded to the several bidders, they shall be severally liable to pay the auction price.
5. All prospective bidders shall declare their participation in a specific auction in accordance with its terms, after having provided the surety referred to in Article 965(1) and electronically submitted the power of attorney referred to in Article 1003(2) and, in cases of joint bids, the power of attorney referred to in paragraph 4 of this Article, no later than 15:00 hours two working days prior to the auction date set. On penalty of nullity, bids must not contain conditions or caveats and are irrevocable. The fee for using e-auction systems shall be paid by the highest bidder. The surety, the fee for using the e-auction system and the auction price shall be exclusively deposited by the auctioneer into a special non-garnishable business account held at a Greek bank. In the case of a joint bid referred to in paragraph 4, the surety and the fee for using [the e-auction system] may be deposited by any bidder, whether acting individually or as the representative of the other bidders. Each prospective bidder and, in the case of a joint bid, the representative of the other bidders, shall, by means of an e-declaration, appoint a process agent domiciled in the district of the court of first instance of the place of enforcement no later than 15:00 hours two working days prior to the auction date set, otherwise the registrar of the court of first instance of the place of enforcement shall be deemed to be the process agent. The preceding sentence applies even when the auction is being conducted in the presence of a notary public from the district of the notarial association of the place of enforcement or from the notarial association of the capital.
6. After the deadline set in the preceding paragraph has lapsed, the e-auctioneer shall check the files submitted, issue a deed ascertaining compliance with the formalities laid down in the preceding paragraphs no later than 17:00 hours on the day prior to the e-auction, and upload a list of the eligible prospective bidders to the e-auction systems.
7. If the attached things are located in the district of several courts of the peace, the auction shall be conducted, at the choice of the expediting party, in the district of any of the aforesaid courts of the peace. If the auction can be conducted electronically in only one of these districts, the district of that specific court of the peace must be selected, and if the auction cannot be conducted in any of these districts, the district of the notarial association of the capital shall be selected. The court of the place of enforcement shall have jurisdiction to resolve disputes arising from how the auction was conducted.
8. E-auctions shall be conducted only on Wednesdays, Thursdays or Fridays that are working days, from 10:00 to 12:00 hours and from 14:00 to 16:00 hours. Where a bid is submitted during the last minute of the e-auction, i.e. from 11:59:00 until 11:59:59 or from 15:59:00 until 15:59:59, an automatic five-minute extension shall be granted. For each bid submitted during the last minute of the extension, a new automatic five-minute extension shall be granted, provided a higher bid was submitted. The extensions may continue for a period no longer than one hour from the time set for the e-auction to end, at which time the bidding process shall end. E-auctions may not be held from 1 August to 31 August and during the week prior to and the week subsequent to elections for members of parliament, members of the European Parliament and local government authorities. This prohibition also applies to run-off elections and only in the districts where such elections are being held, except in cases of ships, aircraft and things that can become spoiled.

9. Ο ηλεκτρονικός πλειστηριασμός είναι ανοικτού πλειοδοτικού τύπου κατά τον οποίο υποβάλλονται διαδοχικές προσφορές. Οι συμμετέχοντες υποβάλλουν συνεχώς προσφορά μεγαλύτερη από την εκάστοτε μέγιστη έως το χρόνο λήξης της υποβολής προσφορών. Στα ηλεκτρονικά συστήματα καταγράφονται όλες οι υποβληθείσες κατά τα ανωτέρω προσφορές.
10. Με την υποβολή της προσφοράς, οι υποψήφιοι πλειοδότες ενημερώνονται αμέσως από τα συστήματα για το ποσό της προσφοράς τους, τον ακριβή χρόνο υποβολής της, καθώς και ότι αυτή έχει καταγραφεί. Ο υποψήφιος πλειοδότης ενημερώνεται για την εκάστοτε μέγιστη υποβληθείσα προσφορά.
11. Όλοι οι υποψήφιοι πλειοδότες που λαμβάνουν μέρος στον ηλεκτρονικό πλειστηριασμό ενημερώνονται αμέσως από τα συστήματα για τυχόν αναστολή, ματαίωση ή διακοπή του πλειστηριασμού, καθώς και για τον λόγο αυτής.
12. Μετά τη λήξη της διαδικασίας υποβολής των πλειοδοτικών προσφορών, ανακοινώνεται το αποτέλεσμα του πλειστηριασμού μέσω των ηλεκτρονικών συστημάτων. Όσοι έχουν λάβει μέρος στον ηλεκτρονικό πλειστηριασμό ενημερώνονται αμελλητί για το αποτέλεσμά του. Ο υπάλληλος του ηλεκτρονικού πλειστηριασμού συντάσσει την έκθεση της παρ. 2 του άρθρου 965, κατακυρώνοντας τα πράγματα στον πλειοδότη.
13. Στον ηλεκτρονικό πλειστηριασμό κινητών, ο υπερθεματιστής έχει υποχρέωση να καταβάλει στον ειδικό τραπεζικό επαγγελματικό λογαριασμό του υπαλλήλου του πλειστηριασμού το πλειστηρίασμα και το τέλος χρήσης το αργότερο την τρίτη εργάσιμη ημέρα από τον πλειστηριασμό. Με την καταβολή του πλειστηριάσματος και του τέλους χρήσης, το κατακυρωμένο πράγμα παραδίδεται στον υπερθεματιστή. Η παράδοση του πράγματος στον υπερθεματιστή δεν μπορεί να γίνει πριν την καταβολή του πλειστηριάσματος και του τέλους χρήσης. Ο υπάλληλος του ηλεκτρονικού πλειστηριασμού οφείλει, το αργότερο την πέμπτη εργάσιμη ημέρα από τον πλειστηριασμό, να καταθέσει το πλειστηρίασμα στο Ταμείο Παρακαταθηκών και Δανείων. Η κατάθεση του πλειστηριάσματος είναι ακατάσχετη, δεν εμπίπτει στην πτωχευτική περιουσία και δεν υπόκειται στις δεσμεύσεις που επιβάλλει το Δημόσιο για τη διασφάλιση των συμφερόντων του. Εντός της επόμενης εργάσιμης ημέρας από την παρέλευση της ανωτέρω προθεσμίας, ο υπάλληλος του πλειστηριασμού αποδίδει το τέλος χρήσης στον οικείο συμβολαιογραφικό σύλλογο του οποίου αυτός είναι μέλος. Εντός τριών (3) εργασίμων ημερών, μέρος του ανωτέρω ποσού, το οποίο καθορίζεται με την απόφαση της παραγράφου 14 του παρόντος, αποδίδεται από τον οικείο συμβολαιογραφικό σύλλογο στο ΤΑ.Χ.ΔΙ.Κ. Οι ειδικότεροι όροι της τήρησης των επαγγελματικών τραπεζικών λογαριασμών των υπαλλήλων των πλειστηριασμών ορίζονται με κοινή απόφαση των Υπουργών Οικονομικών και Δικαιοσύνης.
14. Με αποφάσεις του Υπουργού Δικαιοσύνης, καθορίζονται οι ειδικότεροι όροι λειτουργίας των ηλεκτρονικών συστημάτων πλειστηριασμού, οι λεπτομέρειες υποβολής των πλειοδοτικών προσφορών, η διαδικασία πιστοποίησης και εγγραφής χρηστών στα συστήματα, το ύψος και ο τρόπος καθορισμού, επιμερισμού, είσπραξης και απόδοσης του τέλους χρήσης των συστημάτων, αναπροσαρμογής του τέλους χρήσης και του μέρους αυτού που αποδίδεται στο ΤΑ.Χ.ΔΙΚ., καθώς και κάθε σχετική λεπτομέρεια.

Άρθρα 959Α-961

[Καταργούνται]

Άρθρο 962

1. Αν τα κατασχεμένα πράγματα μπορεί, κατά την κρίση του υπαλλήλου του πλειστηριασμού, να υποστούν φθορά, πλειστηριάζονται αμέσως. Ο υπάλληλος του πλειστηριασμού μπορεί να προβεί σε κάθε κατάλληλη ενέργεια για την εξασφάλιση δημοσιότητας. Αν διαφωνήσει εκείνος υπέρ του οποίου γίνεται ή εκείνος κατά του οποίου στρέφεται η εκτέλεση, αποφασίζει το ειρηνοδικείο του τόπου της εκτέλεσης, που δικάζει κατά τη διαδικασία των άρθρων 686 επ.
2. Τα υποκείμενα σε φθορά ευπαθή προϊόντα, πλειστηριάζονται οποιαδήποτε μέρα, και η κατά την παρ. 6 του άρθρου 959 ανάρτηση στα ηλεκτρονικά συστήματα μπορεί να διενεργείται και αυθημερόν, πριν την έναρξη του πλειστηριασμού, η δε κατά την παρ. 1 του άρθρου 965 εγγυοδοσία δύναται να κατατεθεί και σε μετρητά.

9. E-auctions shall be open competitive procedures during which successive bids are submitted. Participants shall continuously submit bids higher than the highest bid at any given time until the bidding period has ended. All the bids submitted in accordance with the foregoing shall be recorded by the [e-auction] systems.
10. Upon submitting their bids, bidders are immediately notified by the systems with regard to the amount of their bid, the precise time of its submission and the fact that it has been recorded. Bidders are notified of the highest bid at any given time.
11. All bidders participating in the e-auction are immediately notified by the systems if the auction is suspended, cancelled or ends and the reason for this.
12. After the bidding process has ended, the auction result is announced by the [e-auction] systems. Participants in the e-auction are promptly notified of the result. The e-auctioneer shall prepare the report referred to in Article 965(2) and award the things to the highest bidder.
13. In cases of e-auctions of movables, the highest bidder is obligated to pay the auction price and the fee for using [the e-auction systems] into the special business account held by the e-auctioneer no later than the third working day after the auction. Upon payment of the auction price and the fee for using [the e-auction systems], the thing awarded shall be handed over to the highest bidder. The thing may not be handed over to the highest bidder before the auction price and the fee for using [the e-auction systems] have been paid. The e-auctioneer is obligated to deposit the auction price with the Consignment Deposits and Loans Fund no later than the fifth working day after the auction. The auction price which has been deposited is non-garnishable, does not constitute part of the bankruptcy estate and is not subject to freezing orders imposed by the Greek State to safeguard its interests. During the working day after the date on which the aforesaid deadline lapses, the auctioneer shall remit the fee for using [the e-auction systems] to the relevant notarial association to which they belong. Within three working days, part of the above amount, to be specified in the decision referred to in paragraph 14 of this Article, shall be remitted by the relevant notarial association to the Court Buildings Financing Fund. The specific terms on professional bank accounts held by auctioneers shall be laid down in a joint decision issued by the Minister of Finance and the Minister of Justice.
14. The specific terms on the operation of e-auction systems, the details concerning submission of bids, the process for certification and registration of users with such systems, the amount and manner of determination, allocation, collection and remittal of the fee for using such systems, adjustment of the fee for using such systems and the part of that amount to be remitted to the Court Buildings Financing Fund, as well as all relevant details, shall be laid down in decisions issued by the Minister of Justice.

Articles 959A-961

[Repealed]

Article 962

1. If, in the view of the auctioneer, the attached things could become spoiled, they shall be auctioned immediately. The auctioneer may take any appropriate steps to ensure publicity. If the person for whose benefit enforcement is being done or the person enforcement concerns disagrees, the court of the peace of the place of enforcement shall decide, trying the matter under the procedure laid down in Articles 686 *et seq.*
2. Perishable goods which could become spoiled shall be auctioned on any day, and the upload to the [e-auction systems] in accordance with Article 959(6) may also be done on the same day, prior to the commencement of the auction, while the surety referred to in Article 965(1) may also be deposited in cash.

Άρθρο 963

[Καταργείται]

Άρθρο 964

Εκείνος κατά του οποίου στρέφεται η εκτέλεση, ορίζει εγγράφως, εφόσον το επιθυμεί, προς τον υπάλληλο του πλειστηριασμού, τη σειρά με την οποία θα κατακυρώνονται τα κατασχεμένα πράγματα, το αργότερο δύο (2) ημέρες πριν τη διενέργεια του ηλεκτρονικού πλειστηριασμού. Ο υπάλληλος του πλειστηριασμού δύναται να ορίσει ο ίδιος σε περίπτωση μη έγγραφης ειδοποιήσεως του καθ' ου η εκτέλεση την σειρά κατακύρωσης. Ο υπάλληλος του πλειστηριασμού ενημερώνει τα ηλεκτρονικά συστήματα για τη σειρά κατακύρωσης των κατασχεμένων πραγμάτων. Από τη στιγμή που το πλειστηρίασμα καλύψει το ποσό της απαίτησης εκείνου υπέρ του οποίου έγινε η εκτέλεση και των δανειστών που αναγγέλθηκαν, καθώς και τα έξοδα της εκτέλεσης, δεν γίνεται κατακύρωση για τα λοιπά κατασχεθέντα και δεν συντάσσεται ως προς αυτά έκθεση πλειστηριασμού και κατακύρωσης.

Άρθρο 965

1. Η πλειοδοσία αρχίζει με βάση την τιμή πρώτης προσφοράς. Δεν μπορούν να πλειοδοτήσουν ο οφειλέτης, ο υπάλληλος του πλειστηριασμού και οι υπάλληλοί του. Για την από κοινού πλειοδοσία περισσότερων εφαρμόζονται οι παρ. 4 και 5 του άρθρου 959. Ο υπάλληλος του πλειστηριασμού οφείλει, αν προβληθεί εγγράφως πριν την έναρξη της διαδικασίας αντίρρηση από τον επισπεύδοντα ή τον καθ' ού η εκτέλεση ή από οποιονδήποτε πλειοδότη να αποκλείσει από την πλειοδοσία κάθε πρόσωπο εις βάρος του οποίου επισπεύδεται αναπλειστηριασμός, εφόσον το γεγονός αυτό προκύπτει από δημόσιο έγγραφο ή ομολογείται. Κάθε πλειοδότης οφείλει να καταθέτει με μεταφορά πίστωσης στον ειδικό τραπεζικό επαγγελματικό λογαριασμό του υπαλλήλου του πλειστηριασμού ή με εγγυητική επιστολή τράπεζας, διάρκειας τουλάχιστον ενός (1) μήνα, ή με επιταγή που έχει εκδοθεί από τράπεζα ή άλλο πιστωτικό ίδρυμα, εγγυοδοσία ίση προς το τριάντα τοις εκατό (30%) της τιμής της πρώτης προσφοράς. Επί περισσότερων υποψήφιων πλειοδοτών κατά την παρ. 4 του άρθρου 959, η κατάθεση ή η έκδοση της επιταγής μπορεί να γίνει από οποιονδήποτε πλειοδότη είτε αυτός ενεργεί ατομικά είτε ως εκπρόσωπος των λοιπών. Αν υπερθεματιστής αναδείχθηκε άλλος, ή αν η κατακύρωση ματαιώθηκε από οποιονδήποτε λόγο, η εγγυοδοσία επιστρέφεται σε εκείνον που την είχε καταθέσει αμέσως μετά το πέρας του πλειστηριασμού.

2. Τα πράγματα που πλειστηριάζονται κατακυρώνονται στον πλειοδότη που προσφέρει τη μεγαλύτερη τιμή. Ο υπάλληλος του πλειστηριασμού πρέπει να καταχωρίζει στην έκθεσή του όλες τις προσφορές που έγιναν.

3. Ο υπερθεματιστής έχει υποχρέωση να καταβάλει στον υπάλληλο του πλειστηριασμού το πλειστηρίασμα σε μετρητά ή με μεταφορά πίστωσης στον ειδικό τραπεζικό επαγγελματικό λογαριασμό του υπαλλήλου του πλειστηριασμού ή με επιταγή έκδοσης τράπεζας που λειτουργεί νόμιμα στην Ελλάδα, την τρίτη εργάσιμη μέρα από τον πλειστηριασμό και αμέσως μετά του παραδίδεται το κατακυρωμένο πράγμα. Η παράδοση του πράγματος στον υπερθεματιστή δεν μπορεί να γίνει πριν αυτός καταβάλει το πλειστηρίασμα και το τέλος χρήσης.

4. Ο υπάλληλος του πλειστηριασμού οφείλει, το αργότερο τη δέκατη εργάσιμη ημέρα από τον πλειστηριασμό, να καταθέσει εντόκως το πλειστηρίασμα στο Ταμείο Παρακαταθηκών και Δανείων. Οι αναλογούντες επί του πλειστηριάσματος τόκοι υπολογίζονται από το Ταμείο Παρακαταθηκών και Δανείων και αποδίδονται από κοινού με το πλειστηρίασμα με εντολή του επί του πλειστηριασμού υπαλλήλου, σύμφωνα με την κείμενη νομοθεσία. Με απόφαση του Διοικητικού Συμβουλίου του Ταμείου Παρακαταθηκών και Δανείων που δημοσιεύεται στην Εφημερίδα της Κυβερνήσεως, καθορίζονται οι όροι και η διαδικασία και οι αναγκαίες λεπτομέρειες που αφορούν στην απόδοση του πλειστηριάσματος στους δικαιούχους, καθώς και άλλο σχετικό ζήτημα. Η κατάθεση είναι ακατάσχετη, δεν εμπίπτει στην πτωχευτική περιουσία και δεν υπόκειται στις δεσμεύσεις που επιβάλλει το Δημόσιο για τη διασφάλιση των συμφερόντων του.

Article 963

[Repealed]

Article 964

No later than two days prior to the e-auction, the person enforcement concerns shall, if they so wish, specify in writing to the auctioneer the order in which the attached things will be auctioned [and awarded]. If the person enforcement concerns fails to provide notification in writing, the auctioneer may themselves specify the order in which things will be auctioned [and awarded]. The auctioneer shall update the electronic systems regarding the order in which the attached things are to be auctioned [and awarded]. Once the auction price covers the amount of the claim of the person for whose benefit enforcement is being done and of the creditors who lodged claims, as well as the enforcement costs, the remaining attached things shall not be auctioned [and awarded], and no auction and award report shall be prepared concerning those things.

Article 965

1. Bidding shall commence using the starting price. The debtor, the auctioneer and the auctioneer's employees may not submit bids. Article 959(4) and (5) apply to joint bids. If the person procuring enforcement or the person enforcement concerns or any bidder files an objection in writing prior to commencement of the process, the auctioneer is obligated to exclude any person against whom a repeat auction is sought from the bidding, where this fact arises from a public document or is admitted. All bidders are obligated to provide surety equal to 30% of the starting price by transferring that amount into the special business account held by the auctioneer or by providing a bank-issued letter of guarantee with a duration of at least one month or by providing a cheque issued by a bank or other credit institution. In the case of a joint bid referred to in Article 959(4), the cheque may be deposited or issued by any bidder, whether acting individually or as the representative of the other bidders. If a different person was declared to be the highest bidder or the award was cancelled on any grounds, the surety shall be returned to the person who deposited it immediately after the auction has ended.
2. The things being auctioned shall be awarded to the bidder who offers the highest price. The auctioneer must record all bids submitted in their report.
3. The highest bidder is obligated to pay the auction price to the auctioneer in cash or by transferring that amount into the special business account held by the auctioneer or by providing a letter of guarantee issued by a bank lawfully operating in Greece [by] the third working day after the auction, and the awarded thing shall then be immediately handed over to the highest bidder. The thing may not be handed over to the highest bidder before they have paid the auction price and the fee for using [the e-auction systems].
4. The auctioneer is obligated to deposit the auction price, with interest, with the Consignment Deposits and Loans Fund no later than the tenth working day after the auction. The relevant interest on the auction price shall be computed by the Consignment Deposits and Loans Fund and remitted together with the auction price, on instructions of the auctioneer, in accordance with the legislation in force. The terms, procedure and necessary details concerning remittal of the auction price to the entitled persons and other relevant issues shall be laid down in a decision issued by the Board of Directors of the Consignment Deposits and Loans Fund and published in the Government Gazette. The deposited amount is non-garnishable, does not constitute part of the bankruptcy estate and is not be subject to freezing orders imposed by the Greek State to safeguard its interests.

5. Αν ο υπερθεματιστής δεν καταβάλει εμπροθέσμως το πλειστηρίασμα και το τέλος χρήσης, ο υπάλληλος του πλειστηριασμού οφείλει μέσα στις επόμενες δύο (2) εργάσιμες ημέρες να τον οχλήσει με εξώδικη πρόσκληση που επιδίδεται με δικαστικό επιμελητή. Αν ο υπερθεματιστής δεν καταβάλει το πλειστηρίασμα μέσα στις επόμενες από την όχληση πέντε (5) εργάσιμες ημέρες, η κατακύρωση σε αυτόν ανατρέπεται, η εγγυοδοσία που έχει καταθέσει καταπίπτει, καλούνται δε οι επόμενοι πλειοδότες, η προσφορά των οποίων, αθροιζομένη με το ποσό της εγγυοδοσίας που κατέπεσε, είναι ίση με το πλειστηρίασμα, να καταβάλουν σε τακτή ημέρα που ορίζεται στην πρόσκληση το ποσό που είχαν προσφέρει. Η πρόσκληση επιδίδεται με δικαστικό επιμελητή, επί δε κοινής πλειοδοσίας επιδίδεται στον εκπρόσωπο αυτών. Αν εμφανισθούν περισσότεροι ενδιαφερόμενοι συντάσσεται σχετική έκθεση από τον συμβολαιογράφο και η κατακύρωση γίνεται σε εκείνον που είχε προσφέρει κατά τον πλειστηριασμό το μεγαλύτερο ποσόν. Το πλειστηρίασμα συνίσταται στο άθροισμα του ποσού που καταβλήθηκε και της εγγυοδοσίας του αρχικού υπερθεματιστή που κατέπεσε. Αν, κατά την ελεύθερη κρίση του υπαλλήλου του πλειστηριασμού, η κατά τα προηγούμενα εδάφια πρόσκληση των επόμενων πλειοδοτών είναι αδύνατη ή ιδιαίτερα δυσχερής για λόγους που εκτίθενται σε σχετική έκθεση, καθώς και σε κάθε περίπτωση που η διαδικασία αυτή δεν τελεσφόρησε, γίνεται αναπλειστηριασμός κατά τις διατάξεις των επόμενων εδαφίων. Η επίσπευση του αναπλειστηριασμού γίνεται είτε με επιμέλεια του υπαλλήλου του πλειστηριασμού είτε από τον υπέρ ου ή από τον καθ' ου η εκτέλεση ή από κάθε δανειστή που έχει αναγγελθεί με τίτλο εκτελεστό. Ο αναπλειστηριασμός επισπεύδεται με πράξη του υπαλλήλου του πλειστηριασμού ή με δήλωση προς τον υπάλληλο του πλειστηριασμού του υπέρ ου ή του καθ' ου ή του δανειστή, για την οποία συντάσσεται πράξη. Περίληψη της πράξης, η οποία περιέχει και όσα πρέπει να περιλαμβάνονται στο απόσπασμα της κατασχετήριας έκθεσης, δημοσιεύεται με επιμέλεια του υπαλλήλου του πλειστηριασμού στην Ιστοσελίδα Δημοσιεύσεων Πλειστηριασμών του Δελτίου Δικαστικών Δημοσιεύσεων του Ηλεκτρονικού Εθνικού Φορέα Κοινωνικής Ασφάλισης (e-ΕΦΚΑ). Η διάταξη του άρθρου 959 της παρ. 8 εφαρμόζεται αναλόγως και η σχετική προθεσμία υπολογίζεται αφότου συνταχθεί η πράξη. Ο αρχικός υπερθεματιστής, που δεν κατέβαλε το πλειστηρίασμα, δεν μπορεί να πλειοδοτήσει, δικαιούται όμως, έως ότου αρχίσει η πλειοδοσία, να καταβάλει το οφειλόμενο πλειστηρίασμα, με τον τόκο υπερημερίας, καθώς και τα έξοδα του αναπλειστηριασμού και να ζητήσει να του κατακυρωθεί το πράγμα.

6. Αν κατά τον αναπλειστηριασμό δεν επιτευχθεί το ίδιο πλειστηρίασμα, ο πρώτος υπερθεματιστής, που δεν κατέβαλε, ευθύνεται για τη διαφορά εντόκως, με το επιτόκιο υπερημερίας. Η εγγυοδοσία που είχε καταθέσει, με τους τυχόν τόκους της, καταλογίζεται στη διαφορά για την οποία ευθύνεται. Αν απομένει επιπλέον διαφορά, η έκθεση του αναπλειστηριασμού αποτελεί εναντίον του τίτλο εκτελεστό για τη συμπλήρωση. Αν έγιναν περισσότεροι αναπλειστηριασμοί, όλοι οι προηγούμενοι διαδοχικοί υπερθεματιστές, που δεν κατέβαλαν, εξακολουθούν να ευθύνονται εις ολόκληρον για την τυχόν διαφορά μεταξύ του αρχικού πλειστηριάσματος και του πλειστηριάσματος που τελικά επιτεύχθηκε και καταβλήθηκε, χωρίς όμως η ευθύνη του καθενός να υπερβαίνει το ποσόν της διαφοράς από τη δική του οφειλή. Οι εγγυοδοσίες που είχαν κατατεθεί από τους προηγούμενους διαδοχικούς υπερθεματιστές δεν επιστρέφονται έως ότου καταβληθεί το πλειστηρίασμα από τον τελικό υπερθεματιστή, προκειμένου να γίνει ο ως άνω καταλογισμός στην τυχόν διαφορά. Ο υπερθεματιστής που δεν κατέβαλε δεν δικαιούται, αν κατά τον αναπλειστηριασμό επιτεύχθηκε μεγαλύτερο πλειστηρίασμα, να απαιτήσει το επιπλέον.

7. Ο υπάλληλος του πλειστηριασμού μπορεί, αν κρίνει ότι υπάρχει ανάγκη, να ζητεί κατά τη διεξαγωγή του πλειστηριασμού την επιβαλλόμενη από τις περιστάσεις συνδρομή και προστασία αστυνομικού οργάνου, στο οποίο παρέχει τις αναγκαίες οδηγίες και υποβάλλει αιτήματα για την τήρηση της τάξης και την αποκατάσταση της ομαλής διενέργειας και συνέχισης του πλειστηριασμού.

5. If the highest bidder fails to pay the auction price and the fee for using [the e-auction systems], the auctioneer is obligated to place them on notice within the next two working days by means of extra-judicial invitation served by court process server. If the highest bidder fails to pay the auction price within five working days of being placed on notice, the award shall be reversed, the surety deposited shall be forfeited, and an invitation shall be extended to the next highest bidders — whose bid, together with the forfeited amount of surety, must be equal to the auction price — to pay the amount they had offered on a due date specified in the invitation. The invitation shall be served [on them] by court process server and, in cases of joint bids, on the representative of the joint bidders. If several interested parties appear, the notary public shall prepare a relevant report and the things shall be awarded to the person who had offered the highest amount during the auction. The auction price consists of the sum of the amount paid and the forfeited surety paid by the initial highest bidder. If, at the unfettered discretion of the auctioneer, it was impossible or particularly difficult to extend an invitation to the next highest bidders under the preceding sentences for reasons to be set out in a relevant report, and in all cases where this procedure was unsuccessful, a repeat auction shall take place under the provisions set forth in the following sentences. The repeat auction shall be expedited either by the auctioneer or by the person for whose benefit or against whom enforcement was done or any creditor who lodged a claim and holds an enforceable title. The repeat auction shall be expedited by means of an act issued by the auctioneer or a statement made by the person for whose benefit or against whom enforcement was done or the creditor to the auctioneer, who shall prepare a [relevant report]. A summary of the [report], which must contain all the information included in the excerpt of the attachment report, shall be published by the auctioneer on the auctions announcement website of the Court Announcements Bulletin of the e-National Social Security Fund. The provisions of Article 959(8) apply *mutatis mutandis* and the relevant deadline shall be calculated after the [report] has been prepared. The initial highest bidder who failed to pay the auction price may not submit bids, but is entitled, before bidding commences, to pay the auction price due, plus default interest, as well as the repeat auction costs, and request that the thing be awarded to them.

6. If the same auction price is not achieved during the repeat auction, the initial highest bidder who failed to pay is liable for the difference, with interest at the default interest rate. The surety the initial highest bidder had deposited, plus any interest, shall be taken into account when calculating the difference for which they are liable. If an additional difference remains, the repeat auction report shall constitute an enforceable title against the initial highest bidder to pay the supplementary amount. If several repeat auctions took place, all previous successive highest bidders who failed to pay shall remain severally liable for any difference between the initial auction price and the auction price ultimately achieved and paid, but without the liability of each highest bidder exceeding the amount of difference from their own debt. Surety provided by the previous successive highest bidders shall not be reimbursed until the final highest bidder has paid the auction price, so that any difference, as referred to above, can be calculated. If a higher auction price was achieved during the repeat auction, the highest bidder who had failed to pay is not entitled to claim the excess amount.

7. Where deemed necessary and as required under the circumstances, the auctioneer may request assistance and protection from a police officer while conducting the auction, and shall issue the necessary instructions and make requests for order to be kept and for the auction to be conducted and continue in a problem-free manner.

Άρθρο 966

1. Αν δεν παρουσιαστούν πλειοδότες ή δεν υποβληθούν προσφορές, το πράγμα που πλειστηριάζεται κατακυρώνεται στην τιμή της πρώτης προσφοράς σε εκείνον υπέρ του οποίου έγινε η εκτέλεση, αν το ζητήσει. Ο επισπεύδων δανειστής υποβάλλει ηλεκτρονικά σχετική αίτηση, αφού παρέλθει η προθεσμία της παρ. 6 του άρθρου 959 και πριν από την έναρξη του πλειστηριασμού, στον υπάλληλο του πλειστηριασμού, ο οποίος στη συνέχεια την αναρτά στα ηλεκτρονικά συστήματα πλειστηριασμών.
2. Αν δεν υποβληθεί η αίτηση της παρ. 1, ο πλειστηριασμός επαναλαμβάνεται με την ίδια τιμή πρώτης προσφοράς και σε ημερομηνία που ορίζεται από τον υπάλληλο του πλειστηριασμού, μέσα σε σαράντα (40) ημέρες, αναρτωμένης της σχετικής δημοσιεύσεως στις αντίστοιχες ιστοσελίδες δημοσιεύσεως πλειστηριασμών του Δελτίου Δικαστικών Δημοσιεύσεων του Ηλεκτρονικού Εθνικού Φορέα Κοινωνικής Ασφάλισης (e-ΕΦΚΑ) και ΗΛ.ΣΥ.ΠΛΕΙΣ (e-auction).
2Α. Αν και ο πλειστηριασμός της παρ. 2 αποβεί άγονος, διεξάγεται νέος με τιμή πρώτης προσφοράς ίση προς το ογδόντα τοις εκατό (80%) της αρχικώς ορισθείσας τιμής και σε ημερομηνία που ορίζεται από τον υπάλληλο του πλειστηριασμού, μέσα σε τριάντα (30) ημέρες, αναρτωμένης της σχετικής δημοσιεύσεως στις αντίστοιχες ιστοσελίδες δημοσιεύσεως πλειστηριασμών του Δελτίου Δικαστικών Δημοσιεύσεων του Ηλεκτρονικού Εθνικού Φορέα Κοινωνικής Ασφάλισης (e-ΕΦΚΑ) και ΗΛ.ΣΥ.ΠΛΕΙΣ (e-auction).
2Β. Σε περίπτωση που και ο πλειστηριασμός της παρ. 2Α αποβεί άγονος, ο υπάλληλος του πλειστηριασμού τον επαναλαμβάνει μέσα σε τριάντα (30) ημέρες, με τιμή πρώτης προσφοράς ίση προς το εξήντα πέντε τοις εκατό (65%) της αρχικώς ορισθείσας, με ανάρτηση στις αντίστοιχες ιστοσελίδες δημοσιεύσεως πλειστηριασμών του Δελτίου Δικαστικών Δημοσιεύσεων του Ηλεκτρονικού Εθνικού Φορέα Κοινωνικής Ασφάλισης (e- ΕΦΚΑ) και ΗΛ.ΣΥ.ΠΛΕΙΣ (e-auction).
3. Αν και ο νέος πλειστηριασμός έμεινε χωρίς αποτέλεσμα, το αρμόδιο δικαστήριο του άρθρου 933, που δικάζει κατά τη διαδικασία των άρθρων 686 επ., ύστερα από αίτηση οποιουδήποτε έχει έννομο συμφέρον μπορεί να άρει την κατάσχεση ή να διατάξει να γίνει αργότερα νέος πλειστηριασμός με την ίδια κατά την παρ. 2Β τιμή ή και κατώτερη τιμή πρώτης προσφοράς.
4. Αν καταστεί ανέφικτη ή διακοπεί η διενέργεια του πλειστηριασμού, για λόγους τεχνικής αδυναμίας λειτουργίας των ηλεκτρονικών συστημάτων διενέργειας αυτού, η διαδικασία θεωρείται ότι παραμένει σε εκκρεμότητα και συνεχίζεται με εντολή του επισπεύδοντος, κατόπιν ανάρτησης αναγγελίας από τον υπάλληλο του πλειστηριασμού στο ηλεκτρονικό σύστημα δέκα (10) εργάσιμες ημέρες πριν την ημερομηνία συνέχισης. Τυχόν προσφορές πλειοδοτών που είχαν υποβληθεί πριν τη διακοπή της διαδικασίας παραμένουν ισχυρές.

Άρθρο 967

1. Αν τα κατασχεμένα πράγματα είναι από εκείνα που αναγράφονται στο δελτίο του χρηματιστηρίου αξιών, ο υπάλληλος του πλειστηριασμού τα εκποιεί στο χρηματιστήριο.
2. Αν τα πράγματα που πλειστηριάζονται είναι νομίσματα ή άλλα αντικείμενα από χρυσό ή άργυρο, δεν μπορούν να κατακυρωθούν σε τιμή μικρότερη από την αγοραία τιμή του νομίσματος, του χρυσού ή του αργύρου. Στην περίπτωση που αυτό δεν κατορθώθηκε, ο υπάλληλος του πλειστηριασμού τα πωλεί ελεύθερα στην παραπάνω τιμή τους.

Άρθρο 968

Ο πλειστηριασμός των καρπών μπορεί να γίνει είτε μετά είτε πριν από τον αποχωρισμό τους. Ο υπάλληλος του πλειστηριασμού μπορεί να διατάξει να γίνει η συγκομιδή των καρπών πριν από τον πλειστηριασμό.

Άρθρο 969

1. Ο πλειστηριασμός ολοκληρώνεται με την κατακύρωση. Όποιος υπερθεματίζει δεσμεύεται ώσπου να γίνει καλύτερη προσφορά ή ώσπου να ματαιωθεί η κατακύρωση.
2. Έως την κατακύρωση εκείνος κατά του οποίου στρέφεται η εκτέλεση έχει δικαίωμα να εξοφλήσει τα έξοδα και τις απαιτήσεις εκείνου που την επισπεύδει και των άλλων δανειστών που έχουν τίτλο εκτελεστό και αναγγέλθηκαν, καθώς και το τέλος χρήσης του ηλεκτρονικού συστήματος πλειστηριασμού και να αναλάβει τα πράγματα που πλειστηριάζονται. Εκείνος κατά του οποίου έγινε η εκτέλεση έχει δικαίωμα να ενεχυριάζει τα πράγματα που πλειστηριάζονται για να βρει τα μέσα να εξοφλήσει την απαίτηση και να πληρώσει τα έξοδα.
3. Ο υπάλληλος του πλειστηριασμού είναι υποχρεωμένος να τον ενεργήσει, εκτός αν συμφωνούν στην ματαίωσή του ο επισπεύδων την εκτέλεση και όλοι οι αναγγελμένοι δανειστές που έχουν καταθέσει εκτελεστό τίτλο.

Article 966

1. If bidders do not appear or bids are not submitted, the thing being auctioned shall be awarded at the starting price to the person for whose benefit enforcement is being done, if so requested by the latter. The expediting creditor shall submit a relevant application electronically, after the deadline set in Article 959(6) has lapsed and before the auction commences, to the auctioneer, who shall then upload it to the e-auction systems.
2. If the application referred to in paragraph 1 is not submitted, the auction shall be repeated with the same starting price on a date set by the auctioneer within 40 days and with the relevant publication uploaded to the corresponding auctions announcement website of the Court Announcements Bulletin of the e-National Social Security Fund and e-auction system websites.
2A. If the auction referred to in paragraph 2 also proves unsuccessful, a new auction shall be held with a starting price equal to 80% of the initial starting price on a date set by the auctioneer within 30 days and with the relevant publication uploaded to the corresponding auctions announcement website of the Court Announcements Bulletin of the e-National Social Security Fund and e-auction system websites.
2B. If the auction referred to in paragraph 2A also proves unsuccessful, the auctioneer shall repeat the auction within 30 days with a starting price equal to 65% of the initial starting price and with the relevant upload to the corresponding auctions announcement website of the Court Announcements Bulletin of the e-National Social Security Fund and e-auction system websites.
3. If the new auction also proves unsuccessful, the court with jurisdiction under Article 933, trying the matter under the procedure laid down in Articles 686 *et seq.*, following an application filed by any person with a legitimate interest, may reverse the attachment or order that a new auction be held on a subsequent date with the same [starting] price referred to in paragraph 2B or even a lower starting price.
4. If it is not possible to hold the auction or it is interrupted due to technical grounds relating to the e-auction systems, the process shall be paused and shall resume on instructions from the expediting party, after the auctioneer uploads a notice to the e-auction system 10 working days before the date of resumption. Any bids submitted before the process was interrupted shall remain valid.

Article 967

1. If the attached things are among those listed in the stock exchange bulletin, the auctioneer shall sell the things on the stock exchange.
2. If the things being auctioned are foreign currency or gold or silver items, they may not be auctioned at a price lower than the market price of such foreign currency or gold or silver. If this is not achieved, the auctioneer shall freely sell such items at their aforesaid price.

Article 968

Fruit may be auctioned either before or after it has been picked. The auctioneer may order that the fruit be picked prior to the auction.

Article 969

1. The auction is completed upon award [of the things]. The highest bidder shall remain bound [by their bid] until a higher bid is submitted or the award is cancelled.
2. Up to the time the things are awarded, the person enforcement concerns has the right to pay the costs and claims of the person procuring enforcement and other creditors who lodged claims and who hold an enforceable title, as well as the fee for using the e-auction system in full, and take back the things being auctioned. The person enforcement concerns has the right to pledge the articles being auctioned in order to secure the funds necessary to pay the claim in full and pay the costs.
3. The auctioneer is obligated to hold the auction, unless the person procuring enforcement and all creditors who lodged claims and who have deposited an enforceable title agree to cancel it.

Άρθρο 970

Όταν το πράγμα κατακυρώνεται σε εκείνον υπέρ του οποίου έγινε η εκτέλεση, αυτός πληρώνει στον υπάλληλο του πλειστηριασμού το υπόλοιπο του πλειστηριάσματος που μένει, αφού αφαιρεθεί η απαίτησή του και τα έξοδα της εκτέλεσης, εφόσον δεν αναγγέλθηκαν άλλοι δανειστές. Η πληρωμή πρέπει να γίνει μέσα στην επόμενη ημέρα από τη λήξη της προθεσμίας για αναγγελία, και το πράγμα που πλειστηριάστηκε δεν παραδίδεται πριν περάσει αυτή η προθεσμία. Αν αναγγελθούν άλλοι δανειστές οφείλει να πληρώσει ολόκληρο το πλειστηρίασμα.

Άρθρο 971

1. Αν το πλειστηρίασμα αρκεί για να ικανοποιηθούν εκείνος υπέρ του οποίου έγινε η εκτέλεση και οι δανειστές που αναγγέλθηκαν, ο υπάλληλος του πλειστηριασμού, αφού αφαιρέσει τα έξοδα της εκτέλεσης, τους ικανοποιεί την εικοστή ημέρα μετά τον πλειστηριασμό, ή και νωρίτερα, αν συμφωνήσει εκείνος κατά του οποίου έχει στραφεί η εκτέλεση.

2. Εκείνος κατά του οποίου έχει στραφεί η εκτέλεση μπορεί να ανακόψει την αναγγελία μέχρι και την ημέρα της διανομής του πλειστηριάσματος, σύμφωνα με τα άρθρα 933 επ.. Αντίγραφο της ανακοπής επιδίδεται χωρίς καθυστέρηση και στον υπάλληλο του πλειστηριασμού. Κατά της απόφασης που εκδίδεται επιτρέπεται μόνο το ένδικο μέσο της έφεσης.

3. Αν εκείνος κατά του οποίου έχει στραφεί η εκτέλεση ασκήσει ανακοπή, εφαρμόζεται αναλόγως η διάταξη του άρθρου 980 παρ. 2 ως προς τους δανειστές των οποίων τις απαιτήσεις έχει προσβάλει με την ανακοπή.

Άρθρο 972

1. Οι δανειστές εκείνου κατά του οποίου έγινε η εκτέλεση έχουν δικαίωμα να αναγγείλουν την απαίτησή τους. Η αναγγελία επιδίδεται στον υπάλληλο του πλειστηριασμού, σε εκείνον υπέρ του οποίου γίνεται και σε εκείνον κατά του οποίου στρέφεται η εκτέλεση και πρέπει να περιέχει:

α) διορισμό αντικλήτου στην περιφέρεια του πρωτοδικείου, του τόπου της εκτέλεσης, στον οποίο μπορούν να γίνονται όλες οι επιδόσεις και προσφορές που αφορούν την εκτέλεση. Αν δεν οριστεί αντίκλητος, αντίκλητος είναι ο δικηγόρος που υποχρεωτικά υπογράφει την αναγγελία, με την επιφύλαξη τυχόν αντίθετης ειδικής ρύθμισης,

β) περιγραφή της απαίτησης του δανειστή που αναγγέλλεται. Η αναγγελία πρέπει να επιδοθεί το αργότερο δέκα πέντε (15) ημέρες μετά τον πλειστηριασμό και μέσα στην ίδια προθεσμία πρέπει να κατατεθούν τα έγγραφα που αποδεικνύουν την απαίτηση. Τα έξοδα της αναγγελίας βαρύνουν όποιον αναγγέλλεται.

2. Το κύρος της αναγγελίας δεν επηρεάζεται από την αναστολή ή τη ματαίωση του πλειστηριασμού. Αν η απαίτηση του δανειστή που αναγγέλλεται στηρίζεται σε τίτλο εκτελεστό, η αναγγελία έχει τα ίδια αποτελέσματα με την κατάσχεση.

Άρθρο 973

1. Αν για οποιονδήποτε λόγο ο πλειστηριασμός δεν έγινε κατά την ημέρα που είχε οριστεί, επισπεύδεται πάλι με δήλωση που κατατίθεται στον υπάλληλο του πλειστηριασμού και συντάσσεται σχετική πράξη. Η νέα ημέρα του πλειστηριασμού ορίζεται από τον υπάλληλο του πλειστηριασμού δυο (2) μήνες από την ημέρα της δήλωσης και όχι πάντως μετά την παρέλευση τριών (3) μηνών από την ημέρα αυτή. Ο υπάλληλος του πλειστηριασμού εντός πέντε (5) ημερών μεριμνά ώστε να αναρτηθεί η γνωστοποίηση της δήλωσης και η ημέρα του πλειστηριασμού στην ιστοσελίδα δημοσιεύσεων πλειστηριασμών του Δελτίου Δικαστικών Δημοσιεύσεων του Ηλεκτρονικού Εθνικού Φορέα Κοινωνικής Ασφάλισης (e-ΕΦΚΑ).

2. Κάθε δανειστής, εφόσον έχει απαίτηση που στηρίζεται σε εκτελεστό τίτλο και κοινοποίησε σε εκείνον κατά του οποίου στρέφεται η εκτέλεση επιταγή προς εκτέλεση, μπορεί να επισπεύσει τον πλειστηριασμό.

Article 970

Where the thing is awarded to the person for whose benefit enforcement is being done, they shall pay the auctioneer the auction price less their claim and the enforcement costs, provided no other creditors have lodged claims. Payment must be made during the day after the end of the deadline for lodging claims, and the auctioned thing shall not be handed over until said deadline has lapsed. If other creditors lodge claims, the aforesaid person is obligated to pay the auction price in its entirety.

Article 971

1. If the auction price is sufficient to satisfy [the claim of] the person for whose benefit enforcement is being done and [of] the creditors who lodged claims, the auctioneer, after deducting the enforcement costs, shall pay them on the 20th day after the auction or even earlier, with the assent of the person enforcement concerns.

2. The person enforcement concerns may file an opposition against claims lodged up to the date on which the auction price is to be distributed, in accordance with Articles 933 *et seq*. A copy of the opposition shall also be served without delay on the auctioneer. Only the legal remedy of appeal may be filed against the judgment handed down.

3. If the person enforcement concerns files an opposition, the provisions of Article 980(2) apply *mutatis mutandis* with regard to the creditors whose claims were contested by means of the opposition.

Article 972

1. The creditors of the person enforcement concerns have the right to lodge their claim. Lodged claims shall be served on the auctioneer, the person for whose benefit enforcement is being done and the person enforcement concerns, and must:

a) appoint a process agent in the district of the court of first instance of the place of enforcement on whom all documents and bids concerning the enforcement may be served. If a process agent is not appointed, the lawyer obligated to sign the lodgement shall be the process agent, without prejudice to any specific provision to the contrary;

b) describe the claim of the creditor who lodged a claim. The lodged claim must be served no later than 15 days from the auction, and the documents proving the claim must be filed within the same deadline. The lodgement costs shall be borne by the person lodging the claim.

2. The validity of the lodgement shall not be affected by the stay or cancellation of the auction. If the claim lodged by the creditor is based on an enforceable title, lodgement generates the same effects as attachment.

Article 973

1. If for any reason the auction was not held on the day set, it shall be expedited again by means of a declaration filed with the auctioneer, and a new [report] shall be prepared. The auctioneer shall set the new auction date two months from the date of the declaration and no later than three months from that date. The auctioneer shall ensure that the notification of the declaration and the auction date are uploaded to the auctions announcement website of the Court Announcements Bulletin of the e-National Social Security Fund within five days.

2. Any creditor whose claim is based on an enforceable title and who notified an enforcement order to the person enforcement concerns may expedite the auction.

3. Αν ένας δανειστής, άλλος από τον επισπεύδοντα, θέλει να επισπεύσει τον πλειστηριασμό κατά την παρ. 2, πρέπει να το δηλώσει στον υπάλληλο του πλειστηριασμού και να συνταχθεί σχετική πράξη. Αν ο δανειστής αυτός έχει και ο ίδιος επιβάλει κατάσχεση, η δήλωση συνέχισης του πλειστηριασμού επέχει θέση ανάκλησης της δικής του κατάσχεσης. Αντίγραφο της πράξης επιδίδεται μέσα σε τρεις (3) ημέρες από τη δήλωση στον αρχικώς επισπεύδοντα. Ο πλειστηριασμός γίνεται ενώπιον του ίδιου υπαλλήλου. Ο υπάλληλος του πλειστηριασμού εντός πέντε (5) ημερών μεριμνά ώστε να αναρτηθεί η γνωστοποίηση της δήλωσης και η ημέρα του πλειστηριασμού στην ιστοσελίδα δημοσιεύσεων πλειστηριασμών του Δελτίου Δικαστικών Δημοσιεύσεων του Ηλεκτρονικού Εθνικού Φορέα Κοινωνικής Ασφάλισης (e-ΕΦΚΑ).
4. Κάθε δανειστής της παρ. 2 μπορεί να ζητήσει από το αρμόδιο κατά το άρθρο 933 δικαστήριο, που δικάζει κατά τη διαδικασία των άρθρων 686 επ., να του επιτρέψει να επισπεύσει αυτός την εκτέλεση, αν ο πλειστηριασμός ματαιώθηκε για δεύτερη φορά χωρίς σοβαρό λόγο, καθώς και σε κάθε άλλη περίπτωση που από τη στάση του επισπεύδοντος προκύπτει συμπαιγνία ή ολιγωρία. Η ανάθεση της επίσπευσης στον αιτούντα μπορεί να εξαρτηθεί από τη ματαίωση του τυχόν επισπευδόμενου πλειστηριασμού. Ο δανειστής, στον οποίο ανατέθηκε η επίσπευση, οφείλει να προβεί στην κατά την παρ. 3 δήλωση. Ο πλειστηριασμός επισπεύδεται κατά τις διατάξεις της παραγράφου αυτής.
5. Αν στην περίπτωση της παρ. 3 εμφανίστηκαν ταυτόχρονα περισσότεροι δανειστές που θέλουν να επισπεύσουν την εκτέλεση ή, στην περίπτωση της παρ. 4, οι αιτούντες είναι περισσότεροι, το κατά το άρθρο 933 δικαστήριο, ύστερα από αυτοτελή ή παρεμπίπτουσα αίτηση οποιουδήποτε έχει έννομο συμφέρον, δικάζοντας με τη διαδικασία των άρθρων 686 επ., επιλέγει τον καταλληλότερο στον οποίο και αναθέτει την επίσπευση. Ο πλειστηριασμός επισπεύδεται κατά τις διατάξεις της παρ. 3.
6. Αντιρρήσεις για οποιονδήποτε λόγο που αφορά το κύρος της δήλωσης συνέχισης, ασκούνται με ανακοπή μέσα σε προθεσμία τριάντα (30) ημερών από την ημέρα της κατά την παρ. 1 ανάρτησης. Η συζήτηση της ανακοπής προσδιορίζεται υποχρεωτικά μέσα σε εξήντα (60) ημέρες από την κατάθεσή της και γίνεται με τη διαδικασία των άρθρων 686 επ. Κατά της απόφασης που εκδίδεται μέσα σε έναν (1) μήνα από τη συζήτηση της ανακοπής δεν επιτρέπεται η άσκηση ενδίκων μέσων ούτε και αίτηση ανάκλησης. Πρόσθετοι λόγοι ανακοπής μπορούν να προταθούν μόνο με ιδιαίτερο δικόγραφο που κατατίθεται στη γραμματεία του δικαστηρίου προς το οποίο απευθύνεται η ανακοπή, κάτω από την οποία συντάσσεται έκθεση, και κοινοποιείται στον αντίδικο οκτώ (8) τουλάχιστον ημέρες πριν από τη συζήτηση.

Άρθρο 974

Αν το πλειστηρίασμα δεν αρκεί για να ικανοποιηθεί εκείνος υπέρ του οποίου έγινε η εκτέλεση και οι δανειστές που αναγγέλθηκαν, αυτός, όπως και εκείνος κατά του οποίου στρέφεται η εκτέλεση, καθώς και κάθε δανειστής που αναγγέλθηκε έχουν δικαίωμα μέσα σε πέντε ημέρες αφότου λήξει η προθεσμία για την αναγγελία να υποβάλλουν παρατηρήσεις ενώπιον του υπαλλήλου του πλειστηριασμού ο οποίος συντάσσει πράξη. Μέσα σε άλλες δέκα ημέρες αφότου λήξει αυτή η προθεσμία ο υπάλληλος του πλειστηριασμού, αφού λάβει υπόψη και τις παρατηρήσεις που τυχόν έχουν υποβληθεί, συντάσσει πίνακα κατάταξης. Η πέρα του διμήνου από τη λήξη των προθεσμιών αυτών καθυστέρηση σύνταξης του πίνακα αποτελεί για τον υπάλληλο του πλειστηριασμού πειθαρχικό παράπτωμα.

3. If a creditor other than the expediting party wishes to expedite the auction in accordance with paragraph 2, they must declare this to the auctioneer, and a relevant [report] shall be prepared. If the creditor in question has also procured attachment, the declaration of resumption of the auction shall serve as revocation of their own attachment. A copy of the [report] shall be served on the initial expediting party within three days of the [date the] declaration [was made]. The auction shall take place in the presence of the same auctioneer. The auctioneer shall ensure that the notification of the declaration and the auction date are uploaded to the auctions announcement website of the Court Announcements Bulletin of the e-National Social Security Fund within five days.

4. Any creditor under paragraph 2 may petition the court with jurisdiction under Article 933, trying the matter under the procedure laid down in Articles 686 *et seq.*, to allow him or her to expedite enforcement if the auction was cancelled for a second time without a serious reason, and in all other cases where the stance of the expediting party is indicative of collusion or delaying tactics. Assigning the applicant the task of expediting [the auction] may be predicated on cancelling any auction currently being expedited. The creditor to whom the task of expediting [the auction] was assigned is obligated to make the declaration referred to in paragraph 3. The auction shall be expedited in accordance with the provisions of that paragraph.

5. If, in the case referred to in paragraph 3, several creditors who wish to expedite enforcement appeared simultaneously, or, in the case referred to in paragraph 4, there are several applicants, the court referred to in Article 933, following a standalone or incidental application filed by any person with a legitimate interest and trying the matter under the procedure laid down in Articles 686 *et seq.*, shall select the most suitable person and assign them the task of expediting [the auction]. The auction shall be expedited in accordance with the provisions of paragraph 3.

6. Objections on any grounds concerning the validity of the declaration of resumption shall be filed by means of an opposition within a deadline of 30 days from the date of the upload referred to in paragraph 1. The hearing of the opposition must be set within 60 days from the date it is filed, and shall take place in accordance with the procedure laid down in Articles 686 *et seq.* The judgment must be handed down within one month from the hearing of the opposition, and no legal remedies and no revocation application may be filed against it. Additional grounds of opposition may be pleaded only by means of a separate procedural document filed with the registry of the court to which the opposition is addressed, at the end of which a report shall be drafted, and it shall be notified to the opponent at least eight days prior to the hearing.

Article 974

If the auction price is not sufficient to satisfy [the claim of] the person for whose benefit enforcement was done and [of] the creditors who lodged claims, that person, the person the enforcement concerned and any creditor who lodged a claim have the right, within five days of the expiry of the deadline for lodging claims, to submit observations to the auctioneer, who shall prepare a [report]. Within a further 10 days after the expiry of the said deadline, the auctioneer, having taken any observations submitted into account, shall prepare a ranking table. Any delay in preparing the said table by more than two months after these deadlines have expired shall constitute misconduct on the part of the auctioneer.

Άρθρο 975

Η κατάταξη των δανειστών στον πίνακα γίνεται με την εξής σειρά. Αφού αφαιρεθούν τα έξοδα της εκτέλεσης, που ορίζονται αιτιολογημένα από τον υπάλληλο του πλειστηριασμού, κατατάσσονται:

1) Οι απαιτήσεις για την κηδεία ή τη νοσηλεία εκείνου κατά του οποίου είχε στραφεί η εκτέλεση, του συζύγου και των τέκνων του, αν προέκυψαν κατά τους τελευταίους δώδεκα (12) μήνες πριν από την ημέρα διενέργειας του πλειστηριασμού ή κήρυξης της πτώχευσης. Στην ίδια τάξη υπάγονται και οι απαιτήσεις αποζημίωσης δανειστών, λόγω αναπηρίας ποσοστού ογδόντα τοις εκατό (80%) και άνω, με εξαίρεση την ικανοποίηση για ηθική βλάβη, εφόσον προέκυψαν έως την ημέρα διενέργειας του πλειστηριασμού ή την κήρυξη της πτώχευσης.

2) Οι απαιτήσεις για την παροχή τροφίμων αναγκαίων για τη συντήρηση εκείνου κατά του οποίου είχε στραφεί η εκτέλεση, του συζύγου και των τέκνων του, αν προέκυψαν κατά τους τελευταίους έξι (6) μήνες πριν από την ημέρα διενέργειας του πλειστηριασμού ή κήρυξης της πτώχευσης.

3) Οι απαιτήσεις, που έχουν ως βάση τους την παροχή εξαρτημένης εργασίας, καθώς και οι απαιτήσεις από αμοιβές, έξοδα και αποζημιώσεις των δικηγόρων, που αμείβονται με πάγια περιοδική αμοιβή, εφόσον προέκυψαν μέσα στην τελευταία διετία πριν από την ημέρα διενέργειας του πλειστηριασμού ή κήρυξης της πτώχευσης. Οι αποζημιώσεις λόγω καταγγελίας της σχέσης εργασίας, καθώς και οι απαιτήσεις των δικηγόρων για αποζημίωση λόγω λύσης της σύμβασης έμμισθης εντολής κατατάσσονται στην τάξη αυτή ανεξάρτητα από τον χρόνο που προέκυψαν. Στην ίδια τάξη κατατάσσονται απαιτήσεις δικηγόρων από δικηγορικές υπηρεσίες που παρασχέθηκαν κατά υπόθεση στον οφειλέτη, εφόσον προέκυψαν ένα έτος πριν από την ημέρα διενέργειας του πλειστηριασμού. Οι απαιτήσεις του Δημοσίου από φόρο προστιθέμενης αξίας και παρακρατούμενους και επιρριπτόμενους φόρους με τις προσαυξήσεις κάθε φύσης και τους τόκους που επιβαρύνουν τις απαιτήσεις αυτές. Στην ίδια τάξη υπάγονται και οι απαιτήσεις των φορέων κοινωνικής ασφάλισης αρμοδιότητας της γενικής γραμματείας κοινωνικών ασφαλίσεων, οι απαιτήσεις αποζημίωσης σε περίπτωση θανάτου του υπόχρεου προς διατροφή, καθώς και οι απαιτήσεις αποζημίωσης λόγω αναπηρίας ποσοστού εξήντα επτά τοις εκατό (67%) και άνω, εφόσον προέκυψαν έως την ημέρα διενέργειας του πλειστηριασμού ή την κήρυξη της πτώχευσης.

4) Οι απαιτήσεις αγροτών ή αγροτικών συνεταιρισμών από πώληση αγροτικών προϊόντων, αν προέκυψαν κατά τον τελευταίο χρόνο πριν από την ημέρα διενέργειας του πλειστηριασμού ή κήρυξης της πτώχευσης.

5) Οι απαιτήσεις του Δημοσίου και των οργανισμών τοπικής αυτοδιοίκησης από κάθε αιτία, με τις προσαυξήσεις κάθε φύσης και τους τόκους που επιβαρύνουν τις απαιτήσεις αυτές.

6) Οι απαιτήσεις του Συνεγγυητικού κατά του οφειλέτη, εφόσον ο τελευταίος έχει ή είχε στο παρελθόν την ιδιότητα της επιχείρησης παροχής επενδυτικών υπηρεσιών κατά την έννοια του άρθρου 2 του ν. 2396/1996 και οι απαιτήσεις του Συνεγγυητικού έχουν προκύψει εντός δύο (2) ετών πριν από την ημέρα διενέργειας του πλειστηριασμού ή κήρυξης της πτώχευσης.

Άρθρο 976

Οι απαιτήσεις που έχουν προνόμιο επάνω σε ορισμένο κινητό πράγμα ή σε ποσότητα χρημάτων κατατάσσονται με την ακόλουθη σειρά, εφόσον πρόκειται να διανεμηθεί το πλειστηρίασμα του πράγματος ή η ποσότητα χρημάτων,

1) οι απαιτήσεις που προέκυψαν από δαπάνες για τη διατήρηση του πράγματος,

2) οι απαιτήσεις για τις οποίες υπάρχει ενέχυρο,

3) οι απαιτήσεις που προέκυψαν από δαπάνες για την παραγωγή και τη συγκομιδή καρπών.

Άρθρο 977

1. Με την επιφύλαξη της παρ. 3 του άρθρου αυτού, αν εκτός από τις απαιτήσεις του άρθρου 975 υπάρχουν και οι απαιτήσεις του άρθρου 976 αριθμ. 3, προτιμώνται οι πρώτες. Αν υπάρχουν και απαιτήσεις του άρθρου 976 αριθμ. 1 και 2, τότε οι απαιτήσεις του άρθρου 975 ικανοποιούνται έως το ένα τρίτο του πλειστηριάσματος που πρέπει να διανεμηθεί στους πιστωτές και τα δύο τρίτα διατίθενται για να ικανοποιηθούν οι απαιτήσεις του άρθρου 976 αριθμ. 1 και 2. Από τα υπόλοιπα που απομένουν από το ένα τρίτο ή τα δύο τρίτα, μετά την ικανοποίηση των απαιτήσεων των άρθρων 975 και 976 αριθμ. 1 και 2, κατά το προηγούμενο εδάφιο, κατατάσσονται, ώσπου να καλυφθούν, οι απαιτήσεις της άλλης από τις προαναφερόμενες δύο κατηγορίες, που δεν έχουν ικανοποιηθεί.

Article 975

Creditors shall be ranked in the table in the following order. After the enforcement costs, specified with reasoning by the auctioneer, have been deducted, claims shall be ranked [in the following order]:
1) claims concerning the funeral or hospitalisation of the person the enforcement concerned, [or] their spouse [or] children, if such arose during the 12 months prior to the date of the auction or the declaration of bankruptcy. The same class [of claims] shall include compensation claims of creditors due to a disability percentage of 80% or more, except satisfaction for moral damage, provided such claims arose by the date of the auction or the declaration of bankruptcy;
2) claims concerning the provision of the food necessary for the subsistence of the person enforcement concerns, their spouse and children, if such arose during the six months prior to the date of the auction or the declaration of bankruptcy;
3) claims based on employment, as well as claims pertaining to fees, costs and compensation of lawyers paid a periodic retainer, provided such claims arose within the two years prior to the date of the auction or the declaration of bankruptcy; the same class [of claims] shall include compensation due to termination of employment, as well as claims of lawyers for compensation due to termination of retainer contracts, irrespective of when they occurred; the same class [of claims] shall include claims of lawyers arising from legal services provided on a case-by-case basis to the debtor, provided such claims arose within one year prior to the date of the auction; claims of the Greek State pertaining to value added tax and withheld taxes and assessed taxes plus surcharges of any kind and the interest levied on such claims; the same class [of claims] shall include claims of social security organisations under the oversight of the General Secretariat for Social Security, claims for compensation in the case of death of a party liable to pay maintenance, as well as claims for compensation due to a disability percentage of 67%, provided such claims arose by the date of the auction or the declaration of bankruptcy;
4) claims of farmers or farming cooperatives from the sale of agricultural products, provided such claims arose within the year prior to the date of the auction or the declaration of bankruptcy;
5) claims of the Greek State and local government authorities on any grounds, plus surcharges of any kind and the interest levied on such claims;
6) claims of the Athens Stock Exchange Members Guarantee Fund against the debtor, provided the latter is or was an investment firm, within the meaning of Article 2 of Law 2396/1996 and [provided] the claims of the Athens Stock Exchange Members Guarantee Fund arose within the two years prior to the date of the auction or the declaration of bankruptcy.

Article 976

Preferential claims to a specific movable or quantity of monies shall be ranked in the following order, provided the auction price for the [movable] or the quantity of monies is to be distributed[:]
1) claims arising from expenditure for preserving the thing;
2) claims for which there is a pledge;
3) claims arising from expenditure for producing and picking fruit.

Article 977

1. Without prejudice to paragraph 3 of this Article, if, in addition to the claims referred to in Article 975, there are also claims under Article 976(3), preference shall be given to the former. If there are also claims under Article 976(1) and (2), then up to 1/3 of the auction price to be distributed to the creditors shall be used to satisfy the claims under Article 975, and the [remaining] 2/3 shall be distributed to satisfy the claims under Article 976(1) and (2). Following satisfaction of claims under Article 975 and Article 976(1) and (2), in accordance with the preceding subparagraph, preference shall be given to non-satisfied claims belonging to the other of the two categories referred to above, using the balance remaining from the 1/3 or the 2/3 until such claims been covered.

2. Με την επιφύλαξη της παρ. 3 του άρθρου αυτού, αν υπάρχουν περισσότερες απαιτήσεις από αυτές που αναφέρονται στα άρθρα 975 ή 976, η απαίτηση της προηγούμενης τάξης προτιμάται από την απαίτηση της επόμενης τάξης και αν είναι της ίδιας τάξης ικανοποιούνται συμμέτρως. Αν συντρέχουν περισσότερες απαιτήσεις από εκείνες που αναφέρονται στο άρθρο 976 αριθμ. 2, ακολουθείται η κατά το ουσιαστικό δίκαιο σειρά.

3. Αν εκτός από τις απαιτήσεις του άρθρου 975 υπάρχουν και απαιτήσεις του άρθρου 976, καθώς και μη προνομιούχες απαιτήσεις, τότε οι απαιτήσεις του άρθρου 976 ικανοποιούνται έως το εξήντα πέντε τοις εκατό (65%), οι απαιτήσεις του άρθρου 975 έως το είκοσι πέντε τοις εκατό (25%) και οι μη προνομιούχες απαιτήσεις έως το δέκα τοις εκατό (10%) του ποσού του πλειστηριάσματος που πρέπει να διανεμηθεί στους πιστωτές συμμέτρως. Από τα υπόλοιπα που απομένουν από το εξήντα πέντε τοις εκατό (65%) ή από το είκοσι πέντε τοις εκατό (25%) κατατάσσονται, ώσπου να καλυφθούν οι απαιτήσεις της εκάστοτε άλλης από τις δύο προαναφερόμενες κατηγορίες, που δεν έχουν ικανοποιηθεί. Από τα υπόλοιπα που απομένουν από την ικανοποίηση των εγχειρόγραφων δανειστών ικανοποιούνται οι απαιτήσεις του άρθρου 976 και του άρθρου 975 κατά τα οριζόμενα στο δεύτερο εδάφιο της παρ. 1. Αν υπάρχουν απαιτήσεις του άρθρου 976 και μη προνομιούχες απαιτήσεις, οι πρώτες ικανοποιούνται έως το ενενήντα τοις εκατό (90%) και οι δεύτερες έως το δέκα τοις εκατό (10%) του ποσού του πλειστηριάσματος, που πρέπει να διανεμηθεί στους πιστωτές συμμέτρως. Αν υπάρχουν απαιτήσεις του άρθρου 975 και μη προνομιούχες απαιτήσεις, οι απαιτήσεις του άρθρου 975 ικανοποιούνται σε ποσοστό έως το εβδομήντα τοις εκατό (70%) του ποσού του πλειστηριάσματος, που πρέπει να διανεμηθεί στους πιστωτές, ενώ οι μη προνομιούχοι ικανοποιούνται στο υπόλοιπο ποσοστό συμμέτρως. Εάν υπάρχουν και εγχειρόγραφοι δανειστές οι προνομιούχες απαιτήσεις των άρθρων 975 και 976 δεν συμμετέχουν στο δέκα τοις εκατό (10%) ακόμη και εάν δεν ικανοποιήθηκε η απαίτησή τους.

Άρθρο 977Α
Σειρά κατάταξης υπερπρονομιούχων, προνομιούχων και μη

1. Αν μετά την έναρξη ισχύος του παρόντος άρθρου γεννηθούν εξ ολοκλήρου απαιτήσεις και συσταθεί για την εξασφάλισή τους ενέχυρο επί μη βεβαρημένου κατά την ανωτέρω ημερομηνία πράγματος, αυτές κατατάσσονται, με την επιφύλαξη της παρ. 2 και αφού αφαιρεθούν τα έξοδα της εκτέλεσης, με την εξής σειρά:
α) απαιτήσεις του άρθρου 976 αριθμ. 1 και 2
β) απαιτήσεις του άρθρου 975 και απαιτήσεις του άρθρου 976 αριθμ. 3
γ) μη προνομιούχες απαιτήσεις.

2. Απαιτήσεις οι οποίες προέκυψαν πριν από την ημέρα διενέργειας του πλειστηριασμού και αφορούν σε μη καταβληθέντες μισθούς έως έξι (6) μηνών από παροχή εξαρτημένης εργασίας και έως του ποσού το οποίο ισούται ανά μήνα οφειλόμενου μισθού και ανά εργαζόμενο με το νόμιμο κατώτατο μισθό υπαλλήλου άνω των είκοσι πέντε (25) ετών επί διακόσια εβδομήντα πέντε τοις εκατό (275%) ικανοποιούνται προνομιακά πριν από κάθε άλλη απαίτηση (υπερ-προνόμιο) και μετά την αφαίρεση των εξόδων της εκτέλεσης.

3. Σε περίπτωση ύπαρξης περισσότερων βεβαρημένων πραγμάτων, οι απαιτήσεις της παρ. 2 του παρόντος, εφόσον έχουν αναγγελθεί, ικανοποιούνται από το ποσό των πλειστηριασμάτων που πρέπει να διανεμηθούν στους πιστωτές ως εξής:
α) συμμέτρως, εφόσον οι πλειστηριασμοί διενεργήθηκαν ταυτοχρόνως ή
β) κατά τη σειρά διενέργειας των πλειστηριασμών και έως την ολοσχερή εξόφλησή τους, εφόσον οι πλειστηριασμοί διενεργήθηκαν διαδοχικώς.
Στην περ. β' του προηγούμενου εδαφίου, οι ειδικοί προνομιούχοι πιστωτές σε βάρος των οποίων ικανοποιήθηκαν εν όλω ή εν μέρει οι απαιτήσεις αυτές, υποκαθίστανται για το επιπλέον της αναλογίας τους στο πλειστηρίασμα από τον πλειστηριασμό των υπόλοιπων πραγμάτων.

4. Με την επιφύλαξη της παρ. 2 του παρόντος, αν υπάρχουν περισσότερες απαιτήσεις από αυτές που αναφέρονται στα άρθρα 975 ή 976, η απαίτηση της προηγούμενης τάξης προτιμάται από την απαίτηση της επόμενης τάξης και αν είναι της ίδιας τάξης ικανοποιούνται συμμέτρως. Αν συντρέχουν περισσότερες απαιτήσεις από εκείνες που αναφέρονται στο άρθρο 976 αριθμ. 2, ακολουθείται η κατά το ουσιαστικό δίκαιο σειρά.

2. Without prejudice to paragraph 3 of this Article, if there are several claims of the type referred to in Article 975 or Article 976, the claim of the preceding class shall be given preference over the claim of the subsequent class and, if they belong to the same class, they shall be satisfied *pari passu*. If there are several claims of the type referred to in Article 976(2), the order set forth in substantive law shall be followed.

3. If, in addition to the claims under Article 975, there are also claims under Article 976 as well as non-preferential claims, then the claims under Article 976 shall be satisfied using up to 65%, the claims under Article 975 using up to 25%, and non-preferential claims using up to 10% of the amount of the auction price to be distributed to the creditors *pari passu*. Preference shall be given to non-satisfied claims belonging to the other of the two categories referred to above, using the balance remaining from the 65% or the 25% [of the auction price]. The balance remaining from satisfying the claims of unsecured creditors shall be used to satisfy the claims under Article 976 and Article 975 in accordance with the provisions of the second subparagraph of paragraph 1. If there are claims under Article 976 as well as non-preferential claims, the former shall be satisfied using up to 90% and the latter using up to 10% of the amount of the auction price to be distributed to the creditors *pari passu*. If there are claims under Article 975 as well as non-preferential claims, the claims under Article 975 shall be satisfied using up to 70% of the amount of the auction price to be distributed to the creditors, while non-preferential [claims] shall be satisfied *pari passu* using the remaining percentage. If there are also unsecured creditors, the preferential claims under Article 975 and Article 976 shall not be covered by the 10% even if their claim was not satisfied.

Article 977A

Ranking of super-preferential, preferential and non-preferential [claims]

1. If claims arose in their entirety after the entry of this Article into force and a pledge has been established to secure them on a thing which was not encumbered on that date, these shall be ranked in the following order, without prejudice to paragraph 2 and after the enforcement costs have been deducted:

a) claims under Article 976(1) and (2);

b) claims under Article 975 and claims under Article 976(3);

c) non-preferential claims.

2. Claims which arose prior to the date of the auction and which concern up to six months of unpaid employment salaries and up to the amount due per month for salaries owed and per worker at the lawful minimum salary of an employee over the age of 25 multiplied by 275% shall be given preference over any other claim (super-preference) and after enforcement costs have been deducted.

3. Where there are several encumbered things, the claims referred to in paragraph 2 of this Article, provided they have been lodged, shall be satisfied using the amount of the auction price to be distributed to the creditors as follows:

a) *pari passu*, where the auctions were held simultaneously; or

b) in the order in which the auctions were held and until they have been paid in full, where the auctions were held in succession.

In case (b) of the preceding subparagraph, special preferential creditors to whose detriment these claims were satisfied in whole or in part shall be satisfied for their additional portion in the proceeds from auctioning the remaining things.

4. Without prejudice to paragraph 2 of this Article, if there are several claims of the type referred to in Article 975 or Article 976, the claim of the preceding class shall be given preference over the claim of the subsequent class and, if they belong to the same class, they shall be satisfied *pari passu*. If there are several claims of the type referred to in Article 976(2), the order set forth in substantive law shall be followed.

5. Μετά την ικανοποίηση των απαιτήσεων που έχουν προνόμιο, σύμφωνα με τις προηγούμενες παραγράφους, οι μη προνομιούχοι πιστωτές ικανοποιούνται συμμέτρως από το υπόλοιπο του ποσού του πλειστηριάσματος που πρέπει να διανεμηθεί στους πιστωτές.

Άρθρο 978

1. Απαιτήσεις που εξαρτώνται από αίρεση ή αμφίβολες κατατάσσονται τυχαίως. Με την προσκόμιση ισόποσης εγγυητικής επιστολής σε πρώτη ζήτηση τράπεζας που είναι νόμιμα εγκατεστημένη στην Ελλάδα, ο υπάλληλος του πλειστηριασμού υποχρεούται να ικανοποιήσει το δανειστή, η απαίτηση του οποίου κατατάχθηκε τυχαία. Σε περίπτωση που δεν πληρωθεί ο όρος υπό τον οποίο τελεί η τυχαία κατάταξη, ο δανειστής υποχρεούται να επιστρέφει εντόκως το ποσό που εισέπραξε. Απαιτήσεις υπό προθεσμία κατατάσσονται, αφού αφαιρεθεί ο τόκος που αναλογεί έως τη λήξη τους.
2. Όταν απαίτηση κατατάσσεται τυχαίως, ο υπάλληλος του πλειστηριασμού ορίζει στον πίνακα κατάταξης πώς κατανέμεται το ποσό της απαίτησης, με την προσθήκη των αναλογούντων τόκων, αν αυτή παύσει να υφίσταται.

Άρθρο 979

1. Μέσα σε τρείς (3) ημέρες αφότου συνταχθεί ο πίνακας, ο υπάλληλος του πλειστηριασμού καλεί με έγγραφο εκείνον υπέρ του οποίου έγινε και εκείνον κατά του οποίου είχε στραφεί η εκτέλεση και τους δανειστές που αναγγέλθηκαν, για να λάβουν γνώση του πίνακα της κατάταξης. Ο υπάλληλος του πλειστηριασμού οφείλει την επόμενη ημέρα της πρόσκλησης να επιδείξει ή και να χορηγήσει στα ως άνω πρόσωπα τον πίνακα και τα σχετικά έγγραφα.
2. Μέσα σε δώδεκα (12) εργάσιμες ημέρες αφότου επιδοθεί η πρόσκληση της παρ. 1 οποιοσδήποτε έχει έννομο συμφέρον μπορεί να ανακόψει τον πίνακα της κατάταξης, οπότε εφαρμόζονται τα άρθρα 933 επ. Αντίγραφο της ανακοπής επιδίδεται, μέσα στην ίδια προθεσμία, και στον υπάλληλο του πλειστηριασμού. Κατά της απόφασης που εκδίδεται επιτρέπεται η άσκηση όλων των ένδικων μέσων πλην της ανακοπής ερημοδικίας. Η ανακοπή στρέφεται κατά των δανειστών των οποίων προσβάλλεται η κατάταξη. Η συζήτηση προσδιορίζεται υποχρεωτικά μέσα σε εξήντα (60) ημέρες από την κατάθεσή της, αν ο δανειστής είναι κάτοικος ημεδαπής ή μέσα σε εκατόν είκοσι (120) ημέρες από την κατάθεσή της, αν ο δανειστής είναι κάτοικος αλλοδαπής.

Άρθρο 980

1. Αν δεν ασκήθηκε ανακοπή κατά του πίνακα της κατάταξης, ο υπάλληλος του πλειστηριασμού διανέμει αμέσως το πλειστηρίασμα.
2. Αν κάποιος από τους δανειστές άσκησε ανακοπή, ο υπάλληλος του πλειστηριασμού δεν μπορεί να ικανοποιήσει τους δανειστές των οποίων η κατάταξη προσβάλλεται με την ανακοπή, εκτός αν προσκομίσουν ισόποση εγγυητική επιστολή σε πρώτη ζήτηση τράπεζας που είναι νόμιμα εγκατεστημένη στην Ελλάδα. Σε περίπτωση τελεσίδικης ευδοκίμησης της ανακοπής ο δανειστής υποχρεούται να επιστρέψει στον υπάλληλο του πλειστηριασμού εντόκως το ποσό που εισέπραξε.

Άρθρο 981

Κάθε υπάλληλος πλειστηριασμού τηρεί ιδιαίτερο βιβλίο, που ονομάζεται «βιβλίο πλειστηριασμών». Στο βιβλίο αυτό, και σε ιδιαίτερη μερίδα για κάθε πλειστηριασμό, καταχωρίζονται με αύξοντα αριθμό και χρονολογική σειρά τα στοιχεία των εγγράφων που κοινοποιούνται ή κατατίθενται στον υπάλληλο του πλειστηριασμού, καθώς και τα στοιχεία των πράξεων που αυτός συντάσσει. Στο τέλος του βιβλίου τηρείται αλφαβητικό ευρετήριο, όπου σημειώνονται τα ονοματεπώνυμα του επισπεύδοντος την εκτέλεση και εκείνου κατά του οποίου στρέφεται.

5. Once preferential claims have been satisfied in accordance with the preceding paragraphs, [the claims of] non-preferential creditors shall be satisfied *pari passu* using the balance of the amount of the auction price to be distributed to the creditors.

Article 978

1. Conditional or doubtful claims shall be ranked without preference. Upon being provided with a letter of guarantee for the same amount payable on first demand, issued by a bank lawfully established in Greece, the auctioneer is obligated to satisfy the claim of any creditor whose claim was ranked without preference. If the condition leading to ranking without preference is not met, the creditor is obligated to return the amount collected plus interest. Claims subject to a term shall be ranked after the interest payable up to their date of expiry has been deducted.
2. Where a claim is ranked without preference, the auctioneer shall specify in the ranking table how the claim amount will be distributed, plus the corresponding taxes, if the claim ceases to exist.

Article 979

1. Within three days from the date the table was prepared, the auctioneer shall invite in writing the person for whose benefit enforcement is being done and the person enforcement concerns and the creditors who lodged claims, so that they become aware of the ranking table. The day after the invitation, the auctioneer is obligated to show or even provide the table and relevant documents to the aforesaid persons.
2. Within 12 working days of service of the invitation referred to in paragraph 1, any person with a legitimate interest may file an opposition against the ranking table, in which case Articles 933 *et seq.* apply. A copy of the opposition shall also be served on the auctioneer within the same deadline. All legal remedies except opposition against a default judgment may be filed against the judgment handed down. The opposition shall be brought against the creditors whose ranking is being contested. The hearing date must be set within 60 days of the date of filing if the creditor is domiciled in Greece, or within 120 days from the date of filing if the creditor is domiciled abroad.

Article 980

1. If no opposition was filed against the ranking table, the auctioneer shall distribute the auction price immediately.
2. If any of the creditors filed an opposition, the auctioneer cannot provide satisfaction to the creditors whose ranking is being contested by means of said opposition, unless they produce a letter of guarantee for the same amount payable on first demand, issued by a bank lawfully established in Greece. If a *de jure* non-appealable judgment is handed down upholding the opposition, the creditor is obligated to return to the auctioneer the amount collected plus interest.

Article 981

Auctioneers shall keep a special register called the "auctions register". The details of documents notified to or filed with the auctioneer and the details of [reports] prepared by the auctioneer shall be recorded in this register by incremental number and in chronological order, with a separate entry for each auction. An alphabetical index shall be kept at the end of the register noting the full names of the person procuring enforcement and the person enforcement concerns.

ΚΕΦΑΛΑΙΟ Δ'
Κατάσχεση σε χέρια τρίτου.

Άρθρο 982

1. Μπορούν να κατασχεθούν

α) χρηματικές απαιτήσεις εκείνου κατά του οποίου στρέφεται η εκτέλεση κατά τρίτων μη εξαρτώμενες από αντιπαροχή ή απαιτήσεις του κατά τρίτων για μεταβίβαση της κυριότητας κινητών μη εξαρτώμενη από αντιπαροχή,

β) κινητά πράγματά του που βρίσκονται χέρια τρίτου.

2. Εξαιρούνται από την κατάσχεση

α) πράγματα που μπορούν να υποστούν άμεση φθορά,

β) η εταιρική μερίδα σε προσωπικές εταιρίες,

γ) απαιτήσεις διατροφής που πηγάζουν από το νόμο ή από διάταξη τελευταίας βούλησης, καθώς και απαιτήσεις για συνεισφορά των συζύγων στις ανάγκες της οικογένειας,

δ) απαιτήσεις μισθών, συντάξεων ή ασφαλιστικών παροχών, εκτός αν πρόκειται να ικανοποιηθεί απαίτηση για διατροφή που στηρίζεται στο νόμο ή σε διάταξη τελευταίας βούλησης ή για συνεισφορά στις ανάγκες της οικογένειας, οπότε επιτρέπεται να γίνει κατάσχεση έως το μισό, αφού ληφθούν υπόψη τα ποσά που εισπράττει ο υπόχρεος, το μέγεθος των υποχρεώσεων που του δημιουργεί ο γάμος του για αντιμετώπιση των οικογενειακών αναγκών και ο αριθμός των δικαιούχων.

ε) κάθε είδους κοινοτικές ενισχύσεις ή επιδοτήσεις στα χέρια του Ο.Π.Ε.Κ.Ε.Π.Ε. ως τρίτου, μέχρι την κατάθεση τους στον τραπεζικό λογαριασμό των δικαιούχων ή την με άλλο τρόπο καταβολή τους σε αυτούς.

στ) απαιτήσεις που επιδικάζονται σε βάρος του Ελληνικού Δημοσίου από το Ευρωπαϊκό Δικαστήριο Ανθρωπίνων Δικαιωμάτων, κατ' εφαρμογή του άρθρου 41 της Ευρωπαϊκής Σύμβασης για την Προστασία των Δικαιωμάτων του Ανθρώπου, λόγω διαπίστωσης παραβιάσεων της Σύμβασης αυτής ή των Πρωτοκόλλων της, εξαιρουμένων των απαιτήσεων που επιδικάζονται για την παραπάνω αιτία προς αποκατάσταση υλικής ζημίας. Το εν λόγω ακατάσχετο ισχύει όταν η κατάσχεση επισπεύδεται για την ικανοποίηση απαίτησης δανειστή, που ανήκει στο δημόσιο τομέα, όπως ορίζεται στην περίπτωση α' της παρ. 1 του άρθρου 14 του ν. 4270/2014 «Αρχές δημοσιονομικής διαχείρισης και εποπτείας (ενσωμάτωση της Οδηγίας 2011/85/ΕΕ) - δημόσιο λογιστικό και άλλες διατάξεις» (Α' 143).

ζ) απαιτήσεις που προβλέπονται σε ειδικότερους νόμους ως ακατάσχετες.

3. Η εξαίρεση των περ. δ' και ζ' της παρ. 2 ισχύει και όταν η καταβολή του ποσού γίνεται με κατάθεση σε τραπεζικό λογαριασμό του οφειλέτη σε πιστωτικό ίδρυμα. Η εξαίρεση ισχύει μόνο στην έκταση που ο λογαριασμός παρουσιάζει υπόλοιπο που δεν υπερβαίνει, κατά το χρονικό διάστημα από την επιβολή της κατάσχεσης έως και έναν (1) μήνα μετά την καταβολή, το ποσό της εξαιρούμενης από την κατάσχεση απαίτησης.

Άρθρο 983

1. Η κατάσχεση στα χέρια τρίτου γίνεται με επίδοση στον τρίτο και σε εκείνον κατά του οποίου στρέφεται η εκτέλεση, εγγράφου που πρέπει να περιέχει, εκτός από τα στοιχεία του άρθρου 118, και

α) ακριβή περιγραφή του εκτελεστού τίτλου και της απαίτησης, βάσει των οποίων γίνεται η κατάσχεση,

β) το ποσό για το οποίο επιβάλλεται η κατάσχεση,

γ) επιταγή προς το τρίτο να μην καταβάλει σε εκείνον κατά του οποίου γίνεται η εκτέλεση,

δ) διορισμό αντικλήτου που κατοικεί στην περιφέρεια του ίδιου ειρηνοδικείου ή στην έδρα του πρωτοδικείου της κατοικίας του τρίτου, αν εκείνος υπέρ του οποίου γίνεται η εκτέλεση δεν κατοικεί στην περιφέρεια του ειρηνοδικείου της κατοικίας του τρίτου.

2. Το έγγραφο που προορίζεται για εκείνον κατά του οποίου γίνεται η κατάσχεση πρέπει να του επιδοθεί το αργότερο μέσα σε οκτώ ημέρες αφότου γίνει η επίδοση στον τρίτο, αλλιώς η κατάσχεση είναι άκυρη.

CHAPTER IV
Garnishment

Article 982

1.The following may be garnished[:]
a) monetary claims of the person enforcement concerns against third parties for which there is no counter-performance, or claims of that person against third parties concerning transfer of ownership of movables, for which there is no counter-performance;
b) movables in the possession of a third party.
2. The following are exempt from garnishment[:]
a) things that can quickly become spoiled;
b) shareholdings in partnerships;
c) maintenance claims deriving from the law or a testamentary disposition, as well as claims for contributions of spouses for the needs of the family;
d) claims for salaries, pensions or insurance benefits, unless a maintenance claim deriving from the law or a testamentary disposition or for contribution for the needs of the family is to be satisfied, in which case garnishment up to half may take place, having taken account of the amounts collected by the debtor, the size of obligations created for them by their marriage to address family needs and the number of entitled persons;
e) any kind of Community aid or subsidies held by the Payment and Control Agency For Guidance and Guarantee Community Aid as a third party, until deposited into the beneficiaries' bank accounts or otherwise paid to them;
f) claims awarded against the Greek State by the European Court of Human Rights, pursuant to Article 41 of the European Convention on Human Rights, where the Court found that there has been a violation of the Convention or the Protocols thereto, except claims to make good material losses awarded on the above grounds. This exclusion from garnishment applies when garnishment is being expedited to satisfy the claim of a public-sector creditor, as provided for in Article 14(1)(a) of Law 4270/2014 on the principles of fiscal management and supervision (transposition of Directive 2011/85/EU) - public accounting and other provisions (Government Gazette, Series I, Issue 143);
g) claims provided for in more specific laws as being excluded from garnishment.
3. The exclusion provided for in cases (d) and (g) of paragraph 2 also applies when the amount is deposited into a bank account held by the debtor at a credit institution. The exclusion applies only to the extent that the account shows a balance which, during the period from imposition of garnishment until one month after payment, exceeds the amount of the claim excluded from garnishment.

Article 983

1. Garnishment shall take place by means of service of a document on the third party and on the person enforcement concerns, which, in addition to the information required in Article 118, must also contain[:]
a) a precise description of the enforceable title and the claim on the basis of which garnishment is taking place;
b) the amount for which garnishment is being imposed;
c) an order to the third party not to make payments to the person enforcement concerns;
d) appointment of a process agent domiciled in the district of the same court of the peace or the seat of the court of first instance of the place of residence of the third party, if the person for whose benefit enforcement is being done is not domiciled in the district of the court of the peace where the third party is domiciled.
2. The document intended for the person garnishment concerns must be served on them no later than eight days after the date of service on the third party, otherwise the garnishment is null and void.

3. Όταν πρόκειται για απαίτηση από τίτλο εις διαταγήν, η κατάσχεση της παρ. 1 μπορεί να γίνει αφού ο τίτλος αφαιρεθεί κατά το άρθρο 954 παρ. 1 από εκείνον κατά του οποίου στρέφεται η εκτέλεση και παραδοθεί σε εκείνον υπέρ του οποίου γίνεται.
4. Για την κατάσχεση στα χέρια πιστωτικού ιδρύματος ως τρίτου το έγγραφο επιδίδεται στην έδρα του ή σε οποιοδήποτε κατάστημά του.
5. Το απόρρητο των κάθε μορφής καταθέσεων σε πιστωτικά ιδρύματα, καθώς και των άυλων μετοχών που καταχωρίζονται στο Σύστημα Άυλων Τίτλων (Σ.Α.Τ.) του Κεντρικού Αποθετηρίου Αξιών δεν ισχύει έναντι του δανειστή που έχει δικαίωμα κατάσχεσης της περιουσίας του δικαιούχου της κατάθεσης ή της μετοχής. Το απόρρητο αίρεται μόνο για τα χρηματικό ποσό που απαιτείται για την ικανοποίηση του δανειστή.

Άρθρο 984

1. Απαγορεύεται και είναι άκυρη υπέρ του κατασχόντος η διάθεση του κατασχεμένου από εκείνον κατά του οποίου έγινε η κατάσχεση, αφότου του επιδοθεί το κατά το άρθρο 983 έγγραφο, έστω και αν το έγγραφο αυτό δεν έχει ακόμη επιδοθεί στον τρίτο. Η ευθύνη του τρίτου ρυθμίζεται σύμφωνα με την παρ. 3.
2. Απαγορεύεται και δεν παράγει έννομες συνέπειες για τον κατάσχοντα η εξόφληση από τον τρίτο της κατασχεμένης απαίτησης ή ο συμψηφισμός της με μεταγενέστερη απαίτηση, καθώς και η απόδοση σε εκείνον κατά του οποίου έγινε η κατάσχεση ή η διάθεση σε τρίτους του κατασχεμένου, αφότου του επιδοθεί το έγγραφο του άρθρου 983, έστω και αν αυτό δεν επιδόθηκε ακόμα σε εκείνον κατά του οποίου γίνεται η κατάσχεση. Όταν πρόκειται για χρηματικές απαιτήσεις, η απαγόρευση αφορά μόνο το ποσό για το οποίο έγινε η κατάσχεση.
3. Αφότου του κοινοποιηθεί η κατάσχεση, ο τρίτος γίνεται μεσεγγυούχος.
4. Η κατάσχεση που έχει επιβληθεί δεν εμποδίζει εκείνον κατά του οποίου έγινε να στραφεί κατά του τρίτου δικαστικώς ή με αναγκαστική εκτέλεση. Σ' αυτή την περίπτωση, μετά την ενέργεια της εκτέλεσης, και αν πρόκειται για πράγμα που μπορεί να κατατεθεί, κατατίθεται δημόσια, αλλιώς ο δικαστικός επιμελητής ορίζει μεσεγγυούχο για να το φυλάει.
5. Οι διατάξεις του άρθρου 956 παρ. 4 έως 6 εφαρμόζονται και στις περιπτώσεις των παρ. 3 και 4 του άρθρου αυτού.

Άρθρο 985

1. Μέσα σε οκτώ (8) ημέρες αφότου του επιδοθεί το κατασχετήριο, ο τρίτος οφείλει να δηλώσει αν υπάρχει η απαίτηση που κατασχέθηκε, αν έχει στα χέρια του το κατασχεμένο πράγμα και αν επιβλήθηκε στα χέρια του άλλη κατάσχεση και συνάμα να αναφέρει ποιος την επέβαλε και για ποιο ποσό. Όταν η κατάσχεση επιβάλλεται στα χέρια πιστωτικού ιδρύματος, αυτό θα πρέπει να δηλώσει, αν υφίσταται στα χέρια του ακατάσχετη απαίτηση κατά την έννοια των περ. γ', δ' και ζ' της παρ. 2 του άρθρου 982.
2. Η δήλωση της παρ. 1 κατατίθεται εγγράφως στη γραμματεία του ειρηνοδικείου του τόπου της κατοικίας εκείνου που δηλώνει και συντάσσεται σχετική έκθεση. Είναι δυνατή η υποβολή της δήλωσης και με ηλεκτρονικά μέσα. Στην περίπτωση αυτή η σχετική έκθεση συντάσσεται επίσης ηλεκτρονικά. Ο τρόπος υποβολής της δήλωσης και της σύνταξης της σχετικής έκθεσης με Τεχνολογίες Πληροφορικής και Επικοινωνιών, καθώς και κάθε άλλη σχετική λεπτομέρεια καθορίζεται με κοινή απόφαση των Υπουργών Δικαιοσύνης και Ψηφιακής Διακυβέρνησης.
3. Η παράλειψη της δήλωσης εξομοιώνεται με αρνητική δήλωση. Αν η δήλωση παραλειφθεί ή είναι ανακριβής, ο τρίτος ευθύνεται να αποζημιώσει αυτόν που επέβαλε την κατάσχεση.

3. In the case of a claim from a note payable to order, the garnishment referred to in paragraph 1 may take place after the note has been removed, in accordance with Article 954(1), from the person enforcement concerns and handed over to the person for whose benefit enforcement is being done.
4. In the case of garnishment involving a credit institution as the third party, the document shall be served at its registered offices or at any of its branches.
5. The secrecy of deposits of any kind at credit institutions and dematerialised shares entered in the Dematerialised Securities System of the Central Securities Depository shall not apply vis-à-vis any creditor with the right to effect garnishment of the assets of the beneficiary of the deposit or the share. Secrecy shall be lifted only for the monetary amount required to satisfy [the claim] of the creditor.

Article 984

1. Disposal of the garnished thing by the garnishee after the document referred to in Article 983 has been served on them is prohibited and null and void vis-à-vis the garnishor, even if this document has not yet been served on the third party. The liability of the third party is regulated in accordance with paragraph 3.
2. Payment of the garnished claim in full or offsetting of the garnished claim against a subsequent claim, as well as return of the garnished thing to the garnishee or disposal of the garnished thing to third parties after the document referred in Article 983 has been served on said person is prohibited and does not generate legal effects for the garnishor, even if the document has not yet been served on the garnishee. In [cases of] monetary claims, the prohibition shall only apply to the amount for which garnishment was effected.
3. After having been notified of the garnishment, the third party shall become a sequestrator.
4. The garnishment imposed shall not hinder the garnishee from taking steps against the third party either by initiating proceedings or seeking compulsory enforcement. In this case, after enforcement has been effected and if the thing can be deposited, it shall be deposited with the state, otherwise the court process server shall designate a sequestrator for its safekeeping.
5. The provisions of Article 956(4) to (6) also apply in the cases referred to in paragraphs 3 and 4 of this Article.

Article 985

1. Within eight days of the garnishment order being served on the third party, they are obligated to declare whether the garnished claim exists, whether they hold the garnished thing and whether a different garnishment order has [already] been imposed in relation to it, as well as who imposed it and for which amount. When garnishment involves a credit institution, the latter must declare whether it holds a non-garnishable claim within the meaning of Article 982(2)(c), (d) and (g).
2. The declaration referred to in paragraph 1 shall be filed in writing with the registry of the court of the peace of the place where the declarant has their place of domicile, and a relevant report shall be prepared. The declaration may also be submitted using electronic means. In this case, the relevant report shall also be prepared using electronic means. The manner in which the declaration is submitted and the relevant report is prepared using information and communications technologies and all other relevant details shall be set out in a joint decision issued by the Minister of Justice and the Minister of Digital Governance.
3. Failure to make a declaration shall be equivalent to a negative declaration. If the declaration is not made or is inaccurate, the third party shall be liable to compensate the garnishor.

Άρθρο 986

Μέσα σε τριάντα (30) ημέρες από τη δήλωση του άρθρου 985 όποιος επέβαλε την κατάσχεση έχει δικαίωμα να την ανακόψει ενώπιον του κατά τα άρθρα 12 επ. και 23 επ. δικαστηρίου. Με την ανακοπή μπορεί να ζητηθεί και αποζημίωση κατά το άρθρο 985 παρ. 3.

Η συζήτηση της ανακοπής προσδιορίζεται υποχρεωτικά μέσα σε εκατόν είκοσι (120) ημέρες από την κατάθεση της, μπορεί δε να επιδοθεί και στον πληρεξούσιο δικηγόρο που υπέγραψε την προσβαλλόμενη δήλωση. Η ανακοπή εκδικάζεται κατά την ειδική διαδικασία των περιουσιακών διαφορών των άρθρων 614 επ.

Άρθρο 987

Ο τρίτος δεν έχει δικαίωμα να προσβάλει το κύρος της κατάσχεσης παρά μόνο αν το κατασχετήριο δεν περιέχει τα στοιχεία του άρθρου 963 ή δεν κοινοποιήθηκε σε εκείνον κατά του οποίου στρέφεται η εκτέλεση.

Άρθρο 988

1. Αν ο τρίτος δηλώσει πως η απαίτηση που κατασχέθηκε υπάρχει και είναι επαρκής για να ικανοποιηθούν εκείνος ή εκείνοι που επέβαλαν την κατάσχεση, ο τρίτος οφείλει, αφού περάσουν οκτώ ημέρες αφότου η κατάσχεση κοινοποιήθηκε σε εκείνον κατά του οποίου έγινε η εκτέλεση, αν κατοικεί στην Ελλάδα, και αφού περάσουν τριάντα ημέρες, αν κατοικεί στο εξωτερικό ή είναι άγνωστη η διαμονή του, να καταβάλει στον καθένα από εκείνους που επέβαλαν κατάσχεση το ποσό για το οποίο έγινε η κατάσχεση. Αν η κατασχεμένη απαίτηση δεν επαρκεί για να ικανοποιηθούν όλοι όσοι επέβαλαν κατάσχεση, ο τρίτος οφείλει να κάνει δημόσια κατάθεση και η διανομή γίνεται από συμβολαιογράφο που ορίζεται αφού το ζητήσει οποιοσδήποτε έχει έννομο συμφέρον, από τον ειρηνοδίκη του τόπου της εκτέλεσης κατά τη διαδικασία των άρθρων 686 επ. Εάν, για οποιονδήποτε λόγο, δεν είναι δυνατό να ορισθεί συμβολαιογράφος του τόπου εκτέλεσης, αρμόδιος για τη διανομή μπορεί να οριστεί και συμβολαιογράφος διορισμένος στην περιφέρεια του συμβολαιογραφικού συλλόγου του τόπου εκτέλεσης ή, αν και αυτό δεν είναι δυνατό, του συμβολαιογραφικού συλλόγου της πρωτεύουσας του κράτους. Η διανομή σε εκείνους που έκαναν την κατάσχεση γίνεται σύμφωνα με τα άρθρα 974 επ. και η προθεσμία του άρθρου 974 παρ. 1 αρχίζει αφότου γνωστοποιηθεί στο συμβολαιογράφο η απόφαση του ειρηνοδίκη που τον διορίζει.

2. Αν ο τρίτος δηλώσει ότι έχει στα χέρια του το κατασχεμένο πράγμα, γίνεται πλειστηριασμός ενώπιον συμβολαιογράφου που ορίζεται σύμφωνα με την παράγραφο 1. Ο πλειστηριασμός γίνεται κατά τα άρθρα 959 επ. με την εφαρμογή και του άρθρου 955 παράγραφος 2 εδάφιο β', η προθεσμία του οποίου αρχίζει αφότου η απόφαση του ειρηνοδικείου για το διορισμό του γνωστοποιηθεί στο συμβολαιογράφο, ο οποίος και ορίζει το δικαστικό επιμελητή ο οποίος θα ενεργήσει την εκτέλεση.

Εάν, για οποιονδήποτε λόγο, δεν είναι δυνατό να ορισθεί συμβολαιογράφος του τόπου εκτέλεσης, αρμόδιος για τη διανομή μπορεί να οριστεί και συμβολαιογράφος διορισμένος στην περιφέρεια του συμβολαιογραφικού συλλόγου του τόπου εκτέλεσης ή, αν και αυτό δεν είναι δυνατό, του συμβολαιογραφικού συλλόγου της πρωτεύουσας του κράτους.

Άρθρο 989

Η καταφατική δήλωση του άρθρου 988 αποτελεί τίτλο εκτελεστό κατά του τρίτου. Τον εκτελεστήριο τύπο τον δίνει ο ειρηνοδίκης στη γραμματεία του οποίου έγινε η δήλωση.

Άρθρο 990

Αν η ανακοπή του άρθρου 986 γίνει δεκτή, το δικαστήριο με την απόφασή του υποχρεώνει τον τρίτο να καταβάλει το κατασχεμένο ποσό ή να παραδώσει το κατασχεμένο πράγμα, τηρούνται όμως οι διατάξεις του άρθρου 988.

Article 986

Within 30 days of the declaration referred to in Article 985 being filed, the garnishor has the right to file an opposition against [such declaration] before the court referred to in Articles 12 *et seq.* and 23 *et seq.* The opposition may also include a claim for compensation under Article 985(3).

The hearing of the opposition must be set within 120 days of the date from the date it was filed, and [the opposition] may also be served on the authorised lawyer who signed the declaration being contested. The opposition shall be tried under the special procedure on property disputes laid down in Articles 614 *et seq.*

Article 987

The third party does not have the right to contest the validity of the garnishment unless the garnishment order does not contain the information required in Article 963 or was not notified to the person enforcement concerns.

Article 988

1. If the third party declares that the garnished claim exists and is sufficient to satisfy [the claim of] said party or the garnishors, the third party is obligated, after eight days have elapsed from notification of the garnishment to the person enforcement concerns, if they are domiciled in Greece, and 30 days, if they are domiciled abroad or have no known place of residence, to pay the amount for which garnishment is taking place to each of the garnishors. If the garnished claim is not sufficient to satisfy [the claims of] all the persons who procured garnishment, the third party shall be obligated to make a deposit to the state and the distribution shall be carried out by a notary public designated, following a request by any person with a legitimate interest, by the court of the peace judge of the place of enforcement in accordance with the procedure laid down in Articles 686 *et seq.* If a notary public of the place of enforcement cannot be designated for any reason, then a notary public from the district of the notarial association of the place of enforcement may be designated as competent to effect distribution and, if this is also not possible, from the notarial association of the capital. Distribution to the persons who procured garnishment shall take place in accordance with Articles 974 *et seq.*, and the deadline set in Article 974(1) shall commence after the notary public has been notified of the decision of the court of the peace judge appointing them.

2. If the third party declares that they have the garnished thing in their possession, an auction shall be held in the presence of a notary public designated in accordance with paragraph 1. The auction shall be held in accordance with Article 959 *et seq.*, with Article 955(2)(b) also applying, the deadline for which shall commence after the court of the peace decision designating the notary public has been notified to them, and the notary public shall designate a court process server to effect enforcement.

If a notary public of the place of enforcement cannot be designated for any reason, then a notary public from the district of the notarial association of the place of enforcement may be designated as competent to effect distribution and, if this is also not possible, from the notarial association of the capital.

Article 989

An affirmative declaration in accordance with Article 988 constitutes an enforceable title against the third party. The enforcement form shall be given by the court of the peace judge at the registry where the declaration was made.

Article 990

If the opposition referred to in Article 986 is accepted, the court shall hand down a judgment ordering the third party to pay the garnished amount or hand over the garnished thing, on the proviso that the provisions of Articles 988 are applied.

Άρθρο 991

Αν η κατασχεμένη απαίτηση ασφαλίζεται με ενέχυρο ή υποθήκη, εφαρμόζονται και οι διατάξεις των άρθρων 458 και 1312 του Αστικού Κώδικα. Η σημείωση στα δημόσια βιβλία γίνεται μετά την καταφατική δήλωση ή την τελεσιδικία της απόφασης που δέχεται την ανακοπή κατά της δήλωσης του τρίτου.

Άρθρο 991Α

Αν αντικείμενο της κατάσχεσης είναι κινητές αξίες ή χρηματοπιστωτικά μέσα που τηρούνται σε άυλη μορφή και εκποιούνται σε χρηματιστήριο ή άλλη ρυθμιζόμενη αγορά που λειτουργεί στην ημεδαπή, εφαρμόζονται αναλόγως οι διατάξεις των άρθρων 983 επόμενα. Η κατάσχεση θεωρείται ως κατάσχεση πράγματος που βρίσκεται στα χέρια τρίτου. Η εκποίηση των κινητών αξιών ή των χρηματοπιστωτικών μέσων που κατασχέθηκαν γίνεται στο πλαίσιο δημόσιου αναγκαστικού πλειστηριασμού, σύμφωνα με τη διαδικασία που προβλέπεται σε αποφάσεις της Επιτροπής Κεφαλαιαγοράς.

Άρθρο 991Β

Αν αντικείμενο της κατάσχεσης είναι μερίδια οργανισμών συλλογικών επενδύσεων, εφαρμόζονται αναλόγως οι διατάξεις των άρθρων 983 επόμενα. Η κατάσχεση θεωρείται ως κατάσχεση απαίτησης στα χέρια τρίτου και καταλαμβάνει την αξίωση του οφειλέτη για εξαγορά των μεριδίων. Ως τρίτος προς τον οποίον επιδίδεται το προβλεπόμενο στο άρθρο 983 έγγραφο νοείται η εταιρεία διαχείρισης που έχει εκδώσει τα μερίδια.

ΚΕΦΑΛΑΙΟ Ε'
Κατάσχεση ακινήτων, πλοίων ή αεροσκαφών του οφειλέτη.

Άρθρο 992

1. Μπορεί να γίνει κατάσχεση ακινήτου που ανήκει στην κυριότητα του οφειλέτη ή εμπράγματου δικαιώματος του οφειλέτη επάνω σε ακίνητο. Ακίνητο που έχει μεταβιβαστεί από τον οφειλέτη σε τρίτο κατάσχεται στην περιουσία του οφειλέτη από το δανειστή που πέτυχε τη διάρρηξη της μεταβίβασης αυτής ως καταδολιευτικής, κατά τα άρθρα 939 επ. του Αστικού Κώδικα, αφού η απόφαση που απαγγέλει τη διάρρηξη σημειωθεί στο περιθώριο της μεταγραφής της απαλλοτριωτικής πράξης. Οι διατάξεις για την κατάσχεση ακινήτου εφαρμόζονται και για την κατάσχεση δικαιωμάτων στα οποία ισχύουν οι σχετικοί με τα ακίνητα κανόνες, καθώς και για την κατάσχεση πλοίων και αεροσκαφών.
2. Η κατάσχεση ακινήτου εκτείνεται και στα συστατικά του, καθώς και στα παραρτήματά του μόνο αν περιληφθούν σ' αυτήν. Αν τα παραρτήματα δεν έχουν περιληφθεί στην κατάσχεση του ακινήτου, μπορούν να κατασχεθούν σύμφωνα με την διαδικασία της κατάσχεσης κινητών πραγμάτων.
3. Αν το κατασχεμένο είναι ασφαλισμένο, η κατάσχεση ισχύει και για την αποζημίωση που οφείλεται από την ασφάλιση.

Άρθρο 993

1. Η κατάσχεση γίνεται με τη σύνταξη έκθεσης από το δικαστικό επιμελητή μπροστά σ' έναν ενήλικο μάρτυρα. Η κατάσχεση του ενυπόθηκου κτήματος μπορεί να γίνει είτε κατά του οφειλέτη είτε κατά του τρίτου κυρίου είτε κατά εκείνου που νέμεται με νόμιμο τίτλο το ενυπόθηκο κτήμα, αφού κοινοποιηθεί η επιταγή στον οφειλέτη και στον τρίτο. Η προθεσμία του άρθρου 926 αρχίζει από την τελευταία κοινοποίηση.

Article 991

If the garnished claim is secured by a pledge or mortgage, the provisions of Articles 458 and 1312 of the Civil Code also apply. The note shall be made in the public registers after the affirmative declaration [has been made] or after the judgment accepting the opposition against the third party's declaration has become *de jure* non-appealable.

Article 991A

If the garnishment involves transferable securities or financial instruments kept in dematerialised form and sold on a stock exchange or other regulated market operating in Greece, the provisions of Articles 983 *et seq.* apply *mutatis mutandis*. Garnishment shall be deemed to be garnishment of the thing held by a third party. The transferable securities or financial instruments garnished shall be sold in the context of a public forced auction, in accordance with the procedure laid down in decisions of the Hellenic Capital Market Commission.

Article 991B

If the garnishment involves units in collective investment undertakings, the provisions of Articles 983 *et seq.* apply *mutatis mutandis*. The garnishment shall be deemed to be garnishment of a claim in the possession of a third party and shall cover the debtor's claim for acquisition of the units. The management company that issued the units shall be deemed to be the third party on whom the document referred to in Article 983 is served.

CHAPTER V
Attachment of immovables, arrest of ships or aircraft of the debtor

Article 992

1. An immovable owned by the debtor or a right *in rem* of the debtor over the immovable may be attached. An immovable transferred by the debtor to a third party shall be attached as part of the assets of the debtor by the creditor who successfully challenged the transfer as fraudulent in accordance with Articles 939 *et seq.* of the Civil Code, after the judgment pronouncing the successful challenge is noted in the margin of the entry of the alienation deed [in the register]. The provisions on the attachment of an immovable also apply to the attachment of rights to which the rules concerning immovables apply, as well as to the arrest of ships and aircraft.

2. The attachment of an immovable shall also extend to its constituent parts, as well as to its accessories only if they are included in the attachment. If the accessories were not included in the attachment of the immovable, they may be attached under the procedure for the attachment of movables.

3. If the attached thing is insured, the attachment shall also apply to the insurance compensation.

Article 993

1. Attachment shall be done by the court process server preparing a report in the presence of an adult witness. The attachment of a mortgaged property may concern the debtor or the third-party owner or the person possessing the mortgaged property under a legitimate title, after the order is notified to the debtor and the third party. The deadline set in Article 926 shall commence from the date of the most recent notification.

2. Οι διατάξεις των παρ. 1 εδάφιο β' και 2 έως 4 του άρθρου 954 εφαρμόζονται και εδώ, με εξαίρεση τον χρόνο διενέργειας του πλειστηριασμού, ο οποίος ορίζεται υποχρεωτικά σε επτά (7) μήνες από την ημερομηνία περάτωσης της κατάσχεσης και πάντως όχι μετά την παρέλευση οκτώ (8) μηνών από την ημερομηνία αυτή. Εάν η παραπάνω προθεσμία συμπληρώνεται τον μήνα Αύγουστο, τότε για τον υπολογισμό της λαμβάνεται υπόψη ο επόμενος μήνας. Το κατασχεμένο ακίνητο πρέπει, ύστερα από επιτόπια μετάβαση του δικαστικού επιμελητή, να περιγράφεται με ακρίβεια ως προς το είδος, τη θέση, τα όρια και την έκτασή του, με τα συστατικά και τα παραρτήματα που κατασχέθηκαν, ώστε να μη χωρεί αμφιβολία για την ταυτότητά του. Για την εκτίμηση της αξίας του ακινήτου, που κατάσχεται, λαμβάνεται υπόψη η εμπορική του αξία, όπως αυτή προσδιορίζεται κατά τον χρόνο της κατάσχεσης.
3. Για την επιβολή της κατάσχεσης και την περιγραφή του ακινήτου ο δικαστικός επιμελητής έχει το δικαίωμα να εισέρχεται σε αυτό έστω και αν κατέχεται από τρίτο.

Άρθρο 994

Αν μαζί με το ακίνητο κατασχέθηκαν και τα παραρτήματά του, το αρμόδιο κατά το άρθρο 933 δικαστήριο, ύστερα από αίτηση όποιου έχει έννομο συμφέρον, μπορεί, δικάζοντας κατά τη διαδικασία των άρθρων 686 επ., να διατάξει να πλειστηριαστούν χωριστά, κατά τη διαδικασία του πλειστηριασμού κινητών πραγμάτων, εφόσον κρίνει ότι αυτό συμφέρει περισσότερο, οπότε και ορίζει προθεσμία για την επίσπευση του πλειστηριασμού.

Άρθρο 995
Επιδόσεις αντιγράφου ή περίληψης έκθεσης κατάθεσης

1. Αντίγραφο της κατασχετήριας έκθεσης επιδίδεται μόλις περατωθεί η κατάσχεση στον καθ' ου η εκτέλεση, αν ήταν παρών, και, αν αυτός αρνηθεί να παραλάβει το έγγραφο που του επιδίδεται, ο επιμελητής συντάσσει έκθεση για την άρνησή του. Αν είναι απών ή δεν είναι δυνατή η άμεση κατάρτιση του αντιγράφου, η επίδοση γίνεται το αργότερο την επομένη της ημέρας που έγινε η κατάσχεση, εφόσον εκείνος κατά του οποίου στρέφεται η εκτέλεση έχει την κατοικία του στην περιφέρεια του δήμου όπου έγινε η κατάσχεση, διαφορετικά μέσα σε οκτώ (8) ημέρες από την κατάσχεση. Η παράλειψη των διατυπώσεων αυτών επιφέρει ακυρότητα. Ως τιμή πρώτης προσφοράς για τον πλειστηριασμό ακινήτου ορίζεται η εμπορική του αξία, όπως αυτή προσδιορίζεται κατά τον χρόνο της κατάσχεσης κατά το π.δ. 59/2016 (Α' 95).
2. Με ποινή ακυρότητας, αντίγραφο της κατασχετήριας έκθεσης επιδίδεται στον υποθηκοφύλακα (κτηματολόγιο) της περιφέρειας όπου βρίσκεται το κατασχεμένο μέσα σε πέντε (5) ημέρες από την κατάσχεση. Αν πρόκειται για πλοία νηολογημένα στην Ελλάδα, η επίδοση γίνεται σε εκείνον που τηρεί το νηολόγιο, όπου είναι γραμμένο το πλοίο, και αν πρόκειται για αεροσκάφη γραμμένα σε μητρώο που τηρείται στην Ελλάδα, η επίδοση γίνεται σε εκείνον που το τηρεί. Ο υποθηκοφύλακας ή όποιος τηρεί το νηολόγιο ή το μητρώο οφείλει να εγγράφει την ίδια ημέρα την κατάσχεση σε ειδικό βιβλίο κατασχέσεων που τηρείται για το σκοπό αυτό και να παραδώσει μέσα σε προθεσμία πέντε (5) ημερών, αφότου κατά τα προαναφερόμενα του έγινε η επίδοση, το σχετικό πιστοποιητικό βαρών στον αρμόδιο για την εκτέλεση δικαστικό επιμελητή, ενώ ο γραμματέας του ειρηνοδικείου οφείλει αυθημερόν να καταχωρίσει την κατασχετήρια έκθεση σε ειδικό βιβλίο με αλφαβητικό ευρετήριο, με βάση τα ονοματεπώνυμα των καθ' ων η κατάσχεση.
3. Αν πρόκειται για κατάσχεση ενυπόθηκου κτήματος και η κατάσχεση έγινε κατά του τρίτου, κυρίου ή νομέα, πρέπει να επιδοθεί σ' αυτόν και στον οφειλέτη αντίγραφο της κατασχετήριας έκθεσης, αλλιώς επέρχεται ακυρότητα. Αν η κατάσχεση έγινε κατά του οφειλέτη, πρέπει να επιδοθεί στον τρίτο, κύριο ή νομέα, αντίγραφο της κατασχετήριας έκθεσης, αλλιώς επέρχεται ακυρότητα.

2. The provisions of the second sentence of paragraph 1 and the provisions of paragraphs 2 and 4 of Article 954 also apply in this case, except for the time at which the auction is held, which must be set within seven months of the date of completion of the attachment and, in all cases, no later than eight months after that date has elapsed. If the above deadline lapses in August, the following month shall be taken into account for the above calculation. Following an on-the-spot visit by the court process server, the attached immovable must be precisely described in terms of type, location, boundaries and area, including the constituent parts and accessories which were attached, so that there can be no doubts concerning its identity. In valuing the attached immovable, its commercial value, as determined at the time of attachment, shall be taken into account.
3. The court process server has the right to enter the immovable, even if it is under the detentorship of a third party, in order to impose the attachment and prepare the description of the immovable.

Article 994

If the accessories of the immovable were attached together with it, the court with jurisdiction under Article 933 may, following an application filed by any person with a legitimate interest and trying the matter under the procedure laid down in Articles 686 *et seq.*, order that they be auctioned separately under the procedure for the auctioning of movables, where the court considers that this is more advantageous, and shall set a deadline for the auction to be held.

Article 995
Service of a copy or summary of an [attachment] report

1. Once attachment is completed, a copy of the attachment report shall be served on the person enforcement concerns, if present, and if they refuse to take receipt of the document being served, the court process server shall prepare a report on such refusal. If that person is absent or the copy cannot be prepared immediately, service shall be effected no later than the day after the date of completion of the attachment, where the person enforcement concerns is domiciled in the district of the municipality where attachment took place, otherwise within eight days of the date of the attachment. Failure to comply with these formalities shall result in nullity. The starting price for the auctioning of an immovable shall be its market value, as determined at the time of attachment in accordance with Presidential Decree 59/2016 (Government Gazette, Series I, Issue 95).
2. On penalty of nullity, a copy of the attachment report shall be served on the land registrar (cadastral [officer]) of the district where the attached immovable is located within five days of the attachment. In cases of ships registered in Greece, service shall be effected on the person keeping the ship registry in which the ship is registered, and in the case of aircraft registered in a registry kept in Greece, service shall be effected on the person keeping that registry. The land registrar or the person keeping the ship or [aircraft] registry is obligated to enter the attachment/arrest on the same day in a special attachment/arrest register kept for this purpose, and, within a deadline of five days and after having been served in accordance with the foregoing, to deliver the relevant encumbrance certificate to the court process server competent for carrying out enforcement, while the court of the peace registrar is obligated to enter the attachment/arrest report on the same day in a special register with an alphabetical index based on the full names of the persons whom attachment/arrest concerns.
3. In the case of attachment of a mortgaged property where attachment concerned a third party, whether owner or possessor, a copy of the attachment report must, on penalty of nullity, be served on that third party and on the debtor. If the attachment concerned the debtor, a copy of the attachment report must, on penalty of nullity, be served on the third party, whether owner or possessor.

4. Ο δικαστικός επιμελητής οφείλει, μέσα σε είκοσι (20) ημέρες από την κατάσχεση, να καταθέσει στον υπάλληλο του πλειστηριασμού τον εκτελεστό τίτλο, την έκθεση επίδοσης της επιταγής της εκτέλεσης, την κατασχετήρια έκθεση και τις εκθέσεις επίδοσής της στον οφειλέτη, τον τρίτο κύριο ή νομέα και τον υποθηκοφύλακα ή όποιον τηρεί το νηολόγιο ή το μητρώο, το πιστοποιητικό βαρών, καθώς και, σε έντυπη και ψηφιακή μορφή, την έκθεση εκτίμησης του πιστοποιημένου εκτιμητή του π.δ. 59/2016. Ο υπάλληλος του πλειστηριασμού συντάσσει έκθεση για όλα αυτά. Απόσπασμα της κατασχετήριας έκθεσης, που περιλαμβάνει τα ονοματεπώνυμα του υπέρ ου και του καθ' ου η εκτέλεση, καθώς και τον αριθμό φορολογικού μητρώου αυτών και, αν πρόκειται για νομικά πρόσωπα, την επωνυμία και τον αριθμό φορολογικού τους μητρώου, συνοπτική περιγραφή του ακινήτου που κατασχέθηκε κατά το είδος, τη θέση, τα όρια και την έκτασή του, με τα συστατικά και όσα παραρτήματα συγκατάσχονται, καθώς και μνεία των υποθηκών ή προσημειώσεων που υπάρχουν επάνω στο ακίνητο, την τιμή της πρώτης προσφοράς, του ποσού για το οποίο γίνεται η κατάσχεση, τους όρους του πλειστηριασμού, που θέτει ο υπέρ ου η εκτέλεση και που γνωστοποιήθηκαν στον δικαστικό επιμελητή με την εντολή για εκτέλεση του άρθρου 927 και το όνομα και τη διεύθυνση του υπαλλήλου του πλειστηριασμού, καθώς και τον τόπο, την ημέρα και την ώρα του πλειστηριασμού, εκδίδεται από τον δικαστικό επιμελητή και δημοσιεύεται με επιμέλεια αυτού μέχρι την δέκατη πέμπτη ημέρα από την κατάσχεση στην ιστοσελίδα δημοσιεύσεων πλειστηριασμών του Δελτίου Δικαστικών Δημοσιεύσεων του Ηλεκτρονικού Εθνικού Φορέα Κοινωνικής Ασφάλισης (e- ΕΦΚΑ). Στο απόσπασμα περιλαμβάνεται και η βεβαίωση του δικαστικού επιμελητή, σχετικά με την αδυναμία ορισμού συμβολαιογράφου του τόπου εκτέλεσης ή της Περιφέρειας του συμβολαιογραφικού συλλόγου του τόπου εκτέλεσης. Το απόσπασμα επιδίδεται μέσα στην ίδια προθεσμία στον τρίτο κύριο ή νομέα και στους ενυπόθηκους δανειστές. Ο πλειστηριασμός δεν μπορεί να γίνει χωρίς να τηρηθούν οι διατυπώσεις των προηγούμενων εδαφίων, διαφορετικά είναι άκυρος. Ο δικαστικός επιμελητής παραδίδει στον υπάλληλο του πλειστηριασμού, σε ηλεκτρονική μορφή, φωτογραφίες του κατασχεθέντος ακινήτου, τις οποίες λαμβάνει κατά την επιτόπια μετάβασή του σε αυτό. Η λήψη τους από τον υπάλληλο του πλειστηριασμού αναφέρεται στην παραπάνω έκθεση. Τα πληροφοριακά στοιχεία, τα οποία περιλαμβάνονται στο απόσπασμα της κατασχετήριας έκθεσης, καθώς και η έκθεση του πιστοποιημένου εκτιμητή και οι φωτογραφίες αναρτώνται από τον υπάλληλο του πλειστηριασμού στο ηλεκτρονικό σύστημα πλειστηριασμού.

5. Εφόσον δεν ορίζεται διαφορετικά, οι διατάξεις των άρθρων 972 και 973 εφαρμόζονται και εδώ.

Άρθρο 996

1. Μεσεγγυούχος του ακινήτου είναι όποιος το κατέχει όταν γίνεται η κατάσχεση. Αν το ζητήσει οποιοσδήποτε έχει έννομο συμφέρον, ο ειρηνοδίκης της περιφέρειας όπου βρίσκεται το κατασχεμένο μπορεί, δικάζοντας κατά τη διαδικασία των άρθρων 686 επ., να ορίζει άλλο μεσεγγυούχο ή να το αντικαθιστά, καθώς και να αποφασίζει για κάθε αμφισβήτηση που αφορά την μεσεγγύηση. Οι διατάξεις των παρ. 4 και 5 του άρθρου 956 εφαρμόζονται και εδώ.

2. Οι φυσικοί καρποί του κατασχεμένου που συλλέγονται μετά την επιβολή της κατάσχεσης εκποιούνται από το μεσεγγυούχο εκτός αν, ύστερα από αίτηση του δανειστή που επέβαλε την κατάσχεση ή του οφειλέτη, ο ειρηνοδίκης της περιφέρειας όπου βρίσκεται το κατασχεμένο, δικάζοντας κατά τη διαδικασία των άρθρων 686 επ., διατάξει να πουληθούν σε πλειστηριασμό. Το προϊόν της εκποίησης των φυσικών καρπών κατατίθεται δημόσια. Αν το κατασχεμένο αγροτικό ή άλλο προσοδοφόρο ακίνητο είναι εκμισθωμένο, οι φυσικοί καρποί που έχουν συλλεγεί μετά την κατάσχεση ανήκουν στο μισθωτή που έχει υποχρέωση να καταθέσει δημόσια το μίσθωμα.

3. Από την εγγραφή της κατάσχεσης στο βιβλίο των κατασχέσεων ο μεσεγγυούχος εισπράττει και καταθέτει δημόσια τις προσόδους του κατασχεμένου πράγματος που προέρχεται από έννομο σχέση. Ο οφειλέτης από την έννομη σχέση καταβάλλει έγκυρα σε εκείνον κατά του οποίου έχει στραφεί η εκτέλεση πριν εκείνος ο οποίος επέβαλε την κατάσχεση τον ειδοποιήσει εγγράφως για την επιβολή της.

4. Οι διατάξεις του άρθρου 956 παρ. 7 εφαρμόζονται και εδώ.

4. Within 20 days of the attachment/arrest, the court process server is obligated to file with the auctioneer the enforceable title, the enforcement order service report, the attachment/arrest report and the reports on its service to the debtor, the third party, whether owner or possessor, and the land registrar or the person keeping the ship registry or [aircraft] registry, the encumbrance certificate, as well as the valuation report prepared by a certified valuer under Presidential Decree 59/2016, in hard copy and electronic form. The auctioneer shall prepare a report on all the foregoing. An excerpt of the attachment report, containing the full names of the person for whose benefit or against whom enforcement was done, as well as their tax identification numbers and, in the case of legal persons, their corporate names and tax identification numbers, a brief description of the attached immovable in terms of type, location, boundaries and area, including any constituent parts and accessories which were also attached, as well as reference to any mortgages or prenotations of mortgage on the immovable, the starting price, the amount for which attachment is taking place, the auction terms set by the person for whose benefit enforcement is being done and notified to the court process server together with enforcement instructions under Article 927 and the name and address of the auctioneer, as well as the place, date and time of the auction, shall be issued and published by a court process server no later than 15 days after the attachment, on the auctions announcement website of the Court Announcements Bulletin of the e-National Social Security Fund. The excerpt shall also contain confirmation prepared by the court process server on the inability to appoint a notary public of the place of enforcement or the district of the notarial association of the place of enforcement. The excerpt shall be served within the same deadline on the third party, whether owner or possessor, and on the mortgagees. Any auction not held in compliance with the formalities laid down in the preceding subparagraphs is null and void. The court process server shall provide the auctioneer with photographs of the attached immovable, in electronic form, taken during their on-the-spot visit to the immovable. The auctioneer shall note the fact that such photographs were received in the aforesaid report. The information contained in the excerpt of the attachment report, as well as the report prepared by the certified valuer and the photographs, shall be uploaded by the auctioneer to the e-auction system.
5. Unless otherwise provided for, the provisions of Articles 972 and 973 also apply in this case.

Article 996

1. Any person with detentorship of the immovable when attachment takes place shall be the sequestrator. If so requested by any person with a legitimate interest, the court of the peace judge in the district where the attached immovable is located may, trying the matter under the procedure laid down in Articles 686 *et seq.*, designate a different sequestrator or replace them, and rule on any challenge concerning the sequestrator. The provisions of Article 956(4) and (5) also apply in such cases.
2. The natural fruits of the attached immovable collected after attachment had been imposed shall be sold by the sequestrator, unless, following an application filed by the creditor who procured the attachment or the debtor, the court of the peace judge in the district where the attached immovable is located, trying the matter under the procedure laid down in Articles 686 *et seq.*, orders their sale at auction. The proceeds of sale of the natural fruits shall be deposited with the state. If the attached agricultural or other revenue-generating immovable is under a lease, the natural fruits collected after the attachment shall belong to the lessee, who is obligated to deposit the rent with the state.
3. Once the attachment has been entered in the attachment register, the sequestrator shall collect the revenues from the attached thing arising from any legal relationship and deposit them with the state. Any payment made by the debtor under the legal relationship to the person the enforcement concerned before being notified by the person who procured attachment of such imposition shall be valid.
4. The provisions of Article 956(7) also apply in this case.

Άρθρο 997

1. Απαγορεύεται και είναι άκυρη υπέρ εκείνου που επέβαλε την κατάσχεση και υπέρ των δανειστών που αναγγέλθηκαν η διάθεση του κατασχεμένου από τον οφειλέτη· αν πρόκειται για ενυπόθηκο ακίνητο είναι άκυρη η διάθεσή του και από τον τρίτο, κύριο ή νομέα. Μετά την κατάσχεση του ακινήτου η εκμίσθωσή του από τον οφειλέτη ή τον τρίτο κύριο ή νομέα ή η παραχώρηση της χρήσης ή κατοχής του με βάση άλλη έννομη σχέση μπορεί να καταγγελθεί από τον υπερθεματιστή μέσα σε προθεσμία δύο (2) μηνών από τη μεταγραφή της περίληψης της κατακυρωτικής έκθεσης. Με την καταγγελία αυτή η μίσθωση ή άλλη έννομη σχέση λύεται μετά από δύο (2) μήνες και χωρεί η κατά το άρθρο 1005 παρ. 2 εκτέλεση. Δικαίωμα καταγγελίας της μίσθωσης κατά το άρθρο 615 ΑΚ δεν θίγεται και η περίληψη εκτελείται κατά του μισθωτή αφού περάσουν οι προθεσμίες του άρθρου αυτού που αρχίζουν αφότου η περίληψη επιδοθεί στο μισθωτή.

2. Τα αποτελέσματα της παρ. 1 αρχίζουν αναδρομικά:

α) για τον οφειλέτη, αφότου του επιδοθεί σύμφωνα με το άρθρο 995 αντίγραφο της κατασχετήριας έκθεσης ή συνταχθεί η έκθεση, που πιστοποιεί την άρνησή του να παραλάβει το αντίγραφο κατά το πρώτο εδάφιο της παρ. 1 του άρθρου 995, με την προϋπόθεση ότι θα ακολουθήσει η επίδοση του αντιγράφου της κατασχετήριας έκθεσης μέσα σε προθεσμία οκτώ (8) ημερών,

β) για τον τρίτο, κύριο ή νομέα, αφότου του επιδοθεί σύμφωνα με το άρθρο 995 αντίγραφο της κατασχετήριας έκθεσης ή συνταχθεί η έκθεση, που πιστοποιεί την άρνησή του να παραλάβει το αντίγραφο κατά το άρθρο 995 παρ. 1 και 4, με την προϋπόθεση ότι θα ακολουθήσει η επίδοση του αντιγράφου της κατασχετήριας έκθεσης εντός προθεσμίας οκτώ (8) ημερών,

γ) για τους τρίτους, μόνο αφότου η κατάσχεση εγγραφεί κατά το άρθρο 995 στο βιβλίο κατασχέσεων και εφόσον έγιναν οι, κατά τις περ. α' και β' της παραγράφου αυτής, επιδόσεις στον οφειλέτη και τον τρίτο, κύριο ή νομέα.

3. Σε όποιον επέβαλε την κατάσχεση και στους δανειστές που αναγγέλθηκαν δεν αντιτάσσεται η μεταγραφή ή η εγγραφή υποθήκης που έγινε μετά την εγγραφή της κατάσχεσης στο βιβλίο κατασχέσεων σε οποιονδήποτε τίτλο και αν στηρίζεται η υποθήκη. Η τροπή της προσημείωσης σε υποθήκη, που έγινε μετά την εγγραφή της κατάσχεσης, είναι έγκυρη και για το δανειστή που επέβαλε την κατάσχεση και για τους δανειστές που έχουν αναγγελθεί.

4. Αν συμπέσει την ίδια ημέρα εγγραφή κατάσχεσης και μεταγραφή ή εγγραφή υποθήκης στο ίδιο ακίνητο, προτιμάται αυτή που καταχωρίστηκε έστω και ελάχιστο χρόνο νωρίτερα.

5. Μετά την εγγραφή της αναγκαστικής κατάσχεσης στο βιβλίο κατασχέσεων επιτρέπεται να επιβληθεί και άλλη αναγκαστική κατάσχεση επάνω στο ίδιο ακίνητο από άλλο δανειστή του οφειλέτη. Οι διαφορετικές διαδικασίες αναγκαστικής εκτέλεσης διενεργούνται ξεχωριστά, χωρίς να επηρεάζει η μια την άλλη. Δεν επιτρέπεται η αναζήτηση των εξόδων της εκτέλεσης που προκατέβαλε εκείνος ο δανειστής, η εκτέλεση του οποίου δεν περατώθηκε.

6. Ο κατασχών ή ο δικαστικός επιμελητής που επέβαλε την κατάσχεση μπορεί με την επίδειξη αντιγράφου της κατασχετήριας έκθεσης να ζητήσει και να λάβει από τις αρμόδιες Δ.Ο.Υ. αντίγραφα των προ της κατασχέσεως μισθωτηρίων και από τις αρμόδιες πολεοδομίες τον φάκελο του ακινήτου.

Άρθρο 998

1. Το κατασχεμένο ακίνητο πλειστηριάζεται με ηλεκτρονικά μέσα ενώπιον του συμβολαιογράφου της εφετειακής περιφέρειας όπου βρίσκεται το ακίνητο. Εάν, για οποιονδήποτε λόγο, δεν είναι δυνατό να ορισθεί συμβολαιογράφος του τόπου εκτέλεσης (κατάσχεσης), το κατασχεμένο ακίνητο πλειστηριάζεται ενώπιον συμβολαιογράφου διορισμένου στην περιφέρεια του συμβολαιογραφικού συλλόγου του τόπου εκτέλεσης ή, αν και αυτό δεν είναι δυνατό, του συμβολαιογραφικού συλλόγου της πρωτεύουσας του Κράτους. Το άρθρο 959 εφαρμόζεται και στον πλειστηριασμό ακινήτων.

Article 997

1. Disposal of the attached immovable by the debtor is prohibited and null and void vis-à-vis the person who procured attachment and creditors who lodged claims; in the case of a mortgaged immovable, its disposal by the third party, whether owner or possessor, is also null and void. Once the immovable has been attached, its leasing by the debtor or third party, whether owner or possessor, or granting of its use or detentorship under a different legal relationship may be terminated by the highest bidder within a deadline of two months from the date the summary of the award report was entered [in the register]. Following such termination, the lease or other legal relationship shall end after two months, and enforcement under Article 1005(2) shall take place. The right to terminate the lease under Article 615 of the Civil Code shall not be prejudiced, and the summary shall be enforced against the lessee after the deadlines referred to in this Article, which commence after the summary is served on the lessee, have lapsed.

2. The effects referred to in paragraph 1 shall commence retroactively:

a) for the debtor, after the copy of the attachment report is served on them in accordance with Article 995 or the report certifying their refusal to accept the copy is prepared in accordance with Article 995(1), on condition that the copy of the attachment report is subsequently served within a deadline of eight days;

b) for the third party, whether owner or possessor, after the copy of the attachment report is served on them in accordance with Article 995 or the report certifying their refusal to accept the copy is prepared in accordance with Article 995(1) and (4), on condition that the copy of the attachment report is subsequently served within a deadline of eight days;

c) for third parties, only after the attachment has been entered in the attachment register in accordance with Article 995 and provided service was effected on the debtor and the third party, whether owner or possessor, in accordance with cases (a) and (b) of this paragraph.

3. The transcription or registration of a mortgage made after the attachment was entered in the attachment register, irrespective of the title on which the mortgage is based, does not generate effects in relation to any person who procured the attachment and creditors who lodged claims. The conversion of a prenotation to a mortgage done after the attachment was registered shall also be valid for the creditor who procured the attachment and for creditors who lodged claims.

4. If, with regard to the same immovable, attachment was registered and a mortgage was transcribed or registered on the same day, preference shall be given to whichever one occurred even a minimum amount of time earlier.

5. Following registration of the compulsory attachment in the attachment register, a different compulsory attachment may be procured for the same immovable by a different creditor of the debtor. The different compulsory enforcement proceedings shall be conducted separately and one shall not affect the other. The costs of enforcement paid in advance by a creditor whose enforcement was not completed may not be recovered.

6. The person who procured attachment or the court process server who effected attachment may, by producing the attachment report, request and receive copies of lease agreements entered into prior to the attachment from the competent tax offices and the file concerning the immovable from the competent planning departments.

Article 998

1. The attached immovable shall be auctioned electronically in the presence of a notary public within the district of the court of appeal where the immovable is located. If a notary public from the place of enforcement (attachment) cannot be appointed for any reason, the attached immovable shall be auctioned in the presence of a notary public from the district of the notarial association of the place of enforcement or, if this is also not possible, from the notarial association of the capital. Article 959 also applies to the auctioning of immovables.

2. Ο πλειστηριασμός δεν μπορεί να γίνει από την 1η έως και τις 31 Αυγούστου, καθώς και την προηγουμένη και την επομένη εβδομάδα της ημέρας των εκλογών για την ανάδειξη βουλευτών, αντιπροσώπων στο Ευρωπαϊκό Κοινοβούλιο και Οργάνων Τοπικής Αυτοδιοίκησης. Η απαγόρευση αυτή ισχύει και για τις επαναληπτικές εκλογές και μόνο για τις περιφέρειες που διεξάγονται τέτοιες.
3. Η διάταξη της προηγούμενης παραγράφου σχετικά με την απαγόρευση πλειστηριασμού από την 1η έως και τις 31 Αυγούστου δεν εφαρμόζεται, όταν πρόκειται για πλοία και αεροσκάφη.
4. Αν τα κατασχεμένα πράγματα βρίσκονται στην περιφέρεια περισσότερων ειρηνοδικείων, ο πλειστηριασμός διενεργείται, κατ' επιλογή του επισπεύδοντος, στην περιφέρεια οποιουδήποτε εκ των άνω ειρηνοδικείων. Εάν ο πλειστηριασμός μπορεί να γίνει ηλεκτρονικά σε μία μόνο από αυτές, επιλέγεται υποχρεωτικά η περιφέρεια του συγκεκριμένου ειρηνοδικείου, και, αν για οποιονδήποτε λόγο, δεν μπορεί να διενεργηθεί σε καμία από αυτές, τότε επιλέγεται η περιφέρεια του συμβολαιογραφικού συλλόγου της πρωτεύουσας του κράτους. Αρμόδιο για την επίλυση των διαφορών που αναφύονται από τη διενέργεια του πλειστηριασμού είναι το δικαστήριο του τόπου εκτέλεσης.
5. Ύστερα από αίτηση οποιουδήποτε έχει έννομο συμφέρον, το δικαστήριο του άρθρου 933, δικάζοντας κατά τη διαδικασία των άρθρων 686 επ., μπορεί να διατάξει να γίνει ταυτόχρονα η πώληση του κατασχεμένου ακινήτου, ολόκληρου ή τμηματικά, με βάση σχεδιάγραμμα ή σχέδιο μηχανικού ή γεωμέτρηση, που υποβάλλεται μαζί με την αίτηση. Στην περίπτωση αυτή η κατακύρωση τότε μόνο γίνεται τμηματικά σε όποιους πλειοδοτούν τμηματικά, όταν το σύνολο των προσφορών τους είναι μεγαλύτερο από την τιμή που προσφέρεται για να πωληθεί συνολικά.
6. Μετά από αίτηση του οφειλέτη, το δικαστήριο του άρθρου 933, το οποίο δικάζει κατά τη διαδικασία των άρθρων 686 επ., μπορεί να επιτρέψει να πωληθεί ελεύθερα το ακίνητο με τίμημα το οπσοίο ορίζεται από το δικαστήριο. Η πώληση αυτή γίνεται από τον υπάλληλο του πλειστηριασμού το αργότερο δέκα (10) ημέρες πριν από τον πλειστηριασμό με ταυτόχρονη εξόφληση του τιμήματος. Αν η πώληση δεν πραγματοποιηθεί κατά το προηγούμενο εδάφιο, ο πλειστηριασμός διεξάγεται κατά την ορισθείσα ημερομηνία.

Άρθρα 998Α-999

[Καταργούνται]

Άρθρο 1000

Ύστερα από αίτηση του οφειλέτη, η οποία κατατίθεται, με ποινή απαραδέκτου, δεκαπέντε (15) τουλάχιστον εργάσιμες ημέρες πριν από την ημέρα του πλειστηριασμού, το δικαστήριο του άρθρου 933, δικάζοντας κατά τη διαδικασία των άρθρων 686 επ., μπορεί να αναστείλει τη διαδικασία του πλειστηριασμού έως έξι (6) μήνες από την αρχική ημέρα του πλειστηριασμού, αν δεν υπάρχει κίνδυνος βλάβης του επισπεύδοντος και εφόσον προσδοκάται βάσιμα ότι ο οφειλέτης θα ικανοποιήσει μέσα στο χρονικό αυτό διάστημα τον επισπεύδοντα ή ότι, αν περάσει το χρονικό αυτό διάστημα, θα επιτευχθεί μεγαλύτερο πλειστηρίασμα. Η απόφαση εκδίδεται υποχρεωτικά έως τις 12:00' το μεσημέρι της Δευτέρας που προηγείται του πλειστηριασμού και η αναστολή χορηγείται πάντοτε υπό τον όρο της καταβολής:
α) των τυχόν εξόδων επίσπευσης του πλειστηριασμού, τα οποία καθορίζονται κατά προσέγγιση στην απόφαση και
β) του ενός τετάρτου τουλάχιστον του οφειλόμενου κεφαλαίου στον επισπεύδοντα.
Η απόφαση με την οποία αναστέλλεται ο πλειστηριασμός γνωστοποιείται στον υπάλληλο του πλειστηριασμού αυθημερόν με την έκδοσή της. Η καταβολή γίνεται υποχρεωτικά μέχρι την 10.00 πρωινή της ημέρας διεξαγωγής του πλειστηριασμού και αν αυτή δεν γίνει ο πλειστηριασμός διεξάγεται κανονικά.

2. Auctions may not be held from 1 August to 31 August and during the week prior to and the week subsequent to elections for members of parliament, members of the European Parliament and local government authorities. This prohibition also applies to run-off elections and only in the districts where such elections are being held.
3. The provisions of the preceding paragraph on the prohibition of auctions from 1 August to 31 August do not apply to ships and aircraft.
4. If the attached things are located in the districts of several courts of the peace, the auction shall be held, at the choice of the expediting party, in the district of any of the aforesaid courts of the peace. If the auction can be held electronically in only one of these districts, the district of that specific court of the peace must be selected, and if the auction cannot be conducted in any of these districts, the district of the notarial association of the capital shall be selected. The court of the place of enforcement has jurisdiction to resolve disputes arising from how the auction was conducted.
5. Following an application filed by any person with a legitimate interest, the court with jurisdiction under Article 933 may, trying the matter under the procedure laid down in Articles 686 *et seq.*, simultaneously order sale of the attached immovable, in whole or in segments, on the basis of a diagram or plan drawn up by an engineer or land measurement [by a surveying engineer] submitted together with the application. In this case alone, the award shall take place in segments to the highest bidders for segments, when the entirety of their bids exceeds the price offered for sale as a whole.
6. Following an application filed by the debtor, the court with jurisdiction under Article 933 may, trying the matter under the procedure laid down in Articles 686 *et seq.*, allow the immovable to be sold freely at a price set by the court. This sale shall be done by the auctioneer no later than 10 days prior to the auction, with the price being paid in full at that time. If the sale is not done in accordance with the preceding subparagraph, the auction shall be held on the date set.

Articles 998A-999

[Repealed]

Article 1000

Following an application filed by the debtor, on penalty of inadmissibility, at least 15 working days prior to the date of the auction, the court with jurisdiction under Article 933 may, trying the matter under the procedure laid down in Articles 686 *et seq.*, stay the auction procedure for up to six months from the initial date of the auction, if there is no danger of harm being caused to the expediting party and it is reasonably expected that the debtor will satisfy the claim of the expediting party within that period or that a higher auction price will be achieved if the period in question elapses. The judgment must be handed down by 12:00 noon on the Monday prior to the auction, and the stay shall always be granted on condition of payment of:
a) any costs for expediting the auction, set approximately in the judgment; and
b) at least one quarter of the amount owed to the expediting party.
The judgment staying the auction shall be notified to the auctioneer on the same date it is handed down. Payment must be made by 10:00 on the morning of the auction and, if it is not made, the auction shall go ahead as normal.

Άρθρο 1001

Αν με την ίδια έκθεση κατασχέθηκαν περισσότερα ακίνητα που βρίσκονται στην ίδια περιφέρεια, αυτά πλειστηριάζονται χωριστά την ίδια ημέρα. Εκείνος κατά του οποίου στρέφεται η εκτέλεση, εφόσον το επιθυμεί, ορίζει εγγράφως προς τον υπάλληλο του πλειστηριασμού τη σειρά με την οποία θα κατακυρώνονται τα κατασχεμένα πράγματα, το αργότερο δύο (2) ημέρες πριν τη διενέργεια του πλειστηριασμού. Ο υπάλληλος του πλειστηριασμού δύναται να ορίσει ο ίδιος, σε περίπτωση μη έγγραφης ειδοποιήσεως του καθ' ου η εκτέλεση, τη σειρά κατακύρωσης. Από τη στιγμή που το πλειστηρίασμα καλύψει το ποσό της απαίτησης εκείνου υπέρ του οποίου έγινε η εκτέλεση και των δανειστών που αναγγέλθηκαν, καθώς και τα έξοδα της εκτέλεσης, δεν γίνεται κατακύρωση για τα λοιπά κατασχεθέντα ακίνητα και δεν συντάσσεται ως προς αυτά έκθεση πλειστηριασμού και κατακύρωσης.

Άρθρο 1001Α

Σε περίπτωση κατάσχεσης ακινήτων, στα οποία έχουν εγκατασταθεί βιομηχανικές, βιοτεχνικές, ξενοδοχειακές ή τουριστικές επιχειρήσεις ή άλλες παραγωγικές μονάδες, που διαθέτουν εξοπλισμό και αποτελούν οικονομικό σύνολο, εφαρμόζονται οι επόμενες διατάξεις:

α. Το ακίνητο εκτίθεται σε πλειστηριασμό με τα παραρτήματά του εφόσον έχουν κατασχεθεί μαζί. Χωριστή πλειστηρίαση των παραρτημάτων μπορεί να διαταχθεί, σύμφωνα με το άρθρο 994, μόνο αν κατά τον πρώτο πλειστηριασμό δεν επιτεύχθηκε κατακύρωση.

β. Αν έχουν κατασχεθεί με την ίδια έκθεση περισσότερα ακίνητα, πλειστηριάζονται μαζί, εφόσον έχουν λειτουργική ενότητα για την εξυπηρέτηση της επιχείρησης ή της παραγωγικής μονάδας, που έχει εγκατασταθεί σε ένα από αυτά. Αν τα παραπάνω ακίνητα βρίσκονται σε διάφορες περιφέρειες, αρμόδια για την εκτέλεση είναι τα όργανα της περιφέρειας στην οποία βρίσκεται οποιοδήποτε από αυτά κατ' επιλογή του επισπεύδοντος. Η διάταξη του άρθρου 998 παράγραφος 4 εφαρμόζεται αναλόγως.

γ. Η αναστολή κατά το άρθρο 1000 δεν μπορεί να υπερβεί συνολικά τους τέσσερις (4) μήνες.

Άρθρο 1002

1. Ο πλειστηριασμός ολοκληρώνεται με την κατακύρωση. Ο υπερθεματιστής δεσμεύεται ώσπου να γίνει καλύτερη προσφορά ή ώσπου να ματαιωθεί η κατακύρωση.

2. Έως την κατακύρωση εκείνος κατά του οποίου στρέφεται η εκτέλεση έχει δικαίωμα να εξοφλήσει τις απαιτήσεις εκείνου υπέρ του οποίου γίνεται η εκτέλεση και των δανειστών που έχουν τίτλο εκτελεστό και αναγγέλθηκαν, καθώς και τα έξοδα και το τέλος χρήσης του ηλεκτρονικού συστήματος πλειστηριασμού. Στην περίπτωση αυτή ο πλειστηριασμός ματαιώνεται και αίρεται η κατάσχεση.

3. Η παρ. 3 του άρθρου 969 εφαρμόζεται και εδώ.

Άρθρο 1003

1. Το ακίνητο που πλειστηριάζεται κατακυρώνεται σε εκείνον που προσφέρει τη μεγαλύτερη τιμή κατ' εφαρμογή των παρ. 1 και 2 του άρθρου 965.

2. Όποιος υπερθεματίζει για λογαριασμό τρίτου, οφείλει να δηλώσει προηγουμένως στον υπάλληλο του πλειστηριασμού τα πλήρη στοιχεία του τρίτου και να καταθέσει σε αυτόν ειδικό συμβολαιογραφικό πληρεξούσιο, με το οποίο του χορηγείται η σχετική εντολή.

3. Στην έκθεση της κατακύρωσης πρέπει να καταχωρίζονται και οι όροι που τυχόν έθεσε εκείνος προς όφελος του οποίου έγινε η εκτέλεση, όσοι αφορούν την κατακύρωση και δεσμεύουν τον υπερθεματιστή.

4. Οι διατάξεις των άρθρων 965 παρ. 4 έως 7 και 966 παρ. 1 έως 4 εφαρμόζονται αναλόγως.

Article 1001

If several immovables located in the same district were attached by means of the same report, they shall be auctioned separately on the same day. No later than two days prior to the auction, the person enforcement concerns shall, if they so wish, specify in writing to the auctioneer the order in which the attached things will be auctioned [and awarded]. If the person enforcement concerns fails to provide notification in writing, the auctioneer may themselves specify the order in which things will be auctioned [and awarded]. Once the auction price covers the amount of the claim of the person for whose benefit enforcement is being done and of the creditors who lodged claims, as well as the enforcement costs, the remaining attached immovables shall not be auctioned [and awarded], and no auction and award report shall be prepared concerning those immovables.

Article 1001A

In cases of attachment of immovables on which industrial, craft, hotel or tourism enterprises or other production units that have equipment and constitute a single economic entity have been established, the following provisions apply:

a. the immovable shall be placed on auction with its accessories, provided they were made subject to attachment together with the immovable. Separate auctioning of the accessories may be ordered, in accordance with Article 994, only if no award was made during the first auction;

b. if several immovables were made subject to attachment by means of the same report, they shall be auctioned together, provided they constitute a single functional entity in the service of the enterprise or production unit established on one such immovable. If the aforesaid immovables are located in different districts, officers from the district where any such immovable is located shall be competent to effect enforcement, at the choice of the expediting party. The provisions of Article 998(4) apply *mutatis mutandis*;

c. any stay under Article 1000 may not exceed four months in total.

Article 1002

1. The auction is completed upon award [of the immovables]. The highest bidder shall remain bound [by their bid] until a higher bid is submitted or the award is cancelled.

2. Up until the time the award takes place, the person enforcement concerns has the right to pay in full the claims of the person for whose benefit enforcement is being done and those of creditors who lodged claims and hold an enforceable title, as well as the costs and the fee for using the e-auction system. In this case, the auction shall be cancelled and the attachment shall be reversed.

3. Article 969(3) also applies in this case.

Article 1003

1. The immovable being auctioned shall be awarded to the person who places the highest bid, in accordance with Article 965(1) and (2).

2. The person placing the highest bid on behalf of a third party is obligated to have previously declared to the auctioneer the full details of the third party and to have filed a special notarial power of attorney empowering them.

3. The award report must include any conditions set by the person for whose benefit enforcement is being done concerning the award and which are binding on the highest bidder.

4. The provisions of Article 965(4) to (7) and Article 966(1) to (4) apply *mutatis mutandis.*

Άρθρο 1004

1. Στον πλειστηριασμό ακινήτων ο υπερθεματιστής έχει υποχρέωση να καταβάλει στον ειδικό τραπεζικό επαγγελματικό λογαριασμό του υπαλλήλου του πλειστηριασμού το πλειστηρίασμα και το τέλος χρήσης το αργότερο τη δέκατη εργάσιμη ημέρα από τον πλειστηριασμό. Ο υπάλληλος του ηλεκτρονικού πλειστηριασμού οφείλει, το αργότερο τη δέκατη πέμπτη εργάσιμη ημέρα από τον πλειστηριασμό, να καταθέσει το πλειστηρίασμα στο Ταμείο Παρακαταθηκών και Δανείων. Η κατάθεση του πλειστηριάσματος είναι ακατάσχετη, δεν εμπίπτει στην πτωχευτική περιουσία και δεν υπόκειται στις δεσμεύσεις που επιβάλλει το Δημόσιο για τη διασφάλιση των συμφερόντων του. Εντός της επόμενης εργάσιμης ημέρας από την παρέλευση της ανωτέρω προθεσμίας, ο υπάλληλος του πλειστηριασμού αποδίδει το τέλος χρήσης στον οικείο συμβολαιογραφικό σύλλογο του οποίου αυτός είναι μέλος. Εντός τριών (3) εργασίμων ημερών, μέρος του ανωτέρω ποσού, το οποίο καθορίζεται με την απόφαση της παρ. 14 του άρθρου 959, αποδίδεται από τον Συμβολαιογραφικό Σύλλογο στο ΤΑ.Χ.ΔΙ.Κ.

2. Αν ο υπερθεματιστής είναι ενυπόθηκος δανειστής, ο υπάλληλος του πλειστηριασμού μπορεί να επιτρέψει να μην καταβάλει το ποσό του πλειστηριάσματος που αναλογεί στην ενυπόθηκη απαίτησή του ή μέρος του ποσού αυτού, ώσπου να γίνει η οριστική κατάταξη, με εγγύηση ή και χωρίς εγγύηση. Κατά τα λοιπά και σε ό,τι αφορά την κατάθεση του πλειστηριάσματος στο Ταμείο Παρακαταθηκών και Δανείων και τον υπολογισμό της τοκοδοσίας εφαρμόζεται αναλογικά το άρθρο 965 παρ. 4, με εξαίρεση όσα ρυθμίζονται ειδικά στην παρούσα διάταξη.

Άρθρο 1005

1. Από τη στιγμή που ο υπερθεματιστής καταβάλει το πλειστηρίασμα και το τέλος χρήσης, ο υπάλληλος του πλειστηριασμού του δίνει περίληψη της κατακυρωτικής έκθεσης. Με την κατακύρωση, και αφότου μεταγραφεί η περίληψη της κατακυρωτικής έκθεσης, ο υπερθεματιστής αποκτά το δικαίωμα που είχε εκείνος κατά του οποίου έγινε η εκτέλεση.

2. Η περίληψη της κατακυρωτικής έκθεσης είναι τίτλος εκτελεστός. Με βάση αυτή την περίληψη μπορεί να γίνει κατά το άρθρο 943 αναγκαστική εκτέλεση υπέρ του υπερθεματιστή και των διαδόχων του και εναντίον εκείνου κατά του οποίου έγινε η εκτέλεση και των διαδόχων του, εφόσον η διαδοχή επέλθει μετά την εγγραφή της κατάσχεσης στο βιβλίο κατασχέσεων, καθώς και κατά εκείνου που νέμεται ή κατέχει το πράγμα στο όνομα εκείνου κατά του οποίου έγινε η εκτέλεση ή των διαδόχων του, αδιάφορο αν πρόκειται για σχέση εμπράγματη ή ενοχική. Οι διατάξεις του άρθρου 947 εφαρμόζονται και εδώ.

3. Η καταβολή του πλειστηριάσματος από τον υπερθεματιστή επιφέρει απόσβεση της υποθήκης ή προσημείωσης που υπάρχει επάνω στο ακίνητο. Ο υπερθεματιστής μετά την καταβολή του πλειστηριάσματος έχει δικαίωμα να ζητήσει την εξάλειψη των υποθηκών, προσημειώσεων και κατασχέσεων που είναι γραμμένες στο ακίνητο. Αν ο πλειστηριασμός ακυρωθεί, αναβιώνουν αυτοδικαίως οι υποθήκες και οι προσημειώσεις που εξαλείφθηκαν. Ο υποθηκοφύλακας έχει υποχρέωση να κάνει σχετική σημείωση στα ειδικά βιβλία, όταν του προσαχθεί αντίγραφο της ακυρωτικής απόφασης.

Άρθρο 1006

1. Αν ο υπερθεματιστής καταβάλει αμέσως το πλειστηρίασμα και είναι αυτό αρκετό για να ικανοποιηθεί εκείνος υπέρ του οποίου έγινε η εκτέλεση και οι δανειστές που αναγγέλθηκαν, εφαρμόζονται όσα ορίζει το άρθρο 971.

2. Αν δόθηκε προθεσμία για την καταβολή μέρους του πλειστηριάσματος και αυτή έγινε αφού πέρασε η προθεσμία του άρθρου 971 παρ. 1, η ικανοποίηση των δανειστών πρέπει να γίνει μέσα σε δύο ημέρες από την καταβολή του υπολοίπου.

3. Αν το πλειστηρίασμα δεν αρκεί για να ικανοποιηθούν εκείνος υπέρ του οποίου έγινε η εκτέλεση και οι δανειστές που αναγγέλθηκαν, εφαρμόζονται και τα άρθρα 974, 979, 980 και 1007.

Article 1004

1. In cases of auctions of immovables, the highest bidder is obligated to pay the auction price and the fee for using [the e-auction systems] into the special business account held by the e-auctioneer no later than the tenth working day after the auction. The e-auctioneer is obligated to deposit the auction price with the Consignment Deposits and Loans Fund no later than the fifteenth working day after the auction. The auction price which has been deposited is non-garnishable, does not constitute part of the bankruptcy estate and is not subject to freezing orders imposed by the Greek State to safeguard its interests. On the working day after the date on which the aforesaid deadline lapses, the auctioneer shall remit the fee for using [the e-auction systems] to the relevant notarial association to which they belong. Within three working days, part of the above amount, which shall be specified in the decision referred to in Article 959(14), shall be remitted by the notarial association to the Court Buildings Financing Fund.
2. If the highest bidder is a mortgagee, the auctioneer may allow them to not pay the amount of the auction price corresponding to their mortgage-backed claims or part of that amount until the final ranking has taken place, whether with or without surety. In all other respects and with regard to the deposit of the auction price with the Consignment Deposits and Loans Fund and the calculation of interest, Article 965(4) applies *mutatis mutandis*, with the exception of all matters specifically regulated under this provision.

Article 1005

1. Once the highest bidder has paid the auction price and the fee for using [the e-auction systems], the auctioneer shall provide them with a summary of the award report. Once the thing has been awarded and the summary of the award report has been entered [in the register], the highest bidder shall acquire the right previously held by the person enforcement concerns.
2. The summary of the award report is an enforceable title. This summary may serve as a basis for effecting compulsory enforcement under Article 943 for the highest bidder and their successors and against the person the enforcement concerned and their successors, provided succession occurred after the attachment was registered in the attachment register, as well as to the detriment of the person with possession or detentorship of the thing in the name of the person the enforcement concerned or their successors, regardless of whether it concerns an *in rem* or a contractual relationship. The provisions of Article 947 also apply in such cases.
3. Payment of the auction price by the highest bidder shall result in extinguishment of the mortgage or prenotation of mortgage registered on the immovable. After having paid the auction price, the highest bidder has the right to request that mortgages, prenotations of mortgage and attachments registered on the immovable be stricken out. If the auction is cancelled, the mortgages and prenotations of mortgage stricken out shall be restored *ipso jure*. Upon being presented with a copy of the cancellation decision, the land registrar is obligated to make a relevant note in the special registers.

Article 1006

1. If the highest bidder pays the auction price immediately and it suffices to satisfy the claim of person for whose benefit enforcement was done and the creditors who lodged claims, the provisions of Article 971 apply.
2. If a deadline was set for payment of part of the auction price and said payment took place after the deadline set in Article 971(1) lapsed, the creditors' claims must be satisfied within two days of payment of the balance.
3. If the auction price does not suffice to satisfy the claims of the person for whose benefit enforcement was done and the creditors who lodged claims, Articles 974, 979, 980 and 1007 shall apply.

4. Αν η απαίτηση του δανειστή που αναγγέλλεται στηρίζεται σε τίτλο εκτελεστό, η αναγγελία έχει τα ίδια αποτελέσματα με την κατάσχεση, εφόσον επιδοθεί και στον υποθηκοφύλακα της περιφέρειας όπου βρίσκεται το κατασχεμένο και αφότου αυτό σημειωθεί στο περιθώριο της εγγραφής της κατάσχεσης. Αντίγραφο της πράξης του άρθρου 973 παρ. 2 και 3 για τη δήλωση ότι άλλος δανειστής επισπεύδει τον πλειστηριασμό, πρέπει να επιδοθεί μέσα σε πέντε ημέρες από την ημέρα που έγινε η δήλωση στον υποθηκοφύλακα της περιφέρειας όπου βρίσκεται το κατασχεμένο και αυτό να σημειωθεί στο περιθώριο της εγγραφής της κατάσχεσης, αλλιώς επέρχεται ακυρότητα.

Άρθρο 1007

1. Για την κατάταξη των δανειστών εφαρμόζονται τα άρθρα 975 έως 978, εκτός από την διάταξη του άρθρου 976 αρ. 3. Τη θέση των απαιτήσεων του άρθρου 976 αρ. 2 και της παραγράφου 1 του άρθρου 977Α, παίρνουν οι ενυπόθηκες απαιτήσεις. Η απαίτηση υπέρ της οποίας έχει εγγραφεί προσημείωση κατατάσσεται τυχαίως.

2. Αν γίνει χωριστός πλειστηριασμός των παραρτημάτων ενυπόθηκου κτήματος στα οποία εκτείνεται η υποθήκη, η απαίτηση του ενυπόθηκου δανειστή κατατάσσεται σύμφωνα με τις διατάξεις της παρ. 1.

Άρθρο 1008

Αν συναινεί ο ενυπόθηκος δανειστής, ο υπερθεματιστής μπορεί να αναδεχτεί την ενυπόθηκη απαίτηση, οπότε η υποθήκη διατηρείται επάνω στο ακίνητο. Η δήλωση του υπερθεματιστή και η συναίνεση του ενυπόθηκου δανειστή καταχωρίζεται στην κατακυρωτική έκθεση. Ο υπερθεματιστής σ' αυτή την περίπτωση μπορεί να μην καταβάλει ανάλογο μέρος από το πλειστηρίασμα, οπότε εφαρμόζεται το άρθρο 1004 παρ. 2.

Άρθρο 1009

Αν το ακίνητο που πλειστηριάστηκε ήταν μισθωμένο για την άσκηση σε αυτό επιχείρησης, ο υπερθεματιστής έχει δικαίωμα να καταγγείλει τη μίσθωση, οπότε αυτή λύεται μετά την πάροδο έξι (6) μηνών από την καταγγελία. Αν το ακίνητο που πλειστηριάστηκε ήταν μισθωμένο ως κατοικία, ο υπερθεματιστής έχει δικαίωμα να καταγγείλει τη μίσθωση οπότε η μίσθωση λύεται μετά την πάροδο έξι (6) μηνών από την καταγγελία. Στην περίπτωση του προηγούμενου εδαφίου, η καταγγελία δεν είναι δυνατή πριν τη συμπλήρωση του προβλεπόμενου στο άρθρο 2 του ν. 1703/1987 (Α' 78) χρονικού διαστήματος. Στην περίπτωση αυτή η περίληψη της κατακυρωτικής έκθεσης εκτελείται κατά του μισθωτή και του υπομισθωτή, καθώς και κατά οποιουδήποτε αντλεί τα δικαιώματά του από αυτούς ή κατέχει το μίσθιο γι' αυτούς.

Άρθρο 1010

Η ανακοπή για την ακύρωση πλειστηριασμού ή αναπλειστηριασμού ακινήτου είναι απαράδεκτη, αν δεν εγγράφει στο βιβλίο διεκδικήσεων της περιφέρειας όπου βρίσκεται το ακίνητο μέσα σε τριάντα ημέρες από την κατάθεσή της. Σ' αυτή την περίπτωση επιτρέπεται νέα ανακοπή μέσα στην προθεσμία του άρθρου 934.

Άρθρο 1011

1. Στην έκθεση κατάσχεσης πλοίου πρέπει να αναφέρονται και το όνομα και η ιθαγένεια του πλοιοκτήτη, το όνομα του πλοίου, η πράξη της νηολόγησης, καθώς και το διεθνές σήμα του. Η περιγραφή του κατασχεμένου πλοίου πρέπει να περιλαμβάνει τις διαστάσεις και τη χωρητικότητα, το είδος της κινητήριας δύναμης και τη δύναμη της μηχανής, καθώς και τα κατασχεμένα παραρτήματα. Η περιγραφή πρέπει να γίνεται με ακρίβεια σε τρόπο που να μη γεννιέται αμφιβολία για την ταυτότητα του πλοίου.

2. Αντίγραφο της κατασχετήριας έκθεσης επιδίδεται και στο λιμενάρχη του λιμανιού όπου έγινε η κατάσχεση του πλοίου, στον πλοίαρχο και στο Ναυτικό Απομαχικό Ταμείο μέσα σε τρεις (3) ημέρες από την ημέρα που έγινε η κατάσχεση. Η κατάσχεση εμποδίζει τον απόπλου του πλοίου και ο λιμενάρχης, μόλις του επιδοθεί το αντίγραφο της κατασχετήριας έκθεσης, οφείλει να εμποδίσει τον απόπλου.

4. If the claim lodged by the creditor is based on an enforceable title, lodgement generates the same effects as attachment, provided it is also served on the land registrar of the district where the attached [immovable] is located and this is noted in the margin of the attachment entry. On penalty of nullity, a copy of the [report] referred to in Article 973(2) and (3) regarding the declaration that a different creditor is expediting the auction must be served within five days of the date of the declaration to the land registrar of the district where the attached [immovable] is located, and this must be noted in the margin of the attachment entry.

Article 1007

1. Articles 975 to 978, except for the provisions of Article 976(3), apply to the ranking of creditors. Mortgage-backed claims shall take the place of the claims referred to in Article 976(2) and Article 977A(1). Claims for which a prenotation of mortgage was registered shall be ranked without preference.
2. If the accessories of a mortgaged property which are also covered by the mortgage are auctioned separately, the claim of the mortgagee shall be ranked in accordance with the provisions of paragraph 1.

Article 1008

If the mortgagee consents, the highest bidder may take on the mortgage-backed claim, in which case the mortgage on the immovable shall remain in effect. The declaration by the highest bidder and the consent of the mortgagee shall be recorded in the award report. In this case, the highest bidder may opt to not pay the corresponding part of the auction price, in which case Article 1004(2) shall apply.

Article 1009

If the immovable auctioned was leased as business premises, the highest bidder shall have the right to terminate the lease, in which case the lease shall end after six months have elapsed from the date of termination. If the immovable auctioned was leased as a residence, the highest bidder shall have the right to terminate the lease, in which case the lease shall end after six months have elapsed from the date of termination. In the case of the preceding paragraph, termination shall not be possible before the period provided for in Article 2 of Law 1703/1987 (Government Gazette, Series I, Issue 78) has elapsed. In this case, the summary of the award report shall be enforced against the lessee and sublessee, as well as any person deriving rights from the foregoing or with detentorship of the immovable.

Article 1010

An opposition to cancel the auction or repeat auction of an immovable shall be inadmissible if it is not entered in the claims register of the district where the immovable is located within 30 days of the date it is filed. In this case, a new opposition may be filed within the deadline laid down in Article 934.

Article 1011

1. Ship arrest reports must also cite the name and nationality of the owner-operator, the name of the ship, the ship registration decision, as well as its international call sign. The description of the arrested ship must include its dimensions and capacity, the means of propulsion and rated engine power, as well as the accessories subject to arrest. The description must be precise in a manner that ensures that no doubts can arise concerning the identity of the ship.
2. A copy of the arrest report shall also be served on the harbour master of the port where the ship was arrested, the master of the ship and the Seafarers' Retirement Fund within three days of the date of arrest. Arrest shall prevent the ship from setting sail and, upon being served a copy of the arrest report, the harbour master is obligated to prevent the ship from setting sail.

Άρθρο 1011Α

1. Ο πλειστηριασμός πλοίου ορίζεται την πρώτη εργάσιμη Τετάρτη μετά την πάροδο σαράντα (40) ημερών από την κατάσχεση.

2. Οι προθεσμίες του άρθρου 934 παράγραφος 1 περίπτωση α' και β' είναι τριάντα (30) ημέρες από την κατάσχεση του πλοίου και σαράντα (40) ημέρες από τη σύνταξη της έκθεσης πλειστηριασμού αντιστοίχως. Η ανακοπή του άρθρου 954 παράγραφος 4, και η αίτηση αναστολής του άρθρου 1000 ασκούνται με ποινή απαραδέκτου μέσα σε προθεσμία τριάντα (30) ημερών από την κατάσχεση, δικάζονται με τη διαδικασία των άρθρων 686 επ. και η απόφαση δημοσιεύεται μέχρι τις 12.00 το μεσημέρι της Δευτέρας πριν από τον πλειστηριασμό. Μέσα στην ίδια προθεσμία και με την ίδια διαδικασία μπορεί με αίτηση του ανακόπτοντος να διαταχθεί από το αρμόδιο κατά το άρθρο 933 δικαστήριο η αναστολή της αναγκαστικής εκτέλεσης με εγγύηση ή και χωρίς εγγύηση αν κρίνεται ότι η ενέργεια της αναγκαστικής εκτέλεσης θα προξενήσει ανεπανόρθωτη βλάβη στον αιτούντα και πιθανολογείται η ευδοκίμηση της ανακοπής. Επίσης, μπορεί να διαταχθεί να προχωρήσει η αναγκαστική εκτέλεση αφού δοθεί εγγύηση.

3. Με την απόφαση επί της ανακοπής του άρθρου 954 παραγράφου 4 και επί της αίτησης αναστολής του άρθρου 1000 ορίζεται αντίστοιχα ως νέα ημέρα πλειστηριασμού η πρώτη εργάσιμη Τετάρτη μετά την πάροδο τριάντα (30) ημερών από τη δημοσίευση της απόφασης επί της ανακοπής και η πρώτη εργάσιμη Τετάρτη μετά τη λήξη της χορηγηθείσης αναστολής. Κατά τα λοιπά τηρούνται οι προβλεπόμενες διατυπώσεις δημοσιότητας.

4. Αν για οποιονδήποτε λόγο ο πλειστηριασμός πλοίου δεν έγινε κατά την ημέρα που είχε οριστεί, επισπεύδεται σύμφωνα με το άρθρο 973 και νέα ημέρα πλειστηριασμού ορίζεται η πρώτη εργάσιμη Τετάρτη μετά την πάροδο είκοσι (20) ημερών μετά τη δήλωση συνεχίσεως.

Άρθρο 1012

1. Ο πλειστηριασμός του κατασχεμένου πλοίου γίνεται ενώπιον συμβολαιογράφου της περιφέρειας του λιμανιού όπου βρίσκεται το πλοίο κατά την κατάσχεση. Εάν για οποιονδήποτε λόγο δεν είναι δυνατό να οριστεί συμβολαιογράφος του τόπου της κατάσχεσης, ο πλειστηριασμός γίνεται ενώπιον συμβολαιογράφου διορισμένου στην περιφέρεια του συμβολαιογραφικού συλλόγου του τόπου εκτέλεσης ή, αν και αυτό δεν είναι δυνατό, του συμβολαιογραφικού συλλόγου της πρωτεύουσας του κράτους. Η αναστολή του άρθρου 1000 δεν μπορεί να υπερβεί τους τρεις μήνες.

2. Αντίγραφο της κατασχετήριας έκθεσης πλοίου κατατίθεται στον υπάλληλο του πλειστηριασμού.

3. Η κατάταξη των δανειστών στον πίνακα της κατάταξης γίνεται κατά πρώτο λόγο σύμφωνα με τις διατάξεις του Κώδικα Ιδιωτικού Ναυτικού Δικαίου.

4. Σε περίπτωση αναγκαστικής εκτέλεσης κατά ελληνικού πλοίου ή αεροσκάφους, αν αυτό βαρύνεται με υποθήκη σε ξένο νόμισμα, καθώς και κατά αλλοδαπού πλοίου ή αεροσκάφους, σε κάθε περίπτωση, η επιταγή πληρωμής, η εκτίμηση του κατασχεμένου, η κατασχετήρια έκθεση, ο αναγκαστικός πλειστηριασμός και η κατάταξη των δανειστών γίνονται σε ξένο νόμισμα, που ορίζεται από τον επισπεύδοντα. Κάθε δανειστής που έχει έννομο συμφέρον δικαιούται να ζητήσει, με τη διαδικασία του άρθρου 954 παράγραφος 4, τη διενέργεια του πλειστηριασμού σε άλλο ξένο νόμισμα ή, αν η κατακύρωση ματαιώθηκε τουλάχιστον μια φορά, επειδή δεν παρουσιάστηκαν πλειοδότες, και σε ευρώ, σε αυτήν την περίπτωση και από τον επισπεύδοντα. Στην περίπτωση πλειστηριασμού σε συνάλλαγμα, η δημόσια κατάθεση του πλειστηριάσματος γίνεται σε αυτούσιο συνάλλαγμα, μη υποχρεωτικά εκχωρητέο στην Τράπεζα της Ελλάδος. Η διανομή στους δανειστές που έχουν απαιτήσεις σε συνάλλαγμα γίνεται σε αυτούσιο ελεύθερο συνάλλαγμα, ενώ στους υπόλοιπους η διανομή γίνεται σε ευρώ, με την ισοτιμία του χρόνου διανομής.

Article 1011A

1. Ships shall be auctioned on the first working Wednesday after 40 days have elapsed from the date of arrest.

2. The deadlines laid down in Article 934(1)(a) and (b) are 30 days from the date of arrest of the ship and 40 days from the date of preparation of the auction report, respectively. The opposition referred to in Article 954(4) and the application to stay [the auction] referred to in Article 1000 shall be filed, on penalty of inadmissibility, within a deadline of 30 days from the date of arrest and tried under the procedure laid down in Articles 686 *et seq.*, and the judgment shall be handed down no later than 12:00 noon on the Monday prior to the auction. Within the same deadline and under the same procedure, the court with jurisdiction under Article 933 may, following an application filed by the opposing party, order the stay of compulsory enforcement, whether with or without surety, if the court considers that effecting compulsory enforcement will cause irreparable damage to the applicant and considers it likely on the balance of probabilities that the opposition will be successful. The court may also order that compulsory enforcement go ahead after surety has been provided.

3. The judgment on the opposition referred to in Article 954(4) and the application to stay [the auction] referred to in Article 1000 shall set the new auction date as the first working Wednesday after 30 days have elapsed from the date the judgment on the opposition was handed down and the first working Wednesday after the stay granted elapses, respectively. In all other respects, the publicity formalities provided for shall be complied with.

4. If, for any reason, the auction of a ship did not take place on the date set, it shall be expedited in accordance with Article 973 and the the new auction date shall be set as the first working Wednesday after 20 days have elapsed from the date of the declaration of resumption.

Article 1012

1. The arrested ship shall be auctioned in the presence of a notary public from the district of the harbour where the ship was located at the time of arrest. If a notary public from the place of arrest cannot be appointed for any reason, the [ship] shall be auctioned in the presence of a notary public from the district of the notarial association of the place of enforcement or, if this is also not possible, from the notarial association of the capital. The stay [of the auction] referred to in Article 1000 may not exceed three months.

2. A copy of the ship arrest report shall be submitted to the auctioneer.

3. The creditors shall be ranked in accordance [with the order set out] in the provisions of the Code of Private Maritime Law.

4. In cases of compulsory enforcement against a Greek ship or aircraft, if it is encumbered with a mortgage denominated in a foreign currency, [or] against a foreign ship or aircraft, in all cases, the payment order, the valuation of the arrested ship or aircraft, the arrest report, the forced auction and the ranking of the creditors shall take place in the foreign currency specified by the expediting party. Any creditor with a legitimate interest is entitled to request, under the procedure laid down in Article 954(4), that the auction be held in a different foreign currency or, if the award was cancelled at least once due to no-show of bidders, even in euros; the latter may also be requested by the expediting party as well. In the case of an auction held with bids accepted in a foreign currency, the auction price shall be deposited with the state in the same foreign currency for which there is no obligation for assignment to the Bank of Greece. Distribution to creditors with claims in foreign currency shall take place in freely disposable actual foreign currency, while distribution to the remaining creditors shall take place in euros using the exchange rate at the time of distribution.

Άρθρο 1013

Αν το πλοίο που κατασχέθηκε σε ελληνικό λιμάνι είναι αλλοδαπό, ο λιμενάρχης του λιμανιού όπου έγινε η κατάσχεση έχει υποχρέωσή να στείλει χωρίς υπαίτια καθυστέρηση αντίγραφο της κατασχετήριας έκθεσης και την περίληψή της σε εκείνον που τηρεί το νηολόγιο όπου είναι νηολογημένο το πλοίο. Το ίδιο ισχύει και όταν πρόκειται για πλοία ελληνικά, γραμμένα σε νηολόγια που τηρούν ελληνικές προξενικές αρχές.

Άρθρο 1014

1. Στην κατασχετήρια έκθεση αεροσκάφους πρέπει να αναφέρονται και το όνομα και η ιθαγένεια του, ιδιοκτήτη του αεροσκάφους, τα διακριτικά στοιχεία του αεροσκάφους, η πράξη της εγγραφής του στα μητρώα και το διεθνές σήμα του. Η περιγραφή του κατασχεμένου αεροσκάφους πρέπει να περιλαμβάνει τις διαστάσεις και τη χωρητικότητα, το είδος και τη δύναμη των κινητήρων του, καθώς και τα παραρτήματα που κατασχέθηκαν. Η περιγραφή πρέπει να γίνεται με ακρίβεια, σε τρόπο που να μη γεννιέται αμφιβολία για την ταυτότητα του αεροσκάφους.

2. Αντίγραφο της κατασχετήριας έκθεσης επιδίδεται και στο διοικητή του αερολιμένα όπου έγινε η κατάσχεση του αεροσκάφους μέσα σε δύο ημέρες από την ημέρα που έγινε η κατάσχεση. Η κατάσχεση εμποδίζει την απογείωση του αεροσκάφους και ο διοικητής του αερολιμένα μόλις του επιδοθεί το αντίγραφο της κατασχετήριας έκθεσης οφείλει να εμποδίσει την απογείωσή του.

Άρθρο 1015

1. Ο πλειστηριασμός του κατασχεμένου αεροσκάφους γίνεται ενώπιον συμβολαιογράφου της περιφέρειας του αερολιμένα όπου έγινε η κατάσχεση. Εάν για οποιονδήποτε λόγο δεν είναι δυνατό να οριστεί συμβολαιογράφος του τόπου της κατάσχεσης, ο πλειστηριασμός γίνεται ενώπιον συμβολαιογράφου διορισμένου στην περιφέρεια του συμβολαιογραφικού συλλόγου του τόπου εκτέλεσης ή, αν και αυτό δεν είναι δυνατό, του συμβολαιογραφικού συλλόγου της πρωτεύουσας του κράτους.

2. Αντίγραφο της κατασχετήριας έκθεσης επιδίδεται και στον κυβερνήτη του αεροσκάφους και στο διοικητή του αερολιμένα και κατατίθεται στον υπάλληλο του πλειστηριασμού.

3. Η κατάταξη των δανειστών στον πίνακα της κατάταξης γίνεται κατά πρώτο λόγο σύμφωνα με τις διατάξεις των νόμων για την πολιτική αεροπορία.

Άρθρο 1016

Αν το αεροσκάφος που κατασχέθηκε σε ελληνικό αερολιμένα είναι αλλοδαπό, ο διοικητής του αερολιμένα όπου έγινε η κατάσχεση έχει υποχρέωση να στείλει χωρίς υπαίτια καθυστέρηση αντίγραφο της κατασχετήριας έκθεσης και της περίληψής της σε εκείνον που τηρεί το μητρώο όπου είναι γραμμένο το αεροσκάφος.

ΚΕΦΑΛΑΙΟ ΣΤ'
Διατάξεις κοινές για τον πλειστηριασμό κινητών και ακινήτων

Άρθρο 1017

1. Οι διατάξεις του ουσιαστικού δικαίου για την κτήση κυριότητας από μη κύριο εφαρμόζονται και στον πλειστηριασμό κινητού πράγματος.

2. Σε πλειστηριασμό πράγματος κινητού ή ακινήτου δεν υπάρχει ευθύνη για πραγματικά ελαττώματα. Για τα νομικά ελαττώματα υπάρχει ευθύνη μόνο εκείνου που επισπεύδει τον πλειστηριασμό και μόνο αν αυτός γνώριζε κατά το χρόνο του πλειστηριασμού την ύπαρξη του νομικού ελαττώματος. Η ευθύνη από τις διατάξεις του αδικαιολογήτου πλουτισμού δεν αποκλείεται.

3. Τον κίνδυνο από την τυχαία καταστροφή ή χειροτέρευση του πράγματος φέρει ο υπερθεματιστής από την κατακύρωση.

4. Ο υπερθεματιστής παίρνει τα ωφελήματα και φέρει τα βάρη του πράγματος από την κατακύρωση.

Article 1013

If a foreign ship is arrested at a Greek port, the harbour master of the harbour where arrest took place shall be obligated to send a copy of the arrest report and its summary without undue delay to the person keeping the registry in which the ship is registered. This also applies to Greek ships registered in ship registries kept by Greek consular authorities.

Article 1014

1. Aircraft arrest reports must also cite the name and nationality of the aircraft owner, the identification details of the aircraft, its registration documentation and its international call sign. The description of the arrested aircraft must include its dimensions and capacity, the type of engine and engine power, as well as the accessories subject to arrest. The description must be precise in a manner that ensures that no doubts can arise concerning the identity of the aircraft.

2. A copy of the arrest report shall also be served on the manager of the airport where the aircraft was arrested within two days of the date of arrest. Arrest shall prevent the aircraft from taking off and, upon being served a copy of the arrest report, the airport manager is obligated to prevent the aircraft from taking off.

Article 1015

1. The arrested aircraft shall be auctioned in the presence of a notary public from the district of the airport where the arrest took place. If a notary public from the place of arrest cannot be appointed for any reason, the [aircraft] shall be auctioned in the presence of a notary public from the district of the notarial association of the place of enforcement or, if this is also not possible, from the notarial association of the capital.

2. A copy of the arrest report shall also be served on the captain of the aircraft and the airport manager, and shall be submitted to the auctioneer.

3. The creditors shall be ranked in the ranking table in first instance in accordance with the provisions of the civil aviation laws.

Article 1016

If an aircraft arrested at a Greek airport is a foreign aircraft, the manager of the airport where arrest took place is obligated to send a copy of the arrest report and its summary without undue delay to the person keeping the register in which the aircraft is registered.

CHAPTER VI
Common provisions on the auctioning of movables and immovables

Article 1017

1. The provisions of substantive law on acquisition of ownership by a non-owner also apply to the auctioning of movables.

2. In auctions of movables or immovables, there shall be no liability for actual defects. With regard to legal defects, only the person who instituted the auction shall be liable, and only if they were aware of the existence of the legal defect at the time of the auction. Liability under the provisions on unjust enrichment shall not be precluded.

3. Following the award, the risk of accidental destruction or deterioration of the thing shall be borne by the highest bidder.

4. Following the award, the highest bidder enjoys the advantages and bears the charges of the thing.

Άρθρο 1018

Σε περίπτωση που ο πλειστηριασμός ακυρώθηκε και διενεργηθεί νέος, η απαίτηση του υπερθεματιστή του πλειστηριασμού που ακυρώθηκε να αναλάβει το πλειστηρίασμα που διανεμήθηκε κατατάσσεται μετά τα έξοδα της εκτέλεσης του νέου πλειστηριασμού και πριν από τις απαιτήσεις των άρθρων 975, 976, 977Α, 1007, 1012 παρ. 3 και 1015 παρ. 3. Στην ίδια τάξη κατατάσσεται και η αξίωση του υπερθεματιστή για την καταβολή τόκων, που οφείλονται από την ημέρα καταβολής του πλειστηριάσματος, μόνον εάν προαποδεικνύεται ότι δεν έχει εκτελεστεί από αυτόν η περίληψη κατακυρωτικής έκθεσης. Για να ικανοποιηθεί αυτή η απαίτηση, ο υπερθεματιστής μπορεί να επισπεύσει πλειστηριασμό με βάση την απόφαση που ακύρωσε την εκτέλεση και πιστοποίηση του υπαλλήλου του πλειστηριασμού ότι το πλειστηρίασμα έχει καταβληθεί και διανεμηθεί.

Άρθρο 1019

1. *Η κατάσχεση, εφόσον δεν ακολούθησε πλειστηριασμός μέσα σε ένα έτος αφότου επιβλήθηκε ή αναπλειστηριασμός μέσα σε έξι μήνες από τον πλειστηριασμό, ανατρέπεται, αν το ζητήσει οποιοσδήποτε έχει έννομο συμφέρον, με απόφαση του ειρηνοδικείου στην περιφέρεια του οποίου επιβλήθηκε η κατάσχεση, το οποίο δικάζει κατά τη διαδικασία των άρθρων 686 επ. Το δικαστήριο γνωστοποιεί χωρίς υπαίτια καθυστέρηση την απόφαση στον υπάλληλο του πλειστηριασμού που οφείλει να σταματήσει κάθε παραπέρα ενέργεια και να ζητήσει να εγγραφεί σχετική σημείωση στο βιβλίο κατασχέσεων. Η ανατροπή λογίζεται ότι έχει επέλθει ως προς όλους αφότου δημοσιευθεί η απόφαση.*
2. *Στις προθεσμίες που ορίζονται στην προηγούμενη παράγραφο δεν υπολογίζεται το διάστημα από την έκδοση απόφασης σύμφωνα με το άρθρο 966 παρ. 3 και 4, μέχρι την ημέρα του πλειστηριασμού που ορίσθηκε σύμφωνα με αυτήν, το διάστημα αναστολής της εκτέλεσης, η οποία χορηγήθηκε με δικαστική απόφαση ή με κοινή συναίνεση εκείνου που επισπεύδει και του οφειλέτη, η οποία βεβαιώνεται με συμβολαιογραφική πράξη, καθώς και ο χρόνος από 1 έως 31 Αυγούστου.*
3. *Αν πριν από την έκδοση της κατά την παρ. 1 απόφασης, είχαν αναγγελθεί δανειστές με τα προσόντα αυτοτελούς κατάσχεσης, κατά τα άρθρ. 972 παρ. 2 εδάφ. β' και 1006 παρ. 1 εδάφ. α', η ανατροπή επέρχεται ως προς αυτούς μόνο αν οι ως άνω προθεσμίες είχαν συμπληρωθεί και ως προς αυτούς από τις αναγγελίες τους. Διαφορετικά, η κατάσχεση ως προς αυτούς διατηρείται και ισχύει αυτοτελής προθεσμία ανατροπής της από την αναγγελία τους, η προθεσμία όμως αύτη ουδέποτε συμπληρώνεται πριν από την πάροδο εξαμήνου από την ανατροπή.*

Άρθρο 1020

Αγωγή διεκδίκησης του πράγματος που πλειστηριάστηκε πρέπει να ασκηθεί μέσα σε αποκλειστική προθεσμία, για τα κινητά ενός έτους από τότε που παραδόθηκαν στον υπερθεματιστή, και για τα ακίνητα πέντε ετών από τότε που μεταγράφηκε η περίληψη της κατακυρωτικής έκθεσης.

Άρθρο 1021

Όταν σύμφωνα με διάταξη νόμου ή με δικαστική απόφαση ή με συμφωνία των μερών γίνεται εκούσιος πλειστηριασμός ενώπιον συμβολαιογράφου, η διαδικασία αρχίζει με έκθεση περιγραφής, η οποία συντάσσεται από δικαστικό επιμελητή και περιέχει όσα ορίζονται στην παράγραφο 1 του άρθρου 955, αν πρόκειται για κινητό, ή του άρθρου 995, αν πρόκειται για ακίνητο. Ο εκούσιος πλειστηριασμός πραγματοποιείται με τη διαδικασία είτε του άρθρου 959, αν πρόκειται για κινητό, είτε του άρθρου 998, αν πρόκειται για ακίνητο. Περαιτέρω, εφαρμόζονται αναλόγως οι διατάξεις των άρθρων 954 παράγραφος 4, 955 παράγραφοι 1 και 2 εδάφιο β', 965, 966, 967, 969 παράγραφος 1, 995 παράγραφος 4 εδάφιο β', 1002, 1003 παράγραφοι 1, 2 και 4, 1004, 1005 παράγραφοι 1 και 2 και 1010. Ο εκούσιος πλειστηριασμός γίνεται ενώπιον συμβολαιογράφου της περιφέρειας όπου βρίσκεται το κινητό ή το ακίνητο.

Article 1018

Where the auction was cancelled and a new auction is held, the claim of the highest bidder from the cancelled auction to take on the auction price distributed shall be ranked lower than the enforcement costs of the new auction and higher than the claims referred to in Articles 975, 976, 977A, 1007, 1012(3) and 1015(3). The claim of the highest bidder for payment of interest owed from the date of payment of the auction price shall be ranked in the same class only if it is proven in advance that the highest bidder has not enforced the summary of the award report. In order for this claim to be satisfied, the highest bidder may expedite an auction on the basis of the judgment annulling enforcement and a certificate from the auctioneer that the auction price have been paid and the proceeds have been distributed.

Article 1019

1. Provided an auction was not held within one year of the date it was imposed or a repeat auction was not held within six months of the auction, the attachment shall, if so requested by any person with a legitimate interest, be reversed by means of a judgment handed down by the court of the peace in whose district the attachment was imposed, trying the matter under the procedure laid down in Articles 686 *et seq.* The court shall notify the judgment without undue delay to the auctioneer, who is obligated to take no further action and to request entry of a relevant note in the attachment register. The reversal shall be deemed to apply *erga omnes* once the judgment has been handed down.

2. When calculating the deadlines laid down in the preceding paragraph, account shall not be taken of the period from the handing down of the judgment in accordance with Article 966(3) and (4) until the date of the auction set in that judgment, of the period of stay of enforcement granted by court judgment or through common consent of the expediting party and the debtor, attested by means of a notarial deed, as well as of the period between 1 and 31 August.

3. If, prior to the judgment referred to in paragraph 1 being handed down, a claim is lodged by creditors able to request attachment on their own in accordance with the second subparagraph of Article 972(2) and Article 1006(1), the reversal shall take place with regard to the foregoing only if the aforesaid deadlines had also lapsed with regard to them from the date they are lodged. If that is not the case, the attachment shall persist with regard to them and a separate deadline for its reversal shall apply from the date they are lodged; however, this deadline cannot expire before six months from the date of reversal have elapsed.

Article 1020

An action for revendication of a thing that was auctioned must be filed, in the case of movables, within a fixed deadline of one year from the date they were handed over to the highest bidder, and, in the case of immovables, five years from the date the summary of the award report was entered [in the register].

Article 1021

Where a voluntary auction is held in the presence of a notary public in accordance with a statutory provision or court judgment or an agreement between the parties, the process shall commence with a report being prepared by a court process server describing the thing and containing the information required under Article 955(1), in cases of movables, or under Article 995, in cases of immovables. The voluntary auction shall take place under the procedure laid down either in Article 959 in cases of movables, or Article 998 in cases of immovables. Furthermore, the provisions of Article 954(4), Article 955(1) and the second subparagraph of Article 955(2), Article 965, Article 966, Article 967, Article 969(1), the second subparagraph of Article 995(4), Article 1002, Article 1003(1), (2) and (4), Article 1004, Article 1005(1) and (2) and Article 1010 apply *mutatis mutandis*. The voluntary auction shall take place in the presence of a notary public from the district where the movable or immovable is located.

Εάν για οποιονδήποτε λόγο δεν είναι δυνατό να οριστεί συμβολαιογράφος της περιφέρειας όπου βρίσκεται το κινητό ή το ακίνητο, ο πλειστηριασμός γίνεται ενώπιον συμβολαιογράφου διορισμένου στην περιφέρεια του συμβολαιογραφικού συλλόγου του τόπου εκτέλεσης ή, αν και αυτό δεν είναι δυνατό, του συμβολαιογραφικού συλλόγου της πρωτεύουσας του κράτους. Σε περίπτωση διενέργειας εκούσιου πλειστηριασμού με τη διαδικασία του άρθρου 959, με συμφωνία των μερών ή με απόφαση του ειρηνοδικείου της περιφέρειας όπου βρίσκεται το πράγμα ή το ακίνητο, η οποία εκδίδεται κατά τη διαδικασία των άρθρων 686 επ., μπορεί, αν το ζητήσει οποιοσδήποτε έχει έννομο συμφέρον, να οριστεί άλλος τόπος πλειστηριασμού.

ΚΕΦΑΛΑΙΟ Ζ'
Κατάσχεση ειδικών περιουσιακών στοιχείων.

Άρθρο 1022

Κατάσχεση μπορεί να γίνει και σε περιουσιακά δικαιώματα εκείνου κατά του οποίου στρέφεται η εκτέλεση, τα οποία δεν μπορούν να αποτελέσουν αντικείμενο κατάσχεσης κατά τη διαδικασία των άρθρων 953 παρ. 1 και 2, 982 και 992, ιδίως σε δικαιώματα πνευματικής ιδιοκτησίας, ευρεσιτεχνίας, εκμετάλλευσης κινηματογραφικών ταινιών, σε απαιτήσεις κατά τρίτων εξαρτώμενες από αντιπαροχή, εφόσον κατά τις διατάξεις του ουσιαστικού δικαίου επιτρέπεται η μεταβίβαση αυτών των δικαιωμάτων.

Άρθρο 1023

1. Την κατάσχεση δικαιωμάτων του άρθρου 1022 διατάζει ύστερα από αίτηση εκείνου υπέρ του οποίου γίνεται η εκτέλεση, το ειρηνοδικείο, κατά τη διαδικασία των άρθρων 741 επ.
2. Το δικαστήριο μπορεί να μην επιτρέψει την κατάσχεση, αν κρίνει ότι είναι δύσκολο να γίνει η αναγκαστική εκτέλεση ή ότι το αποτέλεσμά της θα είναι ασύμφορο.

Άρθρο 1024

1. Το δικαστήριο με την απόφαση που διατάζει την κατάσχεση ή και με μεταγενέστερη ορίζει τα μέσα που κρίνει πρόσφορα για την αξιοποίηση του δικαιώματος και ιδίως μπορεί να διατάξει να μεταβιβαστεί το δικαίωμα σε εκείνον υπέρ του οποίου γίνεται η εκτέλεση, με πληρωμή ορισμένου τιμήματος ή με συμψηφισμό ολόκληρης ή μέρους της απαίτησής του, ή να διατάξει την ελεύθερη ή με πλειστηριασμό διάθεση του δικαιώματος, και, αν δεν κρίνει πρόσφορα τα μέτρα αυτά, διορίζει διαχειριστή. Διαχειριστής μπορεί να διοριστεί και εκείνος υπέρ του οποίου έγινε η κατάσχεση ή κάποιος από τους δανειστές που αναγγέλθηκαν.
2. Αν η απαίτηση εκείνου κατά του οποίου στρέφεται η εκτέλεση συνίσταται στο να εκπληρώσει ένας τρίτος παροχή εξαρτώμενη από αντιπαροχή, το δικαστήριο επιτρέπει την κατάσχεση και υπό τον όρο να εκπληρωθεί η αντιπαροχή προς τον τρίτο. Σ' αυτή την περίπτωση η αξιοποίηση του κατασχεμένου γίνεται σύμφωνα με την παρ. 1, οπότε αποκλείεται ο διορισμός διαχειριστή και η αξία της αντιπαροχής που εκπληρώθηκε θεωρείται ως έξοδο εκτέλεσης κατά το άρθρο 975.

Άρθρο 1025

1. Η κατάσχεση γίνεται, αν πρόκειται για απαίτηση κατά τρίτου, με επίδοση της απόφασης που επέτρεψε την κατάσχεση σε εκείνον κατά του οποίου στρέφεται η εκτέλεση και στον τρίτο. Αν πρόκειται για δικαίωμα εκείνου κατά του οποίου γίνεται η εκτέλεση, η κατάσχεση γίνεται με την επίδοση της απόφασης σ' αυτόν. Στις περιπτώσεις που για τη σύσταση ή τη μεταβίβαση του δικαιώματος προβλέπεται η τήρηση βιβλίων από δημόσιες αρχές, η κατάσχεση εγγράφεται στο περιθώριο της πράξης και εφαρμόζονται οι διατάξεις των άρθρων 995 παρ. 2 και 977. Οι αρχές αυτές επέχουν θέση υποθηκοφύλακα.

If a notary public from the district where the movable or immovable is located cannot be appointed for any reason, the auction shall be held in the presence of a notary public from the district of the notarial association of the place of enforcement or, if this is also not possible, from the notarial association of the capital. Where a voluntary auction is held under the procedure laid down in Article 959, if requested by any person with a legitimate interest, a different place for the auction may be designated by means of an agreement between the parties or a judgment of the court of first instance of the district where the [movable] thing or immovable is located, handed down in accordance with the procedure laid down in Articles 686 *et seq.*

CHAPTER VII
Attachment of special assets

Article 1022

Attachment may also concern the property rights of the person enforcement concerns, which cannot be attached under the procedure laid down in Articles 953(1) and (2), 982 and 993, particularly regarding copyright, patent rights, exploitation rights for films, claims against third parties contingent on counter-performance, where the transfer of such rights is allowed under the provisions of substantive law.

Article 1023

1. The attachment of rights under Article 1022 shall be ordered, following an application filed by the person for whose benefit enforcement is being done, by the court of the peace under the procedure laid down in Articles 741 *et seq.*
2. The court may refuse to allow attachment if it considers that compulsory enforcement will be difficult or that its result will be disadvantageous.

Article 1024

1. In the judgment ordering attachment or even in a subsequent judgment, the court shall specify the measures it deems expedient for exploitation of the right and, in particular, may order transfer of the right to the person for whose benefit enforcement is being done, with payment of a specific price or offsetting of all or part of their claim, or order the sale of the right freely or at auction and, if it does not consider these measures expedient, shall appoint a manager. The person for whose benefit enforcement is being done or one of the creditors who lodged claims may also be appointed as manager.
2. If the claim of the person enforcement concerns involves performance by a third party contingent on counter-performance, the court shall allow the attachment, on condition that the counter-performance be provided to the third party. In this case, the attached thing shall be exploited in accordance with paragraph 1, and the appointment of the manager shall be precluded and the value of the counter-performance provided shall be deemed to be enforcement costs under Article 975.

Article 1025

1. Where attachment involves a claim against a third party, it shall be done by means of service of the judgment allowing attachment on the person enforcement concerns and on the third party. Where attachment involves a right of the person enforcement concerns, it shall be done by means of service of the judgment on that person. Where the establishment or transfer of the right requires the keeping of registers by public authorities, the attachment shall be recorded in the margin of the [register decision] and the provisions of Articles 995(2) and 977. These authorities shall perform the same function as a land registrar.

2. Αφότου η απόφαση επιδοθεί σύμφωνα με την παρ. 1 σε εκείνον κατά του οποίου στρέφεται η εκτέλεση, απαγορεύεται, και είναι άκυρη υπέρ εκείνου που επέβαλε την κατάσχεση, η διάθεση του κατασχεμένου. Όταν προβλέπεται να γίνει εγγραφή σε βιβλίο, η ακυρότητα ισχύει για τους τρίτους μόνο αν η κατάσχεση είχε ήδη εγγραφεί στο βιβλίο, όταν έγινε η διάθεση.
3. Οι διατάξεις των άρθρων 984 παρ. 1 και 2, 985 έως 987 και 990 εφαρμόζονται και εδώ.

Άρθρο 1026

Αν διατάχθηκε να εκποιηθεί με πλειστηριασμό το κατασχεμένο δικαίωμα, το δικαστήριο του άρθρου 1023 παρ. 1 ορίζει τον υπάλληλο του πλειστηριασμού και εφαρμόζονται οι διατάξεις που ισχύουν για τον πλειστηριασμό κινητών.

Άρθρο 1027

1. Η απόφαση που διορίζει διαχειριστή καταχωρίζεται σε ιδιαίτερο βιβλίο, όπως ορίζουν οι διατάξεις του άρθρου 776, και κοινοποιείται στο διαχειριστή με επιμέλεια εκείνου υπέρ του οποίου γίνεται η εκτέλεση.
2. Ο διαχειριστής οφείλει, μέσα σε οκτώ ημέρες αφότου του επιδοθεί η απόφαση να δηλώσει στη γραμματεία του δικαστηρίου που την εξέδωσε, αν δέχεται το διορισμό. Η παράλειψη της δήλωσης θεωρείται αποποίηση.
3. Ώσπου να αναλάβει ο διαχειριστής τα καθήκοντά του, ασκεί προσωρινά καθήκοντα διαχειριστή εκείνος κατά του οποίου στρέφεται η εκτέλεση ο οποίος οφείλει να λογοδοτήσει στο διαχειριστή.

Άρθρο 1028

1. Ο διαχειριστής ενεργεί όλες τις δικαιοπραξίες ή πράξεις που είναι ενδεδειγμένες για την επωφελή εκμετάλλευση του δικαιώματος και για την επιτυχία του σκοπού της διαχείρισης και παρίσταται στο δικαστήριο για κάθε έννομη σχέση που αφορά τη διαχείριση του δικαιώματος, έστω και αν η σχέση αυτή γεννήθηκε πριν από τη διαχείριση.
2. Ο διαχειριστής δεν μπορεί χωρίς άδεια, που τη δίνει κατά τη διαδικασία των άρθρων 741 επ. το δικαστήριο που εξέδωσε την απόφαση για τη διαχείριση, να καταρτίζει δικαιοπραξίες με διάρκεια μεγαλύτερη από ένα έτος.

Άρθρο 1029

1. Αν το ζητήσει εκείνος υπέρ του οποίου έγινε ή εκείνος κατά του οποίου έχει στραφεί η εκτέλεση ή κάποιος από τους δανειστές που αναγγέλθηκαν, το δικαστήριο του άρθρου 1023 παρ. 1 μπορεί να αντικαταστήσει το διαχειριστή.
2. Κάθε διαφορά που αφορά τη διαχείριση του δικαιώματος λύνεται από το δικαστήριο του άρθρου 1023 παρ. 1, ύστερα από αίτηση εκείνου κατά του οποίου έγινε η εκτέλεση ή του διαχειριστή ή οποιουδήποτε έχει έννομο συμφέρον. Το δικαστήριο μπορεί να ορίζει τον τρόπο που θα γίνεται η διαχείριση και να διατάζει κάθε μέτρο πρόσφορο για το σκοπό αυτό.

Άρθρο 1030

1. Το δικαστήριο του άρθρου 1023 παρ. 1 ορίζει τη μηνιαία αποζημίωση του διαχειριστή.
2. Ο διαχειριστής, αφού αφαιρέσει τα έξοδα, τους φόρους και την αποζημίωσή του για τη διαχείριση, καταβάλλει χωρίς καθυστέρηση στο δανειστή το υπόλοιπο που απομένει, ώσπου να εξοφληθεί η απαίτησή του.
3. Αν υπάρχουν και άλλοι δανειστές, αναγγέλλονται με έγγραφη δήλωση που επιδίδεται στο διαχειριστή και σε εκείνον κατά του οποίου έγινε η εκτέλεση. Ο διαχειριστής κάθε τρίμηνο συντάσσει πίνακα διανομής. Η κατάταξη των δανειστών γίνεται σύμφωνα με τις διατάξεις των άρθρων 975, 977 παράγραφοι 2 και 3, 977Α και 1024 παράγραφος 2. Για την κατάταξη των απαιτήσεων του άρθρου 975, αντί της ημέρας του πλειστηριασμού λαμβάνεται υπόψη η ημέρα που άρχισε η διαχείριση.

2. After the judgment has been served on the person enforcement concerns, in accordance with paragraph 1, disposal of the attached article is prohibited and null and void vis-à-vis the person who procured attachment. Where entry in a register is required, such nullity shall apply to third parties only if the attachment had already been entered in the register when the disposal took place.
3. The provisions of Article 984(1) and (2), 985 to 987 and 990 also apply in this case.

Article 1026

If sale of the attached right at auction was ordered, the court referred to in Article 1023(1) shall designate the auctioneer, and the provisions applicable to the auctioning of movables apply.

Article 1027

1. The judgment appointing a manager shall be recorded in a special register, kept in accordance with the provisions of Article 776, and notified to the manager by the person for whose benefit enforcement is being done.
2. Within eight days of being served the judgment, the manager is obligated to declare to the registry of the court that handed down the judgment whether or not they accept the appointment. Failure to make such a declaration shall be deemed to be a refusal.
3. Until a manager assumes their duties, the person enforcement concerns shall temporarily perform the duties of manager and is obligated to render account to the manager.

Article 1028

1. The manager shall enter into all legal transactions or take all steps appropriate for the beneficial exploitation of the right and achievement of the management objectives, and shall appear before the court with regard to any legal relationship concerning management of the right, even if this relationship arose prior to that person being appointed as manager.
2. The manager may not enter into legal transactions whose duration is longer than one year without permission from the court that handed down the judgment on management under the procedure laid down in Articles 741 *et seq.*

Article 1029

1. The court referred to in Article 1023(1) may replace the manager at the request of the person for whose benefit enforcement is being done, or of the person enforcement concerns, or of any of the creditors who lodged claims.
2. Any dispute concerning management of the right shall be resolved by the court referred to in Article 1023(1), following an application filed by the person enforcement concerns, or by the manager, or by any person with a legitimate interest. The court may specify the manner in which management shall take place and may order any measures that are expedient for this purpose.

Article 1030

1. The court referred to in Article 1023(1) shall specify the manager's monthly fee.
2. After deducting costs, taxes and their management fee, the manager shall pay the creditor the remaining balance without delay until the claim of the latter has been paid in full.
3. If there are also other creditors, they may lodge claims by means of a written declaration served on the manager and the person enforcement concerns. The manager shall compile a distribution table every three months. The creditors shall be ranked in accordance with the provisions of Articles 975, 977(2) and (3), 977A and 1024(2). When ranking the claims referred to in Article 975, the day management commenced shall be taken into account instead of the day of the auction.

4. Μέσα σε πέντε ημέρες αφότου συνταχθεί ο πίνακας διανομής, ο διαχειριστής καλεί εγγράφως εκείνον υπέρ του οποίου έγινε και εκείνον κατά του οποίου στρέφεται η εκτέλεση και τους δανειστές που αναγγέλθηκαν για να λάβουν γνώση του πίνακα.

Άρθρο 1031

Κατά της αναγγελίας δανειστή και κατά του πίνακα διανομής εκείνος υπέρ του οποίου έγινε και εκείνος κατά του οποίου στρέφεται η εκτέλεση καθώς και όσοι άλλοι αναγγέλθηκαν μπορούν να προβάλουν αντιρρήσεις στο δικαστήριο του άρθρου 1023 παρ. 1, μέσα σε δέκα ημέρες από την επίδοση που προβλέπει το άρθρο 1030 παρ. 4. Η άσκηση αντιρρήσεων κατά την αναγγελίας ή κατά του πίνακα διανομής αναστέλλει την καταβολή ως προς το δανειστή κατά του οποίου στρέφονται οι αντιρρήσεις, ώσπου να γίνει τελεσίδικη η απόφαση του δικαστηρίου.

Άρθρο 1032

1. Ο διαχειριστής οφείλει να υποβάλει κάθε έτος, καθώς και όταν περατωθεί η διαχείριση, έγγραφη λογοδοσία σε εκείνον υπέρ του οποίου έγινε και σε εκείνον κατά του οποίου είχε στραφεί η εκτέλεση και στους δανειστές που αναγγέλθηκαν.
2. Ο διαχειριστής ευθύνεται, κατά τις διατάξεις του ουσιαστικού δικαίου, να αποζημιώσει εκείνον υπέρ του οποίου έγινε και εκείνον κατά του οποίου είχε στραφεί η εκτέλεση και τους δανειστές που αναγγέλθηκαν.

Άρθρο 1033

Η διαχείριση του δικαιώματος παύει με τελεσίδικη απόφαση του δικαστηρίου του άρθρου 1023 παρ. 1, όταν το ζητήσει εκείνος κατά του οποίου έγινε η εκτέλεση ή οποιοσδήποτε έχει έννομο συμφέρον
1) αν ικανοποιήθηκαν οι απαιτήσεις εκείνου υπέρ του οποίου έγινε η εκτέλεση και των δανειστών που αναγγέλθηκαν ή αν αυτοί, με έγγραφη δήλωσή τους προς εκείνον κατά του οποίου έγινε η εκτέλεση, παραιτήθηκαν από τη διαχείριση,
2) αν το δικαστήριο κρίνει ότι δεν είναι ενδεδειγμένη η εξακολούθηση της διαχείρισης ή ότι αυτή είναι επιβλαβής για τα συμφέροντα εκείνου κατά του οποίου έγινε η εκτέλεση.

ΚΕΦΑΛΑΙΟ Η'
Αναγκαστική διαχείριση.

Άρθρο 1034

1. Για να ικανοποιηθεί χρηματική απαίτηση του δανειστή, μπορεί να επιβληθεί αναγκαστική διαχείριση ακινήτου ή επιχείρησης του οφειλέτη.
2. Η αναγκαστική διαχείριση επιβάλλεται ύστερα από απόφαση του μονομελούς πρωτοδικείου της περιφέρειας όπου βρίσκεται το ακίνητο ή η έδρα της επιχείρησης του οφειλέτη, αν το ζητήσει δανειστής που έχει τίτλο εκτελεστό και που επέδωσε στον οφειλέτη επιταγή για εκτέλεση. Η απόφαση που δέχεται ή απορρίπτει την αίτηση προσβάλλεται μόνο με έφεση. Η αίτηση και η έφεση δικάζονται κατά τα άρθρα 686 επ. Ο πρόεδρος των εφετών ορίζει την προθεσμία για την εμφάνιση, ενώ το άρθρο 226 εφαρμόζεται και εδώ.
3. Το ακίνητο ή η επιχείρηση βρίσκεται σε αναγκαστική διαχείριση αφότου επιδοθεί στον οφειλέτη η απόφαση που διατάζει την αναγκαστική διαχείριση. Το άρθρο 912 εφαρμόζεται και εδώ.

4. Within five days from the date the distribution table was prepared, the manager shall invite in writing the person for whose benefit enforcement is being done, the person enforcement concerns and the creditors who lodged claims to take cognisance of the table.

Article 1031

The person for whose benefit enforcement is being done and the person enforcement concerns and any other creditors who lodged claims may file objections against the claim lodged by a creditor and the distribution table with the court referred to in Article 1023(1) within 10 days of the [invitation] referred to in Article 1030(4). Filing objections against the claim lodged or the distribution table shall stay payment with regard to the creditor against whom the objections are filed until the judgment handed down by the court becomes non-appealable.

Article 1032

1. Every year and until management has ended, the manager is obligated to render account in writing to the person for whose benefit enforcement is being done and the person enforcement concerns and the creditors who lodged claims.
2. The manager shall be liable under the provisions of substantive law to compensate the person for whose benefit enforcement was done and the person the enforcement concerned and the creditors who lodged claims.

Article 1033

Management of the right shall cease pursuant to a *de jure* non-appealable judgment handed down by the court referred to in Article 1023(1) on a request from the person the enforcement concerned or any person with a legitimate interest[:]
1) if the claims of the person for whose benefit enforcement is being done and the creditors who lodged claims received satisfaction for their claims or the aforesaid persons relinquished management by means of a written declaration addressed to the person the enforcement concerned;
2) if the court considers that continued management would not be appropriate or would be harmful to the interests of the person the enforcement concerned.

CHAPTER VIII
Compulsory administration

Article 1034

1. Compulsory administration may be imposed on the immovable or enterprise of the debtor in order to satisfy a monetary claim of the creditor.
2. Compulsory administration shall be imposed following a judgment handed down by the single-member court of first instance of the district where the immovable or the registered offices of the enterprise of the debtor are located, if so requested by a creditor who holds an enforceable title and who has served an enforcement order on the debtor. The judgment accepting or dismissing the application may be contested only by means of appeal. The application and the appeal shall be tried in accordance with Articles 686 *et seq.* The presiding appeal judge shall set the deadline for entering an appearance, and Article 226 also applies in this case.
3. The immovable or the enterprise shall be placed in compulsory administration after the judgment ordering compulsory administration has been served on the debtor. Article 912 also applies in this case.

Άρθρο 1035

Αναγκαστική διαχείριση ακινήτου ή επιχείρησης δεν επιβάλλεται για έναν από τους ακόλουθους λόγους:
1) αν το δικαστήριο κρίνει ότι από τα εισοδήματα του ακινήτου ή της επιχείρησης δεν μπορεί να ικανοποιηθεί μέσα σε λογικό διάστημα η απαίτηση του δανειστή,
2) αν το δικαστήριο κρίνει ότι το ποσό της απαίτησης δεν δικαιολογεί να τεθεί το ακίνητο ή η επιχείρηση σε αναγκαστική διαχείριση,
3) αν πρόκειται για μικρή επιχείρηση ή για ακίνητο μικρής αξίας και το δικαστήριο κρίνει ότι θα ήταν ασύμφορη η αναγκαστική διαχείριση,
4) αν πρόκειται για επιχείρηση και το δικαστήριο κρίνει ότι συντρέχουν σπουδαίοι λόγοι για να μην τεθεί η επιχείρηση σε αναγκαστική διαχείριση.

Άρθρο 1036

1. Η απόφαση που διατάζει την αναγκαστική διαχείριση, αν πρόκειται για ακίνητο, εγγράφεται, με επιμέλεια του δανειστή που τη ζήτησε, στο βιβλίο κατασχέσεων της περιφέρειας όπου βρίσκεται το ακίνητο, και αν πρόκειται για επιχείρηση, σε ειδικό βιβλίο που το τηρεί η γραμματεία του πρωτοδικείου στην περιφέρεια του οποίου βρίσκεται η έδρα της επιχείρησης.
2. Η εγγραφή της αναγκαστικής διαχείρισης στα σχετικά βιβλία σύμφωνα με την παρ. 1 δεν εμποδίζει τη διάθεση του ακινήτου ή της επιχείρησης, η αναγκαστική όμως διαχείριση εξακολουθεί και μετά τη διάθεση.
3. Αν κατασχέθηκαν το ακίνητο ή τα περιουσιακά στοιχεία της επιχείρησης, η αναγκαστική διαχείριση παύει αφότου γίνει ο πλειστηριασμός. Επίσης παύει η αναγκαστική διαχείριση, αν ο οφειλέτης κηρυχθεί σε πτώχευση. Και στις δύο περιπτώσεις μπορεί να ζητηθεί η εξάλειψη της εγγραφής της παρ. 1.

Άρθρο 1037

1. Με την απόφαση που διατάζει την αναγκαστική διαχείριση διορίζεται συνάμα και διαχειριστής του ακινήτου ή της επιχείρησης. Ο διαχειριστής που διορίζεται πρέπει να είναι πρόσωπο κατάλληλο και προτιμώνται όποιοι ασκούν το ίδιο ή συγγενικό επάγγελμα ή έχουν τις απαιτούμενες ειδικές γνώσεις ή πείρα.
2. Διαχειριστής μπορεί να διοριστεί ο οφειλέτης, αν το δικαστήριο κρίνει ότι αυτό συμφέρει στην εκμετάλλευση του ακινήτου ή τη λειτουργία της επιχείρησης. Όταν διαχειριστής διορίζεται ο οφειλέτης διορίζεται συνάμα και επόπτης του διαχειριστή.
3. Διαχειριστής μπορεί να διοριστεί και ένας από τους δανειστές. Αν ένας αξιόχρεος δανειστής προτείνει για διαχειριστή ή επόπτη ορισμένο πρόσωπο και δηλώνει συνάμα ότι αναλαμβάνει την ευθύνη για τις πράξεις ή τις παραλείψεις του, προτιμάται το πρόσωπο που αυτός προτείνει, κατά την κρίση του δικαστηρίου.
4. Ο διαχειριστής και ο επόπτης που τυχόν διορίστηκε οφείλουν μέσα σε οκτώ ημέρες αφότου τους επιδοθεί η απόφαση να δηλώσουν στο δανειστή που ζήτησε την αναγκαστική διαχείριση, αν δέχονται το διορισμό, αλλιώς, θεωρούνται ότι τον αποποιήθηκαν.

Άρθρο 1038

1. Η απόφαση που διατάζει την αναγκαστική διαχείριση κοινοποιείται, με επιμέλεια του δανειστή που ζήτησε την αναγκαστική διαχείριση, στον οφειλέτη, στο διαχειριστή, στον τυχόν διορισμένο επόπτη και στους ενυπόθηκους δανειστές. Αν ο οφειλέτης αρνηθεί να συμμορφωθεί με την απόφαση, γίνεται αναγκαστική εκτέλεση, κατά τις διατάξεις του άρθρου 947.

Article 1035

Compulsory administration of an immovable or enterprise shall not be imposed where any of the following grounds apply:

1) if the court considers that the revenues from the property or the enterprise cannot satisfy the debtor's claim within a reasonable period of time;

2) if the court considers that the amount of the claim does not justify placement of the immovable or the enterprise in compulsory administration;

3) in the case of a small enterprise or a low-value immovable and where the court considers that compulsory administration would be disadvantageous;

4) in the case of an enterprise, where the court considers that there is a serious reason not to place the enterprise in compulsory administration.

Article 1036

1. In the case of an immovable, the judgment ordering compulsory administration shall be entered by the creditor who requested it in the attachment register of the district where the immovable is located, and, in the case of an enterprise, in a special register kept by the registry of the court of first instance in the district where the registered offices of the enterprise are located.

2. Entry of compulsory administration in the relevant registers in accordance with paragraph 1 shall not hinder sale of the property or enterprise; however, compulsory administration shall persist even after the sale.

3. If the immovable or assets of the enterprise were attached, the compulsory administration shall cease after the auction has been held. Compulsory administration shall also cease if the debtor is declared bankrupt. In both cases, striking out the entry referred to in paragraph 1 may be requested.

Article 1037

1. The judgment ordering compulsory administration shall also appoint an administrator of the immovable or the enterprise. The administrator appointed must be a suitable person, and preference shall be given to those exercising the same or a related profession or possessing the necessary special knowledge or experience.

2. The debtor may be appointed as administrator if the court considers that this would be advantageous for exploiting the immovable or running the enterprise. Where the debtor is appointed as administrator, a supervisor of the administrator shall also be appointed.

3. One of the creditors may also be appointed as administrator. If a solvent creditor nominates a specific person as administrator or supervisor and declares that they shall be liable for the actions or omissions of the person nominated, preference may, at the discretion of the court, be given to the person nominated by said creditor.

4. The administrator and any supervisor appointed is obligated, within eight days of being served the judgment, to declare to the creditor who requested compulsory administration whether or not they accept the appointment, otherwise they shall be deemed to have refused it.

Article 1038

1. The judgment ordering compulsory administration shall be notified by the creditor who requested compulsory administration to the debtor, the administrator, any supervisor appointed and the mortgagees. If the debtor refuses to comply with the judgment, compulsory enforcement shall take place in accordance with the provisions of Article 947.

2. Αφότου η απόφαση που διατάζει την αναγκαστική διαχείριση επιδοθεί στον οφειλέτη, αυτός στερείται τη διαχείριση του ακινήτου ή της επιχείρησης. Ώσπου να αναλάβει τα καθήκοντα του ο διαχειριστής, καθήκοντα διαχειριστή ασκεί προσωρινά ο οφειλέτης και έχει υποχρέωση να λογοδοτήσει στο διαχειριστή.
3. Αν επιβληθεί στο ακίνητο ή στα περιουσιακά στοιχεία της επιχείρησης συντηρητική ή αναγκαστική κατάσχεση, μεσεγγυούχος είναι ο διαχειριστής.

Άρθρο 1039

1. Ο διαχειριστής ενεργεί όλες τις πράξεις που είναι ενδεδειγμένες για την τακτική και επωφελή οικονομική εκμετάλλευση του ακινήτου ή της επιχείρησης και οφείλει να διατηρεί το ακίνητο ή την επιχείρηση σε καλή κατάσταση και να αποφεύγει πράξεις που βλάπτουν την οικονομική τους υπόσταση.
2. Ο διαχειριστής μόλις αναλάβει τα καθήκοντά του ειδοποιεί με έγγραφο τους οφειλέτες εκείνου κατά του οποίου έχει επιβληθεί η διαχείριση και εκείνους που συναλλάσσονται με την επιχείρηση ότι ανέλαβε τη διαχείριση του ακινήτου ή της επιχείρησης και πρέπει σ' αυτόν να καταβάλουν στο εξής τις οφειλές τους και μαζί του να συναλλάσσονται.
3. Ο διαχειριστής ενεργεί κάθε δικαιοπραξία ή πράξη για να πετύχει ο σκοπός της διαχείρισης και έχει το δικαίωμα, για να συνεχιστούν οι εργασίες της επιχείρησης ή της εκμετάλλευσης του ακινήτου, να συνάπτει δάνεια και μπορεί να δίνει και ενέχυρο επάνω στις πρώτες ύλες ή τα προϊόντα της επιχείρησης. Για κάθε έννομη σχέση που αφορά τη διαχείριση, και αν ακόμη η σχέση αυτή γεννήθηκε πριν από τη διαχείριση, στο δικαστήριο παρίσταται ο διαχειριστής. Οι διατάξεις των άρθρων 997 του αστικού κώδικα και 956 παρ. 6 αυτού του κώδικα εφαρμόζονται και εδώ.
4. Ο διαχειριστής δεν μπορεί, χωρίς την άδεια του μονομελούς πρωτοδικείου, που παρέχεται κατά τη διαδικασία των άρθρων 686 επ., να καταρτίζει δικαιοπραξίες με διάρκεια μεγαλύτερη από ένα έτος.

Άρθρο 1040

1. Όταν το ζητήσει ο οφειλέτης ή κάποιος από τους δανειστές, ο διαχειριστής ή ο επόπτης, το μονομελές πρωτοδικείο μπορεί, κατά τη διαδικασία των άρθρων 686 επ., να αντικαταστήσει το διαχειριστή ή τον επόπτη.
2. Κάθε διαφορά σχετική με τη διαχείριση επιλύεται από το μονομελές πρωτοδικείο κατά τη διαδικασία των άρθρων 686 επ., αν το ζητήσει ο διαχειριστής ή ο επόπτης ή ο οφειλέτης ή οποιοσδήποτε έχει έννομο συμφέρον. Το δικαστήριο μπορεί να ορίζει τον τρόπο που θα γίνεται η διαχείριση και να διατάζει κάθε μέτρο πρόσφορο γι' αυτήν.

Άρθρο 1041

1. Το μονομελές πρωτοδικείο, ορίζει τη μηνιαία αποζημίωση του διαχειριστή και του επόπτη. Οι διατάξεις του άρθρου 1034 παρ. 2 εδάφ. δεύτερο, τρίτο και τέταρτο, εφαρμόζονται και εδώ.
2. Αν ο οφειλέτης δεν έχει τα μέσα για τη διατροφή του, το μονομελές πρωτοδικείο ορίζει ένα χρηματικό ποσό που πρέπει να του πληρώνεται κάθε μήνα για τα απαραίτητα έξοδα της διατροφής του και της διατροφής της οικογένειάς του. Οι διατάξεις του άρθρου 1034 παρ. 2 εδάφια δεύτερο, τρίτο και τέταρτο εφαρμόζονται και εδώ.
3. Αν ο οφειλέτης κατοικεί μέσα στο ακίνητο, έχει το δικαίωμα να εξακολουθήσει να κατοικεί εκεί και μετά την επιβολή της αναγκαστικής διαχείρισης.
4. Ο οφειλέτης όταν ορίζεται διαχειριστής δεν έχει δικαίωμα μηνιαίας αποζημίωσης.

2. Once the judgment ordering compulsory administration has been served on the debtor, the latter shall be deprived of management of the immovable or the enterprise. Until such time as the administrator assumes their duties, the debtor shall temporarily perform the duties of administrator and is obligated to render account to the administrator.
3. If preventive or compulsory attachment is imposed on the immovable or the assets of the enterprise, the administrator shall be the sequestrator.

Article 1039

1. The administrator shall take all steps appropriate for the orderly and beneficial financial exploitation of the immovable or the enterprise, and is obligated to keep the immovable or enterprise in good condition and to abstain from all financially harmful acts.
2. Upon assuming their duties, the administrator shall notify in writing the debtors of the person compulsory administration concerns and those transacting with the enterprise that they have assumed administration of the immovable or the enterprise and that such debtors must henceforth pay their debts to and transact with the administrator.
3. The administrator shall enter into any legal transaction or take any steps to achieve the objectives of compulsory administration, and has the right, with a view to continuing the work of the company or exploitation of the immovable, to take out loans, and may also establish pledges on the raw materials or products of the enterprise. The administrator shall appear before the courts with regard to any legal relationship that concerns management, even if this relationship arose prior to compulsory administration. The provisions of Article 997 of the Civil Code and Article 956(6) of this Code also apply in this case.
4. The manager may not enter into legal transactions whose duration is longer than one year without permission from the single-member court of first instance under the procedure laid down in Articles 686 *et seq.*

Article 1040

1. On a request from the debtor or any creditor, from the administrator or from the supervisor, the single-member court of first instance may replace the administrator or the supervisor under the procedure laid down in Articles 686 *et seq.*
2. If so requested by the administrator or the supervisor or the debtor or any person with a legitimate interest, any dispute concerning the compulsory administration shall be resolved by the single-member court of first instance under the procedure laid down in Articles 686 *et seq.* The court may specify the manner in which compulsory administration will take place and may order any measure that is expedient for the compulsory administration.

Article 1041

1. The single-member court of first instance shall specify the monthly fee of the administrator and the supervisor. The provisions of the second, third and fourth subparagraphs of Article 1034(2) also apply in this case.
2. If the debtor lacks the means for their own subsistence, the single-member court of first instance shall specify a monetary amount payable to the debtor every month to cover the costs necessary for their subsistence and that of their family. The provisions of the second, third and fourth subparagraphs of Article 1034(2) also apply in this case.
3. If the debtor resides within the immovable, they have the right to continue residing there even after compulsory administration has been imposed.
4. Where appointed as administrator, the debtor does not have the right to a monthly fee.

Άρθρο 1042

Ο διαχειριστής από τους καρπούς και τα εισοδήματα του ακινήτου ή της επιχείρησης καταβάλλει τις αποδοχές του προσωπικού, τους τακτικούς φόρους και τις εισφορές σε ασφαλιστικούς οργανισμούς που γίνονται απαιτητοί αφού αρχίσει η διαχείριση, εξοφλεί τα δάνεια που πήρε και γενικά καταβάλλει όλα τα έξοδα που χρειάζονται για την εκμετάλλευση του ακινήτου ή τη λειτουργία της επιχείρησης.

Άρθρο 1043

1. Το υπόλοιπο που απομένει, αφού αφαιρεθούν τα έξοδα του άρθρου 1042, ο διαχειριστής το καταβάλλει στο δανειστή ώσπου να ικανοποιηθεί η απαίτησή του.

2. Αν υπάρχουν και άλλοι δανειστές εκτός από εκείνον που ζήτησε την αναγκαστική διαχείριση, αναγγέλλονται με έγγραφη δήλωση που επιδίδεται στο διαχειριστή και σε εκείνον κατά του οποίου στρέφεται η εκτέλεση.

3. Αν αναγγέλθηκαν δανειστές, ο διαχειριστής συντάσσει κάθε τρίμηνο πίνακα διανομής και με βάση αυτόν πληρώνει εκείνον που ζήτησε την αναγκαστική διαχείριση και τους δανειστές που αναγγέλθηκαν. Η κατάταξη των δανειστών στον πίνακα διανομής γίνεται σύμφωνα με τις διατάξεις των άρθρων 975, 976, 977 και 1007. Για την κατάταξη των απαιτήσεων του άρθρου 975 αντί της ημέρας του πλειστηριασμού λαμβάνεται υπόψη η ημέρα που άρχισε η αναγκαστική διαχείριση.

4. Μέσα σε δέκα ημέρες αφότου συνταχθεί ο πίνακας διανομής ο διαχειριστής καλεί εγγράφως τον οφειλέτη και τους δανειστές να λάβουν γνώση του πίνακα.

Άρθρο 1044

1. Κατά της αναγγελίας δανειστή, καθώς και κατά του πίνακα διανομής, ο οφειλέτης και κάθε δανειστής που έχει αναγγελθεί μπορεί, μέσα σε δέκα ημέρες αφότου περάσει η προθεσμία του άρθρου 1043 παρ. 4, να ασκήσει αντιρρήσεις στο κατά άρθρο 933 αρμόδιο δικαστήριο. Η άσκηση αντιρρήσεων κατά αναγγελίας ή κατά πίνακα διανομής αναστέλλει την καταβολή στο δανειστή κατά του οποίου στρέφονται οι αντιρρήσεις, ώσπου να γίνει τελεσίδικη η απόφαση του δικαστηρίου.

2. Όταν περάσει η προθεσμία της παρ. 1, ο διαχειριστής καταβάλλει στους δανειστές με βάση τον πίνακα διανομής.

Άρθρο 1045

1. Ο διαχειριστής οφείλει να υποβάλλει κάθε έτος, καθώς και όταν περατωθεί η διαχείριση, έγγραφη λογοδοσία στον οφειλέτη, σε εκείνον που ζήτησε την αναγκαστική διαχείριση και στους δανειστές που αναγγέλθηκαν.

2. Ο επόπτης του διαχειριστή επιβλέπει και παρακολουθεί τη διαχείριση και έχει δικαίωμα να εξετάζει τα βιβλία και τους λογαριασμούς της διαχείρισης και να ενημερώνεται για τη γενική κατάσταση της διαχείρισης.

3. Σε κάθε περίπτωση που το δικαστήριο του άρθρου 1040 παρ. 2 επιλύει διαφορά σχετική με την αναγκαστική διαχείριση καλείται υποχρεωτικά και ο επόπτης.

4. Ο διαχειριστής και ο επόπτης είναι υπεύθυνοι να αποζημιώσουν τον οφειλέτη και τους δανειστές κατά τις διατάξεις του ουσιαστικού δικαίου.

Article 1042

The manager shall use the fruits and revenues of the immovable or the enterprise to pay staff earnings, ordinary taxes and contributions to social security organisations that fall due after compulsory administration begins, to pay back loans taken out and, generally, to pay all the costs required for exploiting the immovable or running the enterprise.

Article 1043

1. After the costs referred to in Article 1042 have been deducted, the administrator shall pay the balance to the creditor until their claim has been satisfied.
2. If there are also other creditors apart from the creditor who requested compulsory administration, they may lodge a claim by means of a written declaration served on the administrator and on the person enforcement concerns.
3. If creditors have lodged claims, the administrator shall prepare a distribution table every three months, on the basis of which the administrator shall pay the creditor who requested compulsory administration and the creditors who lodged claims. The creditors shall be ranked in the distribution table in accordance with the provisions of Articles 975, 976, 977 and 1007. When ranking the claims referred to in Article 975, the day compulsory administration commenced shall be taken into account instead of the day of the auction.
4. Within 10 days from the date the distribution table was prepared, the administrator shall invite in writing the debtor and the creditors to take cognisance of the table.

Article 1044

1. The debtor and any creditors who lodged claims may file objections against the claim lodged by a creditor and the distribution table with the competent court under Article 933 within 10 days from the date the deadline set in Article 1043(1) has elapsed. [The act of] filing objections against the claim lodged or the distribution table shall stay payment to the creditor against whom the objections are filed until the judgment handed down by the court becomes *de jure* non-appealable.
2. Once the deadline referred to in paragraph 1 has lapsed, the administrator shall pay the creditors on the basis of the distribution table.

Article 1045

1. Every year and until compulsory administration has ended, the administrator is obligated to render account in writing to the debtor, the person who procured compulsory administration and the creditors who lodged claims.
2. The administrator's supervisor shall oversee and monitor compulsory administration, and has the right to examine the compulsory administration ledgers and accounts and to be briefed on the overall status of compulsory administration.
3. In all cases where the court referred to in Article 1040(2) resolves a dispute concerning compulsory administration, the supervisor must also be summoned.
4. The administrator and the supervisor are liable to compensate the debtor and the creditors in accordance with the provisions of substantive law.

Άρθρο 1046

1. Η αναγκαστική διαχείριση παύει με τελεσίδικη απόφαση του μονομελούς πρωτοδικείου της περιφέρειας όπου βρίσκεται το ακίνητο ή όπου εδρεύει η επιχείρηση του οφειλέτη, όταν το ζητήσει ο οφειλέτης ή ο δανειστής ή οποιοσδήποτε έχει έννομο συμφέρον:

α) αν ικανοποιήθηκαν οι απαιτήσεις εκείνου που ζητεί την αναγκαστική διαχείριση και των δανειστών που αναγγέλθηκαν ή αν αυτοί, με έγγραφη δήλωσή τους προς τον οφειλέτη, παραιτήθηκαν από την αναγκαστική διαχείριση,

β) αν το δικαστήριο κρίνει ότι η εξακολούθηση της αναγκαστικής διαχείρισης δεν είναι ενδεδειγμένη ή ζημιώνει τα συμφέροντα του οφειλέτη,

γ) αν ο δανειστής που ζήτησε την αναγκαστική διαχείριση δεν φρόντισε, μέσα σε λογικό διάστημα αφότου επιδόθηκε στον οφειλέτη η απόφαση που διατάζει την αναγκαστική διαχείριση, να αναλάβει τα καθήκοντα του διαχειριστής ή επόπτης.

Οι διατάξεις του άρθρου 1034 παρ. 2 εδάφ. δεύτερο, τρίτο και τέταρτο εφαρμόζονται και εδώ.

2. Αφότου, με βάση την τελεσίδικη απόφαση, εξαλειφθεί η εγγραφή στα ειδικά βιβλία σύμφωνα με το άρθρο 1036 παρ. 1, παύει η αναγκαστική διαχείριση του ακινήτου ή της επιχείρησης.

ΚΕΦΑΛΑΙΟ Θ'
Προσωπική κράτηση

Άρθρο 1047

1. Προσωπική κράτηση διατάσσεται στις περιπτώσεις που ορίζει ρητώς ο νόμος. Μπορεί να διαταχθεί επίσης και για απαιτήσεις από αδικοπραξία. Η διάρκεια της προσωπικής κράτησης ορίζεται με την απόφαση, έως ένα έτος. Η αγωγή για απαγγελία προσωπικής κράτησης μπορεί να ασκηθεί και αυτοτελώς. Στην περίπτωση αυτή εκδικάζεται κατά την ειδική διαδικασία των περιουσιακών διαφορών των άρθρων 614 επ. και υπάγεται στο μονομελές πρωτοδικείο. Η αγωγή αυτή, όταν ασκείται αυτοτελώς, εισάγεται είτε στο δικαστήριο της γενικής δωσιδικίας του εναγομένου, είτε στο δικαστήριο που είναι κατά τόπον αρμόδιο για την απαίτηση. Αίτηση απαγγελίας προσωπικής κράτησης που περιέχεται σε αγωγή για την απαίτηση εκδικάζεται κατά τη διαδικασία στην οποία υπάγεται η αγωγή.

2. Δεν διατάσσεται προσωπική κράτηση για απαίτηση δικαστικών εξόδων που επιδικάστηκαν από πολιτικό δικαστήριο ή για απαίτηση μικρότερη από οκτακόσια ογδόντα (880) ευρώ, εκτός αν προέρχεται από πιστωτικό τίτλο.

3. Αν πρόκειται για νομικά πρόσωπα, εκτός από τις ανώνυμες εταιρίες και τις εταιρίες περιορισμένης ευθύνης, ως προς τα χρέη της παραγρ.1 εδ. πρώτο του άρθρου αυτού, η προσωπική κράτηση διατάσσεται κατά των εκπροσώπων τους, και τις περιπτώσεις του άρθρου 947 παρ. 1 διατάσσεται κατά των νομικών αντιπροσώπων του διαδίκου που τελεί υπό επιμέλεια.

Άρθρο 1048

Προσωπική κράτηση δεν διατάσσεται:

α) κατά των ανηλίκων που τελούν υπό γονική μέριμνα ή υπό επιτροπεία και κατά των προσώπων που έχουν τεθεί σε κατάσταση δικαστικής συμπαράστασης,

β) κατά βουλευτών όσο διαρκεί η βουλευτική περίοδος και τέσσερις εβδομάδες μετά τη λήξη της,

γ) κατά προσώπων που συμπλήρωσαν το εξηκοστό πέμπτο έτος της ηλικίας τους και

δ) κατά κληρικών κάθε βαθμού κάθε γνωστής θρησκείας.

Article 1046

1. On a request from the debtor or the creditor or any person with a legitimate interest, compulsory administration shall cease pursuant to a *de jure* non-appealable judgment handed down by the single-member court of first instance of the district where the immovable is located or the enterprise of the debtor has its registered offices:

a) if the claims of the person who procured compulsory administration and the creditors who lodged claims were satisfied or the aforesaid persons discontinued the compulsory administration by means of a written declaration made to the debtor;

b) if the court considers that continued compulsory administration would not be appropriate or would be harmful to the interests of the debtor;

c) if the creditor who requested compulsory administration did not take steps to have an administrator or supervisor assume duties within a reasonable period of time after the judgment ordering compulsory administration was served on the debtor.

The provisions of the second, third and fourth subparagraphs of Article 1034(2) also apply in this case.

2. Compulsory administration of the immovable or the enterprise shall cease after the entry is deleted from the special registers pursuant to the *de jure* non-appealable judgment, in accordance with Article 1036(1).

CHAPTER IX
Personal detention

Article 1047

1. Personal detention shall be ordered in the cases expressly provided for in law. Personal detention may also be ordered for tortious claims. The duration of personal detention of up to one year shall be set in the judgment. An action requesting personal detention may also be filed independently. In this case, the action shall be filed before the single-member court of first instance and heard under the special procedure on property disputes laid down in Articles 614 *et seq.* When filed independently, this action shall be brought for a hearing either before the general forum of the defendant or the court with jurisdiction *ratione loci* over the claim. An application requesting personal detention contained in an action regarding a claim shall be heard under the procedure applicable to the action.

2. Personal detention shall not be ordered for claims of court costs awarded by a civil court or claims under 880 euros, unless arising from a credit instrument.

3. In cases of legal persons, except for sociétés anonymes and limited liability companies, with regard to the debts referred to in the first subparagraph of paragraph 1 of this Article, personal detention shall be ordered against their representatives and, in the cases referred to in Article 947(1), against the lawful proxies of the party in the proceedings under custodianship.

Article 1048

Personal detention shall not be ordered:

a) against juveniles in the care of their parents or under tutorship and against persons placed under legal guardianship;

b) against Members of Parliament during the parliamentary term and for four weeks after it has ended;

c) against persons who have attained the age of 65; and

d) against priests of any rank and of any known religion;

Άρθρο 1049

1. Η διάταξη για προσωπική κράτηση εκτελείται μόνο αφότου η δικαστική απόφαση που τη διατάζει γίνει τελεσίδικη και αφού προηγουμένως επιδοθεί σ' αυτόν που καταδικάστηκε. Όταν πρόκειται για εκπρόσωπο νομικού προσώπου, η προσωπική κράτηση δεν εκτελείται πριν περάσουν τρεις (3) ημέρες αφότου η απόφαση του επιδόθηκε. Απόφαση που διατάζει την προσωπική κράτηση, σύμφωνα με το άρθρο 1047, δεν εκτελείται αν εκείνος που καταδικάστηκε βρίσκεται κατά το χρόνο της εκτέλεσης σε αδυναμία να εκπληρώσει τη χρηματική οφειλή του.

2. Όποιος καταδικάστηκε σε προσωπική κράτηση συλλαμβάνεται από το δικαστικό επιμελητή, πάντα μπροστά σε μάρτυρα που προσλαμβάνεται για το σκοπό αυτό, και συντάσσεται σχετική έκθεση. Η σύλληψη απαγορεύεται:

α) στον τόπο όπου συνεδριάζει δικαστήριο και όσο διαρκεί η συνεδρίαση,

β) σε καθιερωμένο τόπο ιερουργίας γνωστής θρησκείας και όσο διαρκεί η ιερουργία,

γ) από 1 έως 31 Αυγούστου.

δ) από 23 Δεκεμβρίου μέχρι 7 Ιανουαρίου του επόμενου έτους,

ε) από τη Μεγάλη Δευτέρα μέχρι την Κυριακή του Θωμά και

στ) την προηγούμενη και την επόμενη εβδομάδα των εκλογών για την ανάδειξη βουλευτών, αντιπροσώπων στο Ευρωπαϊκό Κοινοβούλιο και Οργάνων Τοπικής Αυτοδιοίκησης. Η απαγόρευση αυτή ισχύει και για επαναληπτικές εκλογές και μόνο για τις περιφέρειες που διεξάγονται τέτοιες.

Άρθρο 1050

1. Αν όποιος έχει συλληφθεί προβάλει αντιρρήσεις κατά της προσωπικής κράτησης, προσάγεται αμέσως στον πρόεδρο πρωτοδικών στην περιφέρεια του οποίου έγινε η σύλληψη. Αυτός, δικάζοντας κατά τη διαδικασία των άρθρων 686 επ., αποφασίζει για τις αντιρρήσεις που μπορούν να υποβληθούν και προφορικά.

2. Αν δεν προβλήθηκαν αντιρρήσεις ή αν απορρίφθηκαν, αυτός που έχει συλληφθεί οδηγείται στις φυλακές, όπου κρατείται σε χώρο διαφορετικό από εκείνον που προορίζεται για όσους είναι υπόδικοι ή κατάδικοι για αξιόποινες πράξεις. Μόνον ώσπου να τον οδηγήσουν στη φυλακή μπορεί να φυλαχθεί σε οποιαδήποτε άλλη φυλακή ή και σε οποιοδήποτε άλλο χώρο.

3. Ο διευθυντής της φυλακής παραλαμβάνει εκείνον που έχει συλληφθεί μόνο αν του παραδοθεί η απόφαση που διατάζει την προσωπική του κράτηση και αντίγραφο της έκθεσης της σύλληψής του και του προκαταβληθούν, με απόδειξη, για ένα μήνα τα τροφεία που ορίζονται με απόφαση του υπουργού δικαιοσύνης. Στον ίδιο διευθυντή προκαταβάλλονται, με απόδειξη, τα τροφεία κάθε επόμενου μήνα.

4. Η προσωπική κράτηση των στρατιωτικών εκτελείται από τη στρατιωτική αρχή, στην οποία προκαταβάλλονται τα τροφεία, σύμφωνα με όσα ορίζει η προηγούμενη παράγραφος.

Άρθρο 1051

Αποφάσεις προσωπικής κράτησης για την είσπραξη απαιτήσεων προγενέστερες από την έναρξη της προσωποκράτησης που αποτίθηκε, εκτελούνται μόνο αν αυτή δεν κράτησε ένα έτος, και μόνο για το χρονικό διάστημα που μένει για να συμπληρωθεί το έτος. Η προσωπική κράτηση για το χρονικό αυτό διάστημα ενεργείται ως συνέχεια της προηγούμενης ή και μετά την απόλυση του καταδικασμένου. Για να εκτελεστεί στη συνέχεια αρκεί έκθεση του δικαστικού επιμελητή που συντάσσεται μπροστά σε εκείνον κατά του οποίου στρέφεται η εκτέλεση και στο διευθυντή της φυλακής στον οποίο παραδίδεται η απόφαση που εκτελείται και αντίγραφο της έκθεσης και στον οποίο προκαταβάλλονται τα τροφεία σύμφωνα με την παρ. 3 του προηγούμενου άρθρου.

Article 1049

1. The personal detention order is enforceable only after the court judgment ordering it has become *de jure* non-appealable and has been served on the person whose personal detention has been ordered. In the case of a representative of a legal person, personal detention is not enforceable before three days have elapsed from the date the judgment is served on them. A judgment ordering personal detention in accordance with Article 1047 is not enforceable if the person whose personal detention has been ordered [proves that they are] unable to pay their monetary debt at the time of enforcement.

2. Any person whose personal detention has been ordered shall be arrested by the court process server, always in the presence of a witness enlisted for this purpose, and a relevant report shall be prepared. Arrests shall be prohibited:

a) at the place where the court is sitting and for the duration of the sitting;

b) at an established place where ceremonies of a known religion are conducted and for the duration of the ceremony;

c) between 1 and 31 August;

d) between 23 December and 7 January of the following year;

e) between Monday before [Orthodox] Easter and the Sunday after [Orthodox] Easter; and

f) the week prior to and the week subsequent to elections for members of parliament, members of the European Parliament and local government authorities. This prohibition shall also apply to run-off elections and only in the districts where such elections are being held.

Article 1050

1. If the arrested person objects to personal detention, they shall be immediately brought before the presiding judge of the court of first instance in whose district the arrest took place. That judge, trying the matter under the procedure laid down in Articles 686 *et seq.*, shall decide on the objections, which may also be made verbally.

2. If objections were not raised or were dismissed, the arrested person shall be brought to prison, where they shall be detained in an area of the prison distinct from that intended for persons on remand or persons convicted of criminally punishable acts. The arrested person may be held at any other prison or any other facility only until they are committed to prison.

3. The prison governor shall take receipt of the arrested person only if the judgment ordering their personal detention and a copy of the arrest report are delivered to the governor and the fees set in a decision of the Minister of Justice for one month are paid in advance to the governor, and a receipt shall be issued. The prison sustenance expenses for every subsequent month shall be paid in advance to the governor, and a receipt shall be issued.

4. Military personnel shall be detained by military authorities, to which the fees shall be paid in advance, in accordance with the provisions of the preceding paragraph.

Article 1051

Judgments ordering personal detention for the collection of claims that arose prior to commencement of the personal detention time served are enforceable only if the personal detention lasted less than one year and only for the period remaining until one year has elapsed. Personal detention for this period shall be a continuation of the previous personal detention or shall be ordered even after the convicted person has been released. In order [for personal detention] to be subsequently enforced, a report of the court process server shall suffice, prepared in the presence of the person enforcement concerns and the prison governor, to whom the judgment being enforced and a copy of the report shall be delivered and the fees shall be paid in advance, in accordance with paragraph 3 of the preceding Article.

Άρθρο 1052

Ο κρατούμενος απολύεται

α) αν συμπληρώθηκε η διάρκεια της προσωπικής κράτησης που ορίζει η απόφαση,

β) αν κατατεθεί στο Ταμείο Παρακαταθηκών και Δανείων το χρέος για το οποίο επιβλήθηκε η προσωπική κράτηση μαζί με τους τόκους που οφείλονται ήδη και τα έξοδα της εκτέλεσης και κατατεθεί το γραμμάτιο στο γραμματέα του πρωτοδικείου, στην περιφέρεια του οποίου βρίσκεται η φυλακή,

γ) αν συναινέσουν εγγράφως ο δανειστής που επέβαλε την προσωπική κράτηση και κάθε άλλος δανειστής που ζήτησε να παραταθεί η κράτηση,

δ) αν ο κρατούμενος συμπληρώσει το 65ο έτος της ηλικίας του και

ε) αν παραλείφθηκε η προκαταβολή των τροφείων.

Στις περιπτώσεις α', γ' και ε', η απόλυση γίνεται από το διευθυντή της φυλακής. Στις άλλες, με απόφαση του προέδρου πρωτοδικών, στην περιφέρεια του οποίου βρίσκεται η φυλακή, ο οποίος δικάζει κατά τη διαδικασία των άρθρων 686 επ. Στην περίπτωση ε', η απόλυση γίνεται μόλις περάσει η ώρα 12 το μεσημέρι της τελευταίας ημέρας, για την οποία πληρώθηκαν τροφεία και δεν επιτρέπεται νέα κράτηση του οφειλέτη για το ίδιο χρέος.

Άρθρο 1053

Αν ο κρατούμενος είναι ασθενής ή ασθενήσει κατά τη διάρκεια της κράτησής του, ο πρόεδρος πρωτοδικών που αναφέρεται στο προηγούμενο άρθρο, δικάζοντας κατά τη διαδικασία των άρθρων 686 επ., μπορεί να επιτρέψει να κρατηθεί ο κρατούμενος, με δικά του έξοδα, σε νοσοκομείο ή σε ιδιωτική κατοικία, και μπορεί επίσης να επιτρέψει την ελευθέρωσή του αν η ασθένεια είναι τέτοια ώστε να υπάρχει κίνδυνος από την παράταση της κράτησης.

Άρθρο 1054

1. Κάθε διαφορά σχετική με την εκτέλεση της προσωπικής κράτησης υπάγεται, αν δεν ορίζεται διαφορετικά, στην αρμοδιότητα του πολυμελούς πρωτοδικείου στην περιφέρεια του οποίου εκτελείται. Ο πρόεδρος του δικαστηρίου αυτού ορίζει σύντομη δικάσιμο, και την προθεσμία για να κλητευθεί ο αντίδικος εκείνου που προσφεύγει.

2. Η προθεσμία της ανακοπής ερημοδικίας και της έφεσης κατά της απόφασης που εκδίδεται σύμφωνα με την προηγούμενη παράγραφο είναι πέντε ημέρες, αλλά ούτε αυτή ούτε και η άσκηση των ένδικων αυτών μέσων αναστέλλουν την εκτέλεση.

Article 1052

The detained person shall be released if[:]
a) the duration of personal detention set in the judgment elapses;
b) the debt for which personal detention was imposed is deposited with the Consignment Deposits and Loans Fund, together with interest already due and the enforcement costs, and the note is deposited with the registrar of the court of first instance in whose district the prison is located;
c) consent is provided in writing by the creditor who procured personal detention and any other creditor who requested extension of personal detention;
d) the detained person attains the age of 65; and
e) the fees were not paid in advance.
In cases (a), (c) and (e), the detained person shall be released by the prison governor and, in the other cases, pursuant to a judgment handed down by the presiding judge of the court of first instance in whose district the prison is located, trying the matter under the procedure laid down in Articles 686 *et seq.* In case (e), the detained person shall be released after 12:00 noon on the final day for which fees had been paid, and the debtor may not be detained again for the same debt.

Article 1053

If the detained person is ill or falls ill during their personal detention, the presiding judge of the court of first instance referred to in the preceding Article, trying the matter under the procedure laid down in Articles 686 *et seq.*, may allow the detained person to be detained, at their own expense, at a hospital or a private residence, and to allow their release if the illness is such that extending personal detention would give rise to a risk.

Article 1054

1. Unless otherwise provided for, all disputes concerning enforcement of personal detention shall fall under the jurisdiction of the multi-member court of first instance in whose district personal detention is being enforced. The presiding judge of that court shall set a close hearing date and a deadline for summonsing the opponent of the person seeking recourse.
2. The deadline for filing an opposition against a default judgment and filing an appeal against the judgment handed down in accordance with the preceding paragraph is five days, but neither [the act of] filing an opposition nor [the act of filing] such legal remedies shall stay enforcement.

II. ΕΙΣΑΓΩΓΙΚΟΣ ΝΟΜΟΣ ΚΩΔΙΚΑ ΠΟΛΙΤΙΚΗΣ ΔΙΚΟΝΟΜΙΑΣ

Άρθρο 1

Από την εισαγωγή του Κώδικα Πολιτικής Δικονομίας καταργούνται
α) ο νόμος της 2/14 Απριλίου 1834 «περί Πολιτικής Δικονομίας»,
β) ο νόμος της 23 Ιουλίου 1903 «περί Πολιτικής Δικονομίας της Κρητικής Πολιτείας»,
γ) τα άρθρα 315 έως 409 της Κρητικής Πολιτικής Δικονομίας της 25 Ιανουαρίου 1880,
δ) τα άρθρα 50 έως 56 της Ειδικής Δικονομίας των Κρητών της 10 Φεβρουαρίου 1880 ως ίσχυαν μέχρι τούδε
ε) κάθε άλλη διάταξη που είναι αντίθετη σ' αυτόν και
στ) κάθε διάταξη που αφορά θέματα, που ρυθμίζει ο εισαγόμενος Κώδικας, εφόσον δεν συμβιβάζεται με τις διατάξεις αυτού του κώδικα, και δεν ορίζεται διαφορετικά στο νόμο αυτόν.

Άρθρο 2

Με την εισαγωγή του Κώδικα Πολιτικής Δικονομίας δεν επηρεάζεται η ισχύς δικονομικών διατάξεων που στηρίζονται σε διεθνείς συμβάσεις.

Άρθρο 3

1. Στις περιπτώσεις που ειδικοί νόμοι παραπέμπουν σε διατάξεις οι οποίες καταργούνται με το νόμο αυτόν, από την εισαγωγή του Κώδικα Πολιτικής Δικονομίας εφαρμόζονται οι αντίστοιχες διατάξεις του.
2. Στις περιπτώσεις που διατάξεις του Αστικού Κώδικα ή άλλου νόμου παραπέμπουν στην αρμοδιότητα και στην επ'αναφορά διαδικασία γενικά του προέδρου πρωτοδικών ή στη διαδικασία των άρθρων 634 έως 639 της Πολιτικής Δικονομίας ή 564 έως 568 της Κρητικής Πολιτικής Δικονομίας, από την εισαγωγή του ΚΠολΔ είναι αρμόδιο το μονομελές πρωτοδικείο, δικάζοντας κατά τη διαδικασία των άρθρων 686 επ. ΚΠολΔ, εκτός αν ορίζεται διαφορετικά.
3. Στις περιπτώσεις που διατάξεις νόμων παραπέμπουν στην επ'αναφορά διαδικασία ενώπιον του Πρωτοδικείου ή στη διαδικασία των άρθρων 640 έως 645 της Πολιτικής Δικονομίας ή 557 έως 560 της Κρητικής Πολιτικής Δικονομίας, από την εισαγωγή του ΚΠολΔ εφαρμόζεται η διαδικασία τον άρθρων 740 επ., εκτός αν ο νόμος αυτός ορίζει διαφορετικά.
4. [Καταργείται]

Άρθρο 4

Από την εισαγωγή του ΚΠολΔ καταργούνται όλες οι διατάξεις νόμων που καθιερώνουν ειδικές διαδικασίες ενώπιον των πολιτικών δικαστηρίων ή ειδικούς κανόνες για ορισμένες κατηγορίες υποθέσεων που εισάγονται στα δικαστήρια αυτά, εκτός αν ο νόμος αυτός ορίζει διαφορετικά.

Άρθρο 5

1. Όλα τα χρηματικά ποσά που ορίζουν οι διατάξεις του ΚΠολΔ σε δραχμές, επιτρέπεται να αυξομειώνονται με διατάγματα, που εκδίδονται ύστερα από πρόταση του Υπουργού Δικαιοσύνης.
2. Για την εφαρμογή των διατάξεων της παρ.1 λαμβάνεται υπόψη ο χρόνος
α) που ασκήθηκε η αγωγή ή η αίτηση, όταν πρόκειται για την αρμοδιότητα του δικαστηρίου ή την εφαρμογή ειδικών διατάξεων ή ειδικών διαδικασιών,
β) που εκδόθηκε η απόφαση, όταν πρόκειται για το επιτρεπτό ένδικου μέσου και την αρμοδιότητα του δικαστηρίου που το δικάζει,
γ) που επιβλήθηκε η ποινή, όταν πρόκειται για χρηματικές ποινές, και
δ) που γεννήθηκε η έννομη σχέση, όταν πρόκειται για το επιτρεπτό της απόδειξης με μάρτυρες.

II. LAW INTRODUCING THE CODE OF CIVIL PROCEDURE

Article 1

Upon the entry of the Code of Civil Procedure into force, the following are repealed[:]
a) the law of 2/14 April 1834 on Civil Procedure;
b) the law of 23 July 1903 on Civil Procedure of the Cretan State;
c) Articles 315 to 409 of the Cretan Civil Procedure [Code] of 25 January 1880;
d) Articles 50 to 56 of the Special Procedure [Code] of the Cretans of 10 February 1880 in force until now;
e) all other provisions contrary to the Code of Civil Procedure; and
f) all provisions concerning matters regulated under the Code of Civil Procedure being introduced, where incompatible with the provisions of that Code and unless otherwise provided for in this Law.

Article 2

The entry of the Code of Civil Procedure into force does not affect the validity of procedural provisions based on international treaties and conventions.

Article 3

1. Where special laws refer to provisions repealed under this Law, the corresponding provisions of this Law apply from the entry of the Code of Civil Procedure into force.
2. Where provisions of the Civil Code or any other law refer to the jurisdiction and non-contentious proceedings in general under the presiding judge of the court of first instance or the procedure laid down in Articles 634 to 639 of the Civil Procedure [Code] or 564 to 568 of the Cretan Civil Procedure [Code], the single-member court of first instance has jurisdiction from the entry of the Code of Civil Procedure into force, trying the matter under the procedure laid down in Articles 686 *et seq.* of the Code of Civil Procedure, unless otherwise provided for.
3. Where statutory provisions refer to non-contentious proceedings before the court of first instance or the procedure laid down in Articles 640 to 645 of the Civil Procedure [Code] or Articles 557 to 560 of the Cretan Civil Procedure [Code], the procedure laid down in Articles 740 *et seq.* applies, unless otherwise provided for in this Law.
4. [Repealed]

Article 4

Upon the entry of the Code of Civil Procedure into force, all statutory provisions establishing special procedures before the civil courts or special rules for certain categories of cases brought for a hearing before such courts are repealed, unless otherwise provided for in this Law.

Article 5

1. All monetary amounts specified in the provisions of the Code of Civil Procedure in drachmas may be increased or decreased pursuant to decrees issued on a proposal from the Minister of Justice.
2. When applying the provisions of paragraph 1, account shall be taken of the time[:]
a) the action or application was filed, where the jurisdiction of the court or the application of special provisions or special procedures are concerned;
b) the judgment was handed down, where the admissibility of a legal remedy and the jurisdiction of the court trying said legal remedy are concerned;
c) the penalty was imposed, in cases of monetary penalties; and
d) the legal relationship arose, where the admissibility of evidence given by witness testimony is concerned.

Άρθρο 6

1. Ο νόμος 406 της 17/24 Νοεμβρίου 1914 «περί δικαστηρίου συγκρούσεως καθηκόντων» διατηρεί την ισχύ του.

2. [Καταργείται]

Άρθρο 7

1. Από την εισαγωγή του ΚΠολΔ καταργούνται το άρθρο 38 του νόμου 3632 της 17/26 Ιουλίου 1928 «περί χρηματιστηρίων αξιών» και το προεδρικό διάταγμα της 15/15 Απριλίου 1929 «περί εκδικάσεως των χρηματιστηριακών διαφορών», οι παρ.3 επ. του άρθρου 18 του νομοθετικού διατάγματος της 2/10 Νοεμβρίου 1923 «περί χρηματιστηρίου εμπορευμάτων», τα άρθρα 51 έως 63 του Εμπορικού Νόμου καθώς και όλες οι διατάξεις νόμων που καθιερώνουν ειδικά πολιτικά δικαστήρια ή υποχρεωτικές ή αναγκαστικές διαιτησίες για την εκδίκαση διαφορών ιδιωτικού δικαίου, εκτός από εκείνες που ορίζονται στα άρθρα 8 και 46.

2. Οι εκκρεμείς δίκες κατά την εισαγωγή του ΚΠολΔ, ενώπιον των ειδικών πολιτικών δικαστηρίων ή των υποχρεωτικών ή των αναγκαστικών διαιτησιών που καταργούνται με την παρ. 1, συνεχίζονται ενώπιον τους, σύμφωνα με τις καταργούμενες διατάξεις εωσότου εκδοθεί τελεσίδικη απόφαση.

Άρθρο 8

1. Διατηρούνται σε ισχύ οι διατάξεις του άρθρου 10 του νόμου 2345 της 24 Ιουνίου/3 Ιουλίου 1920 «περί προσωρινού αρχιμουφτή και μουφτήδων των εν των κράτει μουσουλμάνων και περί διαχειρίσεως των περιουσιών των Μουσουλμανικών Κοινοτήτων».

2. Οι παρ. 2 και 3 του άρθρου 10 του νόμου 1345 της 24 Ιουνίου 1920 τροποποιούνται ως εξής: «2. Κάθε απόφαση του μουφτή για ζητήματα αμφισβητούμενης δικαιοδοσίας δεν μπορεί να εκτελεστεί, ούτε αποτελεί δεδικασμένο, αν δεν κηρυχθεί εκτελεστή από το μονομελές πρωτοδικείο, στην περιφέρεια του οποίου εδρεύει ο μουφτής που εξέδωσε την απόφαση, κατά τη διαδικασία των άρθρων 741 επ. ΚΠολΔ.

3. Το δικαστήριο της παρ.2 εξετάζει μόνο αν η απόφαση εκδόθηκε μέσα στα όρια της δικαιοδοσίας που έχει ο μουφτής με το νόμο αυτόν και δεν εξετάζει το περιεχόμενο της».

Άρθρο 9

1. Από την εισαγωγή του ΚΠολΔ καταργούνται όλες οι διατάξεις που ορίζουν την καθ'ύλην ή κατά τόπον αρμοδιότητα των πολιτικών δικαστηρίων για την εκδίκαση των υποθέσεων που υπάγονται σ' αυτά.

2. Οι δίκες που είναι εκκρεμείς κατά την εισαγωγή του ΚΠολΔ συνεχίζονται ενώπιον των δικαστηρίων όπου είχαν εισαχθεί' ή είχαν παραπεμφθεί, εφόσον, σύμφωνα με τις διατάξεις που ίσχυαν πριν από την εισαγωγή του είναι καθ'ύλην και κατά τόπον αρμόδια, και αν είναι αναρμόδια, εφαρμόζονται οι διατάξεις του ΚΠολΔ για την αρμοδιότητα.

3. Στις περιπτώσεις της παρ.2 η διαδικασία διεξάγεται σύμφωνα με τις διατάξεις του δικαίου που ίσχυε έως την εισαγωγή του ΚΠολΔ.

Άρθρο 10

1. Τα άρθρα 42 έως 51 του ΚΠολΔ εφαρμόζονται και στις δίκες που εκκρεμούν ενώπιον των πολιτικών δικαστηρίων κατά την εισαγωγή του.

2. Συμφωνία για παρέκταση της αρμοδιότητας που είχε συνομολογηθεί πριν από την εισαγωγή του ΚΠολΔ, σύμφωνα με τις διατάξεις του δικαίου που ίσχυε έως τότε, είναι έγκυρη, αν αφορά την κατά τόπον αρμοδιότητα.

Article 6

1. Law 406 of 17/24 November 1914 on the court with jurisdiction over conflict of duties remains in force.
2. [Repealed]

Article 7

1. Upon the entry of the Code of Civil Procedure into force, Article 38 of Law 3632 of 17/26 July 1928 on stock exchanges and the Presidential Decree of 15/15 April 1929 on the adjudication of stock exchange disputes, Article 18(3) *et seq.* of the Legislative Decree of 2/10 November 1923 on the commodities exchange, Articles 51 to 63 of the Commercial Law and all statutory provisions establishing special civil courts or compulsory or mandatory arbitration for the adjudication of private-law disputes are repealed, except for those provided for in Articles 8 and 46.
2. Proceedings pending at the time of entry of the Code of Civil Procedure into force before special civil courts or under contractually or statutorily mandated arbitration repealed under paragraph 1 shall continue before said courts in accordance with the repealed provisions until a *de jure* non-appealable judgment has been handed down.

Article 8

1. The provisions of Article 10 of Law 2345 of 24 June/3 July 1920 on the provisional grand mufti and muftis of the Muslims in the state and on management of the assets of Muslim Communities remain in force.
2. Article 10(2) and (3) of Law 1345 of 24 June 1920 are amended as follows: "2. No decision issued by a mufti on matters of disputed jurisdiction may be enforced or constitute *res judicata* if it is not declared enforceable by the single-member court of first instance in whose district the mufti who issued the decision is seated, in accordance with the procedure laid down in Articles 741 *et seq.* of the Code of Civil Procedure.
3. The court referred to in paragraph 2 shall only examine whether the decision was issued within the remit of the mufti under this Law and shall not examine its contents".

Article 9

1. Upon the entry of the Code of Civil Procedure into force, all provisions specifying the jurisdiction *ratione materiae* or *ratione loci* of the civil courts to adjudicate cases falling within their jurisdiction are repealed.
2. Proceedings pending at the time of entry of the Code of Civil Procedure into force shall continue before the courts to which they had been brought for hearing or had been remitted, provided that, in accordance with the provisions in force prior the entry of the Code into force, the said courts had jurisdiction *ratione materiae* and *ratione loci* and, if they lack jurisdiction, the provisions of the Code of Civil Procedure on jurisdiction apply.
3. In the cases referred to in paragraph 2, proceedings shall be conducted in accordance with the provisions of the law in force until the entry of the Code of Civil Procedure into force.

Article 10

1. Articles 42 to 51 of the Code of Civil Procedure also apply to proceedings pending before the civil courts at the time of entry of the Code into force.
2. A prorogation of jurisdiction clause agreed prior to the entry of the Code of Civil Procedure into force, in accordance with the provisions of the law in force until that time, shall be valid, if it concerns jurisdiction *ratione loci*.

Άρθρο 11

1. Όλες οι διαφορές που κατά τις διατάξεις του β. διατάγματος 27/27 Μαίου 1957 «περί τροποποιήσεως και συμπληρώσεως των διατάξεων του ενοικοστασίου κλπ. συναφών νόμων κατ' εφαρμογήν του νόμου 3664/57» υπάγονται στην αρμοδιότητα του προέδρου πρωτοδικών ή του ειρηνοδικείου δικάζονται στο εξής οι πρώτες από το μονομελές Πρωτοδικείο και οι δεύτερες από το ειρηνοδικείο κατά τη διαδικασία τον άρθρων 647 έως 662 του ΚΠολΔ.

2. Οι δίκες που είναι εκκρεμείς κατά την εισαγωγή του ΚΠολΔ ενώπιον των αρμόδιων κατά το β. διάταγμα της παρ.1 δικαστηρίων συνεχίζονται στα δικαστήρια αυτά σύμφωνα με τις διατάξεις που ίσχυαν έως την εισαγωγή του.

Άρθρο 12

Στις δίκες που κατά την εισαγωγή του ΚΠολΔ είναι εκκρεμείς στον πρώτο βαθμό, οι διαδικαστικές πράξεις ρυθμίζονται από τις διατάξεις του, όσες όμως είχαν ενεργηθεί πριν από την εισαγωγή του ρυθμίζονται από το προγενέστερο δίκαιο.

Άρθρο 13

1. Οι διατάξεις των άρθρων 144 έως 151 του ΚΠολΔ για τις προθεσμίες εφαρμόζονται, εφόσον η επίδοση ή το γεγονός που αποτελεί την αφετηρία της προθεσμίας συντελέστηκε μετά την εισαγωγή του ΚΠολΔ.

2. Η διάρκεια των προθεσμιών που είχαν αρχίσει πριν από την εισαγωγή του ΚΠολΔ και δεν έχουν λήξει, καθώς και η παρέκτασή τους, κρίνονται σύμφωνα με το δίκαιο που ίσχυε πριν από την εισαγωγή του, η παράταση όμως, η αναστολή και η διακοπή τους εξαιτίας γεγονότων που επήλθαν μετά την εισαγωγή του ΚΠολΔ, κρίνονται με βάση τις διατάξεις του.

3. Οι διατάξεις των άρθρων 152 έως 158 ΚΠολΔ εφαρμόζονται και στις προθεσμίες που είχαν αρχίσει πριν από την εισαγωγή του, εφόσον δεν περατώθηκε η δίκη με αμετάκλητη απόφαση.

Άρθρο 14

1. Οι διατάξεις των άρθρων 173 έως 175 ΚΠολΔ εφαρμόζονται και στις δίκες που είναι εκκρεμείς πριν από την εισαγωγή του.

2. Οι διατάξεις των άρθρων 176 έως 193 ΚΠολΔ εφαρμόζονται και στις δίκες που είναι εκκρεμείς κατά την εισαγωγή του.

Άρθρο 15

Οι διατάξεις των άρθρων 205 και 206 ΚΠολΔ εφαρμόζονται και στις δίκες που είναι εκκρεμείς κατά την εισαγωγή του.

Άρθρο 16

Οι διατάξεις των άρθρων 208 έως 214 ΚΠολΔ εφαρμόζονται και στις αγωγές που είχαν ασκηθεί πριν από την εισαγωγή του και δεν έχουν ακόμη συζητηθεί.

Άρθρο 17

Οι διατάξεις των άρθρων 226 έως 281, 296 και 297 ΚΠολΔ εφαρμόζονται και στις αγωγές που είναι εκκρεμείς κατά την εισαγωγή του.

Article 11

1. All disputes which, under the provisions of the Royal Decree of 27/27 May 1957 amending and supplementing rent control provisions etc. of related laws pursuant to Law 3664/1957, which fall under the jurisdiction of the presiding judge of the court of first instance or of the court of the peace shall henceforth be tried as follows: the former by the single-member court of first instance and the latter by the court of the peace under the procedure laid down in Articles 647 to 662 of the Code of Civil Procedure.
2. Proceedings pending at the time of entry of the Code of Civil Procedure into force before the courts with jurisdiction under the Royal Decree referred to in paragraph 1 shall continue before said courts in accordance with the provisions which were in force prior to the entry of the Code into force.

Article 12

During proceedings pending at first instance at the time of entry of the Code of Civil Procedure into force, procedural steps shall be regulated under the provisions of the Code, while those taken prior to said entry shall be regulated under the law previously in force.

Article 13

1. The provisions of Articles 144 to 151 of the Code of Civil Procedure apply if service [of documents] or the event constituting the starting point of the deadline occurred after the entry of the Code into force.
2. The duration of deadlines which had commenced prior to the entry of the Code of Civil Procedure into force and which have not expired, as well as any extension thereto, shall be adjudicated in accordance with the law in force prior to said entry; however, extensions, stays and discontinuations of such deadlines due to events that occurred after the entry of the Code of Civil Procedure into force shall be adjudicated on the basis of the provisions of said Code.
3. The provisions of Articles 152 to 158 of the Code of Civil Procedure also apply to deadlines that had commenced prior to the entry of the Code into force, provided the proceedings were not completed with an irrevocable judgment being handed down.

Article 14

1. The provisions of Articles 173 to 175 of the Code of Civil Procedure also apply to proceedings that were pending prior to the entry of the Code into force.
2. The provisions of Articles 176 to 193 of the Code of Civil Procedure also apply to proceedings that were pending at the time of entry of the Code into force.

Article 15

The provisions of Articles 205 and 206 of the Code of Civil Procedure also apply to proceedings that were pending at the time of entry of the Code into force.

Article 16

The provisions of Articles 208 to 214 of the Code of Civil Procedure also apply to actions that had been brought prior to the entry of the Code into force and have yet to be heard.

Article 17

The provisions of Articles 226 to 281, 296 and 297 of the Code of Civil Procedure also apply to actions that were pending at the time of entry of the Code into force.

Άρθρο 18

1. Οι διατάξεις των άρθρων 286 έως 312 ΚΠολΔ εφαρμόζονται και στις δίκες που είναι εκκρεμείς κατά την εισαγωγή του.
2. Οι διατάξεις των άρθρων 313 έως 320 και 332 έως 334 ΚΠολΔ εφαρμόζονται και στις αποφάσεις που δημοσιεύθηκαν πριν από την εισαγωγή του.

Άρθρο 19

1. Διατηρούνται σε ισχύ οι ειδικές διατάξεις για διεξαγωγή εξώδικης πραγματογνωμοσύνης ή δειγματοληψίας.
2. Το δικαστήριο εκτιμά ελεύθερα τις γνωμοδοτήσεις πραγματογνωμόνων σύμφωνα με την παράγραφο 1 ή τις αποφάσεις διοικητικών αρχών ή συλλογικών οργάνων της διοίκησης που εκδίδονται με βάση τις γνωμοδοτήσεις αυτές και κάθε αντίθετη διάταξη καταργείται.

Άρθρο 20

Οι διατάξεις των άρθρων 393 και 394 ΚΠολΔ εφαρμόζονται στις δικαιοπραξίες που καταρτίστηκαν μετά την εισαγωγή του.

Άρθρο 21

Οι διατάξεις των άρθρων 415 έως 420 και 421 έως 431 ΚΠολΔ εφαρμόζονται και στις δίκες που είναι εκκρεμείς κατά την εισαγωγή του. Διαδικαστικές πράξεις απόδειξης που έγιναν κατά τις διατάξεις του δικαίου που ίσχυε πριν από την εισαγωγή του ΚΠολΔ κρίνονται κατά το δίκαιο αυτό. Αν πριν από την εισαγωγή του ΚΠολΔ είχε επιβληθεί δικαστικός όρκος, εφαρμόζονται οι διατάξεις του δικαίου που ίσχυε τότε.

Άρθρο 22

1. Οι διατάξεις των άρθρων 432 έως 449 ΚΠολΔ εφαρμόζονται και στα έγγραφα που συντάσσονται από την εισαγωγή του.
2. Οι διατάξεις των άρθρων 450 έως 465 ΚΠολΔ εφαρμόζονται και στα έγγραφα που έχουν συνταχθεί πριν από την εισαγωγή του.

Άρθρο 23

1. Οι αγωγές που έχουν ασκηθεί κατά τις διατάξεις του νομ. διατάγματος της 9/16 Νοεμβρίου 1925 «περί εκδικάσεως των μικροδιαφορών κ.λπ.», όπως το διάταγμα αυτό κυρώθηκε με το νόμο 4204 του 1929, και δεν έχουν ακόμη συζητηθεί έως την εισαγωγή του ΚΠολΔ, δικάζονται κατά τις διατάξεις του ΚΠολΔ.
2. Οι διατάξεις των άρθρων 473 έως 477 του ΚΠολΔ εφαρμόζονται και στις δίκες που είναι εκκρεμείς κατά την εισαγωγή του.
3. Οι διατάξεις των άρθρων 478 έως 494 του ΚΠολΔ εφαρμόζονται και στις δίκες που είναι εκκρεμείς κατά την εισαγωγή του.

Άρθρο 24

1. Το παραδεκτό των ένδικων μέσων, το επιτρεπτό των προβαλλόμενων λόγων και ο χρόνος της άσκησης κρίνονται σύμφωνα με το νόμο που ισχύει κατά το χρόνο που δημοσιεύεται η απόφαση. Στα ένδικα μέσα που είχαν ασκηθεί κατά την εισαγωγή του ΚΠολΔ εφαρμόζονται οι διατάξεις του άρθρου 12.
2. Οι διατάξεις των άρθρων 518 παράγραφος 2, 545 παράγραφος 5 και 564 παράγραφος 3 ΚΠολΔ εφαρμόζονται και στις αποφάσεις που εκδόθηκαν πριν από την εισαγωγή του. Οι προθεσμίες που καθορίζονται από τις διατάξεις αυτές αρχίζουν από την έναρξη της ισχύος αυτού του νόμου.

Article 18

1. The provisions of Articles 286 to 312 of the Code of Civil Procedure also apply to proceedings that were pending at the time of entry of the Code into force.
2. The provisions of Articles 313 to 320 and 332 to 334 of the Code of Civil Procedure also apply to judgments handed down prior to the entry of the Code into force.

Article 19

1. The special provisions on the provision of extra-judicial expertise or sampling remain in force.
2. The court shall freely weigh up the opinions of experts in accordance with paragraph 1 or the decisions of administrative authorities or collective bodies of the Public Administration issued on the basis of such opinions, and all provisions to the contrary are repealed.

Article 20

The provisions of Articles 393 and 394 of the Code of Civil Procedure apply to legal transactions entered into after the entry of the Code into force.

Article 21

The provisions of Articles 415 to 420 and 421 to 431 of the Code of Civil Procedure shall also apply to proceedings that were pending at the time of entry of the Code into force. Procedural steps concerning evidence that were taken under the provisions of the law in force prior to the entry of the Code of Civil Procedure into force shall be ruled upon in accordance with that law. If a judicial oath had been imposed prior to the entry of the Code of Civil Procedure into force, the provisions of the law then in force apply.

Article 22

1. The provisions of Articles 432 to 449 of the Code of Civil Procedure also apply to documents that were drafted after the entry of the Code into force.
2. The provisions of Articles 450 to 465 of the Code of Civil Procedure also apply to documents that had been drafted prior to the entry of the Code into force.

Article 23

1. Actions which had been brought in accordance with the provisions of the Legislative Decree of 9/16 November 1925 on the adjudication of small claims etc., as ratified by Law 4204/1929 and had not been heard until the entry of the Code of Civil Procedure into force shall be tried under the provisions of the Code of Civil Procedure.
2. The provisions of Articles 473 to 477 of the Code of Civil Procedure also apply to proceedings that were pending at the time of entry of the Code into force.
3. The provisions of Articles 478 to 494 of the Code of Civil Procedure also apply to proceedings that were pending at the time of entry of the Code into force.

Article 24

1. The admissibility of legal remedies, the acceptability of the grounds put forth and the time they were filed shall be ruled upon in accordance with the law in force at the time the judgment is handed down. The provisions of Article 12 apply to legal remedies filed at the time of entry of the Code of Civil Procedure into force.
2. The provisions of Articles 518(2), 545(5) and 564(3) of the Code of Civil Procedure also apply to judgments handed down prior to the entry of the Code into force. Deadlines set in these provisions shall commence from the time of entry of this Law into force.

Άρθρο 25

1. Οι διατάξεις των άρθρων 501, 502, 511 έως 517, 538 έως 543, 552 έως 562 ΚΠολΔ εφαρμόζονται στις αποφάσεις που εκδίδονται από την εισαγωγή του.

2. Οι διατάξεις των άρθρων 495 έως 500 ΚΠολΔ, εφαρμόζονται στα ένδικα μέσα που ασκούνται από την εισαγωγή του.

3. Οι διατάξεις των άρθρων 506 έως 510, 524 έως 537, 548 έως 551, 568 έως 582 ΚΠολΔ εφαρμόζονται και στα ένδικα μέσα που είχαν ασκηθεί πριν από την εισαγωγή του.

Άρθρο 26

1. Τα άρθρα 593 έως 597 ΚΠολΔ εφαρμόζονται στις αγωγές που ασκούνται από την εισαγωγή του.

2. Τα άρθρα 592, 598 έως 607 και 611 έως 613 εφαρμόζονται και στις δίκες που είναι εκκρεμείς κατά την εισαγωγή του.

Άρθρο 27

Με την επιφύλαξη των διατάξεων του ουσιαστικού δικαίου δικάζονται κατά τη διαδικασία των άρθρων 593 έως 613 ΚΠολΔ και οι διαφορές που αφορούν το χωρισμό από τραπέζης και κοίτης.

Άρθρο 28

Τα άρθρα 614 έως 622 ΚΠολΔ εφαρμόζονται και στις δίκες που είναι εκκρεμείς κατά την εισαγωγή του.

Άρθρο 29

1. Αν κατά διαταγής πληρωμής χρηματικής απαίτησης δεν ασκηθεί εμπρόθεσμα ανακοπή ή η ανακοπή που ασκήθηκε απορριφθεί τελεσίδικα, η διαταγή πληρωμής αποτελεί τίτλο για εγγραφή υποθήκης.

2. Αν έχει εγγραφεί προσημείωση για να ασφαλιστεί απαίτηση για την οποία εκδόθηκε διαταγή πληρωμής, η προσημείωση μετατρέπεται σε υποθήκη, εφόσον συντρέχουν οι προϋποθέσεις της παραγράφου 1.

Άρθρο 30

Το β. διάταγμα της 29/31 Δεκεμβρίου 1953 «περί κωδικοποιήσεως των ισχυουσών διατάξεων του νομ. διατάγματος της 13/19 Σεπτεμβρίου 1925 περί εκδικάσεως των εκ συναλλαγματικών και εμπορικών ή μη γραμματίων εις διαταγήν διαφορών», όπως το διάταγμα αυτό τροποποιήθηκε και συμπληρώθηκε, καταργείται, οι δίκες όμως που είναι εκκρεμείς με βάση τις διατάξεις του ίδιου διατάγματος κατά την εισαγωγή του ΚΠολΔ εξακολουθούν να δικάζονται έως την έκδοση αμετάκλητης απόφασης κατά τα άρθρα 1 έως 15 του β.δ. που καταργείται.

Άρθρο 31

Το διάταγμα της 24/30 Δεκεμβρίου 1943 «περί κωδικοποιήσεως των διατάξεων του νόμου ΒΧΗ' του 1899 περί εξώσεως δυστροπούντων μισθωτών», όπως το διάταγμα αυτό τροποποιήθηκε και συμπληρώθηκε, καθώς και όλες οι διατάξεις που αναφέρονται στην εφαρμογή των διατάξεών του καταργούνται, οι δίκες όμως που είναι εκκρεμείς με βάση τις διατάξεις του ίδιου διατάγματος κατά την εισαγωγή του ΚΠολΔ εξακολουθούν να δικάζονται έως την έκδοση αμετάκλητης απόφασης κατά τα άρθρα 1 έως 9 του διατάγματος που καταργείται.

Άρθρο 32

Το άρθρο 13 του νόμου 164 της 29/30 Οκτωβρίου 1946 «περί τροποποιήσεως διατάξεων της Πολ. Δικονομίας» καταργείται.

Article 25

1. The provisions of Articles 501, 502, 511 to 517, 538 to 543, 552 to 562 of the Code of Civil Procedure apply to judgments handed down after the entry of the Code into force.
2. The provisions of Articles 495 to 500 of the Code of Civil Procedure apply to legal remedies filed after the entry of the Code into force.
3. The provisions of Articles 506 to 510, 524 to 537, 548 to 551, 568 to 582 of the Code of Civil Procedure also apply to legal remedies that had been filed prior to the entry of the Code into force.

Article 26

1. Articles 593 to 597 of the Code of Civil Procedure apply to actions brought after the entry of the Code into force.
2. Articles 592, 598 to 607 and 611 to 613 [of the Code of Civil Procedure] also apply to proceedings that were pending at the time of its entry into force.

Article 27

Without prejudice to the provisions of substantive law, disputes concerning [legal separation] shall also be tried under the procedure laid down in Articles 593 to 613 of the Code of Civil Procedure.

Article 28

Articles 614 to 622 of the Code of Civil Procedure also apply to proceedings that were pending at the time of entry of the Code into force.

Article 29

1. If an opposition is not filed in good time against an order for payment of a monetary claim or the opposition filed is dismissed by means of a *de jure* non-appealable judgment, the order for payment shall constitute a title for registration of a mortgage.
2. If a prenotation had been registered to secure a claim for which an order for payment was issued, the prenotation shall be converted into a mortgage, provided the requirements laid down in paragraph 1 are met.

Article 30

The Royal Decree of 29/31 December 1953 on codification of the applicable provisions of the Legislative Decree of 13/19 September 1925 on the adjudication of disputes arising from bills of exchange and promissory notes, whether or not commercial, as said Royal Decree was amended and supplemented, is repealed; however, proceedings pending on the basis of the provisions of the selfsame Decree at the time of entry of the Code of Civil Procedure into force shall continue to be tried until an irrevocable judgment is handed down in accordance with Articles 1 to 15 of the repealed Royal Decree.

Article 31

The Decree of 24/30 December 1943 on the codification of the provisions of Law 2608/1899 on the eviction of intransigent lessees, as said Decree was amended and supplemented, and all provisions concerning the application of its provisions, are repealed; however, proceedings pending on the basis of the provisions of the selfsame Decree at the time of entry of the Code of Civil Procedure into force shall continue to be tried until an irrevocable judgment is handed down in accordance with Articles 1 to 9 of the repealed Decree.

Article 32

Article 13 of Law 164 of 29/30 October 1946 amending provisions of the Code of Civil Procedure is repealed.

Άρθρο 33

Το άρθρο 11 του νόμου 3741 της 4/9 Ιανουαρίου 1929 «περί της ιδιοκτησίας κατ' ορόφους» καταργείται, οι δίκες όμως που είναι εκκρεμείς έως την εισαγωγή του ΚΠολΔ, δικάζονται μέχρι την έκδοση αμετάκλητης απόφασης κατά τις διατάξεις του άρθρου που καταργείται.

Άρθρο 34

1. Η περίπτωση 8 του άρθρου 2 του νόμου 4672 της 5/9 Μαΐου 1930 «περί ρυθμίσεως των αγοραπωλησιών καπνού» αντικαθίσταται ως εξής: «8. Κάθε άλλον όρο που δεν είναι αντίθετος προς τους προηγούμενους όρους».

2. Το άρθρο 6 του νόμου 4672/1930 καταργείται, οι δίκες όμως που είναι εκκρεμείς έως την εισαγωγή του ΚΠολΔ δικάζονται έως την έκδοση αμετάκλητης απόφασης κατά τις διατάξεις του άρθρου που καταργείται.

Άρθρο 35

Τα άρθρα 27 έως 32 του νόμου 2475 της 24 Ιουλίου/17 Σεπτεμβρίου 1920 «περί μεταναστεύσεως και αποδημίας» καταργούνται, οι δίκες όμως που είναι εκκρεμείς έως την εισαγωγή του ΚΠολΔ, δικάζονται έως την έκδοση αμετάκλητης απόφασης, κατά τις διατάξεις των άρθρων που καταργούνται.

Άρθρο 36

1. Όλες οι διαφορές οι οποίες κατά τις διατάξεις του β.δ. της 23/23 Σεπτεμβρίου 1948 «περί εκτελέσεως της παραγράφου 2 του άρθρου 4 του ψηφίσματος ΚΗ'/1947 «περί παροχής διευκολύνσεων δια την υπό ιδιωτών ανοικοδόμησιν», όπως το διάταγμα αυτό τροποποιήθηκε, συμπληρώθηκε και επεκτάθηκε, υπάγονται στην αρμοδιότητα του προέδρου πρωτοδικών κατά τη διαδικασία του νόμου ΒΧΗ', από την εισαγωγή του ΚΠολΔ δικάζονται από το μονομελές πρωτοδικείο κατά τη διαδικασία των άρθρων 647 έως 662 ΚΠολΔ. Οι ειδικές δικονομικές διατάξεις του β.δ. διατηρούνται σε ισχύ και αρκεί πιθανολόγηση των πραγματικών ισχυρισμών.

2. Η παράγραφος 4 του άρθρου 3 του β.δ. που αναφέρεται στην παράγραφο 1 καταργείται.

3. Οι διαφορές που αναφέρονται στην παράγραφο 6 του άρθρου 3 και στην παράγραφο 4 του άρθρου 9 του β.δ/τος που αναφέρεται στην παράγραφο 1 δικάζονται από το μονομελές πρωτοδικείο κατά τη διαδικασία των άρθρων 647 έως 662 ΚΠολΔ. Οι ειδικές δικονομικές διατάξεις των άρθρων αυτών διατηρούνται και αρκεί πιθανολόγηση των πραγματικών ισχυρισμών. Η απόφαση του μονομελούς πρωτοδικείου δεν υπόκειται σε τακτικό ή έκτακτο ένδικο μέσο.

4. Η αναστολή εκτέλεσης σύμφωνα με την παράγραφο 5 του άρθρου 3 του β.δ. που αναφέρεται στην παράγραφο 1 χορηγείται από το μονομελές πρωτοδικείο κατά τη διαδικασία των άρθρων 686 επ. ΚΠολΔ και τηρούνται οι ειδικές διατάξεις που αναφέρονται στην παράγραφο αυτή.

5. Οι δίκες που είναι εκκρεμείς στα δικαστήρια που αναφέρονται στις παραγράφους 1, 3 και 4 κατά την εισαγωγή του ΚΠολΔ συνεχίζονται στα δικαστήρια αυτά σύμφωνα με τις διατάξεις που ισχύουν έως την εισαγωγή του ΚΠολΔ.

Article 33

Article 11 of Law 3741 of 4/9 January 1929 on ownership by storeys is repealed; however, proceedings pending until the time of entry of the Code of Civil Procedure into force shall be tried until an irrevocable judgment is handed down in accordance with the provisions of the repealed Article.

Article 34

1. Article 2(8) of Law 4672 of 5/9 May 1930 regulating tobacco purchases and sales is replaced as follows: "8. All other clauses not contrary to the preceding terms".

2. Article 6 of Law 4672/1930 is repealed; however, proceedings pending until the time of entry of the Code of Civil Procedure into force shall be tried until an irrevocable judgment is handed down in accordance with the provisions of the repealed Article.

Article 35

Articles 27 to 32 of Law 2475 of 24 July/17 September 1920 on migration and expatriation are repealed; however, proceedings pending until the time of entry of the Code of Civil Procedure into force shall be tried until an irrevocable judgment is handed down in accordance with the provisions of the repealed Articles.

Article 36

1. All disputes which, in accordance with the provisions of the Royal Decree of 23/23 September 1948 on enforcement of Article 4(2) of decree 28/1947 on the provision of facilitations for reconstruction by private citizens, as said Royal Decree was amended, supplemented and expanded, shall fall under the jurisdiction of the presiding judge of the court of first instance in accordance with the procedure laid down in Law 2608 and, following entry of the Code of Civil Procedure into force, shall be tried by the single-member court of first instance in accordance with the procedure laid down in Articles 647 to 662 of the Code of Civil Procedure. The special procedural provisions of the aforesaid Royal Decree remain in force, and it shall suffice [for the court] to consider the factual assertions likely on the balance of probabilities.

2. Article 3(4) of the Royal Decree referred to in paragraph 1 is repealed.

3. The disputes referred to in Article 3(6) and Article 9(4) of the Royal Decree referred to in paragraph 1 shall be tried by the single-member court of first instance in accordance with the procedure laid down in Articles 647 to 662 of the Code of Civil Procedure. The special procedural provisions of these Articles remain in force, and it shall suffice [for the court] to consider the factual assertions likely on the balance of probabilities. The judgment handed down by the single-member court of first instance shall not be subject to ordinary or extraordinary legal remedies.

4. Stay of enforcement in accordance with Article 3(5) of the Royal Decree referred to in paragraph 1 shall be granted by the single-member court of first instance in accordance with the procedure laid down in Articles 686 *et seq.* of the Code of Civil Procedure, and the special provisions referred to in the aforesaid paragraph shall be complied with.

5. Proceedings pending before the courts referred to in paragraphs 1, 3 and 4 at the time of entry of the Code of Civil Procedure into force shall continue before said courts in accordance with the provisions that were in force prior to the entry of the Code into force.

Άρθρο 37

Το β.δ. της 1/1 Αυγούστου 1920 «περί κωδικοποιήσεως των διατάξεων του νόμου ΓϡΟΔ' περί εκδικάσεως των μεταξύ εργατών και εργοδοτών διαφορών κ.λπ», όπως το διάταγμα αυτό τροποποιήθηκε και συμπληρώθηκε, όλες οι διατάξεις που αναφέρονται στην εφαρμογή των διατάξεών του και όλες γενικά οι διατάξεις που αναφέρονται στην εκδίκαση των διαφορών του άρθρου 663 ΚΠολΔ καταργούνται, οι δίκες όμως που είναι εκκρεμείς κατά την εισαγωγή του ΚΠολΔ δικάζονται έως την έκδοση αμετάκλητης απόφασης, σύμφωνα με τις καταργούμενες διατάξεις.

Άρθρο 38

Όλες οι διατάξεις οι σχετικές με την εκδίκαση των διαφορών που αναφέρονται στο άρθρο 677 του ΚΠολΔ καταργούνται, οι δίκες όμως που είναι εκκρεμείς κατά την εισαγωγή του ΚΠολΔ δικάζονται έως την έκδοση αμετάκλητης απόφασης κατά τις καταργούμενες διατάξεις.

Άρθρο 39

Καταργούνται από την εισαγωγή του ΚΠολΔ όλες οι διατάξεις του δικαίου που ίσχυε έως τότε για προφυλακτικά, προσωρινά ή συντηρητικά μέτρα. Κατ' εξαίρεση διατηρείται η ισχύς των διατάξεων για διορισμό προσωρινού επιτρόπου ή κηδεμόνα, καθώς και οι διατάξεις των άρθρων 24 έως 31 του νόμου ΨΜΒ/1862 «περί συστάσεως φρενοκομείων».

Άρθρο 40

Η μεταρρύθμιση ή η ανάκληση ασφαλιστικών μέτρων που έχουν ληφθεί ή διαταχθεί κατά τις διατάξεις του δικαίου που ίσχυε έως την εισαγωγή του ΚΠολΔ γίνεται κατ' εφαρμογή των άρθρων 682 επ. ΚΠολΔ. Αν το δικαστήριο που διέταξε τα ασφαλιστικά μέτρα είναι ο πρόεδρος πρωτοδικών, αρμόδιο για τη μεταρρύθμιση ή την ανάκλησή τους είναι το μονομελές πρωτοδικείο.

Άρθρο 41

Οι σχετικές με την υποθήκη διατάξεις του ΚΠολΔ εφαρμόζονται και στην προσημείωση, εκτός αν ορίζεται διαφορετικά. Το ίδιο ισχύει και για τις διατάξεις του νόμου για την είσπραξη των δημόσιων εσόδων.

Άρθρο 42

Κάθε παραβίαση από τους διαδίκους των αποφάσεων που διατάζουν ασφαλιστικά μέτρα για την προσωρινή ρύθμιση της νομής ή της κατοχής, ανεξάρτητα από τις άλλες συνέπειές της, τιμωρείται και με την ποινή του άρθρου 169 ΠΚ.

Άρθρο 43

Από την εισαγωγή του ΚΠολΔ, το μονομελές πρωτοδικείο της τοποθεσίας του ακινήτου δικάζει, κατά τη διαδικασία των άρθρων 682 επ. ΚΠολΔ, την αίτηση εξαγοράς που αναφέρεται στο άρθρο 61 ΕνΑΚ.

Άρθρο 44

[Καταργείται]

Article 37

The Royal Decree of 1/1 August 1920 on codification of the provisions of Law 3974 on the adjudication of disputes between workers and employers etc., as said Decree was amended and supplemented, and all provisions concerning the application of its provisions, as well as all provisions in general that refer to the adjudication of the disputes referred to in Article 663 of the Code of Civil Procedure, are repealed; however, proceedings pending at the time of entry of the Code of Civil Procedure into force shall be tried until an irrevocable judgment is handed down in accordance with the repealed provisions.

Article 38

All provisions concerning the adjudication of the disputes referred to in Article 677 of the Code of Civil Procedure, are repealed; however, proceedings pending at the time of entry of the Code of Civil Procedure into force shall be tried until an irrevocable judgment is handed down in accordance with the repealed provisions.

Article 39

Upon the entry of the Code of Civil Procedure into force, all statutory provisions that were in force until that time concerning precautionary, interim or preventive measures are repealed. By way of exception, the provisions on the appointment of an interim tutor or custodian and the provisions of Articles 24 to 31 of Law 742/1862 'on the establishment of mental institutions' remain in force.

Article 40

Interim measures adopted or ordered under the statutory provisions that were in force until the time of entry of the Code of Civil Procedure into force shall be amended or revoked pursuant to Articles 682 *et seq.* of the Code of Civil Procedure. If the interim measures were ordered by the presiding judge of the court of first instance, the single-member court of first instance shall have jurisdiction to amend or revoke them.

Article 41

Unless otherwise provided for, the provisions of the Code of Civil Procedure on mortgages also apply to prenotations of mortgage. The same applies to the provisions of law on the collection of public revenues.

Article 42

Any violation by the parties in proceedings where judgments ordering interim measures for provisional regulation of possession or detentorship were handed down shall, irrespective of any other consequences, also carry the penalty laid down in Article 169 of the Penal Code.

Article 43

Upon the entry of the Code of Civil Procedure into force, the single-member court of first instance of the place where the immovable is located shall try the application for acquisition referred to in Article 61 of the Law Introducing the Civil Code under the procedure laid down in Articles 682 *et seq.* of the Code of Civil Procedure.

Article 44

[Repealed]

Άρθρο 45

Οι διατάξεις των άρθρων 84 έως 86 του νόμου 5325 της 9/16 Μαρτίου 1932 «περί συναλλαγματικής και γραμματίου εις διαταγήν», των άρθρων 64 έως 66 του νόμου 5960 της 23/23 Δεκεμβρίου 1933 «περί επιταγής» και των άρθρων 81 έως 86 του νομ. Διατάγματος της 17 Ιουλίου/13 Αυγούστου 1923 «περί ειδικών διατάξεων επί ανωνύμων εταιρειών» από την εισαγωγή του ΚΠολΔ καταργούνται και σε περίπτωση απώλειας ή καταστροφής τίτλου εις διαταγήν εφαρμόζεται η διαδικασία των άρθρων 843 έως 860.

Άρθρο 46

Οι διατάξεις συμβάσεων για διαιτησία διαφορών ιδιωτικού δικαίου που είναι κυρωμένες με νόμο εξακολουθούν να ισχύουν, όπως και οι διατάξεις των νόμων που τις τροποποιούν ή τις συμπληρώνουν. Στις διαιτησίες που αρχίζουν μετά την έναρξη της ισχύος του νόμου αυτού εφαρμόζονται τα άρθρα 867 επ. ΚΠολΔ, εφόσον δεν είναι αντίθετα προς τις διατάξεις της σύμβασης ή των νόμων που την τροποποιούν ή τη συμπληρώνουν.

Άρθρο 47

1. Τα άρθρα 867 έως 885 ΚΠολΔ εφαρμόζονται και στις συμφωνίες διαιτησίας που συνομολογήθηκαν πριν από την εισαγωγή του, εφόσον κατά τις διατάξεις του δικαίου που ίσχυε πριν από την εισαγωγή του ΚΠολΔ δεν πέρασε η προθεσμία της ισχύος των συμφωνιών διαιτησίας ή της έκδοσης των διαιτητικών αποφάσεων.
2. Τα άρθρα 886 έως 891 του ΚΠολΔ, εφαρμόζονται στις διαιτητικές διαδικασίες που αρχίζουν μετά την εισαγωγή του.
3. Τα άρθρα 892 έως 900 του ΚΠολΔ εφαρμόζονται στις διαιτητικές αποφάσεις που συντάσσονται και υπογράφονται μετά την εισαγωγή του.

Άρθρο 48

Οι διατάξεις για τη διαιτησία των επιμελητηρίων καταργούνται, όπως και κάθε άλλη διάταξη για εκούσια διαιτησία. Αν κατά την εισαγωγή του ΚΠολΔ έχει αρχίσει η διαιτητική διαδικασία, συνεχίζεται σύμφωνα με τις διατάξεις που καταργούνται.

Άρθρο 49

1. Το Δημόσιο μπορεί να συνομολογήσει συμφωνία διαιτησίας μόνο εγγράφως ύστερα από γνωμοδότηση της ολομέλειας του Νομικού Συμβουλίου και απόφαση του υπουργού των οικονομικών και του αρμόδιου υπουργού. Με τον ίδιο τρόπο το Δημόσιο ορίζει τους διαιτητές του.
2. Οι προθεσμίες των άρθρων 873 έως 876 του ΚΠολΔ είναι ενός μηνός, αν πρόκειται για συμφωνίες διαιτησίας που συνομολογήθηκαν από το Δημόσιο.

Άρθρο 50

1. Οι σχετικές με την αναγκαστική εκτέλεση διατάξεις του ΚΠολΔ εφαρμόζονται στις εκτελέσεις που αρχίζουν από την εισαγωγή του. Η αναγκαστική εκτέλεση θεωρείται ότι άρχισε από τότε που επιδόθηκε η επιταγή σε εκείνον κατά του οποίου στρέφεται η εκτέλεση.
2. Οι διατάξεις των άρθρων 1000 και 1009 έως 1012 του ΚΠολΔ εφαρμόζονται και στις εκτελέσεις που έχουν ήδη αρχίσει πριν από την εισαγωγή του. Οι διατάξεις των άρθρων 1034 ως 1046 του ΚΠολΔ εφαρμόζονται και στις αναγκαστικές διαχειρίσεις που επιβλήθηκαν πριν από την εισαγωγή του.
3. Η προθεσμία αναγγελίας κατά τα άρθρα 972 παράγραφος 1 και 999 παράγραφος 4 ΚΠολΔ ισχύει και για την αναγγελία του Δημοσίου και δεν εφαρμόζεται ως προς αυτό η διάταξη του άρθρου 10 του κ.δ. της 26 Ιουνίου/10 Ιουλίου 1944 «περί κώδικος νόμου περί δικών του Δημοσίου».

Article 45

Upon the entry of the Code of Civil Procedure into force, the provisions of Articles 84 to 86 of Law 5325 of 9/16 March 1932 on bills of exchange and promissory notes, Articles 64 to 66 of Law 5960 of 23/23 December 1933 on cheques, and Articles 81 to 86 of the Legislative Decree of 17 July/13 August 1923 on special provisions concerning sociétés anonymes are repealed, and in the event of loss or destruction of a note payable to order, the procedure laid down in Articles 843 to 860 shall apply.

Article 46

The provisions of treaties and conventions on the arbitration of private-law disputes that are ratified by law and statutory provisions amending or supplementing such provisions remain in force. Articles 867 *et seq.* of the Code of Civil Procedure apply to arbitration commencing after the entry of this Law into force, provided they are not contrary to the provisions of the treaty or convention or of the laws amending or supplementing the treaty or convention.

Article 47

1. Article 867 to 885 of the Code of Civil Procedure also apply to arbitration agreements entered into prior to the entry of the Code into force if, under the statutory provisions that were in force prior to said entry, the deadline for the validity of arbitration agreements or the issuance of arbitration awards has not elapsed.
2. Articles 886 to 891 of the Code of Civil Procedure apply to arbitration proceedings commencing after the entry of the Code into force.
3. Articles 892 to 900 of the Code of Civil Procedure apply to arbitration awards prepared and signed after the entry of the Code into force.

Article 48

The provisions on arbitration by chambers [of commerce etc.] and all other provisions concerning voluntary arbitration are repealed. If arbitration proceedings have commenced at the time of entry of the Code of Civil Procedure into force, they shall continue in accordance with the repealed provisions.

Article 49

1. The Greek State may enter into an arbitration agreement only in writing, following an opinion issued by the plenary of the Legal Council [of the State] and a decision of the Minister of Finance and the competent minister. The Greek State shall designate its arbitrators in the same manner.
2. In cases of arbitration agreements entered into by the Greek State, the deadlines set in Articles 873 to 876 of the Code of Civil Procedure are one month.

Article 50

1. The provisions of the Code of Civil Procedure on compulsory enforcement apply to enforcement commencing after the entry of the Code into force. Compulsory enforcement shall be deemed to have commenced from the time the order was served on the person enforcement concerns.
2. The provisions of Articles 1000 and 1009 to 1012 of the Code of Civil Procedure also apply of enforcement that had already commenced prior to the entry of the Code into force. The provisions of Articles 1034 to 1046 of the Code of Civil Procedure also apply to compulsory administration imposed prior to the entry of the Code into force.
3. The deadline for lodging claims under Articles 972(1) and 999(4) of the Code of Civil Procedure also applies to claims lodged by the Greek State, to which the provisions of Article 10 of Regulatory Decree of 26 June/10 July 1944 on the code of laws on proceedings involving the Greek State do not apply.

Άρθρο 51

Από την εισαγωγή του ΚΠολΔ καταργούνται:

1) οι διατάξεις νόμων που προβλέπουν την προσωπική κράτηση ως μέσο αναγκαστικής εκτέλεσης κατά την πολιτική δικονομία για την ικανοποίηση χρηματικών απαιτήσεων, διατηρούνται όμως σε ισχύ οι διατάξεις για την είσπραξη των δημόσιων εσόδων,

2) οι διατάξεις νόμων που ορίζουν ότι τα προνόμια που οι ίδιες προβλέπουν υπερισχύουν από το προνόμιο των εξόδων της αναγκαστικής εκτέλεσης,

3) οι διατάξεις νόμων που αποκλείουν την προσωρινή εκτέλεση κατά νομικών προσώπων δημόσιου ή ιδιωτικού δικαίου, καθώς και οι διατάξεις που ορίζουν ότι η προθεσμία ή η άσκηση αναίρεσης έχει ανασταλτικό αποτέλεσμα για την αναγκαστική εκτέλεση,

4) οι διατάξεις νόμων που επιβάλλουν άδεια του δικαστηρίου για την επιβολή κατάσχεσης στα χέρια τρίτου, αν και ο δανειστής έχει τίτλο εκτελεστό,

5) οι διατάξεις του άρθρου 19 του α.ν. 2514 της 24 Αυγούστου/4 Σεπτεμβρίου 1940 «περί τροποποιήσεως και συμπληρώσεως των περί μεταλλείων διατάξεων»,

6) οι διατάξεις του α.ν. 1519 της 17/19 Δεκεμβρίου 1938 «περί αναγκαστικής εκτελέσεως και συντηρητικών μέτρων επί περιουσίας αλλοδαπών κρατών».

Άρθρο 52

Διατηρούνται σε ισχύ:

1) οι διατάξεις του άρθρου 79 του ν.δ. της 31 Δεκεμβρίου 1923 «περί του καταστατικού νόμου της Αυτοκεφάλου Εκκλησίας της Ελλάδος»,

2) οι διατάξεις των άρθρων 45 έως 57 του ν.δ. 3077 της 6/11 Οκτωβρίου 1954 «περί γενικών αποθηκών»,

3) οι διατάξεις του ν.δ. της 17 Ιουλίου/13 Αυγούστου 1923 «περί ειδικών διατάξεων επί ανωνύμων εταιρειών» που αφορούν την αναγκαστική εκτέλεση για ικανοποίηση απαιτήσεων που ασφαλίζονται με ενέχυρο ή υποθήκη, εκτός από τις διατάξεις των άρθρων 60, 63, 92 και 94, οι οποίες καταργούνται από την εισαγωγή του ΚΠολΔ,

4) οι διατάξεις του νόμου 4332 της 10/16 Αυγούστου 1929 «περί κυρώσεως της μεταξύ ελληνικού Δημοσίου και Εθνικής Τραπέζης της Ελλάδος συμβάσεως κ.λπ», όπως τροποποιήθηκε, που αφορούν την αναγκαστική εκτέλεση για ικανοποίηση απαιτήσεων της Αγροτικής Τράπεζας,

5) οι διατάξεις που αφορούν την αναγκαστική εκτέλεση του ν.δ. 1038 της 10/17 Αυγούστου 1949 «περί κυρώσεως της από 12 Νοεμβρίου 1948 και της τροποποιητικής και συμπληρωματικής ταύτης από 15 Απριλίου 1949 συμβάσεως δια γεωργικά και βιομηχανικά δάνεια και περί ειδικών επί των εν λόγω δανείων διατάξεων», που κυρώθηκε με το ν.δ. 1198 της 9/19 Οκτωβρίου 1949, όπως τροποποιήθηκαν και συμπληρώθηκαν με τις διατάξεις του ν.δ. 2688 της 31 Οκτωβρίου/10 Νοεμβρίου 1953 και με τις διατάξεις του ν.δ. 2941 της 31 Ιουλίου/ 9 Αυγούστου 1954 «περί κυρώσεως των υπ. αριθ. 2/29.3.1952, υπ. αριθ. 3/15.9.1952 και υπ. αριθ. 4/18.6.1954 τροποποιητικών και συμπληρωματικών συμβάσεων δια γεωργικά και βιομηχανικά δάνεια κ.λπ»,

6) οι διατάξεις του ν.δ. 3441 της 12/12 Νοεμβρίου 1955 «περί επεκτάσεως επί του Οργανισμού Χρηματοδοτήσεως Οικονομικής Αναπτύξεως των διατάξεων του ν.δ. περί ειδικών διατάξεων επί ανωνύμων εταιρειών»,

Article 51

Upon the entry of the Code of Civil Procedure into force, the following are repealed:

1) statutory provisions stipulating personal detention as a means of compulsory enforcement under civil procedure for the satisfaction of monetary claims — however, the provisions on the collection of public revenues shall remain in force;

2) statutory provisions specifying that the privileges they contain take precedence over the privilege for the costs of compulsory enforcement;

3) statutory provisions precluding provisional enforcement against bodies governed by public or private law, as well as provisions specifying that the [fact that the] deadline for [filing an application has commenced] or [the act of] filing an application for cassation shall stay compulsory enforcement;

4) statutory provisions requiring that, even though the creditor holds an enforceable title, leave of the court is necessary to impose garnishment;

5) the provisions of Article 19 of Emergency Law 2514 of 24 August/4 September 1940 amending and supplementing the provisions on mines;

6) the provisions of Emergency Law 1519 of 17/19 December 1938 on compulsory enforcement and preventive measures against the assets of foreign states.

Article 52

The following remain in force:

1) the provisions of Article 79 of the Legislative Decree of 31 December 1923 on the statutes of the Autocephalous Church of Greece;

2) the provisions of Articles 45 to 57 of Legislative Decree 3077 of 6/11 October 1954 on general warehouses;

3) the provisions of the Legislative Decree of 17 July/13 August 1923 on special provisions concerning sociétés anonymes with regard to compulsory enforcement for the satisfaction of claims secured by pledge or mortgage, save the provisions of Articles 60, 63, 92 and 94, which are repealed upon the entry of the Code of Civil Procedure into force;

4) the provisions of Law 4332 of 10/16 August 1929 ratifying the agreement between the Greek State and the National Bank of Greece etc., as amended, with regard to compulsory enforcement for the satisfaction of claims of the Agricultural Bank [of Greece];

5) the provisions on compulsory enforcement of Legislative Decree 1038 of 10/17 August 1949 ratifying the agreement dated 12 November 1948 and the agreement dated 15 April 1949 amending and supplementing the aforesaid agreement concerning agricultural and industrial loans and special provisions regarding said loans, ratified by virtue of Legislative Decree 1198 of 9/19 October 1949, as amended and supplemented by the provisions of Legislative Decree 2688 of 31 October/10 November 1953 and the provisions of Legislative Decree 2941 of 31 July/9 August 1954 on ratification of amending and supplementing agreements Nos 2/29.3.1952, 3/15.9.1952 and 4/18.6.1954 concerning agricultural and industrial loans, etc.;

6) the provisions of Legislative Decree 3441 of 12/12 November 1955 on extension of the provisions of the Legislative Decree laying down special provisions concerning sociétés anonymes to the Economic Development Financing Organisation;

7) οι διατάξεις των νόμων που προβλέπουν τη διαδικασία της συντηρητικής ή αναγκαστικής κατάσχεσης καπνού,
8) οι διατάξεις του άρθρ. 15 του β.δ. της 24 Ιουλίου/25 Αυγούστου 1920 «περί κωδικοποιήσεως των νόμων περί ευθύνης προς αποζημίωσιν των εξ ατυχήματος εν τη εργασία παθόντων εργατών ή υπαλλήλων»,
9) οι διατάξεις νόμων που προβλέπουν το ακατάσχετο επιδομάτων ή βοηθημάτων που χορηγούνται σε επαγγελματίες ή πρόσωπα που χρειάζονται βοήθεια,
10) οι διατάξεις νόμων που προβλέπουν την κατάσχεση και τον πλειστηριασμό ή το ακατάσχετο αρχαιολογικών αντικειμένων, ιστορικών κειμηλίων και κτημάτων που διατηρούνται από ιστορικούς ή άλλους λόγους,
11) οι διατάξεις νόμων που προβλέπουν τις προϋποθέσεις με τις οποίες είναι δυνατή η κατάσχεση των απαιτήσεων εργολάβων,
12) οι διατάξεις νόμων που προβλέπουν το ακατάσχετο της εγγυοδοσίας για ειδικό σκοπό,
13) οι διατάξεις του άρθρου 9 του νόμου 1023 «περί ιδιωτικής επιχειρήσεως ασφαλίσεως» που κωδικοποιήθηκε με το β.δ. της 8/10 Οκτωβρίου 1920,
14) οι διατάξεις του άρθρου 11 του νόμου 3632 της 17/26 Ιουλίου 1928 «περί χρηματιστηρίων αξιών»,
15) οι διατάξεις του άρθρ. 16 του νόμου 841/1948 «περί ταχυδρομικών δεμάτων»,
16) οι διατάξεις του άρθρου 11 του ν.δ. 4114/1960 «περί κώδικος περί του ταμείου νομικών» που αφορούν τη δημοσίευση προγράμματος πλειστηριασμού ο οποίος διεξάγεται στην περιφέρεια του τέως δήμου Αθηναίων, και που εφαρμόζονται σε κάθε πλειστηριασμό που διεξάγεται στην περιφέρεια της τέως διοικήσεως πρωτευούσης,
17) οι διατάξεις του άρθρου 8 του διατάγματος της 24/30 Δεκεμβρίου 1943 «περί κωδικοποιήσεως των διατάξεων του νόμου ΒΧΗ/1899 περί εξώσεως των δυστροπούντων μισθωτών», όπως τροποποιήθηκε, ως προς την αναγκαστική εκτέλεση των αποφάσεων που εκδόθηκαν σε δίκες εκκρεμείς κατά την εισαγωγή του ΚΠολΔ,
18) οι διατάξεις των άρθρων 22 ν. 3693/1957, 19 α.ν. 1715/1951, 8 και 22 α.ν. 1539/1938 και 125 και 126 α.ν. 2039/1939,
19) ο νόμος 4112/1929,
20) ειδικές διατάξεις που επιτρέπουν την κατάσχεση και εκχώρηση μισθών, συντάξεων και ασφαλιστικών παροχών,
21) διατάγματα που καθορίζουν το συνηθισμένο τόπο πλειστηριασμού· ο υπουργός δικαιοσύνης εξουσιοδοτείται να τα τροποποιεί και να εκδίδει τέτοια διατάγματα στο μέλλον,
22) οι διατάξεις του άρθρου 6 του ν.δ. 4001/1959.

Άρθρο 53

Τα άρθρα 105 παράγραφος 2, 205, 521, 539, 1275, 1310, 1377, 1473 και 1889 ΑΚ, καθώς και τα άρθρα 126 και 127 του ΕνΑΚ καταργούνται.

Άρθρο 54

Το άρθρο 2025 ΑΚ αντικαθίσταται ως εξής: «Ο κληρονόμος ασκεί τις αξιώσεις της κληρονομίας. Ο εκτελεστής της διαθήκης ασκεί τις αξιώσεις της κληρονομίας και ενάγεται για τις αξιώσεις κατά της κληρονομίας, εφόσον έχει τη διαχείριση της κληρονομίας ή των σχετικών αξιώσεων».

Άρθρο 55

Το άρθρο 606 ΑΚ αντικαθίσταται ως εξής: «Αν τα εισκομισθέντα απομακρύνθηκαν από το μίσθιο και μεταφέρθηκαν αλλού, το νόμιμο ενέχυρο του εκμισθωτή υπάρχει μόνο εφόσον αυτός μέσα σε ένα μήνα αφότου πληροφορήθηκε την απομάκρυνσή τους, τα κατέσχε αναγκαστικώς ή εκτέλεσε απόφαση που διατάζει τη συντηρητική κατάσχεση ή τη δικαστική μεσεγγύησή τους».

7) statutory provisions laying down the procedure for preventive or compulsory attachment of tobacco;
8) the provisions of Article 15 of the Royal Decree of 24 July/25 August 1920 on codification of laws concerning liability to provide compensation to workers or employees involved in occupational accidents;
9) statutory provisions stipulating non-attachability of benefits or aid granted to professionals or persons requiring assistance;
10) statutory provisions stipulating attachment and auctioning or non-attachability for archaeological items, historical relics and properties listed for historical or other reasons;
11) statutory provisions laying down conditions under which contractors' claims are attachable;
12) statutory provisions stipulating non-attachability for provision of surety for special purposes;
13) the provisions of Article 9 of Law 1023 on private insurance companies, codified by the Royal Decree of 8/10 October 1920;
14) the provisions of Article 11 of Legislative Decree 3632 of 17/26 July 1928 on stock exchanges;
15) the provisions of Article 16 of Law 841/1948 on postal packages;
16) the provisions of Article 11 of Legislative Decree 4114/1960 on the Jurists' Fund Code concerning publication of the calendar of auctions held in the district of the former Municipality of Athens and applicable to all auctions held in the district of the former administrative authority of the capital;
17) the provisions of Article 8 of the Decree of 24/30 December 1943 codifying the provisions of Law 2608/1899 on the eviction of intransigent lessees, as amended, with regard to compulsory enforcement of judgments handed down during proceedings which were pending at the time of entry of the Code of Civil Procedure into force;
18) the provisions of Article 22 of Law 3693/1957, Article 19 of Emergency Law 1715/1951, Articles 8 and 22 of Emergency Law 1539/1938 and 125 and 126 of Emergency Law 2039/1939;
19) Law 4112/1929;
20) special provisions allowing the attachment and assignment of wages, pensions and insurance benefits;
21) decrees specifying a usual place for auctions to be held, with the Minister of Justice being empowered to amend and issue such decrees in the future;
22) the provisions of Article 6 of Legislative Decree 4001/1959.

Article 53

Articles 105(2), 205, 521, 539, 1275, 1310, 1377, 1473 and 1889 of the Civil Code, as well as Articles 126 and 127 of the Law Introducing the Civil Code are repealed.

Article 54

Article 2025 of the Civil Code is replaced as follows: "The heir shall bring the claims arising from the estate.
The executor of the will shall bring the claims arising from the estate and may be sued for claims against the estate, provided they manage the estate or relevant claims.".

Article 55

Article 606 of the Civil Code is replaced as follows: "If the things brought into the leased property were removed and transported elsewhere, the lessor's lawful pledge exists only if, within one month of learning of their removal, the lessor imposed compulsory attachment thereon or enforced a judgment ordering their preventive attachment or judicial sequestration".

Άρθρο 56

1. Το άρθρο 1274 ΑΚ αντικαθίσταται ως εξής: «Εγγραφή προσημείωσης υποθήκης γίνεται μόνο ύστερα από δικαστική απόφαση».

2. Το άρθρο 1323 ΑΚ αντικαθίσταται ως εξής: «Απόσβεση της προσημείωσης επέρχεται από τους λόγους που ισχύουν και για την υποθήκη καθώς και

1) με την ανάκληση της απόφασης που διέταξε την προσημείωση,

2) αν μέσα σε ενενήντα ημέρες από την τελεσίδικη απόφαση που επιδικάζει την απαίτηση δεν τράπηκε σε υποθήκη».

3. Το άρθρο 1330 ΑΚ αντικαθίσταται ως εξής: «Η προσημείωση εξαλείφεται

1) με συναίνεση του δανειστή, που παρέχεται όπως και στην εξάλειψη της υποθήκης,

2) αν προσαχθεί απόφαση που ανακαλεί την απόφαση, που είχε διατάξει την εγγραφή της ή απόφαση που διατάζει την εξάλειψή της,

3) αν από την τελεσίδικη επιδίκαση της απαίτησης πέρασαν ενενήντα ημέρες χωρίς η προσημείωση να τραπεί σε υποθήκη».

Άρθρο 57

(Οι παράγραφοι 1-4 έχουν ήδη αντικατασταθεί από το ν. 1329/83)

5. Στο τέλος του άρθρου 1647 Αστ. Κώδικα προστίθεται το εξής «7. να συνομολογεί εξώδικη διανομή».

Άρθρο 58

Τα άρθρα 210, 212, 213, 215, 216, 217 και 218 του κώδικα ιδιωτικού ναυτικού δικαίου καταργούνται.

Άρθρο 59

1. Το άρθρο 65 του νόμου 5017 της 11/13 Ιουνίου 1931 «περί πολιτικής αεροπορίας» καταργείται.

2. Το άρθρο 66 του νόμου 5017/1931 «περί πολιτικής αεροπορίας», στο οποίο αναφερόταν η παράγραφος 2 του προκείμενου άρθρου, καταργήθηκε με το άρθρο 193 ν. 1815/1988 «κύρωση του κώδικα αεροπορικού δικαίου». Με την τελευταία διάταξη καταργήθηκαν και όλες οι άλλες διατάξεις του ν. 5017/1931.

Άρθρο 60

Καταργήθηκε με το άρθρο 77 ν. 1541/1985, ενώ και ο τελευταίος αυτός νόμος καταργήθηκε στη συνέχεια με το άρθρο 55 παράγραφος 1 α' ν. 2169/1993 «αγροτικές συνεταιριστικές οργανώσεις κ.λπ».

Άρθρο 61

Οι διατάξεις των παραγράφων 2 έως 4 και 7 του άρθρου 6 του νόμου 5367 της 7/18 Απριλίου 1932 «περί εκτελέσεως των δημοσίων έργων», στις οποίες αναφερόταν τούτη η διάταξη, καταργήθηκαν με το άρθρο 22 ν.δ. 1266/1972, το οποίο στη συνέχεια καταργήθηκε με το άρθρο 28 παρ. 1 ν. 1418/1984.

Άρθρο 62

Το εδάφ. ΙΙ της παραγράφου 1 του άρθρου 89 του π.δ. της 18/21 Ιουλίου 1931 «περί κωδικοποιήσεως του νόμου 4952/1931 «περί οργανώσεως της κεντρικής πρεσβευτικής και προξενικής υπηρεσίας του επί των εξωτερικών υπουργείου» αντικαθίσταται ως εξής: «ΙΙ. έχουν υποχρέωση να ενεργούν διαιτησίες, αν εκείνοι που έχουν συνάψει τη συμφωνία διαιτησίας είναι Έλληνες».

Article 56

1. Article 1274 of the Civil Code is replaced as follows: "Prenotations of mortgage shall be registered only pursuant to a court judgment.".

2. Article 1323 of the Civil Code is replaced as follows: "A prenotation shall also be extinguished on the grounds applicable to mortgages, as well as:

1) if the judgment that ordered prenotation is revoked;

2) if the prenotation was not converted into a mortgage within 90 days of the *de jure* non-appealable judgment awarding the claim.".

3. Article 1330 of the Civil Code is replaced as follows: "A prenotation shall be stricken out if:

1. the creditor gives consent, which is granted in the same manner as required for striking out a mortgage;

2. a judgment revoking the judgment ordering registration of the prenotation or a judgment ordering its striking out is adduced;

3. if the prenotation was not converted into a mortgage within 90 days from the date the de jure non-appealable judgment was handed down.".

Article 57

(Paragraphs 1 to 4 have been replaced by Law 1329/1983)

5. The following phrase shall be inserted at the end of Article 1647 of the Civil Code: "7. enter into an agreement concerning extra-judicial partition".

Article 58

Articles 210, 212, 213, 215, 216, 217 and 218 of the Code of Private Maritime Law are repealed.

Article 59

1. Article 65 of Law 5017 of 11/13 June 1931 on civil aviation is repealed.

2. Article 66 of Law 5017/1931 on civil aviation to which paragraph 2 of this Article referred was repealed by virtue of Article 193 of Law 1815/1988 on ratification of the Code of Aviation Law. The aforesaid provision also repealed all other provisions of Law 5017/1931.

Article 60

Repealed by virtue of Article 77 of Law 1541/1985, which was also subsequently repealed by Article 55(1)(a) of Law 2169/1993 on farming cooperative organisations etc.

Article 61

The provisions of Article 6(2) to (4) and (7) of Law 5367 of 7/18 April 1932 on the execution of public works, to which this provision referred, were repealed by Article 22 of Legislative Decree 1266/1972, which was subsequently repealed by Article 28(1) of Law 1418/1984.

Article 62

Article 89(1)(II) of the Presidential Decree of 18/21 July 1931 on codification of Law 4952/1931 on the organisation of the central ambassadorial and consular service of the Ministry of Foreign Affairs is replaced as follows: "II. shall be obligated to carry out arbitration, if the parties who entered into the arbitration agreement are Greek".

Άρθρο 63

[Καταργείται]

Άρθρο 64

[Καταργείται]

Άρθρο 65

Οι εκθέσεις που πριν αρχίσει να ισχύει ο νόμος αυτός συντάχθηκαν στη γραμματεία του ειρηνοδικείου, για διορισμό ή ανάκληση ή αντικατάσταση ή παραίτηση αντικλήτου και τα αλφαβητικά κατά επώνυμα ευρετήρια που τηρήθηκαν για τις εκθέσεις αυτές αποστέλλονται χωρίς υπαίτια καθυστέρηση από τη γραμματεία του ειρηνοδικείου στη γραμματεία του πρωτοδικείου όπου υπάγεται το ειρηνοδικείο και αυτή, μόλις τα λάβει, τα καταχωρίζει στο ειδικό αλφαβητικό κατά ονοματεπώνυμο βιβλίο που τηρεί.

Άρθρο 66

Αν ο μισθωτής καθυστερήσει το μίσθωμα από δυστροπία, ο εκμισθωτής έχει δικαίωμα να ζητήσει να του αποδοθεί το μίσθιο όσο διαρκεί η μίσθωση, και αν δεν την κατάγγειλε κατά το άρθρο 597 ΑΚ. Η άσκηση της αγωγής στην περίπτωση αυτή δεν ισχύει ως καταγγελία της σύμβασης.

Άρθρο 67

Στις ανακοπές που ασκήθηκαν εμπρόθεσμα κατά ερήμην αποφάσεων, για τις οποίες δεν έχει εκδοθεί απόφαση έως τη δημοσίευση αυτού του νόμου, καθώς και σε όσες ανακοπές ασκηθούν στο εξής, εφαρμόζεται το άρθρο 501 του ΚΠολΔ όπως τροποποιείται.

Άρθρο 68

Οι διαδικαστικές πράξεις γενικά που ενεργήθηκαν για υποθέσεις εκκρεμείς κατά την 16 Σεπτεμβρίου 1968 είναι έγκυρες, είτε εφαρμόστηκαν οι διατάξεις του ΚΠολΔ είτε οι διατάξεις της πολιτικής δικονομίας που ίσχυσε προηγουμένως. Για τις υποθέσεις αυτές η διαδικασία διεξάγεται στο εξής κατά τις διατάξεις του ΚΠολΔ, εκτός αν ορίζει διαφορετικά αυτός ο εισαγωγικός νόμος.

Άρθρο 69

1. Υποθέσεις εκκρεμείς που δεν συζητήθηκαν εκδικάζονται κατά τις διατάξεις του ΚΠολΔ όπως αυτές τροποποιούνται. Το δικαστήριο όπου εκκρεμούν διατάζει, με απόφασή του που εκδίδεται την ημέρα της ορισμένης δικασίμου, να γραφτούν για άλλη δικάσιμο στο πινάκιο του αρμόδιου δικαστηρίου· η εγγραφή αυτή ισοδυναμεί με κλήτευση για τους διαδίκους που δικάζονται κατ' αντιμωλίαν ή νομίμως ερήμην. Κάθε διάδικος μπορεί, πριν εκδοθεί τέτοια απόφαση, να φέρει με κλήση την υπόθεση για να συζητηθεί.

2. Οι υποθέσεις που συζητήθηκαν στον εισηγητή του άρθρου 296 είτε εκδόθηκε, είτε δεν εκδόθηκε μη οριστική απόφαση, εξακολουθούν να δικάζονται κατά τον ΚΠολΔ όπως ίσχυε πριν τροποποιηθεί. Ο πρόεδρος των πρωτοδικών μπορεί, όσο διαρκεί η αποδεικτική διαδικασία, να ορίσει, αν συντρέχει σπουδαίος λόγος, άλλο δικαστή ως αντικαταστάτη του εισηγητή. Όταν περατωθεί η αποδεικτική διαδικασία, η υπόθεση εισάγεται με κλήση για να συζητηθεί στο πολυμελές πρωτοδικείο, στη σύνθεση του οποίου παίρνει μέρος, αν είναι δυνατόν, ο πιο πάνω εισηγητής. Το άρθρο 297 παράγραφοι 1 και 2 του ΚΠολΔ δεν εφαρμόζεται εδώ.

3. Ανακοπές ερημοδικίας, τριτανακοπές και αναψηλαφήσεις κατά των αποφάσεων του εισηγητή, που εκδόθηκαν ή που θα εκδοθούν, εισάγονται στο εξής για συζήτηση στο πολυμελές πρωτοδικείο.

Article 63

[Repealed]

Article 64

[Repealed]

Article 65

Reports drafted at the court of the peace registry concerning appointment or removal or replacement or resignation of a process agent and the indexes kept in alphabetical order by surname for such reports prior to entry of this Law into force shall be sent without undue delay by the court of the peace registry to the registry of the court of first instance to which the court of the peace is subordinate and the latter, upon taking receipt of such indexes, shall enter them in the special register it keeps in alphabetical order by full name.

Article 66

If a lessee delays payment of rent due to intransigence, the lessor has the right to request return of the leased property for the duration of the lease, even if the lessor did not terminate the lease in accordance with Article 597 of the Civil Code. In this case, bringing an action shall not function as termination of the agreement.

Article 67

Article 501 of the Code of Civil Procedure, as amended, applies to oppositions filed in good time against default judgments for which no judgment had been handed down by the publication of this Law and to any oppositions filed after that date.

Article 68

Procedural steps that were generally taken in cases which were pending on 16 September 1968 are valid, whether the provisions of the Code of Civil Procedure or the provisions concerning civil procedure previously in force were applied. From now on, in such cases, the procedure shall be conducted in accordance with the provisions of the Code of Civil Procedure, unless otherwise provided for in this Law.

Article 69

1. Pending cases that have not been heard shall be adjudicated in accordance with the provisions of the Code of Civil Procedure, as amended. On the hearing date set, the court before which they are pending shall issue an order for entry of a different hearing date in the case register of the competent court. Such entry shall be equivalent to a summons for parties in the proceedings in which both sides are heard or lawfully tried *in absentia*. Any party in the proceedings may, prior to such a decision being issued, bring the case for a hearing by means of a summons.

2. Cases heard before the reporting judge referred to in Article 296, whether or not a non-final ruling was handed down, shall continue to be tried under the Code of Civil Procedure as in force prior to its amendment. For the duration of the taking of evidence, the presiding judge of the court of first instance may appoint a different judge to replace the reporting judge, where there is good cause. When the taking of evidence has concluded, the case shall be brought for a hearing before the multi-member court of first instance, on whose bench the aforesaid reporting judge, if possible, shall sit. Article 297(1) and (2) of the Code of Civil Procedure do not apply in this case.

3. Oppositions against a default judgment, third-party proceedings and applications for re-opening proceedings against judgments handed down or to be handed down by the reporting judge shall from now on be brought for a hearing before the multi-member court of first instance.

Άρθρο 70

Υποθέσεις πτωχευτικές που εκκρεμούν ενώπιον του μονομελούς πρωτοδικείου και δεν συζητήθηκαν, εισάγονται με κλήση για συζήτηση στο πολυμελές πρωτοδικείο και εφαρμόζεται η διάταξη του άρθρου 69 παράγραφος 1 εδάφ. δεύτερο και τρίτο αυτού του ΕνΚΠολΔ. Οι υποθέσεις που συζητήθηκαν εξακολουθούν να υπάγονται στο μονομελές πρωτοδικείο έως ότου αυτό εκδώσει οριστική απόφαση.

Άρθρο 71

Στις εργατικές διαφορές καθώς και στη διαδικασία έκδοσης διαταγής πληρωμής οφειλόμενου μισθού δεν καταβάλλεται το κατά το νόμο ΓϿΟΗ/1912 (Α' 3) δικαστικό ένσημο, για το μέχρι του ποσού της εκάστοτε καθ' ύλην αρμοδιότητας του ειρηνοδικείου αίτημα της αγωγής ή της αίτησης αντίστοιχα.
Στις περιπτώσεις εργατικών διαφορών, καθώς και αιτήσεων για την έκδοση διαταγής πληρωμής οφειλόμενου μισθού, για τις οποίες καταβάλλεται δικαστικό ένσημο, αυτό καθορίζεται σε ποσοστό τέσσερα τοις χιλίοις (4‰) επί της αξίας του αντικειμένου της αγωγής, της αίτησης ή άλλου δικογράφου που υποβάλλεται σε οποιοδήποτε δικαστήριο του Κράτους και υπόκειται σε δικαστικό ένσημο κατά τις οικείες διατάξεις.

Άρθρο 72

[Καταργείται]

Άρθρο 73

1. Αγωγή κακοδικίας κατά δικηγόρου, συμβολαιογράφου, άμισθου υποθηκοφύλακα, διαιτητή, δικαστικού γραμματέα και δικαστικού επιμελητή υπάγεται στο κατά τόπον αρμόδιο, κατά τις διατάξεις του Κώδικα Πολιτικής Δικονομίας, πολυμελές πρωτοδικείο που δικάζει κατά την τακτική διαδικασία.
2. Η αγωγή, που συντάσσεται σύμφωνα με τα άρθρα 118 και 216 εδάφιο 1 του Κώδικα Πολιτικής Δικονομίας, πρέπει:
α) να περιέχει όλους τους λόγους, στους οποίους ο ενάγων στηρίζει την αγωγή κακοδικίας, και
β) να αναγράφει με ακρίβεια όλα τα αποδεικτικά μέσα που επικαλείται για να αποδείξει τους λόγους, διαφορετικά επέρχεται ακυρότητα.
3. Στη αγωγή επισυνάπτονται:
α) τα αποδεικτικά έγγραφα που ο ενάγων επικαλείται για να υποστηρίξει τους λόγους της αγωγής, σε πρωτότυπα η επικυρωμένα αντίγραφα,
β) ειδικό πληρεξούσιο στον δικηγόρο που υπογράφει την αγωγή, αλλιώς είναι απαράδεκτη.
4. Αγωγή κακοδικίας επιτρέπεται μόνο αν στηρίζεται σε δόλο ή βαριά αμέλεια ή αρνησιδικία και ο ενάγων ζημιώθηκε από τέτοιες πράξεις ή παραλείψεις.
5. Δεν επιτρέπεται αγωγή κακοδικίας όταν περάσουν έξι μήνες από την πράξη ή παράλειψη που επικαλείται ο ενάγων.
6. Αν η αγωγή κακοδικίας απορριφθεί για οποιονδήποτε λόγο, δεν επιτρέπεται να ασκηθεί νέα αγωγή για την ίδια υπόθεση, για τους ίδιους ή άλλους λόγους, και ο ενάγων καταδικάζεται να πληρώσει τα έξοδα, και μπορεί να καταδικαστεί και σε χρηματική ποινή κατά το άρθρο 205 του Κώδικα Πολιτικής Δικονομίας.

Άρθρο 74

Ο κώδικας πολιτικής δικονομίας και ο εισαγωγικός νόμος του αρχίζουν να ισχύουν από τις 16 Σεπτεμβρίου 1968.

Article 70

Bankruptcy cases which are pending before the single-member court of first instance and have not been heard shall be brought for a hearing before the multi-member court of first instance, and the provisions of the second and third subparagraphs of Article 69(1) of this Law Introducing the Code of Civil Procedure apply. Cases that were heard shall remain under the jurisdiction of the single-member court of first instance until the latter hands down a final judgment.

Article 71

In cases of labour disputes and the procedure for obtaining an order for payment for unpaid salaries, the judicial stamp duty required under Law 3978/1912 (Government Gazette, Series I, Issue 3) need not be paid for the form of order sought in the action or application, respectively, up to the amount for which the court of the peace has jurisdiction *ratione materiae,* as applicable from time to time.

In cases of labour disputes and applications to obtain an order for payment for unpaid salaries for which judicial stamp duty is payable, this shall be set at 4‰ of the value requested in the action, application or other procedural document that is submitted to any Greek court and is subject to judicial stamp duty under the relevant provisions.

Article 72

[Repealed]

Article 73

1. Actions for miscarriage of justice against a lawyer, notary public, non-stipendiary land registrar, arbitrator, court registrar [or] court process server shall be brought before the multi-member court of first instance with jurisdiction *ratione loci* under the provisions of the Code of Civil Procedure, which shall try the matter under the ordinary procedure.

2. The action, which shall be prepared in accordance with Articles 118 and 216(1) of the Code of Civil Procedure, must:

a) set out all the grounds on which the plaintiff's action for miscarriage of justice relies; and

b) precisely indicate, on penalty of nullity, all the means of evidence relied upon to prove the grounds.

3. The following shall be attached to the action:

a) the documentary evidence relied upon by the plaintiff in support of the grounds of the action, as originals or certified copies;

b) a special power of attorney authorising the lawyer signing the action, otherwise it shall be inadmissible.

4. An action for miscarriage of justice shall be permitted only if it relies on *dolus* or gross negligence or denial of justice and the plaintiff suffered harm due to such acts or omissions.

5. An action for miscarriage of justice may not be brought after six months have elapsed from the act or omission being invoked by the plaintiff.

6. If the action for mistrial is dismissed on any grounds, a new action may not be brought with regard to the same case, on the same or different grounds, and the plaintiff shall be ordered to pay the costs, and may be ordered to pay a monetary penalty in accordance with Article 205 of the Code of Civil Procedure.

Article 74

The Code of Civil Procedure and the Law Introducing the Code enter into force on 16 September 1968.

Άρθρο 75

Με β.δ. που εκδίδεται ύστερα από πρόταση του υπουργού δικαιοσύνης, θα κωδικοποιηθούν σε ενιαίο κείμενο οι διατάξεις του κώδικα πολιτικής δικονομίας και του εισαγωγικού του νόμου, όπως ισχύουν τώρα και όπως τροποποιούνται και συμπληρώνονται από το νόμο αυτόν και θα μεταβληθεί και η αρίθμηση των άρθρων τους.

Άρθρο 76

Αυτός ο νόμος αρχίζει να ισχύει από την 1η Οκτωβρίου 1971, εκτός από την παράγραφο 7 του άρθρου 53, τις παραγράφους 3 και 4 του άρθρου 63 και τα άρθρα 69 και 73, που αρχίζουν να ισχύουν από τις 16 Σεπτεμβρίου 1971.

Article 75

The provisions of the Code of Civil Procedure and the Law Introducing the Code, as currently in force and as amended and supplemented by this Law, shall be codified into a single text and the numbering of their Articles shall be changed pursuant to a Royal Decree issued on a proposal from the Minister of Justice.

Article 76

This Law enters into force on 1 October 1971, except for Article 53(7), Article 63(3) and (4), and Articles 69 and 73, which enter into force on 16 September 1971.

Greek to English Glossary

EL	EN	Notes
Αγωγή	Action	
Αγωγή διάρρηξης δικαιοπραξίας ως καταδολιευτικής	Paulian action	
Αγωγή διεκδίκησης	Action for revendication	
Αγωγή για λογοδοσία	Action for an account to be rendered	
Αγωγή κακοδικίας	Action for miscarriage of justice	
Αγωγή νομής	Action concerning possession	
Άδεια	Permission	
Άδεια (διακοπών, διεξαγωγής δίκης, επίδοσης)	Leave	
Αδικαιολόγητος πλουτισμός	Unjust enrichment	
Αδικοπραξία	Tort	
Αεροσκάφος	Aircraft	
Άθικτος	Intact	
Αίρεση	Condition	
Αίτημα (διαδίκου)	Motion	
Αίτημα της αγωγής	Form of order sought (in the action)	
Αίτηση	Application	See Article 4
Αίτηση	Request	See Article 5(1)
Αίτηση για παραπομπή	Application for remittal	
Αιτία θανάτου (επίρ.)	*Mortis causa*	
Αιτιολογικό (απόφασης)	Reasoning	
Αιτών	Applicant	
Ακατάσχετος	Non-attachable / Non-garnishable	Context-dependent
Ακίνητα	Immovables	See Article 948, Civil Code
Ακυρότητα	Nullity	
Ακύρωση (απόφασης, γάμου)	Annulment	
Αλλοδαπή αρχή	Foreign authority	
Αλλοδαπός	Foreign national/Foreigner	
Άμισθος δικαστικός επιμελητής	Non-stipendiary court process server	
Αμφοτεροβαρής σύμβαση	Bilateral contract	See Articles 374 *et seq.*, Civil Code
Αναβλητική αίρεση	Suspensive condition	
Αναβολή (δίκης, κτλ.)	Adjournment	
Αναβολή (ενεργειών)	Postponement	
Αναγγελία (δικαιώματος ή απαίτησης)	Lodgement	
Αναγκαστική απαλλοτρίωση	Expropriation	
Αναγκαστική διαχείριση	Compulsory administration	

Αναγκαστική εκποίηση	Forced sale	
Αναγκαστική εκτέλεση	Compulsory enforcement	
Αναγκαστική κατάσχεση	Compulsory attachment	
Αναγνώριση	Acknowledgment	See Article 65
Αναγνώριση	Recognition	See Article 17
Αναγνωρισμένο τέκνο	Recognised child	
Αναγνωριστική αγωγή	Action for a declaratory judgment	
Αναδρομική ισχύς	Retroactive effect	
Αναιρεσείων	Cassationer	
Αναίρεση	Cassation	
Αναίρεση υπέρ του νόμου	Cassation of any judgment in the interests of ensuring proper application of the law in the future	
Αναιρεσίβλητος	Cassationee	
Αναιρετήριο	Application for cassation	
Ανάκληση (απόφασης)	Revocation	
Ανακοίνωση (δίκης)	Third-party notice	
Ανακοπή	Opposition	
Ανακοπή ερημοδικίας	Opposition against a default judgment	
Ανάλογη εφαρμογή	Application *mutatis mutandis*	
Αναπαράσταση	Re-enactment	
Αναστολή (εκδίκασης)	Stay	
Αναστολή παραγραφής	Suspension	See Article 255 *et seq.*, Civil Code
Ανασυζήτηση	Re-hearing	
Αναψηλάφηση	Application for re-opening proceedings	
Ανέκκλητη απόφαση	*De facto* non-appealable judgment	
Ανεπίδεκτος εκτίμησης	Incapable of being assessed	
Ανήλικος	Juvenile	
Ανιόντες	Relatives in the ascendant line	
Ανταγωγή	Cross-action	
Ανταίτηση	Cross-application	
Ανταπόδειξη	Counter-evidence	
Αντεισαγγελέας	Deputy public prosecutor	
Αντεκκαλών	Cross-appellant	
Αντέφεση	Cross-appeal	
Αντικείμενο (δίκης)	Subject-matter (of the proceedings)	
Αντίκλητος	Process agent	
Αντίκρουση	Rebuttal	
Αντιπαροχή	Counter-performance	
Ανώνυμη εταιρεία	Société anonyme	

Ανώνυμη ομολογία	Bearer bond	
Αξιόγραφο	Security	See Article 850(1) See Foreword
Αξιωματικός υπηρεσίας	Officer on duty	
Απαίτηση	Claim	
Απαλλοτρίωση	Alienation	See Article 939, Civil Code
Απαράδεκτος	Inadmissible	
Απλή ομοδικία	Permissive joinder	
Απόγραφο	Enforcement precept	
Αποδεικτικά μέσα	Means of evidence	
Αποδεικτική ισχύς	Probative value	
Αποδέκτης επίδοσης	Person served	
Απόδοση	Return / Handing over	
Απόδοση χρήσης μισθίου	Return of use of a leased propety	
Αποδοχή κληρονομιάς	Acceptance of an inheritance	
Αποζημίωση	Compensation	
Αποζημίωση εξαιτίας πταίσματος κατά τις διαπραγματεύσεις	Compensation due to *culpa in contrahendo*	
Αποθετήριο	Depositary receipt	
Αποκλειστική αρμοδιότητα	Exclusive jurisdiction	
Αποκλειστική προθεσμία	Fixed deadline	
Απόλυση	Dismissal	
Αποποίηση κληρονομιάς	Repudiation of an inheritance	
Αποσβεστική προθεσμία	Exclusive deadline	See Article 279, Civil Code
Αποσφράγιση	Unsealing	
Απόφαση	Ruling	See Article 114(2), see Foreword
Απόφαση	Judgment	See Article 114(3), see Foreword
Απόφαση ασφαλιστικών μέτρων	Judgment granting interim measures	
Αποχή	Abstention	
Αργία	Bank holiday	
Άρειος Πάγος	Supreme Court	
Αρεοπαγίτης	Supreme Court Judge	
Αριθμός φορολογικού μητρώου	Tax identification number	
Αρμοδιότητα	Competence	See Article 7, see Foreword
Αρμοδιότητα	Jurisdiction	See Article 3(1), see Foreword
Αρνησιδικία	Denial of justice	
Αρνητική δήλωση	Negative declaration	
Αρνητικό διαφέρον	Reliance damages	

Αρχαιότητα	Seniority	
Αρχείο του δικαστηρίου	Court archives	
Αστυνομικό κατάστημα	Police facility	
Αστυνομικό τμήμα	Police department	
Αστυνομικός σταθμός	Police station	
Ασφάλεια (κοινή, κράτους)	Security	See Article 48
Ασφάλεια	Collateral	See Article 11
Ασφαλισμένος	Insured person	
Ασφαλιστικά μέτρα	Interim measures	
Άτοκο γραμμάτιο πληρωτέο εν όψει	Interest-free promissory note payable on demand	
Άυλη μετοχή	Dematerialised share	
Αυτεπαγγέλτως	*Ex officio*	
Αυτούσια διανομή	Partition *in natura*	
Αυτοψία	Inspection	
Αφαίρεση (κληρονομητηρίου)	Withdrawal	
Αφάνεια	Absence	See Article 40, Civil Code
Βαθμός δικαιοδοσίας	Instance	
Βαριά αμέλεια	Gross negligence	
Βάρος	Charge	See Article 965, Civil Code
Βέβαιη χρονολογία	Timestamp	
Βεβαιωτικός όρκος	Attesting oath	
Βίαιη διακοπή δίκης	Forced discontinuation of the proceedings	
Βιβλίο (νόμου)	Book	
Βιβλίο διεκδικήσεων	Claims register	
Βιβλίο υποθηκών	Mortgage register	
Βιοτέχνης	Artisan	
Γαμικές διαφορές	Matrimonial disputes	
Γάμος	Marriage	
Γενική δωσιδικία	General forum	
Γεωμέτρηση	Survey	
Γνήσιο τέκνο	Legitimate child	
Γονική μέριμνα	Parental responsibility	
Γραμματεία (δικαστηρίου)	Registry	
Γραμμάτιο εις διαταγήν	Promissory note	
Γραμμάτιο κατάθεσης	Deposit note	
Γραφή	Handwriting	
Γραφολογική πραγματογνωμοσύνη	Handwriting expert evidence	
Δανειστής	Creditor	
Δεσπόζον κτήμα	Dominant tenement	

Δευτεροβάθμιο δικαστήριο	Second-instance court	
Δήλωση βούλησης	Declaration of will	See Article 130 *et seq.*, Civil Code
Δήλωση επιλογής	Declaration of choice	See Article 1967 *et seq.*, Civil Code
Δημόσια αρχή	Public authority	
Δημόσια διαθήκη	Public will	
Δημόσια τάξη	Public policy	
Δημοσίευση διαθήκης	Granting of probate	
Δημόσιο	Greek State	See Foreword
Δημόσιο έγγραφο	Public document	
Διαδικαστική πράξη	Procedural step	
Διάδικος	Party in the proceedings	
Διαζύγιο	Divorce	
Διαίρεση κοινού (ακινήτου)	Division of a jointly owned immovable	
Διαιρετό δικαίωμα	Divisible right	
Διαιτητής	Arbitrator	
Διαιτητής πραγματογνώμων	Expert arbitrator	
Διαιτητική απόφαση	Arbitration award	
Διαιτητικό δικαστήριο	Arbitration panel	
Διακάτοχος	Holder of possession	
Διακοπή δίκης	Interruption	See Article 286
Διακοπή παραγραφής	Interruption	See Article 146(1) See Article 260 *et seq.*, Civil Code
Διακοπή συμβίωσης	Cessation of living together in wedlock	
Διάλυση (εταιρείας)	Winding up	
Διαμέρισμα	Apartment	See Article 128(2)
Διαμέρισμα	Dwelling	See Article 827(2)
Διαμεσολάβηση	Mediation	
Διαμονή	Residence	
Διανεμητέο	Partitionable thing	
Διανομή (κοινού πράγματος)	Partition	See Article 478 *et seq.*
Διανομή (εταιρικής περιουσίας, εκπλειστηριάσματος)	Distribution	See Articles 27(2), 957(2)
Διανομή κληρονομιάς	Sharing-out of an estate	See Article 30(1)
Διάσκεψη	Deliberations	
Διαταγή πληρωμής	Payment order	
Διατακτικό (μέρος απόφασης)	Operative part of the judgment	
Διάταξη (νόμου, απόφασης, κτλ.)	Provision	
Διάταξη διαθήκης / τελευταίας βούλησης	Testamentary disposition	

Διατροφή	Maintenance	
Διατυπώσεις δημοσιότητας	Publicity formalities	
Διαφέρον	Damages	
Διαφορά	Dispute	
Διαφορά από αδικοπραξία	Tortious dispute	
Διαχείριση με δικαστική εντολή	Court-ordered administration	
Διαχείριση χωρίς δικαστική εντολή	Non-court-ordered administration	See Article 730 *et seq.*, Civil Code
Διαχειριστής	Manager	See Article 795
Διαχειριστής	Administrator	See Article 614(5)(b)
Διαχειριστής ιδιοκτησίας κατ' ορόφους	Building manager	
Διδάγματα κοινής πείρας	Teachings of common experience	
Διεθνές δίκαιο	International law	
Διεθνές σήμα	International call sign	
Διεθνής διαιτησία	International arbitration	
Διεθνής σύμβαση	International treaty/convention	
Διερμηνέας/Ερμηνέας	Interpreter	
Δικαιόγραφο	Decision incorporating rights	
Δικαιοδοσία	Jurisdiction	
Δικαιοπρακτική δήλωση	Transactional representation	
Δικαιοπραξία	Legal transaction	
Δικαιοπραξία εν ζωή	Legal transaction *inter vivos*	
Δικαιούχος διατροφής	Person entitled to maintenance	
Δικαίωμα	Right	
Δικαίωμα ιδιωτικού δικαίου	Private-law right	
Δικαιώματα	Fees	
Δικαιώματα εκμετάλλευσης κινηματογραφικών ταινιών	Exploitation rights for films	
Δικαιώματα ευρεσιτεχνίας	Patent rights	
Δικαιώματα πνευματικής ιδιοκτησίας	Copyright	
Δικανική πεποίθηση	Judicial conviction	See Article 340(2)
Δικάσιμος	Hearing date	
Δικαστήριο παραπομπής	Remittal court	
Δικαστήριο της κληρονομίας	Court ruling on the inheritance	
Δικαστήριο της ουσίας	Trial court	
Δικαστής μεσολαβητής	Mediator judge	
Δικαστικά έξοδα / δικαστική δαπάνη	Court costs	
Δικαστική μεσολάβηση	Judicial mediation	
Δικαστική αρχή	Judicial authority	
Δικαστική εκκαθάριση	Judicial liquidation	

Δικαστική μεσεγγύηση	Judicial sequestration	
Δικαστική προστασία	Judicial protection	
Δικαστικό τεκμήριο	Judicial presumption	
Δικαστικός λειτουργός	Judicial functionary	
Δικαστικός πληρεξούσιος	Advocate	
Δίκη	Proceedings	
Δικηγορικός σύλλογος	Bar association	
Δικηγόρος	Lawyer	
Δικόγραφο	Procedural document	
Δικονομικός εγγυητής	Third party joined in proceedings as guarantor	
Διοικητής (αστυνομικού τμήματος)	Commanding officer	
Διοικητικές διαφορές	Administrative disputes	
Διοικητικό δικαστήριο	Administrative court	
Διοικητικό πρωτοδικείο	Administrative court of first instance	
Δόλος	*Dolus*	
Δουλεία	Easement	
Δουλεύον κτήμα	Servient tenement	
Δυστροπία	Intransigence	
Δωροληψία	Passive bribery	
Εγγραφή υποθήκης	Registration of a mortgage	
Εγγύηση	Guarantee	See Article 11
Εγγύηση	Surety	See Article 164(3)
Εγγυητής	Guarantor	
Εγγυητική επιστολή	Letter of guarantee	
Εγγυοδοσία	Provision of surety	
Εγχειρόγραφος δανειστής	Unsecured creditor	
Έδρα (δικαστηρίου, σωματείου, κτλ.)	Seat	
Έδρα (εταιρείας)	Registered offices	
Ειδική κατοικία	Special place of domicile	
Ειδικός διάδοχος	Specific successor	
Ειδικός επίτροπος	Guardian *ad litem*	
Ειδικός κηδεμόνας (σχολάζουσας κληρονομίας)	Special curator	See Article 1910, Civil Code
Ειρηνοδικείο	Court of the peace	
Εισαγγελέας	Public prosecutor	
Εισαγγελέας του Αρείου Πάγου	Supreme Court Public Prosecutor	
Εισαγωγή υπόθεσης	Bringing a case [for a hearing]	
Εισαγωγικός Νόμος	Law Introducing the Code of Civil Procedure	
Εισηγητής	Reporting judge	
Εισφορά (σε ασφαλιστικό οργανισμό)	Contribution	

Εκείνος κατά του οποίου γίνεται κατάσχεση είς χείρας τρίτου	Garnishee	
Έκθεση κατάθεσης	Filing report	
Εκκαθάριση (εταιρείας)	Liquidation	
Εκκαθαριστής	Liquidator	
Εκκαλών	Appellant	
Εκκρεμής δίκη	Pending proceedings	
Εκκρεμοδικία	*Lis pendens*	
Εκμίσθωση	Leasing	
Εκούσια δικαιοδοσία	Non-contentious proceedings	
Εκούσιος πλειστηριασμός	Voluntary auction	
Εκποίηση	Sale	
Έκπτωση από δικαίωμα	Forfeiture of a right	
Έκτακτη διαθήκη	Extraordinary will	
Έκταση (ακινήτου)	Area	
Εκτελεστής διαθήκης	Executor of a will	
Εκτελεστικό όργανο	Enforcement officer	
Εκτελεστός τίτλος	Enforceable title	
Εκτιμητής	Valuer	
Ελεγκτικό Συνέδριο	Court of Audit	
Έλεγχος (Αρείου Πάγου)	Review	
Ελεύθερη συμβίωση	Free union	See Foreword
Έλλειψη δικαιοδοσίας	Lack of jurisdiction	
Έλλειψη συμφωνηθεισών ιδιοτήτων	Absence of properties agreed upon	
Εμπράγματη αγωγή	Action *in rem*	
Εμπράγματη ανακοπή	Opposition *in rem*	
Εμπράγματη απαίτηση	Claim *in rem*	
Εμπράγματη σχέση	*In rem* relationship	
Εμπράγματο δικαίωμα	Right *in rem*	
Εναγόμενος	Defendant	
Ενάγων	Plaintiff	
Ένδικο βοήθημα	Form of relief	
Ένδικο μέσο	Legal remedy	
Ενέχυρο	Pledge	
Ενεχυρόγραφο	Warrant	
Ενεχυρούχος δανειστής	Pledgee	
Έννομη σχέση	Legal relationship	
Έννομο συμφέρον	Legitimate interest	
Ένορκη βεβαίωση	Affidavit	
Ενοχική σχέση	Contractual relationship	

Ένσταση αναρμοδιότητας	Plea of lack of jurisdiction	
Εντεταλμένος δικαστής	Delegated judge	
Εντολέας	Principal	
Ενυπόθηκη απαίτηση	Mortgage-backed claim	
Ενυπόθηκος δανειστής	Mortgagee	
Ένωση προσώπων	Grouping of persons	See Article 107, Civil Code
Εξαίρεση (δικαστή)	Exemption	
Εξάλειψη	Striking-out	
Εξαρτημένη εργασία	Salaried labour	
Εξασφαλίσεις	Collateral	See Article 952
Εξέταση	Examination	
Έξοδα	Costs	
Εξουσιοδότηση	Authorisation	
Εξώδικος	Extra-judicial	
Εορτή	Holiday	
Επαναπλειστηριασμός	Repeat auction	
Επαναφορά των πραγμάτων στην προηγούμενη κατάσταση	Restoration of a prior state of affairs	
Επιβλαβής για τα χρηστά ήθη	Injurious to morality	
Επιδιαιτητής	Presiding arbitrator	
Επικαρπία	Usufruct	
Επίκοινο	Jointly owned asset	
Επικοινωνία (με ανήλικα παιδιά)	Access	
Επικουρική δικαστική συμπαράσταση	Assisted legal guardianship	See Article 1676, Civil Code
Επικουρική σώρευση αγωγών	Joinder of actions in respect of their alternative bases	
Επιμέλεια ανηλίκου	Custody	
Επίμορτη αγροληψία	Sharecropping	
Επιταγή	Cheque	
Επιτροπεία	Tutorship	See Article 1589 *et seq.*, Civil Code
Επιτροπευόμενος	Ward	
Εποπτικό συμβούλιο	Supervisory board	See Article 1682, Civil Code
Εργαζόμενος	Worker	
Εργοδότης	Employer	
Ερήμην δίκη	Proceedings held *in absentia*	
Ερημοδικία	Failure to enter an appearance	
Ερμηνευτικός κανόνας	Interpretative rule	
Εσφαλμένη εφαρμογή	Misapplication	

Εσωτερικό δίκαιο	National law	
Εταιρία	Company Partnership	See Article 788 See Article 27(1) See Foreword
Εταιρική μερίδα	Shareholding	
Εταίρος	Partner	
Ετεροδικία	Immunity from jurisdiction	
Ετερόρρυθμη εταιρεία	Limited partnership	
Ευεργέτημα απογραφής	Benefit of inventory-taking	
Ευεργέτημα πενίας	Legal aid	
Ευπαθές πράγμα	Perishable thing	
Ευπρέπεια	Propriety	
Ευρωπαϊκή Διαταγή Δέσμευσης Λογαριασμού	European Account Preservation Order	
Έφεση	Appeal	
Εφεσίβλητος	Respondent [in appeal]	
Εφέτης	Appeal judge	
Ζημιογόνο γεγονός	Loss event	
Ηλεκτρονική απόδειξη παραλαβής	Electronic acknowledgment of receipt	
Ηλεκτρονική επαλήθευση	Electronic verification	
Ηλεκτρονικός πλειστηριασμός	e-auction	
Θέση (ακινήτου)	Location	
Θετός γονέας	Adoptive parent	
Θρησκευτικός όρκος	Religious oath	
Ιδιόγραφη διαθήκη	Holographic will	
Ιδιοκτήτης	Owner	
Ιδιόχειρος	Handwritten	
Ιδιωτικό δίκαιο	Private law	
Ιδιωτικό έγγραφο	Private document	
Ιθαγένεια	Nationality	
Ικανότητα δικαστικής παράστασης	Capacity to appear before the courts	
Ισχυρισμός	Argument	See Article 20(4)
Ισχυρισμός	Assertion	See Article 77
Ισχύς απέναντι σε όλους	*Erga omnes* effect	
Καθ' ύλην αρμοδιότητα	Jurisdiction *ratione materiae*	
Κάθετη ιδιοκτησία	Vertical property	
Καθολικός διάδοχος	Universal successor	
Κανόνας δικαίου	Legal norm	
Κανονισμός δικαστηρίου	Statute of the court	
Κανονισμός ορίων	Determination of boundaries	

Καρπός	Fruit	See Article 961, Civil Code
Κατ' αναψηλάφηση δίκη	Re-opened proceedings	
Κατά τόπον αρμοδιότητα	Jurisdiction *ratione loci*	
Καταβολή ορισμένου ελλείμματος	Payment of a specific shortfall	
Κατακυρωτική έκθεση	Award report	
Κατάλογος εξόδων	List of costs	
Κατάλοιπο λογαριασμού	Account balance	
Καταπιστευματοδόχος	Trustee	
Κατάργηση (δικαιώματος)	Abolition	
Κατάσχεση	Attachment	See Article 707 See Foreword
Κατάσχεση (αεροσκάφους, πλοίου)	Arrest	See Article 709 See Foreword
Κατάσχεση εις χείρας τρίτου / σε χέρια τρίτου	Garnishment	See Article 712 See Foreword
Κατάσχων	Garnishor	
Καταφατική δήλωση	Affirmative declaration	
Καταχρηστικός	Abusive	
Καταψήφιση	Request seeking performance	
Κατιόντες	Descendants	
Κατοικία	Domicile	
Κατοχή	Detentorship	
Κάτοχος	Detentor	
Κεκλεισμένων των θυρών	*In camera*	
Κεφάλαιο (απόφασης)	Head of a judgment	
Κηδεμόνας (σχολάζουσας κληρονομίας)	Curator (of an unclaimed estate)	
Κίνδυνος για την κοινή ασφάλεια	Public security risk	
Κινητό	Movable	
Κληροδοσία	Legacy	
Κληροδότημα	Bequest	
Κληροδόχος	Legatee	
Κληρονομητήριο	Certificate of inheritance	
Κληρονομιά	Inheritance	See Article 263(e) See Foreword
Κληρονομία	Estate	See Article 30(1) See Foreword
Κληρονομική μερίδα	Share in the estate	
Κληρονομικό δικαίωμα	Inheritance right	
Κληρονομικό καταπίστευμα	Testamentary trust	
Κληρονόμος	Heir	

Κλήρος	Lot	
Κλήρωση	Drawing by lot	
Κληρωτίδα	Drawing apparatus	
Κλήση	Summons	
Κοινόχρηστες δαπάνες (κτιρίου)	Building service charges	
Κοινωνία (δικαιώματος)	Community of rights	See Article 785 *et seq.*, Civil Code
Κοινωνική υπηρεσία	Social services	
Κοινωνός	Member of a community of rights	
Κοινωφελής περιουσία	Estate intended for public-benefit purposes	
Κομιστής	Bearer	
Κτήμα	Tenement	
Κυρία διαθήκη	Valid will	
Κύρια διαφορά	Main dispute	
Κύρια παρέμβαση	Main intervention	
Κυριότητα	Ownership	See Article 999 *et seq.*, Civil Code
Κύρος	Validity	
Ληξιαρχική πράξη	Civil registry certificate	
Λιμάνι	Port	
Λιμεναρχής	Harbour master	
Λογοδοσία	Rendering of account	
Μάρτυρας	Witness	
Ματαίωση (πλειστηριασμού κτλ.)	Cancellation	See Article 972(2)
Ματαίωση (συζήτησης)	Inability to go ahead	See Article 260(2)
Μερίδα	Entry	See Article 981
Μερίδα	Share	See Article 480(3)
Μερισματαπόδειξη / Μερισματόγραφο	Dividend coupon	
Μέσα επίθεσης ή άμυνας / Επιθετικά ή αμυντικά μέσα	Pleas	
Μεσεγγυούχος	Sequestrator	
Μεταβατική έδρα	Circuit	
Μεταβίβαση	Transfer	
Μεταβίβαση με λευκή οπισθογράφηση	Transfer with a blank endorsement section	
Μεταγλώττιση	Recast	
Μεταγραφή	Entry	See Article 992(1)
	Registration	See Article 489(2)
	Transcription	See Article 997(3)
Μη οριστική απόφαση	Non-final ruling	
Μη προνομιούχα απαίτηση	Non-preferential claim	
Μητρώο (αεροσκαφών)	Aircraft registry	
Μικροδιαφορά	Small claim	

Μικτή αγωγή	Mixed action	
Μισθίο	Leased property	
Μισθός υπερημερίας	Default salary	
Μίσθωμα	Rent	
Μίσθωση (πράγματος)	Leasing	See Article 574 *et seq.*, Civil Code
Μισθωτής	Lessee	
Μισθωτική σύμβαση	Lease agreement	
Μονομελές εφετείο	Single-member court of appeal	
Μονομελές πρωτοδικείο	Single-member court of first instance	
Μυστική διαθήκη	Sealed will	
Ναυτικό Απομαχικό Ταμείο	Seafarers' Retirement Fund	
Νηολόγιο	Ship registry	
Νομέας	Possessor	
Νομή	Possession	See Article 974 *et seq.*, Civil Code
Νομική βάση	Legal basis	
Νομική προσωπικότητα	Legal personality	
Νόμιμη μοίρα	Reserved portion of an estate	See Article 1825 *et seq.*, Civil Code
Νομιμοποιημένο τέκνο	Legitimised child	
Ολομέλεια	Sitting in full court	
Ομάδα αντικειμένων	Group of things	
Ομοδικία	Joinder	
Ομόδικος	Joined party	
Ομολογία (διαδίκου)	Admission	
Ομολογιακό δάνειο	Bond loan	
Ομόρρυθμη εταιρεία	General partnership	
Ονομαστικός τίτλος (μετοχών)	Registered (share) certificate	
Οργανισμός κοινής ωφελείας	Utility company	
Οργανισμός κοινωνικής ασφάλισης	Social security organisation	
Όριο (ακινήτου)	Boundary	
Οριζόντια ιδιοκτησία	Horizontal property	
Ορισμένη διάρκεια	Fixed duration	
Όρκιση	Oath-taking	
Όρκος	Oath	
Όρος	Proviso	
Οροφοκτησία	Joint ownership [within a building]	
Όροφος	Storey	
Ουσιαστικό δίκαιο	Substantive law	

Οφειλέτης	Debtor	
Όχληση	Notice	
Παράβαση	Breach	See Article 424
	Failure to comply	See Article 159
	Infringement	See Article 15(3)
	Violation	See Article 205
Παράβαση καθήκοντος	Breach of duty	
Παράβολο	Procedural fee (receipt)	
Παραγραφή	Time-barring period	
Παραδεκτό	Admissibility	
Παράδοση (ακινήτου)	Handing back of a property	
Παραίτηση	Waiver	
Παραίτηση (πληρεξουσιότητας)	Relinquishment	
Παράλειψη	Omission	
Παραπομπή	Remittal	
Παραπομπή (υπόθεσης)	Referral of a case	
Παράρτημα (ακινήτου)	Accessory	See Article 956, Civil Code
Παραχώρηση	Granting	
Πάρεδρος	Associate judge	
Παρέκταση αρμοδιότητας	Prorogation of jurisdiction	
Παρεμβαίνων	Intervener	
Παρέμβαση	Intervention	
Παρεμπίπτον ζήτημα	Incidental issue	
Παρεμπίπτουσα αγωγή	Incidental action	
Παρεμπίπτουσα αίτηση	Incidental application	
Παροχή	Performance	
Πελάτης	Customer	
Πελάτης (ξενοδοχείου)	Guest	See Articles 834 to 839, Civil Code
Περιοδικές παροχές	Periodically recurring dues	
Περιουσιακά δικαιώματα	Property rights	
Περιφέρεια (δικαστηρίου)	District	
Πιθανολόγηση	Balance of probabilities	
Πινάκιο	Case register	
Πλαστογραφία	Forgery	
Πλειοδότης	Bidder	
Πλειστηρίασμα	Auction price	
Πλειστηριασμός	Auction	
Πληρεξούσιο (εγγράφο)	Power of attorney	

Πληρεξουσιότητα	Power of representation	
Πλοίαρχος	Master	
Πλοίο	Ship	
Πλοιοκτήτης	Owner-operator	
Πολεοδομία	Planning department	
Πολιτική Δικονομία	Civil procedure	
Πολιτικό δικαστήριο	Civil court	
Πολιτικός όρκος	Secular oath	
Πολυμελές πρωτοδικείο	Multi-member court of first instance	
Πράγμα	Thing	See Article 947 *et seq.*, Civil Code
Πράγμα υποκείμενο σε φθορά	Thing which can become spoiled	
Πραγματική δουλεία	Real easement	
Πραγματικό ελάττωμα	Actual defect	
Πραγματικός ισχυρισμός	Factual assertion	
Πραγματογνωμοσύνη	Expert evidence	
Πραγματογνώμων	Expert	
Πρακτικό δημοσίευσης διαθήκης	Will probate report	
Πρακτικό διαμεσολάβησης	Mediation report	
Προδικασία	Preliminary procedure	
Προδικαστικό ερώτημα	Request for a preliminary ruling	
Πρόεδρος Αρείου Πάγου	President of the Supreme Court	
Πρόεδρος δικαστηρίου	Presiding judge	
Πρόεδρος εφετών	Presiding appeal judge	
Πρόεδρος τριμελούς συμβουλίου (που διευθύνει το δικαστήριο)	President of the three-member management board	
Προθεσμία	Deadline	See Article 20A
Προθεσμία	Term	See Article 682 See Article 210, Civil Code
Προϊστάμενος (δικαστηρίου)	Head of a court	
Προνόμιο ετεροδικίας	Privilege of immunity from jurisdiction	
Προνομιούχες απαιτήσεις	Preferential claims	
Προξενική αρχή	Consular authority	
Πρόξενος	Consul	
Προσεπικαλούμενος	Impleaded party	
Προσεπίκληση	Impleader	
Πρόσθετη παρέμβαση	Permissive intervention	
Πρόσθετοι λόγοι έφεσης	Additional grounds of appeal	
Προσοδοφόρο αντικείμενο	Revenue-generating thing	
Προσωπική δουλεία	Personal easement	

Προσωπική εταιρεία	Partnership	See Article 982(2)(b) See Foreword
Προσωπική κατάσταση	Personal status	
Προσωπική κράτηση	Personal detention	See Foreword
Προσωρινή διαταγή (ασφαλιστικών μέτρων)	Interim order	
Προσωρινή δικαστική προστασία	Interim relief	
Προσωρινός δικαστικός συμπαραστάτης	Interim legal guardian	
Προσωρινός επίτροπος	Interim tutor	
Προφορική συζήτηση	Oral hearing	
Πρωτοδικείο	Court of first instance	
Πρωτοφειλέτης	Principal debtor	
Πταισματοδικείο	Petty offences court	See Foreword
Πτωχευτικός συμβιβασμός	Bankruptcy composition	
Ρητός	Express	
Σιωπηρός	Tacit	
Σκοπός (αστυνομικός)	Guard	
Σπουδαίος λόγος	Serious reason	
Στρατιωτικός	Military personnel member	
Στρεψοδικία	Chicanery	
Συγγένεια	Family relationship	
Συγγένεια εξ αγχιστείας	Relation by marriage	
Συγγένεια εξ αίματος	Relation by blood	
Σύγκληση	Calling	
Συγκρότηση (δικαστηρίου)	Constitution	
Συζήτηση	Hearing	
Συζήτηση κατ' αντιμωλίαν	Hearing having heard both sides	
Σύζυγος	Spouse	
Συλλογική σύμβαση εργασίας	Collective bargaining agreement	
Συμβιβασμός	Settlement	
Συμβιβαστική επέμβαση	Settlement intervention	
Συμβολαιογραφικό έγγραφο	Notarial instrument	
Συμβολαιογράφος	Notary public	
Συμβούλιο διεύθυνσης δικαστηρίου	Court management board	
Συμβούλιο της Επικρατείας	Council of State	
Συμβούλος (ΣτΕ)	Councillor of State	
Σύμμετρη πληρωμή	*Pari passu* payment	
Συμπαιγνία	Collusion	
Συμπαραστατέος	Person to be placed under legal guardianship	
Συμπαραστατούμενος	Person under legal guardianship	
Συμφωνία για διαιτησία	Arbitration agreement	

Συναίνεση	Consent	
Συναλλαγματική	Bill of exchange	
Συναλλακτικές σχέσεις	Dealings	
Σύνδικος πτώχευσης	Bankruptcy administrator	
Συνεδρίαση	Sitting	
Συνεισφορά (κοινωνού)	Contribution	
Συνέλευση	Meeting	
Συνεταιρισμός	Cooperative	
Συνηθισμένο περιβάλλον	Usual environment	
Σύνοικος	Co-habitant	
Συντηρητική κατάσχεση	Preventive attachment	
Συντηρητική κατάσχεση (πλοίου ή αεροσκάφους)	Preventive arrest	
Σύσταση (δικαιώματος)	Establishment	
Συστατικό (ακινήτου)	Constituent part	See Article 953, Civil Code
Σφραγίδα	Seal	
Σχέσεις συζύγων	Relations between spouses	See Article 1386 *et seq.*, Civil Code
Σχετικό έγγραφο (σε δικόγραφο)	Exhibit	
Σχολάζουσα κληρονομία	Unclaimed estate	
Σωματείο	Association	See Article 78 *et seq.*, Civil Code
Τακτικό πολιτικό δικαστήριο	Ordinary civil court	
Τέκνο γεννημένο σε γάμο	Child born in wedlock	
Τέκνο χωρίς γάμο	Child born out of wedlock	
Τελεσίδικη απόφαση	*De jure* non-appealable judgment	
Τηλεδιάσκεψη	Teleconference	
Τηλετύπημα	Telex	
Τίτλος εις διαταγήν	Note payable to order	
Τίτλος παραστατικός αξίας	Security	See Article 164 See Foreword
Τίτλος στον κομιστή	Bearer security	
Τμήμα (Αρείου Πάγου)	Chamber	
Τοκομερίδιο	Interest coupon	
Τριμελές εφετείο	Three-member court of appeal	
Τριτανακοπή	Third-party proceedings	
Τρίτος	Third party	
Τροφεία	Prison sustenance expenses	See Article 22, Correctional Code
Τυπική παράλειψη	Procedural oversight	
Υιοθεσία	Adoption	
Υιοθετημένο τέκνο	Adopted child	

Υπαγωγή	Subsumption	
Υπάλληλος (γραμματείας δικαστηρίου)	Registry clerk	
Υπάλληλος πλειστηριασμού	Auctioneer	
Υπέρβαση εξουσίας	*Ultra vires*	
Υπερημερία αποδοχής	Default of acceptance	
Υπερθεματιστής	Highest bidder	
Υπερπρονομιούχες απαιτήσεις	Super-preferential claims	
Υπόθεση	Case	
Υποθήκη	Mortgage	
Υπομισθωτής	Sublessee	
Υπόμνημα	Memorandum	
Υπόνοια μεροληψίας	Suspicion of bias	
Υποχρέωση	Obligation	
Φύλακας	Custodian	
Φυσικός καρπός	Natural fruit	See Article 961, Civil Code
Χρεόγραφο	Security	See Article 624 See Foreword
Χρηματική απαίτηση	Monetary claim	
Χωρισμός (δίκης)	Splitting of proceedings	
Χωρισμός από τραπέζης και κοίτης	Legal separation	See Foreword
Ψευδής κατάθεση	False testimony	
Ψευδορκία	Perjury	
Ψιλή κυριότητα	Bare ownership	See Article 1142 *et seq.*, Civil Code
Ωφέλημα	Advantage	See Article 962, Civil Code

English to Greek Glossary

EN	EL	Notes
Abolition	*Κατάργηση (δικαιώματος)*	
Absence	*Αφάνεια*	See Article 40, Civil Code
Absence of properties agreed upon	*Έλλειψη συμφωνηθεισών ιδιοτήτων*	
Abstention	*Αποχή*	
Abusive	*Καταχρηστικός*	
Acceptance of an inheritance	*Αποδοχή κληρονομιάς*	
Access	*Επικοινωνία (με ανήλικα παιδιά)*	
Accessory	*Παράρτημα (ακινήτου)*	See Article 956, Civil Code
Account balance	*Κατάλοιπο λογαριασμού*	
Acknowledgment	*Αναγνώριση*	See Article 65
Action	*Αγωγή*	
Action concerning possession	*Αγωγή νομής*	
Action for a declaratory judgment	*Αναγνωριστική αγωγή*	
Action for an account to be rendered	*Αγωγή για λογοδοσία*	
Action for miscarriage of justice	*Αγωγή κακοδικίας*	
Action for revendication	*Αγωγή διεκδίκησης*	
Action *in rem*	*Εμπράγματη αγωγή*	
Actual defect	*Πραγματικό ελάττωμα*	
Additional grounds of appeal	*Πρόσθετοι λόγοι έφεσης*	
Adjournment	*Αναβολή (δίκης, κτλ.)*	
Administrative court	*Διοικητικό δικαστήριο*	
Administrative court of first instance	*Διοικητικό πρωτοδικείο*	
Administrative disputes	*Διοικητικές διαφορές*	
Administrator	*Διαχειριστής*	See Article 614(5)(b)
Admissibility	*Παραδεκτό*	
Admission	*Ομολογία (διαδίκου)*	
Adopted child	*Υιοθετημένο τέκνο*	
Adoption	*Υιοθεσία*	
Adoptive parent	*Θετός γονέας*	
Advantage	*Ωφέλημα*	See Article 962, Civil Code
Advocate	*Δικαστικός πληρεξούσιος*	
Affidavit	*Ένορκη βεβαίωση*	
Affirmative declaration	*Καταφατική δήλωση*	
Aircraft	*Αεροσκάφος*	

Aircraft registry	*Μητρώο (αεροσκαφών)*	
Alienation	*Απαλλοτρίωση*	See Article 939, Civil Code
Annulment	*Ακύρωση (απόφασης, γάμου)*	
Apartment	*Διαμέρισμα*	See Article 128(2)
Appeal	*Έφεση*	
Appeal judge	*Εφέτης*	
Appellant	*Εκκαλών*	
Applicant	*Αιτών*	
Application	*Αίτηση*	See Article 4
Application for cassation	*Αναιρετήριο*	
Application for remittal	*Αίτηση για παραπομπή*	
Application for re-opening proceedings	*Αναψηλάφηση*	
Application *mutatis mutandis*	*Ανάλογη εφαρμογή*	
Arbitration agreement	*Συμφωνία για διαιτησία*	
Arbitration award	*Διαιτητική απόφαση*	
Arbitration panel	*Διαιτητικό δικαστήριο*	
Arbitrator	*Διαιτητής*	
Area	*Έκταση (ακινήτου)*	
Argument	*Ισχυρισμός*	See Article 20(4)
Arrest	*Κατάσχεση (αεροσκάφους, πλοίου)*	See Article 709 See Foreword
Artisan	*Βιοτέχνης*	
Assertion	*Ισχυρισμός*	See Article 77
Assisted legal guardianship	*Επικουρική δικαστική συμπαράσταση*	See Article 1676, Civil Code
Associate judge	*Πάρεδρος*	
Association	*Σωματείο*	See Article 78 *et seq.*, Civil Code
Attachment	*Κατάσχεση*	See Article 707 See Foreword
Attesting oath	*Βεβαιωτικός όρκος*	
Auction	*Πλειστηριασμός*	
Auction price	*Πλειστηρίασμα*	
Auctioneer	*Υπάλληλος πλειστηριασμού*	
Authorisation	*Εξουσιοδότηση*	
Award report	*Κατακυρωτική έκθεση*	
Balance of probabilities	*Πιθανολόγηση*	
Bank holiday	*Αργία*	
Bankruptcy administrator	*Σύνδικος πτώχευσης*	
Bankruptcy composition	*Πτωχευτικός συμβιβασμός*	

Bar association	*Δικηγορικός σύλλογος*	
Bare ownership	*Ψιλή κυριότητα*	See Article 1142 *et seq.*, Civil Code
Bearer	*Κομιστής*	
Bearer bond	*Ανώνυμη ομολογία*	
Bearer security	*Τίτλος στον κομιστή*	
Benefit of inventory-taking	*Ευεργέτημα απογραφής*	
Bequest	*Κληροδότημα*	
Bidder	*Πλειοδότης*	
Bilateral contract	*Αμφοτεροβαρής σύμβαση*	See Articles 374 *et seq.*, Civil Code
Bill of exchange	*Συναλλαγματική*	
Bond loan	*Ομολογιακό δάνειο*	
Book	*Βιβλίο (νόμου)*	
Boundary	*Όριο (ακινήτου)*	
Breach	*Παράβαση*	See Article 424
Breach of duty	*Παράβαση καθήκοντος*	
Bringing a case [for a hearing]	*Εισαγωγή υπόθεσης*	
Building manager	*Διαχειριστής ιδιοκτησίας κατ' ορόφους*	
Building service charges	*Κοινόχρηστες δαπάνες (κτιρίου)*	
Calling	*Σύγκληση*	
Cancellation	*Ματαίωση (πλειστηριασμού κτλ.)*	See Article 972(2)
Capacity to appear before the courts	*Ικανότητα δικαστικής παράστασης*	
Case	*Υπόθεση*	
Case register	*Πινάκιο*	
Cassation	*Αναίρεση*	
Cassation of any judgment in the interests of ensuring proper application of the law in the future	*Αναίρεση υπέρ του νόμου*	
Cassationee	*Αναιρεσίβλητος*	
Cassationer	*Αναιρεσείων*	
Certificate of inheritance	*Κληρονομητήριο*	
Cessation of living together in wedlock	*Διακοπή συμβίωσης*	
Chamber	*Τμήμα (Αρείου Πάγου)*	
Charge	*Βάρος*	See Article 965, Civil Code
Cheque	*Επιταγή*	
Chicanery	*Στρεψοδικία*	
Child born in wedlock	*Τέκνο γεννημένο σε γάμο*	
Child born out of wedlock	*Τέκνο χωρίς γάμο*	

Circuit	*Μεταβατική έδρα*	
Civil court	*Πολιτικό δικαστήριο*	
Civil procedure	*Πολιτική Δικονομία*	
Civil registry certificate	*Ληξιαρχική πράξη*	
Claim	*Απαίτηση*	
Claim *in rem*	*Εμπράγματη απαίτηση*	
Claims register	*Βιβλίο διεκδικήσεων*	
Co-habitant	*Σύνοικος*	
Collateral	*Ασφάλεια*	See Article 11
Collateral	*Εξασφαλίσεις*	See Article 952
Collective bargaining agreement	*Συλλογική σύμβαση εργασίας*	
Collusion	*Συμπαιγνία*	
Commanding officer	*Διοικητής (αστυνομικού τμήματος)*	
Community of rights	*Κοινωνία (δικαιώματος)*	See Article 785 *et seq.*, Civil Code
Company	*Εταιρία*	See Article 788 See Foreword
Compensation	*Αποζημίωση*	
Compensation due to *culpa in contrahendo*	*Αποζημίωση εξαιτίας πταίσματος κατά τις διαπραγματεύσεις*	
Competence	*Αρμοδιότητα*	See Article 7, see Foreword
Compulsory administration	*Αναγκαστική διαχείριση*	
Compulsory attachment	*Αναγκαστική κατάσχεση*	
Compulsory enforcement	*Αναγκαστική εκτέλεση*	
Condition	*Αίρεση*	
Consent	*Συναίνεση*	
Constituent part	*Συστατικό (ακινήτου)*	See Article 953, Civil Code
Constitution	*Συγκρότηση (δικαστηρίου)*	
Consul	*Πρόξενος*	
Consular authority	*Προξενική αρχή*	
Contractual relationship	*Ενοχική σχέση*	
Contribution	*Εισφορά (σε ασφαλιστικό οργανισμό)*	
Contribution	*Συνεισφορά (κοινωνού)*	
Cooperative	*Συνεταιρισμός*	
Copyright	*Δικαιώματα πνευματικής ιδιοκτησίας*	
Costs	*Έξοδα*	
Council of State	*Συμβούλιο της Επικρατείας*	
Councillor of State	*Συμβούλος (ΣτΕ)*	
Counter-evidence	*Ανταπόδειξη*	

Counter-performance	*Αντιπαροχή*	
Court archives	*Αρχείο του δικαστηρίου*	
Court costs	*Δικαστικά έξοδα / δικαστική δαπάνη*	
Court management board	*Συμβούλιο διεύθυνσης δικαστηρίου*	
Court of Audit	*Ελεγκτικό Συνέδριο*	
Court of first instance	*Πρωτοδικείο*	
Court of the peace	*Ειρηνοδικείο*	
Court ruling on the inheritance	*Δικαστήριο της κληρονομίας*	
Court-ordered administration	*Διαχείριση με δικαστική εντολή*	
Creditor	*Δανειστής*	
Cross-action	*Ανταγωγή*	
Cross-appeal	*Αντέφεση*	
Cross-appellant	*Αντεκκαλών*	
Cross-application	*Ανταίτηση*	
Curator (of an unclaimed estate)	*Κηδεμόνας (σχολάζουσας κληρονομίας)*	
Custodian	*Φύλακας*	
Custody	*Επιμέλεια ανηλίκου*	
Customer	*Πελάτης*	
Damages	*Διαφέρον*	
De facto non-appealable judgment	*Ανέκκλητη απόφαση*	
De jure non-appealable judgment	*Τελεσίδικη απόφαση*	
Deadline	*Προθεσμία*	See Article 20A
Dealings	*Συναλλακτικές σχέσεις*	
Debtor	*Οφειλέτης*	
Decision incorporating rights	*Δικαιόγραφο*	
Declaration of choice	*Δήλωση επιλογής*	See Article 1967 *et seq.*, Civil Code
Declaration of will	*Δήλωση βούλησης*	See Article 130 *et seq.*, Civil Code
Default of acceptance	*Υπερημερία αποδοχής*	
Default salary	*Μισθός υπερημερίας*	
Defendant	*Εναγόμενος*	
Delegated judge	*Εντεταλμένος δικαστής*	
Deliberations	*Διάσκεψη*	
Dematerialised share	*Άυλη μετοχή*	
Denial of justice	*Αρνησιδικία*	
Deposit note	*Γραμμάτιο κατάθεσης*	
Depositary receipt	*Αποθετήριο*	
Deputy public prosecutor	*Αντεισαγγελέας*	

Descendants	*Κατιόντες*	
Detentor	*Κάτοχος*	
Detentorship	*Κατοχή*	
Determination of boundaries	*Κανονισμός ορίων*	
Dismissal	*Απόλυση*	
Dispute	*Διαφορά*	
Distribution	*Διανομή (εταιρικής περιουσίας, εκπλειστηριάσματος)*	See Articles 27(2), 957(2)
District	*Περιφέρεια (δικαστηρίου)*	
Dividend coupon	*Μερισματαπόδειξη / Μερισματόγραφο*	
Divisible right	*Διαιρετό δικαίωμα*	
Division of a jointly owned immovable	*Διαίρεση κοινού (ακινήτου)*	
Divorce	*Διαζύγιο*	
Dolus	*Δόλος*	
Domicile	*Κατοικία*	
Dominant tenement	*Δεσπόζον κτήμα*	
Drawing apparatus	*Κληρωτίδα*	
Drawing by lot	*Κλήρωση*	
Dwelling	*Διαμέρισμα*	See Article 827(2)
Easement	*Δουλεία*	
e-auction	*Ηλεκτρονικός πλειστηριασμός*	
Electronic acknowledgment of receipt	*Ηλεκτρονική απόδειξη παραλαβής*	
Electronic verification	*Ηλεκτρονική επαλήθευση*	
Employer	*Εργοδότης*	
Enforceable title	*Εκτελεστός τίτλος*	
Enforcement officer	*Εκτελεστικό όργανο*	
Enforcement precept	*Απόγραφο*	
Entry	*Μερίδα* *Μεταγραφή*	See Article 981 See Article 992(1)
Erga omnes effect	*Ισχύς απέναντι σε όλους*	
Establishment	*Σύσταση (δικαιώματος)*	
Estate	*Κληρονομία*	See Article 30(1) See Foreword
Estate intended for public-benefit purposes	*Κοινωφελής περιουσία*	
European Account Preservation Order	*Ευρωπαϊκή Διαταγή Δέσμευσης Λογαριασμού*	
Ex officio	*Αυτεπαγγέλτως*	
Examination	*Εξέταση*	
Exclusive deadline	*Αποσβεστική προθεσμία*	See Article 279, Civil Code

Exclusive jurisdiction	*Αποκλειστική αρμοδιότητα*	
Executor of a will	*Εκτελεστής διαθήκης*	
Exemption	*Εξαίρεση (δικαστή)*	
Exhibit	*Σχετικό έγγραφο (σε δικόγραφο)*	
Expert	*Πραγματογνώμων*	
Expert arbitrator	*Διαιτητής πραγματογνώμων*	
Expert evidence	*Πραγματογνωμοσύνη*	
Exploitation rights for films	*Δικαιώματα εκμετάλλευσης κινηματογραφικών ταινιών*	
Express	*Ρητός*	
Expropriation	*Αναγκαστική απαλλοτρίωση*	
Extra-judicial	*Εξώδικος*	
Extraordinary will	*Έκτακτη διαθήκη*	
Factual assertion	*Πραγματικός ισχυρισμός*	
Failure to comply	*Παράβαση*	See Article 159
Failure to enter an appearance	*Ερημοδικία*	
False testimony	*Ψευδής κατάθεση*	
Family relationship	*Συγγένεια*	
Fees	*Δικαιώματα*	
Filing report	*Έκθεση κατάθεσης*	
Fixed deadline	*Αποκλειστική προθεσμία*	
Fixed duration	*Ορισμένη διάρκεια*	
Forced discontinuation of the proceedings	*Βίαιη διακοπή δίκης*	
Forced sale	*Αναγκαστική εκποίηση*	
Foreign authority	*Αλλοδαπή αρχή*	
Foreign national/Foreigner	*Αλλοδαπός*	
Forfeiture of a right	*Έκπτωση από δικαίωμα*	
Forgery	*Πλαστογραφία*	
Form of order sought (in the action)	*Αίτημα της αγωγής*	
Form of relief	*Ένδικο βοήθημα*	
Free union	*Ελεύθερη συμβίωση*	See Foreword
Fruit	*Καρπός*	See Article 961, Civil Code
Garnishee	*Εκείνος κατά του οποίου γίνεται κατάσχεση είς χείρας τρίτου*	
Garnishment	*Κατάσχεση εις χείρας τρίτου / σε χέρια τρίτου*	See Article 712 See Foreword
Garnishor	*Κατάσχων*	
General forum	*Γενική δωσιδικία*	

General partnership	*Ομόρρυθμη εταιρεία*	
Granting	*Παραχώρηση*	
Granting of probate	*Δημοσίευση διαθήκης*	
Greek State	*Δημόσιο*	See Foreword
Gross negligence	*Βαριά αμέλεια*	
Group of things	*Ομάδα αντικειμένων*	
Grouping of persons	*Ένωση προσώπων*	See Article 107, Civil Code
Guarantee	*Εγγύηση*	See Article 11
Guarantor	*Εγγυητής*	
Guard	*Σκοπός (αστυνομικός)*	
Guardian *ad litem*	*Ειδικός επίτροπος*	
Guest	*Πελάτης (ξενοδοχείου)*	See Articles 834 to 839, Civil Code
Handing back of a property	*Παράδοση (ακινήτου)*	
Handwriting	*Γραφή*	
Handwriting expert evidence	*Γραφολογική πραγματογνωμοσύνη*	
Handwritten	*Ιδιόχειρος*	
Harbour master	*Λιμεναρχής*	
Head of a court	*Προϊστάμενος (δικαστηρίου)*	
Head of a judgment	*Κεφάλαιο (απόφασης)*	
Hearing	*Συζήτηση*	
Hearing date	*Δικάσιμος*	
Hearing having heard both sides	*Συζήτηση κατ' αντιμωλίαν*	
Heir	*Κληρονόμος*	
Highest bidder	*Υπερθεματιστής*	
Holder of possession	*Διακάτοχος*	
Holiday	*Εορτή*	
Holographic will	*Ιδιόγραφη διαθήκη*	
Horizontal property	*Οριζόντια ιδιοκτησία*	
Infringement	*Παράβαση*	See Article 15(3)
Immovables	*Ακίνητα*	See Article 948, Civil Code
Immunity from jurisdiction	*Ετεροδικία*	
Impleaded party	*Προσεπικαλούμενος*	
Impleader	*Προσεπίκληση*	
In camera	*Κεκλεισμένων των θυρών*	
In rem relationship	*Εμπράγματη σχέση*	
Inability to go ahead	*Ματαίωση (συζήτησης)*	See Article 260(2)

Inadmissible	*Απαράδεκτος*	
Incapable of being assessed	*Ανεπίδεκτος εκτίμησης*	
Incidental action	*Παρεμπίπτουσα αγωγή*	
Incidental application	*Παρεμπίπτουσα αίτηση*	
Incidental issue	*Παρεμπίπτον ζήτημα*	
Inheritance	*Κληρονομιά*	See Article 263(e) See Foreword
Inheritance right	*Κληρονομικό δικαίωμα*	
Injurious to morality	*Επιβλαβής για τα χρηστά ήθη*	
Inspection	*Αυτοψία*	
Instance	*Βαθμός δικαιοδοσίας*	
Insured person	*Ασφαλισμένος*	
Intact	*Άθικτος*	
Interest coupon	*Τοκομερίδιο*	
Interest-free promissory note payable on demand	*Άτοκο γραμμάτιο πληρωτέο εν όψει*	
Interim legal guardian	*Προσωρινός δικαστικός συμπαραστάτης*	
Interim measures	*Ασφαλιστικά μέτρα*	
Interim order	*Προσωρινή διαταγή (ασφαλιστικών μέτρων)*	
Interim relief	*Προσωρινή δικαστική προστασία*	
Interim tutor	*Προσωρινός επίτροπος*	
International arbitration	*Διεθνής διαιτησία*	
International call sign	*Διεθνές σήμα*	
International law	*Διεθνές δίκαιο*	
International treaty/convention	*Διεθνής σύμβαση*	
Interpretative rule	*Ερμηνευτικός κανόνας*	
Interpreter	*Διερμηνέας/Ερμηνέας*	
Interruption	*Διακοπή δίκης*	See Article 286
Interruption	*Διακοπή παραγραφής*	See Article 146(1) See Article 260 *et seq.*, Civil Code
Intervener	*Παρεμβαίνων*	
Intervention	*Παρέμβαση*	
Intransigence	*Δυστροπία*	
Joinder	*Ομοδικία*	
Joinder of actions in respect of their alternative bases	*Επικουρική σώρευση αγωγών*	
Joined party	*Ομόδικος*	
Joint ownership [within a building]	*Οροφοκτησία*	
Jointly owned asset	*Επίκοινο*	

Judgment	*Απόφαση*	See Article 114(3), see Foreword
Judgment granting interim measures	*Απόφαση ασφαλιστικών μέτρων*	
Judicial authority	*Δικαστική αρχή*	
Judicial conviction	*Δικανική πεποίθηση*	See Article 340(2)
Judicial functionary	*Δικαστικός λειτουργός*	
Judicial liquidation	*Δικαστική εκκαθάριση*	
Judicial mediation	*Δικαστική μεσολάβηση*	
Judicial presumption	*Δικαστικό τεκμήριο*	
Judicial protection	*Δικαστική προστασία*	
Judicial sequestration	*Δικαστική μεσεγγύηση*	
Jurisdiction	*Αρμοδιότητα*	See Article 3(1), see Foreword
Jurisdiction	*Δικαιοδοσία*	
Jurisdiction *ratione loci*	*Κατά τόπον αρμοδιότητα*	
Jurisdiction *ratione materiae*	*Καθ' ύλην αρμοδιότητα*	
Juvenile	*Ανήλικος*	
Lack of jurisdiction	*Έλλειψη δικαιοδοσίας*	
Law Introducing the Code of Civil Procedure	*Εισαγωγικός Νόμος*	
Lawyer	*Δικηγόρος*	
Lease agreement	*Μισθωτική σύμβαση*	
Leased property	*Μισθίο*	
Leasing	*Εκμίσθωση*	
Leasing	*Μίσθωση (πράγματος)*	See Article 574 *et seq.*, Civil Code
Leave	*Άδεια (διακοπών, διεξαγωγής δίκης, επίδοσης)*	
Legacy	*Κληροδοσία*	
Legal aid	*Ευεργέτημα πενίας*	
Legal basis	*Νομική βάση*	
Legal norm	*Κανόνας δικαίου*	
Legal personality	*Νομική προσωπικότητα*	
Legal relationship	*Έννομη σχέση*	
Legal remedy	*Ένδικο μέσο*	
Legal separation	*Χωρισμός από τραπέζης και κοίτης*	See Foreword
Legal transaction	*Δικαιοπραξία*	
Legal transaction *inter vivos*	*Δικαιοπραξία εν ζωή*	
Legatee	*Κληροδόχος*	
Legitimate child	*Γνήσιο τέκνο*	

Legitimate interest	*Έννομο συμφέρον*	
Legitimised child	*Νομιμοποιημένο τέκνο*	
Lessee	*Μισθωτής*	
Letter of guarantee	*Εγγυητική επιστολή*	
Limited partnership	*Ετερόρρυθμη εταιρεία*	
Liquidation	*Εκκαθάριση (εταιρείας)*	
Liquidator	*Εκκαθαριστής*	
Lis pendens	*Εκκρεμοδικία*	
List of costs	*Κατάλογος εξόδων*	
Location	*Θέση (ακινήτου)*	
Lodgement	*Αναγγελία (δικαιώματος ή απαίτησης)*	
Loss event	*Ζημιογόνο γεγονός*	
Lot	*Κλήρος*	
Main dispute	*Κύρια διαφορά*	
Main intervention	*Κύρια παρέμβαση*	
Maintenance	*Διατροφή*	
Manager	*Διαχειριστής*	See Article 795
Marriage	*Γάμος*	
Master	*Πλοίαρχος*	
Matrimonial disputes	*Γαμικές διαφορές*	
Means of evidence	*Αποδεικτικά μέσα*	
Mediation	*Διαμεσολάβηση*	
Mediation report	*Πρακτικό διαμεσολάβησης*	
Mediator judge	*Δικαστής μεσολαβητής*	
Meeting	*Συνέλευση*	
Member of a community of rights	*Κοινωνός*	
Memorandum	*Υπόμνημα*	
Military personnel member	*Στρατιωτικός*	
Misapplication	*Εσφαλμένη εφαρμογή*	
Mixed action	*Μικτή αγωγή*	
Monetary claim	*Χρηματική απαίτηση*	
Mortgage	*Υποθήκη*	
Mortgage register	*Βιβλίο υποθηκών*	
Mortgage-backed claim	*Ενυπόθηκη απαίτηση*	
Mortgagee	*Ενυπόθηκος δανειστής*	
Mortis causa	*Αιτία θανάτου (επίρ.)*	
Motion	*Αίτημα (διαδίκου)*	
Movable	*Κινητό*	
Multi-member court of first instance	*Πολυμελές πρωτοδικείο*	

National law	*Εσωτερικό δίκαιο*	
Nationality	*Ιθαγένεια*	
Natural fruit	*Φυσικός καρπός*	See Article 961, Civil Code
Negative declaration	*Αρνητική δήλωση*	
Non-attachable / Non-garnishable	*Ακατάσχετος*	Context-dependent
Non-contentious proceedings	*Εκούσια δικαιοδοσία*	
Non-court-ordered administration	*Διαχείριση χωρίς δικαστική εντολή*	See Article 730 *et seq.*, Civil Code
Non-final ruling	*Μη οριστική απόφαση*	
Non-preferential claim	*Μη προνομιούχα απαίτηση*	
Non-stipendiary court process server	*Άμισθος δικαστικός επιμελητής*	
Notarial instrument	*Συμβολαιογραφικό έγγραφο*	
Notary public	*Συμβολαιογράφος*	
Note payable to order	*Τίτλος εις διαταγήν*	
Notice	*Όχληση*	
Nullity	*Ακυρότητα*	
Oath	*Όρκος*	
Oath-taking	*Όρκιση*	
Obligation	*Υποχρέωση*	
Officer on duty	*Αξιωματικός υπηρεσίας*	
Omission	*Παράλειψη*	
Operative part of the judgment	*Διατακτικό (μέρος απόφασης)*	
Opposition	*Ανακοπή*	
Opposition against a default judgment	*Ανακοπή ερημοδικίας*	
Opposition *in rem*	*Εμπράγματη ανακοπή*	
Oral hearing	*Προφορική συζήτηση*	
Ordinary civil court	*Τακτικό πολιτικό δικαστήριο*	
Owner	*Ιδιοκτήτης*	
Owner-operator	*Πλοιοκτήτης*	
Ownership	*Κυριότητα*	See Article 999 *et seq.*, Civil Code
Parental responsibility	*Γονική μέριμνα*	
Pari passu payment	*Σύμμετρη πληρωμή*	
Partition	*Διανομή (κοινού πράγματος)*	See Article 478 *et seq.*
Partition *in natura*	*Αυτούσια διανομή*	
Partitionable thing	*Διανεμητέο*	
Partner	*Εταίρος*	

Partnership	*Εταιρεία* *Προσωπική εταιρεία*	See Article 27(1) See Article 982(2)(b) See Foreword
Party in the proceedings	*Διάδικος*	
Passive bribery	*Δωροληψία*	
Patent rights	*Δικαιώματα ευρεσιτεχνίας*	
Paulian action	*Αγωγή διάρρηξης δικαιοπραξίας ως καταδολιευτικής*	
Payment of a specific shortfall	*Καταβολή ορισμένου ελλείμματος*	
Payment order	*Διαταγή πληρωμής*	
Pending proceedings	*Εκκρεμής δίκη*	
Performance	*Παροχή*	
Periodically recurring dues	*Περιοδικές παροχές*	
Perishable thing	*Ευπαθές πράγμα*	
Perjury	*Ψευδορκία*	
Permission	*Άδεια*	
Permissive intervention	*Πρόσθετη παρέμβαση*	
Permissive joinder	*Απλή ομοδικία*	
Person entitled to maintenance	*Δικαιούχος διατροφής*	
Person served	*Αποδέκτης επίδοσης*	
Person to be placed under legal guardianship	*Συμπαραστατέος*	
Person under legal guardianship	*Συμπαραστατούμενος*	
Personal detention	*Προσωπική κράτηση*	See Foreword
Personal easement	*Προσωπική δουλεία*	
Personal status	*Προσωπική κατάσταση*	
Petty offences court	*Πταισματοδικείο*	See Foreword
Plaintiff	*Ενάγων*	
Planning department	*Πολεοδομία*	
Plea of lack of jurisdiction	*Ένσταση αναρμοδιότητας*	
Pleas	*Μέσα επίθεσης ή άμυνας / Επιθετικά ή αμυντικά μέσα*	
Pledge	*Ενέχυρο*	
Pledgee	*Ενεχυρούχος δανειστής*	
Police department	*Αστυνομικό τμήμα*	
Police facility	*Αστυνομικό κατάστημα*	
Police station	*Αστυνομικός σταθμός*	
Port	*Λιμάνι*	
Possession	*Νομή*	See Article 974 *et seq.*, Civil Code
Possessor	*Νομέας*	

Postponement	*Αναβολή (ενεργειών)*	
Power of attorney	*Πληρεξούσιο (εγγράφο)*	
Power of representation	*Πληρεξουσιότητα*	
Preferential claims	*Προνομιούχες απαιτήσεις*	
Preliminary procedure	*Προδικασία*	
President of the Supreme Court	*Πρόεδρος Αρείου Πάγου*	
President of the three-member management board	*Πρόεδρος τριμελούς συμβουλίου (που διευθύνει το δικαστήριο)*	
Presiding appeal judge	*Πρόεδρος εφετών*	
Presiding arbitrator	*Επιδιαιτητής*	
Presiding judge	*Πρόεδρος δικαστηρίου*	
Preventive arrest	*Συντηρητική κατάσχεση (πλοίου ή αεροσκάφους)*	
Preventive attachment	*Συντηρητική κατάσχεση*	
Principal	*Εντολέας*	
Principal debtor	*Πρωτοφειλέτης*	
Prison sustenance expenses	*Τροφεία*	See Article 22, Correctional Code
Private document	*Ιδιωτικό έγγραφο*	
Private law	*Ιδιωτικό δίκαιο*	
Private-law right	*Δικαίωμα ιδιωτικού δικαίου*	
Privilege of immunity from jurisdiction	*Προνόμιο ετεροδικίας*	
Probative value	*Αποδεικτική ισχύς*	
Procedural document	*Δικόγραφο*	
Procedural fee (receipt)	*Παράβολο*	
Procedural oversight	*Τυπική παράλειψη*	
Procedural step	*Διαδικαστική πράξη*	
Proceedings	*Δίκη*	
Proceedings held *in absentia*	*Ερήμην δίκη*	
Process agent	*Αντίκλητος*	
Promissory note	*Γραμμάτιο εις διαταγήν*	
Property rights	*Περιουσιακά δικαιώματα*	
Propriety	*Ευπρέπεια*	
Prorogation of jurisdiction	*Παρέκταση αρμοδιότητας*	
Provision	*Διάταξη (νόμου, απόφασης, κτλ.)*	
Provision of surety	*Εγγυοδοσία*	
Proviso	*Όρος*	
Public authority	*Δημόσια αρχή*	
Public document	*Δημόσιο έγγραφο*	

Public policy	*Δημόσια τάξη*	
Public prosecutor	*Εισαγγελέας*	
Public security risk	*Κίνδυνος για την κοινή ασφάλεια*	
Public will	*Δημόσια διαθήκη*	
Publicity formalities	*Διατυπώσεις δημοσιότητας*	
Real easement	*Πραγματική δουλεία*	
Reasoning	*Αιτιολογικό (απόφασης)*	
Rebuttal	*Αντίκρουση*	
Recast	*Μεταγλώττιση*	
Recognised child	*Αναγνωρισμένο τέκνο*	
Recognition	*Αναγνώριση*	See Article 17
Re-enactment	*Αναπαράσταση*	
Referral of a case	*Παραπομπή (υπόθεσης)*	
Registered (share) certificate	*Ονομαστικός τίτλος (μετοχών)*	
Registered offices	*Έδρα (εταιρείας)*	
Registration	*Μεταγραφή*	See Article 992(1)
Registration of a mortgage	*Εγγραφή υποθήκης*	
Registry	*Γραμματεία (δικαστηρίου)*	
Registry clerk	*Υπάλληλος (γραμματείας δικαστηρίου)*	
Re-hearing	*Ανασυζήτηση*	
Relation by blood	*Συγγένεια εξ αίματος*	
Relation by marriage	*Συγγένεια εξ αγχιστείας*	
Relations between spouses	*Σχέσεις συζύγων*	See Article 1386 *et seq.*, Civil Code
Relatives in the ascendant line	*Ανιόντες*	
Reliance damages	*Αρνητικό διαφέρον*	
Religious oath	*Θρησκευτικός όρκος*	
Relinquishment	*Παραίτηση (πληρεξουσιότητας)*	
Remittal	*Παραπομπή*	
Remittal court	*Δικαστήριο παραπομπής*	
Rendering of account	*Λογοδοσία*	
Rent	*Μίσθωμα*	
Re-opened proceedings	*Κατ' αναψηλάφηση δίκη*	
Repeat auction	*Επαναπλειστηριασμός*	
Reporting judge	*Εισηγητής*	
Repudiation of an inheritance	*Αποποίηση κληρονομιάς*	
Request	*Αίτηση*	See Article 5(1)
Request for a preliminary ruling	*Προδικαστικό ερώτημα*	

Request seeking performance	*Καταψήφιση*	
Reserved portion of an estate	*Νόμιμη μοίρα*	See Article 1825 *et seq.*, Civil Code
Residence	*Διαμονή*	
Respondent [in appeal]	*Εφεσίβλητος*	
Restoration of a prior state of affairs	*Επαναφορά των πραγμάτων στην προηγούμενη κατάσταση*	
Retroactive effect	*Αναδρομική ισχύς*	
Return / Handing over	*Απόδοση*	
Return of use of a leased propety	*Απόδοση χρήσης μισθίου*	
Revenue-generating thing	*Προσοδοφόρο αντικείμενο*	
Review	*Έλεγχος (Αρείου Πάγου)*	
Revocation	*Ανάκληση (απόφασης)*	
Right	*Δικαίωμα*	
Right *in rem*	*Εμπράγματο δικαίωμα*	
Ruling	*Απόφαση*	See Article 114(2), see Foreword
Salaried labour	*Εξαρτημένη εργασία*	
Sale	*Εκποίηση*	
Seafarers' Retirement Fund	*Ναυτικό Απομαχικό Ταμείο*	
Seal	*Σφραγίδα*	
Sealed will	*Μυστική διαθήκη*	
Seat	*Έδρα (δικαστηρίου, σωματείου, κτλ.)*	
Second-instance court	*Δευτεροβάθμιο δικαστήριο*	
Secular oath	*Πολιτικός όρκος*	
Security	*Αξιόγραφο* *Ασφάλεια (κοινή, κράτους)* *Τίτλος παραστατικός αξίας* *Χρεόγραφο*	See Article 850(1) See Article 48 See Article 164 See Article 624 See Foreword
Seniority	*Αρχαιότητα*	
Sequestrator	*Μεσεγγυούχος*	
Serious reason	*Σπουδαίος λόγος*	
Servient tenement	*Δουλεύον κτήμα*	
Settlement	*Συμβιβασμός*	
Settlement intervention	*Συμβιβαστική επέμβαση*	
Share	*Μερίδα*	See Article 480(3)
Share in the estate	*Κληρονομική μερίδα*	
Sharecropping	*Επίμορτη αγροληψία*	

Shareholding	*Εταιρική μερίδα*	
Sharing-out of an estate	*Διανομή κληρονομιάς*	See Article 30(1)
Ship	*Πλοίο*	
Ship registry	*Νηολόγιο*	
Single-member court of appeal	*Μονομελές εφετείο*	
Single-member court of first instance	*Μονομελές πρωτοδικείο*	
Sitting	*Συνεδρίαση*	
Sitting in full court	*Ολομέλεια*	
Small claim	*Μικροδιαφορά*	
Social security organisation	*Οργανισμός κοινωνικής ασφάλισης*	
Social services	*Κοινωνική υπηρεσία*	
Société anonyme	*Ανώνυμη εταιρεία*	
Special curator	*Ειδικός κηδεμόνας (σχολάζουσας κληρονομίας)*	See Article 1910, Civil Code
Special place of domicile	*Ειδική κατοικία*	
Specific successor	*Ειδικός διάδοχος*	
Splitting of proceedings	*Χωρισμός (δίκης)*	
Spouse	*Σύζυγος*	
Statute of the court	*Κανονισμός δικαστηρίου*	
Stay	*Αναστολή (εκδίκασης)*	
Storey	*Όροφος*	
Striking-out	*Εξάλειψη*	
Subject-matter (of the proceedings)	*Αντικείμενο (δίκης)*	
Sublessee	*Υπομισθωτής*	
Substantive law	*Ουσιαστικό δίκαιο*	
Subsumption	*Υπαγωγή*	
Summons	*Κλήση*	
Super-preferential claims	*Υπερπρονομιούχες απαιτήσεις*	
Supervisory board	*Εποπτικό συμβούλιο*	See Article 1682, Civil Code
Supreme Court	*Άρειος Πάγος*	
Supreme Court Judge	*Αρεοπαγίτης*	
Supreme Court Public Prosecutor	*Εισαγγελέας του Αρείου Πάγου*	
Surety	*Εγγύηση*	See Article 164(3)
Survey	*Γεωμέτρηση*	
Suspension	*Αναστολή παραγραφής*	See Article 255 *et seq.*, Civil Code
Suspensive condition	*Αναβλητική αίρεση*	
Suspicion of bias	*Υπόνοια μεροληψίας*	

Tacit	*Σιωπηρός*	
Tax identification number	*Αριθμός φορολογικού μητρώου*	
Teachings of common experience	*Διδάγματα κοινής πείρας*	
Teleconference	*Τηλεδιάσκεψη*	
Telex	*Τηλετύπημα*	
Tenement	*Κτήμα*	
Term	*Προθεσμία*	See Article 682 See Article 210, Civil Code
Testamentary disposition	*Διάταξη διαθήκης / τελευταίας βούλησης*	
Testamentary trust	*Κληρονομικό καταπίστευμα*	
Thing	*Πράγμα*	See Article 947 *et seq.*, Civil Code
Thing which can become spoiled	*Πράγμα υποκείμενο σε φθορά*	
Third party	*Τρίτος*	
Third party joined in proceedings as guarantor	*Δικονομικός εγγυητής*	
Third-party notice	*Ανακοίνωση (δίκης)*	
Third-party proceedings	*Τριτανακοπή*	
Three-member court of appeal	*Τριμελές εφετείο*	
Time-barring period	*Παραγραφή*	
Timestamp	*Βέβαιη χρονολογία*	
Tort	*Αδικοπραξία*	
Tortious dispute	*Διαφορά από αδικοπραξία*	
Transactional representation	*Δικαιοπρακτική δήλωση*	
Transcription	*Μεταγραφή*	See Article 997(3)
Transfer	*Μεταβίβαση*	
Transfer with a blank endorsement section	*Μεταβίβαση με λευκή οπισθογράφηση*	
Trial court	*Δικαστήριο της ουσίας*	
Trustee	*Καταπιστευματοδόχος*	
Tutorship	*Επιτροπεία*	See Article 1589 *et seq.*, Civil Code
Ultra vires	*Υπέρβαση εξουσίας*	
Unclaimed estate	*Σχολάζουσα κληρονομία*	
Universal successor	*Καθολικός διάδοχος*	
Unjust enrichment	*Αδικαιολόγητος πλουτισμός*	
Unsealing	*Αποσφράγιση*	
Unsecured creditor	*Εγχειρόγραφος δανειστής*	
Usual environment	*Συνηθισμένο περιβάλλον*	
Usufruct	*Επικαρπία*	

Utility company	*Οργανισμός κοινής ωφελείας*	
Valid will	*Κυρία διαθήκη*	
Validity	*Κύρος*	
Valuer	*Εκτιμητής*	
Vertical property	*Κάθετη ιδιοκτησία*	
Violation	*Παράβαση*	See Article 205
Voluntary auction	*Εκούσιος πλειστηριασμός*	
Waiver	*Παραίτηση*	
Ward	*Επιτροπευόμενος*	
Warrant	*Ενεχυρόγραφο*	
Will probate report	*Πρακτικό δημοσίευσης διαθήκης*	
Winding up	*Διάλυση (εταιρείας)*	
Withdrawal	*Αφαίρεση (κληρονομητηρίου)*	
Witness	*Μάρτυρας*	
Worker	*Εργαζόμενος*	

www.ingramcontent.com/pod-product-compliance
Lightning Source LLC
LaVergne TN
LVHW081942200926
848484LV00009B/2498

* 9 7 8 1 8 3 8 4 1 0 6 4 3 *